The GATE LODGES of LEINSTER: *a gazetteer*

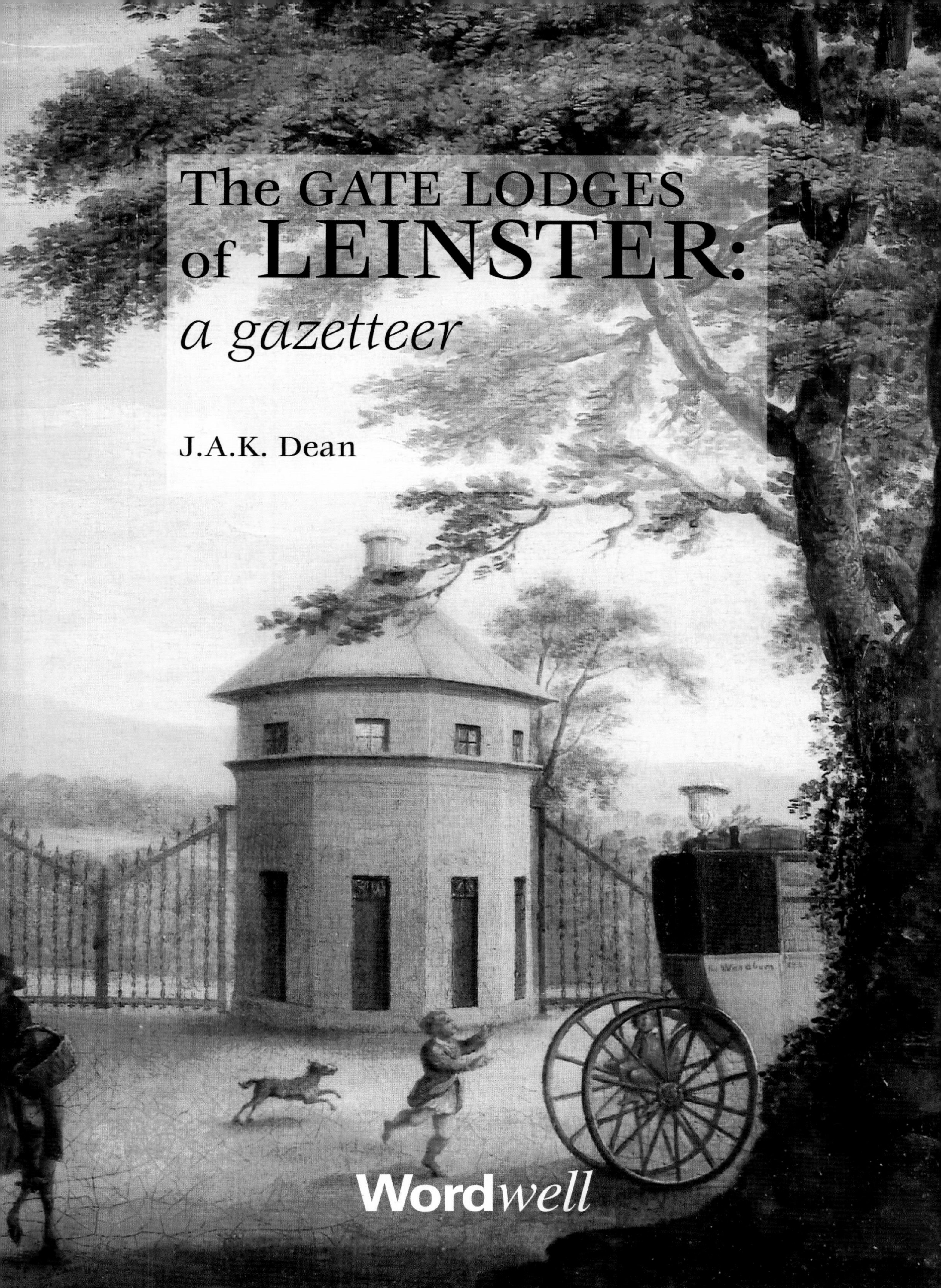
The GATE LODGES
of LEINSTER:
a gazetteer
J.A.K. Dean
Wordwell

In fond memory of Victor Hall.

First published 2016
Word*well*
Unit 9, 78 Furze Road,
Sandyford Industrial Estate, Dublin 18, D18 C6V6
Tel: +353-1-2933568
Email: office@wordwellbooks.com
Web: www.wordwellbooks.com

ISBN: 978 0-9933518-3-9

British Library Cataloguing-in-Publication Data.
A catalogue record for this book is available from the British Library.

Front cover illustration: *Entrance gates to Tinny Park, Co. Kilkenny,* by William Robertson (*c.* 1812), courtesy of the Royal Society of Antiquaries of Ireland.

Other cover illustrations: watercolour views by Edward McFarland (1853) on the Dublin to Howth road. Back flap from top: Clontarf Castle, Howth Castle and Killester House. Front flap: Marino House. All courtesy of the National Library of Ireland.

Title-page illustration: Robert Woodburn's oil painting of the 'turret' gate at Belline, Piltown, Co. Kilkenny (1800), courtesy of David Ker.

The publisher gratefully acknowledges financial assistance from the School of Irish Studies Foundation, the Irish Georgian Society and the Esmé Mitchell Trust.

Typeset in Ireland by Wordwell Ltd.
Copy-editor: Emer Condit.
Book design: Nick Maxwell.

Printed by Turners, Longford.

CONTENTS

FOREWORD

We all know that we should not judge a book by its cover, but the beautiful picture on the front of *The gate lodges of Leinster* draws us like a magnet. All the historic illustrations in this publication help us to empathise with these lovable little buildings before we begin our journey through the treasures within. Dean has done us all a service by raising our awareness of the gate lodge as a particular building type rather than simply an adjunct to the 'Big House', and by highlighting the owners who commissioned the lodges. I like the way he has taken pains to identify, where possible, the gate porters and those who lived in the lodges; they are often the forgotten ones. It is 22 years since the Ulster Architectural Heritage Society published Dean's *Gate lodges of Ulster* and this second volume has been eagerly awaited. *The gate lodges of Leinster* benefits from his continuing careful research and comparisons with gate lodges across Ireland. This book is about much more than the lodges, however, for it provides us with fascinating insights into the 'Big House' as well.

The rate of loss of these buildings is frightening. While we mourn the loss of very special examples like Belline Lodge, described by Dean as 'a national treasure', and many more besides, we celebrate the advent of the Irish Landmark Trust. Over the past 24 years it has rescued buildings like the Batty Langley lodge at Castletown, Celbridge, Co. Kildare, and the Triumphal Arch gate lodge at Colebrooke, Co. Fermanagh, from varying states of dereliction. A book such as this can only help to raise awareness of the importance of the building type, and encourage individuals and organisations to restore them. The ILT's approach ensures that we can all have the opportunity of spending a few days savouring life in these delightful historic buildings—enjoying the retention of quirky details and inconvenient aspects that would drive us mad if we had to face them daily but are simply endearing when on holidays!

We are all indebted to Dean for his travels across Ireland to find the elusive, bramble-covered gate lodges that are such wonderful elements of our architectural heritage. His tenacious dedication in researching the individual buildings is an example to us all; I am sure that he will inspire budding architectural historians and writers to follow in his footsteps. We await with great anticipation the publication of *The gate lodges of Connacht* and *The gate lodges of Munster*, but before then we salute Dean for another fascinating publication, which will take us on journeys of discovery across Leinster, and we thank Lynne for her patience and dedication in helping him to locate these special aspects of our architectural heritage. Our lives are enriched by their collective endeavours.

Primrose Wilson CBE, Hon. RSUA

ACKNOWLEDGEMENTS

This, the second in a series of books on the gate lodges of Ireland, might not have come to fruition were it not for the generous financial contributions of an award from the School of Irish Studies Foundation, grants from the Irish Georgian Society and latterly the Esmé Mitchell Trust that have given me much incentive and sustenance since 1997, for which I am truly appreciative. Disappointingly, overtures from Dúchas and approaches to the Heritage Council came to naught.

I am indebted to various academic institutions and places of public record, first and foremost to the staff of the Irish Architectural Archive, in particular Aisling Dunne for patiently identifying images from a vast source, and Ann Martha Rowan and David Griffin with their encyclopaedic knowledge of Irish architecture, which was readily imparted. Their assistance in attributions was invaluable, as was that of Kevin Mulligan, who gave so freely of his expertise, although they should be absolved from some of my ascriptions.

For their assistance in research and facilities rendered I am grateful to the staff of *Country Life* magazine, the Linenhall Library, Belfast, the National Archives, the Public Record Office, Kew, the Public Record Office of Northern Ireland, the RIBA Drawings Collection in the Victoria & Albert Museum, the Royal Irish Academy and, more specifically, to Stephen Astley of Sir John Soane's Museum, Lynne Dean of Stranmillis University College Library, Alan Phelan of the Erasmus Smith Trust and Donall Mac Giolla Easpaig of the Department of Community, Rural and Gaeltacht Affairs.

The Valuation Office is a rich source for dating building development and I am grateful to the staff for their forbearance, in particular Brendan Robbins for his consideration. Without that essential tool that is the Ordnance Survey of Ireland and the 6in. maps in their various editions this work would not have been possible, so to the map librarians of Trinity College Dublin, Paul Ferguson, and Queen's University Belfast, Maura Pringle, my special thanks for permitting such easy access.

My gratitude is due to library staff throughout the province for their help, namely Honora Faul, Joanna Finnegan, Elizabeth Kirwan, Eilis Ni Dhuibhne and Collette O'Daly (NLI), Diarmaid Bracken (Offaly Co.), Gretta Connell (Westmeath Co.), Mario Corrigan (Kildare Co.), Maura Flanagan (Drogheda), Alan Hand (Louth Co.), Josephine Lacy (Gorey), Patricia Lynch (Laois Co.), Celestine Murphy (Wexford Co.), Gearoid O'Brien (Aidan Heavey, Athlone), Barbara Scally (Meath Co.) and Mary Carleton Reynolds (Longford Co.), but above all to Kieran Swords (South Dublin Co.) who took especial interest, seeking and providing information on areas which extended far beyond his bailiwick.

Especially helpful were Brendan Ward in his familiarity with counties Carlow and Laois, Amanda Pedlow in her role as Heritage Officer for Offaly County Council and John McCullen for imparting his specialist knowledge of the Phoenix Park. James Howley was particularly generous in giving permission to reproduce illustrations from his splendid *The follies and garden buildings of Ireland*.

Invaluable specialist knowledge was provided by many private collections, principal of which were those of Alec Cobbe (Newbridge, north Dublin), Alison Kelly (Coade Stone), David Ker (Belline, Co. Kilkenny), Valerie, Lady Longford (Pakenham Hall, Co. Westmeath), Sister Mary C. Merriman (Gloster, Co. Offaly), Michael O'Dwyer (Belline and Bessborough, Co. Kilkenny), Peter Pearson (Dublin), Lord Rosse (Birr Castle, Co. Offaly), Nigel Temple (architectural pattern-books) and Barry Watson (postcards), all of whom kindly gave permission to reproduce drawings and photographs.

Late in the day I made contact with a kindred spirit in Julian Humphreys, who generously gave me access to, and permission to reproduce illustrations from, his unpublished university thesis on the grand Irish estate entrance, the survey for which was invaluable in dating from the 1970s, when destruction of our architectural heritage was at its height.

To the following I am obliged for encouragement, information and illustrations which, where reproduced, I have acknowledged individually:
Frank Barrett, Bridget Barron, Michael J. Blaney, Dr Paul Bradley, Bernard Browne, Tim Campbell, N. Campion, Kevin Casey, Mr and Mrs Peter Clarke, Joe Clinton, Esmé Colley, Pat Comerford, Ambrose Congreve, John Conlon, Seamus and Caroline Corballis, Diana Cornell, Dr Maurice J. Craig, Nick A. Crawford, Cathal Crimmins, Kathleen Cullen, Iris Mary Cunningham, Joe Curtis, Sir Howard Colvin, Eileen Dalton, Leo Daly, Beryl F. Dean, Count Anthony de la Poer, Pat Dillon, Sylvia Dockeray, Mary Doyle, Jean Egan, William Ellis, Rosemary ffolliott, Mr and Mrs Patrick Finegan, Eileen Fitzharris, Orla Flynn, Margaret Franklin, Alan Gilmer, P.M. Ging, the Knight of Glin, Roger Greene, Hon. Desmond Guinness, Colette Hatton, Margaret Hogan, John R. Holohon, Michael Hurley, Mark Jenkinson, Frank Keohane, Ina Larkin, Elsie Layton, Ishbel Lee, Prof. Ralph Loeber, Joy Mawhinney, Donal McCarthy, John McCullen, Michael McElligott, Margaret Sheil McNally, Fonsie Mealy, Chris

Miller, Esther Molony, William Montgomery, Joe Murray, Martin Nevin, Freddie O'Dwyer, J.J.D. O'Leary, Treasa Orbney, Dr A.J.F. O'Reilly, Padraig Ó Snodaigh, Jimmy O'Toole, Otho and Myra Perrott, Rosalie Pickering, Anita Puigcerver-Rumbold, Ruth and Alan Rankin, Martin Reynolds, John Martin Robinson, the Earl of Roden, Peter Rowan, Bernardine Ruddy, Brendan Scally, Colin Scudds, Joan Sharkey, James Shaw, Elaine Skehan, Sarah Sherlock, Ben Simon, Dr David Sowby, Frank Taaffe, John Tierney, Maura Toler-Aylward, Peggy Walpole, Patrick Walsh, Finola Watchorn, Helena Williams and Maura Windrim.

To this majority of generous individuals who replied to my queries down the years, some of whom have sadly since passed away, my sincere thanks. From a minority I have not yet given up hope of response.

As relief from countless bed and breakfast accommodations I will cherish memories of hospitality from Julia and Tony Cooper and from Veronica and David Rowe. I am doubly indebted to David, and also to Eithne Scallan, for giving so freely of their knowledge of the Wexford country house.

I would like to thank Nick Maxwell for initially taking on this project and for guiding it through the later stages, as well as Emer Condit for her editing work and Cillian Dunne for his work on the illustrations.

But the person to whom I owe so much is Michelle McGaughey, who single-handedly transformed transient handwritten notes into an immaculate word-processed text.

Finally, to my wife Lynne, who has patiently lived with this for many years and will now realise a blessed release, my thanks.

INTRODUCTION

In 1995 the Ulster Architectural Heritage Society published *The gate lodges of Ulster: a gazetteer*, a comprehensive catalogue of that building in the northern province. This was prompted by its alarming and continuing loss and a consequent urgent need to record it for posterity and, in so doing, hopefully encourage awareness of what had become taken for granted. Subsequently the author, in the absence of any reciprocal survey of Connacht, Leinster or Munster, was convinced of the logic of preparing volumes to cover the gate lodges of the whole island. These should likewise be in a format similar to that of Mark Bence-Jones's *A guide to Irish country houses*. Just as these little structures served as introductions to those country houses, so could this series of books be considered as companions to that invaluable work. Besides such motivation, travelling the highways and particularly the byways of the Irish countryside had become an increasing delight in its revelations of hidden treasures, with the expectation around the next corner of a surviving lodge nestling at the secondary gate to a stately home or entrance to a gentry farmhouse. But the reality was that only four out of ten lodges in Leinster indicated on the first-edition Ordnance Survey map of the 1830s or 1840s had survived, and it was realised that a detailed survey and record of this fascinating little building had to be completed in the face of continuing losses, albeit 50 years late.

A further incentive for producing a series of books on the porters' lodges in the four provinces was to right a wrong, for to date they have received scant notice, being in the shadow of the big house—the subject of an endless pre-Christmas release of tomes, some academic. Reference to the lodge is decidedly sparse in publications on general or domestic architecture in Ireland—remarkable, considering the precocity of many. Dr Maurice Craig, for example, that doyen of architectural historians, in his highly acclaimed *The architecture of Ireland* affords but half a page out of 325 to gate lodges. One has to resort to a delightful contribution by Rosemary ffolliott in the *Irish Ancestor* magazine in 1971 and a chapter in James Howley's splendid *The follies and garden buildings of Ireland* to find anything meaningful.

So this is an attempt to give this building type the exposure it deserves: to correct a disparity in print between it and its big house and help grant it the status it deserves in the context of Ireland's architectural heritage and within the greater complex of buildings to which it is, or was, a conspicuous prelude, be it to a noble mansion, gentry villa, farmhouse or rectory, or to a cemetery, workhouse, lunatic asylum, convent, school, hospital or town park.

The same principle applies in an attempt to recognise, in addition to those whom they served, the anonymous 'little people' who inhabited these little structures—the porter, or gatekeeper, identified by name in the main from the mid-nineteenth century in the Griffith Valuation, revealed particularly in the greater Dublin area.

The fieldwork and research for Connacht, Leinster and Munster were progressed concurrently, to permit early comparative analysis. Without that approach the identity, for instance, of the architect for the porters' lodges to Kilmurry (Kilkenny) and Bellegrove (Laois)—or, indeed, the designer of that to Ballindoolin (Kildare)—might not have been known had not *The gate lodges of Ulster* survey already been completed, although that volume did not benefit from such cross-referencing.

As a consequence, such has been the duration of the preparatory work for these books, between when surveys were commenced in 1996 and dates of publication, that inevitably much has altered and any feedback on change of conditions, or indeed omissions or discrepancies, would be welcomed.

To Irish travellers gate lodges were, and remain, an omnipresent architectural form. Whether at the entrances to great houses, villas or institutions, they signalled to the passer-by the wealth, prestige and taste of their creators. That the gate lodge is a distinct building type in its own right is plain to see, located as it is in full public view, exhibiting more than any other a wider spectrum of architectural styles. By 1811 T.D.W. Dearn in his *Designs for lodges and entrances* already considered them, 'although of minor importance on account of their size, [to be] nevertheless of much consequence, when considered as affecting the character of a place, to which they serve as an introduction'. Just like their larger counterparts, to which they are a prelude, this most modest of forms appears as everything from a vernacular manifestation to being clothed in the most extravagant architectural finery. It is extraordinary the variety of guises taken on by this most basic of structures, clad by the expert—or not so expert—hands of countless architects to distinguish one from another throughout the province.

Whilst those lodges identified in Ulster highlighted their greater proliferation relative to numbers in England and Wales, this in no way prepared one for their abundance in Leinster. Statistics can be revealing and relevant; whereas in excess of 2,100 lodges were identified in the northern province, which equated to about one every 10km^2, Leinster far exceeded this in its 4,285 lodges at one per 4.6km^2, more than double the density. While the greater instance of lodges in Ireland as a whole compared to those in Britain can be explained by our relatively complex roads network, particular security needs and, indeed, tradition, Leinster contained in that period, when lodge-building was at its height, the second city of Empire, a capital which was the administrative, political and commercial centre of the country. Hence it held the main concentration of population, major landowners, gentry and aristocracy. There were in excess of 1,600 lodges in the relatively small county of Dublin alone, which shows one per 0.5km^2 compared to a lodge every 7km^2 in the other eleven counties of Leinster, or 38% of the total in the province.

That there was such a profusion of porters' lodges in the Dublin outskirts was already evident by 1813, when John Curwen on tour recorded that 'An attempt even to notice all the splendid residences, and highly ornamental villas, which we have seen in the course of this day's circuit of thirty miles, would fill a volume'. He also, however, went on to observe that 'The contrast between affluence and poverty in this country is a matter of perpetual unpleasant observation. A noble mansion is approached by a dilapidated lodge, tenanted by poverty—it was wonderful that such incongruities can be suffered, and not felt by those who could so easily correct them.' This could well account for the state of many of the late eighteenth-century lodges in the Dublin suburbs and explain their considerable losses. This privation seems to have been addressed, however, if their numerous Victorian replacements are anything to go by. In any case, many of these Georgian properties of the landed gentry were by the mid-nineteenth century broken up into smaller lots to house the expanding professional and merchant classes. Land was at a premium and outlying villages such as Blackrock and Dundrum were developing at an extraordinary rate. Nearby, for example, the townland of Roebuck had become an enclave of villas predominantly of the legal fraternity, with as many as 40 porters' lodges to an equal number of fine residences of attorneys and barristers. In 1836 this had not been entirely to the liking of John d'Alton, who found that 'The beauty of these avenues is, however, overshadowed by the high walls topped with thick hedges, the close, tall wooden gates and concealed gatehouses, that give the whole a sombre unsocial appearance'.

Such areas no longer paint that picture of sombre beauty, more's the pity—walls, gatehouses and most of the villas swept away in a subsequent frantic demand for building land. Nowhere is this more evident than in the vicinity of Rathmines, from the Grand Canal southward, which the *Parliamentary Gazetteer* around 1845 records as 'a beautiful and rather large suburb ... it really commences at Portobello, and extends in a continuous line of nearly two miles in length to the vicinity of the Dodder. Over the greater part of its length, its houses are a continuous series of handsome villas and splendid mansions, of every description of fancy construction, from the modern castellated pile, to the Italianate villa or the modest cottage ornée.' Of these and their obligatory protective porters' lodges almost nothing survives. So was lost almost a lifetime of Georgian lodges; not a single little Classical temple, Gothic cottage or 'inkpot' survives by the Dublin roadside, though there emerged a whole new generation of Victorian lodges for a *nouveau riche*. These assumed less of a defensive role, rather becoming increasingly a status symbol in which to house a coachman or gardener, gate chores being left to a dutiful wife. But the demand for land remained insatiable, as it does to this day, with the consequent loss of many later lodges, the magnitude of which is revealed by statistics. In Dublin city and county south of the River Liffey, 1,109 gatekeepers' lodges identified have been reduced to 330, a loss of 70%, whereas beyond this area the losses range from 'only' 40% in County Wicklow to 52% in counties Longford and Offaly.

On roads radiating out into the country from Dublin city centre one can see clearly the reasons for the demise of the landed estate and its buildings, with the widespread hunger for building land resulting in largely uncontrolled redevelopment in the second half of the twentieth century. Consequential has been the upgrading of the roads network, with realignment severing long-established properties and widening sweeping away stone boundary walls, entrances and their lodges. Beyond in rural Leinster, although the losses are less severe, up to half of lodges have succumbed; many that survive do so in ruinous condition or in various stages of dereliction, having been neglected, perhaps, in hopes of gaining planning approval for a replacement dwelling.

The gate lodge has been a familiar, welcome and once commonplace sight, signalling with its attendant entrance screen and protective walls in wooded setting another landed estate, some of which boasted more than one such access and others having multiple gates. None was more remarkable than the now devastated demesne of Belan (Kildare), the mansion on which was approached via no fewer than a dozen lodges, in the form of six pairs, each octagonal in plan, but of which there is but one forlorn derelict survivor as evidence of a money-sapping folly-building venture of the 4th earl of Aldborough. No less impressive was the Bessborough (Kilkenny) estate for the earls of that name with its ten lodged gates, here rather more functional in being built to house estate workers. The eight lodges to Luttrellstown (Dublin N) and Lough Crew (Meath) largely survive, in the latter case outliving their big house. Whereas landowners in County Monaghan sought to outdo one another in quality and quantity of lodges to their properties, there is no such evidence of this in Leinster. Pakenham Hall (Westmeath) was guarded by nine gatekeepers, perhaps in response to what Arthur Young discovered of the tendency of the lower classes here in 1776: 'They steal everything they can lay their lands on

... Gates will be cut in pieces and conveyed away ... Good stone out of a wall will be taken for a firehearth, etc. ... such was the need for vigilance.' The Anglo-Irish landlord was always at risk from disaffected tenantry, particularly at his gates.

A relative calm which visited the country after the Battle of the Boyne saw the establishment of many of these landed estates or their expansion with attendant lodges, and continued largely unabated despite the tribulations of the 1798 Rebellion and the Act of Union in 1800. In fact, the latter prompted a building programme from 1801 to 1821, when the Board of First Fruits granted monies to assist in a huge improvement in church and rectory stock of the Established Church with their attendant lodges of both sextons and gate porters, although these were of such meagre dimensions and inferior construction that few survive. Although the Great Famine effectively put the brakes on country house-building in the mid-nineteenth century, a slump which put many Irish architects out of business, it was not sufficient to affect gate lodge construction, for this continued undiminished, doubtless along with estate wall-building as a relief measure. Sadly, this did not seem to have the intention of providing accommodation, as many lodges lay vacant over this period—in the townland of Scholarstown (Dublin S), for example, all four lodges to separate holdings in 1849 lay empty.

The big house and its lodged gate in rural Leinster faced problems different from those of their suburban Dublin counterparts. The agricultural depression of the 1880s and consequent agrarian troubles left the nobility and gentry even worse off than they had been in the years which followed the Famine, and they were finally ruined by the later Land Acts. This was followed successively by the uncertain political situation, with the controversy over Home Rule, the Great War (1914–18), the struggle for independence (1919–21) and the Civil War (1922–3), when many Irish country houses were burnt, and finally the abandonment of many a big house in a bid to save on rates. All of this had a dramatic impact on the fate of the gate lodge, which, along with other estate buildings, often perished with its big house.

Examples of such are tragically common throughout the country, seen in the likes of Rathescar Lodge (Louth) and Gaulston Park (Westmeath), which have been lost with all four of their gates lodges, while at Belcamp Park (Dublin N), Landscape (Dublin S) and Camolin Park (Wexford) neither a trace remains of these houses nor of the three lodges at each of their gates.

There are, of course, notable exceptions to this trend where some trace of a once-thriving landed estate does remain; the lost house of Lough Crew (Meath) is survived by all eight of its porters' lodges, but conversely Coolamber Manor (Longford) outlives its four.

Where the gate lodge has not fallen foul of roadworks, urban spread, the ignorance of the planner or the avarice of the developer, then the tinker has got the lead and the vandal or arsonist will finish the job. This greed of the developer or landowner blinds him to the potential for practical rehabilitation and extension of these little structures. True, the meanness of scale of the basic early single-storey standard lodge does not appear to lend itself to restoration and enlarging, but contrary to this common perception it is possible to rehabilitate it to meet modern living standards without compromising its integrity, provided that some simple rules are observed. Modernisation need not be clinical; re-rendering an extension should not mean sharp arises, replacement materials should not be synthetic and, above all, avoid plastic. Extensions need not blindly replicate original materials, detailing or style—some of the more successful and sensitive additions are in completely contrasting styles but crucially to the integrity of the original structure realise a visual break with the new. Sensitivity is the key and there are many professional architects proven in the restoration field prepared to advise on discriminating rehabilitation. There are exemplars in the suburbs of south Belfast which prove that there is no good reason why a modest standard lodge cannot be incorporated into a greater scheme of things. It does, though, take less imagination to extend satisfactorily the later Victorian lodge, with its informal plan, irregular outline and relative generosity of scale.

Alternatively, there are admirable instances of porters' lodges being lovingly and effectively maintained as eye-catchers by the gates or functioning as practical buildings ancillary to the main house. Commendably, just such can be found at Clareen (Offaly), Rathvinden (Carlow) and most admirably in that sweet little lodge to Fosterstown (Meath), which survives in pristine condition despite its thatched roof and considerable antiquity.

After decades of equivocation, and hopelessly late to save many of our finest buildings, the government eventually displayed some concern for the architectural heritage when legislation designed to protect and preserve it was passed in 2000. This made it incumbent upon owners not to endanger selected structures through damage or neglect. Regrettably, thirteen years on, in the financial climate at the time of writing there is no monetary incentive available to back that up and, despite the rare example of an enlightened proprietor, generally the decline in the condition of the gate lodge continues relentlessly. Just how ineffectual such legislation is proving can be appreciated by the recent collapse of the internationally important Belline (Kilkenny) 'Primitive Greek Hut' lodge despite warnings by the Irish Georgian Society of its serious decline eight years in advance.

Nevertheless, it is fervently hoped that this gazetteer will go some way towards raising awareness of the gate lodge and helping to arrest the decline in its numbers.

IMAGE REPOSITORY

The publisher has set up an area on his website to facilitate those who want to see larger, more detailed versions of the images used in the gazetteer of this book. It is not intended as a replacement or an alternative to the book and only the images will be available there. They appear exactly as the author has supplied them.

To view any of the images in the book, you will need the reference number that appears with the entry.

To proceed
First log into http://wordwellbooks.com/gatelodges/ by typing this into the address line of your web browser.

How to find an image
You will need the gate lodge reference number and county name. For example, the gate lodge at Bagenalstown, Co. Carlow, is referenced as No. 2 in the Carlow gazetteer. To view it via this page, you should type **Carlow-2** [CountyHyphenNumber] in the finder window on the page and the image will appear. *Typing **Bagenalstown** will not find the image.*

Where there is more than one entry per site in the book, for instance **29. Duckett's Grove**, the first image that appears in that listing can be found by entering **Carlow-29a**, the second by entering **Carlow-29b** and so on.

For gate lodges in Dublin South, type **Dublin South-**[number]. For gate lodges in Dublin North, type **Dublin North-**[number]. For example, **364. Whitestown, Balbriggan** should be entered as **Dublin North-364**, and for **4. Abbey Ville, Rathfarnham** type **Dublin South-4**.

Copyright notice

A HISTORY OF THE GATE LODGE IN LEINSTER

The gate lodge, in the interests of facility and clarity, can be considered to have developed in three forms: the pierced gatehouse tower; the single sentry-box; twin pavilions.

THE PIERCED GATEHOUSE TOWER

Leaving aside many earlier tenuous precedents for the lodge, the most immediate and relevant source was the medieval gatehouse, which evolved when defensive earthen banks were replaced by tall curtain walls and was created as a highly defended and attended structure at the point of access to the bailey and its keep within. With its battlements and machicolations it was to become a favourite model for Victorian reproductions based on the likes of the medieval gatehouses to the castles of Carlingford (Louth), its gateway framed by lofty rectangular structures, and Ballyloughan (Carlow), with its twin round towers flanking the arched gateway reflected in an entrance to Charleville Forest (Offaly, *c.* 1800). So, too, can the massive gatehouse at Trim Castle (Meath) be seen to have influenced the village entrance to Borris (Carlow, *c.* 1813) 600 years later—a pierced gatehouse tower.

THE SINGLE SENTRY-BOX

But the simplest and most instantly recognisable manifestation of the porter's lodge is, alongside its gate, that two-roomed, three-bay, single-storey cottage [**Fig. 1**], probably derived from the vernacular Irish three-roomed, four-bay peasant cabin [**Fig. 2**] but given a degree of sophistication in an invariably more considered symmetrical main front with central doorway, more often than not hip-roofed. This was to appear in numerous guises in whatever architectural styles were in fashion at that point in time, perhaps worthy of the big house beyond. So, too, was it built as often in a basic unadorned vernacular form at the entrances to properties of the gentry or prosperous farmer, the example at Plantation, Co. Meath [**Fig. 3**] being archetypal, standard and once commonplace. These little buildings were to become over two centuries the most familiar, accessible and admired in the Irish countryside, so common as to be taken for granted.

TWIN PAVILIONS

A precedent for the twin-lodged gate can be traced more readily, however, than its single counterpart. Certainly more pretentious, it was to recur down the years as the most conspicuous estate entrance, as many as one in ten being of that form. A 1738 painting of the access to the

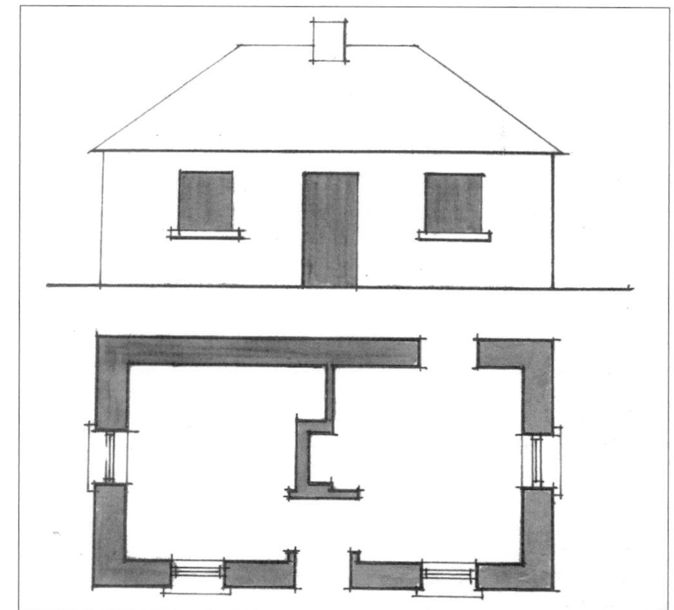

Fig. 1

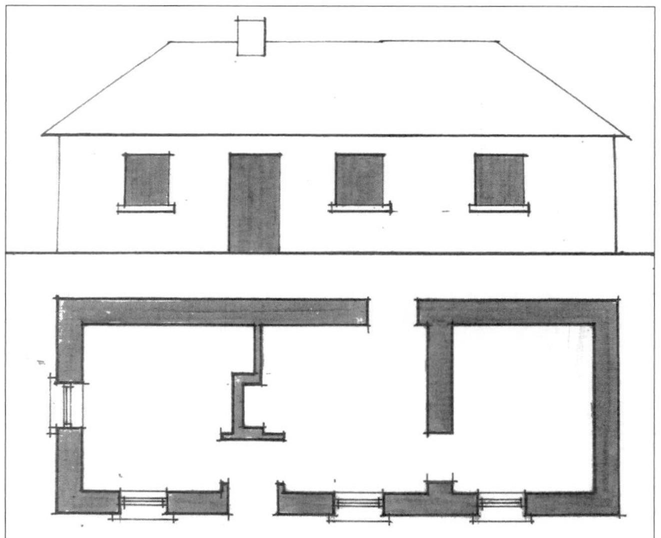

Fig. 2

Fig. 3

Ulster Museum

Fig. 4

Ulster Museum

Fig. 5

forecourt of Carton (Kildare), on an axis with the front door of the Queen Anne mansion, shows a pair of little cubic sentry-boxes with pyramidal roofs flanking the ornamental gateway [**Fig. 4**]. They would appear to be purely decorative garden ornaments were it not for chimney-stacks rising from their side walls, indicating a more permanent function as accommodation. This was the sort of arrangement to be found more frequently in the relative calm which visited the country after the Williamite wars, prior to which, as in England, the evidence for park gate lodges is almost entirely absent in the first quarter of the eighteenth century. Likewise, a bird's-eye view of Stradbally Hall (Laois) of *c.* 1740 reveals another early pair of single-storey hip-roofed structures by the village gate [**Fig. 5**], but here sited on a less formal approach, an arrangement also visible on John Roque's map of 1756 at estates in the vicinity of Swords (Dublin N) at Forrest House, Forrest Town House, Lissen Hall and Little Lissen Hall. All these are things of the past, but at Bellevue (Wexford, *c.* 1740) a pair of very early rustic Palladian lodges now preside ruinous over a field gate.

THE ESTATE WALL

By that date, though, Roque shows the Carton sentry-boxes to have gone, and his later map and vignette of 1760 reveal them to have been replaced by two separate porters' lodges at a distant boundary wall, a clue that by the mid-eighteenth century the aristocracy were expanding and enclosing their estates of many hundreds and thousands of acres with tall, remote stone walls, to contain livestock and deter extraneous elements. In 1738 just such an enclosure was being erected by Sir William Fownes about his Woodstock (Kilkenny) property next to Inistioge village, while the Cox family were building an 11ft-high perimeter wall at nearby Castletown Cox (Kilkenny) at about this time, both conscious that such remote new entrances should be monitored by a permanent presence. Thus was born both a new building type in the gate lodge and a new occupation in the gate porter.

The progression of the gate lodge from its initial function of defence and vigilance to being a fashion statement in the space of 150 years will become apparent.

THE GATE PORTER

It was imperative that this new position be entrusted to a dependable person, preferably a faithful family retainer such as a retired butler. He was required to be vigilant and in permanent attendance, competent to monitor visitors and to recognise those to whom he should open or close the gates. Those gates were there to ensure the retention of livestock and at the same time to deter extraneous elements. The byways of Leinster were constantly frequented by tramps and vagabonds. Arthur Young in 1776 found that Lord Longford at Pakenham Hall (Westmeath) was plagued by the pilfering of local peasantry:

'They steal everything they can lay their hands on, and I should remark, that this is an account which has been very generally given me. All sorts of iron hinges, chains, locks, keys, etc. Gates will be cut in pieces, and conveyed away in many places as fast as built. Trees as big as a man's body, and that would require ten men to move, gone in a night. Lord Longford has had the new wheels of a car stolen as soon as made. Good stones out of a wall will be taken for a fire hearth, etc., though a breach is made to get at them. In short, everything, and even such as are apparently no use to them, nor is it easy to catch them, for they never carry their stolen goods home, but to some bog hole.'

By 1837 things were clearly more relaxed, for Samuel Lewis discovered at Glynsouthwell (Dublin S) 'the seat of C.B. Ponsonby, Esq., by whom the grounds are thrown open for the inspection of visitors', and around 1840 Mr and Mrs S.C. Hall reported from Ballycurry (Wicklow) that 'Mr Tottenham requires that all visitors shall leave their names at his lodge where an order for admission into the glen is given by the lodge-keeper, a kindly and gossiping dame in whose company the stranger may pass a few minutes very profitably'. Not all was sweetness and light by the gate, though, for Whitelaw in his Census of 1821 found that 'Tyrone House of the Marquis of Waterford was inaccessible from the rudeness of the porter'. W.M. Thackeray in 1842 revealed the disadvantages to the proprietor of hospitality at his gates, whereby at Duninga (Kilkenny) 'the good-natured practice of the country admits a beggar as well as any other visitor. To a couple our landlord gave money, to another a little job of work; another he sent roughly out of the premises: and I would judge thus what a continual tax upon the Irish gentleman these travelling paupers must be, of whom his ground is never free.' Twenty years later Thomas Lacy recorded at Hollybrook (Wicklow) 'the fine seat of Sir George F.J. Hodson, Bart., the beautiful demesne of which is open to respectable strangers, on writing their names and addresses in the visitors' book, which is kept at the gate-lodge'. So keeping a visitors' book could be a duty additional to that of receiving deliveries by the gate, such as that from the post-chaise, according to T.D.W. Dearn in 1811, a role 'usually intended, either for an old man, an old woman, or both, or for a mother and daughter; in short for anything but a family group of small children, though occasionally picturesque in a situation like this, is not, on the whole desirable'. This ideal soon fell by the wayside, as many large families were to be raised in the confines of these little two-roomed lodges.

The Georgian and early Victorian gate porter remained largely anonymous, but it was his vulnerability in a location as first line of defence that identified one in tragic circumstances. In March 1798 the occupant of the lodge to Rathgar Mansion (Dublin S), Daniel Carroll, a gardener, was brutally murdered by three men. Whether he was the main target is not clear, but what it does highlight is that the role of gatekeeper there may have been filled by a dutiful wife. Certainly by the second half of the nineteenth century lodges built to the numerous new merchants' villas in the Dublin suburbs were becoming little more than status symbols, being within a stone's throw of the main house and occupied by a gardener, coachman or, in the case of The Ochra (Dublin S), the cook. By then gatekeepers, particularly in the vicinity of the capital, were being identified thanks to the Griffith Valuation of the 1850s, which is revealing. Even given that the surname Byrne was common in Leinster, it must be significant that no fewer than 39 of them were named as gate porters in the greater Dublin area and north Wicklow, suggesting that their role was one of some respectability and pride, becoming a family tradition and probably passed down from father to son. Similarly revealing was that only one of that name was female.

THE EARLY GEORGIAN ENTRANCE

The more prosperous gates of the early eighteenth-century period, mostly then unattended, were of exuberant curvilinear Baroque wrought iron which closed against scroll-topped stops integral with soaring pillars of layers of V-jointed rusticated masonry with exaggerated oversailing cornices. Such surviving ironwork is thin on the ground, but County Kildare can still boast fine examples in the beautiful gatescreen to Castle Martin (*c.* 1745) and those taken from Belan (*c.* 1730) to be re-erected at Carton but separated from their monumental ball-finialled pillars. Remarkable, too, for its survival is the almost intact gatescreen to Shankill Castle (Kilkenny, *c.* 1720), which was significantly lodgeless.

As early as 1740, proprietors were inviting architects of eminence to provide designs for lodges to impress at their gates; most of those commissioned before the end of that century are identified as being of English or Scottish extraction. Home-grown architects tended to remain anonymous and many lodges are the creations of amateurs or jobbing builders. The most notable of these immigrant practitioners with a huge country house practice was the talented Richard Castle, who in the 1740s for the Celbridge Collegiate School and probably nearby Longtown House, both in County Kildare, produced pairs of Palladian pedimented lodges with lunette windows linked by grand carriage archways. Not surviving is his porter's accommodation to the Rotunda Lying-In Hospital (Dublin N, *c.* 1786), which was little more than a convenient function given to one of its grand pavilions to stop one of the colonnades leading from what in essence was a design for one of his grand country mansions. At Russborough (Wicklow, *c.* 1745) his sturdy rusticated triple archway was lodgeless, but not so Kildare (Dublin S, *c.* 1745), where his design to the forecourt incorporated porter's accommodation. This was distinguished on its public face by heavily reticulated masonry much beloved of the period, to be found elsewhere as alternate blocks gracing the early bow-fronted pair of lodges to Lucan (Dublin S, *c.* 1760), the triple archway to the Provost's House (Dublin S, *c.* 1760) and Scottish architect James Gibbs's magnificent entrance pillars at Newbridge (Dublin N, *c.* 1752), from which rise Cobbe family pelicans out of ducal coronets.

THE MID-GEORGIAN ENTRANCE

Many such crests were to crown entrance pillars of the nobility, none better than the Caulfield dragons atop those of the gates to the once-superb Marino (Dublin N, *c.* 1768) demesne designed for the earl of Charlemont by that other leading Scot Sir William Chambers, the friezes to whose pillars also feature wonderful sculpted bucrania. This gatescreen, much admired by George IV on a visit to Dublin, was later to gain a flanking pair of neo-Classical lodges, since removed. Lord Burlington's *c.* 1730 design for chunky piers at the entrance to Castletown Celbridge (Kildare, 1783) as adapted by Chambers displays prominent swag motifs, but without a contemporary porter's lodge. At Mosstown (Longford, *c.* 1760) was a resplendent pair of eagles, but generally finials to entrance pillars in the mid-Georgian period were the hospitable pineapples, pine cones or simple balls on pedestals to be seen on the recently restored exceptionally tall and elegant pillars to Syngefield (Offaly, *c.* 1760), now lodgeless. Similarly popular was the vase, or urn, to be found in extraordinary variety from the clumsy to the dainty, the best of the latter apparent in those that grace the double-lodged entrance to Ravensdale (Kildare, *c.* 1785), which had a twin at Killester Abbey (Dublin N, *c.* 1785), both probably by the Cork-born Thomas Ivory.

THE LATE GEORGIAN ENTRANCE

English architects continued to settle here in the later eighteenth century; those who thrived included James Gandon, Thomas Cooley and Samuel Woolley. Gandon is chiefly known for his public buildings but did have a limited country house clientele. Notable is his Classical archway and precocious flanking twin lodges for the Gleadowe-Newcomen family at Carrigglass (Longford, *c.* 1800), now neglected and overgrown. Still evident in the spandrels of the arch is his trademark draped disc motif, also intended to decorate an arched gateway to Emo Court (Laois, *c.* 1780), designs for which remain unexecuted.

Thomas Cooley, before his early demise in 1784, was no less able a practitioner, his work surviving as rather reticent astylar boxes by his gates to Ardbraccan (Meath, *c.* 1772) and its offspring by Francis Johnston at Rokeby Hall (Louth, *c.* 1788), which contrast with his little Georgian Gothic affair at Mount Kennedy (Wicklow, *c.* 1784), where he acted as executant architect to the eminent James Wyatt, who, for all his involvement in Irish domestic architecture, has no lodges positively attributable to him in the province save perhaps at the devastated demesne of Baronstown (Westmeath, *c.* 1800), which has Wyatt-designed Coade stone urns to the gate pillars of one entrance. Samuel Woolley, the least known of these adopted architects, despite providing his clients with many fine villas about the country will always be remembered for that remarkable lodgeless Classical gatescreen to Glenanea (Westmeath, 1796) for the Smith family, although his source for this was a plate in Robert Adam's *The works in architecture* (1778). Sadly, this showcase for Mrs Coade's stone was truncated in removal to a new site at nearby Rosmead in the same county, where it was subsequently horribly vandalised. Woolley offered the same design unsuccessfully as an introduction to Seaforde House (Down, *c.* 1798).

This newfangled and durable material which was Coade stone became a mass-produced face of neo-Classicism in the late Georgian era, to embellish the façades of buildings throughout the British Isles and beyond. It was similarly embraced by Irish landowners, reducing the call for masons and sculptors, being applied as it was in a huge range of details both to order and off the shelf. Mrs Eleanor Coade of Lambeth's products were imported to be seen in those fine strigillated and festooned urns at Baronstown (Westmeath, *c.* 1800), two beautiful sphinxes which probably adorned entrance piers at Pakenham Hall (Westmeath, 1799), and in more modest applications as draped paterae at Lucan (Dublin S, *c.* 1780) and floral discs on the friezes to pillars at Furness (Kildare, *c.* 1790).

Otherwise the majority of late eighteenth-century estate entrances displayed crisply chiselled examples of the stonemason's craft. Generally these pillars tended to be less monumental than their predecessors (an exception in County Meath being the massive pillars to Headfort) but compensated in embellished friezes, none better than those exhibited by Thomas Cooley's design at Ardbraccan (Meath, *c.* 1772) with its swags and paterae, whilst at Drewstown (Meath, *c.* 1775) for the same Maxwell family they display a Greek key pattern over rusticated shafts, all topped by ball-finialled cappings, much as the architect provided for the archiepiscopal palace (Armagh, 1771). These are all tripartite gateways, whereas entrances of the period were more commonly comprised of a carriage gateway with understated ironwork, with tall pillars flanked by stone or harled straight screen walls containing postilion openings with architraved surrounds.

THE STANDARD LODGE

By the turn of the nineteenth century the Irish countryside was already conspicuous for an instantly recognisable new breed of building by the roadside guarding gates to distant mansions, villas and farmhouses, commonly in the form of a simple harled and limewashed rectangular single-storey cottage with symmetrical three-bay front below a shallow-pitched slated hipped roof with central chimney-stack, generally without any embellishment. These early examples have what was to be a recurring standard plan form of two rooms, for living and sleeping, accessed by a tiny entrance hall, some having ladder access to restricted lofts, but lacking any attached sanitary arrangement. This endured as archetypal for a century or more throughout the country, varying only in dimensions.

Some of the smaller and more spartan lodges, which ironically showed little Christian regard for human comfort, were those built as sextons' or porters' accommodation as part of the great building programme prompted by substantial sums voted from 1801 to 1833 through the Board of First Fruits to the Established Church to complement their churches and rectories.

THE VERNACULAR COTTAGE LODGE

Of a vernacular steeply pitched thatched-roof variant very few remain, owing to their vulnerability to the elements and shoddy maintenance. Those known to have endured seem to have survived thanks to an altruistic attitude of some neighbouring County Meath gentry who favoured the type. At Hamwood (1783) the thatch to the unusually commodious lodge was subsequently replaced by an equally uncommon plain clay tile finish, whilst the frailty of the material is emphasised at Spring Valley (*c.* 1810), where a period of 40 years of neglect has seen the structure of a once-charming landmark return to nature. It is the oldest of this trio, at Fosterstown (*c.* 1750), which ironically remains gloriously intact, sustained by years of loving care. Beyond the county there are other possible examples, subsequently slated but abandoned, at Auburn, Glassan (Westmeath, *c.* 1760), and Pigeon Park (Kilkenny, *c.* 1750), both antique in gate lodge terms with their minuscule openings asymmetrically arranged.

THE DEVIANTS

Practical plan as the rectangle proved to be, early OS maps reveal proprietors to have been at pains to deviate from the commonplace and to seek alternatives with novel and arresting forms by their gates—few of the solutions to which considered the convenience of the gatekeeper, although they did attract affectionate appellations.

Just such was the circular, or drum, lodge. A quaint variant, the impractical plan of the 'inkpot' proved to be its downfall and only one survives in the province, that charming but derelict two-roomed example at Dunkerrin Deanery (Offaly, *c.* 1790), its rareness demanding preservation. Another is recorded in an old illustration as having presided over an entrance by the River Liffey to Luttrellstown (Dublin N, *c.* 1770), complete with a conical thatched roof, which also capped a like lodge at Dangan Castle (Meath, *c.* 1770) that here rather bizarrely sported a sophisticated Doric entrance portico.

Almost as unfeasible, and likewise thin on the ground, was the hexagonal lodge, again there being but one survivor, a late example at Levally (Laois, *c.* 1780). In the same county James Shiel had unsuccessfully proposed a pair to his client at Woodbrook (*c.* 1820), whilst the rare brick-faced two-storey example crowned by a grand lantern at Kilkenny railway station (*c.* 1850) is no more.

Considerably more workable and thus relatively common was the octagonal plan, which can still be seen in single-storey form in a survivor of two originally at Brockley Park (Laois, *c.* 1810) and the sweet little example at Lark Lodge (Kildare, *c.* 1836), and barely surviving in duplicate at Ballyanne (Wexford, *c.* 1790). This was a form popularly flanking many gates in Leinster, with their octahedral roofs, often with central chimney-stacks, being particularly striking in two-storey form at Johnstown Castle (Wexford, *c.* 1825), probably by architect James Pain, once Gothic but now horribly Classicised. By unknown designers are two instances where but one of a pair survives: at Belline (Kilkenny, *c.* 1800), standing alone, its intended twin never having been realised, is a sturdy stone-built gatehouse, whilst the similar example at Belan (Kildare, *c.* 1770) is apparently the sole survivor of no less than six such pairs on the approaches to the earl of Aldborough's mansion. Considerably more convenient in plan is the extended octagon, to be found at Rathvinden (Carlow, *c.* 1820), which might otherwise be seen as a square lodge with canted ends.

The square-planned cubic lodge or 'tea caddy' was often used to conspicuous effect, and an early one survives with its pyramidal roof rising to a central chimney-stack at Furness (Kildare, *c.* 1790). This was a form much beloved of the Arts and Crafts designers of a century later.

A ROOM WITH A VIEW

Generally, however, the simple rectangular format reigned supreme, occasionally given a bow at one end, as at Stacumney (Kildare, *c.* 1790), at both ends at Mullagh (*c.* 1800) and Clonfin (*c.* 1820), Co. Longford, and as a central frontispiece in the hands of Francis Johnston at Lagore (*c.* 1800) and Galtrim (*c.* 1805), Co. Meath, and John Hargrave's Palmerston (Kildare, *c.* 1800). Likewise, his elegant lodges at Ballynegall (Westmeath, 1825) and Clifton Lodge (Meath, *c.* 1832) are very convenient for viewing comings and goings at their gates. Perversely, these convex viewing conveniences are here flanked by blind concave round-headed niches, a popular Classical device to relieve and ornament façades, which can be seen in triplicate on the remarkable now-ruined lodge at New Forest (Westmeath, *c.* 1800). The Victorian architect was soon to completely supplant the difficult-to-roof bow by the canted or semi-octagonal bay.

THE FRONTISPIECE

By far the most commonly employed features to enhance the main front of the standard lodge were a central projecting hall or an entrance breakfront, their gables often in the form of a pediment. This enrichment was taken a stage further to show the influence of the Grand Tour in the application of Classical columns, either engaged or in a portico of Roman or Greek origin in varying degrees of sophistication, depending upon the refinement of the client or the quality of his architect. The best of these can be viewed at Woodtown Park (Dublin S, *c.* 1835) in durable granite by an unidentified architect, Thomas Cobden's chaste designs in County Carlow at St Patrick's College (*c.* 1830) and Browne's Hill (1842), Francis Johnston's at Annesbrook (Meath, *c.* 1821), and William Farrell's identical porters' lodges to Kilmurry (Kilkenny, *c.* 1820) and Bellegrove (Laois, *c.*

1840) with their innovative circular porticos that he had also provided for Ely Lodge (Fermanagh, *c.* 1820), a design which he had borrowed from that known as 'Eagle Lodge' on the Blenheim Palace (Oxfordshire) estate. Also notable are the lodges gracing the entrances to Oakley Park (Meath, *c.* 1839) and Ballindoolin (Kildare, *c.* 1835), both attributable to William Vitruvius Morrison. A delightful and endearing little example of this genre is at Innismore (Dublin S, *c.* 1845), with its pairs of Doric columns flanking the doorway *in antis*. Experimental and eccentric variants in this Classical tradition exist at Killakee (Dublin S, *c.* 1835) and Gigginstown (Westmeath, *c.* 1855), where columns stand in external corner recesses, '*ex antis*' so to speak, an idiosyncrasy more common in Munster to a design by C.F. Anderson.

THE GEORGIAN GOTHIC ENTRANCE

A period between 1780 and 1820 was marked by the emergence of a Gothic Revival which vied with these Classical and astylar lodges for the landowners' affections. Sandwiched between the remarkable and effusive examples of the Batty Langley lodge at Castletown (Kildare, *c.* 1785) and James Pain's octagonal pair to Johnstown Castle (Wexford, *c.* 1825) emerged a considerable number of otherwise relatively modest little standard lodges identifiable by their lancet or pointed-arched openings invariably containing Y-traceried sash windows. The majority of survivors are to be found in County Wexford, engagingly at Hill Castle (*c.* 1805) and that opposite the gates to Bargy Castle (*c.* 1840) with its crenellated parapet. There, too, is a series of related lodges displaying pretty ogee arches to openings containing pretty intricate patterns to glazing and door panels. Those at Raheenduff, Long Graigue, Heathfield and Stokestown from around 1840 seem to descend from another at Ballycurry (Wicklow, *c.* 1825), which, if not attributable to Francis Johnston, must be of 'his school'. The Gothic was not a style confined to the standard single-storey cottage, for it was applied to a charming 1½-storey lodge at Belmount (Laois, *c.* 1800) and can be seen in the two-storey gatehouse to Woodville (Wexford, *c.* 1815). Similarly, the pairs of lodges flanking the gates to Barmeath (Louth, *c.* 1830) and Archerstown House (Westmeath, *c.* 1790) display the fashion. Perversely, most of these Gothic lodges tended to be attended by Classical gatescreens.

But Gothic gatescreens from the turn of the nineteenth century do exist, and impressively, such as those to Charleville Forest (Offaly, *c.* 1845), with its finely carved traceried panels, and, likewise accompanied by a Tudor Gothic lodge, as at Howth Castle (Dublin N, *c.* 1820), where Richard Morrison's lofty cluster-columned pillars delight. This was a design that he also provided for Portumna Castle (Galway, *c.* 1805) and Lismore Cathedral (Waterford, *c.* 1810), surely influenced by plates in Batty and Thomas Langley's *Gothic architecture, improved* (1747). Of the same genre are those at Clonyn Castle (Westmeath, *c.* 1800), here framed by screen walls with lancet postilion openings, and at Leixlip Castle (Kildare, *c.* 1800), where octagonal gate pillars are wrapped around with cluster-columns of pointed arcading which differ from one another only in the treatment of their cappings. These are clearly by the same as-yet-unidentified designer, both entrances sadly minus their original lodges. Later George Papworth was to conceive a spectacular entrance to Mount Jerome Cemetery (Dublin S, *c.* 1837), both gatescreen and lodge being in complementary Gothic.

Papworth was, with the likes of Daniel Robertson, Thomas Cobden and George Wilkinson, an immigrant British architect still plying his trade here, with thriving practices based on domestic commissions, but by the early nineteenth century the home-grown practitioner was realising an identity. Johnston, Farrell, Hargrave, William Robertson, Keane, Murray and Morrison were becoming household names and proving more than capable of competing alongside the intruder.

THE TEMPLE LODGE

But it is to the eminent Scots architect Sir William Chambers that one looks as a pioneer of the most exalted of structures in the Irish countryside. In a sleepy southern corner of County Kilkenny, hidden away remote from the entrance to Belline House is its main lodge (*c.* 1790) in the form of a Greek hut constructed of the most primitive and thus least durable of materials, evidenced by the recent collapse of its portico. Having been abandoned for many years, it urgently seeks a new function, the sporadic attempts thus far to halt its decline proving insufficient. Based upon such a structure illustrated in his *Treatise on civil architecture* and his commissions for the earl of Bessborough it is attributed to Chambers. It was to become the forerunner of a form of gate lodge in which Leinster is rich, there being any number to be seen in varying degrees of sophistication, all thankfully constructed in more lasting materials, for most have survived, though abandoned. Other than the rare Ionic example at Killua Castle (Westmeath, *c.* 1802), this temple lodge appears with little exception as Doric or Tuscan tetrastyle, ranging from the naive interpretations at New Pass (Westmeath, *c.* 1825) and Bennekerry (Carlow, *c.* 1840) through the charming example at Townley Hall (Louth, 1819), surely showing Francis Johnston's influence, to the splendid affair opposite the gates to the lost house of Lough Crew (Meath, 1825), a masterpiece of English architect C.R. Cockerell. But the two purest temples are those, each appropriately elevated on a height, at Castleboro (Wexford, *c.* 1825), probably by Daniel Robertson, and at Castlemorres (Kilkenny, *c.* 1840), doubtless a design of Sir Richard Morrison.

THE SOANE EFFECT

This temple lodge depended for its convincing effect upon the simple two-roomed, single-storey rectangular lodge being turned about 90° to enable a short elevation to become a showfront addressing the avenue. Morrison became an ardent purveyor of this form, developing it into the most innovative, unique and important series of lodges in the country. To what were now side elevations he added secondary projections in an entrance hall and balancing closet, effectively creating a cruciform plan and giving the whole a sense of solidarity. His inspiration was an illustration of a cottage from Sir John Soane's

Fig. 6

Sketches in architecture (1793) [**Fig. 6**], which he was to replicate at Castlecoole (Fermanagh *c.* 1835) and Killruddery (Wicklow, *c.* 1829). He would go on to develop a whole series of variants throughout Ireland, their common denominator being a wide tripartite window, which at Ballyfin (Laois, *c.* 1825) for the Coote family and for the Barrys at Fota (Cork, *c.* 1820) he was to recess behind an elegant neo-Classical frontispiece with a pair of Doric columns *in antis*, a configuration that he also presented at the gates to Somerville (Meath, *c.* 1835). It should be mentioned that the trouble with lodges as temples was that there were no Classical precedents for them being lived in—they needed to have windows and chimney-stacks. It was a problem that continually faced Greek Revival architects but was something that didn't concern the Morrisons greatly; they just condemned the gatekeeper and his family to half-light—a victory of aesthetics over amenity. Later this format was to appear in a series of choice *in antis* lodges, both in north County Dublin, from the board of the Office of Public Works architect Jacob Owen in the two little parapeted sentry-boxes to the National Model Schools (*c.* 1837) and a pair at the King's Inns (*c.* 1837), one of which has been demolished, its counterpart surviving with a tetrastyle entablatured breakfront, the columns with vermiculated bands below a balustraded parapet.

THE REGENCY ENTRANCE

Early in his country house career Richard Morrison had accompanied his porters' lodges with a gatescreen, instantly recognisable as his design, in an extensive low entrance of a pair of inner drum carriage pillars and flanking square postern piers creating a tripartite gateway framed by quadrant walls, as at Hyde Park (Wexford, *c.* 1805). But at the previously noted four properties and at Castlemorres (Kilkenny, *c.* 1840) he was again to reproduce another's design, in this case the distinctive and original composition from J.B. Papworth's *Rural residences* (1818) [**Fig. 7**], with its massive sculptural neo-Egyptian 'pylon' pillars and secondary iron posts recommended to carry the gates. This Morrison unashamedly replicated to the letter, only personalising it with his trademark laurel wreath motif or the proprietor's family crest. This was an arrangement subsequently more loosely interpreted by other local practitioners, particularly John McCurdy at Castleboro (Wexford, 1862) and Harristown (Kildare, 1864). It was no coincidence that the time of Morrison's conversion to the Papworth design around 1825 saw, too, the transition from the delicate wrought ironwork of the Georgian period to that of the chunkier cast iron of the Victorian era, with its less time-consuming manufacture and facility to reproduce complicated and repetitive motifs.

Fig. 7

THE REGENCY LODGE

This period in Ireland after the Union, for about 30 years during the Regency and into the reign of William IV, was one of intense building activity on the domestic scene, when landed estates were becoming profitable and the architecture was reflecting it. This was manifest in a sort of middling lodge, neither plain nor displaying the opulence of the Classical temple already noticed, but what can be labelled the Regency lodge, whereby the standard single-storey three-bay main front was expressed in a simple arcade, the openings framed in arched recesses, with the heads invariably segmental or semicircular, typically at Foulkscourt (Kilkenny, *c.* 1840) and Nurney (Kildare, *c.* 1835)—much as in the gentry villa of that time. At Luttrellstown (Dublin N, *c.* 1835) and the almost identical lodge at Middleton (Westmeath, *c.* 1845) the arched recesses are taken onto pedimented hall projections; they are carried about the faces of a semi-octagonal hall extension at Gaybrook (Westmeath, *c.* 1835), whereas at Landenstown (Kildare, *c.* 1825) the arches define the three-bay elevations of a pair which face each other across the access and their single-bay fronts, addressing the arrivals with perfect symmetry.

Just such balance is apparent in one of the most remarkable estate entrances in the country. But there the similarity ends, revealing a most singular composition wholly constructed with rocks to create a matching pair of square rooms below pyramidal roofs, linked by an archway surmounted by a bellcote bearing a date-stone. It is a sort of double grotto at the gates to Bracklyn Castle (Westmeath, 1821), the most understated of houses, and it significantly foresaw the beginnings of indifference to the old order of things.

This had been hinted at a decade earlier in a gate to the Luttrellstown demesne (Dublin N, *c.* 1810). Not unrelated to its Rustic Arch and certainly of that mood is this eccentric group of structures, bound by a common facing of boulders, two of which seem to have provided gatekeeper's accommodation but significantly distinctly asymmetrical. At Dunsany Castle (Meath, *c.* 1840), seemingly appended to an earlier plain lodge is the sole example in the province of a Romantic Rustic Ruin—built as such and remaining so, it is comprised of a decaying miniature keep alongside two Gothic archways as a gatescreen, reflecting the architecture of the old church of St Nicholas within the estate.

THE EARLY VICTORIAN GATESCREEN

Otherwise late Georgian, Regency and early Victorian gatescreens tended to be of equal spread to their predecessors but were generally of lower elevation. V-jointed rustication was less common, ashlar pillars often terminating in pedimented or gadrooned cappings or—the trend in counties Louth and Meath—concave-topped alternatives. Gone were the tall straight or concave walls sufficient to contain postern openings, to be replaced by triple gateways, their lower flanking walls permitting convex or ogee quadrants. Greater use was also made of cast iron in extensive screens, their railings terminating in spear, palmette or anthemion finials. An effective and conspicuous alternative throughout the country was what may be termed the trabeated gateway, where pedestrian archways double as carriage pillars, typical instances being at Corbollis (Louth, *c.* 1830), Kilmurry (Kilkenny, *c.* 1820) and Warrenpoint (Dublin N, *c.* 1845), where the brick-built gateways are crowned by sphinxes. The lost entrance screen at Baronstown (Westmeath, *c.* 1810) was particularly prominent for its great pedimented ashlar aedicule features, which separated postern and carriage openings.

THE SEARCH FOR SYMMETRY

Quite where the gate lodge should be sited relative to these gates was a dilemma for the Georgian client and his architect, their sensitivities leaning towards order and symmetry. Six out of ten did not address the problem, placing it deferentially within and aside—at least giving the porter a degree of protection, something which was not afforded him when, as was common, the lodge was located opposite on an axis with and facing the gate across the public road. Often, contours permitting, what appears from the entrance to be a standard single-storey cottage on duty is in fact raised off a basement storey, as in the two lodges at Kilknock (Carlow, *c.* 1850). There is no such disguise at Cronybyrne (Wicklow, *c.* 1850), however, where the upper floor is treated as a *piano nobile* and is approached via a flight of steps. Another response to the problem was an attempt to disguise the porter's accommodation as part of a quadrant of the gatescreen, it being pierced by windows monitoring the forecourt. All the surviving examples of this are Georgian Gothic: Neillstown (Dublin S, *c.* 1800), Ashfield (Laois, *c.* 1835) and the charming Rockbrook (Westmeath, *c.* 1800) entrance which is effectively located as a modest vista stop to the road from the village.

An ideal balance was achieved, however, at the accesses to the perfectly delightful gates at Kilranelagh (Wicklow, *c.* 1800), the once-splendid entrance to Ringwood (Kilkenny, *c.* 1790) for Lord Callan, and Decimus Burton's innovative octagonal lodge at the Knockmaroon gate to the Phoenix Park (Dublin N, 1838). Here the lodges are central to their complexes, flanked by pairs of gates and quadrant screens beyond—a logical and impressive solution, mysteriously rarely encountered in the province.

For those who could afford it, the ideal for symmetry, or duality, at their gates was the lodged pair or twin pavilions already noticed, either as an inconvenient 'day and night' arrangement—surely none more tedious for the gatekeeper than the distant detached cubic rooms at Bellevue (Wicklow, *c.* 1800), inviting the popular sobriquet 'salt and pepper'—or, as became more common and more social, twin independent family units. T.D.W. Dearn, despite revealing reservations in his *Designs for lodges and entrances* of 1811 ('It is often remarked, that a building, whether of a single room, stuck at each end of a gate, has something in it too trite and formal to be pleasing'), nevertheless offered four such designs. A recurring solution in the Georgian period, becoming less so in the nineteenth century, it was common to find the lodges linked by a central archway, as at the two entrances to Rossenara (Kilkenny, *c.* 1825) or Carrigglass (Longford, *c.* 1800), whereas the divided unit could be socially connected by a covered archway such as is to be seen at Courtown (Wexford, *c.* 1835). This superior arrangement is but one step away from the most desirable and prestigious grouping, whereby the gatekeeper's quarters are wholly integrated within an archway.

THE TRIUMPHAL ARCHWAY

In scale only to be challenged later by the Tudor Revival castellated gatehouse and a throwback to the grandeur of ancient Rome was this ultimate spectacle of power at the gates of the Irish landowner—the triumphal archway. Independent of its porter's accommodation, the earliest, most precocious and grandest of all graces the entrance to Kilkenny Castle (*c.* 1700) in an otherwise Medieval Revival complex, with its massive Corinthian pilasters, pedimented and swagged in Portland and Caen stone, built for £1,500 probably to designs of Sir William Robinson, all befitting a premier duke of the kingdom. Of little less moment and in the same Corinthian order, worth noticing again, was the ostentatious gateway by Samuel Woolley of almost a century later to Glenanea (Westmeath, *c.* 1796), for the Smiths, no less, now horribly mutilated. In Drogheda, by an unidentified architect stands a most pure archway now apparently superfluous, shorn of its lodge, avenue and demesne—Ballsgrove (Louth, *c.* 1810); it remains proud, with its ovoid niches and Greek key pattern in beautiful limestone ashlar. For sheer extent and portent nothing in the province exceeds the great triple archway to Browne's Hill (Carlow, *c.* 1763), with its endless railed screen, apparently designed by one Peters, lately dismantled stone by stone and rail by rail to be transported and reassembled at the entrance to Lyons (Kildare), leaving behind its little lodge, forlorn and gateless. Likewise receiving welcome care and attention at Saunders Court (Wexford, *c.* 1780) is the soaring cut-stone round-arched carriage opening below a pediment carried on pairs of engaged Tuscan columns, the whole flanked by brick-built screen walls and commodious pavilions—a creation perhaps of John Roberts, which through circumstances never did realise its intended purpose but endures as a forlorn folly.

To achieve convincing three-dimensional effect, however, the architect saw fit to create the porter's lodgings as integral to the structure as a whole. The Morrisons at Oakpark (Carlow, *c.* 1840) did not quite realise this in their giant overture to the Bruens' house, their entablatured archway carried by paired Ionic columns to the approach and Doric to the park raised off vast pedestals, where the accommodation is meagre in the extreme, housing little more than a sentry-box. The architects were later to acknowledge their meanness when presenting the same design for Baronscourt (Tyrone, *c.* 1838) and Castlecoole (Fermanagh, *c.* 1834) but the porters there to be accommodated in detached Classical temples—neither built. Two designs probably by Francis Johnston, one unexecuted at Charleville Forest (Offaly, *c.* 1810) and the other miraculously surviving city sprawl as the Dodder or Ely gate to Rathfarnham Castle (Dublin S, *c.* 1802), are of sufficient depth to afford twin two-storey gate porters' accommodation within the structures. Doubtless many a gatekeeper would have felt privileged to be associated with such prestigious living, so preferable to a peasant hovel. Nevertheless, his comfort remained of little priority; like the gate lodge in general, it was a case of the triumph of pretension—some would say the preposterous—over practicality. Such was the case at Kildare House (Dublin S, *c.* 1745), where Richard Castle's triumphal gateway to the great forecourt had bed space at first-floor level inconveniently complemented by a living room in a single-storey wing. Here the architect and his client were more conscious of public and private appearances, that to the house presenting a refined Tuscan columned front, contrasting with a more rustic Palladian elevation without.

THE 'DETACHED' LODGE

Nevertheless, no such qualms as to symmetry or public expression were of importance to the odd proprietor, there always being exceptions to the rule of the majority of landowners seeking to display their taste, power and affluence by their gates. There was the introvert who orientated his lodge as an object to be enjoyed solely from within his property—a park ornament such as at Clareen (Offaly, *c.* 1825) and Hazelbrook (Dublin N, *c.* 1820), where the lodges turn their backs discourteously upon neighbours, peers, visitors and passers-by. The twin of the latter lodge did, though, have his design rather more politely addressing the avenue to Bohomer (Dublin N, *c.* 1820). But for the ultimate essay in inhospitality the great impenetrable walled entrance to Lisnavagh (Carlow, *c.* 1849) would be difficult to surpass, its pair of lodges behind obscured from public prying.

An age was dawning that demanded ever-increasing architectural diversity, fuelled not least by an urge to upstage the neighbouring landowner, introducing further diverse curiosities into the Irish landscape.

THE PICTURESQUE

Symmetry was a quality that was soon dramatically to become of considerably less consequence. The reign of Queen Victoria in Ireland was to witness an extraordinary revolution in architectural attitudes. These saw the casting off of the old shackles of the Georgian traditions of order and formality and the embracing of a new era of wider choice and experimentation. There was born a more relaxed and informal thinking, aided and abetted by a medieval revival which became known as the Picturesque movement, realised in the resurrection of the Tudor and Jacobean styles manifest in the manners of the English manor house, an ornamental English cottage and the medieval English castle. This was a movement prompted by the thinking of Richard Payne Knight and Uvedale Price and put into practice by the likes of the architect John Nash. He had been pioneering it on the mainland with his, and the Reptons', Blaise Hamlet (Gloucestershire, 1809), with its exquisite decorative cottages, and his sham castles, which he had also designed for far-flung parts of Ireland from as early as 1802 in his Killymoon Castle (Tyrone) and its lodge (*c.* 1803). This movement was to be given further impetus by the phenomenon of the pattern-book.

THE PATTERN-BOOK

The influence of the architectural pattern-book has already been noticed from as early as that of Batty Langley, whose *Gothic architecture, improved* (1747) was the origin of the Conollys' Dublin lodge to Castletown (Kildare, *c.* 1785), and J. Miller's *The country gentleman's architect* (1787), which seems to have been the source for Thomas Owen's Maynooth gate at Carton (Kildare, *c.* 1810). The Kilkenny architect William Robertson was a rare practitioner to have found anything practical in Joseph Gandy's publications to reproduce, but did so in the charming front elevation to his lodges in his adoptive county at Jenkinstown (*c.* 1820), Kilfane (*c.* 1815), Tinny Park (*c.* 1812) and probably two at Castle Blunden (*c.* 1812), taken from Gandy's *Designs for cottages* (1805)

Fig. 8

[**Fig. 8**]. Later in his career Robertson was to turn to the 'standard' three-bay fronted lodge as introduction to his country house commissions, but this early seduction ran parallel to that of his contemporary Richard Morrison, who had initially, as has already been noticed [**Fig. 6**], been inspired by a design from an architect in whose office Gandy was an assistant. The *Sketches in architecture* (1793) of John Soane and J.B. Papworth's *Rural residences* (1818) were the origins for numerous lodges and gates about the country plagiarised by the Morrison office, Sir Richard and his son William Vitruvius, as well as their erstwhile assistant J.B. Keane. Few architects' offices or landowners' libraries were without a pattern-book on their shelves and the Victorian era saw no let-up in their issue, the majority of which now fuelled a passion for this newfangled Picturesque, with all manner of seductive 'chocolate box' perspectives, plans and elevations. Peter Frederick Robinson led the way with six publications which ran to umpteen editions, one of which of particular relevance was his *Designs for lodges and park entrances* (1833). Thomas Frederick Hunt was likewise prolific, and the lodge built at Glendalough (Wicklow, *c.* 1840) is a close interpretation of a design in his *Exemplars of Tudor architecture* (1830), perhaps as mishandled by executant architect Daniel Robertson, while James Thomson's *Retreats* (1827) was the source for the sweet little folly lodge at Newtown (Wexford, *c.* 1830). No pattern-book was more widely referred to by architects, proprietors and jobbing builders than the voluminous work that was John Claudius Loudon's *Encyclopaedia of cottage, farm and villa architecture* (1833), wherein he selected an abundance of designs by lesser-known practitioners, many specifically for cottages or gate lodges. One such can be identified as the quirky affair of W. and H. Laxton once at a gate to Ardgillan Castle (Dublin N, *c.* 1835).

Fig. 9

Conspicuously, all of these popular and influential volumes are from English or Scottish authors. Any that emanated from these shores, for whatever reason, are scarce, and the few that did made little or no impact upon the local architectural scene. Along with proposals for villas, Richard Morrison's *Useful and ornamental designs in architecture* (1793) offered one 'Design for a Gate Way or Entrance to a Park' [**Fig. 9**], a triumphal archway very much influenced by his erstwhile employer James Gandon, and Sir William Chambers before that. Like his contemporary practitioner, the aforesaid English-born William Robertson was unable to practise what he preached, for nothing from his *Designs in architecture* (1800) appears to have been executed, despite his having been a prolific lodge-builder in his numerous domestic commissions. The sophisticated designs therein comprise a couple of predictably symmetrical and grand neo-Classical entrances; one [**Fig. 10**], an octagonal lodge, is central to a pair of postilion

Fig. 10

Fig. 11

openings and carriage gateways, each with an innovative ironwork overthrow containing a lamp; the other [**Fig. 11**] is a triumphal archway, with vase atop, flanked by two bow-fronted porters' lodges. As a provincial architect, it seems that Robertson never attracted an appropriately affluent clientele for such elaborate proposals to be realised. On a more modest scale, the only replica discovered from Arthur Creagh Taylor's *Designs for agricultural buildings suited to Irish estates* (1841), despite an impressive list of subscribers, is the porter's lodge at an inner gateway to Whitewood Lodge (Meath, *c.* 1835).

BUILDING COSTS

Many of these books helpfully appended estimated costs of construction which varied 'depending upon embellishment', ranging from £255 to £490 as quoted by T.F. Hunt in his *Half-a-dozen hints* (1825), whereas Francis Goodwin's *Rural architecture* (1850) specifically advised prices for a Grecian-style lodge as follows:

Brick and Stucco	£380
Brick and Stone Dressing	£420
Stone	£560

Likewise, closer to home, Sir Richard Morrison offered entrances ranging from £150 to £350, to which could be added his professional fees of 5% of the building costs for a full service, with travelling expenses charged at a shilling per mile on top of that.

BUILDING MATERIALS

Goodwin may have been familiar with a ready availability of brick as a building material but in Leinster the common fabric was stone—in rubble form in the humblest of lodges finished in harling or limedash, as a hewn facing on the porter's lodge to a gentleman's park or as ashlar on the prosperous landed estate. Otherwise cut stone was confined to features such as quoins, label mouldings, door-cases or porticoes. This varied from the readily available and durable granite prevalent in the southern counties of Carlow, Wexford and Wicklow and in Dublin south of the Liffey to the local limestone of the midlands, light in colour in Longford and Westmeath and a darker strain in Meath, which lent itself to use as a facing material. Brick was confined, owing to its rarity, to quoins, dressings and as an eaves band in an otherwise rendered wall. The exception was County Louth to the north, where brick, sourced from the Kingscourt region of County Cavan, was in common use as facing.

For roofing, slate prevailed through the era of the gate lodge as the preferred material, in the main imported from north Wales; it was selected principally for its durability but not least because it set the lodge apart from the neighbouring lowly thatched peasant cottage, with which the big landowner had no wish to herald his property (although, as noted above, there were a few notable exceptions to this rule). The thatched roof was in any case vulnerable to fire and bad maintenance.

LOCAL DETAILING

County Louth is also an exception when it comes to identifying localised detailing, showing a partiality for decorative fascia boards, a peculiarity purveyed by the County Surveyor John Neville at Ardee Convent of Mercy (*c.* 1858), having probably been influenced by earlier work in the county by William F. Caldbeck at Williamstown (*c.* 1860) and Beltichbourne (*c.* 1860), whose source may have been the architecture of the Great Northern Railway. Caldbeck was an architect typical of the day, having to prove himself versed in a variety of architectural styles to compete with his peers and attract clientele. With or without the inspiration of the pattern-book he had to learn to adapt to new trends, and this he did with further lodges in a Picturesque bargeboard cottage style at Emo Court (Laois, *c.* 1861), but he would go on to produce a series in the region of south Dublin and Wicklow in the Italianate style, with which he seemed more at ease.

THE MEDIEVAL REVIVAL

The Leinster landowner in embracing the Picturesque movement may or may not have been influenced by good intentions but the result was generally to the social benefit of his tenant. The desired effect required an irregularity in outline, so the basic rectangular cottage demanded the addition of a verandah here or a bay window there, but most importantly the convenience of a closet appendage. Further features included the external expression of a bulky chimney-breast taken up to enliven the roofscape in a cluster of ornamental stacks alongside a gablet to break the eaves of a roof so steeply pitched as to justify attic rooms approached via a staircase, so much more practical than the previous ladder access to contrived loft space in the traditional lodge.

The Tudor Gothic Revival lodge was available in two alternatives fundamentally distinguished by a variation in the treatment of the gable, or more specifically its verge, whereby the roof could either oversail the wall and terminate in ornamental bargeboards or abut it, the wall raised as a cut-stone skew-table invariably rising off moulded kneelers. Whichever alternative was chosen, it featured flat, Tudor or pointed-arched openings, label- or hood-moulded, further distinguished by a decorative squared or latticed glazing pattern in cast iron, a material or method which serendipitously came into its own to simulate the old Tudor manor house leaded light, convincingly divided by mullions and transoms. The ensuing expanse of gable wall, if not relieved by a garret window, was just the place to exhibit a finely chiselled family crest or, hopefully, a date-stone.

THE ENGLISH MANOR HOUSE LODGE

The 'skew-table' or Tudor manor house lodge is to be found in abundance in the province; most single-storey, their attraction derives from an irregular layout, the best being built off an L-, T- or cruciform plan. Such articulation is to be found in the charming examples at Wellington (Wexford, *c.* 1855) and Ballybrack Lodge (Dublin S, *c.* 1845). The same attributes are evident in both lodges to Durrow Abbey (Offaly, *c.* 1837) and that at Bective (Meath, 1852), the two former thought to be by William Murray, an architect who had learnt to diversify from the more familiar Classical style learnt in the office of his cousin Francis Johnston, and the latter by his son W.G. Murray.

THE ENGLISH PICTURESQUE COTTAGE LODGE

In the English Picturesque cottage lodge the Tudor Revival blossomed further, displaying the same cut-stone detailing as its cousin, being instantly recognisable through its distinctive decorative bargeboards applied to main gables, gablets and porches, intricately carved into waves or foiled lengths and perforated with all manner of Gothic motifs—cusps, mouchettes, trefoils and quatrefoils. These rose to stop against hip-knobs with pendants and spiky finials. Sadly, such wooden details were at the mercy of our climate and many have succumbed, but still recognisable are examples at Ashfield Hall (Laois, *c.* 1835), St Catherine's (Kildare, *c.* 1845) and Oaklawn (Dublin S, *c.* 1847), this probably by the Morrison office, proving their eclecticism, and whose influence is clear in the lodge at Hollybrooke (Wicklow, *c.* 1842) created for himself by the gentleman amateur architect Sir George Hodson. Others in varying stages of decay are at Howth Castle (Dublin N, *c.* 1840) and Carstown (Louth, *c.* 1850), whilst the splendid commodious example at Beaulieu (Louth), built in brick and displaying all the attributes of the genre with its rustic post verandah supports, ins and outs and perforated bargeboards, has gone without trace.

This much-loved type remained in demand late into the century and is represented by two remarkably well-tended lodges which announced the now-lost St Anne's (Dublin N, *c.* 1890), one by George C. Ashlin; Joseph Maguire's Eastholme Lodge (Laois, *c.* 1870) is notable for its patterned diaper brickwork, whilst John McCurdy's design at Kilcroney (Wicklow, *c.* 1870) displays the prettiest of fretted bargeboards to a background of polygonal granite facings. The English architect John Birch was rightly proud enough to publish in 1879 his designs for two delicious ornamental cottages at the gates to Glenart Castle (Wicklow, 1875 and 1876) for the Proby family.

THE *COTTAGE ORNÉ* LODGE

In relation to the Picturesque cottage, mention must be made here of its derivative, the *cottage orné*, a rare survival owing to its impermanent materials. An old photograph reveals what may have been Daniel Robertson's contribution to Ramsfort (Wexford, *c.* 1835). Now unrecognisable having lost its steeply hipped thatched roof, its eaves curved to form eyebrow windows off rustic tree trunk supports, dominated by towering chimney-stacks. In contrast is the pristine state of the lodge to the Zoological Gardens (Dublin N, 1833), designed by the versatile W.D. Butler with half-timbered walls, admirably maintained as the first exhibit by the gate.

THE ROMANTIC CASTELLATED LODGE

Before the advent of these pretty cottages in our countryside, this Picturesque Tudor Gothic Revival was already making its presence felt in some of the most spectacular landmarks. The great landowners were embracing the fantasy architecture of the medieval castle and cloaking their Georgian houses accordingly, often creating complementary gatehouses by the roadside. This romantic sham style was, over a period of 60 years, to appear in bewildering variety, duplication being totally absent. These came almost entirely from the drawing boards of native-born architects, most examples attributable to their authors, keen as they must have been to be associated with these designs. They were to prove themselves to be well acquainted with the new and varied architectural vocabulary. The two most eminent local practitioners were already designing in the style in the first decade of the nineteenth century: Francis Johnston produced two entrances for the marquis of Conyngham at Slane Castle (Meath, *c.* 1810) and went on to create the gatehouse to Barrack Bridge (Dublin S, 1812), subsequently re-sited at the Royal Hospital, Kilmainham (Dublin S), whilst Richard Morrison a year later built a convincing barbican at the entrance to Borris (Carlow, *c.* 1813) for the McMorroughs.

While the Picturesque lodge in its three forms represented a considerable spatial improvement over its standard Georgian predecessor, the castellated gatehouse largely contained accommodation contrived to achieve the desired external effect, and in the interests of authenticity the interiors often tended to be confined and ill lit. Those gatehouses which were intended to replicate the medieval keep in miniature—such as those at Donadea Castle (Kildare, 1846), with its authentic Irish crenellations by George Wilkinson, and Daniel Robertson's contemporary Johnstown Castle (Wexford, 1846)—were more social in layout, set as they were alongside their carriage archway. James Shiel, a pupil of Francis Johnston, likewise presented a convincing 'keep' alongside a massive buttressed archway at Dunsany Castle (Meath, *c.* 1840), but that at Pakenham Hall (Westmeath, *c.* 1825) straddled the main archway with gatekeeper's rooms, access to the upper storey being via a feature octagonal spiral stair turret. Attempts to integrate access with the accommodation led to all manner of discomforts, with little more than a ladder approach to a room above the archway or the impracticality of a spiral staircase which rose beyond to give onto ramparts—all the stuff of dreams but hardly functional. Nevertheless, presumably the novelty and a certain kudos placated the gatekeeper when faced with such deprivations.

The robustness and durability of their construction has led to the survival of most of these fantasies, and they continue to delight with their variety of outline and detail, displaying a whole range of forms in towers, turrets and bartizans, every manner of size and shape, containing walls randomly relieved by motifs such as phoney cross arrowloops, quatrefoils and crests mingling with label- or hood-moulded Tudor-arched openings, all below crenellated parapets supported on mock machicolations, the whole generally in rubble facings with cut-stone dressings.

Lodge-building was at its height in the 1840s and 1850s, thus spanning the Famine period, doubtless as relief, some appearing as little more than ornamental screens with accommodation tacked on behind almost as an afterthought, such as at Shaen (Laois, *c.* 1840) or the otherwise impressive entrance to Clongowes Wood (Kildare, 1840). By an unidentified architect, this is a symmetrical composition, as are the conspicuous entrances to Castlebellingham (Louth, *c.* 1850) and Rathaldron (Meath, *c.* 1845), which integrate their porters' quarters. Rather more domestic in scale from the 1840s is a series of castellated complexes thought to be by Sandham Symes in the delightful compositions at Killiney Castle (Dublin S, *c.* 1840), Victoria Castle (Dublin S, *c.* 1840) and Baymount Castle (Dublin N, *c.* 1838), whereas the outstanding Castle Durrow (Laois, *c.* 1835) entrance, which remains unattributed, in like manner has its main porter's lodging rising to three storeys. This was also a style in which the amateur architect would dabble with some success: at Birr Castle (Offaly, 1848) Mary, Countess of Rosse, completed an admirable bridge-approached portcullised bartizan, whilst much earlier M.F. Trench was responsible for the pleasant rustic gatehouse and archway to Heywood (Laois, *c.* 1810), although it subsequently had to be extended to accommodate a family adequately. Two of the most fascinating in this genre can be found on the Killua Castle estate (Westmeath), which already had a Classical temple opposite one of its gates; each is contrasting but both in their own way are quite symmetrical. To one approach, independent of its gates, is the cutest of toy castles (*c.* 1855) in its own right, with a central two-storey square entrance tower linked to like turrets by curtain walls, the whole castellated and containing label-moulded windows and hood-moulded lancets. It has been lately restored and rehabilitated, like its big house. Not so the middle gateway (1828), which lies decaying; its twin-roomed accommodation flanks a tall carriage opening, and its three bays are defined by pilasters rising to crenellated tops, all in coursed facings relieved by moulded string-courses, quatrefoil motifs and clover-leaf crosses. It is flanked by single-storey postilion gateways and screen walls beyond, with its fine ironwork deserving of care and attention. At Knockdrin Castle (Westmeath, 1862) John McCurdy, at a time when he was purveying many little Italianate lodges in the south Dublin area, was proving himself truly eclectic with this exceptional composition dominated by three-storey porter's rooms overlooking the lofty Tudor-arched carriage archway alongside, balanced by a square turret and pedestrian archway beyond, the whole heavily 'machicolated' and exhibiting immaculate dressed stone in uncoursed rubble facings.

This marked an end to fascination with the Romantic Castellated Revival style in the province, but not before it had twelve years earlier reached a climax in the most outrageous of apparitions in the introduction to Duckett's Grove (Carlow, *c.* 1850), conceived by an architect of Irish descent, John McDuff Derick. His two great archways give on to approaches at right angles to one another, linked by massive Irish crenellated curtain walls liberally punctuated by a variety of turrets and buttresses. The main carriageway is crowned by the Duckett arms and flanked by accommodation in unmatching three-storey square towers, one rising to a bartizaned parapet—and much more, in striking crisp granite extending to 240ft. Its scale is such that newcomers could be forgiven for thinking that they had already arrived at the big house.

THE ITALIANATE LODGE

Old habits died hard, however, for the Classical tradition was not totally forsaken in preference for the Picturesque, living on in a Renaissance style, the Italianate finding a place in the hearts of many proprietors and their designers. Disappointingly, as in the rest of the country, there is no evidence of the *villa rustica* of the Tuscan countryside in Leinster, no campaniles and few loggias to be seen—doubtless considered impractical in the Irish climate, although the free-standing two-storey belvedere at the gates to Victoria Hill Park (Dublin S, 1853) comes close. Rather the Italianate became manifest in the form and detailing of the great urban palazzos, with their low-pitched oversailing hipped roofs on conspicuous carved modillion brackets, forthright quoin stones and architraved openings, as popularised by Sir Charles Barry and applied to our minuscule standard porters' lodges. There is but a hint of bravura in the lodge to Mount Wolseley (Carlow, *c.* 1864), with its porticoed front door by the Belfast practice of Lanyon, Lynn and Lanyon, but nothing approaching the flair of that series they designed for the Ulster gentry. Four Dublin-based architects were particularly occupied by the style. Decimus Burton as early as the 1830s, after impressing with his porters' lodges to the London parks, was invited to improve the entrances to the Phoenix Park (Dublin N), which he did with a series of designs, well articulated, entablatured and pedimented, that still grace the perimeter and the main gate to the Viceregal Lodge (1842), with that to the Castleknock entrance (*c.* 1836) being particularly innovative in its massing. George Papworth's *tour de force* was to be the ill-fated Kenure Park (Dublin N, *c.* 1845), with its two spectacular gatescreens and once-matching grand lodges, both of which displayed vermiculated rustication. Both lodges are now destroyed, one through misguided attention, the other through a lack of any. William F. Caldbeck has already been noticed as being a purveyor of Picturesque lodges in the province but was to prove himself as adept in the Italianate manner. Preferring his lodges to be gabled to exhibit shields and verges with brackets carried around as mutules from the eaves, he also had a weakness for Irish pilaster quoins, as at Eaton Brae (Dublin S, *c.* 1860) and two lodges at Grangecon (Wicklow, *c.* 1865). Also attributable to Caldbeck on stylistic grounds is the splendid lodge at Dowth Hall (Meath, *c.* 1865), whereas there is documentary evidence that he was in charge of building at Clonhugh (Westmeath, *c.* 1867), where he employed the same detailing on his lodge but turned it about 90° to address the avenue with a pretty carved wooden verandah porch.

The mid-nineteenth century realised a frantic building programme in the south Dublin suburbs, as the rising merchant class sought property within easy reach of the capital, many of the old estates being broken up to accommodate their new villas. These *nouveaux riches* preferred the *gravitas* of the Italianate style to grace their new parks rather than the flippancy of the Picturesque. John Skipton Mulvany was another designer who dealt mainly in the Italianate; having flirted briefly with the faintly Oriental in his lost lodge to St Margaret's (Dublin S, *c.* 1852), he created an inventive variation in the style at nearby Mount Anville (Dublin S, *c.* 1852), with its heavily pilastered corners, bracketed friezes, arrowhead bay window and conspicuous triple chimney-stack, off an irregular plan—unique were it not for a twin which he presented for a client at Minella (Waterford, *c.* 1862).

Two architects in particular were to benefit from this demand and indulged themselves in a flurry of villa- and lodge-building. Alfred Gresham Jones, erstwhile assistant to Mulvany, in his extensive domestic practice dealt almost entirely in the Italianate, but in two very different interpretations. For his speculative builders he provided a bland standard but well-proportioned lodge depending for impact upon segmentally headed openings, a gabled breakfront and corbelled chimney-stack, such as those in the Ballybrack area (Dublin S, *c.* 1870)—Aughnacloy, Inveruish, Williams Park and St Columba's being attributable. Outside the confines of his developer clients he provided a set of singular lodges for individual patrons which, although separated by a span of around 25 years, all shared irregular and generous plans and singular detailing, probably nurtured by his time with J.S. Mulvany. Conspicuous for their fenestration of round and pseudo-three-centred arches arranged dually and triply with vermiculated voussoirs rising to contrasting keystones, they had corbelled sills containing margined glazed windows, all features to be found in the south Dublin region at Montebello (*c.* 1860), Monkstown (*c.* 1859) and Johnstown Kennedy (*c.* 1880), and at Hollywoodrath (Dublin N, *c.* 1850).

It was John McCurdy, already noticed for his prowess in the neo-Classical, Picturesque Cottage and Romantic Castellated styles, who was to go on to prove himself truly the master eclectic in his handling of the Italianate. As the most prolific of practitioners in the province, he was to create countless examples in a variety of forms. The most common was that which marked many gates to parks of the mid-Victorian merchant—an otherwise standard single-storey hip-roofed affair, but dressed up by McCurdy to leave little stuccoed surface unadorned. He favoured the Irish pilaster quoin and round- and segmentally arched openings, that of the fanlit front door breaking the open pediment of a central frontispiece, the whole liberally embellished with architraves, keystones, corbelled sills and bracketed eaves. This pattern can still be seen in the south Dublin area at Ailesbury (*c.* 1865), Craigmore (*c.* 1873), Homestead (1871), Newtownpark (*c.* 1872) and Bellosguardo (*c.* 1875), and he went on to develop the theme at Prumplestown (Kildare, *c.* 1870), with its fretted gable features, and Rathmore Park (Carlow, *c.* 1865), which has an elegantly carved bracketed entrance canopy. Both of these were accompanied by extensive and pretentious gatescreens.

THE L-PLAN

But McCurdy could and should be remembered as being mainly responsible for introducing and popularising the L-plan gate lodge, with a socially desirable third room for the porter and his family and incidental scope for an ornamental entrance porch or verandah in the internal corner. At Harristown (Kildare, *c.* 1864) for the La Touche family he provided no fewer than three such layouts, each attired differently—Picturesque, Italianate and Ruskinian Gothic. He went on with his partner W.M. Mitchell to design a further two at Pollacton (Carlow, 1873), Lowther Lodge (Dublin N, 1876) and possibly Elm Grove (Meath, c. 1870). But it was at Rockfort, or Tudenham Park (Westmeath, 1865), aided by a wealthy client, that he was able to reveal his ability in this little masterpiece. On a grand scale for a porter's lodge, it is elevated off a cruciform plan in beautifully punched limestone dressed with strapwork balustrade, round-headed openings, oculi and wreath motifs, the portico overlooking the opulent gatescreen containing one delightful marble-shafted column with an exquisitely chiselled floral capital.

COMPATIBILITY

Mention should be made of W.G. Murray's three-roomed luxurious Italianate lodge to Sea Park (Wicklow, *c.* 1870), notable for being the perfect prelude to its big house, their styles being compatible, which epitomised the mid- to late Victorian age, when much new estate development was consistent in style, particularly suburban villas and their lodges. This was much in keeping with the advice of architectural writers of the day. T.D.W. Dearn in his *Designs for lodges and entrances* (1811) considered that 'One of the first objects of improvements, in this line, should be to adapt the character to that of the House; as the effect likely to be produced on the mind of a visitor by a first view, should be duly regarded: for we frequently decide on the Character of places, as well as persons, by first impressions'. This criterion, though, was rarely met by the older landed estates in the countryside which had evolved over the centuries, and the opening up of a new access or the replacing of an old dilapidated Georgian lodge resulted in building in the fashion current at the time. The finest example in the province of an estate entrance being a foretaste of what to expect within was at Ballyanne (Wexford, *c.* 1790), where, being contemporary, the twin lodges with their canted fronts perfectly presaged the like treated bay windows on the big house beyond, which they now survive in a state of ruin. Two other County Wexford estates perfectly portray the extremes: at Johnstown Castle (1846) Daniel Robertson's castellated gateway gives just the right flavour of the pile within, whereas at Rathaspick (1900) at the gate to the sedate Queen Anne mansion is a quite dotty miniature multicoloured French château. For a different reason, what may have been a quite apt introduction to Fosterstown (Meath, *c.* 1750) in its little thatched vernacular cottage has no longer been so since 1843, with the replacement of the old house by the surviving villa.

But the same W.G. Murray, if called on, could be just as flexible and insensitive as his fellow contemporary practitioners to the architecture of the big house in the provision of lodge gates. At Gowran Castle (Kilkenny, 1856), for example, he turned his back on the tasteful façade of William Robertson's Classical house and furnished designs for Tudor Revival entrances duly built by the 3rd Viscount Clifden.

UNREALISED DREAMS

Three years later his abilities apparently were not as appreciated by the 3rd Baron Castlemaine at Moydrum Castle (Westmeath, 1859), where a series of four beautifully presented drawings for alternative proposals for an entrance were not acted upon. Then, as now, it could be impossible to identify or satisfy many a client's desires. Some could be quite promiscuous in the treatment of their architects—Emo Court (Laois) never did realise an entrance worthy of the place, despite grand designs being offered (*c.* 1780) by James Gandon and Thomas Sandby, and by Lewis Vulliamy (*c.* 1835). So, too, at Stradbally Hall (Laois) the Cosby of the time flirted (*c.* 1865) with James Kempster and John Louch before Charles Lanyon was chosen to reconstruct the house. At Carton (Kildare, *c.* 1770) Thomas Ivory must have been put out not to have had at least one of his elegant arched gateway designs executed.

Other designs resting in archives lie unfulfilled, undiscovered or already rased. The Murray Collection contains proposals, probably by William Murray, for an elegant Classical cottage (IAA 1231) obviously intended to oversee gates [**Fig. 12**], and another for a 1½-storey thatched half-hip-roofed brick-built Tudor cottage (IAA 1232) with label-moulded octagonal glazed pattern windows [**Fig. 13**]. Seemingly also unbuilt are two drawings of *c.* 1860 for Italianate-style lodges of contrasting quality by George Wilkinson [**Figs 14 and 15**], who had seen dozens of his workhouse designs executed. So, too, there is a charming plan and elevation for another 1½-storey thatched hip-roofed Tudor Gothic

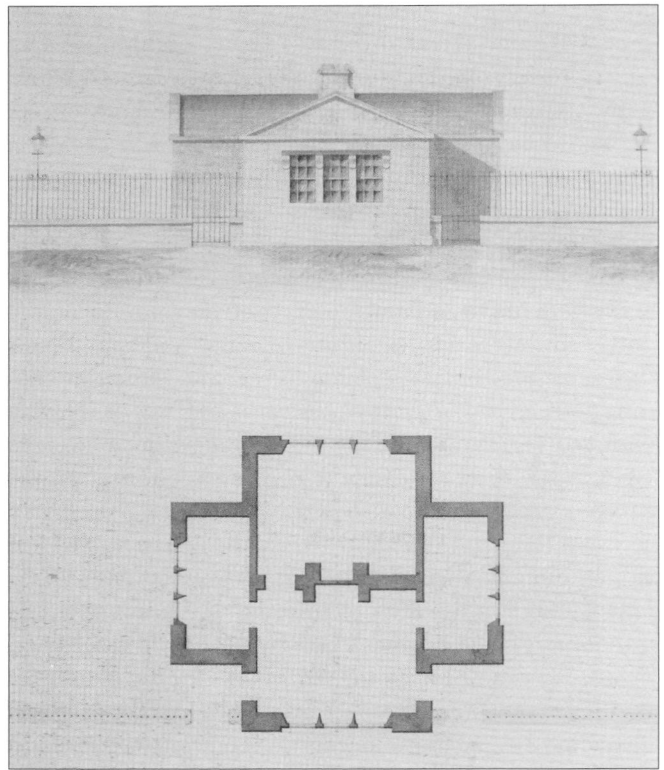

Fig. 12

Fig. 13

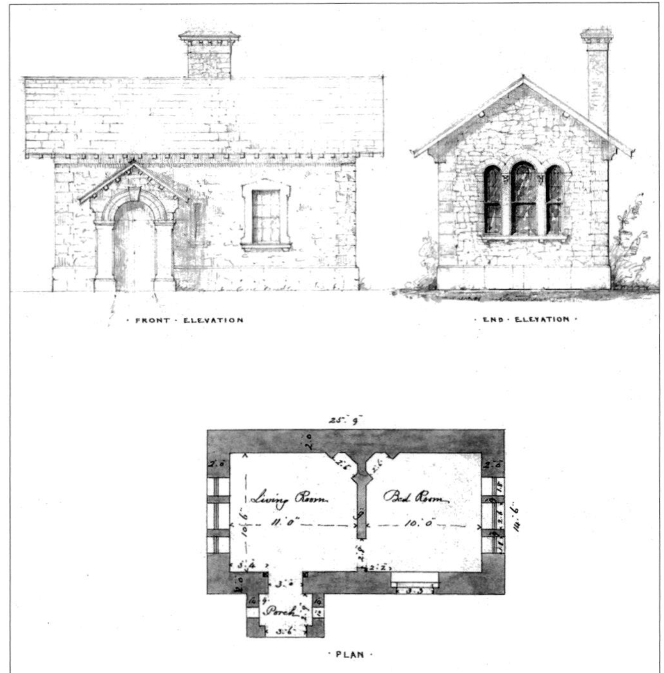

Fig. 14

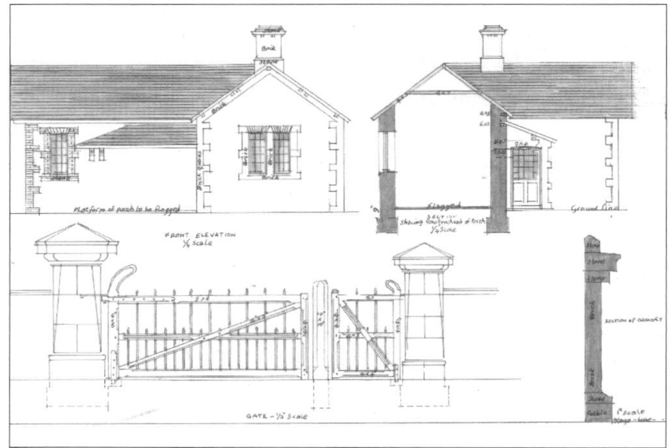

Fig. 15

cottage with tripartite cusped lattice-glazed windows and rustic porch, by Owen Fahy, illustrator in the Morrison practice, which could have been intended for anywhere in the country around 1840 [**Fig. 16**]. From a couple of generations later came two designs which would not have fitted so snugly into the Irish countryside. William Kaye-Parry published in the 1 August 1882 edition of the *Irish Builder* a plan and perspective for a 1½-storey gabled Elizabethan Revival lodge [**Fig. 17**], with all that vocabulary of towering brick cluster chimney-stacks, black-and-white work, tile cladding, jettied attic storey, carved wooden entrance porch and leaded lights 'for a gentleman's residence in the neighbourhood of Dublin'. The same magazine on 15 January 1881 had printed an outrageous proposal for a 'New Principal Entrance To a Demesne' by the English immigrant architect William Isaac Chambers, showing his virtuosity in a sort of Hiberno-Norman mix, the whole dominated by a round tower in the Early Christian manner which was to give access to 'two sleeping apartments above the arched entrance', leading beyond to 'a look-out window in top-room of tower, facing all four cardinal points' [**Fig. 18**]. The anonymous 'well-known landed proprietor' abandoned the idea 'owing to the unsettled state of the country', and its architect returned to his homeland shortly afterwards.

THE HYBRIDS

Such reference to ancient ecclesiastical monuments is not as outlandish as it first seems, for 40 years earlier that

Fig. 16

Fig. 17

Fig. 18

short-lived and precocious practitioner William Vitruvius Morrison had inventively created just such a round tower, albeit a stunted version, to penetrate the roof of his otherwise Tudor-style castellated gatehouse at Clontarf Castle (Dublin N, 1836). This mid-nineteenth-century age of architectural experimentation was not to be satiated by these newfangled options for the Medieval Revival and all its permutations, nor the continuing enthusiasm for its parallel Italianate style. Already had been born, perhaps out of naivety, a sort of hybrid in a combination of the Tudor manor house and the Roman town house. Probably initially in the hands of the amateur architect or jobbing builder came windows with latticed lights and label mouldings, below Classical modillion-bracketed roof soffits of shallow-pitched roofs—a sort of mongrel which nevertheless eventually became accepted as pedigree in such examples as the lodge to Newabbey (Kildare, *c.* 1900) and at Brook Hill (Wexford, *c.* 1850), where the overriding Italianate feel incorporates hood mouldings to its round-arched openings. Even the likes of the otherwise sophisticated *in antis* Classical lodge at Ballindoolin (Kildare, *c.* 1835) seems to have originated with Tudor cast-iron latticed casements.

CURIOSITIES

The Scots Baronial style, unsurprisingly, was not wholly embraced in Leinster, where the Scottish influence was considerably less than in Plantation Ulster. One notable exception is the lodge at Gilltown (Kildare, *c.* 1855), resplendent with its characteristic crow-stepped gables, a design from the Edinburgh architect David Bryce. He was a one-time pupil of that most prolific of his countrymen William Burn, whose work is to be seen in the outstanding and innovative cottage at the gates of Courtown (Wexford, *c.* 1867). The sole instance in the province of a Tyrolean chalet as porter's lodge was to be found at The Orchards (Dublin S, *c.* 1875), its geometric brick polychromy having sought to imitate wooden half-timbering below a characteristic oversailing roof. But again it is worth noticing that wonderful variegated French château lodge at Rathaspick (Wexford, 1900), which surpasses all else in Leinster for sheer absurdity.

THE GOTHIC REVIVAL LODGE

Whilst the Italianate style was to endure in affections until the end of the century, peaking in William Hague's opulent lodge to the Catholic archbishop's palace (Dublin N, 1889) and its Rococo sculpted gate cartouches, interest was reawakened in the Gothic's latest revival as a Continental strain through the teachings of the likes of John Ruskin and A.W.N. Pugin, which after subdued beginnings was to flower in the introduction of new colourful and contrasting building materials combining to create polychromy.

One of the most competent designs of this period,

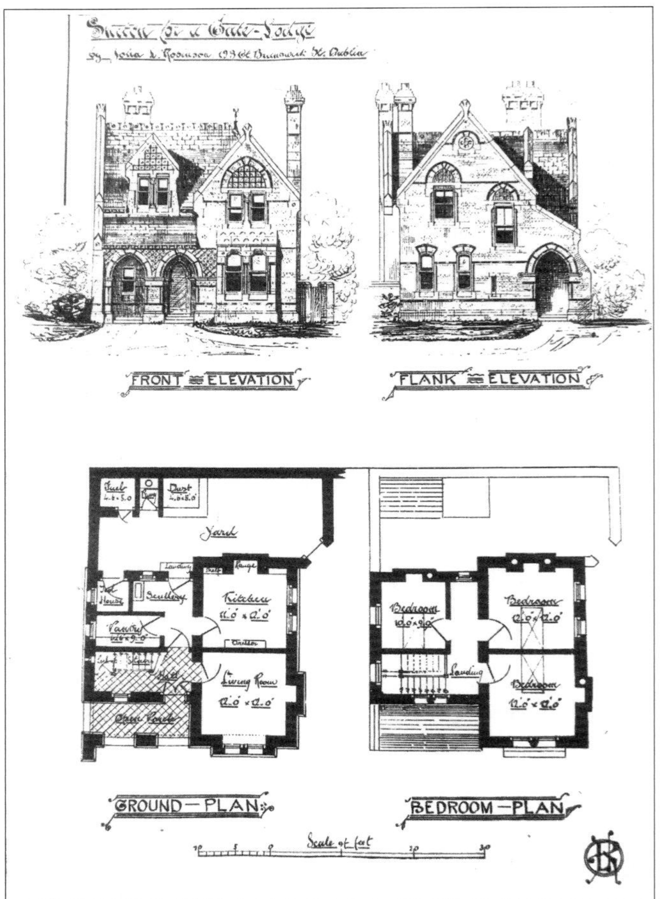

Fig. 19

which seems never to have materialised on site, was a sketch [**Fig. 19**] by John Loftus Robinson, noted more for his ecclesiastical and commercial work about Dublin, published in the *Irish Builder* of 2 March 1874, which was the epitome of the Pugin tradition—a 1½-storey gate lodge exhibiting all the informality of fenestration and variety of materials associated with it.

Initially there were two main exponents indulging themselves in the new vocabulary: Thomas Newenham Deane and his tragically short-lived partner Benjamin Woodward, who complemented all three of their singular villas at St Austin's (Carlow, *c.* 1859), Carrickbrack (Dublin N, 1861) and Clontra (Dublin S, *c.* 1861) with a series of irregularly fenestrated but restrained dormered lodges in a subtle Ruskinian Gothic. By contrast, in the 1860s William Henry Lynn, as he was to do in a design for Cahir Park (Tipperary, *c.* 1863), produced two thoroughly quirky little lodges with distinctively high-pitched roofs and boldly articulated elevations, but notable mainly for their conspicuous use of polychromatic brickwork, red with an imported cream as dressings. These little gems at Mount Temple (Dublin N, *c.* 1865) and Ashurst (Dublin S, *c.* 1863) were to prove forerunners in a twenty-year period in the inventive use of the interplay of materials. Contrasting stone finishes were used to effect at Woodville (Wexford, 1887), probably by A.E. Murray, and spectacularly in the similarly spired, towered variants at Roebuck Castle (1872) and St Patrick's, Dalkey (1869), in the south Dublin suburbs, where architect E.H. Carson, at least in the latter, had also introduced slate banding to his roofs for further effect. These latter two examples by the early 1870s heralded the peak of the High Victorian Gothic, although it was to linger on for a decade in George Ashlin's St George's (Dublin S, 1882) and Alfred Jones's Roebuck Cottage (Dublin S, *c.* 1883) or Ardilea, as it became, the latter with its extensive gatescreen and towering chimney-stacks making theatrical use of stone and brick banding combined.

THE HIGH VICTORIAN LODGE

By now the gate lodge had long been firmly established as a building type of significance. There is no greater evidence of this than its acceptance in 1882 as a suitable subject for a competition sponsored by the *Irish Builder* journal, promoted by architect W.I. Chambers. Although the response was a disappointment, there being but seven entries, the three designs chosen to be illustrated were of high quality. They display ingenuity and inventiveness in a wide range of forms and diversity of materials, but above all a social conscience in generosity of accommodation: 1½ storeys, with two of three bedrooms displaying the exuberance of youth and fine disregard for economy. They display, too, the general confidence of the late Victorian period, and two of the offerings exhibit more than a passing resemblance to the distinctive style of Chambers, who regularly contributed designs to the journal and was one of the judges of the entries. The winner of the first prize [**Fig. 20**] was one J. Whiteside, with a Dublin address, none else of whose work has been recorded for posterity.

This High Victorian Gothic Revival with its structures of bold outline and irregular layout meant well for the comfort of the gatekeeper, and it was to endure in the genesis of a new fancy in a number of manifestations gathered under the umbrella of the so-called Arts and Crafts movement. By far the most popular of these, and remaining so with speculative builders to this day, was an Old English Revival subjected to numerous and various interpretations by the late Victorian and Edwardian architect. It is principally identified by the familiar use of half-timbering or black-and-white work on gables, but in some cases on much else, as can be seen in the likes of the conspicuous Blessington Basin lodge (Dublin N, *c.* 1890) by an unidentified designer, in the hands of W.I. Chambers at Balrath Bury (Meath, *c.* 1880) and in the excesses of Seamount lodge (Dublin N, *c.* 1905), probably by Frederick Batchelor. This 'Stockbrokers' Tudor', as it was christened by Osbert Lancaster, was to appear with some subtlety in O'Callaghan and Webb's delightful example at St Helen's (Wicklow, 1909) and in a sadly unexecuted lodge for Eversham (Dublin S, *c.* 1900) by L.A. McDonnell. He

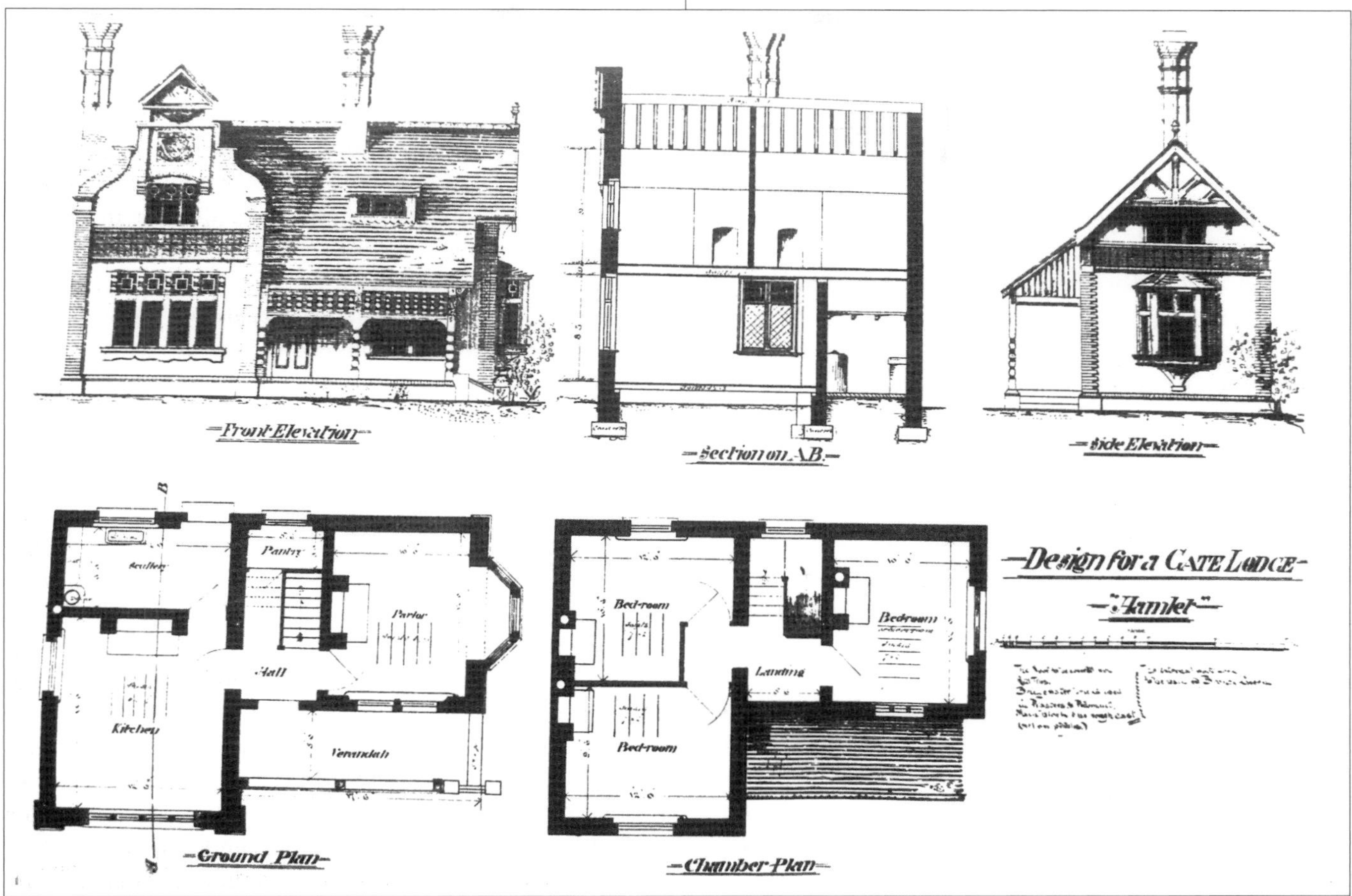

Fig. 20

fully embraced the craze and saw many of his designs built for his clients: at Eyrefield Lodge (Kildare, 1900) and no fewer than three at Knockmaroon (Dublin N, *c.* 1905) for his wealthy Guinness patron. Jettying, ornamental carved porches, leaded lights and Rosemary roof tiles enhanced the effect, commonly allied with red brick, as at Stameen (Meath, *c.* 1895) by W.M. Mitchell, who also created the spectacular entrance lodge and gates to Brownswood (Wexford, *c.* 1890), where he substituted red clay tile-hanging for half-timbering. It was possibly this busy and productive practitioner who was to mix half-timbering and tile-hanging extravagantly at Rahinstown (Meath, *c.* 1890), whilst to Dalguise (Dublin S, *c.* 1881) he introduced fancy fretwork apexes. William Kaye-Parry displayed his command of the style in his unexecuted quintessential design with typical towering articulated brick chimney-stacks, published in the *Irish Builder* of 1 August 1882. T.J. Mellon's innovative little offering at Colonel White's Gate to the Phoenix Park (Dublin N, 1905) is a delight, as is the quirky little rambling affair at the McGeogh Home (Dublin S, *c.* 1900), perhaps by R.F.C. Orpen. Whereas Sir Thomas Manley Deane employed half-timbering to flimsy effect at Bellegrove (Laois, *c.* 1890) and Rockford (Dublin S, *c.* 1882), such reticence is not evident on the part of George Ashlin in his extraordinary bravura at All Saints lodge to St Anne's (Dublin N, *c.* 1890).

THE ARTS AND CRAFTS LODGE

By now, from *c.* 1880 to the 1920s, gate lodge-building had entered its final phase, by which time architects were vying with one another to create designs that would outshine their competitors. To avoid repetition, these came in dramatic variety to woo the clients of the rapidly expanding south Dublin suburbs, there being little call to meld with the landscape. These developed a brashness in the architecture of the late Victorian and Edwardian era in the choice of form, materials and detailing which, though lumped under the Arts and Crafts banner, made styles difficult to categorise. Whereas Old English is easy to identify, not so the likes of Baroque and Queen Anne, whereby architects tended to mix and match details from the past and there was much overlapping of styles, which led to some intriguing concoctions.

There are many unashamedly eye-catching examples that may be labelled neo-Baroque, with a touch of Caroline thrown in, to be seen south of the Liffey, again in W.M. Mitchell's lodge to the Female Masonic School (*c.* 1895) and what is probably William Kaye-Parry's masterpiece at Rathgar Mansion, or Oakland (1893). Each is single-storey on an irregular plan in a vivid red brick finish with contrasting gable ends and displaying part-pedimented tripartite windows, probably influenced by Norman Shaw. Here, too, are conspicuous verandahed entrance porches with white-painted turned post supports. The latter lodge displays a distinctive compressed swan-neck broken pediment feature that is also to be found as gables to the great bulging attic oriel windows of the lodge at Rockfield (Dublin S, *c.* 1895), which borders on the grotesque. This is an ingredient which is altogether more correctly exhibited on a very fine door-case to the enchanting lodge at Stacumney (Kildare, 1911).

Concurrent with this unrestrained concept ran a thoroughly more polite and decorous creation termed 'Queen Anne Revival' (or, more graphically, 'Wrenaissance'), an Arts and Crafts form which was no less effective for its simple symmetrical outline. It found strangely little favour in the province, apart from one quite singular example at Herbertstown (Meath, *c.* 1916) by an as-yet-unidentified and talented designer: an elegant, simple, cubic 1½-storey box, its attic rooms contained in a pyramidal roof and typically lit by flat-roofed dormers, a banded central brick chimney-stack reflecting the channelled quoins which frame pebble-dashed panels with Georgian-style sash windows.

This form of pavilion had already been in evidence in Leinster but very much pared down, its elevations unadorned, almost a sanitised return to the old vernacular cottage. Variants were introduced by eminent mainland architects: firstly by Sir Robert Lorimer at St Marnock's (Dublin N, *c.* 1895), two essays in brick with simple toothed stone dressings and another couple of pure examples at Kilteragh (Dublin S, *c.* 1905), probably by W.D. Caroe, both very much in the vogue of Voysey—leaded lights in chaste white roughcast walls below pyramidal roofs of tiny slates. In like genre is the lodge at The Orchard (Dublin S, *c.* 1911), with similar flat-roofed dormers but here in red clay-tiled finish, its entrance emphasised by a porch with catslide roof. At Clowanstown (Meath, 1908) is a remarkable variant, the roof bellcast over rubble walls, from one of which prominently extends a semicircular lattice-glazed room, to designs of A.E. Murray, showing his versatility. Equally distinguished at Dromin (Wicklow, 1899), Frederick Batchelor, to complement his contemporary Arts and Crafts house, designed a single-storey lodge on an L-plan in plain white finish, accentuating the horizontal emphasis of multipartite leaded windows, to which he applied the whimsy of a Tuscan portico. But a century and a half after its début the standard single-storey form of porter's lodge was not abandoned, for at Kilcoursey (Offaly, *c.* 1911) is an example devoid of any detail but distinguished nevertheless by its simplicity and perfection of proportion, squared casements set in white roughcast walls below a red clay-tiled shallow-hipped roof, showing L.A. McDonnell with a finesse far removed from his Old English Revival period. Accompanying this little masterpiece is a lovely set of wooden carriage gates, the carpenter's craft having become much more in evidence, combined with that of the ironmonger, in this final phase of lodge-building. Built as it was just prior to the Great War, this virtually signalled the end of an era of lodge-building; this trauma, followed by the Civil War and the formation of the Irish Free State, saw a dramatic social restructuring to the detriment of domestic building on a grand scale and the 'Big House' in particular.

THE LAST LODGES

One rare exception was R.H. Byrne's replacement lodge to Shanganagh Castle (Dublin S, 1926), but generally the tradition of lodge-building was only perpetuated by a programme of hospital-building in the country, this invariably in the modern International Style, a type of architecture in which enrichment had no place. It is epitomised in J.V. Downes's two-storey gate lodge to St Luke's Hospital (Kilkenny, *c.* 1940), which is typically devoid of ornament, dependent on massing and fenestration for effect, being a particularly boxy flat-roofed affair, a suitable prelude to the complex beyond.

There are two late examples of gate lodges worthy of mention in Leinster, both in County Kildare. One is an overpowering rustic brick pair flanking a curvilinear gabled carriage archway complete with belfry, looking to have escaped from a stable yard, appropriately enough marking the entrance to Kildangan Stud (1988). The other is a commendable 21st-century neo-neo-Classical affair on the site of a predecessor opposite the grand gates belonging to Browne's Hill (Carlow) but otherwise an appropriate prelude to Sir Richard Morrison's Lyons House within. But these are rare examples indeed, this technological age finally sounding the death-knell for two illustrious centuries of gate lodge-building, effectively replaced by the remote-control security gate.

GUIDE TO THE GAZETTEER

Entries are numbered and listed county by county for ease of reference; Dublin is divided into north and south relative to the River Liffey. Each entry heading gives the *NAME* of the property with its *LOCATION*. This heading (or subheading, where there is more than one lodge) is followed by the *DATE* of the building's construction, its *ARCHITECT* and, should there be little or nothing evident on site, its *CONDITION*. Proposals which remain unexecuted are also indicated. An *ILLUSTRATION* generally precedes the *DESCRIPTION*, and *REFERENCES* complete the entry.

NAME
Title of house, demesne or institution with which a lodge is associated, the name given being that when it was first known to have been 'lodged'; any previous and subsequent titles of a property are cross-referenced.

LOCATION
The nearest town or village.

DATE
Where a date-stone or documentary evidence is lacking, the date of construction is deduced from visual assessment. If a lodge has been demolished, is ruinous or so altered as to be unrecognisable, a date is given as 'pre-' that of the earliest Ordnance Survey map on which it appears. Occasionally, where a gate lodge is referred to in a valuation book offering a more accurate date of erection, this is noted. (For dates of the Ordnance Survey maps and Griffith valuations see the bibliography.)

ARCHITECT
In the absence of a documentary source, attributions are made on stylistic grounds or on the evidence of associated building activities. Such ascriptions are made with varying degrees of certainty, ranging from 'perhaps', through 'possibly' to 'probably'. 'Architect not known' indicates a design sufficiently sophisticated as to suggest the hand of a professional architect or talented amateur but with no positive attribution possible.

CONDITION
This is recorded solely where a lodge within the time-span of the survey (which took place between 1996 and 2006) was discovered to have been demolished. Inevitably more demolitions have occurred since.

ILLUSTRATIONS
Photographs and drawings are by the author unless otherwise credited. Note of the original architect, artist or photographer is followed (in parenthesis) by the owner or holder of such material. Most architecturally significant lodges are illustrated. Some of lesser merit have also been included, as they have been demolished and their record is considered of importance.

DESCRIPTION
Reference to a lodge being 'standard' indicates that its ground-floor main elevation is three-bay symmetrical, the front door flanked by windows. In addition to a physical description of the structure, an attempt has been made to relate it to other building phases on the estate, to the big house and to the family, proprietor or patron responsible. Over 4,000 sites have been visited in the course of this study and some have, of necessity, not been surveyed for some time; changes have thus occurred in the interim, especially in urban areas. Where known, the identities of gate porters have been recorded.

ABBREVIATIONS

APSD	*The dictionary of architecture* (Architectural Publication Society)
BPB	*Burke's Peerage and Baronetage*
CLAHJ	*County Louth Archaeological and Historical Journal*
DB	*The Dublin Builder*
IAA	Irish Architectural Archive
IADS	*Irish Architectural and Decorative Studies*
IAR	*Irish Arts Review*
IB	*The Irish Builder*
IFR	*Irish Family Records*
IGS	Irish Georgian Society
JASCK	*Journal of the Archaeological Society of County Kildare*
LG	*Burke's Landed Gentry*
LGI	*Burke's Landed Gentry of Ireland*
NAOPW	National Archives, Office of Public Works
NIAH	National Inventory of Architectural Heritage
NLI	National Library of Ireland
OS	Ordnance Survey
OSM	Ordnance Survey Memoirs
PRO	Public Record Office, Kew
PRONI	Public Records Office of Northern Ireland
RIBA	Royal Institute of British Architects; Drawings Collection
RSAI	Royal Society of Antiquaries of Ireland
TCD	Trinity College Dublin

COUNTY CARLOW

1. ACLARE, Myshall; post-1839; *demolished.*
A 112-acre holding in the mid-nineteenth century of Michael Gorman, its lodge, remote from the public road, built before 1905.
Griffith 1848–60.

2. BAGENALSTOWN, Bagenalstown; *c.* 1860; architect not known.

At the gate to a modest Georgian villa, originally of the Mercers, are the contrastingly robust mid-Victorian lodge and entrance. Although the property had passed to a branch of the county's numerous Newton family, John, it seems to have been built for his successor, Captain Walter Persse. Set forward of the entrance in its own enclosure of concave wing walls and railed screen is the single-storey ashlar-faced lodge under a hipped roof with exaggerated moulded stone eaves brackets. It is dominated by a semi-octagonal central projection with round-headed windows, a doorway set back to one side. There is a series of gadroon-domed pillars, the entrance screen set off by wide concave quadrants. Occupied.
Slater 1870; O'Dwyer 1999.

3. BALLINTEMPLE, Ardattin; pre-1839; *demolished.*
Both house and lodge are no more, the latter built by Sir Richard Butler, or his son Sir Thomas, of Clogrennan (*q.v.*).
O'Toole 1993.

4. BALLYELLIN, Goresbridge; pre-1839; *demolished.*
A lodge for the Blackney family, who were here between 1781 and 1865. Its demise may date from the house's burning in 1908.
O'Toole 1993.

5. BALLYKEALEY, Ballon; *c.* 1835; architect possibly T.A. Cobden.
Contemporary with, but in contrast to, the Tudor Revival house, opposite the entrance is a standard shallow hip-roofed lodge with high eaves to accommodate loft space. Just discernible through a modern extension and improvements is a series of pilasters suggestive of Thomas Alfred Cobden's familiar Classical style. All for John James Leckey (1799–1878). Occupied.
LGI (1904); Bence-Jones 1988.

6. BALLYREDMOND, Clonegall; *c.* 1839; *demolished.*
A house, described in 1846 as 'the picturesque modern lodge of H. Newton', now known as 'Sandhill'.
Slater 1846.

BEECHY PARK (see BETTYFIELD)

7. BELLMOUNT, Carlow; *c.* 1835.
A standard single-storey lodge with shallow gabled roof having salvaged carved modillion brackets to verges, in Regency manner. All sand/cement-rendered with modern windows, and greatly extended. On one gable is a plaque inscribed 'Mount St Jude'. Built by the Vigors family. Occupied.
Brewer 1825.

8. BENNEKERRY, Carlow; *c.* 1840.
Philip Newton (1796–1856) in 1832 assumed the name and arms of Bagenal after his mother, married in 1838 and soon created this quirky Classical temple design. A tetrastyle portico of slender granite Doric columns supports a grossly oversized pediment. Recessed is a doorway flanked by tiny round-headed sash windows, all framed by Doric pilasters. The later roughcast to tympanum, bargeboards and concrete roof tiles add to the eccentricity. The gatescreen is of granite ashlar walls to low carriage pillars with recessed panels below corniced cappings.
LGI (1904).

9. BENNEKERRY LODGE, Carlow; *c.* 1830.
Not quite opposite its entrance is a once-charming building in rubble stone, single-storey and maintained as a novelty with a wide round-headed doorway flanked by semicircular bows with like-arched narrow windows, all below a hipped roof. The proprietor in 1837, Edward Gorman, was succeeded before 1852 by Beauchamp Colclough.
Lewis 1837; Griffith 1848–60.

10. BETTYFIELD, Rathvilly; pre-1839; *demolished.*
A seat until 1814 of the other Benjamin D'Israeli, it was subsequently renamed 'Beechy Park'.
O'Toole 1993.

11. BORRIS, Borris (5).
What was a plain early eighteenth-century house was, about 1813, given a Tudor Gothic cloak by architects Sir Richard and William Vitruvius Morrison. That commission included not only a family chapel but also a grand entrance to the demesne from the heart of the village, replacing a previous access off the main street further south, the remains of the pillars to which are still to be seen. The client was initially Walter Kavanagh (d. 1813), who was succeeded to the estate by his younger brother Thomas Kavanagh (1767–1837), who oversaw the improvements developing.

Main entrance; *c.* 1813; architects Sir Richard and W.V. Morrison.
Set well back from the street is this Romantic barbican gate in the form of a stone-faced two-storey structure containing two-centre-arched carriage openings, complete with

buttresses, square turrets, label-moulded windows, mock arrowloops, machicolated crenellations and tall octagonal stair tower. To one side is single-storey porter's accommodation, with its battlements taken across buttressed screen walls beyond. An anonymous writer in the *Irish Builder* magazine 75 years later dared to relate that Sir Richard Morrison accepted a consideration from the contractor in return for overlooking a defect in its building. There are similar such gatehouses by the Morrison practice at Thomastown, Co. Tipperary, and Glenarm Castle, Co. Antrim.

Ballyteigelea entrance; pre-1839; *demolished.*

Cottage entrance; *c.* 1835.

Opposite the gates is what was originally a standard 1½-storey gabled cottage with later single-storey flat-roofed hall projection and a single-bay extension to the left-hand side. Not contemporary is the very fine antique entrance screen of four stone pillars with Baroque cushion friezes, deeply moulded cappings and simple ball finials on generous pedestals, all framed by tall concave rubble quadrant walls and dating from around 1730.

Borris Bridge entrance; *c.* 1855.

For Arthur MacMorrough Kavanagh (1831–89), famed for living life to the full despite being born limbless, is this good standard

1½-storey Tudor Revival cottage, gabled with ornamental scalloped bargeboards. Single-storey gabled hall projection flanked by label-moulded, mullioned bipartite casement windows in ashlar walling which is confined to the main front; diagonally set stone chimney-stacks. Fine ashlar entrance pillars and ornamental cast-iron gates with cusped Gothic tracery and foliated finials.

Ballynagrane entrance; *c.* 1890.

At the end of an old public road, long redundant, is a house of generous proportions, so distant from its gate as to suggest a dual role. A gabled 1½-storey three-bay structure in rubble stone having a commodious stairwell and central hall projection with room over; single-storey back return. Now ruinous on its disused avenue. Built for Walter MacMorrough Kavanagh (b. 1856), who succeeded to the property in 1889.

LGI (1904); McParland *et al.* 1989.

12. BRAGANZA, Carlow; *c.* 1820; architect probably T.A. Cobden; *demolished.*

Irish Architectural Archive

Contemporary with the delightful bow-fronted house built for Sir Dudley St Leger Hill (1787–1851) on his return from Portugal and the Peninsular War, to designs of architect Thomas Alfred Cobden, was this equally charming single-storey standard Georgian Gothic lodge with pointed arches to openings and Y-traceried glazing in harled wall below a hipped roof. A sad loss.

The Carlovian Magazine (1949), pp 123–6; IAA photograph (S/506/1).

13. BROOMVILLE, Ardlattin (2).

Both porters' lodges in place by 1839 have been demolished. Probably built by Captain James Butler to the dower house for that family of Ballintemple (*q.v.*).

14. BROUGHILLSTOWN, Rathvilly; pre-1908; *demolished.*

A lodge built after 1839 for the Montmorency family.

15. BROWNE'S HILL, Carlow (3).

Robert Browne was the first of the family to reside here, marrying in 1762 and erecting the Classical mansion in time to house his new bride the following year. To complement it he commissioned a design for a magnificent arched entrance screen to the demesne. An unsigned and undated drawing for it survives and may have been by the same mystery architect called Peters who designed the house.

Main entrance; *c.* 1763; architect possibly —— Peters.

What materialised shows minor variations from the drawing—the pediment surmounting the round-headed carriage opening, rather than being broken by it, is supported by large Doric pilasters instead of squat rusticated piers. Flanking Gibbsian postern gates are crowned by sculpted lions and the whole complex extended in vast concave quadrant railings on dwarf walls. These, the finest and most extensive Georgian gates in the country, were saved from the Land Commission through the influence of the Irish Georgian Society to be acquired, dismantled and re-erected by University College Dublin at Lyons House, Co. Kildare (*q.v.*), where they remain. The original wooden gates were replaced with cast iron.

Main entrance lodge; 1842; architect T.A. Cobden.

Robert Browne's grandson, Robert Clayton Browne, succeeded to the estates on the death of his father in 1840 and replaced the original gatekeeper's lodge to the other side of the entrance with this exquisite neo-Classical single-storey standard lodge. Its hipped roof is part-hidden behind a granite entablatured parapet which extends to support a pediment over the projecting porch, with its square outer pillars and Doric columns *in antis*. Granite is used further to dress the windows with corbelled sills and corner pilasters contrasting with stuccoed panels. Now rather forlorn, shorn of its vast entrance screen, and, although well restored and maintained, it is reduced through the loss of its stone chimney-stack. As Thomas Alfred Cobden, its English architect who had settled in Carlow, died before the lodge's completion, Browne had to look elsewhere for architectural inspiration at other gates.

South gate; *c.* 1845; architect probably George Papworth.

A Tudor Revival composition, single-storey on an L-plan with random stone facings, its avenue gable contains a breakfront bay whilst a small hall projects from the internal angle. Tall finials surmount the skew-table gables which spring from deeply moulded kneelers—identical to those of architect George Papworth's keeper's lodge at Kilkenny Lunatic Asylum (*q.v.*). Adding weight to this attribution is that he is known to have been working around this time at neighbouring Oak Park (*q.v.*), and also for Robert Clayton Browne's father-in-law Hans Hamilton on the Abbotstown estate, Co. Dublin. Furthermore, there is a very similar porter's lodge at Garbally Court, Co. Galway, where Papworth is also known to have been commissioned.

East gate; *c.* 1845; architect probably George Papworth.

A 1½-storey version of the south gate lodge, but in the English Picturesque Cottage idiom with highly decorative bargeboards in the Pugin manner. Roughcast with granite dressings and pretty quatrefoil motif above the doorway.

Both the south and east lodges suffer from modern window intrusions, probably having replaced latticed cast-iron casements.

IGS *Bulletins* (April–June 1961; 1984); Bence-Jones 1988; O'Toole 1993.

16. BURGAGE, Leighlinbridge; pre-1839; *demolished.*

A lodge probably built for Revd Thomas Mercer Vigors (1775–1850), who succeeded to the estate on the death of his father in 1797.

LGI (1904).

17. BURRENDALE, Carlow; pre-1839; *demolished.*

The first OS map indicates that the porter's lodge was little more than a minuscule pillbox structure. A property in 1852 of John Lawrence.

Griffith 1848–60.

18. BURTON HALL, Carlow (3).

'The avenue that leads to this beautiful home is at least an English mile long, and the breadth large. On each side is a far extended wood, cut out with a variety of vistas.' The access to this avenue from the west, about which Philip Luckombe wrote in 1779, survives in the form of a wide-railed entrance screen with six tall Georgian ashlar pillars topped by moulded cappings and ball finials, with a variety of concave and convex pedestals which would seem to have served as models for the other Burton estate at Pollerton (*q.v.*). In contrast is a very plain 1½-storey standard gabled lodge of about 1835 with a single-storey flat-roofed hall projection.

Two other pre-1839 gatekeepers' lodges, one to the north and another in County Kildare, have been demolished. The demise of this once-proud property was hastened by the decline of the family's financial fortunes from the late eighteenth century, William Fitzwilliam Burton (1826–1909) being forced to let the house in 1864 prior to its eventual demolition in 1930.

Luckombe 1780; *LGI* (1912).

19. CARLOW ARMY BARRACKS, Carlow; pre-1839; *demolished.*

A lodge originally built as a guardhouse which later served as a mortuary.

20. CARLOW FEVER HOSPITAL, Carlow; *c.* 1845; *demolished.*

An institution off Dublin Road built after the first OS map of 1839, to be valued by Griffith thirteen years later.

Griffith 1848–60.

21. CARLOW INFIRMARY, Carlow; pre-1839; *demolished.*

A lodge on Hanover Road which had been removed by 1900.

22. CARLOW LUNATIC ASYLUM, Carlow; 1929; architect William Murray.

An asylum built to serve the counties of Carlow, Kildare, Kilkenny and Wexford, at a cost of £22,552, a figure which presumably covered its typically sturdy and severe institutional porter's lodge. A single-storey standard structure with hipped roof,

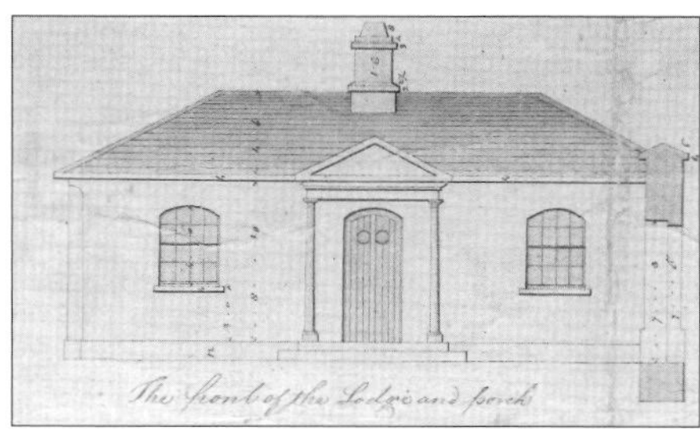

1829 William Murray (134) (IAA)

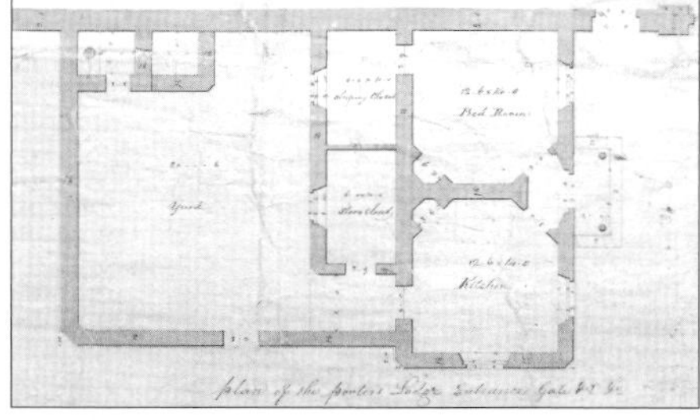

1829 William Murray (134) (IAA)

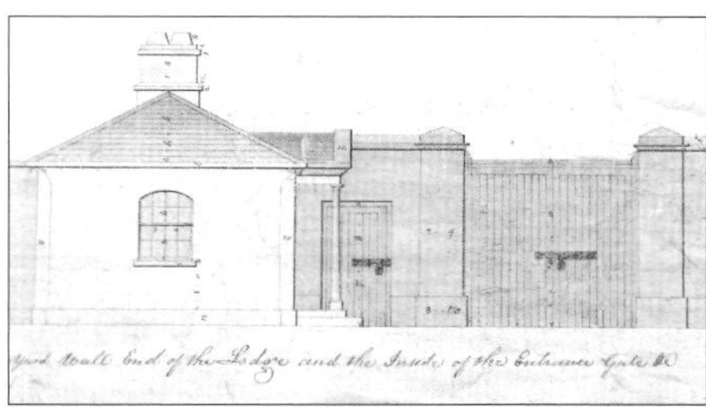

1829 William Murray (134) (IAA)

segmentally arched windows in ashlar walls and a projecting porch, the pediment of which is supported by a plucky pair of slender cast-iron posts. William Murray's drawings for the lodge survive in the Irish Architectural Archive. There is a similar lodge by William Murray to the Armagh Lunatic Asylum, with the same chamfered left-hand corner to accommodate carriage wheels. Edward Drennan was gatekeeper in 1852.

Lewis 1837; Griffith 1848–60; IAA (Murray Collection 134 and 135).

23. CARRICKSLANEY, Ballon; *c.* 1890.

A standard single-storey hip-roofed structure subsequently lengthened to double the size to six bays, the original doorway being converted to a window. Modernised and smartly rendered to pass for a twentieth-century bungalow. A property created in 1890 by Henry Wilson.

24. CASTLETOWN, Carlow; *c.* 1790.

Pre-dating architect Daniel Robertson's *c.* 1835 transformation of the property was a house completed in 1790 by Samuel Faulkner for his steward, Philip Kennedy. Contemporary is this dilapidated Georgian Gothic lodge; single-storey standard with granite-dressed pointed-arched windows flanking a round-headed fanlit doorway set in later roughcast walls below a hipped roof resplendent in a corrugated asbestos finish. Situated by the roadside, linked to its carriage opening by an iron turnstile postilion gate. The house is a ruin.

O'Toole 1993.

25. CLOGRENNAN, Carlow; pre-1839.
A featureless 1½-storey affair with clipped eaves and verges in a roughcast finish. Built by the Rochfort family, whose house has been reduced to a shell.

26. CONVENT OF MERCY, Carlow; pre-1905; *demolished.*
A branch of the Sisters of Mercy was formed here in 1837, their lodge added after 1839.
Slater 1846.

27. CORRIES, Goresbridge; *c.* 1839.

It was Henry Rudkin, described as having extravagant habits, who gradually sold off the property, living on here as a tenant of Robert Hardy until his death in 1846, prior to which the lodge was added. It is a standard 1½-storey design, elevated opposite the entrance, gabled with hip-knobs and replacement ornamental bargeboards, the roof of which extends over the front elevation to form a picturesque verandah carried on four granite Doric columns, punctuated by a gabled canopy to the doorway. Some openings retain their Tudor-style label mouldings, but unfortunately the windows now lack their original octagonal glazing pattern; rendered.
O'Toole 1993.

28. CRANEMORE, Clonegall; pre-1839; *demolished.*
A seat of a branch of the Durdins of Huntington Castle (*q.v.*), its lodge probably built for Robert Atkins Durdin (d. 1841).
LGI (1904).

29. DUCKETT'S GROVE, Carlow (3).
In 1830 the neo-Classical mansion was transformed by Thomas Alfred Cobden into a fairytale Gothic castle. His commission for John Dawson Duckett (1791–1866) extended to the design of contrasting gate lodges at the (then) extremities of the estate.

North entrance; pre-1839/*c.* 1840; architect T.A. Cobden.
What must have been an impressive and innovative neo-Classical temple lodge has been disfigured by later 'improvements'. Still recognisable as original is a pair of 9ft-6in.-high baseless granite Doric columns *in antis* forming part of a portico projecting beyond a three-bay façade with stone-dressed windows and boldly corbelled sills. The roof has latterly been lifted to accommodate an attic storey, and a single-storey hallway sprouts from between the columns, the whole having been cement-rendered and its roof concrete-tiled. Now minus its entrance gates since the old avenue became a public road. The lodge, of which the accompanying drawing is in part conjectural, had a predecessor on the site.

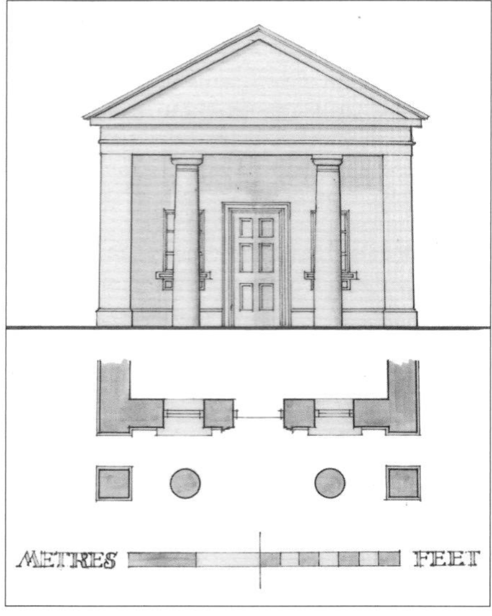

South entrance; *c.* 1835; architect probably T.A. Cobden.
A 1½-storey Tudor Gothic composition on an irregular plan remaining much as built but for nasty recent window replacements and enclosure of the large porch. Strikingly dressed in granite with its fine sculpted hip-knobs, skew-tables, kneelers and plinth. On the avenue gable is a breakfront bay window with its parapet stepping down to show the loft window. Rendered redundant as a gatekeeper's lodge when Duckett extended the demesne boundary to Russellstown crossroads and sought designs for a more pretentious entrance and extensions to the mansion.

Russellstown entrance; *c.* 1850; architect John McDuff Derick.
As Cobden had died in 1840, J.D. Duckett turned to an English-based architect of Irish descent not noted for his subtle creations. Here was no exception, for what materialised was one of the most excessive and extensive neo-Gothic entrance gate complexes in the country, an extravaganza in granite of machicolated castellations, towers, bartizans, buttresses, a variety of slit windows and mock arrowloops to complement an oriel window and a portcullis archway, all too bizarre to describe in brief or in detail. This fantasy fortress contains archways to two avenues, one for family and guests, the other for tenants and staff. Overlooking its huge forecourt are family armorial bearings sculpted by Kelly and Kinsella, once coloured and gilded and set in columned recesses with the mottoes *Je veux le droit* (I will have my right) and *Spectemur Agendo* (Let us be judged by our actions). Sadly, the estate has fallen into advanced decay, and of Derick's folly one archway spans a public road whilst the other, with porter's accommodation, has been blocked up, having been the scene of a series of fruitless ventures, such as a pub and restaurant.
LGI (1904); Bence-Jones 1988; Williams; Lawrence photograph (575 I).

30. DUNLECKNEY, Bagenalstown (2).
Walter Newton (d. 1853) inherited the demesne upon the death in 1832 of his mother, Sarah Bagenal, and engaged Daniel Robertson to design him the Tudor Gothic manor house in limestone ashlar, one of a series of houses for her sons in the county.

29. Duckett's Grove, Russellstown entrance (National Library of Ireland/Lawrence Collection) Inset: the armorial bearings with the mottoes *Spectemur Agendo* and *Je veux le droit.*

West gate; pre-1839; *demolished.*
It seems that the old gate lodge to which he succeeded was never replaced. It is said that the architect also furnished contemporary drawings for a replacement, but that Walter by that stage had run short of funds and the design was adapted for the entrance to Shankill Castle, Co. Kilkenny (*q.v.*). As an alternative, at the main entrance at the foot of a perfectly straight new avenue is a pair of remarkably squat and solid granite pillars with cusped Gothic panels and crenellated cappings.

South gate; pre-1900; *demolished.*
Built sometime after 1839 on a new approach occasioned by the realignment of the county's road, that avenue now itself a public road.

Fraser 1838; *LGI* (1904); Bence-Jones 1988; *IAR* (1999).

31. ERINDALE, Carlow; pre-1839; *demolished.*
The distinctive Georgian Gothic red-brick villa was probably built by Nicholas Aylward Vigors (1755–1828), otherwise of Old Leighlin and Belmont (*q.v.*). His lodge was presumably contemporary.

LGI (1904).

32. EVINGTON, Carlow; *c.* 1835.
Home in 1846 to Revd Henry Hare, who will have known this single-storey standard hip-roofed lodge, now roughcast with Classical carved modillion brackets to its soffit. Derelict.

Slater 1846.

33. FENAGH, Fenagh; *c.* 1890.
Denis Robert Pack-Beresford (1864–1942) inherited the lodgeless property on the death of his father in 1881 and remedied the situation perhaps not coincidentally upon his marriage in 1891. This is a distinctive single-storey standard structure on a square plan in random stone facing, with toothed brick dressings to windows on each side of a flimsy entrance canopy on post supports. The oversailing pyramidal roof rises to a brick chimney-stack. Derelict.

IFR.

34. GARRYHUNDON, Leighlinbridge; 1892.
Situated down a long avenue is this simple single-storey standard rendered hip-roofed porter's lodge with a gabled hall projection; subsequently extended by an unsympathetic bay to left-hand side. An estate of the Butler family, it was recorded in 1780 as 'a most stately seat' but that 'The present proprietor has neglected it', and by 1818 was deserted, having the 'appearance of ancient magnificence, with extended park and gardens'. A certain renaissance of the place seems to have been effected towards the end of the nineteenth century by Sir Thomas Pierce Butler (1836–1909), who had succeeded to it as 10th baronet on the death of his father in 1862.

Luckombe 1780; Atkinson 1815; *BPB* (1929).

35. GRANGE PARK, Tullow; pre-1839.
A modest lodge, single-storey standard roughcast and gabled with a like-roofed projecting hall. Subsequently lengthened by a bay and given galvanised metal windows in a twentieth-century make-over. Originally serving a very simple farmhouse replaced around 1855 by Richard Fenton, who purchased the place after the death of John Whelan.

Griffith 1848–60.

36. HANOVER, Carlow; *c.* 1855; architect not known; *demolished.*

Irish Architectural Archive

Tragically, both the important early eighteenth-century house and its later quirky little pair of Italianate gatekeepers' lodges have been demolished. Each was an irregular single-storey gabled composition, the avenue elevation pedimented over a round-headed, stone hood-moulded bipartite window set in a stuccoed panel framed by rusticated pilaster quoins. To the approach off Burrin Street was a similarly rusticated breakfront containing the door-case with its dressed segmental arch breaking an open pediment. Both pediments were heavily mutuled in the manner of architect William Caldbeck. A property in 1846 of Simeon Clarke, miller and corn merchant of the town.

Slater 1846; IAA photographs (S/579/9 & 11).

HOLLODEN (see MALCOLMVILLE)

37. HOLLYBROOK, Myshall (2).
An estate in the early nineteenth century of Adam Bloomfield Feltus, both of the pre-1839 lodges to which had been demolished by 1908.

Leet 1814; Lewis 1837.

38. HUNTINGDON CASTLE, Clonegall; *c.* 1835/*c.* 1845.

Like the castle, the gate porter's accommodation appears to have evolved over the years. Located outside the entrance with its big spear-topped wrought-iron carriage gates and approached down a lane past estate workers' cottages is an appropriate introduction to the big house within. In the form of a miniature stone tower-house with pilaster quoins carried up its two storeys as mock turrets to a crenellated parapet, its single-bay front sits alongside a 1½-storey gabled adjunct in random rubble finish, the symmetrical three-bay elevation addressing the park. Probably created in two stages for William Leader Durdin (1778–1849), whose family had come by the property through marrying Esmonde daughters.

LGI (1904); Bence-Jones 1988; Williams 1994.

39. JOHNSTOWN, Carlow (2).

Two lodges, probably built by Rt Hon. William Frederick Fownes Tighe (1794–1878), who succeeded to the principal estate of Woodstock, Co. Kilkenny (*q.v.*), and Johnstown on the death of his father in 1816, although the latter was leased in the early nineteenth century to Revd Joseph Bunbury, followed by John Campion.

North gate; pre-1839; *demolished.*

South gate; *c.* 1830.
A pretty little lodge sympathetically extended to the rear to double the accommodation, though losing its chimney-stack in the process. In contrast to the steeply gabled, turreted and tall-chimneyed outline of the Tudor Gothic house, the lodge is a single-storey standard cottage with shallow hipped roof, its casement windows in roughcast walls below basic granite label mouldings, on each side of an entrance recess. The older gate pillars are topped by pineapple finials.

LGI (1904); Bence-Jones 1988; O'Toole 1993.

40. KELVINGROVE, Carlow; *c.* 1820; *demolished.*

A Regency villa, probably built by Thomas Haughton (1788–1851) following his Quaker wedding to Sarah Pim in 1817, his gate lodge presumably contemporary. The first OS map suggests that on plan it was double-fronted with a pair of bow windows, much as the lodge to Bennekerry Lodge (*q.v.*), and a miniature version of many of the gentlemen's villas in the county. It had been removed by 1938.

IFR.

41. KILCARRIG, Bagenalstown; pre-1839; *demolished.*

A property at the turn of the nineteenth century of the Humphreys family, both house and lodge having been removed by 1938.

Taylor and Skinner 1778; 1783 [1969]; Wilson 1803.

42. KILCARRY COTTAGE, Clonegall; pre-1839; *demolished.*

A lodge opposite its gates, which had gone by 1908, to a small holding in 1852 of William Drury, his gatekeeper Moses Doyle.

Griffith 1848–60.

43. KILCOLTRIM, Borris; pre-1839; *demolished.*

An important mid-eighteenth-century house sadly lies in ruin, its entrance marked by a pair of large rustic gate pillars, the lodge having gone by 1874. The property in 1814, and later, of Edmund Hagerty.

Leet 1814.

44. KILCUMNEY, Goresbridge; pre-1839; *demolished.*

An estate in 1852 of John Murphy, leasing from Viscount Beresford.

Griffith 1848–60.

45. KILGRANEY, Goresbridge; *c.* 1870.

A mid-Victorian porter's lodge, Classical in style, with its squared sash windows in recently cement-rendered walls; single-storey on an L-plan below a hipped roof. Alongside a good pair of earlier Georgian stone carriage pillars and a nice little hoop-topped iron postern gate. A property in 1852 of Francis R. Malcomson.

Griffith 1848–60.

46. KILNOCK, Ballon (2).

A property of the Lecky family, who were also to be found at neighbouring Ballykealey (*q.v.*). The house was lodgeless until the occupancy of Mary J. Lecky, who impressively remedied that situation.

East entrance; *c.* 1850.

Opposite a railed entrance screen with concave quadrants and V-jointed granite pillars is the lodge, framed by lower wing walls and pillars. A very solid, apparently single-storey standard affair, in fact raised off a basement storey in random stone facings; its bipartite sash windows and doorway have smooth chamfered dressings, the cut stone extending to quoins and a ground-floor string-course. Wide oversailing eaves to a shallow pyramidal roof, rising to the central chimney-stack in stone with recessed panels. Now all severed from its avenue by road realignment.

West entrance; *c.* 1850.

Almost identical to its eastern counterpart but located by its gateway; likewise of generous accommodation.

Griffith 1848–60; *LGI* (1904).

47. KILLINANE, Leighlinbridge; *c.* 1825.

A plain single-storey standard structure below a hipped roof with wide windows in harled walls. Contrastingly grand entrance screen of four large cut-stone pillars, with four-faced pedimented cappings, containing concave quadrant walls. Probably built by Edward Groome, who had succeeded the Mercer family to the property by 1814.

Wilson 1803; Leet 1814; Lewis 1837.

48. KILMACART, Hacketstown; pre-1839; *demolished.*

An estate in the early nineteenth century of the Hardy family, the lodge to which had been removed by 1908.

Leet 1814; Griffith 1848–60.

49. LEIGHLINBRIDGE RC CHURCH AND PAROCHIAL HOUSE, Leighlinbridge; pre-1839; *demolished.*

Surviving are large square pillars framing the carriage opening and concave quadrant walls, the right-hand one of which contains a flat-arched postilion opening.

50. LISNAVAGH, Rathvilly (3).

Another example in the county of the domestic work of architect Daniel Robertson in his familiar Tudor Gothic mode, here dating from 1847 for William Bunbury McClintock-Bunbury (1800–66), younger brother of the 1st Lord Rathconnel, who in 1846 had taken the Bunbury name and come from Drumcar, Co. Louth (*q.v.*), to reside here.

Main entrance; *c.* 1849; architect possibly D. Robertson.

Replacing an earlier lodge which lay deeper up the avenue is this strange and forbidding introduction in the form of a lofty wide wall

with canted wings relieved by buttresses and the central Tudor-arched carriage gate with hood moulding and sculpted dripstones below a stepped coping. Behind the wooden portcullis gates is screened single-storey porter's accommodation to each side in coursed rubble finish with single and bipartite label-moulded windows, one structure having a canted bay—but neither having an aspect of the road or visitors. Originally flat-roofed with octagonal chimney-flues. A peculiar design either by Daniel Robertson or the Dublin architect John McCurdy who succeeded him here.

School entrance; *c.* 1849; architect possibly D. Robertson.

A replacement opposite its gates for a predecessor further north. A pleasant dual-purpose structure, 1½-storey Tudor Revival with bi- and tripartite label-moulded windows in coursed rubble facings, its roof topped by two pairs of octagonal chimney-stacks rising from skew-table gables. Extending from each side are lower, plainer wings perhaps of later date. Opposite is a concave quadranted sweep with portcullis-type wooden gates.

East entrance; *c.* 1849.
Alongside the gate is a pair of semi-detached cottages, the closer having housed the gatekeeper; 1½-storey in dressed random stone facings with skew-table gables, each having three-bay fronts with smaller flat-roofed hall projections and minuscule windows containing cast-iron latticed glazing.

BPB (1929); *IAR* (1999).

51. THE LODGE, Bagenalstown; *c.* 1825.
A once single-storey standard lodge, stucco-finished with a hipped roof, raised sometime in the twentieth century by a roughcast storey; plain granite dressing to the front door. Of its entrance screen three of the original six monolithic granite posts survive, the same as those at Jenkinstown, Co. Kilkenny (*q.v.*), where architect William Robertson was employed. A property in the early nineteenth century of Matthew Weld.

52. LUMCLOON, Fennagh; *c.* 1860.
A far from pretty single-storey gabled cottage, roughcast on an L-plan with a later porch squeezed into the internal angle. Probably built by Samuel Henry Watson (1823–70), who inherited the estate on his father's death in 1853 and perhaps upon his marriage the following year carried out improvements.

IFR.

53. MALCOLMVILLE, Bagenalstown; *c.* 1750.

Here are the pathetic remains of an antique lodge with its steeply pitched hipped roof display of original tiny slates. Single-storey three-bay but not quite symmetrical, the bipartite casement windows on each side of a later flat-roofed hall projection, all in limewashed thick rubble walls. Vernacular compared with the later Classical gatescreen of six pillars with recessed panels, now lacking their pedestalled ball finials, and wide-railed concave quadrants with low walls. Built for a Mr Mulhadden whose estate subsequently came into the possession of the Vigors family, who renamed it 'Holloden' after their Devon roots. Their house lies in ruins.

ffolliott 1971b; Bence-Jones 1988; IAA photograph (S/141/12 & S/142/1).

54. MILFORD, Leighlinbridge; *c.* 1835.

The late Georgian house and extensive flour mill and malting business of the Alexander family, of whom John (1764–1843) would have built this pleasant Regency lodge. Single-storey standard with segmentally arched openings, its windows wide with bipartite sashes in rubble walls below a very shallow gabled roof with foiled bargeboards and a chunky brick chimney-stack over a finish of replacement corrugated iron. Wide gatescreen with cylindrical carriage pillars.

LGI (1912); O'Toole 1993.

55. MILK PARK, Ballon; pre-1839; *demolished.*
In the early nineteenth century there was an unidentified structure by the entrance to a previous avenue, subsequently abandoned and demolished by 1890 in favour of a new unlodged approach and gate further south. A seat of the Tomlinson family from the late seventeenth century until its sale in 1958.

O'Toole 1993.

56. MILL HOUSE, Tullow; *c.* 1860.
The 1839 OS map shows a cluster of buildings at the entrance to the corn mill and mill-owner's house, in the mid-nineteenth century of William Legett. The surviving gate lodge is of later date. Standard single-storey with a steeply hipped roof and bulky chimney-stack and having segmentally headed openings in rendered walls. From its front door projects the most grotesque flat-roofed addition. Derelict and blocked up. Good contemporary ironwork in carriage gates and matching ogee-railed quadrants. A property now called 'St Francis Farm'.

Slater 1846; Griffith 1848–60.

57. MOUNT LEINSTER LODGE, Borris; pre-1839; architect possibly Daniel Robertson; *demolished.*
Another villa in the county by architect Daniel Robertson for a Newton brother, this for the youngest, Henry (d. 1863), son of Philip Newton of Dunleckney (*q.v.*). His gate lodge has been replaced by a bungalow.

LGI (1904); *IAR* (1999).

58. MOUNT WOLSELEY, Tullow; *c.* 1864; architects Lanyon, Lynn and Lanyon.
Compared to Charles Lanyon's notable *porte-cochère* Italianate lodges of a decade earlier at Dundarave and Moneyglass, Co. Antrim, and Ballywalter and Eglantine, Co. Down, this distinctive porter's lodge is relatively clumsy but an appropriate prelude to the Belfast practice's house built for Sir John Richard A. Wolseley (1834–74), who in 1857

Irish Builder

became the 6th baronet on his father's death. Single-storey standard with a hefty chimney-stack on the shallow hipped roof. Segmentally arched windows flank a bulky projecting porch with its round-headed, keystoned entrance arch, the archivolts springing from a string-course to penetrate an open pediment. All in a rendered finish with stone dressings picked out in a striking paint scheme. Preceded by a highly decorative cast-iron gatescreen, 'off the shelf' from the foundry of Kennan and Sons of Fishamble Street, Dublin, almost precisely as advertised in 1876, though here personalised with the Wolseley monogram: Talbot's head crest as outer finials and, on the carriage pillars, 'out of a ducal coronet' a mysterious acorn device. These gates may post-date the lodge, probably being chosen by Sir Clement James Wolseley, who succeeded his brother.

DB (1 Sept. 1863); *IB* (1 May 1876); *BPB* (1929); Dean 1994.

59. MOYLE, Carlow (2).
An estate of the Bunbury family of Lisnavagh (*q.v.*); their house is now lost but was approached via two lodged avenues, both surviving at each end of what is now a public road—relieved of their duties.

South entrance; *c.* 1835.
A standard 1½-storey plain lodge with tall eaves to its steeply pitched hipped roof. Paired eaves brackets over tiny one-over-one sash windows in cement-rendered walls. Probably built by Thomas Bunbury, who was succeeded on his death in 1846 by his younger brother, Col. Kane Bunbury, who lived on here until 1874, in the interim replacing the other lodge.

North entrance; pre-1839/*c.* 1870; architect probably J. McCurdy.

Located not quite opposite its gates, presumably to facilitate later removal of its predecessor, is this jaunty little building, 1½-storey, its three-bay front not quite symmetrical. Built in rough-textured random granite with smooth dressings to segmentally headed door-case and shouldered bipartite window with a colonette divider. The steeply pitched skew-tabled roof rises from the corbelled eaves to a perforated scalloped red-crested ridge broken by a single spindly circular stone chimney-stack. More than probably the work of Dublin architect John McCurdy, who at this time was working for the family at Lisnavagh (*q.v.*) and in 1865 for Colonel Bunbury at his other estate of Rathmore (*q.v.*).

IB (1 June 1867); *LGI* (1904).

60. MYSHALL LODGE, Myshall; pre-1900; *demolished.*
A Victorian lodge built after 1839 for John Beauchamp Brady or his son John Cornwall Brady, their house likewise lost, burnt in 'the Troubles'.

O'Toole 1993.

61. NEWGARDEN, Carlow; pre-1839; *demolished.*
A property in 1814 of Christopher Williams, the lodge to which had been removed by 1908.

Leet 1814.

62. NEWSTOWN, Ardlattin (3).
A good neo-Classical villa built to designs of architects Thomas Alfred Cobden and James Sands for James Eustace (d. 1831) in 1824–8, incorporating an earlier house. In 1814 A. Atkinson on tour found the demesne 'enriched by beautiful and extensive plantations, and the gates, lodges, and fences, are judiciously disposed for ornament and protection'. Of these earlier gate lodges only that at the main gate remains and probably was not part of Cobden and Sands's commission. A single-storey standard lodge, plain but nicely proportioned, its six-over-six sash windows in rendered walls on each side of the doorway, since converted to a matching window, below a hipped roof. Also dating from around 1810 is the elegant straight entrance screen of tall square Classical granite pillars with triglyphed friezes and ball finials set off by contrasting rendered walls which contain postilion openings, the copings carried across as lintels. All lovingly tended.

Atkinson 1815; *LGI* (1904); Bence-Jones 1988.

63. NURSERYVILLE, Carlow; pre-1839; *demolished.*
The lodge, which had gone by 1938, was situated by the plant nursery after which the house took its name. In 1852 the property of William Whitmore.

Griffith 1848–60.

64. OAKPARK, Carlow (6).
Formerly 'Paynestown', a splendid demesne to which but one of the entrance lodges of the five that existed in 1839 has survived. A. Atkinson in April 1814 wrote: 'The principal part of this extensive demesne, which measures, as I was informed, near eight hundred acres, is enclosed by a wall eight or ten feet high, with gates and lodges, which accommodate and ornament the approaches to the concern'. Both lodges to the deer-park which enclosed a racecourse across the old Castledermot Road have been demolished. Colonel Henry Bruen (d. 1852) had succeeded his father to the property in 1797 as a minor and in 1822 married Anne Wandesford Kavanagh of Borris (*q.v.*), where architects Sir Richard Morrison and his son William Vitruvius had been employed nine years earlier. It was to the latter that the Colonel turned around 1832 to embellish the house and complement it with more imposing entrances.

Carlow Gate; *c.* 1840; architect probably W.V. Morrison.

At this previously lodgeless approach to the house is this magnificent triumphal archway, preceded by a walled carriage turn and series of pillars with outsized cappings. In fine ashlar, its massive entablature is carried on paired columns, Doric to the park and externally Ionic as an overture to the mansion's portico. The Morrisons, father and son, offered this design with flanking gatescreens and complementary temple lodges for Baronscourt, Co. Tyrone, and Castlecoole, Co. Fermanagh, without success; both remained unexecuted. Here the design is adapted to contain a room on each side of the archway as 'day and night' accommodation for a porter in the bulk of the grand pedestals. This must be a design realised posthumously, for W.V. Morrison died in 1838 and it does not appear on the 1839 OS map. Although Lacy in 1861 maintains that the archway was modelled on the Wellington Arch at Hyde Park, London, it is almost identical to the Pershore entrance at Croome Court, Worcestershire, seat of the earls of Coventry, to a design by Robert Adam of 1779.

Castledermot Gate; *c.* 1835; architect probably W.V. Morrison.

Of a pattern employed throughout the country by the Morrison office is this very fine neo-Classical single-storey lodge based on a cruciform plan, its granite features contrasting effectively with otherwise stuccoed surfaces. A tripartite window with fluted dressings is set deep within a recess framed by a pediment supported on stone piers with recessed panels, sculpted modillion brackets, identical to those of plaster in the dining room of the house, and the Morrison's hallmark laurel wreaths. Alternatively, this could be a design by J.B. Keane, who had been employed as assistant in the Morrison practice and was responsible in his own right for the mausoleum on the estate in 1841. It certainly is closer to his variants of this design at Stradone, Co. Cavan, Mount Richard, Co. Tipperary, and Rockgrove, Co. Cork. Despite retaining its avenue front, the lodge has been grotesquely enlarged into a plain two-storey house. The wreath motif, seen also on the portico of the big house, is repeated on the eight pillars of an impressive and extensive railed entrance screen.

Atkinson 1815; Lacy 1863; *LGI* (1904); McParland *et al.* 1989; Dean 1994.

ORCHARD (see WOODLANDS)

65. PARK, Carlow; *c.* 1835; *demolished.*

Opposite its gates is a standard single-storey lodge with tiny slates to a hipped roof having sturdy paired modillion brackets to the soffits of high oversailing eaves. In roughcast walls, sash windows flank a later door-case with a stylised Arts and Crafts open pediment, from which time dated the replacement red-brick panelled corbelled chimney-stack. A property at the turn of the nineteenth century of a Mr Barnes, who was followed here in 1814 by Richard Evans before Richard Dunne had become resident by 1852.

Wilson 1803; Leet 1814; Griffith 1848–60.

66. POLLACTON, or POLLERTON, Carlow (3).

'At Pollacton, nr. Carlow, the seat of Sir C. W. Cuffe Burton, Bart., there has lately been erected a handsome lodge, with large sweep entrance, having four ornamental piers and base course, massive iron gates and side railings. The walls are of finely-chiselled limestone from Royal Oak quarries, near Bagnelstown. The ironwork was supplied by Mr William Turner, Oxmanstown Foundry, Dublin. The designs were furnished by Messrs McCurdy and Mitchell. Mr Joseph F. Lynch, Carlow, was the contractor.' Thus informs an *Irish Builder* magazine of 1873. The fine gatescreen remains intact, its four pillars crowned by ogee-pedestalled ball finials, identical to those at the Burton family's other seat of nearby Burton Hall (*q.v.*), where architect John McCurdy had worked a decade earlier. The lodge, in an Italianate manner, much as those of his designs for Harristown, Co. Wicklow (*q.v.*), is single-storey and gabled on an L-plan; a bow window with its own half-cone roof extends from the avenue wing, with a flat parapeted roof to the hallway in the internal angle. Built in a punched ashlar, with contrasting smooth rusticated Irish pilasters as quoins and topped by an articulated stone chimney-stack, for Sir Charles William Cuffe Burton (1822–1902). It lies derelict but having fared better, thus far, than its big house, which along with its two earlier pre-1839 lodges is a thing of the past, neglect setting in upon the extinction of the baronetcy in 1902.

IB (1 March 1873); *BPB* (1929); McParland *et al.* 1989; O'Toole 1993.

67. RATHCROGUE, Carlow; pre-1839; *demolished.*

A lodge, opposite its gates, built for the Elliott family was by 1938 already a shell but probably eventually fell foul of road-widening.

68. RATHMORE PARK, Rathvilly (3).

A charming house in parkland, previously 'Paulville' of the Paul family, occupied in the early nineteenth century by Charles Putland, in whose time two lodges were in place.

North entrance; pre-1839; *demolished.* A gatekeeper's lodge opposite the gates to the secondary approach which was a shell by 1900.

South entrance; pre-1839/*c.* 1865; architect probably John McCurdy.

On the west bank of the River Slaney lie the fragments of an early single-storey stone lodge near its mid-Victorian successor. By about 1850 Colonel Kane Bunbury had taken up residence and by 1865 employed architect John McCurdy to enlarge and give the old house an Italianate make-over. His commission seems to have extended to a design for this appropriate prelude to the house. Standard single-storey with a moulded chimney-stack crowning a hipped roof with multi-bracketed soffit over segmentally arched keystoned openings with toothed dressings matching the quoins. Three-over-three sash windows flank a double-leafed panelled door in a gabled canopied porch with ornate carved wooden brackets, pendants and spiky hip-knobs. In 1999 this fine lodge was saved from dereliction, greatly extended to the rear, and restored with the unfortunate loss of its original windows and chimney-stack. Nearby is the contemporary ostentatious and extensive gatescreen comprised of balustered concave quadrants on stone plinth walls, contained by four tall stone pillars which flank carriage and postern gates hung on iron piers liberally decorated with foliage and anthemion motifs.

DB (1 Jan. 1865); O'Toole 1993.

69. RATHVINDEN, Leighlinbridge; *c.* 1820.

Another one of Carlow's charming double-bow-fronted villas, here approached via an equally delightful gatekeeper's cottage. A single-storey structure on an elongated octagonal plan with Georgian Gothic lancet openings of latticed glazing and a simple sheeted door in roughcast walls. Although no longer performing its original role, it is well maintained as a garden ornament. Presumably built for Revd Samuel T. Roberts, who is recorded as resident here in 1814 and 1837.

Leet 1814; Lewis 1837.

70. RATHWADE, Leighlinbridge; pre-1839; *demolished.*

A lodge which may have been contemporary with a house, yet another Tudor-style residence by architect Daniel Robertson for one of the sons of Philip Newton of Dunleckney (*q.v.*)—in this case a more rustic design for the third son, Beauchamp Bartholomew Newton.

IAR (1999).

71. RUSSELLSTOWN PARK, Carlow; *c.*

1825; architects probably T.J. Cobden and J. Sands.
A relatively commodious and sophisticated single-storey standard neo-Classical lodge, notable for its wide tetrastyle Doric pedimented portico with responding pilasters framing a recess which further deepens the entrance. On each side in crisp ashlar walls are windows with entablatures on crossettes, and underpanels, details which may point to a date later than the big house. The hipped roof is bound by an entablatured parapet and crowned by a bulky four-flue stone chimney-stack. Well maintained but with unsympathetic modern window replacements. The extensive gatescreen is comprised of six square pillars with unusual fluted and acanthus leaf-decorated friezes, containing railed quadrants and matching iron triple gateway, the carriage meeting rail sporting the family crest of a plume of five ostrich feathers out of a ducal coronet.

The house, which may be contemporary with its entrance, was commissioned in 1824 from architect Thomas Alfred Cobden in collaboration with James Sands by William Duckett (1796–1868), second son of like-named father of neighbouring Duckett's Grove (*q.v.*).

LGI (1904); Bence-Jones 1988; Colvin 2008.

72. ST AUSTIN'S ABBEY, Tullow; *c.* 1859; architect Benjamin Woodward.
When Charles Henry Doyne (1809–67) came to create his new home around 1856, he was seduced into embracing the newfangled Ruskinian Gothic style as pioneered in Ireland by his architects, the practice of Deane and Woodward. The commission included a complementary gate lodge which could almost be described as unique were it not for an almost identical lodge by Woodward at Clontra, Co. Dublin.

Whilst his house lies a tragic ruin, burnt in 1922, its lodge remains intact, as described by Seán Rothery: 'The robust gate lodge survives intact, however, and is an example of Woodward's wonderful

manipulation of geometry to produce arresting architectural forms. Even for a commission as small as a gate lodge the architect gives a unique identity and sense of importance to the building. The steep roof with its asymmetrically placed dormer window sits on top of a solid stone block. The stonework is a finely bonded squared rubble and the quite large stones are bonded without any obvious pattern and without regular quoins, giving a textural effect very different from a formal classical design. The dramatic chimney stack is a contradiction of this with its bold chamfers and ashlar masonry.' Below the tall, boldly corbelled eaves of its hipped roof, the regular three-bay front features a flat-roofed breakfront hallway flanked by bipartite casement windows, with more dressed granite in sills, lintels and mullions.

LGI (1904); Rothery 1997; O'Dwyer 1997b.

ST FRANCIS FARM (see MILL HOUSE)

73. ST MARY'S CEMETERY, Carlow; 1893.
An unprepossessing standard single-storey lodge with steeply pitched hipped roof and two symmetrically placed chimney-stacks to the ridge. Cement-rendered with toothed granite quoins and moulded window surrounds on each side of a hall projection, the gable of which contains a slate plaque bearing the inscription 'Carlow Urban Council 1893 John Hammond Esq. M.P. Chairman'. The graveyard opened on 20 July 1894.

74. ST PATRICK'S COLLEGE, Carlow; *c.* 1830; architect T.A. Cobden.
'The building, which consists of a spacious centre connected with two wings by corridors, is situated in a park comprising an area of 34 acres, nearly in the centre of the town, and enclosed with high walls and well-planted.' Access through these walls described in 1837 is via a splendid gatescreen of lofty rusticated carriage pillars flanked by round-headed postilion openings, all in granite pleasantly contrasting with whitewashed stuccoed concave quadrant walls. The over-ornate modern iron gates and vulgar overthrow sully the effect. This

combination of stuccoed walls and granite detailing is used to further advantage in Cobden's little masterpiece, a delightful single-storey neo-Classical composition, a porter's lodge with pediments, their tympana whitened contrasting with blank shields, that to the avenue spanning almost the full width of a strangely blind façade of an entrance portico comprising two fluted Doric columns *in antis*. Elsewhere liberal use is made of corresponding pilasters, whilst a four-square panelled ashlar single-flue chimney-stack crowns the ridges.

Lewis 1837.

SANDHILL (see BALLYREDMOND)

75. SLIGUFF, Bagenalstown; *c.* 1790.

The sad remains of a single-storey bow-ended rubble-built lodge with vestiges of limewash finish and a slated roof. Known in its heyday affectionately as the 'Teapot House'. A holding in the nineteenth century of the Dunbar family.

Griffith 1848–60.

76. STEWART LODGE, Leighlinbridge; pre-1839; *demolished.*
The 1939 OS map shows the lodge to be already in decline but the entrance arch survives as streetscape. In the form of a tall semicircular walled screen with round-headed openings, the high central carriage archway flanked by lower postern arches. Presumably built for William Richard Steuart.

LG (1863).

77. STRAWHILL, Carlow (2).

South gate; pre-1839; *demolished.*

North gate; *c.* 1830.

An elongated single-storey standard gabled lodge with roof catsliding over the hall projection; plain and cement-rendered. There are the remains of crisp limestone ashlar entrance pillars, two with lanterns. A dower house of the Bruen family of nearby Oakpark (*q.v.*) but occupied down the years by various lessees. Perhaps built in the time here of John Greene (1796–1840) of the Greenville Park (*q.v.*), Co. Kilkenny, family.

LGI (1904); O'Toole 1993.

78. TULLOWPHELIM RECTORY, Tullow; *c.* 1835.

A 1½-storey plain rendered structure, its front elevation asymmetrical with a single-storey gabled hall to the right-hand side. Possibly built during the incumbency (1832–60) of Revd John Beresford Johnston (1792/3–1860), his gatekeeper in 1852 John Hill. The avenue to the glebe house now severed.

Griffith 1848–60; Seymour and Leslie 2012.

79. UPTON, Bagenalstown; pre-1839; *demolished.*

The lost porter's lodge may have been contemporary with the house built for John Gray, to designs by Daniel Robertson, after he had purchased the estate in 1835 from the La Touche family of Marlay, Co. Dublin (*q.v.*).

O'Toole 1993.

80. VIEWMOUNT, Carlow; pre-1839; *demolished.*

The seat until his murder in the 1798 rebellion of Sir Edward Crosbie was thereafter absorbed into the Browne's Hill estate (*q.v.*) and for much of the early nineteenth century was leased to John Bennett.

Leet 1814; Pigot 1824; Brewer 1825.

81. WELLS C. of I. CHURCH, Leighlinbridge; *c.* 1810.

By the gate and fronting the footpath is this simple two-bay single-storey gabled sexton's lodge with a later hip-roofed appendage. Possibly built for the Revd Dean George Maunsell (1752/3–*c.* 1835), incumbent from 1804 to 1822, and contemporary with the building in 1810 of the church, which was demolished in 1963.

Seymour and Leslie 2012.

WOODFIELD, Bunclody (see COUNTY WEXFORD)

82. WOODLANDS, Ardattin; pre-1839; *demolished.*

Both house and gate lodge are survived by an extensive entrance screen of rustic concave quadrant walls stopped by carriage pillars with ball finials. Possibly dating from the time here of the Wolseley family, when the property was known as 'Orchard' at the end of the eighteenth century.

Taylor and Skinner 1778; 1783 [1969]; Wilson 1803.

83. WOODSIDE, Hacketstown; *c.* 1830.

An estate in the nineteenth century of the Jones family, whose gate lodge lies as a shell, recognisable as having been single-storey standard with a not quite symmetrical three-bay front of rubble stone with plain smooth opening surrounds and now minus its hipped roof. Intact is a gatescreen of four octagonal granite posts with convex quadrants of railings with fleur-de-lis finials and matching gates. Sheppard Jones was resident here in 1837 and 1852, perhaps the same as was then to be found at Bellgrove, south Dublin (*q.v.*).

Lewis 1837; Griffith 1848–60.

76. Stewart Lodge, Leighlinbridge

COUNTY DUBLIN (NORTH)

1. ABBEVILLE COTTAGE, Malahide; *c.* 1810.
A property, originally part of the greater Abbeville estate, subsequently renamed 'Cintra', was home in 1841 to Revd Edmond Nugent (1808–54). The lodge along with the house which he leased from the Cusacks is a delightful and, but for its modern squared plastic casements, quintessentially Irish single-storey standard example with a very shallow hipped roof, one end window incorporated into the boundary wall. Nicely rendered and finished in pastel yellow.

Thom's; *LGI* (1904).

2. ABBEVILLE, Malahide (2).
A seat with renowned connections down the years, the first being the Rt Hon. John Beresford, brother of the 1st marquis of Waterford, barrister, commissioner of revenue and taster of wines in the port of Dublin, who in 1790 engaged the prominent Anglo-Irish architect James Gandon to design a dairy, gates and stables, and renovate and extend the house which Beresford had named for his French wife. Both lodges were in place by 1837 and the surviving example can be dated to that busy period of building on the estate. That Gandon would have been bothered with such trifles is unlikely, and Gothic at that.

Inner gate; *c.* 1790.
What was a charming Georgian Gothic building has been shown scant respect over the centuries, despite being upgraded to command what is now the principal entrance, and recently a site of high security. A single-storey two-roomed lodge built off an elongated octagonal plan with a corresponding steep roof over whitewashed rendered walls containing lancet openings. Now almost obscured by luxuriant foliage and suffering a hideous modern flat-roofed hall appendage. Even the delightful ogee-railed gatescreen of about 1845 has shown it little respect in its positioning, although its pretty iron carriage piers are octagonal in section. The sweep terminates in squat stone pillars with ball finials. The gate porter to the 1850 proprietor, Henry Batchelor, was Thomas Hepenstal.

Outer gate; pre-1837; *demolished.*
Nothing remains of what may have been the original main approach or its lodge, which was occupied in 1850 by John Williams.

Griffith 1848–60; *BPB* (1929); McParland 1985; Haughey 1996.

ABBEY LODGE (see MARY VILLA, Castleknock)

3. ABBOTSTOWN, Blanchardstown (7).
The old estate of the Falkiner family which embraced the townlands of Abbotstown and Sheephill had by the late eighteenth century become the site of two big houses, the other having been built by Hans Hamilton and named after the latter townland. This accommodation is explained by an earlier marriage between the families, but following the death of Sir Frederick John Falkiner (1768–1824) his family's connection with the property ceased; their house was removed and that of the Hamiltons adopted the Abbotstown name. It was subsequently developed over the century into its present form by successive Hamiltons, who embellished existing entrances and added new lodges into the twentieth century.

Deanestown gate; pre-1837; *demolished.*
Probably one of the original Falkiner lodges, which was located opposite its gate.

Blanchardstown gate; pre-1837; *demolished.*
Lost in the great earthworks to accommodate the new motorway. The gatekeeper in 1849 was Charles Conlan.

Abbotstown gate; *c.* 1865; architect possibly J.F. Kempster; *demolished.*

A lodge built after 1837, also swept away to make way for roadworks, surviving which are the remnants of a once-magnificent gatescreen to be found at the neighbouring entrance to Elmgreen (*q.v.*). Two of the six original stone pillars with extensive concave railed quadrants have been re-erected there and are identical to a similarly re-sited entrance from Garbally Court in County Galway, which would suggest that the architect was J.F. Kempster of Ballinasloe. The pillars rise in stages with raised-panel rusticated frontispiece to intermediate cappings with dentil courses and heavily mutuled main caps above that again. The lost lodge may have been part of Kempster's scheme commissioned by James Hans Hamilton (1810–63).

Sheephill south gate; pre-1837; *demolished.*
A lodge which had been removed by 1910; its gate porter in 1849 was Robert Thornton.

Dunsink Gate; *c.* 1820.
Opposite its entrance is a plain single-storey standard lodge on a square plan with clipped eaves. Extending flat-roofed hall and modern PVC windows.

Hans Wellesley Hamilton (1886–1942) inherited the estate as 2nd Baron Holmpatrick on the death of his father in 1898 and added two lodges to the extreme north of the property.

Sheephill north gate; *c.* 1900; architects possibly Kaye-Parry and Ross.

A solid and commodious 1½-storey Victorian Italianate composition, with its back separated from the road by a later single-storey lean-to extension. Constructed in pleasant rubble facings embellished with toothed red-brick quoins and dressings to six-over-six sash windows. The fascias return across the gables to form open pediment features with paired bracket supports. To the ridge is a variegated brick chimney-stack and a semblance of the original terracotta fleur-de-lis cresting. Occupied.

Sheephill north-east gate; pre-1837/*c.* 1900; architects possibly Kaye-Parry and Ross.

Replacing an earlier lodge, whose gatekeeper in 1849 was John Murphy, is this single-storey standard gabled successor. Far from standard in appearance is this incredibly brazen and original affair in a variety of materials. Paired brackets decorate eaves and the verges of open pediments to the main gables and that of the hall breakfront, which has an *oeil-de-boeuf* above the front door with its canted arched head and matching drip moulding, a feature repeated above the bipartite margined casement windows. All in roughcast finish with a surplus of red-brick toothed highlighting in dressings and quoins.

Ornamental cresting between the chimney-stacks has fallen foul of the vandals. Strangely abandoned and derelict. Alongside are equally forthright and contemporary quarry-faced stone pillars.

Wilson 1803; Griffith 1848–60; *LGI* (1904); Ball 1995; *BPB* (1949).

4. AIRFIELD, Castleknock; pre-1836/*c.* 1905; architect probably R.F.C. Orpen.

A late Georgian villa in 1837 of the Manders family, from whom by 1849 it had passed to George Frederick Brooke of Colebrooke, Co. Fermanagh. By tradition his grandson of the same name, who was created 1st Baronet Summerton (1849–1926) in 1903, was forced to sell 'Summerton', as it had been renamed, in 1911 through his excessive spending on collecting and hospitality. This intemperance, however, must have extended to improvements and building, for the replacement gate lodge appears on the 1906–7 OS map. The architectural partnership of Orpen and Dickinson is recorded as working on the house for T.K. Laidlaw after 1911, but Orpen may already have been commissioned by Sir George prior to the sale of the place. Unlike its predecessor, this striking Arts and Crafts composition is set back from the roadside on an L-plan, single-storey below a hipped roof, with a smooth rendered frieze and carved eaves brackets. In contrast to otherwise six-over-six sash windows, that to the leading corner is chamfered with small-paned leaded casements, all in a distinctive and typically Edwardian pebble-dash finish. To the internal corner the front door is sheltered by a bracketed flat-roofed canopy. The (now) smooth rendered four-flue chimney-stack pierces a roof finish of Westmoreland green slate. There is a fine contemporary extensive railed gatescreen with antique-style spear tops and ashlar pillars, those to the carriage opening being rusticated, as are their dainty ball finials.

Lewis 1837; *BPB* (1929); Bence-Jones 1988; Williams 1994.

5. AIRFIELD LODGE, Balgriffin; pre-1837; *demolished.*

A property, later known as 'Ayrfield', was home in 1837 to Alderman Sir Edmund Nugent.

Lewis 1837.

6. ALBERT AGRICULTURAL COLLEGE, Glasnevin; *c.* 1900; architect probably J.F. Fuller; *demolished.*

The lodge, presumably by architect James Franklin Fuller, is survived by its huge rusticated granite entrance pillars and inner cast-iron carriage posts.

Williams 1994.

7. ALBERT TERRACE, Jones's Road, Clonliffe; *c.* 1850; *demolished.*

A housing development of John Vincent, solicitor, whose gatekeeper in 1854 was William Hanlon.

Griffith 1848–60.

8. ALDBOROUGH HOUSE/BARRACKS, Portland Row; *c.* 1840.

Irish Architectural Archive

The grand town house built in 1792–8 by Edward Stratford, 2nd earl of Aldborough, which fared considerably better than his country seats, despite being deserted by the family and serving as a school until 1829. A 1796 engraving shows it to have been originally preceded by an elegant railed semicircular gatescreen which by 1821 had been superseded by a tall impenetrable wall to confine the children. Common to these two views and surviving today is the pair of Portland stone carriage pillars with V-jointed rustication but minus their lion tops, incorporated into a new straight screen and accompanied by a gate lodge. Probably more accurately called a guardhouse added when the place became a military barracks, it is a simple two-roomed single-storey structure with a hipped roof, a long, coursed rubble-built four-window bay elevation to the footway, and a three-bay cut-stone arcaded façade keeping watch over the rear of the carriage gates.

Georgian Society Records (Vol. IV).

9. ALLANDALE, Clonsilla; pre-1837; *demolished.*

A seat in the mid-nineteenth century of George Hill.

10. ALLENSWOOD, Lucan; *c.* 1845.

A standard single-storey lodge with plain soffit brackets to a shallow hipped roof. Whitewashed harled walls with a simple clipped verge-gabled hall projection tucked in below the eaves. The most unremarkable of lodges were it not for the pretty hexagonal-pattern cast-iron casement windows. A villa and lodge built by James Cahill. Later extended to the rear into a double pile.

Griffith 1848–60.

ALL HALLOWS COLLEGE (see DRUMCONDRA)

11. ALL SAINTS' CHURCH AND RECTORY, Grangegorman; *c.* 1910.

In stark contrast to the 1828 First Fruits church and other grey buildings in the complex is this red-brick single-storey plain astylar box, almost square in plan, with clipped eaves to its hipped roof which rises to an oversized corbelled chimney-stack. Modern plastic windows below segmental arches and unsightly rear extension. Built during the lengthy (1887–1923) incumbency of Revd Henry Hogan (1840–1923). The old glebe house has been replaced.

Casey 2005; Leslie and Wallace 2001.

ALMS HOUSE (see CARLINGFORD)

12. ANNADALE, Fairview; pre-1837; *demolished.*

A lodge, which by 1907 had gone, to a property in 1837 of William Hone, whose gate porter twelve years later was Anne Downey.

Lewis 1837; Griffith 1848–60.

13. ANNA LIFFEY MILLS, Lucan; *c.* 1845.

Forsaken and forlorn by the banks of the River Liffey is this single-storey standard early Victorian lodge in a mild Italianate manner, the window openings of its avenue front set in segmentally headed recesses mimicking the lodges of neighbouring Dunavarra and Luttrelstown (*q.v.*). The doorway has a moulded architrave in rendered walls below the oversailing hipped roof. Abutting is the contemporary gatescreen of a pair of Classical pillars with recessed moulded panels and corniced cappings, carrying good iron gates with poppy finial to the meeting rails. Like the flour mill-owner's house, built by the proprietor, Richard Rainsford.

Griffith 1848–60.

14. ANNSBROOK, Clontarf; pre-1837; *demolished.*

A property of ever-changing ownership, in 1846 occupied by Robert Brunton, brush-maker.

Slater 1846.

ÁRAS AN UACHTARÁIN (see VICEREGAL LODGE)

15. ARCHBISHOP'S PALACE, Drumcondra; 1889; architect William Hague.

A typically excessive late Victorian response is this complex for the Roman Catholic Dublin archdiocese, both the palace and its contemporary lodge compositions in orange brick and grey stone dressings with Baroque detailing. As an introduction is the ostentatious gatescreen of beautifully chiselled masonry, the main carriage pillars with moulded panels and splendid leafy cartouches, fluted friezes, dentilled cappings and lanterns atop. On each side containing the pedestrian gates the secondary pillars are similarly panelled with paterae to their friezes, and crowned by rusticated balls with their own finials over that again; suitably extravagant ironwork to the gates. Overlooking this is a chunky single-storey standard porter's lodge with a hipped roof displaying terracotta hip and ridge tiles and ball-finialled hip-knobs. The openings have bold moulded surrounds with shoulders and scroll keystones to segmental heads, and bands of stone form an eaves frieze and sill course with a prominent plinth. From the main avenue front projects a hip-roofed hallway, whilst to the road is a semi-octagonal bay with corresponding roof. Commodious, as it extends in like finish to the rear; an appropriate banded chimney-stack with moulded capping tops it off.

IAA.

16. ARDGILLAN CASTLE, Balbriggan (6).
Sometime 'Prospect House', a maritime villa of the 1st earl of Bective of Headfort, Co. Meath (*q.v.*), was transformed from a plain Georgian house in stages into the present rambling castellated affair by his fifth son, the Hon. and Revd Henry Edward Taylor (1768–1852), and the latter's eldest son, Col. Edward Thomas Taylor (1811–83). Although the demesne and its structures have since 1982 been in the care of Fingal County Council, it is sad that the same concern was not shown for its lodges, not one of which remains. Of the five which served the property in 1837, two at the southern approach and the rest on the coast road, photographic record survives of that on the northern approach.

Balbriggan or Harmon's lodge; *c.* 1835; architects W. and H. Laxton; *demolished.*

Joe Curtis

J.C. Loudon

Although the architects for this peculiar design are known, it is doubtful whether they were ever engaged by Revd Taylor; rather it was sourced from J.C. Loudon's *An encyclopaedia of cottage, farm and villa architecture and furniture* (1833), in which it was published complete with working details and specification, with an estimated construction cost of £257.15.7. Faithfully reproduced in its two-storey commodious gabled form, it was an eccentric Tudor castellated affair with an irregular two-bay façade to the avenue, its skew-tabled full-height projection containing the hallway and a bedroom closet over. The front door had a hood-moulded Tudor archway below a label-moulded window with pretty hexagonal glazing pattern and a shield above that again in rendered walls. To the park, strangely hidden from the visitor and spurning the sea view, a main gable was flanked by a pair of two-stage crenellated turrets, with mock arrowslits, intended to house 'light closets'. An appropriate prelude to the big house beyond, it was sadly removed in about 1990.

The coming of the railway in the Dublin–Drogheda branch line in 1842 and the consequent realignment of the coast road spared the Balbriggan lodge but required the demolition of two other porters' lodges, both of which were subsequently replaced but the southernmost of which is recorded in family snapshots.

South coastal lodge; pre-1837/*c.* 1860; architect probably Sandham Symes; *demolished.*

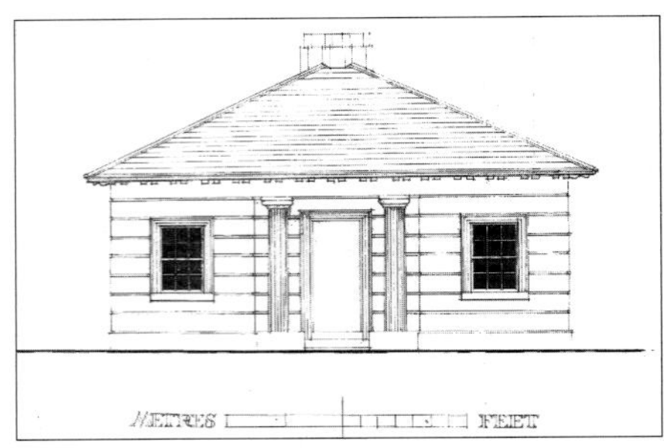

Sandwiched between road and railway at a level crossing and on the site of a predecessor was this very fine neo-Classical lodge. Colonel T.E. Taylor in 1863 had plans drawn up for additions and improvements to the house by Sandham Symes, an architect noted for his Classical banks and castellated villas, so why he seems to have chosen the former style as introduction to the baronial pile makes it a curiosity. Single-storey standard on a square plan beneath a hipped roof rising to a cluster of hexagonal chimney-flues, the eaves emphasised by pairs of carved modillion brackets. The front elevation was treated as horizontal channelled rustication punctuated by six-over-six sash windows with moulded surrounds on each side of a central entrance recess screened by a pair of fluted Doric columns *in antis*. Another lodge that was relatively generous in its four-roomed accommodation and could so easily have been adapted and extended for modern living but was mindlessly removed. The carriage gates had a poppy finial to the meeting rails identical to those at the Anna Liffey Mills entrance (*q.v.*).

Loudon 1833; *LGI* (1904); *BPB* (1929); Keane *et al.* 1995.

17. ARTANE CASTLE, Artane (2).

'The old castle was pulled down in 1825, and on its site and with its materials was erected, by the late Matthew Boyle, Esq., uncle of the present proprietor, U. Callaghan, Esq., a handsome house.' Thus did Samuel Lewis record in 1837 when the two lodges, now both removed, were already in place. In 1848 the porters were John Ryan and Lawrence Halpin as lessees of Matthew Callaghan, whose family's interest in the property ceased in 1870 when it was acquired by the Christian Brothers, who established an industrial school here. At the south entrance all that survives is a conspicuous pair of granite carriage pillars with, on the cappings, remarkable sculpted portions of heraldic wreaths with anthemion motifs to their ends.

Lewis 1837; Griffith 1848–60; Lyons 1993.

18. ARTANE, Artane; pre-1837; *demolished.*
A seat from early in the nineteenth century of Thomas Alley, whose gatekeeper in 1848 was Patrick Bedford.

Lewis 1837; Griffith 1848–60.

ARTANE LODGE (see KILLGRIEF LODGE)

19. ASHBROOK, Blanchardstown; *c.* 1835.
A single-storey lodge with some margined windows and serrated bargeboards, much modernised and extended through time. In 1848 home to Revd William Alexander Neville (b. 1814), later canon of St Canice's Cathedral, Kilkenny. His gate porter was John Woods.

Griffith 1848–60; *LGI* (1904).

20. ASHFIELD, Ashtown; pre-1843; *demolished.*
A seat of William Oldham in 1837 whose lodge had gone by 1907.

Lewis 1837.

21. ASHTON, Ashtown; pre-1837/1891; architect William Hague.

This was in 1837 the seat of attorney Josias Dunne, who was still in residence in 1849, when his gatekeeper was Mary Keating. Later in the century the place was transformed, the house being done up in an Italianate cloak and a new gate lodge built at the other side of the entrance for Alderman Andrew Thomas Moore. His architect was the same as was responsible for the archbishop's palace, Drumcondra (*q.v.*), identified as William Hague, an attribution based on the comparative form of the lodges and the close similarity of these Ashton gate pillars to the secondary ones at Drumcondra. This is a commodious single-storey hip-roofed lodge, rendered with moulded opening surrounds, Irish pilaster quoins, a moulded plinth and bracketed eaves. The hall projects with side entry below a hipped roof with terracotta finials to ridges. Dominating is a four-flue chimney-stack with prominent corniced capping. The opulent gatescreen boasts four grand Classical pillars with vermiculated plinth panels, chamfered shafts, friezes with paterae ornament, and moulded cappings terminating in rusticated ball features with their own finials; equally decorative iron carriage and postilion gates.

Lewis 1837; Griffith 1848–60; *Thom's*.

22. ASHTOWN, Ashtown; pre-1837/*c.* 1906; architect probably Edwin Bradbury; *demolished.*

A thoroughly English Elizabethan Revival cabin with an abundance of 'black-and-white' work. Single-storey and steeply gabled on an L-plan, with a balustraded entrance porch in the internal angle. All in keeping with Bradbury's extensions to the house and adjacent turnstiles, stables and grandstands to the racecourse for the Phoenix Park Race Committee. On the road boundary is an extensive railed enclosure with matching carriage and pedestrian gates hung on three cast-iron pillars, each having a finial of a phoenix rising. All replacing an earlier house and lodge.

IB (3 Nov. 1906); Williams 1994.

23. ASHTOWN LODGE, Blanchardstown; pre-1837/*c.* 1870.

An exceptionally commodious and sophisticated lodge, probably much extended and improved by a Captain Murray about 1870. The early pre-1837 standard single-storey lodge could still be there, refaced in ashlar and flanked by advancing gabled single-bay wings to match the central breakfront. The whole is united by a moulded eaves band with paired brackets continuing about the projections as paired mutules to form three open pediments; unusually narrow windows with recessed surrounds. In 1848 the gatekeeper was John Boles, as tenant of John Croker. Simple railed quadrants with palmette finials as gatescreen.

Griffith 1848–60; Slater 1870.

24. ASHTOWN MILLS, Ashtown (2).
In 1849 the oil mills and house of proprietor Bernard McGarry, of the family business of Michael McGarry and Sons, copper, lead and oil merchants, on 135 acres with two gate lodges, whose porters were John Brannan and James Gorman. Both lodges have been demolished.

Slater 1846; Griffith 1848–60.

25. AUBURN, Killester; pre-1837/*c.* 1870.
A standard single-storey porter's lodge with shallow hipped roof and eaves sailing beyond pebble-dashed walls with bipartite casement windows. Derelict. 'Auburn' inscribed on each of the banded gate pillars, which are framed by modest pebble-dashed ogee quadrant walls. Probably all originally in brick facings to match the villa it served, built for the Walsh family. There was an earlier lodge on the site to an older property in 1848 of Anthony Corcoran.

Griffith 1848–60; *Thom's*.

26. AUBURN, Malahide; pre-1837; *demolished.*
An estate in the early nineteenth century of the Crawford family which by mid-century had passed to the Donnellys.

27. BALCURRIS, Santry; pre-1907; *demolished.*
A property in 1870 of Joseph Kinsey, the gate lodge to which was erected after 1837.

Slater 1870.

28. BALGRIFFIN, Balgriffin; pre-1837; *demolished.*
A very fine demesne of which little evidence remains. Neither the old castle of Richard Talbot, earl of Tyrconnell, nor the replacement house, built by the Walker family with stones from the castle, have survived. The gate lodge was removed before 1906.

Wilson 1803; Lewis 1837; Craig and Fewer 2002.

29. BALHEARY, Swords (2).
Both lodges to a residence of Arthur Baker have gone, when in 1837 at least one was in place. By 1849 his gatekeepers are documented as John Bell and Michael Higgins.

Lewis 1837; Griffith 1848–60.

30. BALLYCOOLEN TOWNLAND, Blanchardstown; pre-1907; *demolished.*
One of two farmhouses in the townland which remained anonymous on the OS maps. A lodge built after 1837, the proprietor of which in 1848 was John O'Connor.

Griffith 1848–60.

31. BALLYCOOLEN TOWNLAND, Mulhuddart; pre-1837; *demolished.*
An anonymous property in 1848 of Edward Reilly, the lodge to which had gone by 1906.

Griffith 1848–60.

32. BALLYGALL, Finglas; pre-1837; *demolished.*
A seat at the turn of the nineteenth century

of Revd William Darley which by 1849 was home to John Dennis, whose gate porter was Patrick Lambe.

Griffith 1848–60; Ball 1995.

33. BALROTHERY RECTORY, Balrothery; *c.* 1890.

The glebe house considerably pre-dates its lodge, having been built in 1815. This is a highly unusual late Victorian composition, 1½-storey and lofty, its high eaves accommodating loft rooms. Faced in roughcast with much red-brick relief in moulded plinth top and eaves band, sill course, pilaster quoins, soldier arches and chimney-stack. The leading elevation has uncommon fenestration, three-bay symmetrical with a central pair of windows; door to rear. Occupied. Built in the incumbency (1887–1909) of Revd John Neuman Lombard (1859–1917).

Lewis 1837; Leslie and Wallace 2001.

34. BASKIN HILL, Cloghan; pre-1837; *demolished.*

A house built by James Saurin (1759–1842) when he was curate of St Doolagh's (1783–1801); he was later elevated to bishop of Dromore. He was succeeded here by the Tymons family, whose gatekeeper in 1848 was Patrick Carey. The lodge had gone by 1906.

Lewis 1837; Griffith 1848–60; Leslie and Wallace 2001.

35. BAYMOUNT CASTLE, Clontarf (2).

The plain late eighteenth-century house, previously called 'Granby Hall' and 'Baymount House', was acquired *c.* 1835 by the solicitor and property developer Robert Warren (1787–1869), who was seduced by the newfangled fantasy Castellated Tudor trend. Whilst half-heartedly cloaking the house in some fairytale trappings, he fully embraced the style in a new entrance at the inland gate. This seems to be the forerunner of similar developments at his residence of Killiney Castle and Victoria Castle (*q.v.*). There is little doubt that his architect both here and later in south Dublin was his nephew Sandham Symes, subsequently known for his Italianate villas and banks but early in his career proving himself a master of the Tudor Picturesque composition.

Mount Prospect Avenue gate; *c.* 1838; architect probably Sandham Symes.

David Griffin

A delightful design comprised essentially of two interlocking ashlar boxes, one containing a lofty parlour with canted bay window to the park, the other a two-storey bedroom tower with tiny bartizan. Both are crenellated

David Griffin

with a hint of mock machicolations, and fenestrated by false arrowloops and single and bipartite windows with label mouldings terminating in sculpted grotesque head dripstones. Abutting is the Tudor-arched carriage gateway flanked by round turrets, and alongside the similarly headed postilion opening with stepped gable containing a shield. The whole is framed by wide concave battlemented quadrant walls stopped by round towers. One should be grateful that this fine entrance lodge is occupied, well maintained and sensitively extended, but not that the great semicircular forecourt has been enclosed by a modern boundary wall and rather selfishly screened and removed from the sight of passing public admiration.

Clontarf Road Gate; pre-1837; *demolished.*

By the shore to what was probably the original main gate was a round lodge, perhaps an 'inkpot', and contemporary with the original house.

The gatekeepers in 1848 are recorded as James Mooney and Thomas Chambers.

Lewis 1837; Griffith 1848–60; *LGI* (1904); Bence-Jones 1988; Fewer 2001.

36. BEACHFIELD, Clontarf; pre-1837; *demolished.*

A residence in 1837 of John Tudor, which by 1848 had passed to Dr John L. Moore, whose lodge lay vacant.

Lewis 1837; Griffith 1848–60.

37. BEAU, Rush; *c.* 1835.

Jim Shaw

Since renamed 'Knockdromin', it was a seat of the Smith family. Their lodge remains as a pretty single-storey standard cottage of that particular Italianate Tudor mix, with its very shallow-pitched hipped roof with a gable formed over the breakfront hall containing a chamfered Tudor-arched doorway with distant hood moulding. Flanking this in harled walls are bipartite square-paned casement windows similarly with chamfered reveals. There is a lofty central, diagonally set, square chimney-stack. Sometime later extended in like manner seamlessly by a bay. There are what appear to be late Georgian ashlar carriage pillars with friezes and moulded cappings, and straight screen walls, lacking postern openings, flanked by convex quadrants beyond.

Leet 1814.

38. BEAUMONT, Beaumont (3).

A once-proud estate now overrun by modern development, the semblance of one lodge remaining of the three in place in 1837, built by Arthur Guinness (1725–1803) and/or his son of the same name (1768–1855) of the famous brewing family and ancestors of future baronets and lords. The surviving south-west entrance lodge is a tatty-looking affair now extended to two storeys, the upper floor clad in haphazard mock-Elizabethan fashion below a hipped roof, the original ground floor in very roughcast finish. In use. Two of the gatekeepers in 1848 were Thomas Lynch and James Nicholson.

Griffith 1848–60; *BPB* (1929).

39. BEECH PARK, Mulhuddart (2).

A small estate in 1848 of Henry B. Clarke, whose gatekeepers were then Nicholas Mulvany and John Clampit, one of whom occupied the most delightful of lodges.

East lodge; pre-1837; *demolished.*

West lodge; *c.* 1820.

Surviving at the main gate is this example of architectural whimsy obscured by laurel. Two-roomed single-storey, its short main front to the avenue is three-bay, the front door flanked by lunettes, all in a recess behind a portico formed by a pair of square posts *in antis* carrying a Classical portico, in the tympanum of which is a Gothic quatrefoil motif. Occupied and finished in stark white harling, it apparently had a twin at nearby Clonsilla House (*q.v.*).

Griffith 1848–60.

40. BEECHWOOD, Portmarnock (2).

A seat in the early nineteenth century of N.J. Trumbull, the pre-1837 lodges to which are both lost. The porters in 1848 were Michael Ryan and Catherine Flaherty.

Lewis 1837; Griffith 1848–60.

41. BELCAMP HALL, Balgriffin (3).

An estate of the eighteenth-century politician Sir Edward Newenham (1734–1814), after whose death it was acquired by Charles Stewart Hawthorne. Of the three lodges to this lofty brick mansion not one survives. One may have pre-dated 1760, as suggested by John Rocque's map, but certainly all were in place by 1837. The remaining gatescreen on the eastern avenue gives some clue as to

the previous grandeur at the entrance. The square granite late eighteenth-century pillars have friezes with fluting which continues through on each side to entablature lintels across the postilion openings. Nice contemporary iron gates, the bowed top of the carriage leaves adapted to accommodate the widened opening. The OS maps show the accompanying lodge to have been spacious, with projecting wings creating a central recess to the road elevation. Its gatekeeper in 1848 was James Byrne.

Lewis 1837; Griffith 1848–60; *LGI* (1904); d'Alton 1976 [1838]; Ferguson 1998.

42. BELCAMP, Balgriffin; pre-1837; *demolished.*
A lost lodge, occupied in 1848 by George Brannagan, to a big house in the nineteenth century of the Chamley family, which itself lies a burnt-out shell.

Griffith 1848–60; Craig and Fewer 2002.

43. BELCAMP HUTCHINSON, Balgriffin; *c.* 1820.
'The seat of the Hon. Francis Hutchinson, a large handsome brick house, beautifully situated, with a fine view of the sea, and adjacent country; the demesne consists of about fifty acres, well cultivated and wooded, and excellent gardens.' Thus did Archer find the place in 1801 and, remarkably, both house and lodge survive. The latter is a plain standard single-storey affair facing the park under a hipped roof, with a segmentally headed doorway in later rendered walls and extended by an extra bay to the left-hand side with modern windows. Probably built by Francis Hely Hutchinson (1759–1827), whose father, the provost of TCD, had erected the house.

Archer 1801; *BPB* (1929).

44. BELCAMP PARK, Balgriffin (3).
Of neither house nor lodges is there a sign, the former having been a seat since 1681 of the Grattan family, later being a property of Sir Henry Meredyth Jervis-White-Jervis (1793–1869), who for most of the mid-nineteenth century let it to George Farren. The lodge on the eastern approach was circular in plan and may have been of the Georgian 'inkpot' variety.

Lewis 1837; Griffith 1848–60; *BPB* (1929); Craig and Fewer 2002.

45. BELFIELD PARK, Artane; pre-1837; *demolished.*
A seat in the early nineteenth century of Major Edward Cottingham (1790–1848), inspector-general of prisons, after whose death it was home to Isaias English, whose gate porter was William Spencer.

Lewis 1837; Griffith 1848–60; *LGI* (1904).

46. BELLE VUE, Finglas; *c.* 1810; *demolished.*
'In the vicinity are three private lunatic asylums', this one of which in 1837 was that of William Gregory MD, whose gatekeeper in 1848 was John Dillon. Prior to this, in 1783 it had been a residence of Mitchell, Esq., although the gatescreen and lodge look later. The porter's cottage was a simple single-storey two-bay affair with tiny windows below a hipped roof with clipped eaves. This leading front, in roughcast finish, was parallel with the straight entrance alongside. Two segmentally headed postern openings flanked a pair of tall carriage pillars raised in quarry-faced stone block to be crowned by fine rusticated ball finials. At the other side to balance the lodge was a railed screen.

Taylor and Skinner 1778; 1969 [1783]; Lewis 1837; Griffith 1848–60.

47. BELLEVUE PARC, Castleknock; pre-1837; *demolished.*
The property in 1837 of Alexander Ferrier, warehouseman, haberdasher and stationer. The lodge was removed about 1865 to make way for the new Victorian replacement which was to serve Knockmaroon Lodge (*q.v.*) beyond.

Lewis 1837; Slater 1846.

48. BELL GROVE, Clontarf; *c.* 1870.
Now severed from the avenue to the house, secreted behind the right-hand entrance quadrant, obscured by later extensions and modernised out of all recognition, is what was a single-storey hip-roofed affair, only the roll-top ridge tiles and dog's tail hip-knobs giving any clue as to original age. A property which had a succession of owners, that in 1870 being John F. Biggs.

Thom's.

49. BELLE VILLE, Phoenix Park; *c.* 1815.

Opposite the Ashtown Gate to the Phoenix Park is the entrance to a seat in 1837 of J. Murphy, the lodge to which remarkably survives, although recent road realignment has laid bare its two-bay window elevation to the back of the footpath. Single-storey and hip-roofed, its main façade with a breakfront containing a segmentally headed tripartite window, below its own hipped roof, faces across the forecourt to monitor visitors. Originally harled with a pleasant white limewashed finish, it has now been modernised with a pebble-dash cloak; crisp new synthetic 'slates' with red concrete hip tiles, and much added to. To the carriage pillars are cast-iron eagles, with urns to those on each side.

Lewis 1837.

50. BELMONT, Raheny; pre-1837; *demolished.*
A small estate in the early nineteenth century of the White family.

51. BELVIDERE, Drumcondra; pre-1837/1911; architects Ashlin and Coleman.

The earlier entrance lodge to the site must have played host to an ever-changing series of proprietors. The early Georgian house initially was fairly settled as the residence of the Coghills, following which, until 1794, it became home to Lord Rokeby, primate of all Ireland, when it was briefly 'Primate's-Hill'. Thereafter it passed to Lord Chancellor Bowes, who had 'a fine entrance from "the great road to Drogheda"'. In 1801 it was 'the seat of the widow Sweetman ... in a demesne of about fifty acres, enclosed with a stone wall'. After 1837 it was acquired by Colonel Duncan McGregor, inspector-general of constabulary, whose gatekeeper in 1848 was John Harvey. After many more comings and goings, Belvidere was purchased by the Vincentians around 1885 and assumed its present role as St Patrick's Training College for teachers, the first architect for the conversion being J.L. Robinson. He was succeeded by George Ashlin, whose contribution is recorded in the *Irish Builder* magazine in 1911: 'A handsome new lodge on the Drumcondra Road at the entrance to St Patrick's Training College is being built by Mr Clarke contractor of Harold's Cross. The inside walls are in brick, the outside in concrete. Ashlin & Coleman, architects.' Had the publication not been so hasty in reporting the occasion, it could have described the pebble-dash finish to a fine single-storey gabled Arts and Crafts composition on an irregular plan with 'black-and-white' work on the gables, that to the avenue advancing to extend over a shallow bow window with leaded lights. In the internal angle is a rustic verandah-cum-entrance porch with bench seating. To the rear the accommodation extends into a double pile, above which is a conspicuous brick chimney-stack—a cluster of octagonal flues, above an earthenware plain tiled roof.

Archer 1801; Wilson 1803; Griffith 1848–60; *IB* (9 Dec. 1911); Ball 1995; Williams 1994.

BETTYGLEN (see RAHENY PARK)

52. BETTYVILLE, Lusk (2).
A property in 1814 of George Wilson which ten years later had passed to Richard Cave.

East lodge; pre-1837; *demolished.*
Replaced by a bungalow.

By 1837 Bettyville had been acquired by the Byrne family, of whom Mark Byrne added another lodged entrance to the demesne.

East lodge; *c.* 1845.
A standard single-storey hip-roofed cottage built in exposed rubble facings, extended to the rear below a catslide roof. Now derelict and ivy-covered. The estate had by 1937 been renamed 'Gerrardstown'.

Leet 1814; Pigot 1824; Lewis 1837; Griffith 1848–60.

53. BEVERSTON, Portrane; *c.* 1880.
A single-storey lodge built off an L-plan with a steeply hipped roof, the canted projection to the avenue having a corresponding semi-octahedral roof. From the internal angle extends a gabled hallway; large red-brick chimney-stack and red earthenware ridge tiles. Extended, modernised but abandoned. A small estate in the townland of Beaverstown in 1890 of Michael Smyth, who succeeded John Daly here.

Land owners in Ireland 1876; *Thom's*.

54. BLACKHEATH, Clontarf; pre-1907; architect perhaps Thomas Drew; *demolished.*
Built in 1879 to replace the old house of 'Grace Ville' is the large, opulent High Victorian villa designed by architect Thomas Drew for Gibson Black. Its lodge may have formed part of that commission.

IB (15 July 1879).

55. BLANCHARDSTOWN RC CHURCH, Blanchardstown; pre-1837; *demolished.*
A lodge which survived into the mid-twentieth century.

56. BLESSINGTON STREET BASIN, Grangegorman; 1811/*c.* 1890; architect not known.

At the head of Blessington Street is an oasis in the form of this public park, created in 1810 from an old reservoir supplying the city and now serving as a duck pond. The original gate lodge of 1811 has been replaced by the present striking late Victorian structure in an Arts and Crafts mock-Tudor style, with its 'black-and-white' gables contrasting effectively with red-brick walls and two soaring ribbed chimney-stacks. Built off an irregular plan of a single storey with segmentally arched quadripartite windows, the roof catslides over an internal angle to form a pretty verandahed porch with coved eaves supported on turned carved wooden posts, between which are similarly treated balustrades. Plain bargeboards rise to spiky hip-knobs. This is preceded at the head of the street by an impressive iron gatescreen.

MacLoughlin 1979.

BOHOMER (see ST DOOLAGH'S)

57. BONNYBROOK, Beaumont (2).
Both lodges to this delightfully named property in the early nineteenth century of the White family have gone. A gatekeeper in 1848 was James Purcell.

D'Alton 1976 [1838]; Griffith 1848–60.

58. BRACKENSTOWN, Swords (2).
The antique demesne of Breckdenston, then so called when it came by marriage to the Molesworth family, of whom Robert, the 1st viscount, his widow and son John restructured the place in the early eighteenth century. They abandoned the original formal axial approach to the mansion in favour of a more intriguing sinuous avenue from a new entrance to the south-west, at which Sir Robert as early as 1716 confirms in a letter to his wife Letitia the provision of a lodge 'house by Dublin gate ... as 'tis done in places of 40 times greater resort all about London and Hampton Court'. Rocque's map records the lodge to have been in place in 1760 and it may have survived until as late as the turn of the twentieth century. The Molesworths' interest in the property gradually waned over the Georgian period and it was Richard Manders who purchased it at the beginning of the Victorian era, possibly building the intermediate gate lodge at an inner enclosure on the main avenue.

Inner lodge; pre-1837; *demolished.*
By 1937 this short-lived structure had been removed.

Richard Manders's long reign here came to an end with his death in 1884, the estate being purchased three years later by Denis Richard O'Callaghan, who added a lodge by the outer gate alongside the ancient Molesworth lodge which it was to replace.

Outer lodge; *c.* 1716/*c.* 1890.
This is a plain single-storey standard cottage with Georgian-style six-over-six sash windows below a hipped roof, a recent flat-roofed glazed porch disfiguring the main front. Its actual date is betrayed by balancing chimney-stacks at each end in twentieth-century bungalow fashion. From the same time is the lovely curvilinear ironwork of the gatescreen and pebble-dash finish to tall convex quadrants and straight walls containing the postern openings. In effective contrast are the six old V-jointed rusticated stone pillars with finely corniced cappings, which may be the early Georgian originals of Sir Robert Molesworth.

In 1913 the great house was destroyed by fire and a replacement erected in 1916 for the new owner, Captain Henry Ussher.

Glin *et al.* 1988; Ferguson 1998; O'Kane 2004.

59. BROADSTONE STATION, Broadstone; *c.* 1850; architect probably J.S. Mulvany.

Dominated by John Skipton Mulvany's monumental Egypto-Greek masterpiece, designed for the Midland Great Western Railway Company in 1841, is what is little more than a sentry-box. Presiding over flanking iron gatescreens on a square plan is a granite box, one bay to front and back pedimented façades, that to the rear rising to a chimney-stack which drew the porter's fire in his living room, over which was presumably sleeping space approached by a ladder. The gatekeeper who enjoyed this accommodation in 1854 was Patrick Cullen. The terminal was abandoned as a railway station in 1931.

Griffith 1848–60; Craig 1980; *IADS* (2000).

60. BROGHAN, St Margaret's; *c.* 1860.
A standard single-storey lodge with quoins, plinth and eaves band to a steeply hipped roof. Now pebble-dashed with new casement windows. A property in 1850 of Edward King.

Griffith 1848–60.

61. BROOKVILLE, Coolock; pre-1837; *demolished.*
All that survives at the entrance are two rusticated limestone gate pillars which used to be accompanied by a pair of lodges that by 1906 had been reduced to a single building. An estate in the early nineteenth century of the banking family of Law, but by 1848 it was the residence of Solomon Watson, to whom they were related by marriage. His gate porter then was James Finnegan.

Lewis 1837; Griffith 1848–60; *LGI* (1904); Craig and Fewer 2002.

BROOMEBRIDGE (see TOLKA LODGE)

62. BROOMFIELD, Lucan; pre-1836; *demolished.*
In 1801 'the seat of Edward North, Esq., a large and elegant house, well situated, with a demesne of about twenty acres, well wooded and watered; the gardens are excellent, and contain a quantity of glass; it is bounded on one side by the river Liffey, and the rest enclosed by a stone wall'. By 1824 the property had passed to Thomas Webb and in 1837 to Revd S. Thompson, who was still there in 1849 when the gate lodge lay vacant, perhaps a result of the Famine.

Archer 1801; Pigot 1824; Lewis 1837; Griffith 1848–60.

63. BROOMFIELD, Malahide; pre-1837; *demolished.*
A small demesne in 1837 belonging to J. Frazier which by 1849 had been acquired by George Cash, whose gatekeeper then was Mary Curtis.

Lewis 1837; Griffith 1848–60.

64. BROOMHILL, Drumcondra; *c.* 1883; architect possibly A.E. Murray; *demolished.*
A development founded in 1883 as 'Garden Farm', which probably refers to its having been built on a portion of the old estate of High Park (*q.v.*). Along with the out-offices, this brash Italianate villa was designed by Albert E. Murray for Robert Paul, and the commission possibly included the ill-fated gate lodge. It preceded the building of the villa, so alternatively it may have served High Park, for it appears on the 1883 *Thom's* map, whereas 'Garden Farm' does not. The property has exploded into a grand hotel, though the villa remarkably retains its identity.

IB (15 April 1883); *Thom's.*

65. BROOMVILLE, Drumcondra; pre-1907; *demolished.*
A lodge built after 1837 to a property which for 50 years after 1840 had six different occupants.

BUSHFIELD (see CUTALDO)

66. BUZZARDSTOWN, Mulhuddart; pre-1906; *demolished.*
A farm in the mid-nineteenth century of the Hoey family on which a gate lodge was added after 1837.

67. BYRON HOTEL, Sutton; pre-1837; *demolished.*
An establishment on Strand Road, the proprietress of which was Miss Louisa Holland in 1849, when her gate porter was John Collins.

Griffith 1848–60.

CABRA DOMINICAN CONVENT (see CABRA, GREAT)

68. CABRA, GREAT, Cabra (4).
Once a grand brick mansion with wings and pavilions, which went under the name of 'Much Cabra' in the time of the Arthur family. Their interest in it seems to have

ceased about 1760, when it became home to Thomas Waite, under-secretary at Dublin Castle, at which time Rocque's contemporary map suggests that there was a lodge opposite its entrance gate at the head of a straight avenue on an axis with the front door. This seems also to have been the situation in 1837; the place had been bought eighteen years earlier as a nunnery and another porter's lodge added to the south. Neither survives. Since then the property in stages has been developed into the huge Dominican Convent complex, the house in the process having been decapitated by a storey and two further lodges built before 1907, one of which remains to be outshone by its magnificent entrance archway. The porter's accommodation has been adapted from the original single-storey hip-roofed lodge into the present nondescript bungalow. The beautifully sculpted ashlar triple archway is on a grand scale in a mild Baroque style, consisting of the central round-headed archivolted carriage opening flanked by pairs of Doric pilasters which carry a segmentally arched entablature crowned by a cross on a plinth with scrolled support. On each side are the secondary pedestrian gates, with flat heads set in round-arched recesses below corniced entablatures with dies containing blank plaques. Probably the work of architect John Bourke, who added Italianate extensions to the old house around 1850. The lost northern gate lodge was built in 1877, perhaps to designs of O'Neill and Byrne. In 1849 a gate porter was Matthew Boyle.

Lewis 1837; Griffith 1848–60; Ball 1995; Ferguson 1998; Craig and Fewer 2002; Williams 1994.

69. CABRA, LITTLE, Cabra; pre-1837; *demolished.*
The other large antique mansion in the townland, in 1801 'the seat of Lord Norbury, a capital house, well situated, with a fine prospect, a demesne well wooded, and well improved gardens, &c.'. In fact this was the 2nd Lord Norbury, who was murdered on his main seat of Durrow Abbey, Co. Offaly (*q.v.*), in 1839, for Cabra was but his occasional residence, leasing from the Segrave family, who had been here from the seventeenth century. They had rented the place out from about 1785 and continued to do so, for in 1849 the lessee was Peter Heany, whose gatekeeper was Philip Franklin, the Segraves having settled at Kiltimon, Co. Wicklow (*q.v.*).

Archer 1801; Brewer 1825; Griffith 1848–60; *LGI* (1904); *BPB* (1929); Ball 1995.

70. CAPPOGE, Finglas; pre-1837; *demolished.*
A property in 1848 of Robert McGarry, whose gate porter was Philip Reilly.

Griffith 1848–60.

CAPPOGE (see HEATHFIELD LODGE)

71. CARLINGFORD, Glasnevin; pre-1837; *demolished.*
A small demesne by the village of Glasnevin in the early nineteenth century of the Crawford family, whose gatekeeper in 1849 was Denis McGrath.

Lewis 1837; Griffith 1848–60.

72. CARRICKBRACK, Howth; 1861; architect Benjamin Woodward.

An example of the genius of Benjamin Woodward, cut down in his prime despite the efforts of his client here, the eminent physician William Stokes, who had acquired the mountain cottage in 1856 from the Widow Harrington. Like the work to the house, Woodward's work has been much diluted over the years, but still apparent of this innovative little single-storey lodge as original is the projecting hallway, with its glazed and timber-strutted leading gable springing from shoulder-high stone plinth walls and containing a sheeted pointed doorway. Perhaps original is the roof with its slated scalloped bands which catslides to the right-hand side to form the roof to a rectangular bay window. From the left-hand gable projects a canted bay with arrowhead windows, probably a later addition, as certainly is the dominant 1½-storey extension to the opposing end. Woodward's creation has also to compete with a rampant *Clematis montana.* The architect was particularly proud of his lodge and, as Dr Stokes related, 'when asked for a design for a gate lodge would say "you may copy the lodge at Carrigbraec, I can do nothing better than that"'. There is a very similar and contemporary porch to Dundrum Schools by Woodward and Deane.

Lewis 1837; Blau 1982; *IAR* (1997); Williams 1994.

73. CASTILLA, Clontarf; pre-1907; *demolished.*
A house and lodge built *c.* 1860 for Sir John Bradstreet.

74. CASTLE FORBES, East Road; pre-1837; *demolished.*
A long-lost property presumably founded by the Forbes family, though by 1907 house and lodge had been removed to make way for a vast timber yard. In 1850 of Edward George Carolin.

Griffith 1848–60; Shaw 1988.

CASTLEKNOCK COLLEGE (see ST VINCENT'S)

75. CASTLEKNOCK LODGE, Castleknock; *c.* 1840; *demolished.*
A lodge built after 1837 to a property in 1848 of Mrs Mary Flanagan, whose porter is recorded then as Richard Kennedy.

Griffith 1848–60.

CASTLEKNOCK RECTORY (see HYBLA)

76. CASTLE MOAT, Cloghran; pre-1906; *demolished.*
A property in 1870 of James McOwen, about when the big house took on its present opulent Italianate mantle. Twentieth-century road realignment and widening brought it closer to public notice and swept away the gate lodge, which was built after 1837.

Thom's.

77. CASTLEMOUNT VILLA, Castleknock; *c.* 1850; architect not known.

A remarkable and exquisite fairytale Tudor Gothic house built on the Strawberry Fields around 1850 by John Schreiber, musical box-, clock- and watchmaker to his Excellency the Lord Lieutenant, which he for a period nostalgically called 'Schlossberg Villa'. He also added an extensive curtain-walled screen to each side of the entrance with its crenellated octagonal carriage pillars. All in a grey roughcast finish relieved by pointed mock arrowloops. The right-hand wall terminates in an octagonal turret, whilst that to the left-hand side is stopped by a round tower, castellated as is the adjacent parapet raised to conceal the porter's accommodation behind, which is of relatively little interest other than in its little cast-iron latticed lancet window keeping an eye out for visitors, across the gates.

Shaw 1988; *Thom's.*

CENTRAL POLICE TRAINING DEPOT (see ROYAL IRISH CONSTABULARY BARRACKS)

CHARTER SCHOOL (see TOWER HOUSE)

78. CHIEF SECRETARY'S LODGE, Phoenix Park (2).
Colonel Sir John de Blacquiere (1732–1812) on becoming park bailiff in 1774 built himself a house and as chief secretary enclosed a demesne of around 35 acres; maps of 1772 and 1773 by Thomas Sherrard show an earlier villa on the site and already a lodged main gate.

Principal entrance; pre-1801/*c.* 1845; architect not known/architect possibly Jacob Owen.

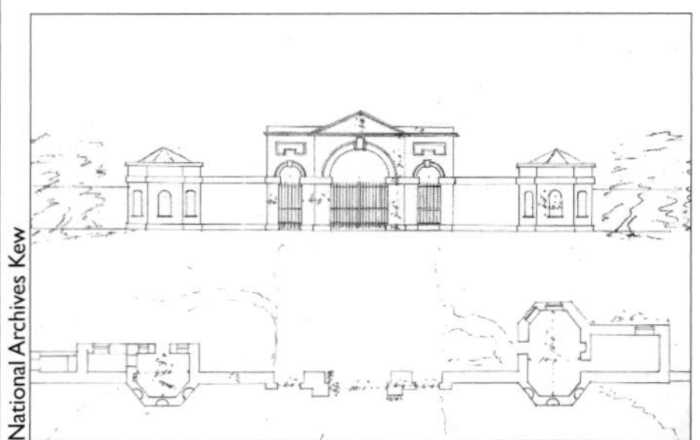
National Archives Kew

In the Abbot Papers held in the National Archives, Kew, London, is a drawing, neither signed nor dated, entitled 'Plan of Lodges & Gates at the Entrance of the Grounds of the Chief Secretary's Lodge, Phoenix Park, Dublin'. Charles Abbot (1757–1829), created 1st Baron Colchester in 1817, was chief secretary in 1801–2 and in his brief office seems nevertheless to have left his mark with this equally short-lived gateway. It indicates a grand triple archway with ground-headed openings, that to the carriageway surmounted by a slim cornice and shallow pediment. The flanking postern gates have relieving plaques above keystoned arches with archivolts that spring from a bold impost band which continues as a coping to wing walls and about the pair of lodges beyond—or rather lodge, for although they both present matching blind canted fronts with round-arched niches on each face to the visitor, that to the right was an elongated octagon containing living accommodation, whilst its counterpart was a truncated version only half the size, perhaps a guardroom. Both octahedral and semi-octahedral roofs were part-concealed by parapets. Beyond stretched additional rooms behind boundary walls. It seems that rather than being a proposal this was a survey drawing of what existed (perhaps by the Board of Works architect of the time, Vincent Waldré) with a view to Abbot commissioning alterations. In any case, it survived unscathed until 1844, when it appears on a map prepared by Decimus Burton, but only three years later a subsequent map by Josiah Parkes shows the lodges which pertain today, for which a badly damaged drawing, without visible signature or date, survives in the National Archives; despite having upper-case annotation resembling the hand of Decimus Burton, it is attributed to Jacob Owen. What this reveals is that the previous archway was simply amended and 'beefed up', the pediment replaced by a die, or heavier blocking course, with the plaques shown to be incised in Soaneian manner. The original accommodation was superseded on the same footprint by a twin pair of single-storey rectangular two-roomed lodges, each presenting to the visitor a single bay of six-over-six sash window framed by hefty piers, all bound by moulded cornices to their parapeted roofs. In roughcast walls, innovatively two-over-two slit sash windows keep watch across the face of the gateway. Quite the most impressive and elegant entrance in the Phoenix Park (*q.v.*), it appears to have been the third on the site, for Sherrard's 1773 map and that of Captain Brown of 1789 show an even earlier pair of buildings flanking the gates of the previous dwelling on the site. The present ironwork is by Richard Turner. The newly installed gatekeeper in 1849 was William Hinds.

Back gate; *c.* 1824; architect not known; *demolished.*
At the access to the farmyard Mary Walsh was the resident porter in 1849 of a lodge, now lost but apparently recorded for posterity in another drawing held in the Public Record Office, Kew. It depicts a nicely proportioned single-storey standard Classical structure, like the main lodges its roof concealed behind a corniced parapet. The central breakfront contained a sidelit and semicircular-arched fanlit doorway flanked by a pair of flat-arched windows.

The demesne has been home to the US Ambassador since 1927.

Griffith 1848–60; Ball 1995; *BPB* (1929); Bence-Jones 1988; *IADS* (2002); Casey 2005; NAIOPW (5HC/2/19); PRO (30/9/10/35/21949); McCullen 2009.

CINTRA (see ABBEVILLE COTTAGE)

79. CLAIRVILLE, Malahide; pre-1837.
A seat in the early nineteenth century of Major St Claire, whose gate lodge now lies an ivy-covered ruin.

CLANABOY (see GRIFFIN LODGE)

80. CLAREGROVE, Balgriffin; pre-1837; *demolished.*
Previously an eighteenth-century property called 'Annesley Lodge' of that family, which in the first half of the following century was home to General Alexander Cuppage, who presumably renamed it after his wife Clarinda.

D'Alton 1976 [1838]; *LGI* (1904).

81. CLAREMONT, Glasnevin (2).
A big house in 1786 of a Mr Flood which by

1816 had been acquired as a home to the Irish National Deaf and Dumb Institution under the patronage of Queen Victoria and the duke of Connaught. Both of its lodges, in place by 1837, have been demolished.

Wilson 1803; *Dublin Penny Journal* (2 April 1836); Lewis 1837.

82. CLAREMONT VILLA, Glasnevin; pre-1906; *demolished.*
A lodge built after 1837 to a property which changed hands often through the nineteenth century, being home to the McDermott family in mid-century followed by Thomas Cassin in 1870.

Thom's.

83. THE CLIFFS, Howth; *c.* 1920.
This remains a remote and private house, having in 1837 been home to William Stewart Bellingham of the Castle Bellingham, Co. Louth (*q.v.*), connection and in whose family it stayed, being largely rebuilt and tenanted in the mid-nineteenth century, but remained lodgeless until a Lady Thompson took up residence around 1920. It is a modest single-storey, mildly Arts and Crafts affair of its time, the two-bay main front in a pebble-dash finish below a hipped roof with sawtooth-pattern asbestos 'slates'.

Lewis 1837; *Thom's.*

84. CLOGHRAN C. of I. CHURCH, Cloghran; pre-1837; *demolished.*
A home in 1848 to John Boles, who also filled the role of churchwarden. The lodge had been removed by 1906 and the church in 1944.

Griffith 1848–60; Leslie and Wallace 2001.

85. CLOGHRAN, Cloghran; pre-1837; *demolished.*
An estate in the early nineteenth century of Samuel Waters, the lodge to which had gone by 1906.

CLONKEEN (see GRANGE, Kill of the Grange)

CLONLEA (see CHAMOUNT)

CLONLEA (see MURPHYSTOWN LODGE)

86. CLONLIFFE, Drumcondra (2).

Main entrance; pre-1837; *demolished.*
A property originating as 'The Grange' which in the mid-eighteenth century became 'Fortrick's Grove' after Tristram Fortrick, its owner, before passing through many hands, one of whom in the early nineteenth century was the theatrical character Frederick E. 'Buck' Jones. Between 1845 and 1857 the house was used by the Revenue Police, whose gate porter in 1849 was Timothy Teen.

Side entrance; *c.* 1860; architect possibly J.J. Bourke.
The grounds now are home to Holy Cross Church and College, the latter a severe grey neo-Georgian complex matched by the little single-storey square lodge below an almost pyramidal roof with tall central chimney-stack. The two main two-window bay fronts, with inappropriate modern replacement casements, are in dull sand/cement rendering in stucco effect, relieved only by bold V-jointed granite quoins. Banished to beyond the boundary across from its contemporary gates.

Griffith 1848–60; Joyce 1912; Ball 1995; Williams 1994.

87. CLONMETHAN RECTORY, Oldtown; pre-1837/pre-1937; *demolished.*
Both the original gate lodge opposite the gates, which may have been contemporary with the 1817 quintessential glebe house built during the incumbency (1813–34) of Revd Thomas Radcliff (d. 1834), and its later replacement within the grounds have gone.

Lewis 1837; Leslie and Wallace 2001.

88. CLONSILLA C. OF I. CHURCH, Clonsilla; *c.* 1820.
Barely recognisable as a gate lodge thanks to successive additions is what may have been a single-storey hip-roofed structure; presumably built during the incumbency of Revd James Reade.

Leslie and Wallace 2001.

CLONSILLA (see LOHUNDA)

89. CLONSILLA HOUSE, Mulhuddart; pre-1837; *demolished.*
Reputedly the lodge was identical to that which survives at nearby Beech Park (*q.v.*). The big house was burnt down about 1980, and both it and its demesne are the site for a development of semi-detached housing, the lodge and gates replaced by a brash new pillared entrance proclaiming 'Porter's Gate'. This was in 1837, until his death ten years later, the seat of Robert Henry French from French Park, Co. Roscommon. In 1848 the lodge lay vacant.

Lewis 1837; Griffith 1848–60; *LGI* (1904); Craig and Fewer 2002.

90. CLONSILLA LODGE, Mulhuddart (2).
Another seat, in 1848, of the French family of adjacent Clonsilla House (*q.v.*), at which time both of its porters' lodges lay unoccupied.

Main entrance; pre-1837; *demolished.*

Secondary entrance; *c.* 1840/*c.* 1910.
An earlier lodge has been replaced by the present 1½-storey gabled Arts and Crafts affair. At ground-floor window-head level is a jettied attic apex and a moulded corbel band; single-storey gabled hall projection and lead-effect windows aping their real predecessors. Occupied.

Griffith 1848–60; *LGI* (1904).

91. CLONTARF CASTLE, Clontarf; 1836; architect W.V. Morrison.

Morrison's expert extension and rehabilitation of an antique Pale keep in the Tudor Revival style has a perfect prelude at its entrance in a beautifully constructed 1½-storey gatehouse in like vein but with the added quirk of the top of an Irish round tower emerging from the parapets. A development for John Edward Venables Vernon (1813–90), who had succeeded his brother to the estate in 1833, the lodge is basically built off an L-plan and contains an integral carriage access with bedrooms over, approached by a hall and stairs in the internal angle. The whole is built in ashlar, with hood mouldings to the Tudor carriage opening and ornamental arrowslits and label mouldings to single, bi- and tripartite windows. The main gables are skew-tabled with kneelers now, like the conical tower roof, lacking their original finials. Elsewhere there are all the other decorative Tudor

National Library of Ireland

91. Clontarf Castle, Clontarf

Gothic devices of crenellated parapets with lion masks, buttresses and a shield with the Vernon bearings. To the rear projects a chunky chimney-breast rising in stages to a cluster of four octagonal stone flues to echo those on the big house. A charming watercolour of 1853 by Edward McFarland brings home how the entrance used to look in its heyday, in context with its crucial curtain walls and grand forecourt, now lost in the interests of entry and exit for what is presently a hotel within, leaving it high and dry and discomposed, with its carriage access converted to living space.

Pike and McDowell 1908; *LGI* (1904); McParland *et al.* 1989; NLI painting (1986 TX 30).

92. CLONTURK, Drumcondra; pre-1837; *demolished.*
A property in 1837 of Thomas Dooley, solicitor, which by 1848 he was letting to Thomas Kelly, whose gatekeeper was then Thomas Hicks. The lodge had by 1907 been removed.

Lewis 1837; Griffith 1848–60.

CLUAIN MHUIRE (see HIGHFIELD, Grangegorman)

93. COLLINSTOWN, Santry; pre-1907; *demolished.*
A seat in the first half of the nineteenth century of the Brangan family, nursery and seedsmen, the lodge to which was built after 1837. The property has been completely absorbed into Dublin airport.

94. CONVENT HOUSE, Clontarf; pre-1837; *demolished.*
A small estate in 1837 of the Hon. Arthur Moore, second justice of the Court of Common Pleas.

Lewis 1837.

95. COOLMINE COTTAGE, Blanchardstown; pre-1837; *demolished.*
The property in 1848 of Thomas Gresham, the lodge to which was opposite its entrance.

Griffith 1848–60.

96. COOLMINE, Blanchardstown (3).
The large farm in 1837 of Alexander Kirkpatrick, who then had three gate lodges, none of which remain.

Lewis 1837.

97. COOLOCK, Coolock; pre-1837; *demolished.*
Home in the early nineteenth century to Henry Daniel Digby Brooke of the Dromvana, Co. Cavan, family, from whom it passed in about 1846 to the Maconchy family of nearby Edenmore (*q.v.*). The site of the lodge has been severed from the house by modern road realignment. In 1848 the gatekeeper was Paul Bardle.

Lewis 1837; Griffith 1848–60; *LGI* (1904).

98. COOLOCK LODGE, Coolock; pre-1837; *demolished.*
A property in 1837 of Thomas Sherrard which by 1848 the family was letting to Sir Edward Borough, whose gate porter was then John Cunningham. The place had been renamed 'St Brendan's' by 1856.

Lewis 1837; Griffith 1848–60.

CORDUFF (see ST VINCENT'S)

99. CORDUFF, Lusk; *c.* 1820
A plain single-storey standard lodge built in stone rubble facings, its skew-table gables with brick chimney-stacks; flat-roofed hall to front door and extended by a bay to right-hand side. In 1801 'the seat of Thomas Baker, Esq., a good plain house and garden, with an extensive demesne of 200 acres, well improved and in high cultivation'.

Archer 1801; Lewis 1837.

100. COTTAGE, Grange (2).
Later known as 'Grangemore', it was in 1824 the estate of Robert Law, both pre-1837 lodges to which have been demolished.

Pigot 1824.

101. COURTDUFF, Blanchardstown; pre-1938; *demolished.*
The property in the mid-nineteenth century of Robert Donovan, from whom it passed around 1860 to the Hogan family. The lodge was erected after 1837.

102. COURTDUFF HOUSE, Blanchardstown; pre-1938; *demolished.*
A seat in the mid-nineteenth century of the Smith family which has been swept away by industrial development.

CRAIGFORD (see OATLEY)

THE CRESCENT (see WARRENPOINT)

103. CROYDON, Marino (2).
The large mid-Georgian house, later home to Jones Stevelly (*c.* 1763–1833), has gone, along with both its pre-1837 porters' lodges. The property by 1848 was owned by Robert J. Stevelly of Glenduff Castle, Co. Limerick, one of whose gatekeepers was then Daniel Byrne.

Griffith 1848–60; *LGI* (1904).

104. CRUISERATH, Mulhuddart; pre-1837; *demolished.*
A property which has been overrun by industrial development was in 1849 home to William Maxwell, whose gate porter was then John Caffrey.

Griffith 1848–60.

105. CUTALDO, Fairview; pre-1837; *demolished.*
A property with armed forces connections. Its occupant in 1841 was a Captain Mayne, who seems to have changed its name to 'Bushfield'. By 1849 he had been replaced by Captain William Neame RN, whose gatekeeper then was Roderick Whelan.

Thom's; Griffith 1848–60.

106. DAMASTOWN, Naul; *c.* 1780.
An ancient seat in 1687 of the Proby family which has been replaced by a modern industrial estate but to which, remarkably, a gate lodge—just—survives. Single-storey with a steeply hipped roof, now covered in corrugated iron to replace the original thatch. Rubble-built, harled, derelict and overgrown.

Craig and Fewer 2002.

107. DAMASTOWN TD, Naul; *c.* 1850.
An anonymous property to which there is a neat single-storey cottage with a steeply hipped roof which catslides over the front door set in a breakfront. Stone-faced with brick dressings and soldier arches. Derelict.

108. DANESFIELD, Dollymount; pre-1837; *demolished.*
A small estate in 1837 of John Campbell.

Lewis 1837.

109. DARNDALE, Coolock (2).
Two lost lodges which were in place in 1837, when Francis Gogarty was proprietor. Twelve years later his gatekeepers were Patrick Reilly and James Byrne.

Lewis 1837; Griffith 1848–60.

DEER PARK (see MARY VILLA, Castleknock)

110. DELVILLE, Glasnevin; pre-1836; *demolished.*
'On the central elevation of this deserted village is Delville House ... A tall close gate and wall conceal it from the view of prying curiosity.' Such was the scene, very different from today, witnessed by d'Alton about 1836. Once the proud early eighteenth-century creation of Mrs Delaney and her husband, the Revd Dean of Down, visited by Swift and Stella. Now the charming garden ornamental temple, beloved house and its gate lodge (bow-fronted to the house) have all gone. The latter was occupied by Margaret Reilly in 1849, when she was gate porter to the Gordon family.

D'Alton 1976 [1838]; Lewis 1837; Griffith 1848–60; Ball 1995.

111. DISWELLSTOWN, Castleknock; pre-1836; *demolished.*
From the middle of the eighteenth century this was home to the Kennan family, in 1801 'the seat of Thomas Kennan, Esq., an elegant, large modern house, pleasantly situated on a rising ground, with a fine prospect of a beautiful improved country. The demesne consists of an hundred acres, highly improved, and well-wooded; the gardens are elegant, and laid out in the first style.' The house remains, as does its entrance screen, comprised of four slender octagonal granite pillars on tall plinths, with fluted friezes and gadrooned cappings, all framed by roughcast quadrant walls. Seemingly of *c.* 1845, there is a similar set at nearby Mary Villa (*q.v.*). Of the lodge, inhabited in 1849 by John Donohoe, there is no trace.

Archer 1801; Griffith 1848–60.

DOLLAND (see KELLYSTOWN)

DOMINICAN CONVENT (see CABRA, GREAT)

112. DONAGHMEDE, Grange; pre-1837; *demolished.*

The seat in 1837 of Arthur King, the lodge to which was far to the south of Kilbarrack Road, an avenue which was severed from its big house in the late nineteenth century. In 1849 the gate porter to Mrs Eliza King was Patrick Clancy.

Lewis 1837; Griffith 1848–60.

113. DONNYCARNEY COTTAGE, Clontarf (2).

A small estate in 1841 of the Atkinson family, with a pre-1837 gate lodge, which by *c.* 1855 had been completely remodelled to see the house greatly enlarged, a replacement lodge built on adjacent property absorbed to the south and all renamed 'St Johnsby' for Henry Davis, solicitor and coroner for the county. Both lodges have been demolished.

Thom's.

114. DONNYCARNEY, Clontarf (2).

In the early eighteenth century this was a seat of Sir John Perceval, later 1st earl of Egmont, which by 1837 had become home, complete with gate lodge, to Abel Labertouche, public notary. By about 1845 Donnycarney was the Dublin residence of Luke White MP, an elder brother of the 1st Baron Annaly of Luttrelstown (*q.v.*), whose main seat was Rathcline, Co. Longford (*q.v.*), and before his death in 1854 he left his mark on the place with the building of a new house and the replacement of the old lodge with one at a new entrance further south. This was a well-proportioned single-storey standard hip-roofed porter's lodge of generous proportions, its projecting hall given *gravitas* by a pediment with mutules continued beyond as eaves brackets. Prior to becoming surplus to requirements to the present golf-club owners and being demolished, it had been covered in bland render with nasty modern window replacements. The ashlar of its chimney-stack is survived by that of the fine gatescreen of contemporary date. Comprised of four bulky pillars, the carriage pair are in that Egypto-Grecian manner pioneered by J.B. Papworth, their tapering pylon breakfronts and moulded recessed panels below friezes with three Tudor rosettes crowned by great oversailing cappings. These have long since been moved to accommodate modern traffic, with the loss of much fine decorative iron railing. The author of all this has not been identified but his work is to be found in the identical entrances to Dartry (*q.v.*) and St Pancra's (*q.v.*) in Rathgar. White's gate porter in 1849 was Catherine Hazard, who may have been retained by the next owner of Donnycarney, Alexander Thom of the invaluable directories.

Papworth 1818; Lewis 1837; Griffith 1848–60; *Thom's*; *BPB* (1929); Ball 1995.

115. DRUMCONDRA CASTLE, Drumcondra (3).

Before it passed *c.* 1880 to the trustees of St Joseph's Asylum for the Male Blind, the house had a succession of occupants—Sir Edward Newenham and Sir James Galbraith, amongst others, prior to its becoming home to Richard Williams, notary of the city, for about twenty years until 1855, in whose time here it may have been castellated. In 1848 his gatekeepers were Henry Harper, John King and Elim Johnston.

North entrance; pre-1837; *demolished.*

Main entrance; pre-1837; architect not known.

A grand complex, of which the lodge may have originated as a plain single-storey standard hip-roofed structure. Around 1845 it was given its present splendid Tudor Castellated cloak of a crenellated parapet, which extends about the hall breakfront and label mouldings to chamfered window openings, all in the manner of Sandham Symes. The walls have recently been rendered in grey stucco-effect cement finish and unfortunate plastic windows inserted. It overlooks the fine granite ashlar gatescreen with its matching crenellations to screen walls which contain label-moulded postern openings flanked by octagonal turrets. The excellent contemporary decorative ironwork gates are not matched by the later overthrow to the carriage opening.

South entrance; pre-1849; *demolished.*

A lodge added to the property after 1837 on Waterfall Avenue.

D'Alton 1976 [1838]; Griffith 1848–60; *Thom's*; Ball 1995.

116. DRUMCONDRA, Drumcondra (3).

The splendid house built in 1727 for Marmaduke Coghill, which passed through marriage to Charles Moore, 2nd Lord Tullamore, and then passed through many hands before it was acquired in 1842 from General Sir Guy Campbell as 'the Roman Catholic Missionary College of All Hallows, the object of which was to educate clergymen for foreign missions'. Subsequent development of the site saw the loss of one porter's lodge and the replacement of another.

Church Avenue North lodge; pre-1837; *demolished.*

A building which was much extended before 1885 but had been removed by 1935.

Grace Park Road lodge; pre-1837/*c.* 1900; architect possibly G.C. Ashlin.

The earlier lodge was superseded by the present structure at the opposite side of the entrance, possibly as part of the commission of architect George Ashlin, who was engaged in 1895 to replace the chapel that had been destroyed by fire. This is a commodious single-storey gabled lodge, finished in rendering with distinctive rustic brick toothed dressings, quoins and a polychromatic chimney-stack in the same material piercing a ridge decorated with perforated earthenware cresting. Built off an L-plan; the one-over-one sash windows are in segmentally headed openings with perforated sheeted features to leading gable apexes; later twentieth-century extension in sympathy. In contrast is a pair of fine Gothic gabled ashlar carriage pillars, with chamfers and recessed Celtic cross motifs, from which hang timber and iron gates of equal quality. Alongside, a screen wall contains a postilion opening with dressed surround and shouldered arch.

The college gate porters in 1848 were John Farrell and John Archbold.

Thom's; Griffith 1848–60; Ball 1995; Bence-Jones 1988; IAA.

117. DRUMCONDRA LODGE, Drumcondra; pre-1837; *demolished.*

A property in the mid-nineteenth century of attorney Edward Levesey. By 1907 the estate had been covered in Victorian terraced housing.

118. DRUMNIGH COTTAGE, Balgriffin; pre-1837; *demolished.*

An estate in 1837 of Mark Farran, whose gatekeeper in 1848 was Peter Byrne.

Lewis 1837; Griffith 1848–60.

119. DRYNAM, Malahide; pre-1837/*c.* 1880.

The old lost house of the Cruise family, whose lodge in 1850 was unoccupied, perhaps prior to its being replaced by the surviving structure. This is a standard single-storey hip-roofed cottage with clipped eaves and fancy late Victorian earthenware poppy hip-knobs. Roughcast with a projecting gabled hall, which has an arrowhead window and perforated wavy bargeboards rising to a spiky turned finial with pendant. To the left-hand side is a tiny bow window. Occupied.

Griffith 1848–60; Craig and Fewer 2002.

120. DUNSINEA CANDLE MANUFACTORY, Castleknock; pre-1837; *demolished.*

A concern of the Rathborne family, whose gate porter in 1848 was Oswald Kearns.

Griffith 1848–60.

121. DUNSINK OBSERVATORY, Blanchardstown; pre-1837; *demolished.*
An establishment founded in 1774 thanks to a bequest of £3,000 and £250 per annum by Dr Francis Andrews, provost of TCD, which financed the provision of a fine gatescreen and attendant lodge. The latter, whose porter in 1848 was Philip Milmore, has been replaced by a twentieth-century bungalow, but big, tall, concave quadrant walls remain with postilion openings, rendered with a stone plinth and plain carriage pillars.

Dublin Penny Journal (15 Aug. 1835); Griffith 1848–60; *Parliamentary Gazetteer.*

EAGLE VILLE (see STRAND VILLE)

122. EDENDALE, Cloghran; pre-1837; *demolished.*
A residence in 1848 of Robert Hickey, whose gatekeeper was James Hunt.

Griffith 1848–60.

123. EDENMORE, Raheny (2).

Formerly called 'Violet Hill', it was the home in the early nineteenth century of the Dick family, followed by John Maconchy (1793–1843). The main approach was from an entrance close to the house.

West gate; pre-1837; *demolished.*
An entrance and lodge which had gone by 1906, having been superseded by a lengthier avenue created by the new owner, solicitor John Maunsell (1824–99), who had relocated here from Rockmount, Dundrum (*q.v.*), about 1870.

East gate; *c.* 1870; architect not known
An Italianate single-storey gabled porter's lodge on an L-plan with a pair of segmentally arched windows set in recessed surrounds in the leading gable. The roof, to which is a band of ornamental fish-scale slates, extends over the internal angle to create a verandah porch. Roughcast and sanitised in modernisation to form doctors' consulting rooms at what is now the entrance to St Joseph's Hospital. The contemporary gatescreen is very extensive, with concave railed quadrants and four fine Classical granite pillars, those to the carriage opening with incised panel shafts and four-sided pedimented cappings with acroteria.

D'Alton 1976 [1838]; *Thom's*; *LGI* (1904).

124. ELLENFIELD, Drumcondra; pre-1907; *demolished.*
A property previously called 'Clonturk Cottage', probably renamed by Fergus Farrell, seed merchant, who is recorded here in 1848 and by 1856 had risen to become lord mayor of Dublin, the lodge perhaps being added then as appropriate to his new standing.

Griffith 1848–60; Shaw 1988; *Thom's.*

125. ELM GREEN, Blanchardstown (2).
Rocque's map of 1760 suggests a porter's lodge here to a property later that century of Richard Malone. In 1837 it was the residence of Francis Dwyer but eleven years later had passed to solicitor Richard A. Simpson.

Ashtown Bridge gate; pre-1837; *demolished.*
Simpson's gatekeeper in 1848 was John Whately.

Dunsink gate; *c.* 1830.
The shell of a single-storey standard hip-roofed structure with clipped eaves over harled rubble walls in which are Tudor label mouldings to windows. To it has been added a later Victorian gabled glazed hall. Its porter in 1848 was James Murphy.

Now a golf club, the entrance to which is graced by a showy gatescreen purloined from neighbouring Abbotstown (*q.v.*).

Lewis 1837; Griffith 1848–60; Ferguson 1998.

126. ELMHURST, Glasnevin; *c.* 1905; architect probably A.G.C. Millar.

A highly decorative Edwardian porter's lodge in the Arts and Crafts tradition of the time. Single-storey gabled and built off an informal plan with a quarry-faced stone plinth, otherwise in red brick with Staffordshire blue engineering brick bands. There is much ornamental and intricate joinery work in the apex and eaves features perforated with quatrefoils and sporting exaggerated hip-knobs. In the leading internal angle is a lean-to porch (now enclosed) with finely fretted spandrel piece and carved exposed joist ends. Probably to designs of Adam Gerald Chaytor Millar for the Eustace family, for whom he worked at the neighbouring Hampstead Lodge (Hillside Farm) (*q.v.*).

IB (16 May 1908).

127. ELM PARK, Artane (2).
Both pre-1837 lodges, to a property that year of Thomas Hutton, coach-builder, have gone. In 1848 one of his gatekeepers was James Connor.

Lewis 1837; Griffith 1848–60.

128. ELM VIEW, Clontarf; *c.* 1820.
A small estate which in the past was the seat of Lords Shannon and Southwell and which by 1837 contained the beautiful gardens of William Chaigneu Colville, who was still resident here in 1848. His lodge was probably a single-storey standard gabled affair, since much altered and extended to left and right, there being a bow to the road and a pedimented portico (now glazed in). Rendered and roofed in modern concrete tiles. The entrance has a good pair of Classical flat-arched pedestrian openings flanked by shallow concave quadrants terminating in granite pillars. By 1870 the place had been renamed 'Yew Park'.

D'Alton 1976 [1838]; Lewis 1837; Griffith 1848–60.

129. EMSWORTH, Balgriffin; pre-1837; *demolished.*
A rare example of a James Gandon villa of 1794, built for James Woodmason. Nothing attributable to the distinguished architect survives at the gates.

McParland 1985.

130. FAIRFIELD, Coolock (2).
A property of the Roper family in the nineteenth century.

East gate; pre-1837; *demolished.*
Although this lodge existed in 1906, by then its avenue was no more.

West gate; pre-1906; *demolished.*
A lodge was built here sometime after 1837.

131. FAIRFIELD, Glasnevin; pre-1837; *demolished.*
A seat in 1837 of Revd Joseph Hutton, the gate lodge to which had gone by 1907. His porter in 1855 was Nicholas Reed.

Lewis 1837.

132. FARMLEIGH, Castleknock (3).
Another great Irish house of the Guinness family, here a transformation of a modest late Georgian villa of Charles Trench (1772–1840), after whose death it passed through the hands of William English and Henry Smythe before being purchased in 1873 from J.C. Coote by Edward Cecil Guinness (1847–1927). Concurrent with his ennoblement as baronet in 1885 and baron in 1891, the 1st earl of Iveagh added to his house in stages, to designs by J.F. Fuller and W. Young. The end result is some very fine interiors but an exterior no more memorable than its porters' lodges.

Phoenix Park gate; pre-1836/*c.* 1900.
So much altered and extended as to be almost incoherent, all that is still recognisable is a single-storey gabled structure on a cruciform plan with Westmoreland green slates and a battered chimney-stack as a hint of Arts and Crafts, which suggests that it may have formed part of William Young's commission in 1895. Built on the site of a previous lodge from the Trench era. The porter in 1848 was Lawrence Fagan.

Hybla gate; pre-1837; *demolished.*
A lodge on a northern approach which had gone by 1907.

Knockmaroon gate; *c.* 1870.
Dwarfed by a bizarre backdrop of the 200ft-high Florentine water-cum-clock tower from

the Palazzo Vecchio, this peculiar hybrid design has pedimented Classical door and window openings below carved English Picturesque foil and wave bargeboards with spiky hip-knobs. Single-storey, rendered and built off an irregular plan, its little entrance hall applied alongside almost as an afterthought. Cast-iron carriage pillars carry gates with husk motifs, having modest concave quadrants beyond with spear-topped railings.

Griffith 1848–60; *LGI* (1904); *BPB* (1929); Bence-Jones 1988; Williams 1994.

133. FARNHAM, Finglas (2).
Once a Dublin seat of the Maxwells of County Cavan, the Lords Farnham, which from 1814 served as one of the three private lunatic asylums in the vicinity of Finglas village. The fine house was demolished in 1954, going the same way as its lodges.

North lodge; pre-1837; *demolished.*
The gatekeeper in 1849 was John McDonagh, whose lodge had gone by 1906.

South lodge; *c.* 1845; *demolished.*
In 1849 the porter was John Barton, listed as lessee of James Duncan MD.

Lewis 1837; Griffith 1848–60; Pike and McDowell 1908; Craig and Fewer 2002.

134. FEMALE ORPHAN HOUSE, Phibsborough (2).
The institution 'was commenced in 1790 by Mrs Edward Tighe and Mrs Este, and, owing in a great measure to the advocacy of the celebrated Dean Kirwan, who preached a succession of sermons for its support, was opened in the present buildings on the North Circular Road, which contain ample accommodation for 160 children and a large Episcopal chapel'.

Early lodge; pre-1837; *demolished.*
Perhaps contemporary with the building of the orphanage itself, it was of considerable longevity relative to its successor.

Late lodge; 1936; architects McCurdy and Mitchell; *demolished.*
Contract drawings, dated 10 November 1937, survive of this short-lived Arts and Crafts bungalow designed for Lynne and Co. It was a single-storey, three-bedroomed, hip-roofed three-bay affair, the right-hand bay extending gabled beside a catslide-roofed porch advancing alongside.

Lewis 1837; IAA (McCurdy and Mitchell Collection: 79/17, Bin III, Roll 16).

135. FIELDSTOWN EAST, Donaghmore; pre-1837; *demolished.*
Described about 1836 as 'a sweet seat of Mr Bourne, intersected by a pretty rivulet', prior to which, in 1814, it was home to Thomas Rowe.

Leet 1814; d'Alton 1976 [1838].

136. FINGLASWOOD, Finglas; pre-1837; *demolished.*
The house and adjoining tannery of the Savage family. By 1907 the ancient house, where James II is reputed to have slept one night, was 'in ruins'.

Lewis 1837.

137. FORREST, GREAT, Swords; pre-1760; *demolished.*
A seat with which many families have been associated, in the early eighteenth century with the Nichols and in 1783 with the Hill family. The Rocque map shows a pair of lodges at the base of a formal avenue to the house, which survived until the turn of the twentieth century.

Taylor and Skinner 1778; 1969 [1783]; Ferguson 1998; O'Kane 2004.

138. FORREST TOWN, Swords; pre-1760; *demolished.*
The Rocque map indicates a pair of lodges placed forward of a semicircular forecourt to the gates, mirrored by the Forrest, Great (*q.v.*) lodges across the road. An early eighteenth-century property of James Hand, which in 1783 was home to Baron Hamilton, 'that true patriot'.

Taylor and Skinner 1778; 1969 [1783]; d'Alton 1976 [1838]; Ferguson 1998; O'Kane 2004.

139. FOSTERSTOWN, Swords; pre-1837; *demolished.*
A property in 1814 and 1848 of Hugh Moran.

Leet 1814; Griffith 1848–60.

140. FOX HALL, Raheny; pre-1837; *demolished.*
Modern housing occupies the gate lodge site and estate of the Foxhall family.

141. FURRY PARK, Killester; pre-1837; *demolished.*
Formerly a seat of the earl of Shannon, by 1837 it was the residence of barrister Thomas Bushe, whose gate porter in 1848 was James Guthrie. His house survives as offices.

D'Alton 1976 [1838]; Lewis 1837; Griffith 1848–60.

142. FURRY PARK, Santry; pre-1837; *demolished.*
Now the site of an industrial estate, the old house, in 1841 of Thomas Brannicke, having been swept away. His gatekeeper in 1848 was John Furlong.

Thom's; Griffith 1848–60.

GARDA HEADQUARTERS (see ROYAL IRISH CONSTABULARY BARRACKS)

GARDEN FARM (see BROOMHILL)

143. GAY BROOK, Malahide (2).
Formerly a property in 1837 of Revd Francis Chamely, of whose lodges in 1850 one was unoccupied, the other staffed by Richard Reilly. Both are no more, having been overrun by modern housing.

Lewis 1837; Griffith 1848–60.

GERRARDSTOWN (see BETTYVILLE)

144. GLASNEVIN CEMETERY, Glasnevin (2).
'Prospect Cemetery', as it was called initially, 'was opened here in 1832, comprising 6 Irish acres, neatly laid out; in the centre is a chapel for funeral service, and the area is enclosed with walls, having at each angle a castellated watch tower'. Lewis in 1837 did not draw attention to the entrance and lodge off Prospect Square, as architect Patrick Byrne did not carry out this commission for the Dublin Cemeteries Committee until some years later.

Prospect Square gate; *c.* 1845; architect Patrick Byrne.

Dominating the square is the handsome Classical carriage archway with archivolted round-headed opening and sculpted cornice rather incongruously crowned by a ball-mounted crucifix. Forming the centre-piece of a segmental railed screen, stopped to the left-hand side by a well-proportioned two-storey three-bay gatehouse with hipped roof concealed by a parapet which reflects the top of the archway, the cornice stopped against a pedimented breakfront, as is the first-floor sill band. Projecting is a single-storey porch, its openings semicircular-arched and detailed as the archway. All now finished in a drab grey stucco-effect rendering.

Increasing demands on the cemetery and its rapid expansion led to the need for greater accessibility, and architect J.J. McCarthy was engaged to design a new entrance on the Finglas Road.

Finglas Road gate; 1876; architect J.J. McCarthy.
What the 'Irish Pugin' came up with was something rather less elegant in this great 1½-storey informal granite Norman-Gothic pile, presenting a gableted front to the

footpath with an array of narrow round-headed windows, relieving arches and corbelled eaves to the steeply pitched hipped roof. Built to accommodate offices and staff quarters, it is revealed to the rear as rising off an L-plan; a skew-tabled single-storey porch projects toward the gates, with a hood-moulded clock in its gable over a pair of round arches meeting and supported on a squat Byzantine column with beautifully sculpted capital—the whole topped off with an Irish cross finial. The pair of gate pillars are suitably monumental, with slender engaged columnettes to chamfered corners, nicely chiselled foliated corbels and surmounted by cast-iron Celtic crosses. Somehow this complex is rendered less ostentatious relative to the backdrop of the towering O'Connell monument.

Lewis 1837; *IB* (15 Dec. 1876); *A guide through Glasnevin Cemetery* (1879); *IGS Bulletin* (April–Dec. 1964); Sheehy 1977.

145. GLASNEVIN, Glasnevin; pre-1837; *demolished.*
A seat in 1824 of Colonel William John Gore (1767–1836), from whom it passed by marriage of his daughter to George Hayward Lindsay. The lodge had gone by 1907.

Pigot 1824; *LGI* (1904); *BPB* (1929).

146. GLENA COTTAGE, Raheny; *c.* 1900; architect not known.

A smart little Edwardian Arts and Crafts composition mainly in red brick for gentleman farmer Patrick McKenna. Single-storey on an L-plan, its steep gables ornamented with carved bargeboards. Subtly raised toothed quoins frame the leading gable with its pair of segmentally headed one-over-one sash windows below a double hood moulding of brick specials. The corbelled stack in like material rises from a roof with red earthenware ridge tiles and decorative bands of scalloped Westmoreland green slates. In the internal angle is a tiny hall below a lean-to roof.

Thom's.

GLENMAROON (see KNOCKMAROON LODGE)

GLENVAR (see HOLLYBROOK LODGE)

147. GRACEFIELD, Artane; pre-1837; *demolished.*
In 1837 the seat of the Eames family, after whom it became home to Captain Francis Charles Forde, whose gatekeeper in 1848 was James Barry.

Lewis 1837; Griffith 1848–60; *LGI* (1904).

148. GRAND CANAL COMPANY, Usher's Quay; pre-1854; *demolished.*
A porter's lodge identified by the valuation but not identifiable on the OS maps.

Griffith 1848–60.

149. GRANGE, Grange; *c.* 1835.
By the roadside is what was a single-storey two-window-bay structure with a hipped roof later extended by a bow-ended addition. Presiding over modern gates to a modern house. A property in 1841 of John Howard and seven years later of Michael Howard, when the lodge was unoccupied.

Thom's; Griffith 1848–60.

150. GRANGE LODGE, Grange; pre-1837; *demolished.*
A seat in 1837 of W. Allen, thereafter with a succession of different owners.

Lewis 1837.

GRANGEGORMAN CHURCH & RECTORY (see ALL SAINTS CHURCH & RECTORY)

GRANGEGORMAN MENTAL HOSPITAL (see RICHMOND NEW DISTRICT ASYLUM)

151. GRANGEGORMAN MILITARY CEMETERY, Grangegorman; 1876.

A typically sturdy mid-Victorian lodge constructed in the same rubble as the boundary wall, coursed and dressed with quarry-faced quoins and cream brick to the bipartite sash windows, which display deep chiselled sills matched by the lintels. Single-storey standard with a high-eaved hipped roof and central gabled entrance breakfront with a hint of an open pediment. Dominating the ridge is an equally solid brown brick chimney-stack. Occupied. At the access are pillars in more quarry-faced stone on pronounced plinths and with conspicuous corbelled cappings. The inner gate pillars are relatively flimsy, with distinctive helically bound shafts. The graveyard was opened in 1876 for burial of British service personnel and their families.

Liddy 1987.

GRANGEMORE (see COTTAGE)

152. GRANGEMOUNT, Balbriggan; *c.* 1840.
A tiny standard single-storey lodge, the hipped roof catsliding centrally over the breakfront entrance. Roughcast with three-over-six squared sash windows and V-jointed toothed stone quoins. Occupied. Pretty railed convex entrance quadrants with the hooped tops containing anthemions. House and lodge built after 1837 by Mason Yates.

Griffith 1848–60.

153. GREENFIELD, Coolock; pre-1837; *demolished.*
A small estate in 1841 held by physician Benjamin Guinness Darley, in whose hands it remained until at least 1870, his gatekeeper in 1848 being Patrick Reilly.

Thom's; Griffith 1848–60.

GREENFIELD (see SEAFIELD)

154. GREENMOUNT, Drumcondra; pre-1837; *demolished.*
A property in 1841 of Thomas Meally, the lodge to which lay vacant in 1850, when the proprietor was John Clarke.

Thom's; Griffith 1848–60.

155. GREENWOOD, Portmarnock (2).
In 1801 'the seat of Richard Sayers, Esq., formerly of Sir William Montgomery, a neat small house and demesne, with good shrubberies, and well planted with all kinds of trees'. A house where Handel is reputed to have visited has now gone, as has its early 1837 gate lodge. The later surviving lodge of about 1845 was built either by W. Shaw, who was here in 1837, or his successor Hans H. Woods (1814–79), later of Whitestown (*q.v.*). It is single-storey with leading canted front, over which projects a gable with later 'Elizabethan' features; subsequent flat-roofed additions to each side. Originally much as the lodge to Abbeville Lodge (*q.v.*) nearby. In 1848 the gatekeeper was Thomas Frazer.

Archer 1801; Brewer 1825; Lewis 1837; Griffith 1848–60; *LGI* (1904).

156. GRIFFIN LODGE, Lucan (2).
Captain Gandon is noted as resident here in 1836, when there was an early lodge to the north. By 1907 this was avenueless and another gave access to a new house on the property, 'Clanaboy'. Neither lodge survives. In the mid-nineteenth century Thomas R. Needham moved here after his main seat of St Edmondsbury (*q.v.*), across the River Liffey, was auctioned off in 1853.

D'Alton 1976 [1838]; Griffith 1848–60; Lyons 1993.

157. HACKETSTOWN, Skerries (2).
'... the property of J.H. Hamilton, Esq., proprietor of the parish, and now the residence of his agent.' Thus recorded

Samuel Lewis in 1837, when both lodges were in place. This was James Hans Hamilton, who moved to the family's main seat of Abbotstown (*q.v.*) upon inheriting it on the death of his father in 1822. House and lodges have gone, leaving only some dilapidated outbuildings.

Lewis 1837; *BPB* (1929); Craig and Fewer 2002.

158. HAMPSTEAD CASTLE, Glasnevin; pre-1837; *demolished.*
The principal residence in a townland which from *c.* 1830 was progressively acquired by the Eustace family as a place for their private lunatic asylum, and later as site of their houses such as 'Hampstead Lodge' (*q.v.*) and 'Elmhurst' (*q.v.*). Hampstead Castle was acquired from John Davys by Sir Richard Steele just before his death in 1785 and remained in the family until the passing of his grandson of the same name, the 3rd baronet (1775–1850), whose gatekeeper in 1848 was John Ryan. By 1906 both big house and its lodge had gone.

Taylor and Skinner 1778; 1969 [1783]; d'Alton 1976 [1838]; Griffith 1848–60; *BPB* (1903); Ball 1995.

159. HAMPSTEAD LODGE, Glasnevin; *c.* 1820/*c.* 1905.
Originating as a tiny single-storey hip-roofed cottage serving what was probably a dower house to the adjacent Hampstead Castle (*q.v.*), by 1906 it had been expanded into a treble pile with red-brick chimney-stacks, earthenware ridges and hipped tile cresting with a roughcast finish, presumably when Hampstead Lodge had been extended and transformed into 'Hillside Farm' in the time of Benjamin Fawcett Eustace. Occupied.

IB (21 Sept. 1907).

160. HAMPTON HALL, Balbriggan (4).
An imposing mansion overlooking the Irish Sea, built *c.* 1775 by George, Baron Hamilton, solicitor general for Ireland. In about 1850 Thomas Lacy noted that the estate 'comprises upwards of 500 acres, and is approached by a spacious avenue, with three separate entrances, at which are characteristic gate-lodges'. Not one of these, nor a fourth within the estate, all in place by 1837, survives. A modern sketch, however, drawn from memory and old photographs, shows the northern, and main, entrance from Balbriggan to have been an impressive introduction. Comprised of four Classical pillars in ashlar with ball finials to the carriage pair and what appear to be braziers to the outer pillars. These were linked by concave railed quadrants on dwarf walls and containing postern gates. Beyond was a 1½-storey gabled cottage, probably in the English Picturesque fashion of *c.* 1830, with small-paned windows and an ornamental chimney-stack.

Young 1780; Lacy 1852; *IFR*.

161. HAMPTON LODGE, Drumcondra (2).
Two pre-1837 lodges to a property in the early nineteenth century of M.A. Williams. One of the gatekeepers of his widow in 1848 was Thomas Hanly. Both have been demolished.

Lewis 1837; *Parliamentary Gazetteer*; Griffith 1848–60.

162. HANSFIELD, Clonsilla; pre-1837/*c.* 1860.
Now called 'Ongar', a house in 1862 'approached by an avenue, with handsome gate entrance and lodge', the latter presumably then newly built as a replacement; what survives is a substantial rendered 1½-storey gabled gatehouse on an L-plan, still in occupation. A Thomas Williams is recorded as proprietor in 1837 and as late as 1860; his gate porter in 1849 was Peter Hanlon.

Lewis 1837; Griffith 1848–60; Lyons 1993.

163. HARTFIELD, Finglas; pre-1837; *demolished.*
In 1848 James Cassidy occupied the gate lodge as porter to William J. Lynch, proprietor of a private lunatic asylum which the house, previously of N.J. O'Neill in 1837, had become.

Lewis 1837; *Thom's*; Griffith 1848–60.

HARTSTOWN (see SHAMROCK LODGE)

164. HAYSTOWN, Rush; *c.* 1835.
A plain single-storey standard hip-roofed cottage with like hall projection. Much modernised and extended into a double pile in the process. The gatekeeper in 1852 was Francis Cosgrave, to Abel Onje, whose family is noted here in 1783 and also to be found at Newberry Hall (*q.v.*).

Taylor and Skinner 1778; 1969 [1783]; Griffith 1848–60.

165. HAZELBROOK, Portmarnock; *c.* 1820.

Irish Architectural Archive

A once-delightful lodge identical to that at nearby St Doolagh's (*q.v.*) but this is in terminal decline. A seat in the early nineteenth century of James Frazer, its lodge is a standard single-storey gabled Classical Regency affair, the main front to the park an arcade of segmentally arched recesses containing bipartite casement windows flanking the front door in a harled finish below an all-embracing pediment. Impolitely it presents its (now-derelict) rear to the visitor. In 1848 it was a proud home to James Vaughan.

Lewis 1837; Griffith 1848–60; IAA photograph (S/860/12).

166. HEATHFIELD LODGE, Finglas (2).
The house, now taking the name of its townland, 'Cappoge', has lost both its lodges, whose occupants in 1848 were Bernard Rorke and Thomas Lynch, gate porters to John Martin. Only the lodge to the eastern gate is identifiable on the 1837 OS map.

Griffith 1848–60.

167. HIGHFIELD, Drumcondra; *c.* 1845; architect not known.

Captain Thomas Aiskew Larcom (1801–79) in 1828 was appointed administrator in the Ordnance Survey at Mountjoy House, where he remained until 1846, about which time he built himself the house and its contemporary porter's lodge on nine acres at Drumcondra. His stay here was short, as in 1853 he was appointed under-secretary for Ireland, with use of the Under-secretary's Lodge (*q.v.*) as his residence. His lodge is charming: single-storey, built off an L-plan below a hipped roof with decorative foiled fascia boards. The principal feature is the right-hand of the three bays of the avenue front, which is a verandahed recess containing the doorway behind cast-iron post supports. Set in whitened harled walls are pretty bipartite round-headed casement windows with margined and Y-traceried glazing pattern. The brick chimney-stack is a late Victorian rebuild. There is a similar gate lodge at Warrenpoint, Clontarf (*q.v.*), conceivably by Larcom's contemporary at the Phoenix Park, Jacob Owen.

Griffith 1848–60; OSI 1991; Lalor 2003.

168. HIGHFIELD, Grangegorman; 1875; architect not known.

On the North Circular Road, looking for all the world like an early Victorian creation, is this Picturesque English Country Cottage, its date only betrayed by the blue earthenware fleur-de-lis cresting to its steeply pitched gabled roofs. Single-storey standard with a back return and little central entrance hall with slit side windows and a segmentally arched fanlit doorway incongruously sporting a Classical moulded architrave in a smooth rendered wall, which clashes with the otherwise mainly brick finish. Mainly that is because construction seems to have been contemplated in rubble stone with large boulder quoins, abandoned in favour of brickwork at an early stage. To the roofs are canted slate bands and perforated wavy bargeboards with hip-knobs. On the road gable is a semi-octagonal bow window with equivalent roof monitoring the gates, which have railed screens and plain rough-finished stone carriage pillars. The big Classical house within, of *c.* 1860, now known as 'Cluain Mhuire', originated as a semi-detached pair built for their senior employees by the Midland and Great Western Railway Company.

169. HIGHPARK, Drumcondra (2).
Both pre-1837 lodges, to a property in that year of George Gray, have gone. In 1848 one of the gatekeepers was Joseph Sullivan, when the house was the residence of Captain Robert Hillard. At the south entrance survive three Classical pillars in channelled rustication and shallow concave quadrant walls.

Lewis 1837; Griffith 1848–60.

170. HILLBROOK, Blanchardstown (2).
An old seat in the mid-eighteenth century of the Sampson family which by 1824 was the property of Joseph Spencer and later that century of the Taylors. Both lodges, one pre-1837 and that which superseded it further west, have gone, to be replaced at one gate by a remarkable gatescreen purloined in part from the neighbouring Abbotstown (*q.v.*), another two pillars having found their way to Cherry Cottage, Westport, Co. Mayo. In 1848 a gate porter was David English.

Pigot 1824; *Thom's*; Ball 1995.

HILLSBORO (see MOUNT PLEASANT)

HILLSIDE FARM (see HAMPSTEAD LODGE)

171. HOLLYBROOK LODGE, Killester; pre-1837; *demolished.*
A property in 1824 and 1846 of Nathaniel Low.

Pigot 1824; *Thom's*.

172. HOLLYBROOK PARK, Killester; *c.* 1830.
A modest single-storey standard lodge on a square plan, its shallow pyramidal roof rising to a central chimney-stack; stucco-effect walls with exposed rafter toes to the eaves. Boarded up but an amazing survival. Two basic carriage pillars alongside to a property in 1837 of George Symes.

Lewis 1837.

173. HOLLYWOODRATH, Ward; pre-1837/*c.* 1850; architect probably Alfred G. Jones.

A seat in the late eighteenth century of the Garnet family which passed by the marriage in 1793 of Mary Garnet to her cousin Major William Thompson of Clonfin, Co. Longford (q.v.), who lived here until his death in 1850, following which it was his son Thomas who replaced the gate lodge they inherited with the surviving singular specimen. Not unique, for there are others in south Dublin, such as at Montebello (*q.v.*), Monkstown House (*q.v.*) and Johnstown Kennedy (*q.v.*), with like detailing, and its similarity to that at the latter makes it safely attributable to architect Alfred G. Jones. In a peculiar Italianate style, it is single-storey gabled, on an irregular plan, with a single-bay front extending to the avenue, its tripartite window with round-headed arches below an open pediment. To the road is a wide window with depressed arch, like the others with bracketed sill and hood mouldings, the keystone and voussoirs of which have a reticulated finish springing from fluted scrolled brackets. In the internal angle was a flat-roofed entrance portico with Doric columns and pilasters, now enclosed. In a smooth rendered finish, with plinth and bands to corners and eaves, all topped off with a tripartite chimney-stack. Equally distinctive is the gatescreen with its unusual granite pillars, those to the carriage openings with incised panel shafts tapering to a frieze with discs below a capping bearing scrolls and palmette motifs. These are linked to outer drum pillars with more discs below gadrooned cappings and 'bap' finials by chunky iron railings with further palmette and floral features.

LGI (1904).

HOLY CROSS CHURCH AND COLLEGE (see CLONLIFFE)

174. HOUSE OF INDUSTRY, Grangegorman; *c.* 1800; architect probably Francis Johnston; *demolished.*
A workhouse for beggars and vagrants which, like its gate lodge, has gone. Presumably also designed by the Johnston office, a surviving floor-plan drawing shows porter's accommodation clearly shoehorned into a restricted site off North Brunswick Street. Built against an existing structure, it was single-storey and two-roomed, probably below a lean-to roof, with chamfered ends extending to a storeroom behind the left-hand quadrant of a triple gateway with two octagon carriage pillars.

Casey 2005; IAA (Murray Drawing Collection: 398).

175. HOWTH CASTLE, Howth (3).
The extraordinary property of the St Lawrences, earls of Howth, which can boast of being uninterruptedly inhabited by the same family for over 800 years and which has the added curiosity of having remained lodgeless until the mid-nineteenth century. In all that time the castle survived without any outer 'defences', and even when the 3rd earl, Thomas St Lawrence (1803–74), inherited the estate in 1822 the porters' lodges that he built were essentially decorative and convenient. Thomas proved particularly promiscuous with his architects, engaging many of the best-known Irish practitioners of the time, of whom only Richard Morrison can be identified as meeting with his client's approval in seeing many of his plans executed for alterations to the castle, its stables and the entrance gates off the Howth Road, and perhaps its gatekeeper's lodge.

Main entrance; *c.* 1840; architect probably R. Morrison; *demolished.*

On the northern approach is this wonderful Gothic gatescreen with its four pillars, each of cluster-columns, octafoil in section with foliated friezes and concave capping, which used to be crowned with floral finials. Pairs of these are linked by screen walls containing arched postilion gates. Attribution to Richard

175. Howth Castle, Howth, main entrance.

Morrison is prompted by there being an almost identical screen at Lismore Cathedral, Co. Waterford, the design drawing for which by Owen Fahy, his assistant, survives. The source, however, may well have been another example at Portumna Castle, Co. Galway. If Morrison was not responsible for it too, his client would certainly have been aware of it, perhaps from as early as his courtship of Lady Emily de Burgh, daughter of the 13th earl of Clanricarde of Portumna, whom Thomas took as his first wife in 1826. In any case, all seem to have been influenced by Batty and Thomas Langley's *Gothic architecture, improved by rules and proportions* (1747). The author of the once attendant lodge is not so clear, for the only illustration surviving is in a delightful painting of 1853 by Edward McFarland, which depicts a charming Tudor Revival cottage with a pair of diagonally set stone chimney-stacks, sawtooth slating, hip-knobs and fretted bargeboards to its steeply pitched roofs; 1½-storey and two-bay to the avenue, that to the left-hand side as a gabled breakfront containing the front door below a gabled porch. McFarland shows quaintly creeper-clad walls, which are now reduced to an overgrown pile of rubble, but sufficient remains to suggest that there was an oriel window to the road gable.

South entrance; pre-1906; *demolished.* Off the Carrickbrack Road was a short-lived lodge built after 1837 but survived by a mid-Georgian gatescreen of grand granite

V-jointed rusticated pillars with ball finials and beautifully chiselled festooned friezes. Incongruously accompanied by a twentieth-century bungalow.

East entrance; 1872/*c.* 1920; architect Joseph Maguire.

'... a neat gate-lodge has been completed near the deer park, Howth Castle, the seat of the Rt Hon. the earl of Howth. Mr Joseph Maguire, archt.' Thus ran the *Irish Builder* entry of 1872 for a standard single-storey cottage with a hipped roof covered in scalloped slates. No other original features are discernible, for it is disfigured to the front by a hideous flat-roofed projection and dominated to the rear by an attached twentieth-century two-storey roughcast hip-roofed structure identified by the 1906–7 OS map as a lodge in its own right.

Langley and Langley 1747; McFarland painting (NLI 1986 TX 13); *IB* (15 Dec. 1972); *BPB* (1929); McParland *et al.* 1989; IAA photograph (2/23Z3).

176. HOWTH LODGE, Howth; pre-1906; *demolished.*

A residence in the mid-nineteenth century of Charles Kohler, tailor and draper in the city, the lodge to which was built after 1837.

Griffith 1848–60; Shaw 1988.

177. HUNTSTOWN, Finglas (2).

Both lodges to a property in 1837 of Owen Coghlan have been demolished.

Lewis 1837.

178. HUNTSTOWN LOWER, Mulhuddart (2).

A seat of Henry McFarlane (1767–1851) which had a single lodge in 1837, to which his son, Henry James McFarland (1817–1901), added another, neither of which remain.

LGI (1904).

179. HUNTSTOWN UPPER, Mulhuddart; pre-1837; *demolished.*

A residence in 1848 of William Morrison.

Griffith 1848–60.

180. HYBLA, Castleknock; pre-1836; *demolished.*

'Mount Hybla', as it became known, was home to rectors of Castleknock parish, of whom Revd George O'Connor was incumbent from 1809 to 1843 in succession to his equally long-serving father, Revd John O'Connor, rector from 1767.

Leslie and Wallace 2001.

181. IRISHTOWN, Dunboyne; pre-1837; *demolished.*

A property in 1849 of William Inglis Clyde.

Griffith 1848–60.

182. JAMESTOWN, Finglas; pre-1906; *demolished.*

A lodge built after 1837 on an estate in the mid-nineteenth century of the Shaw family.

JOHNSTOWN (see LAWDON TOWER)

183. KELLYSTOWN, Mulhuddart; *c.* 1810/*c.* 1840.

The most peculiar of lodges, or rather assembly of lodges, seemingly of sundry periods. What appears to have been an ordinary standard single-storey three-bay hip-roofed structure (now with its door sealed) was later flanked by a striking pair of identical wings which extend to the avenue to present pedimented fronts, each comprised of toothed granite quoins framing a three-bay façade of tiny cast-iron latticed windows on either side of granite Doric pilasters which mirror the door-case of the panelled door. An amusing exercise in duality, with some sophisticated detailing in otherwise limewashed harled walls. This may be a neat solution of the Kennedy family to provide accommodation for more than one family of their estate workers, much as at Coolmore, Co. Cork. At the entrance is a pair of late Georgian carriage pillars with fluted friezes and resplendent eagles over, probably of an age with the original lodge, whilst the gates and their matching ogee-railed quadrants with palmette motifs are contemporary with the later building period, when the place had become 'Dolland'.

184. KENURE PARK, Rush (6).
The once-proud estate known as 'Rush' of the Palmer family would not today be recognised as such were it not for the survival of the grand portico to their spacious and handsome mansion, which stands forlorn with two of its gate lodges in varied conditions of dereliction and misguided revamping. What remains is the work of architect George Papworth, who was engaged in 1842 to reface 'Rush House, a handsome antique structure', by Sir William Henry Roger Palmer (1802–69), the 4th baronet, who had succeeded to the property on the death of his father two years earlier. Of the six porters' lodges, two of which were in place in 1836, three survive.

North entrance; pre-1836/*c.* 1845; architect George Papworth.

On the site of a predecessor is this notable and unusual Classical lodge. Single-storey standard of generous proportions, its hipped roof hidden behind a solid parapet, built in a stucco finish having openings with moulded architraves below architraves, the doorway contained in a breakfront with alternate reticulated quoins and a relieving panel below a crowning pediment. The windows to opposing ends are contained in segmentally arched recesses. The lodge lies abandoned and windowless behind an impressive gatescreen of more alternate reticulated giant blocks to pillars with rusticated ball finials atop. These are linked by wide, shallow, concave quadrant walls. A sorry sight.

South entrance; *c.* 1845; architect George Papworth.
At the Rush gate, this was essentially the same composition as at the northern approach, differing only in its gatesweep being extended by central straight railed screens of contemporary ironwork with a

pair of additional grand pillars. Within is the extraordinary apparition of the lodge, occupied and maintained but stripped of its stuccoed cloak and decorative detailing to reveal its fabric of brick seconds at the mercy of the elements, like a skinned rabbit caught in headlights—a situation not irreversible by the authority responsible.

Church entrance; *c.* 1870; architect J.E. Rogers.
Opposite the gate to Rogers's little Church of Ireland church is this single-storey four-bay structure which also served as a schoolhouse. Constructed in rubble facings, with punched stone quoins and brick-dressed openings, rising to hipped gables. All for the 5th baronet, Sir Roger William Henry Palmer (1832–1910), after whose death the baronetcy became extinct and the property's decline began.

D'Alton 1976 [1838]; *BPB* (1903); Williams 1994; Craig and Fewer 2002; NIAH.

185. KILBARRACK CEMETERY, Sutton; 1876; architect Joseph Maguire.
Boundary and gate lodge were built by Richard Campbell, contractor, of Howth, to plans by Joseph Maguire; a block plan and grave-plot layout drawing survives in the Irish Architectural Archive. It is a modest single-storey standard structure, with roughcast walls framed by Irish pilaster quoins below a hipped with wooden eaves brackets. The gabled central entrance breakfront is flanked by stone-dressed windows. To the ridge is a big brick stack with plinth and corbelling. Derelict, 'In its lonely churchyard sleep many who, in times more perilous for seafarers, were cast up by the waves'.

IB (1 Sept. 1876); Joyce 1912; IAA (Workhouse Drawings Collection 85/138.105).

186. KILBARRACK, Raheny (2).
From the early nineteenth century a seat of the Law family, both pre-1837 lodges to which have been demolished. An old photograph of that to the southern gate shows a humble if commodious rustic 1½-storey structure with limewashed rubble walls, slated with clipped eaves and verges.

187. KILDONAN, Finglas (2).
Both the big house, recorded in 1837 as being 'in ruins', and its gate lodge were rebuilt thereafter, but even the replacement for the latter, opposite the gates, has gone. In 1848 the proprietor was Revd John Courtney and in 1870 M.F. Byrne, who may briefly have resurrected the place.

Griffith 1848–60; *Thom's*.

188. KILLESTER ABBEY, Killester; pre-1837; *demolished.*
A property in 1841 of William Nugent, whose gatekeeper in 1849 was John Segrave.

Thom's; Griffith 1848–60.

189. KILLESTER, Killester (3).
The important early eighteenth-century single-storey mansion was owned late in the century by William Gleadowe, who by 1781 had become Sir William Gleadowe-Newcomen through being created a baronet that year and having previously assumed the additional surname after marrying Charlotte, sole child and heiress of Charles Newcomen of Carriglass, Co. Longford (*q.v.*). She became a viscountess in her own right in 1803. Their only son, Sir Thomas Newcomen, inherited Killester on his father's death and his mother's title on her death in 1817, enjoying the property for another eight years until his own demise, after which it was a seat of General Thomas P. Luscombe until about 1850. Of the three lodged entrances at least one appears to have been built by Sir William. None are evident on the 1760 Rocque map.

Malahide Road gate; pre-1837; *demolished.*

Inner gate; pre-1837; *demolished.*

Howth Road gate; *c.* 1785; architect possibly Thomas Ivory; *demolished.*
A very fine Palladian entrance was in the form of a pair of single-storey lodges placed well forward of their gatescreen and connected to them by convex walled quadrants. The leading fronts were blind but not lacking in interest, each having a round-headed niche with plaque over, set in a depressed arched recess below a parapet crowned by an urn. The channelled rusticated finish was continued back through the screen walls to the shafts of the carriage pillars, which had swagged friezes and urns atop to match those to the lodges. All very elegant, and a description which would not have been possible without the survival of a charming watercolour painting by Edward McFarland in 1853 of the entrance with a wooded backdrop, two venerable trees in the foreground, an elderly gentleman availing of rest in one of the niches and a coach emerging from between the grand carriage pillars. What the painting also reveals is that the remaining gatescreen at Ravensdale, Co. Kildare, is identical, which raises the common denominator of architect Thomas Ivory, who is known to have worked there and to have designed the Newcomen Bank. In 1801: 'Killester, the seat of Sir William

National Library of Ireland
189. Killester, Killester.

Gleadowe Newcomen, with a spacious house, a demesne of nearly forty acres, well wooded; the walks are judiciously laid out so far as to form a compleat country residence, though situated within a mile and a half of the capital. The gardens are elegantly disposed, a large extent of glass well furnished with pines, grapes &c. of the first flavour.' This whole evocative scene is a thing of the past and wiped from the map.

Archer 1801; NLI painting (1986 TX 8); Burke's *Dormant and extinct peerages* (1883); Bence-Jones 1988; IAA.

190. KILL GRIEF LODGE, Artane; pre-1837; *demolished.*
A seat in 1841 of Edward C. Irvine, whose gatekeeper seven years later was Robert Little. The property was later renamed 'Artane Lodge'.

Thom's; Griffith 1848–60.

191. KILMARTIN, Dunboyne (2).
Both pre-1837 lodges to a property in 1837 of J. Hoskins have gone.

Lewis 1837.

192. KILMORE, Artane; pre-1837; *demolished.*
An estate in 1837 of H. Hutton.

Lewis 1837.

193. KILMORE LODGE, Artane; post-1837; *demolished.*
The residence in 1849 of Revd John Hare (1796–1871), when his gate porter was John Donaldson. Hare was incumbent of the Free Church, Great Charles Street, Dublin (1828–71). He had married well in 1826 to Henrietta, daughter of the Pakenham family of Tullynally Castle, Co. Westmeath (*q.v.*), which may have financed building of the lodge.

Griffith 1848–60; *BPB* (1929); Leslie and Wallace 2001.

194. KILREESK, Swords; pre-1836; *demolished.*
A house and lodge in the early nineteenth century of the Greene family. By 1937 the house was 'in ruins' and the lodge gone.

195. KILROCK, Howth; *c.* 1885; architect J.F. Fuller.

Overlooking Balscadden Bay and Howth Harbour is a big mid- to late Victorian red-brick house built in phases in 1875 and 1888 for the Rt Hon. Gerald Fitzgibbon, justice of appeal. Initially the work of architects James Edward Rogers and James Franklin Fuller, who shared an office address in the city, and later of the latter alone, Rogers having returned to London in 1816. The lodge is an appropriate prelude to the house, being in a like brick finish. Chunky in outline, single-storey and built off a T-plan, the downstroke extending beyond its boundary wall and gatescreen, a canted bay window projecting further into the carriageway. Like the one-over-one sash window openings, the front door is segmentally arched below a high-eaved hipped roof from which rises at the ridge intersection a big brick stack with bands and sawtooth corbelling. On the otherwise blind avenue front is a relieving pair of decorative ceramic tiles. To the leading corner is a protective buttress, whilst alongside is a pair of brick carriage pillars with sandstone dressings, an intermediate band inscribed 'Kilrock House' and broaching to decorative octagonal cappings. The lodge has a twin at Broomville, South Dublin (*q.v.*).

IAA.

196. KILRONAN, Cloghran; pre-1837; *demolished.*
A property in the mid-nineteenth century of Robert Dawson, whose gatekeeper in 1848 was James Murphy.

Griffith 1848–60.

197. KILSHANE, St Margaret's; *c.* 1840.
A modest roughcast single-storey standard gabled structure, with modern windows, located opposite the gates. Vacant; probably doomed to removal to accommodate road-widening. A property in 1848 of James Blake.

Griffith 1848–60.

198. KING'S INNS, Constitution Hill (4).
From 1795, when James Gandon's designs were approved, the building proceeded painfully, and the designs were not realised until after the architect's resignation from the commission and his retirement. The addition of entrances and porters' lodges proved equally fitful in execution.

Henrietta Street gate; *c.* 1820; architect Francis Johnston.

Johnston, as architect to the Board of Works from 1805, carried out alterations to the complex and completed the cupola of the building to Gandon's design. In 1819 his scheme for 'Gate, Sweep Wall, and Frontispiece, entering into the society's Ground, to their Dining Hall, the Registry Office, and other buildings to be built, according to a Plan and Estimate to be approved of by the Society, and that the Expense should be defrayed jointly by Government, and the Society, as will be the principal Entrance into their said Concerns from Henrietta-Street', was successful and by August 1820 approval had been given for the works, which were to include a gate lodge, all to commence for a sum of £1,123.3s.5d. Based on Gandon's gateways to the screens at the Four Courts, this is a grand triple triumphal archway with a pair of subsidiary arched openings to side courts. The main carriage opening is semicircular-arched in rusticated granite, flanked by a pair of similarly headed postilion gates with recessed panels as a relief over, all below a parapet and central die which is crowned by the royal arms. The cornice continues in a curve above tall round-headed recesses containing pedestrian doorways, the right-hand one of which was monitored by Johnston's little porter's lodge shoehorned in behind, almost as an afterthought, with no apparent effort to integrate it into the general scheme of things. Two-roomed, single-storey, hip-roofed and modest in the extreme, it surprisingly is still put to use.

The society had resolved to open up the building to Constitution Hill and by 1833 had acquired sufficient land along that frontage to commission a lengthy entrance screen and gatekeeper's lodge.

North lodge; *c.* 1837; architect Jacob Owen; *demolished.*

Kearns

Owen, architect to the Board of Works, was charged with providing an entrance gateway and a lodge, the cost of which was not to exceed £200, a task in which he clearly failed, for the lodge was obviously of sophisticated detailing and materials. Built in ashlar, it was a distinguished single-storey two-roomed neo-Classical box, with a short front to the avenue comprised of a single opening set in a recess screened by a pair of square Doric columns *in antis*. Its hipped roof was concealed by a balustraded parapet. Sadly, it no longer stands guard over its gatescreen, having been removed in 1953 owing to its being 'in bad repair'. Alongside, the gates survive in the form of a pair of flat-arched postern gates on each side of short railed screens and tall carriage pillars which sported lanterns. This was linked by an extensive tall boundary wall to an identical gatescreen to the south.

South lodge; 1845; architect Jacob Owen.

It was probably always the building committee's intention to balance the Constitution Hill boundary with a matching lodge when land became available. At the city gate, what at a glance they appear to have achieved is identical in outline with the same balustraded parapet. For some reason, however, Owen chose an alternative and more opulent principal front. Here to a six-over-six sash window he applied a breakfront with two pairs of Tuscan columns having alternate vermiculated drums flanked by channelled ashlar, which turns the corner to contain round-headed niches. This fine building has had a more charmed existence than its erstwhile companion, having survived the surveyor's scrutiny to remain maintained and occupied. Probably also by Owen, at the National Model Schools (*q.v.*) is a similar pair of truncated *in antis* lodges, little more than sentry-boxes.

A mysterious early lodge seems to have existed in 1794, for there is a record of porter's wages having been paid out. This may have been created by the Society's treasurer and amateur architect William Caldbeck, although there is no sign of it on early maps.

Craig 1980; Kearns1995; Duffy 1999.

199. KINSALEY HALL, Kinsaley; *c.* 1825.
A good mid-eighteenth-century gentleman farmer's house, which passed from the Taylor family through marriage of a daughter Penelope in 1784 to Edward Mapother, who is noted here in 1814 and may have added the gate lodge. Thereafter it was home to John Neill, whose gatekeeper in 1850 was Martin Maguire. The lodge is a single-storey cottage in stucco-effect finish that has canted short elevations, below an equivalent steeply pitched roof, one of which faces the road to be flanked by two gatescreens, one of old granite Georgian pillars. About 1870 a new access was created in the form of ogee-railed quadrants; the lodge was reoriented, with a tiny new gabled hall tucked in below the eaves with ornamental bargeboards to what had been the rear of the lodge, now facing the realigned avenue.

Leet 1814; Griffith 1848–60; *LGI* (1904).

200. KINSALEY, Kinsaley; pre-1906; *demolished.*
A short-lived lodge built after 1837 to a property in 1848 of Terence Gorman, who was followed here by Lawrence Neill about 1862.

Griffith 1848–60; *Thom's.*

KNOCKDROMIN (see BEAU)

201. KNOCKMAROON, Castleknock (4).
The delightful small leafy estate by the Strawberry Beds on the banks of the Liffey has a big plain Georgian house, in 1783 residence of the archbishop of Dublin, followed in about 1790 by Robert Watson Wade. There were two gate lodges in place by 1837, both of which were replaced during extensive improvements to the property in 1905 after it had been purchased, following the long occupation of Walter Brinkley (1826–84), by the 1st Baron Iveagh for his third son, the Rt Hon. Walter Edward Guinness (1880–1944), later created 1st Lord Moyne. Whilst the old house escaped relatively unscathed, the building works included a new stable block and four gate lodges, most in a 'Stockbroker Tudor' manner almost identical to a gate lodge at Eyrefield Lodge, Co. Kildare (*q.v.*), and a similar one to Lumville Farm (*q.v.*) in the same county.

Tower Road gate; pre-1837/*c.* 1905; architect probably L.A. McDonnell.
A distinctive 1½-storey gable-fronted two-bay English Arts and Crafts cottage, its two

front windows in a red-brick finish with outer chamfered entrance corners over which the regular attic storey cantilevers on carved decorative brackets to create triangular porches. The upper floor is pebble-dashed with a half-timbered-effect apex over twinned tripartite square-paned casement windows installed flush with the wall finish in southern English fashion. The earthenware-tiled roof is crowned by a red-brick chimney-stack, the bargeboards with applied dentil pattern. Spacious and occupied, it replaced a Georgian lodge on the site.

Carpenters Road gate; pre-1837/*c.* 1905; architect probably L.A. McDonnell.

Identical to the above and likewise having had an earlier predecessor.

College Road gate; *c.* 1905; architect probably L.A. McDonnell.
Much as the foregoing lodges but even more generous in accommodation, the avenue front three-bay with a central doorway, and windows occupying the chamfered corners.

Lower Road gate; *c.* 1900.
By the river on a height, this lodge monitored the footbridge crossing to a boat-house on the southern bank. Now totally derelict and overgrown is a single-storey hip-roofed structure built in quarry-faced masonry with cream brick dressings, quoins and eaves band off a T-plan, the downstroke to the road containing a dominant canted bay window in the same brick, as is the massive brick stack at the meeting of the ridges.

Taylor and Skinner 1778; 1969 [1783]; *BPB* (1949); Craig and Fewer 2002; IAA.

202. KNOCKMAROON LODGE, Chapelizod (3).
A property with the most strange and confusing recent history. D'Alton about 1837 describes 'on the ascent from Chapelizod to Knockmaroon Hill, the residence of Colonel Colby is seen at left, in a delightful concentration of charming prospects. The entrance to it is from the Phoenix Park, over a bridge thrown across the high road which divides them.' This was Lieut. Col. Thomas Frederick Colby (1784–1852), who was appointed in 1824 to head the mammoth task of preparing the first Ordnance Survey of Ireland, upon the completion of which, in 1846, he retired. His office was Mountjoy House in the Phoenix Park, only a short walk north from his house but separated by the public road. The 'Pond Gate Lodge', so called on the 1837 OS map, and the bridge thereto may have been created for his convenience or for earlier occupants of Knockmaroon Lodge.

Pond gate lodge; pre-1837/*c.* 1880; *demolished.*
What occupies this site today are the outbuildings to the great half-timbered pile that is Glenmaroon House, built in 1905 for the Hon. Arthur Ernest Guinness to designs of L.A. McDonnell and which bizarrely is linked by the same footbridge to the present Knockmaroon Lodge. Attached to these outbuildings is what seems to be a gate lodge to Glenmaroon in the shape of a single-storey hip-roofed structure on an L-plan with stucco-effect finish and conspicuous carved brackets to the oversailing eaves. The red-brick chimney-stacks suggest a late nineteenth-century date. Modernised with plastic windows failing to look like original six-over-six timber sashes.

By 1843 Knockmaroon Lodge had been acquired by a Dublin draper for whom business clearly prospered, as by 1862 the *Dublin Builder* announced: 'large mansion in course of erection for Mr Gilbert Burns, to be entitled Knockmaroon House. It is in the Italian style with a campanile centrally placed over the principal entrance, D.C. Ferguson archt.' To his new house Burns created two new approaches, both with lodges.

Bellevue Parc gate; *c.* 1865; architect probably D.C. Ferguson.

To the west of Knockmaroon Hill, Burns procured the old entrance to Bellevue Parc (*q.v.*) and extended that avenue to his new house, retaining the Classical gatescreen with its concave quadrants and postern openings below stone soldier arches, and, regardless, replaced the old lodge with one in a transitional style somewhere between early Victorian English Picturesque Cottage and High Victorian Gothic. Built off an L-plan, 1½-storey with very steeply pitched roofs to give generous attic accommodation, the gables and gablet decorated with fancy carved perforated continuous bracket bargeboards and hip-knobs. The crude roughcast walls contain chamfered stone-dressed and label-moulded surrounds to mullioned and transomed windows with pretty hexagonal glazing pattern. To the eaves are serrated fascia boards and in the internal angle is a lean-to single-storey hall with a delightful pointed-arched, hood-moulded doorway.

Phoenix Park gate; *c.* 1865; architect probably D.C. Ferguson.

On the eastern side of Knockmaroon Hill, next to the Knockmaroon gate to Phoenix Park, Burns created a new entrance on a grander scale with richer detailing and materials. Here is the same fancy glazing pattern but with cut-stone mullions and transoms in ornate hexagonal granite-faced walls. The hip-knobs, bargeboards and eaves pendants are in top-quality joinery work, whilst the buttressed chimney-stacks, with mock cross arrowloop motifs, dominate. Of unusually generous scale, wide tripartite windows predominate, and in the internal angle is a long single-storey porch and hallway below a catslide roof. Preceding this is an opulent Classical gatescreen with banded rusticated stone pillars with moulded cappings and pedestalled ball finials, set off by railed concave quadrants. This entrance was purloined by the Guinness family when they built their house of Glenmaroon.

D'Alton 1976 [1838]; *Thom's*; *DB* (15 May 1861 and 1 Feb. 1862); Williams 1994.

203. KNOCKNAGIN, Gormanstown; *c.* 1720.
Not what one would perceive as a conventional gate lodge but rather as a rare 1½-storey vernacular Irish thatched cottage of such generous accommodation as to suggest that it originated as an independent house in its own right, before in the nineteenth century certainly assuming the role of a porter's lodge sited forward of its entrance gates. This is an extraordinary and

delightful survivor, presenting a traditional linear four-bay ground-floor front, with tiny two-over-two sash windows in thick walls and even more minuscule attic windows in the form of eyebrow dormers in the thatch and to the half-hipped gables. Harled and whitewashed correctly but with a later gabled trellised porch to the entrance half-doors and a straw cock pheasant to the ridge in English Picturesque manner. Recently admirably restored, it may be of an age with its more formal Classical big house, which in 1783 was home to one Martin Esq. and was named 'Seaview' when occupied in the nineteenth century by the O'Reillys of Knock Abbey, Co. Louth (*q.v.*). A remarkable example of Ireland's heritage, the survival of which should be extended by removal of traffic to the new north–south motorway.

Taylor and Skinner 1778; 1969 [1783].

204. KNOCKSEDAN, Swords; pre-1836.
A pleasant mid-eighteenth-century Georgian gentry house in fine condition, which contrasts with its ruinous lodge. Set well back from the modest entrance, it was a single-storey harled brick and rubble-built structure, now the site of a compost heap. A seat in the early nineteenth century of the Aungier family.

D'Alton 1976 [1838].

205. LA MANCHA, Malahide; pre-1837; *demolished.*
Both the lodge and its house have gone to make way for a twentieth-century housing estate. The eighteenth-century seat was home in 1837 to Michael Martin O'Grady MD, whose gatekeeper in 1850 was James Kerr.

Lewis 1837; Griffith 1848–60.

206. LARCH HILL, Santry; pre-1837; *demolished.*
A property in the mid-nineteenth century of James Kerr, china and glass merchant of Anglesea Row in the city.

Shaw 1988; *Thom's.*

207. LARK HILL, Coolock; pre-1837; *demolished.*
A seat in 1837 of Edward Hickson which by 1848 had been acquired by Conolly Norman, whose gate porter was then James Duff.

Lewis 1837; Griffith 1848–60.

LARK HILL (see MARY VILLE, Finglas)

208. LAUREL LODGE, Blanchardstown; pre-1938; *demolished.*
A house built *c.* 1870 by Patrick Manly, whose family was here until the end of the

century. Its short-lived lodge may have been built by Revd Stephen Fennelly, proprietor around 1900.

209. LAWDON TOWER, Finglas; pre-1837; *demolished.*
An estate in 1848 of Robert William Law.
Griffith 1848–60.

210. LIFFEYBANK, Islandbridge; pre-1837.
The lodge is now a two-storey structure below an oversailing hipped roof but may have originated as single-storey. In the mid-nineteenth century a premises on Conyngham Road of William Smith.
Griffith 1848–60.

211. LIME HILL, Balgriffin; *c.* 1840.
The quintessential basic Irish gate lodge, built somewhat later than its appearance suggests. Single-storey standard below an oversailing shallow hipped roof without any pretensions, with square rectangular-paned casement windows on each side of a simple sheeted door in walls now roughcast. The moulded cornice to the oversized chimney-stack capping gives a clue to its later date. To an older house *c.* 1800 of a Mr Druitt, by the 1840s the proprietor was Charles Cox, presumably the lodge-builder.
Wilson 1803; *Thom's.*

212. LINENHALL, Yarnhall Street; pre-1760.

The great complex created to facilitate the sale of cloth was erected initially in 1728 and eventually extended to over four acres. The gatehouse, identified by the 1850 valuation as the accommodation of John Nulty, can be located on a map of 1816 by John Parke as being at the entrance to the first court of the Yarn Hall at the head of the street of that name. It still remarkably survives, though much altered and in use alongside a sophisticated granite carriage archway of two free-standing Roman Doric columns framing a semicircular arch with prominent voussoirs rising to a female head as keystone. Above is a bold mutuled entablature with a die over, probably once informative but now blank. Attributed to Thomas Cooley *c.* 1784, the year of his death. The gates and their overthrow ironwork are later. The plain two-storey gatehouse with single-bay elevation to the approach formed an integral part of a row of thirteen stalls interrupted by the 'Chamberlain of the Hall's House'. This northernmost enclosure of the court along with the gateway is shown on Rocque's map of 1756. The rise of the port of Belfast badly affected trade in Dublin, and the Linenhall ceased functioning as a market in 1828, thereafter serving as a barracks before meeting an ignominious fate, being burnt down in the Rising of 1916.
Maxwell 1956; Craig 1980; Ferguson 1998; IAA (Edward Parke map).

213. LISSENHALL, GREAT, Swords; pre-1760; *demolished.*
An old property in 1783 of John Hatch but which features on Rocque's map of 1760 with what seem to be a pair of lodges at its entrance opposite that to Little Lissenhall House (*q.v.*). Sadly, all that survive at the gates are a modern bungalow and a gatescreen of *c.* 1845, when the proprietor was Thomas Cuffe.
Taylor and Skinner 1778; 1969 [1783]; Archer 1801; Griffith 1848–60; Ferguson 1998.

214. LISSENHALL, LITTLE, Swords; pre-1760; *demolished.*
A seat in the late eighteenth century of the Gordon family, to which there appear, from the Rocque map of 1760, to have been a pair of lodges at the gates, which by 1837 had been reduced to a single cottage.
Taylor and Skinner 1778; 1969 [1783]; Ferguson 1998.

215. LOHUNA PARK, Mulhuddart; *c.* 1860.
A remarkable survivor in this sea of frantic redevelopment is a single-storey standard roughcast lodge below a hipped roof, now with modern concrete tiles but retaining its paired soffit brackets. A hip-roofed hall extends to the avenue with a round-headed window; prominent plinth. Extended to the left-hand side, it remains in use. The property, previously called 'Clonsilla', was the seat in 1870 of Michael Beatty.

LONG COTTAGE (see ROSEMOUNT, Artane)

216. LOWTHER LODGE, Balbriggan (2).
The Lowther family was here until about 1790, when the estate was acquired by Townley Patten Filgate of Lisrenny, Co. Louth (*q.v.*). After his death the place became second home to his only surviving child and heiress and her husband, George Macartney of Lissanoure, Co. Antrim, who had married in 1828. Upon the coming of age of their second son, Townley Patten Hume Macartney-Filgate, in 1862, he assumed that Filgate name by royal licence and inherited Lowther Lodge.

North gate; pre-1837/1876; architects McCurdy and Mitchell.
The first OS map shows what may have been a pair of lodges to the property, probably

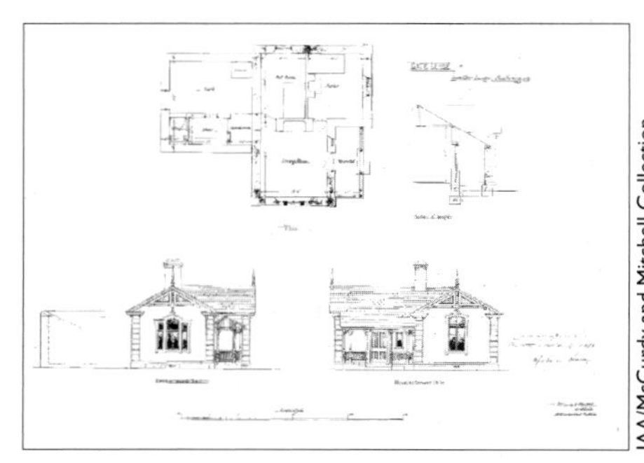

IAA/McCurdy and Mitchell Collection

dating from the Lowthers' time here. It was T.P.H.M. Filgate who made changes to the place, adding a replacement gate lodge to designs by the prolific Dublin architectural practice of McCurdy and Mitchell. Their dated contract drawing survives, indicating a decorative Italianate-style structure as built. Single-storey gabled on an L-plan built off a stone plinth, with rendered walls set off by raised rusticated Irish pilaster quoins and elaborate window surrounds with keystones and sill brackets, that to the road front a tripartite Venetian opening. The gables were decorated with carved woodwork to their apexes, whilst there was more fancy joinery work to a pretty entrance verandah in the internal corner below a catslide roof with bracketed posts and balustrades. The eaves brackets were repeated to the chimney-stack capping. This admirable design was subsequently sympathetically extended to the rear, but a more recent one has not seen the same sensitivity and it has been lost in modernisation. On a brighter note, pencil jottings on this contract drawing have identified that the architects presented a watered-down version of this lodge, which was built at Doobeg, Co. Sligo.

South lodge; *c.* 1860.
A rather more modest secondary lodge, single-storey standard with a pair of symmetrically placed chimney-stacks to the ridge of a steeply hipped roof, below the eaves of which is tucked a delightful rustic gabled porch with scalloped slates and a pair of chunky wooden pole supports. On each side in roughcast walls are tall six-over-six sash windows. Occupied but dilapidated.
Taylor and Skinner 1778; 1969 [1783]; Wilson 1803; *LGI* (1904); IAA (McCurdy & Mitchell Collection 79/17, Bin VIII, Roll 17).

217. LUCAN VILLA, Lucan; *c.* 1840.
The archetypal Classical Regency lodge, displaying the twenty-year time-lag of architectural fashions from the mainland, it is in a style favoured by the gentry and aristocracy of the neighbourhood, there being similar examples at Luttrellstown Castle (*q.v.*) and Anna Liffey Mills (*q.v.*). A nice, rendered, single-storey standard structure with its (now modern) openings framed in segmentally arched recesses below oversailing eaves with carved paired soffit brackets to its hipped roof. Built for Thomas Smullen, pawnbroker in the city. The property was renamed 'Ounavarra' *c.* 1870 by John Woodford Stanford.
Lewis 1837; *Thom's.*

218. LUSK RECTORY, Lusk; *c.* 1821.
A typically modest Church of Ireland gate lodge, single-storey, gabled and rubble-built. Ruinous and overgrown, in 2001 it was the subject of a planning application for replacement. Presumably contemporary with the glebe house which was built in 1821, to which the Board of First Fruits gave £400 and a loan of the same amount. The rector was then Revd Roseingrave Macklin (1793–1865), incumbent from 1816 until 1835.

Lewis 1837; Leslie and Wallace 2001.

219. LUTTRELLSTOWN CASTLE, Lucan (8).
A castle of the Pale, ancestral home to the Luttrell family of notorious memory. In 1800 General Henry Luttrell, 2nd Lord Carhampton, sold a demesne 'much the largest and most beautiful in the County of Dublin or within the same distance from the city on any side' to the wealthy Luke White (1740–1824), a self-made man, who obtained a property (the name of which he changed to 'Woodlands') that already boasted many fascinating features in a mock ruin, artificial lake, hermitage, shell house, wooded glen and rustic lodge, all within a walled 400 acres. White continued the transformation of the old castle into a fairytale Tudor Castellated mansion, to whose designs is not known. Although there is similarity with the work of Richard Morrison, there is no documentary evidence; the same mystery surrounds later gate lodges to the place, built for Thomas White, who succeeded his father Luke and lived here until his death without issue in 1847, when he was followed by his younger brother Henry (1789–1873), who was created Baron Annaly in 1863.

River gate; *c.* 1770/*c.* 1835; architect not known.

IAA/Jonathan Fisher

An aquatint by Jonathan Fisher in *Scenery of Ireland*, dated 1792, shows an old wooden bridge thrown across the River Liffey by the Luttrells to give access to the property known as The Hermitage (*q.v.*). It also depicts this entrance to Luttrellstown as having a little Georgian 'inkpot' lodge, a simple single-storey drum-shaped structure with a conical roof, probably limewashed and thatched. Not on Rocque's map of 1760, it survived until about 1835 before its replacement by the present lodge to what was the main entrance, as suggested by its wide, imposing gatescreen. This consists of six ashlar pillars containing extensive railings in outer concave quadrants, inner screens with postilion gates and carriage gates to match, with spear tops aplenty. The Classical lodge looks to pre-date the gates by about ten years. Single-storey standard, built in a stucco-effect finish below a hipped roof with tall eaves which have paired carved soffit brackets. All the openings, including the lattice-paned bipartite casement windows and the doorway in the pedimented frontispiece, are set in segmentally arched recesses. On the ridge, in the typical early Victorian confusion of styles, is a conjoined pair of diagonally set chimney-stacks in the Tudor manner. This may be the entrance over which Prince Pückler-Müskan, on a tour of Ireland in 1828–9, enthused that its 'open park gate' was yet another example of Ireland resembling 'the continent, where every proprietor, from the King to the humble country gentleman, enhances his own enjoyment by sharing with the public!' The same welcome is no longer extended. The wooden bridge has long since been swept away in a flood.

Broomfield gate; pre-1760; *demolished.*
Opposite the entrance to Broomfield House (*q.v.*) was an early lodge to the estate which had gone by 1836.

Flour mills gate; pre-1836/pre-1907; *demolished.*
Neither the earlier lodge nor its successor to the other side of the gateway, on the south-western approach, survives.

Westmanstown gate; pre-1836/*c.* 1855.
A bulky single-storey standard affair, with a back return and a steeply hipped roof having chunky paired carved soffit brackets. Plastic windows in a stucco-effect wall finish. A replacement for an earlier lodge by the roadside, on the western avenue.

North gate; *c.* 1810.
A plain 1½-storey shallow-gabled structure with lean-to wings. This avenue was discontinued, to be succeeded *c.* 1845 by the new approach from the Clonsilla gate.

Clonsilla gate; *c.* 1845; architect not known.

At the head of a fine tree-lined avenue is this good Classical lodge, much like that at the river gate, with the same pedimented breakfront and segmentally arched recess,

but the windows six-over-six sashes. The impressive contemporary gatescreen is composed of two tall stone carriage pillars with moulded cornices and four-pediment-faced cappings of the period. To each side the straight rubble walls contain postern openings cased with Doric pilasters supporting stone lintels, whilst beyond are convex-walled quadrants terminating in further stone pillars.

Kellystown gate; pre-1836; *demolished.*
On the eastern approach the first OS map indicates a square lodge, which by 1906 had been replaced or much extended.

Rustic lodge; *c.* 1810.

So named on the 1836 OS map is this quaint eye-catcher of the same spirit, and perhaps age, as the rustic arch within the demesne. At a road junction, constructed of barefaced boulders, is a one-up/one-down gabled gatehouse with lancet openings now sealed up with iron Y-tracery to reflect its lost Gothic windows. Alongside are sheeted carriage doors with ornamental strap hinges repeated on the tiny postern gate, beyond which is a crenellated single-storey tower, again with lancet openings and a chimney-stack, which implies that this also formed part of primitive and unsocial gatekeeper's accommodation. It is extraordinary that this curiosity has stood the test of time.

The valuation of 1849 reveals that the gate porters to lodges within the Woodlands townland were Lawrence Weldon, Fanny McMahon, James Doolan, James Fannin and Patrick Dunne.

Archer 1801; Curwen 1818; *Parliamentary Gazetteer*; Griffith 1848–60; Joyce 1912; Ball 1995; *BPB* (1929); Guinness and Ryan 1971; Malins and Glin 1976; Howley 1993; Ferguson 1998; O'Kane 2004.

McKEE BARRACKS (see MARLBOROUGH BARRACKS)

220. MALAHIDE CASTLE, Malahide (4).
The spectacular castle, which remained in the possession of the same family for 800 years, originated in 1174, when it was built by Richard Talbot. Gradually down the centuries it became less of a stronghold and more of a family home, with gate lodges being built on the park perimeter, three being in place by 1837. All of these were replaced at these entrances and a fourth added by Richard Wogan Talbot, 5th Lord Talbot of Malahide (1846–1921), who succeeded to the estate on the death of his father in 1883.

Mabestown gate; pre-1837/*c.* 1890.
The gatekeeper in 1850, Bryan Casey, may have seen the erection of the present gatescreen, which looks to date from *c.* 1860 and would have accompanied his lodge. It is comprised of four V-channelled rusticated stone pillars and moulded corniced cappings, with straight railed screens of decorative ironwork having spear and anthemion motifs matching the carriage gates, which are hung on secondary cast-iron piers with gadrooned caps. The late Victorian lodge may have originated as a single-storey standard symmetrical three-bay cottage with gabled ends, a brick stack to each apex and a brick eaves band with corbelled gutter brackets. Simple bipartite casement windows flank a panelled door and rectangular fanlight in plain roughcast walls. To the left-hand side is a gabled bay, probably added later, with delicate perforated foiled bargeboards which may then have been added to the road gable. To the rear is a hipped roof which may be part of the previous lodge, perhaps incorporated.

Swords gate; pre-1837/1893; architect not known.
Replacing an earlier lodge at this entrance, the porter of which in 1850 was James Markey, is this structure, which has the appearance of a later council labourer's cottage. Single-storey standard with a steeply hipped roof which makes much use of red brick in its toothed quoins and dressings to four-over-four margined sash windows, chimney-stack, corbelled eaves course and the gabled breakfront, with its segmentally headed fanlit doorway with a date and the monogram 'T.D.M.' over, above which again are wavy bargeboards. In mint condition with its otherwise rubble finish. Big contemporary cast-iron ornamental gate posts.

Malahide gate; pre-1837/*c.* 1900; architect possibly F.G. Hicks.

By far the most ostentatious of the lodges is this distinctive building, with some beautifully crafted detailing. Single-storey, built off a square plan in rough uncoursed

rubble facings with punched stone dressings. The pyramidal roof rises with its small slates and secret hips to a hefty ashlar chimney-stack with a moulded capping. From the avenue front advances a central gabled breakfront with skew-table and kneelers, in the apex of which is a plaque containing a coat of arms and the monogram *Forte et Fidele*. Below this is a bipartite transomed and mullioned window with leaded lights, whilst to one side is a tripartite version of the window and to the other side a deep recess forms the entrance porch, with chunky turned post supports. To the road elevation is a wide sexpartite window. The equally striking gatescreen has two grand pillars with intricately sculpted frieze and elegant pedestalled ball finials, upon which hang fine cast-iron decorative gates. To one side a pedestrian gate with overthrow. An innovative design which may be by the long-lived architect Frederick George Hicks (1870–1965). The gatekeeper of the previous lodge on the site in 1850 was John Dodd.

Back gate; *c.* 1890.
A smart single-storey standard gabled and roughcast lodge with red-brick highlights as opening dressings, corbelled eaves band taken about the end elevations, and chimney-stack. Segmentally arched windows with two-over-two sashes flanking a sheeted door with mouth-organ fanlight.

Griffith 1848–60; *BPB* (1929); de Breffny 1977.

221. MALHENEY, Lusk; pre-1837; *demolished.*
A seat in 1814 of Revd Henry Johnson, whose family by 1852 had let their property to Thomas Baker, whose gate porter was Patrick Newman.

Leet 1814; Griffith 1848–60.

222. MALLAHOW, Naul; pre-1837.
Here are the ruins of a tiny three-bay structure to an estate in 1814 of Henry Baker and by 1837 of his son Revd Thomas Baker (1783–1857), vicar of Hollywood and Naul from 1837 until his death.

Leet 1814; Lewis 1837; Leslie and Wallace 2001.

223. MANTUA, Swords; pre-1837; *demolished.*
The residence in 1783 of Keene Esq., which a few years later had passed to a Mr Bunbury, whose family then let it in the early nineteenth century to the Dalys. The fine house and its lodge have gone.

Taylor and Skinner 1778; 1969 [1783]; Wilson 1803; Leet 1814; Lewis 1837.

224. MARINO, Clontarf (3).
The magnificent demesne that was Marino, the creation in the main of James Caulfeild, 1st earl of Charlemont (1728–99), is no longer an entity, having been broken up in the twentieth century for development. This was a decline which began after his death; even in 1825 Brewer wrote that 'we regret to observe that this very attractive demesne is, at present, subject to considerable neglect'. Charlemont never lavished much expense on the exterior of his house, which remained plain; rather he concentrated on its interior, on his town house and on embellishing the estate, most notably with the internationally important Casino, which alone of the buildings on the property happily survives, along with two elegant gatescreens but none of the lodges to its three entrances.

Fairview gate; *c.* 1810; architect not known; *demolished.*

224. Marino, Dublin, Fairview gate (Chambers' sketch)

Snodin

Georgian Society Records

National Library of Ireland

224. Marino, Clontarf, Fairview gate.

Samuel Lewis in 1837 informs us that Marino 'is entered from the Strand road, near Fairview, by an elegant semi-circular gateway of hewn granite, which attracted the notice of his late Majesty, George IV, who pronounced it to be the most perfect structure of the kind in his dominions'—praise indeed from one of such discernment. The king's visit to Dublin was in 1821 and it would be interesting to know whether the pair of lodges were then in place, for they do not look to have formed part of Sir William Chambers's scheme of things, sitting as they did rather awkwardly with his grand gates. Lord Charlemont met Chambers after his Grand Tour of 1754, following which he and the famous Scottish architect became firm friends for twenty years, a partnership which produced the wonderful Casino. About 1766 they put their minds to an appropriate entrance to Marino, as revealed by a rough sketch by Chambers, on the inside of an envelope, for a triumphal archway, a design which it seems was not developed further. This shows a round-headed opening flanked by Roman Doric columns (as on the Casino) supporting a 'Doric Mutule Cornice' with guttae below a pediment. This was to have been flanked by railed screens terminating in squat piers as bases for feline sculptures holding shields. The whole was to have been 62ft wide, with a carriage opening 20ft high by 10ft wide. What transpired on site was considerably different, the archway being discarded in favour of a pair of noble pillars crowned by the shields which survive from the preceding sketch, supported now by spectacular Caulfeild dragons couchant in Portland stone, below which are friezes with swags draped over the Charlemont monograms. The V-jointed rusticated granite shafts support grand spear-topped wrought-iron carriage gates to a pattern repeated in the postern openings in concave quadrant walls. These are framed by moulded architraves topped by lintels of Greek key pattern below dies with the Caulfeild motto, *Deo juvante, ferro comitante* ('With God as my guide, and my sword by my side'). Beyond, the sweep terminated in secondary pillars with friezes also having swags chiselled in Portland stone, crowned by gadrooned vases supported by quatrepods on the elegant moulded cappings. Thanks to the survival of correspondence from Chambers to Charlemont the gates can be accurately dated, for on 25 August 1767 designs were sent for the gates 'done in the manner your Lordship desires. My clerk has misunderstood my sketch and committed a mistake or two in the drawing which I have endeavoured to correct in the margin as there is not time this post for drawing it correctly. I fancy the smith will understand it sufficiently.' Later the architect sent Cipriani's drawing of the 'dragons of the gate' on 9 February 1768. This was Giovanni Batista Cipriani, a London-based Italian decorative painter and engraver (1727–85). The gatescreen has been restored and re-erected nearby and out of harm's way, but sadly not the lodges. A photograph of *c.* 1910 in the *Georgian Society Records* shows the gates with, ominously in the background, an early sign of the breakup of the demesne in the looming Christian Brothers' School. This rather pointedly does not show the lodges, but they have been recorded for posterity in one of a series of delightful watercolours painted on 'a Drive from Howth returning by Clontarf in 1853' by Edward McFarland. This depicts a matching pair of single-storey pediment-fronted cottages, each of a single bay comprised of a tripartite transomed and mullioned casement window set in a rectangular recess. Just sufficient of them appears in the later photograph to detect that they were stone-built and hip-roofed to the rear. Neither were considered of sufficient quality to salvage.

Middle gate; pre-1837; *demolished.* An entrance in close proximity to the house on the eastern approach which seems to have been lost without any record.

North gate; pre-1837; *demolished.*

Whilst the plain lodge was removed in the mid-twentieth century, its fine gatescreen survives on a new site as an appropriate introduction to the Casino. Probably also by William Chambers, the slenderness of the carriage pillars curiously contrasting with the squatness of the outer pillars. There is something in the form of the latter to suggest that the architect's unexecuted design, already described, was in fact intended for this access. They are raised off a square plinth, with plain panels created by frames of deeply vermiculated masonry crowned by crisply chiselled cappings. These are now linked by low, concave quadrant walls to the main pillars, which are built up in similarly vermiculated stonework to impressive cappings with friezes adorned in triglyphs and metopes with alternate bucrania and disc motifs, over which are wide cornices supporting paltry gadrooned urns resting on swagged bases.

The valuation of 1848 lists four gate porters of the 2nd earl of Charlemont: Andrew Cunningham, John Dixon, Henry Jessop and Michael Byrne, two of whom were presumably housed at the main gate.

Brewer 1825; Lewis 1837; d'Alton 1976 [1838]; Griffith 1848–60; *Georgian Society Records* (Vol. V); *BPB* (1929); *IGS Bulletin* (July–Sept. 1965); NLI painting (1986 TX 2); *Country Life* (4 and 11 Feb. 1988); Snodin 1996; O'Connor 1995; IAA.

225. MARLBOROUGH BARRACKS, Grangegorman; *c.* 1895; architect probably J.T. Marsh.

Now McKee Barracks off Blackhorse Avenue, this great red-brick cavalry barracks was completed in 1893 to the designs of a virtually unknown Captain J.T. Marsh, who may have been responsible for this diminutive lodge, which is little more than a sentry-box but still displays a chimney-stack and symmetrical three-bay front. Single-storey with two narrow four-over-four sash windows on each side of the doorway, sheltered below a lean-to canopy with wooden bracket support; steep tiled hipped roof. Entrance pillars in like red brick, with battered bases, panelled shafts and sandstone square cappings broaching to octagonal lantern bases.

Williams 1994.

226. MARY VILLA, Castleknock; pre-1836; *demolished.*

In a region suffering dramatic redevelopment survives an octagonal pillar with fluted frieze and gadrooned capping, just like those at Diswellstown (*q.v.*). A property in the early nineteenth century of the Roycrofts, which was subsequently renamed 'Abbey Lodge'.

Griffith 1848–60.

227. MARY VILLA, Phoenix Park; pre-1837/*c.* 1900; architect not known.

A property later called 'Deer Park' was in the late nineteenth century a residence of Maurice Flanagan. An exercise in polychromatic brickwork of English bond, mainly in a yellow calcium silicate brick liberally highlighted with red toothed quoins, dressings, plinth, eaves band and chimney-stacks. Single-storey on an L-plan with a flat-roofed entrance hall in the internal corner; one wing is hipped whilst that leading is gabled, with red sandstone skew-table and kneelers, having an ornamental roundel to the apex over a pair of nine-over-one sash windows. A predecessor on the site had in 1848 Richard Kennedy as porter to Mrs Mary Flanagan.

Griffith 1848–60; Slater 1870.

228. MARYVILLE, Drumcondra; pre-1837; *demolished.*

A seat in 1837 of J.J. Finn, in whose time the place was renamed 'Lark Hill'. By 1846 it was home to Henry Alley, whose gatekeeper two years later was William Daly.

Lewis 1837; *Thom's*; Slater 1846; Griffith 1848–60.

229. MARYVILLE, Killester; pre-1912; *demolished.*

A lodge built after 1837 to a property which until his death in 1822 was the seat of the 1st Viscount Frankfort de Montmorency, which thereafter had a succession of owners until occupied in the 1870s by Thomas and William Fayle.

Parliamentary Gazetteer; Slater 1870; *BPB* (1929).

230. MAYNE LODGE, Baldoyle; pre-1837; *demolished.*

A lodge to the property in 1848 of Peter Byrne, whose gatekeeper was then James Wade. It had gone by 1910.

Griffith 1848–60.

231. MERCHAMP LODGE, Clontarf; pre-1837; *demolished.*

A small estate in 1824 of Sir B.W. Burdett which by 1837 was a property of one E. Shaw, from whom in 1848 it passed to Hans Blackwood Hamilton, whose gatekeeper was his namesake James. In 1862 there were grand redevelopment plans for the place, as previewed in the *Dublin Builder* magazine. 'The extensive premises known as "Mercamp" [*sic*] situated in Vernon Avenue, Clontarf, at the intersection of the Green Lanes, have been taken by Mr George Tickell, and are by him about to be converted into two distinct and spacious dwellings with architectural exterior and commodious outbuildings, the portion of the existing entrance to be preserved in a modified form, and with new lodge for one, and a gateway and lodge to be formed in Seafield Avenue for the other. J.J. Lyons, archt.' In reality 'Merchamp' was joined by 'Rosetta', but neither of the new lodges transpired.

Pigot 1824; Lewis 1837; Griffith 1848–60; *DB* (1 June 1862).

232. MERTON, Balgriffin; pre-1837; *demolished.*

A residence in 1848 of John Faris, solicitor.

Griffith 1848–60; Shaw 1988.

233. MEUDON, Swords (2).

Both lodges in place by 1836, to a property in 1814 of a Major Campbell, have been demolished.

Leet 1814.

234. MIDDLETOWN LOWER, Cloghran; *c.* 1830.

A plain single-storey standard gabled roughcast cottage with a projecting gabled hall, which was home in 1848 to Thomas Boylan, gate porter of Thomas McOwen.

Griffith 1848–60.

235. M.G.W.R. COMPANY OFFICE, Inns Quay; pre-1850; *demolished.*

There is no trace of a surviving gate lodge at the premises of the Midland Great Western Railway and Royal Canal Company which is identified by the 1850 valuation in Blessington Street.

Griffith 1848–60.

236. MILVERTON, Skerries (6).

For a demesne of such relatively modest extent it is extraordinarily well endowed with gate lodges, and all, it seems, built by the one proprietor, the long-lived George Woods (1786–1876), who is recorded as living here as early as 1814. This penchant for lodge-building must be explained by his connections to other landed families with just such a tradition. In 1812 George had married Sarah, daughter of James Hans Hamilton (from whom he came by the place) of Abbotstown (*q.v.*), and in 1840 his son, and inheritor of Milverton, Hans Hamilton Woods took as his second wife Louisa Catherine Taylor of the adjacent Ardgillan Castle (*q.v.*), two estates liberally provided with porters' accommodation. His architect for the later cottages here, and probably at Woods's previous property of Whitestown (*q.v.*), was almost certainly Sandham Symes (1807–94), for he not only had a commission at Ardgillan but is also recorded as working for George Woods in carrying out improvements to dwellings in Naul village. His client was clearly a man with few pretensions, as all his lodges display architectural restraint, principally created to house his estate workers. The entrances, named after townlands, are described commencing with that to the north, advancing clockwise about the estate.

Baltrasna gate; pre-1837; *demolished.*
Surviving is an impressive gatescreen, apparently of about 1835, of concave railed quadrants contained by four stone pillars of V-jointed rustication below corniced cappings. The lodge is likely to have been contemporary, located opposite them, but now replaced by a chalet bungalow.

Milverton gate; *c.* 1845; architect probably Sandham Symes.

On the eastern approach is a single-storey standard lodge with stucco-effect walls below a shallow hipped roof with oversailing eaves and paired carved soffit brackets. New small-paned casement windows on each side of the main architectural feature—a flat-roofed porch projection with facing of limestone pilasters supporting an entablature of like material, the same as that to the 'School' lodge. Here is the grandest of the entrance screens, much as at the Baltrasna gate but with the carriage pillars carrying terracotta pots and the concave railed screen with palmette tops.

Courtlough gate; *c.* 1855; architect possibly Sandham Symes.
At the base of the southern avenue is a delightful single-storey standard hip-roofed

composition with, again, carved paired soffit brackets. The rendered walls contain segmentally headed openings, the three-over-nine sash windows flanking a double-leafed doorway in a similarly arched recess. The gatescreen has V-jointed stone pillars with concave cappings containing shallow concave rubble quadrants.

School gate; *c.* 1837; architect probably Sandham Symes.

Flanking the entrance is what appears to be a pair of lodges, both of which are on the first OS map but avenueless, perhaps just constructed in expectation of the new approach from the south-west being formed. The buildings do not match. To the left-hand side is a single-storey five-bay structure with harled walls containing a projecting flat-roofed porch, exactly like that at the Milverton gate but flanked on each side by two three-over-nine sash windows. Hip-roofed but with clipped eaves, it is sufficiently spacious to have accommodated two classrooms. To the right-hand side of the gateway is a plain single-storey standard lodge, again harled, with clipped eaves to its hipped roof and three-over-nine sash windows on each side of a sheeted door having a later decorative canopy over with scalloped slates and spandrel boarding. Presumably its occupant combined the roles of schoolteacher and gatekeeper. Good V-jointed ashlar pillars with concave cappings.

Grange gate; *c.* 1865.

A plain but pretty creeper-clad cottage at the western entrance. Single-storey standard, roughcast with smooth surrounds to doorway and its two-over-two mid-Victorian sash windows. Hipped roof with high unadorned eaves.

Margaretstown gate; *c.* 1860.

Opposite the entrance with its concave capped pillars is a modest single-storey standard lodge with hipped roof over segmentally headed openings, the doorway with a bracketed mono-pitch canopy, flanked by windows recently given a Tudor lead effect.

Leet 1814; d'Alton 1976 [1838]; *DB* (15 Jan. 1866); *LGI* (1904).

237. MOATFIELD, Coolock; pre-1837; *demolished.*

An estate before 1837 of M. Staunton, from whom it passed *c.* 1840 to Charles White, whose gate porter in 1848 was James Sherlock.

D'Alton 1976 [1838]; Lewis 1837; *Thom's* (1841); Griffith 1848–60.

238. MORGAN'S AND MERCER'S SCHOOLS, Phoenix Park (2).

Adjacent schools founded by bequests of a Mr Morgan and a lady called Mercer for boys and girls respectively, 'for educating, clothing, maintaining, and apprenticing ... supported from the produce of lands bequeathed'. Before 1837 the schools were accessed via parallel approaches on each side of an early lodge off the Royal Canal towpath to the north. With the coming of the MGW Railway this was swept away and a new avenue and lodge created about 1850 to the south from the Dunboyne road. This too has gone.

Parliamentary Gazetteer.

239. MOUNT DILLON, Artane; pre-1837; *demolished.*

A property in 1837 of the Cooper family which by 1841 had been acquired by John Hollway, whose gatekeeper eight years later was Patrick White.

Lewis 1837; *Thom's*; Griffith 1848–60.

MOUNT HYBLA (see HYBLA)

240. MOUNT PLEASANT, Lucan; *c.* 1780.

Here are the pathetic remains of a Georgian Gothic lodge dating from the time here of the Macfarlane family of Huntstown (*q.v.*). Once a single-storey standard gabled cottage, its main front alongside the gates facing the visitor, with two little lancet windows on each side of the doorway in harled rubble walls. The screen wall linking it to the right-hand square limestone carriage pillar contained a postern opening which at some time was to give access to an extension to the lodge, probably created when the property was leased to Thomas Flood in the mid-nineteenth century and its name changed to 'Hillsboro'.

Taylor and Skinner 1778; 1969 [1783]; Slater 1846; Griffith 1848–60; *LGI* (1904).

241. MOUNT SACKVILLE, Castleknock; pre-1837/*c.* 1845.

In 1801 'the seat of Thomas Kemmis, Esq., a very good house, and pleasantly situated, with a good garden and a demesne of about fifty acres'. From Kemmis, probably of that family of Shaen Castle, Co. Laois (*q.v.*), it had passed by 1837 to John Hawkins, by whom it was later leased in the mid-nineteenth century to William G. Walmsley, whose gate porter in 1848 was a Mrs Bracken. There does not appear to be much at the entrance surviving from the early nineteenth century. What does remain is a dramatic make-over or a replacement from Walmsley's stay which has suffered much from later modifications. Recognisable architecturally is a pedimented gable to a single-storey structure advancing to the avenue, its tympanum having carved mutule brackets which extend about the eaves. Otherwise bland in refenestration. There is a contemporary gatescreen lacing its central carriage pillars and postilion gates to leave concave railed spear-topped concave quadrants contained by Classical granite pillars with recessed moulded panels and cappings with dentil courses.

Archer 1801; Lewis 1837; Griffith 1848–60.

242. MOUNT TEMPLE, Clontarf (3).

A seat in the first half of the nineteenth century of the agents of the earls of Charlemont of neighbouring Marino (*q.v.*) that had two early lodges, the gatekeepers to which in 1849 were John Dixon and Patrick Carroll. By 1863 a grand new Jacobean-style mansion with curvilinear gables was under construction to designs of the Belfast practice of Lanyon, Lynn and Lanyon for the sister of the 3rd earl of Charlemont, Lady Margaret Zoë Caulfeild, and her husband, whom she had married in 1848, the future 4th baronet of Tynan Abbey, Co. Armagh, John Calvert Stronge. Built with stone dressings to a largely red-brick finish, materials reflected in its outstanding gate lodge.

Malahide gate; *c.* 1865; architects Lanyon, Lynn and Lanyon.

Whilst the house reflects the favoured style of Lanyon's assistant Thomas Turner, this lodge is clearly by his partner, William Henry Lynn, in a High Victorian Gothic manner, with the emphasis on polychromatic brickwork for effect, much as that to Ashurst (*q.v.*), south Dublin, and a stone version at Cahir Abbey, Co. Tipperary. A wonderfully eccentric composition, single-storey on a T-plan, with steeply pitched hipped gables rising to ridges with serrated cresting, a battered chimney-stack and rows of sawtooth slates. The red-brick walls are relieved by cream highlights of banding and alternate voussoirs to segmental pointed arches to openings. In the internal angle is a catslide-roofed entrance hall and to the leading gable, rising from a staged plinth, is an arrowhead bay window with an extraordinary semi-pyramidal roof of its own, culminating in a decorative knob. This quirky little lodge is unfortunately not matched by its bland replacement gatescreen.

Both early lodges have been demolished.

Griffith 1848–60; *DB* (15 May 1863); Williams 1994; O'Connor 1995.

243. NATIONAL BOTANIC GARDENS, Glasnevin (2).

'... the Botanic Gardens of the Royal Dublin Society, a most interesting object, situated where was once the demesne of Tickell the poet ... This place was purchased subject to a ground rent, for the sum of £2000, from his representatives, for the scientific objects to which it is devoted. The entrance lodges and connecting gates were erected by a donation of £700 from Mr Pleasants, and are very handsome.' Thus wrote d'Alton about 1836 of an institution opened to the public in 1800 and its lodges added fifteen years later. These would seem to have replaced an earlier porter's lodge, perhaps that to the original house on the 30-acre site, flanked by twin entrances.

Early entrance; 1815; architect perhaps Edward Parke; *demolished.*

Handsome indeed were this pair of matching Classical single-storey lodges with their backs to the gardens located forward of their gates, each presenting a symmetrical three-bay front with a central pedimented breakfront which contained a tripartite window below a segmental relieving arch. The windows would seem to have had banded surrounds, all below corniced parapets to the hipped roofs. The carriage pillars behind were crowned by urns and linked to the lodges by concave-walled quadrants, with postilion openings. The architect Edward Parke worked for the Dublin Society from 1796 to 1840 and may have been retained to design this elegant entrance. Already by 1837 the first OS map suggests that the restricted access between lodges has resulted in the removal of one. In any case, by about 1870 both had gone, to be replaced by the present complex.

Existing entrance; *c.* 1880; architect possibly J.H. Owen.

The architect for the replacement lodged gateway was clearly influenced by its predecessor, for here again is a pair of lodges, three-bay with pedimented frontispieces containing tripartite sash windows flanked by six-over-six sashed openings below hipped roofs, but now with more serviceable oversailing bracketed eaves to two-storey gatehouses—villas in their own right and widely spaced. Their rather drab grey rendering is in summer obscured by luxuriant wisteria. The great banks of banded and corniced chimney-stacks help in the dating. One of this pair of dignified houses no doubt once accommodated a gatekeeper to attend to the straight connecting gatescreen of granite pillars and railings with pedestrian gates. Perhaps designed by James Higgins Owen, who was architect to the Board of Works in the 1880s.

D'Alton 1976 [1838]; Nelson and McCracken 1987; Lohan 1994; IAA.

244. NATIONAL MODEL SCHOOLS, Marlborough Street (2); *c.* 1837; architect probably Jacob Owen.

Previously the site of Tyrone House, the town house designed about 1740 by Richard Castle for Sir Marcus Beresford, later earl of Tyrone. There is no sign of gatekeeper's accommodation on John Rocque's map of 1756, although a rather miffed Whitelaw in 1821 records: 'Marlborough Street, 27, Marques of Waterford; the house was inaccessible from the rudeness of the porter'. Like most other Dublin mansions of the aristocracy, Tyrone House in 1835 was bought by the government and became the headquarters of the Board of National Education; the site was considerably redeveloped, with a pair of lodges added at the centre of the extensive screen to Marlborough Street, probably built to designs by Jacob Owen, appointed in 1832 as architect and engineer to the Board of Works. These used to face each other across the carriage entrance, each conventionally two-roomed, but sometime later in the century they were parted and rebuilt in part at each extreme of the street boundary as little more than single-roomed sentry-boxes. Their chaste neo-Classical façades survive, each as a pair of granite fluted Greek Doric columns *in antis*, between pilasters carrying a plain entablatured parapet, if anything reflecting the grand portico of the pro-cathedral across the street rather than the Castle town house. Owen's *in antis* lodges to the King's Inns (*q.v.*) are more commodious and considerably less restrained.

Irish Georgian Society Records 1969 [1911] Vol III; Craig 1980; Ferguson 1998; Pearson 2000.

245. NEWBERRY HILL, Santry; pre-1837/*c.* 1870.

An estate in 1837 of an A. Onj, who may have been the Abel Onje listed in 1814 at Kiltrea Lodge, Co. Wexford, and whose main seat seems to have been Haystown (*q.v.*). The early lodge was replaced by the surviving single-storey standard gabled mid-Victorian brick-built structure, probably built by solicitor James W. O'Reilly, who had acquired the property around 1870.

Leet 1814; Lewis 1837; *Thom's.*

246. NEWBRIDGE, Donabate (4).

Charles Cobbe I (1686–1765) acquired Newbridge in 1736, and after being enthroned as archbishop of Dublin in 1743 was planning himself a grand mansion worthy of a primate of all Ireland, to which elevation he expected promotion in due course. He was to be disappointed and had to settle for something less palatial in the noble villa we see today. His architect for this and the grander scheme has recently been dramatically identified as being James Gibbs, the leading British practitioner of his generation, none of whose work had previously been discovered in Ireland. The house was substantially complete by 1750, but neither John Rocque's map of 1760 or Charles Frizell's survey of 1776 suggest that there was a contemporary lodge, nor does there seem ever to have been one worthy of the place, for the one design of significance which would have impressed and amused appears never to have been built.

Unexecuted lodge; 1791; architect John Bruce.

Cobbe Collection

A delightful and quirky proposal by a presumably amateur architect, son of the steward at Newbridge of the same name, which may have been intended to accompany the main entrance gates. To be built integral with the demesne wall alongside, its main symmetrical front to face the road with three lancet openings—or rather two openings, for the central doorway was to be a dummy, complete with mock knocker! On a grand lofty scale, 'Height to top of Blocking course 14′3″ ', its parapet, accommodating a family coat of arms with foliated decoration above the sham door, is broken by a plinth carrying a fine crest of a pelican rising from a ducal coronet. To each corner of the parapet was to have been an elegant Classical urn, one of which was to have served as a chimney-pot. Framed at each corner by prominent toothed V-jointed quoins and moulded cornice, its two rooms were to have been entered from the sides, the plan indicating that front and rear elevations were basically to have matched.

What did materialise by the main gates was considerably plainer.

Main entrance; *c.* 1835; *demolished.*

Cobbe Collection

Cobbe Collection

Old photographs show a single-storey gabled structure breaking the estate wall, its main front monitoring the outer face of the gatescreen with its projecting gabled hall which contained a Cobbe shield above a label-moulded doorway, probably built by Charles Cobbe III (1781–1857). The magnificent triple gateway is comprised of four articulated granite pillars rusticated with alternate deeply vermiculated blocks, rising to moulded cappings. The taller carriage pillars are crowned by the family crest, just as intended by Bruce on his gate lodge, whilst the secondary pillars had ball finials rusticated with the same vermiculated finish. The design all originated from a James Gibbs illustration in his *A book of architecture* of 1728, which was realised at his St Mary's Gate House, Derby. An undated drawing that survives for the gates is thought to be by George Semple, who acted as executant architect for Gibbs. Although the gateway is often dated to around 1752, when the archbishop extended the boundaries of his demesne, John Rocque's map suggests that this may not have happened for another ten years.

Castle gate; pre-1837; *demolished.*
Off the same Dublin road was another impressive gatescreen for which survive what appear to be undated and unsigned sketches, selected details from which add up to that erected; certainly the ironwork pattern was identical. Of the four pillars connected by straight railed screens, the carriage pillars were comprised of V-jointed rusticated masonry with unusual frieze motifs of plaques with guttae and ball pendants. Atop were moulded cappings with coronets from which probably issued more Cobbe pelicans, as proposed by the anonymous design of about 1815. The lodge may have been contemporary. Perhaps twenty years later John Bruce was still purveying inventive designs.

West gate; pre-1837/*c.* 1880; *demolished.*

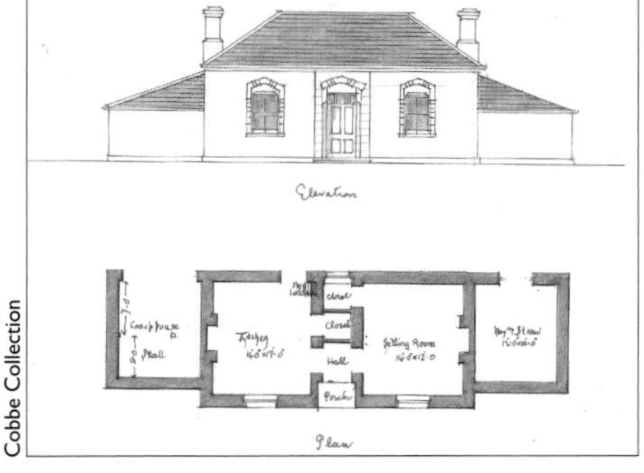
Cobbe Collection

An image of *c.* 1968 shows a double pile structure, very plain and dilapidated, awaiting removal. It appears that a mid-Victorian single-storey standard hip-roofed affair with two-over-two sash windows in harled rubble walls had been built across the face of its predecessor, similarly with a hipped roof. The new front door was framed by a gabled surround as a modest frontispiece. There is in the Cobbe Archive an anonymous undated drawing for a proposed lodge which may have been intended as a replacement here. It indicates a single-storey standard layout with a hipped roof accommodating attic bedroom space with access unsocially by ladder. To each end were intended matching wings containing a hay and straw shed and a coach-house. As a cost-cutting compromise, these may have been omitted in favour of retaining the old lodge as an annexe. An improvement probably instigated by Charles Cobbe IV (1811–86), as was that on the eastern approach.

Donabate gate; *c.* 1860.
On Church Drive is this unprepossessing single-storey standard gabled lodge, with two-over-two sashes on each side of a little latticed porch. Occupied, it stands with its back to the park.

The house and demesne have recently been admirably restored by Dublin County Council with the Cobbe family's cooperation and are now a treasure accessible to the public.

LGI (1904); ffolliott 1970; *Country Life* (4 Oct. 2001 and 24 Jan. 2002); Cobbe and Friedman 2005; Cobbe Archive; IAA photographs.

247. NEWGROVE, Grange (2).
Two pre-1837 lodges, both demolished, in 1848 occupied by John McDaniel and James Rodney as porters to John Cochrane. The big house, in 1841 the seat of John Somers Dawson, has also gone.

Thom's; Griffith 1848–60.

248. NEWPORT, Swords; *c.* 1770.
A seat, in 1760 called 'Ballinadrought', which in 1783 was occupied by the Mercer family, who would have known this antique porter's lodge. Now derelict, it is a simple single-storey, shallow-gabled, harled, rubble-built structure with high eaves over a three-bay main front, its doorway to the right-hand side. Attached to a gable is the basic tall screen wall and gate pillars with naive ball finials on crude pedestals.

Taylor and Skinner 1778; 1969 [1783]; Ferguson 1998.

249. NEWTOWN, Balbriggan; *c.* 1835.
Prominently sited outside its gates at a right-angled bend in the road is this single-storey, harled, rubble-built affair below an oversailing hipped roof finished in scalloped slates. Wider-than-high windows in a now-derelict lodge which in 1852 was to a property of Richard McNally.

Griffith 1848–60.

250. NEWTOWN, Finglas (2).
A seat in the nineteenth century to a succession of occupants—Patrick Colclough in 1814 and Barnett Shaw in 1837—and which is now given over to use as a golf club.

East lodge; *c.* 1835.
A long, low, single-storey standard lodge with a hipped roof, wide windows and chamfered door surround in a projecting gabled hall; roughcast walls. Perhaps later extended to the left-hand side.

West lodge; pre-1837.
A single-storey, roughcast, low, plain gabled structure which has developed its present T-plan through much evolution over the years.

Leet 1814; Lewis 1837.

251. NEWTOWN, Swords; pre-1836; *demolished.*
A residence of a Mr Lyons in 1814, followed a decade later by D.H. Ginn.

Leet 1814; Pigot 1824.

252. NORTH DUBLIN UNION AUXILIARY WORKHOUSE, Cabra; *c.* 1880.

In stark contrast to the backdrop of the big Classical institution is this dear little single-storey hip-roofed lodge in rubble facings with segmental brick-arched openings; tiny hallway in like finish. Since 1892 the Daughters of Charity have run the establishment as St Vincent's residential home.

253. OATLANDS, Castleknock (2).
The seat in the early nineteenth century of John Godley, who until about 1865 let it to Lt. Col. Philip Hill, whose gatekeeper in 1849 was Michael Martin.

East lodge; pre-1836/*c.* 1880/*c.* 1920.

Replacing an earlier lodge on the site is this charming twentieth-century pebble-dashed single-storey lodge, built off an L-plan. Originating on a simple rectangular plan with hipped roof and soffit brackets, it was subsequently extended by a gabled projection to the avenue containing a diamond-pattern motif to its clipped verge apex over a flat-roofed, leaded bow window overlooking the gate. In the internal angle is a flat-roofed porch. Occupied.

West lodge; *c.* 1880.
A simple single-storey standard lodge with the appearance of something older were it not for its steeply pitched hipped roof and two-over-two sashes in roughcast walls. Regency-style soffit brackets.

The cores of these two lodges probably date from the arrival at Oatlands of Captain Leslie Martin *c.* 1880, with the later alterations at the hands of Frederick Koenigs, wine merchant.

Lewis 1837; Griffith 1848–60; *Thom's*; *LGI* (1904).

254. OATLEY, Artane; pre-1837; *demolished.*
A residence in 1837 of G. Farran Esq., which by 1841 was home to the Horsham family, whose gate porter in 1849 was Thomas Holland. Subsequently called 'Craigford'.

Lewis 1837; *Thom's*; Griffith 1848–60.

255. O'BRIEN'S INSTITUTE, Marino; *c.* 1881; architect probably J.J. O'Callaghan; *demolished.*
A charitable orphanage built for the trustees of a Miss O'Brien, won in architectural competition by John Joseph O'Callaghan from eight others in 1880. Within a stone's throw of the wonderful Casino but in an insensitive High Victorian Tudor Gothic style, its lost gate lodge was doubtless in like manner but fell foul of twentieth-century road requirements.

Williams 1994; IAA.

256. OLDTOWN, Coolock; pre-1837; *demolished.*
A seat in 1814 of the Boden family which later changed hands frequently.

Leet 1814.

ONGAR (see HANSFIELD)

257. ORDNANCE SURVEY OFFICE, Phoenix Park; *c.* 1891; architect possibly J.H. Pentland.

Luke Gardiner's early Georgian house, 'Castleknock Lodge', was passed to the government *c.* 1780 for use as a barracks. In 1825 it became the nucleus of the headquarters of the Ordnance Survey, the complex gradually growing thereafter until map stores were added in 1891 to designs of John Howard Pentland. He, as first senior surveyor of buildings to the Board of Works, may also have been responsible for the first gate lodge on the site. It is a single-storey Classical design in raw red brick, dressed with stone in its skew-table gables and kneelers forming open pediments and chamfered surrounds to its three-bay avenue front of segmentally arched openings. This main elevation of two-over-two sash windows and doorway to the right-hand side is sheltered by a flat-roofed cast-iron canopy supported by clusters of slender columns. To the leading gable is a tall aedicule window and on the ridge is a dainty red-brick chimney-stack with stone band and moulded capping.

IADS (2002); Casey 2005.

OUNAVARRA (see LUCAN VILLA)

258. PACEFIELD, Mulhuddart; pre-1837; *demolished.*
Francis MacFarlane was the proprietor here in the early nineteenth century and had brothers living in the vicinity at Stirling, Co. Meath (*q.v.*), Huntstown (*q.v.*) and Mount Pleasant (*q.v.*).

LGI (1904).

259. PELLETSTOWN, Cabra; pre-1837/*c.* 1865; architect not known.
A lodge of some distinction, which tragically lies abandoned and boarded up. Richard Allen is recorded here in 1849 with his gatekeeper John Kelly, after which the property lay vacant until the coming of the Lowe family *c.* 1860, who replaced the existing lodge with this desirable single-storey gabled mid-Victorian lodge. Built off a T-plan, the downstroke of which advances towards the avenue, terminating in a canted bay window below its own corresponding

roof with a decorative roundel in the apex over. On each side of this projection, in the interests of symmetry, is a little hall in the internal angle, extending to an open porch under a flat-cum-hipped roof sporting fish-scale slates, all supported by a decorative turned post. The perforated scalloped terracotta ridge tiles are broken by a squat articulated chimney-stack. A splendid composition which overlooks a twentieth-century gatescreen of crenellated pillars and concave quadrant walls.

Griffith 1848–60; *Thom's*.

260. PELLETSTOWN HOSPITAL, Cabra; *c.* 1950.
A single-storey lodge on an L-plan in Flemish bond brickwork, with the shallow bow windows to each wing extending below the soffits of its steeply pitched hipped roof, crowned by a hefty four-flue chimney-stack. To the internal angle is a like-roofed porch, latterly enclosed as an entrance hallway. On the Navan Road, a remarkable survival given the loss of the hospital buildings and the encroachment of later housing. Built for the Dublin Board of Assistance.

261. PHIBBLESTOWN, Clonsilla; 1910.
The much older house, of J. Reade Clarke in the mid-nineteenth century and later of John Hunt, was not complemented by a porter's lodge until as late as 1910, and then built in the manner of a century earlier, by Henry J. Rooney. Remote from its gate; single-storey standard hip-roofed in rendered finish with Irish pilaster quoins. Extending to an L-plan with a gabled glazed porch. Derelict, the big house gone, the site is waiting to be overrun by modern housing development.

Thom's.

262. PHOENIX PARK, Phoenix Park (9).
This great legacy to the people of Dublin from Charles II was created as a royal deer-park and was opened to the public in 1747 by Lord Chesterfield, the then viceroy. Enclosed by an 11km boundary wall with eight carriage gates, its 707 hectares was greater in area than the sum of the London parks, and it is appropriate that when, at the beginning of the nineteenth century, the park had deteriorated through neglect the Office of Woods and Forests should turn to a young English architect to ascertain the condition of the park's 'Lodges, Gates, Boundary Walls, Internal Fences, Drives, Plantations and Herbage' and make recommendations for its improvement. Decimus Burton (1800–81) had already commended himself through his work at the royal parks in London and his

landscaping scheme for the Zoological Gardens (*q.v.*) in the Phoenix Park. His report was scathing of some of the existing porters' lodges and proposed their replacement. What he discovered were several lodges erected by William Dodson, who was responsible for building the walled enclosure of the park in the early 1660s, thus making them the earliest recorded in Ireland. Charles Brooking's map of 1728 reveals a lodge at Parkgate Street, whilst Rocque in 1760 shows further gatekeepers' lodges at the entrances of Castleknock, Chapelizod and Knockmaroon, and by 1772 Thomas Sherrard's map indicates a further two at Backhorse Lane (Cabra gate) and Islandbridge. The fact that Burton came to act upon his own suggestions is a mystery, considering that Jacob Owen had been appointed architect and engineer to the Board of Works in 1832. He nevertheless was to provide designs for most of the lodges that existed, having found them to be unsatisfactory in appearance, too large for their purpose and 'mean of character'. He identified the Knockmaroon, Ashtown and Castleknock gates as being particularly ugly. His advice was to produce buildings of 'solid yet handsome character, and even if required to be simple and void of embellishment, yet good proportions should be studied'. This he achieved between 1832 and 1849.

Parkgate entrance; pre-1728/1811; architect Francis Johnston.

This is the main lodge on the Dublin approach which Burton found the 'least offensive'—hardly surprising, as it was the work of Ireland's leading architect of the time, Francis Johnston, and was built just twenty years previous to his remarks. He did, however, propose that a grand entrance be built with gates set back 300 yards from their then location, and 'that two lamps, at least, should be erected at each of the gates and should be lighted nightly by the respective gatekeepers'. Johnston's great drum pillars in stone with his favourite gadrooned domed cappings were in fact provided with lanterns, and in the twentieth century were eventually repositioned as per Burton's suggestion. The pair of lodges in a restrained Classical manner do not match, that to the left being little more than a sentry-box, presumably manned only by day. It is single-storey and gabled, its front to the avenue a single bay in the form of a fanlit doorway set in a segmentally arched recess which breaks the tympanum to form an open pediment. Finished in stucco effect, with a granite date-stone above the door marked in Roman numerals: 'MDCCCIX'. Across the avenue is a standard single-storey three-bay lodge, in like finish below a clipped hipped roof broken by a pedimented hall frontispiece with a mouth-organ fanlight below a matching date-stone. To each side is an eight-over-eight sash window, and a hefty staged chimney-stack breaks the ridge. There is a very similar lodge to Carton, Co. Kildare (*q.v.*). Ironwork was by Robert Mallet.

Islandbridge entrance; pre-1772/*c.* 1810/*c.* 1833; architect probably Jacob Owen.

Christopher Machell

NLI/S.F. Brocas

This has proved to be the best documented of the park gates, with elevated ground nearby affording an excellent vantage point for artists seeking views towards Kilmainham and the city beyond, with the entrance in the foreground shown at various stages of its development down the years. Christopher Machell in 1804 reveals the previous antique lodge to have been a rustic single-storey steeply hip-roofed affair, probably rubble faced, commodious and

NLI/S.F. Brocas

rambling. Unlike its successor, it is located to the left of its gate, which is marked by a simple flat-headed carriage archway. A charming view of about ten years later by Samuel Frederick Brocas shows the new gatehouse and its predecessor still *in situ*, separated by a screen wall containing a postilion opening and a pair of hefty circular carriage pillars. In September 1834 Burton reported various landscape improvements completed since August 1832, which included the Islandbridge gate lodge repaired and decorated in the *cottage orné* style and the ground in its immediate environs planted with trees. He did not reveal who was responsible for its transformation, but the unsatisfactory proportions do not accord with some of his delightful English villa creations in the Picturesque Tudor Cottage style. G.N. Wright's 1831 view of Dublin from the Phoenix Park clearly shows the replacement lodge in its previous state as a simple three-bay gatehouse on a square plan with pyramidal roof rising to a tall central chimney-stack, and a single-storey gabled porch or hall extending from the left-hand side. This Jacob Owen, or whoever, cloaked to form gables with regulation perforated decorative bargeboards and outsize hip-knobs, and applied Tudor label mouldings to windows. To the left-hand side he added a projecting two-storey wing, alongside which the roof catslides down to form an arched entrance verandah, with a fancy dormer giving light to the attic formed. To the road the upper floor jetties past the park wall over the footpath, a foiled Tudor Gothic device relieving the apex over a tripartite chamfered and label-moulded window. This overlooks an extensive railed screen with octagonal ashlar carriage pillars alongside, which is an innovative pedestrian gate or turnstile in the form of a revolving cage with an informative plaque explaining its operation and the manufacturer J. & C. McGloughlin Ltd, of Great Brunswick Street, 'Patent applied for'.

Chapelizod entrance; pre-1760/1836; architect Decimus Burton.

Here Burton had the old lodge demolished and replaced by the most inspired of his

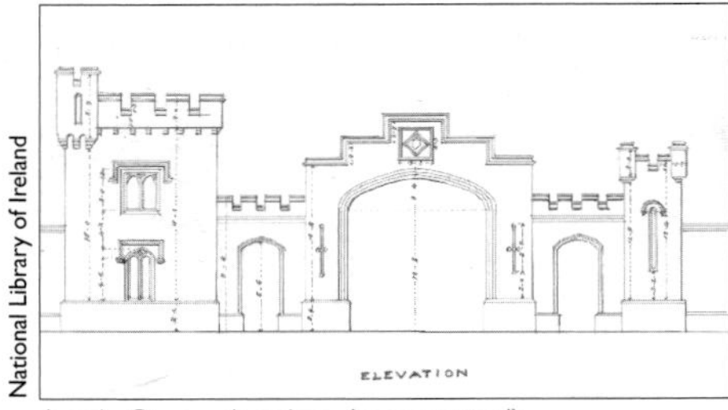

Jacob Owen drawing (unexecuted).

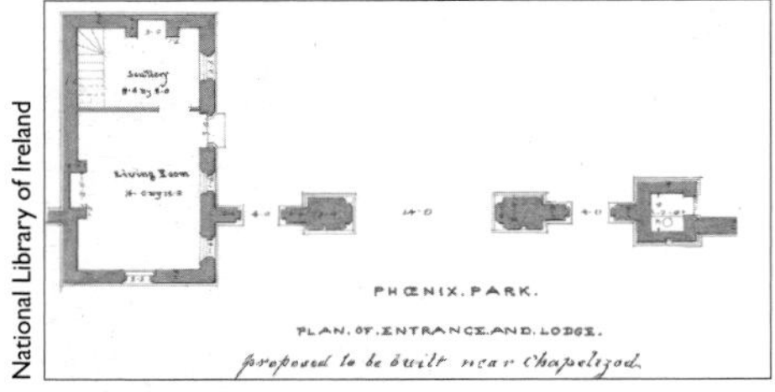

Jacob Owen drawing (unexecuted).

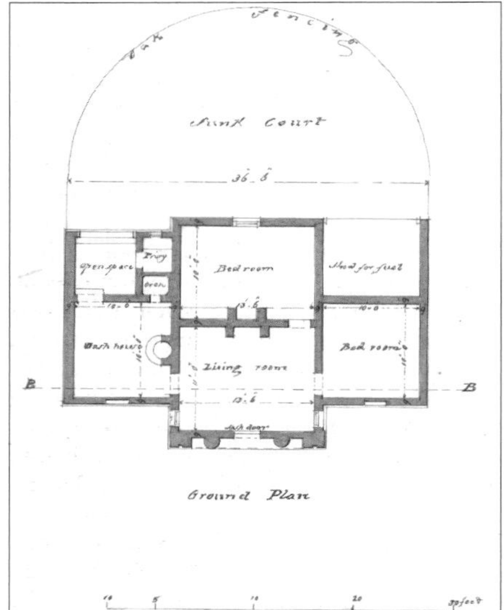

'Design for Chapelizod Lodge ...'
Decimus Burton, 31 Jan. 1822 (National Archives).

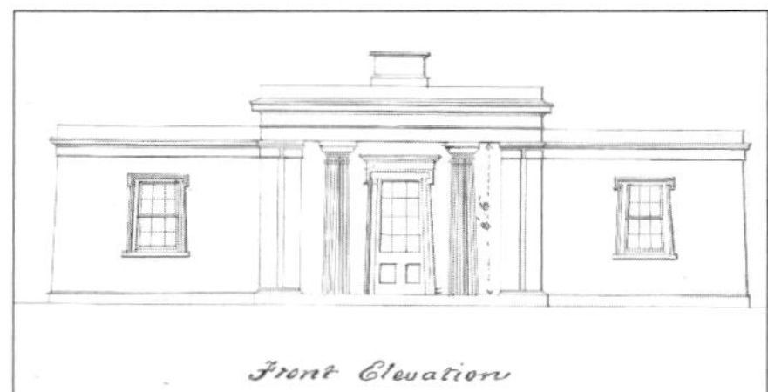

'Design for Chapelizod Lodge ...'
Decimus Burton, 31 Jan. 1822 (National Archives).

Classical gatekeeper's lodges to the park, resembling those he designed for Hyde Park in London. That this had a long gestation period is clear from his early drawing, undated, showing an extensive Tudor Castellated scheme with a two-storey gatehouse, two up/two down, having a crenellated and machicolated parapet broken by a bartizan and, below, bipartite label-moulded Gothic windows. Attached was to have been a triple gateway with a central stepped gable decorated with a Tudor plaque and mock cross arrowloops. Beyond would have been a square turret containing a rather

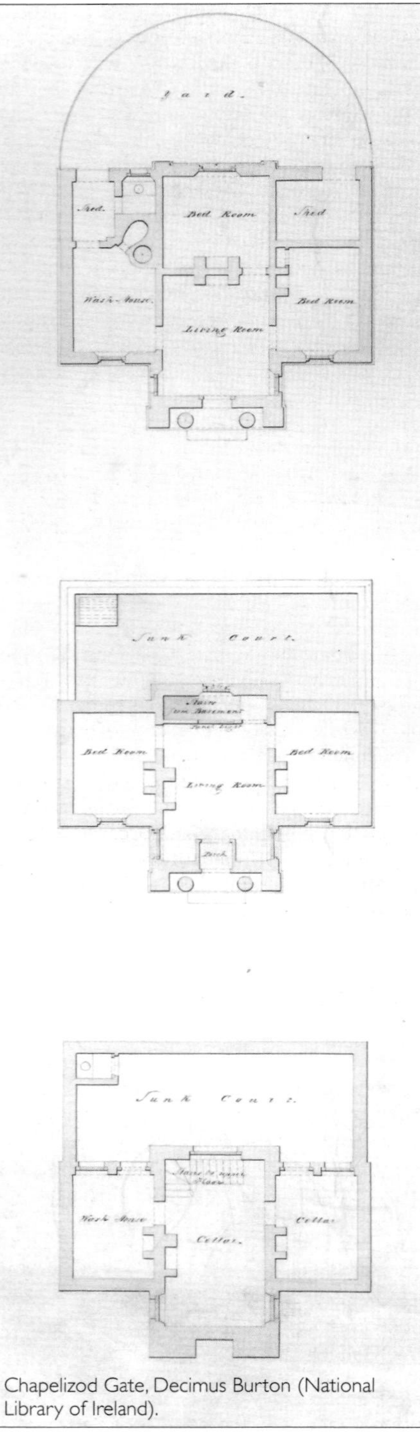

Chapelizod Gate, Decimus Burton (National Library of Ireland).

remote closet. His alternative design, and almost that adopted, dates from 31 January 1833 and shows a single-storey three-bay lodge on a cruciform plan with parapeted roofs. The main body of the building advanced to the avenue with a pair of engaged fluted Doric columns *in antis* framed on each side by double pilasters. Within the portico is a doorway with a tapering Egyptian-style case, repeated on the windows to the lower wings, the sliding operation of the six-over-six sash windows to which would have been problematical. The accommodation comprised in the main body a bedroom and living room, which gave on to another bedroom and wash-house in the wings, behind which were intended a roofed yard with 'privy' and a fuel shed. To the rear was to have been a semicircular 'sunk court' screened by oak fencing. There followed an intermediate design with minor amendments, where the columns became free-standing and a simple semicircular yard replaces the sunken court. This was priced at £600 by Messrs Carolin and Co., contractors. By 19 March 1836 Burton produced a final design, not as built and differing from the preceding sketches in being single-storey over a basement: the 'Plan as proposed to be reduced in size in consequence of adding a basement story'. The lodge as built sees the columns with smooth shafts and, sadly, the loss of the Egyptian-style openings and double pilasters, but all crafted beautifully in limestone ashlar with Killiney granite as dressings, and prominent quoins, all as per the intermediate proposal at a cost of £680 by Henry, Mullins and McMahon. Accompanying this is an extensive straight railed screen and triple gateway contained by eight square stone pillars, the central pair of which were to have carried lanterns, the whole being centred about an axis with the Hibernian Military School within.

Knockmaroon gate; pre-1760/1838; architect Decimus Burton.

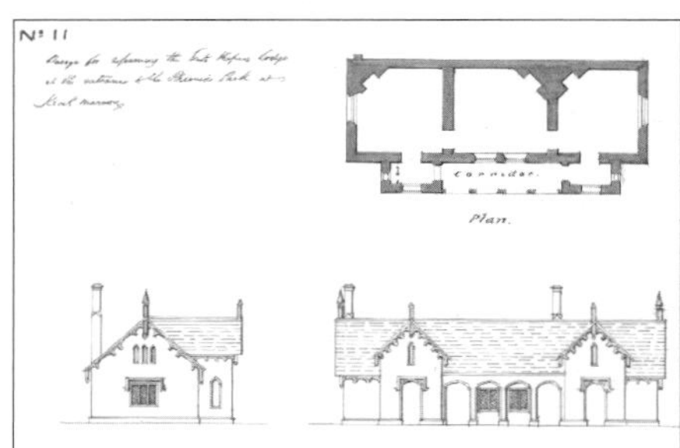

'Design for reforming the gatekeeper's lodge at Knockmaroon', J. Owen (National Archives).

Along with the Ashtown gate, Burton in his survey was most critical of this entrance and lodge, describing it as being 'extremely ugly and in bad order' and having 'a mean and wretched appearance'. As at Islandbridge, Jacob Owen intended to 'reform' it, for a drawing dated 21 March 1834 shows his proposal to turn what looks to have been little more than a three-roomed traditional linear cottage into a pleasant Picturesque English Tudor affair. The scheme envisaged the addition of tall gabled porches flanking an arched arcade or verandah in monastic fashion. Gables were to sport perforated foiled bargeboards, hip-knobs and pendants, whilst the windows were to be leaded with label mouldings. Very pretty, but discarded for Decimus Burton's novel proposal. Not for him a lodge sited deferentially to one side of the gates but rather one placed forthrightly as the central feature symmetrically between matching gatescreens in the simple but striking form of a single-storey octagonal structure with a parapet roof concealing a polygonal cluster chimney-stack. Finished in lime stucco rendering, with deep horizontal channelled rustication and Golden Hill granite to keystones and a spring band to semicircular arched openings with spoked sash windows. Burton's original scheme envisaged the whole to be carried out in limestone with Killiney granite dressings, but this was priced at £1,700 by the contractor, John Butler; the alternative finishes saw the estimate reduced to £1,050. The four main gate pillars are similarly octagonal in section with lofty lanterns and contain sets of triple gateways with spear-topped gates and secondary iron pillars. The lodge is contained to the fore by a low segmental railed enclosure; to the rear it was extended in like manner in 1865.

Colonel White's gate; pre-1837/1905; architect T.J. Mellon.

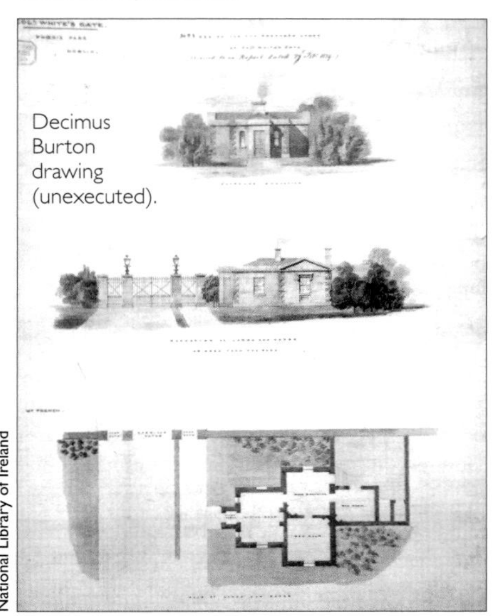
Decimus Burton drawing (unexecuted).

National Library of Ireland

So called after Thomas White of Woodlands, or Luttrellstown (*q.v.*), who had this as his own private entrance. Of the five gateways to the park for which Burton is known to have submitted gate lodge designs to the Board, for whatever reason this was the only one never built. His plans dated January 1839 indicate a fully worked-up scheme for another distinctive single-storey neo-Classical lodge and gateway with surrounding shrubbery. The main body of the building was to have had pedimented gables above six-over-six sash windows with underpanels and bracketed entablatured heads, all framed by

262. Phoenix Park, Colonel White's gate.

reticulated toothed quoins, a type of masonry finish he had already used in his Cumberland Lodge, Hyde Park, London. Projecting to the avenue was intended a hip-roofed living room, with parapeted eaves, lit by a round-headed slit window on each side of a further extension in the shape of a 'close porch'. Strangely, a bedroom back return does not complete a perfectly symmetrical cruciform plan but is positioned off-centre. Another eccentricity is that both bedrooms are accessed off a 'wood & potatoes' store. Adjacent is a smart triple gateway of spear-topped ironwork and four square pillars, the central pair of which were to carry splendid lanterns. The old gatekeeper's lodge was not to be replaced for another 65 years, by which time architectural taste had changed dramatically, and what materialised is like no other lodge in the park. This is a thoroughly quirky little creation in the Arts and Crafts manner on a rambling plan. It is single-storey in a nice, mellow, orange rustic brick in English bond, below a bewildering roofscape of flat, hipped and gabled forms with a finish of Westmoreland green slates. To the apexes is black-and-white work, the eaves ornamented with a bracketed soffit, a bow window to one external corner, a nice wooden glazed hallway and a hefty brick four-flue chimney-stack. Mellon from 1900 was one of three principal surveyors of the Office of Public Works.

Castleknock entrance; pre-1760/*c.* 1836; architect Decimus Burton.

The visitor in the early 1830s was met by a lodge 'of straggling and extensive dimensions', according to Burton's report to the Board. A preliminary proposal for its replacement was prepared by Jacob Owen on 21 March 1834, in a distinctive Italianate style comprised of a hip-roofed two-storey centre, containing a palatial bedroom lit by a solitary tripartite high-level window, over an arcaded porch through which light was expected to filter to the living room behind. To one side was a single-storey parapeted hip-roofed bedroom, with a balancing wing to the opposing side which would have been little more than a screen wall to a lean-to shed and privy. These intended wings had no front windows but rather mock 'openings' with shouldered and moulded surrounds and terminating in recessed panel pilasters—an attractive but impractical design remedied by what materialised on site. Presumably by Burton, this is an amazing exercise in block massing on a small scale, developed from Owen's original scheme. The attic bedroom is reduced in size, lit by a wide rectangular window subdivided by a sequence of miniature Doric stone mullions, below a parapeted roof crowned by the final block—a squat four-flue chimney-stack. At ground-floor level the central block is flanked by single-bay wings and fronted by a projecting block from which a Doric pilastered entrance porch extended yet further to the avenue. Built by Butler and Co. in limestone ashlar dressed in Killiney Hill granite, with smooth entablatured surrounds to windows now reduced to plastic look-alike six-over-six sashes. More than any other of Decimus Burton's lodges to the park, it fulfils his aim that 'the buildings should be designed of a solid but handsome character, and even if required to be simple and void of embellishment, yet good proportions should be studied'—and innovatively too. It seems, however, that the gatekeeper, Mr Bryan, was less than enamoured with his new abode, for in 1838 he found the accommodation inconvenient, erecting an 'unsightly' wooden shed in his sunken court. The architect was annoyed and insisted that it be removed and that all the gatekeepers be served with notices not to make alterations without permission. He also demanded that Bryan take down during the day the shutter of the entrance sash door, which he had previously refused to do. He did concede that the sunken court could be turned into a pantry and an iron wicket gate be placed across the front door. Alongside is a fine triple gateway, much as Burton had intended for Colonel White's gate, with six stone pillars, the carriage pair carrying tall iron lanterns.

Ashtown gate; pre-1837/1838; architect Decimus Burton.

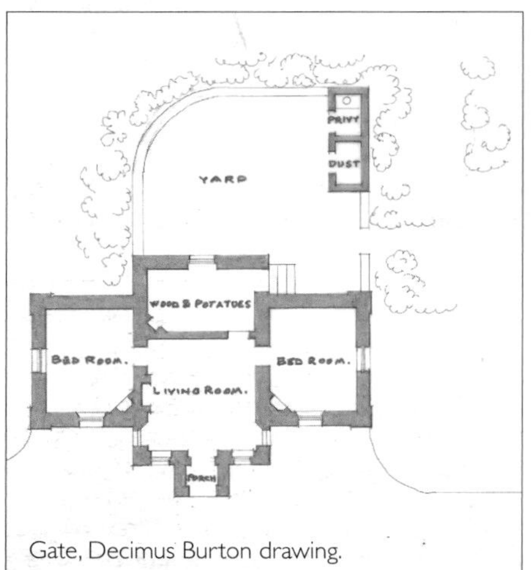

Gate, Decimus Burton drawing.

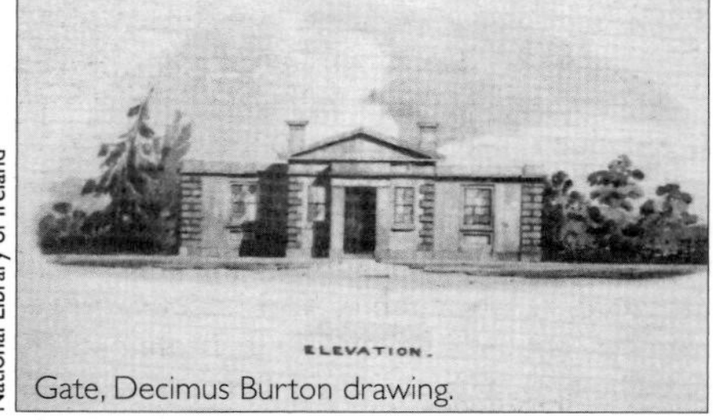

Gate, Decimus Burton drawing.

National Library of Ireland

Like the Knockmaroon gate, the entrance here was described by Burton as 'extremely ugly and kept in bad order'. The existing substandard structure to the left-hand side of the entrance he proposed replacing, on the other side of the avenue, with a relatively conventional Classical lodge. The architect's drawing of January 1838 shows the building as built unusually in a brick finish, probably influenced by the previous excesses at the Chapelizod and Castleknock gates, with lime stucco dressings. Single-storey three-bay with a parapeted roof, the central bay breaks forward below a pediment with narrow four-over-four sash windows on each side of a flat-roofed porch projection. Whilst the breakfront has traditional toothed quoin stones, the main ones are as Irish pilasters, something Burton must have absorbed in his stay. The bedroom windows to the avenue are six-over-six sashes in architraves with underpanels. Internally the ill-lit living room is flanked by a pair of bedrooms and extends to the rear to form a cruciform plan, with the obligatory room for 'Wood & Potatoes'. In June 1839 Arthur McKenna and Sons submitted an account for £720 in respect of

262. Phoenix Park, Ashtown gate lodge.

work carried out on the entrance.

By 1848 Burton's lodge had been converted for use as a police barracks and complemented across the access by a new lodge to match, in the same Flemish bond brickwork, to form a pair, linked by another of Burton's six-pillared triple entrance screens with carriage lanterns, but widened by intermediate straight railings and further extended by tall wing walls.

Cabra gate; pre-1772/1839; architect Decimus Burton.

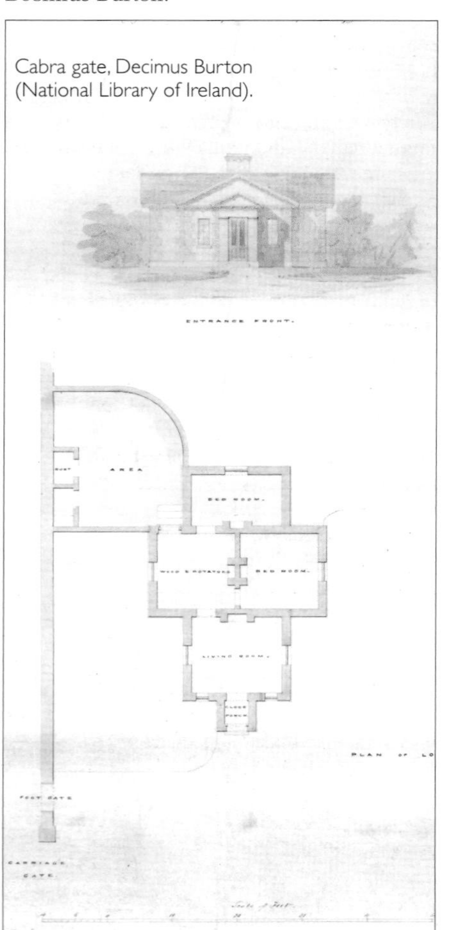
Cabra gate, Decimus Burton (National Library of Ireland).

National Library of Ireland

Much as he proposed for Colonel White's gate but here a gabled version on a perfectly cruciform plan, Burton's drawing of January 1839 recommended that his client locate his Classical design a lot further west of the old lodge. In reality it was sited further west but only at the other side of the entrance to its predecessor, which was a long rectangular structure built against the park wall. Single-storey and pedimented on its three main fronts, from the living room projects a lower, similarly treated 'close porch' or hall, all with mutules to tympanums carried on as eaves brackets. Roughcast-finished, framed by toothed stone quoins, its bedrooms are accessed via the required 'Wood & Potatoes' room. The distant railed entrance screen has the imperative lantern lights atop plain granite pillars which here are secondary to cast-iron carriage posts. The contractor was again Arthur McKenna and Sons.

Circular Road gate; *c.* 1816; architect probably F. Johnston.

Not unlike the Parkgate lodge, which

262. Phoenix Park, North Circular Road gate.

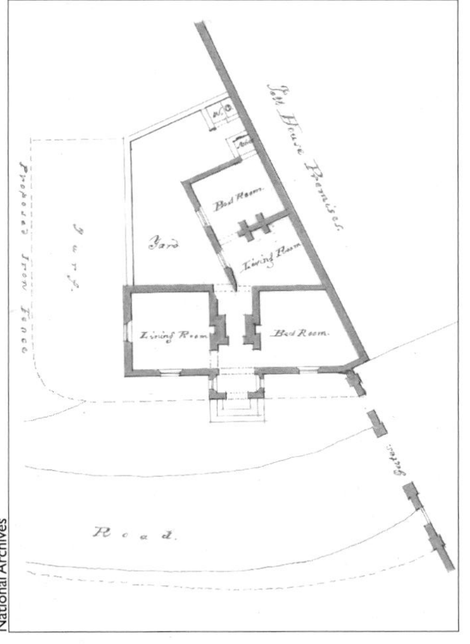

National Archives

similarly escaped Decimus Burton's broom. He did, though, furnish a plan in January 1844 for alterations to it, which appear not to have been carried out. Originally an elongated single-storey standard hip-roofed lodge with a pedimented hall projection, the front door to which was subsequently moved to one side. Flanking are two-over-two sash windows, later replacements in 'improvements' which also saw the addition of their Classical Victorian surrounds. Conspicuous toothed quoins in roughcast walls are in contrast with the cluster of four polygonal Tudor-style chimney-pots. A building distinguished in 1890 as a meeting place which saw the foundation of Bohemians Football Club. The elaborate and extensive gatescreen from the turn of the twentieth century is comprised of five grand cast-iron pillars, three of which display copper lanterns to illuminate the double carriageway gates.

Decimus Burton, within the constraint of a £15,000 budget, more than fulfilled his employers' expectations to 'render the park more attractive' with his landscaping and architectural professionalism. Whether the wearing of livery by the gatekeepers, as envisaged by Burton, was realised is not known. Those identified by the valuation of 1849 could have told us: Richard Mooney, Edward Hind, James Goodman, Peter Farrell, William Goddin, Owen McCarthy, Martin Ryan and William Fallon.

Wright 1831; Griffith 1848–60; Lawrence photo (5442C); Institute of Landscape Horticulture of Ireland (1988:2); *IGS Bulletin* (1995); *IADS* (2002); Casey 2005; NAIOPW drawings (13170/03); NLI drawings (AD 2121, 2123, 2126, 2127, 2128); McCullen 2009.

263. PORTMARNOCK, Portmarnock; pre-1837; *demolished.*
A property for the greater part of the early nineteenth century of Luke Plunkett, whose gatekeeper in 1848 was John Keenan. Like the lodge, its big house has gone.

Lewis 1837; Griffith 1848–60; *LGI* (1904).

264. PORTMARNOCK RECTORY, Portmarnock; pre-1848; *demolished.*
To a rectory dating back to 1791 the porter's lodge was added by the perpetual curate Revd George Cole Baker (1796–1880), during whose incumbency (1830–59) the gatekeeper was Henry Donnelly.

Lewis 1837; Griffith 1848–60; Leslie and Wallace 2001.

265. PORTRAINE, Donabate; pre-1837/*c.* 1880.

In 1844 a 'sumptuous demesne of George H. Evans' with 'a spacious square structure composed of brick'. Its surviving gate lodge dates from another generation, George Evans having replaced an earlier one to the other side of the avenue. This is a pleasant single-storey late Victorian cottage in red brick, three-bay below a hipped roof dominated by a semi-octagonal central bay window and equivalent roof. The entrance doorway is to the left-hand side, fast becoming enveloped in Virginia creeper. For relief are Irish pilaster quoins to the walls and rows of scalloped slates to the roof. Occupied. There is a very fine cast-iron gatescreen from perhaps twenty years earlier, with fleur-de-lis and anthemion tops to railings and gates, and pillars rose-enriched and ivy-entwined.

Pigot 1824; *Parliamentary Gazetteer*; *Thom's*.

266. PORTRAINE LUNATIC ASYLUM, Portrane; *c.* 1900; architect probably G.C. Ashlin.

A massive red-brick complex, a small town in its own right, on the outskirts of which is a vaguely Tudor-style 1½-storey lodge in matching materials with red sandstone dressings as skew-tables and kneelers to its leading gable. Built off an L-plan with otherwise hipped roofs, there are special bricks to the eaves course and bands at first-floor and ground-floor sill levels. In English bond brickwork which contains an odd mix of sash and casement windows below segmental arches; big bold chimney-stacks.

Williams 1994.

267. PRIMROSE CASTLE, Coolock (2).
This was a seat in the mid-nineteenth century of John Graham, who altered its name to 'Shrubs Cottage' and replaced the earlier lodge with one further south. Both have gone.

Griffith 1848–60; *Thom's*.

268. PRIORSWOOD, Santry; pre-1837; *demolished.*
An estate which passed in the mid-eighteenth century by marriage from Joseph Sherwood to the Evans family. On the death of Francis Evans in 1834 it was purchased by another barrister, Thomas Cosgrave, whose home it remained for twenty years.

Lewis 1837; *Thom's*; *LGI* (1904).

269. PRIVATE SECRETARY'S LODGE, Phoenix Park; pre-1837; *demolished.*
Now known as 'Ratra House' and previously

as 'Little Lodge', in its days as home to British government representatives it was appropriately abutting the Viceregal Lodge (*q.v.*). From an 1830s map prepared by Decimus Burton in his improvement plans, the porter's lodge appears as a simple rectangular cottage to the left of the gates which survived until the mid-twentieth century. The gate porter in 1849 was James Gahan.

Griffith 1848–60; NAIOPW drawings (13170/03).

PROSPECT (see ARDGILLAN CASTLE)

270. PROSPECT POINT, Swords; pre-1837; *demolished.*

A seat in 1824 and 1837 of a Captain Purcell.

Pigot 1824; Lewis 1837.

271. RAHENY COTTAGE, Raheny; *c.* 1830.

In 1836 'the pretty cottage and well enclosed parks of Mr D'Arcy'. This John D'Arcy, a brewer, was still here in 1851, three years before which his gate porter is recorded as Edward Travers, who was privileged to live in this decent Regency lodge, now rendered astylar through modern improvements. Single-storey standard below a hipped roof broken by a gabled hall frontispiece. Later extended to an L-plan with new windows in smooth rendered walls. Tucked in behind the left-hand convex railed quadrant of a gatescreen with four good Classical granite pillars, with recessed shafts and semicircular pedimented cappings, containing spear-topped gates and screens.

D'Alton 1976 [1838]; Griffith 1848–60; *Thom's*.

RAHENY (see RATHMORE)

272. RAHENY PARK, Raheny (2).

A good red-brick villa, like its two gate lodges a thing of the past, was home for the greater part of the nineteenth century to Thomas M. Gresham, senior and junior, whose gatekeepers in 1848 were John Tracey and Denis Mayland.

North lodge; pre-1837/*c.* 1870; *demolished.*

A photograph of *c.* 1961 shows a traditional single-storey hip-roofed lodge, one end of which broke the tall boundary wall with the entrance alongside of two plain square roughcast pillars. This had replaced an earlier cottage within the curtilage of the Howth road, the widening of which led to the demise of its successor.

South lodge; pre-1837/*c.* 1910; architects probably Batchelor and Hicks.

At the shore road entrance the early lodge to the old house was replaced by the present Arts and Crafts bungalow. In 1910 Andrew Jameson of the whiskey family developed the site for his new mansion of 'Bettyglen' to designs by Batchelor and Hicks, part of whose commission must surely have included this lodge. It is a striking pebble-dashed affair in a sort of Queen Anne Revival manner, with a steeply pitched hipped roof and exaggerated oversailing soffit to cover two canted bay windows with leaded casements and a similarly projecting hall, beyond the eaves of which it extends further as a flat-roofed canopy supported on carved wooden brackets. An effort has been made to extend it sympathetically although it is now dominated by oversized dormer windows and modern concrete tiles.

Lewis 1837; Griffith 1848–60; *Thom's*; *IB* (3 Sept. 1910); Joan Sharkey photograph; Williams 1994.

273. RAHENY RECTORY, Raheny; pre-1837; *demolished.*

Both the old glebe house and its lodge were swept away in favour of modern housing.

274. RATHBEALE HALL, Swords (2).

An important mansion given its Palladian cloak *c.* 1751 by Hamilton Gorges. It was briefly called 'Catherine's Grove' before the family's interest in it waned. By the early nineteenth century it was let to Matthew Corbally, whose brother Elias bought it in 1832 and built the first of its lodges.

West gate; *c.* 1835.

A novel little single-storey hip-roofed lodge with a short front to the avenue comprised of a chamfered tripartite window, framed by toothed stone quoins, to the road side of which is a recessed porch whose roof is carried on a fluted wooden Doric column. Otherwise in a plain render, it monitors a splendid gatescreen, much as that to Portraine House (*q.v.*), with cast-iron carriage pillars ornamented with rose and honeysuckle motifs and scrambling ivy.

East gate; *c.* 1870.

Elias T. Corbally died in 1846, to be succeeded by his only son Matthew James Corbally (1837–1907), a minor, who added a secondary lodge on the main road from Swords not long after reaching his majority. It is a single-storey cottage built off an L-plan with a shallow hipped roof. The simple rendered walls are enhanced by brick toothed quoins and dressings to a series of tripartite casement windows. Occupied but run down, with an unsightly walled entrance screen.

Taylor and Skinner 1778; 1969 [1783]; Leet 1814; *LGI* (1912); *Country Life* (24 Aug. 1972); Bence-Jones 1988.

275. RATHMORE, Raheny; pre-1907; *demolished.*

Previously 'Raheny House' or the 'Manor House', erected by the Grace family, it was for much of the nineteenth century a seat of the Sweetmans, who built a lodge sometime after 1837, on the site of which is now a car showroom.

Lewis 1837.

276. REYNOLDSTOWN, Naul; *c.* 1800.

A neat example of how to solve the Georgian dilemma of achieving symmetry at the gate. Facing the road is a single-storey standard Gothic cottage with a hipped gable roof and a pair of lancet windows in harled walls. This is flanked by two carriage entrances with tall plain pillars, the whole framed by sloping whitewashed rustic quadrant walls, all creating an impressive forecourt. A place which doubtless originated as a Reynolds property but in 1814 was a residence of William Barry, from whom it had passed to William W. Yates by 1837.

Leet 1814; Lewis 1837.

277. RICHMOND HOUSE OF INDUSTRY, Grangegorman; *c.* 1810; architect probably F. Johnston; *demolished.*

Part of the vast complex of institutional buildings which came and went over a period of 300 years, both the House of Industry and its porter's lodge have been removed. The latter was probably located on one of the alleys off North Brunswick Street, and its outline is revealed by an undated and unsigned plan in the Murray Drawings Collection. It was squeezed into a restricted site, probably as a lean-to against an earlier structure. Single-storey, two-roomed with a canted front, it lay behind a gatescreen of two octagonal carriage pillars and postern gate openings in walls which extended at angles to accommodate storerooms on each side.

IAA (Murray Drawings Collection 398); Casey 2005.

278. RICHMOND LUNATIC ASYLUM, Grangegorman; 1855; architect probably Sir G.F. Hodson; *demolished.*
The original Lunatic Asylum was designed in 1810–15 by Francis Johnston, whose commission did not extend to providing a gate lodge. The complex was enlarged in 1851 and porter's accommodation was added soon after. Strangely, this appears to have been drawn up by the amateur architect Sir George Frederick Hodson of Hollybrooke, Co. Wicklow (*q.v.*). His forte was designs in the Tudor Picturesque English Cottage style, but here he put his hand to a simple astylar single-storey two-bay box, with quoin stones framing squared bipartite casement windows below a high-eaved pyramidal roof rising to a central chimney-stack. His preliminary sketch shows a lean-to housing an entrance 'porch', store and privy.

Casey 2005; IAA (Hodson Drawings Collection 87/55; 29/1).

279. RICHMOND DISTRICT LUNATIC ASYLUM (NEW), Grangegorman; pre-1870; *demolished.*
Now part of St Brendan's Hospital, the gate lodge to which may have been contemporary with the building of the vast complex designed in 1848–54 by the architectural firm of Murray and Denny. Early maps indicate a structure with an L-plan off Grangegorman Lane. At the main entrance are fine gates removed from Santry Court (*q.v.*).

O'Dwyer 1997a.

280. RICHMOND, Drumcondra; pre-1837; *demolished.*
A property which in the nineteenth century had a bewildering turnover of occupants, one of whom in 1848 was William Auchinleck Dane of Killyhevlin, Co. Fermanagh, an attorney in the city, whose gate porter to his Dublin seat was Patrick Carroll.

Griffith 1848–60.

281. RIVERMOUNT, Finglas; pre-1837; *demolished.*
The seat in 1846 of Daniel Magan, solicitor in chancery, whose gate lodge three years later lay vacant.

Slater 1846; Griffith 1848–60.

282. RIVERSDALE, Finglas; *c.* 1840; *demolished.*
A residence in 1837 of C. Stewart Esq., from whom by 1849 it had passed to Horatio Nelson Walker, at which time his newly built porter's lodge lay empty.

Lewis 1837; Griffith 1848–60.

283. ROCKFIELD COTTAGE, Artane (2).
The pre-1837 porter's lodge close to the house was unoccupied in 1848, perhaps prior to being superseded by that on the Malahide road, which too has gone. This was a property in 1843 of John Atkinson, after which it was home to a succession of residents, principal among whom were Edward Moore, a railway contractor in the 1850s and '60s, and Charles Reilly, farmer and limekiln contractor, from about 1870 to 1890.

Griffith 1848–60; *Thom's.*

284. ROGANSTOWN, Swords; *c.* 1855.
An estate of the Aungier family, whose lodge is a plain standard single-storey structure, roughcast with modern windows on each side of a gabled hall projection, the ridge of which is below the eaves of the main steeply hipped roof. Derelict.

Pike and McDowell 1908.

285. ROSE HILL, Finglas; pre-1837; *demolished.*
A remarkable survival in the village is this early eighteenth-century house, occupied in 1848 by Patrick Corbally, renting from Richard Shaw. The lodge, whose porter then was Patrick McGuinness, has gone.

Griffith 1848–60; Craig and Fewer 2002.

286. ROSEMOUNT, Artane; *c.* 1865/*c.* 1905.
'Long Cottage' or 'Rosemount Cottage', as it became known in the mid-nineteenth century, was later replaced with the present house by Walter Cyrus Warner, complete with a short-lived porter's lodge, which in turn was superseded by the present structure, probably by one A.E. Wood, the proprietor in 1910. This survivor is a single-storey, unostentatious, vaguely Arts and Crafts affair in English bond red brick with a hipped roof, the eaves of which extend to cover the central breakfront to the public footway, which contains a wide small-paned casement window flush with the brickwork in English fashion and with moulded sill brackets. The doorway of the two-bay front to the avenue is protected by a later flat-roofed glazed hall.

Thom's.

287. ROSEVALE, Killester; pre-1837; *demolished.*
A property in 1841 of Joseph Kinsey, whose gate lodge in 1848 lay vacant.

Thom's; Griffith 1848–60.

288. ROTUNDA LYING-IN HOSPITAL, Parnell Street; *c.* 1786; architect probably James Gandon; *demolished.*
'The building consists of a centre and two projecting pavilions connected with it by curved colonnades; the whole of the façade extends 125 feet in length; the principal entrance leads into a spacious hall, and a broad flight of steps leads from the hall to the

Malton

chapel. The western pavilion forms an entrance to the porter's lodge, and the eastern to the rotunda.' Thus did Samuel Lewis in 1837 reveal the layout of architect Richard Castle's maternity unit, built in the form of a grand Palladian country mansion. Sadly, much has changed down the years, not least the loss of the left-hand pavilion and its porter's accommodation. James Malton's view of 1795 shows its main front, probably remodelled by James Gandon, on the back of the footway to what was Great Britain Street, linked by a wide railed screen to the twin façade of the entrance to the later Assembly Rooms—the Rotunda to which the hospital owes its name. This fine elevation was short-lived, for by *c.* 1839 Bartlett shows it remodelled and raised by a storey. It had a two-stage blind façade of three bays, the central one of which was recessed, containing a double-leafed panelled doorway flanked by pairs of Roman Doric columns framed by rusticated outer bays with round-headed niches. The upper stage above the entablature was relieved by swagged panels on each side of a semicircular relieving arch, over which the corniced parapet had a central die as base for a squat crowning urn. The eastern pavilion remains as a sad reminder of its lost twin.

Lewis 1837; Wright 1839; Malton 1978; McParland 1985; Ferguson 1998; Casey 2005.

289. ROWLESTOWN, Swords; pre-1836; *demolished.*
The estate at the turn of the nineteenth century of the Smith family, from whom it passed by marriage in 1820 to John William Stubbs (1790–1851), probably the builder of the lost lodge.

LGI (1904).

290. ROYAL HIBERNIAN MILITARY SCHOOL, Phoenix Park; *c.* 1820.
A nondescript long, single-storey, hip-roofed building with six-over-six sash windows and a small catslide-roofed projection to the avenue; plain gatescreen. Rather less

distinguished than the residential school established in 1766 for the children of deceased soldiers and those abroad, which was enlarged about 1810 to designs by Francis Johnston, to whom it would be difficult to attribute the lodge. The gatekeeper in 1848 was John Smullen. Now St Mary's Hospital.

Casey 2005.

291. ROYAL IRISH CONSTABULARY BARRACKS, Phoenix Park (3).

In 1832 the Englishman Jacob Owen was appointed to the Board of Works as their chief architect and engineer, and this Royal Irish Constabulary Barracks (now the HQ of An Garda Síochána) was the single largest complex constructed under his supervision in the park. Built in 1841–3 by Messrs Carolin, contractors, behind an extensive straight railed screen, at the extremities of which are outer lodges that could be considered a matching pair were they not so far apart. Each is a grey-rendered single-storey rectangular two-roomed box projecting beyond the screen as a single-window bay elevation set in a recess flanked by mock gunloops. Below a shallow pediment to the side are pairs of round-headed gunslits monitoring the boundary in Italianate manner. Presumably by Owen.

Central guardroom; *c.* 1900; architect possibly J.H. Pentland.
Looking to date from the turn of the twentieth century is this bland exercise in duality. Single-storey, built in two-tone brickwork, rising to a tall-eaved hipped roof with projecting bays to each side of the entrance doorway. Perhaps designed by John Howard Pentland, principal surveyor to the Board.

Lohan 1994; *IADS* (2002).

292. ROYAL MILITARY INFIRMARY, Phoenix Park; pre-1837; *demolished.*
'The Royal Military Infirmary was completed in 1788, at the expense of £9,000 after plans of Mr William Gibson.' The early lodge is survived by a later nasty, single-storey, flat-roofed affair cowering behind the boundary wall of what is now the Department of Defence.

Brewer 1825.

RUSH (see KENURE PARK)

293. ST ANNE'S, Clontarf (4).
Here, occupying most of the townland of Heronstown, was a large Georgian house called 'Thornhill', once of the Eustace family and in 1835 of Hugh O'Reilly, which two years later was absorbed into the great Guinness empire when it was purchased by the brothers Arthur Lee Guinness and Benjamin Lee Guinness. Following the death of the latter in 1868, his son, Sir Arthur Edward Guinness (1840–1915), having married in 1871, commenced a most extensive development of house and demesne, from 1873 creating his ostentatious Italianate marine mansion to designs of architect James Franklin Fuller and extending the property into adjacent townlands. Guinness was ennobled in 1880 as Lord Ardilaun, spreading his stout-fuelled building excesses to the lakeside castle of Ashford, Co. Galway, as well as new stables and estate buildings at St Anne's. For these works he also had the services of George Coppinger Ashlin—no one architect could cope with his demands. Here, too, he formed new entrances to the property, adding porters' lodges as well as remodelling those he had inherited, two of which survive as outstanding examples of late Victorian Picturesque.

Thornhill lodge; pre-1837; *demolished.*
One of the original lodges to the old house on the property which was retained by Ardilaun but removed in the mid-twentieth century. Its gatekeeper in 1849 was James Anderson.

Blackbush lodge; pre-1907; *demolished.*
Another entrance, created after 1837, off the old Blackbush Lane (now Mount Prospect Avenue) which was short-lived and was taken down with the demise of the big house.

Sealawn lodge; pre-1837/*c.* 1875; architect possibly J.F. Fuller.

A charming composition, on the old southern approach off the shore road, which seems to incorporate an early single-storey gabled cottage to which was applied a 1½-storey extension in the English Tudor Picturesque manner. To the road front is a single-storey gabled hallway with perforated decorative wavy bargeboards and hip-knobs above the doorway, with its hood-moulded four-centred archway all tucked in below a fancy carved fascia board. The main delight is in the avenue elevation, with its steeply pitched gable of more carved, ornate cusped bargeboards above lattice-paned French doors, with stone dressings and label mouldings, which open onto a wide balcony with quatrefoil-motif balustrade, which in turn rests on a glazed ground-floor canted bay window. Breaking the main ridge is a rectangular brick chimney-stack with three bulbous octagonal terracotta and brick-built pots. Otherwise the plain grey roughcast is softened by ivy, beautifully setting off the striking woodwork. Lovingly maintained and well restored but for the modern glazed front door.

All Saints Lodge; *c.* 1890; architect G.C. Ashlin.

In 1885 Lord Ardilaun paid for the replacement of the old Raheny parish church as a final resting place for himself and his wife, George Ashlin's commission extending to this superlative sexton's lodge that also gave onto the ilex-lined avenue which led south to the house. Single-storey, built off a cruciform plan in half-timbered work with rendered infill, opposing hipped gables jetty out over canted, glazed bay windows. To the avenue projects a gabled verandahed porch with bosses to bargeboards above an ornamental apex extending over an ornate coving intricately carved with foliation, rose and sunflower motifs framing a shield displaying intertwined Ardilaun monograms. Below is the arcaded porch with turned post support. The roof has rows of canted slates with earthenware cresting and hip-knobs.

In 1968 the mansion was demolished after being given scant protection from escalating vandalism.

Griffith 1848–60; *BPB* (1929); Williams 1994; Sharkey 2002.

ST ANN'S (see BROOMHILL)

ST BRENDAN'S (see COOLOCK LODGE)

ST BRENDAN'S HOSPITAL (see RICHMOND DISTRICT LUNATIC ASYLUM)

ST CATHERINE'S PARK (see COUNTY KILDARE)

294. ST DOOLAGH'S, Balgriffin; *c.* 1825.

A Regency lodge, single-storey standard but with main three-bay avenue façade embraced by a gable in the form of a pediment, its openings set in segmentally arched recesses containing cast-iron latticed bipartite casements—a dear little whitewashed harled lodge in caring hands which, if it were not, might have deteriorated to the condition of its twin at nearby Hazelbrook (*q.v.*). Probably built by the husband of a Mrs Grace Shaw who was living here in 1837, whose gate porter eleven years later was Patrick Farrell. The property was renamed 'Bohomer' *c.* 1860.

Lewis 1837; Griffith 1848–60.

295. ST DOOLAGH'S LODGE, Balgriffin; pre-1837; *demolished.*
An old seat of the Rutherford family, the lodge to which seems later to have served the new property of St Doolagh's Park (*q.v.*), created further north in about 1845.

Wilson 1803; d'Alton 1976 [1838].

296. ST DOOLAGH'S PARK, Balgriffin; *c.* 1845.

A development of big house, outbuildings and contemporary gate lodge by Francis and Christopher Savage. This is a decent Regency-style building, single-storey standard with segmentally headed openings, the door set in a similarly arched recess in rendered walls below an oversailing hipped roof with a cut-stone chimney-stack. Of an age is a set of six Classical pillars with V-jointed stone shafts, containing a triple gateway and quadrant walls with railings and matching iron gates. The property by 1857 had been acquired by Nathaniel Hone (1807–80), who moved from, and demolished, Wellfield Cottage (*q.v.*) to the rear, and he absorbed it into his new park, extended the old avenue and utilised his old lodge. The 1870 high sheriff of Dublin seems also to have purloined the porter's lodge of neighbouring St Doolagh's Lodge (*q.v.*) on an extended southern avenue.

Thom's; *IFR*.

297. ST FINTAN'S GRAVEYARD, Howth; *c.* 1840.
An unprepossessing single-storey hip-roofed lodge with later gabled back return having scalloped bargeboards; harled rubble walls with a stone eaves band. Derelict. Dating from about the foundation of the cemetery.

298. ST FINTAN'S, Howth; *c.* 1840.
A standard single-storey roughcast lodge with an oversailing hipped roof and a hefty chimney-stack. Extended by a bay to the right-hand side in unsympathetic modernisation, which included the blocking up of the original doorway. Built for Captain John King, whose gate porter in 1850 was Lawrence Kealy. Now 'Sutton Park School'.

Slater 1846; Griffith 1848–60.

299. ST HELENA, Finglas; pre-1837; *demolished.*
In 1837 this was a property of Dr William Harty run as a private lunatic asylum, but by 1848 it was let to a George Nesbitt, whose gate lodge lay vacant.

Lewis 1837; *Parliamentary Gazetteer*; Griffith 1848–60.

300. ST HELEN'S, Malahide; pre-1837; *demolished.*
A seat in 1814 of the Macartney family, whose descendant in 1849, Clotworthy Macartney (also noted at Bloomville, South Dublin), had a gatekeeper in Mary Savage.

Leet 1814; Griffith 1848–60.

ST ITA'S HOSPITAL (see PORTRAINE LUNATIC ASYLUM)

ST JOHN'S (see DONNYCARNEY COTTAGE)

301. ST JOSEPH'S DEAF AND DUMB INSTITUTION, Cabra (2).
Both lodges, both sadly demolished, formed part of a large complex designed in 1864 by Charles Geoghegan and were probably constructed in like materials of rubble stone with red-brick dressings.

Williams 1994.

ST JOSEPH'S MALE BLIND ASYLUM (see DRUMCONDRA CASTLE)

ST JOSEPH'S NATIONAL SCHOOLS (see ST MARY'S CONVENT OF MERCY)

302. ST MARNOCK'S, Portmarnock (2).
The only identified Irish work of the famed Scottish Arts and Crafts architect Sir Robert Lorimer in his remodelling and additions to an earlier house for John Jameson, who no doubt selected him owing to his own family's Scottish ancestry. In a faintly Queen Anne

Revival style the two lodges reflect it.

North lodge; *c.* 1895; architect probably Sir R. Lorimer.
A restrained 1½-storey steeply gabled bungalow in red brick with toothed stone dressings to openings which have square-paned casements, their heads at soffit level. Two big channelled granite pillars with moulded cappings.

South lodge; *c.* 1895; architect probably Sir R. Lorimer.
A more distinguished 1½-storey lodge at the principal gate. Standard symmetrical in materials as per the north lodge but with an oversailing hipped bellcast roof with Westmoreland green slates and hip-roofed dormers, crowned by a chunky brick chimney-stack. Squared casement windows on each side of a double-leaved glazed panelled door. Wide brick screen wall broken by two carriage pillars to match those to the north lodge but crowned by ball finials and carrying gates with some pretty Arts and Crafts foliated ironwork.

Savage 1980; Williams 1994.

303. ST MARY'S COLLEGE, Clontarf; *c.* 1940; architect not known.

A mid-twentieth-century exercise in the Classical Revival style. Single-storey standard and generous in scale, with a Westmoreland green slated hipped roof. Faced in granite ashlar and framed by recessed panel pilasters with disc motifs as capitals, a feature repeated as square column support to the central porch, spanned by a lintel with Greek key pattern below a pediment, the mutuled tympanum of which contains a Celtic cross. On each side is a tripartite mullioned window with rectangular panes and bracketed sills. Tall chimney-stacks at each end emphasise the symmetry. All preceded by an extensive entrance screen of great channelled rusticated granite pillars with ball finials. Also the Marino Institute of Education.

ST MARY'S HOSPITAL (see ROYAL HIBERNIAN MILITARY SCHOOL)

304. ST MARY'S CONVENT OF MERCY, Grangegorman; *c.* 1870; architect possibly G.C. Ashlin.

Alternatively and additionally over the years leading to the House of Refuge, the Stanhope Street Convent Schools of the Religious Sisters of Charity and the St Joseph's National Schools is this pleasant group of mid-Victorian Gothic Revival buildings. A triple entrance archway of a pair of lancet postern gates flanks the segmental pointed-arched carriage opening, all hood-moulded below a stepped parapet ascending to a Celtic cross. Alongside is a 1½-storey gatehouse, having a steeply pitched gable with sculpted kneelers, skew-tables and shamrock hip-knob over a lancet attic window and a pair of the same to the ground floor. This street front is in random uncoursed squared rubble with contrasting dressings, but this all lapses into grey rendered walls to the secondary elevations, which contain a mixture of stone-dressed openings with shouldered lintels and a grand first-floor Venetian Gothic tripartite window in accommodation rather too commodious to house a gatekeeper alone. Architect George Ashlin may have added this complex when the church was built in the 1870s.

Casey 2005; IAA.

305. ST MICHAN'S CHURCH, Oxmanstown; *c.* 1825.

A church of Norse foundation, which now dates largely from *c.* 1685, was 're-roofed and thoroughly repaired in 1828, at a cost of about £1,500'. This drastic restoration may have included the provision of this rather obtrusive gatekeeper's lodge in the shape of a square two-storey gatehouse with a parapeted hipped roof and a lofty unsightly chimney-stack vying with the church tower. Two-bay to the road with lancet-headed windows, this may once have been acceptable but it has now lost its Y-traceried windows, been coated in drab grey rendering and imposed upon by later hideous additions. As a prelude is a good pair of stone entrance pillars with moulded cappings and pedestalled ball finials, probably of mid-

eighteenth-century origin. The long-serving incumbent from 1809 until his death was Revd John Rowley (1777–1845).

Lewis 1837; Killanin and Duignan 1962; Leslie and Wallace 2001.

ST PATRICK'S TRAINING COLLEGE (see BELVIDERE)

306. ST VINCENT'S, Castleknock (3).

In 1834 the Revd John McCann purchased, on behalf of the Vincentian Order, the old residence of the Warren family known as 'Corduff'. A school was established which today is Castleknock College. They also acquired with the estate a gate lodge which was to serve well into the twentieth century, its gatekeeper in 1848 being Mary Cavanagh.

South lodge; pre-1837/*c.* 1912; architects probably Ashlin and Coleman.

By the site of its predecessor is this dapper Arts and Crafts lodge, as perfect as the day it was built. Standard 1½-storey, built off a square plan in coursed quarry-faced stone with smooth dressings to quoins, bipartite mullioned casement windows and projecting door-case. The roof rises as a perfect pyramid covered in Westmoreland green slates to a square chimney-stack and is broken by a contemporary flat-roofed central dormer window. Triple gateway with similarly underplayed ashlar pillars with lanterns and gate ornament continuing the square theme.

North lodge; pre-1836/*c.* 1900.

So-called 'Farm Lodge' is now four-bay single-storey, perhaps extended from standard form towards the road when it was modernised with rendered window surrounds and scalloped bargeboards with fretted trefoil motifs. Blocked-up window to road.

Wilson 1803; d'Alton 1976 [1838]; Griffith 1848–60; Pike and McDowell 1908; *IB* (16 March 1912).

307. ST VINCENT'S CONVENT, Drumcondra; pre-1837/*c.* 1905.

Now St Vincent's Hospital, it was previously a Female Lunatic Asylum run by nuns of the Presentation Order. The present modest lodge is a replacement. Two-storey hip-roofed in red brick, with a later, central, full-height flat-roofed hall projection.

ST VINCENT'S HOME (see NORTH DUBLIN UNION AUXILIARY WORKHOUSE)

308. SANTRY COURT, Santry (5).

Little more than pathetic fragments remain of this once-noble demesne, and nothing of the great Classical brick mansion created in 1703 by the 3rd Lord Barry of Santry and later extended by his son in the mid-eighteenth century. The estate gates and lodges have fared little better. Of these at least three were added after 1850, probably by Sir Charles Compton William Domvile (1822–84), who inherited the property in 1857. His mother, Lady Helena Sarah Domvile, was a gifted amateur designer; she not only published an architectural pattern-book but also was responsible in 1840 for the model village of eleven English Picturesque cottages at Santry village, sadly a thing of the past. Whether she had a hand in any of the lodges is not known. Of the two early porters' lodges the occupants in 1841 and 1848 are recorded as John Dunbar and John Anderson. Both were located off Santry Avenue.

'Glasnevin Gate Lodge'; *c.* 1830.

A plain single-storey standard rendered affair with a hipped roof and clipped eaves. Later hip-roofed extension to the road and a central glazed flat-roofed hall. Occupied.

'Dublin Gate Lodge'; pre-1837; *demolished.*

From the first OS map this appears to have been a sizeable lodge with a central projecting hallway.

The 1906 OS map shows three additional lodged entrances, perhaps by architect Sandham Symes, who in 1863 and

1871–2 prepared gate lodge designs for Sir C.C.W. Domvile.

'Blackwood Gate Lodge'; post-1837; *demolished.*

This would appear to have superseded the old 'Glasnevin Gate Lodge' as a new western approach.

'Dublin Gate Lodge'; post-1837; *demolished.*

Again this seems to have replaced the earlier entrance of the same name. At Santry village on the main road it became the main approach, with an appropriately grand gatescreen presumably relocated from an earlier entrance, for it looks to be mid-eighteenth-century. Surviving is a pair of granite gate pillars in V-jointed rusticated blocks with festooned friezes. These are framed by extensive concave quadrant walls in brick as an appropriate introduction to the big house.

Santry Bridge lodge; post-1837; *demolished.*

Another entrance created on the Swords Road to a new serpentine approach from the north-east.

Eighteenth-century gates were removed from a Santry Avenue entrance in the 1940s and re-erected at the St Brendan's, Grangegorman (*q.v.*), complex for long-term hospital care. A sorry story.

Thom's; Griffith 1848–60; *BPB* (1929); Bence-Jones 1988; Craig and Fewer 2002; Casey 2005; IAA.

309. SANTRY HALL, Santry (2).

A seat in the early nineteenth century of the Martins, both pre-1837 lodges to which have gone. Their porters in 1848 are recorded as Thomas Farquaher and John McGuinness.

Lewis 1837; Griffith 1848–60.

310. SANTRY LODGE, Ballymun; *c.* 1840.

A building that originated as a charter school under the Incorporated Society, in which about 30 children were clothed, maintained and educated in the 1840s under the superintendence of John Dockeray. The gate lodge with short elevation to the approach is single-storey, roughcast and hip-roofed but now surrounded by flat-roofed indiscretions.

Lewis 1837; Griffith 1848–60.

311. SAUCERSTOWN, Swords; pre-1937; *demolished.*

A seat in the nineteenth century of the Lawless family, the lodge to which was built after 1836.

SCHLOSSBERG VILLA (see CASTLEMOUNT VILLA)

312. SCRIBBLESTOWN, Castleknock (3).

A residence in the early nineteenth century of Alexander Holmes which by 1848 was occupied by Christopher Coffey, when the valuation identifies three gate porters, Michael Doyle, James Kelly and Matthew Smith, although only two lodges are obvious on the OS maps.

East lodge; pre-1837; *demolished.*

South lodge; pre-1837/*c.* 1865; architect possibly E.P. Gribbon.

On the site of its predecessor, built for James Vokes Mackey, is this smart mid-Victorian Classical composition. Single-storey standard below a hipped roof with fish-scale slate band, surmounted by a prominent chimney-stack with plinth and moulded capping. In a stucco-effect finish, the round-headed fanlit front door is contained in a gabled projection flanked by a pair of chamfered pilasters with fluted friezes, each supporting a chunky open pediment. The architect Edward P. Gribbon was the neighbour in Scripplestown House (*q.v.*) at this time.

Pigot 1824; Lewis 1837; Griffith 1848–60; *Thom's.*

313. SCRIPPLESTOWN, Castleknock (2).

Neither of the lodges built before 1837 survives, nor does the replacement one at the southern entrance. In 1848 William Rathbone, the proprietor, had gatekeepers in Matthew Coyle and John Whateley. The architect Edward P. Gribbon is recorded as living here in 1856, but four years later was responsible for extensive improvements to the property for the widow of the 1st Baron Clanmorris (1777–1865). This commission may have included the new gate lodge. A place that was later called 'Scribblestown Park', which, like its lodges, has gone, having been consumed by fire in 1976.

Griffith 1848–60; *Thom's*; *BPB* (1929); IAA.

314. SEAFIELD, Clontarf; pre-1837; *demolished.*

A property in 1837 of T. Gresham Esq., which by 1841 had become home to John Allingham, whose gatekeeper in 1848 was Henry Dignam.

Lewis 1837; *Thom's*; Griffith 1848–60.

315. SEAFIELD, Howth; pre-1837; *demolished.*

Later renamed 'Greenfield', in 1837 this was a house of Colonel George Grogan, whose gate porter eleven years later was Michael Farrell.

Lewis 1837; Griffith 1848–60.

316. SEAFIELD, Swords (2).

Two families have been associated with this grand house: the Arthurs, who built it in the Palladian style in the mid-eighteenth century, and the Hely-Hutchinsons, of whom John (1836–1919) purchased it *c.* 1865 and added the extraordinary Italianate campanile wing. Strangely, neither family seems to have seen the value of a fitting lodged entrance.

East gate; pre-1837/*c.* 1855.

Replacing the earlier Arthur lodge opposite the entrance is a single-storey standard hip-roofed affair, facing the park and secreted with its back to the demesne wall in a derelict overgrown state. With cut-stone quoins to the main body of the structure, there is a central gabled hall projection and a flat-roofed extension to the avenue.

West gate; pre-1837/*c.* 1855.

This is either a replacement for, or a reworking of, an earlier lodge on the site, set back from the most modest of entrance screens, its plain roughcast pillars and crude cappings with inelegant ball finials. The ironwork in contrast is good, with chunky palmette motifs. The lodge is a perfectly decent little single-storey standard example with rendered walls, peculiar later window-head features and toothed quoins, below a hipped roof with red-brick chimney-stack having corbelled cappings.

BPB (1929); Bence-Jones 1988.

317. SEAMOUNT, Malahide; *c.* 1905; architect probably F. Batchelor.

The big house was rebuilt after a fire in 1904, when John George Jameson (b. 1855) took the opportunity of adding a gate lodge to the property, presumably also to the design of his architect Frederick Batchelor. This is a remarkable apparition in the Elizabethan Revival Arts and Crafts mode, with its riot of 'black-and-white' work to a generous form. Single-storey raised on a tall plinth, it has a symmetrical three-bay entrance front with a flat-roofed bracketed canopy to the front door. Towering red-brick chimney-stacks rise from a sea of plain red Rosemary tiles covering its high hipped roof, from which, at opposing side elevations, project blind gables. It lies strangely abandoned and overgrown, its multi-paned transomed and mullioned casement windows rotting.

Williams 1994.

318. SEA PARK, Clontarf; pre-1837; *demolished.*
The lodge is survived by a good mid-Georgian gatescreen comprised of four V-jointed rusticated pillars with moulded plinths, sculpted swagged friezes and ball finials on moulded cappings, all contrasting with plain, shallow, concave, roughcast quadrants and contemporary wrought-iron carriage gates. The early OS maps show the lodge to have been a large square building to a property in 1841 of Robert Warren, probably the same as had about then acquired the neighbouring Baymount Castle (*q.v.*). Seven years later, James Logan was gatekeeper to the next proprietor, Judge Louis Perrin.

Thom's; Griffith 1848–60.

319. SEATOWN, Swords; pre-1837; *demolished.*
A lodge built after 1837 to a property which passed from the Balheary family to the McKennas, who were here in the mid-nineteenth century.

D'Alton 1976 [1838]; *Thom's*.

320. SELLA LODGE, Artane; pre-1837; *demolished.*
A property in the early nineteenth century of Martin Curwen.

Lewis 1837.

321. SHAMROCK LODGE, Mulhuddart; pre-1837; *demolished.*
The property, subsequently named 'Hartstown' after the townland, occupied in 1849 by Robert Cooper, whose gatekeeper was Patrick Kerr.

Griffith 1848–60.

SHRUBS COTTAGE (see PRIMROSE CASTLE)

322. SHRUBS, Beaumont; pre-1837; *demolished.*
A seat of William White (1801–57), fifth son of Luke White of Luttrellstown Castle (*q.v.*), also known as 'Shrubs Hill'. White is noted here as early as 1836, his gatekeeper thirteen years later being Thomas Corcoran.

D'Alton 1976 [1838]; Griffith 1848–60; *BPB* (1929).

323. SION HILL, Drumcondra; *c.* 1840; *demolished.*
A gate lodge built sometime between 1837 and 1848, when the proprietor Hugh Boyd's gate porter was Cyrus Metcalf.

Lewis 1837; Griffith 1848–60.

324. SOMERVILLE, Swords; pre-1837; *demolished.*
A small estate in the mid-nineteenth century of John Hartley.

Griffith 1848–60.

325. SOUTH VALE AND WOOLLEN MILLS, Glenmaroon; pre-1837; *demolished.*
A premises in the mid-nineteenth century of Daniel Miller, who in 1846 is listed as a coppersmith and brass-founder. In 1848 his gate lodge was vacant. House and mills had been swept away by 1907.

Slater 1846; Griffith 1848–60.

326. SPRINGFIELD, Phoenix Park; 1874; *demolished.*
A development in 1873 by John O'Brien, who sold the property the following year to Christiana Pierce.

327. SPRING HILL, Balgriffin (2).
On a long and winding lane approach were outer and inner porters' lodges, both extant in 1837, when the proprietor was H. Parsons Esq. They survived for at least another century before their removal.

Lewis 1837.

328. STAPOLIN, Baldoyle (2).
Two pre-1837 lodges to an estate in 1814 of Mrs Dodh which by 1841 had passed to Charles R. Frizell, one of whose gatekeepers in 1848 was Christopher Carpenter. Both have been demolished.

Leet 1814; *Thom's*; Griffith 1848–60.

329. STOCKHOLE, Cloghran; pre-1837; *demolished.*
A seat in 1850 of Jonathan Alley.

Griffith 1848–60.

330. STRAND VILLE, Clontarf; pre-1837; *demolished.*
In 1837 this was a relatively rural villa occupied by William Minchiner, commission agent, on a site which by mid-century was being developed, the house subsequently occupied by a succession of residents and renamed 'Eagle Ville'.

Lewis 1837; Slater 1846; *Thom's*.

SUMMERTON (see AIRFIELD)

331. SUTTON, Howth; *c.* 1895; architect probably Alfred Derbyshire.

A bizarre pile of a house, designed by the Manchester architect Alfred Derbyshire for Andrew Jameson (1855–1940), chairman and managing director of the great distilling firm of John Jameson and Son Ltd from 1905 until his death. Derbyshire's commission doubtless extended to include this striking gatehouse. Commodious and 1½-storey,

originally on an L-plan, from a deep brick band rises an attic storey clad in black-and-white work which continues as coved eaves, broken by hip-roofed bracketed oriel gablets. The hipped roof is covered in red Rosemary tiles with earthenware cresting and a tall red-brick chimney-stack. In the internal angle is a single-storey gabled hall projection with a shouldered arched opening, probably a later addition like an extension to the right-hand side. The rendered ground floor has mullioned tripartite casement windows, one in a quirky rectangular bay window set at 45° across an external corner. Nearby is a contemporary gatescreen, its four square red sandstone pillars having chamfered shafts, reticulated panels, friezes with trefoil motifs and cappings with cusped Gothic motifs below lanterns.

IFR; Williams 1994.

332. SWORDS, Swords; pre-1837/*c.* 1850; *demolished.*
A big house of the Taylor family, a glimpse of which in an old photograph also shows what was a single-storey standard hip-roofed gate lodge, with toothed quoins and tripartite windows on each side of a projecting gabled hall with carved decorative bargeboards over a hood-moulded lancet doorway. Probably a make-over of an earlier lodge carried out for James Joseph Taylor.

Griffith 1848–60; IAA (Photograph S/555/12).

333. SYBIL HILL, Clontarf (2).
Two pre-1837 lost lodges, perhaps contemporary with the 1808 house built for James Barlow to designs of Frederick Darley. John Barlow's gate porters in 1848 were Christopher Meehan and Catherine Flinn. The property was absorbed into the burgeoning estate of St Anne's (*q.v.*) in 1876.

Griffith 1848–60; Bence-Jones 1988.

334. TALAVERA, Baldoyle; pre-1907; *demolished.*
A lodge built after 1837, probably for Captain Norbury K. Furnace.

Thom's.

335. TANKARDVILLE or TANKERVILLE, Balbriggan; *c.* 1840.
A single-storey standard gatekeeper's lodge, built off an almost square plan, with a hipped roof rising to a central chimney-stack. Square sash windows all around in stuccoed walls with toothed stone quoins, and a pretty canted bay window to one end below an equivalent roof of its own. Neat and tidy but now at the entrance to a modern housing development. A property in 1837 of Thomas Swan Croker.
Lewis 1837.

336. THORMANBY LODGE, Howth; *c.* 1880; architect not known.

A chunky late Victorian lodge, single-storey standard but not quite symmetrical, with the segmental arch to its recessed porch almost central between two pairs of narrow round-headed one-over-one sash windows. Distinctive with its red-brick toothed dressings, arches and quoins in grey rendering below a hipped roof, with further brick to eaves band and a sawtooth corbelled chimney-stack. The roof is further enhanced with a scalloped contrasting slate band and the remains of a fleur-de-lis cresting. Recently extended to the rear in like manner in a huge unintegrated addition. Probably built by James Wilson, barrister.

337. THORNDALE, Artane; pre-1837; *demolished.*
A seat of David Henry Sherrard, land agent and secretary to the Street Commissioners, who is recorded here in 1837 and whose gatekeeper seven years later was John Armstrong.
Lewis 1837; Griffith 1848–60.

338. THORNHILL, Clontarf; pre-1835; *demolished.*
A property in 1783 of a Colonel Eustace which by 1837 had been sold to the Guinness family by Hugh O'Reilly and absorbed into the St Anne's estate (*q.v.*). The lodge appears, irregular in outline, on a map by Brassington and Gale of 1835.
Taylor and Skinner 1778; 1969 [1783]; Lewis 1837; Sharkey 2002.

339. THORNTONS, Swords; *c.* 1850.
A single-storey gabled plain and derelict structure with a corrugated asbestos roof and rendered, with a flimsy flat-roofed hallway. A property in 1848 of Joseph Kensey.
Griffith 1848–60.

340. THORNTOWN LODGE, Swords (2).
Despite going under the previous unpropitious name of its townland of 'Dunmucky', this was clearly a house of some importance given the quality of its surviving gate lodge, although the house has gone the way of the other lodge.

North lodge; pre-1836; *demolished.*

South lodge; *c.* 1835; architect possibly Sir Richard and W.V. Morrison.

This was a sophisticated little building, single-storey standard below a hipped roof, with square openings (now windowless) having architraved surrounds set in equivalent recesses in stuccoed walls flanking a pedimented frontispiece with two wooden Doric columns *in antis.* These screen, just like the lodges at Ballindoolin, Co. Kildare (*q.v.*), and Modreeney, Co. Tipperary, a semicircular open porch containing two doors which were the unsocial link between the two main rooms. Perhaps significantly, an identical design for the Baronscourt estate in County Tyrone emanated from the Morrison office but stayed unexecuted. Can this be a lost lodge by Sir Richard Morrison or his son William Vitruvius? If so, it was for the proprietor in 1837, John T. Armstrong. It lies in terminal decline, a hole in the roof where once was the chimney-stack.
Lewis 1837; Dean 1994.

341. TOLKA LODGE, Cabra; pre-1837; *demolished.*
A property in 1849 of Charles Meredith which by 1857 had been renamed 'Broomebridge'.
Griffith 1848–60; *Thom's.*

342. TOLKA LODGE, Finglas; pre-1837; *demolished.*
The residence in 1837 of John W. Bayley.
Lewis 1837.

343. TOLKA PARK, Finglas (2).
A seat in the early nineteenth century of the Savage family. Both pre-1837 lodges have gone, the occupant of one of which in 1848 was Anne McGrath, porter to John E. O'Moore, barrister.
Pigot 1824; Griffith 1848–60.

344. TOLKA VALE AND PAPER MILLS, Tolka; pre-1837; *demolished.*
The house and premises in 1849 of Edward Hanlon.
Griffith 1848–60.

TOWER (see SANTRY LODGE)

TURNERVILLE (see WALSHESTOWN)

345. TURVEY, Donabate (2).
The ancient lost seat of the Barnewalls, Viscounts Kingsland, largely demolished in 1987, neither of the lodged entrances to which have fared better. Rocque's map of 1760 shows a long avenue linking the mansion westwards to the main Dublin road, at which was a pair of lodges or a gatehouse, probably superseded by the later porter's lodge on the Donabate road indicated near the house on the 1837 OS map.
D'Alton 1976 [1838]; Bence-Jones 1988; Ferguson 1998.

TYRONE (see NATIONAL MODEL SCHOOLS)

346. TYRRELSTOWN, Mulhuddart (2).
A property in the early nineteenth century of the Rorke family, both of whose pre-1837 lodges have been removed.

347. UNDER-SECRETARY'S LODGE, Phoenix Park; pre-1803/1803/*c.* 1845.

Originating as a medieval castle which was incorporated into the mid-Georgian villa of 'Ashtown Lodge', to be purchased by the government as a residence of the under-secretary for Ireland. It was recently demolished, to be surprisingly survived by one of the least assuming of gate lodges in the Phoenix Park. Having had a predecessor, it would formerly have been a modest two-roomed cottage, single-storey, roughcast and hip-roofed; its single-bay main short

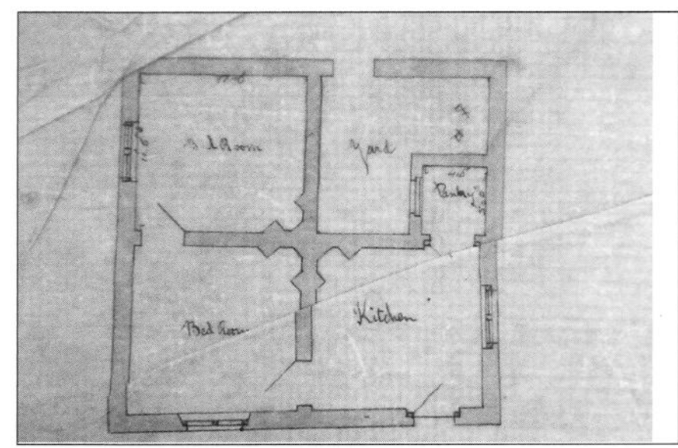

National Archives

elevation now lies forward of its gatescreen, with toothed stone quoins framing a simple casement window vying with a plastic external electricity-meter cupboard. An undated and unsigned drawing survives, seemingly in the hand of Jacob Owen, which proposed the addition of a back return as executed, but also its apparent 'Tudorisation' with gables and label-moulded bipartite lattice-paned casement windows—a transformation not realised. Alongside, cast-iron carriage posts with gadrooned cappings are linked to masonry pillars with raised panel mouldings and the obligatory Park lanterns on tall standards. The first OS map shows this to be a replacement gatescreen. Built during the tenure (1801–6) of Under-Secretary Alexander Marsden. A successor (1846–52), Thomas Nicholas Redington, had as his gatekeeper Philip Hughes. The period 1832–4 saw the removal of stone boundary walls about the demesne, to be replaced by a 'sunk wall and turfed slope' (or ha-ha), as recommended by architect Decimus Burton.

Griffith 1848–60; Reilly 1993; McCullen 2009.

348. UNION LODGE, Fairview; pre-1837; *demolished.*

A residence in 1837 of J. English Esq., which was in 1849 leased by Mrs Anne E. English (probably his widow) to Thomas Drury, whose gatekeeper was James Lunny.

Lewis 1837; Griffith 1848–60.

UNITED STATES AMBASSADOR'S RESIDENCE (see CHIEF SECRETARY'S LODGE)

349. THE VICEREGAL LODGE, Phoenix Park (5).

Áras an Uachtaráin—or the residence of the president of Ireland, as it has been since 1937—has at its core 'Phoenix Lodge', the villa which the Rt Hon. Nathaniel Clements as park ranger, banker, politician, developer and amateur architect designed and built for himself in 1751 and in which he lived until his death in 1777. That very year his son, Robert Clements, later the 1st Lord Leitrim, sold it as a residence for the lord lieutenant, from which time began its evolution towards its present appearance, coming about in stages at the whim of various viceroys. A Bartlett view of the house in 1783 shows what may have been an early lodge in a three-by two-bay single-storey structure with a hipped roof which also served as the right-hand pavilion of the house, to which it was linked by a curved quadrant, and overlooked a gatescreen adjacent to the forecourt. In 1807 Charles Lennox, 4th duke of Richmond (1764–1819), accepted the appointment as lord lieutenant, having only succeeded to the dukedom on the death of his uncle the previous year. On his arrival he wasted little time in commissioning an appropriate grand entrance to the demesne.

Duke's gate; 1808; architect probably John Nash.

The prince regent's eminent architect had been employed by the 3rd duke of Richmond to carry out undefined works at his family seat of Goodwood House, Sussex, just prior to his death, and Nash later furnished his nephew with a design for a villa. That there is an almost identical pair of lodges by Nash, dated 1812, at Caledon House, Co. Tyrone, makes attribution of this less refined forerunning design sound. Each single-storey structure presents to the approach a pedimented single-bay façade in the form of a tripartite window of six-over-six sashes divided by mullion boxes with fluted scrolled brackets to flat heads, all set in an equivalent rectangular recess. A charming contemporary naive drawing by Michael Dowling confirms that this apparently twin pair of lodges is not all it seems. The left-hand 'lodge' was in fact created as a single-roomed dairy, whilst its counterpart was a three-roomed porter's lodge, a bedroom forming its back return and a symmetrical three-bay elevation mirroring its twin across the avenue. Linking them is a tripartite gateway, the postern gates in architraved openings in ashlar screen walls with Greek key-patterned dies to copings, much as on the old main entrance to Marino House (*q.v.*)—was Nash aware of William Chambers's much-admired gateway? The grand rectangular bow-fronted carriage pillars rise from splayed gadrooned or claw feet to be crowned by lanterns. A later addition to the lodge has seen the right-hand postern gate becoming a window and the wall raised to accommodate a date-stone inscribed 'MDCCCVIII'. The gate porter in 1849 was Richard Smith.

Rear gate; *c.* 1803.

Otherwise 'Buggy's Lodge', this is a modest single-storey hip-roofed rendered cottage having an arrowhead end (with a cast-iron latticed casement window), the point of which continues as a screen wall containing a simple postilion gate opening. From the ridge rises a lofty chimney-stack, heightened in search of draw. Its gatekeeper in 1849 is recorded as Susan Abraham.

The Phoenix gate; 1842; architect Decimus Burton.

The young English architect Decimus Burton had endeared himself to the authorities in his recommendation for landscaping the greater park and his designs for the various new

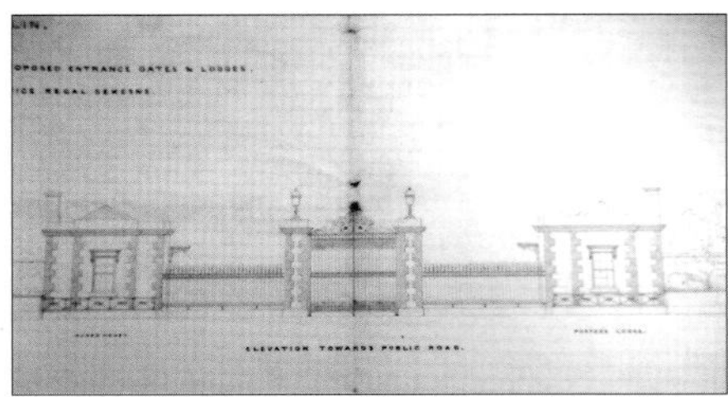

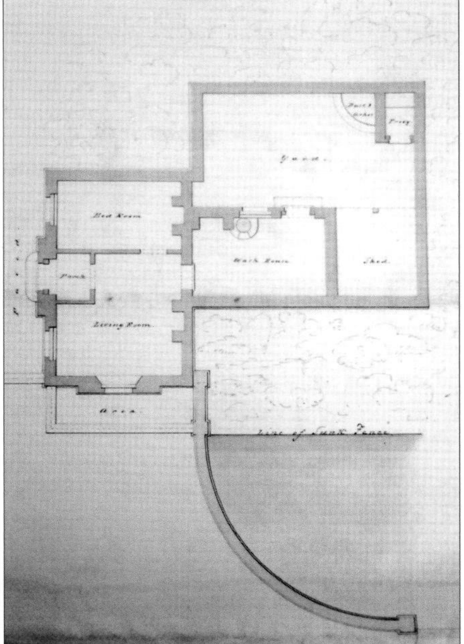

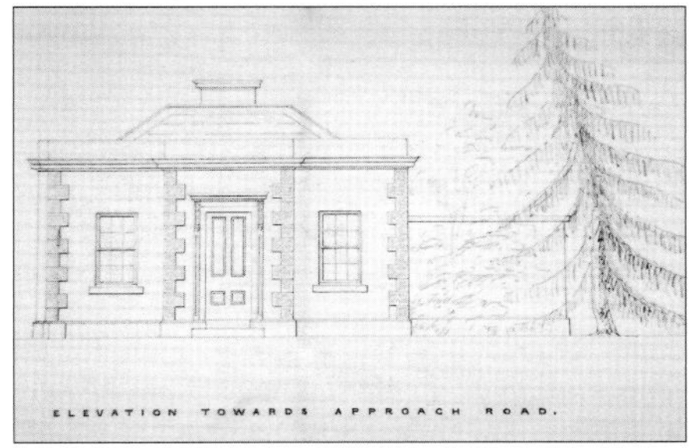

Above—Designs for proposed entrance gates and lodges to Viceregal demesne by Decimus Burton, 1842 (National Archives).

lodges about its perimeter in the 1830s. His drawings for a new entrance to the viceregal demesne are dated 20 June 1842 and were realised, and remain, almost as intended. As a pair of lodges (the left-hand one was in fact a single-roomed 'Guard Room' with 'Sleeping Bench'), each presents a single-storey one-bay front to the visitor, their six-over-six sash windows with bracketed entablatures set in breakfronts. Within, they confront one another below parapeted hipped roofs as three-bay symmetrical ashlar façades, the front doors again in breakfronts with bracketed entablature lintels. Burton had intended that the latter extended to form sheltering canopies. Where he also probably made amendments was in the omission of vermiculation to a plethora of quoin stones to lodges and carriage pillars which rise off moulded plinths to be crowned by pretty cast-iron lanterns. Linking railed screens and ornate carriage gates are as Burton envisaged. All remains in pristine condition, in use as

349. The Viceregal Lodge, Laundry lodge.

the main entrance. The gatekeeper in 1849 was Thomas Guilslenan. Burton's ensemble may have been preceded by a simpler unlodged gatescreen by Francis Johnston, for which an undated drawing shows a pair of octagonal dome-capped carriage pillars flanked by wing walls containing flat-arched postern openings.

Laundry gate; *c.* 1900; architect probably T.J. Mellon or Edward Kavanagh. A surprising and, in its context, incongruous Arts and Crafts 'Stockbroker Tudor' affair. Commodious and 1½-storey, it displays a brick lower storey and plain rosemary earthenware tiling to a vast catsliding roof and apex cladding. Hefty banded chimney-stacks and ornamental ridge ventilator display a surfeit of red clay finish, contrasting dramatically with the half-timbered work of its upper storey and a hideous flat-roofed dormer window (probably not original). To the road front below the catslide roof are a glazed hallway and small-paned curved corner window much like that on the White's gate entrance (*q.v.*) to Phoenix Park. Presumably a design by either T.J. Mellon or Edward Kavanagh, who were principal surveyors to the Office of Public Works around the turn of the twentieth century.

Lewis 1837; Griffith 1848–60; *IB* (15 April 1900); Dean 1994; *IGS Bulletin* (1995); Mansbridge 1991; *IADS* (2002); Casey 2005; Colvin 2008; IAA (Dowling photograph C6/116); NAOPW drawings (13170/03); NLI drawings (AD2121, 2123, 2126, 2127 & 2128); NLI (Bartlett view); McCullen 2009.

350. VICTORIA PARK, Donnycarney; *c.* 1890; *demolished.*
A short-lived lodge to a property in 1890 of Thomas Byrne, agent.

Thom's.

351. VILLA PARK, Cabra; pre-1837; *demolished.*
A small estate in 1850 of John Doyle, whose lodge then lay vacant.

Griffith 1848–60.

352. VIOLET HILL, Tolka; pre-1837; *demolished.*
Patrick Daly was gatekeeper in 1849 to John Robertson, who seems to have altered the name of the place to 'White Hall'.

Griffith 1848–60.

VIOLET HILL (see EDENMORE)

353. WALMER COTTAGE, Raheny; pre-1837; *demolished.*
Home to William Bryan in 1848, when his gate porter was Michael Duggan.

Griffith 1848–60.

354. WALSHESTOWN, Naul; *c.* 1845.
A single-storey standard lodge with oversailing shallow hipped roof and plain soffit brackets. Now roughcast, it has been much abused in 'improvements', with modern windows inserted and its original wide, segmentally arched porch recess, which probably contained a side- and fanlit front door, now disfigured by a new glazed screen. The new gatescreen is in keeping with these alterations. Originally built by the Hon. St John Butler (1808–78), third son of the 13th Baron Dunboyne, who owned the property for much of his adult life.

BPB (1929).

355. WARREN, Sutton; pre-1837.
A property in the mid-nineteenth century of the Piers family of neighbouring Warren Lodge (*q.v.*), by whom it was leased to Andrew Vance in 1848, when his gatekeeper was Patrick Quirk. The lodge is now a two-storey gabled three-bay house with a symmetrical three-bay main front and a central gabled hall projection. The first-floor rooms have gabled peaks to their windows. All in smart painted roughcast, there is a later hip-roofed wing extending from the right-hand side. It is not clear whether this is a replacement structure or whether the original lodge is in there somewhere.

Griffith 1848–60.

356. WARREN LODGE, Sutton; pre-1906; *demolished.*
Edward Piers, solicitor, is recorded here as early as 1846, but the valuation of two years later suggests that his lodge had yet to be built. By 1862 the property had been acquired by John Farley.

Slater 1846; 1856; Griffith 1848–60; *Thom's.*

357. WARRENPOINT, Clontarf; *c.* 1845; architect not known.

A very fine terrace development of six Georgian-style houses, probably built as a speculative venture by the Warren family, who occupied No. 1 for many years. To emphasise the exclusive nature of the project, a fine gatescreen in the Classical manner was added, accompanied, in contrast, by a little lodge with Tudor Revival details, recognising that newfangled fashion. A most attractive design, single-storey and two-bay, below shallow oversailing eaves with pretty carved foiled fascia boards, the windows bipartite round-headed casements embraced by label mouldings in stucco-effect walls. The right-hand bay comprises a verandahed recess as an entrance porch, the doorway tucked into the internal corner, with the roof carried on three slender posts. From the ridge rises a spindly brick chimney-stack, perhaps giving a clue as to the lodge's original finish, for the nearby gatescreen was comprised of a pair of brick-built postilion openings, with segmental arches surmounted by fine Coade stone sphinxes on stone cappings, both of which served as carriage pillars, the right-hand one of which has been unfortunately reduced to a lone pillar. The lodge, of which there is another in similar vein at Highfield, Drumcondra (*q.v.*), has been immaculately restored. It was home in 1849 to Robert Sherwood, leasing from Mrs Christine Margaret Warren, china and glass merchant.

Griffith 1848–60; Slater 1856; Kelly 1990.

358. WELLFIELD COTTAGE, Balgriffin; pre-1837; *demolished.*
A seat of the Hone family which had been removed by 1906, Nathaniel Hone having built his new house of St Doolagh's Park (*q.v.*) nearby and employed his old gate lodge, occupied in 1848 by James Byrne, at his new back entrance.

Thom's; Griffith 1848–60.

WELLFIELD (see ST DOOLAGH'S PARK)

359. WESTMANSTOWN PARK, Leixlip; pre-1837/*c.* 1845.
What originated as a single-storey standard lodge with an oversailing hipped roof and carved soffit brackets has been much modernised, losing much of its character in the process. The footprint has been increased and the roof accordingly, the original chimney-stack losing contact with the new ridge and appearing from a concrete tiled finish. Replacement windows in roughcast

walls and little gabled canopy over the front door. The striking gatescreen escaped improvements unscathed. It is an extensive iron affair, with wide ogee quadrant hoop-topped railings and matching carriage gates hung on ornate pillars with anthemion motifs. An earlier lodge was located at the other side of the entrance, presumably replaced by Henry B. Clarke, who was here in 1849 but by 1851 had moved to Beechpark (*q.v.*), to be followed by Edward M. Keon.

Griffith 1848–60; *Thom's.*

360. WESTOWN, Naul (4).
A historic estate which was in the seventeenth century a property of the Bellew family, from whom it passed by marriage to Peter Hussey, whose descendants lived on here until Richard Hussey died unmarried in the early nineteenth century and Westown was bequeathed to his cousin Gerald Strong, who assumed the Hussey surname. His grandson, Malachi Strong Hussey (1815–80), in 1859 inherited the place and its early lodged entrances, which are clearly shown on the John Rocque map of 1760 and survived at least until the publication of the first OS map in 1837. The eastern entrance seems to have been the grander, for it was marked by a pair of lodges set forward of and linked to the carriage entrance by concave quadrants. To the western approach was a single lodge. M.S. Hussey must have found both outdated, for he replaced them at new locations several yards south of their predecessors.

Main gate; *c.* 1860; *demolished.*
This entrance is testament to how a once-fine estate can deteriorate; like its big house, it is a thing of the past.

Rear gate; *c.* 1865.
Situated out of harm's way is this surprising survivor of the general devastation, complete with gates but leading nowhere. A sizeable single-storey standard mid-Victorian porters' lodge, with an elongated front elevation in roughcast framed by Irish pilaster quoins; modern windows flank a central projecting gabled porch, now glazed in. All the gables sport mutuled verges, with eaves highlighted by prominent carved soffit brackets. The chimney-stack rises off the back wall. The entrance screen is comprised of four good ashlar Classical pillars with bold moulded cornices to cappings and contemporary ironwork to gates and matching straight screens.

Parliamentary Gazetteer; *LGI* (1904).

361. WESTPARK, Glasnevin; pre-1837; *demolished.*
A residence in 1848 of Thomas Haslem,

agent and actuary to the Savings Bank; his gate porter was then Patrick McGurk, whose lodge by 1871 had already gone.

Griffith 1848–60.

362. WHITE HOUSE, Santry; *c.* 1850; *demolished.*
A lodge built between the survey for the first OS map of 1837 and the 1850 valuation, when the proprietor is recorded as James Reilly and whose lodge was unoccupied, perhaps having been recently completed.

Griffith 1848–60.

363. WHITEHALL, Drumcondra; pre-1837; *demolished.*
Originally a seat of the White family, it was let for many years to Charles Sloane, whose lodge in 1849 lay vacant.

Griffith 1848–60.

WHITE HALL (see VIOLET HILL, Tolka)

364. WHITESTOWN, Balbriggan (2).
The development of this estate post-dates the 1837 OS map and was the creation of Hans Hamilton Woods (1814–79), probably in preparation for his wedding in 1840 to Louisa Catherine Taylor of nearby Ardgillan Castle (*q.v.*). He was correct in predicting that he might have a time to wait before inheriting the family seat of Milverton Hall (*q.v.*), for his father lived on there until 1876. There is little doubt that Sandham Symes was his architect, for he had already been employed by his father and there are in any case almost identical porters' lodges to the one here at Lisnabin Castle (*q.v.*) and Ladywell (*q.v.*), both in County Westmeath, where Symes worked. A third in the same county can be attributed to him at the property of H.H. Woods's brother-in-law, Middleton Park (*q.v.*). The feature which is a common denominator to all is the wide recessed panel or 'blind window'.

Main entrance; *c.* 1840; architect probably Sandham Symes.

A single-storey standard harled hip-roofed lodge, distinguished by its pedimented breakfront, tripartite windows with brackets to sills and mullions, and of course blank recessed panels to opposing end elevations. It lies sadly decaying.

Secondary entrance; *c.* 1840.
Unlike its senior counterpart, this basic little rustic lodge is in pristine condition. Without any architectural ornamentation, but no less attractive for that, is this single-storey standard structure with clipped eaves to hipped roof over whitewashed harled walls and three-over-three sash windows, which may be original.

LGI (1904).

365. WILLSBOROUGH, Santry; pre-1760; *demolished.*
An antique seat in 1783 of one Sheppy Esq., which by 1907 was in ruins. The Rocque map of 1760 appears to indicate the gate lodge identified on the first OS map of 1837.

Taylor and Skinner 1778; 1969 [1783]; Ferguson 1998.

366. WINTER LODGE, Balrothery; *c.* 1800; *demolished.*
An early house of the Woods family, from whom descended those at Milverton Hall (*q.v.*) and Whitestown (*q.v.*), which seems to have been on the site of an even earlier one called 'Hayestown' or 'Hestown', in 1783 of Fownes, baronet. In any case, the porter's lodge was late Georgian, dating from the time here of John Woods (1738–1826). Originally a quintessential little rustic single-storey standard structure with a steeply pitched hipped roof. Rubble-built with limewashed harled walls, it had square windows on each side of the front door, sheltered by a flat-roofed porch projection. It was later considerably enlarged by an extra bay to the right-hand side before its demolition. There was an appropriate basic harled entrance with concave quadrant walls.

Taylor and Skinner 1778; 1969 [1783]; *LGI* (1904); Ferguson 1998.

367. WOODFORD, Santry (2).
A property in 1837 of F.W. Edwards, then only with the eastern lodge, by whose family it was let in 1848 to Daniel F. Beere, whose gatekeepers were then George Keating and Patrick Barry. By 1907 the western lodge had been removed, to be followed by the other later in the century.

Lewis 1837; Griffith 1848–60.

374. Zoological Gardens, Phoenix Park.

WOODLANDS (see LUTTRELLSTOWN CASTLE)

368. WOODLANDS, Santry; *c.* 1830.
Originating as the important early Georgian house called 'Clinshogh', built by Revd Dean John Jackson, whose friend Dean Swift was a visitor here. Neither would have known a porter's lodge here, as what survives is from a century later than the house and was probably built by the proprietor in 1837, Colonel A. Thompson, CB. This is a modest single-storey standard cottage with stucco-effect walls, with modern windows below a hipped roof with clipped eaves. Although plain, it is given prominence by facing the road, flanked by low, shallow, convex wing walls, with the entrance to the right-hand side. By 1848 Michael Mahony was gate porter to a new owner, Charles S. Archer.

Lewis 1837; Griffith 1848–60; Bence-Jones 1988.

369. WOODLAWN, Santry; pre-1837; *demolished.*
An estate in the early nineteenth century of the Logan family.

370. WOODVILLE, Artane; pre-1837; *demolished.*
A property in 1837 of John Cornwall, land agent.

Lewis 1837; Slater 1846.

371. WOODVILLE, Killester; pre-1837; *demolished.*
The residence in 1848 of Lt-General Alexander Armstrong, whose gatekeeper was Christopher Ward.

Griffith 1848–60.

372. WOODVILLE LODGE, Blanchardstown; pre-1837; *demolished.*
This was home to Edmund Grehan in 1849; the lodge had gone by 1938.

Griffith 1848–60.

373. WYANSTOWN, Oldtown; pre-1837; *demolished.*
An old seat, in 1837 of Richard Rooney.

Lewis 1837.

YEW PARK (see ELM VIEW)

374. ZOOLOGICAL GARDENS, Phoenix Park; 1833; architect W.D. Butler.
A 30-acre site in the Phoenix Park was given over in 1830 by the 3rd duke of Northumberland, as lord lieutenant, to the Dublin Zoological Society. They commissioned Decimus Burton to produce a report and plans, which he submitted in 1832 as proposals for the new Zoological Gardens. How closely the Society followed his recommendations is not clear, as his plans are lost, or whether he furnished a design for the gatekeeper's lodge which has been popularly attributed to him. It is in fact by William Deane Butler, a council member of the Society. This is a delightful *cottage orné* which lies a redundant curiosity but beautifully restored in 1971 and since maintained as the first exhibit in its own railed enclosure as an alien introduction. Single-storey on a T-plan in striking black-and-white work with rustic timbers under a heavy thatched roof, which undulates organically over the gables to form eyebrows and bows over the doorway to form a porch supported on tree trunks. In the opposing front is a rectangular tripartite oriel window

with latticed glazing pattern. The chimney-stack offers no competition, barely breaking the ridge.

Dublin Penny Journal (29 Aug. 1835); Reilly 1993; *IGS Bulletin* (1995); Casey 2005.

COUNTY DUBLIN (SOUTH)

1. ABBEYLANDS, Ballybrack; *c.* 1880.
A development of about 1870, as was much else in the region of Killiney, of stockbroker Joshua D. Chaytor, here apparently originating as a semi-detached pair of houses. Its gate lodge was added after 1871 as a rustic granite-faced single-storey cottage, its shallow main gables and that to the pretty porch with its scalloped slates having perforated geometric carved bargeboards and delicate hip-knobs. Lately developed into a double pile with a 1½-storey addition to the rear. Boulder-topped quarry-faced granite carriage pillars.

Thom's; Pearson 1998.

2. ABBEY VIEW, Dalkey; pre-1871; *demolished.*
Both the house, where Thomas Steele is recorded as occupant in 1851, and its lodge post-date 1837.

Thom's.

3. ABBEY VIEW, Kill of the Grange (2).
Both lodges have been removed, that to the south the earlier, built between 1814 and 1837. A property in the mid-nineteenth century of Charles Butler, whose gatekeeper in 1849 was Patrick Halpin.

NLI/Longfield; Griffith 1848–60.

4. ABBEY VILLE, Rathfarnham; pre-1837; *demolished.*
Eventually absorbed into the neighbouring Loreto Convent (see Palliser's Park) complex, this modest property was the residence of Augustine Holland in 1849, when his porter's lodge lay vacant.

Griffith 1848–60.

5. ABILENE, Galloping Green; pre-1837/*c.* 1880.

Thomas Dixon was proprietor here in 1837 and also of the adjoining house of Maestwyllydd (*q.v.*) to the north, even though his lodge was shared by Eversham (*q.v.*) to the south, being flanked by the two gatescreens. In 1849 Dixon was still in residence but the lodge lay vacant. Townley W. Hardman occupied Abilene by 1870 and must have been responsible for the surviving lodge, detached from the Eversham lodge replacement. Quaint and single-storey on an L-plan, located outside its gates, mildly Italianate with its shallow pitched roof and the suspicion of an open pediment to the park gable, it nevertheless has contradictory perforated Picturesque bargeboards to the road front. It has suffered in modernisation, with smooth rendering and shuttered plastic leading window. The peculiar gate pillars would seem to remain as contemporary with the original lodge, being slender round posts with ill-fitting granite gadrooned square caps. The chunky decorative gates are later.

Lewis 1837; Griffith 1848–60; *Thom's.*

6. ADELAIDE CONVALESCENT HOME, Rathfarnham; *c.* 1905; architect probably George P. Beater.

Built in the old grounds of 'Newtown Cottage' from the bequest of a Miss Fetherston-Haugh as a convalescent home of the Adelaide Hospital. Its architect in 1893 was George Palmer Beater, whose institution is an exercise in polychromatic brickwork and red terracotta in the Flemish manner. Beater was retained into the twentieth century as architect to the Adelaide Hospital, so, although documentary evidence is lacking, it was probably he who was displaying his eclecticism in this later gatekeeper's lodge. It is a fine Arts and Crafts composition in red English garden wall bond brickwork on an irregular plan. A 'canted' theme permeates the design in the carved perforated bargeboard overlays, roof slate bands and the apex tile-hanging which projects on decorative corbelled brick specials. Little expense has been spared on the bellcast roof and the joinery of gable brackets and beautifully turned posts to the little hip-roofed entrance porch in an internal angle. Plain modern wooden casement windows may have replaced leaded lights. There is an extensive ornate iron gatescreen of an age, to what is now a Theological College of the Church of Ireland.

Pike and McDowell 1908; Williams 1994.

7. ADELAIDE, Merrion; pre-1837; *demolished.*
A seat in 1841 of Henry Goodisson which seven years later was home to Thomas Johnston, whose gatekeeper was Stephen Cleary.

Thom's; Griffith 1848–60.

8. AGHDERRIG FARM, Lucan; *c.* 1840.
An ivy-covered shell of stone rubble, the remains of a lodge built perhaps for John Rourke, who was resident in the mid-nineteenth century.

Griffith 1848–60.

9. AILESBURY, Merrion; *c.* 1865; architect probably John McCurdy.

An excellent Italianate-style lodge of a type common in the south Dublin suburbs, so akin to those at Newtownpark (*q.v.*) and Craigmore (*q.v.*) as to make attribution to architect John McCurdy safe. Built along with the big villa for Timothy O'Brien, a baker and corn merchant. Originally single-storey three-bay standard, it was later extended by a bay to the right-hand side in like manner. The walls in stucco-effect rendering have highlights in Irish pilaster quoins and moulded surrounds to segmentally arched openings with two-over-two sashes and a fanlit double-leafed panelled door; the latter is set in a gabled hall projection with an open pediment having carved modillion brackets which continue boldly about the soffit of its shallow-pitched hipped roof, from which rises a stout chimney-stack with plinth and moulded cornice capping. Immaculately maintained as entrance to what is now the Spanish Embassy. The contemporary gatescreen has hefty granite pillars with simple incised panels, moulded cappings and chunky cast-iron gates and railings of the period.

Slater 1856; *Thom's.*

10. AIRFIELD, Donnybrook; *c.* 1810.
A much-modernised gate porter's cottage with a two-bay elevation to the avenue below a hipped roof now containing attic accommodation. Modern windows in crisply rendered walls hidden behind the left-hand of two tall screen walls in stucco-effect rendering, relieved by moulded surround plaques which tell us nothing, unlike those to St Ann's (*q.v.*) down the road. These are flanked by four good V-jointed rusticated granite pillars with fluted friezes. A property in 1837 of Charles Hogan, who by 1841 was letting it to Leathum Blacker, whose gatekeeper eight years later was William Black.

Lewis 1837; *Thom's*; Griffith 1848–60.

11. AIRFIELD, Drummartin; pre-1837/*c.* 1900.

To a property which changed hands often in the nineteenth century is this lodge reflecting just that, in appearance a late Victorian Arts and Crafts cottage which evolved over the years. Single-storey, it may incorporate, in that portion next to the road, the early standard three-bay gabled structure. Now much elongated, with a varied roofscape of red Rosemary tiles and earthenware perforated ridge tiles to catslides, gables and mono-pitched gablets having exposed rafter toes and a criss-cross wooden feature in the gabled door canopy. This transformation was probably carried out for Trevor Overend, a Dublin solicitor who purchased the property and its old eighteenth-century farmhouse in 1894. The early gatescreen of *c.* 1835 survives, with its six gadroon-capped granite pillars containing a pair of postern openings with rudimentary pediments over, flanked by short railed quadrants probably erected by the Palmer family.

Pearson 1998.

AIRFIELD (see RATHCREEDAN)

12. AIR HILL, Loughlinstown; pre-1837; *demolished.*
Later renamed 'Kilbrae', this was a seat in 1837 of one W. Hall. By 1849 it had been acquired by Edward Kennedy, whose gate porter was James Brady.

Lewis 1837; Griffith 1848–60.

13. AIRLAWN, Terenure; pre-1837; *demolished.*
A small estate in 1849 of Patrick Regan, whose lodge then lay empty. A property now called 'Triffan'.

Griffith 1848–60.

14. AIRLIE, Lucan; *c.* 1880.
Pretty single-storey standard with oversailing eaves and verges and a chimney-stack to each gable; two-over-two sash windows in rendered walls, and half-timbered-effect feature to the apex of the projecting hall. A farm in the late nineteenth century of Patrick Barr.

Thom's.

15. AIRPARK, Woodtown; pre-1837; *demolished.*
In 1849 the lodge was occupied by Patrick Whelan, gatekeeper to Mrs Catherine Delany, presumably the widow of the proprietor in 1837, John Delany. The pleasant mid-eighteenth-century villa was removed recently to make way for a motorway. The pleasant spear-topped gates and plain granite carriage pillars are contemporary with the house.

Lewis 1837; Griffith 1848–60; Pearson 2002.

16. ALBANY COTTAGE, Rathgar; pre-1837; *demolished.*
A suburban villa in 1841 of Arthur Greene, whose gate porter seven years later was Patrick Reilly. By 1907, although it was still standing, its frontage to Rathgar Road was built up and the lodge consequently removed.

Thom's; Griffith 1848–60.

17. ALBANY LODGE, Templeogue; pre-1837; *demolished.*
A residence in 1850 of William Henry Ellis, barrister, who had moved here from Ashfield, Rathfarnham (*q.v.*).

Griffith 1848–60.

ALBERTA (see CYPRESS GROVE)

ALDBOROUGH (see PROBY PARK)

ALMA (see SEAFIELD)

18. ALTADORE, Glenageary; pre-1837; *demolished.*
A fine villa designed by Sandham Symes in 1844 for wine merchant John Aylmer and which replaced a house with a much greater footprint on the site. Succeeding OS maps suggest that the lodge, removed to make way for modern housing on the frontage, was itself a replacement. Aylmer's gatekeeper in 1849 was James O'Donnell. Peter Pearson records that the old granite gate pillars were surmounted by cast-iron stags with antlers, presumably the crest of a later owner.

Griffith 1848–60; Williams 1994; Pearson 1998.

ALTAMORE (see CASTLEDAWSON)

19. ALTON GRANGE, Foxrock; *c.* 1904; architect not known.
An impressive late Victorian 'Stockbroker Tudor' house built for Sir John G. Barton, commissioner of valuation. At the gate on a butterfly plan is this single-storey gabled chip off the main block, quite symmetrical in roughcast with black-and-white work to the

apexes and steel multi-paned casement windows. Across the internal angle is the entrance hall, the front door below a bracketed gabled canopy, whilst to the ridge are diagonally set brick chimney-stacks in Elizabethan Revival style. Very attractive, occupied and well tended.

Thom's.

20. ALTONA, Galloping Green; pre-1907; *demolished.*
A lodge built after 1871 for the McCrea family.

Thom's.

21. ANGLESEY, Rochestown; pre-1837; *demolished.*
John Thomas Papworth in 1929 exhibited a perspective view of a design for 'Anglesey, the seat of F.C. Parker', probably of plans by his father George, whom he had just joined as assistant. By 1851 the house was occupied by William E. Hughes, who then had as his gate porter James Byrne.

Griffith 1848–60; IAA.

22. ANNAGHANOON, Killiney; *c.* 1870; architect probably T.N. Deane; *demolished.*
A big Jacobean-style house built *c.* 1869 for William Allen Exham QC (1820–81), almost certainly to designs of Thomas Newenham Deane, which he very soon after renamed 'Court-na-Farraga'. Sadly, 'the red brick gate-house' has been removed but the house lives on as the 'Court Hotel'.

Thom's; O'Dwyer 1997b.

23. ANN MOUNT, Drummartin; pre-1837.
Still standing is this single-storey standard rendered lodge with a steeply hipped roof, visible despite the later surrounding flat-roofed additions which frustrate dating of the original. The property may have been named after Mrs Ann O'Connor, who is recorded here in the mid-nineteenth century, in 1849 taking in lodgers and with Patrick Byrne as her gatekeeper.

Griffith 1848–60; *Thom's.*

24. ANNA FIELD, Dundrum; pre-1837; *demolished.*
A property in 1850 of Anne Hayes, whose gate porter was John McDonnell; it was later raised to the grandeur of 'Manor House', probably by Bartholomew Clifford QC around 1862, when the house was dramatically enlarged.
Griffith 1848–60; *Thom's.*

25. ANNA VILLA, Windy Arbour; pre-1837; *demolished.*
This was home from as early as 1822 for about 30 years to silk and poplin manufacturer Sir George Whiteford, as he became after serving as lord mayor of Dublin in 1833–4. In 1849 his gate lodge lay vacant.
Griffith 1848–60; Ball and Hamilton 1895; Pearson 1998.

ANNEFIELD (see ST ANN'S)

ANNEMOUNT (see MOUNT ALTON)

26. ANON, Dundrum; pre-1837; *demolished.*
A property, which included a laundry, was let in 1850 by George Meyler of nearby Laurel Lodge (*q.v.*) to engineer William T. Mulvany before he moved on to the neighbouring Dundrum Lodge (*q.v.*). The porter was then Lawrence Flanagan, at an entrance from the Churchtown Road junction which gave onto a long avenue running south to the house parallel to Main Street.
Griffith 1848–60.

ARBOURFIELD (see WINDY ARBOUR)

27. ARBUTH, Rathmines; *c.* 1845; *demolished.*
Richard Gibson in 1850 was gate porter to Rodolphus Burke, whose villa is one of many on the eastern side of Rathmines Road to have been swept away by later development.
Griffith 1848–60.

ARCHBISHOP RYAN PARK (see MERRION SQUARE GARDENS)

28. ARDAVON, Rathgar; pre-1869; *demolished.*
A house that appears in the directories around 1850 on the creation of the Orwell Road extension south of the Dodder River, linking Rathgar and Churchtown. Built by solicitor Joseph Hanley when it was initially spelt 'Aardeven', it had a lodge shown to be substantial and was presumably contemporary.
Thom's.

29. ARD BRUGH, Dalkey (2).
A property created after 1871 with the development of the Ardbrough and Cunningham roads by A. O'Neill JP.
North gate; *c.* 1880; *demolished.*
South gate; *c.* 1880.
A late Victorian interpretation of the Tudor Picturesque is this single-storey symmetrical three-bay lodge. Gabled with plain bargeboards rising to turned hip-knobs stopping trefoil-perforated earthenware cresting. Rendered, with wide multi-paned

transomed and mullioned casement windows below label mouldings with pendant dripstones. There is a heraldic shield to the leading road gable rather than that to the central hall projection, which has a side entrance with a discordant modern glazed door; fish-scale slate bands to the roof and a central banded chimney-stack. The flat-roofed extensions to each end are not too intrusive. Pretty, decorative Gothic cast-iron gates and carriage posts sandwiched between brutal quarry-faced stone pillars.
Thom's.

ARDGLAS (see FARMLEY)

ARDILAUN (see BRAY COTTAGE)

ARDILEA (see ROEBUCK COTTAGE)

ARDLUI (see MAESGWYLLYDD)

ARDMEEN (see NEWTONPARK COTTAGE)

ARDMORE (see BELLVIEW LODGE)

ARDNABEL (see FARRANBOLEY COTTAGE)

30. ARDNAGRENA, Rathgar; *c.* 1880; *demolished.*
A late Victorian development which by 1890 was a girls' school.
Thom's.

ARDTONA (see LYNDHURST)

31. ARDVARNA, Shanganagh; *c.* 1894; architect probably C.H. Townsend.
A house designed for F.W. Meredith, solicitor for oaths, by the English architect Charles Harrison Townsend in 1894. Its commodious gate lodge was probably part of that commission. Much modernised and extended, it was an Arts and Crafts design, 1½-storey with a hipped roof and a catslide, with hipped gablets, built off an L-plan. Roughcast, with inappropriate replacement windows and a red clay-tiled roof. Now a property, 'Cloneybrien', in its own right.
Thom's; Williams 1994.

32. ARNOLD VILLE, Monkstown (2).
Both lodges, built before 1837, were at the entrance to a property of the Newcomen family in 1849, when one lay vacant and the other was staffed by Malachy Byrne. Neither survives; the big house was removed in 1977.
Griffith 1848–60.

ASHFIELD (see PRIESTHOUSE [2])

33. ASHFIELD, Rathfarnham (2).
Two lost lodges to a Georgian house, originally a clergy property, which was owned in the early nineteenth century by Sir William Cusack Smith (1766–1836), baron of the court of exchequer in Ireland from 1801 until his death. The lodges may have been built by him, but by 1849 Michael Collins was one porter to William Denis Tottenham, who lived here until 1869.
Griffith 1848–60; *LGI* (1904); *BPB* (1929); Bence-Jones 1988.

34. ASHFIELD, Rathmines; pre-1837; *demolished.*
Home in 1841 to Revd James Read, by 1907 its lodge had gone, to give way to redevelopment.
Thom's.

35. ASHGROVE, Kill of the Grange; pre-1837; *demolished.*
A seat in 1837 of J. Murphy Esq., which had passed to George Williamson by 1849, when the lodge lay unoccupied.
Lewis 1837; Griffith 1848–60.

36. ASHGROVE, Rathmines; pre-1837; *demolished.*
George Watson, clerk in the court of exchequer, was here in 1837 and thirteen years later, when his porter's lodge was vacant. By 1907 its site had been built over.
Lewis 1837; Griffith 1848–60.

37. ASHGROVE LODGE, Glenageary; *c.* 1860.
Remarkably, the house, which was demolished in 1986 to make way for a church, is survived by its gate lodge. Standard single-storey, with modern window and door inserted in rubble walls below a hipped roof. The proprietor in the mid-nineteenth century was John Sullivan.
Thom's; Pearson 1998.

38. ASHTON PARK, Monkstown; pre-1837/*c.* 1877; architects possibly Millar and Symes; *demolished.*
A mid-eighteenth-century house, in 1797 residence to Robert Ashworth, which, like its lodge, has gone, although the latter was probably replaced about 1877, when architects Millar and Symes are recorded as providing a complete new complex of villa, stables, offices and gate lodge for John Hone. In the interim the property belonged to Andrew Thunder, whose gatekeeper in the old lodge was Edward Murphy.
Lewis 1837; Griffith 1848–60; Pearson 1998; Glin *et al.* 1988; IAA.

ASHURST (see MOUNT MERRION [1])

39. ASHURST, Killiney; *c.* 1863; architects Lanyon and Lynn.
A great High Victorian pile in orange brick designed in 1860 by William Henry Lynn of the Belfast practice of Lanyon and Lynn for the Hon. William Carey Dobbs (1806–69) of Castle Dobbs, Co. Antrim, judge of the landed

estate court. Whilst the big house is severe and institutional in feel, its little gate lodge is a delightful caprice, in polychromatic brickwork like the big house but with cream highlights in verge and eaves corbels, quoins, Gothic arch voussoirs, string-course and a diaper feature. Single-storey and built off an L-plan with very steeply pitched gables, that to the road containing a large window with a segmental pointed arch. The avenue gable is taken up with a canted bay window with equivalent roof over, whilst advancing alongside is a little gabled hallway with a stone diagonal buttress. On the ridge is a big chimney-stack with the same theme. Lynn designed lodges in a similar vein at Mount Temple, north Dublin (*q.v.*), and a stone version at Cahir Abbey, Co. Tipperary.

DB (1 Dec. 1860, 15 Feb. 1861 and 15 Jan. 1863); *LGI* (1904).

THE ASKE (see OAKLAWN)

40. ASKE COTTAGE, Little Bray; *c.* 1845.
A pleasant, modest harled cottage, which probably was once even more so, originating as a single-storey standard structure built by James Cahill, whose gatekeeper in 1849 was William Brien. The property was alternatively known as 'Crinken Cottage' but about 1865 became 'St James Parsonage', which was probably when a steeply gabled attic floor was added to the lodge, raised off the old stone eaves band, and the previous small-paned casement windows were heightened when Revd John Winthrop Hackett (1804–88) arrived from Lordello (*q.v.*), he having been the incumbent of St James, Crinken (1840–83). Occupied.

Lewis 1837; Griffith 1848–60; *Thom's*; Leslie and Wallace 2001.

41. ATHGOE PARK, Rathcoole; pre-1837; *demolished.*
A mid-eighteenth-century house of the Locke family, who doubtless built the lodge, their connection with the property ending with the death of Peter Warren Locke in 1833.

Bence-Jones 1988; Craig and Fewer 2002.

42. AUBRAY, Shankill; *c.* 1862/*c.* 1890
An Italianate villa built about 1862 for John J.W. Quin of the neighbouring family of Claremont (*q.v.*) by the eminent contractor Gilbert Cockburn. The valuation book of that time records a gate lodge but, for whatever reason, this was deleted *c.* 1877. Certainly what survives, opposite the gates, looks to date from the end of the century, by which time Aubray had become home to Captain Robert Lefroy (1834–1907) of the 97th Regiment. In a style to reflect the house, this is a single-storey standard lodge below a hipped roof with a bold eaves band of corbels carried about the tympanum of an open pediment to the central hall projection, which contains the doorway with a round-arched fanlight. The main front is in facing brickwork with inappropriate modern door, windows and louvre shutters.

Thom's; *IFR*; IAA.

43. AUBURN VILLA, Rathgar; pre-1849; *demolished.*
A lodge identified by the Griffith valuation though not obvious on any of the OS maps or on site, assumed removed. In 1849 the lodge was leased to Michael Tracey by John Houston and the house to Sarah Hardman, who ran a 'ladies seminary'.

Griffith 1848–60; *Thom's.*

44. AUGHNACLOY, Ballybrack; *c.* 1875; architect possibly A.G. Jones.

A dapper Italianate-style lodge, of which there is an identical example at Inveruish (*q.v.*) next door and one similar at Williams Park (*q.v.*) nearby, all three properties on Seafield Road, a development by William Field, grocer of Ballybrack, probably in association with architect Alfred Gresham Jones. A single-storey standard hip-roofed structure with a gabled hall projection containing a semicircular-arched fanlit doorway in a recessed surround, as are the segmentally headed two-over-two sash windows. The rendered walls have Doric pilasters to the main external corners and to the ridge is a central chimney-stack with a Classically corniced capping and plinth. The first owner was Captain H. Hewetson (later Major in 1890). There are also like lodges to Lordello (*q.v.*) and St. Columba's (*q.v.*).

Thom's; Pearson 1998.

45. AVONDALE, Rochestown; pre-1837; *demolished.*
A property in 1837 of C. Hughes Esq., let in 1848 by his widow, Charity, to Charles Sohan, whose gate porter was Thomas Redmond.

Lewis 1837; Griffith 1848–60.

46. AVONMORE, Foxrock; *c.* 1870; *demolished.*
A victim of road-widening was this delightful single-storey standard hip-roofed lodge with two-over-two casements, in stucco-effect rendered walls, on each side of a panelled doorway within a charming hip-roofed porch carried by octagonal posts from

Sylvia Dockeray

which sprouted abundant curved bracket supports. Alongside was a beautifully ornate fretwork external doorway in a screen wall. Thomas W. Adams in 1870 occupied Avonmore, which was renamed 'Lisballaly' in the twentieth century.

Thom's.

AYESHA CASTLE (see VICTORIA CASTLE)

47. BADGER HILL, Rathcoole; pre-1937; *demolished.*
A lodge built sometime after 1837, opposite its entrance, by the Morgan family.

48. BAGGOTRATH, Sandymount; *c.* 1870; architect not known; *demolished.*

This was a very fine mid-Victorian lodge with much sophisticated Classical detailing. Single-storey standard below a shallow hipped roof which oversailed on three sides, supported by six cast-iron posts to form a charming verandah. One-over-one sash windows and doorway in rendered walls had moulded surrounds with ornamental entablatures carried on acanthus-leafed console brackets with decorative floral motifs to friezes. The three main façades were framed by pilasters with more acanthus leaves as capitals. Sadly unprotected, it was eventually squeezed out by greedy modern development. Although Baggotrath first appears in the directory of 1856 as home to William Graham, the lodge appears more likely to date from the time here of Richard Sawyer, gold and silver manufacturer in the city.

Slater 1856; *Thom's.*

49. No. 73 BAGGOT STREET LOWER; *c.* 1800; architect not known.

Irish Architectural Archive

Just across Herbert Place from the Grand Canal was an uncommon end-of-terrace garden entered via a rare urban lodged gate in the shape of a day-and-night lodge—a room on each side of a segmentally arched carriage opening and linked by a busy parapet of dies and a central debased pediment with anthemion acroteria. In contrast with the three-storey brick house it was finished in rendering, each bay defined by plain pilasters with overpanels displaying laurel wreaths. Over the three segmental arches are ornamental carved spandrels. Latterly, the right-hand window and carriage opening have been blocked up. All contained behind a low wrought-iron screen of spear-topped railings and gate.

IAA photo (53/10Z1).

50. BALDONNELL, Baldonnell; 1909.
Philip Grierson, after occupying an older house in the townland, in 1869 built himself a new one on a virgin site in an eccentric newfangled High Victorian Gothic manner, probably to designs of Thomas Newenham Deane. Approached by a ramrod-straight avenue, which was not supplemented with a porter's lodge until much later, in the time here of Revd Dean Dickinson. Already this is in a woebegone state, being dilapidated and ivy-covered with some corrugated iron to the roof. Rather less imaginative than the house, it is in a tame Elizabethan Revival style. Single-storey on an L-plan, rendered with mock half-timbered work to gables and mildly ornamental bargeboard toes. The date of construction is displayed on the avenue gable and a big banded chimney-stack rises from the remains of the roof.

Thom's; O'Dwyer 1997b.

51. BALGADDY, Clondalkin; pre-1837; *demolished.*
A seat in the mid-nineteenth century of William Masterson.

Griffith 1848–60.

BALLAWLEY PARK (see BELLEWLEY PARK)

BALLINACOR (see BALLYBRACK LODGE)

52. BALLINCLEA, Cabinteely (2).
A good late Georgian villa of the Talbots of Malahide Castle (*q.v.*), removed in the 1950s, to which one gatekeeper's lodge survives.

South lodge; pre-1837/*c.* 1860.
An early lodge at the gate was replaced on

the same site probably by the Hon. Richard Gilbert Talbot (1810–79), who succeeded to Ballinclea after the death in 1855 of his aunt, whose stepdaughter he had married in 1847. It is an asymmetrical 1½-storey gabled cottage in smooth rendering with plain modern wavy bargeboards and delicate turned hip-knobs. Six-over-six sash windows survive to the attic storey with some label mouldings. The full-height projecting gabled hall advances further as a later single-storey addition below a label moulding to the original front door. To the right-hand side is a glazed canted bay window with equivalent roof. Occupied. There is a fine and extensive fleur-de-lis-topped gatescreen with Classical carriage pillars having recessed moulded panels. Architect Sandham Symes is thought to have carried out work at Ballinclea. In 1849 the gate porter of the Hon. Eliza Lyster Kaye (née Talbot) was William Lyons.

North lodge; pre-1837; *demolished.*
This entrance originally served the neighbouring property of Plasnewydd (*q.v.*) but between 1871 and 1907 the avenue was diverted towards Ballinclea.

Lewis 1837; Griffith 1848–60; *BPB* (1929); Pearson 1998.

53. BALLINTEER COTTAGE [1], Ballinteer; pre-1837; *demolished.*
A property in 1849 of a Mrs Keane which by 1870 had been upgraded to 'Ballinteer Villa'.

Griffith 1848–60; *Thom's.*

54. BALLINTEER COTTAGE [2], Ballinteer; pre-1869; *demolished.*
A lodge probably built after the estate passed from farmer Matthew Ennis about 1855 to the Gillespie family.

Griffith 1848–60; *Thom's.*

55. BALLINTEER HALL, Ballinteer; pre-1837/*c.* 1907; architect possibly J.H. Webb.
There would seem to have been a gate lodge here as early as 1760, although the surviving gatescreen is late Georgian, in the shape of a pair of plain granite carriage pillars with fluted friezes, a feature repeated in the lintels over the flanking postern openings. 'Ballintyre Hall', as it became known, was for much of the mid-nineteenth century home to the Hon. Mrs Townsend, after which until 1891 it was the residence of Sir Edward Grogan. Arthur Vesey Fitzherbert (1845–1926) of Black Castle, Co. Meath (*q.v.*), had settled as a young man in Uruguay but returned to see out his days in Ireland, purchasing Ballintyre Hall *c.* 1907, when he commissioned architect J.H. Webb to carry out 'large and extensive alterations'. This work may have included the surviving lodge. Standard 1½-storey gabled in rubble facings with brick dressings to wide windows on each side of a gabled open porch. To the eaves is a rendered band, the gables having ornamental bargeboards with quatrefoil perforations. Abandoned and blocked up, awaiting redevelopment.

Thom's; Ball and Hamilton 1895; *IB* (16 Nov. 1907); *IFR*; Ferguson 1998.

BALLINTYRE HALL (see BALLINTEER HALL)

56. BALLYBODEN RESERVOIR, Ballyboden; *c.* 1880; *demolished.*

57. BALLYBRACK GROVE, Ballybrack (2).
A property acquired *c.* 1857 from Japhet Alley by James West, who Gothicised the house and gave it two gate lodges. Alas, nothing of them survives. Before its demise it was renamed 'Shanganagh Grove'.

Thom's.

58. BALLYBRACK, Ballybrack; *c.* 1845.

A seven-headed hydra, perhaps belonging to the Du Bedat family (Fairbairn 1986, 38/5).

Crammed in behind the right-hand entrance quadrant is a fascinating little Tudor-style lodge, its single-bay main gabled front having a skew-table and minimal kneelers over a wide label-moulded opening which now contains an unfortunate modern pair of glazed French windows flanked by original cast-iron latticed sidelights, all set in crude roughcast walls. Probably built by barrister Alderman Charles Palmer Archer. Quite whose the crest is in the gable is not clear but it looks to have been inserted later. It appears to be a seven-headed hydra, perhaps belonging to the Du Bedat family, of whom William George, stockbroker, lived here from *c.* 1860 to 1884. The chamfered granite carriage pillars have been moved back from the road's edge to effectively hem in the lodge.

Thom's.

59. BALLYBRACK LODGE, Ballybrack; *c.* 1845; architect not known.

A perfectly delightful little single-storey Tudor Gothic composition built off an informal plan with a variety of label-moulded transomed and mullioned windows, probably divested of their latticed glazing pattern. Stucco-effect walls rise to skew-table gables with deep kneelers, that to the avenue elevation stepping to a semicircle broken by an untopped carved stone hip-knob. From this gable projects a tiny skew-tabled hallway with chamfered Tudor arched doorway and round-headed slit side windows; staged chimney-stack with octagonal earthenware pots. Squat chamfered granite gate pillars are framed by ogee-walled quadrants. Long may this little gem survive the developers. Built in the time here of Captain D.O. Batley to a property which was renamed 'Egremont' by Thomas Jameson *c.* 1857, and more recently 'Ballinacor'. The porter in 1849 was Thomas Whiteside.

Griffith 1848–60; *Thom's.*

60. BALLYBRIDGE COTTAGE, Little Bray; pre-1837; *demolished.*

A seat in 1837 of the Hon. Randal Edward Plunkett (1804–52) until his succession in 1848 as 15th Baron Dunsany. The gatekeeper in 1849 was Robert Atkins.

Lewis 1837; Griffith 1848–60; *BPB* (1929).

61. BALLYCORUS GRANGE, Golden Ball; *c.* 1870; architect possibly Charles Geoghegan.

The manager's house for the leadworks of the Irish Mining Company is, with its lodge, a late Victorian replacement. Like the house, the lodge is faintly Italianate in flavour but

here the similarity ends, for this is an innovative composition. Finished in rendering with distinctive brick toothed surrounds to the windows, it is single-storey on an irregular plan, the main front to the road presenting on one side a gabled projection with an open pediment, below which is a pair of round-headed three-over-two sash windows. To the right-hand side is an elongated octagonal element below an equivalent roof, the wall faces alternating with wide and slit windows. Between these two components was an open porch to the front door, now blocked up in poor taste. The informality of the plan extends commodiously to the rear below a hipped roof. Now severed from its big house, it was presumably also by architect Charles Geoghegan, who prepared plans for the house in 1862. What is notable from the directories is a brisk turnover of managers to the lead mines.

Thom's; Pearson 1998; IAA.

62. BALLYCORUS LEADWORKS, Golden Ball; *c.* 1865; architect probably Charles Geoghegan.

The concern run by the Irish Mining Company operated from *c.* 1807 to 1913, and this entrance is testimony to its mid-Victorian confidence and solidarity. Two very tall, plain ashlar carriage pillars are flanked by screen walls, terminated by a round turret on one side and on the other by a substantial two-storey gabled gatehouse on an elevated site, its two-bay main front overlooking the entrance, inside and out. Built in a satisfying rubble with blocked granite dressings to two-over-two sash windows, the main concession to architectural extravagance being the first-floor window on its leading front, with its bipartite sash below an arrowhead arch. Still in use.

Pearson 1998; IAA.

63. BALLYFERMOT CASTLE AND GRAVEYARD, Ballyfermot (3).

Towards the close of the eighteenth century a school was kept in the castle by William Oulton Prossor, but by 1837, when occupied by a Captain Lamplin, it was already in decline, for by 1907 it had become the 'Site of Castle'. Despite that, the early pre-1837 lodges were joined by a third, though none now survive.

Lewis 1837; Ball 1995.

64. BALLYFERMOT COTTAGE, Ballyfermot; pre-1837; *demolished.*

A property, later renamed 'The Grange', was home in 1846 to barrister George Godfrey Place, whose lodge three years after lay vacant.

Slater 1846; Griffith 1848–60.

65. BALLYFERMOT, Ballyfermot; pre-1837; *demolished.*

A property in the mid-nineteenth century of John Molloy, no trace of house or lodge remains.

66. BALLYMAN, Old Connaught; *c.* 1870.

A standard plain lodge with two-over-two sash windows in harled walls below a steeply hipped roof rising to a crested ridge and tall slender chimney-stack. Occupied. Equally plain roughcast entrance pillars and concave quadrants. Presumably built by Philip Sydney Barrington of the Fassaroe, Co. Wicklow (*q.v.*), family.

Thom's.

67. BALLYMOUNT CASTLE, Clondalkin; *c.* 1860; *demolished.*

What was probably an early nineteenth-century house built in the shadow of the castle, its gatehouse being for much of that century a seat of Michael J. Smith.

Griffith 1848–60; *Thom's*; Joyce 1912.

68. BALLYOWEN COTTAGE, Esker; pre-1836; *demolished.*

A small estate in 1849 of Thomas Carr, whose gatekeeper was Walter Edmond. It may have been the property recorded in 1837 as 'Ballyowen Lodge' of J. Cathrew Esq.

Lewis 1837; Griffith 1848–60.

69. BALLYOWEN, Esker; pre-1836; *demolished.*

The residence in 1849 of John Fitzpatrick, whose gate lodge then lay vacant.

Griffith 1848–60.

70. BALLYOWEN VILLA, Palmerston; pre-1836; *demolished.*

An antique estate of the Nottinghams which by the early nineteenth century had passed to the Rochfort family, of whom J.S. Rochfort by 1849 was letting it to William Masterson. This may be the property at which in 1914 architects Millar and Symes carried out additions and alterations to lodge, dwelling house and farm houses.

Griffith 1848–60; Ball 1995; *IB* (18 July 1914).

71. BALLYROAN COTTAGE, Ballyboden; pre-1837; *demolished.*

A property in 1837 and for another twenty years of Andrew Reilly.

Lewis 1837; *Thom's.*

72. BALLYROAN HOUSE, Ballyboden (2).

Joshua Watson, maltster, corn factor, tea and general merchant, was the wealthy proprietor here as early as 1841. Within eight years he had added a porter's lodge at the Ballyboden Road gate, occupied by William Cooper.

East entrance; *c.* 1845; architect not known.

If what is surviving is that recorded in the 1849 valuation then this is a precocious composition, looking to date from about

1870. Single-storey standard below a gabled roof in Italianate style. Sadly abandoned, with its openings sealed up, the windows have shouldered moulded surrounds in rendered walls flanking a pedimented breakfront doorway set in a recess leading to the hall, which has a round-arched niche. Both eaves and main verges are bound by a plain frieze with corbel brackets. A proud little lodge lying derelict, vandalised and vulnerable, deserving of a better fate.

West entrance; *c.* 1875.
An additional lodge to a lengthy new western approach from the Knocklyon Road, probably built by Henry Watson after he succeeded to Ballyroan around 1870. Pleasantly shrouded in assorted creepers is this 1½-storey standard roughcast gabled lodge with brick quoins and dressings. To one end is a single-storey bay window below main serrated bargeboards rising to delicate turned hip-knobs, whilst entry is through a later single-storey brick gabled hallway projection. Nice iron carriage gates with hooped anthemion motifs look earlier, salvaged from elsewhere.

Griffith 1848–60; *Thom's*; NIAH.

73. BALROTHERY PAPER MILL AND HOUSE, Balrothery; *c.* 1830; *demolished.*

Patrick Healy

Opposite the gates of what was later to be known as 'Bella Vista' House and paper mill, framed by a row of Scots pines, was this quintessential little Regency lodge with some applied newfangled Tudor detailing. Single-storey standard, built off a square plan with a pyramidal roof rising to a central chimney, its windows were bipartite casements, possibly once lattice-glazed, below label mouldings in rendered walls. Probably built by Joseph McDonnell, whose brother and cousins were all paper-mill proprietors. Its occupant in 1850 was gatekeeper Charles Byrne.

Griffith 1848–60; Healy 2004.

BARLEY FIELD (see EDENBROOK)

74. BARLEY HILL, Willbrook; pre-1837; *demolished.*
Before its demolition in 1979, latterly better known as 'Orchardton', this was a seat associated with the Bushe and Deane families. In 1849 George Deane's porter is listed as William Cooper, which is either a coincidence or a valuer's error, as Griffith records a gatekeeper of that name at neighbouring Ballyroan House (*q.v.*).

Griffith 1848–60; *LGI* (1904); Healy 2005.

BARNCLOSE (see OLD ABINGTON)

75. BARN ELM(S), Dundrum; pre-1869; *demolished.*
A lodge built after 1837 on the site of the previous house before its replacement. In 1851 it was a property of John O'Connor, followed in 1870 by Patrick Mason.

Thom's; Slater 1870.

76. BARN HILL, Dalkey; pre-1837; *demolished.*
A small estate of Andrew Johnston (1770–1833), president of the Royal College of Surgeons from Kilmore, Co. Armagh, who lived here until his death. His widow Sophia remained here, her gatekeeper in 1849 being Thomas Wright.

LGI (1904); Griffith 1848–60.

BARRACK BRIDGE (see ROYAL HOSPITAL)

77. BARTON LODGE, Willbrook; pre-1837; *demolished.*
A seat of William Conlan in 1837, which he was leasing to Arthur Netterville by 1849, when the gate lodge lay vacant.

Lewis 1837; Griffith 1848–60.

78. BARTRA HALL, Dalkey; *c.* 1850.
A standard single-storey hip-roofed lodge with a chunky extending pedimented hall flanked by windows with granite surrounds in pink-finished rendered walls. Much added to on each end. Along with the impressive Italianate marine residence, probably built not long after the marriage in 1839 of Francis Blake Knox (d. 1851) to Elizabeth Mary Hutchinson of nearby Bullock Castle. His gatekeeper in 1849 was John Neal.

Griffith 1848–60; *LGI* (1904).

79. THE BAWN, Carrickmines; pre-1907; *demolished.*
A short-lived gate lodge, probably contemporary with the house of 1903 built for George Panter.

Pearson 1998.

BAWNVILLE (see MOUNTAINVIEW)

BAYLY'S CABIN (see KILGOBBIN CASTLE HOUSE)

80. BAYVIEW, Dalkey; pre-1837; *demolished.*
An early nineteenth-century house and lodge, in 1849 the residence of Thomas Connolly, whose gate porter was then Edward Byrne.

Griffith 1848–60.

81. BEAUCHAMP, Little Bray (2).
A house probably built by the delightfully named Captain Sir Lovelace Stamer (1797–1860) about 1828, when he married and presumably added a contemporary lodge.

North gate; pre-1837; *demolished.*
The lodge, once back to back with that to the neighbouring St James's Parsonage (*q.v.*), was removed before 1938.

The surviving lodge was built by the Bookey family, who acquired the property after Lady Stamer's death in 1872.

South gate; *c.* 1875; architect perhaps J.S. Mulvany.

Although of a single-storey standard format, it has a highly elaborate front elevation typical of its mid-Victorian origin. Below a shallow-pitched hipped roof, projecting from a stucco-effect wall are flat-roofed canted bay windows with two-over-two sashes, on each side of a porch with an open pediment (containing a heraldic shield) carried by two pairs of Roman Doric columns and corresponding pilasters resting on Classical wing walls with recessed panels. There are sufficient similarities to the lodge at Mountainville House (*q.v.*) to suggest the work of architect John Skipton Mulvany. The gatescreen has gone but the lodge remains occupied and well maintained. In 1849 it was manned by James McEvoy.

Lewis 1837; Griffith 1848–60; *Thom's*; *BPB* (1929).

82. BEAUFIELD, Stillorgan (2).
A house of the Regency period, probably built along with its lodges by Henry Darley, who was living here in 1837. Twelve years later he was leasing the seat to John Sweetman, whose brother Patrick, of the brewing family, was resident across the road at Stillorgan Priory (*q.v.*). His gatekeepers were then Patrick Cooke and James Walsh. Both house and lodges have been demolished.

Lewis 1837; Griffith 1848–60; Pearson 1998.

83. BEAUFORT, Rathfarnham (2).

Willbrook Road entrance; pre-1837; *demolished.*
The designer of these innovative granite pillars was clearly familiar with those at the Duke's Gate of the Viceregal Lodge (*q.v.*) in the Phoenix Park, north Dublin, reproducing the gadrooned or claw feet to bow fronts (here updated with moulded recessed panels) and fluted friezes. The particular finials may have had as their source those at Artane Castle (*q.v.*), north Dublin, resembling kegs with ends sculpted into palmettes. With

its concave railed quadrants, the entrance appears to be of *c.* 1855, thus post-dating its lost lodge. John McNamara was gate porter in 1849.

Grange Road entrance; pre-1837/*c.* 1925; *demolished.*
A complex consciously created to complement and mirror that of the old Loreto Convent (see Palliser's Park) across the road, its lodge having only lacked a twin. The triple gateway is contained by like pillars with fluted friezes framing rosettes, the carriage pair crowned by urns. Unlike its counterpart, there seems never to have been a pair of lodges. All that survives is another blind façade exactly as opposite, probably a twentieth-century concoction dating from when the Beaufort property was acquired by the Loreto nuns about 1925. A pair of round-headed recesses is framed by V-jointed rusticated granite, surmounted by a frieze with roundels and fluted panels below an articulated parapet. The property has been home to a college since the departure of the Hodgens family, resident here for much of the nineteenth century, their gatekeeper here in 1849 being James Dillon.

Lewis 1837; Griffith 1846–60.

BEAUMONT (see VIEWMOUNT)

84. BEAUMONT, Williamstown; pre-1837; *demolished.*
A house built for himself in 1810 by Sir Henry Cavendish, but by 1834 Arthur Ormsby had commenced Waltham Terrace on its approach in the form of 38 semi-detached villas. In 1849 he was still landlord when Richard Fleming occupied the gate lodge.

Griffith 1848–60; Pearson 1998.

85. BEECHGROVE, Glenageary; pre-1907; *demolished.*
A property called 'Lower Prospect' in the mid-nineteenth century had been renamed by 1870 and a gate lodge built by 1907. Whoever was responsible—and there was a bewildering turnover of owners—did not foresee the imminent development of their front garden, for by 1936 it had succumbed to new housing on Glenageary Road.

BEECHGROVE (see BEECHWOOD)

86. BEECH HILL, Donnybrook (2).
A seat in 1841 of Joseph Wright, one of whose gate porters in 1849 was William Tobyn. Both lodges have been demolished, that to the east entrance having gone as early as 1869.

Thom's; Griffith 1848–60.

87. BEECHLANDS, Loughlinstown; *c.* 1895; architect not known.

Although in a standard single-storey format, this is a striking late Victorian lodge of red brick in a strange bond of headers every sixth course. It has a substantial feel, with a high plinth wall surround to a canted course at sill level which continues as copings to entrance wing walls supporting chamfered posts that carry a gabled canopy with carved woodwork. This projects from a steeply pitched hipped roof with perforated earthenware cresting broken by a brick chimney-stack with matching plinth and corniced capping. Two-over-two sash windows below segmental arches flank the round-headed fanlit doorway. 'Ranville Lodge' can be accurately dated through its twin at Desmond (*q.v.*) but by the same unidentified architect working for Edward O'Farrell, who acquired a property that had lain vacant for years after the departure of the Carter family.

BEECH PARK (see FERNEY)

90. BEECHWOOD, Loughlinstown; pre-1837; *demolished.*
Once a renowned public house in Georgian times known as 'Owen Bray's Inn', it had by 1817 become a private house of the O'Toole family. In 1849 it was leased by Mrs O'Toole to Arthur Baker, probably the same of Balheaery (*q.v.*) in north Dublin, whose gateman was John Brannan. In the later nineteenth century the house was renamed 'Beechgrove' and was demolished in the 1970s.

Griffith 1848–60; d'Alton 1976 [1838]; Ball 1995; Pearson 1998.

91. BEGGAR'S BUSH BARRACKS, Beggar's Bush; 1827; architect not known.

It was '... erected for the accommodation of four companies of infantry' in 1827, and became the scene of many executions. It now presents a more benign and welcoming air, despite the survival of its monumental triumphal entrance archway, raised mainly in V-jointed rusticated masonry to piers, and the inner round-headed carriage opening with its bold voussoirs, all crowned by a corniced entablature with large central die. To each side spread tall rubble walls containing panelled pedestrian doors in stone surrounds. These lead past a pair of triple-arched arcades which face each other across the approach and form part of twin commodious guardhouses. Each is single-storey, faced in mellow Flemish bond brickwork below a roof hipped to the curtain wall but gabled to the rear main elevation, with a wide pediment embracing two stone door-cases flanking a central Wyatt window. Now all adapted to residential use, the grassy forecourt is lined with cannons as bollards, chain-linked.

D'Alton 1976 [1838]; Liddy 1987.

92. BELFIELD, Booterstown (2).

In 1801 'the seat of Ambrose Moore, Esq., an excellent new house, just finished; the demesne lately planted, and promises to be a handsome seat'. By 1849 it was owned by Thomas Wallace, one of whose lodges lay vacant while the other was occupied by John Wright, both having been in place by 1837 but since demolished. The house remains, handsome, having been acquired *c.* 1948 as part of the UCD complex.

Archer 1801; Griffith 1848–60.

93. BELFIELD, Roebuck; *c.* 1865.

Although the eighteenth-century villa was removed in 1984, its lodge miraculously survives along with the gatescreen. Belfield was sold on the death of Daniel Kinahan (1797–1859), after which it was home to Robert Exham Turbett, who moved from the family home of Owenstown (*q.v.*) nearby. He was probably the builder of this modest mid-Victorian cottage. Single-storey standard, modernisation has deprived it of its chimney-stack on the hipped roof, which retains its chunky carved soffit brackets. The roughcast walls have segmentally arched openings lacking their original windows. The gatescreen, with its roughcast concave quadrant walls and tapering carriage pillars with corniced cappings, may be earlier, from the time here of the Kinahans.

Thom's; *IFR*; Pearson 1998.

94. BELFORT, Blackrock; *c.* 1875.

A standard single-storey lodge below a hipped roof and similarly roofed pretty porch projection with carved post support; segmentally headed openings in rendered whitened walls. Now stunted, the original appearance of its chimney-stack can be seen in a twin lodge to Melfield (*q.v.*) opposite as being tall with plinth and corbelled capping. Graves Swan Warren (1822–1907), second son of the prolific developer and solicitor Robert Warren of Killiney Castle (*q.v.*), is noted here in 1878. Belfort now forms part of a school complex.

Thom's; *LGI* (1912); Pearson 1998.

95. BELGARD CASTLE, Belgard (2).

An ancient property originally of the Talbots which passed by female heirs through a succession of families to the Dillons and then the Trants, who leased it for many years to Francis H. Cruise, a noted miser, which may explain the vacancy of his two lodges in 1849. Both have since been demolished, that to the southern gate having been built by him after 1837, but the other to the northern avenue preceding that date.

D'Alton 1976 [1838]; Lewis 1837; Griffith 1848–60; Ball 1995.

BELGROVE (see PRIESTHOUSE [2])

BELLAVISTA (see BALROTHERY HOUSE AND PAPER MILL)

96. BELLE VILLE, Blackrock; *c.* 1845; *demolished.*

A mid-eighteenth-century house and small park which about 1845 was acquired after the death of the Hon. John Radcliff LLD by Henry William Talbot, whose gatekeeper in 1849 was John Brady. Sadly, the house, alternatively known as 'Rosefield', was removed in 1983 after being home to the Kelly family for over a century.

Thom's; Griffith 1848–60; Pearson 1998.

97. BELLE VUE, Belgard; *c.* 1880; *demolished.*

A mid-Victorian house and lodge, a property in 1883 of John Barr.

Thom's.

98. BELLEVUE, Merrion; pre-1837; *demolished.*

Jackson-Stops

Up a secret laneway which also led to the rear entrance of Nutley (*q.v.*) lay a charming porter's lodge which in 2002 became the site for a spanking new executive house. Much altered over the nineteenth century by various owners, it was single-storey, presenting a single window to the visitor alongside its iron gatescreen, and a peculiar cranked four-bay elevation within, probably extended by a bay to the left-hand side, below a hipped roof with two hefty banded and corbelled late Victorian chimney-stacks. Built in harled rubble, the main attraction was a tall crenellated parapet, a flimsy Romanticisation probably of twentieth-century origin. Bellevue was home in the early nineteenth century to the McGauley family, by whom it was leased from *c.* 1845 to Charles French, whose gatekeeper in 1849 was James Pluck.

Thom's; Griffith 1848–60.

99. BELLEVUE, Booterstown; pre-1837; *demolished.*

A seat in 1837 to John Gillman, whose porter's lodge on Cross Avenue had been removed by 1907. Prior to his residence it was occupied by a Captain Tisdall after the death of the countess of Brandon in 1789.

Lewis 1837; Smyth 1994.

100. BELLEVUE, Drummartin; pre-1871; *demolished.*

An early Victorian Italianate villa, occupied between 1849 and 1854 by Mrs Henrietta Crawford, the gate lodge to which was erected after 1837, perhaps by the following owner, barrister Philip Lawless.

Thom's.

101. BELLEVUE PARK, Killiney (2).

A fine neo-Classical villa of 1836, an early work of J.S. Mulvany for banker client Alexander Boyle, approached from north and south via lodged entrance gates.

Glenageary gate; *c.* 1835.

A sturdy standard two-storey three-bay gatehouse with a hipped roof and full-height central breakfront with pedimented gable supported by a pair of brackets, below which a segmentally headed recess contains the doorway. A first-floor sill course embraces the roughcast Regency building, the modern windows to which probably replaced tripartite originals, the ground-floor sills of which are bracketed.

Ballinclea gate; *c.* 1835.

In contrast to the house is this Tudor Picturesque 1½-storey standard gabled cottage, now lacking much of its original detailing, with its plain casement windows minus label mouldings, probably lost in sanitising rendering. It does retain mildly decorative bargeboards to steeply pitched main gables and that to the central breakfront with its segmentally headed doorway and slit attic window. Surviving is the distinctive cluster of four diagonally set chimney-flues on a square plinth where the ridges meet. There is a good cast-iron gatescreen with palmette feature, fleur-de-lis-topped rails and ornate iron pillars with intertwining foliate shafts climbing to anthemion tops.

Outside this entrance is 'Bellevue Park Lodge' of about 1875, a very decorative 1½-storey Picturesque double cottage with perforated foiled bargeboards and other Tudor motifs, probably built as estate workers' accommodation. Although both porters' lodges look to be contemporary with Mulvany's work to the house, there is little apparently attributable to him.

Slater 1846; Pearson 1998; *IADS* (2000).

102. BELLEWLY PARK, Sandyford (2).
Alternatively 'Ballawley', this was a late Georgian villa, home in the early nineteenth century to Faithful William Fortescue until 1824 and thereafter owned by Robert Maunsell, the ninth of eleven sons of Daniel Maunsell (1795–1876) of Ballywilliam, Co. Limerick, and Sarah Meares. Said by Pearson to have had an entrance in the form of a tall Gothic gateway, all that remain at the southern entrance are four big square pillars with concave quadrant walls, and at the northern entrance fine cast-iron gates and pillars of foliage climbing to hoop-topped anthemion motifs. Maunsell's gatekeepers in 1849 were Edward Kane and Francis Baker.

LGI (1904); Ball and Hamilton 1895; Pearson 1998.

103. BELLGROVE, Chapelizod; pre-1837; *demolished.*
A seat in 1837 of Major Watts and twelve years later, when the gate lodge lay vacant, of Sheppard Jones, a name also to be found at Woodside, Co. Carlow (*q.v.*), at that time.

Lewis 1837; Griffith 1848–60.

104. BELLOSGUARDO, Galloping Green (3).

Latterly, before its demolition, called 'Ardagh Park', the house was originally approached by two avenues, but both their early lodges, at Carysfort Avenue and Newtown Park Avenue, have gone. A property then of Robert Powell, in 1849 one of his lodges was occupied by Anne Killeen and the other lay vacant. Bellosguardo was inherited by Nathaniel Robert Powell and he had the place made over in Italianate style, which is reflected in the new contemporary lodge dating from about 1875. Now shorn of its big house and demesne, it is an independent dwelling, a very smart little composition in proud, caring hands. It has much in common with almost identical structures at Craigmore (*q.v.*), Newtownpark House (*q.v.*), Ailesbury (*q.v.*), Homestead (*q.v.*) and Tibradden (*q.v.*), and can be attributed to architect John McCurdy. It varies from the others only in its prominent keystones to segmentally arched openings with moulded surrounds. Single-storey standard with rendered walls and conspicuous Irish pilaster quoins highlighted in an effective colour scheme to main corners and those of the entrance frontispiece, which contains a double-leaf doorway, below an open pediment. About the eaves are bold console brackets to the hipped roof, which rises to a bulky chimney-stack with moulded corniced capping. A happy survival.

Lewis 1837; *Thom's*; Griffith 1848–60; Pearson 1998.

105. BELLVIEW LODGE, Booterstown; pre-1849; *demolished.*
Robert Harrison, physician and surgeon, is recorded here between 1841 and 1856 and added a lodge to the old house sometime after 1837, his porter in 1849 being Thomas Nowlan. About 1865 a new house was built to designs of John McCurdy and the property renamed 'Ardmore'.

Thom's; Griffith 1848–60.

106. BELMONT, Galloping Green; pre-1837; *demolished.*
The house had become a boarding school for 'the sons of the nobility, clergy, and gentry, including preparation for the English and Irish universities, naval, military, and engineering colleges, &c.' by 1841, when the principal was Dr John Smyth. The gatekeeper in 1849 was James Fox.

Thom's; Griffith 1848–60; Shaw 1988.

107. BELVILLE, Kill of the Grange (2).
A good Georgian house in the early nineteenth century of the Cash family, from whom it passed by marriage in 1835 to Revd Henry Humbertson Jones Westby, whose gate porters in 1849 were Thomas Brady and William Doyle.

Pottery Road gate; pre-1837; *demolished.*
A lodge on the northern approach which by 1871 was already avenueless and had been removed by 1940.

Rochestown Avenue gate; pre-1837; *demolished.*
The first OS map shows a circular lodge, or 'inkpot', suggestive of a mid- to late eighteenth-century structure. The site is now occupied by a twentieth-century bungalow with hipped gables and a three-bay symmetrical front in gate lodge format. The property was renamed 'The Cedars' and now forms part of Our Lady of Lourdes Hospital of the Sisters of Mercy.

Pigot 1824; Griffith 1848–60; *LGI* (1904); Pearson 1998.

108. BERMUDAVILLE, Cullenswood; pre-1848; *demolished.*
A lodge identified by the Griffith valuation as occupied by Thomas Marsh as gatekeeper to Daniel Moore MD; not obvious on any maps or on site, assumed demolished.

Griffith 1848–60.

109. BERNARDVILLE, Rathmines; pre-1837; *demolished.*
As with all the porters' lodges on the western side of Rathmines Road, this is a thing of the past. A map of 1876 shows it to have had a canted front to the avenue approach to a villa in 1841 of John Colclough, salesmaster of Smithfield. His gatekeeper nine years later was Peter McEvoy.

Thom's; Griffith 1848–60.

110. BESSBOROUGH, Terenure; *c.* 1830.
James Gaffney, gate porter in 1849 to Peter Blackburne, occupied this tiny single-storey standard lodge with chimney-stacks to each of its skew-tabled gables and big gutter corbels to the eaves; two-over-two sashes in rendered walls. Prior to Blackburne's residency Bessborough was home to John Smith, solicitor.

Slater 1846; Griffith 1848–60; Shaw 1988.

111. BETTY FORT, Clondalkin; pre-1837; *demolished.*
A residence in 1850 of Michael Smith, whose gate porter was then John Rooney.

Griffith 1848–60.

112. BEVERSTON, Rathmines; *c.* 1840; *demolished.*
A lodge built after 1837 that was occupied in 1850 by William Connor, who was gatekeeper to Richard John Hicks, paper manufacturer. It must have been Hicks who added it to a property previously known as 'Elm Mount'.

Slater 1846; Griffith 1848–60.

113. BEVERSTON, Roebuck; pre-1837; *demolished.*
The lodge was occupied in 1849 by William McCormack, despite the villa within lying vacant.

Griffith 1848–60.

114. BIRCH GROVE, Kill of the Grange; pre-1837; *demolished.*
A seat in 1837 of G. Williamson Esq., which by 1849 had passed to Richard Johnston, whose gatekeeper was John Plunkett.

Lewis 1837; Griffith 1848–60.

115. BLACKROCK COLLEGE, Williamstown; 1904; architect P.H. McCarthy.

A great expanse of open space owes its survival to the foundation of this famous school and the gradual acquisition for its use of four adjoining landed estates: Castle Dawson in 1860, Williamstown Castle in 1875, Clareville in 1899 and Willow Park in 1924, all with the subsequent loss of their individual porters' lodges. In about 1900 the present main entrance was formed off the Rock Road, the new approach entailing the removal of Williamstown Avenue and the loss of at least ten houses which lined it. The new triple gateway and railed quadrants are contained by six grand Gothic stone pillars, the carriage pair supporting an elaborate ironwork overthrow announcing 'Blackrock College'. Tucked in behind is a faintly Tudor-style lodge built off an irregular plan.

Single-storey in quarry-faced uncoursed masonry, it displays skew-table gables with deep kneelers, a glazed lean-to porch in an internal angle and the dreaded modern plastic window replacements. An old photograph of *c.* 1904 shows a gang of workmen posing to a backdrop of the newly completed lodge before returning to demolish Williamstown Avenue. Joining them is the gatekeeper's wife. Lodge and gates were designed by Patrick Harnett McCarthy.

IB (14 Jan. 1905); Gorham 19[...] Pearson 1998.

116. BLACKROCK, Blackrock; *c.* 18[...]
A big brick maritime residence of *c*[...] built by Sir John Lees and frequent[...] place of relaxation by many of his [...] cronies. After his death in 1811 [...]

entablatured door-cases under the inscription 'Blackrock House'. The gates are heavily ornate, with palmette and Gothic motifs. Unusually and politely, the entrance presents its best face to the public, it being in rubble to the rear. The fortunate gatekeeper in 1849 was Thomas Christy.

Archer 1801; Griffith 1848–60; Ball 1995; *BPB* (1929).

117. BLENNER VILLE, Monkstown; pre-1837; *demolished.*
This was the Dublin seat of the Blennerhassett family of a place of the same name in County Kerry. John Blennerhassett, solicitor, had by 1846 changed the name of the place to 'Greenville', presumably after the immediate lessor Molesworth Green. His gate porter in 1849 was Joseph Harris.

Slater 1846; Griffith 1848–60; *LGI* (1904).

118. BLOOMFIELD, Merrion; pre-1837; *demolished.*

An estate in 1837 [...] 1788), sixth son [...] (*q.v.*). His [...] whose lo[...] triple[...] ce[...]

121. BLOOMVILLE, Windy Arbour (2).
Front entrance; pre-1837/*c.* 1890; architect J.F. Fuller.

The house, dating from *c.* 1830, was the residence in 1841 of Clotworthy Macartney, who also held St Helen's, north Dublin (*q.v.*), and whose gatekeeper eight years later was James McCabe. By 1869 Bloomville had been acquired by the Robertson family and renamed 'Gledswood'. Their descendants later replaced the old lodge on the same site by the present red-brick structure, attributable to architect James Franklin Fuller on the strength of its twin lodge at Kilrock, [...]th Dublin (*q.v.*). Single-storey and [...] on a T-plan below a steeply hipped [...]wnstroke culminating in a canted [...] overlooking the entrance. [...]

125. BOHERNABREENA RESERVOIR, Friarstown (2).
'Admission to the pathway, which is practicable for cycles, leading by the river and reservoir lake to Castlekelly ... runs close to the river ... A caretaker's cottage marks the commencement of the lower lake, and a similar cottage, sheltered by evergreens, is passed as we ascend to the level of the upper lake.' Thus did Weston St John Joyce guide visitors in 1912 past the lodges of the waterworks of the Rathmines and Rathgar township.

Outer gate; *c.* 1900; *demolished.*
The lodge has been replaced by a bungalow but surviving is an entrance screen with recessed panel, tapering pillars and a postilion gate.

Inner gate; *c.* 1900.
Raised from a basement is a single-storey three-bay gabled lodge with a like roofed hall projecting from the left-hand side. These roofs have a mix of tiled skew-tables, perforated wavy bargeboards and scalloped earthenware crested ridges. To main gables are half-timbered-effect apexes. In use, with new plastic window inserts.

Joyce 1912.

126. BOLBROOK PAPER MILL, Ta
pre-1837; *demolished.*
An establishment in 18
Williams which

its rectangular fanlight framed by a moulded entablature on a pair of Classical console brackets. The shallow hipped roof was crowned by a pair of bulky brick chimney-stacks on plinths.

Thom's; IAA photograph (S/491/5&6).

128. BOLTON HALL, Ballyboden; pre-1837; *demolished.*
Although a house is shown on the site in 1760, that which survives is late Georgian; its lost lodge was probably contemporary with it and built by Philip Jones, who is recorded here in 1837 and later in 1849, when his gate porter was Michael Murray. Also remaining is a mildly Classical gatescreen of unadorned outer granite pillars and smaller inner carriage pillars with tapering recessed panels and oversailing cappings containing railed screens and matching gates, looking to be of *c.* 1845.

Lewis 1837; Griffith 1848–60; Healy 2005.

BOOTERSTOWN RECTORY (see MARINO)

129. BRAY LODGE, Little Bray; pre-1837; *demolished.*
uccessively the residence of Mr Wray, ain Mason, Alfred Sothern and in 1846 ard Orr, who three years later had ing the lodge vacant and the house f his 'representatives'.
bitant 1907; Slater 1846;

Cabinteely; *c.*
ably George

left-hand side with an Irish pilaster quoin and three-over-three sash window in a rectangular recess, whilst that to the right-hand side contains a portico with a pair of Roman Doric columns *in antis* and corresponding pilasters. This and the leading window have hopelessly inappropriate modern inserts. Also dating from the early Victorian make-over is a prominent chimney-stack with moulded capping and recessed panel shaft defining the three flues. The lodge is sited forward of, and presides over, a most sumptuous gatescreen of carriage and postern gates hung on cast-iron pillars with anthemion tops framed by great rusticated granite pillars with wreath carvings to their cappings and flanked by short concave quadrants with moulded recessed panels, terminating in outer pillars crowned by elegant Portland stone urns, each banded in Greek key pattern. The design shows the influence of J.B. Papworth through his brother George, who is recorded as working here for Joseph Pim in 1842. The gatekeeper of George Pim in 1849 was Michael Branagan.

Pigot 1824; Lewis 1837; Griffith 1848–60; IAA.

BROOKFIELD (see JOBSTOWN)

131. BROOKFIELD, Williamstown; pre-1837; *demolished.*
A house semi-detached with 'Brook Lawn' (*q.v.*), the gate lodge to which was occupied 1849 by William Malone, porter of a Annesley and perhaps previously of arstin in 1841.
hom's; Griffith 1848–60.

ROOKLAWN, Dolphin's Barn; pre-
lemolished.
erty off what was Love Lane South, onore Avenue, in 1846 of Thomas Copeland, wood engraver.
later 1846.

ROOKLAWN, Ballsbridge; pre-1837;
shed.
ıse with a frequent turnover of nts, the gate lodge to which in 1849 ome to Denis Whelan. The house, nce in 1841 to Robert Belton, shared an nce and pair of lodges with 'Mary Ville') next door, off what was Beggar's Bush d but which by 1870 had become lbourne Road.

Thom's; Griffith 1848–60.

134. BROOKLAWN, Kimmage; pre-1837; *demolished.*
William Whelan was gatekeeper of James Hyland in 1849 to a property that included a flour mill.

135. BROOKLAWN, Palmerston (2).
An eighteenth-century house of the Brooke family, after whom it was presumably named, on the southern bank of the Liffey. Of the two pre-1837 lodges the remnants of one seem to have survived.

West lodge; *c.* 1780/*c.* 1860.
Intriguingly, parts of an antique single-storey lodge appear to have been preserved in a now two-storey square gatehouse with a pyramidal roof. In the east and south fronts, incorporated for posterity, are two sophisticated Classical façades, each in the form of a tall, blank, keystoned, round-headed archway rising into an open pediment and flanked by a pair of lower windows, all linked by a continuous sill. A mix of rubble, roughcast and brick dressings, united by a common paint finish.

East lodge; pre-1837/*c.* 1890.

A replacement late Victorian Picturesque lodge built off an L-plan. Single-storey gabled in pebble-dash finish with stone quoins, the leading avenue projection boasts ornamental apex woodwork whilst the roof catslides alongside to form an entrance verandah now housing a later glazed bay window. The roof has scalloped slate courses and trefoil-perforated earthenware cresting broken by corbelled red-brick chimney-stacks, to be found also in the neighbouring lodge at 'Quarryvale' (*q.v.*). Replacement lead-effect lattice casement windows. An improvement for one John Reddy.

One gatekeeper in 1850 is recorded as Simon Slattery, porter to Michael Hackett. The property is now home to King's Hospital School. Plain entrance pillars have elegant vases atop.

Taylor and Skinner 1778; 1969 [1783]; Wilson 1803; Griffith 1848–60; *Thom's*.

136. BROOKLAWN, Stradbrook (2).
A house built in 1847 in the grounds of 'Stradbrook House' (*q.v.*) by merchant tailor Richard Allen, one of the old pre-1837 lodges which he acquired. Both have gone, to be replaced by twentieth-century dwellings, that to Stradbrook Road a good gate-lodge look-alike.

Thom's; Pearson 1998.

137. BROOK LAWN, Williamstown; pre-1837; *demolished.*
The house is semi-detached with 'Brookfield' (*q.v.*), in 1837 occupied by J. McCullagh Esq., and twelve years later by William Furlong, whose gatekeeper was Patrick Byrne. Surviving is one solitary concave quadrant of a once-extensive gatescreen in V-jointed rusticated masonry with an architraved pedestrian opening, all contained by a pair of pillars, with decorative panels, looking to date from *c.* 1865.

Lewis 1837; Griffith 1848–60.

138. BURTON HALL, Sandyford; pre-1837; *demolished.*
A house built in 1730 by Samuel Burton whose demesne has been ravaged by new commercial developments and its entrance swept away in new road requirements. Across that road was 'Rockland House' (*q.v.*), built by Samuel's brother Richard, the gate lodge to which has suffered a similar fate.

Flanagan 1991.

139. BUSHY PARK, Terenure (3).
Formerly 'Bushe's Park', built before 1700 by Arthur Bushe of County Kilkenny, by 1801 it had become 'the seat of Abraham Wilkinson, Esq., a very large elegant house, with a beautiful prospect of a well improved neighbourhood. The demesne consists of about forty acres, well improved, laid out in great taste, and enclosed with a stone wall.' Wilkinson gave it as a dowry to his only child, Maria, by whose marriage in 1796 it passed to the family of her husband, Sir Robert Shaw (1774–1849). At the time of his death the gate porters were Denis Byrne, Lawrence Byrne and Mrs Marley. Of their three pre-1837 lodges not one survives.

Archer 1801; Carr 1806; Griffith 1848–60; Ball 1995; *BPB* (1929).

140. BUTTERFIELD, Rathfarnham (2).
Neither the lodge shown on the 1837 OS map as next to the house then occupied by James Wright nor that built further east after 1869 has survived. By 1841 the property had passed to Charles M. Bunn, whose gate porter eight years later was Robert Leggett. The later lodge was probably created by the Marlowe family, who were here after 1870.

Lewis 1837; *Thom's*; Griffith 1848–60.

141. CABINTEELY, Cabinteely (3).
A house created about 1770, probably to designs of Thomas Cooley, for Robert, first and last Earl Nugent and Viscount Clare, which he initially called 'Clare Hill'. He bequeathed the place to the Byrne family, of whom Robert in 1799 was succeeded by his widow and, after her death, by his three daughters, 'Misses Byrne; the latter are almost always absentees, though they have a fine house here, and certainly the most strongly enclosed demesne in the country'. Thus noted d'Alton about 1836. The wall, which took around five years to build, remains fairly intact to this day and in 1837 had one lodged break in it, to which the situation has reverted.

Main entrance; pre-1837/*c.* 1880.
What survives is a replacement lodge built on the site of its predecessor. Single-storey and hip-roofed on an L-plan, the leading wing to the avenue has a canted glazed bay window and a flat-roofed hall in the internal angle. To the corners are broad Doric pilasters but otherwise in a drab grey rendered finish. This is preceded by a rather older and impressive gatescreen, probably of about 1830 and perhaps contemporary with the original porter's lodge. Tall stucco-effect concave quadrant walls contain architraved postilion openings and are stopped by plain square granite pillars; good chunky spear-topped iron gates.

The three gate lodges which appear on the 1907 OS map may have formed part of a spruce-up of the estate, which was owned from the late 1860s for about twenty years by William Richard O'Byrne.

South entrance; pre-1871; *demolished.*
A lodge built sometime after 1837.

North entrance; post-1871; *demolished.*

The place is now a pleasant public park.

Archer 1801; d'Alton 1976 [1838]; *Thom's*; Ball 1995; Pearson 1998.

CAERLEON (see GORTMORE)

142. CALLAGNUS, Booterstown (2).
Alternatively spelt 'Collegnes' after the place in France whence the D'Olier family hailed, the property is now 'St Andrew's College'.

Gardiner's Row lodge; pre-1837; *demolished.*
The sole lodge in the early nineteenth century was home in 1849 to Joseph Wright, porter to Isaac D'Olier.

Grotto Avenue lodge; *c.* 1875.
A modest single-storey hip-roofed cottage, lately extended to an L-plan, with modernisation apparent in its concrete roof tiles and missing chimney-stack. Built by Merrick Lloyd.

Griffith 1848–60; *Thom's*; Pearson 1998; Craig and Fewer 2002.

CALLY PARK (see SALLY PARK)

143. CAMPFIELD, Dundrum; pre-1837/*c.* 1880.
The original lodge may be incorporated in the present structure, which surprisingly survives the devastation wrought by development of this fine park and the loss of the old house. It was probably built by Samuel Boxwell, who died at Campfield in 1852. Known as 'Taney Lodge', it is now a five-bay gabled lodge with like projecting hall flanked by a verandah supported on brick piers. Basic wavy bargeboards and round-headed windows with banded toothed dressings. Much modernised and in use as an office. Probably built or improved by Walter Henry Rooney, who succeeded John Stokes here about 1870, they having been partners as West India merchants in the city.

Lewis 1837; Slater 1856; *Thom's*; Ball and Hamilton 1895; Pearson 1998.

144. CAMPOBELLO, Rathmines; *c.* 1830.
A villa presumably named by James Del Vecchio, print and statuary seller, plaster of Paris and Roman cement manufacturer, who was its immediate lessor in 1850 to Hugh Duffy, whose gatekeeper was Eliza Hartford. On the Dartry Road is this charmed survivor, with a tall window to each face of its canted main avenue front below a corresponding roof which is hipped to the rear. Single-storey and roughcast with two-over-two

sashes, it seems to have been severed from the lodge of neighbouring Woodpark (*q.v.*), to which it appears from the early maps to have been once joined, or back to back. Occupied, with a variety of modern additions to its original minuscule floor plan, it nestles avenueless and independent. By 1851 the house had been renamed 'Clare Ville'.

Slater 1846; Shaw 1988; Griffith 1848–60; *Thom's*.

145. CANONBROOK, Lucan; *c.* 1830.
A house notable for its association with the renowned architect James Gandon, who retired to Canonbrook in 1806 and lived there until his death in 1823. He would not have known the lodge that survives, dating as it does from the time here of his only son, of the same name. Single-storey standard and hip-roofed, its eaves have carved Classical paired soffit brackets but most else is, or was, Tudor in flavour. Whilst a pair of diagonally set chimney-flues survive, lost in 'improvements' were latticed casement windows and label mouldings rendered over. It now lies derelict. Nearby are four good granite rusticated entrance pillars with fluted friezes, linked by shallow concave railed quadrants—probably contemporary with the lodge. In 1849 Canonbrook was leased to George Huband, whose gate porter was Lawrence Downey.

Griffith 1848–60; Duffy 1999.

146. CAPPAGH, Clondalkin; pre-1836; *demolished.*
A property in 1850 of James Singleton, the lodge to which had gone by 1906.

Griffith 1848–60.

CAPPAGHMORE (see ROSEBANK)

147. CAREW, College Green; pre-1728; *demolished.*
Originally built on the site of a nunnery dissolved by Henry VIII by Sir George Carew (1555–1629), president of Munster and lord high treasurer of Ireland, it became the town house of Lord Deputy Sir Arthur Chichester (1563–1625), being renamed 'Chichester House'. From 1661 it served briefly as accommodation for parliament, when it is recorded as having 'a gatehouse next the street, with several rooms and a spacious garden, containing a large banqueting-house'. By 1727 it had become neglected, gone to ruin, and the following year was demolished to make way for Sir Edward Lovett Pearce's masterpiece.

O'Flanagan 1870; Craig 1980.

CARNACLOUGH (see MULBERRY PLACE)

148. CARRAIG-NA-GREINE, Dalkey; *c.* 1855; architect not known.
A large, austere, cut-stone house built around 1830 by Charles Leslie, who was to live on here for another 40 years. For much of this time the main approach was from a lodgeless gate from Loreto Avenue to the north. The entrance eventually created on Leslie Avenue shows a similar severity with a simplicity of

detailing in neo-Classical style. The lodge is in immaculate ashlar granite, single-storey standard with a back return below a hipped roof. The pedimented frontispiece contains an open porch with round-headed opening, relieving discs in the spandrels over piers with recessed panels. To each side are similarly arched narrow windows in like recesses taken to ground level, repeated in end walls of inferior materials. The pediment entablature continues as an eaves course about the structure. The splendid postern opening is flanked by great pylon pillars with recessed panels and solid plinths tapering upwards and containing good chunky ironwork to railings and gates. At a distance was the carriage gate, at the time of my visit ominously dismantled to admit construction machinery. These pillars contained recessed panels with the name of the property inscribed in Gaelic and, above, a wrought-iron archway.

Thom's; Pearson 1998.

149. CARRICKBRENNAN LODGE, Monkstown; *c.* 1830; architect possibly W. Farrell; *demolished.*

Irish Architectural Archive

A scene outrageously destroyed despite vigorous protests was the vista down the delightful approach from Monkstown Road stopped by a splendid and unusual little Classical lodge taken down in 1987. Single-storey, it had a long symmetrical front elevation, the central bay of which was a wide recessed porch screened by a pair of Doric columns *in antis* flanked on each side by single six-over-three sash windows framed by Doric pilasters, all below a hipped roof with two chimney-stacks carefully positioned for balance. This lodge was very much akin to that at Ballyhaise House, Co. Cavan, reminiscent of the work of William Farrell, here presumably working for Edward Atkinson, whose gatekeeper in 1849 was Thomas Sullivan. Alongside is the entrance to the neighbouring property of 'Dalguise' (*q.v.*), whilst at the Monkstown Road is what may have been porter's accommodation in a 1½-storey gabled affair of the late nineteenth century or early twentieth century in roughcast with banded surrounds to openings; called 'Easton Lodge'.

Thom's; Griffith 1848–60; Dean 1994; Pearson 1998; IAA photo (46/24).

CARRICKMINES CASTLE (see CLAREMOUNT)

150. CARRIGLEA, Kill of the Grange (2).
Two pre-1837 lodges, neither of which remains, belonged at that time to a property of Revd Thomas Goff of Carrowroe Park, Co. Roscommon. After his death in 1844 it became a seat of his eldest son, Thomas William Goff (1829–76), one of whose gate porters in 1849 was Lawrence Kavanagh.

Lewis 1837; Griffith 1848–60; *LGI* (1904).

151. CARYSFORT, Blackrock (3).
A tall, plain house built in 1803 by John Joshua Granville-Leveson Proby, 2nd Baron Carysfort (1751–1828), also of Glenart Castle, Co. Wicklow (*q.v.*), who may also have created at that time a suitably grand entrance, some of which can still be seen incorporated into the later screens.

Principal gate; *c.* 1803/*c.* 1845; architects not known.

Retained are the front elevations of a pair of lodges, each in the form of a blind segmentally arched recess surmounted by a corniced parapet. These are joined to the screen of four pillars by tall concave quadrant walls in similar granite ashlar. Behind the left-hand façade is a single replacement porter's lodge built by Mark Anthony Saurin, solicitor to the excise and attorney-general, who succeeded to the property in 1839, his father, the Rt Hon. William Saurin, having been leased the place in the early nineteenth century by Lord Carysfort. This is a single-storey standard lodge below a shallow oversailing hipped roof. In rectangular recesses are a panelled door with pretty fanlight, flanked by margined sash windows, all in grey rendering framed by granite quoins. The

triple gateway has ironwork contemporary with the later lodge; the outer pillars carry urns whilst the carriage pillars have what may be hawks of the Deasy family atop. Saurin's gatekeeper in 1849 was Mrs McLoughlin.

Secondary gate; pre-1837; *demolished.* An entrance, also off Carysfort Avenue, which led to the outbuildings.

Rear gate; 1885.
About 1865 Carysfort was bought by the Rt Hon. Rickard Morgan Deasy, baron of the exchequer and lord justice of the appeal. He died in 1883, to be succeeded by his younger son Henry Hugh Peter Deasy (1866–1947), who during his brief tenure created a third entrance off the newly constructed Avoca Avenue to the north. This is a plain single-storey affair, built off an L-plan below a hipped roof with a lean-to hallway in the internal angle which is joined to a doorway in the screen wall surmounted by a semicircular lintel. The gate pillars are inscribed with a date and 'Sisters of Mercy', to whom Deasy sold the place for a convent and educational establishment in 1891, which it remains to this day, having been acquired by University College Dublin a century later.

Thom's; Griffith 1848–60; *BPB* (1929); *IFR*; Flanagan 1991; Pearson 1998.

152. CARYSFORT LODGE, Stillorgan; pre-1837; *demolished.*
Both the Georgian villa and its lodge are lost. A seat in 1837 of Thomas Goold, who by 1849 had been succeeded by Thomas Beasley, whose porter then was John Fennell.

Lewis 1837; Griffith 1848–60.

153. CASINO, Dundrum (2).
Both pre-1837 lodges have been demolished. George Stapleton was resident here in 1837, but by 1849 James Dillon Meldon had moved here from nearby Rosemount (*q.v.*), his gate porters being Edward Colgan and James Stapleton. The place is better known for its connections with the Emmet family, whose home this was in the late nineteenth century.

Lewis 1837; Griffith 1848–60; Pearson 1998.

154. CASTLE BAGOT, Baldonnel; pre-1837/pre-1937; *demolished.*
A large three-storey late Georgian pile of the Bagot family, lately rehabilitated. Both the pre-1837 lodge, when the seat was called 'Kilmactalway' after its townland, and its replacement have gone, to be survived by very fine Classical pillars, expertly restored. The V-jointed rusticated shafts, moulded

corniced cappings and beautifully chiselled swagged friezes contrast dramatically with hideous new concrete-block quadrant walls and stunted outer pillars, perhaps since rendered as more acceptable. Both pillars and original lodge probably date from the time of James John Bagot.

Ball 1995.

155. CASTLE DAWSON, Williamstown; pre-1837; *demolished.*
A lost lodge to a house built for James Massy Dawson about 1762, since when it has passed through a variety of owners, in 1807 becoming a boarding school under Revd Alexander Leney before reverting to a dwelling of the Rt Hon. Edward Litton, MP for Coleraine between 1849 and 1858, when his gatekeeper was Mary McDonnell. He renamed the place 'Altamore' after his main seat in County Tyrone before, in 1860, it was acquired by the French Fathers who founded Blackrock College (*q.v.*).

Thom's; Griffith 1848–60; Smyth 1994; Pearson 1998.

156. CASTLEFIELD, Knocklyon; pre-1907; *demolished.*
For much of the mid-nineteenth century this was a property of Patrick Maguire, the lodge to which was added after 1869, probably in the time here of Marcus C. Sullivan in the 1880s and '90s.

Thom's.

157. CASTLE LODGE, Kilgobbin; pre-1837.
A very plain porter's lodge, over the years raised in alteration and extended. Roughcast, with one bay to the road under a hipped roof, it remains occupied. A property in 1849 of a Mrs Cuthbert, whose splendidly named porter was Christopher Shakespeare.

Griffith 1848–60.

158. CASTLE PARK, Dalkey; *c.* 1825; architect not known.

Built *c.* 1820 as 'Perrin Castle' by Alderman Arthur Perrin, it is difficult to believe that its impressive entrance screen and the modest

lodge are contemporary. Despite their being attached, they are not an integrated composition. Single-storey standard roughcast and hip-roofed, with an exceptionally wide central breakfront containing a large round-headed arch which may once have been an open porch, now blocked up. At the meeting of the ridges is an obese chimney-stack. The cottage, subsequently extended into a triple pile to the rear, abuts the rear of the left-hand screen wall of the great symmetrical Picturesque castellated entrance, comprised of a chamfered Tudor carriage archway with an Irish battlemented parapet. To each side the tall crenellated screen walls, once with circular arched postilion openings, are stopped by sturdy round towers with more Irish battlements over. This fine design, intended as an appropriate prelude to the big house with its similar detailing, has been visited by all manner of uneducated abuse, the pleasant rubble finish having been cloaked in a grim grey cement rendering, the left-hand pedestrian opening blocked up, the right-hand curtain wall gouged out hideously to permit separate vehicular access and egress, and the main gates gone—all quite ironic, given that this now introduces a place of learning. The shoddy, ill-placed sign sums it all up. In 1849 the whole was controlled by William Mangan, porter to the Hon. John Richards, baron of the exchequer, to whom the house was then leased.

Lewis 1837; Griffith 1848–60; Pearson 1998.

159. CASTLE VIEW, Roebuck; pre-1837; *demolished.*
Like much else in Roebuck townland, this was a house associated with the legal profession; in the early nineteenth century of Joseph McDermott (d. 1837), solicitor, it was acquired as 'Castle View' by Charles Hogan, barrister of the Four Courts, who left it *c.* 1860 called 'Charlton'. His gatekeeper in 1849 was Patrick Adams.

Thom's; Griffith 1848–60; Ball and Hamilton 1895.

160. CATHERINE PARK, Ballyboden; pre-1837/1874; architect J. Maguire; *demolished.*
'A gate lodge and entrance at St Catherine's Park, Ballyboden, Co. Dublin for William Russell. Joseph Maguire, archt., Mr Fegan, Rathgar, contractor.' Russell seems to have come here about 1856, canonised the place and created a new entrance as late as 1874. Before his tenure it was home to many, in 1849 to John Teeling, whose gate porter in the earlier lodge was James McCormick.

Thom's; Griffith 1848–60; *IB* (1 Oct. 1874).

161. CEDARMOUNT, Mountanville; pre-1837; *demolished.*
A seat of the West family, previously called 'Mountanville Cottage', its gate porter in 1849 was William Keegan, serving John West.
Griffith 1848–60; *Thom's.*

THE CEDARS (see BELVILLE)

162. CENTRAL LUNATIC ASYLUM, Windy Arbour; *c.* 1850; architect probably Jacob Owen.

A great stone-built institution behind a forbidding boundary wall, built in 1847–50 to designs of Jacob Owen of the Board of Works as a criminal asylum, now known as the 'Central Mental Hospital'. Marginally more conspicuous is the less formal single-storey gate lodge built off an L-plan in uncoursed rubble with punched granite dressings rising to skew-table gables, the leading one of which contains the remains of a rectangular bay window with its own hipped roof now butchered to provide a glazed reception kiosk. Alongside, the original gabled porch extends toward the avenue, whilst from the road eaves rises a tall (rebuilt) staged brick chimney-stack. Remarkably still in use in its original role after a century and a half.
O'Dwyer 1997a; Pearson 1998.

163. CHAMOUNT, Ballinteer (2).
A house built in the 1840s for the Tilly family of 'Chantilly', by whom it was let in 1849 to Abraham Sweeny. In 1870 it was home to Captain Robert Ashworth Studdert when the gate lodge lay opposite the gates, but by 1883, renamed 'Clonlea', it was taken by Studdert's fellow Taney churchwarden Robert Henry Tilly, who replaced the porter's lodge with one on the same side of the road. Neither survives.
Griffith 1848–60; *Thom's*; Ball and Hamilton 1895.

CHARLEVILLE (see NEWTOWNPARK VILLA)

164. CHARLEVILLE, Churchtown; *c.* 1850; *demolished.*
A house and its lodge that formed a development by Charles S. Young, which he probably named after himself.
Thom's.

CHARLTON (see CASTLE VIEW)

165. CHEEVERSTOWN, Saggart (2).
The Cheevers had by the mid-nineteenth century forsaken their family seat with its pre-1837 gate lodge and it became home to Joseph Fishbourne. After lying vacant towards the end of that century, it was taken in 1908 by the Clayton family, who five years later extended the avenue towards the Naas road and built an inner lodge. Both the house and its lodges have been demolished.
Thom's.

166. CHERBURY, Booterstown; *c.* 1865; architect probably C. Geoghegan; *demolished.*
A house that existed in 1762 as 'Herbert Lodge', probably a dower house of the Pembroke estate, by 1864 belonged to Robert Millner, wool merchant, who enjoyed the place until the end of the century, having engaged the architect Charles Geoghegan to enlarge the house and create new outbuildings. This commission seems to have included design of the gate lodge which appears on the 1871 OS map, although the evidence has gone.
DB (1 Oct. 1864); Smyth 1994; Pearson 1981.

167. CHERRYFIELD, Templeogue; pre-1837; *demolished.*
An estate in 1814 and 1837 of Peter A. Lawless, who probably added the lodge to a property once called 'Cherrytree'. Henry Littlewood was in residence by 1849, when his gatekeeper was George Geathings. Both house and lodge have gone.
Leet 1814; Lewis 1837; Griffith 1848–60; Healy 2004.

168. CHERRYWOOD, Loughlinstown; pre-1837; *demolished.*
In 1751 the house became the rectory of Rathmichael parish and remained so for about a century, Revd Dr John P. Hunt (1786–1866) being rector from 1825 until his death, the gate lodge in 1849 lying unoccupied. The place seems to have reverted to a private residence after his death.
Griffith; *LGI* (1904); Pearson 1998; Leslie and Wallace 2001.

169. CHESTERFIELD, Booterstown; pre-1837; *demolished.*
A property which in the nineteenth century had a rapid turnover of owners. A map of *c.* 1830 shows there to have been no gate lodge then, so it can only have been added either by Nathaniel Sneyd, MP and wine merchant, who lived here until being murdered in 1833, or by Revd William Betty, who succeeded him. By 1849 it was home to Miss Eliza Cox, whose gate porter was Mary Devans.
Griffith 1848–60; Pearson 1998; Smyth 1994.

CHICHESTER (see CAREW)

CHRISTCHURCH (see TANEY CHURCH OF IRELAND CHURCH)

170. CHURCHTOWN, Dundrum; pre-1837; *demolished.*
An unimpressive neo-Classical house, in 1837 a seat of J. Busby Esq., who was survived here in 1849 by the Misses Busby, whose gate porter was George Thompson.
Lewis 1837; Griffith 1848–60; *Thom's.*

171. CHURCHTOWN HOUSE, Dundrum; *c.* 1845; *demolished.*
A seat in 1837 of the Corbett family, for whom John Flannagan was gatekeeper in 1849 to Miss Susan Corbett. The house later became 'Glenbower'.
Lewis 1837; Griffith 1848–60.

CHURCHTOWN LODGE (see LYNDHURST)

172. CHURCHTOWN PARK, Dundrum; pre-1869; *demolished.*
A lodge built after 1837 probably for Thomas Moyers, solicitor.
Thom's.

173. CHURCH VIEW, Booterstown; pre-1837; *demolished.*
A property in 1837 of Henry Higginbotham, who was leaving it to Charles Hope eleven years later, when the gatekeeper was Murtagh Ennis. The site was redeveloped in 1856 as 'Glenvar' (*q.v.*).
Lewis 1837; Griffith 1848–60.

174. CLAREMONT, Shanganagh (3).
A house built originally about 1832 by Thomas Clarke, who by 1837 had added two lodges to his property. William Charles Quinn had acquired the house by 1849, with gatekeepers in Lawrence Byrne and Lawrence Lawless.

Main gate; pre-1837; *demolished.*
With the arrival of the Dublin South-Eastern Railway around 1853 the old access was severed, but its lodge remained as a dwelling by the Dublin Road well into the twentieth century.

Secondary gate; pre-1837; *demolished.*
A lodge which monitored the entrance to outbuildings off Corbawn Lane but was likewise removed in the twentieth century.

About 1875 the place was acquired by John McCall, who greatly extended the house and transformed it into 'Dorney Court', named after the Tudor house in Berkshire, but it was a later owner, Charles T. Wallis, who gave it an appropriate new lodged entrance around the turn of the century.

Dorney Court gate; *c.* 1900; architect probably L.A. McDonnell.

A thoroughly Edwardian 'Stockbroker Tudor' composition, having much in common with the lodges to Knockmaroon, north Dublin (*q.v.*), and Eyrefield Lodge, Co. Kildare (*q.v.*), though here a single-storey version. Its main avenue front displays a wide mock half-timbered gable, which may have had a datestone (now roughcast over), and bargeboards with delicate dentil trim. Below is a tripartite multi-paned window in a quarry-faced stone wall, flanked by corner recesses with wooden post and carved bracket supports. To the roof is a red pantile-effect covering and a chunky stone stack. The gatescreen looks earlier, with main carriage pillars having moulded recesses and 'Dorney Court' inscribed in the cappings. Framing are convex iron-railed quadrants, spear-topped to match the gates. All this survives the house, which was demolished in 1984.

Lewis 1837; Griffith 1848–60; *Thom's*; An Old Inhabitant 1907; Pearson 1998.

175. CLAREMONT, Sandymount; *c.* 1850; *demolished.*
A house built along with its lodge in the mid-nineteenth century by Robert Lovely, slate and general merchant.

Thom's.

176. CLAREMOUNT CASTLE, Carrickmines; pre-1838; *demolished.*

Irish Architectural Archive/Kevin Fox

A property that by 1871 had been renamed 'Carrickmines Castle', and later still 'Hollywood Castle', was a wonderful Castellated Tudor Gothic jumble, which has evolved over the years with an ill-defined history but may have originated as someone's romantic vision about 1810. Built on the roadside with an extent of rustic battlements, buttresses, towers and a bartizan with mock cross arrowloops, as had the round carriage gate turrets. Sadly, the outline of the lodge from old photographs remains vague, but it was a rectangular single-storey structure with castellated wall to the road next the carriage gate and a segmentally headed postilion opening between, in harled rubble walls. Later maps suggest that the lodge was linked to the main house to form an enclosed yard. Certainly the new entrance has been moved southwards to create something rather less evocative. Occupied in 1849 by Patrick Fennell and later in the century by the architect Richard Millar.

Griffith 1848–60; Pearson 1998; IAA photographs (C8/375 & 376).

177. CLAREMOUNT, Carrickmines; *c.* 1865.
What otherwise appears as an early nineteenth-century plain single-storey standard lodge with white rendered walls has its true age revealed by one-over-one sash windows and chimney-stacks to both main gables. But chiefly it is betrayed within its gabled breakfront porch by its sophisticated mid-Victorian door-case with recessed panel

pilasters and acanthus-leafed console brackets carrying a moulded entablature with rectangular fanlight over, all framing a four-panelled door. The modest roughcast entrance screen, comprised of tall convex quadrant walls, one containing a postern opening, is older. A seat in the mid-nineteenth century of the Harris family, previously called 'Clareview'.

Thom's.

CLAREVIEW (see CLAREMOUNT)

178. CLAREVILLE, Booterstown; pre-1837; *demolished.*
Like neighbouring Castle Dawson (*q.v.*), a house built *c.* 1752 by Thomas Keating but, unlike it, not surviving its acquisition by Blackrock College (*q.v.*). It became a popular seaside demesne convenient to the city, occupied successively from 1756 by Ellen Weld, Alexander Marsden, William Kenny and until 1838 by Sir Ross Mahon (1763–1835) of Castlegar, Co. Galway, and his widow, one of whom must have been the lodge-builder. In 1849 James Quinn was gate porter to Michael O'Donnell.

Griffith 1848–60; *BPB* (1929); Smyth 1994.

CLAREVILLE (see CAMPOBELLO)

CLIFFE LODGE (see WILLMOUNT)

179. CLIFTON, Shanganagh; pre-1907; *demolished.*
A lodge built after 1871, probably by the Rt Hon. Charles Hare Hemphill of Rathkenny, Co. Tipperary, solicitor-general for Ireland (1892–5) and MP for County Tyrone.

Thom's; *LGI* (1904).

180. CLONARD, Killiney; *c.* 1880; architect not known.

A distinctive and innovative Arts and Crafts lodge, part of a development with the house for John Crosbie Goff (b. 1840) of the Carrowroe Park, Co. Roscommon, family. Substantial single-storey on a perfectly square plan, giving a pyramidal roof which rises from coved eaves to the central chimney-stack. The leading corner is recessed as a verandah porch with the support of a square pier and a pair of carved wooden posts. Alongside to the avenue is a glazed canted oriel window, the sill line of which carries about the structure as a string-course, relieving the rendered finish. Understated gatescreen of four pillars of channelled rustication containing carriage gates and matching concave railed quadrants. John Crosbie Goff's father and eldest brother, Thomas William Goff, lived at Carriglea (*q.v.*).

Thom's; *LGI* (1904).

181. CLONARD, Kimmage; pre-1907; *demolished.*
A short-lived porter's lodge and Edwardian villa built about 1900 by Edward Carolin, merchant and Russian vice-consul.

Thom's.

CLONARD (see MOREEN LODGE)

CLONASLEIGH (see WILMOUNT)

182. CLONBURRIS COTTAGE, Clondalkin; pre-1836; *demolished.*
A small estate in 1837 of M. Pearson Esq., which was the residence of John Ledwith by 1850, when his lodge lay vacant.

Lewis 1837; Griffith 1848–60.

183. CLONFADDA, Blackrock; *c.* 1890.

A single-storey standard late Victorian lodge in Flemish bond orange brickwork below a shallow oversailing hipped roof with a gabled porch simply formed by projecting piers, its only pretension being subtle raised brick quoins. The front elevation has recently been unbalanced in refenestration and modernisation, which also saw the reinstatement of its arrow-headed doorway but not its chimney-stack. Also surviving the entrance to a modern housing development are contrasting big tapering granite 'pylon' pillars with quarry-faced panels and oversized brackets to the cappings. A property in the late nineteenth century of William Carter, carpenter and builder.

Thom's.

CLONKEEN (see GRANGE)

184. CLONMORE, Kilmacud (2).
Both lodges, built between 1837 and 1871 for Henry Fulton, physician, have been demolished. One was distant on the Brewery Road by the reservoir, whilst that to the

north-west approach, shared by Westbury (*q.v.*), made way for a roundabout.

Thom's.

185. CLONSKEAGH CASTLE, Roebuck (3).
A plain late Georgian house built by Henry Jackson, proprietor of the nearby ironworks, who left for America after taking part in the 1798 rebellion. His successor, George Thompson (1769–1860) of the Oaklands, Co. Meath (*q.v.*), family, gave the house its symmetrical castellated cloak about 1825, adding at least one entrance lodge in matching manner.

Main entrance; *c.* 1825; architect not known; *demolished.*

On the Clonskeagh Road was a wholly appropriate prelude to the house in a like symmetrical castle style, in the form of a great round-arched carriage gateway with toothed dressings and quoins surmounted by Irish crenellated 'ramparts', relieved by mock medieval arrowloops. On each side were matching 'day and night' lodges presenting blind elevations to the visitor, both single-bay with round-headed recesses below plain parapets and rectangular plaques between. All this was preceded by a vast forecourt with convex walled quadrants, the area no better for its removal. For whatever reason, this is identical to that surviving at Burton Park, Co. Cork.

Inner gate; pre-1837; *demolished.*
A lodge to an inner enclosure by the mill-race to the north.

West gate; pre-1837; *demolished.*
A lodge on the Dundrum Road which has suffered the same fate as the others.

Two of George Thompson's gate porters in 1849 were Michael Connor and John Bryan. The house thankfully survives relatively unscathed, although creeping modern development inexorably claims the fine demesne.

D'Alton 1976 [1838]; Lewis 1837; Griffith 1848–60; Ball and Hamilton 1895; *LGI* (1904); Pearson 1998.

186. CLONTRA, Shankill; *c.* 1861; architects Deane and Woodward.
The wonderful Ruskinian Gothic villa designed for the renowned Dublin lawyer James Anthony Lawson (1817–87) by the office of Thomas Newenham Deane and Benjamin Woodward not long before the latter's premature death in 1861. Despite being relatively muted, the lodge formed part of that extended commission. Built in the same pleasant rubble facings, it is similarly 1½-storey and has an exaggeratedly steeply pitched hipped roof along with a lofty

chimney-stack, but with gabled dormers to the attic rather than gablets. The roof catslides to form a pretty entrance porch with pointed arches in fretted screens actually more ornate than the latticing on the verandah of the house. There is a beautiful pedestrian Gothic iron gate reflecting the conservatory. Unfortunately, the modern window replacements are insensitive. A very similar lodge is to be found at another Deane and Woodward creation at St Austin's Abbey, Co. Carlow (*q.v.*).

Country Life (29 May 1975); Blau 1982; Williams 1994.

187. CLORAGH COTTAGE, Ballyboden; pre-1837.
There is a rubble structure with mono-pitched roof on the site, in use as a shed. A property in the mid-nineteenth century of surgeon William Henry Porter as his country retreat.

Griffith 1848–60; *Thom's*; Shaw 1988.

188. CLORAGH, Ballyboden; pre-1849; *demolished.*
The seat in 1837 of Charles Davis to which a lodge had been added by 1849, when his porter was Mark Russell.

Lewis 1837; Griffith 1848–60.

189. CLOVERHILL, Clondalkin; pre-1836; *demolished.*
A residence in 1837 of D. Kinahan Esq., which by 1848 had been acquired by wine merchant Ninian Boggs McIntyre, whose gate porter was Patrick Ferguson.

Lewis 1837; Slater 1846; Griffith 1848–60.

190. CLYDA, Donnybrook; pre-1837; *demolished.*
A lodge, which in 1848 lay unoccupied, on Coldelow Lane (later Belmont Avenue) to a residence of Lawrence Redmond, since at least 1841.

Thom's (1841); Griffith 1848–60.

COBURG (see WARREN LODGE)

COLLEGNES (see CALLAGNUS)

191. COLLINSTOWN, Palmerston; pre-1836; *demolished.*
An estate in the late eighteenth century of the Wilson family, which in 1823 passed through marriage to Michael Mills. By 1850 Richard Mills was letting Collinstown to Deane Wilson, whose gatekeeper was then Peter Larkin. A property notable for its association with John Betjeman, who rented it briefly.

Lewis 1837; Griffith 1848–60.

192. CONSTANTINE, Greenhills; pre-1837; *demolished.*
A seat in 1850 of Patrick Dunne.

Griffith 1848–60.

193. COOLDRINAGH LODGE, Leixlip; pre-1836; *demolished.*
An early nineteenth-century villa, in 1849 belonging to Bartholomew Delany. There is a replacement house on the site of its gate lodge.

Griffith 1848–60.

COOLGRANEY (see ANNA FIELD)

194. CORK ABBEY, Little Bray; pre-1837; *demolished.*
An estate in 1783 of the Barry family, which in 1802 the Hon. Col. Edward Wingfield (1772–1859), third son of the 3rd Lord Powerscourt, purchased from the Rt Hon. Theophilus Jones and remained there until the end of his days. D'Alton in 1836 writes of the wooden gate to the property and 'a straight and noble avenue, overhung with elms, beeches, sycamores, and some fine walnut trees'. Similarly in 1801 Archer was impressed with the large and elegant house, 'which, for situation, can hardly be equalled', grounds for Wingfield's contentment with the place. His gate porter in 1849 was James Richardson. The house was lost in the 1950s.

Taylor and Skinner 1778; 1969 [1783]; Archer 1801; d'Alton 1976 [1838]; *BPB* (1929); Pearson 1998.

CORK LODGE (see WOODLAWN)

195. CORKAGH, Clondalkin (2).
A magnificent demesne now saved as a public park for the enjoyment of the people of Clondalkin, the grand mansion of the Finlays having been demolished in the 1960s by a subsequent owner—just one of a sequence of crimes committed on the property, including the loss of much of the fine estate wall and both of its porters' lodges.

Main entrance; pre-1760/*c.* 1835; *demolished.*
At the base of the venerable oak avenue by the Naas Road in 1760 was a pair of lodges that the trees may have seen. Probably built by the first of his family to settle here, Thomas Finlay, who died in 1776, they were replaced by his grandson of the same name, who had succeeded to the estate on the death of his father in 1823 but only enjoyed his inheritance for fourteen years. The new lodge was single-storey standard below an

oversailing hipped roof, in render with bold V-jointed toothed quoins. An old photograph shows its most attractive feature to have been a highly ornate hexagonal cast-iron glazing pattern to casement windows in moulded surrounds. The contemporary gatescreen was comprised of four pillars with recessed panels containing ogee quadrant rails with palmette tops and carriage gates to match. Thomas Finlay's eldest son, Revd John William Finlay (1805–79), was in residence in 1850, when his gatekeeper was Henry Dowling.

Secondary entrance; *c.* 1800; *demolished.*
At the St John's Road gate to the north of the house was a single-storey gabled lodge in a harled finish and, as revealed in an old photograph, a round-headed window with Georgian Gothic Y-traceried glazing pattern.

A third gate lodge was in fact to the neighbouring property of Kilmatead (*q.v.*), the Corkagh dower house.

Griffith 1848–60; *LGI* (1904); Ferguson 1998; Devine 2003.

196. CORRIG CASTLE, Dun Laoghaire; pre-1837; *demolished.*
The rambling mock castle with a copious display of crenellations was probably created about an earlier house, perhaps by a Major Langley who was resident in 1835, although he was followed here in 1837 by Christopher N. Duff, whose gate porter in 1849 was Hugh Corr. Like its lodge, the 'castle' is a thing of the past.

Lewis 1837; Griffith 1848–60; Pearson 1981.

197. CORRIG, Dun Laoghaire (2).
Both the big house and its two lodges, built before 1849, have been removed. The gatekeepers then were John Kelly and Lawrence Devereux to a William Dee or Deey. Only one of the lodges is apparent on the 1837 OS map, when the proprietor was named O'Callaghan.

Thom's; Griffith 1848–60.

198. COSEY LODGE, Terenure; pre-1837/*c.* 1889; architect probably J.H. Pentland.
Now St Joseph's Presentation Convent, which it had become by 1866, its surviving lodge is a five-bay single-storey irregular hip-roofed structure with canted red-brick clipped eaves and two-over-two sash windows in sand/cement stucco-effect finished walls. Architect John Howard Pentland carried out work here, with this probably forming part of his brief. The old lodge was clearly found wanting by the new regime and replaced. The gatekeeper in 1849 was Thomas Deneef, porter to Mrs Sarah Henneky. Prior to becoming a convent the house was briefly called 'Netherby'.

Griffith 1848–60; *Thom's*; *IB* (1 April 1889).

199. COTTAGE PARK, Murphystown; pre-1871; *demolished.*
Before the addition of the lodge after 1837 the house had been 'Lilliput'; it was renamed by Joseph Huband Smith in about 1850 and yet again altered to 'Park House' in the early twentieth century before becoming, more grandly, 'Lisieux Hall'.

Slater 1846; *Thom's*.

COURT-NA-FARRAGA (see ANNAGHANOON)

200. CRAIGMORE, Blackrock (2).
William Hogg, Quaker and tea merchant with Thomas Bewley and Co., acquired this virgin site in 1863 for his new house to designs by John McCurdy at a cost of £6,000. This may have included the building of the first porter's lodge.

Temple Road gate; *c.* 1863; architect perhaps J. McCurdy; *demolished.*
Initially the sole approach to the house, which it remained for a decade.

Temple Hill gate; *c.* 1873; architect probably J. McCurdy.

A classy little Italianate lodge of a pattern common in south Dublin, to be found at Ailesbury, Bellosguardo, Homestead, Newtownpark and Tibradden. Single-storey standard below a hipped roof, it displays the Classical detailing in its open pedimented breakfront with paired console bracket supports continued about the eaves. To the external corners are Irish pilaster quoins in plain grey rendered walls, the one-over-one sash windows framed with toothed dressings whilst the double-leafed front door has a segmentally arched fanlight with keystone. To the ridge the chimney-stack has a plinth and a moulded corniced capping; the entrance screen has been removed.

Thom's; *DB* (15 April 1863); Pearson 1998; Smith 2001.

CRICKEN COTTAGE (see ST JAMES'S PARSONAGE)

201. CRINKEN, Shanganagh; pre-1837/*c.* 1880.
An example of one of those delightful Regency single-storey-over-basement villas with *piano nobile* built *c.* 1825 by a William White, perhaps the same William White (1801–57) of Shrubs (*q.v.*), north Dublin, fifth son of Luke White of Luttrellstown Castle (*q.v.*), who had married in 1824. Its gate lodge, which was probably contemporary, was vacant in 1849 and by 1871 had gone altogether. White's widow lived on here until about 1866, following which Crinken was occupied for many years by a Miss Holmes, who must have had the surviving replacement structure built. This is a pleasant single-storey standard lodge with a hipped roof, in granite rubble with cream brick dressings. Subsequently extended by a bay to the left-hand side, the original doorway sealed and a new projecting gabled hall added.

Griffith 1848–60; *Thom's*; *BPB* (1929); An Old Inhabitant 1907; Pearson 1998.

202. CROMLECH, Loughlinstown; pre-1871; *demolished.*
Since overrun by suburban development, a house and lodge of 1850 on the newly created Shanganagh Road for Adam D. Stewart. Both are survived by the neighbouring chamber tomb after which the property was named.

Griffith 1848–60; *Thom's*.

203. CROMWELL'S FORT, Crumlin; pre-1837; *demolished.*
A property at Oliver's Corner in 1841 of Eugene Sweeny, coach-builder.

Thom's.

204. CRUMLIN, Crumlin (2).
'The Purcell family long held the manor as well as much the larger part of the other lands of the parish; and the mansion which they inhabited is a substantial structure, not very agreeably situated.' This fine mid-eighteenth-century house today occupies no more salubrious a setting than it did in 1845, being surrounded by twentieth-century housing. Neither of its lodges has survived the extraordinary development of the area.

South gate; pre-1837/*c.* 1880; *demolished.*
The 1837 OS map indicates a cruciform-plan structure at the gate but no avenue, and by 1869 the lodge also had gone. In 1907 the avenue had been reinstated from Kimmage Road West with an attendant porter's lodge. This was an attractive building in a Tudor Revival style, single-storey with a single-bay leading front comprised of a multi-paned casement window below a steeply pitched skew-table gable with deep kneelers. A little gabled hallway projected towards the road. Presumably built for the Hollwey family, who came to the property soon after 1870, when Francis John Purcell was in residence.

North gate; pre-1837; *demolished.*

Finola Watchorn

Situated on the approach from the old Captain's Lane was a lodge that is shown on an old photograph to have been a single-storey cottage below a hipped roof, with eaves perhaps high enough to accommodate loft rooms. To the avenue advanced a gabled hall from an elevation that appears to have been otherwise blind. Although for much of its history an estate of the Purcell family, it was held from *c.* 1814 until at least 1837 by William Collins, who may have added the lodge. The gatekeeper in 1849 to Ignatius Francis Purcell was James Gallagher.

Lewis 1837; *Parliamentary Gazetteer*; Griffith 1848–60; *Thom's*; Watchorn 1985.

CUILIN (see HIGHNAM LODGE)

CULMORE (see PARK VIEW)

205. CYPRESS GROVE, Templeogue (2).

Patrick Healy

Along with neighbouring Templeogue House (*q.v.*), this formed a territory in the eighteenth century of the Domvile family of Santry Court (*q.v.*), north Dublin. They let it out over the decades as a temporary home to a succession of notables: Sir William Cooper, and then a dowager countess of Clanbrassil, who left the old irregular buildings, with small grounds laid out in exquisite taste, to her nephew Robert Jocelyn, who may have been here until his succession as the 2nd Lord Roden in 1797. Thereafter it was the residence of John Orr in 1814, followed in 1837 by John Duffy, one of whose gatekeepers thirteen years later was Martin Boland. Both lodges were in place by 1837 but both have gone, one having by 1869 been replaced at the entrance to Templeogue Lodge (*q.v.*), a property created from part of the Cypress Grove plot. All that survives is an old blurred photograph of the western gatescreen. This was a dignified neo-Classical entrance from *c.* 1820 of four square ashlar pillars with plain friezes, containing spear-topped carriage gates and flanking matching iron screens with postilion gates. By 1907 the place had been renamed 'Alberta' and the fine park has been broken up for modern housing, although the big house remarkably remains as home to a missionary order.

Leet 1814; Lewis 1837; Griffith 1848–60; *Thom's*; Ball 1995; Craig and Fewer 2002; Healey 2007.

206. DALGUISE, Monkstown; *c.* 1881; architect William M. Mitchell.

'Richmond Cottage' had a succession of different owners, from Robert Gray in 1841 to a Mrs Redmond in 1870, and was not quite grand enough to warrant a lodge at its gate. In 1880 all that changed with the arrival of a

Irish Builder

Unexecuted design by W.M. Mitchell.

Mrs Hart, who transformed the cottage into a substantial house and altered its name. Her architect almost certainly was William Mansfield Mitchell, for the property was also given the *gravitas* of a gate lodge, for which a perspective view by him was published in the *Irish Builder* magazine. This showed a very elaborate Arts and Crafts design, single-storey on an L-plan in brick with a low-pitched roof and having half-timbered effect and decorative fretwork to the gables. To the avenue gable was intended a canted bay window and a porch in the internal angle with carved woodwork. Mrs Hart clearly found Mitchell's proposal to be deficient in accommodation, for what transpired is considerably larger. Double-fronted with a pair of canted windows on each side of the doorway and beautiful intricate fretwork to apexes and supporting the hip-knobs, all painted white to contrast starkly with red Flemish bond brickwork. In addition to the conspicuous ribbed chimney-stacks, this emphatic little lodge has another surprise in an eccentric rectangular bay window angled across the left-hand corner below an unusual pediment with decorated tympanum and turned finial supported by a console bracket. Whilst it is lovingly tended, its fine erstwhile older companion lodge to neighbouring Carrickbrennan Lodge (*q.v.*) has gone, both having shared a common approach from Monkstown Road.

Thom's; *IB* (1 Nov. 1881); Williams 1994; Pearson 1998.

207. DANUM, Rathgar (2).

An Edwardian development, home in 1910 to Ernest Bewley.

Zion Road entrance; *c.* 1905; architect not known.

The main approach is announced by an impressive red-brick gatescreen of four grand articulated Classical pillars crowned by corniced stone cappings with ball finials. Flanking the carriage opening, tall straight walls contain round-headed pedestrian openings and on one side a plaque with

'DANVM' inscribed. Beyond this formality is a little single-storey Arts and Crafts lodge in matching material below a hipped roof with a bulky chimney-stack. The three-bay avenue front in contrast is informal, with a glazed, flat-roofed canted bay window to one side of the entrance portico, its entablature carried by a pair of miniature Roman Doric columns raised on pedestals. Subsequently extended to form an L-plan.

Orwell Road entrance; *c.* 1910; architect not known.

The secondary lodge is none the worse for being a plainer version of that at the main gate. Single-storey standard in a mellow rustic brick below an earthenware pantiled hipped roof.

Thom's.

208. DARTRY, Rathmines; pre-1837/*c.* 1850; *demolished.*

A house that belonged to the proprietor of the adjacent woollen cloth mills, until *c.* 1848 of William and Thomas Willans. Thereafter they were let to the Drury family, who replaced the previous lodge with another at the opposite side of the access and complemented it with a fine new gatescreen. This survives but has been removed to a new site nearby, as entrance to the modern housing development of 'Orwell Woods', though it lacks its carriage gates. The sturdy granite pillars are neo-Classical with a touch of Egyptian in the recessed panelled tapering shafts and even Tudor with the roses to friezes. The outer pillars are plainer, with suitably chunky contemporary postilion gates and railings. There are identical pillars at Donnycarney, north Dublin (*q.v.*), and something similar at nearby St Pancra's (*q.v.*). In 1850 the gate porter was Mrs Verder.

Thom's; Griffith 1848–60.

209. DAWSON GROVE, Beggar's Bush; pre-1837; *demolished.*
A terrace of four houses with a common entrance at which the gatekeeper in 1850 was Henry O'Hara, to the landlord Robert Ruskell.

Griffith 1848–60.

210. DEAN'S GRANGE CEMETERY, Kill of the Grange; 1865; architect possibly Richard Hastings Frith.

A graveyard created in the early 1860s on the site of an old gravel pit to which this substantial caretaker's lodge was in place by 1869, built for the sum of £517 by contractor M. Gahan; 1½-storey and raised off a cruciform plan with hipped gables, carved wooden eaves features and exposed rafter toes, it may have originated with rubble facings, of which chamfered stone dressings survive with the odd label moulding. The avenue projection contains what was a bipartite pointed-arched opening to a recessed porch with a central incongruous Doric column. In an inept late twentieth-century make-over this has been closed by an unsightly screen, plastic windows inserted elsewhere, ugly flat-roofed dormers introduced and the whole covered in a drab sand/cement rendering. Below the leading attic window is a peculiar 'inverted' trefoil motif. Inspired by the newfangled Ruskinian Gothic enthusiasm, though in less able hands than such as Deane and Woodward. The 1931 entrance screen, with its quarry-faced pillars and ogee railed quadrants, is by Patrick Harnett McCarthy.

IB (1 Aug. 1931); Pearson 1998; O'Donoghue 2007.

DEAN'S GRANGE (see GRANGE)

211. DEANSRATH, Clondalkin; pre-1837; *demolished.*
A mid-eighteenth-century farmhouse, the grounds of which have been overrun by modern housing. A residence in the early nineteenth century of the Hughes family.

Craig and Fewer 2002.

212. DELAFORD, Firhouse; pre-1837; *demolished.*
An old wayside inn, converted *c.* 1800 into a private house by Alderman Bermingham, which was acquired in 1820 by B.J. Ottley. His family let it to George Shepherd in 1849, when the lodge lay vacant. Delaford was demolished about 1977.

Lewis 1837; Griffith 1848–60; Bence-Jones 1988; Craig and Fewer 2002; Healy 2004.

213. DESMOND, Killiney; pre-1837/1895; architect not known.

A property now known as 'Padua', its pretty lodge on the Killiney Hill road called 'Linden Cottage' in its own right. Single-storey standard below a hipped roof, it originally displayed red-brick facings, now rendered over but can be seen as intended in its twin lodge to Beechlands (*q.v.*). Distinguished by a high plinth to sill level which gives it an air of permanence, the round-headed fanlit front door is sheltered by a canopied porch with ornamental joinery and chamfered post support. To each side are segmentally arched windows, whilst the roof is highlighted by canted slate courses; the chimney-stack, with plinth and corniced capping, retains its brick finish on a ridge of perforated, serrated earthenware cresting. Obligingly, the date '1895' reveals this to be a replacement lodge built for barrister Robert Jebb, probably when the house was enlarged. One year later the house is listed as being vacant. The predecessor on a slightly different site may, like Desmond, have dated from the early 1830s. In 1849 a Major Fitzgerald rented the place to John Wall, whose gatekeeper was James Kennedy.

Griffith 1848–60; *Thom's.*

214. DR STEEVENS'S HOSPITAL, Steevens's Lane; pre-1837; *demolished.*
Commenced in 1719 to designs of Thomas Burgh and opened in 1733. The porter's lodge appears on the first OS map but the only image otherwise is a tantalising glimpse of the hipped roof of a single-storey structure in an early nineteenth-century photograph. Perhaps contemporary with an adjacent V-jointed rusticated pillar of *c.* 1800, which terminated a tall boundary wall containing a small pedestrian opening. Beyond, across the face of the hospital, is an extensive railing and a pair of mid-nineteenth-century cast-iron 'Chinese stove' carriage posts.

Harvey 1949.

DOMINICAN CONVENT, Dún Laoghaire (see ECHO LODGE)

215. DOMINICAN PRIORY, Tallaght; *c.* 1865; architect possibly J.J. McCarthy; *demolished.*
Site of the ancient castle of Tallaght, the materials of which in 1729 were incorporated into the country residence of the Protestant archbishops of Dublin. Falling into ruin by the early nineteenth century, its grounds were leased in 1842 to the Dominicans, who established the Gothic Revival monastery of St Mary's, designed by J.J. McCarthy in 1863. His commission may have included the provision of the porter's lodge that appears on the 1870 OS map.

Joyce 1912; Williams 1994.

216. DONNYBROOK CASTLE, Donnybrook; pre-1837; *demolished.*
The ancient castle had become in the early nineteenth century a residence of the Downes family, who by 1837 were letting it as a boarding school run by John Madden. By 1870 it had been adapted as an asylum of St Mary Magdalene. The valuation of 1849 places its porter's lodge on the main street, but there may have been another off Coldblow Lane (now Belmont Avenue), neither now apparent.

Wilson 1803; Lewis 1837; *Thom's*; Griffith 1848–60.

217. DONNYBROOK COTTAGE, Donnybrook; pre-1837; *demolished.*
A property, subsequently renamed 'St Margaret's', which was home from about 1816 until just before his death of the eminent surgeon Abraham Colles (1773–1843). It was purchased *c.* 1841 by the Hon. Patrick Plunkett (1799–1859), after whose death his widow lived on there.

Ball and Hamilton 1895; *Thom's.*

DORNEY COURT (see CLAREMONT)

218. DRIMNAGH CASTLE, Drimnagh; pre-1837; *demolished.*
The now splendidly restored ancient manor of the Barnewall family had by the early nineteenth century become the property of the marquis of Lansdowne, who then let it to the farming family of Cavanagh, of whom a Mrs Cavanagh continued to work the land until at least 1862. The lodge had been removed by 1938.

Lewis 1837; Ball 1995; *Thom's.*

219. DRIMNAGH LODGE, Drimnagh; pre-1837; *demolished.*
A property in the mid-nineteenth century of Robert McMicken, the gate lodge to which lay vacant in 1849.

Griffith 1848–60.

220. DRIMNAGH PAPER MILL, Drimnagh; pre-1837; *demolished.*
'The little river, that filled the fosse, has been in more modern times deepened into a reservoir for the uses of a paper-mill, whose busy voice alone disturbs the silence of a pretty glen immediately adjacent. This factory is kept by Mrs Sullivan, and employs about twenty-five persons of both sexes.' Thus was d'Alton captivated in 1836 by the scene which remained well into the twentieth century by the River Cammock and its mill-race. The concern remained in Sullivan family hands for well over a century.

D'Alton 1976 [1838].

221. DRUMMARTIN CASTLE, Drummartin (2).
In common with much else in this area of south Dublin, which became commuter-land for the legal profession, this fine late Georgian villa was home to barristers. Resident in the early nineteenth century was Henry Dawson (1782–1833) and in 1837 his widow, when both lodges were in place. Thereafter it was occupied for many years by Henry Birch (1806–82) of like calling. Sadly, both the house and its two lodges have been demolished.

Lewis 1837; *Thom's*; Ball and Hamilton 1895; Pearson 1998.

DRUMMARTIN HILL (see ANNMOUNT)

222. DRUMMARTIN, Drummartin; *c.* 1820.
A remarkable survival is this little lodge to a residence in the early nineteenth century of John Curry, who died here about 1837. This is the simplest of standard single-storey examples but with an unusually steep hipped roof, lacking its chimney-stack. The roughcast walls contain small two-over-two sash windows on each side of a nice sheeted door. Occupied and maintained. The basic gatescreen looks to be of an age.

Lewis 1837; Ball and Hamilton 1895.

223. DRUMMARTIN LODGE, Drummartin; pre-1869; *demolished.*
A gate lodge built sometime after 1837 probably by John Robert Brereton (1817–71), barrister, who is recorded here in 1849.

Griffith 1848–60; *IFR*.

224. DUBLIN CASTLE GARDEN, Dublin Castle; *c.* 1830; architect not known.

Across the Lower Castle Yard from the castle is a relatively unostentatious entrance screen in the form of a pair of substantial two-storey gatehouses, doubtless principally providing gardener's accommodation. In the form of cubes below pyramidal roofs with central chimney-stacks, they are simply rendered behind whilst to the visitor they each present, in coursed rubble, a single-bay front of a doorway with a little bipartite mullioned window over, both linked by a large segmentally arched carriage gateway. This wide three-bay screen is defined by dividing full-height pilasters, or piers.

225. DUBLIN TURF GAS COMPANY; 1823; architect W. Murray; *demolished.*
The entrance to the city's Gas Works off Great Brunswick Street (now Pearse Street) was once marked by a pair of buildings in the

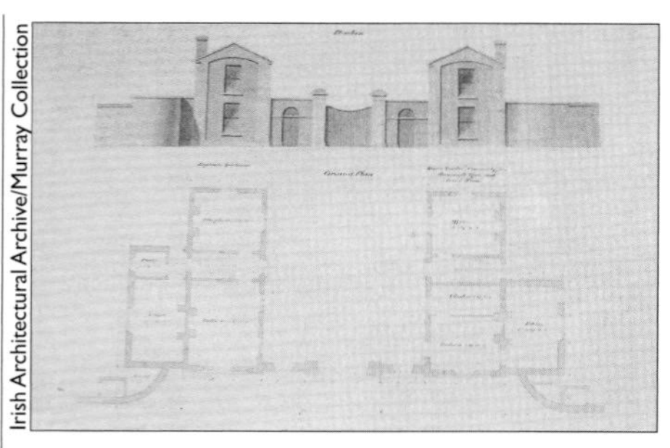

Irish Architectural Archive/Murray Collection

guise of two-storey gatehouses. From an undated drawing by architect Patrick Byrne they were in fact designated as engineer's apartments to one side and keeper's accommodation, offices and boardroom to the other. Each structure was to have had a single-storey kitchen back return behind convex entrance quadrants which framed single-bay fronts of six-over-six sash windows in segmentally arched recesses, each breaking the suggestion of an open pediment. These were intended to flank a pillared carriage opening with wooden sheeted gates and similar postern doorways to each side with round-headed panels over, divided by spring courses. From the 1837 OS map it would appear that a subsequent design of 9 July 1823 by William Murray was adopted by the Board; it differs little in form, other than the single-storey rear accommodation running full width and simpler, more assured front elevations which dispense with recesses and display full pediments. The postern doors lose their fussy over-panels and concave quadrant walls are substituted. On the drawing is an overlay to the left-hand gatehouse of a less elegant elevational treatment which would have been unfortunate were it carried out—although now rather irrelevant, as all has been swept away, the area today being site to a residential development.

IAA drawings (Murray Collection 92/46: 709–710).

DUNAMASE (see LOTA)

226. DUNARDAGH, Blackrock (2).
George Orr Wilson (1830–1902), a Belfast merchant, acquired a portion of the old estate of Rockfield (*q.v.*) around 1865 and almost certainly commissioned the practice of Lanyon, Lynn and Lanyon to design his new house in the Italianate style. It bears a very close resemblance to their Mount Wolseley, Co. Carlow (*q.v.*), and some Ulster houses by the practice. Wilson originated from Daramona, Co. Westmeath (*q.v.*), being one of four brothers, two of whom at their properties of Coolcarrigan, Co. Kildare (*q.v.*), and Currygrane, Co. Longford (*q.v.*), pointedly employed different architects. Here, unusually, he agreed with the Hoggs of neighbouring Craigmore (*q.v.*) to create and share an extensive entrance screen to serve two adjacent avenues.

Templehill lodge; *c.* 1865.
On an elevated site on the northern approach is this strangely bland porter's lodge, subsequently much extended and modernised. Single-storey standard and rendered below a hipped roof now sporting a concrete tiled finish. About 1873 Hogg and Wilson jointly engaged John McCurdy to design the rather more sophisticated Italianate lodge at the opposite side of the entrance (see Craigmore). Late twentieth-century road works necessitated the re-siting of the gatescreen.

Newtownpark Avenue lodge; *c.* 1875; architect not known.

Wilson may have had second thoughts about sharing a main entrance to his property, for he formed this new access to the south of the house about ten years later. It may also have been prompted by the death of his friend William Hogg. A particularly forthright mid-Victorian Italianate design which probably originated on an L-plan but has been latterly much extended and abused with the insertion of a shop window in the road front, its avenue discontinued. Single-storey gabled in stucco finish on a stone plinth, each of the main gables being open pediments, that to the old avenue broken by the roof of a canted bay window with boldly bracketed eaves and guttering which extended about the lodge. The once 'feature' chimney has been rendered featureless. Surviving are good Classical pillars with recessed panels and 'Dunardagh' in glazed tiles to the cappings; fine contemporary ironwork.

Thom's; *DB* (15 April 1863); Pearson 1998; Smith 2001.

227. DUNDRUM CASTLE, Dundrum (2).
Home to barrister John Walsh, who is recorded here in 1837 and remained until close to his death in 1886. Although the valuation of 1849 lists him as having two gatehouses, only one is obvious on the OS maps. His porters were Patrick Casey and John Geraghty. The lodge, which survives the old house built near the Pale castle ruins, is a replacement probably erected by C. Luscombe-Tooke, who took the place after it had lain vacant for a few years. On the site of its pre-1837 predecessor is this neat single-storey late Victorian lodge of *c.* 1890 below a hipped roof, in an orange brick laid to Flemish bond with a variety of sash windows below segmental arches, some tripartite. All intentionally slightly asymmetrical, with its chimney-stack and gabled front projection

off-centre, it has an ornamental truss as an apex feature and foiled bargeboards. There is a cut-stone plinth and some rubble wall integrated in a side elevation, perhaps part of the original structure. Also surviving modern alterations is a tall, crenellated entrance screen wall.

Lewis 1837; Griffith 1848–60; *Thom's*; Ball and Hamilton 1895.

228. DUNDRUM, Dundrum; pre-1837; *demolished.*
A property in 1846 of George Meyler, as was the neighbouring Laurel Lodge (*q.v.*). In 1849 its lodge lay vacant.

Slater 1846; Griffith 1848–60.

229. DUNDRUM LODGE, Dundrum (2).
Both lodges, built before 1837, have been demolished. A seat by the mid-nineteenth century of William Blackburne, one of whose gate porters in 1850 was William Flaherty. Thereafter briefly of William T. Mulvany, who then moved to Wykham (*q.v.*) across the road.

DUNEDIN (see MONKSTOWN VIEW)

DUN EMER (see RUNNYMEDE)

230. DUNFILLAN, Rathgar; *c.* 1865; architect probably C. Geoghegan; *demolished.*
A good villa residence which first appears in a directory of 1857 as home to seedsman David Drummond. About ten years later he had engaged architect Charles Geoghegan to carry out alterations and additions to it, but it is not clear from what building stage its gate lodge dated. Surviving is an entrance screen with striking stone drum pillars like squat Doric columns with oversized cappings.

Thom's; *DB* (15 May 1865).

231. DUNSTAFFNAGE LODGE, Galloping Green; pre-1837/pre-1907; *demolished.*
A small demesne, home to a frequent turnover of different occupants, in 1837 of R.H. Sheehan; twelve years later it had been acquired by Joseph Hynes, whose gate porter was then Thomas Colgan. No gate lodge is indicated on the 1871 OS map, which suggests that the original was subsequently replaced and it too demolished.

Thom's; Griffith 1848–60.

232. EASTBOURNE, Terenure; pre-1837; *demolished.*
A long-removed gate lodge which had gone by 1869, never to be replaced. Perhaps the proprietor in 1851, music-seller Henry Shade, knew it.

Thom's.

233. EASTON LODGE, Monkstown; pre-1837; *demolished.*
Major-General Sir John Montague Burgoyne (1796–1858) resided here until about 1846, when he was succeeded by J. Greenwood Pim, whose gatekeeper in 1849 was Thomas Keys.

Thom's; Griffith 1848–60.

234. EASTWOOD, Dundrum; *c.* 1890.

With lodgeless 'Westerton' forming a late Victorian pair of semi-detached houses occupied in 1895 by the stockbroker John Low. Contemporary is this tidy little single-storey standard gate lodge, recently sensitively extended and modernised but for its synthetically slated hipped roof with red concrete ridge and hip tiles. Built in polygonal stone facings with red-brick quoins, dressings to two-over-two sash windows and projecting gabled hall which sports lacy perforated foiled bargeboards, iron hip-knob and pretty round-headed archway with glazed and herringbone-sheeted door. The gatescreen looks older, presumably salvaged from elsewhere, with its railed quadrants and pair of octagonal granite carriage pillars with peculiar chevron-sculpted friezes, much as at Mount Jerome Cemetery (*q.v.*).

Thom's.

235. EATON BRAE, Shanganagh; *c.* 1860; architect probably W.F. Caldbeck.

A very fine Italianate villa and complementary gate lodge, both in the manner of architect William F. Caldbeck (1825–72), presumably a cousin of the developer of the site, Thomas Fulton Caldbeck (1821–91). Single-storey standard but boldly detailed, with prominent moulded brackets to eaves and verges of gables, both main and that of the entrance breakfront, which contains a round-headed fanlit doorway in a similar recess. The segmentally arched two-over-two sash windows on each side are similarly treated in stucco-effect walls framed on main corners by conspicuous quarry-faced stone quoins. The park gable is relieved by a semicircular arched niche. There are lodges akin to this at Grangecon, Co. Wicklow (*q.v.*), and like details on Caldbeck's lodge to Clonhugh, Co. Westmeath (*q.v.*).

Thom's; *LGI* (1904).

236. ECHO LODGE, Dún Laoghaire; pre-1837/*c.* 1850; *demolished.*
The original house on the site, called 'Myrtle Lodge', dated from before 1816. In 1847 it

Irish Architectural Archive

Irish Architectural Archive

passed from the Leathley family to the Dominicans, who incorporated it into their new convent, probably to designs of architect John Bourke. He may have been responsible for the eccentric and gauche gate lodge, either as a rework of an existing structure or as a replacement. It was single-storey standard below a parapeted flat roof. Centrally was a five-panelled front door with rectangular fanlight in a pilastered and pedimented door-case. This was flanked, quirkily, by a pair of breakfronts containing six-over-six sash windows in rectangular recesses, each of which rose above the main parapet. Nearby was a rather more correct and sophisticated triple-arched triumphal gateway. The main round-headed carriage opening was framed by pairs of Doric pilasters on plinths and supporting a chaste entablature which was repeated on the smaller auxiliary postern arches. There were railed quadrant screens. In 1849 the gatekeeper was Andrew Dooley. The whole complex was recently demolished to make way for a shopping centre.

Lewis 1837; *Thom's*; Griffith 1848–60; *DB* (1 Jan. 1861); Williams 1994; Pearson 1981; IAA.

237. EDEN COTTAGE, Kimmage; pre-1837; *demolished.*
A property in 1850 of Thomas Dillon, let by the previous owners, the Brunton family. James Maguire was then the gate porter. By 1862 the house had been acquired by Edward Rothwell, who changed its name to 'Meeanee Villa'.

Griffith 1848–60; *Thom's.*

238. EDEN, Harold's Cross; *c.* 1910.
An Edwardian lodge, single-storey and steeply gabled, its short elevation to the avenue. Roughcast-finished with red-brick highlights in a diamond motif to the apex, plinth and a chimney-stack emerging from the earthenware-pantiled roof finish. Modernised with an unfortunate lean-to hall, road extension and new windows. An old Cromwellian house, now a pub, it was from the 1850s home to the Barton family.

Thom's; Craig and Fewer 2002.

239. EDENBROOK, Willbrook; pre-1837; *demolished.*
A seat in 1837 of Edmund Conlan, which by 1849 he was letting to Patrick Regan, whose gatekeeper was Richard Ruttledge.
Lewis 1837; Griffith 1848–60.

EDENFIELD (see EDEN PARK)

240. EDEN PARK, Dundrum; pre-1837; *demolished.*
A small estate in 1837 of Lawrence Finn. Subsequently renamed 'Edenfield'.
Lewis 1837.

241. EDEN VILLE, Dún Laoghaire (2).
A property of James Sheridan on the main street of Glasthule in 1837, when at least one gate lodge was in place. Ralph J. Newcomen was the proprietor by 1849, when his gate porter was John Redmonds, one lodge lying vacant. In 1851 the place was also being run as a dancing and fencing academy, but twenty years later the house had been replaced by terraced housing and its lodges subsequently removed.
Lewis 1837; Griffith 1848–60; *Thom's.*

242. EDMONDSTOWN, Ballyboden; pre-1837; *demolished.*
A modest late Georgian farmhouse in 1837 of C. McGrane Esq., whose widow was probably in occupation in 1849. Mrs McGrane's gatekeeper was then Robert Walsh.
Lewis 1837; Griffith 1848–60; Crofton 1980.

243. EDMONDSTOWN PARK, Ballyboden; pre-1837; *demolished.*
The pleasant Georgian gentry villa was in 1849 the property of Daniel Watson, whose gate porter was James Magee. For the rest of the century it was owned by William Armstrong Hayes.
Lewis 1837; Griffith 1848–60; Crofton 1980.

EGREMONT (see BALLYBRACK LODGE)

244. EL DORADO, Galloping Green; *c.* 1860; *demolished.*
A house built *c.* 1860 for insurance agent Charles Fox Goodwin, its lodge probably contemporary. Later renamed 'St Petroc'.
Thom's.

245. ELLEN LODGE, Dalkey; pre-1837; *demolished.*
A gate lodge which had gone by 1871 was occupied in 1849 by Richard McCormick, porter to Timothy Byrne, hosiery warehouseman and glove manufacturer.
Slater 1846; Griffith 1848–60.

246. ELLERSLIE, Little Bray; pre-1837; *demolished.*
A delightful small estate and Picturesque late Georgian villa in 1837 of William Bigger. The entrance is now marked by a bungalow.
Lewis 1837.

ELM CLIFF (see FORT LISLE)

247. ELMFIELD, Milltown; pre-1837; *demolished.*
In 1837 'the residence of the Misses Hunt, partly the repaired edifice of Milltown Castle', which it remained into the 1870s, by which time the property had become 'Elm Hall'. Miss Charlotte Hunt's gatekeeper in 1850 was Thomas Nevin.
Lewis 1837; Griffith 1848–60; *Thom's.*

248. ELM GROVE, Stillorgan; pre-1837; *demolished.*
A seat in the early nineteenth century of the Richards family, whose gate lodge had gone by 1907. Its occupant in 1849 was Thomas Brady, gatekeeper to J.W.C. Richards.
Lewis 1837; Griffith 1848–60.

ELM GROVE (see TERENURE)

ELM MOUNT (see BEVERSTON)

249. ELM PARK, Ballinteer; pre-1837; *demolished.*
A demesne, also known in the past as 'Elm Grove', in 1837 of P. Morgan Esq. The late eighteenth-century house was still in the family in 1849, when John Kinsella was gate porter to Robert Morgan. There is a modern 'gate lodge' nearby.
Lewis 1837; Griffith 1848–60; Pearson 1998.

250. ELM PARK, Merrion; pre-1837; *demolished.*
A property in 1837 of Joseph Watkins, who was still there eleven years later, when his gatekeeper was Thomas Lyons. Now St Vincent's Hospital complex.
Lewis 1837; Griffith 1848–60.

251. ELM PARK, Terenure; pre-1837; *demolished.*
Loan banker Parker Molloy was living here in 1846 and three years later, when the porter's lodge lay vacant. By 1851 he had moved on to Newbawn (*q.v.*). Both house and lodge had been swept away by 1907.
Slater 1846; Griffith 1848–60.

ELMS (see ROCKVILLE)

252. ELM VILLA, Sandymount; pre-1871; *demolished.*
A lodge added on Serpentine Avenue after 1837 to an older house, either by auctioneer William Young or merchant William Leckey, who succeeded him here about 1860.
Thom's.

253. ELMVILLE, Terenure; pre-1837; *demolished.*
James Geraghty was gatekeeper in 1849 to Sir Thomas Whelan, who was preceded here by James Moore. What appears to have been a sizeable lodge was swept away by the formation of the Kenilworth Park junction with Harold's Cross Road, the Elmville site being redeveloped by 1907.
Thom's; Griffith 1848–60.

254. ELY CLOTH FACTORY, Rathfarnham; pre-1837; *demolished.*
In 1779 the 'Widow Clifford's Mill', it was by 1836 kept by Mr Murray, who employed 'about fifty persons', or 'about 100 persons' according to Lewis a year later. In 1850 this Thomas Murray employed James Timmons as his gatekeeper. By 1880, after it had become a flour mill, the concern was closed and the buildings by the River Dodder subsequently demolished.
D'Alton 1976 [1838]; Lewis 1837; Griffith 1848–60; Healy 2005.

255. ERITH LODGE, Irishtown; pre-1837; *demolished.*
In 1841 this was the residence of Revd Richard Henry Wall DD, chaplain of the Royal Chapel of St Matthew, his gate porter seven years later being listed as Thomas Snow. The porter's lodge had gone by 1907.
Thom's; Griffith 1848–60.

256. ERRIGAL, Rathgar; *c.* 1890.
A plain single-storey four-bay structure with a hipped roof to the road, gabled to the park and with a catslide over the front door projection. Lodge and house built by barrister D.M. Wilson. Recently the Russian Embassy.
Thom's.

257. ESKER, Esker; pre-1836.
At the entrance to the Georgian house is a good cast-iron late Victorian gatescreen alongside the sad remains of a butchered gate lodge now sporting a mono-pitched roof. A seat in 1824 of a Captain Ellis, thirteen years later of John Cash and by 1849 of Captain Edmund Wynne, whose gatekeeper was Michael Daly.
Pigot 1824; Lewis 1837; Griffith 1848–60.

258. ESKER LODGE, Esker; pre-1836; *demolished.*
Perhaps the 'Esker Cottage' recorded in 1814 of a Captain Godfrey, by 1837 it was home to Major Wills. Matthew Reid was in 1849 the gatekeeper of John Wills, who remained here until *c.* 1860, when he moved to nearby Willsbrook (*q.v.*).
Leet 1814; Lewis 1837; Griffith 1848–60; *Thom's.*

259. ESKER NEW CEMETERY, Esker; *c.* 1860.
A 1½-storey four-bay gabled lodge, roughcast with stone quoins and tall eaves over a gabled single-storey breakfront hall. Occupied. Probably contemporary with the graveyard's formation.

260. ESKER RECTORY, Esker; pre-1836; *demolished.*
A lodge perhaps built during the incumbency (1795–1820) of Revd Dr Edward Berwick (1754–1820). Revd Henry Stewart was rector by 1848, when his gate porter was John Toner.
Griffith 1848–60; Leslie and Wallace 2001.

261. ESKER VILLA, Esker; pre-1836; *demolished.*
Also known as 'Esker Hall', it was home to

Thomas Berry in the mid-nineteenth century, his gate porter in 1848 being John Green.
Thom's; Griffith 1848–60.

262. EVERGREEN LODGE, Ballybrack; pre-1837; *demolished.*
A property in 1849 of John P. Smith.
Griffith 1848–60.

263. EVERSHAM, Galloping Green; *c.* 1830/*c.* 1900; architect probably L.A. McDonnell.

Like its immediate neighbour 'Abilene' (*q.v.*), this is one of those many charming single-storey-over-basement villas which sprang up south of Dublin in the 1830s, built for merchants and lawyers, within easy reach of the city. Both houses had little contemporary lodges back to back and shared a common entrance screen. The first owner would appear to have been William Minchin (1793–1843) from Annagh, Co. Tipperary, who is recorded here in 1837. Eversham was leased by his widow and cousin, Georgina, to Henry McGeough by 1849, when the gatekeeper was John Thornton. The property then had a succession of occupants before Henry Seymour Guinness (1858–1945), politician and governor of the Bank of Ireland, and also of Burton Hall (*q.v.*), took up residence and made improvements to the place, which included the replacement of the old gate lodge with a fine new bungalow in the Arts and Crafts style. This is stylistically akin to lodges at Knockmaroon, north Dublin (*q.v.*), Eyrefield Lodge, Co. Kildare (*q.v.*), and Claremont, Shanganagh (*q.v.*), which suggests the involvement of architect Lawrence Aloysius McDonnell. Single-storey with, as at those other examples, a wide gabled main front containing a substantial living-room window, here with an entablature and pediment, once flanked by a pair of corner recesses, one of which was the entrance porch, each probably having had ornamental post and bracket support. These have been enclosed in modernisation with an insensitive hodgepodge of unrelated glazing patterns. The quarry-faced stone walls are topped by the roughcast gable to a roof of red clay interlocking tiles with a crested ridge

L.A. McDonnell proposal.

broken by a corniced red-brick chimney-stack. That this may be a comprehensive work-over of its predecessor rather than a replacement is suggested by a seductive perspective drawing, which shows a more conventional bungalow with conspicuous leading half-timbered gables and verandahed porch, entitled 'Proposed Alterations and Additions to the Gate Lodge for H.S. Guinness Esq.', undated but signed by L.A. McDonnell MRIAI—clearly not seductive enough.
Lewis 1837; *Thom's*; Griffith 1848–60; *LGI* (1904); Smith 2001; *IFR*; IAA.

264. FAIRBROOK, Willbrook; pre-1837; *demolished.*
A seat in 1837 of Thomas Murphy which by 1849 had been acquired by John Dennis, whose gate porter was then Michael Egan. Both lodge and house have gone.
Lewis 1837; Griffith 1848–60.

265. FAIRFIELD, Rathgar; *c.* 1840.
An early Victorian house and lodge of Charles Cooney, starch manufacturer, which by 1849 was leased to William Ross, whose gatekeeper was Bartholomew McNamara. Remarkably, the lodge survives amongst modern development as a tiny single-storey hip-roofed cottage.
Thom's; Slater 1846; Griffith 1848–60.

FAIRHOLME (see MONKSTOWN RECTORY)

266. FAIRVIEW, Clondalkin; pre-1837; *demolished.*
A property in 1849 of William M. Russell, the lodge to which had gone by 1906.
Griffith 1848–60.

FAIRY HILL (see MERRYVILLE)

267. FAIRYLAND, Milltown; pre-1837; *demolished.*
The gatehouse in 1850 lay vacant to a home of solicitor William C. Hogan. The property by 1870 had been renamed 'St Philip's'.
Griffith 1848–60; *Thom's.*

268. FAIRYLAND, Monkstown; *c.* 1845; *demolished.*
A late Georgian brick villa built for himself in 1804 by architect John Semple. Its lodge is later, being recorded in the valuation of 1851, when its occupant was Thomas Clements, porter to Revd Edward Semple. A property now known as 'St Helen's'.
Griffith 1848–60; IAA.

269. THE FARM, Stillorgan; pre-1837; *demolished.*
Alternatively called 'Farmleigh', in 1841 it was a seat of Robert R. Guinness, barrister, whose gatekeeper in 1849 was Mary Staunton. The Georgian villa and its lodge have both gone.
Thom's; Griffith 1848–60.

270. FARMHILL, Dundrum (2).
Both lodges were in place by 1837, when the proprietor was James Pratt. Twelve years later William Booth was here, and his gate porters were listed as Matthew Duncan and Patrick Lee. House and lodges had been removed by the 1970s to make way for modern private housing.
Lewis 1837; Griffith 1848–60; Craig and Fewer 2002.

FARMLEIGH (see THE FARM)

271. FARMLEY, Dundrum (2).
A property in 1837 of J.T. Underwood which by 1849 had been acquired by John T. Lloyd, barrister, one of whose porters was then James North.
Ballinteer Road gate; pre-1837/*c.* 1875.
Lloyd died in 1853, so this replacement lodge was built either by Joseph William Coppinger (1807–83), solicitor, who was here in 1870, or his successor, stockbroker John Low, who also changed the name of the place to 'Lynwood'. This is a big two-storey gatehouse in rubble construction with red-brick toothed dressings and quoins and a bull's-eye first-floor window to the road, below a hipped roof.
Sandyford Road gate; pre-1837; *demolished.*
Late in the nineteenth century a portion of ground to the east was sold off to be occupied by 'Ardglas', which thus acquired the old lodge and access.
Lewis 1837; Griffith 1848–60; *Thom's*; Ball and Hamilton 1895.

272. FARRANBOLEY COTTAGE, Windy Arbour; *c.* 1845; *demolished.*
A Robert Billing, solicitor, and presumably his son of the same name are associated with the property in 1843 and in 1872. In 1849 the gate porter is recorded as John Bryan. The house was briefly renamed 'Ferndale' around 1869 and finally 'Ardnabel' thereafter, when Miss Harriett Billing was in residence.
Thom's; Griffith 1848–60; Ball and Hamilton 1895.

FARRANBOLEY (see OAKLAWN)

FAUNAGH (see ORWELL)

273. FERNBANK, Dundrum (2).
The house and one lodge originated in the grounds of 'Woodville' (*q.v.*) about 1860, when merchant John Webb was the first owner. Another lodge was added sometime between 1869 and 1907, probably in the time here of John M. Green. Both have been demolished.
Thom's.

FERNDALE (see FARRANBOLEY COTTAGE)

FERNDALE (see SHANGANAGH COTTAGE)

274. FERNDENE, Stradbrook; pre-1837; *demolished.*
The house was built *c.* 1870 by Henry J. Allen, woollens importer and clothier, next door to another family house of Brooklawn. Ferndene seems to have shared the old eastern access to Rock Villa (*q.v.*), so the attendant gate lodge may originally have related to the latter.

Thom's.

275. FERNEY, Galloping Green; pre-1837; *demolished.*
A lovely late Georgian bow-fronted villa, in 1804 the home of Eleanor Taylor but for many years thereafter of Henry Scovell, whose gatekeeper in 1849 was Michael Quigley. Latterly it was known as 'Beech Park' and became a special school for deaf boys.

Lewis 1837; Griffith 1848–60; Flanagan 1991; Pearson 1998.

276. FERN HILL, Sandyford (2).
An estate established in the early nineteenth century, probably around 1812, if the date-stone on a gate lodge is any indication, by Alderman Frederick Darley, one of a family of builders, architects and stonemasons. More significantly for Fern Hill, it was a legal man, the long-lived Judge William Frederick Darley, who from 1860 added to it and created a renowned garden.

North lodge; *c.* 1812/*c.* 1895; architect not known.

Judge Darley remodelled the house in 1893 and doubtless this lodge formed part of the architect's commission. Single-storey Arts and Crafts with a wide gabled three-bay symmetrical front in pebble-dash finish with minimal black-and-white work to the apex, which frames a date-stone presumably salvaged from its predecessor on the site. Below is a gabled hall projection, whilst the roof has a red earthenware tiled finish, perforated ornamental cresting and bargeboards with carved dentil decoration.

South lodge; pre-1837; *demolished.*
The OS maps reveal an unusually long, narrow structure, which survived into the twentieth century.

Apart from a short period about 1837 when the place was let to John McCasky, the Darleys were here for over a century before it was sold to the Walker family.

Lewis 1837; *Thom's*; Joyce 1912; Williams 1994; Pearson 1998.

FERNSIDE (see ILLERTON)

277. FETTERCAIRN, Belgard; pre-1837/*c.* 1896; *demolished.*
A farm of 58 acres in 1850 of Mrs Janet Gregg, its lodge first being valued in 1896, perhaps as a replacement for Patrick Mooney.

Griffith 1848–60.

278. FIELD VILLA, Blackrock; pre-1837; *demolished.*
A seat in 1837 of Henry Casey Field, physician and surgeon, who lived here until about 1860, his gate porter in 1849 being Patrick Kane.

Lewis 1837; Griffith 1848–60; *Thom's.*

279. FINNSTOWN, Esker; *c.* 1820.
The quintessential little late Georgian gate lodge of single-storey standard format below a hipped roof with paired soffit brackets. The Classical panelled front door is flanked by simple bipartite plastic casement windows in harled walls, now delightfully cloaked in *Cotoneaster horizontalis.* A side window with segmental head and Y-tracery suggests a date perhaps contemporary with the house, where John Rourke is recorded in 1814. In 1849 John Rourke's gatekeeper was George McGrane. The entrance screen has been crudely rebuilt and roughcast; wide concave quadrant walls contain postilion openings tight to eagle-finialled carriage pillars. The outer pillars have basic ball finials. Now a country house hotel and golf-course.

Leet 1814; Griffith 1848–60; Pike and McDowell 1908.

280. FINNSTOWN LODGE, Esker; *c.* 1830.
A typical Irish Regency lodge with a confusion of styles, having Classical paired soffit brackets and Tudor label mouldings to windows. Single-storey standard now in new-rendered walls with obviously plastic windows below an oversailing hipped roof, its chimney-stack rising off the rear wall. Later extended by a bay to the right-hand side. In 1837 a residence of S. Bell Esq., but by 1849 it was a seat of Henry Phillips, whose gatekeeper was James Bradley.

Lewis 1837; Griffith 1848–60.

281. FIRHOUSE CONVENT, Firhouse; *c.* 1830.
A house built in the late eighteenth century by the Fieragh family which was purchased in 1827 by the nuns, who added a chapel and schoolhouse in the grounds and perhaps this modest single-storey roughcast hip-roofed gate lodge. James Doran was the gate porter in 1850 to superioress Mrs Maginness.

Griffith 1848–60; Craig and Fewer 2002.

282. FLORAVILLE, Clondalkin; *c.* 1825.
The seat in 1837 of Francis Smith, whose gate lodge thirteen years later lay vacant. Surprisingly, unlike its big house, which was demolished in 1973, it survives well preserved and tended. Plain single-storey standard with roughcast walls below clipped eaves to the steeply pitched hipped roof with an off-centre chimney-stack. Modern windows.

Lewis 1837; Griffith 1848–60.

283. FLORAVILLE, Donnybrook (2).
A property in 1837 of M. Fitzgerald Esq., when it shared the townland with a huge hat manufactory which was then in terminal decline.

Brookvale Road gate; pre-1837; *demolished.*
This entrance was the sole approach to the house from the south by the bank of the Dodder.

By 1869 the factory had gone, to be replaced by villas that were accessed from the new Eglinton Road, from which another entrance was created to Floraville.

Eglinton Road gate; *c.* 1865.

A lodge sufficiently presumptuous to ensure its survival amongst modern housing. A striking single-storey standard Classical lodge below a hipped roof with tall eaves having a frieze that continues into the open pediment of the entrance breakfront, which contains a chamfered three-centred archway. To each side the window openings are crowned by entablatures carried on scrolled console brackets, all framed by high Doric pilasters to the external corners. The two octagonal chimney-pots which squinch off square plinths are more Picturesque than Classical, and the modern contributions of dull grey rendering, plastic casements and Arts and Crafts double doors are unfortunate. Probably built by barrister Edward Thomas Wright (1810–81), who in 1832 had married his cousin Charlotte Wright of nearby Beech Hill (*q.v.*). His brother Joseph William Wright set up home at Kilrock, north Dublin (*q.v.*).

Lewis 1837; *Thom's*; *IFR.*

284. FLOWERGROVE, Rochestown; pre-1837; *demolished.*
A distinctive mid-Georgian villa with alterations and additions of *c.* 1820, from when the gate lodge may have dated. A residence in 1837 of Hervey de Montmorency, 4th Viscount Mountmorres (1796–1872), from 1850 dean of Achonry, whose house has recently been converted into flats and its grounds developed.

Lewis 1837; *BPB* (1929); Pearson 1998; Craig and Fewer 2002.

285. FONTHILL ABBEY, Willbrook; pre-1837; *demolished.*
A distinctive house, now removed, like its lodge, saw a succession of owners over the

centuries. John Thomas Moran was resident here in 1841 but eight years later it was home to Richard Hughes, whose gate porter was James Carberry.

Thom's (1841); Griffith 1848–60; Healy 2005.

286. FONTHILL, Palmerston; *c.* 1850; *demolished.*
A house and lodge built after 1837 for John Godley, probably the same who was previously at Oatlands, north Dublin (*q.v.*).

Griffith 1848–60; *Thom's.*

287. FORTFIELD, Rathgar; pre-1837; *demolished.*
A porter's lodge occupied in 1850 by a Mrs Kelly had been demolished by 1869 to make way for Fortfield Terrace. It was then, as thirteen years previously, a property of Patrick Boylan.

Lewis 1837; Griffith 1848–60.

288. FORTFIELD, Terenure (2).
A magnificent Palladian mansion was sadly demolished in 1934—like its two gate lodges, both in place by 1834, a thing of the past. Built in 1785 by Barry Yelverton (1736–1805), who was created Viscount Avonmore in 1800. By 1849 it was let by the representatives of a subsequent owner, the late 3rd Baron Clanmorris, to the widow of Sir William McMahon (1776–1837), whose gate porters were Philip Cooke and Michael Lamb.

Griffith 1848–60; Ball 1995; *BPB* (1929); Bence-Jones 1988.

289. FORTFIELD LODGE, Templeogue; pre-1837; *demolished.*
A property in 1837 of barrister William Crozier, whose gatekeeper in 1849 was Patrick Shea.

Lewis 1837; Griffith 1848–60.

290. FORT LISLE, Blackrock; pre-1837; *demolished.*
An old house, built about 1762 by the 1st Lord Lisle, occupied by Admiral Moore, which subsequently fell from grace, or rather to Mrs Maria Grace, who ran it in the first half of the nineteenth century as 'Elm-Cliff Boarding House'. Her gatekeeper in 1849 was Peter Murray. By 1907 the house had gone, with its grounds having been incorporated into Vauxhall Gardens.

Thom's; Griffith 1848–60; *Hill's guide to Blackrock*; O'Kane 2004.

291. FORTWILLIAM, Mount Merrion; *c.* 1860.
A modest house, which previously had access from Mount Merrion Avenue, subsequently entered from Stillorgan Road, with a new gate lodge probably built in the time here about 1857 of a Captain O'Sullivan or his successor, Humphreys Peare of the Bank of Ireland. It is a plain 1½-storey hip-roofed structure, rendered and much altered.

Thom's.

292. FOUNDLING HOSPITAL, James Street; pre-1837; *demolished.*
Originally founded in 1703 as a workhouse, in 1727 it was reconstituted as the Foundling Hospital, with a history, in part, 'of unspeakable horror'. It was described in 1837 as 'a very extensive establishment in James Street, for the reception of this description from all parts of Ireland, for many years afforded an asylum to 2000 deserted children within its walls'. Its gate lodge may date from modifications carried out to the great hall in 1798 by Francis Johnston.

Lewis 1837; Craig 1980.

293. FOXROCK, Foxrock; *demolished.*
The house, which was demolished in 1976, was comprised of a single-storey villa attached to an earlier two-storey structure, perhaps work carried out in the mid-nineteenth century for solicitor Bernard Lynott which would have included the provision of a porter's lodge.

Thom's; Pearson 1998.

294. FOXROCK LODGE, Foxrock; pre-1837; *demolished.*
The early lodge to a property in 1851 of a Miss Thompson had gone by 1907. By 1927 C.J. Rutherford was in residence and commissioning a replacement to designs by W.M. Mitchell and Sons, which seems never to have been built. The drawings show an Arts and Crafts three-bedroomed bungalow with an irregular three-bay front having two multi-paned canted glazed bay windows below a hipped roof. Thereafter the place became part of a Loreto school.

Thom's; Pearson 1998; IAA drawing (McCurdy & Mitchell Collection 79/17, Bin III, Roll 30).

295. FRANKFORD LODGE, Windy Arbour (2).
Two porters' lodges occupied in 1849 by William Heeney and Alexander Rogers serving William Booth, who is also recorded here three years earlier.

Dundrum lodge; pre-1837; *demolished.*

Rosemount lodge; *c.* 1820.
On the northern approach survives a single-storey standard lodge below a hipped roof presenting a side elevation and that of its double-pile extension to the main road. It also has a two-bay addition to the opposing front, its main door being sealed in the process; two-over-two sashes in roughcast walls survive. There are also the remains of a pair of channelled rusticated carriage pillars and a distant postilion opening.

Alternatively called 'Frankfort Castle'.

Slater 1846; Griffith 1848–60; *Thom's.*

296. FRESCATI, Blackrock; pre-1837; *demolished.*
Historically one of the most unfortunate architectural losses to the county, its demolition accompanied by a furore whilst its porter's lodge passed without a whisper, despite Lord Edward Fitzgerald's being familiar with it. Long associated with the Leinster family as their marine residence from its purchase in 1766, it was home in 1849 to John Plunkett, whose porter at the gate was James Barnes. The house was subsequently divided into separate units before its 1983 demise.

Griffith 1848–60; Joyce 1912; Pearson 1998; O'Kane 2004.

297. FRIARSLAND, Roebuck; *c.* 1845; *demolished.*
A lodge in Classical style built after 1837, its gatekeeper in 1849 being William Stewart as porter to Henry William Curran, commissioner of insolvent court. The house is attributed to architect J.S. Mulvany, whose commission may have included the lodge.

Griffith 1848–60; *Thom's*; Pearson 1998.

298. FRIARSTOWN, Friarstown (2).
An estate in the early nineteenth century of Ponsonby Shaw (1784–1871), a Dublin banker who spent much money and thought on it, reclaiming and planting the grounds, converting them into a pretty wooded glen with winding walks, grottoes and miniature waterfalls. He was so discouraged by having much of his work swept away by the bursting of the artificial lake he had formed that he abandoned the place to become wilderness. His porters' lodges, occupied in 1850 by Anne Kinshela and Andrew Collins, survive after a fashion.

South lodge; *c.* 1830.
The ruins of a three-bay single-storey cottage, with door to the left-hand side, in harled rubble and a brick-on-edge eaves band.

North lodge; *c.* 1840.
Originally a standard single-storey hipped roof lodge extended by a bay to the right-hand side. Now all refaced horribly in twentieth-century silver-grey concrete brick, permitted by the oversailing soffit, of which the old carved brackets are grotesquely just discernible; new lean-to hall projection and aluminium windows.

Griffith 1848–60; *LGI* (1904); Joyce 1912.

299. GALLANSTOWN, Ballyfermot; pre-1836; *demolished.*
A farm in 1850, home to John West.

Griffith 1848–60.

300. GARDEN HILL, Old Kilmainham; pre-1837; *demolished.*
A property of William Moore in 1841 and 1854.

Thom's; Griffith 1848–60.

301. JOSEPH GARRATT AND CO., The Coombe; 1878; architects McCurdy and Mitchell; *demolished.*
A firm of tea and sugar merchants, whose main premises were in Thomas Street, engaged architects McCurdy and Mitchell to design an enclosed courtyard comprising carriage park, stables, hayloft and a gatehouse, all of which presented to the street a pair of matching single-bay two-storey elevations, each with windows only to the upper floor below hipped roofs linked by a tall screen wall and carriage doors. The surviving dated drawing for the scheme does not indicate either materials or embellishment.

Thom's; IAA drawing (McCurdy & Mitchell Collection, Bin IX, Roll 24).

302. GAYFIELD, Donnybrook; pre-1837; *demolished.*
A property in 1837 and 1851 of General Thomas P. Luscombe, who was also to be found around this time at Killester House, north Dublin (*q.v.*). By 1907 the place had been developed as St Mary's College and the gate lodge removed.
Lewis 1837; *Thom's.*

303. GEORGE'S QUAY COAL AND IRON STORES, George's Quay; pre-1837; *demolished.*
A business premises in 1824 of George Lawler, 'Coal and Culme [*sic*] merchant', which was in ruins by 1850 but four years later had been resurrected by Thomas Hilton.
Pigot 1824; Shaw 1988; Griffith 1848–60.

304. GERALDVILLE, Rathgar; *c.* 1851; *demolished.*
One of the first sites to be developed when the Orwell Road was extended about 1850, it being occupied the following year by Cheyne Brady, solicitor.
Thom's.

305. GLASTHULE, Dún Laoghaire; pre-1837; *demolished.*
A pretty Regency villa belonging in 1837 to Robert Meekins, whose gatekeeper in 1849 was John Myers.
Lewis 1837; Griffith 1848–60.

GLEDSWOOD (see BLOOMVILLE)

306. GLENAGAREY HILL, Glenageary; pre-1837; *demolished.*
John Walsh was in 1849 gate porter to Captain John Dillon, who is also recorded here twelve years previously. Two years later the place was the residence of Harry Leachman, who renamed it 'Greythorn'.
Lewis 1837; Griffith 1848–60; *Thom's.*

307. GLENAGEARY, Glenageary (3).
All three lodges on Ballynoggin Road, Rochestown Avenue and Glenageary Road Upper were in existence in 1837 to a fine estate, the house to which was subsequently remodelled in the mid-nineteenth century by stockbroker Halliday Bruce but was sadly demolished by 1987 along with its lodges.
Lewis 1837; Pearson 1998.

GLENAGAREY LODGE (see PROSPECT)

308. GLENAGAREY LODGE, Glenageary; pre-1837.
The original house on the site dated from around 1830, its occupant in 1849 being Robert Chambers, whose gate porter was Patrick King. In the early 1850s the property was upgraded to 'Glenageary Hall' by stockbroker Edward Fox, who built himself a highly ornamental Italianate villa. This was disgracefully demolished in 1978 but it is a pity that its lodge did not suffer the same fate, for it has been incorporated into a hideous transformation which looms over the elegant early railed gatescreen with its palmette tops and concave-capped square and round pillars.
Griffith 1848–60; *Thom's*; Slater 1856; Pearson 1998.

309. GLENAGAREY PARK, Glenageary; pre-1837; *demolished.*
A lodge which had to make way for a spanking new roundabout was occupied in 1849 by Alexander Ellis, gatekeeper to Richard Browne.
Griffith 1848–60.

GLENALBYN (see JANEVILLE)

310. GLENAMUCK, Stepaside; pre-1837; *demolished.*
An estate in 1837 and 1854 of Joseph Strong.
Lewis 1837; *Thom's.*

311. GLENAULIN HOUSE AND FLOUR MILLS, Chapelizod; pre-1837; *demolished.*
A property in 1841 of James Macken, corn merchant, baker and flour merchant, whose gatehouse in 1849 was manned by Patrick Brennan.
Thom's; Slater 1846; Griffith 1848–60.

312. GLENBROOK, Willbrook; pre-1837; *demolished.*
Situated across a bridge over the River Owendoher was the gate lodge run between 1836 and 1847 as a dispensary by the proprietor, Thomas A.A. Kirkwood MD, surgeon. A modern housing estate now occupies the property.
Lewis 1837; Healy 2005.

313. GLENCAIRN, Sandyford; *c.* 1860; architect Benjamin Woodward.

A fine estate that owes its present splendour to the efforts of two owners. In 1859 solicitor George Gresson (1802–76) purchased lodgeless Murphystown House on 36 acres and employed Benjamin Woodward to design him a new house in the Tudor style nearby, where he lived on until his death. In 1904 it was sold on to Richard Welstead 'Boss' Croker (1841–1922), a wealthy returning Irish-American. He had the cosy house transformed into the present Baronial Castellated pile, much against the better judgement of his architect, James Franklin Fuller. Both phases of the building development are reflected at the entrance gate. Woodward's gate lodge is a surprising deviation from his more familiar Ruskinian Gothic style, as at Clontra (*q.v.*). Single-storey standard but sturdy on a square plan, in granite facings with a string-course at sill level, its steep pyramidal roof rises to a central stone cluster stack with a peculiar

hefty corbelled brick capping, for which the architect is noted in his earlier works. The plastic casement window pattern reflects that of the original, flanking a flimsy porch with a roof canopy bellcasting from the main roof to be supported on pairs of plain wooden posts. Fuller's grand entrance screen is dominated by a central triple archway; the great carriage opening with its hood-moulded three-centred arch is crowned by a crow-stepped gable mirroring many of those on the big house. In uncoursed cut granite, it is supported by a pair of shouldered, flat-arched pedestrian gates. Decorative ironwork to the gates extends into ogee quadrant railings and is continued in crenellated curtain walls. All well tended as home to the British Embassy.
IB (24 Sept. 1904 and 14 Jan. 1905); Williams 1994; O'Dwyer 1997b.

314. GLENCULLEN, Kiltiernan; pre-1837; *demolished.*
A pretty, small estate with an original modest farmhouse to which was added *c.* 1800 a new single-storey front with a neo-Classical portico, sufficiently chaste for it to be popularly attributed to Francis Johnston. A seat in 1837 of Christopher Fitzsimon, in whose family it remained for another century. Its gate lodge may have dated from that period of improvement.
Lewis 1837; Pearson 1998.

315. GLENDRUID HOUSE AND COTTAGE, Cabinteely; pre-1837/*c.* 1860.
A single-storey symmetrical five-bay cottage with hipped roof from which extends a gabled hall with scalloped bargeboards; big ugly chimney-stack off-centre. Either a replacement or transformation of the earlier cottage. In 1849 its occupant was William Simmons, porter to Manliff Barrington, who lived on here until the 1870s and whose family had built the house in 1808. By 1938 the pretty Glendruid Cottage had been removed.
Griffith 1848–60; *Thom's*; Pearson 1998.

GLENGARA LODGE (see LONGFORD LODGE)

GLEN-NA-GERAGH HALL (see GLENAGAREY LODGE)

GLENGOWER (see CHURCHTOWN [2])

316. GLEN-NA-SMOIL, Rathmines; *c.* 1880; *demolished.*
Merchant Edmund Johnstone Figgis acquired

Veronica Rowe

this suburban plot for his new villa on Darty Road, complete with a fine contemporary obligatory porter's lodge in a typical late Victorian fusion of styles. Single-storey standard rendered with a shallow hipped roof in traditional manner, with Classical detailing in its Irish pilaster quoins, segmentally headed window and carved modillion brackets to the soffits. This was in contrast to a highly ornamental gabled wooden porch, its decorative joinery and later trellised work a delight. Sometime later the accommodation was doubled to a double pile, with a twin pair of miniature tripartite windows to the footpath. Each ridge had a lofty chimney-stack raised to give draw in this once-wooded setting. After Figgis's death the property was acquired in 1908, along with neighbouring 'Palmerston' (*q.v.*), to form 'Trinity Hall' as residential quarters for lady students of TCD. The lodge was removed in 2002.

Thom's; *IB* (22 Aug. 1908).

GLENSAVAGE (see LANDSEND)

317. GLENVAR, Booterstown (2).
Whether either or both of the porters' lodges, built by 1871 on Mount Merrion Avenue and Cross Avenue, reflected the quirkiness of architect J.S. Mulvany's big house, with its oriental detailing, may never be known. They could well have been akin to his other lost lodge at St Margaret's (*q.v.*)—both have gone. Mulvany exhibited his design proposal at the RHA in 1856 as a villa for George McMullin Esq., although by 1862 it was already occupied by John Barrington. There was previously a house called 'Church View' (*q.v.*) on the site.

Thom's; Pearson 1998; *IADS* (2000).

318. GLENVILLE, Priesthouse; pre-1837; *demolished.*
A property alternatively called 'Granville' was home in 1841 to Joseph M. McGeough, whose gate lodge eight years later was unoccupied.

Thom's; Griffith 1848–60.

319. GLYNSOUTHWELL, Ballinteer; pre-1837; *demolished.*
In 1837 'the seat of C.B. Ponsonby Esq., by whom the grounds are thrown open for the inspection of visitors', visitors who would have been monitored in 1849 by gatekeeper James Rothery. Charles B. Ponsonby had come by the property, also known as 'Little Dargle', through marriage into the family who built the eighteenth-century house, the Southwells.

Lewis 1837; Griffith 1848–60; Ball 1995; *BPB* (1929).

GOLDENBRIDGE CEMETERY (see RICHMOND CEMETERY)

320. GOLDENBRIDGE, Goldenbridge; pre-1837/*c.* 1880; architect not known.

James Barry in 1849 was gate porter to Thomas J. Lynch in a lodge that gave way to the present extraordinary replacement around the turn of the twentieth century. This innovative structure, built for the Sisters of Mercy at the gate to their St Vincent's Reformatory, is a composition in red brick dominated by high eaves to its steeply pitched hipped roof to accommodate its attic floor, lit by six-over-six sash windows which pierce the distinctive, deep-coved, white plastered soffit. The symmetrical three-bay entrance front has an ornamental gabled canopy to the front door with carved bargeboards and bracket support. To each side are tall, segmentally arched six-over-six sash windows, and both gables have dominant towering battered and corbelled cluster chimney-stacks. The contemporary gatescreen is represented by a sole surviving integral pillar with a nice sculpted foliated cross to the capping.

Griffith 1848–60; *Thom's*.

321. GOLDENBRIDGE PAPER MILLS, Goldenbridge; pre-1837; *demolished.*
A concern in 1841 of Bartholomew Sullivan and in 1849 of Daniel Payton Sullivan, paper manufacturer, whose gate porter was Patrick O'Hara. By 1890 the place lay vacant.

Thom's; Griffith 1848–60.

GONZAGA COLLEGE (see SANDFORD COTTAGE)

322. GORTLEITRAGH, Dún Laoghaire; pre-1837; *demolished.*
Originally a square villa of the Stewart family, agents of Lords Longford and De Vesci, with its own gate lodge in beautifully manicured terraced gardens. It was given grandeur in a mid-Victorian facelift, with Classical detailing and the addition of wings by James Robert Stewart (1805–89). All unceremoniously removed in 1955 to make way for flats.

Thom's; *LGI* (1904); Pearson 1981.

GORTMHUIRE (see GORTMORE, Ballinteer)

GORTMORE (see PLANTATION)

323. GORTMORE, Ballinteer (3).
The previous modest house on the site had a porter's lodge slightly north of its replacement built prior to 1837. About 1858 solicitor Richard Atkinson (1818–71) redeveloped the property, probably to the recommendations of architect J.S. Mulvany, building a new neo-Classical house and adding two new gate lodges.

Main entrance; *c.* 1865; architect not known.

This is marked by a highly decorative gatescreen effectively located at a kink in the road, with chunky iron-railed screens on ogee dwarf walls and octagonal cut-stone pillars squinching off square bases and terminating in elaborate iron lanterns. Behind is a distinctive little mid-Victorian Italianate lodge in render highlighted by a spring-course to the little banded round-headed windows. Single-storey standard with a hipped roof of scalloped slates, from which projects a central gabled hall projection containing a three-centred arched opening to a fanlit double-leaf door. Emphasising the eaves and verge are carved brackets, and to each external corner is an ornamental bracket. Surveying the gateway on the end elevation is a striking little Venetian window. Now all somewhat relieved by road realignment but severed from the demesne.

Secondary entrance; *c.* 1840.
On the northern approach is what was a modest single-storey standard lodge with plain window surrounds in roughcast walls below a hipped roof. All rather difficult to date, as it has become a display for all manner of artefacts and architectural salvage in the likes of huge console brackets applied

to the shallow-gabled glazed hall projection; occupied. Nearby are the remains of a Georgian gatescreen with an elegant ball-finialled carriage pillar and a simple postern opening alongside. Possibly moved from the original entrance to the property.

Thom's; *LGI* (1904); Williams 1994; *IADS* (2000).

324. GORTMORE, Ballybrack; *c.* 1865/*c.* 1895.

A mid-Victorian development by Captain John Shuldham, which after about 30 years seems to have been remodelled under the new name of 'Caerleon'. A standard single-storey hip-roofed porter's lodge with a gabled breakfront hall having distinctive bracketed verge supports. Doorscreen and two-over-two sash windows have segmentally arched heads in rendered walls with simple banded quoins, high plinth and dressings. To the ridge is a red-brick chimney-stack with stone panels emerging from a scalloped slate roof finish. This could alternatively be a replacement lodge for a short-lived predecessor which the new proprietor, wine merchant Frederick Trouton, found wanting. The modest gatescreen is from the earlier period of simple roughcast screen walls and rusticated pillars. Subsequently called 'Kylemore'.

Thom's; Pearson 1998.

325. GRACEFIELD, Blackrock; pre-1837/*c.* 1865.

A detached house secluded behind the semis of Waltham Terrace, in 1841 the residence of Captain Bernard O'Reilly. By 1871 the outline of its porter's lodge had grown considerably from that on the first OS map, by which time the property had been in the hands of solicitor John Fitzgerald and from *c.* 1865 of his wife. The modest gatescreen of about that date is comprised of four posts with recessed panels containing a triple gateway. A house occupying the site of the lodge displays ornamental bargeboards, perhaps reflecting a feature of its predecessor.

Thom's.

GRANADA (see RIVERSDALE)

326. GRAND CANAL COMPANY OFFICES, Canal Harbour; *demolished.*

James Street harbour, completed in 1785 as terminus at the head of the Grand Canal, today lies waste, but in 1854 it was a thriving complex with a porter's lodge identified by the valuation.

Griffith 1848–60; Pearson 2000.

327. GRANGE CASTLE, Lucan; pre-1836; *demolished.*

A lodge situated off the Grand Canal towpath, in 1850 occupied by Francis Walsh, porter to Peter Rourke.

Griffith 1848–60.

328. GRANGE COTTAGE, Ballinteer; pre-1837; *demolished.*

A seat in 1837 of J. Whaley Esq., which by 1849 lay vacant but with its porter's lodge occupied by Patrick Ward.

Lewis 1837; Griffith 1848–60.

329. GRANGE, Kill of the Grange; pre-1836/*c.* 1860; architect possibly J.S. Mulvany; *demolished.*

The earlier house and demesne with gate lodge had by 1849 been acquired by Henry Perry, whose nephew, James Perry Jr, subsequently had the whole redeveloped by 1863 with the new name of 'Dean's Grange', a new stuccoed Italianate villa in the manner of architect J.S. Mulvany and a replacement porter's lodge at the other side of the entrance to its predecessor. This presumably formed part of the architect's commission. Prior to the lot being cleared by 1988 it had again been renamed 'Clonkeen'.

Pearson 1998; *IADS* (2000).

THE GRANGE (see BALLYFERMOT COTTAGE)

330. THE GRANGE, Galloping Green; pre-1837; *demolished.*

A fine Georgian house, removed in the 1960s, which had strong links with alcoholic drink. Before being home to a Miss Guinness in the 1860s, it was owned as early as 1837 by Henry Darley, proprietor of the adjacent Stillorgan Brewery of Darley and Co., 'purveyors of ale and table beer'. Twelve years later his gatekeeper was William Browne.

Lewis 1837; Griffith 1848–60; *Thom's*; Pearson 1998.

331. THE GRANGE, Kill of the Grange; pre-1871; *demolished.*

A large Victorian house built in 1864, probably by the McComas family. The site has been redeveloped and its gate lodge removed but survived by its prominent gatescreen of four tall square pillars and quadrant walls, one of which contains a segmentally arched postilion gateway.

Pearson 1998.

GRANGEWOOD (see WOODPARK COTTAGE)

332. GRANITE HALL, Dún Laoghaire; *c.* 1825; architect not known.

A fine, severe neo-Classical house built for himself *c.* 1821 by George Smyth, a stone contractor. Both the house and its excellent little lodge had entrances with pairs of Doric columns *in antis*, although those to the latter are fluted and Greek, flanking the single-bay pedimented leading front with V-jointed rusticated outer piers. Whilst the house was regrettably removed in the 1950s, remarkably

its little lodge survives, much altered and forming the centre-piece of a twentieth-century bungalow. Plain gate pillars carry good contemporary carriage gates with quatrefoil motifs and scroll-topped meeting rails.

Pearson 1981.

333. GRANITEFIELD, Cabinteely; *c.* 1830; *demolished.*

A property of Sir John Macartney, presumably until his death in 1812, after which it was home to the Spear family, John Flynn being gate porter in 1849 to Miss Caroline Spear. Drawings dated 1929 for alterations to the lodge for Charles Deane Oliver by the office of McCurdy and Mitchell reveal it to have been a single-storey standard gabled affair with skew-tables, a Tudor-style pair of diagonally set flues and later one-over-one sash windows.

Lewis 1837; Griffith 1848–60; Ball 1995; *BPB* (1929); Pearson 1998; IAA McCurdy & Mitchell drawings collection (79/17–20).

GRANVILLE (see GLENVILLE)

334. GREENBANK, Monkstown; pre-1849; *demolished.*

A house built around 1845 for Jonathan Pim, whose gatekeeper in 1849 was Dermod Delany. It was demolished in 1977 along with neighbouring Yapton (*q.v.*).

Griffith 1848–60; Pearson 1998.

335. GREENFIELD, Kilgobbin (2).

A property apparently of little significance until the arrival of John Milner, patent lamp and lustre manufacturer, oil and candle merchant, ornamental brass-founder and gas-fitter, whose improvements included the addition of two gate lodges.

Ballyogan Road gate; *c.* 1845; *demolished.*

A lodge occupied in 1849 by Kevin Pluck, the avenue to which was redundant by the 1930s.

Kilboggin Road gate; *c.* 1845.

A fine early Victorian lodge in typical melded styles of its time. Single-storey standard in durable granite facings with wide

windows set in segmentally headed recesses on each side of a Tudor-arched doorway, all openings with inappropriate modern inserts. The chunky banded stone chimney-stack crowns the hipped roof. 'Greenfield House' is inscribed in the friezes of contemporary granite carriage pillars. The gatekeeper in 1849 was William Hadaway.

Slater 1846; Griffith 1848–60.

336. GREENFIELD LODGE, Priesthouse; *demolished.*
Subsequently called 'Moylurg', this was a seat in 1841 of bookseller Philip Dixon Hardy, whose gate porter eight years later was John Lane.

Thom's; Slater 1846; Griffith 1848–60.

337. GREENHILL, Killiney; *c.* 1880; *demolished.*
One of the cluster of four innovative marine houses designed by the practice of Deane and Woodward around 1860, Greenhill being for the eminent concert singer Joseph Robinson, although it went through a succession of occupants before the end of the century, one of whom must have added the modest lodge. It was a simple two-roomed single-storey standard affair below a steeply pitched hipped roof with a gabled entrance breakfront, the open pediment of which boasted foiled bargeboards. The sheeted door was flanked by one-over-one sash windows with carved eaves brackets over; toothed quoins. Architects McCurdy and Mitchell surveyed the lodge in 1918 prior to W.M. Mitchell and Sons proposing alterations to it five years later for Charles Bell. A property latterly called 'Cliff'.

O'Dwyer 1997b; Pearson 1998; IAA McCurdy & Mitchell Collection (79/17, Bin II, Roll 16).

338. GREENMOUNT, Harold's Cross; pre-1837; *demolished.*
A substantial house in 1837 of James Webb, associated with the adjacent spinning manufactory, which by 1850 had been acquired by the Sisters of Charity as a convent and thereafter became Our Lady's Hospice for the Dying. Surviving is a magnificent granite Classical gatescreen.

Lewis 1837; *Thom's.*

339. GREENMOUNT, Milltown (2).
A residence in 1843 of Thomas Kirk, at that time with a single lodged entrance, supplemented by another before 1871 off Prospect Lane, probably added by solicitor William Thompson. Both removed.

Thom's.

340. GREENMOUNT, Terenure; pre-1837.
A property in 1837 of J. Turbett Esq., which had become home to Revd Alexander King by 1849, when his gate porter was Bartholomew Feeny. The lodge survives as a plain single-storey structure with a later Victorian chimney-stack replacement; much modernised. Probably once a rectory, having been owned by the ecclesiastical commissioners.

Lewis 1837; Griffith 1848–60.

341. GREENVILLE, Rathmines (2).
A seat in 1837 of John Chadwick, which four years later had become a residence of Colonel Charles Pepper. In 1849 Greenville was occupied by Walter Lindsay, barrister, whose gatekeepers were Eliza Collins and Christopher Ryan. Whilst the former's lodge was in place by 1837, the other dated from around 1845. Both have gone.

Lewis 1837; *Thom's*; Griffith 1848–60.

GREYTHORN (see GLENAGAREY HILL)

GRIFFITH BARRACKS (see RICHMOND PENITENTIARY)

342. GROSVENOR, Rathmines; *c.* 1845; *demolished.*
A small suburban seat in 1849 of William Henry Mallins, poplin manufacturer, whose lodge then lay vacant.

Slater 1846; Griffith 1848–60.

343. GROVE COTTAGE, Rathfarnham; pre-1837; *demolished.*
An antique early eighteenth-century house, removed in the 1950s, residence of Augustin Holland in 1852, the lodge to which then lay vacant.

Griffith 1848–60; Healy 2005.

344. GROVE COTTAGE, Stillorgan (2).

A smallholding in the mid-nineteenth century of Robert McDonnell formed from the breakup of the greater Stillorgan House estate (*q.v.*). In 1837 there was a porter's lodge opposite the entrance which had gone by 1871, its deterioration such that it was unrecorded in the valuation of 1849. At the gate now stands an attractive and singular cottage, or gatehouse, perfectly symmetrical, the main body of which is 1½-storey. Its hipped roof has bracketed eaves broken by a pair of gablets flanking a central chimney-stack with multiple pots, below which extends a single-storey projection culminating in an open-pedimented gable containing a canted bay window. A building of *c.* 1875.

Griffith 1848–60; *Thom's.*

GROVE (see MOUNT PROSPECT)

345. GROVE, Rathmines; pre-1837; *demolished.*
The property served as a school in the 1830s before becoming the town house in the mid-nineteenth century of Henry Grattan MP of Moyrath, Co. Meath (*q.v.*), younger son of a famous father. The place was also known as 'Portobello Grove' and was subsequently acquired around 1870 by Samuel H. Bolton, who established here his builder's yard of Portobello Works (*q.v.*).

Thom's; *IFR*; Kelly 1995.

346. GROVE, Stillorgan (2).
An estate in 1837 of John James Hughes, in whose family it remained until later in the century. Both its lodges have been demolished; that at the northern gate, in place by 1837, was occupied in 1849 by Joseph Carter. The property was renamed 'Tigh Lorcain Hall' about 1900.

Lewis 1837; *Thom's*; Griffith 1848–60; Ball 1995.

347. GULISTAN, Rathmines; pre-1837; *demolished.*
A lost house which from the 1840s until around 1870 was the residence of the incumbent of St Nicholas's Without and St Luke's in the Coombe, Revd Hickman Rose Halahan (1800–88).

Thom's; Kelly 1995; Leslie and Wallace 2001.

348. HADDINGTON, Dalkey; *c.* 1845; *demolished.*
A lodge lost to 1930s redevelopment which in 1851 was occupied by Patrick Feeny, gate porter to Isidore Burke, prior to which in 1841 it had been a property of Lady Blayney.

Thom's; Griffith 1848–60.

HALDANE GRANGE (see KILMARNOCK)

THE HALL (see RICHVIEW)

349. HARCOURT LODGE, Goldenbridge; pre-1837; *demolished.*
A house in 1841 of John Stokes, engineer to the Grand Canal, which eight years later lay vacant but with its lodge occupied by Edward Frayne.

Thom's; Griffith 1848–60.

350. HARCOURT TERRACE, Adelaide Road; *c.* 1830; *demolished.*
This is in fact a street of semi-detached Regency houses built as a speculation in 1830 by Jean Jasper Joly, at the access to which was the gate lodge for a caretaker who is listed in 1849 as Patrick Nolan.

Griffith 1848–60; Casey 2005.

351. HARLECH, Roebuck; pre-1837; *demolished.*
Located in a townland of fine Georgian villas in their verdant demesnes much beloved of the Dublin legal profession, Harlech was perhaps renamed by its owner in 1841, William Lewis, a solicitor, whose gate porter in 1849 was John Luff. Unlike its gate lodge, the house, remarkably, survives.

Thom's; Griffith 1848–60.

352. HAROLD'S CROSS CONVENT, Harold's Cross; pre-1837; *demolished.*
A foundation that also comprised a female orphan house in 1841 under superioress Mrs Atkinson.

Thom's.

353. HARROW, Ballybrack; pre-1849; *demolished.*

An establishment of about 1845 which seems to have been set up principally as 'Harrow School' by Davis Tate, whose porter's lodge in 1849 lay unoccupied. The impressive gatescreen to the property was to be found in 1990 at an architectural salvage yard in County Kilkenny. Comprised of rock-faced ogee quadrants containing a pair of postern gates over which the copings arched, and smooth stone pillars with rock-faced cappings and plinths, and the inscription 'Harrow House' thereon; good ironwork with rosette motifs and fleur-de-lis finials contemporary, of around 1865, when the place became solely a private house of George Towell or his successor by 1870, Robert Heron.

Griffith 1848–60; *Thom's.*

354. HAWTHORN LODGE, Blackrock; pre-1837; *demolished.*
Mrs Anne Hunt is recorded as living here between 1841 and 1862, in which time a new house was built to replace that on the boundary with Carysfort Avenue, which itself seems to have become porter's accommodation for its successor. All succumbed in 1987 to modern housing development.

Thom's; Pearson 1998.

355. HAYFIELD, Ballyboden; pre-1837; *demolished.*
A property in 1837 of W. Scott Esq., which by 1849 was home to Thomas Higginbotham, whose gate lodge, like the three others in Scholarstown townland, lay vacant, perhaps owing to the effects of the Famine. By 1869 a neighbouring house of the brickworks proprietor had assumed the name 'Hayfield', the old house becoming 'Woodfield'. The avenue is now disused and overgrown.

Lewis 1837; *Thom's*; Griffith 1848–60.

356. HAZELBROOK, Terenure; pre-1837/*c.* 1850.

Located on an axis with the entrance opposite, with some of its original pillars removed, is an Italianate porter's lodge built for the Rt Hon. Maziere Brady as a replacement for a predecessor, more suitable for a lord high chancellor of Ireland. Single-storey standard with a hipped roof, it is of appropriate scale, having a gabled breakfront with chamfered corners to reflect the reveals of openings in rendered walls. The round heads to bipartite one-over-one sash windows are echoed over the panelled front door. The minimal carved-block verge brackets continue about the eaves. The gatekeeper in 1849 was William Lynch.

Slater 1846; Griffith 1848–60; *Thom's.*

357. HERBERT COTTAGE, Ballsbridge; pre-1837; *demolished.*
A house, which had gone by 1907, was the residence in 1841 of Henry Charles, builder and slater, whose gate lodge in 1848 lay vacant.

Thom's; Griffith 1848–60.

358. HERBERT HILL, Dundrum; *c.* 1840.
A single-storey hip-roofed structure, its single-bay main front to the avenue with a tripartite casement window in roughcast walls. A flat-roofed entrance hall extends to the road. A property in the mid-nineteenth century of James Robinson.

HERBERT (see CHERBURY)

359. HERBERTON, Williamstown; *c.* 1890; *demolished.*
A house which first appears, avenueless, on the 1871 OS map but seems to have been much enlarged later in the century and a short-lived lodge added, perhaps by Joseph McCann.

Thom's.

360. HERMITAGE, Booterstown; pre-1837.
A standard single-storey hip-roofed structure with modern additions; occupied. A property in 1837 of W. Folliott Mostyn and twelve years later of Folliott Thornton Mostyn, whose gate porter was William Corcoran.

Lewis 1837; Griffith 1848–60.

361. THE HERMITAGE, Haroldsgrange; pre-1837/*c.* 1890.
The elegant late eighteenth-century house of the Hudson family and its fascinating demesne of Celtic follies, one of which is the so-called 'Emmet's Fort', a miniature star-shaped fort said to have housed a gate porter, but surely not, as none of the OS maps indicate the semblance of a carriage gate adjacent. The primary entrance lies to the north, where the original lodge dated from before 1837 and was built either by the Hudsons or their successor here, the Rt Hon. Richard Moore (1783–1857), 43rd justice of her majesty's court of queen's bench, who came here about 1835 but was almost certainly responsible for the impressive gatescreen of *c.* 1845. It has as its carriage pillars a pair of grand round-headed granite postilion arches, each surmounted by lions couchant, all flanked by rubble-built concave quadrant walls terminating in tall cut-stone square pillars and punctuated by quirky tapering pilasters. The property was

subsequently home to Major Richard Doyne, followed in the late nineteenth century by merchant George Campbell and his wife. The lodge looks to be a replacement and may date from when the place became St Enda's School in 1910, occupying the site of its predecessor. This is a sturdy single-storey standard structure on an L-plan, its roof almost pyramidal, with bulky chimney-stacks rising off the side pitches. Finished in stucco-effect rendering below bracketed eaves, two arrowhead-arched casement windows flank a glazed hall projection with shallow-pitched carved bargeboards and spiky hip-knob. In 1849 Judge Moore's gatekeeper was Thomas Clonan.

Thom's; Griffith 1848–60; *LGI* (1904); Bence-Jones 1988; Howley 1993; *Garden History* (Summer 2000).

362. HERMITAGE, Roebuck; pre-1837/*c.* 1940.
A seat until his death in 1834 of William McCaskey and until around 1860 of James McCaskey, whose gatekeeper in 1849 was Edward Curran. On the site of the early lodge is a mid-twentieth-century bungalow, three-bay symmetrical with a steeply hipped roof and tripartite windows with stone mullions.

Griffith 1848–60; *Thom's*; Ball and Hamilton 1895.

363. HERMITAGE PARK, Lucan (2).
In 1801 'the seat of Colonel Handfield, a good house pleasantly situated, commanding an extensive view on the banks of the river Liffey, and enclosed with a stone wall. The demesne consists of about eight acres, and is well wooded; there are good gardens, and the whole laid out to advantage.' Archer failed to mention the (then) sole entrance to a property still in the Colonel's hands in 1824.

East gate; pre-1837/*c.* 1930.
This has the form of a standard single-storey

lodge with chimneys to each gable of a century earlier, but the thinness of its walls suggests it to be a twentieth-century replacement, extended and occupied. The gates look to be of around 1840.

West gate; pre-1906; *demolished.*
The secondary entrance may have been added by Sir John Kingsmill, to whom this was home in 1837. As John Woodham he had, in 1824, married Elizabeth Catherine Bruce-Kingsmill and took the additional name. She and their daughter and son-in-law lived on here after his death in 1859. One of Sir John's gatekeepers in 1850 was Nicholas Collins.

Archer 1801; Pigot 1824; Lewis 1837; Griffith 1848–60; *Thom's*; *LGI* (1904).

HEUSTON STATION (see KINGSBRIDGE STATION)

364. HIBERNIAN MARINE SCHOOL, Sir John Rogerson's Quay; pre-1854; *demolished.*
An establishment of the Hibernian Society of Dublin, 'For Maintaining, Educating and Apprenticing Orphan Children of Decayed Seamen'. An important Classical building designed by either Thomas Ivory or Thomas Cooley, completed in 1773 but now lost, as is its gate lodge. Quite where this was is not clear from the OS maps, but its existence is identified by the 1854 valuation.

Slater 1846; Griffith 1848–60; Craig 1980.

HIBERNIAN MILLS (see SUSAN VALE)

365. HIGHFIELD, Haroldsgrange; pre-1837; *demolished.*
A demesne and late Georgian house, in 1838 the residence of John Whitcroft, who was here until about 1849, when his gatekeeper was John Coleman. The property, sometime also known as 'Ifield', has been completely built over.

Lewis 1837; Griffith 1848–60; Pearson 1998.

366. HIGHNAM LODGE, Old Connaught; *c.* 1855; *demolished.*

A gate lodge which is probably a considerable architectural loss, judging by the quality of the surviving entrance screen and the remodelling of the old 'Moatfield Cottage', in 1837 a seat of Captain C. Johnstone. This work was probably carried out for Charles Toole of neighbouring Wilfort (*q.v.*), although the place for the remainder of the nineteenth century was home to Hans Blackwood Hamilton, his widow and their daughters, he having moved from Merchamp (*q.v.*), north Dublin. The gatescreen is comprised of four tapering 'pylon' pillars with moulded recessed panels and corniced cappings. These contain ogee quadrants, their railings with palmette finials like the carriage gates, which are reassuringly gripped by cast-iron fists.

Lewis 1837; *Thom's*; Pearson 1998.

367. HIGH THORN, Monkstown; pre-1837; *demolished.*
A villa, in 1837 of J. Meara Esq., was removed in 1979, the site of its gate lodge now a busy road junction. The proprietor by 1846 was solicitor John Orpen, whose gatekeeper three years later was William Moore.

Lewis 1837; Slater 1846; Griffith 1848–60; Pearson 1998.

HILLCOT (see KILMASHOGUE)

HILLCOURT (see INNISMORE)

368. HILTON, Ballinteer; *c.* 1830.
Although the seven-acre property lost many of its fine trees in 1990 road-widening, remarkably the gate lodge survives along with the house. This is a nice single-storey standard affair, its hipped roof oversailing paired carved soffit brackets. A flat-roofed hall projection is flanked by good new squared-pane windows; occupied. Some basic granite entrance pillars remain with ogee cappings. A seat in the mid-nineteenth century of the O'Neill family.

Thom's; Craig and Fewer 2002.

369. HILTON, Rathmines; pre-1837; *demolished.*
In common with the many villas that lined the western side of Rathmines Road Lower in the early nineteenth century this gate lodge has gone, having lain vacant in 1850. John Dogherty, merchant, is noted here between 1841 and 1856.

Thom's; Griffith 1848–60.

370. HILTON LODGE, Rathmines; pre-1837; *demolished.*
In 1837 the proprietor was Joseph Grant, by 1841 replaced by wine merchant Thomas Saunders, whose gate porter nine years later was Patrick McCaffrey. Gone like that of its neighbour Hilton (*q.v.*).

Lewis 1837; *Thom's*; Griffith 1848–60.

371. HIRSEL, Rathfarnham; *c.* 1910; architect H.J. Lundy.
A house built for himself on a greenfield site off Butlerfield Avenue by Henry James Lundy (1871–1964) in 1909. In contrast with his informal Arts and Crafts villa is this single-storey standard smooth-rendered lodge with moulded architrave surrounds to openings and central gabled porch with carved brackets and post support, reflecting the verandah on the house but not repeating any of its half-timbered work, the roof being hip-gabled with a red earthenware tiled finish. Well restored and much extended. Lundy as early as 1912 must have become disenchanted with architecture, giving it up to farm in Canada.

IAA.

372. HOLLYBROOK, Drimnagh; pre-1837; *demolished.*
Both the house and its lodge were in close proximity, located by the Naas Road, to which they succumbed. A property in 1850 of Christopher Warren, whose lodge then lay empty.

Griffith 1848–60.

373. HOLLY PARK, Taylorsgrange (2).
In 1801 'the seat of L. Foote, Esq. The house is excellent and pleasantly situated, the demesne laid out with great judgement, contains about ninety acres, and is well wooded and watered; the gardens are valuable and extensive, and well laid out.' Lundy Foote, a snuff manufacturer, was the son of the builder of the fine Classical villa, Jeffery Foote (1704–73), and it was his grandson Simon who sold the place with its two gate lodges in 1849 as a home to St Columba's public school. Both have gone.

West gate; pre-1837; *demolished.*
Removed in 1911, its gatekeeper of 1849 who had to undergo the traumatic transition from the graceful living of the Foote family to that of exuberant youth was Thomas Byrne.

East gate; pre-1837; *demolished.*

R.C. Orpen

Taken down in 2000 to make way for the M50 motorway, the gatescreen was moved to its new site off Kilmashogue Lane minus its gate lodge, which has at least been captured in a pretty watercolour painting of 1918 by the architect Richard Caulfield Orpen, who had been working on additions to the school. It was a simple single-storey hipped-roof structure facing the park, with its blind back to the road and an *oeil-de-boeuf* window in the right-hand concave quadrant wall supervising the entrance forecourt. The four transplanted granite pillars now lack their graceful urns. The gate porter in 1849 was Joseph Mulvey, his lodge being occupied up until 1957.

Archer 1801; Griffith 1848–60; *LGI* (1904); Williams 1994; ffolliott 1970.

374. HOLLYPARK, Goatstown; pre-1837; *demolished.*
An elegant Georgian villa, the name of which was altered to 'Hollywood' probably by solicitor Thomas Babington, whose gatehouse in 1849 was occupied by Owen Dempsey.

Griffith 1848–60.

375. HOLLYVILLE PARK, Blackrock; pre-1837; *demolished.*
A demesne off Newtownpark Avenue in 1824 of W. Harcourt Carter, who by 1849 was leasing it to Valentine O'Connor, merchant,

whose gate porter was James Cullen. All that survive are four good mid-Georgian granite pillars with scroll-topped stops, fluted friezes and moulded corniced cappings, linked by railed quadrants. An inscribed plaque giving the new name of the property is extraordinarily insensitively positioned on the left-hand carriage pillar.

Pigot 1824; Griffith 1848–60.

HOLLYWOOD CASTLE (see CLAREMOUNT)

HOLLYWOOD (see HOLLYPARK)

376. HOLMSTON, Monkstown (3).
A house built *c.* 1835 which became associated with the Reid family; Peter Reid, an eminent banker, is recorded here in 1849 and 1865.

Glenageary Road Lower gate; *c.* 1835/*c.* 1880.
The surviving lodge is clearly a replacement built for John Hamilton Reid, who is noted at Holmston from 1870. Standard single-storey, its hipped roof with exposed rafter toes catslides over a rectangular bay window to left-hand side. Panelled fanlit front door and two-over-two sash windows. Slender Greek stela-type entrance pillars.

Glenageary Road Upper gate; pre-1849; *demolished.*
Remaining are more gate pillars like those at the rear gate, with the inscription 'Glenageary Woods'.

Holmston Avenue gate; pre-1871; *demolished.*
The latest of the three lodges located within along the back approach.

In 1849 one lodge was vacant and another occupied by Lawrence Byrne.

Griffith 1848–60; *Thom's.*

377. HOLYWELL COTTAGE, Drummartin; pre-1837; *demolished.*
Later raised to the grandeur of 'Holywell Park', a property which had a succession of occupants, an early one of whom was W. Walsh Esq. in 1837, followed in the mid-nineteenth century by Beauchamp B. Hill.

Lewis 1837; Slater 1846; Griffith 1848–60.

378. HOME, Loughlinstown; *c.* 1830; architect probably George Papworth.

With adjacent New Brighton (*q.v.*), an early nineteenth-century speculative development of two Regency villas and their identical gate lodges, probably to designs of George Papworth. Despite the loss of its central chimney-stack, conversion of doorway to a

window and the substitution of steel squared casements for original sashes, this retains its appearance as a substantial chaste building. Once single-storey standard in stucco effect below a shallow oversailing hipped roof with plain paired soffit brackets, its front elevation framed by suitably stout Doric pilaster quoins carrying a deep eaves band. There is a later canted bay window to the park front. The seven-acre property was home to Revd Edward F. Day in 1849, when his gatekeeper was Thomas McGrath. Half the contemporary gatesweep remains, gateless, in the form of a railed screen contained by a particularly sturdy squat gate pillar with recessed moulded panels and a smaller outer version. The property was renamed 'St Brendan's' and has since been built over.

Griffith 1848–60; IAA.

379. HOLMES-VILLE, Rathmines; pre-1837; *demolished.*
A Georgian enclave of six houses facing a communal grassed triangle, probably built by a John Holmes but all now swept away for modern development. Until recently there existed at the access to the laneway a tiny plain cottage for a gate porter.

Thom's; Kelly 1995.

380. HOMESTEAD, Dundrum; 1871; architect probably John McCurdy.

One of a series of very similar Italianate lodges in the south Dublin area all attributable to architect John McCurdy, the others at Ailesbury, Bellosguardo, Craigmore, Newtown Park and Tibradden. Now startlingly exposed by the removal of its boundary wall for road realignment, the lodge is rendered even more conspicuous by a forthright colour scheme emphasising the architect's bold detailing. Single-storey standard with a shallow hipped roof having a soffit with carved brackets which continue about the verge of an open-pedimented breakfront hall containing a doorway with moulded surrounds to a round-headed fanlight. To each side is a segmentally arched two-over-two sash window with moulded surround and bracketed sill, all framed by striking Irish pilaster quoins with deeply channelled rustication. At a distance is what appears to be an earlier gatescreen of square granite carriage pillars with moulded cappings, 'Homestead'-inscribed friezes below and modern lanterns atop. To each side are segmentally headed postern openings, all framed by rebuilt concave rubble quadrants. This probably dates from the occupancy in the 1860s of Joseph Woodlock but the lodge was added for Henry McComas in 1871, the year that saw the death of the demesne's previous resident, Mrs Elizabeth Rockwell, widow of Richard Rockwell of Rockfield, Co. Meath (*q.v.*).

Thom's; *LGI* (1904).

381. HORTON, Terenure; pre-1837; *demolished.*
A seat in 1849 of John Robinson Byrne, whose gatekeeper was Patrick Walsh.

Griffith 1848–60.

382. HOSPITAL FOR INCURABLES, Donnybrook (3).
'The Hospital for Incurables, near Donnybrook-road, was founded by the Musical Society, who disposed of the produce of each year's subscription for this praiseworthy object: the undertaking commenced on the 23rd of May, 1744, in Fleet-street, and was removed to its present site in 1792.' Slater's 1846 *Directory* failed to mention that the new site was that of a large country house called 'Buckingham', which was incorporated into the hospital complex.

Early lodge; pre-1809; *demolished.*
At the head of Bloomfield Avenue to the right-hand side of the gates was a lodge that may have been associated with the old house. Hospital records give a comprehensive insight into the specific duties of their gatekeeper. From 31 March 1809: 'the porter, who also got an allowance of coals and candles and lived in the gate lodge, and was paid £25 per annum'. He was responsible for ensuring that patients did not leave the hospital without permission: 'he shall take care that the patients shall on no account absent themselves from the hospital except at regulated times and that they shall go out by no passage except by the gate'. Drs Robert and Edward Perceval were asked by the governors to draw up a list of the porter's duties at the end of 1817. These were presented to the board and accepted by January 1818. Among the other duties were the following: 'he shall carefully attend the gate and not open it after 8 p.m. until 8 a.m. from 1st October to 1st March, from 1st March to 1st October he shall close the gate at 9 p.m. and open it at 6 a.m. He shall not permit any stranger to enter the hospital except by a written order of a member of the Board of the Medical Gentlemen.' He was also meant to ensure that 'no spirits or drink of any kind whatsoever be carried to the patients by their friends'. The porter in the years 1847–9, Thomas Teeling, seems to have had a cut in salary, for he was then paid £18.9.3d per annum. This may have been subsequently increased, for around 1875 the

gatekeeper's duties were further defined: 'to keep the Entrance Book at the lodge and to take account of every person passing in and out and to see that the orders of the Board are strictly adhered to; to assist in the garden and in lifting patients and act generally as required by the Matron'.

Later lodge; *c.* 1890; architect possibly J. Rawson Carroll.

Replacing the predecessor at the opposite side of the gate, this is a modest astylar single-storey three-bay hipped-roof affair, with a central hip-roofed hall projection with its door to the side. Plastic windows in stucco-effect rendering. The architect J. Rawson Carroll was in 1889 working on additional wards for the hospital. The entrance screen of 1880 was designed by William Kaye-Parry; its tall, square granite carriage pillars, moulded and pedimented, are crowned by lanterns and linked by a round-arched metal overthrow proclaiming 'The Royal Hospital Donnybrook', as it had become.

Latest lodge; *c.* 1910; architects possibly Batchelor and Hicks.

An Arts and Crafts bungalow which may have been added, where the early lodge sat, to provide accommodation for staff with increasingly onerous tasks by the gates. Single-storey gabled with a slated roof relieved by canted bands and intermittent terracotta cresting. The walls are finished in Flemish bond red brick with serrated tile hanging in the gables. Original wooden squared casement windows replaced by plastic 'look-alikes'. Architects Batchelor and Hicks provided plans and specifications for a new mortuary in 1908, their commission perhaps extending to include this design.

Slater 1846; Griffith 1848–60; *IB* (15 Aug. 1880 and 27 June 1908); Burke 1993.

IDRONE (see NEWBAWN)

IFIELD (see HIGHFIELD)

383. ILLERTON, Killiney; *c.* 1871.

Now called 'Alloa', the house, originally taken by William Bewley, was one of a group of four designed by architects Deane and Woodward in 1861, which with neighbours Fernside and Green Hill (*q.v.*) shared a common entrance and then, around ten years later, a porter's lodge. It is a relatively unprepossessing single-storey three-bay structure below a hipped roof in pleasant rubble stone with brick quoins and dressings to two-over-two sash windows, distinguished by a central triangular brick bay with windows giving sight of the gates and down the avenue, the roof over which emphasises the inflexibility of the replacement concrete-tiled finish. 'Fern Cottage', as it is now called, may have been conceived with a rendered finish; occupied and extended.

O'Dwyer 1997b; Pearson 1998.

384. INCHICORE, Kilmainham (2).

Both lodges, built before 1837, have been demolished; their occupants in 1848 were James Walsh and William Abbott. A property that apparently housed staff of the Royal Hibernian Military School across the River Liffey, in 1841 Captain Foss.

Thom's; Griffith 1848–60.

385. INNISCORRIG, Dalkey; *c.* 1875; architect not known.

A house established in 1847 by physician Dominic J. Corrigan, who was later knighted as a Catholic MP. He subsequently developed it into a rugged Tudor Baronial pile on the shoreline and squeezed in an appropriate porter's lodge on this restricted site behind the right-hand convex entrance quadrant. Single-storey, raised off an L-plan in granite rubble, its roof hipped to the road but skew-table gabled to the two-bay avenue elevation, comprised of a wide cut-stone mullioned and transomed tripartite window with a segmentally arched opening to the porch recess; above that is a mock arrowloop. Within reach is a pair of chunky entrance pillars with four-pedimented cappings.

Thom's; Pearson 1998.

386. INNISMORE, Glenageary; *c.* 1845; architect not known.

A fine development of Classical house and matching gate lodge probably for Geoffrey Barcroft, a timber merchant, whose gatekeeper in 1849 was William Smith. It is a tiny single-storey standard structure in white rendering below a shallow hipped roof, distinguished by an outstanding temple breakfront of a shallow pediment over the panelled front door, which is flanked by pairs

of fluted Greek Doric columns *in antis*. On each side are bipartite casement windows with geometric glazing patterns, with tripartite versions to each side elevation. A surprising and welcome survivor, which has been developed into a double pile to the rear and is immaculately maintained. In 1919 the place became 'Hillcourt', a school that absorbed the neighbouring property of Tudor Cottage (*q.v.*), the lodge to which remains.

Thom's; Griffith 1848–60; Pearson 1998.

387. INVERUISH, Ballybrack; *c.* 1875; architect possibly A.G. Jones.

An excellent Italianate-style porter's lodge that sits back to back with its twin to the adjacent Aughnacloy (*q.v.*). Single-storey standard with a hipped roof broken by a gabled entrance breakfront containing a round-headed fanlit doorway. On each side are two-over-two sash windows with moulded surrounds and segmental arches, the whole framed by a prominent plinth and Doric corner pilasters. To the ridge is a plinthed and corniced Classical chimney-stack, just as those to Strathmore (*q.v.*), where architect Alfred Gresham Jones was employed. Here he probably worked with property developer William Field, who was associated with William's Park (*q.v.*) and St Columba's (*q.v.*), which have like lodges. The Hon. Frederick R. Falkiner QC was resident in 1883.

Thom's.

388. IRISHTOWN, Palmerston; pre-1837; *demolished*.

A 130-acre farm in 1850 of John Lenehan.

Griffith 1848–60.

389. ISLANDBRIDGE, Islandbridge; *c.* 1900; architect not known.

In the early nineteenth century this was the premises of William Henry, cotton manufacturer and calico printer, which later in the century had become woollen mills and the house of Francis Moore Scott, before both

fell vacant in 1890. There appears to have been a gate lodge on the site in 1871 but what survives is later and was probably built by Major-General Gossett CB, who is recorded here in 1900, the old mills having been converted into 'Bellevue Maltings'. This is an excellent Arts and Crafts Elizabethan Revival lodge, 1½-storey with a gabled half-timbered upper storey with Queen Anne-style windows over what may have been a brick-faced lower floor, now rendered. Adjacent are older massive stone gate pillars.

Thom's.

IVANHOE (see LANSDOWNE)

390. IVEAGH GARDENS, Harcourt Terrace; *c.* 1910; architect not known.

At the rear entrance to what were Ninian Niven's Winter Garden Grounds to the fore of the Dublin Crystal Palace of 1863 is this 1½-storey commodious gabled Arts and Crafts caretaker's lodge. Built off an L-plan with Edwardian six-over-one sash windows in a red-brick ground floor and the roughcast upper storey, which displays half-timbered effect to main gable and those of the gablets; tall banded and corniced chimney-stacks break the red plain clay-tiled finish of an otherwise hipped roof. In the internal angle the front door is sheltered by a lean-to canopied porch. This seems to have replaced an earlier lodge at the rear entrance, although the two proposed off Earlsfort Terrace seem never to have materialised.

Liddy 1978; Casey 2005.

391. JAMESTOWN, Drimnagh; pre-1837; *demolished.*

A property in 1849 of Paul Reynolds, both house and lodge of which had gone by 1936.

Griffith 1848–60.

392. JAMESTOWN, Kilternan; *c.* 1850; *demolished.*

Now the site of a public golf-course, this was a seat from the late eighteenth century of the Rourke family. The lodge, opposite the gates and distant from the road, was a standard single-storey hipped-roof structure of Regency appearance. Bipartite casement windows were set in rectangular recesses to ground level in walls that were latterly finished in stucco-effect rendering. Prior to its demolition in 2003 it had suffered all manner of indignities. Granite octagonal gate pillars opposite. Probably built by John H. O'Rorke.

Thom's; Pearson 1998.

393. JANE VILLE, Stillorgan (2).

A good late Georgian villa which was home in 1837 to Mrs Wilson, possibly née Jane Stewart, who in 1795 had married her cousin Walter Wilson, surviving him by 42 years, dying in 1849, by which time Jane Ville was occupied by Mrs Louisa McCaskey, whose gatekeepers were then John McCann and Michael Smith. The place was renamed 'Glen Albyn' in the twentieth century and is now a community centre, both lodges having been demolished.

Lewis 1837; *Thom's*; Griffith 1848–60; *LGI* (1904).

394. JANEVILLE COTTAGE, Mount Merrion; pre-1837; *demolished.*

A property in 1849 of Charles J. Bond, whose gate porter was then Michael Cooper. A house later called 'Shanavaun'.

Griffith 1848–60.

395. JANEVILLE, Peter Place; pre-1837; *demolished.*

A house, gatehouse, offices, garden and lawn in 1854 of Revd Matthew Peter on a site that has been commercially developed.

Griffith 1848–60.

396. JOBSTOWN, Tallaght; pre-1837; *demolished.*

A property on the first OS map named after the townland but, before and since, alternatively 'Brookfield'. In 1814 the proprietor was Michael Roe and just before his death Admiral Sir James Hawkins-Whitshed (1762–1849) of Killincarrig, Co. Wicklow (*q.v.*), whose gatekeeper was William Manly.

Leet 1814; Griffith 1848–60; Wikipedia.

397. JOHNSTOWN, Ballyfermot; *c.* 1845; *demolished.*

The lodge was built sometime after 1837 and was noted in the 1850 valuation as home to Michael Brennan, gate porter to Robert S. Findlater, who had succeeded to a property in 1837 of T. Daly Esq.

Lewis 1837; Griffith 1848–60.

398. JOHNSTOWN, Foxrock; *c.* 1810.

A single-storey gate lodge on the footpath's edge, to which it is totally blind, presenting its three-bay fenestration to the park and with a bowed end, half of which creates a convex quadrant to the right-hand side of an elegant straight entrance screen. The walls are roughcast like the lodge but with sophisticated stone dressings and granite ashlar pillars with fluted friezes and gadrooned cappings, flanked by sheeted postilion doors framed by moulded architraves and unusual fluted keystones. The intricate decorative iron gates are later. A seat with a frequent turnover of proprietors, in 1778 of Love Hiatt followed by a Mr Williams, Major Armstrong in 1801 and Sir John Browne by 1824.

In 1849 the gatekeeper was Denis Doyle as porter to Revd Dr Richard Ardill (1801–58), curate (1828–57) of St Kevin's.

Archer 1801; Pigot 1824; Griffith 1848–60; Ball 1995; Leslie and Wallace 2001.

399. JOHNSTOWN-KENNEDY, Rathcoole (4).

R.A. Gray design (*Irish Builder*).

R.A. Gray design (*Irish Builder*).

A great gaunt Georgian house of the Kennedy family, recently removed, part of its fine park given over as a golf-course and its set of porters' lodges much reduced.

East gate; pre-1837; *demolished.*

South gate; *c.* 1800.

A single-storey standard hip-roofed structure with big slates, now extended by a long bay to the right-hand side and plastic windows installed in faintly stucco-effect walls; occupied.

The gatekeepers in these two early lodges, each recorded as containing an office, in 1849 were John Golding and Thomas Marsh, employed by Sir John Kennedy (b. 1785), created 1st baronet in 1836, who had in fact died in 1848.

West gate; pre-1837; *demolished.*

A lodge that was located in Huttonread townland in County Kildare.

Sir John was succeeded by his eldest son, Sir Charles Edward Bayly Kennedy (1820–80), as 2nd baronet, who immediately before his death commissioned a design for a new gate lodge from architect R.A. Gray, which was featured in the *Irish Builder* of 15 August 1879 with two perspective views: 'The material will be Dalkey granite with limestone dressings ... of an ornate character'. If anything, an over-ornateness accounted for its never materialising, for it was to have been in ostentatious High Victorian Gothic style with a wealth of detailing. Single-storey, arranged on an irregular plan, with steeply pitched skew-table gables and hipped gables with curly iron hip-knobs and decorative cresting. All the window openings were to have shouldered arches, some, like that to the triangular bay window, with Gothic colonnette mullions. Elsewhere there were to have been pointed relieving arches and, in an internal angle, the entrance doorway below a wooden arcaded verandah porch with catslide roof. The roofs were to have been further highlighted with sawtooth slate course and elaborate chimney-stacks. Whether Sir Charles and Gray disagreed over style or money is not clear, but the client almost certainly turned to Alfred Gresham Jones, for what was executed has identical detailing to the lodges at Monkstown House (*q.v.*) and Montebello House (*q.v.*), both clearly by Jones on his own or when he was assistant to J.S. Mulvany. There is similarly a lodge to Hollywoodrath House, north Dublin (*q.v.*), identical in form and detailing.

North gate; 1880; architect probably A.G. Jones.

Single-storey gabled on an L-plan in Italianate style, with the most innovative of detailing to a variety of paired, bipartite and

tripartite windows, all with corbelled sills and extraordinary hood mouldings and keystones sculpted with almost tropical flora and foliage in granite set off by plain rendered walls and containing round-headed sash windows with margined glazing. Above, the open pediments frame a date-stone and family bearings on chiselled plaques, one with the monogram 'CEK' and another displaying their crest of a dexter arm embowered in armour holding an oak branch over a left hand signifying the baronetcy. In the internal angle is a flat-roofed porch with a deep dentilled entablature carried on a monolithic square granite pillar, and corresponding pilasters framing a pair of slender fluted and cabled columns and delicately fretted Greek iron railing. Expensively extended in like manner but sadly missing its entrance screen.

IB (15 August 1879); Griffith 1848–60; *BPB* (1929).

400. JOHNVILLE, Saggart; pre-1837; *demolished.*

By 1905 the family home of the Roes, known for their distillery, was already a shell. The demise of its gate lodge may already have started by 1850, as it then lay vacant.

Griffith 1848–60; Joyce 1912.

401. JUBILEE HALL, Old Connaught; pre-1837; *demolished.*

Dr Ryan around 1810 acquired 'Jubilee-lodge' from Edward Smyth and transformed it into a delightful castellated Tudor Gothic fantasy, perhaps with the guidance of his near neighbour, architect Sir Richard Morrison. There is no knowledge of whether the gate lodge reflected the big house but it is survived by appropriate turreted entrance pillars with crenellated caps. The property passed out of Ryan hands *c.* 1850, when the gate lodge lay empty.

Wilson 1803; Leet 1814; Griffith 1848–60; Pearson 1998.

402. KILBOGGET, Cabinteely; *c.* 1830; architect not known.

A splendid single-storey standard Classical lodge with a shallow-pitched hipped roof oversailing long, carved soffit brackets which extend as mutules into the tympanum of a pedimented portico, distyle with monolithic granite Greek Doric columns. Otherwise it is rendered with inappropriate wide, squared casement window replacements; extended by a bay to the right-hand side. Surviving is a pair of octagonal granite entrance pillars with corniced cappings. In 1849 Andrew Tracey was gate porter to Thomas Sherrard, who may well have built the elegant Regency villa onto an older farmhouse about twenty years earlier, with the same Doric columns and soffit bracket features as displayed on its lodge.

Slater 1846; Griffith 1848–60.

KILBRAE (see AIR HILL)

403. KILDARE, Kildare Street; *c.* 1745; architect Richard Castle.

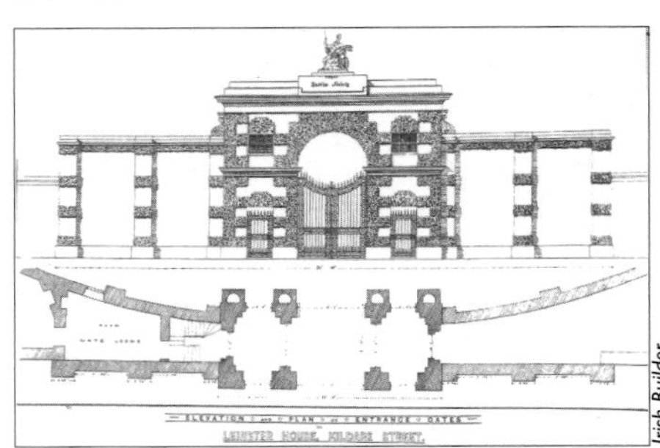

James Fitzgerald, 20th earl of Kildare (1722–73), who inherited the title in 1744, commissioned the design of his Dublin town house from the architect Richard Castle. Built in the form of a country house, it required a secure boundary to its grand forecourt to protect it from the street, and this was created in the form of a double wall; the space

National Library of Ireland

James Henry Brocas 1818

between them, on an axis with the front door, was straddled by a triple entrance archway in the form of a giant cube. Its opposing façades were in stark contrast to one another. That enjoyed by the grandees was elegant, of three bays defined by giant engaged Ionic columns dividing round-headed archways, the tall carriage opening surmounted by a pediment, the postilion gates lower with relieving plaques over. The street elevation was altogether more defensive, with bold rusticated stone quoins, dressings, voussoirs and lintels to the flat-arched postilion doors and the windows over that lit the upper-storey porters' accommodation, which was accessed from their ground-floor rooms, screened by tall curtain walls with rusticated pilasters. In 1814 Leinster House, as it had become, was purchased from Augustus Frederick Fitzgerald, 4th duke of Leinster, by the Dublin Society, who crowned the Kildare Street front with an inscribed die and a statue of Minerva. In 1887 the *Irish Builder* magazine published for posterity a plan and front elevation of the archway prior to its 'removal by the "crowbar" brigade'. It made way for the present railed screen by Thomas Newenham Deane and his son, Thomas Manly Deane, with its central pair of sentry-boxes at the entrance to what is now the Irish parliament, and terminal gates which give access to the National Library and the National Museum, all of 1890.

IB (15 June 1887); *BPB* (1929); Griffin and Pegum 2000, NLI photograph.

404. KILGOBBIN CASTLE HOUSE, Kilgobbin; *c.* 1840.

Veronica and David Rowe

The sad shell of a little standard lodge, in 2000 the skeleton of its hipped roof exposed, its harled walls being engulfed in ivy, a small canted bay window poking out to the park. The single-storey-over-basement villa, previously more aptly named 'Bayley's Cabin', in 1849 was occupied by Emmanuel J. Bayley, whose gatekeeper was Anne Gill.

Griffith 1848–60; Pearson 1998.

405. KILGOBBIN COTTAGE, Kilgobbin; *c.* 1840.

An exceptionally plain single-storey standard hip-roofed roughcast lodge with its doorway blocked up. Well positioned to also monitor the entrance to Clay Farm alongside. A property in the mid-nineteenth century of the Bourne family.

Thom's.

406. KILL ABBEY, Kill of the Grange; pre-1837; *demolished.*

A house of ancient foundation which was 'the country residence of the deans of Christ Church, Dublin, and is part of the estate of Kill of the Grange of Clonkeen, but has been held by lease for above 120 years by the Espinasse family'. Such was the case in 1837 and twelve years later it was the seat of Richard Espinasse, whose gate porter was Mary Hackett.

Lewis 1837; Griffith 1848–60.

407. KILLACOONA, Ballybrack; *c.* 1890; architect not known.

A development of the late nineteenth century for Frederick Wrench, chief land commissioner, the gate lodge to which he added somewhat later. This is a very good English Arts and Crafts 1½-storey cottage with rendered attic storey over red brickwork in English garden wall bond. The roof, covered in earthenware plain tiles, has hipped gables extending above a rectangular breakfront to the road. To the park elevation is a single-storey canted glazed bay window, and to the avenue two wide multi-paned tripartite segmentally arched casements. In contrast is a Classical gatescreen of concave-walled quadrants contained by brick pillars of channelled rustication below ball-finialled corniced stone cappings. Now a convent school.

Thom's; O'Sullivan 1987.

408. KILLAKEE, Killakee (4).
Another tale of woe is the history of this once-proud estate, of which little survives architecturally but for the stable block and two outstanding gate lodges of the original four. These both date from the time here of Samuel White, who, before his death without issue in 1854, improved the house with the addition of a conservatory by ironmaster Richard Turner in 1843 and the demesne with the replacement of two of the gate lodges. Turner was known to put his hand to design buildings other than conservatories and he may have been responsible. Alternatively, his collaboration about this time with Decimus Burton in the Palm House at Kew Gardens may be significant; Killakee itself could well pass for one of the latter's London villas.

South lodge; pre-1837; *demolished.*
An entrance to that portion of the property lying west of the public road opposite the demesne proper.

Middle Lodge; pre-1837; *demolished.*

North Lodge; *c.* 1835; architect possibly R. Turner.

An exceptional porter's lodge, single-storey, built off a cruciform plan below an oversailing square hipped roof carried at each recessed porch by fluted Greek Doric columns. Central to the avenue front projects a canted bay window with, in contrast to the general Classical symmetry, a Picturesque hexagonal glazing pattern, below which are recessed panels to match those of the squat square chimney-stack. To complement the lodge is an equally unique iron gatescreen of ogee spear-topped quadrants meeting at extraordinary gate pillars in the form of intertwined corkscrews spiralling to skep cappings—Turner at his most innovative?

East lodge; *c.* 1835; architect possibly R. Turner.

Another distinctive replacement lodge, single-storey standard below an exaggerated oversailing shallow-pitched hipped roof with, in rendered walls, architraved casement windows on each side of a projecting hip-roofed hall. To the road front under the extensive soffit is a canted bay window, like the other lights displaying a margined latticed leaded glazing pattern, admirably restored. To the ridge is a pair of Tudor-style diagonally set chimney-stacks. The entrance screen exhibits more invention, again with spear-topped ogee railed quadrants contained by iron pillars with Greek key pattern to the shafts and crowned by elegant anthemion motifs. In common with the northern gatescreen there is a continuous perforated band.

In 1849 James Mallen, John Fogarty, Benjamin Fitzpatrick and William Doyle were Colonel Samuel White's gate porters. Following his death, Killakee passed through the marriage of his youngest sister Matilda to the Massy family. The 8th baron, Hugh Hamon Charles John Massy, saw out his days in penury, living in one of his own gate lodges before his death in 1958, the big house being subsequently demolished.

Griffith 1848–60; Joyce 1912; *BPB* (1929); Bence-Jones 1987.

409. KILLEEN, Walkinstown; pre-1836; *demolished.*
In 1837 'An extensive paper manufactory belonging to Messrs McDonnel and Sons, in which from 70 to 80 persons are generally employed, is carried out at Killeen. Within the enclosure of this establishment, which resembles a small town, are dwelling-houses for the workmen and their families; the house of the proprietor is pleasantly situated in some tastefully ornamented grounds.' Nothing tasteful or ornamental has survived the arrival of the modern industrial estate.

Lewis 1837.

410. KILLINEY CASTLE, Killiney (2).

Robert Warren (1787–1869) was a Dublin solicitor who, having acquired Killiney Castle, embarked on a second career as a speculative builder, giving his new home a Romantic Castellated outline and adding a suitable prelude at the main gate in a manner which he also introduced to his ventures at Victoria Castle (*q.v.*) nearby and probably Baymount Castle, north Dublin (*q.v.*). His architect is thought to have been his brother-in-law Sandham Symes, although there is no known documentary evidence and there is also a contender in William Warren, of whom there was more than one of that name in the family, who was adept in this style, one of his works being Augher Castle, Co. Tyrone.

Main gate; *c.* 1840; architect probably Sandham Symes.
This is an impressive entrance in granite dominated by the porter's accommodation in the shape of a battlemented two-storey octagonal 'keep', with a variety of windows below a bold machicolated and crenellated

parapet broken by a chimney-stack corbelled out at first-floor level, treated as a bartizan. Located forward of the gatescreen, it monitors the semicircular forecourt, with its curtain walls having one postern opening and a pair of square turreted carriage pillars. Closing the composition is a slim octagonal tower, the whole bristling with mock arrowloops. To the left-hand side is later much-needed additional space for the gatekeeper behind a screen wall in like style.

Secondary gate; *c.* 1840; *demolished.*

The 1849 valuation identified three gatekeepers in Michael Kenny, Edward Healy and Christopher Keating, although only two lodges are obvious on the OS maps. The place is now a hotel.

Griffith 1848–60; *LGI* (1904); Lyons 1993; Pearson 1998.

411. KILLINEY PARK, Killiney (2).
A property in the early nineteenth century of the Waterhouse family and subsequently in 1837 of Sir Nicholas William Brady (1791–1843) of Willow Park (*q.v.*). Of his house and the lodges which pre-dated 1837, only the overgrown ruin of one of the latter remains at the Killiney Hill Road gate.

Lewis 1837; *BPB* (1929); Pearson 1998.

KILMACUD (see ST MARGARET'S)

412. KILMARNOCK, Ballybrock; *c.* 1860; architect Charles Geoghegan.

A property in the mid-nineteenth century of the Porter family which was purchased by John David Fitzgerald (1816–89), who was advanced to the dignity of Baron Fitzgerald of Kilmarnock. He extended and refaced the house and added a gate lodge in a grand Italianate style, all as befitting an attorney-general for Ireland. His architect was Charles Geoghegan. Single-storey stucco-faced rubble construction with glazed canted windows to each of its open-pedimented gables, in imitation of the big house, and a pair of round-headed windows to the avenue elevation. Now much extended and rehabilitated with alien modern materials. The house was for much of the twentieth century renamed 'Haldane Grange'.

Thom's; Pearson 1998.

413. KILMASHOGUE, Whitechurch; pre-1837; *demolished.*
A seat in 1849 of George Murray, whose gate porter was Thomas Murphy. By 1907 the house had become 'Hillcot'.

Griffith 1848–60.

414. KILMATEAD, Clondalkin; *c.* 1780; *demolished.*

Irish Architectural Archive

Previously the demesne of 'Little Corkagh', dower house of the Arabin family of neighbouring Corkagh (*q.v.*), at which in 1837 Samuel Lewis found 'some gunpowder mills, established a century since, but not used since 1815; one of them has been converted into a thrashing and cleaning mill, capable of preparing 100 barrels daily'. An old photograph shows a most peculiar structure at the gate, seemingly single-storey, its roof hipped to the rear but presenting a single-bay front gable of a two-over-two window above which is a lunette, the sill of which continues as a stone string-course about a pair of rectangular flat-roofed 'flankers' that presumably had a defensive role, for they are blind but for a segmentally headed door opening within the recess. In a simple harled finish, the lunette window suggests this to be a lodge of relative antiquity. Prior to its removal it had been severed from the demesne by realignment of the Dublin–Naas road.

Lewis 1837; IAA (photograph 5/33/2).

415. KILNAMANAGH CASTLE, Clondalkin; pre-1837; *demolished.*
An old-fashioned house, built on the site of an ancient castle, which was home to Patrick Farrell for much of the nineteenth century.

Thom's; Joyce 1912.

416. KILNAMANAGH, Clondalkin; *c.* 1850; *demolished.*
A lodge first valued in 1855 when occupied by John McCormack, porter to Charles Blackham.

KILRONAN (see SIMMONSCOURT [2])

417. KILTALOWN, Saggart (2).
Both lodges built before 1837 have gone, that to the south being demolished by 1937; its deterioration may have begun by 1850, for it then lay vacant. Its counterpart was manned by Thomas Reid, porter to John Robinson, who had acquired the place from James Jackson *c.* 1830. Today it is a community activity centre.

Leet 1914; Lewis 1837; Griffith 1848–60.

418. KILTERAGH, Foxrock (2).
A great rambling Arts and Crafts mansion created in 1905 for the Rt Hon. Horace Curzon Plunkett (1854–1932), of the Dunsany Castle, Co. Meath (*q.v.*), family, by his close contemporary, the London architect William Douglas Caroe, whose commission presumably extended to designs for the more regular porters' lodges.

Foxrock gate; *c.* 1905; architect probably W.D. Caroe.

In the Voysey manner is this whitened roughcast 1½-storey lodge built off a square plan, its pyramidal roof rising to a hefty unadorned roughcast chimney-stack. From the Westmoreland green slated finish break flat-roofed dormers with leaded casements. The asymmetrical three-bay front has a central quadripartite leaded window flanked by a narrow light and a projecting flat-roofed bowed hallway. All beautifully maintained and sympathetically extended.

Leopardstown gate; *c.* 1905; architect probably W.D. Caroe.
Originally much as the above, though with a gabled hall projection. Considerably added to in like materials but with a loss of form and its secret hips.

The house was burnt in 1923 by republicans and subsequently rehabilitated as six dwellings, its lodges given their independence.

IB (29 July 1905); *BPB* (1970); Williams 1994; Colvin 2008.

419. KILTERNAN ABBEY, Kilternan; pre-1837.
A site originally belonging to the monks of St Mary's Abbey, Dublin, which thereafter passed through the hands of various families, until in 1801 is noted 'the seat of Captain Anderson, a good house, beautifully situated, commanding a great prospect of the sea, and adjacent country, and a demesne of an hundred acres well planted'. With the Anderson family it remained for the remainder of that century; in 1849 the gatekeeper was James Byrne, employed by Richard Anderson. A local landmark in the shape of the entrance screen remains, comprised of massive ball-finialled carriage pillars with channel-rusticated shafts, a finish which can still be detected as quoins or Irish pilasters on the gate lodge, which, like the big house, lies in ruins. Now home to Kilternan and Balally Water Works.

Archer 1801; Lewis 1837; Griffith 1848–60; Ball 1995; Pearson 1998.

KILTERNAN GRANGE (see KINGSTON LODGE)

420. KILTERNAN LODGE, Kilternan; *c.* 1865.
An old house occupied in the first half of the nineteenth century by Samuel Moss, owner of the adjacent cotton mills. Its lodge is later, with much of the appearance of a twentieth-century labourer's council cottage, but more elaborate. Single-storey standard in

roughcast below a hipped roof, it abounds with red-brick embellishment in the toothed quoins, dressings and segmental arches to the two-over-two sash windows, sawtoothed bands to eaves finial and chimney-stack and surround to the semicircular fanlit front door, which breaks the open granite pediment of the hall breakfront. Occupied, in a pretty garden setting.

Lewis 1837; *Thom's*.

421. KILVARE, Templeogue; pre-1837; *demolished.*
A big house, in 1837 the Dublin residence of John Sealy Townsend of Myross Wood, Co. Kerry, located by the roadside behind a lofty boundary wall which extends eastwards to the old main entrance, marked by four grand Classical pillars with V-jointed rusticated stone shafts and plain friezes which frame contrasting roughcast concave quadrants containing sheeted postilion doors. The entrance lies redundant, its carriage opening walled up. Behind, the long-lost lodge was a rectangular structure with a wide central bow to the avenue. Townsend, one of the masters in the Irish court of chancery, lived here until his death in 1852, three years previous to which his gatekeeper was Michael Byrne. The place has lately become a convalescent home.

Lewis 1837; Griffith 1848–60; *IFR*.

422. KIMMAGE LODGE, Terenure; pre-1837; *demolished.*
Samuel Parke was living here in 1846 but three years later it had been acquired by Edmund Davy, professor of chemistry, whose gate porter was Martin Brunton.

Slater 1846; Griffith 1848–60.

423. KIMMAGE MANOR, Terenure (3).
None of the lodges to this once-fine estate survive. About 1830 it passed from Alderman Exshaw to Sir Frederick Shaw (1799–1876), recorder of Dublin, and he remained there until 1869, when he succeeded his brother to Bushy Park (*q.v.*). The two pre-1837 lodges, which he probably inherited, one on Fortfield Road and the other within, were manned in 1849 by Edward Grace and Thomas Harris respectively. The impressive entrance off Whitewell Road was extensive, with a semicircular forecourt, but remained lodgeless until sometime between 1849 and 1869.

Pigot 1824; Lewis 1837; Griffith 1848–60.

424. KINGSBRIDGE STATION, Kilmainham; *c.* 1850.
Just as at Broadstone Station in north Dublin (q.v.), so too Heuston Station (as it is now known) has its diminutive porter's lodge alongside, dwarfed by architect Sancton Wood's fantastic palazzo designed in 1845–6 as terminus of the Great Southern and Western Railway. Little more than a one-roomed, flat-roofed sentry-box but with its own chimney-stack on the leading elevation, rather discourteously reserving its distyle Classical portico to the rear, out of public view. Two square Doric pillars with

exaggerated entases support an entablature carried beyond as the roof parapet. All now in a drab grey cement finish, it shares none of the scale or flamboyance of its companion. In contrast, on each side is a series of latticed chinoiserie gates hung on cylindrical iron pillars in the form of stunted Doric columns with 'military helmets' as cappings.

Craig 1980; Williams 1994.

425. KINGSTON, Ballyboden; pre-1837; *demolished.*
This house, along with that of neighbouring Newbrook, was initially associated with the adjacent paper mills, which were founded in 1763 by John Mansergh. They seem to have shared this generous-sized gate lodge, which in 1849 was occupied by Robert Strong, porter to a Bryan Leary, one of a succession of residents from the early nineteenth century who were unrelated to the business. Kingston was demolished in the 1970s.

Thom's; Griffith 1848–60; Craig and Fewer 2002; Healy 2005.

426. KINGSTON, Kiltiernan; pre-1837; *demolished.*
A seat in 1837 of Revd M. McNamara and years thereafter of his widow.

Lewis 1837; *Thom's*.

427. KINGSTOWN, Ballinteer; pre-1907; *demolished.*
A property in the early nineteenth century of William Innis which remained lodgeless until it was acquired *c.* 1880 by James Sheill.

Lewis 1837; *Thom's*.

428. KINGSTOWN LODGE, Kiltiernan.
A very fine gate lodge of two periods, both from the time here of the Brennan family. The earlier, pre-1837 lodge appears to have been a simple single-storey hip-roofed rectangular affair, to which was added *c.* 1845 a more sophisticated structure extending towards the avenue to form a T-plan. From this projects a pedimented breakfront with a tripartite window having a decorative

octagonal glazing pattern. Flanking this frontispiece in whitened rendered walls are elegant round-headed Classical niches. Some fluted octagonal gate posts survive. The gatekeeper in 1849, John Boshell, may have been the first to enjoy this extended accommodation as porter to John Brennan. The house, at some time being similarly refronted, was renamed 'Kiltiernan Grange'.

Lewis 1837; Griffith 1848–60.

KINGSTOWN SCHOOL (see WELLINGTON LODGE)

429. KINGSWOOD COTTAGE, Kingswood; pre-1837.
A single-storey standard roughcast gabled porter's lodge, extended by a bay to the right-hand side, with a chunky battered chimney-stack and corbelled canopy to the front door. Much overhauled in the twentieth century, with plastic windows inserted. An estate in 1814 of Richard Rinkle which subsequently became home to the Walsh family for the remainder of the century.

Leet 1814; Lewis 1837; *Thom's*.

KNOCKLINN (see SEAVIEW)

430. KNOCKLYON [1], Firhouse; pre-1837; *demolished.*
A seat for much of the nineteenth century of Daniel P. Ryan, whose gate lodge lay vacant in 1849.

Griffith 1848–60; *Thom's*.

431. KNOCKLYON [2], Firhouse (2).
Later renamed 'Prospect', it was an estate of W. Dunne Esq. in 1837, when two lodges were in place, one of which was replaced in Edwardian times, probably for Miss S. Roe.

West lodge; pre-1837; *demolished.*

East lodge; pre-1837/*c.* 1900; architect not known.

An Taisce

A simple and effective little Arts and Crafts 'Stockbroker Tudor' composition, single-storey in Flemish bond orange brick, the leading gable of which is in black-and-white half-timbered effect, below which is a multi-paned canted bay window with red plain tiled roof finish, as that of the main roof, which catslides to one side over the hall projection. To the ridge is a bold brick chimney-stack with plinth and corniced capping. Conspicuously located at a turn in the Knocklyon Road, a replacement for a predecessor on the site.

Francis Cotton was in residence in 1849, when his gate porters were Patrick Gahan and Michael Browne.

Lewis 1837; *Thom's*; Griffith 1848–60.

KNOCKRABO (see MOUNTANVILLE HOUSE)

432. KNOCKSINNA, Stillorgan; 1873; architect John Holmes; *demolished.*

Alan Gilmer

The *Irish Builder* in 1873 reports: 'At Stillorgan, Co. Dublin, a mansion is being erected for Robert Smyth, with gate lodge, ornamental entrance gates, stables, &c. Mr Holmes, architect, J. & W. Beckett, contractors'. The second OS map of 1871 shows building to have commenced somewhat earlier for the 'wine merchant and high class grocer', to designs of a little-known architect whose gate lodge shows him to have been of some competence. Single-storey standard gabled with rendered walls and an almost symmetrical front elevation of multi-paned tripartite casement windows on each side of a glazed and carved wooden gabled porch. To each corner were Irish pilaster quoins, stopped at a frieze containing carved soffit brackets that turned the corners to form open-pedimented gables. The chimney-stack had disc motifs to a frieze band. All quite handsome and lovingly maintained but gone for all that, having fallen foul of widening of the Stillorgan Road.

IB (15 Oct. 1873); Pearson 1998.

KYLEMORE (see CAERLEON)

433. LABURNUM LODGE, Sandymount; pre-1837; *demolished.*
A villa by the eminent architect James Gandon in the 1780s for artist William Ashford. Frustratingly, there seems little way of knowing whether its gate lodge was also by him. A property, in the mid-nineteenth century of William Segrave and subsequently his widow, which was renamed 'Rosslyn Park'.

Thom's; Griffith 1848–60; McParland 1985.

434. LAKEFIELD, Merrion; pre-1849; *demolished.*
A gate lodge identified by the Griffith valuation as occupied by Thomas Hughes as gatekeeper of William McKay. There is no evidence of its location on site or on the OS maps of this Strand Road property.

Griffith 1848–60.

435. LAKELAND, Kilmacud; pre-1837; *demolished.*
Also known as 'Lakelands', it was the residence in 1837 of 'druggist' Simon Boileau, who was succeeded here in 1848 by architect John Skipton Mulvany, whose gate lodge one year later lay vacant.

Lewis 1837; Slater 1846; *IADS* (2000).

436. LAKELANDS, Sandymount (2).

In 1837 'the residence of Mrs Williamson, situated in grounds tastefully laid out and commanding fine sea and mountain views'. These views were enjoyed from about 1840 by the Wolseley family before the property, along with its early gate lodge off what was Cottage Park Avenue, was acquired *c.* 1855 by the Sisters of Charity, who over the years created St Mary's Orphanage and Industrial School attached to the Convent of the Immaculate Conception. To this they added a new entrance and gate lodge off the newly formed Gilford Road. Dating from *c.* 1890, this is a thoroughly pleasant and functional little building. Single-storey, built off an L-plan in Flemish bond red brick below a hipped roof, its walls relieved by Staffordshire blue engineering brick as string-courses and alternate voussoirs to segmentally arched one-over-one sash windows with chamfered reveals. The bold plinth is repeated on the chimney-stack, with its prominent corbelled and moulded capping of special bricks, which also feature about the projecting eaves. The brick ogee quadrant walls to the smart entrance screen contrast with stone plinth, cappings and five chamfered pillars, from the fifth of which is hung a pedestrian gate to the left-hand side. Beyond are rubble boundary walls. Architect Charles Geoghegan is recorded as having carried out (undated) work to the convent and this may have formed part of his commission. The early gate lodge to the house has been demolished.

Lewis 1837; *Thom's*; IAA.

437. LAKELANDS, Terenure; *c.* 1865; *demolished.*
A dwelling that seems to have been formed from the outbuildings of Terenure House (*q.v.*) after the foundation of the college here in 1860. Its occupant in 1870 was Thomas Butler.

Thom's.

438. LAKELANDS PARK, Terenure; *c.* 1870; *demolished.*
A mid-Victorian housing development of two pairs of semi-detached villas, exclusive in having their own lodged gate, but by 1936 the porter's lodge was surplus and had made way for terraced housing to the Templeogue Road.

Thom's.

439. LANDSCAPE, Churchtown (3).
Neither the big house, built in the late eighteenth century by Sir George Ribton (1740–1807), nor its three pre-1837 gatekeepers' lodges survive. Following H. O'Callaghan's residence here in 1837 it became home to brewer Robert Manders until the 1870s. His porters in 1849 were Felix Farrington, Michael Ryan and John Carr.

Lewis 1837; *Thom's*; Griffith 1848–60; Ball 1995.

440. LANDSEND, Stillorgan; pre-1837; *demolished.*
A property occupied for much of the mid-nineteenth century by Henry Maunsell MD of the Royal College of Surgeons. Its gate lodge and entrance were shared by the neighbouring house of Carysfort Lodge. About 1865 it was renamed 'Glensavage' by new owner Charles Kenney.

Thom's.

441. LANSDOWNE, Ballsbridge; 1884; architect not known.

A splendidly proportioned late Victorian single-storey standard lodge, very much a pared-down and subtler version of John McCurdy's more extrovert rendered Italianate examples in south Dublin, for which it is none the worse. Stone Irish pilasters enhance main corners and those of the hall, the gable of which projects from the main hipped roof. Otherwise it is faced in Flemish bond brickwork, its doorway and two-over-two sash windows having well-detailed brick segmental arches over. Situated on what was Haig's Avenue (now Lansdowne Road). Originally called 'Mary Villa', its lodge was added by building contractor and owner George Carolin, who renamed the property 'Ivanhoe'.

442. LARAGH, Killiney; *c.* 1880.
A plain roughcast single-storey standard hip-roofed affair with recent plastic windows installed; occupied. A development by Captain Edward Pakenham Stewart, son of James Robert Stewart of Gortleitragh (*q.v.*).

Thom's; *LGI* (1904).

443. LARCH HILL, Ballyboden (2).
A late eighteenth-century house built by the Caldbeck family which, like its lodges, is no more. The property was leased in the mid-nineteenth century to William H. Clarke, a solicitor, whose gatekeeper in 1849 was James Boothe. The second lodge, identified by the valuation of that year, then lay vacant but is not apparent on any OS maps.

Thom's; Griffith 1848–60; Healy 2005.

444. LARKFIELD, Palmerston (2).
James Hamilton is recorded as resident here in 1837 and, indeed, thirteen years later, when the gatekeeper to his south lodge is

noted as Bryan Berryman. Both pre-1837 lodges have been demolished; that to the north lay at the end of a long tree-lined approach which had gone by 1907.

Lewis 1837; Griffith 1848–60.

445. LARKFIELD MILLS, Harold's Cross; pre-1871.
A lodge built after 1837 probably by Francis Tuite, who was the proprietor of the flour mills in 1851.

Thom's.

446. LARK HILL, Rathmines; pre-1837; *demolished.*
An early nineteenth-century house which for much of the middle of that century was the Dublin home of William Wilson of Daramona, Co. Westmeath (*q.v.*). His gate porter in 1849 was John Barrows. By 1890 the property had become a college for boys of the Holy Ghost Fathers. Like all the numerous gate lodges to the west side of Rathmines Road Lower, this has succumbed to later development.

Griffith 1848–60; *LGI* (1904); Kelly 1995.

LAUGHTON (see STONE VILLE)

447. LAUREL HILL, Blackrock; pre-1837; *demolished.*
Semi-detached with its immediate neighbour, 'Field Villa', it had the edge in having a lodge by its gate, which in 1849 was manned by Alexander Beasley, porter to William F. Bentley, one in a succession of various owners.

Griffith 1848–60.

448. LAUREL HILL, Woodtown; pre-1837.
What was a single-storey gabled structure is now dwarfed by a modern extension. A property in 1837 of W. Bourk Esq., which had been acquired by James Horan by 1849, when the gate lodge lay vacant.

Lewis 1837; Griffith 1848–60.

449. LAUREL LODGE, Dundrum; pre-1837; *demolished.*
George Meyler was here in 1837 and as late as the 1860s. In 1849, when he also owned neighbouring Dundrum House (*q.v.*), his gatekeeper was Loughlin Flanagan. Prior to Meyler, Thomas Sherlock was in residence.

Lewis 1837; Griffith 1848–60; *Thom's.*

450. LAUREL LODGE, Glenageary; pre-1837; *demolished.*
A residence of Richard Fletcher in 1849, when his gate porter was Andrew Cavanagh; by 1880 it had been renamed 'Laurel Hill'.

Griffith 1848–60; *Thom's.*

451. LAUREL LODGE, Terenure; pre-1837; *demolished.*
A suburban villa that was home to an ever-changing series of owners. In 1849 it was owned by John Wilson, whose man at the gate was Patrick Toomey.

Griffith 1848–60.

LAURELTON (see THE WILLOWS)

452. LEINSTER LODGE, Rathmines; pre-1890; *demolished.*
A villa built around 1850, the first occupant of which was John F. McMullan, presumably the same as listed further along Leinster Road at No. 31 in 1846, secretary to the Grand Canal Company. Its gate lodge, built after 1837, was a replacement for a predecessor on the site that had overseen the gates to Leinster Road (*q.v.*).

Slater 1846; *Thom's.*

453. LEINSTER ROAD, Harold's Cross (2).
Frederick Jackson had by 1837, preparatory to building work, laid out Leinster Road across lands of Mould's Farm, with gate lodges already in place at each end to what were originally gated accesses. Both have gone. William Montgomery was gate porter in 1849 at the Rathmines Road access, leased by John Butler, architect and developer of Leinster Square, the lodge being superseded by that to Leinster Lodge (*q.v.*).

Griffith 1848–60; Kelly 1995.

454. LEOPARDSTOWN, Leopardstown (3).
A dwelling created *c.* 1845 from the farmyard of Leopardstown Park (*q.v.*) by Anthony Hawkins, who complemented it with a gate lodge on the Leopardstown Road at the head of an old avenue. These were followed by the construction of approaches from new lodged accesses on the distant Ballyogan Road to the south and Foxrock to the east, probably by the Benedictine Fathers who ran a model farm here until 1888, when the racecourse was established. All the lodges have been removed.

Slater 1846; Griffith 1848–60; Pearson 1998.

455. LEOPARDSTOWN PARK, Leopardstown; pre-1837; *demolished.*
Founded in 1796 by Charles Henry Coote, 7th Lord Castlecoote, from whom in 1802 the estate was inherited by his nephew, Eyre Coote, whose son of the same name sold it in 1830 to Fenton Hort, whose family remained here until 1837. Whether the lodge remained in its original form prior to its demolition is not known, but the house certainly was completely refaced in 1861–2 by architect J.S. Mulvany for the widow of Joseph Malcomson of Portlaw, Charlotte.

Archer 1801; Lewis 1837; Flanagan 1991; *IADS* (2000).

456. LINDEN, Stillorgan; pre-1871; *demolished.*
Previously 'Limeville' in 1837 of H.B. Reeves, who remained here until at least 1850; the lodge may have been added by Henry Jackson, resident in 1862. The Sisters of Charity purchased it two years later as a convalescent home, subsequently absorbing the neighbouring Stillorgan Park Cottage.

Lewis 1837; *Thom's*; Flanagan 1991.

457. LISANISKEA, Blackrock; pre-1849; *demolished.*
Originally a ranger's cottage, it was much altered and enlarged *c.* 1748 by Lady Arabella Denny, who had followed William Metcalf when it was called 'Peafield Cliff'. None of the nineteenth-century OS maps seem to show a lodge, but its existence is recorded in the 1849 valuation, when it was occupied by Patrick Trawley as porter to James Wright, who was the proprietor from 1848 to 1854 and may have built it, if the gatescreen is an indicator. Sturdily executed in granite with equally chunky ironwork, having pillars in the manner of Greek stelae with tapering panels containing Soaneian key patterns and anthemion chiselled acroteria to cappings which are crowned by elaborate lanterns—all of about 1845.

Griffith 1848–60; *Thom's*; Smyth 1994.

LISBALLALY (see AVONMORE)

458. LISLE, Crumlin; pre-1837; *demolished.*
An early eighteenth-century Queen Anne house built by the Hon. Joseph Deane, chief baron of the exchequer, from whom it was inherited by his son-in-law, John Lysaght, created 1st Baron Lisle in 1758, after whom the property was named. Following his death in 1781 it had a succession of uses, serving as a Classical Academy and for a while in the mid-nineteenth century as a female lunatic asylum, when the place was owned by William Hayes from 1814 until his death in 1888. His gate porter in 1850 was Patrick Conroy. A twentieth-century sketch suggests his lodge to have been the most modest of single-storey hip-roofed cottages.

Griffith 1848–60; *Thom's*; *BPB* (1929); Watchorn 1985.

459. LISSENFIELD, Rathmines; pre-1837; *demolished.*
A seat in 1837 of George Taylor Jr, which by 1846 was the residence of John Geoghegan, whose gatekeeper in 1850 was Peter Duffy. Like the plentiful line of gate lodges to villas on the western side of Rathmines Road it has gone, as has its big house.

Lewis 1837; Slater 1846; Griffith 1848–60.

460. LOCKSLEY, Shankill; *c.* 1860.

With neighbouring Rosedale (*q.v.*), one of twin villas built by a brewer-cum-property developer called Perry overlooking the sea, each with the added appeal of its own porter's lodge. It is a single-storey standard building with high eaves to its hipped roof, which is finished in scalloped slates. Giving it some accent is a central breakfront of a pair of piers supporting an open-pedimented gable containing a round-arched fanlit doorway. Now coated in coarse roughcast, with inappropriate modern wide casement windows and slip sills. The first occupant of Locksley in 1862 was merchant William H. Fry.

Thom's; Pearson 1998.

461. LODGE PARK, Dún Laoghaire; pre-1849; *demolished.*
A gate lodge that is apparent neither on site nor on any of the OS maps but was identified by the valuation of 1849 as occupied by Denis Cuddy as porter to Revd Bartholomew Sheridan, who had arrived in the 1820s as a wealthy priest at St Michael's Church and built himself Lodge Park.

Griffith 1848–60; Pearson 1981.

462. LONGFORD LODGE, Dún Laoghaire; pre-1837; *demolished.*
The old entrance gates have been moved closer to the house but, sadly, not the gate lodge, which was in existence prior to a major rebuilding of the house to designs of Sandham Symes around 1850, commissioned by either Richard Wordsworth Cooper (1801–50) or his widow Emilia, who lived on here until her death in the 1870s. Their gatekeeper in 1849 was Thomas Ward. A property subsequently renamed 'Glengara Lodge'.

Griffith 1848–60; *LGI* (1904); Pearson 1998.

463. LORDELLO, Shankill; pre-1837/*c.* 1870; architect possibly A.G. Jones.

A neat lodge of mildly Italianate appearance which may be a mid-Victorian revamp of an earlier building on the site, a seat in 1837 of P. Morgan Esq. and which would have been familiar to Revd John Winthrop Hackett (1804–88), from 1840 incumbent of St James's, Crinken, whose gatekeeper in 1849 was Frederick Thomas. He had gone to live at St James's Parsonage (see Aske Cottage) by 1870, when Lordello was occupied by Peter Du Bedat, who may be largely responsible for the lodge's present appearance. Single-storey standard below a hipped roof, a central gabled hall breakfront has a segmentally headed doorway in a like recess with, on each side, a similarly arched two-over-two sash window. Within the hall is a nice semicircular-arched niche, possibly of Regency date. Differing rendered finishes suggest more than one date. Subsequently extended by a bay to the left-hand side. Lovingly tended by the present owners. Attributable to architect Alfred Gresham Jones through its similarity to the lodges at Aughnacloy (*q.v.*), Inveruish (*q.v.*) and Williams Park (*q.v.*).

Lewis 1837; Griffith 1848–60; *Thom's*; Leslie and Wallace 2001.

464. LORETO CONVENT, Dalkey; *c.* 1842; *demolished.*

The surviving entrance screen is almost a perfect reflection of the 'nunnery' as built—almost, in that the convent turrets are octagonal but the four screen pillars are square, with bold corbelled crenellated cappings. These frame stucco-effect concave quadrant walls, each containing postilion openings with stone chamfered dressings. The date over the front door would seem to date the whole complex to 1842, built by Revd Mother Ball of Loreto Abbey, Rathfarnham, whose gate porter in 1849 was John Toole. Work attributed by Jeremy Williams to architect Patrick Byrne.

Griffith 1848–60; Williams 1994; Pearson 1998.

LORETO CONVENT, Rathfarnham (see PALLISER'S PARK)

465. LOTA, Booterstown; *c.* 1845.

A delightful and surprising survivor on Cross Avenue is this single-storey standard hip-roofed lodge with Tudor Picturesque detailing. In smooth rendered finish, its toothed quoins frame a front elevation of a gabled breakfront hall with decorative foiled bargeboards and a chamfered front door below a label moulding terminating in dripstones. On each side are similarly treated windows with modern casements and latticed lead effect, which probably reflect cast-iron predecessors. Beautifully maintained. The occupant in 1849, and probably its first, was John Walsh, gatekeeper to chemist Henry Bewley, who may have added the lodge to the late eighteenth-century house upon acquiring it around 1845. The place now goes under the name of 'Dunamase'.

Slater 1846; Griffith 1848–60.

466. LOUGHLINSTOWN, Loughlinstown (2).
In 1752 Mrs Delany found 'an estate and seat just by the inn [see Beechwood], the house old and ruinous and ingeniously situated to avoid one of the sweetest prospects I ever saw'. This was the house that the Domviles had built in the mid-seventeenth century, lost interest in and neglected in favour of Santry Court, north Dublin (*q.v.*). Thereafter it was lovingly tended by tenants, Revd Dr Thomas Leland (1723–85), rector of Bray from 1768 to 1773, and then Justice Robert Day from 1796 until his death in 1841. The property has been cruelly decimated, first by the intrusion of a motorway and later by housing development, each of which saw the removal of a gate lodge. The gatekeepers in 1849 were Catherine Bonny and Henry McGraine, employed by the then proprietor Jacob West.

Brewer 1825; Griffith 1848–60; Ball 1995; Pearson 1998; Leslie and Wallace 2001.

LOUGHNAVALE (see PAKENHAM LODGE)

LOWER PROSPECT (see BEECHGROVE)

467. LOWVILLE, Merrion; pre-1837; *demolished.*
John McCarthy in 1849 was gate porter to Robert Murray, resident in a house probably founded by the Lows of Merrion Castle.

Griffith 1848–60.

468. LUCAN, Lucan (4).
A charming Palladian-style villa, appropriately now the Italian Embassy, which is located in a pleasant 40-acre estate bounded in part by the River Liffey. It was created by Agmondisham Vesey, whose father of the same name had come into the property through marriage to a Sarsfield niece, and the only two lodged entrances of any architectural merit can also be credited to him, before he died in 1785.

Main entrance; *c.* 1780.

A single-storey hip-roofed cottage with traditional limewashed harled walls, one of the longer of which forms a blind boundary with the town. Within are Georgian Gothic Y-traceried windows, three-bay to the park and single-bay to the avenue. Between is an unusual chamfered corner that must have

housed the original front door. The need for additional protection from the elements called for a later entrance hall, which takes the form of a most odd protuberance with a bowed end containing a bipartite latticed casement window below a semi-conical roof. Alongside is a pair of contemporary late eighteenth-century granite V-jointed rusticated carriage pillars, each with a frieze displaying a round acanthus-leafed Coade stone patera with sculpted drape over. The dereliction of the lodge and inappropriate entrance gates are unworthy.

Stables entrance; *c.* 1760.

Irish Architectural Archive

A delightful introduction to the demesne, which appears to pre-date the house, is this rustic pair of lodges contained by four Palladian rusticated pillars built up in alternate river-pitted blocks, those to the carriage gateway rising to finely chiselled fluted and gadrooned urns. These may well have been repeated on the outer pillars, doubling as flues to corner fireplaces of the single-storey lodges, although there are now standard stacks in place. These little buildings are of irregular plan forward of the gatescreen, their public elevations also forming convex harled rubble quadrants, at least one of which contained a doorway with Y-traceried Georgian Gothic lancet fanlight. Flanking the carriage pillars are twin pointed-arched postern doorways with the same singular rustication as dressings, which continue as alternate voussoirs and keystones. It may be no coincidence that at Newbridge House, north Dublin (*q.v.*), is the same pitted rustication feature to the main entrance gates, which are to a design by James Gibbs, and a lodge proposal indicated a corner fireplace, the flue of which issued via an ornamental urn on the parapet.

After his uncle's death, Colonel George Vesey succeeded to the property, and his widow Emily after his passing until 1856. Her gatekeepers in 1849 were James Murphy at the main lodge, Anne Johnston and Thomas Colquhoun at the twin lodges, and Lawrence Doran and Bridget Lonard in the Leixlip Road lodges.

Middle entrance; pre-1836.

A plain gabled two-storey gatehouse forming part of the demesne wall and a twentieth-century structure tacked on.

Leixlip Bridge entrance; pre-1836/*c.* 1875.

Two miles distant, to the extreme west of the estate at the end along the riverside approach from Leixlip, is a disappointing jumble of a building, the core of which is a single-storey gabled structure with a polychrome brick stack of mid- to late Victorian origin but any other revealing features obscured by rendering and *Pyracantha*. Presumably built by Charles Vesey Colthurst-Vesey (1826–85), who inherited Lucan upon the death of his grandmother. To the rear is what may have been the single-storey hip-roofed earlier lodge and to the left-hand side a two-storey twentieth-century addition.

Archer 1801; Griffith 1848–60; *Thom's*; *LGI* (1904); Bence-Jones 1988.

469. LUCAN LODGE, Lucan; pre-1836; *demolished.*

Although probably built as a dower house by the Veseys of Lucan House (*q.v.*), with which it is linked by a passage below the Leixlip Road, it was nevertheless rented out over the centuries. In 1814 it was home to a Mrs Hamilton, ten years later to a Captain Clynch and in 1837 to Captain T.P. Poe before his move to Mountainview (*q.v.*).

Leet 1814; Pigot 1824; Lewis 1837.

470. LUCAN RECTORY, Lucan; *c.* 1875.

Regrettably, proximity to the town centre left the property at the mercy of modern urban sprawl and the glebe land has been invaded by executive dwellings, with the fine old rectory demolished. Surprising survivals are much of the boundary wall and an unusually commodious and, for a rectory, late gatehouse, which had a distinctly commercial appearance. Two-storey two-bay gabled to the roadside, it was roughcast-finished with toothed brick quoins and window dressings to two-over-two sashes. Latterly stripped to reveal its rubble construction, a shopfront now faces the footpath. The incumbent from 1871 to 1911 was Revd Charles Maunsell Benson (1840–1917).

Mulhall 1996; Leslie and Wallace 2001.

471. LUDFORD PARK, Ballinteer; pre-1837; *demolished.*

Now the home of Wesley College, in 1837 it was a seat of George Hatchell.

Lewis 1837.

472. LYNDHURST, Churchtown; *c.* 1845.

What was probably a single-storey standard lodge when occupied by Patrick Connor as gatekeeper in 1849 to its builder, John William Read. Now it is extended to four bays, having lost its chimney-stack, realised an unsightly flat-roofed hall projection with hideous plastic door, and been cloaked in sand/cement rendering with raised toothed quoins and dressings to one-over-one sash windows. Surviving this twentieth-century facelift is a band of scalloped slates to its hipped roof and conspicuous carved wooden brackets to the oversailing eaves. About 1855 the property was acquired by the Malone family and renamed 'Churchtown Lodge' and later in the century it became 'Ardtona', so called by Edmund William Waller.

Griffith 1848–60; *Thom's*; Ball and Hamilton 1895.

473. McGEOGH HOUSE, Rathmines; *c.* 1900; architect possibly R.F.C. Orpen.

Although the delightful High Victorian Gothic complex was designed *c.* 1875 by J. Rawson Carroll 'for ladies of good character', its gate lodge is of a later generation, being an inventive and quirky creation in an Edwardian Elizabethan Revival Arts and Crafts manner. Single-storey and built in red Flemish bond brickwork, it is essentially hip-roofed but for a half-timbered black-and-white gambrel which dominates the avenue front. From one corner projects a glazed canted hall, from which extends further a pedimented canopy with dentil bands, carried on carved modillion brackets. Typical of the period are casement windows, transomed and mullioned, with multi-glazed upper lights. The red earthenware-tiled ridge is interrupted by a solid square brick four-flue chimney-stack. The stone carriage pillars squinch from square shafts to octagonal cappings and probably date from Carroll's commission, whereas the lodge could conceivably be by Richard Francis Caulfield Orpen, who is recorded as working here as late as 1928.

IB (7 Jan. 1928); Williams 1994.

474. MAESGWYLLYDD, Galloping Green; pre-1837; *demolished.*

A villa in 1837 of Thomas Dickson, whose gatekeeper twelve years later was John Bourne. By 1857 John Cameron seems, understandably, to have renamed the place 'Springfield', and a few years later 'Ardui'. By 1873 the property was in the hands of William James Perry, a wealthy brewer, who transformed the house in the Italianate style to designs of John McCurdy. Whether he was also engaged to upgrade the porter's lodge is not clear, for both it and the big house have gone.

Lewis 1837; Griffith 1848–60; *Thom's*; *IADS* (2000).

MANOR HOUSE (see ANNA FIELD)

475. MARGARETTA, Roebuck (2).

Both the pre-1837 lodge, which lay vacant in the time here in 1849 of Thomas M. Scully, and that on the northern approach, probably added by Gregory Kane, have been demolished.

Griffith 1848–60; *Thom's*.

476. MARINE VILLA, Dún Laoghaire; pre-1837; *demolished.*
A property in 1841 of James Duggan, whose gate porter eight years later was Edward Kiernan.

Thom's; Griffith 1848–60.

477. MARINO, Killiney; *c.* 1830.
The original house dated from the 1830s, in 1837 being occupied by a Mrs King. Thereafter for much of the nineteenth century it was home to the Chaytor family, of whom Joshua D. Chaytor, a stockbroker and developer, had in 1849 Peter Moore as his gatekeeper, whose lodge remarkably survives as a plain single-storey hip-roofed cottage, its short gabled front to the avenue with six-over-six sash windows in roughcast walls. Subsequently extended to an L-plan. Marino was completely rebuilt in 1909 for stockbroker Lawrence A. Waldron, following which it was renamed 'Abbey Lea' by Lady Talbot de Malahide; it now serves as the Australian Embassy.

Lewis 1837; Griffith 1848–60; *Thom's*; O'Sullivan 1987; Pearson 1998.

478. MARINO, Booterstown (2).
For many years a residence, whilst he was perpetual curate of St Philip and St James Church of Ireland church, of Revd Robert Herbert Nixon (1782–1857) until his death, and for a period thereafter of his widow. In 1849 one lodge lay vacant whilst the other was manned by Alexander Meade.

East lodge; pre-1837; *demolished.*

West lodge; pre-1837/*c.* 1875.
What remains is a replacement for that at the other side of the entrance, which was probably built by Richard W. Boyle after half the site was hived off for an official Booterstown Rectory. It rests back to back with the lodge to Rockville (*q.v.*); single-storey standard, hip-roofed and rendered, with a central gabled hall projection.

The east lodge consequently became the access to the rectory before its demise.

Lewis 1837; Griffith 1848–60; *Thom's*; Leslie and Wallace 2001.

479. MARINO LODGE, Killiney; 1894; architect not known.

A striking 1½-storey symmetrical ornamental cottage, a cross between Elizabethan Revival with its half-timbered-effect gables and Rustic Picturesque in the pretty trunk and branch lattice work of the front porch, which is repeated as eaves supports to the recessed corner windows. Finished in pebble-dash with red-brick chimney-stacks to each gable of a red roll-tiled roof; date-board to the entrance porch. Although the house dates from the mid-nineteenth century, the lodge was built in the time here of a Mrs Symes.

Thom's.

480. MARLAY GRANGE, Rathfarnham; *c.* 1875.
In 1864 the banking family of La Touche sold off their interest in the Marlay House estate (*q.v.*) to Robert Tedcastle, who in turn divided the property, the northern portion of which was purchased by the Hon. Hercules Langford Boyle Rowley (1828–1904) of Summerhill House, Co. Meath (*q.v.*). This acquisition included the approach and lodged entrance from Whitechurch Road, which assumed the avenue to his new house, erected in 1872 in a pleasant informal Tudor Gothic style, probably to designs of John McCurdy. To this he added a second access off the Grange Road and a strangely nondescript gatehouse. Two-storey roughcast and gabled, with short elevation to the avenue and a wing to the park, so bland as to be of indeterminate age. The concave quadranted entrance screen is badly damaged but four plain rendered pillars survive, those to the carriage opening having granite ball finials.

LGI (1904); *Land owners in Ireland 1876*; IAA; O'Dwyer 1997b.

481. MARLAY, Rathfarnham (3).
As 'The Grange', the property was acquired from the Taylor family in 1764 by the Rt Hon. David La Touche, of banking fame, who renamed it after his wife's maiden name, and it remained in his family for precisely a century. In 1801 the house was 'extremely elegant, and the farmyard and offices very commodious; the gardens are handsome and extensive, and contain a great deal of glass; the whole abounding with a variety of fruit, &c. The demesne consists of upwards of 300 acres, and is beautifully laid out with fine walks, well wooded, remarkably well watered, and skilfully planted, and the whole well enclosed with a good stone wall.' And so, thanks to the County Council, it remains, available for public enjoyment to this day. Things here were not always sweetness and light, however, nor were the La Touches always in residence, for during the 1798 Rebellion a Mr Humphrey Minchin and his aged father-in-law were tenanting the place and, as Protestants, were threatened with having their throats cut by rebels who included the gardener and the gatekeeper and his wife, no less. This is probably the Humphrey Minchin who moved on to Roebuck Lodge (*q.v.*).

North entrance; pre-1837; *demolished.*
Surviving is the gatescreen in the form of two granite V-jointed rusticated carriage pillars with scroll-topped stops and corniced blocked cappings, from which spring an iron overthrow proclaiming 'Grange Golf Club'. Tall, straight screen walls terminate in delicate pillars with fluted friezes. Prior to formation of the golf-course in 1910, the entrance served Marlay Grange (*q.v.*) from about 1870. In 1849 the gatekeeper was George Keogh.

East entrance; *c.* 1825.
Off the Grange Road is a nondescript long, low, single-storey, pebble-dashed hip-roofed lodge with an eaves band and three blocked-up segmentally arched windows facing the park—an overgrown abandoned shell. Its porter in 1849 was Richard Rainsford. Alongside are later grand quarry-faced granite gate pillars with prominent corniced cappings.

South entrance; *c.* 1835.

A commodious example of the newfangled Tudor Picturesque style that was embraced by landowners in the Regency period. Located off Ballinteer Avenue is this two-storey roughcast gabled gatehouse with paired brackets to soffits and the verges of open-pedimented end elevations. The upper floor is expressed by an embracing stone string-course, whilst the lead-effect, previously latticed cast-iron casement windows have label mouldings in the Tudor manner, also to be seen in the pair of octagonal stone chimney-pots which squinch off a rectangular base. The short avenue front has a symmetrical three-bay ground-floor façade recessed behind a pretty arched screen of banded posts with cusped trefoil spandrels; to the park elevation a gablet breaks the eaves. Recently smartly rehabilitated. The privileged keeper in 1849 was John Maginn. Affording impressive protection is a tall, rubble-built boundary wall with ogee quadrants, one of which contains a modest postern doorway, stopped by a pair of noble Classical granite carriage pillars of V-jointed rustication and pedestalled ball finials.

A distant lodge on the western approach from the Whitechurch Road is considered under Whitechurch Church of Ireland church and the schoolhouse with which it is closely associated.

Archer 1801; Musgrave 1801; Pearson 1998.

482. MARLFIELD, Cabinteely; pre-1837; *demolished.*
Once a house of the Byrnes of Cabinteely House (*q.v.*), who leased it to John Dwyer; he rebuilt it *c.* 1794 and it was occupied for much of the nineteenth century by Miss Catherine Jessop of Doory Hall, Co. Longford (*q.v.*), until she died unmarried in 1891. Her gate porter in 1849 was James Leech, on the site of whose lodge is a twentieth-century bungalow.

Griffith 1848–60; *Thom's*; *LGI* (1904); Craig and Fewer 2002.

MARY VILLA (see LANSDOWNE)

483. MARY VILLA, Booterstown; pre-1837; *demolished.*
A property in 1841 of Mrs O'Brien, whose gate lodge strangely was never replaced, having been removed about the time that a 'spacious mansion with red brick front' was built on the site for goldsmith and jeweller Joseph Johnson to plans by John McCurdy in 1862.
Thom's; *DB* (1 Nov. 1862).

484. MARYVILLE, Beggar's Bush; pre-1837; *demolished.*
Both this lodge and that to neighbouring Brooklawn (*q.v.*) appear to have formed a pair and shared a joint entrance. Occupied by James Gee as porter to Mrs Anne Parker in 1849, both lodges and houses had gone by 1907.
Griffith 1848–60.

MARYVILLE (see MERRYVILLE)

MARYVILLE (see SIMMONSCOURT [2])

485. MASONIC FEMALE ORPHAN SCHOOL, Ballsbridge; *c.* 1895; architect probably W.M. Mitchell.

A great brick and terracotta composition by architects McCurdy and Mitchell of 1882 in a mainly Tudor manner, with just a touch of Queen Anne Revival, which predominates in its lively Arts and Crafts single-storey gate lodge added a few years later, after John McCurdy's death. Essentially raised off an L-plan in polychromatic Flemish bond brickwork, buff with red-brick and sandstone dressings, toothed to the leading tripartite wooden pedimented window, set in a three-centre-arched recess with sill apron and earthenware fluted keystone below a pedimented gable which is contained by ball finials on brick piers. Otherwise the roof is steeply hipped, crowned by a grand chimney-stack and catsliding to form a highly ornamental wooden porch with carved Jacobean posts supporting a continuous bracket arch below bracketed eaves. Now independent, put to office use and under siege by cars.
Williams 1994; IAA.

486. MAYFIELD, Ballinteer; pre-1869; *demolished.*
A short-lived porter's lodge built after 1837 and which, like its big house, had gone by 1907. A property in the 1840s of George A. Purdon, leasing from the Curran family.
Thom's; Griffith 1848–60.

487. MEADOWBANK, Terenure; pre-1837; *demolished.*
Patrick Fitzgerald was in 1849 gatekeeper to George Thorpe, who was leasing from Mrs Margaret Wharton, presumably wife of John Lee Wharton Esq., also of Sweetmount House (*q.v.*), who in 1837 was letting to one T. Copperthwaite. The early lodge was superseded by a replacement further west and the original site occupied by another to 'The Willows' (*q.v.*).
Lewis 1837; Griffith 1848–60.

488. MEADOWBROOK, Dundrum (2).
A 100-acre farm and house in 1846 of Thomas Byrne. Three years later his gatekeepers are listed as Robert Kevett at the main entrance and Hugh Byrne in the back lodge. Both lodges have gone, having been far too close and vulnerable to the explosion that has been Dundrum.
Slater 1846; Griffith 1848–60.

489. MEATH HOSPITAL, Long Lane; pre-1871; *demolished.*
The institution moved from the Coombe to this site in 1822, although a porter's lodge was not added until after 1837, perhaps to designs of Frederick Darley, who was responsible for a children's ward in 1865.
Lewis 1837; Pearson 2000; IAA.

490. MEATH INDUSTRIAL SCHOOL, Blackrock; *c.* 1890; architect not known.

A substantial 1½-storey standard gabled affair built in uncoursed random rubble facing with contrasting cream brick as toothed quoins and dressings and canted single-storey bay windows to end elevations. From the main front projects the hallway, with room over. To the gables are decorative perforated bargeboards with canted motifs repeated as earthenware crestings to the ridge, which is broken by a great red-brick four-flue cluster chimney-stack; modern lead-effect casement windows and an unfortunate new flat-roofed glazed porch to the front door. Built at the entrance to the Meath Protestant Industrial School for Boys, as it was in 1875.
Pearson 1998.

MEEANEE (see EDEN COTTAGE)

491. MELFIELD, Blackrock (2).
One of the earliest and more elegant villas in the area, associated from 1792 with the Atkinson family, who kept an interest in it until about 1870, when it was acquired with two porters' lodges by Michael Frederick Crowe, part of the property being sold off to accommodate the rather less elegant Belfort House (*q.v.*).
Stradbrook Road gate; pre-1837; *demolished.*
This entrance and lodge were abandoned in the late eighteenth century and thereafter seemed to serve Ferndene (*q.v.*). The lodge lay vacant in 1849.
Newtownpark Avenue gate; pre-1837/*c.* 1870.

A fine little single-storey standard replacement for an earlier lodge on the site whose porter in 1849 was John Doyle. Hip-roofed with a similarly treated porch roof carried on carved wooden posts and brackets. Finished in stucco effect with segmentally arched windows in shouldered banded surrounds. Above is a tall corbelled chimney-stack. Badly damaged by fire, unlike its twin lodge across the forecourt; both were part of a comprehensive development and division of the site, but both they and their big houses are now reunited in a school complex.
Thom's; Griffith 1848–60; Pearson 1998; Smith 2001.

492. MERRION CASTLE, Merrion; *c.* 1820.
The ancestral home of the Fitzwilliam family until 1704, after which it passed to the Herberts, earls of Pembroke, by whom it was leased for the first half of the nineteenth century to Francis Lowe, whose gatekeeper in 1848 was John Quinn. The gatehouse survives as a two-storey gabled structure, a one-bay short elevation to the avenue, roughcast and crowned by the semblance of a pediment. Despite much alteration and a monstrous extension to rear and side, it manages to retain some of its original late Georgian character. The property in 1866 became St Mary's Asylum for the Blind, which it remains to this day.
Brewer 1825; Lewis 1837; *Thom's*; Griffith 1848–60; Joyce 1912; Smyth 1994.

493. MERRION HALL, Merrion; pre-1837; *demolished.*
A property in 1837 of Richard Davis, beautifully located on Strand Road.
Lewis 1837.

494. MERRION SQUARE GARDENS; pre-1838; *demolished.*
A rare illustration shows but a glimpse of what appears to have been a sizeable single-storey structure with a large chimney-stack to its hipped roof. Largely obscured by the ultimate in sophisticated rear elevations in the Rutland Fountain, a screen in granite with Portland stone dressings and Coade stone ornamentation. Built in 1792 at the instigation

of Charles Manners, duke of Rutland, to designs of Francis Sandys, it probably preceded the lodge behind by a few years, planting and railed enclosure being completed in 1794. Now Archbishop Ryan Park.

Casey 2005.

495. MERRYVILLE, Stillorgan; pre-1837; *demolished.*
A lodge and entrance shared by Fairy Hill. Solicitor Lloyd H. Thomas is recorded in 1837 as resident of 'Maryville', his gate porter twelve years later being Alexander Walsh.

Lewis 1837; Griffith 1848–60.

496. MERTON PARK, Ranelagh; pre-1850; *demolished.*
The lodge may date from *c.* 1845, when Falconer Myles acquired the property from the Sandford family. His gatekeeper in 1850 was William Blake.

Thom's; Griffith 1848–60.

497. MERVIEW, Williamstown; pre-1837; *demolished.*
A property in 1837 of Thomas Clinch which thereafter saw a frequent change of residents.

Lewis 1837.

498. MERVILLE [1], Booterstown (2).
Now forming part of the great UCD complex, this venerable brick mansion has outlived its porters' lodges, which, for all the evidence that remains, could have been built by any one of a succession of noble proprietors. Built *c.* 1750 by the Rt Hon. Judge Anthony Foster MP (1705–78), who was succeeded here by his equally pre-eminent son, John Foster (*c.* 1740–1828), 1st Lord Oriel and last speaker of the Irish House of Commons. It was then acquired by Sir Thomas Lighton as his home until his death in 1805, when it became the estate of the Rt Hon. William, Baron Downes, until his 1826 demise. It was then briefly the residence of R. Manders Esq., but from *c.* 1840 until his death it was occupied by Henry Edwards Hall (1789–1875), who in his time here rose from the rank of colonel to lieutenant-general. Both of the lodges were certainly in place by 1837 and occupied in 1849 by William Keegan and William Fitzpatrick. Surviving at the Foster's Avenue entrance is an extensive gatescreen of two granite carriage pillars with fluted friezes, flanked by tall roughcast concave quadrant walls containing architraved postilion openings (now blocked up).

Archer 1801; Lewis 1837; Griffith 1848–60; Ball and Hamilton 1895; Ball 1995; *BPB* (1929).

499. MERVILLE [2], Galloping Green; pre-1837; *demolished.*
In 1801 'the seat of Richard Bolton, Esq., a neat house, beautifully situated, with a small demesne, good gardens, and a beautiful green-house'. By 1837 it had been acquired by William James McCausland, perhaps through marriage, for his son was Sir Richard Bolton McCausland. The gate lodge in 1849 lay vacant.

Archer 1801; Lewis 1837; Griffith 1848–60; *LGI* (1904).

500. MESPIL, Ranelagh; *c.* 1770; *demolished.*
In 1751 this was 'Barry House', as it was named by its builder, eminent Dublin physician Edward Barry, who created it as his rural idyll. It was overcome in the mid-twentieth century by city sprawl, but an early photograph shows the house and its entrance in leafy suburbs. A pair of square carriage pillars are flanked by straight screen walls containing postern doorways. Behind is a glimpse of the tiny single-storey hip-roofed porter's lodge, with smoke issuing from a tall stack rising off its rear wall.

Kelly 1995 (Father Browne photograph).

501. MILLMOUNT HOUSE AND CLOTH MILL, Rockbrook; *c.* 1800.

Already a narrow site on which to build a mill and owner's house between the road and the River Owendoher, there was little left to accommodate a porter by the gates. The result is a crude but charming solution. Single-storey, its walls follow the outline of the road and continue as the left-hand convex entrance quadrant forming a bowed end, in a harled finish containing two wide windows which may originally have been tripartite. One can imagine the roof appropriately thatched to complement the eccentric plan, but rather than displaying a fine example of the slater's art the curve is handled unsatisfactorily and angularly with a series of hips. A subsequent lean-to extension to the avenue resulted in the postern gate becoming a window—unlike the mills, remarkably still in use. A concern in the late eighteenth century of Benjamin Nunn which passed early in the following century to Mssrs R.P. Dollard and Co., paper manufacturers and stationers.

Archer 1801; Griffith 1848–60; Healy 2005.

502. MILLMOUNT LODGE AND FLOUR MILL, Milltown; pre-1837; *demolished.*
A concern of James Henderson in 1849, which by then had been adapted to become a sawmill, its porter's lodge lying empty.

Griffith 1848–60.

503. MILLTOWN CASTLE, Milltown; pre-1837; *demolished.*
The residence in 1843 of the Misses Hunt, the gatekeeper to which in 1850 was James Keogh. Now part of Mount St Anne's Convent.

Thom's; Griffith 1848–60.

504. MILLTOWN HILL, Milltown; pre-1837; *demolished.*
A property in the mid-nineteenth century of tobacco and snuff manufacturer George Cowell, who changed its name *c.* 1850 to 'Prospect'.

Slater 1846; *Thom's*.

505. MILLTOWN, Milltown (2).
Both lodges now demolished, one pre-dating 1837 to an estate in 1850 of Michael W. Montserratt, one of whose gatekeepers was then Thomas Perry. The place was united with Milltown Castle (*q.v.*) to form Mount St Anne's Convent.

Griffith 1848–60; Craig and Fewer 2002.

506. MILLTOWN LODGE, Milltown (2).
Two lost lodges, occupied in 1849 by Elizabeth Gerrard and Constantine Maguire, porters to John Duffy.

Griffith 1848–60.

507. MILLTOWN PARK, Milltown; pre-1837; *demolished.*

In 1801 'the residence of Baron George, a good house well situated, a small demesne, well wooded, good gardens, and all well enclosed with a stone wall'. This was the Hon. Denis George, baron of the exchequer, who had acquired the place previously known as 'Coldblow' and occupied by Sir William Fortick in the 1780s. Surviving are plain-walled entrance quadrants with granite carriage pillars having fluted bands and, although much altered, two extraordinary iron gates, each leaf displaying arrows radiating towards an oval floral patera. In 1858 the Jesuit Order took over the property.

Kelly 1995; Pearson 2002.

508. MILLTOWN WOOLLEN MANUFACTORY, Milltown; pre-1837; *demolished.*
A concern of Sir Robert Alexander (1769–1859) in 1850, when the gate lodge lay vacant. In 1837 it had been a cloth mill but by 1869 had become a flour mill and finally a laundry in 1907.

Griffith 1848–60; *BPB* (1929).

509. MINNOWBROOK, Terenure; pre-1837; *demolished.*
A snug little property next to the village of Roundtown, home in 1849 to Jonathan Leech

MD, who two years later had flitted across the road to Laurel Lodge (*q.v.*). His gate porter was John Martin.

Griffith 1848–60; *Thom's*.

510. MOATFIELD, Little Bray; pre-1837; *demolished.*
By 1906 both house and lodge had gone, incorporated into the greater Old Connaught (*q.v.*) property by the 4th Lord Plunket. In 1816 it had been the seat of Hartley Hodson (1759–1839), followed by a Mr Clarke. It was owned by Charles Toole of neighbouring Wilfort (*q.v.*) by 1849, when the gate porter was Andrew Hyland. The old entrance became the third lodged gate to Old Connaught.

Griffith 1848–60; An Old Inhabitant 1907; *BPB* (1929).

511. MOAT HILL, Lucan; *c.* 1890.
A gatehouse, now known as 'Moat Lodge' in its own right and serving as B&B accommodation, which seems to have been built at the entrance to the local curiosity of a ringfort, with souterrain discovered by James Gandon of neighbouring Canonbrook (*q.v.*). It is much altered and extended to offer 'bedrooms en suite' but exhibiting black-and-white work, white roughcast, red-brick chimney-stacks and clay roof tiles suggestive of the turn of the twentieth century.

Lewis 1837; Killanin and Duignan 1962.

512. MONKSTOWN CASTLE, Monkstown; *c.* 1830; architect perhaps G. Papworth; *demolished.*
In 1837 'the residence of Linden [*sic*] Bolton, Esq., a modern house'; along with its gate lodge, it was purchased the following year by James Pim Jr (1796–1856) of the Dublin and Kingstown Railway. His gatekeeper eleven years later was Mrs Ennis. Frederick O'Dwyer has attributed the original house to George Papworth, who may also have been responsible for its lodge, as architect to Lyndon Bolton.

Lewis 1837; Griffith 1848–60; *IADS* (2000).

513. MONKSTOWN COTTAGE, Monkstown; pre-1837; *demolished.*
The seat in 1841 of Benjamin Grant, whose gatekeeper in 1849 was Mrs Acton.

Thom's; Griffith 1848–60.

MONKSTOWN HILL (see RICHMOND PARK)

514. MONKSTOWN, Monkstown (2).
A property until his death in 1821 of Alderman Henry Gore Sankey, lord mayor of Dublin in 1791, which by 1841 had been acquired by Thomas Pim. It seems to have served that family of merchants and cotton-spinners adequately until inherited by William Hervey Pim, who redeveloped the site, replacing both the house and its gate lodge in 1859 to designs of Carmichael and Jones.

Front entrance; pre-1837/1859; architect A.G. Jones.

Mary Doyle was gatekeeper to Thomas Pim in 1849, but it is doubtful that she enjoyed the generous replacement accommodation of ten years later. A striking Italianate design that exhibits much of the detailing seen on other lodges at Montebello (*q.v.*) and Johnstown-Kennedy (*q.v.*) and Hollywoodrath, north Dublin (*q.v.*), attributable to architect Alfred Gresham Jones, the latter two of which also display the same basic form. This is single-storey, built off a cruciform plan below shallow gabled roofs, with what was an open entrance porch in an internal angle, the catslide roof of which is carried on elaborate columns with helically bound barley-twist shafts and imaginative 'hoop' capitals. Smooth rendered walls are relieved by narrow round-headed window openings with banded surrounds rising to conspicuous fluted scrolled brackets from which spring vermiculated voussoirs and keystones. To the leading avenue gable is a rectangular glazed bay window with straight arches and margined sashes, all under its own hipped roof. A round plaque to one gable confirms the date of construction.

Back entrance; pre-1907; *demolished.*
An old garden pathway which led south-eastwards to be stopped by what may have been a summer-house was, sometime after 1871, extended to form a new approach from a lodged access off the Mount Town road. This was to be short-lived, having to make way for a traffic roundabout.

Thom's; Griffith 1848–60; *DB* (1 May 1859); *LGI* (1904); Pearson 1998; *IADS* (2000).

515. MONKSTOWN PARK, Monkstown; *c.* 1835; architect not known; *demolished.*

Peter Pearson

A house and lodge erected by the scholar and humanitarian Charles Haliday, who resided here until his death in 1866. His very fine Classical gate lodge was tragically demolished in 1983 after a fire. It was in effect two-storey, with the appearance of being single-storey built off a basement to a cruciform plan. Rendered and generously detailed with pedimented gables, the projecting hallway had an architraved door and Doric pilasters, whilst the multi-paned windows, at least one of which was tripartite, were below bold bracketed entablatures. The number of rooms was perhaps revealed by three double-flue chimney-stacks. Haliday's gatekeeper enjoying the accommodation in 1849 was Margaret Golding.

Griffith 1848–60; Ball 1995; Pearson 1998.

516. MONKSTOWN RECTORY, Kill of the Grange; pre-1814/*c.* 1880.
A glebe house built in 1797 during the incumbency (1791–9) of Revd John William Dudley Ryves (1716–1801), the gate lodge to which may have been contemporary, as it appears on John Longfield's map of 1814. Its occupant in 1849 was Robert Foster as porter to Archdeacon Charles Lindsay. This remained the rectory of Monkstown Parish until 1870, transferring thence to that of Kill for the next six years. Thereafter it became a private residence called 'Fairholme' and the porter's lodge appears to have been replaced, probably for Roland R. Scovell, who was here in 1883. Despite having been modernised with concrete tiles to its oversailing hipped roof and multi-paned windows and doorscreen, it still retains the feel of a single-storey standard gatekeeper's lodge with rendered walls and late Victorian brick chimney-stack. The railed gatescreen has distinctive cast-iron 'Chinese stove'-type carriage pillars with foliated ornament and rosette motifs. Alterations were carried out to the lodge in 1925 to plans of W.M. Mitchell and Sons but seem to have been for little more than the installation of a WC and drainage.

Griffith 1848–60; *Thom's*; Murphy 2003; Leslie and Wallace 2001; IAA (McCurdy & Mitchell Drawing Collection 79/17, Bin I, Roll 52).

517. MONKSTOWN VIEW, Monkstown; pre-1837/*c.* 1885.

The residence in 1837 of Captain E.S. Kirwan, whose gate porter in 1849 was Daniel Byrne. He seems to have lived on here for another couple of years before it became the property of James Pim, to whom it was home until the 1870s, after which it lay vacant before the site was developed to become 'Dunedin' and a new lodge built at the other side of the entrance. This is single-storey and Italianate in style, with a high hipped roof and pedimented hall breakfront, on each side of which are three-over-one sash windows with moulded surrounds in grey stucco-effect rendered walls framed by raised toothed quoins; extended in a catslide outshot to the road elevation. Probably built for R.E. Turbett, who chose to retain the previous gatescreen, which has a pair of Greek stela-type carriage pillars with tapering recessed panels and good contemporary iron gates of *c.* 1830. The lodge is now independent and avenueless, its big house having gone.

Lewis 1837; Griffith 1848–60; *Thom's*; Pearson 1998.

518. MONTEBELLO, Killiney; *c.* 1860; architect A.G. Jones.

A property created in 1860 for the wealthy barrister and Italophile Daniel Connolly, the villa in the manner of architect J.S. Mulvany. It must, however, be the work of his erstwhile assistant Alfred Gresham Jones under the influence of his employer, for the contemporary gate lodge is uniquely Jones's, displaying identical detailing to that at Monkstown House (*q.v.*) of a year earlier.

Single-storey standard and gabled in a stucco finish boldly detailed with a deep multi-bracketed eaves band, which continues about the verges and forms capitals to the pilasters of an open-pedimented hall projection. The double-leaved front doorway is delightful, with its round-headed glazing a feature repeated in triplicate in the three-over-three sash windows framed by moulded lugged surrounds and bracketed sills. To the avenue front is a pair of narrow semicircular-arched lights with margined glazed sashes in banded surrounds and fluted brackets, from which spring reticulated voussoirs and keystones—just as on the Monkstown House lodge and similar to the examples at Johnstown-Kennedy (*q.v.*) and Hollywoodrath, north Dublin (*q.v.*). In the gable over is a shield sculpted with the Connolly family crest displaying three scallop shells. A splendid little building, which rather than being subordinately sited to the entrance boldly addresses it from an elevated position. The gatescreen is suitably bold in chunky contemporary ironwork from the Murphy Manufactory of Church Street, Dublin; highly elaborate, with rosettes, palmettes, anthemion motifs and an abundance of foliage in the carriage pillars. It seems that Mr Connolly had little time to enjoy his idyll, for by 1870 it was home to Joseph Kirkwood.

Thom's; *IADS* (2000).

519. MONTPELIER, Monkstown (3).

The OS map of 1837 indicates lodged entrances from Monkstown and Stradbrook Roads to a once-elegant house in 1841 of a Captain Jackson. Eight years later he was leasing the place briefly to Hans Hamilton, whose porter at the northern gate was James Mooney. In 1842 architect Arthur Creagh Taylor exhibited a gate lodge design for Montpelier at the RHA, which may not have been executed. The property subsequently fell on hard times, being auctioned in 1852, and passed through a succession of hands before being acquired in 1885 by S.S. McCormick, who renamed the house 'Shandon' and added the only surviving lodge. Next to Montpelier Terrace on the Monkstown Road is a little single-storey rendered gabled cottage with Classical moulded window surrounds and raised toothed quoins. From the main two-bay body of the structure a lower room projects to the road, with a later glazed porch squeezed into the internal angle. There is an incongruous roof covering of plain terracotta tiles with scalloped bands and perforated crestings. This is now all that remains of the property, it all having been redeveloped, the big house demolished after suffering all manner of indignities over the years, unrecognisable as the elegant structure portrayed in an 1802 engraving.

Thom's; Griffith 1848–60; Lyons 1993; Pearson 1998.

520. MONTROSE, Priesthouse (2).

The house, built *c.* 1836 by distiller James Jameson, surprisingly survives but not so its two lodges, one of which was manned in 1849 by Morgan Castles as porter to William Jameson, who had succeeded to the property upon his father's death two years before.

Griffith 1848–60; *LGI* (1904).

MOOREFIELD (see SARAVILLE)

521. MOORFIELD, Roebuck (2).

A seat in 1837 of Patrick Curtis which four years later had been acquired by flour merchant William Haughton (1799–1877), the tenth of twelve brothers, whose gatekeepers in 1849 were John Byrne and Patrick Dunne. Both lodges, in place in 1837, have been removed from their sites on Roebuck Road.

Lewis 1837; Griffith 1848–60; *IFR*.

522. MOREEN, Sandyford (2).

The 1803 *Post chaise companion* records that 'with great industry and expense, is erected a neat compact house, with lawns, gardens, plantations and suitable office belonging to William McKay, Esq.', but makes no mention of porters' lodges, both of which were built by 1837. The two gatekeepers in 1849 were Hugh Doyle and Matthew Reilly, who would have been at their busiest during the annual steeplechase held here. The property is now home to a bank, for whom house and lodges were surplus to requirements.

Wilson 1803; Griffith 1848–60.

523. MOREEN LODGE, Sandyford; pre-1837; *demolished*.

The previous house on the site was substantially altered in 1853 by wine merchant Henry Thompson and renamed 'Clonard'. At the turn of the twentieth century the new owner, M. Barrington Jellett, had commissioned architect R.M. Butler to alter and extend the gate lodge, and by 1912 that work was being undertaken by Messrs Bolger and Doyle.

IB (16 Sept. 1911 and 25 May 1912); Pearson 1998; *IADS* (2000).

524. MOUNTAIN VIEW, Oldbawn; pre-1837; *demolished.*
A property which by the mid-nineteenth century was home to J.R. Burkett MD, whose gate porter in 1849 was Christopher Kelly. Thirty years later proprietor and gatekeeper were James Furlong and Joseph Little, by which time the place was called 'Bawn Ville'.

Griffith 1848–60.

525. MOUNTAINVIEW, Terenure (2).
The previous house on the site was a residence in 1837 of W. Deane Esq. which four years later was home to Captain Thomas P. Poe, whose gate porter in 1849 was Michael Smith. A decade later the *Dublin Builder* magazine was to report that 'an elegant villa has recently been raised by Mr W. Vincent, facing Sir Robert Shaw's demesne, with a beautiful unique gate-lodge and handsome terrace. Mr E.P. Gribbon, archt.' This new lodge replaced that to the north of the road frontage, the property being renamed 'Wasdale'. Sadly, the lodge's uniqueness was no guarantee of its survival.

Lewis 1837; *Thom's*; Griffith 1848–60; *DB* (1 Dec. 1859).

526. MOUNT ALTON, Knocklyon; pre-1869; *demolished.*
Sometime between 1851 and 1854 the property ceased to be 'Annemount' and probably then gained a porter's lodge when the new proprietor was Sheffield Betham, who had moved from Prospect Hill (*q.v.*).

Thom's.

527. MOUNT ALVERNO, Dalkey; pre-1837; *demolished.*
Perversely, when the Regency villa, in 1851 of Revd P. Smyth, was transformed into a Baronial mansion *c.* 1900 by Alexander Conan its lodge was removed, not to be replaced.

Thom's; IAA.

MOUNT ANVILLE COTTAGE (see CEDARMOUNT)

528. MOUNT ANVILLE, Roebuck (3).
Originally a late eighteenth-century house built by Baron Trimlestown; he sold it in 1799 to Thomas Kemmis, in whose family it remained for many years but leased to a number of owners: Daniel Beere from 1802 to 1824, and the Hon. Judge Charles Burton (1760–1847), who was here until his death and latterly seems to have shared the property with John Beatty West, whose widow Eliza lived on here until 1851. Her gatekeepers in 1849, occupants of the two pre-1837 lodges, were James Meegan and Patrick Kearney. These lodges were swept away with the coming in 1851 of the railway, road and canal entrepreneur William Dargan

(1799–1867), who set about rejuvenating the demesne, transforming the villa into an Italianate mansion complete with a belvedere tower and creating a new grand entrance and lodge off Mount Anville Road at the end of a new and lengthy serpentine avenue. Dargan's architect is revealed as J.S. Mulvany, the lodge being almost identical to his design for that at Minella, Co. Waterford. This is a very distinctive and commodious single-storey structure of *c.* 1852, raised in cut granite off a cruciform plan with shallow Italianate gables in the form of open pediments carried on corner pilasters and enhanced with bold mutules taken about the eaves as corbels, a detail beloved of Mulvany. To opposing elevations are pairs of narrow round-headed windows, whilst the avenue projection, flanked symmetrically by lean-to arcaded porches, contains an arrowhead bay window with flat-arched chamfered openings. Emphasising the boldness of the composition is a cluster of three chimney-stacks in a row. Equally extraordinary and innovative is the extensive entrance screen of wide, shallow concave quadrants in coursed random cut granite, like the lodge, with a coping supported by moulded console brackets, a feature repeated about the cappings of a pair of postilion arches which resemble pillboxes, on each side of the carriage opening. The survival of this monument is to be welcomed whilst lamenting that it was parted from its lodge and re-erected closer to the house, which Dargan sold fifteen months before his death to the Sacred Heart nuns.

Griffith 1848–60; Ball and Hamilton 1895; Pearson 1998; *IADS* (2000).

529. MOUNTANVILLE PARK, Roebuck (3).
A property in 1837 that was home to Edward Butler, the western gate to which was then manned and twelve years later occupied by Lawrence Tobin, porter to the new owner, James Gray. From *c.* 1854 until 1863 it was the residence of Robert Orme of Owenmore, Co. Mayo, but it was his successor, Henry Roe Jr, who in his time here to the 1880s transformed the place, employing architects W. and T.K. Louch in 1868 to plan extensive alterations and extensions to the house and presumably to design two new gate lodges.

West gate; pre-1837/*c.* 1868; architects probably W. and T.K. Louch.

Replacing the previous porter's lodge at the other side of the entrance is this single-storey standard hip-roofed structure, commodious, on a grand scale, with a heavily articulated main front of raised toothed quoins framing a pair of glazed semi-octagonal bay windows with their own hipped roofs, flanking a central entrance breakfront which contains a segmentally arched doorway with hood moulding below a heraldic shield in the open-pedimented gable. Smooth-rendered with a tall plinth and a bracketed eaves band, there is a pair of symmetrically placed chimney-stacks with bold corniced cappings. In 2000 abandoned by the Bank of Ireland, and vandalised. Unsuccessfully protecting it is a vast gatescreen of shallow concave quadrants in coursed random cut granite containing postilion openings and all framed by stone pillars on massive plinths, their shafts chamfered to octagonal cappings crowned by iron lanterns. The gates are suitably chunky and decorative. There is a similar lodge to Beauchamp (*q.v.*).

East gate; *c.* 1870.
Considerably less fussy is this single-storey two-bay lodge below a hipped roof, the left-hand bay of which breaks forward to the avenue in a gable with the suspicion of an open pediment. All in a drab grey render with banded segmentally headed sash windows and corbelled chimney-stacks. Derelict.

Both sets of gate pillars are inscribed with the name 'Knockrabo', which the property became in the twentieth century.

Lewis 1837; Griffith 1848–60; *Thom's*; *IB* (15 March 1868); Ball and Hamilton 1895; *IADS* (2000).

530. MOUNT ARGOS, Harold's Cross; pre-1837; *demolished.*
A seat in the first half of the nineteenth century of the Byrne family which in 1857 was acquired as the House of Blessed Paul Retreat of the Passionists, for whom the old gate lodge was surplus to requirements. At the gate *c.* 1910 was created an ostentatious entrance screen of five cut-stone pillars containing a quadruple gateway and supporting a double iron overthrow archway rising to a central cross. Possibly to a design by Charles B. Powell.

Thom's; Liddy 1987.

531. MOUNT BROWN, Kilmainham; pre-1837; *demolished.*
Presumably a foundation of the Brown family which from the mid-nineteenth century was a house, gate lodge, offices, orchard and land of nurseryman Patrick Savage but by 1940 had become the site of a housing development.

Griffith 1848–60.

MOUNT CARMEL CONVENT (see MOUNT DILLON)

532. MOUNT DILLON, Roebuck; pre-1837; *demolished.*
A property which changed hands regularly: in 1837 occupied by Revd Dr Thomas Prior and four years later by the Hon. Major Arthur Southwell, who had risen to the rank of lieutenant-colonel by 1849, when his gatekeeper was Henry Nowlam. In 1883 it had become the Carmelite Convent of Mount Carmel, with the lodge being avenueless and having received its independence as 'Mount Carmel Cottage' in its own right. By 1974 both the old house and its lodge had gone.

Lewis 1837; Griffith 1848–60; *Thom's.*

533. MOUNT EDEN, Little Bray (2).
Originally there was an old eighteenth-century house of the Roberts family on the estate, with two lodged gates, the ownership of which passed on the death of John Roberts through the marriage in 1801 of his daughter and heir Anne to Charles Riall. On the latter's death in 1855 it descended to their eldest son Phineas (1803–84), who put his stamp on the place, rebranding it 'Old Conna Hill' and building a grand new High Victorian Tudor-Gothic house *c.* 1860 to designs of the Belfast practice of Lanyon, Lynn and Lanyon. There is no evidence that they influenced either of the entrances; rather they dated from the Roberts era.

North entrance; pre-1837; *demolished.*
Surviving is a gatescreen of *c.* 1845, of some extent with ogee dwarf-walled quadrants and contemporary railings meeting a pair of good Classical carriage pillars in V-jointed granite rising to fluted friezes below gadrooned capping with moulded cornices.

South entrance; *c.* 1830.
To the left-hand side of the secondary gate is a pair of semi-detached steeply gabled whitewashed cottages, each symmetrical, with brick soldier arches over cast-iron latticed casement windows and tiny hall projections, their gables fitted in below the main eaves. Now 1½-storey.

In 1849 Miss Martha Roberts's gatekeepers were John Allison and James Carberry. The property is now a school.

Griffith 1848–60; *Thom's*; *LGI* (1904); Bence-Jones 1988.

534. MOUNT ERROL, Donnybrook; pre-1871; *demolished.*
A lodge built after 1849 probably by Inspector General of Militia Colonel Edward Selby Smyth, after he acquired the property *c.* 1860 from the widow of Sir Richard Baker.

Griffith 1848–60; *Thom's.*

535. MOUNT HAROLD, Harold's Cross; pre-1837; *demolished.*
The lodge to a property apparently occupied jointly in the mid-nineteenth century by John C. Evans and Mrs Jane Gibton.

Thom's.

536. MOUNT JEROME CEMETERY, Harold's Cross; *c.* 1837; architect probably G. Papworth.

Irish Architectural Archive

A property that initially belonged to the earl of Meath, upon which was built a house by Abraham Wilkinson; his son sold it to John Keogh, from whose descendants the 'beautifully picturesque demesne has lately been purchased by the Dublin Cemetery Company. This cemetery comprises 25 acres of gently elevated ground … Under the direction of the company … provision will be made for the interment of persons of all religious denominations … The plan also embraces the erection of monuments and cenotaphs … the whole is enclosed by a wall.' Thus wrote Lewis of the cemetery's creation in 1835, to a layout devised by architect George Papworth, on the strength of which, it seems, is attributed the design of the gate lodge. Although John Howard Louch was to present plans for an approach, gates and lodge in 1849, this may have been for a secondary unexecuted building, as Lawrence Tobin (there is a keeper of that name at Mountanville Park the same year—father and son?) is already recorded as being in residence that year. Had Papworth, who was as adept in the Classical as the Tudor-Gothic style, known the preponderance of neo-Classical funerary monuments that was to ensue he might have had second thoughts on his proposal. All in all, this is a highly individual exercise in the Tudor-Gothic, its extensive railed gatescreen with double in-and-out carriage gates and spear-topped rails (originally ogee-finished to the gates) nicely setting off the octagonal stone pillars rising to chevroned cappings (much as at Eastwood (*q.v.*)) with pretty poppy finials in church-pew fashion. The gatehouse, in like manner, is suitably commodious, as befitted the extended duties of its caretaker occupant, being two-storey, three-bay with a moulded gabled parapet and diagonal buttresses which on the projecting left-hand bay rise to terminate in poppy finials, just as the gate pillars. All the openings have chamfered reveals below label mouldings, and the left-hand first-floor double doors give onto an arrowhead balconette to the roof of the wooden, glazed, full-height bay window below, which monitored the gates. The Tudor-arched doorway to the right-hand side has been converted into a window in recent rehabilitation which saw the lodge saved from dereliction, being re-covered in stucco effect but losing its square casements and fleur-de-lis crestings in the process. A late Victorian photograph showing an excellent 'turnout' on the forecourt reveals the lodge in its original glory, displaying a splendid rectangular crenellated first-floor oriel window to the approach gable and a fine crowning row of four barley-twist chimney-flues, all sadly removed. There is the suggestion here of the influence of his brother J.B. Papworth, purveyor of such like in his pattern-books.

Lewis 1837; *Parliamentary Gazetteer*; Griffith 1848–60; Ball 1995; Williams 1994; IAA photograph.

537. MOUNT MERRION [1], Booterstown; pre-1837/*c.* 1905; architect probably F.C. Caldbeck.

The early lodge on the site off Mount Merrion Avenue was to a property in 1837 of solicitor Henry Staines, from whom it passed *c.* 1845 to barrister Ebenezer Hore Hatchell, whose gate porter four years later was Michael Kennedy. For much of the remainder of the century the place became 'Palermo' and home to a Miss Hudson before being subsequently renamed 'Ashurst' by J.B. Burton *c.* 1895. The delightful replacement Arts and Crafts porter's lodge was probably the work of architect F.C. Caldbeck, who was resident here in 1906. Single-storey on a square plan, with a porch recess in the leading corner (now glazed in), its road and avenue elevations single-bay with small-paned casement windows, one in the form of a little bracketed oriel overlooking the gates; roughcast below a shallow pyramidal roof which rises to the central chimney-stack, quirkily having gambrels to all four faces. Occupied and creeper-clad.

Lewis 1837; Slater 1846; Griffith 1848–60; *Thom's*.

538. MOUNT MERRION [2], Stillorgan; pre-1837; *demolished.*

Both the attractive house of the Murphy family and its lodge have gone, the latter manned in 1849 by Thomas Mulvey as porter to William Murphy.

Griffith 1848–60; Pearson 1998.

539. MOUNT MERRION [3], Stillorgan (4).

In 1711 the Viscounts Fitzwilliam forsook Merrion Castle for their new-built house nearby but for the following century they were mostly absentees, letting it to a succession of unrelated worthies or leaving it to the occupancy of their agents. It is clear from Jonathan Barker's 1762 map that the property had until then been lodgeless; indeed, the north avenue was to remain so, although its gatescreen with ball finials to the pillars has been re-erected at the entrance to Willow Park (*q.v.*). William Ashford's map of 1806, however, which accompanied his album of twenty views of the estate commissioned by Richard, 7th Viscount Fitzwilliam (1745–1816), founder of the Fitzwilliam Museum, Cambridge, reveals porters' lodges to have been built by then.

East entrance; pre-1806/*c.* 1835; *demolished.*

Erected after 1762, the original lodge was located forward of, and to the right-hand side of, an extensive gatescreen much praised by Edwardian writers. Sometime between Thomas Sherrard's map of 1830 and that of the 1837 Ordnance Survey this lodge was superseded by a replacement within and to the left-hand side of the avenue. Being of cruciform plan it may have been of some presence, built for Robert Henry Herbert, 12th earl of Pembroke and Montgomery (1791–1862), on inheriting the estates in 1827, his family having come into the property through marriage in 1733. The lodge, like its predecessor, is lost.

West entrance; pre-1806/pre-1912; *demolished.*

William Ashford's album of 1806 shows a

O'Kane

539. Mount Merrion, west entrance.

distant view of the lodge by the Mount Anville or Deer Park approach, apparently of two-storey construction with a crenellated parapet. Built after 1762, it is shown to be rather more articulate in outline than the square plan indicated by the early Ordnance Survey maps. Rather remote from the public road access, it may have monitored an inner fence enclosing the deer-park. In any case, by 1912 it had been replaced, presumably by Sydney Herbert, 14th earl of Pembroke and Montgomery (1853–1913), who belatedly took up brief residence in 1905.

Although the modest house survives, not so its lodges and little of its 10ft-high boundary wall.

Ball 1995; Smyth 1994; Pearson 1998; O'Kane 2012.

540. MOUNT MICHAEL, Ballyboden; pre-1837.

A ruinous gabled structure, in 1849 home to John Somers as gatekeeper to haberdasher Michael Walsh, who was also the proprietor twelve years earlier.

Lewis 1837; Griffith 1848–60.

541. MOUNT PLEASANT SQUARE, Ranelagh (2).

Gracious late Georgian terraced housing on three sides about a green, commenced in 1807 and largely completed in 1827 by developer Terence Dolan. It was a development sufficiently exclusive to warrant the cachet of two porters' lodges, neither of which, with their relatively mean accommodation, survives. One lay vacant in 1849.

Griffith 1848–60; Kelly 1995; Dublin City Council 2006.

542. MOUNT PROSPECT, Milltown; pre-1837; *demolished.*

In 1849 the porter's lodge lay vacant to a property in the mid-nineteenth century of the Georges family, which by 1907 had become 'Grove House'.

Griffith 1848–60; *Thom's*.

543. MOUNT ST JOSEPH'S MONASTERY, Clondalkin; pre-1837; *demolished.*

A lost and forgotten lodge which may have been contemporary with another establishment that was founded in 1813 under 'a prior and several brethren, with a chaplain, who support themselves by their own industry. Some of them conduct a day and boarding school for such as can afford to pay ...'.

Lewis 1837.

544. MOUNT SAVILLE, Rathmines; pre-1837; *demolished.*

A seat in 1837 of W. Shine Esq., which by 1849 had passed to Horatio T. Jude, whose gatekeeper was Richard McGrath.

Lewis 1837; Griffith 1848–60.

545. MOUNT TALLANT COTTAGE, Rathmines; pre-1837; *demolished.*

Home in 1837 to Emanuel Hutchinson Orpen, it was a residence of John Reddick twelve years later, when the gate porter was Edward Dalton. The surviving gatescreen dates from their time. It consists of very chunky ornate iron railings and granite pillars with recessed moulded panels, Tudor roses chiselled in the friezes below exaggerated oversailing cappings—identical to those at Dartry (*q.v.*). A property later renamed 'St Pancra's'.

Lewis 1837; Griffith 1848–60; *Thom's*; *LGI* (1904).

546. MOUNT TALLANT, Rathmines; pre-1837; *demolished.*

A property in 1837 of P. Whelan Esq., by whose widow in 1849 it was leased to William Hayes (later of Edmondstown Park (*q.v.*)), whose gatekeeper was John McLorinan. By 1907 the place was home to St Teresa's Monastery.

Lewis 1837; Griffith 1848–60.

547. MOUNT TEMPLE, Blackrock; pre-1837; *demolished.*

A fine late eighteenth-century villa in 1841 of William Garrett which was occupied eight years later by a Mrs Thorpe, whose porter was Peter Byrne.

Thom's; Griffith 1848–60.

548. MOUNT TOWN, Monkstown; *c.* 1845; *demolished.*

Patrick Cunningham was gatekeeper in 1849 to William Flood, who may have been the builder of both the house and its lodge a few years previously.

Griffith 1848–60.

549. MOUNT VENUS, Woodtown; pre-1837; *demolished.*

Little remains of this once-fine estate, in 1790 of the Cullen family and by 1837 of Henry R. Armstrong, other than the lofty gate piers noted by travellers down the years. It seems that by 1850 the decline was well advanced, for no lodge is recorded in the valuation and it had gone by 1907.

Lewis 1837; Joyce 1912; Craig and Fewer 2002.

550. MOYLE PARK, Clondalkin (2).
An estate from the eighteenth century of the Caldbeck family to which there was an early porter's lodge to the right of the entrance gates from as far back as 1810, when Mrs Elizabeth Caldbeck, daughter-in-law of William Caldbeck (1733–1803), ran it as a school until her death in 1840. Thereafter for four years it was her daughter that managed it and it may have been in her time that the surviving lodge was built on the left-hand side, where James Adams was gatekeeper in 1850. This seems to have originated as a single-storey standard hip-roofed affair extending in a back return as an L-plan. Somewhat later in the century it assumed its present appearance, being extended into a double pile with a gabled addition to the rear, a flat-roofed hallway in the internal angle and the loss of the original front door. To the park is a pretty cast-iron hexagonally glazed window, but plain wooden casements to the avenue in roughcast walls from the late nineteenth century. All quite plain, considering the family's architectural aspirations and connections. Both lodges continued in harness flanking the gates until at least 1937.

Griffith 1848–60; *LGI* (1904).

MOYLURG (see GREENFIELD LODGE)

551. MULBERRY PLACE, Dolphin's Barn; pre-1837; *demolished.*
A lodge at the entrance to a quarry, limekiln, house, offices and 28 acres in the mid-nineteenth century of stonemason John Bond, leasing from John Hall, who by 1870 was in residence himself and had changed its name to 'Carnaclough'.

Slater 1846; Griffith 1848–60; *Thom's.*

552. MURPHYSTOWN LODGE, Murphystown; *c.* 1845; *demolished.*
The lodgeless property, in 1837 known as 'Belmont Lodge', of Arthur Park Neville and Son, land and city surveyors and estate valuators, who by 1849 had added porter's accommodation, although it was still vacant. It in part remains as nondescript rubble walls. After the Espinasse family lived here in the 1850s, the place was renamed 'Clonlea' by William C. Hastings about 1890.

Slater 1846; Griffith 1848–60; *Thom's.*

553. MYERSVILLE, Stradbrook; pre-1837; *demolished.*
A seat of the architect Christopher Myers until his death in 1789 which retained the family name until the turn of the twentieth century, when it was erased in favour of 'Wynberg', its lodge surviving until later in the century.

Ball 1995.

554. NANGOR, Clondalkin; pre-1837; *demolished.*
The old castle of Nangor, embodied in a Queen Anne house by John Falkiner, survives in the thick of modern housing. It had become the residence of the Rourke family in the first half of the nineteenth century, its gate lodge of Peter C. Rourke lying vacant in 1850.

Leet 1814; Griffith 1848–60; Ball 1995.

555. NEILLSTOWN, Clondalkin; *c.* 1800.

P.M. Ging

The medieval seat of the Neills; come the Reformation it was owned by the O'Rourke clan, who as the Rourkes built themselves a late eighteenth-century house which is survived by its unusual porter's lodge. Single-storey gabled, the clues to its existence are two tiny lancet windows piercing the left-hand pebble-dashed concave-walled entrance quadrant and peeking across the forecourt. These were probably Y-traceried in Georgian-Gothic fashion but were replaced in improvements that saw the loss of the original iron gates and carriage pillars and considerable modernisation of and extensions to the lodge, which remarkably remains occupied. The proprietor in 1837 was Lawrence Rourke.

Lewis 1837.

556. NEPTUNE, Blackrock; pre-1837; *demolished.*
A very fine cut-granite-fronted villa built *c.* 1767 by James Dennis, lord chief baron of the exchequer, later Lord Tracton, after whose death in 1782 it passed to John Scott (1739–98), 1st earl of Clonmell, who changed its name to 'Temple Hill'. A decline in its fortunes seems to have begun in the early nineteenth century; it served for a while as a boarding house before coming into the hands *c.* 1845 of Robert Gray, who permitted development in its grounds. His gatekeeper in 1849 was George Byrne.

Griffith 1848–60; Ball 1995; *BPB* (1929).

557. NEWBAWN, Knocklyon; pre-1837; *demolished.*
A good gentry house of *c.* 1780, in 1814 occupied by a Mr Delany, from whom it had passed to Samuel Percy Lea by 1837. Parker Molloy was in residence in 1849, when his gate lodge lay vacant. Having come from Elm Park (*q.v.*), he renamed the place 'Idrone'.

Leet 1814; Lewis 1837; Griffith 1848–60.

558. NEW BRIGHTON, Loughlinstown; *c.* 1830; architect probably George Papworth; *demolished.*
This is doubtless, along with its mirror-image villa of 'Home' (*q.v.*) next door, the housing development recorded as the work of George Papworth 'now erecting' in 1829. Although its porter's lodge is no more, the surviving counterpart adjacent is a twin of what was here. Surviving is a pair of entrance pillars, their cappings with placid lions atop. William Graves, secretary to the Bank of Ireland, is noted as the resident in 1837 and twelve years later, when his gatekeeper was John Flynn. The property was subsequently renamed 'Lurganbrae'.

Lewis 1837; Griffith 1848–60; IAA.

NEWBROOK HOUSE AND PAPER MILLS (see KINGSTON)

559. NEWCASTLE, Newcastle; *c.* 1845.
This is a modest rendered single-storey standard structure with an almost symmetrical main front and a shallow gabled roof on the point of collapse. Probably built for Alexander Graydon, the proprietor in the mid-nineteenth century.

Griffith 1848–60; *Thom's.*

560. NEWLANDS, Belgard (2).
Here was a handsome mid-Georgian mansion, in 1787 until his untimely demise in 1803 of Arthur Wolfe MP, of the Forenaghts, Co. Kildare (*q.v.*), family, afterwards 1st Viscount Kilwarden. Thereafter it was home to the Rt Hon. George Ponsonby (1755–1817), lord chancellor of Ireland, before P. Crotty Esq. is recorded as resident in 1837. From a mere glimpse of it in a photograph of 1963 the lodge appears to date from the mid-nineteenth century. It shows a single-storey structure with a canted end and equivalent roof on banded eaves above a small-paned window looking across the outside of and stopping a fine tripartite gatescreen with a pair of tall stone ball-finialled entrance pillars flanked by matching postern gates in straight screen walls. An overthrow archway spanning the carriage opening proclaimed 'Newlands Golf Club', which the demesne became in 1956, with the inevitable tragic consequences—both house and lodge had gone by 1982. This lodge, perhaps dating from the time here of Francis Arthur Trench (1816–68) from 1856 until his death, had a pre-1837 predecessor further south, off the road to Tallaght.

Leet 1814; Lewis 1837; *BPB* (1929); Bence-Jones 1988; Lyons 1993.

561. NEW PARK, Blackrock (2).
A property in 1837 of Willoughby Henry Carter, whose two gatekeepers twelve years later were William Leeson and John Molloy, but of their lodges nothing survives, nor is there evidence of the entrance from the Stillorgan Road. The splendid gatescreen on Newtownpark Avenue remains, however, in a fine display of mid-nineteenth-century ironwork comprised of carriage posts with fancy lanterns and tripartite gates extending to wide, shallow, railed ogee quadrants terminating in stone pillars with gadrooned 'baps' as finials.

Lewis 1837; Griffith 1848–60.

562. NEWPARK LODGE, Foxrock; pre-1907; *demolished.*
A short-lived lodge, built sometime after 1871 for James Quigley.

563. NEWSTEAD, Roebuck; *c.* 1845; *demolished.*
A property created to the rear of Roseville by solicitor Patrick Scott in the townland of Roebuck, perhaps more appropriately 'lawyerland'. The contemporary gate lodge was manned by Charles Lynch.
Griffith 1848–60.

564. NEWTOWN, Blackrock; pre-1837/*c.* 1885; architect not known.

Peter Pearson

A Georgian villa in Newtown Avenue given a mid-nineteenth-century neo-Classical facelift alternatively attributed to George Papworth and J.S. Mulvany. An early gate lodge was replaced somewhat later by the surviving sturdy late Victorian structure next to the gate for the proprietor Arthur Andrews. Modestly hidden by a high wall and hedging is this pleasant single-storey standard porter's accommodation below a hipped roof, in mellow brickwork with bipartite round-headed one-over-one sash windows flanking a central pedimented entrance breakfront in a contrasting rendered finish, with doorway in a semicircular arched recess, laurel wreaths embossed on its spandrels. Raised on a stone plinth, there is a flat-roofed canted bay to one gable with segmentally headed lights. The roof is relieved by scalloped slate bands and crowned by an outsized polychromatic brick chimney-stack with diamond-motif inserts.
Thom's; Pearson 1998; *IADS* (2000).

NEWTOWN (see PALERMO)

565. NEWTOWN, Rathfarnham; pre-1837; *demolished.*
A seat in 1837 of 'John Kirby, Esq., LLD, M.D., in the grounds of which there are some very fine evergreens'. That gentleman was still there as late as 1851 but the property then disappears from the directories, and by 1869 neither house nor lodge are to be found on the OS map. The surgeon's gate porter in 1849 was George McCoy.
Lewis 1837; *Thom's*; Griffith 1848–60.

566. NEWTOWN CLARKE, Palmerston; pre-1836; *demolished.*
A 34-acre farm of the Clarke family, alternatively known as 'Riversdale', on the banks of the Liffey, which was leased in 1850 to Henry Shaw, whose gate porter was Patrick Foley. It survives as a nursing home, the grounds partly built over.
Griffith 1848–60; Lyons 1993; Craig and Fewer 2002.

567. NEWTOWNPARK COTTAGE, Blackrock; *c.* 1835.
A large two-storey gabled structure on a T-plan with a canted wing below a semi-octahedral roof, which may owe its undistinguished appearance to 'improvements' and to the fact that it served in the mid-nineteenth century as a schoolhouse, run in 1849 by Sarah Markam at the gates to a property of Charles Doyne, who is noted here as early as 1837. Plain and roughcast with insensitively placed soil and rainwater pipes, there is a rather more sophisticated front door-case with console brackets. There is a good iron gatescreen, with a spear-topped railed entrance having open carriage posts with pineapple finials. Framed by convex-walled quadrants, one of which extends to yet another postern opening. The house was subsequently renamed 'Ardmeen' and the gatehouse relieved of its duties, becoming 'Belclare' in its own right.
Lewis 1837; Griffith 1848–60; *Thom's.*

568. NEWTOWNPARK [1], Blackrock (2).

A fine house, sufficiently sophisticated to be associated with the work of architects James Gandon and Richard Morrison by Bence-Jones. Probably built for Ralph Ward, there survives an excellent contemporary late eighteenth-century gatescreen, divorced from its lodge but faithfully re-erected further along Newtonpark Avenue. Framed by simply rendered tall concave quadrants is a pair of granite ashlar carriage pillars with finely chiselled moulded cappings above friezes of swagged paterae and bands of Greek key pattern in the manner of Thomas Cooley. By 1837 banker Henry Samuel Close, of the Elm Park, Co. Armagh family, had begun a long association with the place, but the gate lodges of his two porters in 1849, John Beamish and John Gaskin, are long gone. It was his second son, Robert Barry Close, who *c.* 1872 replaced one of the early lodges with the remaining Italianate example, attributable on stylistic grounds to John McCurdy, with its similarity to that at Craigmore (*q.v.*). Single-storey standard in a rendered finish below a shallow-pitched hipped roof, from which projects an open-pedimented breakfront with a blank shield above the segmentally arched fanlit architraved front door. As at the main corners, this is framed by Irish pilaster quoins. The window openings have moulded surrounds rather spoiled by modern plastic intrusions, just as modernisation has seen the loss of the original Classical moulded chimney-stack to a plain substitute. Nicely positioned on a slightly elevated site, approached by a flight of steps but missing its gatescreen. There are also very similar lodges at Ailesbury (*q.v.*), Tibradden (*q.v.*), Homestead (*q.v.*) and nearby Bellasguardo (*q.v.*).
Lewis 1837; Griffith 1848–60; *Thom's*; *LGI* (1904); Bence-Jones 1988; Pearson 1998.

569. NEWTOWNPARK [2], Blackrock; pre-1837; *demolished.*
A demesne long associated with the Perry family, of whom Richard Perry was in residence in 1837, followed twelve years later by William Perry, whose gatekeeper was then John Byrne.
Lewis 1837; Griffith 1848–60.

570. NEWTOWNPARK VILLA, Blackrock; pre-1837; *demolished.*
A villa occupied in 1849 by Mrs Mary Thomson, whose gatekeeper was James Lawless. Subsequently called 'Charleville' when it was given a late Victorian Italianate make-over by barrister Francis John Howard. Later still converted into semi-detached properties.
Griffith 1848–60.

571. NEWTOWN VILLA, Churchtown; *c.* 1855; *demolished.*
A lodge and detached house built off Braemor Road which was subsequently divided into semis, apparently all a speculative development by Robert Manders on his property of Landscape (*q.v.*).

572. NULLAMORE, Rathmines; pre-1837; *demolished.*
A seat in 1837 of W.H. Flemyng, whose family later leased it to Lieutenant-Colonel William Miller, who was resident here in 1846. Four years later his gate lodge lay vacant. Surviving is a good gatescreen of *c.* 1845 with fluted friezes to four rustic granite pillars.
Lewis 1837; Slater 1846; Griffith 1848–60.

573. NUTLEY, Priesthouse (4).
Whilst the house built at the beginning of the nineteenth century by George Roe

remarkably survives at the heart of Elmpark Golf Club, none of his gate lodges do. The valuation of 1849 records their occupants as Margaret Collins, William Ledwidge, Patrick Haydon and John Maguire.

Lewis 1837; Griffith 1848–60; Craig and Fewer 2002.

574. NUTGROVE, Rathfarnham; pre-1837; *demolished.*
In 1912 Joyce informs us of 'the dilapidated locality known as "The Ponds", where a large square-formed gateway stood until last year, bearing the inscription "Nutgrove School, Established 1802", and leading into a pretty avenue shaded by a row of tall trees. The schoolhouse was in former times the dower house of Rathfarnham Castle, and its grounds are now utilized as a flower farm.' Philip Jones is recorded here in 1837 and he remained principal of the school until 1866, being succeeded by Mrs Anne Jones before it closed ten years later, reverting to a private house, subsequently being demolished. The gate porter in 1849 was Patrick Tierney.

Lewis 1837; Griffith 1848–60; Joyce 1912; Healy 2005.

575. OAKFIELD, Harold's Cross; pre-1837; *demolished.*
A property in 1850 of John Holmes, tax collector, the site of which by 1871 had been cleared for new housing.

Shaw 1988.

OAKLANDS (see RATHGAR MANSION)

576. OAKLANDS, Sandymount; pre-1837; *demolished.*
A house off Serpentine Avenue, which was in 1841 the residence of cheese factor Thomas Bacon. Seven years later Mrs Sarah Bacon, presumably his widow, is recorded here, with Edward McCabe as her gate porter.

Thom's; Griffith 1848–60; Slater 1846.

577. OAKLAWN, Little Bray; *c.* 1835/*c.* 1847; architect possibly Sir R. Morrison.

A darling little cottage is this 1½-storey standard lodge in the Tudor Picturesque manner, having the most delicate of decorative curved bargeboards with their fleur-de-lis ornament, hip-knobs and foiled fascias. Lovingly maintained in a livery of whitened walls and black joinery, the projecting central porch with chamfered Tudor entrance archway is flanked by tripartite casement windows. To the road gable is a pretty canted bay window with intricate round-arched margined glazing below a tiny attic casement light. Mysteries surround its date and the architect responsible. Stylistically it is the perfect introduction to the gabled villa within but seems to post-date it by at least a decade. The property was created around 1835 by William Garde, but the gate lodge shown on the 1837 OS map has an L-plan, whereas when the place was offered for auction in 1855 as an incumbered estate an accompanying map indicates the existing structure. Although Garde was recorded as being in residence again at that time, 'The Aske' (as it was renamed *c.* 1860) was occupied in the late 1840s by tenant Alexander Hamilton, in whose time the original lodge seems to have been replaced. Responsibility for this delight seems to rest with the Morrison practice, for the general form of the cottage and its details are to be found on the lodges to Ballymacool and Drumboe Castle in County Donegal and Milltown Lodge in County Tyrone, the latter being positively attributable to William Vitruvius Morrison. But the Oaklawn example post-dates his death in 1838, so may well have been by his father, Sir Richard, who was in any case a near neighbour at Walcot House. In 1849 its gatekeeper was Pat Roche. The railed entrance quadrants are contained by octagonal stone pillars reflecting the gable hip-knobs.

Griffith 1848–60; *Thom's*; An Old Inhabitant 1907; Lyons 1993; Dean 1994; Pearson 1998.

578. OAKLAWN, Windy Arbour (2).
A seat in the 1840s of Francis Codd, corn merchant, whose lodge at the eastern gate, now demolished, was occupied in 1849 by Patrick Forde. By 1857 Codd had moved on, to be replaced by James Turbett Jr of the Owenstown (*q.v.*) family. The surviving lodge at the western entrance facing the road alongside is a structure of *c.* 1895. Single-storey and four-bay below a steeply hipped roof with perforated scalloped earthenware cresting and brick chimney-stacks with corbelled cappings. The roughcast walls contain two-over-two sash windows and a projecting gabled porch (now glazed) with hip-knobs and ornamental apex work supported on carved turned wooden posts. The new owner and builder of the later lodge with materials to hand was Maurice Brooks, builders' merchant.

Thom's; Griffith 1848–60.

579. OAKLEY PARK, Stradbrook; pre-1837; *demolished.*
A seat in 1837 of R. Everard Esq., presumably from Randlestown, Co. Meath (*q.v.*).

Lewis 1837.

580. OATLANDS, Stillorgan (2).
A big eighteenth-century house of the Pollock family, who were resident here for all of the following century and whose country seat was probably that of the same name in County Meath (*q.v.*).

South entrance; pre-1837; *demolished.* The first OS map shows this to have been a large square lodge with a back return and central front projection. Colonel Matthew Pollock is recorded here in 1837 and twelve years later his gate porter was William Henderson.

North entrance; *c.* 1890; architect not known.

A singular and innovative 1½-storey Arts and Crafts creation in a typical confusion of styles, Classical and neo-Elizabethan. Its upper floor jetties beyond a rubble wall with a tripartite oriel window having panelled ogee corbel support and a pediment over, flanked by half-timbered work with herringbone brick infill panels. Built for James J. Pollock.

Thom's; Griffith 1848–60.

OBELISK COTTAGE (see ST GERMAIN'S)

OBELISK HILL (see VICTORIA HILL PARK)

581. OBELISK PARK, Stradbrook (2).

The seat in 1837 'of H. Perry, Esq., so-called from a lofty obelisk erected in the grounds by Lady Pierce, for the employment of the poor during the scarcity of 1741'. In 1829 Henry and James Perry had acquired the property, originally an estate of the Allen family, from Richard Sinclair, and it was to remain in the hands of those Quaker businessmen and their descendants until the twentieth century. Of the early pre-1837 gate lodge on the northern approach there is no sign. William James Perry in 1873 passed the house on to his daughter Hannah and her husband Marcus Goodbody, who wasted little time in completely transforming the house in heavy Italianate style to plans by architect Thomas Drew. The later lodge to the south, next to Sir Edward Lovett Pearce's obelisk, was added as late as 1896 for the recorded and unlikely sum of £165. Apparently the Goodbody family, in the persons of brothers Marcus II and Henry Perry, third and fourth sons of nine of Marcus I (who had died in 1885), had kept faith with the very elderly and, by then, benighted Drew. Here, at the age of 86, he was wearing his Arts and Crafts hat. This is a commodious 1½-storey gatehouse of whitened rendered walls and stark red terracotta-tiled roof of informal outline, part-hipped and part-gabled, with an Elizabethan Revival half-timbered attic storey and a lower floor with Georgian-style six-over-six sash windows in moulded surrounds. To one side the main roof catslides to form a single-storey hall projection. Some red-brick relief is repeated in the bulky corbelled chimney-stack. Derelict but ripe for rehabilitation.

Lewis 1837; *Thom's*; Flanagan 1991; Pearson 1998; *IADS* (2000).

582. THE OCHRA, Little Bray; *c.* 1905.

Opposite but slightly removed from its entrance gates and at right angles to the road is this neat single-storey standard lodge, each of its main gables and that of the breakfront entrance having rudimentary half-timbered ornamentation to their apexes in a typical Edwardian manner; eight-over-two sash windows set off roughcast walls, whilst a pair of symmetrically placed red-brick chimney-stacks break the ridge. Contemporary with the big house built by Thomas O'Meara. The principal roles of recent occupants of the lodge were cook and gardener.

583. OLD ABINGTON, Loughlinstown; pre-1837.

The lodge is a much improved and extended single-storey hip-roofed structure next to its delightful early nineteenth-century house. A property in 1851 of solicitor Robert Tilly. Subsequently renamed 'Barnclose'.

Thom's.

584. OLDBAWN AND PAPER MILLS, Tallaght (2).

Both porters' lodges, in place before 1837, have gone without trace, but what is even worse is that only photographs survive of one of Ireland's few Jacobean manor houses. Built around 1635 by William Bulkely, archdeacon of Dublin, it became associated in the Georgian period with the Tyntes before being acquired by the McDonnell family, who operated the adjacent paper mills in the Victorian era. In 1849 Michael McDonnell's gatekeepers were Denis Moore at the northern gate and, on the main approach through a great avenue of trees, Michael Keegan in the eastern lodge. All of this and the large plantations, deer-park, orchards and gardens have gone, the big house having been removed by 1975.

Griffith 1848–60; Ball 1995; Craig and Fewer 2002.

OLD CONNA HILL (see MOUNT EDEN)

585. OLD CONNAUGHT, Little Bray (3).

The previous house on the estate of the Walsh family was burnt down in 1776 and the property was purchased seven years later by the Rt Revd William Gore, bishop of Limerick, who commenced a new house but died before its completion. Subsequent to this it was finished in the present imposing Classical institutional form by William Conyngham Plunket (1765–1854), possibly to mark his elevation to the peerage in 1827, from which time at least one of the lodges may date.

Old Connaught Avenue gate; pre-1837; *demolished.*

John Redmond was gate porter in 1849.

Ferndale Road gate; *c.* 1830; *demolished.*

Uncatalogued Lawrence postcard.

An old photograph of around 1890 shows a tranquil sylvan scene as setting for a pleasant creeper-clad single-storey standard porter's lodge with an oversailing hipped roof and tall chimney-stack. Flanking the front door were Wyatt-style tripartite sash windows. The privileged keeper in 1849 was Daniel Rorke.

Dublin Road gate; pre-1890; *demolished.*

Built after 1841 at the old entrance to Moatfield (*q.v.*) but now swept away to accommodate a huge roundabout.

Griffith 1848–60; Lawrence photograph (uncatalogued postcard); Ball 1995; *BPB* (1929).

586. OLDORCHARD COTTAGE, Willbrook; *c.* 1800.

A tiny, gabled, plain porter's lodge lies below the level of the avenue, wedged between the Ballyboden Road and the Owendoher River, which runs parallel. Probably dating from the early nineteenth century, judging by an ogee-arched wall opening which pre-dates the gatescreen of *c.* 1845 probably built by William D. Ferguson who was here in 1841, having succeeded John Sweeney who was resident four years earlier. Ferguson, whose gatekeeper in 1849 was Thomas Neill, also changed the name of the place to 'Rosebank', which is inscribed on the gate pillars. These are Tudor-Gothic with recessed panels and steeply gabled cappings to all four faces and sculpted with foiled arches.

Lewis 1837; *Thom's*; Griffith 1848–60.

587. OLIVEMOUNT, Windy Arbour; pre-1837; *demolished.*

In 1849 Patrick Doran was gate porter to Revd Bernard Kirby, founder and chaplain of the Olivemount Institute of the Good Samaritan and RC chapel.

Slater 1846; Griffith 1848–60; *Thom's.*

588. OLNEY, Terenure; pre-1837; *demolished.*

A house of *c.* 1800 which by 1841 was home to Revd John B. Finlay, who was succeeded eight years later by John Foster Grierson, whose gatekeeper then was Samuel Simmons. Neither the big house nor its lodge survive.

Thom's; Griffith 1848–60.

589. ORCHARD, Clondalkin; pre-1836; *demolished.*

A fine late eighteenth-century farmhouse, occupied in the first half of the nineteenth century by a Captain Poe, perhaps the same as was to be found later at Lucan Lodge (*q.v.*) and Mountainview (*q.v.*).

590. THE ORCHARD, Shankill; *c.* 1911; architects probably Batchelor and Hicks.

The *Irish Builder* magazine in 1911 advised that 'One of the finest villa residences in Bray district has just been completed by J. & W. Stewart contractors ... from plans and specifications of Batchelor and Hicks. In red brick and cutstone.' This was for Miss Kate Darley, and her architects' commission must have extended to the provision of a fine porter's lodge: 1½-storey, built off a square plan in a Queen Anne Arts and Crafts style without any cut stone but in roughcast, the only red brick being in the hefty square four-flue chimney-stack, to which rises a pyramidal roof covered in red plain terracotta tiles pierced by flat-roofed dormers with small-paned casements lighting the attic space. The eaves are marked by exposed rafter toes, and to the centre of the avenue front projects a bellcast catslide roof carried on carved posts to form the entrance porch, which is flanked by casement windows in moulded surrounds.

IB (9 Dec. 1911); *Thom's*.

591. THE ORCHARDS, Rathmines (2).

Irish Architectural Archive

A development of about 1865, originating as 'Hamville' for barrister William Tighe Hamilton (b. 1807) of the Hamwood, Co. Meath (*q.v.*), family, built on the site of the ancient castle of Rathmines in Palmerston Park. Both of its lodges have gone, that to the north having been the earlier of the two. Of that off Temple Road, photographic record reveals a unique two-storey gatehouse, built off a cruciform plan as a Swiss chalet, which swapped the timber construction of the Alps for solid Irish brickwork, omitting the balconies and verandahs but retaining the typically shallow-pitched roofs with the familiar outrageously oversailing eaves and verges. The Flemish bond brickwork was polychromatic, with the introduction not only of horizontal sill head and floor bands but also of vertical strips as quoins and continuation of the window reveals to create an unusual pattern of rectangles. The tall perimeter wall in similarly bonded brickwork was relieved by openings with latticed iron railings, a pattern repeated in the carriage gates. Dating from *c.* 1875.

LGI (1904); Joyce 1912; *Thom's*; IAA photograph (60/57x1).

592. ORCHARDSTOWN, Rathfarnham; pre-1837; *demolished.*

The old Georgian villa on Butterfield Avenue survives, a property in 1849 of Thomas Kirkwood MD, which he probably also ran as a private lunatic asylum. His gatekeeper was Hugh Reilly.

Griffith 1848–60.

ORCHARDTON (see BARLEY HILL)

ORCHARDTON (see SWEETMOUNT)

593. ORLAGH, Woodtown; pre-1837; *demolished.*

A house built as 'Footmount' around 1790 by the snuff manufacturer Lundy Foote (1735–1805), who, having come from Holly Park (*q.v.*), also gave it a setting of fine woods. In the early nineteenth century it was acquired by Nathaniel Caldwell, governor of the Bank of Ireland; he sold it on in 1836 to Andrew Carew O'Dwyer, whose gate porter thirteen years later was Edward Hand, who would have been busy with the comings and goings at a place then renowned for its hospitality, which would have been in stark contrast to the atmosphere of an Augustinian novitiate, which it became around 1870.

Griffith 1848–60; Joyce 1912; Craig and Fewer 2002.

ORMONDE (see WHITECHURCH VICARAGE)

594. ORWELL, Rathgar; *c.* 1850; architect probably W.F. Caldbeck.

In 1850 the architect William Francis Caldbeck exhibited at the RHA designs for a William Todd, who from 1851 until *c.* 1880 is listed here in directories. The gate lodge is an excellent Tudor Revival cottage, showing the young architect working in a style that contrasts with his later Italianate preference. Single-storey standard with skew-tables to main gables and that of the steeply pitched projecting hallway with its prominent sculpted stone hip-knob and bold kneelers. The main door opening is chamfered with a Tudor arch and the hall lit by a fanlight and narrow lancets, which alone retain their original cast-iron latticed lights. To each side is a bipartite label-moulded cut-stone casement window, whilst each gable is relieved by a lozenge motif with quatrefoil carving, all unfortunately let down by a drab sand and cement rendered finish. Also remarkably surviving are octagonal entrance pillars with layered cappings. A property that was latterly renamed 'Faunagh'.

Thom's; IAA.

595. OWENSTOWN, Roebuck; pre-1837; *demolished.*

The late Georgian house was successively a residence of livery lace manufacturer Nathaniel Creed (1766–1848), Walter Bourne (1766–1848) and wine merchant James Exham Purefoy Turbett (1790–1868), whose gatekeeper in 1849 was Hans Geary.

Griffith 1848–60; *Thom's*; Ball and Hamilton 1995; Pearson 1998.

596. PAKENHAM LODGE, Merrion; pre-1837; *demolished.*

A seaside villa on Strand Road of the Pakenham family, the lodge to which lay unoccupied in 1848 during the letting to a Mrs Dotson. The place was by 1854 renamed 'Loughnavale' by its resident, William Forde.

Griffith 1848–60; *Thom's*.

597. PALERMO, Little Bray; *c.* 1820; architect possibly William Farrell.

In 1801 'the seat of Sir Francis Hutchinson, Bart.; the house is large and pleasantly situated; the demesne between fifty and sixty acres, indifferently cultivated; shrubberies well planted and laid out; gardens large and handsome'. This scene was complemented by a little Regency porter's lodge, conceivably to plans of William Farrell, for the architect is recorded as having prepared (undated) designs for additions, offices, outbuildings and conservatory for Sir Samuel Hutchinson. This was Revd Sir Samuel Synge Hutchinson (1756–1846), who succeeded to the baronetcy in 1807 as merely Revd Samuel Synge, assuming the additional surname six years later. Upon his death he left the place to his daughter, Frances Synge Hutchinson (1788–1869), who remained unmarried; in 1849 her gatekeeper was James Pollard. This is a single-storey standard rendered cottage with carved paired soffit brackets to its hipped roof and diagonally set chimney-stack. Each bay is set in a segmentally arched recess, that of the central doorway in a hall projection. In 2000 it lay derelict, with replacement imminent. By the road are tall concave-walled quadrants with postilion openings, framed by pillars with applied panel mouldings.

Archer 1801; Griffith 1848–60; *BPB* (1906); *IFR*.

598. PALERMO, Milltown; pre-1869; *demolished.*

A house and lodge built after 1837 probably for Thomas Gowland, who had by 1890 renamed it 'Newtown'.

Thom's.

599. PALLISER'S PARK, Rathfarnham; *c.* 1825/*c.* 1910.

At the head of a formal treeless avenue is the splendid early Georgian Classical red-brick mansion built by William Palliser, now flanked by a variety of 'heavies' in contrasting High Victorian and Edwardian institutional stone buildings, built by the Loreto Order, which acquired the property in 1821, but now beyond their means. At the base of the avenue at Grange Road is porter's accommodation in the shape of a pair of tiny 'day and night' lodges forming part of a greater entrance complex comprising an

amalgam of ages. A noble pair of mid-Georgian lofty granite carriage pillars, with friezes of fluting and sunflower paterae below undersized dainty vase finials, are linked by decorative late Victorian iron gates and postern screens to the lodges. These, judging by their round-headed spoke-topped sash windows, date from the time of the coming of the nuns. These single-storey gabled units have two-bay fronts facing each other across the access, each with basic entablatured door-cases, but address the road with peculiar screen walls in V-jointed rusticated granite with pairs of semicircular-arched recesses, or blind 'openings', below friezes which display what may be salvaged fluted panels and basic roundels, all crowned by stepped gables culminating in plain central chimney-stacks, apparently of twentieth-century origin when Beaufort (*q.v.*) was absorbed into the complex and its lodge fronted to match. Palliser's Park, after it passed from the ownership of king's printer George Grierson, became known as Loreto Abbey for almost 200 years. The lodges lay vacant in 1849.

Lewis 1837; *Thom's*; Ball 1995; Healy 2005.

600. PALMERSTON, Palmerston; pre-1836/*c.* 1875; architect probably John Lanyon.

The land around, named after the noble family of Temple, was purchased in 1763 by the Rt Hon. John Hely Hutchinson, secretary of state for Ireland and provost of TCD, who built the great mansion which still forms the core of the Stewart Institution, into which it was absorbed as the first Irish hospital for the mentally handicapped or, more specifically, 'For Idiotic Imbecile Children'. The property had been offered for sale as an incumbered estate on behalf of Richard John Hely Hutchinson, 4th earl of Donoughmore, in 1860 and was in the hands of William Cherry from 1862 until 1870 before assuming its present role. The architect engaged in 1874–8 was John Lanyon, whose commission must have included plans for the new gate lodge to replace that at the other side of the entrance. Like the great complex, it is in a forthright Italianate style. Single-storey standard and hip-roofed, with lofty eaves given a horizontal emphasis with an eaves band, and string-courses at sill level and that of the spring of the arch to the open-pedimented porch, which, like the one-over-one margined sash windows, has distinctive corbelled shouldered heads. Now divorced from the entrance, it rests on an elevated site in a smooth rendered finish on a plinth, its bulky chimney-stack much simplified.

Archer 1801; Ball 1995; *BPB* (1929); Lyons 1993; O'Dwyer 1997.

601. PALMERSTON, Rathmines; pre-1837/*c.* 1870.

A large house built in 1861 for merchant Benjamin J. Fawcett to designs by Alfred Gresham Jones on lands of Rathmines Castle Old (*q.v.*), the gate lodge to which may have been adapted and reorientated to serve Palmerston. It appears to have been a single-storey standard three-bay cottage, now with irregular fenestration and extended by a bay to the right-hand side; sand/cement-rendered in stucco effect below a hipped roof with paired carved soffit brackets. There are four quarry-faced granite-panelled entrance pillars, very much like those at Russellstown, Co. Kilkenny (*q.v.*), where Jones worked. Their beautiful wood and iron Arts and Crafts gates look to be later. Along with neighbouring Glen-na-smoil (*q.v.*), Palmerston was absorbed to create 'Trinity Hall', accommodating female students of TCD.

DB (1 May 1861); *Thom's*.

602. PALMYRA, Whitechurch; pre-1837; *demolished.*

Far removed from the Syrian desert, Thomas Bewley about 1830 created from an old paper mill what became known as Whitechurch Laundry close by his house. In 1849 his gatekeeper was John Fox. The establishment remained in his family until 1880.

Lewis 1837; Griffith 1848–60; Healy 2005.

603. PARC-NA-SILLA, Loughlinstown; pre-1907; *demolished.*

A property in the mid-nineteenth century of the Stanley family, to which a porter's lodge was built opposite the gates after 1869, perhaps in the time here of Captain Sullivan RN, who *c.* 1880 changed the name from 'Parc-na-grier'.

Thom's.

PARK (see KILLINEY PARK)

PARK (see STILLORGAN)

604. PARK, Tallaght; pre-1837; *demolished.*

An old villa, occupied for much of the nineteenth century by the Jordan family, sited next to Oldbawn (*q.v.*), for which it may have been a dower house and shared the lodge on the eastern approach. This was first valued in 1895, perhaps as a replacement or significant rebuild.

Thom's.

THE PARK (see RATHFARNHAM PARK)

605. PARK VIEW, Palmerston; pre-1837; *demolished.*

Barrister Reuben Norton was proprietor in 1846 and his gate lodge lay vacant two years later. By the turn of the twentieth century the property was named 'Culmore'.

Slater 1846; Griffith 1848–60.

606. PEAFIELD, Blackrock; pre-1837; *demolished.*

Revd Parnell Neville Kearney (b. 1804) is recorded as living here in 1841, his gate porter seven years later being John Boland.

Thom's; Griffith 1848–60; Leslie and Wallace 2001.

607. PEOPLE'S PARK, Dún Laoghaire; 1890; architect W.M. Mitchell.

An example of municipal muted Arts and Crafts style is this bulky gabled 1½-storey house built off an informal plan, sufficient to

accommodate the living and working of a gate-cum-park-keeper and his family. An essay in relentless red: red sandstone dressings and mullions to tripartite windows in English garden wall bond, red brick below red plain earthenware-tiled roof with red serrated cresting. Over the internal angle a vast expanse of roof catslides to form a shady verandahed entrance porch. Liberally adorned with plaques proclaiming the contribution of many worthies and a record of the opening of the public park on 29 September 1890. In contrast are four grand channel-rusticated granite entrance pillars with ball finials and contemporary iron gates with overthrows. Building contractor: George Dixon. Architect: William Mansfield Mitchell.

IB (19 March 1910); Johnston 1989.

608. PILOT VIEW, Dalkey; *c.* 1845.
A plain rendered single-storey standard hip-roofed cottage with rusticated quoins, to a marine villa in the mid-nineteenth century of Abraham Wellington Studdert of the Bunratty Castle, Co. Clare, family.

Thom's; *LGI* (1904).

609. PLANTATION, Dún Laoghaire; *c.* 1820.
A Regency property playfully named by its owner, William Plant MD, surgeon at the neighbouring Rathdown Fever Hospital, who also ran a dispensary at his own gate in the form of this little gate lodge which no longer fills either role but remarkably remains well tended. Single-storey with high eaves to a hipped roof and a two-bay main avenue front of windows set in rectangular recesses with toothed brick dressings in rubble walls which are pleasantly rustic but may originally have been harled. To the ridge is a pair of diagonally set Tudor-style stacks on a rectangular base, now rendered over the previously exposed brick. The granite carriage pillars are bowed back and front, with the new name of 'Gortmore' applied. Dr Plant was still in residence in 1870.

Thom's; Griffith 1848–60; Pearson 1998.

610. PLASNEWYDD, Killiney; pre-1837; *demolished.*
A property, along with neighbouring Beechwood (*q.v.*) and Ballinclea (*q.v.*), in the early nineteenth century of the Talbots of Malahide in the person of the Hon. Eliza Lister Kaye. Its long approach from the lodged entrance to the north-west had been discontinued by 1871 and was later purloined as a third gate to Ballinclea. The house has latterly been called 'Rock Lodge'. The gatekeeper in 1849 was Charles Byrne.

Griffith 1848–60; *BPB* (1929).

611. PLEASANT VIEW TERRACE, Donnybrook; pre-1837 ; *demolished.*
A once-prestigious six-house terrace with the status of a porter's lodge at its extensive semicircular entrance forecourt, the gatekeeper in 1848 being George Keon, to landlord John Donnelly. By 1907 this entrance off Merrion Road had been swept away and 'Glenholme' built on the site.

Griffith 1848–60.

612. PLUNKETT LODGE, Dún Laoghaire; pre-1837; *demolished.*
A residence in 1837 of Henry Plunkett, probably of the Louth Hall (*q.v.*), Co. Louth, Plunkett family. After it had been the home for a while of the Hon. Mrs Sydney Sophia Plunkett, it seems to have been renamed 'Rochelle' by its new owner, Dr John Woodroofe, whose gatekeeper in 1849 was Charles Dunne.

Lewis 1837; Griffith 1848–60; *Thom's.*

613. POYER PARK, Ballinteer; pre-1869; *demolished.*
The lodge was built after 1837, probably *c.* 1860 by the then proprietor, Francis Davis. The 1907 OS map shows the lodge to have outlived its big house.

Thom's.

614. PRIESTHOUSE [1], Booterstown; pre-1837; *demolished.*
Subsequently renamed 'Ashfield', located north of the Stillorgan Road, it was a seat in 1850 of Charles Miller, whose gatekeeper was William Burke.

Griffith 1848–60.

615. PRIESTHOUSE [2], Priesthouse; pre-1837; *demolished.*
A property south of the Stillorgan Road, by 1869 renamed 'Belgrove', which was occupied in 1849 by James Keegan, whose gate porter was Michael Loughlan. The estate was acquired *c.* 1954 by UCD but with its lodge having succumbed to road-widening.

Griffith 1848–60; *Thom's.*

616. PRIMROSE COTTAGE, Lucan; pre-1836; *demolished.*
Otherwise 'Primrose Hill', in 1814 the residence of General Buchanan and ten years later of Augustus Heron MD, whose gate porter in 1849 was Hugh Monaghan.

Leet 1814; Pigot 1824; Griffith 1848–60.

617. PRIORY COTTAGE, Kilmacud; pre-1837; *demolished.*
Edward Kelly in 1849 was gatekeeper to Ford Leathley in a lodge which outlived a house that was ruinous in 1907.

Griffith 1848–60.

618. PRIORY, Ballyboden; pre-1837; *demolished.*
Formerly 'Holly Park', a modest farmhouse largely created by John Philpot Curran in 1786; he lived there until his death in 1817, after which it was home to George Hatchell, by whom it was let in 1849 to William Hall, whose gatekeeper was Patrick Heavy.

Lewis 1837; Griffith 1848–60; Healy 2005; Craig and Fewer 2002.

PRIORY (see RICHVIEW PRIORY)

619. PROBY PARK, Dalkey; *c.* 1890.

A distinctive single-storey lodge, its three-bay avenue front embraced by a wide gable, the central bay with tall oriel window set in a breakfront with squared casements and lozenge overpanels. To the rear is a 1½-storey return, the whole rendered and immaculately maintained. Built for solicitor and land agent Thomas Kift, who acquired in about 1870 what had been known as 'Aldborough'.

Thom's.

620. PROSPECT HALL, Roebuck; pre-1837; *demolished.*
In the early nineteenth century a seat of Sir Robert Way Harty (1799–1832), created 1st baronet the year before his death, having served as lord mayor of Dublin. In 1849 it was leased by his widow to Richard Watkins, whose gate porter was Peter Duffy.

Griffith 1848–60; Ball and Hamilton 1895; *BPB* (1929); Pearson 1998.

621. PROSPECT HILL, Woodtown; *c.* 1820.
Now derelict is this most basic of standard single-storey hip-roofed lodges to a property in 1837 of John Dodd, who by 1849 was leasing it to Sheffield Betham, whose gatekeeper was then Michael Devitt.

Lewis 1837; Griffith 1848–60.

PROSPECT (see KNOCKLYON)

PROSPECT (see MILLTOWN HILL)

622. PROSPECT, Blackrock (2).
Both lodges, to Temple Road and Brookfield Lane, have been demolished, but the splendid entrance screen on the former survives. Of *c.* 1845, the sweep is made up of double carriage gate openings contained by a series of tall stone pillars with oversized pedimented cappings sporting laurel wreaths. The gates are hung on secondary iron posts, all flanked by postern gates in decorative ironwork that extends in matching railed quadrants on dwarf walls. 'Prospect' by 1841 was already serving as a boarding and day school under Revd Daniel William Cahill before reverting to domestic use by 1849, when Charles Cavanagh's gatekeeper at the Temple Road entrance was Thomas Wilson. The Vincentian Order purchased the place in 1873 and it remained

as St Joseph's College for boys for a century. The lodge off Brookfield Avenue (as it became) was only recently removed.

Thom's; Griffith 1848–60; Pearson 1998.

623. PROSPECT, Dolphin's Barn; pre-1837; *demolished.*
In 1850 Prospect was a herd's house on eleven acres of land with a gate lodge manned by James McKenna as porter to Thomas Etchingham, grocer and spirit dealer.

Griffith 1848–60; Slater 1856.

624. PROSPECT, Glenageary; pre-1837; *demolished.*
A property in 1849 of George Baker, whose gatekeeper was Garrett Byrne. Renamed 'Glenagarey Lodge' by 1907.

Griffith 1848–60.

625. PROSPECT, Terenure; pre-1837/*c.* 1875.
A seat in 1837 of James Fagan, whose early porter's lodge was lying vacant twelve years later, in the time here of Thomas William Madden, presumably an indication of its condition, for it was replaced in the 1870s during the residence of William M. Campbell. It is a pleasant single-storey standard hip-roofed structure with a gabled hall projection. Constructed in brick facing brick, red as the chimney-stack, but now painted over. Occupied.

Lewis 1837; Griffith 1848–60; *Thom's*.

626. PROSPECT VILLA, Rathgar; pre-1849; *demolished.*
A residence in 1841 of John Houston, who was leasing it to George Birnie eight years later, when the gatekeeper was Thomas Higgins. In 1851 the lodge seemed also to have served as a post office. It had gone by 1907.

Thom's; Griffith 1848–60.

627. PROVOST'S HOUSE, Grafton Street; pre-1837; *demolished.*
Lurking against the tall, impenetrable, 310ft-long curtain wall, built sometime after 1791, was a simple single-storey porter's lodge, architecturally insignificant in comparison with the Palladian-style town house of the Trinity College provost, built in 1759 across the forecourt in a rusticated limestone, its round-headed arcading reflected in recesses of the screen wall which frame keystoned postern openings, their doors, like those of the carriage entrance, contained by four grand pillars, now lacking their urn finials.

Malton 1978; Craig 1980.

628. QUARRYVALE, Palmerston; pre-1836/*c.* 1890; architect not known.
A house which rather curiously never seems to have had a lasting relationship with a family, perhaps owing to its siting by the road rather than next to the River Liffey, which the 53-acre estate and townland bounds to the north. The impressive gatehouse stands at the opposite side of the entrance from its predecessor. In a late Victorian English Picturesque style with decorative carved

bargeboards, it rises to 1½ storeys off an L-plan in a pebble-dash finish with bold toothed stone quoins. In the internal corner is a square entrance tower with a pyramidal roof and ornamental fascia boards to match the barges. To one gable is an original single-storey rectangular bay window, whilst that to the avenue displays a modern double-storey glazed affair, part of modernisation which includes a large gabled wing, in sympathetic detail, to the rear. The corbelled red-brick chimney-stacks, perforated earthenware cresting, scalloped slate bands and general finishes match the lodge to the adjoining property of Brooklawn (*q.v.*), suggesting a common architect. A seat in 1850 of Patrick Tiernan, whose lodge was replaced in the residency of Henry Fitzgibbon.

Griffith 1848–60; *Thom's*.

629. RANISKEY, Milltown; pre-1837; *demolished.*
A seat of Bartholomew C. Russell for much of the mid-nineteenth century, the porter's lodge to which had gone by 1937.

630. RATHCOOLE, Rathcoole; pre-1837; *demolished.*
A property in the early nineteenth century of James Sheil, the big house on which lies derelict.

631. RATHCREEDAN, Rathcoole; *c.* 1930.
Previously 'Airfield' and lodgeless, home to the Kilbee family, its lodge looks to be of twentieth-century origin, three-bay standard below a hipped roof, the centre bay an entrance doorway with slit sidelights in a roughcast finish with quoins—a bungalow.

632. RATHFARNHAM CASTLE, Rathfarnham (3).
A magnificent property that has led an uncertain existence down the centuries since its foundation in 1585 by Adam Loftus, lord chancellor and archbishop of Dublin. His castle still clearly forms the nucleus of the surviving structure, now happily restored and in the safe hands of the state. After passing from the possession of the Loftus family in 1692, it was redeemed by them in 1767 when purchased by Henry Loftus (1709–83), 4th viscount and 1st and last earl of Ely of the second creation. Upon his death the estates devolved upon his nephew, the Rt Hon. Charles Tottenham (1738–1806), who assumed the surname and arms of Loftus and was in 1801 created marquis of Ely. It is to these two enlightened gentlemen that credit is due for much of the Georgian improvements to the property: to the former for engaging leading architects of the day in James 'Athenian' Stuart and Sir William Chambers to modernise the interiors, and to the latter for inspired improvements in landscaping the park and adding significant entrances to it. Charles may well have approached his uncle's architect, but it could be that Chambers was too involved in the likes of Somerset House to be bothered and he probably recommended his assistant and clerk of works, the little-known Willey Reveley, to provide plans, for an undated design attributable to him survives.

Castellated gate; *c.* 1790; architect probably W. Reveley; *unexecuted.*
Had this design been selected it would have been stylistically more appropriate as an introduction to the castle than what was realised. The drawing, formerly in the collection of the Jesuits in Rathfarmham Castle, was sold at auction and shows an elevation for a gatescreen in the Castellated Picturesque manner, with a central pointed-arched carriage opening flanked by a pair of round towers with arrowslits, all embraced by a machicolated, crenellated parapet. To each side stretch symmetrically a lancet-arched postilion gate with square turret alongside and another terminating a castellated curtain wall beyond, intended to

632. Rathfarnham Castle drawn by W. Reveley.

Irish Architectural Archive

632. Rathfarnham Castle, Dodder gate (National Library of Ireland).

have been 18ft 6in. in height to frame the 30ft-high central archway and flankers. It is not clear at what approach this was intended to be the prelude or whether porter's accommodation was to be incorporated.

Dodder or Ely gate; *c.* 1802; architect Francis Johnston.

Thomas Walmsley/Crookshank and Glin

Charles Tottenham Loftus was further elevated to a peer of the UK in 1801 as Baron Loftus of Long Loftus, Yorkshire, as reward for his vote and influence in connection with the Act of Union, for which, significantly, he also received £45,000, which may go a long way towards dating this dignified gateway, much admired and illustrated down the years by tourists. Archer was here in 1801 and it is perhaps relevant that he noticed only 'a remarkable high wall', whereas Brewer in 1825 remarked upon the demesne being 'entered from the Rathmines road by a splendid gateway ranking among the best productions of this species of architecture to be witnessed in Ireland'. What is not in doubt

The Dodder gate is a reproduction of a design by the architect James Wyatt which stands at the entrance to Canterbury Quad, Christchurch College, Oxford (Oxford University Archive).

is that the entrance was in place by 1806, for artist William Walmsley, who died in this year, depicts it in his painting of Rathfarnham Castle. Nor is there speculation any longer as to Baron Loftus's architect, for a pen and watercolour elevation of it by Francis Johnston has recently come to light, a revelation which in retrospect should have come as no surprise. It is in fact a reproduction by Johnston of an original design by the eminent English architect James Wyatt which stands at the entrance to Canterbury Quad, Christchurch College, Oxford. The common denominator in this connection is Richard Robinson, Baron Rokeby and archbishop of Armagh, who had funded its building in 1773–83 and later became the young Johnston's benefactor, sending him in 1778 to Dublin as a pupil of Thomas Cooley, and from 1784 onwards Johnston worked for the archbishop in Armagh and at his Irish seat of Rokeby Hall, Co. Louth (*q.v.*). Wyatt's original design, described by Curl as 'a fine essay showing the trabeated and arcuated forms mingled', equally applies here in this monumental example of a Roman triumphal archway, executed in fine granite masonry and unsocially containing integral porter's accommodation—'an inhabited archway' (Howley 1993). Three-bay in form, the sole opening being the central semicircular double-height arch, flanked on the front façade by a pair of part-engaged Roman Doric columns with equivalent pilasters to outer corners which frame round-arched niches with square panels, or blind openings, over. The whole is crowned by a deep entablature with balustraded parapet (in which it differs from the Oxford original) with gadrooned urns over. The rear elevation to the park is rather more detailed in having triglyphs to the frieze, *oeil-de-boeuf* niches substituted for the square panels and a wonderful hirsute head of a Roman god as a central keystone in Coade stone, illustrated as standard in the Lambeth catalogues from as far back as the 1770s. Access to the porter's split quarters is at least covered via doors below the barrel vault, but the rooms were lit merely by single square windows to opposing side elevations. The pretty scrolled Georgian ironwork to the gates looks too delicate but is original. The extensive banded ashlar concave quadrants and end pillars with their ball finials (now missing) look to be a later rebuild. This splendid archway, which once gave onto the northern approach, with its Romantic avenue traversing the meandering stream five times and passing a Classical rotunda temple, now lies abandoned and removed from the context of its demesne, marooned on an island, having been disgracefully severed by a new road system. A home in 1849 to porter Patrick Reddy.

Village gate; *c.* 1800/*c.* 1860.

Irish Architectural Archive

Probably of an age with the Ely gate and possibly also by Johnston was a Georgian entrance in the Gothic style. Now thrown down, it addressed the visitor as an extensive segmental forecourt with a tall walled screen dominated by a central lofty carriage opening with a pointed arch, almost Hindu in form, it and the curtain walls having the suggestion of a machicolated coping, the latter pierced by lancet-arched postern openings and relieved by piers crowned by incongruous but beautifully chiselled ball finials, rusticated with Greek key-patterned bands, one of which survives with a small portion of wall in brick construction finished in crude roughcast. An old photograph shows a similarly doomed and contemporary lodge against the rear of the right-hand quadrant wall. Single-storey, it had parapeted eaves to the avenue façade, with two lancet lights and a later semi-octagonal bay window applied. With the passing of the 1st marquis of Ely in 1806, the property suffered through neglect by his successor, who favoured Ely Lodge, Co. Fermanagh, and it was tenanted for many years. D'Alton in 1836 paints a bleak picture: 'the once beautiful grounds of Rathfarnham Castle, but they are now all eloquently waste, the undulating hills covered with rank herbage, the rivulet stagnant and sedgy, the walks scarce traceable, the ice-houses open to the prying sun, the fish-pond clogged with weeds, while the mouldering architecture of the castle, and the crumbling, unsightly offices in its immediate vicinity, even more loudly proclaim those evils of absenteeism ... A direct avenue leads from the castle to the village, through an ugly, lofty gate ...' Salvation was to come after the death of the 2nd marquis in 1845, in the person of the Rt Hon. Francis Blackburne (1782–1867), lord chief justice and lord chancellor, who purchased the place. He clearly considered the lodge that he inherited at the village gate inadequate, and at the other side of the 'ugly, lofty gate' he built the surviving pretty Picturesque cottage. Sited behind the sad remnants of the left-hand quadrant, it is smooth-rendered, 1½-storey and raised off a T-plan, with decorative carved bargeboards over transomed and mullioned casement windows, that on the leading gable in a breakfront below a narrow round-headed slit attic window, alone retaining its cast-iron latticed light. Awkwardly set in an internal angle below a very shallow-pitched gabled roof is the front door, below a three-centred archway with a chamfered surround. Occupied. Matthew Moore was gatekeeper in 1849. The Blackburne family remained in possession of the castle until it was acquired by the Society of Jesus.

Archer 1801; Brewer 1825; d'Alton 1976 [1838]; Lewis 1837; Griffith 1848–60; Harrison 1890; Ball 1995; *LGI* (1904); Joyce 1912; *BPB* (1929); ffolliott 1970; Bence-Jones 1988; Kelly 1990; Crookshank and Glin 1994; Colvin 1995; Howley 1993; Pevsner and Sherwood 2002; Curl 1993; Healy 2005; IAA photographs (2/8 R1+N); Kieran Swords photo; NLI drawing (AD.1913); Mealy's auction catalogue (2 May 2006).

633. RATHFARNHAM, Rathmines (2).
A property that had disappeared by 1907, along with its pre-1837 porters' lodges at Rathmines Avenue and Rathmines Road Upper, its imminent demise perhaps indicated by their being vacant in 1849, when the house was occupied by solicitor Thomas Keller.

Griffith 1848–60.

634. RATHFARNHAM PARK, Ballinteer; pre-1837; *demolished.*
A seat, also known singly as 'The Park', in 1837 of John Davis, whose gatekeeper twelve years later was Patrick McGuinness. Overrun by modern housing.

Lewis 1837; Griffith 1848–60.

635. RATHGAR, Rathgar; pre-1837; *demolished.*
By the bridge over the River Dodder were the house and adjacent mills in 1837 of Patrick Waldron, who was proprietor until *c.* 1853. His gate porter in 1849 was Mary Hughes.

Lewis 1837; Griffith 1848–60.

636. RATHGAR, Terenure; pre-1837; *demolished.*
In 1849 Thomas Shaw was gatekeeper to Edward Quinton in a lodge on Bushy Park Road, which twenty years later had gone.

Griffith 1848–60; *Thom's.*

637. RATHGAR MANSION, Rathgar (2).
A property about which unusually early details of a gate lodge and its occupant have come down the years, thanks to tragic circumstances recorded in the *Freeman's Journal* of 17 March 1798.

Highfield Road gate; pre-1798/*c.* 1830.
'Yesterday morning, about two o'clock, a numerous banditti, said to be forty in number, attacked the country house of Charles Farren, Esq., which is situated near Rathmines Road, adjoining the avenue that leads to Rathfarnham Road. They first entered the gardener's lodge, in which was a poor man, in service of Mr Farren, named Daniel Carroll who giving what resistance he could to the barbarians, they cruelly put him to death, and which we since understand was the chief purpose for which they came to that place.' The murderers were subsequently apprehended and hanged. The surviving lodge looks to be a Regency replacement for the unfortunate Carroll's, but even it is barely discernible through twentieth-century efforts to transform it into a bungalow. It was a standard single-storey hip-roofed structure with paired carved soffit brackets and a central hipped-roof hall projection. Now extended by a bay to the left-hand side, with larger window openings gouged out and reroofed with roll-profiled concrete tiles. The new gatekeeper in 1849 was Bryan Brennan, serving Joseph Farran, the last of that family to live here, the place being taken over about 1855 by Henry W. Todd, merchant, who built a new house on the site called 'Oakland', possibly to designs of Charles Geoghegan, and added a handsome new gatescreen further up the avenue. This is in the form of railed ogee quadrants on dwarf walls of roughly hewn masonry framing a pair of iron carriage pillars, like Chinese stoves, with incongruous modern electric lanterns over. After being in the hands of the Brown family for the 1870s and '80s it was purchased by Samuel Parker, whose stay, though short, was architecturally significant.

Orwell Park gate; 1893; architect probably William Kaye-Parry.

Parker had a 'Shoes and Boot Manufactory to Her Majesty, the Prince of Wales and the Irish Court', the offices of which were at 35 Dame Street, an address shared in the 1890s by the architect William Kaye-Parry, and there is little doubt that Parker turned to him to design a new entrance to Oakland off the newly created Orwell Park south of the house. The gate lodge, though considerably removed from its gates, behind the later houses fronting the public road, is splendidly ostentatious in its quintessential late Victorian Arts and Crafts Queen Anne style, an essay in red clay materials of Flemish bond brickwork with bold specials to eaves and verges, plain Rosemary roof tiles with sawtoothed bands and crowning serrated cresting. Single-storey and raised on an L-plan, its two main gables and that of a breakfront to the side elevation each sport all manner of fancy details. To the half-hipped gable is a wooden tripartite window of squared casement lights and a little pediment, the tympanum of which contains the date of construction. On the main avenue gable is a glazed canted bay window with its own ogee roof, over which is a prominent family coat of arms in red sandstone. To the breakfront gable the window has a delightful scrolled pediment and another sandstone plaque with a monogram. The internal angle contains a little hallway and verandah porch with post support to the catslide roof. Inexcusably, this little architectural gem lies neglected, boarded up and derelict, seemingly an embarrassment to the hospital

that now occupies the site.

Interestingly, all the family bearings displayed on the lodge and gates are of Charles Wisdom Hely, who acquired the property in 1895 and added his monogram, arms and crest to the (perhaps) partially completed entrance. On the distant gateway the Hely crest of 'In hand, coupled at wrist, a buck's horn' adorns the meeting rail of the carriage gates, and further down more monograms in highly decorative ironwork hung, like the flanking pedestrian gates, on a pair of lofty stone pillars with raised panels of 'pockmarked' rustication and friezes with 'Oakland' in relief.

Lewis 1837; *Thom's*; Griffith 1848–60; Joyce 1912; IAA.

RATHLEIGH (see ROSETTA)

638. RATHMINES CASTLE, Rathmines; *c.* 1840/1934; architect W.A. Griffith.
A pleasant 'modern' castle, created *c.* 1820 in the rambling Tudor Castellated manner from what was described in 1813 as his 'charming villa' by Robert Wynne (1760–1838) of the Hazelwood, Co. Sligo, family. The valuation of 1850 records a gatehouse occupied by William Irvine when John Purser, brewer of Arthur Guinness Sons and Co., was the proprietor. This appears to have been built after 1837, but the big dreary 1½-storey gatehouse with its back to the road is no doubt the replacement of 1934 for Sir John Purser almost a century later, his architect being William A. Griffith. A neat little chamfered, granite-dressed, round-headed postilion opening in a concave quadrant wall looks to be a survivor of the original development. Now the Church of Ireland College of Education.

Curwen 1818; *Dublin Penny Journal* (14 Sept. 1833); *Parliamentary Gazetteer*; Griffith 1848–60; *Thom's*; *LGI* (1904); IAA.

639. RATHMINES CASTLE OLD, Rathmines; pre-1837.
A seventeenth-century castle built by Sir George Radcliffe, the district around which in the early eighteenth century came into the possession of the Temple family. Viscount Palmerston's gatekeeper was James Lock in 1850, about when the old estate was beginning to be broken up, the castle removed and exclusive villas developed on the site, such as 'The Orchards' (*q.v.*) and Palmerston House (*q.v.*), which appears to have purloined the gate lodge.

Griffith 1848–60; Ball 1995; Joyce 1912.

640. RATHMINES TRAMWAY DEPOT, Rathmines; *c.* 1910; architect possibly P.F. O'Sullivan.

An attractive single-storey Arts and Crafts Elizabethan Revival lodge, with its front on the Dartry Road footpath to a backdrop of great tram sheds. Two tall red-brick banded and capped chimney-stacks enliven the main hipped roof, from which projects a gable with half-timbered effect over a canted oriel window in roughcast walls with brick pilaster quoins, all on a quarry-faced stone plinth. Alongside, in the internal angle below a catslide roof was the entrance porch, now enclosed; in use. Patrick F. O'Sullivan is recorded as carrying out work here in 1905.

IAA.

641. REDESDALE, Stillorgan (2).
A very fine mid-eighteenth-century Palladian-style villa—sadly, along with its two pre-1837 gate lodges on Lower Kilmacud Road, lost. The eastern lodge had been demolished before 1869, and perhaps twenty years earlier, for the 1849 valuation only notices one, occupied by Michael Ryan, porter to the Rt Hon. and Most Revd Richard Whateley (1787–1863), archbishop of Dublin. Previously Sir Michael Smith, master of the rolls, had sold it in 1799 to Sir John Mitford (1748–1830), ancestor of the noted sisters. He was appointed lord chancellor of Ireland in 1802, elevated as 1st Baron Redesdale after his Northumberland seat and renamed his Irish seat accordingly. Later called 'St Kevin's Park'.

Griffith 1848–60; *BPB* (1929); Flanagan 1991; Leslie and Wallace 2001.

642. RIALTO LODGE, Kilmainham; pre-1837; *demolished.*
A seat in the mid-nineteenth century of Robert Smyth.

RICHELIEU (see RICHVIEW, Merrion)

643. RICHMOND CEMETERY, Goldenbridge; *c.* 1830/*c.* 1890.
'The first general cemetery was established here in 1829 by a grant of £1,000 from the Catholic Association funds. It is chiefly used by Roman Catholic families, and is tastefully arranged and planted; it is surrounded by high walls, and in the centre is a chapel for funerals.' Fourteen years before this 1851 description, Samuel Lewis reported that two years after its opening the graveyard was nearly filled, 1,200 having been interred within. By the end of the century the sexton's and gatekeeper's accommodation had also been found inadequate; one of these positions was held in 1849 by William Reed, employed by the Richmond Cemetery Company. The replacement is a commodious house built in polychromatic brickwork, the main buff facings contrasting subtly with red toothed dressings and quoins. Two-storey and gabled with a minimum of wooden apex ornament, it turns its back on the cemetery with a symmetrical three-bay front to the footway of two-over-two sash windows divided by a first-floor string-course. The roof displays red terracotta cresting to a ridge broken by two sturdy chimney-stacks with corbelled cappings. At right angles to the rear is what may be the original entrance of a double archway, probably with the function of a lych-gate. The segmental arches are highlighted by bold stone voussoirs, above which is a plaque with the inscription 'D.O.M.'

Lewis 1837; *Thom's*.

RICHMOND COTTAGE (see DALGUISE)

644. RICHMOND COTTAGE, Goldenbridge; pre-1837; *demolished.*
A property in 1841 of Charles Hutton.

645. RICHMOND HILL, Bray; pre-1871; *demolished.*
A boarding house run by a Mrs Pemberton in

the mid-nineteenth century, when it acquired its gate lodge. Also called 'Kilcrony' in some directory entries.

Thom's.

646. RICHMOND HILL, Monkstown; *c.* 1835; *demolished.*
An exclusive development in 1841 of four houses, which had increased some years later to eight, with the added *gravitas* of its own gate lodge at the entrance to the cul-de-sac off Carrickbrennan Road.

Thom's.

647. RICHMOND PARK, Monkstown; *c.* 1875; *demolished.*
In 1874 Sydenham Davis built the present smart Italianate house to replace an earlier villa on the site called 'Monkstown Hill'. The solicitor complemented this with a gate lodge at the end of a tortuous avenue leading from the village.

Pearson 1998.

RICHMOND PENITENTIARY (see WELLINGTON BARRACKS)

RICHMOND TOWER (see ROYAL HOSPITAL)

648. RICHVIEW, Merrion; pre-1837; *demolished.*
A marine residence on Sydney Parade Avenue in 1846 of Francis Rea, whose gate porter two years later was Jeremiah Preston. A property previously called 'Richelieu'.

Slater 1846; Griffith 1848–60.

649. RICHVIEW, Milltown (2).
A house of *c.* 1790 built by the Powell family, who remained here in the person of Michael Powell until about 1845.

Main entrance; *c.* 1825.
A square two-storey gatehouse, well maintained and modernised without loss of its Regency character. Commodious below a shallow hipped roof with carved soffit brackets, its single-bay avenue front in crisp rendering containing a flat-roofed, square-paned glazed canted bay window. Unobtrusive recent single-storey extension to one side. Very plain stone entrance pillars and quadrant walls.

Secondary entrance; pre-1837; *demolished.*
A lodge that was sited opposite its gates in the grounds of Springfield House.

John Duffy, who was the proprietor by 1849, then had as his gatekeepers Constantine Maguire and George Pope. Since 1980 the property of UCD.

Lewis 1837; *Thom's*; Griffith 1848–60; McCartney 1999.

650. RICHVIEW, Monkstown; pre-1837; *demolished.*
Little remains of the fine neo-Classical house of around 1825 or its park, other than its huge portico, which has been retained as an eye-catcher in the new apartment development. The gate lodge may have been contemporary to what was in 1837 until about 1855 a seat of solicitor Richard Jordan. The place was called 'St Grellan's' from 1880, and alternatively 'The Hall'.

Lewis 1837; *Thom's*; Pearson 1998.

651. RICHVIEW PRIORY, Monkstown; *c.* 1835; architect not known.

Irish Architectural Archive

Originally a delicious 1½-storey English Picturesque Cottage, as if plucked from a P.F. Robinson pattern-book, on an informal plan with typically steep gables and gablets ornamented with carved bargeboards, that to the main entrance breakfront having a series of quatrefoil perforations to a corbelled jettied attic storey over a Gothic panelled doorway with chamfered Tudor archway. To one side is a single-storey semi-octagonal bay window with small-paned sashes and its own rooflet below a pretty gablet with slit window and foiled carved bargeboards. In 1987 it lay neglected and derelict but was subsequently rebuilt in like manner and enlarged, with its roof raised. Probably built for Richard Jordan of neighbouring 'Richview' (*q.v.*), the Priory was occupied in 1841 by Sir Richard St George, succeeded eight years later by Colonel A. Kearney, whose privileged porter was Christopher Byrne.

Lewis 1837; *Thom's*; Griffith 1848–60; IAA photograph (S/779/11).

RIDDESDALE (see REDESDALE)

RIVERDALE (see RIVERVIEW)

RIVERSDALE (see NEWTOWN CLARKE)

652. RIVERSDALE, Galloping Green; pre-1837; *demolished.*
A villa built in the 1770s as part of the division of the great Allen estates and which had a frequent turnover of owners down the years. In 1837 it was home to John Wilson Barlow, followed in 1849 by attorney Edward Reynolds, whose gate porter was Mary Hanly. In 1954 the house was transformed into 'Granada' and given a delightful Tudor Castellated cloak by the St John of God Brothers.

Lewis 1837; Griffith 1848–60.

653. RIVERSDALE, Dundrum; pre-1837; *demolished.*
A lodge on a confined site behind a rubble wall between river and driveway that had gone by 1907. Occupied in 1849 by Patrick Byrne as gatekeeper of Henry Thomas Price, of the 'Railway Company', who had succeeded leather merchant John Alcorn as proprietor.

Slater 1846; Griffith 1848–60.

654. RIVERSDALE, Monkstown; *c.* 1875; *demolished.*
At the head of the Queen's Park loop was the short-lived lodge at the entrance to the remarkable High Victorian Gothic brick house of the Egan family, wealthy wholesale grocers, built around 1870.

Pearson 1990.

RIVERSDALE (see SALLYMOUNT)

655. RIVERSDALE, Templeogue; pre-1837.
Richard Keefe was gate porter in 1849; his lodge survives, barely discernible through an envelopment of flat-roofed extensions in conversion to its new role as a health clinic. A single-storey hip-roofed structure within suggests that it dates from the building of the house by William Pidgeon about 1830.

Thom's; Griffith 1848–60.

656. RIVERVIEW, Terenure; pre-1837; *demolished.*
A residence in 1837 of Michael T. Kelly, the name of which was altered to 'Riverdale', being located on the banks of the Dodder.

Lewis 1837.

ROCHELLE (see PLUNKETT LODGE)

657. ROCHESTOWN, Rochestown; pre-1837; *demolished.*
Today's Rochestown Avenue served as the grand driveway to the antique mansion of the Mapas family, which, along with its numerous offices, brewery, pigeon house, great gateway and gate lodge, is a thing of the past. The latter was occupied in 1849 by John Williams, porter to Joseph Matthew O'Kelly. Peter Pearson believes that some of its entrance pillars are to be found at the Temple Hill gateway to Rockfield (*q.v.*).

Griffith 1848–60; Ball 1995; Pearson 1998.

658. ROCK, Dalkey; pre-1871; *demolished.*
A marine villa and its porter's lodge built on the Coliemore Road by William Holden around 1850.

Thom's.

659. ROCKBROOK, Rockbrook; *c.* 1790; *demolished.*
The very fine Palladian-style mid-Georgian house of the Campbells, earls of Glenavy, and subsequently for many years in the mid-nineteenth century home to Charles Byrne, whose gatekeeper in 1849 was Mary Rooney. Until recently at the roadside attached to outbuildings, it was in contrast to the big house as a most basic single-storey vernacular cottage, a chimney-stack to its gable and latterly a tarred roof over an asymmetrical three-bay main front of whitewashed roughcast finish on rubble construction. The property is now a school.

Griffith 1848–60; *Thom's*; Healy 2005; NIAH.

660. ROCKFIELD, Dundrum; pre-1837/*c.* 1870; *demolished.*

An old house of clothier Joseph Hone (1747–1803), inherited by his second son of the same name (1775–1857), which by 1849 had been acquired by attorney John Rose Byrne, with James Kavanagh as his gate porter. That lodge was replaced by James R. Byrne, a very neat little Italianate building which itself has been removed to make way for a modern development of apartments. Single-storey standard below a hipped roof with an open-pedimented hall projection containing a moulded-surround round-headed fanlit doorway. On each side in rendered walls were similarly arched one-over-one sash windows with toothed banded dressings. There was a later extension to the right-hand side with an impressive arcaded tripartite window in like style.

Lewis 1837; Slater 1846; Griffith 1848–60; *Thom's*; *IFR*.

661. ROCKFIELD, Stradbrook; 1905; architect probably L.A. McDonnell.

One of the older and larger of the landed estates in the vicinity of Blackrock village, which gradually, from the time here of Viceroy Lord Townshend in the mid-eighteenth century, was subdivided and sold off to accommodate the merchant villas of Dunardagh (*q.v.*) and Craigmore (*q.v.*), where gate lodges were a status symbol. Despite its importance and size, the maps of Rocque (1760) and the first editions of the Ordnance Survey show the demesne to have remained lodgeless at its entrances until the early twentieth century with the arrival of W.P. Geoghegan. And what an unusually bold and gauche example presents itself, bizarrely preceded by auspiciously lofty and elegant mid-eighteenth-century granite entrance pillars with their moulded plinths, recessed panels, scroll-topped stops and pointy pineapple finials, said to have been brought here from the doomed Rochestown House (*q.v.*). In a sort of Queen Anne Edwardian Arts and Crafts style, it is 1½-storey below a hipped roof, the front bracketed eaves of

which are broken by a pair of grotesque tripartite small-paned oriel gablets carried on carved brackets with swan-neck scrolled pediments over. The attic storey is expressed in a roughcast finish over the red-brick ground floor, from which projects a single-storey pedimented entrance hall with date-stone. The outer corners are chamfered to contain angled windows, the floor over supported on bulky wooden brackets with pendants and continuous bracket profiles. This is a feature to be found at Lumville

Newtownpark Avenue entrance.

Farm, Co. Kildare (*q.v.*), and Kilmaroon House, north Dublin (*q.v.*), and suggests the work of architect Laurence Aloysius McDonnell. This would seem to be despite William Mansfield Mitchell's having worked here five years earlier for Geoghegan. Further south, at the present, and probably original, main entrance, is a splendid pair of carriage pillars of *c.* 1760 in the Batty Langley manner, their shafts displaying pointed niches and similarly arcaded friezes below moulded cappings with delightful crocketted cone finials like jesters' hats. In durable granite, they once carried sturdy wooden doors rather than the present flimsy ironwork.

Ball 1995; Ferguson 1998; Pearson 1998; IAA.

662. ROCKFORD, Stradbrook; pre-1837/*c.* 1882; architects probably T.N. Deane and Son.

From being a relatively modest house in 1837 of G.P. Wallace, albeit with its own porter's lodge, it was transformed in two stages into its present manifestation as a great rambling granite late Victorian neo-Tudor pile. In 1849 Andrew Kennedy was gatekeeper in the early lodge to the then owner Joseph Atkinson. Atkinson was succeeded around 1855 by Molyneux Betham, builder of a new house which in turn was found inadequate by William Robert Bruce (1833–1902), who purchased the place in 1881 and immediately engaged the leading architectural practice of Thomas Newenham Deane and Son to carry out initial alterations and additions to cost £7,290, probably chiefly to the designs of the son, Thomas Manly Deane. Surprisingly, the description with sale of Rockford boasted that 'The house is approached from the high road by a handsome carriage drive, with an excellent two-storey gate-lodge at entrance', suggesting that the present Elizabethan Revival gatehouse is a make-over of its predecessor, unless it was rebuilt before 1881. It is a strikingly lofty 1½-storey structure, having exaggerated steep gables and overhangs with exposed rafter toes, and a pointy gablet in the same vein. The walls display a modest quantity of decorative timbers, the ground floor otherwise in rendered finish, the attic storey having red-brick infill. To the leading gable is a single-storey lean-to projection. What remains of the ornamental earthenware cresting and the sturdy brick corbelled stack point to a rebuild of Bruce's occupation. The house is now in flats.

Lewis 1837; Griffith 1848–60; *Thom's*; Williams 1994; O'Dwyer 1997; Pearson 1998; IAA.

663. ROCKLANDS, Sandyford; pre-1837; *demolished.*

Like Burton Hall across the road, Rocklands was a Burton family creation of the eighteenth century which by 1837 was the seat of solicitor John Henry Dunne, who was still in residence twelve years later, when the lodge lay vacant.

Lewis 1837; Griffith 1848–60; Flanagan 1991.

ROCK LODGE (see PLASNEWYDD)

664. ROCKMOUNT, Dundrum; pre-1837; *demolished.*

A property in 1837 of Thomas Courtenay which subsequently had a succession of owners, one of whom was William Blackburne in 1849, when his gate porter was William Flaherty.

Lewis 1837; Griffith 1848–60; *Thom's.*

665. ROCKVILLE, Booterstown; *c.* 1830.

Occupied in 1849 by Nicolas Tevelin as gatekeeper to John Vance, the lodge remarkably survives its big house, with which it was contemporary, both built for Christopher Hope. Modest and rendered but well proportioned, it is single-storey standard with, now, one-over-one sash windows on each side of a projecting hallway, its gable extending from the hipped roof; hefty brick chimney-stack. Strangely, this Rockville lodge forms a double pile, back to back with that to Marino (*q.v.*). The gatescreen to Mount Merrion Avenue also remains relatively unscathed, with its roughcast quadrant walls framing plain granite ashlar pillars with modern globe lights over, like ball finials, and 'Elms' painted on the friezes, a name given to the property about 1870 by the then resident William Williamson. It has now been overrun by apartments.

Lewis 1837; Griffith 1848–60; *Thom's.*

666. ROCKVILLE, Kilternan; pre-1837/*c.* 1890.

A fine mid-eighteenth-century gentry farmer's house, the property in 1837 of Charles W. Roche. Its early porter's lodge was replaced by the surviving late Victorian cottage. On an elevated site, it is solid single-storey three-bay symmetrical with bipartite one-over-one sash windows in random uncoursed granite facings below a steeply hipped roof with clipped eaves and brick chimney-stacks to each end; occupied. Probably built for C. Byrne, dairy farmer.

Lewis 1837; *Thom's*; Pearson 1998.

667. ROCKVILLE or ROCK VILLA, Stradbrook (2).

A small demesne in the early nineteenth century of Samuel Bewley, and subsequently of Thomas Bewley, which featured notable gardens and tropical orchard houses. Neither of the pre-1837 gate lodges survives, the site much built over. Thomas's gatekeepers in 1849 were James White and Michael Doyle.

Thom's; Griffith 1848–60; Pearson 1998.

668. ROEBUCK CASTLE, Roebuck (3).

The historic sixteenth-century castle of the Barnewalls, Barons Trimlestown, in which family the property remained until *c.* 1800, when it was purchased by James Crofton, on whose death in 1828 it passed to his son, Arthur Burgh Crofton. The valuation a year before his death in 1850 records him as having Judith Timmins as gatekeeper, the pre-1837 gatehouse apparently located off the public road by the out-offices at the rear of the house. In 1856 the property was sold to Edward P. Westby (1830–93), who did not rush into improving the place, but when he did in 1872 he transformed the house and added one of the more recognisable architectural delights of the south Dublin area.

Main entrance; 1872; architect probably E.H. Carson.

A remarkably ostentatious set piece on Roebuck Road in a High Victorian Gothic style, conspicuous for its bold outline and polychromatic materials of fair-faced granite with strongly contrasting red sandstone highlights of string-course and alternating voussoirs. Completed two years earlier than work to the house if the respective datestones are to be believed, it is basically 1½-storey built off an L-plan, with an integral carriage archway and a dominant three-storey buttressed entrance tower in the internal angle topped by a spire which terminates in a wrought iron finial, its eaves broken by gablets with beautifully sculpted ornamentation, one of which sports Westby's monogram and the date of construction. The mason's skill is also to be seen in some exquisite foliated banding and a roundel in the front door overpanel carved with the family crest of a martlett holding in its beak a stalk of wheat, and their motto: *Nec Volenti Nec Volanti.* The skew-tabled gables with moulded kneelers display bipartite chamfered windows with overpanels containing trefoils, whilst the whole is framed by concave crenellated quadrants terminating in chamfered pillars with more splendid foliage and layered pyramidal cappings. Clearly attributable to Edward Carson on the grounds of its similarity in form and fenestration to his lodge at St Patrick's, Dalkey (*q.v.*). The present proud owners have carried out a splendid restoration and unobtrusive additions, to include conversion of the carriage opening to a spectacular living room.

Secondary entrance; *c.* 1875.

Considerably more modest in its siting and architecture is this 1½-storey gabled three-bay lodge with doorway to the right-hand side below a bracketed lean-to canopy, its square-headed windows set in lancet-arched brick surrounds. To the road gable an ornamental wooden truss sits above a bipartite attic window with one-over-one sashes in rendered walls.

Lewis 1837; Griffith 1848–60; *Thom's*; *LGI* (1904); *BPB* (1929); Bence-Jones 1988; Williams 1994; Pearson 1998.

669. ROEBUCK COTTAGE, Roebuck; pre-1837/*c.* 1883; architect A.G. Jones.

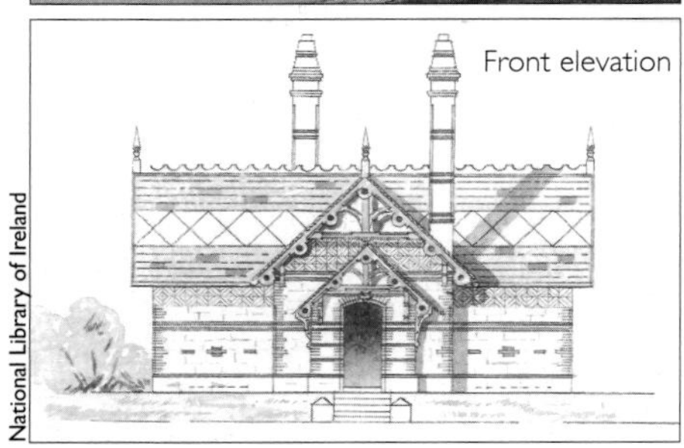

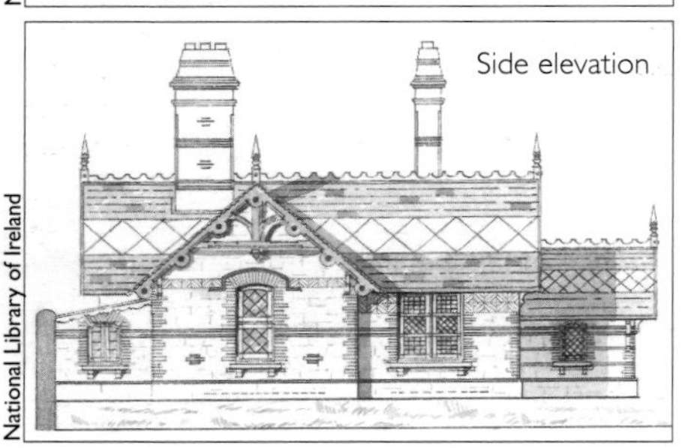

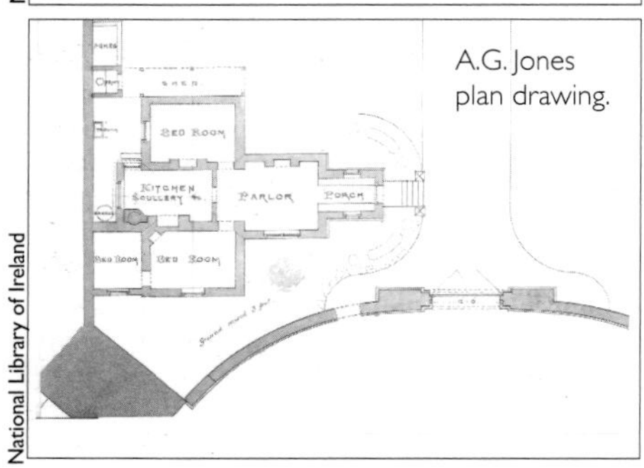

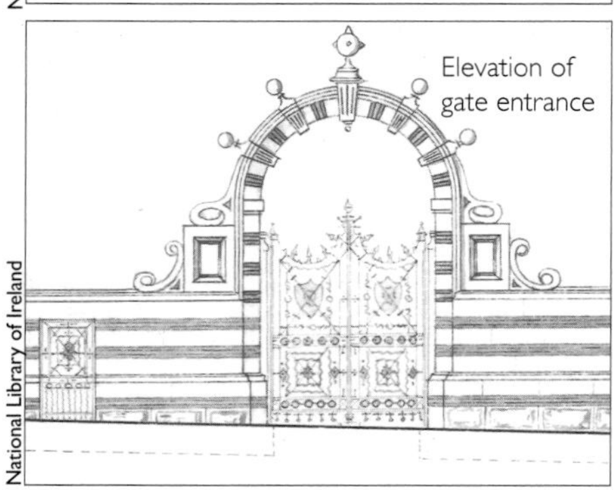

A most conspicuous High Victorian exercise in Polychromatic Picturesque is this single-storey gabled lodge and its extensive gatescreen. Basically built off a cruciform plan that seems to owe much in layout to Decimus Burton's lodges at Phoenix Park, north Dublin (*q.v.*), with the entrance hall projecting further from the main gable towards the avenue. White granite contrasts starkly with cream, blue and red brickwork as banding, quoins and toothed dressings to segmentally headed openings and on the chimney-stacks, which soar from the polychromy of roofs with bands of scalloped Westmoreland green slates and red earthenware sawtooth cresting. The gables are decorated with carved bargeboards and ornamental trusses with spiky hip-knobs. This was commissioned by hardware merchant John C. Parkes from Alfred Gresham Jones, an architect who was then in his sixties and was soon to emigrate to Australia, where he lived on into his nineties. His beautiful presentation drawings survive, much as built but for the intended preposterous round-headed carriage archway with pronounced voussoirs and ball finials and outer piers with graceful urns over. Surviving as designed is the wide segmental forecourt with the backdrop of curtain walls, with a quarry-faced plinth and brick banding over in granite ashlar, which meet in tall entrance pillars with discs to friezes and boldly bracketed cappings. In the left-hand quadrant is a solitary postern opening. Parkes had purchased the property in 1882 from its previous owner, Edmund D'Olier, who around 1860 had replaced the old Georgian cottage with a new villa and renamed it 'Ardilea'. In 1841 it was home, with its pre-1837 gate lodge, to Antony Dempsey before being acquired before 1849 by solicitor Henry Deane Edwards, whose gatekeeper was then Michael Colfer.

Thom's; Griffith 1848–60; Rothery 1997; Williams 1994; NLI (A.G. Jones album 2006 TX 78, 79, 80 & 83).

ROEBUCK GROVE (see ROEBUCK [2])

670. ROEBUCK GROVE [1], Roebuck (3).
A charming single-storey-over-basement villa of *c.* 1840 in a hybrid Italianate-cum-Greek Revival style built by John Goddard Richards (1794–1846), barrister, of Ardamine, Co. Wexford (*q.v.*). The development was approached by three tortuous approaches from Beech Hill Road, Stillorgan Road and a laneway leading to Rosemount House (*q.v.*), each lodged and manned in 1849 by William Cullen, Catherine Dunne and Patrick Kavanagh. Richards had little time to enjoy his Dublin seat, which was also known as 'White Oaks' and in 1949 was purchased by UCD to become the official residence of its president. Sadly, all three lodges proved to be surplus to requirements.

Thom's; Griffith 1848–60; *LGI* (1904).

671. ROEBUCK GROVE [2], Roebuck; pre-1837; *demolished.*
One of three houses of the same name in close proximity, this in Friarsland townland, in 1837 a small demesne of John Cumming, from whom it was acquired *c.* 1845 by solicitor Charles Pickering, whose gate porter in 1849 was Edward Moore.

Lewis 1837; *Thom's*; Griffith 1848–60.

672. ROEBUCK HALL, Roebuck (2).
D'Alton in 1836 opined on the byways of Roebuck: 'The beauty of these avenues is, however, overshadowed by tall wooden gates and concealed gate-houses that give the whole a sombre unsocial appearance, Mr Blackburne's villa opening the only exception to the remark'. This was the Rt Hon. Francis Blackburne (1782–1867), the distinguished lawyer who held the appointments of attorney-general, master of the rolls, lord chief justice, lord justice of appeal and lord high chancellor. His very fine late Georgian villa survives but not its two pre-1837 gate lodges, one of which in 1849 was staffed by Patrick Reddy. Blackburne also employed two gate porters at Rathfarnham Castle (*q.v.*), which he had purchased in 1845.

D'Alton 1976 [1838]; Lewis 1837; Griffith 1848–60.

673. ROEBUCK [1], Roebuck; pre-1837; *demolished.*
One of many gentry houses in the townland of Roebuck which at some stage of their existence went under the name of Roebuck House. This one on the junction of Foster's Avenue, Roebuck Road and Mountanville Road belatedly became 'Roebuck Hill' to avoid confusion around 1860. In 1849 the lodge was occupied by Michael Healy, gate porter to John Charles Lyons, inevitably a solicitor, who had moved here a few years earlier from neighbouring Woodfield (see Rosevale).

Griffiths 1848–60; *Thom's.*

674. ROEBUCK [2], Roebuck; pre-1837; *demolished.*
Located with its entrance off the north of Roebuck Road, its lodge stood back to back with that to Hermitage (*q.v.*), latterly renamed, confusingly, 'Roebuck Grove' in common with other big houses in the townland. It was built in 1792 and demolished in 1980 by UCD, having been home for much of the nineteenth century to the Brewster family.

Pearson 1998.

675. ROEBUCK [3], Roebuck; *c.* 1830.
A remarkable survivor in this area of architectural carnage is this standard single-storey roughcast lodge below a hipped roof with paired carved soffit brackets, now with a modern gate sweep but the old estate avenue now gone. A property in Farranboley townland in the early to mid-nineteenth century of whiskey magnate Sir John Power (1771–1855) for over 40 years, its entrance situated off the west of Clonskeagh Road.

Thom's; *BPB* (1929).

676. ROEBUCK [4], Roebuck; pre-1837; *demolished.*
At the junction of Clonskeagh Road and Wynnsward Drive was the lodge occupied in 1849 by Joseph Williams, porter to merchant John Ennis, who was living here as early as twelve years previously. Around 1870 Captain John Wynne (1799–1884) of the Rathmines Castle (*q.v.*) family came here and renamed the property 'Wynnstay'.

Lewis 1837; Griffith 1848–60; *Thom's*; *LGI* (1904).

677. ROEBUCK LODGE, Roebuck; pre-1837; *demolished.*
According to Lewis in 1837, 'formerly the manor-house, and about 50 years since the only house in the district with the exception of the castle', which was home in his latter years to Humphrey Minchin (1750–1830), who came here from Marlay House (*q.v.*), and thereafter until about 1849 to John Elliott Hyndman, either of whom may have been builder of the porter's lodge, on the site of which is a modern bungalow.

Lewis 1837; *Thom's*; Ball and Hamilton 1895.

678. ROEBUCK PARK, Roebuck (2).
A well-proportioned Regency villa built by Daniel Kinahan (1756–1827) which was lodgeless until his son George, wine and spirit merchant, inherited.

Goatstown Road gate; *c.* 1845; *demolished.*
On the approach from the nearest public road was a lodge occupied in 1849 by porter Anthony Lelis.

George Kinahan (1791–1853) was succeeded in the property by his eldest son Daniel, who only outlived him by seven years, to be followed by his brother George Kinahan (1823–1903), who created a new and lengthy avenue to the south.

Taney Road gate; *c.* 1870; architects possibly Millar and Symes.

A once-decorative little lodge, now overgrown and in an advanced stage of dereliction. Single-storey on an L-plan with hipped roof to the road and gabled to the avenue, with a moulded clipped verge and raised toothed quoins framing a glazed canted bay window, with its own roof, overlooking the gateway. Advancing alongside in the internal corner is a gabled hallway with architraved door and a pretty floral roundel in the apex. Of the contemporary entrance there are only the pathetic remains of one pillar of quarry-faced rusticated granite masonry and a small portion of quadrant in polygonal rubble facing. This lodge and entrance may well be the work of architects Millar and Symes, who are recorded as carrying out additions and alterations to Roepark Park, undated.

Lewis 1837; Griffith 1848–60; *IFR*; IAA.

ROEBUCK VILLA (see ROSEVALE)

679. ROOKVILLE, Rathmines; pre-1837; *demolished.*
The suburban seat in the early nineteenth century of the Codd family, which with its lodge was built over by architect/developer John Butler with terraced housing in the 1850s, swept away like all those Georgian villas on the western side of Rathmines Road Lower.

Lewis 1837; *Thom's*; Kelly 1995.

ROOKWOOD (see SPRINGFIELD)

680. ROSEBANK, Clondalkin; *c.* 1830.

A small estate recorded as the home of William Bayly in 1837 which had been acquired thirteen years later by Robert Heffernan, whose gatekeeper was then Thomas Reddy. In 1870 the property had been renamed 'Cappaghmore', probably by William Whitton, who may have been responsible for the bizarre addition to what was a plain single-storey standard harled porter's lodge with a chimney-stack to each gabled end. To the centre of the avenue elevation has been applied an entrance hall, its front door flanked by canted sidelights which are reflected in a six-planed 'pyramidal' roof independent of the main one; derelict. Slender Classical carriage pillars with recessed panel shafts in a modest triple gateway, the screen extended by limestone quadrant walls.

Lewis 1837; Griffith 1848–60; *Thom's.*

ROSEBANK (see OLD ORCHARD COTTAGE)

ROSEFIELD (see BELLE VILLE)

ROSE HALL (see RUSINA VILLA)

681. ROSE HILL, Stillorgan; pre-1837; *demolished.*
On Carysfort Avenue was this property of the Drevar family, in 1841 of George and seven years later of Henry, whose gatekeeper was Patrick Osborne.

Thom's; Griffith 1848–60.

682. ROSEMOUNT, Booterstown; *c.* 1825.

A modest but well-proportioned, and durable, little single-storey standard lodge with a shallow hipped roof and a central pedimented breakfront entrance hall, its door set in a rectangular recess. On each side are unfortunate modern casement windows in plain rendered walls. There is evidence of this lodge being built in that period when the Tudor Revival was becoming popular in the pair of tall, joined, diagonally set chimney-stacks rising from a rectangular base on the ridge. There is a good contemporary gatescreen with tall roughcast concave-walled quadrants, one with an architraved postern gate, framing a pair of carriage pillars with 'Rosemount' plaques, carrying early nineteenth-century spear-topped iron gates. C. Smith Esq. was the proprietor in 1837 and had been succeeded twelve years later by magistrate of police Hugh O'Callaghan, whose gate porter was then James Kane. A property now home to the Medical Missionaries of Mary.

Lewis 1837; Griffith 1848–60; *Thom's.*

683. ROSEMOUNT [1], Roebuck; pre-1837; *demolished.*
The once-vibrant house and grounds, in the nineteenth century of three generations of the Corballis family, are no more, the fine villa having been acquired and demolished in the 1980s by UCD. It was probably created around the time of his 1791 marriage by Richard Corballis (1769–1847), who complemented it with a porter's lodge that two years after his death was occupied by James McGarry, gatekeeper to his barrister younger son, John Richard Corballis.

Griffith 1848–60; *IFR*; Pearson 1998.

684. ROSEMOUNT [2], Roebuck; pre-1837; *demolished.*

A property that in the nineteenth century had a rapid turnover of occupants. In 1841 it was James Dillon Meldon, an attorney who moved on to Casino (*q.v.*) and by 1849 had been succeeded by Lewis Edward Leipsitt MD, whose gatekeeper was William Hoey. A fine pair of cut-granite carriage pillars survive from *c.* 1830, each with a tapering front incised in Soaneian Greek key pattern, stela-fashion. The cappings are inscribed 'Trimlestown', probably from around 1860, when the then proprietor, Edward Armstrong Vicars, altered the name of the place to 'Trimlestown Lodge'. The attendant porter's lodge had gone by 1907 and the forlorn avenueless pillars are now accompanied by a modern farm gate and mounting rubbish.

Thom's; Griffith 1848–60.

685. ROSENDALE, Shankill; *c.* 1860.
With Locksley (*q.v.*), one of a pair of neighbouring twin villas built by a property developer called Perry, who complemented them with matching porters' lodges. Single-storey standard below a high-eaved hipped roof with scalloped slates, the rendered walls having Irish pilaster quoins and to the main front an entrance frontispiece of a semicircular fanlit door flanked by piers carrying an open-pedimented gable. Extended by a bay to the left-hand side, its wide windows suffering the intrusion of ugly modern casements. The first occupant of Rosendale (subsequently reduced to 'Rosedale') was Thomas Fry.

Thom's; Pearson 1998.

686. ROSENEATH, Sandymount; pre-1871; *demolished.*
A house that appears in the directory of 1851 as the property of John Richardson, its lodge probably contemporary.

Thom's.

ROSEPARK (see ROSY PARK)

687. ROSETTA, Ballybrack; pre-1837/*c.* 1915.
One of the earliest residences in the Ballybrack area, of sufficient import to warrant a gate lodge. It may have been particularly basic, for about 1860, when Hugh Ferguson built himself a new house on the site, which he rebranded 'Rathleigh', he removed the old porter's lodge. Despite passing through a succession of owners thereafter, the property remained lodgeless until the twentieth century. The neat cottage that exists may have been added by the proprietor in 1910, a Dr Woods. It is a small, square, single-storey standard structure in red-brick facings, with a pyramidal roof rising to a central stack. Three-over-three sash windows flank the central sheeted door, which incorporates a tripartite 'fanlight'.

Thom's.

688. ROSEVALE, Roebuck (2).
Both lodges, now demolished, were in place by 1837 at each end of that portion of the avenue running parallel to Goatstown Road. Dr Lewis Edward Leipsitt is recorded here in 1837, but had flitted to Rosemount (*q.v.*) next door by 1849, when Rosevale was briefly taken by merchant John William Gillespie, one of whose gatekeepers was Samuel Jones. In the 1860s the property was renamed 'Roebuck Villa' before finally becoming 'Woodfield' about 1870.

Lewis 1837; *Thom's*; Griffith 1848–60.

ROS MÓR (see SABINEFIELDS)

689. ROSNEY COTTAGE, Glenageary; *c.* 1845; *demolished.*
The house was probably extended and given a romantic Gothic cloak at the same time as the porter's lodge was added to the property by banker Alexander Boyle. His gatekeeper in 1851 was William Whelan.

Griffith 1848–60; Pearson 1998.

ROSSLYN PARK (see LABURNUM LODGE)

690. ROSY PARK, Kill of the Grange; pre-1837; *demolished.*
A seat in 1837 of R. Brown Esq. which twelve years later had been acquired by solicitor Philip Lynch, with Abraham Holmes as his gate porter.

Lewis 1837; Griffith 1848–60.

691. ROYAL COLLEGE OF SURGEONS, St Stephen's Green; pre-1854; *demolished.*
The 'porter's lodge' identified in the Griffith valuation is not evident from the 6in. OS maps but may have been located off York Street and perhaps contemporary with architect Edward Parke's original building of 1806.

Griffith 1848–60.

692. ROYAL HOSPITAL, Kilmainham (3).
The masterpiece of Sir William Robinson, surveyor-general for Ireland, 'the earliest large-scale exercise in architectural classicism in the country' (Craig), built in 1680 for aged war veterans as the first of its kind in the British Empire. Its two main approaches seem not to have been lodged until the nineteenth century.

Western gate; pre-1837; *demolished.*
A gate lodge at the head of the great lime-tree-lined axial avenue at the South Circular Road in Bully's Acre graveyard, whose standing was rather usurped by the arrival of the present grand gateway salvaged for the other entrance.

Barrack Bridge gate; 1812; architect Francis Johnston.

By the old Bloody Bridge or Barrack Bridge, at the eastern end of Victoria Quay on the River Liffey, guarding the Military Road approach, stood this fine example of a gatehouse in the Romantic Castellated style, about which Brewer in 1825 had reservations: 'a tower-gateway, lately erected after a design of Francis Johnston, Esq. ... This crenellated gate possesses considerable beauty, but it may be doubted whether the adoption of the ancient style of military architecture was, in this instance, entirely judicious, as the object to which the gate conducts is in a different mode of design, and of a date comparatively recent as the seventeenth century.' Known in the early nineteenth century as the 'Richmond Guard Tower', after the lord lieutenant at the time of its erection. A composition not quite symmetrical about the central Tudor carriage archway and tripartite sash window above, with machicolated ramparts over that again having Irish crenellations. To three corners of the main block are narrow, buttressed square turrets, whilst the fourth displays a dominant circular stair-cum-flagstaff tower with mock arrowloops and machicolated parapet. To each side of the main archway are tiny lancet windows, one converted from a postern opening when the whole was moved to its new site. In 1846 the structure was relocated to this western gate, being rebuilt limestone block by limestone block at the expense of the Great Southern and Western Railway after the opening of Kingsbridge Station, which had created traffic disruption. In its rebuilding the gatehouse appears to have lost the original latticed casement windows and a great wooden portcullis gate. On its dismantling it was discovered that the architect had secreted his own coat of arms behind a perishable wooden cover, to be revealed in the course of time but prematurely thwarted by events.

Military Road gate; *c.* 1850; architect not known.

The arrival of the railway seems also to have resulted in the creation of this approach from the east, the gatescreen that marked the western gate being re-sited here. The ashlar carriage pillars are surmounted by lead trophies of arms dating from 1708 by William Kidwell; to one side a lower postilion gateway with mid-nineteenth-century ironwork complements the main gates. Across the road, suitably divorced from the greater architectural scheme of things, is this most eccentric of Italianate buildings. Essentially built off an L-plan with the most extraordinary of roofscapes, perhaps contrived thus to achieve attic headroom at a later date. The leading wings have shallow-pitched gables, one over a Venetian window, whilst in the internal angle is a mono-pitch-roofed arcaded porch, its walls with channelled rustication. To cap all this is a very fine stone-built 'Vanbrugh' bridged chimney-stack. All quite appealing but sadly abandoned and boarded up.

Brewer 1825; *Irish Penny Journal* (20 Feb. 1841); Craig 1980; 1982; Kenny 1995; Casey 2005.

ROYAL HOSPITAL FOR INCURABLES (see HOSPITAL FOR INCURABLES)

693. RUBY HALL, Kill of the Grange; pre-1837; *demolished.*
A seat in 1846 of James O'Brien which three years later had been acquired by William Foot, whose gate lodge then lay vacant.
Slater 1846; Griffith 1848–60.

694. RUBY LODGE, Blackrock; pre-1837; *demolished.*
A porter's lodge that had already gone by 1871 and in 1849 lay vacant, in the time here of merchant and money-broker Thomas Bradley. Surviving is a most singular entrance of a triple gateway formed by eight pillars, each with a round-headed recessed panel and moulded gadrooned capping, which contain four concave quadrants. Now St Catherine's Training College.
Thom's; Griffith 1848–60.

695. RUNNYMEDE, Dundrum; pre-1837; *demolished.*
An old eighteenth-century house, until his death in 1817 'of a fever, while attending his professional duty on circuit at Trim', the residence of Judge William Ridgeway. By 1837 it was the seat of J. Fitzpatrick Esq. and twelve years later of Captain John Mayne RN, whose gate porter was William Grace. Both house and lodge have gone, the former having been renamed 'Dun Emer' about 1903, when a guild promoting handmade carpets and printed books was established there.
Lewis 1837; Griffith 1848–60; Ball and Hamilton 1895; Pearson 1998.

696. RUSINA VILLA, Templeogue; pre-1837; *demolished.*
A small estate and house of *c.* 1830 of B. Brunton Esq., whose trustees had let it to Thomas Dillon by 1849, when the gatekeeper was James Maguire. By 1869 the property was called 'Rose Hall'.
Lewis 1837; Griffith 1848–60.

697. RUTLAND, Dolphin's Barn (2).
The whole area of this estate is lost to post-WWII housing. The early pre-1837 gate lodge on the northern approach from what is now Parnell Road was occupied in 1849 by Owen Brady, porter to Joseph Barnes, long-lived barrister. He added a second lodge to the west off Rutland Avenue before 1870. Both have been demolished.
Griffith 1848–60; *Thom's.*

698. SABINEFIELDS, Ballyboden (2).
A farm in 1849 of Patrick J. Moran, both of whose lodges, built before 1837, were then vacant, in common with most others in the vicinity. By 1869 the place had been renamed 'Beech Park' and more recently 'Ros Mór'.
Back lodge; pre-1837; *demolished.*
The rear avenue running into Knocklyon townland had been removed by 1907.
Front lodge; pre-1837/*c.* 1910.
What survives is a replacement structure. Single-storey in rough uncoursed granite, built off an L-plan with a gable to the avenue which may have had mock half-timbering, now roughcast over. The roof is otherwise hipped; occupied.
Griffith 1848–60.

699. SAGGART CEMETERY, Saggart; *c.* 1830.
A basic single-storey hip-roofed cottage with wide windows and door to the left-hand side of the three-bay road elevation. Sited opposite St Mary's RC church.

SAGGART (see TASSAGGART)

700. SAINTBURY, Killiney; *c.* 1825.
An eccentric marine villa, in the early nineteenth century home to Frederick Saintbury Parker. The porter's lodge is a modest single-storey cottage with its gable end to the road. Attached to the lodge of its neighbour, St Anne's (*q.v.*).

701. SAINTVILLE, Killiney; 1886.
A marine villa that originally had a shared access off Killiney Hill Road but gained another winding approach from the newly formed Station Road and this porter's lodge to monitor the distant gate. It is a tiny single-storey gabled roughcast two-bay cottage, its entrance doorway in a flat-roofed projection from the left-hand side. Modern casement windows and a concrete tiled roof spoil the Picturesque effect. The corbelled brick chimney-stack betrays its age; built by William Wallis Harris.

702. ST ALBAN'S, Monkstown; *c.* 1830.
Confined by the driveway and the Monkstown Road–Albany Avenue junction is the nucleus of a basic early nineteenth-century single-storey standard porter's lodge, amusingly given a late twentieth-century Classical facelift by the addition of a parapet raised to the centre to accommodate a sophisticated 'cash-and-carry' pedimented door-case set in a background of sand/cement rendering and flanked by a pair of extremely narrow plastic windows. Would the 1849 gatekeeper, James Madden, and his employer, Revd George Hazelwood, have approved? The gate pillars, contemporary with the lodge, have recessed panels and later sawtoothed brick bands to the cappings.
Thom's; Griffith 1848–60.

703. ST ANDREW'S, Rathmines; *c.* 1868; architect probably A.G. Jones.

A very smart and solid mid-Victorian Italianate lodge that probably formed part of a commission of architect Alfred Gresham Jones, which in the main was a 'dwelling house and premises for Andrew Armstrong' in 1867–8—a commission which ended in acrimony, the client suing his architect for negligence. Single-storey standard with an oversailing hipped roof, there is much innovative detailing in the plasterwork. The minimal entrance breakfront with its keystoned round-headed doorway has bead mouldings on the corners, a feature repeated on the main quoins, which stones have intermittent rather than alternate toothing blocks. There is further originality in the window surrounds, with shouldering to the heads repeated in the upper panes of what were two-over-two sashes. A plinth to sill level has been crudely re-rendered. To the ridge is a dapper chimney-stack with moulded capping and base.
IB (1 Jan. 1870); IAA.

704. ST ANNE'S, Killiney; *c.* 1860.
One of a number of big houses built in the vicinity by the speculative builder Joshua D. Chaytor, this being taken by William G. Du Bedat of Ballybrack House (*q.v.*) nearby, one of a family of stockbrokers in the city. Its porter's lodge, like that to Saintbury (*q.v.*), with which it is placed back to back, is particularly plain, being a single-storey cottage with a gable to the road.
Thom's; Pearson 1998.

705. ST ANN'S, Donnybrook; *c.* 1790/*c.* 1860; architect not known.

A property that originated as 'Annefield', so named to mark the marriage of the first owner Robert Perceval (1756–1839) and Anne Brereton. They would have built the late eighteenth-century gatescreen, which survives and consists of a pair of V-jointed rusticated Classical carriage pillars framed by stucco-effect concave quadrant walls containing low architraved postilion gateways. Beyond, to the back of the footway, is a pair of blind 'pavilions' with plain entablatures carried on pilasters, the walls relieved by moulded plaques, just as those to nearby Airfield (*q.v.*), with the name 'St Ann's' to each. The first OS map suggests that the left-hand 'pavilion' may well have screened an early lodge. What adds weight to this is the valuation of 1849, which identifies a lodge here, occupied by John Murray, whereas what survives is clearly mid-Victorian and must surely be a replacement. This would have been built well after the property was inherited on his father's death by his only son, Revd William Perceval (1787–1880) of Kilmore Hill, Co. Waterford, who too, in 1809, had taken an Anne as bride. She was the daughter of John Waring Maxwell of Finnebrogue, Co. Down, and thus was born the Perceval-Maxwell dynasty. Their fine Classical porter's lodge is single-storey standard with a hipped roof oversailing carved soffit brackets, the eaves being broken by an open-pedimented breakfront which contains a segmentally arched fanlit doorway with moulded surround. From the plinth rise plain corner pilasters that frame wide openings, which sadly now display hideous modern steel windows. On the ridge is a chimney-stack typical of the period, with a plinth and moulded corniced capping. In 1908 unrecorded alterations were carried out to the lodge, to designs and specifications of architect A.E. Murray.

Lewis 1837; Griffith 1848–60; *LGI* (1904); *IB* (3 Oct. 1908).

706. ST AUBYN'S, Ballybrack; *c.* 1860.

A single-storey standard lodge with a chimney-stack to each gable, finished in stucco effect with raised toothed quoins and dressings to small rectangular-paned casement windows. The projecting hallway has a keystone below the open pediment. Two carriage pillars with recessed moulded panels and 'St Aubyn's' on each. With the house a mid-nineteenth-century development, probably for Commander Aaron Stack Symes, the first entry for the property in the 1862 directory.

Thom's.

707. ST BERNARD'S, Carrickmines; *c.* 1865.

A tiny modest single-storey standard gabled porter's lodge, its front door off-centre, in stucco-effect sand/cement-rendered finish below a moulded eaves band; modernised. A property of the 1840s occupied by Hamilton Lane, although the lodge probably dates from the residency of Henry Garbois, professor of dancing.

Griffith 1848–60; *Thom's.*

ST BERNARD'S (see BERNARDVILLE)

ST BRENDAN'S (see HOME)

ST BRIDGET'S (see SPRINGFIELD)

708. ST BRIGID'S, Stillorgan; *c.* 1840.

Making up a pleasant collection of buildings with the church of *c.* 1712 and schoolhouse is this simple standard single-storey hip-roofed gatekeeper's cottage with roughcast walls, plain but for the blocked masonry door-case.

Pearson 1998.

ST CATHERINE'S (see CATHERINE PARK)

ST CLOUD (see VERNEY)

709. ST COLUMBA'S, Ballybrack; *c.* 1870; architect possibly A.G. Jones.

A standard single-storey hip-roofed lodge with contemporary back return and gabled breakfront containing a segmentally arched fanlit doorway flanked by bipartite casements in plain rendered walls. Looking very much like the lodges to Aughnacloy (*q.v.*), Inveruish (*q.v.*) and William's Park (*q.v.*), where, as here, the Classical chimney-stack with coved corbelling to its curved cappings is a common feature and identical to those on Strathmore House (*q.v.*), where architect Alfred Gresham Jones was employed. Here, too, he may have worked with the developer William Field, who is recorded as living here in the 1890s, although its first occupant was solicitor Charles Harte.

Thom's.

ST COLUMBA'S SCHOOL (see HOLLY PARK)

710. ST EDMONDSBURY, Lucan (2).

In 1801 'an elegant house, pleasantly situated, with a charming view of the surrounding country. The demesne consists of about sixty acres, is well wooded and highly improved; bounded by the river Liffey on one side, and the remainder enclosed with a stone wall. The gardens are elegant, with extensive glass for grapes, pines, peaches, &c.' The house had evolved in stages from its mid-eighteenth-century foundation to the present Regency appearance and function as a private hospital. Its two early lodges were built for either or both of the Rt Hon. Viscount Edmond Sexten Pery (1719–1806), who created the park, and his successor Thomas R. Needham, proprietor until 1853, whose gatekeepers three years earlier were John Carty and Michael Moore.

West gate; pre-1836; *demolished.*

The site of the secondary lodge is now occupied by a bungalow.

East gate; pre-1836/*c.* 1905; architects possibly Batchelor and Hicks.

The main entrance lodge occupies the site of its predecessor as an informal and jaunty 1½-storey composition with roughcast walls and a ground-floor sill course. To the park elevation is a pair of round-headed arched openings with an attic window over. The gabled roof has eaves sufficiently lofty to accommodate a decorative wooden gabled porch alongside a wide label-moulded window of the two-bay avenue front. Successive mid-Victorian owners carried out alterations to the big house: the Hon. Judge Walter Berwick in 1862 with J.S. Butler as his architect and, eight years later, William Moran to designs of Charles Geoghegan. On the strength of this little porch, however, it appears that the lodge dates from the turn of the twentieth century when the property became a private hospital, the firm of Batchelor and Hicks being engaged to carry out alterations from *c.* 1902. A relic of the time here ten years earlier of R.F. Butler may be the splendid eagles atop the carriage pillars—the Butler crest. These fine pillars, with their channelled masonry and reticulated blocks, framed by extensive shallow concave quadrant walls in stucco-effect finish, each pierced by a postilion gate, are much earlier and probably from the Pery era. The lodge lies pathetically abandoned and boarded up, going the way of its predecessor.

Archer 1801; Griffith 1848–60; *DB* (1 April 1862); *IB* (1 Jan. 1870); Ball 1995; *BPB* (1929); ffolliott 1970; Bence-Jones 1988; Lyons 1993; IAA.

ST ENDA'S (see THE HERMITAGE)

ST GABIEN'S (see WILLBROOK FLOUR MILLS)

711. ST GEORGE'S, Killiney; 1882; architect G.C. Ashlin.

In 1871 George Coppinger Ashlin (1837–1921) had been practising architecture for only eleven years before creating this home for himself and his wife Mary (Polly). It is little wonder that it deviated little from the

preachings of that great Gothicist A.W.N. Pugin, for in 1867 he had married his daughter, who was also sister to his partner E.W. Pugin. The red brick and some detailing from Ashlin's conspicuous High Victorian composition appears on the obligatory gate lodge, opposite the gates. Two-storey but appearing as single-storey to the road, with a striking off-centre gabled breakfront containing a pair of windows bound by a granite string-course and lintels trimmed by a blue engineering brick which also forms the architect's monogram over, framed by hefty ornamental wooden bargeboards rising from corbelled eaves features to an apex with a carved trefoil motif clasping a shield. Alongside is a peculiar blind wall in Flemish bond brickwork relieved by wide recesses. Another gable terminates in a half-hip, whilst the perforated red earthenware-crested ridge is broken by a channelled and sawtooth corbelled red-brick chimney-stack. Its date of construction is considerately set in mosaic.

Williams 1994; Pearson 1998; IAA.

712. ST GERMAIN'S, Ballybrack; *c.* 1880.
A lodge modernised, altered and extended since it probably originated as a single-storey standard hip-roofed affair built in the time here of Richard Holmes. Subsequently it realised its present L-plan with the addition of a projection from the right-hand bay and a canted hall built in the internal angle thus formed; occupied. A property once known as 'Obelisk Cottage', much enlarged and renamed in the mid-nineteenth century, the lodge survives its big house, back to back with that to neighbouring Ballybrack Lodge (*q.v.*).

Thom's.

ST HELEN'S (see SEAMOUNT)

713. ST HELEN'S, Lucan; *c.* 1840.
A residence in 1837 and 1851 of William Gorman, in which period was built at the entrance to the outbuildings a pair of plain harled gabled semi-detached estate workers' cottages; derelict.

Lewis 1837; *Thom's.*

ST HELEN'S (see FAIRYLAND)

ST ITA'S (see STILLORGAN RECTORY)

ST JAMES'S HOSPITAL (see FOUNDLING HOSPITAL)

714. ST JAMES', Milltown; *c.* 1865.
The quintessential south Dublin Italianate porter's lodge, now unrecognisable as such through much twentieth-century meddling.

Irish Architectural Archive

An old photograph shows it to have been single-storey standard and hip-roofed, with exposed rafter toes and a central gabled entrance breakfront hall containing a round-arched fanlit doorway, flanked by a pair of one-over-one sash windows with segmental heads and moulded surrounds in stucco-effect walls. Subsequently extended by a bay to the right-hand side and latterly by another, losing much detail in 'improvement' along with its scalloped roof slates. The original quarry-faced carriage pillars and chunky contemporary iron gates were framed by shallow rubble ogee quadrant walls. A development created by James Boswell, now lost in a modern apartment complex.

Thom's; IAA photograph (67/72 CSI).

ST JAMES'S PARSONAGE (see ASKE COTTAGE)

ST JOHN OF GOD HOSPITAL (see STILLORGAN CASTLE)

715. ST JOHN'S, Terenure; pre-1837; *demolished.*
In 1849 James Carroll was gate porter to Mrs Darley, who was probably the widow of William Darley, the proprietor twelve years earlier.

Lewis 1837; Griffith 1848–60.

ST JOHN'S (see PROSPECT)

716. ST JOHN'S, Inchicore.
One of a pair of semi-detached houses and its lodge built *c.* 1870 to accommodate senior personnel of the Great Southern and Western Railway in the halcyon days of that mode of transport, now all swept away for a modern road system.

Thom's.

ST JOSEPH'S COLLEGE (see PROSPECT)

717. ST JOSEPH'S CONVENT, Ranelagh; pre-1837/*c.* 1890.
The early porter's lodge may have served the big house of the locality—Willbrook, which was for some time the residence of a bishop of Derry. The surviving replacement lodge was built by the Carmelite nuns, who established their convent, a chapel and a girls' school here in 1788. A plain rendered single-storey standard structure, gabled, as is its hall projection, with a diamond-shaped window in the apex. A red-brick stack rises off-centre from the earthenware-crested ridge and synthetic slated roof with canted bands. Cowering behind a now-redundant bridge, the railway on which perhaps necessitated the rebuilding. In 1849 the gatekeeper was Francis Moore in the lodge that straddled the boundary of two townlands.

Lewis 1837; Griffith 1848–60; Joyce 1912; Kelly 1995.

ST JOSEPH'S CONVENT (see COSEY LODGE)

ST KEVIN'S (see BLOOMWOOD)

ST KEVIN'S PARK (see REDESDALE)

718. ST KEVIN'S PARK, Rathmines; pre-1850; *demolished.*
A house and its gatehouse built after 1837 for Frederick W. Conway, proprietor of the *Dublin Evening Post.* In 1850 the gatehouse lay vacant, its site today occupied by a two-storey red-brick gabled structure of *c.* 1890.

Slater 1846; Griffith 1848–60.

ST LUKE'S HOSPITAL (see RATHGAR)

719. ST MAELRUAIN'S CHURCH, Tallaght; *c.* 1770.

In total contrast to the characteristic spiky buttressed architecture of John Semple's replacement church of 1829 is this little rustic cottage, its whitewashed harled walls distinct against the masonry backdrop which it considerably pre-dates. Single-storey standard with tiny square windows, like its simple sheeted door, below segmental arches; still put to use but no longer housing a sexton/gatekeeper, it has now a shallow hipped roof with clipped eaves band which, curiously, in the twentieth century replaced the original gable ends. A charming survivor. The modest cut-stone carriage pillars, contemporary gates and pedestrian picket gates of an age with the church replaced the earlier entrance screen, when the old pillars were flanked by alternative accesses in a postilion doorway to one side and a stepped stile to the other. Work probably dating from the incumbency (1769–83) of Revd John Elton (1722–83).

Lewis 1837; Ball 1995; Leslie and Wallace 2001; Healy 2004.

ST MARGARET'S (see DONNYBROOK COTTAGE)

720. ST MARGARET'S, Stillorgan; pre-1837/*c.* 1852; architect probably J.S. Mulvany; *demolished.*
A fine late Georgian villa, seat in 1837 of iron merchant Thomas Mooney, whose

J. Nolan

gatekeeper twelve years later was Andrew Magrane. By 1852 the property had been acquired by the Hoey family, both James and Robert being recorded here in mid-century. They renamed the place 'Kilmacud' and almost certainly commissioned architect James Skipton Mulvany to carry out improvements, which included a grand new neo-Classical entrance portico and a replacement gate lodge. This he clearly felt need not be a stylistically appropriate prelude to the house; rather he indulged himself in a peculiar sort of Italianate Picturesque manner with oriental overtones, which he had been then offering to his other clients, the most remarkable feature of which was a bellcast roof, here particularly pronounced on such a small-scale building. This was further accentuated by hefty eaves and verge corbels, the ridges crowned by a pair of octagonal chimney-flues on a rectangular base and bound by a common capping. Single-storey, built off an irregular plan in rendering with narrow windows below round-headed hood mouldings and fancy dripstones. From the leading gable projected a canted bay, which contained the front door, below its own bellcast 'lid'. The gables sported shields with carved bearings. For a century a delightful and beloved landmark on the Lower Kilmacud Road, outrageously removed in the 1960s.

Lewis 1837; Griffith 1848–60; *Thom's*; Nolan 1982; *IADS* (2000).

721. ST MARK'S, Palmerston; pre-1836; *demolished.*
A property in 1837 of a Captain Foss of the Royal Hibernian School, who may have been the same Christopher V. Foss who was leasing the place to Thomas Conroy by 1850, when the gatekeeper was John Byrne.

Lewis 1837; Griffith 1848–60.

ST MARY'S COLLEGE (see GAYFIELD)

ST MARY'S (see WESTHAMPTON)

722. ST MARY'S LODGE, Ballsbridge; pre-1871; *demolished.*
A house and lodge first recorded in 1862 with William Graham as proprietor.

Thom's.

723. ST MARY'S CONVENT, Donnybrook (2).
The site of the old Donnybrook Castle, birthplace of Lord Chief Justice Downes, which by 1837 had become a boarding school, the grounds of which subsequently contained the convent and asylum run by the Sisters of Charity.

Rear entrance; pre-1837; *demolished.* Off the old Coldblow Lane, now Belmont Avenue, was a lodge to the old castle, now marked by the entrance screen of good iron gates and railings framed by large pillars topped by grand swagged stone urns.

Front entrance; *c.* 1910; architect not known.

A substantial two-storey gabled Edwardian gatehouse, three-bay in roughcast finish, with red-brick toothed quoins and dressings. To the main avenue front the eaves are broken by three conspicuous gablets with heart motifs to the apexes over square-paned casement windows, which are repeated on the lean-to glazed hall below, alongside the open porch, positioned asymmetrically. Otherwise windows are four-over-one sashes; obligatory Edwardian half-timbered effect to the main gables and two big red-brick chimney-stacks, symmetrically placed. The fine gatescreen looks to be mid-Victorian: six channel-rusticated corniced cut-stone pillars frame rendered convex quadrant walls and tripartite gateway with postilion openings having moulded surrounds. The remains of one decorative iron lantern tops one pillar.

Lewis 1837; *Thom's.*

724. ST MARY'S CONVENT, Harold's Cross; pre-1837; *demolished.*
Thomas Dunne was gate porter in 1849 to the then superioress, Mrs Mary Clifford, at the gates to the convent and female orphan house run by the Sisters of Charity.

Griffith 1848–60; *Thom's.*

ST MARY'S PRIORY (see TALLAGHT)

725. ST MICHAEL'S, Ballsbridge; *c.* 1870; architect perhaps J.J. McCarthy.

The 'sumptuous Italian Romanesque villa' may be attributable to the 'Irish Pugin', J.J. McCarthy, and perhaps also the striking entrance complex. All dating from about 1870, built for Alderman Michael Meade, the lodge is a neat essay in polychrome brick, though now all covered and highlighted by paint. Picked out are the toothed quoins and dressings to segmentally headed chamfered keystoned windows and the round-arched door opening set in a gabled projection. Single-storey standard and gabled, its brick stack out of reach of the decorator. On a plinth, the later wing to the right-hand side in like manner, with paired windows in matching surrounds. The conspicuous tripartite gateway is distinguished by a series of crisply chiselled granite drum pillars and chunky contemporary iron gates and railed quadrants.

Thom's; Williams 1994.

ST PANCRA'S (see MOUNT TALLAN COTTAGE)

726. ST PATRICK'S CHURCH OF IRELAND CHURCH, Dalkey; 1869; architect E.H. Carson.

Irish Builder

The *Irish Builder* magazine of 1 September 1870 is hugely revealing: 'Our illustration with this number represents a new Gate Lodge and School-house recently erected in connection with Dalkey Church. The building contains a large classroom or lecture-hall, and infant schools, together with apartments for the sexton. It is built in the most substantial manner of granite quarried on the site, and, as a specimen of wrought granite work is well worthy of a visit. The interior is fitted up in a superior manner. The lecture-hall has an open timber roof, stained and varnished. The entire cost (over £1,000) of the building was defrayed by the munificence of Charles Leslie, Esq., who has given it as a free gift to the trustees of the

church. The gas fittings were supplied by Messrs Curtis; the iron work by Maguire and Son; and the tiling by Sibthorpe and Son; the rest of the building was executed by day work under the superintendence of Mr Edward H. Carson, F.R.I.A.I., architect and C.E., 25, Harcourt-street.' Post-dating the church by 30 years, it is understandably commodious and in a matching manner of High Victorian Gothic Revival, basically raised off an L-plan, with a back return in uncoursed random masonry as pristine as the day it was built. It is 1½-storey and steeply gabled, with skew-tables over mainly chamfered pointed-arched openings with Y-tracery and a nice little cusped attic window; to the avenue front is a paired mullioned light below a label moulding, whilst from the leading wing extends a single-storey canted bay window. All very much as Carson would have completed it but for the once-dominant square two-storey entrance tower, originally containing an open porch but now shorn of its main feature—a lofty and acutely angled roof in French Renaissance manner with slated bands which rose to ornamental wrought-iron railings, decapitated to leave a ludicrous flat-roofed replacement lid, thus seriously damaging the architect's composition, even if it does reflect the church tower. To the road are double wooden gates and octagonal stone pillars with layered cappings. Despite the main benefactor having been Charles Leslie of nearby Carraig-Na-Greine (*q.v.*), over the entrance archway is the inscription 'Eric Birch Leslie J.P.'.

IB (1 Sept. 1870); Williams 1994; Pearson 1998.

727. ST PATRICK'S PARK, Bride Street; *c.* 1905; architect not known.

This is 1½-storey over a basement in pink facing brick with a stone band and canted single-storey bay window with stone roof facing the park as part of an informal three-bay front. Gabled with faintly foiled bargeboards, sawtooth earthenware cresting and long plain chimney-stack. Built to monitor a park laid out in 1903 as part of a redevelopment by the Iveagh Trust, which swept away old tenements next to the cathedral.

Pearson 2000.

728. St Stephen's Green Park.

ST PETROC (see EL DORADO)

ST PHILIP'S (see FAIRYLAND)

728. ST STEPHEN'S GREEN PARK, St Stephen's Green; 1880; architect J.F. Fuller.
A highly ornate 1½-storey Arts and Crafts Elizabethan Revival composition on an irregular plan in red brick with clay tiles to roof and serrated specials hung on dormer and gable apexes. To the ridge is perforated earthenware cresting and a towering corbelled brick chimney-stack. The sumptuously carved bargeboards are

influenced by those from Ford's Hospital, illustrated by A.W.N. Pugin in his *Ornamental gables.* The main roof catslides over the single-storey front, which contains heavily mullioned and transomed windows with part-leaded and part-squared lights. Designed to be viewed from every angle by James Franklin Fuller for Lord Ardilaun, principally as gardener's accommodation. It hardly cost any less to construct than the estimate of £2,256; the builder was Thomas Millard.

Pugin 1839; *IB* (1 Aug. 1880); IAA.

ST TERESA'S MONASTERY (see MOUNT TALLANT)

729. ST THOMAS, Whitechurch; pre-1837; *demolished.*
A house occupied in 1837 by Mrs Unthank, who was by 1849 succeeded here by Mrs Mary Fox, whose gate porter was Roger Mahon.

Lewis 1837; Griffith 1848–60.

730. SALEM, Rathmines; pre-1837; *demolished.*
A suburban villa in 1846 of merchant Samuel Lindsay, whose lodge lay vacant three years later and by 1907 had gone.

Slater 1846; Griffith 1848–60.

731. SALLYMOUNT, Willbrook; pre-1837.
A single-storey rubble-built cottage, a chimney-stack to each gabled end, now derelict and overgrown. Located at the base of a long avenue, laid out in 1770, which leads to the modest house now known as 'Riversdale', latterly the final home of W.B. Yeats. In 1837 it was occupied by J. Watson Esq., and twelve years later by Captain John Butler, whose gate porter was Peter Brien.

Lewis 1837; Griffith 1848–60; Joyce 1912; Craig and Fewer 2002.

732. SALLY PARK, Firhouse; pre-1837; *demolished.*
The seat in 1814 of Matthew Handcock, who in his time here planted 7,000 trees. His son, William Elias Handcock, had inherited the property by 1837; his gate porter in 1849 was James Ruth. The house, originally built *c.* 1770 by the first earl of Clanwilliam, is now a nursing home. A twentieth-century bungalow has replaced the gate lodge.

Leet 1814; Lewis 1837; Griffith 1848–60; Craig and Fewer 2002.

733. SALTHILL, Dún Laoghaire; pre-1837; architect J.S. Mulvany; *demolished.*
A house which had been appropriated by the Dublin and Kingstown Railway as a hotel by 1836, when architect J.S. Mulvany was commissioned to make alterations and additions, as well as providing two new gates and a lodge. In 1841 the establishment went under the name of 'Messrs Lovegrove's', but six years later the proprietor was Daniel Jones, with William Dowling as gatekeeper. The hotel was burnt and demolished in 1972.

Thom's; Griffith 1848–60; *IADS* (2000).

734. SANDFORD CHURCH OF IRELAND CHURCH, Ranelagh; 1826.

Samuel Lewis in 1837 tells us much of what we need to know: 'The name of this place is derived from the circumstance of Lord Mount-Sandford having, in 1826, erected and endowed an Episcopal chapel ... sympathising with a large population destitute of any place of worship for Protestants, his lordship liberally expended about £5,000 in building a church, parsonage, and school-houses, besides securing an endowment of £50 per annum to the chaplain. These buildings occupy a very interesting site ... Each school contains about 60 children of each sex, one half of whom are Roman Catholics; there is a lending library attached to the establishment.' The second OS map designates the right-hand one of these delightful and identical schoolhouses, which faced each other across the entrance, as also being a gate lodge. This development was all carried out during the incumbency (1825–58) of the Revd Henry Irwin (1773–1858). In 1868 the church was given a spanking new and eccentric cut-stone façade, and sometime later the left-hand schoolhouse was sadly removed, the only consolation being that their perfect symmetry no longer laughed at Lanyon, Lynn and Lanyon's design. The survivor is a five-bay single-storey structure with stacks to each distant gable. The central projecting entrance hall is similarly gabled in the form of a skew-tabled open pediment over a segmentally arched recess containing, as elsewhere, a mullioned casement window, like the rest now lacking its original charming latticed lights. The doorway is positioned to the side of the hall in stucco-effect walls. The straight railed screen and entrance gates which linked the two buildings survive, with the carriage pillars having tapered recessed panels but now minus their impressive lofty lanterns. Lewis, it seems, should also have given credit for this complex to Robert Newenham of neighbouring Sandford Cottage (*q.v.*).

Lewis 1837; Costello 1989; Leslie and Wallace 2001; IAA photo (S/9189/21-27).

735. SANDFORD COTTAGE, Ranelagh; pre-1849/*c.* 1870.

A Dublin property for many years of a branch of the Newenham family of Coolmore, Co. Cork, who were here until the death of bachelor Thomas Newenham (1813–52). Their lodge, noted in the valuation of 1850, was replaced by the survivor, perhaps for George Moorehead, a private tutor recorded here in 1870. This is a good mid-Victorian rendered lodge on an informal L-plan, gabled with deeply carved ornate bargeboards and a roof, with a three-flue cluster chimney-stack, which catslides over the internal angle to form a glazed entrance hall and porch carried on chamfered wooden posts. To the avenue gable is a semi-octagonal bay window with equivalent roof, whilst to the park gable, on this otherwise Picturesque-style cottage, is a Classical window with entablature on a pair of console brackets, and over, despite the fancy bargeboards, fascias which return on modillion brackets to form an open pediment.

Thom's; Griffith 1848–60; *IFR*.

736. SANDFORD GROVE AND SANDFORD HILL, Ranelagh; pre-1837; *demolished.*
Two villas built in the 1830s by Joseph Bewley, whose family lived on in them for a century before they were absorbed into the Jesuit Gonzaga College in 1949. The gate lodge, occupied in 1850 by John Casdell, would appear to have served both dwellings.

Griffith 1848–60; *Thom's*; Kelly 1995.

737. SANDFORD PARK, Ranelagh; pre-1837/*c.* 1895; architect not known.
An excellent late Victorian Arts and Crafts Elizabethan Revival 1½-storey cottage built off an L-plan in English garden wall bond red brick, with attic storeys clad in 'black-and-white' work. The lower wing contains an open entrance porch in the internal angle, its

plain earthenware-tiled roof supported by decorative turned wooden posts on dwarf walls. Erected for himself, along with a new house, by building contractor James Philip Pile, the property now accommodates Sandford Park School. Previously it was a seat of George Sandford, 3rd Baron Mount Sandford, who presumably built the earlier superseded lodge. Following his death in 1846 the place was acquired by Robert N. D'Esterre.

Griffith 1848–60; Kelly 1995.

738. SANDFORD TERRACE, Ranelagh; *c.* 1825; *demolished.*
A terrace made up of semi-detached and detached elegant Regency villas, with the exclusivity of its own porter's lodge.

Kelly 1995.

739. SANDYCOVE, Sandycove; *c.* 1845; *demolished.*
A lodge in 1851 of recent construction, which nevertheless then lay vacant, probably built by Hugh O'Reilly.

Griffith 1848–60.

740. SANDYMOUNT PARK, Sandymount; pre-1837; *demolished.*
A lodge on Newgrave Avenue where William Kiely in 1848 was gatekeeper to Michael Dillon, whose family was resident here for much of the nineteenth century.

Thom's; Griffith 1848–60.

741. SAN ELMO, Dalkey; *c.* 1875; *demolished.*
A development of a new house and gate lodge in the 1870s for wealthy tanner Henry Hayes, who had previously built Stratford (*q.v.*) in Rathgar to designs of Joseph Maguire. A short-lived lodge, reputed to have been a 'dormered cottage'; demolished *c.* 2004.

Thom's; Pearson 1998.

742. SANS SOUCI, Booterstown; pre-1837; *demolished.*
One of the earliest seats of the city's suburbs, built in the 1750s by Humphrey Butler, 1st earl of Lanesborough (*c.* 1700–68), which after the marriage of the 3rd earl in 1781 to Elizabeth Latouche became associated with that Huguenot banking family, who were resident here until the death of James Digges Latouche in 1827. Prior to this, his father, William Digges Latouche (*c.* 1803), had commissioned architect Richard Morrison to carry out additions and alterations to the house, which was demolished in 1948, preceded nine years earlier by its gate lodge. The entrance screen in part survives at the

end of Rosemount Terrace, now giving access to St Helen's (see Seamount), a function that it seems originally to have fulfilled for both estates. A tripartite gateway, described as noble in 1903, in rustic work, now sadly lacking its central carriage overthrow, which appears to have been a Tudor-style archway, built in antique brickwork, its chamfered reveals repeated in the flanking postern openings which are dressed in granite in rubble walls, suggesting that they may be of later date. In 1849 its gate lodge was manned by Andrew Crigley as porter to Richard P. O'Reilly, whose main seat was Castle Wilder, Co. Longford (*q.v.*).

Wilson 1803; Griffith 1848–60; Ball 1995; *LGI* (1904); *BPB* (1929); McParland *et al.* 1989; Smyth 1994; Pearson 1998.

743. SARAHVILLE, Ballybrack; pre-1871; *demolished.*
A lodge probably built *c.* 1857 by Crown Solicitor Stephen Seed, who had then succeeded to the property, now called 'Moorefield', after Edward Murphy.

Thom's.

744. SARZEY, Rathgar; pre-1837; *demolished.*
A property in the early nineteenth century of the Fleming family which by the turn of the following century had been built over.

Slater 1846.

745. SCHOLARSTOWN, Ballyboden; pre-1837; *demolished.*
A lodge that in 1849, in common with all four in this townland of the same name, mysteriously lay vacant. An ancient property, first of Bishop Adam Loftus in 1588, and in the mid-nineteenth century home to Mrs Dunne.

Griffith 1848–60; *Thom's*; NIAH.

746. SEAFIELD, Booterstown; pre-1837/*c.* 1900.
A small demesne in the early nineteenth century of Thomas Beasley, who was followed here *c.* 1847 by solicitor Thomas Crozier, whose gatekeeper was Christopher Rivers. This early lodge has been replaced by the present single-storey Arts and Crafts jumble known as 'Glenomena Lodge', with roughcast walls, half-timbered gables and multi-paned windows, all lurking shyly behind a tall stone wall and doors, barred to the Stillorgan Road; perhaps built by Captain Frederick Hardy RN, resident here in 1890.

Lewis 1837; *Thom's*; Griffith 1848–60.

747. SEAMOUNT, Booterstown (3).

Subsequently better known as 'St Helen's', as it was renamed in 1838 by Colonel Henry White, probably after Ellen, his wife since 1828. He was to remain here until 1851, having inherited Luttrelstown, north Dublin (*q.v.*), in 1847 on the death of his brother. His gatekeepers in 1849 of three lodges, in place by 1837, were George Mahon, Cornelius Guilfoyle and Samuel Smith. White, subsequently created 1st Baron Annaly, was but one of a succession of distinguished residents of St Helen's since its building as a brick mansion in 1754 by Thomas Cooley MP, most of whom seem to have had a part in its present sumptuous balustraded Italianate Portland stone-clad manifestation as a luxury hotel. Not least of these worthy occupants was Field Marshal Hugh Gough (1779–1869), later 1st Viscount Gough, who employed architect John McCurdy to carry out extensive alterations and additions to the house in 1863. Not one of its gate lodges survives, although its two splendid gatescreens on the Stillorgan Road can still be seen, one only as a photographic image. This was the most northerly of them, illustrated in Francis Elrington Ball's *A history of the county of Dublin* as having an extensive segmental forecourt to tall concave-walled stone quadrants with a pair of postilion doorways with keystoned and moulded surrounds, all framed by four lofty slender pillars with elegant pedestalled ball finials. At the entrance opposite Foster's Avenue is another conspicuous Classical screen, comprised of two very fine carriage pillars with channel-rusticated shafts, 'St Helen's' inscribed on each, Greek key bands, festooned friezes, oversailing moulded cappings and ball finials, all set off by modern iron railings and gates, a combination of new and salvaged material. A fourth gate and lodge seem to have been shared with its neighbour, Sans Souci (*q.v.*), on what was Gardiner's Row.

Griffith 1848–60; *DB* (18 Feb. 1863); Ball 1995; *BPB* (1929); Flanagan 1991; Smyth 1994; Heaney 1999.

748. SEA VIEW, Old Connaught; pre-1837/*c.* 1890.
A property in the early nineteenth century of the Smith family, of whom George Smith's gate porter in 1850 was John Ellis. That lodge was replaced by this surviving late Victorian structure, probably built by the proprietor in 1890, the wine merchant Edmund D'Olier, who had come from Roebuck Cottage (*q.v.*). Single-storey standard hip-roofed in a bland grey sand/cement render, it is lifted by a

quaint gabled porch with carved woodwork carried on posts off dwarf walls, its ridge, as the main one, decorated with perforated scalloped earthenware cresting. The segmentally headed openings now contain modern casement windows. The arrival of D'Olier and the new lodge may have heralded the change of name of the house to 'Knocklinn'.

Leet 1814; Griffith 1848–60; *Thom's*; Pearson 1998.

749. SEDBERGH, Merrion; *c.* 1850; *demolished.*
A property on Strand Road created in the mid-nineteenth century from land of the neighbouring Pakenham Lodge (*q.v.*), in 1862 occupied by a Captain Upton. Now obliterated by late twentieth-century development.

Thom's.

750. SHAMROCK COTTAGE, Dalkey; *c.* 1825.
A tiny standard single-storey hip-roofed cottage with a basic frontispiece of two piers carrying a gable over the front door; modern bipartite casement windows in stucco-effect sand/cement-rendered walls. Occupied in 1849 by Richard Fegan, porter to John Wilmott, renting from solicitor Terence O'Reilly, who was recorded as living here in 1837.

Lewis 1837; Griffith 1848–60.

751. SHAMROCK HILL, Donnybrook; pre-1837.
An old single-storey standard lodge, now thoroughly sanitised and extended by a bay, or completely rebuilt, at the entrance to a new townhouse development labelled 'Donnybrook Castle'. Hip-roofed and now chimneyless, it was in 1849 occupied by Denis Ryan as gatekeeper to snuff and tobacco manufacturer Patrick Nolan, also recorded here eight years earlier.

Slater 1846; *Thom's.*

SHANAVAUN (see JANEVILLE COTTAGE)

SHANDON (see MONTPELIER)

752. SHANGANAGH CASTLE, Little Bray (4).
'Corinken, the seat of Major Cockburne, a fine house, which commands an extensive view, with a demesne of an hundred acres, well planted and improved.' This is Archer's description in 1801 of the property to be transformed into the present castellated

fantasy by the same proprietor, soon to be advanced to the standing of General Sir George Cockburn, with some assistance from architect Sir Richard Morrison. A soldier in the Napoleonic wars, he also extended the house to accommodate his collection of Roman relics. He was probably responsible for building the three early lodges to the estate, photographic records of only one of which survives. One of these seems to have been accompanied and 'distinguished by a large gothic gate, which guards the approach to the concern', as recorded by A. Atkinson in the winter of 1814.

Sea lodge; pre-1837; *demolished.*
Removed before 1871, probably to make way for the development of Locksley (*q.v.*). In 1849 it already lay vacant.

North lodge; *c.* 1830; *demolished.*

Irish Architectural Archive

A delightful and tiny single-storey standard lodge with eccentric stepped gables, that to the road rising to form the chimney-stack. Roofed in minute slates over roughcast walls containing round-headed tripartite casement windows on each side of a later glazed porch, which obscured the front door. Sideways to the footpath, with a hip-roofed wing to one side and screen wall to the other, which contained a studded pedestrian doorway with surround part-Classically blocked and part-Tudor label-moulded. Alongside were the tall walled roughcast quadrants with sawtooth bands to copings and ball-finialled carriage pillars. Occupied in 1849 by gatekeeper Patrick Redmond.

South lodge; pre-1837/1926; architect R.H. Byrne.

The original gate lodge is shown by the OS maps to have bounded the roadside and to have been extensive, staffed in 1849 by Daniel Luff as gatekeeper to Phineas Cockburn, who had succeeded to the place on the death of his father two years previously. The demesne next passed to the Rowan-Hamilton family through marriage to Phineas's sister Catherine. By 1925 one W. Allen was in residence and had engaged Ralph Henry Byrne to design a replacement lodge at the main gate. He created a 'Tudoresque' composition, 1½-storey standard with hipped gables over attic windows. To the main front are chamfered mullioned tripartite windows with toothed dressings below label mouldings which flank a two-storey breakfront with granite quoins, a skew-table gable with finials and the door, an unfortunate 'cash-and-carry' Classical affair, under a label moulding stepped over the inscribed gate. All on a pronounced plinth in a grey render, with a chunky quoined chimney-stack breaking the ridge. A building now severed from the main property, independent, its original gatescreen of tall, castellated mock-Tudor piers having been removed in 1979.

Archer 1801; Atkinson 1815; *Parliamentary Gazetteer*; Bence-Jones 1988; McParland *et al.* 1989; IAA photograph.

SHANGANAGH COTTAGE (see BALLYBRACK COTTAGE)

753. SHANGANAGH COTTAGE, Little Bray; pre-1837; *demolished.*
A small six-acre holding in the shadow of Shankill House which had a succession of different occupants: in 1849 Mrs Eleanor Norman, whose gate porter was Mrs M. Doyle. By the mid-nineteenth century the property had become 'Shankill View', and later in the century 'Ferndale'.

Griffith 1848–60.

754. SHANGANAGH, Shankill (2).
A house thought to have been built in 1823 by William Hopper, who was still recorded here in 1857 and must have been responsible for the early entrance lodge.

North gate; pre-1837; *demolished.*
The first OS map indicates a long structure alongside the road.

South gate; *c.* 1870.

A lodge added to the property either by Matthew P. D'Arcy, who was briefly in residence around 1870 before flitting to Kilconrey, Co. Wicklow (*q.v.*), or his successor here, one Samuel Boyd. This is a neat little asymmetrically planned lodge below a regular shallow-pitched gabled roof with just a hint of the Italianate. Single-storey, two openings of its three-bay front set in a porch recess, its eaves supported on a pair of slender iron posts. Unusual one-over-two sash windows with granite sills and plain brackets in rendered walls.

Lewis 1837; *Thom's*; Pearson 1998.

755. SHANKILL CASTLE, Little Bray; pre-1837; *demolished.*
An ancient castle to which the Lawless family added an early Georgian house; it was acquired in the nineteenth century by the Domviles, who were leasing it to Washington Greville in 1849, when the place was a considerable holding. His gatekeeper was Thomas Byrne but both lodge and main house were already approaching dereliction, for the former had gone by 1871 and twelve years later the latter lay vacant.

Taylor and Skinner 1778; 1969 [1783]; Griffith 1848–60; *Thom's*; Pearson 1998.

756. SHANKILL, Little Bray; pre-1837; *demolished.*
In 1801 'the seat of Counsellor Roberts, beautifully situated on a hill above old Connaught; a fine house, which commands a most enchanting view of the whole surrounding country, the sea, town, and harbour of Bray, with its shipping, &c. and for planting shrubberies, garden, &c., stands unrivalled'. Sadly, none of this survives, the house having been cleared by 1871 to be outlasted by its lodge, which itself had succumbed by 1907. Robert Maddock was the proprietor in 1837, his gate porter twelve years later being Thomas Purcell.

Archer 1801; Lewis 1837; Griffith 1848–60.

SHANKILL VIEW (see SHANGANAGH COTTAGE)

SHEEP HILL (see ABBOTSTOWN)

757. SHERRINGTON, Little Bray (2).
A pleasant Georgian house, which was demolished in 1978, was the seat in 1814 of John Farran, followed in 1837 by J. Harvey Esq.

South lodge; *c.* 1830.
A plain structure, with its two-bay shallow gabled elevation to the avenue in recent stucco-effect sand/cement rendering. To the park a three-bay front of bipartite casements; on the ridge later sawtooth earthenware cresting. Its occupant in 1849 was David Quinn, porter to Judge Henry Martley, upon whose death in 1859 it passed to the Hon. John Plunket, and by 1870 it had become home to Wentworth Erck, who probably added the secondary lodge.

North lodge; pre-1907; *demolished.*

Leet 1814; Lewis 1837; Griffith 1848–60; *Thom's*; An Old Inhabitant 1907; Pearson 1998.

758. SILVERACRE, Rathfarnham; pre-1837; *demolished.*
Michael Rourke in 1849 was gatekeeper to Colonel William Miller, who had acquired the property from the Sweetman family and changed its name to 'Silverton', from which it reverted around 1870 in the residency of Charles H. Todd QC, LLD.

Brewer 1825; Slater 1846; Griffith 1848–60; *Thom's*; Healy 2005.

SILVERMOUNT (see SYLVANMOUNT)

759. SIMMONSCOURT CASTLE, Donnybrook; pre-1837; *demolished.*
Alternatively known as 'Simmonscourt Hall'

in 1837, when it was the seat of George Howell, by 1848 it had been acquired by Henry Forde, whose gatekeeper was then John Deighan. Subsequently in the 1850s and '60s it became home to the splendidly named Bartholomew Moliere Tabuteau.

Lewis 1837; Griffith 1848–60.

760. SIMMONSCOURT [1], Donnybrook; pre-1837; *demolished.*
A residence in 1837 of P. Madden Esq., which by 1848 had passed to Revd William Trocke, whose gate porter was Thomas Argue.

Lewis 1837; Griffith 1848–60; Slater 1856.

761. SIMMONSCOURT [2], Donnybrook (2).
A property now going under the name 'Kilronan' was during the later nineteenth century called 'Maryville'. Its two pre-1837 lodges had John Murphy and John Murray as gatekeepers to Nicholas M. Mansfield.

Simmonscourt Avenue gate; pre-1837; *demolished.*

Here is a very fine gatescreen in the Rococo manner, its pedestrian gates with dies over with the inscription 'Simmonscourt Lodge' and voluptuous fruit-laden urns to the carriage pillars.

Anglesea Road gate; pre-1837/1879; architect not known.

On a site not far removed from its predecessor is this pretty and precocious little lodge in a High Victorian Picturesque style, secure and selfishly hidden behind security gates and tall modern quadrant walls. Single-storey standard in a mellow maroon brick finish on a stone plinth, its steep main gables and that to the breakfront hall sporting chunky scalloped bargeboards with foiled perforations and spiky finials. The breakfront is bolstered by diagonal buttresses on each side of the doorway, fanlit with, like the casement windows to each side, chamfered reveals and segmental arches. The eaves have bold carved moulded wooden brackets with a brick sawtooth band between, a pattern repeated in the slating of the roof, which is crowned by a brick four-flue chimney-stack with chamfers and channels. Built in 1879 for William Nolan, who had acquired the property ten years earlier.

Griffith 1848–60; *Thom's.*

762. SION HILL, Booterstown (2).
A seat in the 1830s of stockbroker and agent Henry Lanauze, who by 1849 was leasing it to the Dominicans as a convent and school.

Main gate; pre-1837; *demolished.*

In 1849 the gate porter was Michael Devereux, but by 1871 his lodge had been removed. This entrance remained the principal access and now displays, on the junction of Mount Merrion Avenue and Cross Avenue, a pair of ostentatious beautifully carved granite carriage pillars with recessed panels containing cartouches and cappings crowned by crosses. To each side are straight grey-rendered wing walls, one having a pedestrian opening below a coping with dentil course. Perhaps part of the commission of architect John Loftus Robinson, who was engaged in alterations to the convent buildings in 1893, or J.J. McCarthy in 1880.

Secondary gate; pre-1940; *demolished.*
Further east was the shortest-lived of porter's lodges, built after 1907.

Lewis 1837; Griffith 1848–60; *Thom's*; Smyth 1994; IAA.

763. SION HILL, Glenageary; *c.* 1845; *demolished.*
Thomas Byrne was porter in 1849 to Robert Chambers, the lodge having been built after 1837.

Griffith 1848–60; *Thom's.*

764. SIR PATRICK DUN'S HOSPITAL, Grand Canal Street; *c.* 1825; *demolished.*
An institution founded in memory of a Scottish doctor in the city, the building of which was long and drawn out in the period 1803–16 to designs of Sir Richard Morrison. Its distinguished main front is now exposed to the street, having originally been obscured by an extensive high wall, which is clear from an illustration in the *Dublin Penny Journal* of 1835. This also reveals the hipped roofs of a pair of rectangular single-storey gate lodges, removed in the late twentieth century and remembered as having been otherwise plain. They are not shown in a view of 1818 and can thus be quite accurately dated.

Warburton *et al.* 1818; *Dublin Penny Journal* (17 Oct. 1835); McParland *et al.* 1989.

765. SKEAGH, Newcastle; pre-1937; *demolished.*
A lodge added after 1837 to this steward's property, possibly in the 1840s, when the Hon. Edward Lawless (1816–69) was in residence. In 1853 he inherited nearby Lyons, Co. Kildare (*q.v.*), on becoming 3rd Baron Cloncurry.

Griffith 1848–60; *BPB* (1929).

766. SLADEMORE, Rathcoole; pre-1837; *demolished.*
Another property of the Kennedys of nearby Johnstown-Kennedy (*q.v.*).

767. SOMERSET, Blackrock; pre-1837; *demolished.*
The seat in 1837 of W. Disney Esq., having previously been the summer residence of the Bourkes, earls of Mayo. Thomas Disney's gatekeeper in 1849 was James McKernal, his lodge, like the fine villa, being a thing of the past.

Lewis 1837; Griffith 1848–60; Pearson 1998.

768. SOMERTON, Esker; pre-1837; *demolished.*
Edmond Powell was gate porter in 1849 to John Smyth, the lodge perhaps contemporary with the pretty late Georgian cottage residence.

Griffith 1848–60.

769. SOMERTON LODGE, Sallynoggin (2).
A delightful rambling Georgian villa associated in the late eighteenth century with the Stowell family, who could have been responsible for both of its lodges. After their departure the property never had any settled occupants; Simon Foote of the Holly Park (*q.v.*) family was resident in 1837, and twelve years later Pentony O'Kelly, whose gatekeepers were Thomas Byrne and Thomas Kane.

East lodge; pre-1837; *demolished.*

West lodge; *c.* 1780.
Here are the sad ruins of a Georgian 'inkpot' lodge, single-storey circular with Gothic lancet windows in harled walls below a conical roof with corbelled eaves, its square wing like the rest a crumbling and overgrown shell. There was a gatescreen of four octagonal granite pillars with the property's name incorporated into the wrought-iron postern gates.

Lewis 1837; Griffith 1848–60; Pearson 1998.

770. SOMERVILLE, Edmondstown; pre-1837; *demolished.*
A house and cotton mill in 1837 of Francis Sommers. By 1849 he was leasing the property to John Reid and Sons, woollen cloth manufacturers, whose gatekeeper was Bartholomew Loughlin.
Lewis 1837; Griffith 1848–60; *Thom's.*

771. SORRENTO TERRACE, Dalkey; *c.* 1950.
A single-storey structure on an irregular plan with parapeted hipped roof and integral garage in a smooth rendered finish, probably built in the mid-twentieth century to augment the magnificently sited exclusive terrace of a century earlier.

772. SOUTH HILL, Booterstown; *c.* 1825/*c.* 1890.
James Apjohn MD, FRS, in the 1890s effected extensive alterations to the eighteenth-century house, home to his family for 30 years. These works also seem to have encompassed a major transformation of the gate lodge. Still discernible is its previous appearance as a single-storey standard hip-roofed structure with squared bipartite casement windows and chimney-stacks to each end, recognisable to the 1837 proprietor, A. Beytagh Esq., and its 1849 owner, William Pennefather, whose porter was Sylvester Fannell. It is now a smart four-bay two-storey villa in crisp rendering with one-over-one upper-floor sash windows in moulded surrounds below a shallow hipped roof. From the same make-over is a fashionable late Victorian gabled porch with ornamental carved bargeboards. Surviving intact and immaculately maintained is the elegant late eighteenth-century gatescreen bounding the semicircular forecourt with high concave quadrant walls contained by V-jointed rusticated block pillars, the outer topped by ball finials, the inner having narrow swagged friezes.
Lewis 1837; Griffith 1848–60; *Thom's*; Pearson 1998.

773. SOUTH HILL, Rathgar; pre-1837; *demolished.*
A seat in 1837 of John Elliott, wine merchant and Hanoverian consul, whose gatekeeper in 1850 was John Tobin. The fine bow-fronted Georgian house around 1939 went the way of its gate lodge.
Lewis 1837; Slater 1846; Griffith 1848–60; Pike and McDowell 1908; Glin *et al.* 1988.

774. SPAFIELD, Ballsbridge; pre-1837; *demolished.*
A terrace of four houses off Merrion Road which had the cachet of their own gate lodge, on a site by 1907 completely built over.

775. SPIRE VIEW, Rathmines; pre-1837; *demolished.*
The porter's lodge in 1849 lay vacant, its immediate lessor then Frederick Jackson, solicitor and renowned property developer. The adjacent creation of Grosvenor Road West doubtless hastened its demise.
Griffith 1848–60.

776. SPRINGBANK, Ballyboden; pre-1837; *demolished.*
A house in 1837 of Thomas J. Wyse, alternatively known as 'Springfield', was twelve years later home to Thomas Thornhill, leasing from the Wyse family, the porter being John McGrath. About 1860 the property was acquired by barrister John C. Hodgens, who changed its name to 'Rookwood', which it remains.
Lewis 1837; *Thom's*; Griffith 1848–60.

777. SPRINGFIELD, Golden Ball; pre-1837; *demolished.*

In 1837 Lewis notes 'the residence of T. Thompson, Esq., a handsome modern mansion'. This Thomas Thompson had as his porter in 1849 Edward Mallen; eleven years later the property was sold as an incumbered estate, the sales advertisement stating that 'the entrance to the Demesne consists of a handsome Iron gate with gate-keeper's lodge adjoining'. Regrettably it no longer adjoins, having been replaced by a football pavilion, but is survived by the remains of its highly distinctive and unusual gatescreen, comprised of four pillars built up in alternate sections of deeply vermiculated blocks which continue as banding to the quadrant walls. Iron railings and gates are replaced with hideous shiplap boarding.
Lewis 1837; Griffith 1848–60; Lyons 1993.

778. SPRINGFIELD, Roebuck; pre-1837; *demolished.*
An eighteenth-century house purchased in 1806 by Matthew Franks of Jerpoint, Co. Kilkenny (*q.v.*), which was occupied until his death by his brother, Sir John Franks QC (1769–1852), who by 1843 had changed its name to 'St Bridget's'.

779. SPRING HILL, Dalkey; pre-1851; *demolished.*
A lodge identified by the valuation as occupied by William Maguire as gatekeeper to Thomas Deighan in 1851.
Griffith 1848–60.

780. SPRINGMOUNT, Little Bray; pre-1837/*c.* 1890.

Lawrence Kelly was gate porter in 1849 to Henry J. Hughes, occupying the early lodge which was replaced in the late nineteenth century by Patrick Ross Murphy. This successor nestles snugly below road level behind the demesne wall. Irregular in plan and outline, with a gablet to the road, catslide roofs and, over the canted bay window avenue front, a gable with half-timbered effect. The good granite octagonal gate pillars with layered cappings look to be earlier.
Griffith 1848–60; *Thom's.*

781. SPRINGMOUNT, Woodtown; pre-1837; *demolished.*
Solicitor Daniel Molloy's gate lodge in 1849 lay vacant. Leasing from Minchin Lucas, he may be the same Daniel Molloy of Clonbela, Co. Offaly, who died in 1856.
Griffith 1848–60; *LGI* (1904).

782. SPRINGVALE, Ballyboden; pre-1871; *demolished.*
Robert Sherlock is recorded here as early as 1837, his lodge being built after that date. A Robert Alexander Sherlock of Springvale is noted as wadding manufacturer of the neighbouring Edmonstown Mills in 1870.
Lewis 1837; *Thom's.*

STEEVENS'S HOSPITAL (see DR STEEVENS'S HOSPITAL)

STEWART'S INSTITUTION (see PALMERSTON)

783. STILLORGAN CASTLE, Stillorgan (2).
The old Wolverston House on the site was replaced as 'Mount Eagle' around the turn of the nineteenth century and was first occupied as such by the young historian and philologist William Monck Mason (1775–1859). He either inherited or built the early lodge located behind the right-hand entrance quadrant, but by 1871 it had gone, to be

superseded by that surviving opposite the gates. Looking to date from *c.* 1830, it may have been erected by the next occupant of the house, the lawyer and wit Henry Deane Grady KC, MP (1765–1847), of Lodge, Co. Limerick. He also probably romanticised the house by the addition of the Tudor label mouldings and crenellated parapet with mock bartizans, and renamed it 'Stillorgan Castle'. The gatehouse, which d'Alton in 1836 considered 'very handsome', is two-storey with a symmetrical three-bay ground floor and two-bay upper storey, with roughcast walls and V-jointed quoins below a hipped roof. Grady's gatekeeper in 1849 was John Doyle. In 1882 the house ceased to be a private residence when it was sold by David Sherlock QC, MP (1816–84), to the Brothers of St John of God as the Maison de Santé, St Patrick's House. The Brothers enlarged it as a hospital for 'invalid gentlemen' and promptly reinstated the lodge on their side of the road, but it fell victim to road-widening and realignment in the late twentieth century.

D'Alton 1976 [1838]; Griffith 1848–60; *Thom's*; *LGI* (1904); Ball 1995; Flanagan 1991.

784. STILLORGAN, Stillorgan (3).
From 1695 Colonel John Allen MP, the future 1st viscount, created one of the finest and most extensive demesnes in County Dublin, but after the family's male line died out two generations later in 1745 the property's fortunes fluctuated in other hands. Sir Edward Lovett Pearce's famous obelisk survives in a park of that name (*q.v.*), resulting from the breakup of the place into smaller lots. Archer in 1801 laments its fate: 'at present inhabited by Nicolas Lefevre, Esq. the estate of Lord Carysfort. This house and demesne, when in the hands of Lord Carysfort, was one of the most beautiful seats in Ireland; but at present it is to be subdivided, that it loses its former splendour. The original demesne, when united contained upwards of an hundred acres, finely wooded and watered, with elegant gardens, &c.' The coming of John Verschoyle (1752–1840) in 1803 saw a revival, albeit in reduced size, and it may have been his improvements which saw the building of lodged entrances, perhaps to designs of George Papworth around 1811.

'Back lodge'; pre-1837; *demolished.*
So called in the 1849 valuation, when it lay unoccupied. Only yards north of the main gate on the Stillorgan Road, it served the approach to the out-offices.

Front lodge; pre-1837; *demolished.*
A pair of lodges, in 1849 separate homes to Joseph Hall and Michael Murray, working for the new landlord Arthur Lee Guinness (1797–1862), who, after taking the estate following Verschoyle's death, built up its reputation as a place of lavish hospitality. The stout funding seems to have dried up, however, to the extent that after his passing the demesne and house suffered a relapse, it being demolished *c.* 1880. Although this entrance by 1871 was already avenueless and redundant, the lodges survived well into the twentieth century and were described nostalgically by Samuel Beckett: 'But the wall was unbroken, and smooth and topped uninterruptedly with broken glass, of a bottle green. But let us cast a glance at the main entrance, wide enough to admit two large vehicles abreast and flanked by two charming lodges covered with Virginia creeper and occupied by large deserving families, to judge by the swarms of little brats playing nearby, pursuing one another with cries of joy, rage and grief.' The eventual demise of this entrance was probably brought about by the demands of the motor vehicle.

A new villa was built on the site, 'Park House' or 'Stillorgan Park', in the 1880s for Henry James Monahan, who also erected a third lodge on the rear approach from Ulster Terrace, which has suffered the same fate as its counterparts.

Archer 1801; Griffith 1848–60; *Thom's*; Ball 1995; *BPB* (1929); Beckett 1958; Bence-Jones 1988; Flanagan 1991.

785. STILLORGAN PRIORY, Stillorgan; pre-1837; *demolished.*
'... a handsome residence in the Elizabethan Style built in 1833 near the site of the old abbey' by the Rt Hon. Anthony R. Blake, who may also have given the place the gate lodge on the Stillorgan Road alongside elaborate castellated gates, now all swept away. From the late 1840s for upward of 30 years it became home to Patrick Sweetman (1803–85), whose country seat was Longtown, Co. Kildare (*q.v.*). With his brother John, who lived across the road at Beaufield (*q.v.*), he was partner in the brewing business of P. and J. Sweetman. The gate porter in 1849 was William Staunton.

Lewis 1837; Griffith 1848–60; *LGI* (1904).

786. STILLORGAN RECTORY, Stillorgan (2).
Eventually becoming a private house, 'St Ita's', in the later nineteenth century, when it was considered on Newtownpark Avenue too remote from the parish church of St Brigid's (*q.v.*). It was home in 1837 to Revd Rawdon Griffith Green (*c.* 1790–1862), perpetual curate to the parish (1815–39).

Back lodge; pre-1837; *demolished.*
The porter in 1849 to the rector Revd John Grant was 'Widow' Dooling.

Front lodge; *c.* 1830.
Now 'Chestley Lodge', it was a single-storey standard structure, the hipped roof having paired carved soffit brackets in the Regency manner. It now has a new house added on and its front elevation sullied with a skin of concrete brickwork. The 1849 gatekeeper was Hugh Byrne.

Lewis 1837; Griffith 1848–60; Leslie and Wallace 2001.

787. STILLORGAN RESERVOIRS, Stillorgan; *c.* 1885; architect probably Parke Neville.
A sturdy and substantial structure in a Tudor Revival style, built in quarry-faced uncoursed granite rubble. Two-storey with skew-table gables, informal in plan, three-bay

with a gabled breakfront right-hand bay and a central single-storey hallway projection. Well served by chunky chimney-stacks, doubtless designed by the waterworks engineer Parke Neville, who also created a conspicuous octagonal pump-house.

Pearson 1998; Williams 1994.

788. STONEHENGE, Killiney; pre-1907; *demolished.*
A house, and presumably its lodge, built *c.* 1880 for Lieutenant-Colonel James Graham, subsequently renamed 'Susquehanna'.

Thom's.

789. STONEHOUSE, Booterstown; *c.* 1845; *demolished.*

John Barton is recorded here in 1837 and again as late as 1870. He had added a gate lodge to the property by 1849, when his porter was Patrick Donnelly. Surviving is a good entrance screen dominated by a pair of granite ashlar postilion arches with entablatures, the dies on which have the inscriptions 'Stone' and 'House'.

Lewis 1837; Griffith 1848–60; *Thom's.*

790. STONE VIEW, Dún Laoghaire; *c.* 1821; *demolished.*
Along with Granite Hall (*q.v.*), one of a pair of neo-Classical villas built around 1821 by stone contractor George Smyth, this one for his son Samuel, who had passed on by 1851, when the gatekeeper was John Delany. His gate lodge was equally short-lived, having gone by 1871, overrun by Clarinda Park.

Griffith 1848–60; Pearson 1981.

791. STONE VILLE, Rochestown; pre-1837.
In 1801 'the seat of Colonel Pratt, a good house, with a fine view, and a well improved demesne of twenty-six acres, and a good garden'. This was presumably the noted military topographer Colonel Charles Vallencey Pratt (1789–1869), who succeeded his father here and whose gate porter in 1849 was Denis Doyle. What may have been a plain single-storey hipped-roof cottage, its short front to the avenue, has been much extended and modernised. Inaccessible, there are granite entrance pillars with garage doors set into the right-hand concave rubble quadrant. By 1870 the new owner, Captain Frederick Wise, had renamed the property 'Laughton'.

Archer 1801; Griffith 1848–60; *Thom's*; Crookshank and Glin 1994.

792. STRADBROOK HALL, Stradbrook; *c.* 1907; architects probably Millar and Symes.
A house built *c.* 1850 for Francis Codd, known then as 'Strickland', which remained lodgeless until the turn of the twentieth century, when architects Millar and Symes were carrying out alterations and adding a verandah to the house for Richard Pim. The two-storey gatehouse, set well back from the gate, presented its single-bay front to the avenue, with a canted oriel first-floor bedroom window carried, like the jettied gable over, on a pair of wooden brackets. Probably once a lot more decorative, it is now finished in a roughcast rendering with undistinguished modern plastic windows.

Thom's; IAA.

793. STRADBROOK, Stradbrook (3).
A property in the first half of the nineteenth century of Ulster King at Arms Sir William Betham, who may have built all of the lodges.

North lodge; *c.* 1830.
Now 'Oakdene Lodge' but originally a simple two-roomed single-storey cottage, a short gabled elevation addressing the avenue with two tiny sidelights flanking the entrance doorway, which now sports a jaunty, faintly oriental bracketed canopy over. The whole has been extended with a wing to the road and elongation to the rear. A remarkable survivor. By 1849 Daniel Kavanagh was the porter to J.J. Murphy, to whom the place was being leased by Betham.

South-east lodge; pre-1837; *demolished.*
Around 1850 'Brooklawn' (*q.v.*) was built in the grounds, thereby purloining this secondary entrance off Stradbrook Road.

South-west lodge; pre-1837; *demolished.*
A building that survived into the twentieth century, minus its entrance and avenue off Newtownpark Avenue.

Thom's; Griffith 1848–60.

794. STRATFORD, Rathgar; *c.* 1865; architect possibly Joseph Maguire.
A development on Orwell Road probably for Henry Hayes, who by 1873 was already commissioning architect Joseph Maguire to design a new conservatory and various other alterations and additions. The lodge is certainly modest enough to have been by him. Single-storey standard and hip-roofed with a gabled breakfront hall, the apex to which is now boarded, the walls otherwise smooth-rendered; alongside a mansard-roofed 1½-storey extension. Henry Hayes shortly afterwards, *c.* 1875, was to be found living at San Elmo, Dalkey (*q.v.*).

Thom's; *IB* (15 Oct. 1873).

795. STRATHMORE, Killiney; *c.* 1870; architect possibly A.G. Jones.
A good Italianate villa designed by Alfred Gresham Jones and built around 1871, on a virgin site with superb sea views over Killiney Bay, for retired wine merchant William Henry. The lodge is a much-abused two-storey mid-Victorian gatehouse with very little of its original character or detailing showing through, other than stone moulded brackets to the first-floor jettying.

Thom's; Pearson 1998; IAA.

796. SUMMERHILL, Killiney; *c.* 1890.

A villa of *c.* 1860, previously 'Santa Severino', of Mrs Ladaveze Aldecron until it was acquired and renamed by Sir John Barrington, lord mayor of Dublin in 1865 and 1879. After his death in 1887 the property was purchased by George F. Stewart, who presumably added this outstanding Arts and Crafts Elizabethan Revival-style gatehouse. Commodious and built off an L-plan, part-two- and part-1½-storey with steep gables, one with a canted attic oriel window on carved brackets below a half-timbered-effect apex. The upper storey is defined in roughcast, with a bold bellcast over the brick-faced ground floor with its small-paned casement windows and an open porch with post support. Surviving much modernisation are some curved ornamental bargeboards and serrated red cresting broken by a rebuilt red-brick chimney-stack.

Thom's.

797. SUMMERVILLE, Windy Arbour; *c.* 1870.
A standard single-storey hip-roofed lodge with brick highlights as segmental arches to openings, toothed dressings, keystones and quoins, all picked out in black and white paint. In the mid-nineteenth century a house of ever-changing residents, the house perhaps enlarged and lodge added during the occupancy of George Heather.

Thom's.

798. SUSANVALE, Kilmainham (2).
A property which in 1837 encompassed 'The Hibernian Mills, established in 1812 by Messrs Willans, for the manufacture of the finest woollen cloths, which trade they have successfully pursued, and having greatly extended their establishment, it affords employment to nearly 500 persons, for whose residence the proprietors have erected suitable dwellings, and also a place of worship for the Independent denomination'. Thomas Willans was the proprietor in 1849, when the porters in his two pre-1837 gate lodges on Inchicore Road were Charles Harvey and Dudley McEvoy. Both have gone.

Lewis 1837; Griffith 1848–60.

SUSQUEHANNA (see STONEHENGE)

799. SWASTIKA LAUNDRY, Ballsbridge; 1914; architect F. Hayes; *demolished.*
'The new lodge for the Swastika Laundry, Ballsbridge is now completed. It has a slated roof, red brick plinth to the exterior of the walls, the remainder being pebbledashed. Mr Frederick Hayes M.R.I.A.I., is architect and Messrs Jones & Sons, Stephen's Green the builder.'

IB (3 Jan. 1914).

800. SWEETMOUNT, Dundrum; *c.* 1820; *demolished.*

IAA/Craig Collection

A sweet and minuscule lodge, single-storey standard with simple casement windows in vernacular whitewashed harled walls below a distinctively bellcast hipped roof with a finish of tiny slates; the chimney-stack was out of sight, probably rising off the rear wall. Nestling behind cut-stone gate pillars with recessed panels and gadrooned caps, looking somewhat later. A seat in 1837 of W. Nolan Esq., renamed 'Orchardton' around 1860. In 1849 the lodge lay unoccupied in the time here of Revd Bernard Kirby.

Lewis 1837; Griffith 1848–60; *Thom's*; IAA (Craig photograph 1/968B).

801. SWEETMOUNT HOUSE, Dundrum; pre-1869; *demolished.*
A lodge probably built by solicitor John Lee Wharton after 1837, when the proprietor was M. Ryan Esq. Wharton's gatekeeper in 1849 was Thomas Kavanagh.

Lewis 1837; Griffith 1848–60; *Thom's.*

802. SWIFTBROOKE, Saggart; pre-1837; *demolished.*
Formerly a residence of Dean Swift, where in 1836 'Mr John McDonnel has two paper factories, employing nearly 200 persons'.

D'Alton 1976 [1838]; Lewis 1837.

803. SWIFT'S HOSPITAL, Kilmainham (3).
Alternatively known as 'St Patrick's Hospital', begun in 1749 and opened in 1757,

a dignified building which was approached from two lodged gates at Bow Lane and Steeven's Lane, both in place before 1837. These little buildings, neither of which survive, in hard times past were pressed into service as billets for ward maids and extended accordingly. They were also the scene of deaths from such diseases as typhoid, prompting the installation of WCs. In 1882 Sandham Symes was succeeded as architectural adviser to the hospital board by James Rawson Carroll, who amongst other alterations and additions in 1892 designed the grand new entrance and porter's lodge. Across the meeting of the lanes, flanked by tall granite ashlar quadrant walls, is a tripartite gateway comprised of four rusticated pillars, each with four-sided pediment caps, the outer with ball finials, the inner crowned by ornamental iron lanterns. Within is a Classical lodge in cut granite, single-storey standard but raised from the ordinary by an all-embracing pediment to the three-bay front and the doorway sheltered by a heavy entablature on a pair of Roman Doric columns, lacking entases, flanked by windows whose lugged moulded surrounds rest on a prominent sill band. The casement lights are mullioned and transomed, like the rest somewhat less than delicate.

IB (1 April 1897); Malcolm 1989; Casey 2005.

804. SYDNEY LODGE, Merrion; pre-1837; *demolished.*
A property in 1841 of John Hall, closely followed by solicitor Richard Charles McNevin, whose lodge seven years later lay empty.

Thom's; Griffith 1848–60.

805. SYLVANMOUNT, Shankill; pre-1837; *demolished.*
Alternatively known as 'Silvermount', it was a seat in 1837 of G. Hillas Esq. and twelve years later a property of Robert Tilly of neighbouring Chantilly, whose gate porter was then John Graham.

Lewis 1837; Griffith 1848–60.

806. TALBOT LODGE, Stillorgan; pre-1837; *demolished.*
The Dublin seat in 1837 of Captain Newenham, probably of the Coolmore, Co. Cork, family, later taken by the Sankeys, whose lodge in 1849 lay unoccupied. The house has likewise gone.

Lewis 1837; Griffith 1848–60; *Thom's.*

807. TALLAGHT COTTAGE, Tallaght; *c.* 1860; *demolished.*
A lodge built by Patrick Hudson, who had acquired the property in 1856 from John McDougell, in so doing building a new house.

808. TALLAGHT, Tallaght; pre-1837; *demolished.*
An estate that carries an inglorious architectural history. The castle commenced here in 1324 by Archbishop Alexander de Bicknor was eventually completed by 1349 but quickly fell into disrepair; it was demolished in 1729 by Archbishop Hoadley, who replaced it with a palace 'spacious, but long and narrow, and destitute of pretentions to architectural beauty'. This was pronounced surplus to Church needs and sold in 1822 to Major Palmer, who demolished it and replaced it with a decent Regency mansion, perhaps complete with a contemporary gate lodge. By 1825 it had been acquired by John Francis Nicholas Lentaigne (1803–86), whose gatekeeper in 1849 was Christopher Fay, but in 1856 he sold the place to the Dominicans, the house serving as the priory until a new one was built; thereafter it was unceremoniously absorbed into a great retreat house and is now unrecognisable.

Brewer 1825; d'Alton 1976 [1838]; Griffith 1848–60; *IFR*; Healy 2004.

809. TANEY CHURCH OF IRELAND CHURCH, Dundrum; *c.* 1824; architect possibly William Farrell.

Flanking the wide gravelled forecourt of the church, built in 1818, is what appear to be a pair of Georgian Gothic cottages. That to the left-hand side was in fact erected around 1836 as a Sunday School. As for that opposite, 'At the Easter Vestry in 1824, Mr James Crofton, the outgoing church warden, presented his account, amounting to £90, for building the sexton's lodge, and finishing the vestry-room'—a very generous price from the proprietor of Roebuck Castle (*q.v.*) for this four-bay single-storey hip-roofed roughcast structure, having the most elegant squared sash windows with Y-traceried heads below four-centred arches. The designer may have been the diocesan architect William Farrell, who had prepared plans for the church six years earlier. All work carried out during the incumbency (1818–51) of Revd Archdeacon John Torrens (1768–1851). A layout reminiscent of that at Sandford Church (*q.v.*).

D'Alton 1976 [1838]; Lewis 1837; Ball and Hamilton 1895; Leslie and Wallace 2001.

810. TANEY HILL, Dundrum (2).
This was in 1837 the seat of Walter Bourne (1766–1848), whose gate porters were, in the year of his death, John Logan and Peter Cullen, who, the OS maps suggest, occupied pre-1837 semi-detached accommodation by the entrance, at which but a solitary cut-granite carriage pillar remains.

Lewis 1837; Griffith 1848–60; Ball and Hamilton 1895.

811. TANEY LODGE, Ballinteer (2).
In 1837 a gate lodge lay on Ballinteer Road at the junction of a cul-de-sac leading to Taney Lodge and Ballinteer Cottage beyond. By 1869 the former had its own porter's lodge, probably built by Henry Parsons, who had acquired the property. The 1907 OS map shows Taney Lodge to have been demolished but survived by its lodge. Ballinteer Cottage, home to the Ruskell family, had by 1870 been elevated to 'Villa' status. Both inner and outer lodges have been demolished.

Griffith 1848–60; *Thom's.*

812. TANEY LODGE, Dundrum; pre-1837; *demolished.*
An estate in 1837 of William Corbett, whose gatekeeper twelve years later was Thomas Moore. By 1856 the property had passed to confectioner Adam Woods and its name altered to 'Woodlawn'. The entrance is remembered for enormous wrought-iron gates hung on granite pillars but almost obscured by a pair of gigantic chestnut trees.

Lewis 1837; Griffith 1848–60; Slater 1856; Nolan 1982.

813. TASSAGGART, Saggart; *c.* 1850/*c.* 1990; architect not known.
An excellent neo-Classical composition, all the more praiseworthy for being a modern twentieth-century replacement for a mid-Victorian predecessor built originally for John James Verschoyle (1805–91), son of John Verschoyle of Stillorgan House (*q.v.*), who acquired the property from the Smith family. Single-storey standard smooth-rendered, with a hipped roof part-concealed behind an

entablature parapet carried on Doric pilaster quoins to the main corners and framing the central entrance recess and the two-over-two sash windows set in their own moulded surrounds. The road elevation has a bipartite window in like manner with a mullion sash box, set off by paired pilasters off a stone plinth. The stone stack with corniced cappings suggests that the original lodge is in there still. It would be right to give credit where due but no information was forthcoming.

Lewis 1837; *Thom's*; *LGI* (1904).

814. TEMORA, Mount Merrion; pre-1837; *demolished.*
The house, home in 1849 to Richard Purdy, whose gate porter was Andrew Corrigan, has gone the way of its lodge.

Griffith 1848–60.

815. TEMPLEHILL CEMETERY, Stradbrook; *c.* 1900.
A Quaker graveyard established in 1860 to which 'Arbutus Lodge' was added later—a single-storey roughcast mildly Arts and Crafts hip-roofed bungalow on a square plan, much altered and extended.

TEMPLE HILL (see NEPTUNE)

TEMPLE HILL (see TEMPLEHOWELL)

816. TEMPLEHOWELL, Terenure; pre-1837; *demolished.*
The residence in 1846 of barrister Edward H. Scriven and his physician son of the same name, whose gatekeeper three years later was Farrell Keogh.

Slater 1846; Griffith 1848–60.

817. TEMPLEOGUE, Templeogue; pre-1837; *demolished.*
The ancient seat of the Domvile family, whose medieval castle was taken down in the early eighteenth century in favour of a Queen Anne mansion, which in turn fell to ruin when the family eventually abandoned it in favour of Santry Court, north Dublin (*q.v.*). A replacement house was, from the beginning of the nineteenth century, home to a succession of tenants, one of whom was John Burke in 1849, when the gatekeeper was Michael Fagan.

Griffith 1848–60; Joyce 1912; Ball 1995.

818. TEMPLEOGUE LODGE, Templeogue; *c.* 1855; *demolished.*
A villa built in the grounds of Cypress Grove about 1855 for barrister Charles Taaffe. The contemporary gate lodge is survived by its fine entrance screen, comprised of a triple gateway formed by four tall stone pillars having recessed panels with bold plinths and heavy corniced cappings with the inscriptions 'Templeogue' and 'Lodge'. The decorative iron gates are matched by the railings on convex quadrant walls. All now prelude to a suburban garden.

Thom's.

819. TEMPLE VILLE, Templeogue; pre-1837; *demolished.*
John Lawlor was porter in 1849 to apothecary Michael Donovan.

Griffith 1848–60.

820. TERENURE, Terenure; pre-1837; *demolished.*
A property in 1841 of F. Greene Esq., which eight years later was occupied by Mrs Cecilia Byrne, whose gate lodge then lay vacant. By 1871 the house was called 'Elm Grove' and appears to have had a pair of lodges.

Thom's; Griffith 1848–60.

821. TERENURE HOUSE, Terenure (4).
The great house of the district was built by Major Joseph Deane after he was granted the Barnwall estate around 1671. Here his descendants remained for over a century before selling the property to Abraham Wilkinson, who promptly sold it about 1789 to Robert Shaw, and it was he who altered the house to give it its present appearance. The three lodges on the Templogue Road may have dated from the turn of the nineteenth century when that road was constructed to split the estate in two and in 1806 prompted Shaw's son of the same name to remove to Bushy Park (*q.v.*) and sell Terenure to Frederick Bourne, who greatly improved the demesne with the help of the noted landscape architect James Fraser. These lodges have all gone, as well as that off the Fortfield Road that served the outbuildings and farmyard that became Lakelands House (*q.v.*) in its own right after the estate was acquired by the Carmelites to establish Terenure College in 1860. The 1849 valuation identifies but one gatekeeper, Luke Farrell, probably at the main entrance, as porter to Henry Bourne.

Taylor and Skinner 1778; 1969 [1783]; Lewis 1837; Griffith 1848–60; Ball 1995; Bence-Jones 1988; Nolan 1982.

822. TERENURE VILLE, Terenure; *c.* 1845.
A mid-nineteenth-century property created for James Bennett, whose lodge lay vacant in 1849. It survives as a modest single-storey standard hip-roofed cottage, with a gabled entrance breakfront flanked by wide windows in plain rendered walls. The otherwise ordinary carriage pillars are topped by dome features with Greek key-pattern banded bases.

Griffith 1848–60.

823. THORNCLIFF, Churchtown; *c.* 1865; *demolished.*
All that remains of a fine lodged entrance screen is a lonesome squat neo-Classical granite carriage pillar, its tapering shaft with recessed panel, topped by an exaggerated oversailing capping. Contemporary with a development made possible by the Orwell Road's being extended east of the River Dodder and created for John Wardell, merchant.

Slater 1870.

824. THORNFIELD, Donnybrook; pre-1837; *demolished.*
A small estate in 1837 of attorney William Potts, at the entrance to which survive two good pillars of V-jointed rusticated granite blocks and friezes with 'Thornfield' inscribed. Of *c.* 1800, they probably date the missing lodge, which has been replaced by a modern 'gate lodge' of long, low appearance, single-storey below a hipped roof, rendered with a wide breakfront in rendering with three-over-three sashes. In 1841 ironmonger John Newson was in residence and eight years later his gate porter was George Owens.

Lewis 1837; Slater 1846; Griffith 1848–60; *Thom's.*

825. THORNHILL, Ballinteer; pre-1871; *demolished.*
Thomas H. Parr was resident here in 1846 and 1851, in the house which pre-dated a lodge built after 1837. Both had gone by 1907.

Slater 1846; *Thom's.*

826. THORN HILL, Little Bray; *c.* 1830.
'... a large and elegant house ... the demesne is small but highly and picturesquely improved with shrubberies, gardens, &c. This beautiful seat, from a wild uncultivated spot, was built on and improved by Mr Mason.' Archer wrote this in 1801 just after the Rt Hon. John Monck Mason MP had moved on, to be succeeded not long afterwards by William Westby (1753–1835), followed after his death by Francis Leigh, who was still here in 1856, his gatekeeper seven years earlier having been Michael Slater. The lodge may date from Westby's time here, though the gatescreen alongside looks to be a replacement of *c.* 1855. Fronting the footpath, the gabled roughcast single-bay elevation has a little canted bay window from which to view the gates. From single-storey it has been extended rearwards, sideways and upwards. At a distance is the splendid gatescreen of four pillars with recessed panel shafts and friezes topped by gadrooned caps, all containing ogee railed quadrants and chunky iron gates hung on secondary iron pillars, as recommended by Papworth.

Archer 1801; Leet 1814; Papworth 1818; Lewis 1837; Griffith 1848–60; *LGI* (1904).

827. THORN HILL, Stillorgan; pre-1837; *demolished.*
A villa in 1837 of barrister John George, who twelve years later was leasing to Cornelius Creagh, with Bridget Killeen as his gatekeeper.

Lewis 1837; Griffith 1848–60.

828. TIBRADDEN, Whitechurch; pre-1849/*c.* 1861; architect Joseph Maguire.

Norman Campion

In 1859 Mary, daughter and heiress of Charles Davis of Tibradden and nearby Cloragh (*q.v.*), married Thomas Hosea Guinness (1831–88), great-grandson of *the* Arthur Guinness. They built a new house and gate lodge to designs of Joseph Maguire where the previous lessee, William Henry Prosser, was in residence on the 42-acre property with an earlier lodge, which in 1849 lay vacant. Its replacement is a beautiful little Italianate composition, single-storey standard below a hipped roof in stucco-effect finish with conspicuous sturdy Irish pilaster quoins to main corners, and the entrance breakfront with its bold open pediment emphasised by chunky carved modillion brackets which are carried about the oversailing soffit projecting from an eaves band. Above the plinth are segmentally headed windows and to the ridge a suitably hefty chimney-stack. Impressively located on an elevated site, the effect is impaired by a hideous modern sun porch erected across the front door. There is an inappropriate but pretty wooden picket fence and octagonal gateposts, on one of which is hung a steel farm gate. This is a design which would seem to have been the source of many such lodges in south Dublin, at Ailesbury (*q.v.*), Homestead (*q.v.*), Bellosguardo (*q.v.*) and Craigmore (*q.v.*), all attributable to John McCurdy.

Griffith 1848–60; *DB* (1 Dec. 1861); *IFR.*

TIGH LORCAIN HALL (see GROVE)

829. TIVOLI VILLA, Dún Laoghaire; pre-1837; *demolished.*
An entrance opening off Tivoli Road onto an exclusive avenue to the house, in 1835 the residence of Alderman Arthur Perrin. By 1871 Kingstown was spreading and the house had been joined by semis and terraces fronting what had become Tivoli Terrace East. The lodge, removed by 1907, was followed 70 years later by the house.

Pearson 1981.

830. TOURVILLE, Rathmines; pre-1837; *demolished.*
One of many villas and their porters' lodges lining the western side of Rathmines Road in the nineteenth century which by the turn of the next had gone. This in 1846 was of John Boswell, and three years later of Mrs Mary Murphy, whose gatekeeper was then Patrick Reilly.

Slater 1846; Griffith 1848–60.

831. TRANQUILLA, Rathmines; pre-1837.
A plain single-storey gabled structure to a villa in 1841 of a Mr Hogan which became a convent of the Sisters of Carmel, of whom the superioress in 1850 was Mrs Fitzgibbon and the gate porter Michael Jordan.

Thom's; Griffith 1848–60.

832. TRAVERSLEA, Glenageary; 1897; architect Cecil Orr.
A development for the artist Nathaniel Hone the younger (1831–1917), both his house and lodge a study in red of brick and sandstone dressings. The 1½-storey lodge serves as an introduction to details on the house, with its heavily expressed open-pediment gables, tripartite sash windows and bold corbelled chimney-stacks. Of the three-bay avenue front the two right-hand windows are below a catslide roof, the other in an internal angle rising to an unsightly later flat-roofed 'gablet'. The gatescreen continues the theme of red brick in the ogee quadrant walls, one of which contains a wicket opening, and four pillars, the central pair having 'Traverslea' in relief on each. All to designs of architect Cecil Orr.

Pearson 1998; IAA.

833. TRIMLESTON, Booterstown; pre-1837/pre-1871/*c.* 1915; architects probably W.M. Mitchell and Sons.

A familiar landmark on the Rock Road is this conspicuous lodge, which seems to have had two predecessors on the site at an entrance which initially served Trimleston House, with its lodge well set back from the gate on the left-hand side. This was a big house, noticed in 1825 by Brewer as the seat of Lord Trimleston, which received a mid-Victorian make-over, perhaps when a new porter's lodge was built to the right-hand side of the gates, probably replacing that of Peter Quin, gatekeeper in 1849 to William Hayes. About that time this access seems to have also served Trimleston Cottage, a residence that latterly became known as 'Dornden'. In 1915 the architects W.M. Mitchell and Sons were engaged by Thomas Atkinson to carry out alterations to the lodge, whose block plan indicates a structure with a symmetrical three-bay front to the avenue and a possible

proposal for a WC to be added to the road gable. It seems that this work was not carried out; rather the client opted for the present replacement in a twentieth-century sumptuous interpretation of the Tudor Revival style. Single-storey, basically built off an L-plan, with two main skew-tabled gables descending to a parapet, with ball and gadrooned vase finials galore, which continues about a flat-roofed entrance hall in the internal angle. Mainly faced in quarry-faced masonry raised off a plinth and relieved by string-course, smooth quoins and dressings. Both gable apexes sport blank shields, one in a roundel, the other contained by a semicircular hood moulding. The excess of decoration spreads to the roof, with a contrasting slate band, red perforated scalloped cresting and a dominant stone chimney-stack with reticulated punched panels and a boldly bracketed moulded capping. Sadly, the complementary gatescreen with its carved pillars and beautifully delicate fretted railings has gone.

Brewer 1825; Griffith 1848–60; *Thom's*; Smyth 1994; Pearson 1998; IAA (Murray Collection 82/49,43).

TRIMLESTON LODGE (see ROSEMOUNT [2])

834. TRINITY COLLEGE DUBLIN, Lincoln Place; pre-1854/1908; architect R.J. Stirling.

On this site where building ground is at a premium it was inevitable that a gate lodge and its entrance screen would become surplus to requirements, to be replaced by a flimsy sentry-box and barrier. The valuation of 1854 identifies a lodge to this gate, but in 1908 the *Irish Builder* magazine reports that 'A new gate lodge is being constructed in Lincoln Place for Trinity College Estate. Messrs G.W. Scott & Co. are builders and the works are from the designs of, and under the superintendence of Mr Robert J. Stirling, B.E., F.R.I.A., architect to Trinity College Estate.' What must have been a replacement for a short-lived predecessor built after 1837 was a distinguished structure; its short three-bay symmetrical front to the avenue had a handsome Tuscan frontispiece, its mutuled pediment carried on engaged columns, square outer and round inner, all with exaggerated entases framing one-over-one sash windows and fanlit doorway. The granite-faced structure continued in plain ashlar to side elevations below a corbelled eaves band. This fine building had ignominious final years, occupying a construction site before being dismantled and taken away for storage amidst assurances as to the University's awareness of its architectural significance and good

intentions to re-erect it at a suitable alternative location, so far unrealised. Much of the gatescreen was removed in the 1960s to facilitate passage of construction traffic. This splendid granite triple gateway of 1852 is an early work of John McCurdy, the college architect, probably contemporary with the first lodge on the site, which was at the other side of the gateway and may have formed part of McCurdy's commission. Four massive pillars with bold plinths and capping cornices had moulded recessed shafts with round heads to match those to the little postilion openings with their moulded surrounds and keystones. The ironwork was suitably rich and elaborate.

Griffith 1848–60; *IB* (25 July 1908); *Irish Times* (8 July 1998); O'Dwyer 1981.

835. TUDOR COTTAGE, Glenageary; *c.* 1835; architect not known.
The house by 1871 had become 'Tudor Lodge' before its demolition last century. The gate lodge is a pleasant 'Tudor' cottage in its own right. Single-storey standard with steep main gables and that to its projecting hall, the doorway in which has a chamfered surround. To each side is a bipartite casement window with latticed cast-iron glazing and a tripartite version to the road façade. To each gable is a blank shield and ribbons. There are clues to its earlier Picturesque appearance in remains of hip-knobs to missing fancy bargeboards; plain replacement chimney-stack. All very

trim in whitened finish to rendered walls, it now adorns the grounds of 'Hillcourt', previously known as 'Innismore' (*q.v.*). The first proprietor would seem to have been woollen draper Alexander Comyns, whose porter in 1849 was Michael McDonnell.

Slater 1846; Griffith 1848–60.

836. TUDOR, Dalkey; pre-1871; *demolished.*
An appropriately named villa, built around 1845 for Dr Richard Parkinson, its grounds much reduced by intrusive development that condemned the gate lodge.

Thom's; Griffith 1848–60.

837. TUDOR LODGE, Glenageary; pre-1837; *demolished.*
A porter's lodge, which sat back to back with that to Glenageary House (*q.v.*), probably contemporary with its big house, built in the 1830s in the Picturesque Tudor bargeboard style. Home in 1849 to Revd John A. Millett, whose gatekeeper was Patrick Barrett, by 1871 it had become 'Tudor House' and in 1965 it was put to use as a school.

Griffith 1848–60; Pearson 1998.

838. TUDOR LODGE, Killiney; pre-1871; *demolished.*
A development which just post-dated the 1849 valuation, probably built for Geoffrey Barcroft, who is recorded here in 1862.

Griffith 1848–60; *Thom's*.

839. TULLAMAINE VILLA, Ranelagh; pre-1880; *demolished.*
A property possibly created by Sir Bernard Burke (1814–92), Ulster King of Arms, who moved here between 1870 and 1878. It is now the site of a hotel.

Thom's.

TURF GAS COMPANY (see DUBLIN TURF GAS COMPANY)

840. TYMON LODGE, Firhouse; pre-1837; *demolished.*
The gate lodge stood at the base of an exceptionally straight tree-lined 500yd-long avenue leading through the 35-acre farm in 1849 of Peter McGrath, whose gatekeeper was Thomas Byrne.

Griffith 1848–60.

UNIVERSITY LODGE (see ROEBUCK GROVE)

841. VALETTA, Dún Laoghaire; pre-1848; *demolished.*
A villa in 1837 of Captain Edward Ward Drewe, who died here about 1865 a colonel. His gate porter in 1848 was Jonathan Holt.

Lewis 1837; Griffith 1848–60; *Thom's*.

842. VALLOMBROSA, Bray (2).
A villa in 1814 of the Walker family, showing none of the style its name implies; rather it is in the English fancy bargeboard manner. It had two porters' lodges, one beyond the county boundary.

Wicklow gate; pre-1838; *demolished.*
By all accounts this was also a pretty English Picturesque cottage.

Dublin gate; *c.* 1820.

Retained as a garden shed is this minuscule single-storey structure, square on plan with a pyramidal roof, now felted, from which projects a gabled canopy to the round-headed front door behind a pair of plain supporting posts—a single-bay avenue front in whitened rendering. By 1849 its occupant was James Toole, porter to Mrs Eliza McBride, who was leasing the big house from the Walkers.

Leet 1814; Griffith 1848–60.

843. VERGEMOUNT, Clonskeagh (2).
Both lodges, built before 1837, have been demolished, one replaced by a flat-roofed twentieth-century bungalow in the same manner as the hospital block which now occupies the grounds. In 1837 this was the seat of Revd John Clark Crosthwaite (1801–74), who in 1844 left as vicar choral of Christchurch Cathedral to become rector at an English parish; Vergemount passed to his brother-in-law, Revd James Henthorn Todd (1805–69), one of whose gatekeepers was Richard Harrison. By 1854, however, the property had been sold as an incumbered estate to one J. Donegan, in whose family it remained until 1884. In 1904 the place was acquired as the 'Vergemount Isolation Hospital', which from the 1960s was known as 'Clonskeagh Hospital'.

Lewis 1837; *Thom's*; Griffith 1848–60; Lyons 1993; Leslie and Wallace 2001.

844. VERNEY, Kiltiernan; pre-1837.
Fronting the road is a three-bay single-storey lodge which may be contemporary with the 1820s farmhouse, though much altered down the years, the right-hand bay being a gabled projection. Later wide windows have keystone features in roughcast walls with toothed quoins. Eccentrically, one main gable is skew-tabled, the other hipped. Occupied. Alongside is a pair of vernacular gate pillars. A property in 1849 of Edward Keegan.

Griffith 1848–60.

845. VEVAY, Ballybrack; *c.* 1850.
The appearance of villas on Church Road, of which Vevay was one, commenced in the

1830s, but the 1849 valuation suggests that 'Anneville', as it was then called by Brindley Hone (1796–1862) after his cousin whom he had married in 1823, was lodgeless until mid-century. This was remedied either by him or by his four bachelor sons, who lived here after his death. The original structure is much disguised by extensions and modifications but it can be seen to have been single-storey, a shallow-pitched gabled short elevation to the avenue and to the rear a clue to its previous appearance in a label-moulded Tudor-style opening with modern latticed lead-effect glazing indicative of an original pattern in cast iron.

Griffith 1848–60; *Thom's*; *IFR*; Pearson 1998.

846. VICAR'S LODGE, Dolphin's Barn; pre-1837; *demolished.*

A property bounded by the old Richmond Penitentiary (see Wellington Barracks), the Grand Canal and the South Circular Road, which was occupied in 1846 and 1856 by optician George Yeates, whose lodge had gone by 1871.

Slater 1846; 1856.

847. VICTORIA CASTLE, Killiney (2).

'... the first stone of the new town [Killiney] has been laid, nay, the first building ... no less a building than Victoria-castle, has been actually erected. Like most modern would-be castles, it has towers and crenellated battlements, and large windows in abundance, and is upon the whole as unlike a real old castle as such structures really are. It is, however, a picturesque and imposing structure of its kind, and what is more consequence to its future occupants, a cheerful and commodious habitation, which is more than can be said of most genuine castles ...' This description in the *Parliamentary Gazetteer* of 1846 could as easily have been of its equally romantic neo-Norman main entrance lodge in like granite ashlar, a wholly appropriate prelude to the fairytale house with its stunning views over Killiney Bay. Built by the solicitor-turned-property developer Robert Warren (1787–1869), who named it after his newly crowned queen and seems to have employed his grandson, Sandham Symes (1807–94), as his architect. He promptly sold it to Revd Humphrey Lloyd (1800–81), later provost of Trinity College Dublin, probably to mark the latter's marriage in 1840.

Victoria Road gate; *c.* 1840; architect probably Sandham Symes.

A delightful and much-loved landmark that once gave onto the private avenue but the carriage archway of which since 1924 has spanned the public road. Approached on each side by tall rubble-built walls with Irish crenellations and relieved by a little round turret and similar miniature bartizan, the now-gateless carriage archway, with bold corbelled shoulders, is flanked by a pair of square turrets with cross arrowloops, one of which contains the postern opening below a flagstaff bartizan that links it to the machicolated and castellated two-storey circular porter's 'keep', with its little

847. Victoria Castle, Killiney, Victoria Road gate (Lawrence Collection, National Library of Ireland).

shouldered slit windows. A charming composition, testament to the eclecticism of its creator, best known for his Italianate banks.

Vico Road gate; *c.* 1855; architect possibly Sandham Symes.

Opposite the entrance, giving the impression of a three-bay symmetrical single-storey lodge to the visitor, it in fact sits on a basement and is thus two-storey to the rear, as dictated by the steep contours. A characterful little structure in uncoursed

granite facings rising to a crenellated parapet that crow-steps up an entrance breakfront, with battered base, which contains a blank shield over a Tudor-arched recess, or porch, to the front door. On each side are similarly arched narrow lattice-patterned windows. Across the road is a complementary castellated entrance screen with pedestrian gates only, which suggests that the entrance dates from before the Vico Road was opened to carriage traffic.

A property later renamed 'Ayesha Castle'.

Parliamentary Gazetteer; *LGI* (1904); Lyons 1993; Williams 1994; Pearson 1998; NLI/Lawrence photograph (3964 C).

848. VICTORIA HILL PARK, Killiney (2).

Back gate; pre-1890; *demolished.*

Built after 1837, a lodge on a square plan with a central projection to its main front.

Front gate; 1853; architect probably Sandham Symes.

Lawrence Collection, Nat. Library of Ireland

A one-up/one-down sentry-box, like a detached campanile, Italianate and square on plan, raised in uncoursed granite with toothed quoins and plain surrounds to openings. To the upper floor are round-headed windows resting on a string-course at sill level and corbel brackets repeated where the chimney-breast emerges. This is all capped by a shallow pyramidal roof rising to a hip-knob finial, its oversailing soffit decorated with carved modillion brackets. Two lofty ashlar carriage pillars have fluted bands and finely moulded cappings with ball finials. A photograph from the turn of the twentieth century shows plain contemporary gates to match the surviving railings, rather than the inappropriate modern decorative replacements. The park, noted for its views and 1740s obelisk, was a proposed site for a mansion in 1790 of Lord Clonmel, which went unrealised. The developer Robert Warren in the 1840s settled at neighbouring Killiney Castle (*q.v.*) and he may well have built the Italianate lodge, to designs of

Sandham Symes, to guard a new approach to his house. The crash of his empire in 1870, however, quashed any further ambitions in the district. The hill was eventually purchased as a public park and opened in honour of Queen Victoria's golden jubilee by the prince of Wales in 1887, when the lodge briefly had a tea room attached.

Ball 1995; Pearson 1998; NLI/Lawrence photograph (1182C).

849. VICTORIA, Dalkey; pre-1837/1908; architect G.F. Beckett.
Martin Burke, proprietor of the Shelbourne Hotel, lived here in 1849, when he had as gatekeeper William Downes. The house saw a succession of different owners in that century before it was greatly altered and enlarged in 1907 to designs of George Francis Beckett for Richard W. Booth of Booth Bros, tool warehouse and engineering works. Beckett's commission extended a year later to providing plans for the replacement porter's lodge. This is a pleasant standard 1½-storey Edwardian Arts and Crafts building below a gabled roof, the deep eaves band to which carries across the double-leaved panelled fanlit front door and beyond over the multi-paned canted bay windows, which project from nice polygonal stone-faced walls with brick dressings. To one side of the concave railed entrance quadrants at the rear of the footpath is a contemporary pedestrian gateway, with flanking walls framing a Classical moulded lugged surround crowned by a small pediment on a pulvinated frieze containing an uninformative plaque.

Griffith 1848–60; *IB* (18 May 1907 and 25 July 1908); *Thom's*; Pike and McDowell 1908.

850. VICTORIA LODGE, Ballybrack; pre-1907; *demolished.*
The pretty Regency *cottage orné* has sadly gone. After 1871 its avenue was extended and an entrance created off Wyattville Road. The accompanying gate lodge, probably built for John D'Arcy, is similarly a thing of the past.

Thom's.

851. VIEWMOUNT, Lucan; *c.* 1854; *demolished.*
A property that had a bewildering turnover of residents down the nineteenth century. An entry in the valuation book for 1862 records the gate lodge to have been 'Built about 8 years', probably during the occupancy of the O'Farrells. Around the turn of the twentieth century the house was renamed 'Beaumont' by a Miss Coyne.

Thom's.

852. VILLA NOVA, Williamstown; pre-1837; *demolished.*
Another small suburban park, its villa and lodge lost to modern development. Home in 1841 to James Henry Blake QC, briefly to Mrs Alicia O'Keefe before she moved to nearby Woodview (*q.v.*) and in 1849 to Thomas John Ryan, whose gate porter was Edward Grumley.

Thom's; Griffith 1848–60.

853. WAINSFORT, Terenure; pre-1837; *demolished.*
An estate in 1837 of Captain Theodore Norton which twelve years later had been acquired by Revd William Stannard, whose gate porter was John Neille.

Lewis 1837; Griffith 1848–60.

854. WALTHAM TERRACE, Booterstown; *c.* 1836; *demolished.*
An early gated development created from an old estate called 'Beaufort' by lawyer and speculator Arthur Ormsby, a pleasant avenue of detached and semi-detached villas given added respectability by the gate lodge, near which a gate pillar bears the date '1836'.

Pearson 1998.

855. WALWORTH, Usher's Quay; pre-1837; *demolished.*
A house and lodge of the proprietor of the Jameson and Robertson Distillery, in 1843 Walter Boyd. All now totally vanished.

Griffith 1848–60; Pearson 2000.

856. WARREN LODGE, Bray; *c.* 1850; *demolished.*
By the bank of the Bray River, which is the county boundary with Wicklow, Thomas Miller took this pleasant place in the mid-nineteenth century, gave it a porter's lodge and renamed it 'Coburg'.

WASDALE (see MOUNTAIN VIEW)

857. WELL PARK, Stepaside; pre-1837; *demolished.*
A small farm in 1849 of John Dale, leasing from Arthur Todd, the lodge to which had gone by 1907.

Griffith 1848–60.

858. WELLINGTON BARRACKS, Dolphin's Barn; pre-1837/*c.* 1890.
Initially built as a remand prison, known as the Richmond Male Penitentiary, or Bridewell, on the site of the Grimswood Nurseries in 1813 to designs of Francis Johnston, who may also have been responsible for an early porter's lodge. In 1887 it was transferred to the War Department and named after the duke of Wellington. The present replacement guardhouse looks to date from that time. In contrast to Johnston's severe grey institution is this late Victorian polychrome affair in red brick with granite dressings; an irregular six-bay hip-roofed building, the left-hand portion of which has a three-bay regular elevation below a hipped roof. To the right-hand side are three high-level windows in walls highlighted by eaves with a cream brick, repeated in the two-tone chimney-stack. On 11 April 1922 the complex was handed over to the Irish army and renamed Griffith Barracks, which it remained until vacated in 1987, subsequently being put to use as a school.

Liddy 1987; IAA.

859. WELLINGTON LODGE, Dún Laoghaire; pre-1837; *demolished.*
A private house, presumably dating from the immediate post-Waterloo period, which by 1837 had a schoolhouse attached and had become 'Kingstown School' under the principal Michael McCaul. He was succeeded by Charles W. Farrell and in 1849 Revd W.C. Stackpoole was the headmaster, with Matthew Tormey as gatekeeper. By 1907 his lodge had gone, to be soon followed by the big house.

Lewis 1837; *Thom's*; Griffith 1848–60; Pearson 1981.

860. WESTBOURNE, Terenure; pre-1837.
What may have been a basic single-storey two-bay hip-roofed cottage, a remarkable survival much disguised by alterations and extensions. Alongside are its rendered carriage pillars, with plinths, friezes and cornices. A large villa in 1841 of solicitor John Richardson Dickinson.

Thom's; Slater 1846.

861. WESTBURY, Kilmacud (2).
Now St Raphaela's Convent, the core of which is a very fine early nineteenth-century villa, in 1837 the seat of Edmund O'Beirne, extended and improved by Thomas Wilson in the 1850s, when he also added a new primary entrance to the demesne.

East gate; pre-1837; *demolished.*
A lodge swept away in the formation of a traffic roundabout. Its gate porter in 1849 was Bernard Solan.

West gate; *c.* 1850; *demolished.*

In a splendid setting of mature trees remains the wide iron entrance screen of shallow railed concave quadrant and triple gateway with four 'Chinese stove' pillars of luxuriant intertwined foliage and anthemion tops.

Both entrances also served the Wilsons' sister house of Clonmore (*q.v.*).

Lewis 1837; *Thom's*; Griffith 1848–60; Flanagan 1991; Pearson 1998.

862. WESTFIELD, Rathmines; pre-1837; *demolished.*
A residence in 1841 and 1851 of John Tomlinson, who in 1849 was leasing to John Browne, whose gatekeeper was Charles Hickey. By 1907 the property was all redeveloped.

Thom's; Griffith 1848–60.

863. WESTHAMPTON, Rathmines; pre-1837; *demolished.*
A property in 1841 of John Radley, probably the proprietor of Radley's Hotel, College Green. By 1849 it had passed to Thomas Harrison, whose gatekeeper was Terence Dunne in a lodge not clear on the OS maps.

Thom's; Griffith 1848–60.

864. WESTMANSTOWN, Newcastle; pre-1837; *demolished.*
A 76-acre farm in 1849 of Peter Rourke, whose gate lodge then lay vacant.
Griffith 1848–60.

865. WESTON COTTAGE, Dundrum; pre-1837; *demolished.*
A property sometime associated with the Franks family but in the mid-nineteenth century occupied by John Blake, whose gate porter in 1849 was Ellen Kavanagh.
Griffith 1848–60; Nolan 1982.

866. WESTON LODGE AND MILLS, Leixlip (2).
Delightfully situated by the Salmon Leap on the River Liffey were the flour mills established by Messrs Reid and Co., and nearby their beautiful thatched cottage of the early nineteenth century. Both the gate lodges, one to the north in Cooldrinagh townland and the other on the southern approach in Backwestonpark townland, have gone, the latter manned in 1849 by Henry Lyons, when the concern was being run as a paper mill by Michael and William McDonnell.
Lewis 1837; Griffith 1848–60; Pike and McDowell 1908.

867. WESTONPARK, Leixlip (2).
An estate in the early nineteenth century of the Marley family that by 1837 had been acquired by J. Hamilton Reid.
Principal gate; pre-1837; *demolished.*
By 1906 this avenue had been made redundant in favour of the other approach.
Secondary gate; pre-1837.
What was a plain single-storey hip-roofed structure, much obscured by twentieth-century additions, now attends on the main access. In 1849 the gatekeeper was James Brady as porter to Andrew Reid.
Leet 1814; Lewis 1837; Griffith 1848–60.

868. WHEATFIELD, Palmerston; pre-1836; *demolished.*
A 62-acre farm of William E. O'Callaghan in 1850, when his gate porter was Charles Dawson. House and lodge have now gone.
Griffith 1848–60.

869. WHITECHURCH CHURCH OF IRELAND CHURCH, Whitechurch; *c.* 1826.
In contrast to architect John Semple's spiky pointed stone edifice, consecrated in 1827, outside the gates and still in use is this modest vernacular single-storey standard hip-roofed cottage with tiny windows in harled walls. Both buildings were erected during the short time here (1824–8) of perpetual curate Revd Lundy Foot (1793–1873).
Lewis 1837; Costello 1989; Leslie and Wallace 2001.

870. WHITECHURCH VICARAGE, Ballinteer; *c.* 1875; *demolished.*
Like the distant church, probably also built on land donated by the La Touche family of Marlay Grange (*q.v.*), possibly when they sold off the estate in 1864. A house initially called 'Ormonde' on Grange Road, it was by 1878 home to Revd James Anderson Carr (1835–1900), incumbent of Whitechurch Parish from 1871 until his death.
Thom's; Leslie and Wallace 2001.

871. WHITE HALL, Belgard; *c.* 1800.
A property certainly not notable for the quality of its architecture but rather for its survival, and in the late nineteenth century for its literary associations. In the time here of Andrew Cullen Tynan and his talented daughters, Katherine and Norah, his modest thatched farmhouse was a magnet for visits by the likes of Douglas Hyde, John O'Leary, 'A.E.' Russell and W.B. Yeats, who may have noticed the unremarkable gate lodge *en route.* Possibly built in the time here of Robert Beauchamp around 1814, it is a single-storey hip-roofed cottage with a door and window to the avenue front, its walls now roughcast and roof chimneyless and covered in corrugated iron. Now very derelict, its occupant in 1850 was Peter Mahon as porter to Richard Cummins, farming 45 acres.
Leet 1814; Griffith 1848–60; *Thom's.*

872. WHITE HALL PARK, Blackrock; pre-1837; *demolished.*
A house that in the early nineteenth century had become a boarding school run by the Misses Hughes in 1849 had reverted to a residence of James Mark. His gatekeeper was Patrick Nowlan.
Thom's; Griffith 1848–60.

WHITEOAKS (see ROEBUCK GROVE)

873. WHITESTOWN, Tallaght; 1878; *demolished.*
A farm in the mid-nineteenth century of William Fox, the lodge to which he added in distant Tallaght townland. Its gatekeeper in 1890 was Patrick Stoney.
Griffith 1848–60.

874. WILFORT, Little Bray (2).
A late eighteenth-century gentry farmhouse and lands which in 1814 were run as nurseries by Charles and Luke Toole. Both pre-1837 gate lodges have gone; in 1849 that to the north was occupied by John McGarry at the entrance to the market gardens, whilst that to the main gate lay vacant. The latter is now the scene of a traffic roundabout and new gates as the access to 'Wilford'.
Leet 1814; Lewis 1837; Griffith 1848–60; Pearson 1998.

WILLBROOK (see ST JOSEPH'S CONVENT)

875. WILLBROOK, Willbrook; *c.* 1845.
A development of a plain villa but singular gate lodge, both built after 1843 seemingly for one John Strong, recorded as resident here in 1846. Within three years it was home to bookseller, printer and stationer John Chambers, whose man at the gate was Edward Dwyer. The lodge is comprised of a tall gabled centre-piece, from which projects a semi-octagonal canted bay window, flanked by lower single-bay gabled wings. All in roughcast with simple clipped eaves and verges, plain but effective, derelict and blocked up, awaiting its fate. Contemporary concave railed quadrants are framed by drab chamfered pillars with recessed panels; the carriage gates are modern.
Slater 1846; Griffith 1848–60; *Thom's.*

876. WILLBROOK FLOUR MILLS, Willbrook; pre-1837; *demolished*
Noted in 1836 as 'Egan's Flour Mills', possibly misspelt fourteen years later when William Evans is recorded as the proprietor, with Peter Brennan as his gatekeeper. The following year, 1851, the owner was Robert Gibney. By 1883 the business had failed and the miller's house was subsequently renamed 'St Gabien's' and occupied by J.E. Madden.
D'Alton 1976 [1838]; Griffith 1848–60; *Thom's*; Healy 2005.

877. WILLFIELD, Sandymount; pre-1837; *demolished.*
A property in 1837 of the Clarke family, its lodge removed by 1935 in the creation of Willfield Road.
Thom's.

878. WILLIAM'S PARK, Ballybrack; *c.* 1875; architect possibly A.G. Jones.

A speculative development by the Ballybrack grocer-cum-developer William Field. He clearly employed the same designer responsible for the almost identical gate lodges to Inveruish (*q.v.*) and Aughnacloy (*q.v.*) further along Seafield Road, St Columba's (*q.v.*) and possibly Lordello (*q.v.*). This is a competent Italianate composition, single-storey standard in smooth rendering below a hipped roof with oversailing eaves, and a gabled breakfront which contains a segmentally headed doorway in a similar recess, arched as the flanking windows. All this is framed by broad Doric corner pilasters, whilst the ridge is crowned by a central Classically moulded chimney-stack capping identical to those on Strathmore (*q.v.*) by architect Alfred Gresham Jones. All beautifully maintained and extended to one side in like manner.
Pearson 1998.

879. WILLIAMSTOWN CASTLE, Williamstown; *c.* 1800; *demolished.*
As backdrop to a photograph of the fine fellows of the 1882–3 French College first XI cricket team is this charming little building in the castellated Georgian Gothic style as the perfect prelude to the big house within,

which was built in 1780 by Councillor William Vavasour, after whom the place was known, as was the local village. His stay here was nevertheless brief and the property became home to a bewildering succession of owners and lessees, before in 1875 it was acquired by the Holy Ghost Fathers and became the second large house in the vicinity to form part of what was to become Blackrock College (*q.v.*) and appears as a vast romantic crenellated castle. Its minuscule lodge was single-storey standard below a hipped roof largely concealed by the tall castellated parapet, under which the avenue front displayed lancet windows with Y-traceried sashes below hood mouldings which continued as a string-course and stepped over the front door head. All in smooth rendering, as was what was probably one of two square turrets with a mock cross arrowloop flanking the front. The fortunate occupant in 1849 was John Archbold, gatekeeper to Stephen Melyn, leasing the property from Revd Richard Vavasour.

Griffith 1848–60; Smyth 1994; Pearson 1998.

880. WILLINGTON, Templeogue; pre-1837; *demolished.*
In 1849 William Seely was porter at the gate to Charles McDonnell, a reverend of the same name being recorded as living here twelve years previously in a house that appears on the Rocque map of 1760.

Lewis 1837; Griffith 1848–60; Ferguson 1998.

881. WILLMOUNT, Ballyboden; pre-1837/pre-1869; *demolished.*
A small estate of the Rt Hon. Joseph Radcliffe QC, of that family of Willmount, Co. Meath (*q.v.*), who was here in the mid-nineteenth century, with a break when he let it to magistrate Francis Thorpe Porter around 1849, the gatekeeper then being John Delaney. On his return in the 1850s Radcliffe altered the name of the property to 'Cliffe Lodge' and a new lodged approach was created further north. Neither this nor its predecessor survives.

Thom's; Griffith 1848–60; Healy 2005.

882. WILLOWMOUNT, Terenure; pre-1837; *demolished.*
A seat in 1837 of W. Hodges Esq. which four years later had been acquired by Thomas Molloy, who in turn by 1849 was leasing it to John Hayes, whose gatekeeper was Alexander Byrne.

Lewis 1837; *Thom's*; Griffith 1848–60.

883. WILLOW PARK, Williamstown (2).
One of the original great marine residences in south Dublin, built in 1766 by Christopher Deey, who lived here for 24 years until he leased it to Hugh, Lord Carlton, from whom it had passed by 1801 to Alderman Alexander, who enjoyed 'a good house, a demesne of about eighteen acres, well planted and improved; fine gardens, with a good deal of glass, and all well enclosed with a stone wall'. The house then passed in succession to Francis Hervey de Montmorency, 3rd Viscount Mountmorres (1756–1833), followed by the earl of Belvedere and the Brady family until 1825, when it was purchased by James Ferrier of the Ferrier and Pollock clothing concern, who remained here for 34 years. Ferrier would have come to a property with one gate lodge at the main approach off Rock Road and another at the secondary access from Booterstown Avenue.

Rock Road gate; pre-1837; *demolished.*
John Sweetman was gatekeeper here in 1849 but his lodge and its gatescreen have gone, the latter to be replaced in 1925 by a new gateway created from a pair of magnificent carriage pillars salvaged from the Mount Merrion House [3] demesne (*q.v.*) when the place became the fourth property in the vicinity acquired to form Blackrock College (*q.v.*). Of mid-eighteenth-century granite construction, they have moulded plinth tops and corniced cappings with ball finials. Flanked by a pair of simple pedestrian gates of mid-nineteenth-century ironwork.

Booterstown Avenue gate; *c.* 1875.

A commodious single-storey standard hip-roofed lodge, two-roomed and three-bay symmetrical, its walls stuccoed, with a niche to the park front and heavily vermiculated quoin stones framing the avenue elevation, with its central arched porch flanked by windows now missing their round-headed bipartite casements. Roofed with alternate rows of canted slates and fleur-de-lis cresting for little boys to throw stones at. The once impressive gatescreen lies redundant and blocked up.

Archer 1801; Griffith 1848–60; *BPB* (1929); Smyth 1994; Pearson 1998.

884. WILLOW TERRACE, Williamstown; *c.* 1825.

An elegant row of tall, early nineteenth-century brick town houses approached through a triple gateway of octagonal granite pillars, two with lanterns atop. The typical single-storey Regency-style gate lodge, now in contrasting rendered finish, has its short front addressing the visitor, with a single wide segmentally arched window, perhaps once tripartite in Morrison manner, set in an equivalent recess. Now flanked by flat-roofed additions. The porter in 1849 was John Downey, his employer James Ferris. A delightful architectural group, all the more satisfying for surprisingly having survived so relatively unscathed.

Griffith 1848–60; Pearson 1998.

885. THE WILLOWS, Terenure; *c.* 1900; architect not known.
On Bushy Park Road this new lodge was built at the old entrance to 'Meadowbank' (*q.v.*), in the grounds of which this late nineteenth-century development of a pair of semi-detached houses was formed. This is a Picturesque single-storey Edwardian lodge in Flemish bond red brick, with bold quarry-faced stone quoins and half-timbered-effect apexes to gables ornamented with fretted bargeboards. Raised off an L-plan with segmentally headed openings, two-bay to the avenue, the doorway in the internal angle (now a window) below a little catslide

canopy. On the road front extends a flat-roofed multi-paned canted bay window overlooking the gateway. The roof is highlighted by perforated scalloped red earthenware cresting, broken by the corbelled brick chimney-stack. Probably built for Richard Pope Froste, solicitor and commissioner for oaths.

Thom's.

886. WILLSBROOK, Lucan; *c.* 1845; *demolished.*
A lodge built after 1836, its occupant recorded in 1849 as Thomas Bennett, porter to Major John Wills, who was previously to be found at Esker Lodge (*q.v.*).

Griffith 1848–60.

887. WILMOUNT, Shanganagh; pre-1871; *demolished.*
A house and lodge built after 1837 which first appear in directories in 1862 as of one — Fry, Esq. Eight years later it was the residence of both a Mrs Sherrard and the Hon. Francis Raymond de Montmorency (1835–1910), a barrister and second son of the 4th Viscount Mountmorres. In the twentieth century the place was renamed 'Clonasleigh' by the Merediths but eventually made way for a shopping complex.

Thom's; *BPB* (1929); Pearson 1998.

888. WILTON, Merrion; *c.* 1880; *demolished.*
A property created after 1871, there being reference in 1881 to a proposed house for John W. Brien by architect W.M. Mitchell, which but four years later was home to William Fry Jr, solicitor and land agent.

Thom's; IAA.

889. WINDSOR, Monkstown; pre-1837; *demolished.*
A villa, probably built in the late eighteenth century by builder and developer John Sproule, occupied until 1832 by the Lane family, who sold it to brewer Michael Thunder, who, if the same of Lagore House, Co. Meath (*q.v.*) (1802–79), acquired it as a home for himself and his new wife of 1834. It may have been Thunder who greatly enlarged the house and perhaps added its gate lodge before selling all before 1841 to jeweller and goldsmith Matthew Law, whose gatekeeper eight years later was Myles Mullins.

Thom's; Griffith 1848–60; *LGI* (1904); Pearson 1998.

890. WINDY ARBOUR, Windy Arbour; *c.* 1845; *demolished.*
William Bibby is recorded here in 1846 but three years later he was dead and the house lay vacant, although Patrick Rourke remained as gate porter, awaiting the imminent arrival of William Stanley Purdon as his new landlord.

Slater 1846; Griffith 1848–60; *Thom's*.

891. WOOD LODGE, Kill of the Grange; pre-1837; *demolished.*
James Carroll was gatekeeper in 1849 to Stephen Sheffield Cassini.

Griffith 1848–60.

WOODBINE LODGE (see WOODTOWN LODGE)

WOODBROOK ESTATE OFFICE (see WOODLAWN, Little Bray)

892. WOODBROOK, Little Bray (2).
An ancient property, variously called in the past 'Old Cork' (1760) and 'Little Cork' (1783) before becoming by 1801 Woodbrook of — Webb Esq.; it was home to a Mr Bourchier in 1814 and thereafter associated with the Hodsons, before around 1830 the Ribton family settled here in the person of the long-lived Sir John Sheppey Ribton (1797–1877). He dramatically improved and enlarged the house to designs of George Papworth, who may well have created a new and extensive entrance screen about a semicircular forecourt and perhaps, as is suggested by the 1871 OS map, a new gate lodge with projecting centre-piece. Sir John's son and widow (his second wife) lived on here until at least 1890, before the property was purchased by Henry Cochrane (1836–1904), later the 1st baronet, of Cantrell and Cochrane fame. It was his fourth son, Sir Stanley Herbert Cochrane (1877–1949), who initiated further extensive additions to the house and, as a cricket fanatic, founded a ground complete with pavilion, a bandstand to the seaward side of the house and its own lodged independent approach from the main road.

North gate; pre-1837/*c.* 1840/*c.* 1905; architect probably F.G. Hicks.

Immensely striking but scarcely beautiful is this imaginative Edwardian interpretation of the Picturesque style. A replacement for what was probably a replacement, it is a single-storey building, not quite symmetrical, with a steeply pitched hipped roof having exposed rafter toes broken by a pair of triple-banked corbelled chimney-stacks and gabled

892. Woodbrook, north gate.

breakfront. This displays a wooden apex and bargeboards variously perforated with quatrefoils, ivy leaves, etc. Below this is a distinctive finish of dogtooth ceramic tiles, under which is the doorway alongside a quadripartite window in roughcast walls with a broad string-course that extends beyond past the flanking tripartite windows. All at an apologetic distance from its extensive gatescreen, with elegant ashlar pillars topped by rusticated ball finials, containing a triple gateway and matching railed quadrants.

South gate; pre-1837/*c.* 1905; architect possibly F.G. Hicks.
A gabled and simple variant of the main lodge in like finish and detailing—the same bargeboards with ivy leaf perforations, and in the road gable a blank stone shield in a roundel set off with brick dressing. Much modernised and extended, seemingly built to monitor the newly formed avenue to the cricket ground. It does seem to have had a predecessor on the site, for the 1849 valuation records two gatekeepers, Michael Donagh and John Waldron, although the nineteenth-century OS maps indicate it to have been avenueless, probably merely at a field gate.

Both lodges are attributable to Frederick George Hicks, who was designing extensive additions and glasshouses in 1905 for Mr Stanley Cochrane before his unexpected elevation to a title on the death of his two older brothers.

Taylor and Skinner 1778; 1969 [1783]; Archer 1801; Griffith 1848–60; *Thom's*; *BPB* (1861); *IB* (25 Feb. 1905); *BPB* (1929); An Old Inhabitant 1907; Ferguson 1998; Pearson 1998.

WOODFIELD (see HAYFIELD)

WOODFIELD (see ROSEVALE)

893. WOODLAWN, Ballinteer (2).
The earlier house of the name was located by Ballinteer Avenue, its pre-1837 lodge further east, the property in 1849 of barrister Abraham Jones Sweeny, thereafter home to James Digges La Touche and John Pearson, before William Carroll (1819–90), lord mayor of Dublin in 1868–9, built a new house on the site appropriate to his status and complemented it with a replacement porter's lodge at an alternative entrance by the old house. The lodges have been demolished, as have both big houses.

Griffith 1848–60; *Thom's*.

WOODLAWN (see TANEY LODGE)

894. WOODLAWN, Little Bray; pre-1837; *demolished.*
A property in 1837 of William Henry Magan, whose main seat was Clonearl, Co. Offaly (*q.v.*). His widow Elizabeth lived on here, and in 1849 her gate porter was Hugh Martin. After her death the place, which had assumed the name 'Cork Farm', at the turn of the twentieth century became attached to neighbouring Woodbrook (*q.v.*) as 'Woodbrook Estate Office', losing its gate lodge in the process.

Lewis 1837; Griffith 1848–60; *Thom's*; *LGI* (1904).

895. WOODLEY PARK, Kilmacud; *c.* 1845; architect possibly C.P. Brassington; *demolished.*
A plain Georgian seat, in 1837 of P.A. Leslie Esq., which had remained lodgeless until the arrival in the 1840s of Charles P. Brassington, who created a new curving approach from the north and Goatstown Road, where 'the main entrance was graced by a cut-stone gate-lodge'. The porter is recorded in 1849 as John Downey and its designer may well have been Brassington himself, as he was a partner in the long-established firm of valuers and land agents, Brassington and Gale, in the city.

Lewis 1837; Griffith 1848–60; Pearson 1998; IAA.

896. WOODPARK COTTAGE, Kill of the Grange; pre-1837; *demolished.*
The residence in 1848 of a Dr Davis, whose gatekeeper was Matthew Hennesey. The property by 1871 had become 'Grangewood', its lodge gone by 1907.

Griffith 1848–60; *Thom's*.

897. WOODPARK, Rathgar; pre-1837; *demolished.*
Thomas Patrick Hayes, stockbroker and notary, was proprietor here in 1837 and as late as 1854. His gate lodge in 1850 lay unoccupied. By 1936 it had gone.

Lewis 1837; Griffith 1848–60; *Thom's*.

898. WOODPARK [1], Rochestown; pre-1837; *demolished.*
A seat in 1837 of Daniel Corneille (1799–1865), whose widow and mother lived on here after his death. In 1849 his gate porter was James Nangle. The property became known as 'Pairc-na-Coille' in the early twentieth century, located to the north of Rochestown Avenue.

Lewis 1837; Griffith 1848–60; *Thom's*.

899. WOODPARK [2], Rochestown; pre-1837; *demolished.*
South of Rochestown Avenue stood a villa built prior to 1787 but removed in the 1990s. In 1837 its occupant was J.J. Kirk Esq., who had given way to John Crosthwaite by 1848, when the lodge lay vacant.

Lewis 1837; Griffith 1848–60; Pearson 1998; Craig and Fewer 2002.

900. WOODPARK [3], Rochestown; pre-1837; *demolished.*
Sited on Sallynoggin Road was this property in 1837 of Mrs Stepney, whose gatekeeper in 1849 was Michael Harvey.

Lewis 1837; Griffith 1848–60.

901. WOODTOWN, Woodtown (3).
The estate of a Mrs Collins in 1837, when the sole approach from the north-east was guarded by two porters' lodges.

Outer gate; pre-1837.
In 1849 inhabited by Thomas Lester, gatekeeper to the new owner, Thomas H. Wilkens. Ruinous.

Inner gate; pre-1837; *demolished.*
Classified on the 1837 OS map as a gate lodge but is valued as a steward's house in 1849. Replaced by a bungalow, itself derelict.

Southern gate; pre-1890; *demolished.*
Built after 1849, probably by John Hayes, who was landowner for much of the remainder of the nineteenth century.

Lewis 1837; Griffith 1848–60; *Thom's*.

902. WOODTOWN LODGE, Woodtown; pre-1837; *demolished.*
Alternatively known as 'Woodbine Lodge', it was in 1837 the residence of Thomas Benjamin Smithson and from around 1850 it was home to tax-collector Thomas Hayes. From about 1880 it was run as a private asylum by a Mrs Hayes, presumably his widow.

Lewis 1837; *Thom's*.

903. WOODTOWN PARK, Woodtown (2).
A Queen Anne house, seemingly that known as 'Mount Pleasant' on the 1760 Rocque map, which around 1800 was acquired by George Grierson, who had left his previous home of Palliser's Park (*q.v.*) upon receiving £100,000 as compensation for the loss of his job as king's printer as a result of the Union. Here he created 'a wonderful farming establishment ... where he raised prize cattle', Woodtown being in 1801 'a large and elegant house, well situated, with a pleasant view of a good neighbourhood. The demesne consists of about an hundred acres, improved to the highest state of perfection, by draining, liming, &c. There are good gardens, and every attention is paid to render it a charming retreat.' The next improver to come to the place was Henry Joy, who was chief baron of the Irish exchequer between 1831 and his death at Woodtown in 1838. About 1830 he carried out extensive alterations to the house, which became known as 'Joy's Villa', and added a very fine porter's lodge to grace its main entrance.

North gate; *c.* 1835; architect perhaps Decimus Burton.
A highly sophisticated composition, the finest Classical porter's lodge in the county, admirably and rightly restored and extended into a double pile. Single-storey standard, its hipped roof partly concealed by an entablatured parapet broken by the central entrance frontispiece, its pediment, like the rest of the detailing in finely chiselled granite, carried on a pair of Roman Doric columns *in antis* between two square equivalents, repeated as corner pilasters to frame six-over-six sash windows in stucco-effect rendered walls. The panelled front door is surmounted by a detached mouth-organ fanlight, whilst the ridge is crowned by a hefty chimney-stack with panelled sides, some details perhaps redolent of the work of Decimus Burton, who had recently arrived in Ireland to work on the Phoenix Park, north Dublin (*q.v.*). The entrance screen is comprised of limewashed convex-walled quadrants contained by ashlar corniced pillars framing an iron-railed triple gateway. The gate porter in 1850 was Nicholas Murphy.

903. Woodtown Park, north gate.

South gate; pre-1837; *demolished.*
A relatively plain lodge at the secondary entrance to the out-offices, which in 1850 lay vacant.

Archer 1801; Griffith 1848–60; Ball 1995; Joyce 1912; Lyons 1993; Ferguson 1998.

904. WOODVIEW, Priesthouse; pre-1837; *demolished.*
Just one of many late Georgian villas which lined the Stillorgan Road occupied in the main by the legal profession, here in 1837 by barrister Edmund John Nolan, who by 1846 had been followed by the Rt Hon. Thomas Francis Kennedy, whose gatekeeper three years later was John Mason.

Lewis 1837; Slater 1846; Griffith 1848–60.

905. WOODVIEW, Stillorgan; pre-1837; *demolished.*
A seat *c.* 1800 of Alderman Nathaniel Warren, MP for Dublin. Directories between 1837 and 1856 list it as the residence of druggist George Wilson Boileau, with James Begley as his gate porter in 1849.

Lewis 1837; *Thom's*; Slater 1846; Griffith 1848–60; Ball 1995.

906. WOODVIEW, Williamstown (2).
A home down the nineteenth century to a stream of various owners, in 1837 Lady Waller, probably Elizabeth, the widow from 1826 of Sir Robert Waller, 2nd baronet, of Newport, Co. Tipperary. This pre-1837 lodge was sited somewhat distant from its Mount Merrion Avenue access and in 1849 was occupied by Patrick O'Shaughnessy, gatekeeper to Mrs Alicia O'Keefe, who only six years earlier was resident in nearby Villa Nova (*q.v.*). The surviving lodge is a replacement of *c.* 1875 by the road probably built for wine merchant William B. Brett. Back to back with the lodge to neighbouring Brookfield (*q.v.*), it is a faintly Italianate affair, single-storey on an L-plan, with mutules to its verges and a catslide roof to the entrance hall in the inner angle; roughcast, plain and occupied.

Lewis 1837; Griffith 1848–60; *Thom's*; *BPB* (1929).

907. WOODVILLE, Churchtown; pre-1837; *demolished.*
Mark Rawson was gatekeeper in 1849 to Arthur Jacob, a physician.

Griffith 1848–60.

908. WOODVILLE, Lucan (2).
The elegant villa and its flanking pavilions was erected for the Rt Hon. Henry Theophilus Clements in the mid-eighteenth century but was sold in 1799, when it became an academy run by the Revd Dr Gilbert Austin. It was acquired before 1824 by John Aldercorn, who by 1837 had sold it to Major-General Sir Hopton S. Scott, whose gate porters in 1850 were Lawrence Ball and Matthew Doyle. Their lodges, both in place by 1836, have, like the big house, been demolished.

Taylor and Skinner 1778; 1969 [1783]; Wilson 1803; Leet 1814; Pigot 1824; Lewis 1837; Griffith 1848–60; Ball 1995; Malcomson 2005.

909. WYCKHAM, Dundrum; *c.* 1820.
Originally built by the Hon. John Butler as 'Primrose Hill' about 1770; when he died in 1789 it passed to barrister John White. By 1837 it was the residence of W. Farran Esq. and his 'richly stored museum of natural curiosities'. The next owner was stockbroker Leonard Bickerstaff, whose gatekeeper was Thomas McKnight in 1849. His lodge survives as a generously proportioned two-storey hip-roofed gatehouse, much altered in the twentieth century. Roughcast with stone toothed quoins, its main avenue front has probably been refenestrated and its central gable feature has acquired a half-timbered effect. Alongside is an extensive and handsome triple gateway terminating in short concave-walled quadrants and plain pillars. The carriage pillars are inscribed 'Wickham' but strangely are dominated by intermediate pillars with round-headed recesses crowned with chaste pedimented cappings complete with mutules and the spandrels below relieved by sunflower

paterae, these chiselled in Portland Stone, the shafts and the rest in granite ashlar. The property in 1925 became home to the Simpson's Hospital.

Lewis 1837; Griffith 1848–60; Ball 1995; *BPB* (1929); Nolan 1982; Pearson 1998.

WYNBERG (see MYERSVILLE)

WYNNSTAY (see ROEBUCK [4])

910. WYVERN, Killiney; *c.* 1865; architect possibly Sandham Symes; *demolished.*
An Italianate villa attributable to architect Sandham Symes in style and for its first occupant having been barrister Robert Warren Jr (1820–94), his cousin. The contemporary lodge may also have been in brick with stone dressings.

Thom's; *LGI* (1904).

911. YAPTON, Monkstown; pre-1837; *demolished.*
An attractive villa demolished in 1977, probably built *c.* 1835 for Warick Hyndman, who by 1849 was leasing it to stockbroker Thomas Hone, whose gate porter then was John Harper.

Thom's; Griffith 1848–60; Pearson 1998.

COUNTY KILDARE

1. ALLAN'S GROVE, Celbridge; *c.* 1855.
Secreted behind the left-hand convex quadrant wall of the entrance and terminating the greater stable yard complex, alongside the road, the gate lodge is a plain structure in exposed rubble, its main front with a clipped gable containing, in the apex, a high-level slit window below a tall sloped ceiling. Derelict. A property in 1851 of George Warburton.

Griffith 1848–60.

2. ANNFIELD, Athy; pre-1837; *demolished.*
A seat of the Vesey family, Viscounts de Vesci, the lodge to which had gone by 1939.

3. ANNFIELD, Kilcullen; pre-1837; *demolished.*
On the first OS maps the gate lodge is shown in outline only, unhatched, suggesting that it was under construction or was a shell awaiting replacement. A property in the early nineteenth century of John Dexter, which may have been named after his wife, Anne Fish; it passed by marriage to the Breretons of nearby New Abbey (*q.v.*) in the mid-nineteenth century.

Leet 1814.

4. ARDINODE or ARDENWOOD, Ballymore Eustace (2).
The John Rocque map of 1760 shows a straight formal avenue leading to the road, with a structure by the entrance to the right-hand side, probably an early lodge. By about 1780, in the time here of the Borrowes family, a more fashionable and subtler approach had been formed from further west.

Main entrance; *c.* 1790.

Deep, tall, concave, harled wall quadrants containing rusticated granite postilion openings are framed by four typical late Georgian V-jointed rusticated ashlar pillars with moulded cappings and ball finials, the carriage pillars having fine Greek key-pattern bands and swagged friezes. In contrast to this rustic sophisticated Classicism is a Gothic gate lodge, perhaps of a few years later. Placed forward of the gates on the road verge, it is a single-storey structure with steeply hipped roof, its front displaying two squat lancet windows with plain granite surrounds which may originally have flanked a similarly arched doorway, now sealed up and rendered over. Inappropriate modern casements. Occupied and extended as a double pile.

Secondary entrance; *c.* 1840.
To the east, opposite the gates, is a simple single-storey hip-roofed roughcast structure with a two-bay front. Occupied. Built in the time here of William Brownrigg.

Taylor and Skinner 1778; 1969 [1783]; Wilson 1803; ffolliott 1970; Ferguson 1998.

5. ARDMORE COTTAGE, Athy; 1886; *demolished.*
A property improved in 1865 by the Cross family, their gate lodge added later by Frederick Cross.

6. ARDMORE, Athy; post-1837; *demolished.*
A seat in the mid-nineteenth century of James Butler.

Griffith 1848–60.

7. ARDREIGH, Athy; *c.* 1800.

A pleasant single-storey Georgian cottage with some fine surviving original features in six-over-six sash windows in rendered walls and tiny slates to the hipped roof. Long and commodious enough to suggest that it may previously have been the miller's house. There is a later two-bay gabled central extension of about 1840 with cast-iron latticed casements and wooden brackets to the verge, which are taken about the eaves. A John Hill Farange is recorded as living here in 1814, but the property is later associated with the Haughton family, mill-owners.

Leet 1814; *IFR*.

8. ATHGARVAN LODGE, Newbridge (2).
Griffith in 1853 notes two lodges, one of which was vacant. One at least existed in 1837, while the other is not evident on the OS maps or on site. Both assumed to have been demolished. Home in 1837 to the Hon. Frederick George Ponsonby (1815–95), who in 1880 succeeded his brother as 6th earl of Bessborough, Co. Kilkenny. It later became a property of Allen McDonagh in the mid-nineteenth century.

Lewis 1837; Griffith 1848–60; *BPB* (1929).

9. ATHY UNION WORKHOUSE, Athy; *c.* 1845; architect probably George Wilkinson.
One of architect George Wilkinson's numerous workhouses, in this case a mild Tudor Revival-style complex, opened for first admissions on 9 January 1844 to 600 persons. Built in facing stone which may have been the original finish of its gate lodge, in the same manner but blandly rendered. Single-storey five-bay with central hall projection, all gables having prominent skew-tables and deep kneelers. Horribly disfigured by the insertion of modern casement windows. In use. Now St Vincent's Hospital.

O'Connor 1995.

10. BALLAGHMOON, Castledermot (2).
A seat in 1852 of Thomas Eager.

East lodge; pre-1852; *demolished.*

West lodge; *c.* 1850.
Not quite opposite the gates is a standard gabled structure with matching projecting hall. Roughcast with a chimney-stack to each end. Extended, modernised and occupied.

Griffith 1848–60.

11. BALLINA or BALYNA, Johnstown Bridge (2).

The ancient seat of the O'More family, from whom it passed through a late nineteenth-century marriage to the O'Ferralls, of whom Ambrose built a Regency house here, the pre-1837 gate lodge to which was opposite the gates. This would seem to have been replaced prior to the destruction by fire of the big house in 1878 and its subsequent rebuilding. This is a singular 1½-storey Tudor Gothic gatehouse, set well back and elevated from the entrance. Built off a T-plan in nice mellow brick, with stone dressings in its plinth, minimal skew-tables and opening surrounds. The latter are very fine, being a variety of single, bipartite and tripartite mullioned, label-moulded windows and lancet doors. From the main front the central projection widens on the ground floor through lean-to hallways to front and rear doors, a seemingly unique device in Irish gate lodges. This dates from about 1860, when Roger More O'Ferrall (1797–1880) employed architect J.S. Butler to design the nearby churches of Broadford and Cloughnarinka. The fleur-de-lis crestings look to be of later date.

IFR; Williams 1994.

12. BALLINDOON, Edenderry; *c.* 1835; architect probably W.V. Morrison.

In 1838, on the death of his talented architect son, Sir Richard Morrison carried on William Vitruvius's unfulfilled commission at Baronscourt, Co. Tyrone, by offering James Hamilton, 2nd marquis of Abercorn, three designs of varied grandeur for entrances to the estate. One could feel sympathy for the architect when none of these proposals were realised. It seems, however, that one of these schemes had already been built a few years earlier here at Ballindoon, for although it did not sufficiently impress the marquis it clearly found favour with Humphrey Bor. Identical in plan and elevation, this is a very fine little Greek Doric lodge in ashlar. Single-storey standard under a hipped roof with a moulded stone eaves band carried up as part of the pediment to its projecting frontispiece, which is carried on a pair of columns *in antis* that lead to a canted internal porch, through which passage was expected between the principal rooms. Flanking the breakfront are bipartite casement windows with cast-iron latticed lights in Tudor manner, all framed with moulded surrounds. The back return contained a storeroom and a closet. The gatescreen differs from that intended for Baronscourt, other than in having recessed panels to the pillars and anthemion motifs. Otherwise there is no other building on the property that would be attributable to Morrison. There are very similar lodges at Thornton Lodge, Co. Dublin (*q.v.*), and Modreeny, Co. Tipperary.

Dean 1994.

13. BALLINDOOLIN TOWNLAND, Edenderry; pre-1837; *demolished.*
An anonymous property in 1853 of Jane Payne, the lodge and entrance to which were opposite the gates to Ballindoolin House and of which there is no longer any trace.

Griffith 1848–60.

14. BALLINTAGGART, Colbinstown (2).
In 1892 Francis Bonham died and was succeeded by his younger brother, Colonel John Bonham (1834–1928), who set about extending the demesne by realigning the public road away from the site of old Ballintaggart Lodge, to replace it with a new mansion and adding two pretty gate lodges, probably to the designs of a young Richard Francis Caulfield Orpen, who chose an early nineteenth-century Tudor Picturesque style with steep ornamental gables and lofty chimney-stacks.

Principal lodge; *c.* 1895; architect Richard Orpen.

A 1½-storey standard structure built in rubble facings with brick dressings and a pair of diagonally set flues. Both main gables and the projecting porch, which rests on carved wooden posts, have highly decorative fretted scrolled bargeboards with spiky finials at eaves and apex. Sadly derelict and heavily shrouded in ivy. There is an extensive and disused entrance screen of shallow concave quadrants in rubble stone, with square carriage pillars broaching to create octagonal cappings in contrasting ashlar.

Secondary lodge; *c.* 1895; architect Richard Orpen.

A single-storey version of the above but with cut-stone dressings and a canted bay to the leading gable. Modern windows.

There are two very similar lodges at Mount Nebo, Co. Wexford (*q.v.*), which can be explained by the brothers' sister, Margaret Louisa Wyatt, chatelaine of that place, having employed Orpen there.

LGI (1958); Bence-Jones 1988; IAA photograph (65/17a).

BALLYFAIR (see NORMANBY LODGE)

15. BALLYGORAN, Maynooth; *c.* 1850.
Developed into a twentieth-century bungalow, only the lion masks to the eaves betray its age. A seat in 1851 of William Browne.

Griffith 1848–60.

16. BALLYHAGAN, Carbury; pre-1911; *demolished.*
Opposite the gates was a gate lodge built after 1838; in 1851 a seat of William Foote.

Griffith 1848–60.

17. BALLYNAKILL, Johnstown Bridge; pre-1838; *demolished.*
The porter's lodge to a seat in the early nineteenth century of Thomas Kearney had gone by 1911.

18. BALLYROE, Athy; pre-1909; *demolished.*
William Fife was resident here in 1852.

BALLYSAX RECTORY (see KNOCKNAGARM)

19. BALLYSHANNON, Calverstown; pre-1837; *demolished.*
A mid-eighteenth-century seat, built by the Annesleys, passed to the Palmers before being purchased in 1800 by the Kennedy family. The lodge had gone by 1939.

BALYNA (see BALLINA)

20. BARBERSTOWN CASTLE, Straffan; pre-1837; *demolished.*
An early thirteenth-century tower-house and later attached Georgian house with a succession of owners down the centuries, which about 1805 passed to a Joseph Atkinson after the death of Hugh Carncross.

Wilson 1803; Leet 1814.

BARN HALL (see PARSONSTOWN)

21. BARN HALL, Leixlip; pre-1837; *demolished.*
Probably previously the home farm to the Conolly's Castletown, Celbridge (*q.v.*), nearby, the house having taken its name from the 'Wonderful Barn' in the grounds. It was in the possession of the Cooper family from the mid-eighteenth century.

JCKAS (1891–5).

BARODA (see CONNELLMORE)

22. BARRETTSTOWN CASTLE, Ballymore Eustace (2).
Two identical disappointing early twentieth-century two-storey gatehouses with lean-to porches, in roughcast with half-timbered effect to the gables. Both occupied. Neither can be attributed to architect Michael Scott, who altered the house for Elizabeth Arden after it passed from the Borrowes family of Gilltown (*q.v.*).

Williams 1994.

23. BARRETTSTOWN, Newbridge; *c.* 1860.

As introduction to the multi-gabled Picturesque mansion within is this excellent single-storey standard Tudor Revival cottage, a rare and remarkable example of the bricklayer's craft, the facings extending to moulded specials as label mouldings and chamfered surrounds to Tudor arches of the projecting hall. All gables are enhanced by ornamental carved bargeboards. The gateway continues the theme, with Tudor-arched

recessed panels to screen walls and pillars topped by pineapple finials. All presumably for George De Pentheny O'Kelly on the death of his elder brother in 1859.

LGI (1958).

24. BARROWFORD, Athy; *c.* 1810.

A modest standard gabled affair with clipped verges, harled and whitewashed. Flat-roofed front hall. Occupied. In 1814 of 'Benjamin Braddell, a well-improved and handsome place'.

Mason 1814–19.

25. BELAN, Moone (12).

A grand Palladian mansion, a rebuild of 1743 to designs by Richard Castle and Francis Bindon for John Stratford, created earl of Aldborough in the year of his death in 1777, which was set in a once-prosperous and decorative demesne. This had every imaginable accoutrement befitting early Georgian leisure grounds: an ornamental canal, fish-ponds, bridges, obelisks, grotto, shell house, hermitage, dovecote, temples and remarkably, according to contemporary sources, no fewer than six lodged avenues. George Powell, agent to Edward Stratford, the 2nd earl, recorded in the rent-roll of 1786: 'The mansion House of Belan is most Magnificent as is also the Demesne thereto, containing 12 porters lodges Erected by the present Earl at the six Approaches'. According to a Mrs Sartoris, the pairs of lodges were adjoined by low white walls, with trees at the back, and were circular or, more precisely, if the single survivor is anything to go by, octagonal. What is as extraordinary is that only one of these twelve structures is apparent on the first OS map of 1837, testament to the tragically rapid decline of the demesne at the hands of the 4th earl, Benjamin Stratford (d. 1833), who brought it to its knees, squandering the family fortunes and, with his absentee gambling excesses, frittering away the improvements of his father and eldest brother, Edward Stratford (d. 1801), the 2nd earl. The location of one of the missing pairs is revealed by a local resident reminiscing in the late nineteenth century: 'the grand entrance was approached from Moone by a long avenue, with a wide piece of grass on either side, with trees at the back, very handsome, and about a mile in length. At either side, quite that distance from the entrance, stood two small houses, white and slated ... This avenue was ended by a very high and beautiful iron gate, on either side of which were low, white circular walls, with trees at the back. On the right was a white circular lodge ...' This iron gate would appear to be the fine ornamental Rococo one which now marks a disused access to Carton demesne (*q.v.*). Of any entrance pillars there

is no trace; indeed, already by 1814 Atkinson on a visit here considered that 'The approach to this place, from Ballitore, is injudicious—it comprises a short avenue running a straight line through mutilated piers, which convey to the mind of the beholder rather the impression of a place deserted and in ruins, than the handsome habitation of a resident nobleman'. The surviving lodge, at the head of a short drive axial with the doorway of the lost house, is the right-hand of a pair shown on a 1774 estate map, perhaps then not long built. It is a substantial two-storey shell, now lacking its octahedral roof, which sprang from the cut-stone corbelled eaves course, the octagon plan giving rise to a brick fabric, the whole finished in rendering with applied quoins. Openings on all faces, some blind, are flat-headed, apart from the doorway, which is set in a segmentally arched recess. A durable structure, now home to luxuriant plant life.

Atkinson 1815; Burke's *Dormant and extinct peerages* (1883); *JCKAS* (1891–5 and 1904); Malins and Glin 1976; Lightbown 2008.

BELLAVILLE (see LONGTOWN)

26. BERT, Kilberry (2).

A great house of the de Burgh family, earls of Downes, had two lodged entrances, one of which made a considerable impression on an 1855 visitor.

South lodge; pre-1837; *demolished.*

'It is approached by a noble avenue of about half a mile in length, of ample width and great regularity, which, with the striking and handsome curving entrance, and the unique gate-lodge, in front of which are laid out tasteful flower-beds, command the admiration of the visitor.' The unique lodge has gone without trace.

Village entrance; *c.* 1820.

A tiny modest two-bay gabled structure, extended and rendered in modernisation. Occupied. Built for Ulysses de Burgh, the 2nd Lord Downes (1788–1864), upon whose death the estates passed to his son-in-law, James, Lord Seaton.

Lacy 1852; *IFR*.

27. BISHOPSCOURT, Kill (4).

A very fine Classical mansion built by William Brabazon Ponsonby (1744–1806) on succeeding to the estate after his father's death in 1787. It seems to have had a contemporary gate lodge, the middle of three entrances from the north.

Early lodge; pre-1838; *demolished.*

East lodge; post-1838.

A lodgeless approach which has nevertheless the grandest of the demesne's gatescreens, comprised of six granite pillars with moulded recessed panels and cappings, set amongst ogee railed quadrants.

West lodge; *c.* 1850.

A modest standard gabled structure lies derelict at an entrance more noticeable for its gate sweep. Of an age with the lodge, with four cast-iron inner pillars, flanked by ogee quadrants terminating in outer stone pillars with round-headed recesses and layered pyramidal cappings.

South lodge; *c.* 1850.

The lodge is like that to the west gate but improved and occupied. Ogee railed sweeps enclosed by squat granite pillars with recessed panels, the carriage ones with ball finials.

The latter three approaches were created by John Ponsonby, the 2nd baron, before his death in 1855.

BPB (1929); Bence-Jones 1988.

28. BLACKHALL, Clane; *c.* 1840.

An estate of the Wolfe family which has had a remarkable late twentieth-century facelift, extending to the creation of a new lodged entrance in a less than subtle English Tudor Picturesque manner. The original lodge has had a like make-over and extension, replicating many of its features in modern materials. Probably previously single-storey standard with steep ornamental bargeboards and decorative hip-knobs, now having synthetic scalloped 'slates', a projecting gabled hallway, lead-effect windows and a canted bay facing the park. Roughcast walls, sporadic modern cresting and a crisp red-brick chimney-stack. Large extension to the road, at right angles to the old structure. Built by Peter Wolfe (1776–1848).

LGI (1904).

29. BOSTON, Kill; *c.* 1850/1905.
A two-storey gatehouse, roughcast with pierced and carved bargeboards. Two-bay upper floor and projecting single-storey hallway. The dated shield in the gable probably gives the time of its being raised a storey. A property in 1853 of Thomas Burton.

Griffith 1848–60.

BROOKLAWN (see PRESTONBROOK)

30. BRYANSTOWN, Maynooth; *c.* 1900.
A single-storey roughcast five-bay gabled affair with three-over-three sash windows. Projecting hallway with clipped verges in the form of an open pediment. Three conspicuous chimney-stacks. Derelict. An estate in the nineteenth century of the Malone family.

BURTON HALL (see COUNTY CARLOW)

BURTOWN (see POWERSGROVE)

31. CALVERSTOWN, Calverstown; pre-1837; *demolished.*
A property that had a succession of occupants: Messrs Levinge (1783), Cuffe (1804), North (1814) and Borrowes (1838); the lodge had gone by 1910.

Taylor and Skinner 1778; 1969 [1783]; Wilson 1803; Leet 1814; Fraser 1838.

CANNYCOURT (see KENNYCOURT)

32. CARDINGTON, Athy; pre-1837; *demolished.*
A gatekeeper's lodge which was built either by Captain Thomas J. Rawson, who was resident here whilst his property of Glassely (*q.v.*) was being restored until his death in 1814, or Captain Benjamin Lefroy of the Carrigglass Manor (*q.v.*) family (1782–1869), who succeeded to the estate.

JCKAS (Vol. 7, July 1914).

CARNALWAY (see NEWBERRY)

33. CARNALWAY RECTORY, Kilcullen; *c.* 1850.
Clearly this parish was a prosperous living, judging by the substantial rectory in Tudor Revival style with an appropriate contemporary English Picturesque Cottage introduction. Single-storey off an L-plan, with ornamental carved bargeboards to main gables and that of the hall, which projects from the internal angle. Rendered, occupied and greatly extended. The fortunate incumbent from 1832 until his death was Revd Thomas Henry Torrens (1801–58), benefiting from a development probably funded by John La Touche of nearby Harristown (*q.v.*).

Leslie and Wallace 2009.

Ulster Museum

34. CARTON, Maynooth (7).
Johann van der Hagen's bird's-eye view of Carton of *c.* 1730 (*above*) reveals the very fine William and Mary mansion of the Ingoldsby family and evidence of its Jacobean predecessor of the Talbots, earls of Tyrconnell, with its vast semicircular forecourt and radiating avenues, the central one of which, on an axis with the front door, was flanked by two great carriage pillars, each crowned by ball finials, which were linked by railings to a pair of pillboxes, prototypes of the gate lodge. Each was simply square on plan, with toothed quoins and pyramidal roof. By 1738 Robert Fitzgerald, 19th earl of Kildare, had purchased the lease and set about transforming the unfashionable house with a Palladian facelift to designs of Richard Castle, and by 1760 a vignette view by John Rocque shows the forecourt and its lodges to have been swept away in favour of a 'natural' landscape. Work on the grounds had begun in 1744, the year that James Fitzgerald, the future 1st duke of Leinster, succeeded to the property. He was to acquire almost 1,000 acres in forming a new demesne enclosed by nearly five miles of boundary walls, which was complete by 1757. In 1747 the young 20th earl had married Emilia Mary Lennox, daughter of the 2nd duke of Richmond, and she until 1774 devoted herself to the improvements, which included the creation of three lodged entrances to the demesne and beyond. One of those creations survives.

Village gate; 1757.

A modest and charming single-storey standard lodge with steeply hipped roof rising to a later lofty brick chimney-stack. In roughcast rubble walls two wide bipartite casement windows flank the doorway with a quirky applied imitation rendered fanlight over. Probably the oldest inhabited gate lodge in the country, it survives, lovingly maintained, in the village of Maynooth at the head of a 600yd avenue of noble and ancient lime trees, planted between 1756 and 1760, which leads to the demesne proper.

Maynooth gate; *c.* 1750/*c.* 1810; architect possibly Thomas Owen.

Thomas Ivory drawing (Irish Architectural Archive).

The original lodge here, to the west, built sometime between 1744 and 1756, was short-lived, having proved inappropriate to a principal entrance that deserved something grander. A suitable replacement must have provoked much debate, for many designs were produced and discarded, including two fine schemes by Thomas Ivory, noted for his Blue Coat school and Newcomen Bank in Dublin, and who had already designed a bridge over the Ryewater in the demesne in 1763. His drawings of *c.* 1770 both proposed a central pedimented semicircular archway and screen walls containing postilion openings, but one showed gatekeeper's accommodation in a pair of lodges with canted fronts, blind with round-headed niches displaying elegant urns to each face. Ivory must have been succeeded as architect to the Fitzgeralds prior to his death in 1786 by Thomas Owen, a proposal of whose survives for a pair of lofty lodges with hipped roofs and corniced clipped eaves. These

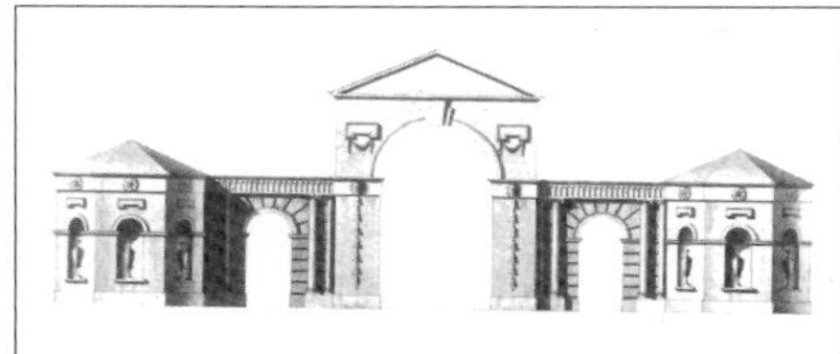

Thomas Ivory drawing (Irish Architectural Archive).

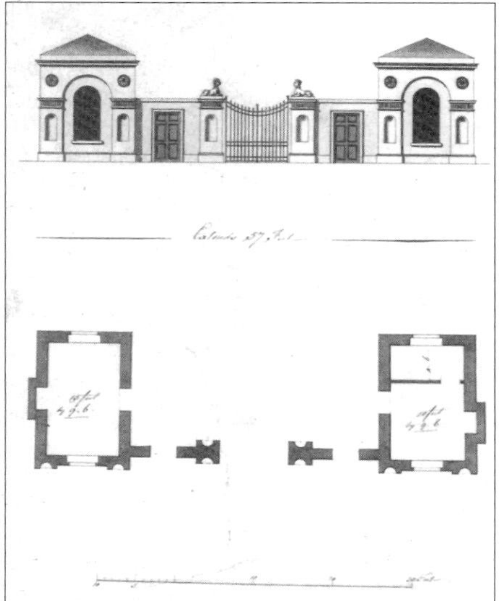

Thomas Owen drawing.

Irish Architectural Archive/W. Ryan

flanked screen walls with pedestrian doorways and carriage gates carried on piers with sphinxes on top. Owen must have had sight of a pattern-book of one J. Miller, *The country gentleman's architect*, the first edition of which is thought to date from 1787, just a year before Owen's death, in which Design No. 30 bears a striking resemblance to Owen's unexecuted proposal. All these plans had a recurring common theme of semicircular arched niches, perhaps a weakness of Emilia's and apparent in what eventually supplanted the old lodge on the left-hand side of the entrance. Although looking more early nineteenth-century than late eighteenth-century, what transpired owes much to the Owen/Miller designs, though the lodges are two-storey gatehouses with oversailing eaves, the same tall arched recesses back and front and niches, but pedimented cappings substituted for sphinxes on the gate pillars with their fluted supporting scrolls. The whole in a sandstone ashlar is very impressive but partly derelict.

Dublin gate; pre-1756/1816; architect probably Francis Johnston.

The previous gate lodge here at the south and main approach, another of the original three to the demesne, was located forward of the gates and again proved relatively short-lived. After Emilia left Carton in 1774 for Frescati House, south Dublin (*q.v.*), with William Ogilvie, there was a period of almost 40 years during which few changes were made to the park, her son William Robert Fitzgerald, the 2nd duke of Leinster, seemingly having devoted much of his attention to politics. His son Augustus Frederick, the 3rd duke (1791–1874), who succeeded in 1804, revived improvements on a major scale, extending and refacing the mansion to designs of Sir Richard Morrison in 1812; he realigned the road by the Dublin gate and in doing so replaced the porter's accommodation with something more fashionable behind the demesne wall. This is a standard single-storey hip-roofed Classical lodge, with rendered walls contrasting with limestone highlights in the blocked rusticated opening dressings, plinth, banded chimney-stacks and pediment to the hall breakfront, which has the date 'MDCCCXVI' in its tympanum. Replacement six-over-six sash windows and panelled door below a mouth-organ fanlight. Occupied. Strangely, this lodge bears an uncanny resemblance to Francis Johnston's at the main gate to the Phoenix Park, north Dublin (*q.v.*), of five years earlier. Tall limestone ashlar carriage pillars with moulded plinths and corniced cappings. Secondary lower pillars and postilion gates. Contemporary early Georgian ironwork. Within is a pretty iron pedestrian turnstile.

Kellystown gate; *c.* 1775.

From the far east of the demesne is this approach created by the 2nd duke sometime between his succession to the title in 1773 and its appearance on a 1788 estate map. The contemporary two-storey gatehouse, located forward of the gates, is constructed of rubble stone, harled, under a hipped roof. Modernised with wider windows inserted. Plain and occupied. Corniced square stone gate pillars with scroll-topped gate stops.

Dunboyne or Old Carton gate; *c.* 1810.

When the new boundary wall to the demesne was built in the mid-eighteenth century, the only original avenue to survive was this approach from the north, but it remained lodgeless until the early nineteenth century. Its chimney-stack and entrance screen suggest that they were built when the Dublin gate was reconstructed. This is a single-storey hip-roofed lodge with a gabled hall projecting from one end, its main front to the avenue comprised of two big tripartite mullioned and transomed cast-iron latticed casement windows with cut-stone chamfered surrounds in pleasant rubble walls. Here the carriage pillars have rusticated ball finials and replacement gates.

Blakestown gate; *c.* 1855.

The only Victorian porter's lodge, built by the 3rd duke, is a pretty English Picturesque cottage with beautifully carved ornamental bargeboards, hip-knobs and eaves pendants to main gables and that to the central projecting hallway. Single-storey standard with toothed dressings to squared casement windows in roughcast walls. Occupied.

Moygaddy gate.

One of the original accesses, long redundant, seems never to have had a lodge.

Miller 1789; *BPB* (1929); *IGS Bulletin* (April–Sept. 1975); Malins and Glin 1976; Fitzgerald 2000; O'Kane 2004.

CASTLE BROWNE (see CLONGOWES WOOD COLLEGE)

35. CASTLE MARTIN, Kilcullen (2).
The glory of this estate is the magnificent gatescreen, seemingly of an earlier century to its gate lodge and apparently of *c.* 1730, after the property had been purchased from the builder of the house a decade earlier, a Dublin banker called Harrison, by Captain Henry Boyle Carter. It was his grandson, William Henry Carter (1783–1859), who erected the very fine Regency porter's lodge.

Main entrance; *c.* 1820; architect not known.

A simple single-storey two-roomed structure below an oversailing shallow pyramidal roof with chunky soffit brackets. Stuccoed walls contain as the principal front to the avenue a tripartite casement window, the mullions with recessed panels under a pronounced moulded lintel and all set in a segmentally headed recess. Now much modernised and extended sympathetically. The entrance gates and screen extend as railings to contain postilion gates and terminate in ashlar pillars. The carriage gates have a profusion of spear-topped rails and scrolls, which extends to a majestic overthrow displaying a crest, in the form of an armoured arm wielding a Danish battleaxe, of the Blacker family. This device and the immaculate condition of the ironwork suggest that it may date from a century later than it first appears. Thomas Samuel Blacker, who bought Castle Martin in 1854, was descended from the Carrick Blacker family of County Armagh and would have been familiar with the very similar and genuinely early Georgian entrance gates to Richhill Castle nearby. Dating from 1745 by the Thornberry brothers, they in turn were probably inspired by James Gibbs's *A book of architecture* (1728).

Secondary entrance; pre-1837; *demolished.*
Of the other gate lodge closer to Kilcullen there is no trace.

Gibbs 1728; *LGI* (1904); Bence-Jones 1988; Dean 1994.

36. CASTLEMITCHELL, Stradbally (2).

Front entrance; pre-1837; *demolished.*
Surviving is a gatescreen with four square pillars having Greek key pattern and rusticated ball finials. The gate lodge opposite served in the early nineteenth century as a police station when the estate was Chapman property.

Rear entrance; *c.* 1850.
A single-storey hip-roofed building with flat-roofed hall projecting from the left-hand side, containing cast-iron latticed lights probably salvaged from the main structure in recent modernisation. Rendered with otherwise modern casements. Occupied. Built by Patrick Charles Doran, who was here in the mid-nineteenth century.

37. CASTLEROE LODGE, Castledermott; pre-1909; *demolished.*
A lost lodge to an earlier house *c.* 1825 of the Keogh family.

38. CASTLESIZE, Sallins (2).
Two gate lodges built either by George Chace or his successor to the property, Isaac Manders.

Front entrance; *c.* 1825.
A nicely proportioned standard single-storey lodge with a hipped roof. Harled with square windows, the central doorway now converted into a window. Square ashlar entrance pillars with basic unmoulded cappings but having splendid pineapple finials.

Side entrance; *c.* 1830.
Roughcast and creeper-clad asymmetrical building, shallow-gabled, with the roof projecting over central bay flanked by recesses to each side, with doorway in that of left-hand side. Occupied.

Leet 1814; Lewis 1837.

39. CASTLETOWN, Celbridge (5).
'This is I believe the only house in Ireland to which the term palace may be applied.' Thus opined Richard Twiss in 1775, and it remains so to this day. Whichever of the three approaches he made to the great 1722 house of the Conollys he would have passed through a lodged entrance, as is made clear by Rocque's map of 1760. Just as responsibility for creation of the house lies with Speaker William Conolly (1662–1729), so we have to thank two women for most of the development of the demesne: his wife Katherine Conyngham, to whom he devised the property on his death, and his nephew Thomas's wife, Lady Louisa Augusta Lennox, daughter of the 2nd duke of Richmond, who, like her sister Emilia at Carton (*q.v.*), devoted herself during her marriage and long widowhood to improving the place, its upkeep and the welfare of the tenants. So for almost a century, between William's death in 1729 and Louisa's in 1821, the aesthetic tastes and ambitions were almost solely theirs. In 1764 Louisa wrote, 'I am in the midst of pleasant improvements in and out of doors', and it is clear that she owed much to a knowledge of architectural pattern-books.

Celbridge entrance; pre-1760/*c.* 1810/*c.* 1890.
The splendid and substantial Classical gate

pillars facing the village have vermiculated rusticated shafts, Greek key patterns, swagged paterae to friezes and sphinxes resting on their cappings, all as adapted by Sir William Chambers in his *Treatise on civil architecture* (1759) from an original design by the 3rd earl of Burlington for himself at Chiswick House, Middlesex, around 1730 but not completed here until 1783. Louisa was pleasantly surprised at the skill of local masons, for she recorded in a letter to her sister: 'what is rather extraordinary to say of Paddy workmen in general is, that the stone cutters work and ironwork are so well finished for the sort of materials that they are done in that it is quite pleasant'. The main subject of her admiration was John Coates, stonecutter of Maynooth, who charged £16.18s.6d for the 'two sphynkes'. Whilst the provenance, date and quality of the gates are manifest, the same cannot be said for the gatekeeper's accommodation to the left-hand side of the entrance screen, which is an undistinguished and unworthy jumble of buildings, probably of three periods, only one of which is obvious. To the rear of the gatescreen is a late Victorian two-storey gatehouse of generous proportions, with roughcast walls contrasting with red-brick dressings to the two-bay first floor above symmetrical three-bay ground-floor fenestration. A shallow gabled roof extends forward of the entrance over an intermediate structure of indeterminate age attached to a taller gabled affair from which projects a bowed construction with semi-conical roof. This, or part of it, may be the 'porter's lodge' marked on John Rocque's map of 1760. On the other hand, as its location is not made clear, it could be a replacement of *c.* 1810, its predecessor having been supplemented to the right-hand side of the gates by the Church of Ireland church erected in 1806. This disparate complex has now pluckily been rehabilitated as accommodation by the Irish Landmark Trust.

West or Pond Field gate; *c.* 1765; *demolished.*
A gatekeeper's lodge presumably dating from between 1760 and *c.* 1768, as it does not

appear on the Rocque map but is faintly outlined on a later demesne plan. It survived until at least 1935.

Leixlip gate; *c.* 1760.

Remote to the north of the demesne at the head of Gay's Avenue is this plain gable-ended two-storey gatehouse with harled walls and some windows set in segmentally arched recesses. Alternatively named 'Shepherd's Lodge' in *c.* 1768 and 'Castletown Lodge' in 1837, it lies derelict alongside its contemporary and rather grander gatescreen. Comprised of flat-arched postilion openings with keystones to each side of a pair of splendid limestone ashlar carriage pillars with scroll-topped gate stops, moulded plinths and corniced cappings and 'bap' finials.

Kelly's lodge; *c.* 1765; *demolished.*

So called on the demesne map of *c.* 1768, it does not appear on the earlier Rocque map and, indeed, had disappeared by 1837. Situated within the estate on the avenue from the Dublin gate, it may have been gateless and accommodated the land steward of the time, after whom it was probably named.

Dublin gate; *c.* 1760/1772/1785.

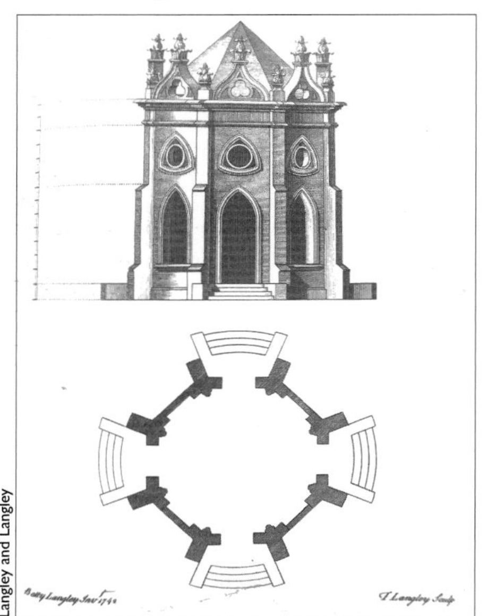

Langley and Langley

A building which evolved over the mid-eighteenth century and has become affectionately known as the 'Batty Langley Lodge' but which Louisa Conolly knew and referred to as 'the Cottage'. She personally directed its improvement, documented in 1772, and was later responsible for orientating it to face the park to be viewed and appreciated from within rather than by the visitor, the most important of whom would, in any case, have approached from the village. To an existing two-storey gatehouse in 1785 she applied a canted extension to one end, each of its three faces separated by three-tier buttresses rising to a corniced parapet decorated with an array of crocketed pinnacles on three crowning ogee gablets perforated by trefoils. The main lancet-headed window openings have Y-traceried sashes, with one retaining its original pretty octagonal glazing pattern. Above these are spherical triangular lights with decorative floral inserts. This is a faithful impression of plate XVII of a Gothic temple in Batty Langley's *Gothic architecture improved by rules and proportions* (1742), a copy of which may have been in the Castletown library. In contrast to this delayed piece of Strawberry Hill Gothic is the robust Classical gatescreen, which would be contemporary with the original pre-1760 gatehouse. Blocked rusticated pillars support similarly treated ball finials; rather more delicate mouldings to plinth, cappings and scroll-topped gate stops. Linked to the lodge by a keystoned postilion opening.

Langley and Langley 1747; Chambers 1862; Twiss 1776; *LGI* (1904); *IGS Bulletin* (Oct.–Dec. 1968); *Country Life* (27 March, 3 April and 10 April 1969); Mowl and Earnshaw 1984; Ferguson 1998; O'Kane 2004.

40. CASTLEWARDEN, Kill; pre-1911; *demolished.*

An estate that passed in the early nineteenth century from the Wolfe family to the Pallisers, who probably built the gate lodge, after 1838.

41. CELBRIDGE ABBEY, Celbridge; pre-1837; *demolished.*

Beloved of Swift, this Georgian Gothic house was also known as 'Marlay Abbey', having been built by Dr Richard Marlay (*c.* 1730–1802), bishop of Waterford. It was tenanted in the early nineteenth century but passed by marriage to the Grattans from the Marlay family. Although there is an attractive Georgian Gothic entrance screen next to the house off the Clane road, its lodged gate had been approached by a bridge over the River Liffey from the Sallins road.

LGI (1904); Bence-Jones 1988; Leslie and Knox 2008.

42. CELBRIDGE COLLEGIATE SCHOOL, Celbridge (2).

Castletown House is at the centre of radiating avenues, two of which are stopped as vistas by the extraordinary giant obelisk to the north-west and the Wonderful Barn to the north-east. A mile and a half to the south-west is the earliest of the three buildings, the Collegiate School. Endowed by Speaker William Conolly and built following his death in 1729, it did not reach completion until after 1737. There has been much unresolved speculation as to whether it was a posthumous work of Thomas Burgh or Edward Lovett Pearse, or by one of their assistants, Isaac or Michael Wills or Richard Castle. What does seem likely is that the design of the entrance to the complex had not been finalised in the initial scheme and that the fine triumphal archway and its attendant lodges are by Castle. In 1740 he was working for William Conolly's widow Katherine in designing the obelisk.

Inner gate; *c.* 1740; architect possibly Richard Castle.

Giving access to the school forecourt is this dignified Palladian composition comprised of a triple archway, the central ashlar carriage opening being a round-headed arch crowned

39. CASTLETOWN, Celbridge, Dublin gate (*Country Life*).

by a pediment raised on Doric pilasters. Beyond the postilion gates the flanking single-storey cubic porters' lodges are similarly pedimented with, back and front, lunette windows in dressed stone pleasantly contrasting with roughcast walls. In the walls forward of the gateway are spyholes or gunloops. There was an almost identical entrance screen at Longtown House (*q.v.*) nearby, the archway of which survives.

Outer gate; *c.* 1820.
Somewhat less dignified is this plain little single-storey hip-roofed structure built off an L-plan, its back turned to the road and its main three-bay symmetrical front facing up the avenue.

Lewis 1837; *Country Life* (3 April 1969); Craig 1982; McParland 2001.

CELBRIDGE HALL (see OAKLEY PARK)

43. CELBRIDGE PARSONAGE, Celbridge; *c.* 1880.

An Taisce

Remarkably, the rectory and its gate lodge were a late Victorian establishment, for the latter looks to date from a half-century earlier, with its typical Regency-style paired eaves brackets to a shallow hipped roof, and segmentally arched recesses for the tripartite sash windows, the lower portion of which have latticed glazing. Single-storey standard, its raised chimney-stack and walls finished in roughcast, as were the quadrant walls to the entrance screen, which had tall corniced ashlar carriage pillars flanked by a pair of flat-arched postilion openings. Spear-topped ironwork. Probably work initiated with the arrival in 1881 of the Revd Charles Irvine Graham, who remained as incumbent for a further 30 years until his death. The house has since been branded 'Celbridge Lodge'.

Leslie and Wallace 2001.

44. CHRISTIANSTOWN, Rathangan; pre-1837; *demolished.*
Like neighbouring Newington (q.v.), a nineteenth-century seat of the Neale family.

45. Clongowes Wood College, front entrance (National Library of Ireland/Lawrence Collection).

45. CLONGOWES WOOD COLLEGE, Clane (3).
Previously a private house called 'Castle Browne', it was rebuilt in 1788 as a symmetrical Gothic castle by Thomas Wogan Browne, an amateur architect who was commissioned by other big landowners. To this house there was one lodged entrance.

Rear entrance; pre-1837; *demolished.*
Situated up a lengthy drive from the Celbridge road to the east.

In 1812 Thomas Wogan Browne took his own life; two years later his younger brother, Lt-Gen. Michael Wogan Browne, sold the property and it was 'opened as a college for the education of the sons of the Catholic nobility and gentry'. It was greatly extended to fulfil its new function, but it was not until 1840 that the main front approach between a long straight avenue of ancient limes was improved and an impressive entrance archway and lodge added under the direction of the rector of the time, Father Robert Haly.

Front entrance; 1840; architect not known.

This is an impressive sham Tudor Castellated composition, unusually symmetrical but perfectly reflecting the main front of Wogan Browne's old house beyond. Like a stage set, but none the worse for that, it has sadly lost its original rubble facings behind a later bland coat of render. The central carriage opening has a four-centred arch with hood moulding, now lacking its portcullis, and a machicolation contained in crenellated ramparts, all between tall slender towers complete with blank shields, label-moulded mock arrowloops and phoney machicolations which extend above what appears to be a pair of flanking lodges. In fact, that to the right is just a screen, although the other does front a rambling single-storey lodge in the same manner, with a liberal application of square turrets and castellated parapets. Now blocked up, it had the dual function of a post office. The complex extends further in battlemented curtain walls to terminate in circular turrets.

Clane entrance; pre-1939; *demolished.*
Another lodge to the west, built by the Jesuits, of which there is no trace.

LGI (1904); Joyce 1912; Lawrence photograph (3994R).

46. CLONKEERAN, Carbury; *c.* 1800.
A derelict single-storey hip-roofed structure to a property in 1800 of a Mr Borman.

Wilson 1803.

47. CONNELLMORE, Newbridge; *c.* 1875; architect probably W. Mansfield Mitchell.

A highly characterful late Victorian single-storey lodge on an L-plan in pleasant mellow brickwork contrasting with the stone chamfered lintels carried on columnettes to bipartite sash windows and steep skew-tables and kneelers. To the leading gabled windows are polychromatic round relieving arches with decorative stone inserts, above

which, in the apex, is a roundel in the same idiom. From the internal angle projects an ornamental carved wooden porch having a hipped gable with pretty scrolled iron hip-knob. Robust cast-iron downpipes and hoppers; to the ridges earthenware cresting between dominant single and paired brick chimney-stacks. The gatescreen is much earlier, of *c.* 1845, with chunky ironwork of that period in its ogee quadrants and gate piers, which have anthemion motifs repeated in the cappings of the outer stone pillars. The entrance screen originally gave access to 'Great Connell Lodge', as the house was known in the early nineteenth century, when it was the seat of the Poole Eyre family, followed by the Powells. In 1872 a Colonel Gray, who had considerably enlarged the place, sold it to James Cox. Cox engaged architect W.M. Mitchell to carry out further works, which must have included the gate lodge. Subsequently, about 1951, the property became home to the deposed maharaja of Baroda and its name changed accordingly.

JCKAS (1896–9); IAA.

48. COOLCARRIGAN, Timahoe (2).
A mid-Victorian seat of the Wilson family, descended from that of Daramona, Co. Westmeath (*q.v.*), which has two lodged gates.

North entrance; *c.* 1850.
A plain single-storey structure with a three-bay road frontage below a hipped roof. Occupied and extended, having the additional function of a post office.

South entrance; *c.* 1845.
A standard single-storey hip-roofed porter's lodge having tall eaves, perhaps subsequently raised to accommodate loft rooms, with paired modillion brackets continued as support to an open pediment to the hall breakfront. On each side a slender round-headed window, with plastic windows, in roughcast walls. Much extended and occupied. Its entrance screen is of later date, perhaps *c.* 1880, of chamfered ashlar pillars with moulded cappings on which are decorative iron finials terminating in ball features. Gates and matching Gothic railings with quatrefoil and cusped-arch motifs. Probably the work of architect Sir Thomas

Drew, whose obituary records him as having carried out additions to the house for Robert Mackay Wilson.

LGI (1904); *IB* (19 March 1910).

49. COURTOWN, Kilcock (2).
A property in the late eighteenth century of the Foster family which was acquired and a new house built upon it *c.* 1815 by the Aylmers. It had originally one lodged entrance gate.

Courtown lodge; *c.* 1880.
A single-storey standard lodge with steeply pitched roof and two symmetrically placed stacks, its gabled hall projection with round-headed fanlight to entrance door flanked by two-over-two sash windows with brick toothed dressings repeated as quoins in white rendered walls. Occupied.

Kilcock lodge; pre-1837/1882.

Replacing an earlier structure on the site and altogether more pretentious is this entrance near the village, now isolated by road improvements. In finishes as above but rather ungainly, the windows segmentally headed and arranged as a pair to the leading gable of an L-plan structure, single-storey with high eaves and paired modillion brackets. High in an apex is a roundel with date-stone. Large red-brick banded and corbelled chimney-stack which has escaped the black gloss paint applied liberally elsewhere. Mightily impressive contemporary cast-iron gatescreen, tall and impenetrable, a fine robust example of the iron-founder's craft, in this case by the Murphy Foundry of Dublin. All commissioned by Michael Aylmer (1831–85) but barely enjoyed by him.

LGI (1904); Bence-Jones 1988.

50. CROTANSTOWN, Newbridge; pre-1837; *demolished.*
An early nineteenth-century estate of the Ryan family.

51. CURRAGH GRANGE, Newbridge; *c.* 1905; architect probably R.C. Orpen.

A house built in 1904 for Captain Joseph Henry Greer, whose architect was Richard Caulfield Orpen. Whilst it is in Queen Anne style, by way of variety the outbuildings form a veritable village of half-timbered work, extending in a riot of black-and-white work into the single-storey gabled gate lodge, built off an irregular plan with red earthenware plain roof tiles, cresting and fancy hip-knobs and red-brick chimney-stacks, in stark contrast to the monochrome walls and squared Arts and Crafts casement windows.

Williams 1994.

52. DAFFY LODGE, Rathmore; pre-1837; *demolished.*
A property in 1863 of Timothy Griffin.

Griffith 1848–60.

53. DERRY LEE, Monasterevin; pre-1939; *demolished.*
A nineteenth-century estate of the Fleming family.

54. DONADEA CASTLE, Donadea (4).
The once-fine, ancient and imposingly walled estate of the Aylmer family eventually fell victim to the Wyndham Land Act of 1903, since when much has been made of its care by Coillte, with little concern shown for its architecture—the mansion lies a sad ruin, its important gate lodges similarly neglected. Sir Gerald George Aylmer (1798–1878) succeeded his father, Sir Fenton, in 1816 as the 8th baronet and inherited a property that had already fallen on hard times. He set about restoring its fortunes and built a reputation as an improver and amateur architect, although it is clear from the lodges that he was not above seeking professional help.

Chough gate; *c.* 1816; architect possibly Richard Elsam.
Hidden away at the base of a 400yd-long approach from the east, a wide avenue flanked by magnificent and venerable lime trees, was a sophisticated neo-Classical design in a pair of single-storey 'day and night' lodges, each an 11ft-square room with a corner fireplace, pyramidal roof behind a parapet and clad in ashlar and stucco finish. This is possibly a design of Richard Elsam, either directly or adapted from an illustration in his *An essay on rural architecture* (1803).

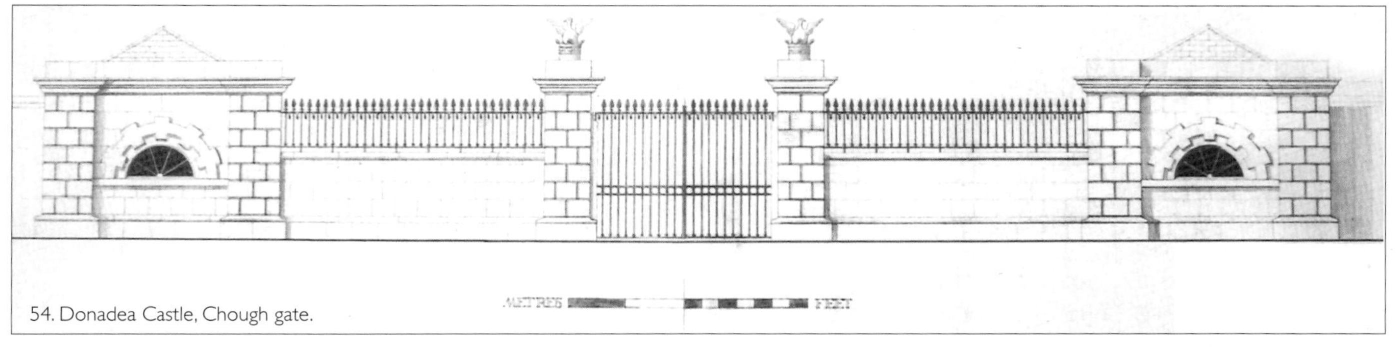

54. Donadea Castle, Chough gate.

He was an Englishman of dubious reputation who came to Ireland and led a peripatetic existence, for whatever reason, between 1808 and 1818 before returning home. The common features of lunette windows with rusticated alternate voussoirs and the gate pillars repeated as pilasters on the lodges are striking. They do not appear to be the work of Sir Richard Morrison, who is thought to have worked on the house, although there is a pair of lodges at Mote Park, Co. Roscommon, with similar lunette windows, a house which Morrison designed. This entrance lies forgotten, ruinous and overgrown; its gate finials of the family crest of a Cornish chough rising out of a ducal coronet probably now adorn someone's back garden.

Kilcock gate; pre-1837/1846; architect George Wilkinson.

The best-known output of the workaholic George Wilkinson is most of the workhouses in the country, but it emerges that after leaving public service he had quite a considerable private practice of mainly domestic work. This he pursued along with his pastime of studying the ancient architecture of his adoptive land. Here, on the northern approach to the demesne, is a product of his middle years in this gatehouse as 'medieval keep'. Two-storey square and indestructible, with a lofty correct Irish crenellated parapet, built in random rubble with narrow chamfered openings. Rising to the rear is a taller square outshot tower with 'arrowloops', which contains a spiral staircase leading to another 12ft-square room and a door to the roof ramparts. Alongside in like manner is a Tudor-arched carriage gateway beside a baby postilion opening. Beyond that, completing the composition is a slender square turret. Ironically, lying as it does an abandoned shell adds to the archaeological effect. To the left-hand side of the avenue survives a hip-roofed single-storey cottage, one of a pair of lodges which flanked the entrance. Now much altered and extended, it also functioned as a dispensary. Its companion was replaced by Wilkinson's creation in 1846.

54. Donadea Castle, Kilcock gate, drawn by Geo. Wilkinson (National Library of Ireland).

Dunmurraghall lodge; pre-1837; *demolished.*

A lodge to the western boundary built on the demesne wall.

Glebe or Kilamoragh lodge; *c.* 1850; *demolished.*

The latest of Donadea Castle's lodges, located at a south-east entrance.

Elsam 1803; *BPB* (1929); Bence-Jones 1988; Colvin 2008; *Journal of the Donadea Local History Group*, Vol. 1, No. 2 (1995); NLI drawings (A.D. 3588/114 & 115).

55. DONAGHCUMPER, Celbridge; pre-1837/*c.* 1870.

A house, previously called 'Rockfield', which was enlarged in the Tudor style in the 1830s for William Kirkpatrick (1769–1844). Its early lodge was replaced by the present structure, which is a very fine Picturesque 1½-storey cottage built in uncoursed quarry-faced stone, with relieving arches to windows and steeply pitched roofs with fancy carved bargeboards, earthenware crestings and tiled finish with canted and serrated bands. To the leading gable is a pretty single-storey canted bay window below a Chinese-style bellcast roof; nice Gothic trellised rustic porch. Concave entrance screen quadrants in matching masonry to lodge, with rockwork outer pillars, ashlar inner, and good wood and iron gates. All by the English architect Philip Charles Hardwick for Alexander Richard Kirkpatrick (1814–91).

Lewis 1837; Slater 1870; *LGI* (1958); Colvin 2008.

56. DONORE, Prosperous; pre-1837; *demolished.*
The late eighteenth-century house of the Hussey de Burghs is ruinous, its lodge gone, but the contemporary gatescreen survives. Big rustic roughcast ogee quadrants and plain carriage pillars with original wrought-iron spear-topped main gates and postilions.

57. DOWDINGSTOWN, Newbridge; *c.* 1840.
A standard single-storey cottage with hipped roof oversailing harled walls. Derelict. A seat in the mid-nineteenth century of Thomas Kirkpatrick.

Griffith 1848–60.

58. DOWDSTOWN, Maynooth; pre-1837; *demolished.*
A property belonging to a succession of owners in the late eighteenth and early nineteenth centuries.

59. DOWNINGS, Prosperous (3).
The estate, which passed *c.* 1810 from the Kemmis family to the Burys, had two early lodges.

East entrance; pre-1837; *demolished.*
Surviving are deep convex quadrants and cut-stone carriage pillars with plinths and cornices.

South entrance; *c.* 1810.
A plain single-storey standard lodge with roughcast walls beneath a hipped roof with clipped eaves. Extended by a bay to the left-hand side with a gabled end. Occupied. Two plain stone carriage pillars with shallow ogee quadrants.

North entrance; pre-1911; *demolished.*
The more recent and shortest-lived of the lodges, built in the time here of Charles Bury.

60. DUNFIERTH, Johnstown Bridge; pre-1838; *demolished.*
A house and lodge in the early nineteenth century of Sir Francis McDonnell.

61. DUNSHANE, Kilcullen; *c.* 1845.
A standard lodge with hipped roof; much modernised. Built between 1837 and 1853 for John Hickie.

Griffith 1848–60.

62. EYREFIELD LODGE, Kilcullen; pre-1837/1900; architect probably L.A. McDonnell.
Replacing a predecessor on the same site is this generous and striking composition typical of the Arts and Crafts movement in its combination of styles, Elizabethan and Classical. Located opposite the gates, this 1½-storey lodge is dominated by a wide gabled front, its three-bay symmetrical lower storey in red brick, with a central projecting single-storey hall having a segmental pediment-fronted roof flanked by multi-paned tripartite casement windows, a feature repeated as a pair of oriels to the attic floor, set in contrasting pebble-dash finish below a half-timbered-effect apex. There is a large corbelled red-brick stack on the ridge of the red tiled roof. Occupied. Added to the property at the turn of the twentieth century by Henry Beasley, who had come in succession to a plethora of previous owners. There are very similar lodges at Knockmaroon House, Co. Dublin (*q.v.*), and a like one to nearby Lumville Farm, prompting attribution of the design to Lawrence Aloysius McDonnell.

Costello 1996; IAA.

63. FARMHILL, Newcastle; *c.* 1810.
Originally a standard single-storey porter's lodge with a hipped roof, now modernised and extended to form an L-plan. A holding in 1814 of Mathew Reade.

Leet 1814.

64. FIRMOUNT, Clane; *c.* 1800.
A two-storey square gatehouse in harled rubble with irregular fenestration below a pyramidal roof, unusually commodious for its age. A property in the late eighteenth century of the Shaw family, which by 1814 was in the possession of Richard Dease.

Taylor and Skinner 1778; 1969 [1783]; Wilson 1803; Leet 1814.

65. FONTSTOWN RECTORY, Fontstown; pre-1837; *demolished.*
In 1837 the glebe house is noted as having been built in 1810 for £500, with later additions costing £600. The latter cost may have included provision of its gate lodge opposite the gates during the long incumbency (1807–54) of Revd John Bagot (1783–1856).

Lewis 1837; Leslie and Wallace 2001.

FORENAGHTS (see FURNESS)

62. Eyrefield Lodge, Kilcullen.

66. FORENAGHTS HOUSE, Naas (2).
In 1816 Revd Richard Wolfe (1787–1841) inherited an already sizeable family mansion on the death of his brother John and began enlargements and improvements on the estate, which included the building of two unusually ample gatekeepers' lodges.

West gate; *c.* 1830.

A standard single-storey lodge with a hipped roof and Regency features of segmentally arched recesses containing its openings in a symmetrical façade, improved and cloaked in modern rendering. Occupied.

East gate; *c.* 1830.

An extensive single-storey five-bay structure below a hipped roof with bellcast eaves. Its principal feature is a cut-stone frontispiece door-case of recessed panel pilasters supporting a stylised pediment with acroteria, framing a panelled door with sidelights and segmentally headed fanlight. Built in pleasant uncoursed rubble, with chiselled quoins and dressings to the windows of an asymmetrical elevation. All rather crudely rehabilitated with imitation sash windows, mouth-organ sidelights, spoked fanlight and synthetic slates.

LGI (1904); Bence-Jones 1988.

67. FOREST FARM, Athy (2).

North entrance; *c.* 1875.
A single-storey gabled three-bay lodge with door to the left-hand side, built in good coursed rubble with punched ashlar dressings to large square windows below a brick eaves course. Ladder access to loft space over right-hand room. Derelict.

South entrance; *c.* 1875.
Single-storey four-bay lodge in random stone facings and roof with clipped gables. Recently sympathetically restored and extended to rear to form a double pile.

A property acquired and developed from about 1870 by David Taylor.

68. FREEPARK, Ballitore; pre-1838; *demolished.*
A property in 1814 of John Thomas.

Leet 1814.

69. FURNESS, Naas (2).
Built *c.* 1740 for Richard Nevill, probably by architect and artist Francis Bindon, this very fine Palladian house was enlarged by his descendant Richard Jones Nevill, who also between *c.* 1780 and his death in 1822 landscaped the estate and added the two entrance lodges.

North lodge; *c.* 1820.
A standard single-storey hip-roofed Regency building in roughcast finish with all three openings set into round-headed recesses. Good granite entrance pillars with plinths, cornices and V-jointed rustication.

South lodge; *c.* 1790; architect not known.

A quite sophisticated little Classical cube, as if to imitate the main house, looks as if it should, or did, form one of a pair, set forward of, and rather ineptly linked to, a grand semicircular entrance screen. Sitting on a tall stone plinth, its main stuccoed front contains a blind lunette, over which is a frieze with

triglyphs and plain metopes below a pyramidal roof rising to a fluted cylindrical stone chimney-pot. The elevation observing the approach has two six-over-six sash windows. The main carriage pillars with their V-jointed rusticated shafts have friezes part-fluted and containing inadequate Coade stone paterae below cappings which cry out for finial finishes. The lodge has later additions from the time here of the Beauman family, who bought the property *c.* 1830.

LGI (1904); Bence-Jones 1988; Kelly 1990.

70. GARRISKER, Johnstown Bridge; *c.* 1825.

Opposite the gates is a caricature Classical temple lodge built for Christopher Nangle. Single-storey, its main front is comprised of a portico with exaggerated steep pediment supported by four plucky octagonal cast-iron columns, or posts, behind which is a window with peculiar canted head, which may originally have been the doorway. Much extended to the rear and rendered plain. Gatescreen of four octagonal stone pillars.

71. GERALDINE, Athy; pre-1837; *demolished.*
A property occupied in the early nineteenth century by Colonel Thomas Fitzgerald.

72. GILLTOWN, Kilcullen (4).
The estate of the Borrowes family for 300 years until its sale in 1925 had four lodged entrances, only one of which to the eighteenth-century house existed prior to the first Ordnance Survey.

Early lodge; pre-1837; *demolished.*
This was opposite the gates on an eastern approach and was in existence as late as 1940.

After the death in 1814 of the 6th baronet, Sir Erasmus Dixon Borrowes, the estate was managed and occupied by his younger brothers and after 1850 by his nephew, Major Robert Higginson Borrowes (1826–1901), who appears to have been responsible for three later lodges.

South lodge; *c.* 1860.

An unremarkable single-storey gabled affair built off an L-plan, rendered with quoins, squared casements and rectangular bay window to the leading front; a panelled chimney-stack on a hipped roof. Contemporary granite gate pillars with exaggerated cornices.

East lodge; *c.* 1850.

A remarkable single-storey standard lodge which has suffered much twentieth-century alteration. On either side of a recessed entrance porch with spindly columns *in antis* below a gablet are glazed canted bay windows, each under a hipped roof projection. Rendered with quoins and plinth. Much extended to the rear.

'Front lodge'; *c.* 1855; architect David Bryce.

An extraordinary apparition in the Irish countryside is this example of a miniature Scots Baronial castle by the most celebrated exponent of the style, Scotsman David Bryce (1803–76). It is 1½-storey, built off an L-plan with very steeply pitched crow-stepped gables, one wing having its attic storey perched on corbels and a cylindrical base, the other containing a single-storey canted, parapeted bay window. From the internal angle, at 45°, projects a single-storey hall with canted stone door surround, blank plaque over and skew-table decorated with five stylised thistle finials. The windows are a variety of squared sashes in rendered walls dressed in granite. Later single-storey back return and extensive railed entrance screen and tall iron carriage posts.

BPB (1929); ffolliott 1971b; Colvin 2008; Williams 1994.

73. GLASSELY, Fontstown; pre-1837; *demolished.*

The old house of the Rawsons was burnt out in the 1798 rebellion and it was not until 1818 that it, and possibly the gate lodge, which was not quite opposite the gates, was rebuilt by Robert Lawson. A decent gatescreen with curved quadrants and pillars with moulded cappings survive.

JCKAS (Vol. 7, July 1914).

74. GLENMONA, Moone; *c.* 1840.

At the entrance to the house and old corn mills in 1837 of Ebenezer Shackleton is a cottage that appears older than its actual date, which is betrayed by the windows with their original mid-nineteenth-century octagonal-pattern cast-iron casements. Single-storey standard in roughcast below a shallow hipped roof, it was later extended by a bay to the left-hand side. The most unprepossessing of rubble carriage pillars support early nineteenth-century gates with delightful scrolled finials to its meeting rails. Adjacent is the lodge to Park Cottage (*q.v.*).

Lewis 1837.

75. GRANGEBEG, Dunlavin; pre-1838; *demolished.*

An early nineteenth-century seat of James Critchley.

76. GRANGEWILLIAM, Maynooth (2).

Obelisk lodge; *c.* 1870.

A plain single-storey gabled structure with matching breakfront hall, the front door having a segmentally headed fanlight. Roughcast; occupied.

Canal lodge; *c.* 1870.

A four-bay single-storey lodge faced in big uncoursed masonry with brick dressings and soldier arches and a projecting brick gabled hall. Occupied. Huge cement-rendered carriage pillars with four-pedimented caps. Concave quadrants and grand gates with overthrow.

A home to Bartholomew Ellis in 1853.
Griffith 1848–60.

GREAT CONNELL LODGE (see CONNELLMORE)

77. GREESE MOUNT, GREESE BANK AND MILL, Ballitore; pre-1838; *demolished.*

Houses and flour mill in 1852 belonging to George Shackleton, the tiny gate lodge to which had gone by 1909.

Griffith 1848–60.

78. HALVERSTOWN, Kilcullen (2).

'Well, then, we drove through a neat lodge-gate, with no stone lions or supporters, but riding well on its hinges, and looking fresh and white; and passed by a lodge, not Gothic, but decorated with flowers and evergreens, with clean windows, and a sound slate roof ...' This idyllic scene related by Thackeray on a visit in 1842 was at 'The new and highly improved seat of Peter Purcell', as reported by Brewer four years earlier. Both lodges were in place in 1837 but to which one Thackeray was referring is not clear, for both have gone, the front entrance having been swept away in road-widening.

Brewer 1825; Thackeray 1879.

79. HARRISTOWN, Kilcullen (5).

These lands were purchased about 1768 by a member of the Dublin banking family of La Touche, whose grandson of the same name, John La Touche (1814–1904), inherited them on his father's death in 1844, along with two early gate lodges. These he replaced at a time when the family's finances were said to be in decline, and he must also have been distracted by the infamous relationship between his young daughter Rose and John Ruskin. He nevertheless commissioned architect John McCurdy to design three new porters' lodges, all sizeable and contrasting in style, but one of which Ruskin would have approved.

Brannockstown gate; 1864; architect John McCurdy.

An Taisce

'A grand entrance and gate lodge in the Bysantine style have been erected at Brannoxstown, Co. Kildare for John La Touche. Materials used were green stones of the locality, with granite dressings and red brick bands having ornamental slate roofs, with turrets, etc., the whole forming a rich and pleasing contrast. John McCurdy, archt., Joseph H. Lynch, Carlow, builder.' Thus ran a contemporary account in the *Dublin Builder* magazine. Described by Jeremy Williams as Ruskinian Gothic but uninspired, this is nevertheless a striking and opulent affair. The turrets referred to in the architect's design, which intended a spiky belfry straddling the ridge, were unrealised, but it has lofty granite chimney-stacks with brick bands; single-storey with steep skew-table gables and kneelers, ornamented with hewn cartouche, trefoil and quatrefoil features. Built off a T-plan, extending as a double pile to one side, with a canted bay window projecting from the avenue gable and relatively flimsy lean-to porch in the internal angle; the roof is decorated with fleur-de-lis cresting and bands of contrasting scalloped slates. The extensive entrance screen is equally extravagant, with heavy decorative ironwork to carriage and postilion gates and extending over the inner quadrant walls. The cut-stone pillars have foliated friezes below layered cappings with sawtooth bands and containing armorial bearings in the shape of pierced five-pointed mullets. The composition extends still further by shallow concave outer quadrant walls, banded like the lodge, with quatrefoil perforations. Replacing an early lodge, whose gatekeeper in 1853 was Mary Malone.

Carnalway gate; 1864; architect John McCurdy.

The *Dublin Builder* again enthuses: 'At Carnalway, for same proprietor, a grand entrance and gate-lodge, in the Italian style, have been lately finished. The entrance having sweep walls with pairs of solid granite, finely chiselled on both sides; elaborate centre piers clustered, with Portland stone and granite. The lodge has granite dressings with cantilever corbelled eaves etc., and built on a sloping terrace. John McCurdy, archt., Joseph F. Lynch, Carlow, builder.' The architect must have relished this commission, allowing him the scope to display the extent of his eclecticism. Essentially this lodge is much as that to the Brannockstown entrance but built off an L-plan, here having a very shallow pitched roof, giving it an Italianate flavour which extends to the conspicuous paired moulded corbels to bargeboards and fascias. Finished in rendering with toothed granite quoins and dressings, a flat-roofed porch with carved wooden posts projects from the internal angle. From the avenue gable projects a canted bay window, and that to the road contains a plaque with a bull's head, crest of the Beaumont family, who acquired the estate in 1946. The stone entrance pillars of extraordinary bulk in the form of Greek stelae are based on a design in J.B. Papworth's *Rural residences* (1818), complete with secondary iron posts which carry carriage and pedestrian gates. Greek key-pattern bands and La Touche mullets embellish the cappings.

Harristown gate; *c.* 1864; architect probably John McCurdy.

To the northern entrance, by way of further variety, is a lodge that is an essay in the Picturesque English style, on a secluded minor road and unrecorded by the *Dublin Builder*. Again single-storey on an L-plan but in polychromatic brickwork, gabled with ornamentally carved bargeboards, octagonal brick chimney-stack and a verandah as porch in the internal angle. The Picturesque effect is enhanced by fleur-de-lis cresting and hexagonal-pattern cast-iron casement windows. To each of the leading gables is the La Touche crest of a mullet of six points pierced and the motto below: 'Quid Verum Atque Decens Curo Et Rogo' [*sic*]—it seems the mason was not a Latin scholar. Extended into a double pile somewhat later. The contemporary gates are hung on square pillars with moulded plinths and capping having scroll-topped stops and quarry-faced masonry to shafts and quadrant walls. Two additional plain, two-storey, roughcast gatehouses with hipped roofs were built in the twentieth century, unworthy of the property.

Papworth 1818; Griffith 1848–60; *DB* (1 Aug. 1864); *LGI* (1904); IAA photograph (38/2).

80. HARTWELL CASTLE, Kill; pre-1837; *demolished.*
An early nineteenth-century house built around an earlier castle, its gate lodge certainly survived until 1853 to a property then of James Flanagan, but had gone before 1938.

Griffith 1848–60.

81. HERBERTSTOWN, Newbridge; pre-1837; *demolished.*
An estate belonging in the early nineteenth century to the Brunton family.

82. HILLSBOROUGH, Newbridge; pre-1837; *demolished.*
A property that had a succession of owners in the first half of the nineteenth century and was subsequently renamed 'Mount Crawley'.

83. HORTLAND, Johnstown Bridge (2).
A very fine house designed for the Rt Revd Josiah Hort by Richard Castle, the lodges to which were built either by his son, the 1st baronet, Sir John Hort (1735–1807), or by his grandson, Sir Josiah William Hort (1791–1876).

Rear entrance; pre-1838; *demolished.*
By the twentieth century the property was in decline, the back avenue and its lodge had gone, to be followed not long after by the big house.

Front entrance; *c.* 1800.
A modest single-storey standard gatekeeper's cottage, roughcast with clipped verge gables and an arrowhead arch to the front door set in a gabled breakfront. Lean-to wing to the left-hand side; derelict. Secondary iron carriage posts between good outer pillars with recessed panel shafts, friezes with paterae, dentil courses and pedimented cappings.

BPB (1929); Bence-Jones 1988.

84. HYBLA, Monasterevin; *c.* 1850; *demolished.*
Home to Thomas Exshaw (1806–86) for over 40 years, it is now in ruins, the gate lodge gone.

IFR.

85. INCHAQUARE COTTON FACTORY, Ballitore; pre-1837; *demolished.*
An extensive concern in 1837 of Leonard Greenham and by 1853 of William Fotheral, whose gatekeeper was Julia Brien.

Lewis 1837; Griffith 1848–60.

86. JIGGINSTOWN, Naas; *c.* 1750.
The extraordinary brick-built palace commenced by Thomas Wentworth, earl of Strafford, *c.* 1636 when lord deputy of Ireland, left unfinished, deserted and going to ruin by 1783. What appears to have been its porter's lodge is more durable. Alongside the gates is this gabled single-storey structure with loft over, having a four-bay squared sash window façade in roughcast finish. Attached at right angles is a two-storey structure which seems to have been an old toll-house.

Taylor and Skinner 1778; 1969 [1783]; Lewis 1837; Bence-Jones 1988.

JOHNSTOWN (see COUNTY DUBLIN)

87. KEARNEYSTOWN, Newcastle; *c.* 1840.
A minuscule standard single-storey gabled structure in roughcast rubble construction, with tiny windows and door in banded surrounds. Very derelict. The gate lodge to a house in 1853 of Richard McKenna.

Griffith 1848–60.

88. KENNYCOURT or CANNYCOURT, Kilcullen; *c.* 1855.
An impressive stretch of mid-Victorian cast ironwork greets the visitor in an entrance screen of ogee railings and foliar inner pillars with fine urns, all stopped by outer granite pillars. Totally upstaged by a huge, venerable and perhaps contemporary purple beech is a sturdy single-storey standard lodge with a shallow hipped roof; its bipartite two-over-

two sash windows in white rendered walls flank a stone door-case with moulded entablature above a depressed arch spanning a concave recess. Built for Joseph Kilby.

89. KERDIFFSTOWN, Sallins (2).
The property of the Kerdiff family passed to the Henricks, who presumably built the lodges.

Rear entrance; pre-1837; *demolished.*
Front entrance; pre-1837; *demolished.*
Greek stela-style pillars probably contemporary with the twentieth-century bungalow that occupies the gate lodge site.

Brewer 1825.

90. KILCOO, Athy; pre-1837; *demolished.*
An estate in the mid-nineteenth century of William Mather.

Slater 1846.

91. KILCULLEN RECTORY, Kilcullen; pre-1900; *demolished.*
A lodge built after 1837 to what ceased to be a glebe house when the parish was united with that of Carnalway in 1922, following which it became a private house known as 'Lios Cluana'.

Leslie and Wallace 2009.

92. KILDANGAN CASTLE, Monasterevin (3).
A place with an old Fitzgerald castle and later a thatched villa of the O'Reilly family, which had one lodged entrance from the east. The property passed in 1849 to Edward More O'Ferrall on his marriage to Susan O'Reilly, but it was his only son, Dominick More O'Ferrall, who succeeded to the estate in 1875, and initiated extensive improvements, including a new mansion and gate lodge. These did not meet with the approval of the *Irish Builder* in 1881: 'Extensive stables court-yard, &c., buildings are being commenced at Kildangan, Co. Kildare, for D. More O'Ferrall, Esq., from designs &c., by an English architect!! and being carried out by an English Clerk of Works!! (no Irish need apply). Tender of Mr Samuel H. Bolton, builder, of the city, was accepted. The bricks specified are to be English red stock. So much for home produce.'

West lodge; *c.* 1885; architect probably W.J. Hopkins.

A 1½-storey cottage with a distinctly English feel, its high-pitched gables having a variety of pretty carved and pierced bargeboards. Built of red brick lain in Flemish garden wall bond off an L-plan, a main roof catslides over the internal angle to form an arcaded porch with perforated spandrels and herringbone-pattern brick panels below. The leaded light transomed and mullioned windows have segmental pointed arches. Perforated earthenware crestings and tall brick chimney-stacks. Clearly by the Worcester-based and maligned architect William Jeffrey Hopkins (1820/1–1901). Modern brick gatescreen.

South lodge; post-1837; *demolished.*
Replaced by a modern bungalow.

East lodge; pre-1837/1988; architects Hunter Price.

The original little granite lodge has been replaced by a startling modern composition in new neo-Jacobean style in the form of a pair of commodious 1½-storey gatehouses, with arcaded recessed porches flanking and forward of a vast central segmentally headed double archway surmounted by curved gables, like the lodges with skew-tables and kneelers, and crowned by a delicate 'belfry' to the ridge. The whole ensemble in rustic brickwork with contrasting string-courses and features in reconstituted stone, as is a prominent round date-stone. Now forming the entrance to an Arab-owned stud farm and designed by an English practice—the editor of the *Irish Builder* will be turning in his grave!

IB (1 June 1881); *LGI* (1904); Bence-Jones 1988; Williams 1994.

93. KILDONAN, Timahoe; *c.* 1860.
A plain 1½-storey gabled affair with a lean-to hall over the right-hand bay. Derelict. In the mid-nineteenth century an 88-acre holding of James Little when the concern was enlarged.

Griffith 1848–60.

94. KILGLASS, Johnstown Bridge; *c.* 1825.

Opposite the gates, a standard single-storey lodge below a hipped roof with high eaves having carved paired brackets. Basic sheeted door in a sophisticated Classical stone architrave with keystone in the form of a console bracket. On each side a square window opening with moulded sill set in limewashed harled rubble walls. Derelict and boarded up. Across the road simple contemporary gates, railings and stone pillars with fine pineapple finials on tall pedestals. An estate in the early nineteenth century of Daniel Higgins, followed by the Shaw family.

95. KILKEA CASTLE, Kilkea (3).
The medieval seat of the Fitzgeralds, who forsook it in the 1740s for Carton (*q.v.*). For a century it was left in the care of tenants, a period which culminated in its burning in 1849, when the 3rd duke of Leinster took it in hand, restoring it as the family dower house, and added a gate lodge at the southern approach which superseded a pre-1837 lodge on an avenue from the east.

Castledermot lodge; *c.* 1850; architect probably William Deane Butler.

A pleasing 1½-storey neo-Tudor cottage with skew-table gables and sculpted kneelers to steeply pitched roofs. Built in random uncoursed rubble facings with cut-stone quoins and dressings to openings with cast-iron latticed casements. From the left-hand side of the avenue front projects a single-storey hall with round arches. To the ridges are fleur-de-lis crestings and a cluster of four brick chimney-pots on a square stone base. The architect may have been William Deane Butler, who had been engaged by the 3rd duke in 1849 on works to the castle. The gatekeeper in 1852 was Terence Mulligan.

Kilkea lodge; *c.* 1863; architect probably J.J. McCarthy.

Essentially a simple two-up/two-down 1½-storey box, enlivened by the Picturesque devices of a single-storey rectangular bay to the leading gable, a gablet breaking the main eaves and a lean-to arched verandah carried on carved wooden posts to two façades, stopped by a tall gabled porch to the front door. Constructed in pleasant coursed rubble with cut-stone quoins and dressings below beautifully fretted bargeboards. Well restored, although the original cast-iron latticed lights have been replaced by lead-effect modern windows. The main chimney-stack has disappeared. This may well be a rare example of domestic work by J.J. McCarthy, the 'Irish Pugin', as he was employed by the earl of Kildare, the future 4th duke of Leinster, to design the village church and its rectory in the 1860s.

Griffith 1848–60; Bence-Jones 1988; Williams 1994.

96. KILL CHURCH OF IRELAND CHURCH, Kill; *c.* 1840.

The parish church dates from 1821 and has stone entrance pillars with gadrooned caps, much favoured by architect Francis Johnston. There is a gate lodge attributable to him at nearby Palmerston (*q.v.*), the seat of Lord Mayo, who was a benefactor of the church. The porter's or sexton's lodge opposite the gates is of later date, built during the long incumbency (1814–78) of Revd John Warburton (1786–1878). Standard single-storey under a hipped roof, rendered and grotesquely disfigured with the insertion of two picture windows in conversion to offices.

Lewis 1837; Leslie and Wallace 2009.

97. KILL RECTORY, Kill; post-1837; *demolished.*

A lodge built during the incumbency of Revd John Warburton (see Kill Church of Ireland church).

98. KILLADOON, Celbridge (2).

Externally at least, this modest big three-storey Georgian house was built soon after his marriage in 1765 by Robert Clements (1732–1804), who was to be created the 1st Lord Leitrim and owned huge properties in counties Cavan, Donegal and Leitrim. It was either he or his son Nathaniel, the 2nd earl, who added two gate lodges to the property before 1837, neither of which survives.

Outer entrance; pre-1837; *demolished.*

Inner entrance; pre-1837/*c.* 1885; architect probably Sir Thomas Drew.

A highly ornamental late Victorian Arts and Crafts design, 1½-storey of irregular outline, its attic storey in red brick with applied half-timbered effect and a six-light window, over a roughcast ground floor. The massive front gable catslides over a single-storey projection from which at right angles extends a lean-to canopied porch with decorative carved wooden posts and brackets and dwarf flanking walls. To the roof a dormer, lofty brick stack and earthenware cresting. Sir Thomas Drew is recorded as working here in 1885 for Robert Bermingham Clements, 4th Lord Leitrim (1847–92), who inherited on his uncle's murder in 1878. This replaced an earlier porter's lodge on the site, the gatescreen to which survives in the shape of grand late Georgian pillars and postilion openings, all in V-jointed rusticated ashlar. There is a similar lodge to another Clements house of Ashfield Lodge, Co. Cavan.

BPB (1929); Dean 1994; *Country Life* (15 and 22 Jan. 2004); IAA; O'Kane 2004.

99. KILLASHEE, Naas; pre-1837; *demolished.*

A gate lodge built for the old house of the Graydon family, who were here until the mid-nineteenth century. Thereafter in 1860 it was transformed into the present Jacobean-style edifice for Richard Moore by the Belfast firm of Lanyon and Lynn, the work being supervised by the young Thomas Drew. The present approach, to what is now a hotel, bears no relation to its original course, the grounds also having been severed by public road realignment.

DB (1 Aug. 1859).

100. KILLYBEGS, Prosperous; pre-1837; *demolished.*

Although the name probably derives from the Brooke family, who also had land in County Donegal, the gate lodge was more likely to have been built for Edward Fitzgerald, in 1847 destined to become 3rd baronet of Carrigoran, Co. Clare, who acquired the property about 1810. There survives a modest gatescreen of four plain stone pillars and a postilion opening in roughcast quadrants.

Wilson 1803; Leet 1814; *BPB* (1908).

101. KNOCKANALLY, Johnstown Bridge (2).

The neo-Classical villa is of *c.* 1850, but there was a house here of William Coates as early as 1814 which had a gatehouse of that period.

North lodge; *c.* 1800.

A two-storey three-bay house with a shallow hipped roof and single-storey central breakfront having a round-headed fanlit doorway with a rusticated surround. Occupied. Extended to right-hand side as gabled addition.

South lodge; *c.* 1870; architect not known.

Barry Watson postcard.

A singular 1½-storey composition with Italianate features in fascia boards continued into gables to form open pediments and round-headed, keystoned paired windows. Originally finished in a variety of stone, it has now been rendered over, leaving some panels of quarry-faced masonry and sculpted eaves course, plinth and dressings. To the park is a charming ogee-roofed single-storey canted bay which used to be leaded, but the main dominant feature is the tall semi-octagonal stair-hall which projects, below a semi-octahedral roof, to the avenue. To the rear is a single-storey return and a lofty cut-stone chimney-stack with moulded and banded capping. Originality spreads to the Classical gatescreen which abuts the stair-hall, the eaves band continuing as copings to the pedestrian gate and its balancing blind panel, and into the grand carriage pillars, built in a vermiculated rusticated block of contrasting stone with scroll-topped gate stops, rising to dentilled cappings. Over the pedestrian gate and its equivalent blind panel are perforated friezes divided by triglyph blocks. Unusually, from the road front projects a less ornate secondary gatescreen. All quite unique. Similarly built for a William Coates, Jeremy Williams sees work in the house reminiscent of the work of architects W.D. Butler and J.S. Mulvany, but the lodge and gates would appear to be too late to be attributable to either.

Leet 1814; Williams 1994.

102. KNOCKFIELD, Castledermot; pre-1837.
Occupied and so much modernised as to make dating difficult. Single-storey and gabled with a picture window, at the base of an antique beech-lined avenue to a house in 1852 of 'the late' Michael Browne, whose gatekeeper had been Phelim Cassidy.

Griffith 1848–60.

103. KNOCKNAGARM, Kilcullen (2).

West lodge; *c.* 1800.
A plain standard hip-roofed cottage with clipped eaves built in harled rubble. Derelict. This was the lodge built to what was Ballysax Rectory, the long-serving (1792–1830) vicar of which was Revd William Tew (1770–1830).

East lodge; post-1837; *demolished.*
Replaced by a monstrous brick house.

The place became a private house, presumably after the parish was joined with Ballysonnan parish in 1877.

Leslie and Wallace 2009.

104. THE KNOCKS, Naas; *c.* 1780.

Beautifully sited by the Grand Canal is this survivor from Georgian times. A pleasant unpretentious single-storey three-bay asymmetrical lodge finished in limewashed harling to rubble construction, with brick dressings to tiny windows and a generous doorway. Clipped verges to gables and to the ridge an octagonal chimney-stack which may be a later addition. A property in 1800 of the Montgomery family, who owned nearby flour mills.

Wilson 1803.

105. LANDENSTOWN, Clane; *c.* 1825; architect not known.
A very fine pair of Regency lodges, twin standard single-storey three-bay, facing each other behind the gatescreen, with bipartite cast-iron latticed casements in smooth white rendered walls flanking flat entablatured stone porticos with pairs of Tuscan columns. The visitor is met by a pair of single-bay

façades of quadripartite latticed casement windows set in segmentally headed recesses framed by toothed V-jointed quoins below oversailing hipped roofs with paired carved soffit brackets. These are linked by a straight entrance screen with stone copings taken across as postilion opening lintels. The big ashlar carriage pillars with recessed panels carry decorative iron gates with spear tops, palmette, helical rails and Vitruvian scroll motifs. Built for J.W. Digby to an equally attractive Palladian house.

Leet 1814; Bence-Jones 1988.

106. LARAGH, Maynooth; *c.* 1845; *demolished.*
A house built in the early eighteenth century by Lord Trimleston had a succession of occupants before Nicholas John Gannon added a gate lodge sometime between inheriting the place in 1837 and its being recorded in 1851.

Griffith 1848–60; *LGI* (1875); Bence-Jones 1988.

107. LARK LODGE, Kildare (2).
A small estate in the mid-nineteenth century of William Disney.

North lodge; pre-1837; *demolished.*

South lodge; *c.* 1836.

A delightful 'tea caddy' lodge, impressively sited on an elevation with a wooded backdrop and approached up a pathway through a pretty garden. Up close is revealed a tiny octagonal cottage with one downstairs room and one over, lit by a skylight, in the octahedral roof, now felt-covered, rising to a ball finial. Finished in whitewashed harling. The entrance is through a minuscule gabled hall, its doorway segmentally arched. Conspicuously shy of windows. The chimney-stack rises in tiers from one face and a rustic buttress lends support nearby. The proud occupant enjoys a crucial later extension to the rear. Its unhatched representation on the first OS map suggests that it was then under construction.

IAA photograph (S/112/6).

108. LEINSTER LODGE, Kilkea (2).
A hunting lodge of the duke of Leinster of nearby Kilkea Castle (*q.v.*) and Carton (*q.v.*), it was, at least between 1824 and 1856, occupied by an agent, James Perrin.

West lodge; pre-1837; *demolished.*
Taken down in the 1990s, this was a standard single-storey structure with a hipped roof and canopied gabled porch carried on a pair of iron pillars. Two basic square gate pillars survive, with cut-stone cornices and big unpedestalled ball finials.

East lodge; *c.* 1845.
A single-storey roughcast cottage below a hipped roof with modern concrete roll-tile finish. Occupied.

109. LEIXLIP CASTLE, Leixlip (2).
A medieval castle in origin; although owned by the Conollys of Castletown (*q.v.*) between 1728 and 1914, they leased it over most of this period to a succession of eminent tenants. Legend has it that there was a gate lodge here during the occupancy of the viceroy, Lord Townsend, in 1767, but those that survived into the twentieth century looked to be of early nineteenth-century date. Perhaps significantly, the leaseholder then was the Hon. George Cavendish (1766–1849), who was here in the 1820s until his death, and as secretary to the lords of the treasury in Ireland it is recorded in 1837 that the castle was modernised and greatly improved by him.

Rear entrance; *c.* 1825.
A plain single-storey affair, roughcast, presenting a short principal front with clipped verge gables, and with a lower extending gabled hall. Now with wide windows as part of many subsequent alterations. Occupied.

Front entrance; *c.* 1825/*c.* 1985; *demolished.*

An inferior late nineteenth-century photograph shows a standard single-storey hipped-roof lodge, which was removed to be superseded by the present structure. In 1958 Leixlip Castle was acquired by that great promoter of Ireland's architectural heritage the Hon. Desmond Guinness, and his first wife Mariga, and their taste is evident in this impressive piece of neo-Gothic, raised prudently on a crepidoma. It is a 1½-storey gatehouse having parapets with crenellations continued up the main front gable, which contains lancet-headed openings with Y-tracery framed by tiered diagonal buttresses. Surviving from an earlier age is a fine pair of mid-Georgian octagonal stone gate pillars decorated with cluster-columns rising to pointed arches on each face below moulded cappings with domed tops. There are very similar examples at Clonyn Castle, Co. Westmeath (*q.v.*).

Lewis 1837; *BPB* (1929); Guinness and Ryan 1971.

110. LEIXLIP, Leixlip; pre-1837; *demolished.*
A property in the late eighteenth century of General Brady which was acquired by John Downing Nesbitt of Tubberdaly, Co. Offaly (*q.v.*), after marrying Brady's daughter in 1800. Nothing remains of the original entrance but it is home to magnificent gates salvaged from French Park, Co. Roscommon.

LGI (1904).

111. LEVITSTOWN, Castledermot; pre-1837; *demolished.*
An estate in the early nineteenth century of William Caulfeild, its lodge had gone by 1909.

LIOS CLUANA (see KILCULLEN RECTORY)

112. LISHEEN, Kilkea; *c.* 1850.
A 1½-storey gabled lodge, rendered with high eaves above two-bay window elevation to the road. Occupied. A property in the mid-nineteenth century of George Lawler.

Griffith 1848–60.

113. LODGE PARK, Straffan (3).
Main entrance; pre-1837/*c.* 1870.

A most eccentric concoction, which may be of two dates. The original single-storey gabled lodge, probably contemporary with the late Georgian gatescreen, forms a wing of the later 1½-storey gabled structure, which has a full-height semi-octagonal projection to the avenue, its eaves broken by oriel gablets supported on carved wooden brackets. Finished in stucco with toothed stone quoins, on the road gable is a single-storey triangular hallway below a hipped roof with what was the doorway, a decorative wooden gabled arbour. At the rear is another single-storey gabled wing. The gatescreen has two very fine stone carriage pillars, with toothed rustication and swagged friezes clearly influenced by those at Castletown (*q.v.*) by Chambers. Beyond are shallow walled quadrants containing postilion openings. An entrance started by Hugh Henry, who also built the house about 1775, and completed by his grandson, Frederick Hugh Henry (1815–88).

West entrance; *c.* 1880; *demolished.*
Strangely, the most recent of the demesne lodges has fared worst.

East entrance; *c.* 1825.

A sophisticated Georgian-style porter's lodge not looking its best, coated in unflattering modern roughcast, being boarded up and abandoned. Single-storey standard with large square window openings on each side of the doorway with its semicircular fanlight. To the road elevation is a bowed projection with window to view the gate. All, unusually, below a parapeted flat roof. Good squat square carriage pillars with plain friezes and projecting corniced cappings in granite; outer stuccoed convex quadrants.

LGI (1904); Bence-Jones 1988.

114. LONGTOWN, Clane (3).
A large, plain early eighteenth-century mansion, originally called 'Bellaville', at the main entrance to which were lodges of two dates.

Inner entrance; *c.* 1740/*c.* 1840.

At the base of a lengthy approach off the public road the visitor is confronted by a very fine ashlar archway that was flanked by a pair of lodges; although long gone, their appearance may be seen by viewing those surviving at Celbridge Collegiate School (*q.v.*), for the archway there is almost identical to this in its dimensions and differing in design here only in its pediment, which has a part-broken entablature and pitch. The generous Doric pilasters carry the pediment and frame the carriage archway, which is round-headed with keystone and imposts, as are the lower postilion openings alongside which used to link to the lodges, now lost. The similarity to the Celbridge entrance suggests that they are either contemporary early Georgian and possibly both designed by Richard Castle, or that this is a later copy built for George Burdett.

Either way, Michael Sweetman (1779–1852), who acquired the property about 1829, sadly must have considered the pair of lodges unsocial and replaced them with more commodious single accommodation in the shape of a single-storey standard lodge below a hipped roof with wooden soffit brackets extending as support to the verge of the central gabled breakfront, in the apex of which is a stone shield with the Sweetman crest of a griffin and their motto, 'Spera in Deo'. Paired one-over-one sash windows are set in bland grey roughcast walls. It now lies deserted and derelict.

Outer entrance; *c.* 1850.
At the head of the approach is the most recent gatekeeper's cottage on an elevated site. Single-storey standard with a hipped roof having high eaves with carved modillion brackets, below which is a gabled hall projection. Rendered with quoins; occupied.

IFR.

115. LUMVILLE FARM, Newbridge; 1923; architects probably McDonnell and Dixon.
A distinctive Edwardian 1½-storey Arts and Crafts lodge with a Queen Anne Revival flavour. Notable for its mansard roof gable,

roughcast and containing a wide eight-light window, four of which are spanned by a small pediment. This all rests on a brick lower storey with chamfered corners and curved brackets, apparently to support the first-floor attic. An idiosyncratic characteristic though not unique, as there are similar quirks to lodges at Knockmaroon (*q.v.*) and Rockfield (*q.v.*), both in County Dublin, and a comparable building at nearby Eyrefield Lodge. A development of home, gate lodge, steward's lodge and offices for Lady McCalmont.

116. LYONS, Newcastle (4).
The magnificent mansion built by Nicholas Lawless and his son Valentine Browne Lawless, 1st and 2nd Lords Cloncurry, latterly to 1802–5 designs by Richard Morrison, seems not to have had a contemporary lodge built worthy of it.

West entrance; pre-1760; *demolished.*
The previous house here of the Aylmer family was approached by a straight formal avenue from the main entrance that had a pair of lodges flanking concave quadrants, which had survived until at least 1838 but all evidence of which had gone by the twentieth century.

South entrance; pre-1838; *demolished.*
All that remain are stone cylindrical gate pillars, the lodge replaced by a bungalow.

Canal entrance; *c.* 1860.

On the towpath is a quite sombre single-storey three-bay symmetrical affair, with a parapeted roof over an elongated front in V-jointed rusticated granite, just like that on the big house, but with rubble construction to the underside of the sills of two-over-six sash windows. Its dimensions suggest that it may have had the double function of a school.

North entrance; *c.* 1830; *demolished.*

Now the main access to the demesne, there was opposite an unprepossessing single-storey standard porter's lodge, square and generous on plan, below a shallow oversailing hipped roof with carved eaves brackets. Central to the main front was a skew-tabled hall projection. This lodge rather incongruously since the 1960s had faced the majestic entrance archway and railed screen that had been relocated from Browne's Hill, Co. Carlow (*q.v.*). Dr Tony Ryan has effected a wonderful revival of the house and demesne, a programme that eventually extended to a replacement 'lodge'. This is secreted behind a wide segmental screen wall, to mirror the gatescreen, and is broken only by an elegant frontispiece in the shape of a Classical temple with a pair of Ionic columns *in antis* carrying a pediment and displaying Roman wreaths in the manner of Morrison. A 21st-century creation by architects de Blacam and Meagher, sufficiently convincing to fool the NIAH survey into dating it at *c.* 1830—worthy of the place.

BPB (1929); *IGS Bulletin* (1984); McParland *et al.* 1989; Ferguson 1998.

117. MARTINSTOWN, Kilcullen; pre-1837; *demolished.*
The Picturesque cottage shooting-box built in the early nineteenth century by Augustus Frederick Fitzgerald, 3rd duke of Leinster, had lost its lodge by 1939.

118. METCALFE PARK, Johnstown Bridge; *c.* 1855.
To a large mid-Georgian house of the Metcalfe family is this plain standard single-storey steeply gabled lodge, with similar hall projection having a round-headed sidelight; two-over-two sash windows in grey rendered walls; deserted. Gates and railings with a nice quatrefoil motif. All for Francis Metcalfe.

119. MILLICENT, Sallins (2).
Although the house was built by the Keating family and is best known for being the childhood home of Richard Griffith of the *Valuation*, its lodges were built by subsequent occupants.

East entrance; *c.* 1830.
A two-storey hip-roofed gatehouse in roughcast finish with cast-iron square-paned casements. Two-bay upper storey above three-bay ground floor, its central door converted to a window and a nasty later brick hall obscuring the left-hand bay. Derelict. Built for a Dublin barrister, Bryan Arthur Molloy, who came to the property *c.* 1810.

West entrance; *c.* 1850; architect not known.

Millicent was acquired from Molloy by Thomas Cooke Trench of the Ashtown, Co. Galway, family about 1850, but he died a year later, to be succeeded by his eldest son, Thomas Richard Frederick Cooke Trench (1829–1902). Father or son added this good Italianate lodge, originally a standard single-storey construction, gabled with high ceilings and lofty eaves to accommodate a gabled hall projection. In rendered walls, openings all round-headed to single, bipartite windows and tripartite on the hip-roofed rusticated rectangular bay extending to the road, over which is a bulls-eye window lighting the recently formed attic storey. Margined glazing with keystoned hood mouldings to windows and semicircular arched fanlit doorway. Sensitively extended. Big square stone carriage pillars and gates with wonderful detailing, including a middle rail of rose, thistle and shamrock motifs of the three kingdoms and in the firm grip of cast-iron hands as hinges.

BPB (1929); Bence-Jones 1988.

120. MOATFIELD, Clane; pre-1939; *demolished.*
A property in 1853 of Stephen Carney.

Griffith 1848–60.

121. MOONE ABBEY, Moone; pre-1838; *demolished.*
A seat until the mid-nineteenth century of the Yates family, the lodge to which had gone by 1909 but is survived by its fine gatescreen of *c.* 1770, a pair of quoined carriage pillars surmounted by ball finials with curious rope-like banding, whereas those atop the

magnificent monumental pillars at the village entrance have more conventional Greek key-pattern rustication, a gateway which seems always to have been lodgeless.

Lewis 1837.

122. MOORE ABBEY, Monasterevin (5).
The great Georgian Gothic mansion was built in 1767 by Charles Moore, 6th earl and 1st marquis of Drogheda (1730–1821), and either he or his eldest son Edward (d. 1837) was probably responsible for two early gatekeepers' lodges to the estate.

East entrance; pre-1838; *demolished.*
A lodge located opposite the gates that survived until at least 1939.

Inner lodge; pre-1838; *demolished.*
Originally located some distance off the main street on a northern approach, this lodge was probably removed on the creation of the two present town entrances in the mid-nineteenth century.

The three surviving lodges to the estate were part of extensive improvements by Henry Francis Moore, 8th earl and 3rd marquis of Drogheda (1825–92), which did not commence until after his coming of age, he having succeeded his uncle to title and lands at the age of twelve. He commissioned architect John Howard Louch to design alterations to the house in 1845, plans which were never realised, but it is possible that he was retained to furnish drawings for gate lodges to the demesne.

Grange Farm lodge; *c.* 1855.
To the southern boundary is a relatively plain standard 1½-storey structure, gabled with clipped eaves, as is its open porch, built in rubble, with cut-stone quoins, dressings and chimney-stack. Occupied.

Town entrance; 1855; architect possibly J.H. Louch.

'A new gateway, with an ample semi-circular sweep, and an elegant gate-lodge, in the true Elizabethan style, were being erected, and in a forward state, when I paid my visit.' Lacy would have discovered this little building in its original state, single-storey on an irregular T-plan, perhaps with rubble facings, skew-table gables and mullioned, lattice-paned windows, all as part of a Tudor-Gothic design. Sadly, these features have been removed in a hideous modern make-over and partly obscured by a prominent flat-roofed extension. Some previous stone highlights survive in a blind lancet niche to the leading gable and label-moulded windows with chamfered reveals, which frame twentieth-century casements in roughcast walls. To the extensive iron-railed quadrants are tall granite octagon Tudor-Gothic carriage pillars with ornamental finialled cappings.

Kildare gate; *c.* 1855; architect possibly J.H. Louch.
To the east of the town is this hugely impressive and conspicuously sited single-storey Tudor-Gothic castellated composition. Framed by wide curtain walls, perfectly symmetrical with a hood-moulded Tudor carriage archway in a massive central crenellated square tower with dentil course above Gothic arcaded 'machicolations'. To each side is gatekeeper accommodation, with tripartite lancet slit windows to the front, extending to bulky round towers, and to the rear two bays, each of label-moulded casements and topped by square turrets which, like the rest, are crowned by battlements in beautiful ashlar which contrasts with the coursed rubble below. By the gateway is affixed a marble plaque to the memory of the great Irish tenor Count John McCormack, who leased Moore Abbey as his family home from 1927 to 1939 and who died in 1945—but not as a centenarian, as the inscription proclaims.

Lacy 1852; *BPB* (1929); Bence-Jones 1988; Bunbury and Kavanagh 2004; IAA.

123. MOOREFIELD, Newbridge (2).
Both lodges dating from before 1837 have been swept away by modern development. Built either by Ponsonby Moore or his son of the same name (1786–1868), who succeeded to the property on his father's death in 1819.

BPB (1929).

124. MOORHILL, Kilcullen (2).
A seat of the Brownrigg family, whose mid-nineteenth-century lodges have both been removed, that to the front entrance replaced by a modern bungalow.

125. MOUNTCASHELL LODGE, Ballymore Eustace; *c.* 1800.
A property of the earls of Mountcashell, this little porter's lodge was probably built for the 2nd earl, Stephen Moore (1770–1822), who succeeded to the title in 1790, when the

122. Moore Abbey, Kildare gate.

house was called 'Broomfield'. Single-storey gabled with modest skew-tables; built in roughcast rubble walls, the two-bay road elevation is comprised of a pair of Georgian Gothic lancet windows with stone rusticated dressings. Derelict. The shallow concave quadrant walls to the entrance contain architraved postilion openings.

Taylor and Skinner 1778; 1969 [1783]; *BPB* (1873).

MOUNT CRAWLEY (see HILLSBOROUGH)

126. MULGEETH, Johnstown Bridge; *c.* 1810.

The quintessential Irish vernacular gate lodge, single-storey standard, perfectly proportioned in harled rubble below a hipped roof. Tiny and derelict. A minor estate in 1837 of E. Ruthven.

Lewis 1837.

127. MUSIC HALL, Leixlip; pre-1837; *demolished.*

A property that passed about 1810 from the Glascocks to Pierce Hacket.

Wilson 1803; Leet 1814.

128. NAAS PROTESTANT CEMETERY, Naas; *c.* 1860.

'... in 1782, Lord Naas bequeathed to the inhabitants a burial ground, which is subject to burial fees.' The benefactor was John Bourke (1705–90), who was created baron of Naas in 1776 and elevated further as Lord Mayo, of nearby Palmerstown (*q.v.*), in 1785. In that year of 1782 the area was surrounded by a tall stone wall, within which most of the aristocracy in the neighbourhood was to be buried. There is a very fine granite cut-stone entrance archway with Doric piers supporting the segmentally headed opening below an entablature. Alongside is a later caretaker's and gatekeeper's lodge in the form of a standard, plain 1½-storey gabled structure with similarly roofed single-storey central hall projection.

Lewis 1837; *BPB* 1929.

129. NARRAGHMORE RECTORY, Ballitore; pre-1909; *demolished.*

Although the glebe house dates from 1818, its lodge was of much later construction, perhaps being built during the incumbency (1867–73) of Revd Frederick Smith Fitzgerald (1827–86). Surviving are four phallic entrance pillars.

Lewis 1837; Leslie and Wallace 2001.

130. NEWABBEY, Kilcullen (2).

An estate of the Brereton family from 1779 to 1909, both lodges, though built many years apart, may have been for the long-lived Captain William Robert Brereton (1816–1906).

Newabbey lodge; pre-1853; *demolished.*

Occupied by gatekeeper John Maguire in 1853, when the property was leased by Captain William Tuthill, the lodge's location is not clear from the early OS maps, being identified by the valuation.

Nicholastown lodge; 1870/*c.* 1900.

This extensive single-storey porter's lodge was built in two stages latterly when major work was being carried out to the house. Looking mid-Victorian, it is an Italianate-style structure, smooth-rendered with prominent plinth, stone quoins and label mouldings below a gabled roof with conspicuous bracketed eaves which return to form open pediments to the gables. Extensive and very fine contemporary cast-iron railed screen, carriage piers and gates with repetitive Gothic motifs.

Griffith 1848–60; *IFR*; Bence-Jones 1988.

131. NEWBERRY HALL, Edenderry (2).

The elegant mid-eighteenth-century Palladian house of the Pomeroys, Viscounts Harberton, the early lodge to which was built by Henry Pomeroy, 2nd viscount (1749–1829), the first of three brothers to hold the title.

Main entrance; *c.* 1820.

At a T-junction on the western approach is a single-storey roughcast hip-roofed structure with oversailing eaves. Three-bay with door to the right-hand side, it lies derelict. Later gate pillars, with tiered cappings minus finials, built into earlier concave quadrants.

After the death of the 4th viscount, the estate was sold *c.* 1835 to Edward Wolstenholme, who added another lodged gate.

North entrance; *c.* 1850.

A now-ruinous single-storey cottage built in rubble stone, with brick dressings to a two-window bay front to the road.

BPB (1929); Bence-Jones 1988.

132. NEWBERRY, Kilcullen; *c.* 1830.

A property originally called 'Carnalway', in the first half of the nineteenth century owned by the La Touche family of nearby Harristown (*q.v.*), which had a succession of tenants, one of whom, William Caldwell, in 1853 had as his gate porter Joseph Croen. Opposite the gates is a single-storey five-bay lodge, gabled with similar entrance breakfront. Modernised, pebble-dashed and occupied.

Griffith 1848–60.

133. NEWINGTON, Rathangan; pre-1837; *demolished.*

An estate in the early nineteenth century of Samuel Neale.

134. NEWPARK, Kilcullen; *c.* 1790.

A two-storey gabled gatehouse with Georgian Gothic latticed lancet windows in roughcast walls, at least one of which may not be in its original location, as the building has been much altered, raised a storey and extended over the years, having served for a while as a schoolhouse. The main avenue front has a three-bay first floor over four bays below. Occupied and lovingly maintained. A property associated with the Annesley family in Georgian times.

135. NEWPARK LODGE, Kilmeage (2).

The sad remains of a once-proud demesne of the Pim family, their big house a ruin and lodges gone.

Main entrance; pre-1837; *demolished.*

Surviving is a fine Georgian gate sweep of ashlar carriage pillars with exaggerated moulded cornices over friezes containing plaques inscribed 'Newpark' and 'Lodge'. In contrast are roughcast quadrants with postilion openings and to the right-hand side a beautifully sculpted tablet with, in bas-relief, a pair of cherubs, the inscription '1st July 1744 John Pim' and his head in the guise of a Roman emperor complete with laurel wreath.

Secondary entrance; post-1837; *demolished.*

136. NEWTOWN, Castledermot (2).
The 1837 OS map shows two structures by the entrance, one opposite, to a property in 1814 of John Leonard.

Leet 1814.

137. NEWTOWN, Maynooth; pre-1900; *demolished.*
An estate in the mid-nineteenth century of Valentine Cullen, its lodge erected after 1837.

138. NEWTOWN HILL, Leixlip; *c.* 1810.
The simplest of single-storey gabled lodges in harled rubble construction with an eaves band. In 2000 roofless after a fire. Carriage pillars with pineapple finials. In 1824 this rustic Palladian villa with wings and pavilions belonged to Revd Charles Otway.

Pigot 1824.

139. NEWTOWN VILLA, Kilcullen; *c.* 1845; *demolished.*
A property in the mid-nineteenth century of John J. Turner, whose gate porter in 1853 was Andrew Byrne. Replaced by a bungalow.

Griffith 1848–60.

140. NORMANBY LODGE, The Curragh (2).
A small estate, previously and now called 'Ballyfair', was a property of the Wynne family which was 'occupied during the races by his Excellency the Lord-Lieutenant'. In 1837 this was Constantine Henry Phipps, 1st marquis of Normanby (1797–1863), lord lieutenant from 1835 to 1839. Both of the lodges, one of which was opposite the gates, are things of the past.

Lewis 1837; *BPB* (1929).

141. NURNEY, Nurney (2).
A demesne in the late eighteenth and early nineteenth centuries of the Bagot family, who sold it about 1835 to James W. Fitzgerald, who is most likely to have been builder of at least one of its lodges.

Main entrance; *c.* 1835.

A typical Irish Regency-style gate lodge located opposite its gates. Standard 1½-storey, steeply hip-roofed with tall eaves; notable for its wide windows set in segmentally arched recesses, all framed by toothed quoins conspicuous in black paint on white rendered walls. There is an unfortunate central modern gabled glazed porch with scalloped bargeboards taken beyond as a fascia feature. Remains of flanking quadrant walls; occupied. There is a similar lodge at Foulkscourt, Co. Kilkenny (*q.v.*).

Secondary entrance; pre-1837; *demolished.*

Lewis 1837; *JCKAS* Vol. 7, July 1914.

142. OAKLY PARK, Celbridge; *c.* 1820.

Irish Architectural Archive

A fine house built for Revd Arthur Price (1678–1752), vicar of Celbridge and later archbishop of Cashel, about 1724, when the property was called 'Celbridge Hall'. Its relatively nondescript lodge is of about a century later, when the owner was Richard Maunsell (1785–1886). Built off an L-plan below a hipped roof; single-storey with a two-bay elevation to the avenue, originally having six-over-six sash windows. Big square carriage pillars flanked by postilion openings, its sweep continued as railed quadrants on low walls.

LGI (1904); IAA photograph (29/37Z 1+N); Bence-Jones 1988; Leslie and Wallace 2009.

143. OLDCONNELL, Newbridge; pre-1837/*c.* 1900.
A property in the early nineteenth century of Edward J. Odlum, its original lodge has been replaced by one much closer to the main road. To 'Oldconnell Stud' is this single-storey early twentieth-century structure in roughcast with red-brick quoins, plinth and chimney-stack to a gabled roof. Projecting hall in same manner. Recently extended to form a pair of semis.

144. OLDTOWN, Naas; pre-1837/*c.* 1907; architect probably R.C. Orpen.
To replace an earlier predecessor on the site is this commodious 1½-storey Arts and Crafts design, with a red-brick attic storey divided from its roughcast ground floor by a moulded brick band. The long elevation to the road has a gablet window relieving the extensive eaves line; projecting brick toothed dressings and quoins. To the avenue entrance gable is an ornamental wooden apex feature in Elizabethan Revival manner. Alongside in limestone ashlar is a grand triple archway

making a rather awkward junction with the lodge. Looking much older, the central carriage archway, like its flanking postilion openings, is round-headed with curved buttress features, which are later adaptations, supporting the understated pediment. Although the ancestral home for centuries of the de Burgh family, the *Irish Builder* in 1906 notes a tender of C.E. Mellon, Brighton Building and Engineering Works, Rathgar, accepted by Col. Wogan Browne, for building of his new residence, Oldtown, Naas, Co. Kildare. R. Caulfield Orpen, archt.

IB (24 March 1906).

145. OVIDSTOWN, Straffan; *c.* 1860.
A simple single-storey gabled porter's lodge, its principal front with two windows and entry via a lean-to projection to the right-hand side. Rendered, with bracketed bargeboards. Derelict. A property in 1870 of Andrew Fortune, the big house of similar age.

Slater 1870.

146. PAINESTOWN, Kill; *c.* 1875.
A plain single-storey standard gatekeeper's cottage in sand/cement render below a steeply hipped roof. A small estate in 1853 of Gerald Turner.

Griffith 1848–60.

147. PAINESTOWN, Straffan; pre-1837; *demolished.*
A property of the Aylmers, of which family the brothers Robert, William and Gerald were in successive occupation in the early nineteenth century.

LGI (1904).

148. PALMERSTOWN, Kill (2).
A large house dating from a 1923 rebuild of that destroyed by fire, itself erected after 1872 by public subscription in fond memory of the 6th earl of Mayo, then viceroy of India, who was assassinated there that year.

Naas entrance; *c.* 1875; *demolished.*
A pair of lodges that may have formed part of that mid-Victorian building phase, placed at the south-western approach, where ball-finialled gate pillars survive with flanking postilion gates as introduction to a twentieth-century bungalow.

Kill entrance; *c.* 1800; architect possibly John Hargrave.
An impressive late Georgian gatescreen comprised of tall granite carriage pillars with fluted friezes and concave quadrants beyond. Secreted behind is this very fine contemporary single-storey cottage below a hipped roof, its three-bay avenue front dominated by a central bow with

sophisticated Wyatt window and flanked by six-over-six sashes in limewashed harled walls. The entrance doorway is on the short road elevation. Although there is no record of his having worked here, this has the feel of John Hargrave about it, being similar to the lodges at Ballynegall, Co. Westmeath (*q.v.*), and Clifton Lodge, Co. Meath (*q.v.*), and, if so, commissioned by John Bourke, 4th earl (1766–1849), after succeeding to the title in 1794. An alternative attribution could be to Francis Johnston.

BPB (1929); Bence-Jones 1988.

149. PARK COTTAGE, Moone; 1901; architect not known.
By the Glenmona (*q.v.*) entrance on an elevated site is this very decent Arts and Crafts design; perfectly symmetrical single-storey standard below a steeply hipped roof with carved soffit brackets to exaggerated oversailing eaves and further conspicuous for its tall plinth. Bipartite casement windows with rectangular panes on each side of a double-leaved door of chevron sheeting. Associated in the valuation book with E. Shackleton and Son.

150. PARSONSTOWN, Leixlip; pre-1837; *demolished.*
Previously called 'Barn Hall', it was a property in 1814 of Sir Hugh O'Reilly.

Leet 1814.

151. PEOPLES' PARK, Athy; *c.* 1845; architect possibly Frederick Darley.

A lofty 1½-storey Tudor-Gothic Revival lodge built off a T-plan, with single-storey rectangular bay window to the side elevation and a little porch projecting from an internal angle with its big kneelers and Tudor-arched opening. All steeply pitched gables with skew-tables and gablets breaking the eaves. Built in coursed rubble with cut-stone chamfering to a variety of flat-arched windows, lancet light and quatrefoil apex feature. Frederick Darley (1799–*c.* 1889) seems to have had a monopoly on commissions around Athy, being associated with the Church of Ireland church, the Methodist church, the Model school and possibly the library; in addition, having had the patronage of the 3rd duke of Leinster, working at his Kilkea Castle (*q.v.*), he may have been responsible for this distinctive lodge.

Williams 1994.

152. PICKERING FOREST, Celbridge; *c.* 1830.

A pretty little 1½-storey cottage, standard with steeply pitched gables and a sheeted door with arrowhead arch to match. Roughcast prettily creeper-clad. Occupied. A property in 1814 of Lewis P. Thomas.

Leet 1814.

153. PIERCETOWN, Newbridge; pre-1837; *demolished.*
A seat in the early nineteenth century of Thomas Mangan, the lodge to which, set well off the main road, had gone by 1939.

Leet 1814.

154. PITCHFORDSTOWN, Kilcock; *c.* 1800.
A fine mid-Georgian house, originally of the White family, which passed by marriage to George Frederick Nugent, 7th earl of Westmeath, who was probably responsible for building the lodge after his succession to the title in 1792. A four-bay single-storey structure, now in exposed rubble below a slated roof with hipped gables. Door to left-hand side. Modern replacement windows and doors. Occupied. Now separated from the house by the intervention of a new bypass road.

BPB (1929).

155. POPLAR HALL, Ballitore; pre-1837; *demolished.*
A property in the first half of the nineteenth century of the Farmer family, whose gatekeeper in 1852 was Julia Brien. The lodge had been removed by 1910.

Griffith 1848–60.

156. POWERSGROVE, Ballitore; pre-1838; *demolished.*
A Power residence that by 1909 was named 'Burtown' and had lost its porter's lodge.

157. PRESTONBROOK, Rathangan; pre-1837; *demolished.*
A ruined house, once of the Preston family, which by 1910 was called 'Brook Lawn'.

158. PRUMPLESTOWN, Castledermot; *c.* 1870; architect John McCurdy.

An impressive composition by the eclectic John McCurdy, here in his Italianate mood, with a wealth of detail applied to a simple single-storey standard lodge. Perfectly symmetrical, its fascia boards with ogee cast-iron guttering, carried on a deep frieze with boldly carved brackets, combine to form the open pediment to its central advancing entrance hallway and repeated on the end elevations as breakfront gablets, all three projecting from the hipped roof with pretty fretted wooden panels to their apexes. Below, roughcast walls, raised on a stone plinth, have smooth-rendered toothed quoins and dressings to flat-arched window openings with bracketed sills and keystones containing two-over-two and three-over-three sashes with round heads. The panelled door has a moulded architrave with segmentally arched head, and on the ridge is a conspicuous chimney-stack with bracketed corniced capping. Complementing this is a contemporary stone entrance sweep in the form of extensive ogee stone quadrants with red-brick bands and ironwork over. More elaborate iron gates hung on carriage pillars with alternate smooth and quarry-faced masonry rustication. McCurdy's client was William Johnson (land and general agent, Carlow), with whom he also had financial dealings.

Slater 1870.

159. QUARRY FARM, Athy; *c.* 1870.
A modest single-storey hip-roofed structure in whitewashed rubble with an unsightly flat-roofed extension to the front. A property in 1852 of John Dunne.

Griffith 1848–60.

160. RAHIN, Edenderry (2).
An old estate of the Palmer family to which the first OS map shows two gate lodges, neither of which has survived.

North entrance; pre-1837; *demolished.*
On the site is a derelict labourer's cottage.

South entrance; pre-1837/*c.* 1875.
Built by Charles Colley Palmer, who inherited the place in 1849 at the age of four, is this replacement 1½-storey gabled lodge off an L-plan, one roof catsliding over the internal angle to form a porch, now enclosed. Rendered walls with stone quoins, the roof having perforated earthenware crestings and canted slate bands. Occupied.

LGI (1904).

161. RATHANGAN, Rathangan; pre-1837; *demolished.*

A seat in the early nineteenth century of the Hon. George Francis Pomeroy (1797–1879), third son of the 4th Viscount Harberton of Newberry Hall (*q.v.*), who assumed the surname Colley in 1830.

BPB (1929).

162. RATHBRIDE, Kildare (2).
Two gate lodges built by the Orford family after 1837 have gone; that to the north ironically is survived opposite the gates by its predecessor, albeit as a very derelict shell. It was single-storey with a clipped verge to the gable and a two-window bay main front, presiding over a disused approach.

163. RATHCOFFEY, Straffan (2).
The old castle of the Wogans was purchased and remodelled by Archibald Hamilton Rowan about 1790 and he may have added the two gate lodges.

East entrance; pre-1837; *demolished.*
Called 'Brook Lodge' on the 1911 OS map.

West entrance; *c.* 1790.
A large two-storey hip-roofed five-bay symmetrical roughcast gatehouse with a back return. Occupied and sadly now missing its squared sashes. It seems to have also served as a schoolhouse, which would account for its size. The big house by 1837 was already described as being 'now comparatively deserted' and is today a ruin.

Lewis 1837; Bence-Jones 1988.

164. RATHMORE, Rathmore; pre-1837/*c.* 1880.
Remaining is this derelict replacement lodge, probably built by Algernon Ambrose Michael Aylmer (1857–1933). It is a single-storey square building with a shallow, almost pyramidal roof rising to a red-brick stack, a material also employed in toothed quoins and soldier arches in roughcast walls. There is a nasty later addition in a lean-to hall to the left-hand side.

LGI (1904).

165. RATHMORE RECTORY, Rathmore; pre-1837; *demolished.*
The lodge may have dated from 1821, when the glebe house was built during the time as vicar, from 1814 until his death, of Revd Thomas Tucker (1770–1829).

Lewis 1837; Leslie and Wallace 2001.

166. RATHSIDE, Ballitore; 1857.
A standard single-storey roughcast gabled affair with stone quoins. Modernised with concrete roof tiles and the dreaded later flat-roofed projecting hall. Occupied. Contemporary with the house and offices when it was created as a fresh development in 1857 by Thomas B. Wakefield.

167. RAVENSDALE, Maynooth (2).
An estate that belonged to David Nixon, which passed by marriage of his daughter Catherine to Nehemiah Donnellan and later, after his death in 1784, to William Morgan, the likely builder of the lodges.

East entrance; *c.* 1785; architect possibly Thomas Ivory.
From within are apparent a simple pair of Georgian cottages, single-storey harled and hip-roofed, with eaves extending over paired soffit brackets. These are coupled with, for effect, the elegant Palladian screen to the road, making this a significant entrance, not just for its architectural sophistication but for its being a very rare instance of a design of this age having had an identifiable twin elsewhere, for there was a matching pair at Killester Abbey, Co. Dublin (*q.v.*), a property of the Newcomens, sadly long removed. This is a very fine composition, though now much the worse for wear and neglect; how it must have looked in its heyday can be seen from McFarland's delightful painting of the Killester entrance. Forward of the gates, the lodge fronts are in the guise of pavilions in ashlar with blind harled (now roughcast) elliptically arched recesses below parapets with graceful stone vases. These are linked by tall convex wing walls to the gatescreen of splendid V-jointed rusticated ashlar Classical carriage pillars with fluted friezes and matching vases aloft, flanked by straight walls pierced by flat-arched pedestrian gate openings. All attributable to architect Thomas Ivory, who is recorded as working here and who designed the Newcomen Bank in Dublin.

167. Ravensdale, Maynooth, east entrance (Irish Architectural Archive).

West or Kellystown gate; *c.* 1800.
In contrast to a pair of ashlar gate pillars with ball finials on elegant pedestals to the right of a postilion opening, and approached within by a flight of steps, is an elevated harled two-storey gatehouse with an unparalleled view of approaching visitors. Below its hipped roof is the most unassuming of two-bay façades, the lower door and window having segmental heads. Occupied, there is a tripartite window to the road and a later single-storey lean-to rear return.

Taylor and Skinner 1778; 1969 [1783]; Wilson 1803; Colgan 2005; Wikipedia.

168. RIVERSTOWN LODGE, Maynooth; pre-1821; *demolished.*
An elegant small Georgian house, dating from the 1760s and the oldest of the properties to be bought and incorporated into the St Patrick's College (*q.v.*) complex in 1802 for £1,000; in 1795 it was occupied by Mrs Craddocks. An 1821 Carton estate map shows its gate lodge to have been a square structure with a canted elevation, set well back from its gatescreen with concave quadrants.

Healy 1895; Corish 1995.

169. ROBERTSTOWN, Robertstown; *c.* 1880.
A sad little unprepossessing boarded-up hodgepodge of a lodge, its appearance not helped by a rendering of sand and cement; 1½-storey, gabled, with clipped main verges but bargeboarded to the projecting central hallway, with its crudely label-moulded window below an attic opening. Strangely, this main front is blind on each side, the ground-floor rooms lit to side and rear. Built by the Ireland family.

170. ROCKFIELD, Athy; pre-1837/post-1872; *demolished.*
An early porter's lodge built opposite the gates in the time of Edward Pilsworth had gone by 1872. A later structure that was in place in 1939 has met the same fate.

171. ROSEBORO, Johnstown; *c.* 1845.
A modest standard rendered hip-roofed gatekeeper's lodge, still occupied, seems to have been built by the Hon. Samuel Crichton (1811–63), a grandson of the 1st earl of Erne of Crom Castle, Co. Fermanagh.
Griffith 1848–60; *BPB* (1929).

172. ROSE LAWN, Celbridge; *c.* 1835.

A symmetrical single-storey lodge with a hipped roof having carved modillion brackets to the eaves carried about the semi-octagonal hall projection, which has slit windows to its canted faces. Rendered, whitewashed and occupied. The gate sweep has four square pillars with moulded recessed panels, surmounted on the cappings by gadrooned 'baps'. Seemingly dating from the occupancy of Joseph Henry Doran.
Slater 1846.

173. ROSETOWN, Newbridge; *c.* 1860.
A mid-Victorian lodge of the Bateman family, plain, single-storey and ruinous. Situated remote from the road and forward of its gates.

174. RYEVALE, Leixlip; pre-1837; *demolished.*
A fine villa built by Robert Law in the late eighteenth century and originally called 'Robertsville', later home to the Otway and Ryan families.
Colgan 2005.

175. ST CATHERINE'S PARK, Leixlip (6).
A once-prosperous estate straddling the boundary with County Dublin by the River Liffey has had a succession of owners since the beginning of the eighteenth century, the principal of whom have been the wealthy banking family of La Touche and the Trenches, both contributing most to the architectural heritage of the demesne. The Rt Hon. David La Touche (1729–1817) of Marlay, Co. Dublin (*q.v.*), purchased the property in 1792, and two of his daughters lived here with their husbands, the 3rd Lord Lanesborough and Colonel George Vesey of Lucan House, Co. Dublin (*q.v.*), before he commissioned architect Francis Johnston from 1798 to castellate the house, which came to nothing, and to design at least two porters' lodges in contrasting styles.

Wood Cottage; 1802; architect Francis Johnston; *demolished.*

Irish Architectural Archive

A remarkable instance of the architect in playful mood with this rare and delightful rustic cottage design, so flimsy in construction as to make its survival into the 20th century extraordinary. Single-storey and three-roomed on a square plan with a pyramidal thatched roof rising to a central stack, there were tree trunks to each corner and a pair as support to the gabled front porch with its chevron-design tympanum, and seats to each side of the sheeted front door with its arrowhead arch. On either side were tiny traceried Gothic windows in lancet openings, and from a side elevation projected a canted bay with leaded lights. To the rear a catslide roof extended over the rear porch and closet.

Stable lodge; 1798; architect Francis Johnston.

Irish Architectural Archive

A most peculiar gabled two-storey gatehouse built in rubble stone with brick dressings and an irregular stepped crenellated parapet only to the leading arrowhead elevation, some of the windows with pointed heads and ornamental hexagonal glazing pattern in Y-tracery. The elevation within the stable yard was in limewashed harling and linked by a castellated curtain wall with decorative cross arrowloop motif to a grand Tudor-style archway flanked by square turrets in limestone ashlar. This whole rather eccentric castellated ensemble now has blocked-up openings and lies behind a palisade fence as protection against the feral class.

Canal entrance; pre-1837; *demolished.*
At the entrance to the northern approach from the Royal Canal was a pair of lodges, one of which and the grand avenue had gone by 1939, thanks to the intervention of the Midland Great Western Railway.

Eastern or Coldblow gate; pre-1837; *demolished.*

Lucan or Bleach Green gate; *c.* 1830.
A two-storey square gatehouse, two-bay with an oversailing hipped roof, the eaves having carved paired brackets, repeated on the single-storey canted bay window which faces the park. New windows and the roughest of modern roughcasts. Occupied.

Leixlip lodge; *c.* 1845; architect not known.

Built by John Trench (1776–1858) is this most delightful Tudor Picturesque-style English cottage, with all the trappings of the Romantic movement; 1½-storey main block under a steeply gabled roof with scalloped slates and decorative carved bargeboards with spiky hip-knobs and pendants, and a pair of brick diagonally placed stacks rising off a rectangular base. Stuccoed walls contained charming label-moulded bi- and tripartite Tudor Gothic windows with pointed heads and latticed glazing patterns in cast iron. To one side was a lean-to entrance structure. Now replaced by a soulless facsimile in synthetic modern materials, none of the original seemingly salvageable. All apparently necessitated by structural faults in the original. There is a twin building alongside. Mrs Emily Vesey lived in this lodge after being widowed in 1829.

Griffith 1848–60; *LGI* (1904); Ball 1995; Joyce 1912; *BPB* (1929); *IGS Bulletin* (July–Dec. 1969); IAA (Murray Drawings Collection).

176. ST CORBAN'S CEMETERY, Naas; *c.* 1880.

Built off an L-plan is this pleasant single-storey gabled lodge with skew-tables and moulded kneelers. The leading gable has a pair of two-over-two sash windows in a smooth rendered surround in otherwise roughcast walls. Above the internal angle the roof catslides to form an open porch with support from a wooden post and carved bracket. Two chimney-stacks with corbelled cappings break earthenware-crested ridges. Nearby is a lych-gate opening and, opposite, a mortuary chapel, all in a sea of tarmacadam.

177. ST DAVID'S CHURCH OF IRELAND CHURCH, Naas; *c.* 1800.

Irish Architectural Archive/An Taisce

Situated off the main street is a perfectly symmetrical and quirky two-storey gatehouse doubling as sexton's accommodation, with three-bay ground floor and single upper-storey window to match those below, with small rectangular-paned casements below shouldered arches, all in roughcast walls below a hipped gable. Four-panelled central doorway. Built when the rector (1789–1830) was Revd James Slater (1756–1830).

Leslie and Wallace 2009; IAA photograph (29/27)

178. ST JOHN'S CHURCH OF IRELAND CHURCH, Kilcullen; pre-1837.

Elevated from its entrance to church and graveyard is this occupied lodge, so altered as to make it difficult to date but perhaps originating from 1836, when the church was being enlarged with the addition of transepts during the incumbency from 1820 until his death of Revd John Hardy (1785–1838). Roughcast single-storey five-bay symmetrical below a hipped roof with gabled breakfront doorway.

Lewis 1837; Leslie and Wallace 2001.

179. ST PATRICK'S COLLEGE, Maynooth; 1960.

'In October 1795, the college was opened for the reception of 50 students', since when it has evolved into the huge complex of today. At the turn of the nineteenth century it was comprised of the neighbouring private demesnes of 'Riverstown Lodge' (*q.v.*) and 'Stoyte House' (*q.v.*); the latter of the duke of Leinster's agent was offered along with 54 acres and a lodge entrance, the necessity for the replacement of which was recognised at an early stage. A lithograph of 1855 based on a drawing by A.W.N. Pugin shows, in a bird's-eye perspective, replacement lodges to both original gates, each approached via bridges. That to the main gate was to span an existing sunken ditch before a two-storey steeply gabled Gothic gatehouse with pointed windows and breakfronts front and back containing arched openings that would have been restricted. To the Riverstown gate a bridge over the Royal Canal leads to a pointed-arched, double-leafed doorway, alongside which is shown a single-storey gabled structure with a tripartite window. In fact, the old main gate to Stoyte House served as entrance to the College until 1960, when gatescreen and lodge were replaced by the present substitutes, which are both inadequate and unworthy. At the northern entrance are fine wrought-iron gates taken from the Dangan Castle estate, Co. Meath (*q.v.*).

Lewis 1837; Atterbury 1995; Corish 1995; Healy 1895; O'Dwyer 1996; Horner 2005.

ST VINCENT'S HOSPITAL (see ATHY UNION WORKHOUSE)

180. ST WOLSTAN'S, Celbridge (2).

The present mansion is the creation of Richard Cane in an early nineteenth-century remodelling of an original house built on priory lands by Sir John Alen a century earlier. The main lodge at least, however, may have been erected in the time here of Revd Dr Thomas Barnard, bishop of Killaloe and Limerick, when the place served as an academy.

Celbridge Road gate; *c.* 1790.

A simple single-storey Georgian Gothic cottage alongside the entrance gateway. Gabled, with a two-bay road front of lancet-headed window and doorway. Now semi-detached with a later structure. John Rocque's map of 1760 suggests that there may have been an earlier lodge on the site.

Leixlip Road gate; pre-1837; *demolished.*

A lodge that was located up what is now a sad, unprepossessing, potholed approach.

Taylor and Skinner 1778; 1969 [1783]; Wilson 1803; Lewis 1837; Ferguson 1998.

181. SALISBURY, Athy; *c.* 1860.

A plain single-storey standard lodge with roughcast walls and hipped roof extending to a gable end over the back return and finished in modern concrete tiles. Unsightly later central flat-roofed hall projection. Occupied. The builder was probably Thomas Beasley, who acquired the property, which until *c.* 1824 was known as 'Shrowland', from the Lawler or Lalor family.

Pigot 1824; Lewis 1837; Slater 1856.

182. SALLYMOUNT, Kilcullen (2).

A house built *c.* 1770 to designs of Francis Sandys for Revd Marmaduke Cramer. Either he or his son, Rev. John Cramer-Roberts (who assumed his wife's maiden name), added gate lodges to the property.

South gate; pre-1837; *demolished.*

Like the big house, this lodge is a thing of the past, survived by large octagonal gate pillars with ball finials.

East gate; pre-1837/*c.* 1870.

Either a replacement or a development of the original is this single-storey symmetrical five-bay porter's accommodation. Finished in stucco effect with toothed quoins and dressings below a hipped roof, there is a half-hipped canopy over the front door supported by carved wooden ornamental brackets. Work presumably initiated by Charles Torin Cramer-Roberts (1837–77), who inherited the estate in 1852.

Brewer 1825; *LGI* (1904).

183. SEASONS, Ballymore Eustace; *c.* 1875.

A conspicuous 1½-storey building, its ground floor an L-plan with regular gabled attic storey over, forming an entrance porch recess with corner post support. Most remarkable for its wall covering of scallop shells with bullnosed brick dressings and quoins. Occupied. For many years a property of the O'Brien family but in 1874 in the possession of Edward Fitzgerald.

Land Owners in Ireland 1876.

184. SHAMROCK LODGE, Athy; *c.* 1790.

A delightful survival, for, although vacant, this lodge is maintained by its owners as an important vernacular building in the countryside, although not of architectural significance. Single-storey with its end gable

in limewashed harling, rising to a minuscule brick chimney-stack, forming part of the entrance screen. Standard three-bay to the avenue, its little square windows actually painted security boarding on each side of a taller doorway. Earthenware canted ridge cresting is later, as is the back return, which breaks the right-hand of the extensive shallow-walled quadrants. Four fine round granite pillars with monolithic shafts and cone cappings frame the carriage and flanking postilion gates of spear-topped ironwork. A demesne in the first half of the nineteenth century of Thomas O'Meara.

SHROWLAND (see SALISBURY)

185. SKERRIES, Fontstown (2).

This property in Skerries North passed in 1822 after the death of Charles Dowling Medlicott to Joseph Lapham. He does not seem to have redeveloped the place until about 1830, a programme of building which included the addition of at least one of the porters' lodges.

Outer gate; pre-1837; *demolished.*

Located on the western approach opposite its gates and divided from the demesne proper by two public roads, this lodge was removed about 1963.

Inner gate; *c.* 1830.

A standard single-storey gatekeeper's lodge which would be unremarkable were it not for its front façade being deeply recessed within a wide elliptical archway. All was finished in harling, now removed in modernisation to reveal a fabric of rubble and brick dressings. Previously with squared casement windows flanking a segmentally fanlit doorway, all these openings have been remodelled and the hipped roof re-covered in synthetic slates. Not unique, for there is a similarly eccentric building at Springfield House, Co. Kilkenny (*q.v.*). In 1852 the gatekeeper here was Patrick Brophy, leasing from Joseph Lapham Beasley, who had inherited the property from his grandfather Joseph Lapham.

Griffith 1848–60; unpublished history of the Flynn family and Skerries by Michael P. Flynn.

186. SPRINGFIELD, Celbridge (2).

West lodge; *c.* 1860.

A 1½-storey gabled building in roughcast with Tudor-style label mouldings and diamond motif to one gable.

East lodge; *c.* 1860.

A single-storey standard version of the above, in smooth rendering with label mouldings and a quatrefoil feature to the leading gable. Simple replacement foiled bargeboards to main gable and that of the projecting hallway, which has side entry. Modernised and occupied.

Both probably built as part of improvements to the estate after the 3rd earl of Leitrim of nearby Killadoon (*q.v.*) had acquired it, his tenant of the time being John Tottenham Langrishe (1807–88) of that family of Knocktopher Abbey, Co. Kilkenny (*q.v.*).

BPB (1929); Malcomson 2009.

187. STACUMNY, Celbridge (3).

A later Georgian house of Sir Michael Cromie, Bart, in whose time the demesne boasted two gatekeepers' lodges, north and south, both of which were replaced by the Hon. Richard Anthony Nugent (1842–1912), fourth son of the 9th earl of Westmeath, who had acquired the property after the death of Sir John Valentine Bradstreet (1815–89). The latter had added in his time here a third, and middle, lodge, which has not survived.

North entrance; pre-1837/1911; architect not known.

A characterful single-storey Edwardian lodge built off a T-plan in a distinctive mix of red brick and roughcast. Otherwise gabled, one end elevation is canted, echoed on the main front by a similar bay window. The main delight is the extraordinary Baroque-detailed door-case, below a gablet, crowned by a swan-neck open pediment which frames a mysterious crest and coat of arms not related to any of the above-mentioned families. Red-brick corbelled chimney-stack and terracotta ridge tiles, hip tiles and hip-knobs.

187. Stacumny, Baroque-detailed door-case.

Middle entrance; post-1837; *demolished.*

South entrance; pre-1837/1906.

An altogether less prepossessing lodge; although constructed in the same materials, these are now lost in an all-over paint scheme. A single-storey standard Picturesque affair, with pretty perforated foiled

bargeboards to main gables and that of the breakfront, which boasts the date-stone. Brick toothed dressings, quoins and dentilled chimney-stack. Older, modest stone gate pillars and tall concave quadrant walls.

Burke's *Dormant and extinct peerages* (1844); *BPB* (1903 and 1929).

188. STACUMNY LODGE, Celbridge; *c.* 1790.

Much improved but retaining its Georgian character is this delightful single-storey lodge located well in advance of its entrance gates, distinctive for its bow end to the road below an equivalent roof with tiny slates. Much extended to the rear, there are squared Georgian-effect windows in roughcast walls with a high plinth. Occupied and proudly maintained. Probably another property of the Cromie family, in the mid-nineteenth century it was occupied by Captain Richard Whitmore.

Griffith 1848–60.

189. STONEBROOK, Ballymore Eustace (2).
East entrance; pre-1837; *demolished.*
West entrance; *c.* 1830.

A single-storey gabled structure, much modernised and extended into a double pile, and more.

Both lodges and house would seem to have been contemporary and built by David O'Connor-Henchy (1810–76).

LGI (1904).

190. STONEBROOK LODGE, Kilcullen; *c.* 1850.
A mid-nineteenth-century single-storey hip-roofed lodge extended by a bay with a gable end facing the park. Rendered and occupied. An estate then of the Thompson family.

191. STOYTE, Maynooth; *c.* 1790; *demolished.*
In 1795 the offer of Mr Stoyte's house in Maynooth as a site for the future St Patrick's College (*q.v.*) was accepted. John Stoyte was a steward of the duke of Leinster and he had just built his house at the recently laid-out western end of the main street. The house survives as part of the complex but lodge and entrance screen have gone. An 1818 description notes the ornaments on the piers in the form of two sphinxes to the entrance pillars, flanked by outer lions couchant and urns. These went in about 1958, although they were then close to disintegration. The porter's accommodation was a modest single-storey hip-roofed structure with an asymmetrical three-bay elevation to the avenue.

Warburton et al. 1818; Lacy 1852; Corish 1995.

192. STRAFFAN, Straffan (2).
John Joseph Henry was one of the wealthiest men in the country when he succeeded to Straffan, but he led a life of profligacy and squandered his fortune in a love of fine wines, which forced him to sell the estate. Ironically, the purchaser in 1831 was Hugh Barton (1766–1854) of the Tipperary family, who had made his money from the French wine trade. He set about extending the house to designs of Frederick Darley of Dublin, who may have been responsible for the two gate lodges to eastern and western approaches, although the demesne was already surrounded by a high stone wall, as recorded by Brewer in 1825. Further improvements were effected to both house and lodges, probably by Hugh Barton's grandson, Hugh Lynedoch Barton (1824–99), after he inherited on his father's death in 1867.

192. Straffan, front entrance.

Rear entrance; pre-1837/*c.* 1867.
Providing extraordinarily generous accommodation is this two-storey standard gabled gatehouse with a central gablet feature containing a tiny lancet light. Small bipartite casement windows, now with modern lead-effect glazing, probably replacing original cast-iron latticed lights, those on the ground floor flanking a projecting single-storey gabled hall with simple wavy bargeboards. This symmetrical composition is enhanced by balancing 1½-storey wings. All now smooth-rendered with string-courses and toothed quoins. Immaculate and occupied. Very tall carriage pillars with 'bap' cappings are matched by the outer pillars, between which are quadrant walls containing round-headed postilion openings.

Front entrance; pre-1837/*c.* 1867; architects probably Lanyon and Lynn.
A big mid-Victorian single-storey gabled Italianate-style lodge, rendered smooth with large moulded plinth and toothed quoins and dressings to a series of eight-over-six bipartite sash windows with round heads. The eaves have distinctive carved paired brackets extending to the main front bargeboards that rise over the canted bay, which projects beyond the gatescreen to the road, ornamented with rendered strapwork. The ridge is broken by two tall chimney-stacks rising off bases and terminating in moulded cappings. On stylistic grounds this may be a replacement and can be ascribed to the Belfast architectural practice of Lanyon and Lynn, an attribution strengthened by a drawing for an unexecuted conservatory design for the house by the firm. Alongside the lodge, in contrast, is a rubble-built gatescreen of pedestrian gate openings flanking a pair of tall carriage pillars with prominent moulded cappings and dainty ball finials.

The property is now a vast country club and golf-course.

Brewer 1825; *LGI* (1904); Bence-Jones 1988; Williams 1994.

193. STRAFFAN RECTORY, Straffan; *c.* 1835.
A Georgian house in 1824 of the curate, Revd Newcomen Whitelaw (1763–1828), whose widow lived on there when the property became 'Straffan Lodge'. There is a minute one-bay Tudor-style brick-built single-storey gabled lodge, with label mouldings to the sidelighted doorway and the wide window with chamfered stone below a gablet. To the inner gable is a paired chimney-stack. Well maintained and occupied.

Pigot 1824; Lewis 1837; Leslie and Wallace 2001.

194. SUNNY HILL, Kilcullen; *c.* 1880.

Detailed in typically forthright late Victorian manner, with its use of materials contrasting in colour and texture. Single-storey and three bay, with its doorway to the right-hand side below a steeply pitched hipped roof. Occupied and extended into a double pile to the

197. Turnings, Straffan.

rear. Built for Thomas Waldron in rubble stone with polychromatic red and cream brickwork to chimney-stack and toothed opening dressings, a moulded brick being employed for chamfered reveals and corbelling to chimney capping and eaves. To the corners are reticulated quoin stones. Modest modern gateway alongside.

Griffith 1848–60.

195. TONLEGEE, Athy; pre-1837; *demolished.*
Replaced by a modern bungalow; two V-jointed rusticated pillars survive with large rustic ball finials. An estate in 1851 of Thomas Fitzgerald.

Griffith 1848–60.

196. TULLYLOST, Rathangan; *c.* 1840.
A roughcast single-storey gabled gatekeeper's lodge with two-window bay elevation to the avenue and doorway to the road now enclosed by a nasty later flat-roofed hallway. Opposing elevation extended by a bay, terminating in a hipped roof to the park. Large paired wooden eaves brackets. A seat in the early nineteenth century of Charles F. Johnston.

Lewis 1837.

197. TURNINGS, Straffan; *c.* 1840.
Standard single-storey roughcast hip-roofed lodge, with small two-over-two sash windows on each side of a projecting gabled hallway with spoked fanlight to the sheeted front door and minuscule arrow-headed slit lights to its sides. Derelict. Built for Samuel Mills.

198. WELLFIELD, Ballymore Eustace; pre-1837.
In the early nineteenth century the property of Richard Doyle, whose lodge is now a modernised 1½-storey house.

199. WHEELAM, Rathangan; pre-1837; *demolished.*
A seat until 1830 of Robert Clibborn, upon whose death it then passed by marriage to William Cope Cooper (1793–1874) of Cooper's Hill, Co. Laois (*q.v.*). By 1910 the gate lodge had gone.

LGI (1904).

200. WHITELEAS, Ballymore Eustace; pre-1837/*c.* 1910.
The early lodge, opposite its contemporary gatescreen with anthemion motifs of *c.* 1830, has been replaced by a remarkable gabled corrugated-iron bungalow. The property in 1814 of Matthew Lynch, by 1836 it was 'the residence of Mr James Lynch, who has built a very fine house and noble offices upon it, and otherwise greatly improved it by winding walks, plantations and a judicious appropriation of the waters of a little rivulet that flows through the grounds'.

Leet 1814; d'Alton 1976 [1838].

201. WILLIAMSTOWN, Edenderry; pre-1837; *demolished.*
The porter's lodge to this fine Palladian-style house, probably by the amateur architect Nathaniel Clements for the Williams family, had gone by 1910.

Bence-Jones 1988.

202. WILLOWBROOK, Ballitore; pre-1838; *demolished.*
The gate lodge to a property in 1814 of John Butler, which by 1851 had passed to Garrett Cullen (*c.* 1773–1845), had disappeared by 1909.

Leet 1814; Griffith 1848–60.

203. WOODBINE COTTAGE, Athy; pre-1838/*c.* 1850.
The previous porter's lodge at the original (and present) entrance of the time of Thomas Rawson's ownership was replaced with this solid successor by John Barrett. Single-storey, hip-roofed with high eaves, in good limestone facings had square windows with pairs of rectangular-paned casements. Three-bay to the road; a hideous flat-roofed draught-hall projects from the right-hand side. There is a later extension to the rear forming a double pile. Occupied. Its entrance has now reverted to the original position to the east.

Leet 1814; Griffith 1848–60.

204. YEOMANSTOWN, Naas (2).
Both pre-1837 lodges, including that to the eastern approach that presided over the long straight tree-lined avenue to the front door of the fine house, have gone. The estate of the Eustaces was inherited by the Mansfield family.

LGI (1904); Bence-Jones 1988.

COUNTY KILKENNY

Note
Kilculliheen parish, north of the River Suir, has been transferred several times between counties Waterford and Kilkenny; properties therein are listed here.

1. ABBEY CHURCH AND GRAVEYARD, Waterford; pre-1837/*c.* 1855.

On the banks of the Suir at Ferrybank by the Abbey Church is this fine two-bay lodge, each bay a pair of round-headed windows with keystone and surround, much as at Leoville on the Passage East road out of Waterford. Single-storey below an overhanging hipped roof with sparse bracket support; a similar but single window to a side elevation surveys the gate approach. In smart black and white livery, the central stack has a variety of square and diamond motifs. All within a railed enclosure. It would seem to have existed in 1839 but was probably given a facelift when the property was acquired by John and Samuel Waring from the Nevins about 1855.

Slater 1846; 1856.

2. ANNMOUNT, Waterford; pre-1839; *demolished.*
A demesne lying on the north bank of the Suir that was probably named after Anne Alston, proprietor in the mid-nineteenth century.

Griffith 1848–60.

3. ANNSBOROUGH, Carrick-on-Suir; pre-1839; *demolished.*
A property that passed from the Osborne family to Richard Sauce sometime between 1790 and 1814.

Wilson 1803; Leet 1814.

4. AUT EVEN, Kilkenny; *c.* 1896; architect William Scott; *not executed.*
Ellen Bischoffheim, second wife of the 4th earl of Desart, on being widowed in 1898 commissioned William Scott to design her house, the model village of Talbot's Inch, a church and gate lodge, though the 1945 OS map suggests that the latter was never built.

BPB (1929); Williams 1994.

5. BALIEF CASTLE, Urlingford; pre-1839; *demolished.*
The seat in the early nineteenth century of Robert St George.

Leet 1814; Lewis 1837.

6. BALLEVEN, Kilmanagh; pre-1839; *demolished.*
A lodge that had gone by 1902, presumably built by Joseph Evans, the last of that family to live here. He died in 1818, making bequests to institutions in Kilkenny city and setting up the Evans' Asylum (*q.v.*).

LGI (1904); Lanigan and Tyler 1987.

7. BALLINABARNEY, New Ross; *c.* 1850.
A bulky single-storey structure built off a square plan with a pyramidal roof of twentieth-century asbestos slates in sawtooth pattern rising to a central red-brick chimney-stack; a not-quite-symmetrical three-bay front elevation with plastic windows in rendered walls. Occupied and recently modernised. Probably built by James Bolger on a property described in 1837 as being an ancient residence of his family, on the water's edge, 'a romantic and richly wooded spot'.

Lewis 1837.

BALLYCARRAN (see BORRIS BIG)

8. BALLYCASTALANE COTTAGE, Carrick-on-Suir; pre-1839; *demolished.*
A seat in the early nineteenth century of R.B. Osborne, like the neighbouring estate of Annsborough (*q.v.*) of that family and likewise minus its gate lodge.

9. BALLYCONRA, Ballyraggett (2).
On a now-bare demesne, its house exposed and dominated by a huge dairy concern, was a property of the Butlers, earls of Mountgarrett, though occupied for much of the nineteenth century by their agents, Michael Richard Cahill and his descendants.

North lodge; *c.* 1835.
Now totally overgrown, it is a standard single-storey hip-roofed building with diagonally placed chimney-stack and a carved fish-scale fascia board about the eaves. Roughcast walls. The entrance gatescreen opposite has been lost in road-widening.

South lodge; *c.* 1850; *demolished.*
Surviving is a fine limestone Classical gatescreen, like its avenue badly in need of a planted setting.

In 1849 the gatekeepers were Edward Dowling and Margaret Burke.

Griffith 1848–60; *IFR.*

10. BALLYDUFF, Inistioge; pre-1839; *demolished.*
The gate lodge had gone by 1903 but is survived by two granite ashlar pillars with deep V-jointed rustication. The house was occupied in 1814 by Revd Richard Cooke, to whom the architect William Robertson inscribed a view of the house and who may have been responsible for building work on the property.

Robertson 1800; Leet 1814.

BALLYHENEBERY (see COOKSTOWN)

11. BALLYHIMMIN, Castlecomer; *c.* 1830.
A modest little single-storey three-bay asymmetrical cottage, harled and limewashed, off an L-plan below a hipped roof. To a house and bleach mill in 1849 of Nathaniel Hayes.

Griffith 1848–60.

BALLYLINCH (see MOUNT JULIET)

12. BALLYQUIN, Mullinavat; pre-1839; *demolished.*
A property in the early nineteenth century of the Dillon family.

13. BALLYRAGGET LODGE, Ballyragget; 1790.
The sad remains of a Georgian Gothic lodge, single-storey below a hipped roof with lancet-headed openings, forward of a Classical gatescreen of four pillars with moulded corniced caps, framing carriage gates and two postilion openings in tall roughcast concave quadrant walls. Built about the time when the estate passed by marriage from the Butlers, earls of Ormonde, to the Kavanaghs of Borris, Co. Carlow (*q.v.*).

LGI (1904); *BPB* (1929).

14. BALLYSPALLEN, Johnstown; pre-1839; *demolished.*
A property in 1814 of Charles Byrne.

Leet 1814.

15. BALLYTOBIN, Dunnamaggan; *c.* 1835.

Irish Architectural Archive

Below a hipped roof is a single-storey symmetrical lodge with an unusually extensive and pleasant front façade, with bipartite latticed casement windows on either side of a matching double-leaved panelled glazed doorway, all recessed and framed by end piers, and deep eaves band supported on two intermediate Doric columns. Opposite is a very fine and wide straight gatescreen, its ornate ironwork with fleur-de-lis, palmette and quatrefoil motifs to carriage gates and matching side railings with postilion gates. The whole framed by stone pillars with recessed panel shafts and moulded cornice cappings. Rubble quadrants beyond that again. Built for Abraham Whyte Baker, who in 1837 had 'a place of considerable antiquity, ... situated in a fine demesne abounding with timber of aged growth, with a deer park attached'.

Lewis 1837; IAA photograph (54/12 Z1).

BANSE GLEBE (see KILMANAGH RECTORY)

16. BARRAGHCORE, Goresbridge (2).
North lodge; *c.* 1835.

A singular sturdy lodge with the most forthright of detailing. Below a hipped roof with chunky paired brackets to high eaves is this single-storey three-roomed lodge sitting on a T-plan, each of its leading harled façades containing wide low-level tripartite windows with six-over-six sashes framed by solid stone uprights with corbels carrying lintels, projecting to match the sills. Internally the windows are set into segmentally arched recesses. Contrasting is the similarly treated doorway with a tall head. Where the ridges intersect is a relatively dainty octagonal chimney-stack. Derelict but sufficiently spacious to lend itself to extension and modern living. The six squat Classical granite entrance pillars with recessed panels and plain corniced cappings contrast with cruder stone screen walls.

South lodge; pre-1839; *demolished.*
The property in the first quarter of the nineteenth century of John Handy, one of whose gatekeepers in 1850 was John Merlin.
Griffith 1848–60

17. BARROWMOUNT, Goresbridge; pre-1839.
Little more than a shell remains of a large gable onto the avenue, accompanied by two very fine square ashlar corniced pillars with ball finials atop, perhaps erected by the Butler family or their successors here, the Gores.

Taylor and Skinner 1778; 1969 [1783]; Bence-Jones 1988.

18. BAYSWELL, Johnstown; pre-1839; *demolished.*
A modern bungalow is on the site of a lodge built by either William Butler or the Byrne family, who succeeded in the early nineteenth century.

19. BEECH HILL, Ballyraggett (2).
The lodges from before 1839 have gone, both probably dating from the time of Revd Francis Lodge (1769–1854), vicar of Kilmocar parish.

Leet 1814; Leslie and Wallace 2009.

20. BELLINE, Piltown (2).
'... an elegant villa built by Peter Walsh, surrounded with a beautiful demesne, almost all of his own creation, for when he began there, the ground was naked and swampy, with only a few oaks scattered over it.' Thus wrote Mason in 1814 of the son of John Walsh of Fanningstown (*q.v.*), who as agent to the earl of Bessborough built the grand house here, complete with its peculiar detached drum pavilions, in 1785 and graced the demesne with what is a porter's lodge unique in these islands.

Rustic temple lodge; *c.* 1790.

Michael O'Dwyer

Michael O'Dwyer

In a property of surprises, situated discreetly up the driveway remote from the public road is this 'Primitive Greek Hut' forerunner to the columned temple, similar to an illustration in Sir William Chambers's *A treatise on the decorative part of civil architecture* (1759). The architect was employed by the 2nd earl of Bessborough, Walsh's immediate neighbour, at his English seat of Parksted in 1760, and it is most likely that this was influential in the conception of this special building. It differs particularly from the Chambers original in lacking a platform or stylobate to support the single-storey lodge with its tetrastyle prostyle portico of baseless tree trunk columns, which are continued to each side elevation as six semi-engaged pseudoperipterally. All have a capital comprising square stone abacus and echinus in the form of a rope. The walls are in harled rubble, over which the continuous entablature, made up of hefty timbers as architrave supporting end-on frieze planks, embraces the structure as both eaves and base to the pediment. The latter is heavily mutuled, its tympanum plastered with an oculus lighting the roof space. On the ridge of the slated roof is a brick chimney-stack that rises from the fireplace wall dividing the front living room from two tiny bedrooms behind. Two almost contemporary mid-Victorian photographs show it in its heyday, one with an earlier thatch; probably attended by the same lady gatekeeper at its original gate. Occupied until as recently as the 1980s, this national treasure now lies derelict and at risk.

'Turret' gate; *c.* 1800; architect not known.

David Ker

To the south-west extremity of the property is another intriguing gate lodge, originally intended to be one of a pair, as illustrated by Robert Woodham's charming oil painting of 1800. The 1839 OS map, however, reveals only one. The artist must have based his subject on an architect's proposals. His view depicts the two-storey lodges each as massive octagonal gate pillars linked by carriage gates and flanked by postilion gates and small walled screens with piers crowned by handsome urns. What was to have been the left-hand porter's lodge is in V-jointed rusticated ashlar in two tiers defined by a moulded upper sill course to shallow windows on each face. The ground-floor openings are part-blind. An octahedral roof rises to a chimney-stack in like form. To the rear is a contrasting crude single-storey extension to a sophisticated structure now depressingly run-down and neglected.

Chambers 1862; Mason 1814–19; Bence-Jones 1988; Lyall 1988; Howley 1993; Colvin 2008; Harris and Snodin 1997.

BELMOUNT COTTAGE (see GRAIGUE LODGE)

21. BELMOUNT, Waterford; pre-1839/*c.* 1890.

The previous lodge to the property was built before 1839, by either Pierce George Barron (1793–1864) or his cousin, Sir Henry Winston Barron (1795–1872), after whose death it was replaced by the present gawky 1½-storey late Victorian affair with naive rendered features in the form of moulded pediments above the windows and rectangular panel over where the later single-storey hall has been ineptly added. Nasty modern windows and giant Irish pilaster quoins. Now St Vincent's Novitiate.

Pigot 1824; Lewis 1837; *IFR*.

22. BELVIEW or BELLEVUE, Waterford; pre-1839; *demolished.*
The gate lodge was probably built by Patrick Power of the Faithlegg, Co. Waterford, family, who bought Bellevue about the time of his marriage in 1811.

Leet 1814; *IFR*.

23. BERRYHILL, Inistioge; *c.* 1925.
The perfectly delightful Picturesque cottage residence of the Dyer family had remarkably survived lodgeless until the early twentieth century, when it was belatedly complemented by a most peculiar and unworthy of concoctions. Single-storey, of two rectangular structures with steeply hipped roofs, barely attached at right angles to one another to form an irregular L-plan. Both three-bay, one surprisingly displaying a wide tripartite window from another age, placed asymmetrically in roughcast walls. Occupied.

NIAH.

24. BESSBOROUGH, Piltown (10).
'Handsome and commodious drives, at the entrances to which are likewise neat lodges, with persons in attendance to open and close the gates, branch off in various directions in front of the house.' So found Lacy in 1862 on what was then, with eight, the most lodged property in the country, as was befitting of the second-largest landowner in County Kilkenny, with an inner demesne of 500 acres. Frederick Ponsonby, 3rd earl of Bessborough (1758–1844), who succeeded his father to the estates in 1793, was an absentee landlord; it is his eldest son and eventual successor, John William as Lord Duncannon, who is credited with much of the improvements in the 1830s. None of the lodges built in this period that remain are architecturally prepossessing, although an exception may have been that to the main entrance.

Grand entrance; pre-1839/*c.* 1860; *demolished.*

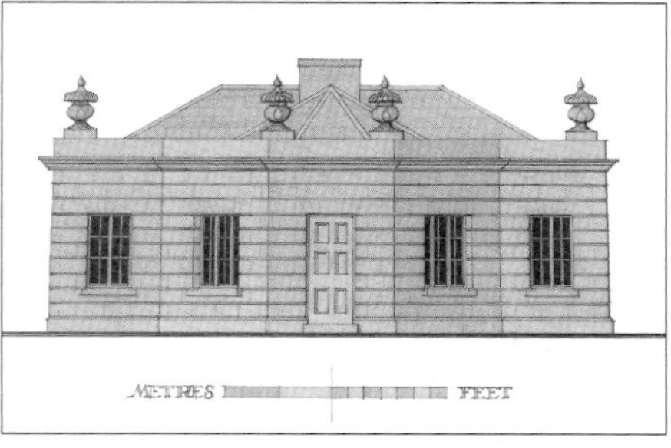

An appropriately extensive tripartite gatescreen that seems, on the evidence of contrasting stonework, to have evolved down the years to its present extent and displays a variety of finials: pineapples to the tall late eighteenth-century carriage pillars, balls to outer pillars, while vases crown intermediate pillars containing alternate rails and walls. These vases were complemented by those on the parapet of the now-lost attendant mid-Victorian lodge, noticeable, too, for its dominant semi-octagonal central hall projection and heavily rusticated masonry. Quite why this characterful and conspicuous structure gave way to the present bland twentieth-century bungalow is a mystery, as before was its creation to supersede a predecessor on the same site which must have been notable in its own right to justify being named on the first OS map as 'Grand Gate Lodge'. The drawing is based on an old photograph.

North lodge; *c.* 1800.
A basic single-storey structure with a harled two-window bay elevation to the road below a hipped roof. Abandoned. Alongside the remains of a more sophisticated gated entrance of square pillars with moulded plinths, their cappings missing.

South lodge; pre-1839/*c.* 1870; architect not known.
An earlier lodge to the right-hand side was replaced to the other side of the entrance by this good, almost symmetrical, 1½-storey Tudor Revival Picturesque cottage. The slit window to attic space on each main gable is repeated on the front gablet above the central single-storey canted bay window, which is

flanked by a bipartite casement window and a studded panelled front door below a fanlight. Whitened rendered walls contrast nicely with quarry-faced stone quoins. Above it all a fine coupled chimney-stack. Probably missing original ornamental bargeboards like those on the contemporary main inner lodge.

North-east lodge; *c.* 1800.
The oldest surviving lodge to the demesne is this agreeable little limewashed hipped-roof single-storey cottage, with its Gothic lancet windows in the central bow projection under a semi-conical roof.

North inner lodge; *c.* 1845.
A modest roughcast standard lodge, gabled with a similar central hall projection.

River lodge; *c.* 1840.
In the heart of the demesne at a natural river boundary are the sad ruins of a standard single-storey cottage with harled rubble walls under a shallow hipped roof, its rafters exposed.

Piltown gate; *c.* 1860.
To the western perimeter of the demesne is a single-storey gabled lodge in cut random uncoursed rubble with tiny squared window casements. Hopelessly inappropriate flat-roofed front projection. Two V-jointed rusticated grand limestone gate pillars with contrasting crude ball finials.

West inner lodge; post-1839; *demolished.*
Only 200 yards up the main avenue at an inner enclosure, a lodge lost without trace.

Farmyard lodge; *c.* 1870.
To the eastern boundary is a much-altered single-storey building in excellent random punched ashlar, its front elevation to the avenue of three bays arranged eccentrically below the gables of a double pile. Occupied.

Main inner lodge; *c.* 1870; architect not known.

Located far up the main avenue at the innermost gate in a boundary to exclude deer is this pretentious and perky lodge built off a cruciform plan; 1½-storey Tudor Picturesque with minute loft windows, with similar features to the contemporary south lodge in its coupled chimney-stack and quoins of a conspicuous quarry-faced finish, which here extends to the canted bay window surrounds. The studded panelled front door has, like the windows, chunky pointed-arch heads to its fanlight. Replacement hip-knobs and ornamental perforated bargeboards carried about as fascias. Immaculately maintained but unoccupied.

These three later lodges, built by John George Brabazon Ponsonby, who succeeded as 5th earl on his father's death in 1847, brought the total here to ten, exceeding the eight of the Shirley family at their County Monaghan estate of Lough Fea Castle. This may be explained by the family's social conscientiousness to house their tenantry and the complex network of roads surrounding the property.

Parliamentary Gazetteer; Lacy 1863; *BPB* (1929); Costello *et al.* 1995.

25. BIRCHFIELD, Kilkenny; pre-1839/*c.* 1840; architect not known.

A property created by the Birch family, who had a gate lodge which was replaced to the other side of the entrance by John Smithwick of Kilcreene Cottage, who had acquired the estate about 1840. A delightful single-storey English Picturesque cottage built off an L-plan; a pair of very steeply pitched gables with basic perforated wavy bargeboards advance to the avenue, that to the left containing a lancet-headed doorway to the hall. White rendered walls with openings picked out with banded surrounds. Contrasting brick stacks with peculiar triangular motifs on their plinths. Sometime later extended towards the road, and later again tragically gutted by fire.

LGI (1904).

BISHOP'S GROVE (see SION LODGE)

26. BLANCHVILLE, Gowran; pre-1839; *demolished.*
An estate of the Kearney family to which a fine entrance gate survives. Square limestone pillars with recessed panel shafts flanked by railed screens terminating in convex quadrant walls. Its gatekeeper's lodge, which had gone by 1902, pre-dated architect Daniel Robertson's work here in the 1840s.

O'Dwyer 1999.

27. BORRIS BIG, Jenkinstown; pre-1839; *demolished.*
In the mid-nineteenth century a property of Thomas Harman, a century later it was called 'Ballycarran', without its lodge.

Griffith 1848–60.

28. BORRISMORE, Urlingford; pre-1839; *demolished.*
The place was previously known as 'Marymount', when Garrett Neville named it after his wife on their marriage in 1765.

LGI (1904); Bence-Jones 1988.

29. BRANDONDALE, Graiguenamanagh; *c.* 1825.
Facing the road, its gates alongside, is this single-storey standard gabled lodge with chimney-stack to each peak. The doorway has the most basic of stone hoods over, on simple bracket supports. On each side the tiny windows are framed in segmentally arched recesses, reflecting those on the big house. Built by David Burtchaell, agent of Lord Clifden.

Fraser 1838.

30. BRENAR, Piltown; pre-1839; *demolished.*
A house, occupied in the mid-nineteenth century by Misses Julia and Jane Burke, whose lodge had gone by 1903.

Griffith 1848–60.

31. BROOKEVILLE, Freshford; *c.* 1835.
A tumbledown single-storey rubble cottage with a gabled low-pitched roof, which was occupied by James Costigan as gatekeeper in 1849; his landlord was Edward H. Williams, who in turn leased from Revd Nesbitt Lodge.

Griffith 1848–60.

32. BROWNSFORD, Inistioge; pre-1839; *demolished.*
Surviving is a pair of square granite gate pillars with heavily corniced cappings supporting pedestalled ball finials. To each side spear-topped concave railed quadrants. Built by the Garvey family, probably by Thomas, who was in residence in 1814.

Leet 1814.

BURNCHURCH (see DANESFORT RECTORY)

33. BURNCHURCH, Burnchurch; *c.* 1900.

Located opposite its gates, the avenue of which within was previously the old public road before its realignment, and seemingly disinterested, its main asymmetrical three-bay front at right angles to it. Single-storey and rendered below a hipped roof, with the round-headed entrance porch to the right-hand side sheltering a nice wooden sheeted door. Looking to be from a century earlier.

34. CASTLE BAMFORD, Kilkenny; pre-1945; *demolished.*
A lodge for the Sullivan family, built after 1839.

35. CASTLE BLUNDEN, Kilkenny (2).
The Blunden family is still in residence here after centuries, but both their gate lodges, on the northern and eastern avenues, are lost without trace. Thanks to A. Atkinson's record of his tour, it is clear that both lodges were in place by 1814; he described one as being a 'light and ornamental gate-house' and noted that both 'had been copied' from that to nearby Tinny Park. Hence they were more than likely to have been to a design by William Robertson for Sir John Blunden, the 2nd baronet (d. 1818), who had inherited the estate from his father in 1783 and whose gatekeepers in 1850 were Matthew Mulrooney and Nicolas O'Hara. Surviving on the eastern approach, however, are two gatescreens of note, separated by a lengthy avenue. The inner entrance is comprised of low concave limestone quadrants, now lacking their iron railings, contained by four V-jointed rusticated cut-stone pillars with neatly moulded cappings, the inner carriage pillars having fluted bases to missing finials. Pretty modern gates. The outer entrance is a less refined version of its counterpart, with rubble quadrants retaining their ironwork with pretty shamrock finials, leading to a pair of V-jointed rusticated stone carriage pillars. Both gatescreens look to be contemporary with their lost lodges of *c.* 1810.

Atkinson 1815; Griffith 1848–60; *BPB* (1929); Bence-Jones 1988.

36. CASTLECOMER, Castlecomer (2).
Of this grand rambling house very little remains. It was from early times the seat of the Wandesforde family, but that male line died out and the property passed on the death in 1784 of the first and last earl of Wandesforde to his only daughter, Lady Anne, who had married the future 17th earl of Ormonde and Ossory. It was not until after her husband's death and the town and old house were burnt in the 1798 rebellion that she commenced major improvements on the demesne, which included rebuilding the mansion house and the provision of a gate lodge.

Early lodge; *c.* 1810; *demolished.*

Fonsie Mealy

A late Victorian photograph shows a typically modest single-storey late Georgian lodge below a hipped roof with symmetrical three-bay façade to the avenue of squared sash windows on each side of a wide front door. Built off an L-plan, a back return extends parallel with the road, secreted behind a tall rubble screen wall, alongside which was a pair of tall ashlar carriage pillars with corniced cappings crowned by pretty globe gas lamps on ornamental iron stands. Another photograph of 1914 shows the lodge awaiting its imminent fate, forlornly facing its successor across the avenue.

Later lodge; 1912; architect George F. Beckett.

A highly conspicuous and commodious Arts and Crafts composition, single-storey over a basement built off a H-plan. From its steeply hipped main roof projects a distinctive gabled half-timbered porch with four carved wooden post supports. To each side is a canted bay with chamfered mullioned leaded lights and parapeted flat roof walls in an early stone-effect concrete blockwork. To the roof are two pairs of octagonal stone chimney-stacks, a feature repeated in the four layered gate pillars linked by the ornamental ironwork of carriage gates and quadrants. Built for Richard Henry Prior Wandesforde (1870–1956), who succeeded to the property in 1892, it now lies a shell, having been gutted by fire.

Parliamentary Gazetteer; *LGI* (1958); *BPB* (1929); Bence-Jones 1988.

37. CASTLECOMER RECTORY, Castlecomer; pre-1849; *demolished.*
A gate lodge identified by the Griffith valuation as being off High Street is no longer to be found. Perhaps built during the long incumbency of Revd Robert O'Callaghan.

Griffith 1848–60.

38. CASTLEFIELD, Bennettsbridge; pre-1839; *demolished.*
The lodge may have dated from the time of John Bourke O'Flaherty's Gothicisation of the house and demesne improvements of *c.* 1790, or later, when the property passed by marriage to Henry J. Willet.

Corballis 1996.

CASTLE HALL (see ROSSENARA)

39. CASTLE MORRES, Kilmaganny (2).
Gone is Francis Bindon's magnificent mid-eighteenth-century mansion for the Morres family, to be survived by the much later excellent lodged entrance built by Major Harvey Randall Saville Pratt de Montmorency (1782–1859), to whom the estates had come by convoluted descent.

Main entrance; *c.* 1840; architect probably Sir Richard Morrison.
A chaste Classical temple lodge, nobly raised on a five-stepped stylobate leading beneath the finely chiselled square ashlar columns of the tetrastyle prostyle portico to the moulded

39. Castle Morres, main entrance (Irish Architectural Archive, de Montmorency Collection).

surround door-case. The deep entablature embraces the stuccoed side elevations, which are each of three bays of six-over-six sash windows with moulded surrounds. There is a horrible later Victorian roof extension to provide attic rooms, which almost spoils the overall effect. Occupied. The equally grand gatescreen is dominated by huge squat Greek stelae carriage pillars with wreath motifs, copied from J.B. Papworth's *Rural residences* (1818) [Fig. 7, p. 7], a design habitually replicated by Sir Richard Morrison throughout the country, here with the latter's characteristic laurel wreaths added. The heavily ornamental iron carriage and postilion gates are carried, as recommended by Papworth, on iron piers, all with a proliferation of palmette and floral motifs. The whole ensemble is completed by secondary stone pillars that contain extensive convex quadrants of nicely contrasting rubble stone. An identical entrance screen is to be found at Somerville, Co. Meath (*q.v.*), which reinforces the attribution.

Rear lodge; *c.* 1840.
Well off the public road is this modest standard rubble-built structure under a hipped roof.

Papworth 1818; *BPB* (1929); *IFR*; IAA photograph (3/25).

40. CASTLETOWN COX, Piltown (2).
One of the most beautiful houses in Ireland, the masterpiece of Davis Duckart, built in 1767–71 for Michael Cox, archbishop of Cashel, which in the *Post chaise companion* of 1803 was described as having 'a very extensive demesne and remarkably fine plantations of 700 acres of fertile land, enclosed with a stone wall eleven feet high'. It would have had two lodged entrances worthy of it, one of which remains.

East gate; *c.* 1770; architect not known.

Situated impressively on an axis with the public road approach to a gatescreen of two grand replacement limestone ashlar carriage pillars, pristine in contrast with their original gadrooned, fluted vase finials with flames issuing forth; smaller secondary postilion pillars to each side, extending in straight railings beyond. Forward of this is the single-storey lodge, reputedly, and conceivably, contemporary with the house, with a hipped roof to lofty eaves with peculiar iron soffit brackets. The main façade to the approach is simply two-bay, each with modern Y-traceried Gothic casement windows in limestone surrounds with keystones, in contrasting stucco-effect whitewashed walls strikingly framed by ashlar pilaster quoins. Recently rehabilitated.

West Gate; *c.* 1780/1911.

Of the original pair of lodges to this avenue the only clue to their appearance is in the pretty gabled standard replacement lodge, which incorporates three Georgian Gothic Y-traceried lights to the windows and door fanlight salvaged from its predecessors. Over the front door is a limestone keystone with the inscriptions '1911' and 'WQ', confirming its builder to have been Colonel W.H. Wyndham-Quin, who bought the estate in 1909 but left in 1926 upon inheriting Adare Manor, Co. Limerick.

Wilson 1803; *LGI* (1904); *BPB* (1929); Bence-Jones 1988.

41. CASTLE VIEW, Kilkenny; *c.* 1845; *demolished.*

The property in 1849 of Sampson Carter Jr (*c.* 1804–60), the city and county surveyor, an unhappy man when he died in tragic circumstances. The gate lodge, for which he could conceivably have been responsible, then lay vacant. Surviving are octagonal stone carriage pillars with cone-like cappings.

Griffith 1848–60; Slater 1856; O'Donoghue 2007.

42. CHAPELIZOD, Dunnamaggan (2).

A fine old house of the Izod family lying ruinous, with one of its gate lodges barely surviving.

North lodge; pre-1834; *demolished.*

Remaining is a good Georgian gatescreen of V-jointed rusticated square pillars with fluted friezes. Wide, low convex quadrants.

South lodge; pre-1839.

A most peculiar building sitting forward of, and at right angles to, the gates, owing its eccentric appearance to twentieth-century alterations. The original structure has had a new front façade added, with a round gable containing a brick-dressed oculus over a window framed by semicircular engaged pillars which merge into a stylised corbelled entablature. Derelict. The 1839 OS map shows the lodge to have had extensive outbuildings in its own right.

43. CLIFDEN, Gowran; pre-1850; *demolished.*

A residence in the early nineteenth century of Patrick Blanchfield, whose gatekeeper in 1850 was Martin Costigan.

Griffith 1848–60.

44. CLONE, Freshford; pre-1839; *demolished.*

In 1837 'The ancient manor-house of Clone, formerly the residence of Sir Toby Caulfeild, ancestor of the earl of Charlemont, and now in the occupation of H. Nixon, Esq. ...'. It had passed to James Arundel Nixon by 1849, when the gate porter was William Stapleton.

Lewis 1837; Griffith 1848–60.

45. CLONMORAN, Kilkenny; pre-1839; *demolished.*

A lodge, which had gone by 1945, to a property in the nineteenth century of the Hyland family, leasing from the Blundens of neighbouring Castle Blunden (*q.v.*).

Griffith 1848–60.

46. CLONMORE, Mooncoin; *c.* 1850.

Set well back from its gates is a single-storey three-bay lodge below a hipped roof. Roughly harled, with lugged window surrounds, crude pilaster quoins and frieze band to the high eaves. Remarkable stone quatrefoil cluster gate pillars with ball finials. Built by the Morris family.

47. CLONMORE RECTORY, Fiddown; pre-1839.

To a delightful 1817 rectory are the remains of an overgrown single-storey cottage at the gates, due for demolition to make way for road-widening.

Lewis 1837.

48. COOKSTOWN, Piltown (2).

South lodge; pre-1903; *demolished.*

North lodge; *c.* 1845.

Standard 1½-storey lodge with hipped gables, roughcast with smooth render strip quoins. Margined windows flanking a modern conservatory porch.

A property called 'Ballyhenebery', in the early nineteenth century of the Burnett family.

49. COOLAGHMORE, Dunnamaggan; *c.* 1830.

A small single-storey standard cottage with tiny cast-iron latticed windows in harled rubble walls below a low-eaved hipped roof with minuscule slates. An early nineteenth-century seat of the Cormack family.

50. COOLMORE, Inistioge; *c.* 1835; architect possibly William Robertson.

A Regency house and lodge built for Peter Connellan (1806–85), the lodge sensitively rehabilitated in 1998. A distinctive single-storey two-bay building of wide windows, tripartite and newly margined, with Classical moulded surrounds, both framed by a stone plinth, heavily recessed panel pilasters and curved soffit cornice to an oversailing low-pitched hipped roof. Spear-topped gates and railings with hooped posts having faintly chinoiserie framework.

LGI (1904).

51. COOLROE, Graiguenamanagh; *c.* 1825; architect possibly William Robertson.

Elevated on a tall plinth, a two-bay single-storey structure, the window of its main front set in segmentally arched recesses, smooth-rendered in contrast to roughcast surrounds. Shallow low-pitched hipped roof. All very similar to the gate lodge to Johnswell (*q.v.*). Derelict. Pretty later iron gates. A seat of Henry Burtchaell in the mid-nineteenth century.

Griffith 1848–60.

52. DANESFORT RECTORY, Bennettsbridge; pre-1839; *demolished.*

On Skeaghaturrish glebe, the lodge was perhaps contemporary with the building of the rectory in 1815, which cost £1,600 during the incumbency of Revd Richard Butler. It subsequently became 'Burnchurch House'.

Lewis 1837.

53. DANGAN COURT, Thomastown; pre-1839.

Well short of a large carriage-arched entrance is a nondescript harled rubble-built tall gabled structure. An early Victorian property of Sydenham Davis.

Pigot 1824.

54. DANGAN, Kilmacow; *c.* 1840.

Looking about 50 years older is this delightful little standard single-storey one-roomed cottage facing the road forward of its gates. Tiny lancet latticed cast-iron Gothic windows set in walls recently sand/cement-rendered below a hipped roof of twentieth-century diagonally fixed asbestos slates. Unoccupied. Strangely not shown on the 1839 OS map. A nineteenth-century property of Martin Hoban.

Griffith 1848–60.

55. DESART COURT, Callan (5).

This noble Palladian mansion became one of Ireland's greatest architectural losses, its once-fine demesne of more than 400 acres now unkempt and the surviving gate lodges doing little to lighten the gloom.

Inner lodge; pre-1839; *demolished.*

South lodge; pre-1839; *demolished.*

North lodge; *c.* 1810.

A sizeable single-storey harled cottage with a hipped roof which bellcasts centrally over a bow to the main three-bay front. Modernised with nasty new casement windows and synthetic slates to the roof. Harled walls; occupied. Built for John Otway Cuffe, 2nd Lord Desart (1788–1820); he was succeeded by his only son, Otway O'Connor Cuffe (1818–65), who was responsible for the two replacement lodges to the east of the demesne.

North-east lodge; pre-1839/*c.* 1840.

Replacing an earlier lodge opposite the gates is this Picturesque cottage, three-bay asymmetrical with cast-iron latticed windows, brick-dressed in pleasant random stone walls under a gabled roof with small slates. Unoccupied.

South-east lodge; pre-1839/*c.* 1840.

Similarly a replacement for its predecessor opposite. A pleasant standard single-storey lodge, its front elevation, of tripartite latticed cast-iron casement windows on each side of the double-leafed sheeted door, recessed behind a verandah formed by four slim iron columns *in antis* carrying a wooden fascia beam. Gabled roof above roughcast walls in pretty pink pastel paint. Occupied.

Lewis 1837; *BPB* (1929); Bence-Jones 1988.

56. DUNGARVAN RECTORY, Dungarvan; pre-1839; *demolished.*

A lodge, which had disappeared by 1902, probably contemporary with the 1813 glebe house, built by Revd Peter Roe with the aid of a £400 gift and a £400 loan from the Board of First Fruits.

Lewis 1837; Leslie 1933.

57. DUNINGA, Paulstown (2).

William Makepeace Thackeray visited the property of the Bookey family in 1842 as recommended, to find it rented out to George Percy, as 'The gentleman who built and owns the house, like many other properties in Ireland found his mansion too expensive for his means and has relinquished it'. He continues: 'There are lodge-gates at both ends of the demesne; but it appears the good-natured practice of the country admits a beggar as well as any other visitor'. Thackeray would have seen the lodge to the north, which survives, but would not have recognised that at the southern gate.

North lodge; *c.* 1835.

A standard three-bay rendered cottage with steeply pitched roof, lying deserted. Granite pillars with recessed panels like those at neighbouring Barraghcore (*q.v.*).

South lodge; pre-1839/*c.* 1845.

Another standard building, single-storey in stone below a hipped roof; either a replacement or a reworking of a predecessor on the site. Derelict.

The Bookey family's circumstances must have improved for they were back in occupation by 1876.

Thackeray 1879; Somerville-Large 1995.

58. DUNKITT, Waterford (2).

Early entrance; *c.* 1800.

Off the beaten track is this once-impressive entrance comprised of a pair of square two-storey gatehouses under pyramidal roofs, one bay to the road, their doorways facing each other distantly across the face of the walled screens, which are now minus their carriage pillars and gates. In harled finish, their one-over-one-roomed accommodation supplemented by single-storey extensions to each of their opposing side elevations. The left-hand pavilion is now extended to the rear and modernised with smart quoins applied, all in stark contrast to its right-hand companion, which lies decaying. Probably built by Tobias Budd.

Later entrance; *c.* 1840.

With its cast-iron latticed lights, lancet-headed openings and dilapidation, this little lodge looks earlier than its age, having been built by Joseph P. Budd probably as compensation for a new road driven through his property in 1839. Rubble-built single-storey standard, with an oversailing hipped roof which is repeated on the projecting front hallway.

Leet 1814; Griffith 1848–60.

59. DUNKITT RECTORY, Kilmacow; pre-1839; *demolished.*

Situated on a glebe of 23¾ acres, its rectory—noted as being out of repair in 1799—was rebuilt in 1817 by way of a gift of £200 and a loan of £600 from the Board of First Fruits for the Hon. Revd George Theobald Bourke. The lodge that may have been contemporary with that rebuilding is a thing of the past, perhaps owing to its basic anti-social accommodation and construction, as was the case with many of those to the rectories of the Established Church.

Lewis 1837; Leslie 1933.

60. DUNMORE, Jenkinstown; pre-1839/*c.* 1845.

The first OS map suggests that this solid lodge is a replacement for an earlier structure on the site. Single-storey standard, built of large blue-grey limestone blocks below a very steeply pitched hipped roof. Derelict. A James Doyle is recorded here in 1849.

Griffith 1848–60.

61. DYSERTMORE, Inistioge; *c.* 1890.

A fine mid-Georgian house of the Lambert family, previously named 'Newgrove', seems not to have had a gate lodge for its first century of existence, an omission which was remedied by Nicholas Henry Lambert. An eccentric 1½-storey standard gabled lodge, with high eaves to accommodate the roofs of the two dinky canted bay sash windows and that of the projecting hall. Roughcast with red-brick dressings in the form of toothed quoins and surrounds to wide ground-floor gable window, over which is a loft light with an arrowhead arch which nicely reflects the bay window roofs. Sympathetically modernised.

LGI (1904).

62. EDEN HALL, Ballyraggett; pre-1839; *demolished.*

A house, originally of the Purcell family, which was in ruins when acquired by Gerald (or Garret) Brenan, who rebuilt it and perhaps erected a replacement gate lodge before his death in 1836.

IFR.

63. EVANS' ASYLUM, Kilkenny; *c.* 1820; architect possibly William Robertson.

The benevolent Joseph Evans of Balleven House (*q.v.*), who died in 1818, bequeathed money for support of a parochial school and a dispensary in the city, as well as for the founding of this almshouse on the site of an old barracks. The development included this minuscule piece of streetscape, a two-bay gate lodge in limewashed harling off an L-plan below a shallow hipped roof. The right-hand window bay, with its elliptically arched recess, advances beyond the door and the neighbouring attached three-storey property. Modernised in the early twentieth century with artificial slate and terracotta ridge tile replacement. A remarkable and welcome survival.

Lewis 1837; Lanigan and Tyler 1987; NIAH.

64. FANNINGSTOWN, Piltown; pre-1839; *demolished.*
To a property of the Walsh family is this vulgar Edwardian gatescreen of ostentatious balustraded ogee quadrants to round cement-rendered gate pillars with urn finials.

65. FARMLEY, Burnchurch; pre-1839; *demolished.*
A gate lodge built either by Robert Flood or by his cousin and predecessor, the Rt Hon. Henry Flood.

LGI (1904).

66. FIDDOWN RECTORY, Fiddown; *c.* 1840.
A rather grand glebe house built in 1817 at a cost of £1,600 by Revd Joseph Sandys. The gate lodge, however, dates from the lengthy incumbency of Revd William Gregory. A single-storey standard gabled building with steeply pitched roof and modest ornamental bargeboards. Small squared sash windows in harled walls. Occupied. The property now called 'Rathmore'.

Lewis 1837; Leslie 1933.

67. FIRGROVE, Inistioge; *c.* 1810.
A tiny single-storey gate lodge with low hipped roof. Two-window bay front to the avenue, its door in an outshot to the rear. Harled walls with basic pilaster features. Built by Joseph Robbins.

68. FLOOD HALL, Thomastown; *c.* 1835.
An extraordinarily durable structure that has lain derelict for decades. Single-storey standard with a back return under a hipped roof with clipped eaves and faintly pedimented projecting hall. Built in

uncoursed random limestone facings with label-moulded large openings. A grand chimney-stack rises off the rear wall. Erected by John Flood, son of another of that name of Farmley (*q.v.*). Recently at last rehabilitated and extended.

LGI (1904).

69. FOULKSCOURT, Johnstown; *c.* 1840.

A typical Regency-style gate lodge, built either by Gorges Hely, who died in 1842, or his younger brother Charles, when the old ruined house was replaced by the present mansion. Situated opposite the gatescreen, as is an identical lodge to Nurney, Co. Kildare (*q.v.*), is this standard single-storey structure under a hipped roof with lofty eaves to accommodate three segmentally arched recesses containing distinctive rectangular casement windows, with ornate hexagonal-pattern cast-iron glazing, and central doorway. Harled with toothed quoins and a crude stone plinth. Contemporary gatesweep with square ashlar pillars.

Parliamentary Gazetteer; *LGI* (1904).

70. FOYLE, Freshford; pre-1839; *demolished.*
The late Georgian house of the Phillips family and their gate lodge opposite its gates have gone.

71. FRAZER'S HALL, Waterford; pre-1839; *demolished.*
A 95-acre property in 1849 of Thomas Lannigan whose lodge and entrance were recently obliterated to make way for a motorway.

Griffith 1848–60.

72. GARRYNAREA, Piltown; pre-1839; *demolished.*
A property of the Briscoe family in the early nineteenth century.

73. GARRYRICKEN, Mullinahone; *c.* 1825.
In County Tipperary on the road's edge is this single-storey standard Regency lodge in an advanced stage of dilapidation, its tall hipped roof over elliptically arched openings in harled rubble walls. Built by one of the Ormonde Butlers to the property that served as a dower house or home to the eldest son.

74. GLASS, Waterford; *c.* 1880.
A plain roughcast single-storey three-bay gabled building with similarly roofed projecting hall. Deep fascias and open pediment features all redone in plastic. A seat until the mid-nineteenth century of John Hackett to which the lodge was added by Paul Anderson.

Griffith 1848–60.

75. GORESGROVE, Urlingford; pre-1839; *demolished.*
An estate in 1814 of John Mitchell, at the entrance to which some decaying pillars remain, the lodge having gone by 1902.

Leet 1814.

76. GOWRAN, Gowran (3).
Henry Welbore Agar, 2nd Viscount Clifden (1761–1836), in 1816 saw fit to replace his 'stately seat' with the surviving elegant Classical house designed by Kilkenny architect William Robertson. This had two gate lodges, which were later replaced by his successors, who clearly felt that they need not reflect the architecture of the house, for both, in addition to a third, are in a sort of Tudor Revival manner.

South lodge; 1856; architect William George Murray.

IAA/Murray Collection

IAA/Murray Collection

According to the architect, the primary function of this lodge was to house the estate forester, and the generous accommodation of its 1½-storey Picturesque Tudor style would bear this out were it not for the large wooden mullioned and transomed oriel window which projects, at first-floor level below a hipped gable, beyond the demesne wall to look out for visitors to the gate nearby, betraying its other role as a gate lodge. Built in random coursed stone with dressed and

76. Gowran, south lodge.

label-moulded bi- and tripartite windows, a single-storey parapet-roofed hallway extends from the internal corner of an L-plan and contains a pretty sheeted door with decorative strap brackets, below a Tudor archway. The roof displays fine stone octagonal chimney-pots to best Tudor manor-house effect, and the ornamental perforated foiled bargeboards lend that cottage feel. Occupied and well maintained. On 19 December 1853, before his Christmas break, Murray had produced the most delightful set of drawings for Henry Agar (1825–66), who had succeeded as 3rd viscount on the death of his grandfather. He was suitably seduced and working details were duly prepared and countersigned by the builder, John J. Nolan of Dublin, on 23 May 1856. What was constructed differs from the original design in the substitution of a peaked for a hipped gable.

Town lodge; *c.* 1870; architect perhaps John McCurdy.

Conspicuously located at the head of the main street, with an impressive and extensive railed screen with octagonal stone pillars, is this whimsical little single-storey building built off an irregular plan with a double pile of steeply pitched gabled roofs, one of which extends over the rectangular bay window projection with recessed porch alongside and subtle half-timbered effect in the apex. Otherwise in uncoursed random stone finish contrasting with toothed quoins, opening dressings and mock arrowloops to the gables. On the back ridge is a fine ashlar chimney-stack. An old photograph shows the missing fancy hip-knobs which once graced all the gables. Although similar in style to the south lodge, they have no details in common, which suggests another architect, and there is the feel of the hand of John McCurdy. This possible change of loyalty may be explained by the early death of W.G. Murray, whose last recorded work was in 1869, by which time his client had passed away three years previously, at an equally early age. Thus the client must have been his widow, for the 4th viscount was a minor, born in 1863. Sadly ramshackle.

North lodge; *c.* 1870; architect perhaps John McCurdy.

Originally in its own right a period piece, which recent owners have almost successfully converted into a characterless modern bungalow, a transformation that will be complete when the stone-dressed gable mock arrowloops have been banished from sight.

BPB (1929); Bence-Jones 1988; IAA (Murray Collection 4/870).

77. GRAIGUE, Kilmanagh; *c.* 1830.

A standard single-storey lodge with a steeply pitched pyramidal roof rising to the chimney-stack off a square plan. Harled rubble walls. Like the house, derelict and overgrown, its avenue gone. An early nineteenth-century property of the Hartford family.

78. GRAIGUE LODGE, Waterford; pre-1839; *demolished.*

Also known as 'Belmont Cottage', it was another property of the Barrons of nearby Belmount (*q.v.*).

79. GRANGE, Ballyraggett; *c.* 1825; architect probably William Robertson.

A charming house, demesne and lodged entrance of the Stannard family. The lodge dates from the time of John Lannigan Stannard, who must have employed as his architect William Robertson of Kilkenny, for

it is in form and proportions akin to those at Woodstock (*q.v.*) and Gracefield Lodge, Co. Laois (*q.v.*), where he is known to have worked. Standard single-storey with a clipped-eaves hipped roof over harled walls with latticed casement windows that are wider than high. All embowered within its own railed enclosure. The gate porter in 1850 was Jeremiah Comboyne. A rather grander but contemporary wide entrance screen of four V-jointed rusticated ashlar pillars framing delightful carriage and postilion gates, ironwork and harled concave-walled quadrants.

Griffith 1848–60; *IFR*.

80. GRANGE, Cuffesgrange; pre-1839; *demolished.*

Surviving is a very fine pair of Georgian V-jointed rusticated carriage pillars in ashlar with corniced cappings carrying pedestalled ball finals. In contrast are crude low convex quadrants. Built by the Shearman family.

81. GREENVILLE, Kilmacow; pre-1839.

A ruined 1½-storey limewashed rubble-built gabled gate lodge with single-storey gabled hall projection. A seat of the Greene family.

82. GREENVILLE MILL HOUSE, Kilmacow (2).

North lodge; pre-1903; *demolished.*

South lodge; *c.* 1880.

A two-window-bay 1½-storey lodge, much modernised, gabled and coated in sand/cement rendering. New serrated earthenware cresting. Occupied.

A property by the River Blackwater of John Mosse Browne in 1884.

Bassett 1884.

83. GREENVILLE PARK, Kilmacow (2).

An early nineteenth-century estate of the Fleming family, which later went under the name of 'Kilcronagh' or 'Kilcroney', has two well-kept gate lodges.

South lodge; *c.* 1800/*c.* 1870.

What may originally have been a typical standard single-storey Georgian Gothic lodge of *c.* 1800 has been considerably extended in

late Victorian times into this large square structure incorporating the early lancet-headed windows and given an embracing verandah carried on carved wooden posts, over which the pyramidal roof projects and rises to a central chimney.

North lodge; *c.* 1860.

A Tudor Picturesque-style cottage, gabled off an irregular plan, the main block 1½-storey, at right angles to which is a single-storey outshot. Openings with label mouldings in rendered walls. Extended to one side to form a double-pile roof, it may previously have had ornamental bargeboards. Good ironwork entrance screen with a palmette motif.

84. GRENAN LODGE, Thomastown; pre-1839; *demolished.*
A house that had a succession of different occupants over the centuries, its gate lodge having gone before 1948.

85. JENKINSTOWN, Jenkinstown (3).
Once one of the finest parks in the country, with a delightful long winged and pavilioned Georgian Gothic mansion, lies broken up with very little of its architecture surviving, the avenues now public roads and lodgeless. The decline seems to have set in when George Bryan (1796–1848) and, later, his son started to replace the old house in a piecemeal way, which suggests that there were problems with finances and, indeed, their architect, C.F. Anderson. Most of the early development dates from about 1820, when Major George Bryan (1770–1843) commissioned William Robertson to design the house and a gate lodge.

Tower lodge; *c.* 1820/*c.* 1845; architects William Robertson and probably C.F. Anderson; *demolished.*
Situated beyond the crossing of the River Dinan to a luxuriant sylvan backdrop, replacing a predecessor on the site, was a Picturesque Castellated Tudor composition, in the manner of Nash and Repton, which provided an appropriate and romantic introduction to the big house up the tree-lined avenue. Comprised of a tall, round,

Irish Architectural Archive

85. Jenkinstown, tower lodge

three-storey tower gatehouse with bipartite latticed casement windows and an even taller square stair-tower attached to the rear, abutting a battlemented carriage gateway with hood-moulded Tudor archway. The ensemble extended as castellated screen walls to terminate in round two-storey turrets. The archway survived the early 1940s demolition to be salvaged for re-erection at St Kieran's College, Kilkenny, its fine limestone ashlar finish having contrasted with the render finish of the gatehouse. The building served briefly as an RIC station. There is a similar entrance at Shankill Castle (*q.v.*). All presumably to designs of C.F. Anderson, who had been employed in ill-fated alterations to the house for George Bryan II (1796–1848).

Gragara School lodge; *c.* 1820.

Mai McElroy

Another building with a dual role, albeit temporarily, was this fine schoolhouse with its distinctive bows, under semi-conical roofs, linked by a verandah with latticed bi- and quadripartite windows in harled walls. When Gragara bridge was built over the Dinan River about 1836, a new entrance to the demesne was opened up and the school served as a gate lodge. Now converted into a private dwelling.

Ballyraggett entrance; *c.* 1820; architect William Robertson; *demolished.*

Irish Architectural Archive

Behind a graceful gatescreen of tall V-jointed rusticated Classical stone carriage pillars with fluted friezes nestled a contrasting and captivating little rustic porter's lodge in a limewashed harled finish. Single-storey with a bellcast hipped roof with big slates, its short elevation to the avenue was recessed behind a wide arch to form a sheltered sitting-out area. Within, by the door, was a rectangular high-level window. Not unique, for there is an identical lodge surviving to the Kilfane estate (*q.v.*), although that to Tinny Park in the county has suffered a similar fate. Robertson clearly had in his library a copy of Joseph Gandy's *Designs for cottages, cottage farms, &c.* [Fig.6, p. 7], for here he replicated the front elevation of the author's plate I, complete with porch and bench seat. The old photograph shows a gate pillar with a bell activated by the visitor outside.

Gandy 1805a; *LGI* (1904); Bence-Jones 1988; Williams 1994; Meagher 1998; IAA photographs (31/16 Z3&4).

86. JERPOINT, Thomastown; pre-1839.
A modest single-storey hipped-roof rubble-built lodge set well back from the gateway, built by the Hunt family.

JOHNSWELL (see NORELANDS)

87. KELLS RECTORY, Kells; *c.* 1830; architect probably William Farrell.

A distinctive lodge built for long-time incumbent Revd Christopher Lovett Darby of the Leap Castle, Co. Offaly (*q.v.*), family. His architect may well have been William Farrell there being a similar lodge at Hilltown, Co. Meath (*q.v.*). Single-storey standard with an exaggerated oversailing shallow-hipped roof, its chimney-stack relegated to rising off the rear wall. Openings in rectangular recessed rendered surrounds starkly contrasting, in renovation, with rubble walls, the windows heavily transomed and mullioned with ornamental glazing bars; six-panelled door. Vacant. Rubble convex quadrant walls framing cut-stone octagonal gate pillars.

LGI (1904); Leslie 1933.

88. KILCORAN, Kells (2).
Previously a seat of the Bakers, in whose time it was lodgeless, which was remedied with the advent of Harvey Mervyn Pratt de Montmorency (d. 1899) after his marriage to Louisa Reade of Rossenara (*q.v.*) in 1853.

Main lodge; *c.* 1870.
Standard 1½-storey gabled, in coursed quarry-faced dark stone with contrasting red-brick toothed dressings and chimney-stack. Projecting single-storey gabled hall. Now to let as holiday accommodation. The entrance screen looks older, of *c.* 1845, with its carriage and postilion gates hoop-topped, a

feature repeated in the stone pillars, which have pretty anthemions crowning their recessed panels.

Secondary entrance; *c.* 1870.
Single-storey standard off a square plan, the pyramidal roof catsliding over the front door breakfront. Rendered, plain and occupied, its avenue gone.

LGI (1904).

89. KILCREENE, Kilkenny; *c.* 1840.
The magnificent William and Mary house of Sir William Evans was inexcusably demolished in the 1950s. Survived by its unprepossessing later gate lodge, located opposite and obliquely to its gatescreen; it was a standard single-storey hipped-roof building, much altered over the years with an additional bay, a basic canopy over the front door and a flat-roofed garage alongside. Rendered and occupied. The straight entrance screen has some semblance of sophistication surviving in its four limestone pillars with ogee-headed recessed panels, which at some later date have been raised in mirror image with walling between, perhaps to replace railings. Moulded cappings and plinth remain. The original pair of carriage openings flanking a postilion gate have been blocked up and roughcast over, to leave the pillars appearing as pilasters. Probably built for Edmond Smithwick, who lived here in the mid-nineteenth century.

LGI (1904); Bence-Jones 1988.

90. KILCREENE LODGE, Kilkenny (2).
In 1865 John William Smithwick, funded by his family's great brewing concern, employed architect Charles Geoghegan to greatly enlarge the house and improve the property, adding the two gate lodges.

West lodge; *c.* 1865; *demolished.*

East lodge; *c.* 1865.
Only one elevation survives as a continuation of the surviving gatescreen alongside.

DB (1 Sept. 1865).

KILCRONAGH or KILCRONEY (see GREENVILLE PARK)

91. KILFANE, Thomastown (2).
'We went to Kilfane, Mr Power's very pretty seat ... very neat Porters lodge all be rosed ...' So found Revd Daniel Augustus Beaufort on a visit in June 1819, and his accompanying sketch shows the lodge to have been trellis-decked, a tradition that remarkably survived until recently.

Main gate; *c.* 1815; architect William Robertson.

A perfectly charming little building that has fared rather better than its twin at Jenkinstown (*q.v.*). A low single-storey structure below an oversailing shallow-hipped roof, its main short whitewashed three-bay front of two high-level latticed bipartite casement windows and door to one side recessed behind an archway, forming a rustic sitting area. Architect William Robertson based this rustic porch on plate I of Joseph Gandy's *Designs for cottages, cottage farms, &c.* [Fig. 6, p. 7] and almost certainly designed the entrance for Gervase Parker Bushe II, from whom it was inherited by his sister Harriett and her husband, John Power of Tullamaine, Co. Tipperary, who in 1836 became 1st Viscount Power of that place. Occupied and snug behind the quadrant wall leading to a tripartite gatescreen of four good ashlar pillars with recessed panels containing spear-topped iron gates. The roses have been replaced by a bed of magnificent red-hot pokers. There were like lodges by Robertson at Jenkinstown and Tinny Park in the county.

Church gate; *c.* 1875.
There had been an avenue leading northwards to the parish church at least since that edifice was built in 1832, but it was not until Sir John Power's grandson, Sir Richard Crampton Power (1843–92), succeeded to the property on his father's death in 1873 that the gate was to be manned. This is a beautifully renovated sedate single-storey standard cottage below a steeply hipped roof with eaves sufficiently lofty to permit a little

gabled brick breakfront hall, flanked by six-over-six sash windows in harled walls.

Gandy 1805a; *Parliamentary Gazetteer*; *LGI* (1904); TCD MS 4037; Bence-Jones 1988; Walsh 2009.

92. KILFANE RECTORY, Thomastown; *c.* 1845; architect possibly James Pain.

A sizeable 1½-storey gabled lodge in the Picturesque English Cottage manner, with label mouldings to openings and replacement decorative bargeboards. Built by Revd Archdeacon Crimes Irwin, perhaps to the design of the diocesan architect, James Pain. The rectory itself dates from 1807, with which the rusticated ashlar gate pillars may be contemporary.

Lewis 1837; Slater 1856.

93. KILKENNY CANAL WALK, Kilkenny; 1849; architect possibly C.F. Anderson.

The Mall, as it was called in 1837, remains a public promenade, originally commenced in an ambitious scheme as towpath to a canal to Inistioge but never completed. The striking gatekeeper's lodge perched on the banks of the River Nore is a whimsical affair, castellated, as is appropriate to the castle backdrop, and built in good-quality punched limestone ashlar. Consisting of a two-storey square 'keep' and single-storey wing attached, with label-moulded doorway and bipartite windows, mock arrowloops and crenellated parapets, that to the tower heavily machicolated. A shield added in 1885 informs the visitor that the lodge's erection in 1849 was funded by Robert Cane, physician, during his second term as mayor of Kilkenny. Its contemporary and complementary decorative iron gatescreen, complete with fancy lanterns, has been removed, seemingly to accommodate more unsightly car-parking. If this is a design by C.F. Anderson, who had succeeded the elderly William Robertson to much work in Kilkenny and its environs, then it could be his last work in Ireland, as he was forced to emigrate to the USA in 1849.

Lewis 1837; Bassett 1884; Lanigan and Tyler 1987; Costello *et al.* 1995.

94. KILKENNY CASTLE, Kilkenny; *c.* 1690; architect probably Sir William Robinson.

Giving entry to the grand quadrangle is this noble Classical gateway, now looking slightly incongruous after William Robertson's controversial 1826 restoration of the castle, which left the old pile of the Ormonde Butlers rather more Victorian than medieval castellated Gothic. Some disagreement amongst experts exists as to the gateway's exact date, but the general consensus is that it was built to a design of Sir William Robinson for either the 1st duke of Ormonde (1610–88) or his son, the 2nd duke, both James Butler, sometime between 1680 and 1700. As such, it would be 'the earliest substantially fully classical piece of architecture in the country'. Not all were convinced that it was fitting, for on a visit in 1709 Dr Thomas Molyneux found that 'The Gate House and new range of buildings belonging to the Castle are mighty ugly, crooked and very expensive; tho' not yet finished the gatehouse having already cost, as we are tould, 15 hundred pounds'! It

displays a magnificent frontispiece in its soaring set of Corinthian pilasters, which frame the three bays of semicircular-headed arches to the carriage gateway, and flanking niches all with archivolts and keystones. Above, set in the Kilkenny limestone, is a band of Caen marble forming the fine Corinthian capitals and swag ornamentation between. Crowning the central bay is an open pediment. Today the great wooden panelled doors with over-panel and fly door see the passing of thousands of tourists who, within, can read a framed 1913 notice which gives an insight into the onerous task of the lodge-keeper.

Luckombe 1780; *BPB* (1929); *IGS Bulletin* (Oct.–Dec. 1963); Craig and Glin 1970; de Breffney 1977; Loeber 1981.

95. KILKENNY COUNTY INFIRMARY, Kilkenny; *c.* 1870.

Somewhat later in date than the main building, opened in 1767, is this standard single-storey lodge with a central gabled hall projection and a chimney-stack to each main gable. Rendered. The big quarry-faced limestone entrance pillars and screen wall with postilion opening alongside suggest a mid-Victorian date.

Lewis 1837.

96. KILKENNY COUNTY GAOL, Kilkenny; *c.* 1830; architect probably C.F. Anderson.

The 48-cell penitentiary was demolished in the 1950s, but an old photograph shows its great brooding battlemented stone gatehouse, of irregular design with a defensive sparsity of windows. A tall square staircase tower rises to the right-hand side of the round-

headed access doorway, over which was a prominent mock machicolation. Although locally based architect William Robertson is credited with its design, Anderson claimed responsibility in a list of his works. It may well be that he added the gatehouse, for there is a feel of the Pains about it, for whom he was an assistant in Cork for a period.

Lewis 1837; Lanigan and Tyler 1987; Costello *et al.* 1995.

97. KILKENNY LUNATIC ASYLUM, Kilkenny; *c.* 1850; architect probably George Papworth.

In contrast to the vast neo-Elizabethan institution is its lodge, tiny but in like style: 1½-storey with rectangularly glazed cast-iron windows in random rubble-faced walls with cut-stone chamfered openings, skew-tables and weighty moulded corbel kneelers. It has suffered in comparison with the little chapel tacked on alongside in matching manner and materials but which is considerably better maintained.

Williams 1994.

98. KILKENNY MILITARY BARRACKS, Kilkenny; *c.* 1800; architect not known.
The barracks originally housed four companies of foot-soldiers of fifteen officers and 558 non-commissioned officers and privates. It is described as having 'a light and elegant appearance, possessing an extensive area and enclosed by a good stone wall', which is entered through an impressive ashlar carriage archway with segmental head, over which is an entablatured top with die. Flanking are tall screen walls, each containing Gibbsian postilion gates, now

blocked up. To the left-hand side is an extensive guardhouse. Single-storey gabled, within it presents an arcaded front of three recesses with round-headed arches off a spring course. All in finely chiselled limestone ashlar, in contrast to its gable to the road, skew-tabled above a similar recess, but blind, its public face crudely roughcast. Built during the period 1800–3 to a design standard to the British Board of Works by the Kilkenny contractor James Switzer. There were identical barracks at Templemore (*q.v.*) and Mullingar (*q.v.*). In use.

Pigot 1824; Lewis 1837; Lanigan and Tyler 1987.

99. KILKENNY RAILWAY STATION, Kilkenny; *c.* 1850; *demolished.*

Clearly not intended originally to be anything more than a shelter at the gate, an 1861 illustration shows a toy-town two-storey one-up/one-down hexagonal sentry-box with a hefty lantern atop its hexahedral roof, but with no chimney-stack. A later photograph shows it to have been in fancy brickwork, with round-headed openings and stone string-course defining the floors. By then it had acquired more accommodation in the shape of a lean-to extension and lofty stack rising independently of the main block and as high, fit for habitation. Now all swept away, along with typical railway wooden picket fencing and gates. Conceivably by Sancton Wood, architect to the Great Southern and Western Railway and the Irish South Eastern Railway.

Lanigan and Tyler 1987; Costello *et al.* 1995.

100. KILLARNEY, Thomastown; pre-1839.
A pair of majestic mid-eighteenth-century 15ft-high ashlar gate pillars, with finely moulded plinths and cornices terminating in grand pedestalled ball finials, grace the entrance to an old house of the Myhills of Cromwellian origin. Alongside, in total contrast and equally remarkable, is a mysterious single-storey rubble-built circular structure with conical stone roof. Of doubtful

function, it may have been a primitive lookout, with its solitary room 13ft 3in. in diameter. It has fared rather better than a more sizeable building in front, indicated on the first OS map, which may have been more traditional, replacement porter's accommodation. Possibly built by one of the Dollard family, who had succeeded to the property.

101. KILLASPY, Waterford; pre-1839; *demolished.*
A seat of the Sherlock family, whose decorative railings of *c.* 1820 remain at the entrance.

102. KILMACOW CONVENT, Kilmacow; *c.* 1870.
A modest 1½-storey gabled structure.

103. KILMANAGH RECTORY, Kilmanagh; *c.* 1850; *demolished.*
The gate lodge to Banse glebe house, as it was more commonly known, was probably built by Revd Hans Caulfeild, a wealthy incumbent who was descended from the earls of Charlemont.

BPB (1929).

104. KILMURRY, Thomastown (2).
A property inherited from his father in 1795 by the great orator and advocate Charles Kendal Bushe (1767–1843), appointed chief justice of Ireland in 1822, who added to and improved Kilmurry in the period 1814–30. At least one of his architects was William Farrell of Dublin, on the strength of the gate lodge at the early main gate.

Main entrance; *c.* 1820; architect William Farrell.

There are almost identical gate lodges at Bellegrove, Co. Laois (*q.v.*), and, more significantly, at Ely Lodge, Co. Fermanagh, where Farrell had a large commission. There he copied 'Eagle Lodge' from the entrance to Blenheim Palace near Woodstock, the home town of his client's young wife. Single-storey standard below a hipped roof, this is a more rustic version, with harled walls substituted for ashlar and dispensing with the pilasters

of the other three examples, but repeating the distinctive circular entrance portico with bowed roof over carried by two granite columns, within which is a half-round recess containing two external doors leading to the two front rooms. The semi-sophistication of this charming lodge is personified by only one of its bipartite latticed casement windows retaining its moulded Classical surround. Particularly pertinent for the accreditation to Farrell is that, in common with the other three lodges, unusually the fire flues are gathered in one stack to be taken centrally off the rear wall. Occupied. The striking contemporary gatescreen, now no longer the main approach, is in the form of a pair of Classical trabeated postilion arches acting as pillars to the main carriage opening. This is of a type that is common around Cork city and to be seen at Rath, Co. Carlow, Drenagh, Co. Londonderry, Knappagh, Co. Armagh, and Cranaghan, Co. Cavan.

South entrance; *c.* 1845; architect possibly William Farrell.

A highly individualistic pair of temple lodges located outside the demesne at a crossroads formed by the southern approach road, which they flank and which is on an axis with the avenue opposite. Each was originally a tall single-storey one-roomed structure below a shallow hipped roof; its main front, facing the entrance screen, has a sidelight front door in a recess, or pronaos, behind two spindly granite columns *in antis* that contrast nicely with the plainer limestone rubble walls. Both have been extended individually with varying degrees of sensitivity, that to the left-hand side faring considerably better, with its respectful balancing wings. This fine entrance probably post-dates Judge Bushe's death and may have been created for his widow Anne, who lived until 1857, and his daughter Katherine, who made Kilmurry her home with her family before selling out to the Butlers.

LGI (1904); Bence-Jones 1988.

105. KILREE, Dunnamaggan; pre-1839; *demolished.*

An estate in the late eighteenth century of the Wrays, followed by the Shaw family, the gate lodge of which had gone by 1948 to be replaced by a modern bungalow.

106. KILRUSH, Freshford; *c.* 1820.

In contrast to the handsome early nineteenth-century villa built by Arthur J. St George is a rather unprepossessing single-storey gate lodge, gabled on an L-plan with a strange orientation, its standard three-bay front facing the demesne and extending in a return to the road with bipartite casement windows in roughcast walls. Two tall square gate pillars of Kilkenny limestone with unusual finials of small pinecones on generous sculpted pedestals.

Bence-Jones 1988.

107. KILTORCAN, Ballyhale; *c.* 1835.

A plain single-storey standard lodge with steeply pitched gables and a later hall projection. A property in the mid-nineteenth century of Richard Hutchinson.

Griffith 1848–60.

KNOCKANE VILLA (see MOUNT MISERY)

108. KNOCKTOPHER ABBEY, Knocktopher; *c.* 1840.

A lodge built as a replacement for a predecessor on the site by Revd Sir Hercules Richard Langrishe, 3rd baronet (1782–1862). Opposite earlier Georgian gate pillars is a once-pretty Picturesque English Cottage-style 1½-storey gabled building built off an L-plan. The effect is rather spoiled by the intrusion of modern windows and a nasty flat-roofed hall extension in the internal angle.

BPB (1929).

109. LACKEN MILLS, Kilkenny; pre-1837; *demolished.*

A gatehouse to the flour and corn mills in the early nineteenth century of Michael Sullivan.

110. LODGE PARK, Freshford (2).

West lodge; pre-1839; *demolished.*

East lodge; *c.* 1830; architect not known.

A very fine single-storey standard lodge, with untoothed Kilkenny limestone dressings and keystones contrasting nicely with whitened harled walls below a shallow hipped roof. Neat and solid square limestone corniced entrance pillars with concave quadrants railed to match the gates. Long the seat of the Warrens, the lodges were probably built for Pooley Abel Warren (1806–34) during his short lifetime, having inherited the place as a minor in 1816.

LGI (1904).

111. LORETO CONVENT, Kilkenny; *c.* 1900.

On Church Lane is this late Victorian or early Edwardian 1½-storey lodge with tall eaves to a steeply hipped roof and pair of gablets over a two-bay main front of square window openings with two-over-two bipartite sashes with round-headed inserts in roughcast walls. To the right-hand side is a single-storey flat-roofed later hall extension. Occupied. Long ago this was the site of Viscount Clifden's town house, to which the Loreto nuns came in 1868 to start a girls' school, since when the place has been steadily expanded into the Good Shepherd Centre.

Lanigan and Tyler 1987; NIAH.

112. LYRATH, Kilkenny; pre-1839; *demolished.*

There was a gate lodge to the old seat of the Wheelers long before the house was transformed in 1862 by architect John McCurdy for Sir Charles Frederick Denny Wheeler-Cuffe. Whether his commission extended to replacing the lodge may never be known. The gatekeeper in 1850 was John Todd.

Griffith 1848–60; *BPB* (1929).

MARYMOUNT (see BORRISMORE)

113. MOUNTAIN VIEW, Waterford; *c.* 1830.

Raised above the road are the ruins of a gabled 1½-storey porter's lodge with harled walls, its roof catsliding over the front hall projection. Octagonal gate pillars with fluted friezes. A property in 1846 of the Pope family.

Slater 1846.

114. MOUNT ELAND, Ballyraggett; pre-1839; *demolished.*

Opposite the gates of a property of the Mossom family its gate lodge has gone without trace.

115. MOUNT JULIET, Thomastown (4).

The magnificent house built in 1760–85 by Somerset Hamilton Butler, 1st earl of Carrick, and its estate are now a hotel leisure complex and golf-course. None of its gate lodges are as antique.

Thomastown gate; *c.* 1830.

The earliest of the estate lodges is this modest single-storey Regency building below a hipped roof, the three-bay avenue façade having its door to the left-hand side and its openings label-moulded in roughcast walls. The gatescreen, in a sparkling granite ashlar, is a puzzle in looking mid-Georgian whilst perhaps actually dating from *c.* 1820, for it is

identical to a limestone version at Sligo cemetery which may have been taken from Hazelwood demesne as a gift from J.A. Wynne of that place. His sister Anne had in 1811 married Somerset Richard Butler, 3rd earl of Carrick (1779–1838), who had inherited Mount Juliet on his father's death in 1813, so it seems that the gates were erected in that period and that their architect may have been the Sligo-based John Lynn. The fine pillars have friezes decorated with delicate floral paterae, and the postilion gates are flanked by piers to the main pillars.

Ballylinch gate; *c.* 1950.

Remote from and forward of the gate sweep is a bulkier version of the Thomastown lodge, with similar main elevation facing the road in smooth rendering. The earlier gatescreen is grand; its ashlar pillars have prominent cornices above fluted friezes and panelled shafts in tapering stela or pylon fashion; the carriage and postilion gates are hung independently on secondary iron posts, all clearly influenced by a J.B. Papworth pattern-book. The lodge was added when the old neighbouring Ballylinch demesne was absorbed into the Mount Juliet property last century.

Middle gate; *c.* 1905; architects probably Batchelor and Hicks.

By the turn of the twentieth century the home and demesne were rented by General Sir Hugh McCalmont, who was later to purchase the property; he commissioned the Dublin architects to draw up plans for alterations to the house and presumably this pair of semi-detached estate workers' houses

opposite the gates. Sturdy, gabled and 1½-storey, their squared casements form with gablets a single bay each to the road. To the main gables are single-storey flat-roofed hallways. The prominent chimney-stacks and walls are in stone-effect concrete blocks which even a century of weathering has failed to disguise. Occupied.

There is a fourth entrance lodge, which is shared with the Norelands demesne (*q.v.*).

IB (26 Aug. 1905); *BPB* (1929); MacDonnell 2002.

116. MOUNT LOFTUS, Goresbridge; *c.* 1830.

On an axis with the Gowran road approach is a magnificent main entrance sweep of four Classical pillars in ashlar, friezed and entablatured, with iron carriage and postilion gates, the whole continued by tall concave quadrant walls beyond. In contrast, the lodge has been rendered featureless by modernisation and extension, but seems to have been a commodious single-storey standard affair on a square plan under hipped roof. There is still evidence of its openings having been framed in rectangular recesses. Probably built for Lt. Col. Sir Nicolas Loftus, 2nd baronet, who succeeded his father to the property in 1818 and died fourteen years later.

IFR.

117. MOUNT MISERY, Waterford; pre-1839; *demolished.*

The first OS map indicates a substantial building set well back from the entrance. Laurence Forestall was here in 1849. The name of the house on the property had, not surprisingly, been changed to 'Knockane Villa' by 1884.

Griffith 1848–60; Bassett 1884.

118. MOUNTROTHE, Paulstown; pre-1839; *demolished.*

A lodge built either by the Rothe family or their successors here, the Bartons. The gatekeeper in 1850 was William D'Arcy.

Griffith 1848–60.

119. MULLINABRO, Waterford (2).

A seat for many centuries of the Jones family.

North lodge; pre-1839.

Opposite the gates is a ruin of the lodge, just sufficient to reveal a standard three-bay symmetrical elevation in rubble stone.

South lodge; pre-1839; *demolished.*

The 1848 valuation tells us that the gate porter was Patrick Healey.

Griffith 1848–60.

NEWGROVE (see DYSERTMORE)

120. NEWPARK, Waterford (2).

East lodge; pre-1839; *demolished.*

There is a modern house on the site of the gate lodge.

West lodge; pre-1839.

The sad remains of a large gate sweep in the form of two forlorn square V-jointed rusticated square pillars. A very basic derelict gabled gate lodge lies behind the left-hand convex quadrant wall.

Originally an estate of the Newports, by 1848 gatekeepers John Denn and Michael Wall were leasing from the then proprietor William Fitzgerald, whose house was burnt down in 1932.

Griffith 1848–60; Lyons 1993.

121. NEWPARK LODGE, Kilkenny; *c.* 1901; architects probably Carroll and Batchelor.

The delightful Picturesque Gothic villa, which has now been engulfed by a modern hotel, remained lodgeless until the turn of the twentieth century. The lodge is in itself charming, as a standard single-storey steeply gabled essay in startling red brick with segmentally headed openings. The road elevation has a gabled rectangular bay window; both it and the main roof over it display ornamental continuous bracket bargeboards. Now associated with Kilkenny College next door. Contrastingly rustic gate pillars.

Williams 1994.

122. NEWTOWN, Kells; *c.* 1835.

A property that has been through a succession of owners, in 1837 the home of Revd Benjamin Morris (1790–1846), who in 1822 married the heiress Elizabeth, daughter of Maurice Nugent O'Connor of Mount Pleasant, Co. Offaly (*q.v.*), whose fortune may have funded the gate lodge. It is single-storey built off a T-plan with harled walls, the room to the road projecting from the main block with a door on each side for symmetry. The very tall eaves to the hipped roofs have modillion brackets to the oversailing soffits. These contain very tall ceilings rather than accommodating any loft rooms. Derelict.

Lewis 1837; *LGI* (1904).

123. NORELANDS, Thomastown; *c.* 1820; architect possibly William Robertson.

A pleasant single-storey Regency lodge below a hipped roof, its main avenue elevation of two bays, door and bipartite casement window framed by elliptically arched recesses in harled walls. Not unlike the lodge at Coolroe (*q.v.*). There are two contemporary gatescreens of square lichen-clad granite pillars with fluted friezes, those

across the road with pretty floral paterae. Gates with spear-topped rails. Built by William Bayley, the property was also known as 'Johnswell', and an avenue from this entrance also served as an approach to neighbouring Mount Juliet (*q.v.*). The gatekeeper in 1850 is listed as being Eliza Nowlan.

Griffith 1848–60.

124. ORCHARDTON, Kilkenny; pre-1839; architect possibly William Robertson; *demolished.*

The lodge has gone but is survived by a Tudor-style entrance archway, its carriage openings having a hood-moulded four-centred head with label-moulded shield motifs in the spandrels. Around the corner is a similarly treated little gate postilion opening. William Robertson is recorded as having worked here and the house may have been built for Sarah, dowager Lady Carrick,

the widow of the 2nd earl, between 1813 and 1841.

Lewis 1837; *BPB* (1929).

125. PAULSTOWN CASTLE, Paulstown; *c.* 1845.

A standard 1½-storey gabled Picturesque cottage in pleasant random stone. Further gables to two dormer windows and a breakfront hall. Plastic windows spoil the effect. Basic carriage pillars with ball finials on outsized pedestals. There seems to have been an earlier lodge outside the gates. This successor would have been built by William Flood (1818–85), who inherited upon his father Henry's death in 1840.

LGI (1904).

126. PIGEON PARK, Burnchurch; *c.* 1750.

What subsequently became home to a succession of farmers was originally the elegant mid-Georgian dower house of the Weyms family of nearby Danesfort, and its gate lodge would be contemporary. A rare survivor for its time, its age revealed by the two diminutive windows which relieve the leading front in limewashed harled rubble walls; single-storey and gabled, the pitch sufficiently steep to have once been thatched. Situated forward and to one side of a basic semicircular gatescreen, its sole doorway opens to the rear.

POWER HALL (see SNOWHILL)

127. PROSPECT, Waterford; pre-1839; *demolished.*

A property in 1837 of John Hackett, whence he appears to have moved to nearby Glass (*q.v.*).

Lewis 1837.

128. PROSPECT PARK, Kilkenny; pre-1839; *demolished.*

A property that had a succession of early nineteenth-century owners, John P. O'Shee of Sheestown Lodge (*q.v.*) being in residence by 1850.

Griffith 1848–60.

129. RATHCLOGH, Bennettsbridge; *c.* 1860.

A single-storey hip-roofed structure, hopelessly abandoned and overgrown, built by the Doyle family, who owned the estate in the mid-nineteenth century.

130. RATHCULLIHEEN, Waterford; pre-1839; *demolished.*

Of the entrance to this demesne of the Wyse family of Waterford all that remain are the pathetic remnants of a fancy cast-iron gate screen, rusting and overgrown. The gatekeeper in 1848 was John Roe.

Griffith 1848–60.

RATHMORE (see FIDDOWN RECTORY)

131. RATHPATRICK, Crosspatrick; *c.* 1850.

Nearly opposite the gates is a nondescript single-storey hip-roofed cottage. Of the entrance screen only a pair of sculpted gable-topped Gothic-style cappings survive on concrete posts. A seat in 1849 of William Ringwood.

Griffith 1848–60.

132. RICHVIEW, Kilkenny; *c.* 1845.

A charming 1½-storey rendered gabled cottage with tall eaves over a two-bay façade, the left-hand one of which is a Romantic rustic sitting-out recess with a wide elliptical archway. Now lying abandoned behind a fine concave entrance quadrant of spear-topped railings on a dwarf wall contained by octagonal limestone ashlar pillars with corniced cappings. The old avenue, which immediately bridges over the Kilkenny–Maryborough and Mount Mellick railway line, is now a public road. This was the newly built property in 1850 of Thomas Bradley, whose gate porter was then John Purcell.

Griffith 1848–60.

133. RINGVILLE, Glenmore; *c.* 1800.

Imposingly located at a bend in the public road is what was once an impressive entrance complex formed by a pair of gate lodges, of which only a few walls of that to the right-hand side survive, along with the two main carriage pillars of blocked ashlar rustication. Built for Nicholas Devereux, upon whose death in 1803 the estate passed to his niece Letitia, the dowager Lady Esmonde.

BPB (1929).

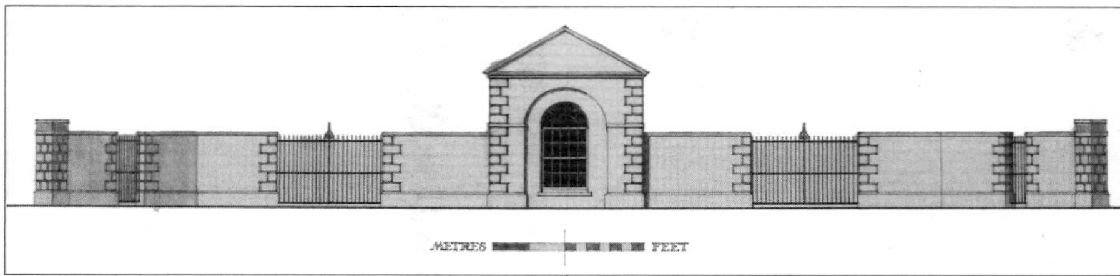

134. RINGWOOD, New Ross; *c.* 1790.
A grandiose and extensive Classical entrance complex (*above*) that cleverly solved the Georgian dilemma of how to relate a single gate lodge to its entrance without placing it opposite and still create symmetry. Here the once-splendid lodge stands as centre-piece, with its tall round-headed window in similar recess, all with granite highlights of spring course, toothed quoins and crowning pediment. It is framed by a carriage gate on each side in straight screen walls that cant forward to contain postilion gate openings, and the whole terminated in V-jointed rusticated ashlar pillars with fluted friezes. The entire composition is in a sorry state but well worth saving from complete ruin. Created by George Agar (1751–1815), perhaps to mark his elevation as Lord Callan in 1790, a title that became extinct upon his death.

BPB (1929).

135. RIVERVIEW, Waterford; *c.* 1835.

Standard single-storey, with high eaves to the shallow-hipped roof which extend over the central hall projection. Rendered with plain strip pilaster quoins and tall plinth. Insensitively modernised with new windows and flat-roofed additions. Good octagonal limestone ashlar gate pillars with moulded recessed panels and replacement wooden picket gates. The house was occupied in the mid-nineteenth century by Revd Alexander Alcock, rector of the nearby Abbey church, who changed the name of the property to 'Tower Hill'.

Slater 1846.

136. ROCHESTOWN, Glenmore; pre-1839; *demolished.*
A seat in the early nineteenth century of the Forestall family.

137. ROCHESTOWN, Mullinavat; pre-1839; *demolished.*
A nineteenth-century property of the Malone family.

138. ROCKLAND, Waterford; pre-1839.
A 1½-storey symmetrical and gabled structure so modernised as to make precise dating difficult. The surviving outer pillars of the gate sweep are square granite with 'bat's wing' features to the cappings of *c.* 1825 and to be found at many properties in County Waterford, by an unknown architect. The house was home to the Snow family in the nineteenth century.

139. ROCKSHIRE, Waterford; pre-1839; *demolished.*
Originally the fine late eighteenth-century seat of the Waterford banking family of Newport, which appears from the first OS map to have had an appropriately imposing and substantial pair of gate lodges by the entrance.

Bence-Jones 1988.

140. ROSE HILL, Kilkenny; *c.* 1830; architect William Robertson.
It is a shame that this gate lodge has not survived, if it reflected the delightful Picturesque villa designed by William Robertson for himself. Even it has been shown little respect in its conversion to a hotel.

Lanigan and Tyler 1987.

141. ROSSENARA, Kilmaganny (3).
A fine pavilioned Palladian-style mansion, said to have been by James Hoban, architect of the White House, Washington, but probably reworked in 1824 when William Morris of Harbourview, Co. Waterford, had inherited the estate from the Reade family, assumed their name and arms and added two fine sets of gate lodges, appropriately pretentious in their own right.

West gate; *c.* 1825; architect possibly William Robertson.

An excellent pair of single-storey two-roomed lodges, with carved eaves brackets to shallow-hipped roofs, they and their screen walls in whitewashed finish contrasting strikingly with ashlar dressings to the postilion openings and the toothed quoins. Each lodge presents a single bay to the visitor, its window, originally a latticed casement, framed in a recess with segmental arch which reflects that of the splendid central ashlar carriage archway, which springs from a moulded spring course

with distinctive voussoirs. The heavy entablatured top is ably restrained, held off the screen walls by beautifully sculpted decorative scrolled buttresses. Nice spear-topped gates in understated ironwork of its time. Over all the openings are unidentified foliar motifs. Occupied and well maintained.

East gate; *c.* 1825; architect possibly William Robertson.
Identical to the above but derelict.

Rear gate; *c.* 1850.
In contrast is this plain single-storey gabled three-bay rendered structure.

LGI (1904); Bence-Jones 1988.

142. RUSSELLSTOWN, The Rower; *c.* 1835.

A modest standard single-storey building with a hipped roof, rendered walls and simple smooth strip quoins. Built for Anthony Charles French. The gates are more recent and remarkable, being late Victorian wooden in robust cross pattern, both postilion leaves and that to the carriage opening hung on big quarry-faced pillars with pedestalled finials, those to the carriage pillars particularly fine with gadrooned cups. These probably date from *c.* 1880 and could be one of Alfred Gresham Jones's last Irish works before he emigrated to Australia in his mid-sixties. His client was John Howlett.

NLI (2006TX).

143. ST CANICE'S COTTAGE, Kilkenny; pre-1839; *demolished.*
A residence in the mid-nineteenth century of John Wade, whose gatekeeper in 1849 was Martin Mullen.

Griffith 1848–60.

ST CANICE'S HOSPITAL (see KILKENNY LUNATIC ASYLUM)

144. ST LUKE'S HOSPITAL, Kilkenny; *c.* 1940; architects Downes and Meehan.

Like the County Hospital, which dates from 1936–42, in complementary and contemporary no-frills International Style. Smart two-storey parapeted on an L-plan in roughcast, with a slit stairwell window emphasising the vertical. The doorway is tucked into the internal corner with projecting concrete case.

O'Dwyer 1997a.

145. ST PATRICK'S INDUSTRIAL SCHOOL, Kilkenny; *c.* 1855; architect probably Frederic Darley; *demolished.*
Of the lodge to this big limestone neo-Jacobean institution nothing remains, but it was probably in a style similar to that which survives at Darley's other Model Farm Institute in Cork City.

146. SCOTSBOROUGH, Callan; pre-1839.
The gate lodge lies a ruin by the road, forward of the gates. The Walsh family succeeded the Millets here in the early nineteenth century.

147. SEVILLE LODGE, Kilkenny; *c.* 1870; architect not known.

A solid mid-Victorian lodge in the Italianate manner built by Eugene Shine. Single-storey with hipped roofs to main block and projecting front room, having a continuous eaves band with corbel features that also appear below window-sills. Horizontal emphasis is repeated in embracing courses to sills and springs of the round-headed openings with intrados. The masonry, large chimney-stack apart, all in smooth painted rendering. Drum carriage pillars in V-jointed rustication and carved conical cappings with dainty ball finials.

148. SHANKILL CASTLE, Paulstown (2).
An early house built by the Aylward family has largely been replaced, but there are the remarkable remains of its original early eighteenth-century gatescreen, straight and railed with Baroque scrolled iron gates and their contemporary rusticated stone carriage pillars on an axis with the distant front doorway. Lodgeless, it and its avenue were a century later abandoned in favour of a Romantic lodged approach to the new home.

Main entrance; *c.* 1830/*c.* 1835; architects William and Daniel Robertson.
A landmark on the Kilkenny to Carlow road is this impressive castellated entrance complex (*above*), its archway and gatehouse clearly by different hands, the former commissioned from architect William Robertson by Nicolas John Patrick Aylward. Differing from the gatehouse in materials, detailing and design, the relatively flimsy crenellated Tudor-style entrance screen has a hood-moulded four-centred carriage arch below a corbelled parapet, the spandrels containing shields with sculpted Aylward

crests. Probably originally a symmetrical composition with flanking octagonal turrets and label-moulded postilion openings in lower wing walls, only one of which survives, that to the right-hand side removed to make way for the lofty gatehouse. Tradition has it that James Kearney Aylward (1811–84), who succeeded on his father's death in 1832, acquired the stonework and design for a gatehouse for Dunleckney Manor, Co. Carlow (*q.v.*), where Walter Newton, having completed his new house to the plans of architect Daniel Robertson, had exhausted his building budget, and the design was realised at Shankill Castle, the existing gateway being partly demolished to accommodate it. In limestone ashlar of considerably higher quality than the archway, which contrasts effectively with the granite features of machicolations and window dressings, particularly the first-floor oriel window with its crenellations, bipartite round-headed window and label mouldings. Basically rectangular on plan, from which a full-height canted front advances to the road, one ground-floor window of which is angled to view the gateways alongside. The entrance screen extends further on each side, with ashlar niches and rubble convex quadrant walls. Good contemporary iron gates. Occupied. There is a similar gatehouse also by Daniel Robertson at Johnstown Castle, Co. Wexford (*q.v.*).

Side entrance; pre-1839/*c.* 1855; architect probably William Deane Butler.

A good asymmetrical Tudor Revival 1½-storey lodge with a two-bay front comprising a pointed-arched doorway alongside a bipartite mullioned window. The entrance screen wall, which extended at right angles, has been removed. Another recent alteration saw the sealing of the wide doorway central to the leading gable elevation, which was flanked by and surmounted by round-headed slit windows. In crude coursed masonry with finer cut-stone dressings and skew-tables with kneelers and octagonal hip-knobs. Sadly, the soaring paired red-brick chimney stack was lowered and blandly rendered over in the 1989 restoration, which at least saved the lodge from dereliction. There was an earlier structure on the site.

Rear entrance; *c.* 1875.

James Kearney Aylward had inherited a single farmyard, to which he somewhat later added a supplementary courtyard complete with its own monitored entrance only a matter of metres from the side lodge. Compared to its neighbour, this is an architecturally modest but relatively commodious 1½-storey standard gabled cottage with twin brick chimney-stacks and clipped verges. Rough rendered walls contain Georgian-style squared sash windows below rudimentary stone hoods on each side of a single-storey gabled entrance breakfront below its clipped eaves.

ffolliott 1970; de Breffney and ffolliott 1975; Bence-Jones 1988; O'Dwyer 1999.

149. SHANKILL CHURCH OF IRELAND CHURCH, Paulstown; *c.* 1830.

A standard single-storey hip-roofed building, the occupant of which may have been the church sexton.

150. SHEESTOWN LODGE, Bennettsbridge (2).

Inner gate; *c.* 1850.

Within the park, remote from the gate, is a 1½-storey gabled lodge in rubble with brick dressings; canted bay to the avenue and clipped eaves now broken by modern gablets. Built by John Power O'Shee, who in 1837 was recorded as being but an occasional resident—presumably spending some time at his other property of Prospect Park (*q.v.*).

Outer gate; pre-1839; *demolished.*

An earlier lodge was situated closer to the entrance.

Lewis 1837; *LGI* (1904).

151. SHIPTON or SHEEPTOWN, Kilmanagh; *c.* 1835.

A standard single-storey hip-roofed lodge. The chimney-stack has been removed and the walls rendered over in modernisation, but the nice punched limestone quoins have escaped 'improvement'. The entrance screen is comprised of roughcast ogee quadrant walls framing V-jointed rusticated gate pillars. All for James Sandiford Lane.

Lewis 1837.

152. SILVERSPRING, Fiddown (2).

Front entrance; pre-1903; *demolished.*

A good straight gatescreen survives.

Rear entrance; *c.* 1840.

A well-proportioned standard single-storey lodge with renewed oversailing hipped roof, its eaves at a height sufficient to permit a little shallow-pitched gabled hall projection, on each side of which is a six-paned square casement window. Rendered walls on a plinth. Located opposite the entrance. A seat of the Osborne family.

153. SION HILL, Waterford (2).

A villa in 1837 of Richard Pope dating from *c.* 1825, splendidly positioned on a height overlooking the city of Waterford. One of the pre-1839 gate lodges survives—just, unlike the house and gardens not having been visited by the hand of the restorer. Single-storey three-bay below a hipped roof with squared Georgian sash windows in white rendered walls, it lies derelict and overgrown. By the main road and of an age lies a reconstructed gatescreen comprised of limestone ashlar pillars, the carriage pillars being chamfered or octagonal, the other ones square, but all having a gadrooned or bat's-wing 'splash' on the cappings, a feature much favoured by the gentry to their estate entrances about County Waterford and suggestive of the work of George Richard Pain. Fleur-de-lis-topped railings.

Lewis 1837; NIAH.

154. SION LODGE, Waterford (2).

An early nineteenth-century seat in 1837 of Charles S. Tandy on the north bank of the River Suir overlooking Waterford. Both of its pre-1839 gate lodges have been demolished. Later renamed 'Bishop's Grove'.

Lewis 1837.

155. SNOWHILL, Waterford; *c.* 1825.

A primitive single-storey gabled lodge, overlooking its relatively sophisticated entrance screen with corniced ashlar gate pillars. A depressing sight: the lodge derelict, pillars askew, and the big house, also known as 'Power Hall', doomed. Both built for Nicholas Power.

An image from the late nineteenth-century Poole Collection mysteriously purports to be Captain O'Neill Power's entrance to the property. The triple gates look to be those that survive, but here shown hung on late Victorian brick gate pillars with Power crests atop, and a single-storey harled steeply hip-roofed lodge indicated at the other side of the access from the present ruin.

LGI (1904); NLI photograph (PIMP 929).

156. SPRINGFIELD, Waterford; *c.* 1830.

The sad shell of a standard single-storey hip-roofed porter's lodge with an uncommon harled rubble elevation, its openings contained in a wide elliptically arched recess. Unique, were it not for an almost identical feature on a lodge to Skerries House, Co. Kildare (*q.v.*). This may not be a coincidence, for Springfield belonged to Samuel and John Waring in the early nineteenth century and they may have known Joseph Dunn Lapham, merchant of Waterford, whose father had owned the Kildare property. The house is a ruin.

Leet 1814; Lewis 1837.

157. SUMMERHILL, Thomastown; *c.* 1845; *demolished.*

A 1947 photograph shows a single-storey gatekeeper's lodge with very high eaves to its hipped roof, probably containing loft space. A main front of two windows in segmentally headed recesses, a feature common in the county, but here with banded surrounds. Built by William Davis. Replaced by a modern bungalow. Good hexagonal gate pillars with snake-like features to gates and railings.

158. SWEET HILL, Freshford; pre-1839; *demolished.*

In 1849 the property of Henry Nixon, its lodge vacant; now, along with the entrance, gone without leaving a trace.

Griffith 1848–60.

159. SWIFTE'S HEATH, Jenkinstown; 1874; architect Joseph Maguire.

The splendid boyhood home of Dean Swift, in 1839 its formal avenue, on an axis with the front door, was lodgeless. About 1845 a new main approach was formed from the south by Godwin Meade Pratt Swift (d. 1864) in the new and fashionable subtle Picturesque manner but announced by a dramatic Classical archway. In ashlar with three round-headed arches, two postilion openings in wing walls flanking that of the carriage gate in the great frontispiece, which is framed by tall Doric pilasters upholding a giant pediment, a composition that suffers from being two-dimensional, like a stage set. It was not accompanied by a porter's lodge until his younger brother, William Richard Swifte (d. 1890), commissioned Joseph Maguire, whom he may have met through having his Dublin house of Whitechurch Lodge, Dundrum (*q.v.*). It is an unostentatious single-storey standard roughcast lodge with hipped roof and gabled entrance breakfront of stone with matching plain quoin strips and limestone toothed dressings to bipartite six-paned casement windows. Mr Meehan of Kilkenny was the contractor.

IB (1 Oct. 1874); *IFR*; Bence-Jones 1988.

TALBOT'S INCH (see AUT EVEN)

160. THREE CASTLES, Jenkinstown; pre-1839; *demolished.*
'... the surrounding scenery ... is also enlivened by the seat of L.S. Ball, Esq.' But no longer, for the fine mid-Georgian villa was demolished in the 1980s, to follow its gate lodge into oblivion.

Lewis 1837.

161. TINNY PARK, Kilkenny; *c.* 1812; architect William Robertson; *demolished.*
If there has been any doubt as to the authorship of the neo-Classical villa with its twin pavilions and linking wings it can be scotched by a charming watercolour painting of its porter's lodge from a notebook of Kilkenny architect William Robertson (*below and cover*). To a formula he based upon a design by Joseph Gandy in his *Designs for cottages, cottage farms, &c.* [Fig. 6, p. 7], which Robertson was also to reproduce at the entrances to Jenkinstown and Kilfane in the county. Single-storey, a short three-bay front addresses the avenue; rustically recessed and framed by advancing ivy-clad piers and a hipped roof, this idyllic roadside scene, once common to the Irish traveller, also reveals the lost ironwork of its gates extending beyond as railings on dwarf convex quadrant walls. One such traveller suitably enchanted was A. Atkinson, who in the summer of 1814 considered that 'The lodge and gate which guard the approach to this demesne (and from which I heard those of Castle Blunden had been copied) are extremely beautiful'. This commission of Robertson's was for Major Michael Den-Keatinge (1775–1829), who had inherited the property in 1811.

Gandy 1805a; Atkinson 1815; Miller 1789; *IFR.*

Royal Society of Antiquaries of Ireland

162. ULLARD RECTORY, Graiguenamanagh; pre-1839; *demolished.*
The gatekeeper's lodge opposite the gates to the fine early eighteenth-century rectory has gone.

163. UPPER COURT or UPPER WOOD, Freshford (2).

East entrance; pre-1839; *demolished.*
A lodge probably built by one of the Mountmorres baronets, the third and last of whom reverted to the original surname of de Montmorency. They had inherited the property by marriage to the co-heiress of the Ryves family. Only a pair of corniced square ashlar gate pillars survive, located well within.

North lodge; pre-1902; *demolished.*
By the 1870s the estate had been purchased by Thomas Eyre, who in 1875 engaged the famous ecclesiastical architect J.J. McCarthy to draw up plans for alterations and additions to the house and gate lodges. Whether one of these materialised at this entrance is not clear, for only part of a rear wall remains.

IAA (Acc. 96/128/1,2); *BPB* (1929); Bence-Jones 1988.

164. VIEWMOUNT, Paulstown; pre-1839; *demolished.*
A porter's lodge probably built by John Flood, descended from that family of nearby Paulstown Castle (*q.v.*). Replaced by a modern bungalow, the avenue now a public road.

LGI (1904).

165. VIOLET HILL, Johnstown; pre-1839; *demolished.*
The lodge, which had gone by 1902, was built for one of a succession of Gorges Helys who lived here in the late eighteenth and early nineteenth centuries, one of whom also resided at nearby Foulkscourt (*q.v.*).

LGI (1904).

166. VIPERKELLS TOWNLAND, Kells; pre-1839/*c.* 1845.
At the base of a long straight avenue is this single-storey standard cottage with a steeply hipped roof that catslides to roof the hall projection, which is flanked by fine six-over-six sash windows in harled walls nicely whitewashed. Extended by an extra bay to the left-hand side in like manner. Occupied. There would appear to have been an earlier lodge on the site. A property in 1849 of Denis and William Dunne.

Griffith 1848–60.

167. WEST COURT, Callan; *c.* 1840; *demolished.*
A house that served as Callan rectory during the incumbency of Revd Charles Butler Stephenson, who may have added the gate lodge, which in 1849 was occupied by Patrick Moran.

Lewis 1837; Griffith 1848–60.

168. WHITE'S WALL, Galmoy; pre-1839; *demolished.*
A property in 1849 occupied by Webb Nowlan. By 1902 its lodge had gone.

Griffith 1848–60.

169. WILLMOUNT, Piltown; *c.* 1835.

A charming 1½-storey standard lodge with two prominent gablets, which may be a subsequent enlargement when the two-over-two sash windows were inserted. Steeply gabled with clipped eaves and verges and a brick stack to each peak. Roughcast with a back return and later single-storey extension to the right-hand side. Occupied. Two good squat ashlar gate pillars with moulded plinths and cornices, topped by simple ball finals. Built for George Briscoe, whose gate porter in 1850 was James Feely.

Griffith 1848–60.

170. WILTON, Urlingford; pre-1839; *demolished.*
A late eighteenth-century house, the gate lodge to which was built by John Butler or, after his death in 1831, his son, William Francis Butler.

IFR.

171. WOODSGIFT, Urlingford (2).
A very large Georgian house and estate that

were presented to the St George family by a Lieutenant Wood.

South gate; *c.* 1750/*c.* 1845.

Here is the vestige of a very early pair of lodges to the old main entrance. The ivy-covered ruin of a harled rubble wall with a bowed front to the road continues to the gate opening as a screen wall containing a round-headed niche. This seems to have been repeated to the left-hand side to form the pair which must have fallen into early dereliction, for their successor lies across the road in the form of a dilapidated single-storey standard cottage of harled rubble and a hipped roof with lofty eaves and high ceilings. Nasty modern replacement window, which matters little as it approaches the state of its predecessors.

North gate; *c.* 1830.

Two-storey single-bay hip-roofed gatehouse with quoins, opposite a good gatescreen with four square ashlar pillars and spear-topped Georgian wrought-iron straight railings.

The big house was acquired about 1850 by Michael Den-Keatinge from Tinny Park (*q.v.*), which failed to arrest the deterioration of this once-proud estate, the big house being burnt and demolished by 1914.

LGI (1904); Bence-Jones 1988.

172. WOODSTOCK, Inistioge (4).

A magnificent demesne, much of the credit for which is due to Sir William Fownes (d. 1778), who commenced its creation in 1737, engaging the artist/architect Francis Bindon to design a Palladian mansion, provide an early instance of enclosure of a landed estate with boundary walls and construct a lodged entrance by the village.

Point Road gate; *c.* 1740/*c.* 1830.

Mr and Mrs S. C. Hall

That the original lodge was superseded almost a century later is evident from an illustration in Mr and Mrs S.C. Hall's *Ireland—its scenery and character* (1843) captioned 'Lodge School' and which depicts a delightful 1½-storey English Picturesque cottage with carved ornamental bargeboards and an oriel window above the hood-moulded front door. This dual-function building was beautifully situated by the River Nore and, as a Female National School, its schoolmistress in 1850 was Miss Honoria D'Arcy. Today this would be unrecognisable had not some salvaged stone quoins, label mouldings to windows and exposed rafter toes survived subsequent additions and 'improvements'. Alongside is a pair of contemporary Classical stone gate pillars with moulded panels, and gates.

The estate passed on Sir William's death to his son-in-law, William Tighe (1738–82) of Rossana, Co. Wicklow, but it was his son of the same name (1776–1816) who continued improvements on the property, commissioning Kilkenny architect William Robertson and his partner Thomas Costello to add wings to the house, build a new stable block and furnish designs for a grander and more appropriate lodged entrance.

172. Woodstock, 'Grand Gates.'

'Grand Gates'; 1800; architects Robertson and Costello.

A squat single-storey standard lodge below a hipped roof, built in granite ashlar with prominent monolithic window surrounds, keystones and more subtle toothed quoins. Flanking the now-blocked-up doorway are unusually wide six-over-twelve sash windows, the fenestration and proportions

very much akin to the gate lodges at Gracefield Lodge, Co. Laois (*q.v.*), where Robertson was also employed, and at The

Grange (*q.v.*). The excellent gatescreen continues the horizontal emphasis with pronounced block rustication to screen walls, which contain the postilion openings, and the carriage pillars with their moulded corniced cappings as bases for sculpted Tighe wolves, whose ears have suffered the ravages of time. The outer piers support fine rusticated ball finials; good contemporary sturdy iron gates.

New Ross gate; *c.* 1800.

On the southern approach is this relatively undistinguished 1½-storey standard roughcast cottage with modern windows, flat-roofed single-storey hall projection and chimney-stack to one of its clipped verge gables. Good granite gate pillars.

Today the park and gardens, along with the remarkable Turner conservatory, neglected for much of the twentieth century, have seen a rebirth, apparently too late to save Bindon's house, which lies an overgrown shell.

Hall 1841–3; Griffith 1848–60; *IFR*; Bence-Jones 1988; Whyte 2007; Lawrence photograph (7789C).

173. WOODVIEW, Castlecomer; pre-1839; *demolished.*

To a nice late Georgian villa is a contemporary whitewashed roughcast rustic gatescreen, but reflecting the taste of the period with a symmetrical pair of flat-arched postilion gateways flanking the gate pillars of the main carriage opening. A property of the Brennan family in the early nineteenth century.

COUNTY LAOIS

1. ABBEYLEIX, Abbeyleix (4).
A magnificent demesne graced by a mansion built to the design of the eminent English architect James Wyatt in 1773 for Thomas Vesey when 2nd Baron Knapton. Raised to the title of Viscount de Vesci three years later, either he or his son built what was then the sole gate lodge at the southern approach before 1839. But it was the socially conscious 2nd, 3rd and 4th viscounts who from 1845 until the end of the century employed a succession of architects to add numerous generously proportioned cottages for their estate workers. Principally it was another member of the great architectural dynasty to whom the family turned in Thomas Henry Wyatt (1807-80) to update the house and furnish the park.

Bluegate lodge; *c.* 1860; architect probably T.H. Wyatt.

A pleasant and commodious 1½-storey English Tudor Picturesque cottage which once doubled as an infant school, accounting for its size. Gabled with ornamentally carved fretted wavy bargeboards and harled walls, the variety of label mouldings and windows suggesting that it may have been extended at one time. Intricately glazed bi- and tripartite cast-iron lights with margined latticed panes to casements. Irregular main elevation with a gabled breakfront alongside, which projects a single-storey hallway with a charming latticed Gothic fanlit doorway. Two chimney-stacks, one with four flues. Occupied.

Home Farm lodge; *c.* 1880.
Built onto the rear of an earlier harled house of *c.* 1800 is this extensive 1½-storey gabled structure, perfectly symmetrical in attractive

coursed rubble with cream calcium silicate brick dressings. The central projection has a big round-headed square-paned window under a tiny similarly arched attic light. To each side are wide flat-arched bipartite small-paned casements. Decorative fretted wave and foil bargeboards. Presumably this served as rather more than gate porter's accommodation, perhaps also of the farm manager.

Grallow lodge; *c.* 1855; architect possibly T.H. Wyatt.

Were it not for its decorative Tudor-style serrated bargeboards with lovely carved pendants to apexes and eaves, this would be an Italianate design, with its low-pitched gables and carved verge and soffit brackets. It is 1½-storey with a pair of gablets to the side elevation over innovative bipartite horizontally sliding sashes with latticed lights, and to the loft of the main front is a tripartite version, below which is a recessed porch behind three chunky chamfered granite pillars. A later lean-to extension to one side contains the relocated front door. A very pretty cottage, not helped by a recent bland cloak of grey rendering. There is an identical lodge at Grantstown (*q.v.*).

Killamuck Wood lodge; pre-1839/*c.* 1880; architect not known.
Yet another extensive gatekeeper's lodge which perhaps incorporates an earlier building on the site. Hideously 'improved' in the twentieth century, its great bulky corbelled brick stack, though rendered over,

still betrays a late nineteenth-century origin. It is 1½-storey gabled, its main single-bay front dominated by an embracing attic pediment with a tripartite window in the tympanum, which is now wooden-sheeted. This jetties out to be carried on long conspicuous moulded soffit brackets, which extend about the building, and a central rectangular bay window in chamfered stone but shorn of its intermediate mullions to accommodate a modern metal light. The verandah to one side is now enclosed with nasty later windows and door. Modern rendering to walls and concrete roof tiles spoil the original effect.

All four lodges and the many estate cottages reveal the consideration of the de Vescis in the provision of such rare commodious accommodation, confirming their reputation for being improving landlords.

BPB (1929); ffolliott 1971b; Guinness and Ryan 1971.

2. AGHABOE RECTORY, Aghaboe (2).
A prosperous living was 'Keelough Glebe', as it was known, having been built in 1820 for £1,450 thanks to a gift and loan from the Board of First Fruits. Both the early lodge, which may have been contemporary with the rectory building but had gone by 1909, and a later lodge further west to 'Glebe Farm' have been demolished.

Lewis 1837.

3. AHARNEY, Durrow; pre-1839; *demolished.*
The house of the Marum family lies a ruin, its gate lodge gone.

4. ANNEGROVE ABBEY, Shanahoe; pre-1839; *demolished.*
The lodge, probably built by James Edmund Scott, was located opposite the gates.

5. ASHFIELD HALL; *c.* 1835; architect not known.
The most exceptional of Tudor Gothic English Cottage lodges in the P.F. Robinson manner but shamefully neglected, except by the vandals. It lies derelict and desirable, 1½-storey on an irregular plan, gabled, now with plain bargeboards. The harled walls have

5. Ashfield Hall.

well-chiselled chamfered stone dressings to a variety of openings with mixed glazing patterns. To the front projection is an attic oriel carried on chunky corbel blocks, and to the park elevation a single-storey flat-roofed rectangular bay window with narrow round-headed sashes. Elsewhere are fancy latticed hexagonal cast-iron window panes, and to the panelled front door a Tudor archway. Relieving the rear façade is a pretty gablet, and crowning it all, on the ridge, is a three-flue chimney-stack of tall octagonal, round and diagonally set pots. Inspirationally built by Peter Gale, a sleeping fairy-tale cottage awaiting its Prince Charming.

6. ASHFIELD, Ballybrittas; pre-1839/*c.* 1850.
A place named after the Ash family, of whom either Sir Thomas Ash or his successor here, the Very Revd Thomas Trench (1761–1834) of nearby Glenmalyre (*q.v.*), dean of Kildare, probably built the earlier lodge on the site.

Certainly the latter rebuilt the house in about 1810. The present striking landmark on the Dublin–Limerick road seems to date from the time here of his sons, Revd Frederick Steuart Trench and Henry Trench, and perhaps took the Gothic features from its predecessor. Forming most of the left-hand entrance quadrant, it is 1½-storey and gabled, and its unique concave front contains three tall Y-traceried latticed lancet sash windows below high eaves in white rendered walls, stark in their backdrop of mature trees. To the ridge is red earthenware cresting perhaps dating from *c.* 1870, when John Leland Maquay was resident. Alongside is a pair of carriage pillars with pedestalled ball-finialled cappings.

Mason 1814–19; Griffith 1848–60; Slater 1870; *LGI* (1904).

7. ATTANAGH RECTORY, Attanagh; *c.* 1825.
What began as a single-storey standard lodge, dating probably from that period when the church was rebuilt and the glebe house greatly enlarged in the 1820s during the incumbency (1813–32) of the wealthy rector Revd the Hon. Arthur Vesey (1773–1832), second son of the 1st Viscount de Vesci of nearby Abbeyleix. Subsequently raised and gabled to provide attic space.

Leslie 1933.

8. BADGER HILL, Mountrath; pre-1909; *demolished.*
A property in 1850 of William Flood.

Griffith 1848–60.

BALLINTAGHER (see SALLY PARK)

9. BALLYFIN, Mountrath (6).
'This magnificent demesne contains above 1200 acres, all walled in; there are two capital approaches from the Mountmelick and Maryborough roads, and a back approach from Mountrath. That from Maryborough is, perhaps, laid out with as much elegant taste and happy design as can be seen; 'tis certainly in the grandest style possible. The approach from Mountmelick is also very fine, but not so modern; the former being but lately finished, after Mr Pole's own design.' It is not clear from these observations by Sir Charles Coote in his 1802 survey of the county whether William Wellesley-Pole (1763–1845), proprietor of Ballyfin, brother of the great duke of Wellington, also designed his own gate lodge or whether it was the work of his predecessor and distant cousin, William Pole, whom he had succeeded to the place on the latter's death in 1781.

Mountmellick entrance; *c.* 1780; architect possibly W. Wellesley-Pole.

This is a single-storey standard hip-roofed lodge, unusually capacious. The sum of its sophisticated parts—Doric tetrastyle pedimented portico with corresponding pilaster and flanking Wyatt windows—do not add up to a particularly elegant whole, suggestive of the hand of an amateur, or even that of his landscape gardener and architect, John Webb. Do the windows show the designer to have been influenced by James Wyatt directly, for the eminent architect is recorded as having had some involvement in the early house? The overall impression is not helped by a cloak of dreary sand/cement rendering and the fact that it lies derelict, boarded up and deprived of its gatescreen. This was removed to adorn the Mountrath entrance probably in the mid-nineteenth century. A triple gateway of very fine ashlar Classical pillars with projecting corniced cappings and fluted friezes, containing spear-topped wrought ironwork with husk motifs to main carriage gates and those of the postilions, set in like straight railings. It cannot be a coincidence that this screen is to be found in identical form and detail at Lawnsdown (*q.v.*), William Pole having in 1748 married Lady Sarah Moore of that place.

William Wellesley-Pole, as chief secretary of Ireland and chancellor of the Irish exchequer, previously of Dangan Castle, Co. Meath (*q.v.*), had by 1812 become disaffected with Ireland, or it with him, resigned his positions and sold Ballyfin to Sir

Charles Henry Coote, 9th baronet (1794–1864). The new owner seems initially to have made do with his purchase, for there is no record until 1820 of alterations to the house commencing to plans of the Galway architect Dominick Madden. Despite considerable progress being made, as at Mount Bellew, Co. Galway, Madden's services were dispensed with in favour of the Morrisons, Sir Richard and his son William Vitruvius, who by 1826 had helped the baronet expend over £20,000 in altering the grounds and creating 'The grandest and most lavishly appointed early 19C Classical house in Ireland' and complementing it with a suitable lodge and entrance gates.

Maryborough entrance; *c.* 1825; architect Sir Richard Morrison.

Morrison senior was so enamoured of plate I in Sir John Soane's *Sketches in architecture* (1793) [Fig. 6, p. 7] that he adapted the design for use as porters' lodges at Castlecoole, Co. Fermanagh, Baronscourt, Co. Tyrone (unexecuted), and Killruddery, Co. Wicklow (*q.v.*), but at Fota, Co. Cork, and here at Ballyfin it metamorphosed into a temple variant, the common element being a tripartite sash window to the main short avenue front recessed behind a pair of fluted Doric columns *in antis*. Single-storey but of deceptively noble scale, the high ceilings below shallow-pitched hipped roof, its oversailing soffits displaying coffers and prominent brackets over a frieze of laurel wreaths—a Morrison trademark. Built in beautifully chiselled limestone, of a cruciform plan created by balancing and opposing projecting hallway and closet to three-bay side elevations with flanking blind 'windows'. As elsewhere with this format, the architect accompanied his lodge with a gatescreen faithfully replicating that in J.B. Papworth's *Rural residences* (1818) [Fig. 7, p.7] in the shape of huge stone stela or pylon main carriage pillars, again with laurel wreath motif (repeated on the house) but here with the family Cootes perched above. The triple gates are hung on secondary iron pillars, as Papworth recommended. Beyond are extensive concave-walled quadrants.

Mountrath entrance; *c.* 1850; architect Sir Richard Morrison.

Irish Architectural Archive

A replica of the Maryborough lodge, presumably post-dating Morrison's death in 1849 but accompanied by the gatescreen removed from the Mountmellick gate, all probably erected under the supervision of Messrs Henry, Mullins and McMahon.

North-west entrance; pre-1839; *demolished.*

Indicated on the first OS map as a police barracks.

West entrance; pre-1839.

Ruinous, with only a single-bay harled wall standing from what was a 1½-storey lodge on an L-plan, a solitary gate pillar marking a disused approach.

Deer-park entrance; *c.* 1850.

Located two miles south-west of the demesne is a ruined lodge and entrance screen of modest rustic appearance but with pretty ironwork which gave access also to the farmyard and sawmills.

The property was given up for sale by the Cootes in the 1920s to become a Patrician college before its recent salvation as a high-class hotel.

Soane 1793; Coote 1802; Papworth 1818; Brewer 1825; *BPB* (1929); Bence-Jones 1988; *Country Life* (13 and 20 Sept. 1973); McParland *et al.* 1989; *IADS* (Vol. III); IAA photograph (4/40 CS 20b).

BALLYGRAN (see GRANTSTOWN)

10. BALLYKILCAVAN, Stradbally; pre-1839; *demolished.*

A fine house of the Walshes, baronets, its long straight avenue on an axis with the front door and apparently extended by the public road, to be stopped by the parish church in the distance but no longer interrupted by the gate lodge, which had gone by 1909.

Bence-Jones 1988.

11. BALLYMANUS, Stradbally; *c.* 1910.

An unusual early twentieth-century single-storey structure, of the then newfangled corrugated-iron construction, having ornamental half-timber effect to the apex of its leading single-bay avenue front. Built by John Harvey Dunne.

12. BALLYMEELISH, Borris-in-Ossory (2).

A property in 1814 of Joseph Thacker, neither of the gate lodges to which is intact.

South gate; pre-1839; *demolished.*

The lodge, situated opposite the entrance, had gone by 1909.

North gate; *c.* 1820.

A once-delightful rubble-built single-storey gatekeeper's accommodation, now an overgrown roofless and incomplete shell; four-roomed symmetrical below a hipped roof, its central three-bay bowed living room having round-headed openings. Set well back from a complete gatescreen of outer octagonal pillars linked by convex spear-topped railings to inner postilion and carriage pillars with reeded panels to shafts.

Leet 1814.

BALLYSHANDUFF (see THE DERRIES)

13. BECKFIELD, Rathdowney; *c.* 1860.

Following the residency of the Roe family, Robert Palmer came to live here in the mid-nineteenth century and built this three-roomed lodge of minuscule proportions. Single-storey standard, its three-bay stone front below a hipped roof. Now derelict, overgrown and dominated by a gatescreen of four brutally quarry-faced stone pillars with four-sided pediment caps, on ogee quadrants. The latter probably built *c.* 1880 by Walter D. Cox.

Slater 1856; 1870; Griffith 1848–60.

14. BELLEGROVE, Ballybrittas (3).

A seat occupied in the late eighteenth/early nineteenth century by the Fitzgerald family but leased by the much-propertied dean of Kildare, the Very Revd Thomas Trench, also of Glenmalyre (*q.v.*) and Ashfield (*q.v.*). George Adair then inherited the place by marrying, in 1822, the dean's second daughter and set about rebuilding the house and adding some porters' lodges.

South lodge; *c.* 1840; architect probably William Farrell.
A familiar sophisticated Classical design (*above*), to be found also at Kilmurry, Co. Kilkenny (*q.v.*), and significantly as 'Eagle Lodge' at Blenheim Palace, Oxfordshire, where it originated as a design by Thomas Hakewill, to be copied at Ely Lodge, Co. Fermanagh, by the Dublin architect William Farrell, who must surely have been commissioned by Adair here. Single-storey standard under a hipped roof with high eaves projecting as a semicircular portico carried on a pair of granite Doric columns, with equivalent pilasters repeated on the external corners. The portico is mirrored as a recess containing the front door, all now enclosed by the most unfortunate of modern glazed screens. The panels formed by the pilasters, plinth and frieze are now rendered in the roughest of roughcast, probably replacing stuccowork, the moulded architraved openings with casements replacing the original Georgian-style sashes. The plan reflects exactly those of the other examples, of three rooms and triple stack rising off the party wall common to the back return.

Middle lodge; *c.* 1850.
A standard lodge in random stone with brick dressings, surround to round-headed doorway and corbelled eaves band below a shallow-hipped roof.

North lodge; pre-1839/*c.* 1890; architect probably Sir Thomas Manly Deane.

An extraordinary incongruity in the Irish countryside is this half-timbered, or rather quarter-timbered, impression of an Elizabethan English cottage, its flimsy woodwork arranged in a variety of cross and chevron patterns. Both the main 1½-storey block and its single-storey wing at right angles have their own verandahs supported by carved posts and perforated wavy bargeboards over big latticed leaded lights in tripartite windows. Like the big house, it now lies totally derelict. Presumably designed by Thomas Manly Dean, who was employed in 1887 to add a conservatory to the big house, then called 'Rathdaire', for John George Adair, notorious for the tenant evictions on his other estate of Glenveagh Castle, Co. Donegal.

Taylor and Skinner 1778; 1969 [1783]; Wilson 1803; Mason 1814–19; *LG* (1863 and 1882); Glin *et al.* 1988; Dean 1994; Williams 1994.

15. BELLMOUNT, Rathdowney; *c.* 1800.
A delightful and unusual standard 1½-storey Georgian Gothic cottage, with a bellcast hipped roof of tiny slates and tall eaves to accommodate loft space lit by small end windows. In harling, its three-bay front has little lancet windows with Y-tracery on each side of a front door with narrow sidelights, recently admirably saved from complete

dereliction. Very basic rubble quadrant walls and carriage pillars with lions couchant to cappings. Up the short avenue is the charming villa residence in 1801 of Chambré Brabazon Ponsonby (1762–1834).

Coote 1802; *IFR*.

16. BLACKFORD, Stradbally; *c.* 1845.

A nice standard 1½-storey early Victorian gabled cottage with two-over-two sashes in harled walls, tall eaves and steeply pitched roof. Occupied. Wide concave-walled quadrants with missing carriage pillars, the surviving outer ones with dentilled cappings and dainty pineapple finials. A seat in the mid-nineteenth century of Andrew Graves.

Lewis 1837; Griffith 1848–60.

17. BLANDSFORT, Ballyroan; pre-1839.
A demesne of the Blands, at the entrance to which remains a plain single-storey harled hipped-roof cottage with a three-window-bay elevation to the road—the derelict survivor of a pair of lodges.

18. BORRIS CASTLE, Borris-in-Ossory; pre-1839; *demolished.*
Originally a pair of lodges flanked the approach to a residence in 1814 of Charles White, one of many different occupants over the years.

Leet 1814.

19. BRITTAS, Clonaslee (3).
Of the three early pre-1839 lodges to 'a neat lodge, with a large demesne', in 1819 of General Edward Dunne, none remain. The main architectural developments on the property date from the time here of Major-General the Rt Hon. Francis Plunkett Dunne and the daughters of his nephew, three of the property's heirs having died between 1874 and 1878. Initially the Major-General commissioned architect John McCurdy to build the castellated mansion in 1868, but at least one of the surviving lodges dates from the time of the additions to the house carried out by Millar and Symes in 1876.

Village gate; pre-1839/*c.* 1876; architects Millar and Symes.

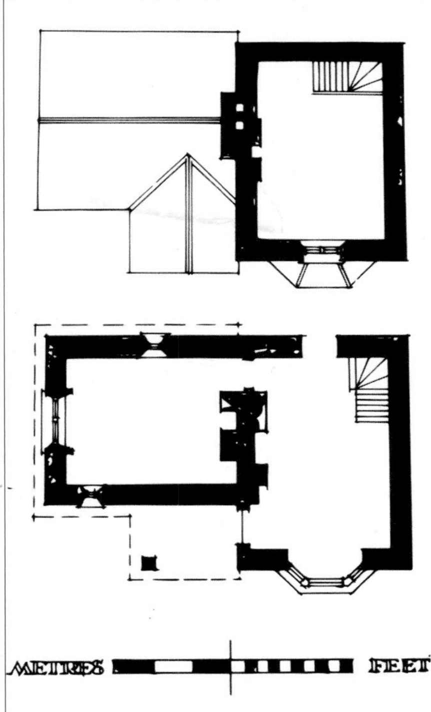

A flamboyant late Victorian Picturesque lodge built off an irregular plan, with a tall battered chimney-stack at the junction between the single-storey wing and the 1½-storey main block, which contains a single-storey canted bay window below a bipartite light with hooded lancet heads under foiled bargeboards and an apex feature in the heavy wood-carving popular at that period. From the internal angle projects a much-altered hallway and, alongside, the avenue wing with scalloped bargeboard and a variety of arched openings in roughcast walls. To the road and avenue is a dwarf wall with good contemporary decorative ironwork and stone pillars with four-pedimented cappings and floral curved iron finials. This is all a replacement for the previous porter's lodge, shown on the 1839 OS map at the head of an eastern approach from the village.

Country gate; pre-1839/*c.* 1870.

An altogether less ambitious lodge, much sanitised in twentieth-century improvements although retaining its intricate ornate fretted bargeboards, hip-knobs, chamfered opening reveals and toothed quoins. Single-storey gabled with modern rendering, inappropriate windows and synthetic slates, it replaced one of the earlier lodges to the estate on the western approach. The original tall rubble concave quadrants survive with the stumps of cut-stone pillars.

Rear gate; pre-1839; *demolished.*

Mason 1814–19; *IB* (1 June 1868 and 15 April 1879); *LGI* (1904); Williams 1994.

20. BROCKLEY PARK, Stradbally (4).

A once-proud demesne of the Jocelyns, of whom Robert in 1771 was created 1st earl of Roden and built himself the mansion in 1768 on the site of an earlier house, to the designs of the Italian architect Davis Duckart. The family's interest here was brief, for after his death in 1797 the place was leased to Revd Thomas Kemmis of Shaen Castle (*q.v.*), who may have been responsible for the earliest of the lodges.

East lodge; *c.* 1810.

A charming single-storey structure, seemingly once octagonal on plan, with an umbrello roof rising to a central stack. It assumed rather more generous proportions *c.* 1860 with the addition of a back return and a gabled hall breakfront with chamfered stone corners and elliptically fanlit doorway below fancy scrolled bargeboards and a little turned hip-knob. Otherwise rendered with modern windows and later banded chimney-stack. Occupied.

The estate was acquired after Revd Kemmis's death in 1827 by William Dent Farrer, who added another lodge nearer the town.

Church Lane lodge; *c.* 1835.

Built as a regulation Regency lodge, standard single-storey under a shallow-hipped roof with paired soffit brackets over harled walls and cast-iron latticed casements. All now sanitised for modern living, with plastic windows, fascias and bargeboards, a new gabled porch and synthetic slates.

Garran Crossroads lodge; *c.* 1810/*c.* 1870.

Single-storey standard Regency-style building under a hipped roof with central gabled hall projection. Constructed in random coursed limestone rubble with toothed brick quoins and dressings.

Modernised with lead-effect bipartite casements, curved bargeboards and a back return. There is a fine earlier gatescreen, probably contemporary with a previous octagonal lodge, comprised of coursed rubble concave-walled quadrants contrasting with good ashlar carriage pillars having moulded plinths, scroll-topped gate stops and pronounced moulded cappings.

Athy Road lodge; pre-1839/pre-1900; *demolished.*

This twentieth-century bungalow appears to be the third building on the site, the intermediate one being apparently a replacement by William Young.

Sadly, the estate is now all broken up for modern development and the big house has been demolished since 1944, which makes the lodges' survival all the more remarkable.

Wilson 1803; Slater 1870; *LGI* (1904); *BPB* (1929); Bence-Jones 1988.

21. CAPARD, Mount Mellick (3).

'... the seat of John Pigott, Esq. The house is one of the most extensive in the kingdom, the front exceeding upwards of two hundred feet, and one of the most beautiful, being built of the quarries on this estate, and mostly hewn, which gives the whole a magnificent appearance; it is situated on a lofty eminence, as the name denotes, in the midst of an extensive demesne, well-wooded, particularly near the house, and to which the proprietor is daily adding large plantations, as well as on the adjacent hills, which form a magnificent background. The approach to this magnificent seat, which has one of the most extensive views in the kingdom, comprising many towns and parts of different counties, is through a well cultivated demesne, and by a beautiful shrubbery laid out with much taste; and the porter's lodge, on the entrance from Rosenallis, is a handsome specimen of the Gothic architecture; it is embattled, and appears to be an antique castle.' Such was the situation in about 1786 as described in the *Post chaise companion*, but poor Pigott's idyll was shattered by the unrest in 1798, for in 1802 Coote had to report that "... Mr Pigot, after discharging the duties of an active magistrate and gallant yeoman, disgusted with the ingratitude and villainies of the neighbouring peasantry, has abandoned this beautiful seat for ever, and gone to reside in England', where he stayed until his death in 1826. Of the early gatehouse that so impressed Wilson nothing seems to have survived intact. It may have been a victim of the disturbances, for there is little evidence of it on the 1839 OS map, and the surviving northern lodge could be its replacement.

Rosenallis gate; *c.* 1830.

A standard single-storey hipped-roof lodge with rendered walls containing openings with chamfered stone surrounds, including the doorway with a round-headed fanlight, latticed and set in a gabled breakfront with a suggestion of an open pediment. Plain gatescreen but for, to one side, a postilion opening with pointed archway, perhaps left over from the previous castellated Gothic porter's lodge, and a cute turnstile with ironwork by 'Hill & Smith of Brierley Hill'. All presumably a replacement by John Pigott's son of the same name upon the family's return to the property.

Skerry lodge; pre-1839; *demolished.*
Originally located opposite the gates on the western approach, its gatekeeper in 1851 was Thomas Savage.

Schoolgate lodge; pre-1839.
The early lodge probably also functioned as a school within the curtilage of the demesne at the southerly access, but by 1909 had been replaced by separate buildings without. There is now a modern bungalow on the site of the replacement lodge.

Wilson 1803; Coote 1802; Griffith 1848–60; *LGI* (1904).

22. CAPPALOUGH, Killeigh (2).
The two lodges to the property have both gone without trace, that well within the demesne having been removed before 1910. Presumably built by an early proprietor, Richard Goodbody (1743–1814), or his successor, Christopher Bailey.

IFR.

24. Castle Durrow, Durrow gate.

23. CASTLECUFFE, Clonaslee; pre-1839.
Home for most of the first half of the nineteenth century to Revd John Baldwin, leasing from Sir Charles Coote. Its porter's lodge has been much altered from the original simple single-storey standard gabled affair. Sometime in the late nineteenth/early twentieth century it was extended to the right-hand side and a hall projection added, with a half-timbered-effect gable, and naive rendered quoins applied. Occupied.

24. CASTLE DURROW, Durrow (2).
The very fine early Georgian mansion of the Flower family, to which Henry Jeffrey Flower (1776–1847), as the 4th Viscount Ashbrook, in the 1830s carried out repairs and additions, as well as building an impressive main estate entrance.

Durrow gate; *c.* 1835; architect not known.
A familiar landmark on this busy thoroughfare is, with the parish church alongside, this splendid extensive piece of townscape facing the square. The three-storey gatehouse is Tudor Castellated in style, square on plan with a circular stair-tower to one corner, all in white rendering contrasting effectively with limestone features of the first-floor canted oriel windows, corner buttresses and crowning mock-machicolated battlements. On each side are separate gates with octagonal turrets as carriage pillars and label-moulded postilion openings in flanking crenellated curtain walls. Immaculately maintained.

Bishop'swood gate; *c.* 1850.
On the western approach in faintly Tudor Revival manner is this standard 1½-storey steeply gabled lodge, plain but in pleasant random rubble facings with a variety of openings, including a narrow arrowhead attic window over an elliptically arched fanlit doorway in the projecting central hallway. On each side, below the eaves, are peculiar blind tripartite 'openings'. Modern plastic, lead-effect inserts do not quite spoil the effect. Probably built by the 5th viscount (1806–71), also Henry Jeffrey Flower, who succeeded to the property in 1847.

Fraser 1838; *BPB* (1929); Bence-Jones 1988.

25. CASTLEFLEMING, Errill; *c.* 1790.
Offered for sale in 2006 with the property as a 'Substantial Gate Lodge' and appropriately located forward of its modern entrance gates is this structure in the form of a vernacular farmhouse, not much smaller than its 'big house'. Pleasant two-storey gabled in whitened harling, originally three-bay standard, it subsequently gained a single-bay extension to the left-hand side and, later still, a single-storey hall projection. Probably built by the Fleming family, the property in the nineteenth century was acquired by the Hamilton Stubbers of nearby Moyne (*q.v.*). Immaculately maintained.

26. CASTLEGROGAN, Rathdowney; pre-1900; *demolished.*
A mid-nineteenth-century lodge opposite the gates built by the Fisher family.

27. CASTLEWOOD, Durrow (2).

North entrance; pre-1839; *demolished.*

South entrance; pre-1839.
Opposite the gates is a sturdy two-storey gabled house, with V-jointed Irish pilasters, which is purported to incorporate the old lodge.

An estate that had a succession of proprietors in the late eighteenth and early nineteenth centuries, with the Lawrinson family here in 1837 and 1850.

28. CHARLEVILLE, Borris-in-Ossory; pre-1839; *demolished.*
A lodge, which fell victim to road-widening, that may have been built by Charles White (1747–1802) to a demesne previously called 'Raheen' prior to his inheriting it from his uncle in 1771.

LGI (1904).

29. CLARA HILL, Clonaslee; *c.* 1880.

Opposite the entrance is a delightfully quirky 1½-storey gabled porter's lodge in roughcast, with smooth rendering used to effect as window surrounds and pediment features applied over the corner recessed porch with its hefty chamfered support. Within there is an angled front door, and alongside, at high level, is a little arrowhead window with shelf sill, lighting the stairwell—like a piscina. Occupied. A nineteenth-century property of the Meredith family.

30. COOPER'S HILL, Ballickmoyler; *c.* 1830.
A single-storey three-bay structure with doorway to the left-hand side, below a steeply pitched hipped roof. Its remoteness opposite the gates ensured its escape from road-widening, but it lies derelict. A pair of gate pillars with peculiar ogee cappings remain. Probably built for William Cope Cooper (1795–1874) upon his succeeding to the place on the death of his father in 1830.

LGI (1904).

31. COTTAGE, Ballylinan; pre-1839; *demolished.*
A house later called 'Ballyadams', in the grounds of the castle of the same name, was a property in the first half of the nineteenth century of Captain Edward Butler.

32. CREMORGAN, Timahoe; pre-1839; *demolished.*
To 'the handsome seat of Lewis Moore' (1801–80) only some good V-channelled ashlar pillars survive at the entrance.

Fraser 1838; *LGI* (1904).

33. THE DERRIES, Ballybrittas (2).
To a property alternatively known as 'Ballyshanduffe', the house on which was built in 1810 by William Johnson Alloway. Neither of its lodges, dating from before 1839, are apparent on the 1909 OS map.

LG (1882); Bence-Jones 1988.

34. DISTRICT LUNATIC ASYLUM, Port Laoise; *c.* 1831; architect William Murray.

Built in 1831, 'The District Lunatic Asylum for the King's and Queen's counties and those of Westmeath and Longford is established here; it was erected at an expense, including the purchase of the land and furniture, of £24,172 ... an enlargement of it is in contemplation ...' Whether the gate lodge was part of the original scheme or a later addition is not clear, but it is of the same pattern as those at Armagh and Carlow asylums (*q.v.*), although here not afforded the luxury of a portico. It is a simple single-storey standard building below a hipped roof but in fine punched ashlar facing with segmentally headed openings, a chamfered corner with squinched top to avoid damage from carriages, and a banded stone chimney-stack. It still serves the purpose for which it was built, though it now lacks its entrance gates and has suffered the intrusion of inappropriate modern casement windows. The porter in 1850 was Robert Lewis.

Lewis 1837; Slater 1846; Griffith 1848–60.

35. DOOLOUGH, Portarlington; pre-1838; *demolished.*
A home in the early nineteenth century of the Dames family, the gatekeeper's lodge to which had gone by 1910.

36. DUNMORE, Durrow (5).
'The demesne is capitally enclosed, with an excellent stone wall; but the mansion house is very old ...' Such was the situation in 1801 and the wall remains largely intact, although increasingly being breached for access to executive dwellings, but the once-beautiful property of the Staples family is now almost completely shorn of its architecture: the early Georgian house and its pre-1839 east, west and walled garden lodges are all gone. Those that survive are equally doomed.

South lodge; *c.* 1820.
A three-bay single-storey lodge, now hideously adapted for forestry use, with a new mono-pitch roof and clad in modern roughcast.

North lodge; *c.* 1860.
An irregular single-storey lodge built off an L-plan created by a back return with steep gables; gablet to the rear having a one-over-one sash window and a projecting bay to the avenue with the remains of a tripartite window, in rendered walls. Now totally derelict, approaching ruin and its avenue impassable.

Coote 1802; Bence-Jones 1988.

37. DUNRALLY, Vicarstown; pre-1839; *demolished.*
Within Dunrally Fort was a pretty shooting-lodge of the Rt Hon. James Grattan MP of Tinnehinch, Co. Wicklow (*q.v.*), by the River Barrow, over which he erected a handsome bridge nearby, complete with toll cottage—along with the porter's lodge, things of the past.

Lewis 1837; Griffith 1848–60.

38. EASTHOLME, Rathdowney; *c.* 1870; architect Joseph Maguire.
An unexpected exercise in the English

Picturesque Cottage style in this Irish village square. An extravagant and substantial mid-Victorian 1½-storey lodge built off a T-plan in grey coursed quarry-faced rubble in contrast with red-brick chamfered dressings to once-margined windows. To the avenue gable is a single-storey canted bay window, which viewed the entrance. Steeply pitched earthenware-tiled roofs with intricately carved decorative foiled bargeboards, and tall, clustered, diagonally placed red-brick chimney-stacks rising from rectangular breasts with blue-brick diaper work, a feature repeated on the entrance screen wall, which has unusual gaps with stepped copings. Impressive octagonal brick carriage pillars crowned with stone ogee Tudor-Gothic cappings. With a new house and stables, built on the back of Robert Perry's adjacent booming ale and porter brewing business. His architect was Joseph Maguire, here showing considerable flamboyance not evident in his other gate lodges at Howth Castle, Co. Dublin (*q.v.*), and Swifte's Heath, Co. Kilkenny (*q.v.*).

IB (15 Aug. 1870); Slater 1870; Williams 1994.

39. EDGE HILL, Clonaslee; pre-1839; *demolished.*
A lodge opposite the gates to a property of the Corbett family.

40. THE ELMS, Portarlington; pre-1838; *demolished.*
A property of the Stannus family, also known as 'Kilnacourt', the lodge to which had gone by 1910.

41. EMO COURT, Portarlington (4).

John Dawson (1744–98) married in 1778 and the following year succeeded his father as 2nd Viscount Carlow, inheriting the demesne of 'Dawson's Court'. The old house was clearly unfit for his new status and, despite his own aspirations as an amateur architect, he sought designs for its replacement from two friends and professionals in Thomas Sandby and James Gandon, the latter of whom was to contribute so greatly to Dublin's public architecture under Carlow's patronage. Thus commenced a protracted design gestation period of a decade before work commenced to Gandon's plans in 1790. Dawson, who was advanced to the title of earl of Portarlington in 1785, was not to see his plans reach completion, for this had to wait until about 1860, thanks to the exertions of his grand-nephew, who succeeded to the title in 1845. In the interim his eldest son, namesake and 2nd earl had frittered away the family fortune, which may also explain why so many grand proposals for Classical entrance gates to the estate never went beyond the drawing board.

Design no. 1; *c.* 1780; architect probably Thomas Sandby; *unexecuted.*

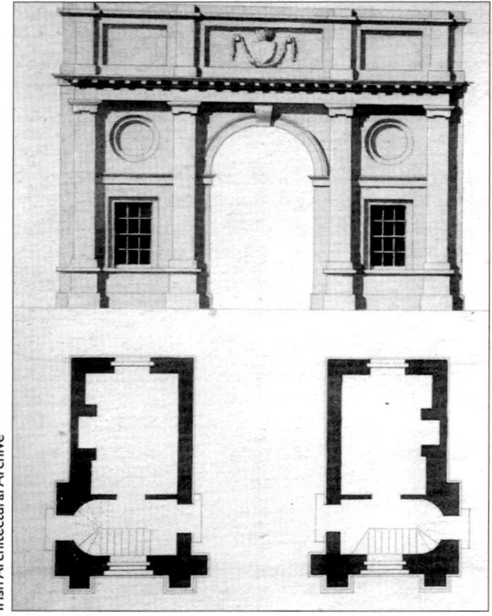

Irish Architectural Archive

A grand Doric pilastered triumphal archway, its tall round-headed carriage opening below a parapet with shield and festoons, and one-up/one-down porter's accommodation very much clapped on behind.

Design no. 2; *c.* 1780; architect probably Thomas Sandby; *unexecuted.*

Irish Architectural Archive

A pair of one-roomed single-storey lodges with semicircular-headed windows in equivalent recesses under parapets crowned by urns, their hallways embodied in a central archway with blind *oeils-de-boeufs*, niches and round-headed opening with heavily mutuled pediment.

Design no. 3; 1780; architect James Gandon; *unexecuted.*

Irish Architectural Archive

Signed, dated and entitled 'Elevation for a Park Gate No. 1', the proposal shows another semicircular-arched carriage opening but with a mutuled entablature supporting a sculpted coat of arms. In the spandrels are Gandon's hallmark paterae with husk-chain drapes. Alongside are piers with round-headed niches, repeated beyond with urns over and separated by railed screens on dwarf walls.

Design no. 4; 1780; architect James Gandon; *unexecuted.*

Irish Architectural Archive

Signed, dated and entitled 'Elevation for a Park Gate No. 2', this differs from design no. 3 only in substituting single-storey lodge accommodation with moulded window surrounds for the railed screens, and smoking chimney-pots to replace the urns.

These proposals were prepared whilst Gandon was still resident in England prior to his Irish career blossoming in the Irish public sector, and are only partial evidence of a search for an acceptable introduction to his friend's mansion; further sketches survive for a twin-lodge solution, in plan form only. All these designs which never bore fruit may show frugality on the part of the 1st earl, and this, allied to his son's preference to spend money on things other than building, probably accounts for the lack of any early gatekeepers' lodges appropriate to a property of this importance. Two lodgeless entrances survive from the 1830s, both rather fine, one of two grand pillars with recessed panels below undersized ball finials, and another with like shafts, also in ashlar, with good ironwork to carriage gates and the flanking postilion archways, an anonymous drawing for which is in the IAA. The only early lodge to the estate survives at the village gate.

Emo gate; *c.* 1780; architect possibly James Gandon.

A modest and antique single-storey lodge, perhaps having served Dawson's Court. Built in rubble stone, harled, below a very shallow hipped roof, it is sited partly forward of its gates, two window bays behind the screen comprised of wide openings with bipartite cast-iron latticed casements from the 1830s. One bay was previously a doorway. Plain stone entrance pillars carry ironwork with husk motifs—a humble introduction to such a grand house. Conceivably this is what remains of one of Gandon's designs.

Both his father and his long-suffering practitioners having passed away, the 2nd earl (1781–1845) persisted in the tradition of commissioning designs for estate entrances, turning to another English architect, Lewis Vulliamy, who also was engaged in abortive schemes for which unsigned drawings survive, two of which warrant notice.

Design no. 5; *c.* 1835; architect probably Lewis Vulliamy; *unexecuted.*

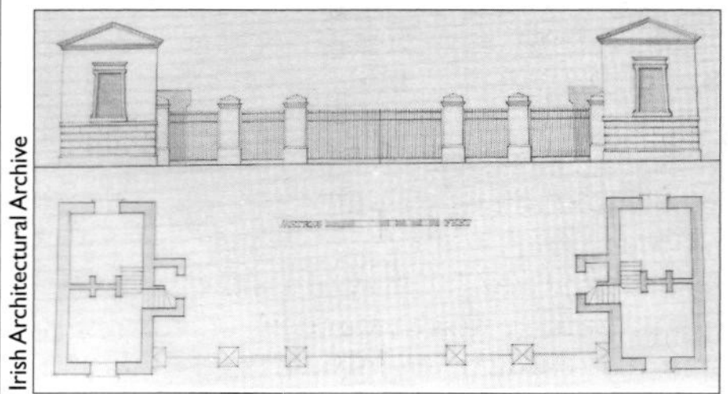

Irish Architectural Archive

Had this scheme materialised it would have formed a fitting prelude to the big house, not only for its exceptionally wide, straight, six-pillared railed gatescreen but also for the distant pair of three-roomed, part-single-storey, part-two-storey twin pavilion lodges raised on 5ft-high rusticated bases, their single-bay main fronts displaying architraved tapering windows, entablatured below pedimented gables. Each split-level accommodation was to have been approached via flights of stairs in little attached hall projections. The drawing is based on Vulliamy's original.

Design no. 6; *c.* 1835; architect probably Lewis Vulliamy; *unexecuted.*

This scheme would have realised a chaste pair of two-up/two-down two-storey Classical boxes, pedimented to the visitor, the elevation below identical to those facing one another across the carriageway, dominated by full-height semicircular-arched recesses broken by moulded string-courses, each with segmentally headed first-floor window over an entablatured living-room light—all the like of which Wyatt and Adam

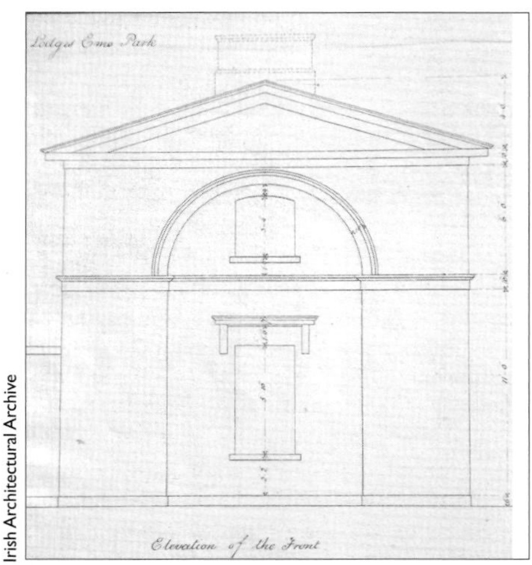

Irish Architectural Archive

were purveying in the time of Sandby and Gandon.

Henry John Reuben Dawson (1822–89) succeeded his uncle in 1845 as 3rd earl of Portarlington, completing the house that his predecessor had commenced 70 years previously and eventually furnishing the estate with gatekeepers' cottages, all to the same pattern by the Dublin-based architect William Caldbeck.

South lodge; *c.* 1861; architect probably William F. Caldbeck.

A decorative design in the English Picturesque cottage manner, single-storey standard below a steeply pitched roof with ornate cresting and fancy fretted foiled bargeboards to main gables and that of the projecting hallway, with its round-headed fanlit doorway. Built in quarry-faced rubble with toothed brick quoins and dressings to bipartite casement windows with margined glazing patterns. To one gable is an arrowhead oriel window supported on intricately carved brackets.

North lodge; *c.* 1861; architect probably William F. Caldbeck.

Identical to the south lodge but for having tripartite casement windows and for lying derelict.

'Deer Lodge'; *c.* 1861; architect probably William F. Caldbeck.

Differing from the north and south lodges in being constructed in contrasting bricks and its roof finished in scalloped slates. Immaculately maintained, with one surviving Tudor-style terracotta chimney-pot. Contrasting classical gate screen.

DB (15 Aug. 1861); *BPB* (1929); *IGS Bulletin* (Oct.–Dec. 1973); *Country Life* (23 and 30 May 1974); IAA drawings (91/101).

42. ERKINDALE, Rathdowney; *c.* 1825.

Seemingly detached from comings and goings opposite, the lodge lies lower than, and curiously at an oblique angle to, the road. It is a standard single-storey cottage with a hipped roof over harled walls, the front door flanked by narrow sidelights. Probably built by the Owen family, it was extended by a bay to the rear and given fancy carved fascia boards *c.* 1870 in the time of Charles Paulette White (1821–95). It lies sadly derelict.

LGI (1904).

43. EVERTON, Carlow; *c.* 1830.

An agreeable little single-storey lodge, its principal short elevation three-bay symmetrical, having a round-headed panelled front door flanked by six-over-six Georgian-style sash windows in roughcast walls under a steeply hipped roof with clipped eaves. Beautifully refurbished. Contemporary pillars to carriage and postilion gates of monolithic granite shafts with recessed panels. A seat in the early nineteenth century of the Thomas family.

44. FARMLEY, Abbeyleix; *c.* 1865; *demolished.*

A short-lived lodge built in the mid-Victorian period for the Pigotts or a later occupant, Revd William Cosby of the Stradbally Hall family.

45. FOREST, Mountrath; pre-1839; *demolished.*

The lodge was opposite the entrance gates to an estate in the first half of the nineteenth century of John Hawksworth.

46. GLENMALYRE, Ballybrittas; pre-1839; *demolished.*

A seat of the Very Revd Thomas Trench (1761–1824), dean of Kildare, and his son Henry (1806–88), the lodge to which has been replaced by a twentieth-century bungalow.

LGI (1904).

47. GRACEFIELD LODGE, Ballylynan (2).

Set in beautiful John Sutherland parkland is this villa by the prince regent's architect, John Nash, commissioned *c.* 1815 by Alicia Grace, the widow of Morgan Kavanagh. The design was rather watered down by the executant architect, William Robertson, but the main entrance and lodge are by the Kilkenny man.

Main entrance; *c.* 1820; architect William Robertson.

A pretty single-storey standard lodge having a shallow-pitched hipped roof with carved paired soffit bracket to its oversailing eaves. Wide bipartite cast-iron latticed casement windows on each side of a double-leaved door glazed in chinoiserie style. Rendered with proportions much as at Robertson's lodges at The Grange (*q.v.*) and Woodstock, Co. Kilkenny (*q.v.*). The fine gatescreen is comprised of four stone pillars with recessed panels and extended cornices below gadrooned cappings. The extensive railings and matching carriage gates in iron with spear, quatrefoil and husk motifs are identical to those at the outer gate to Lawnsdown (*q.v.*).

Secondary entrance; *c.* 1880.
A late Victorian single-storey lodge built off an L-plan in coursed random ashlar with brick toothed dressing under steeply pitched gables with banded stone chimney-stacks. Sympathetically extended, with new mildly ornamental bargeboards and rectangular-paned casement windows. Dating originally from the time here of John Dowell FitzGerald Grace (1821–97), also of Mantua, Co. Roscommon.

Brewer 1825; *LGI* (1904); Bence-Jones 1988.

48. GRAIGAVERN, Ballybrittas (2).
North lodge; *c.* 1810.

National Inventory of Architectural Heritage

A quintessential porter's lodge, single-storey standard below a hipped roof with cut-stone eaves band. Tiny window openings to main front with two-over-two sashes and Georgian lancet window to the road elevation, in stuccoed walls. Derelict.

South lodge; pre-1839/*c.* 1870.
A single-storey plain late Victorian affair, gabled with roughcast walls, opposite the gates. A replacement for an earlier lodge on the site.

An estate in the 1800s of the Armstrong family.

49. GRANTSTOWN, Rathdowney (2).
A demesne, later renamed 'Ballygran', in 1814 noted as of William Hayes but 23 years later as belonging to Robert Vicars, one of whom must have built the early lodge.

East lodge; *c.* 1820.
A single-storey standard gabled structure with harled rubble walls. Derelict.

West lodge; *c.* 1845; architect possibly T.H. Wyatt.

Identical to Grallow Lodge on the Abbeyleix estate is this generous 1½-storey gatehouse, a hybrid design combination of Italianate, with its shallow-pitched gables, and Tudor Picturesque ornamental bargeboards and latticed windows. The principal front has a tripartite attic window projecting to form a recessed porch below, behind three capable square pillars. The two-bay side elevation features a pair of gablets with bipartite windows. Now much modernised and extended, not wholly to the good, with its concrete-tiled roof and replacement plastic and lead-effect glazed windows for the previous cast-iron horizontal sliding sashes. New roughcast walls and original stone quoins. Built in the time here of Peter Roe.

Leet 1814; Lewis 1837; Griffith 1848–60.

50. GRANTSTOWN or GRANSTON MANOR, Rathdowney (2).
An estate, previously known as 'Oldglass' when occupied by the Drought family, did not possess gate lodges until the advent of Robert White (1787–1862) and his successor, John Wilson Fitzpatrick, 1st Lord Castletown (1811–83).

Main entrance; *c.* 1860/*c.* 1870.
What was a standard single-storey lodge built in coursed rubble facings below a hipped roof was considerably enlarged with the addition, to the rear, of a two-storey cubic block in like materials, also having a hipped roof which extends as a catslide over a single-storey wing. The original structure in this process had its doorway sealed and gained a hefty new banded and corbelled chimney-stack. Two pleasant buildings in their own right but a most peculiar combination. Occupied.

Secondary entrance; *c.* 1870.

A 1½-storey gabled structure built in coursed rubble with some brick dressings; three-bay front elevation, that to the left-hand side having a single-storey gabled hall projection that looks like an afterthought. The roof with tall eaves is finished in earthenware tiles and cresting, with a chimney-stack of the same design as those to the main lodge. Derelict.

BPB (1929); Bence-Jones 1988.

51. HARRISTOWN, Rathdowney (2).
Two lodges dating from before 1839, both demolished, that to the east having gone by 1908. A property of a succession of owners in the nineteenth century, one of whom was Michael Head Drought in 1837 and noted here in the 1850 valuation, the date of his death.

Lewis 1837; Griffith 1848–60.

52. HEYWOOD, Ballinakill (4).
An estate in 1763 of Revd Frederick Trench, who already had then '24 Acres Walled round 10 feet high', was to be transformed by his son, Michael Frederick Trench (1746–1836), a competent architect in his own right who had, with some help from James Gandon, designed himself a new house in 1773. He set about creating a Romantic landscape by forming lakes, moving hills and building bridges, a Temple of the Winds, a Gothic ruin, estate cottages for their tenantry and a castellated entrance to the 250-acre demesne.

Abbeyleix gate; *c.* 1810; architect probably M.F. Trench.
An exercise in the Picturesque Castellated manner being popularised at this time by the likes of John Nash, pioneer of the style, with whose work in Ireland and beyond Frederick Trench would have been familiar. Consisting of a four-centred arched carriage gateway, with moulded surround, and a crenellated and machicolated parapet also crowning the right-hand of the two flanking octagonal towers, which rises to three storeys and initially housed the porter's accommodation. The left-hand tower, of two storeys, has a simple corbelled battlemented parapet and

52. Heywood, Abbeyleix gate. Lithograph after F.W. Trench 1821: private collection.

seems only to have contained pedestrian access. The whole is built in rubble stone relieved by a variety of openings, some with Tudor label mouldings. An undated building account for this entrance lists:

'Mason-work Daly
Arch, Battlement, side wall opposite Gate: mortar 4 perches @ 13d: 14.1
facing of sunk fence opposite Gate; dry 16 perches: 10.0'.

This latter entry refers to the ha-ha at the opposite side of the road. A print of *c.* 1819 reveals changes to the structure down the years: the loss of original Irish crenellations, a slender square bartizan to the right-hand parapet, a mock cross arrowloop in an archway spandrel to be replaced by a very fine cut-stone but unidentified achievement, and a bell suspended from a bracket high above the archway to alert the gatekeeper to visitors, its death-knell doubtless hastened by passing ragamuffins. There have since been various single-storey Victorian additions to enhance the gatekeeper's accommodation. Occupied.

Ballinakill gate; *c.* 1810; architect possibly M.F. Trench.

H.Trench drawing c.1810

A pair of rather ungainly 1½-storey gabled lodges forward of the town gates, squinting at each other across the approach, in smart modern roughcast with label-moulded minuscule windows. An old illustration in a book of prints shows the lodges as they looked originally from within the demesne, with their *oeil-de-boeuf* attic windows, latticed, glazed, and presumably pivoting, below hood mouldings. Again undated but signed 'H. Trench', doubtless Helena Sarah, a noted artist and daughter of M.F. Trench, who inherited the property on the failure of the male line, it passing to the family of her husband, Sir Compton Pocklington Domvile of Santry Court, north Dublin (*q.v.*).

Masslough gate; *c.* 1810.
A two-storey three-bay substantial hip-roofed house with open flat-roofed porch and lancet-headed postilion gates flanking. Probably the building referred to on the 1839 OS map as a school.

South lodge; pre-1908; *demolished.*
A short-lived lodge, presumably built in the time here of the Domviles.

Coote 1802; *Country Life* (4 and 11 Jan. 1919); *LG* (1863); *BPB* (1929); Malins and Glin 1976; Friel 2000.

53. HOLLYMOUNT, Carlow; *c.* 1810.

Recently admirably saved from dereliction is this Georgian Gothic cottage, standard single-storey with a steeply pitched hipped roof, built with wide pointed heads to openings in rubble walls perhaps once harled. Coote records Charles Ward 'about to build a capital mansion house', although Robert M. Fishbourne was here by 1814.

Coote 1802; Leet 1814.

54. HUNTINGTON, Portarlington; *c.* 1825.

A standard single-storey hip-roofed porter's lodge which displays the transition between the Georgian and Regency periods, with Y-traceried lancet sash windows set in semicircular-headed recesses on each side of a doorway with pointed head. The new rendered finish probably replaced original harling. Modern 'improvements' have seen the loss of its central chimney-stack, conversion of its doorway into a window and an unfortunate flat-roofed extension to one side. There survive limestone entrance pillars with Gothic-headed recesses. John Eccles was noted here as late as 1816, but the lodge may have been built for Col. Chidley Coote (1798–1876) of the Ash Hill, Co. Limerick, family, who was living here in 1824.

Mason 1814–19; Pigot 1824; *BPB* (1929).

JOHNSTOWN GLEBE **(see RATHDOWNEY RECTORY)**

55. KELLYVILLE or KELLAVIL, Stradbally (3).
'The handsome seat of Rev. Thomas Kelly' in 1838. Two of the lodges may have been built by him or his father, the Rt Hon. Judge Thomas Kelly.

West entrance; pre-1839; *demolished.*
A lodge that had gone by 1909.

East entrance; pre-1839.
A 1½-storey gabled structure, much improved and probably a replacement for an earlier structure. Surviving are the semblance of a mid-Georgian ashlar carriage pillar with a scroll-topped gate stop and moulded cornice, and a solitary concave quadrant with stone-framed postern doorway.

North entrance; *c.* 1870.
A basic single-storey structure with a shallow-pitched gabled roof and single-bay elevation to the avenue. Much added-to. Presumably erected for William Downes Webber, originally of Leekfield, Co. Sligo, who inherited Kellyville through his mother, Frances Kelly, and on his 1873 marriage to the widow of Lord Kingston added Mitchelstown Castle, Co. Cork, to his properties.

Fraser 1838; *LGI* (1904).

56. KILLEANY, Shanahoe; pre-1909; *demolished.*
Situated opposite the gates was this short-lived gatekeeper's lodge, built either by James L. Nolan or by his successor here, Seymour Mobray.

Griffith 1848–60; Slater 1856.

57. KILLEEN, Mountmellick (3).
Not one of the lodges to this estate of the Kemmis family has survived, one built before 1839, the other two added by 1850 for Thomas Kemmis (1798–1844), whose main seat was Shaen (*q.v.*) nearby.

Griffith 1848–60; *LGI* (1904).

58. KILMARTIN, Borris-in-Ossary; *c.* 1845.

A striking porter's lodge and gatescreen built for Henry Smith, who had recently acquired the estate from the long-time owners, the Brereton family. A single-storey standard affair with shallow hipped roof but rising off a cruciform plan with gabled projections back and front, the latter a pedimented hall with mini-entablature to the door recess. Architraved windows in roughcast walls, that to the road a tripartite opening; banded chimney-stack. Derelict. Good straight ironwork screens to match the carriage gate, with palmette motifs at low level and alternating anthemion and fleur-de-lis features to top the railings. Four stone pillars, those to the carriage opening with recessed panel shafts, roundels to the friezes and pedimented cappings.

Griffith 1848–60; *LGI* (1904).

59. KILMORONY, Ballylynan; pre-1839.
'... the improved and handsome residence of the Very Rev. Dean Trench.' This is the same much-propertied Thomas, dean of Kildare (1761–1834), of Glenmalyre (*q.v.*), who had also associations with Ashfield (*q.v.*) in the county. His interest here was through his 1786 marriage to Mary Weldon, whose family had been, and would be, resident here for a century. The original lodge has been lost in a transformation into a bungalow, but four of its six octagonal brick entrance pillars survive, with good iron-railed concave quadrants of about 1835.

BPB (1929).

60. KNAPTON, Abbeyleix (2).
A fine house built onto an earlier structure on the Abbeyleix estate by Colonel George Pigott *c.* 1773. It must have been his eldest son, Sir George Pigott, who added at least one of the porters' lodges to the demesne before his death in 1844.

Front entrance; *c.* 1840; architect not known.

A delightful and uncommon two-storey gatehouse of Georgian proportions but with idiosyncratic chinoiserie features in its lattice-effect glazing to all the openings. Three-bay standard below a shallow-hipped roof, the main front has a Classical door-case and segmentally arched and trellised fanlight all set in a deep concave niche-like recess, very much in Morrison villa manner. This is flanked by wide tripartite casements below bipartite equivalents, between which is a central *oeil-de-boeuf* light. These are nicely set off by roughcast walls in a striking English mustard finish, all immaculately refurbished but for an ill-positioned soil pipe detracting from the overall effect.

Rear entrance; pre-1909; *demolished.*
A lodge on the southern approach, which mysteriously is not shown on an 1890 map.

Coote 1802; *BPB* (1929); Bence-Jones 1899.

61. KNIGHTSTOWN, Mountmellick; pre-1839; *demolished.*
The lodge may have been contemporary with the gate pillars, which had urns and swag ornamentation of Coade stone probably of late eighteenth-century date and thus erected by Joshua Kemmis (1755–1818), who inherited the place on his father's death in 1774.

LGI (1904); Kelly 1990.

62. KNOCKBEG COLLEGE, Carlow; pre-1908; *demolished.*
The lodge must have dated from after 1847, when St Patrick's College moved to this site from Carlow, having acquired the 200-acre estate of the Carruthers family. Later, in 1901, Moore and Aylward, engineers and architects of Dublin, won a competition for work to the institution.

Lewis 1837; Griffith 1848–60; *IB* (13 March 1901).

63. KNOCKFIN, Rathdowney; pre-1908; *demolished.*
A property with a succession of different occupants in the first half of the nineteenth century but which was home in 1837 and 1850 to the Mosse family.

Lewis 1837; Griffith 1848–60.

64. LACCA MANOR, Mountrath; *c.* 1845.
A 1½-storey gabled, rendered structure with a tiny canted-head loft window. Occupied and paying little heed to its entrance. An early nineteenth-century seat of John Pim.

65. LAMBERTON, Port Laoise; pre-1839/*c.* 1860.

A property which had impressed Coote in 1801: 'Lamberton, Sir John Tydd ... the entrance to the demesne is elegant, and the offices are planned with so much convenience as I have not seen before ... I think Lamberton altogether the neatest and best laid down demesne in the county.' The late Georgian gatescreen that impressed Coote was built by Sir John Tydd or his predecessor, a Mr Sherlock, who was here in 1783. It has a pair of 'quoined' V-jointed ashlar carriage pillars with carved swagged friezes. On each side the straight-walled screens contain postilion openings and the whole is framed by more rustic convex quadrants. The early lodge has a replacement, which lies hidden and remote from its entrance, probably built by Michael James Sweetman of Longtown, Co. Kildare (*q.v.*), who succeeded the Moore family on the estate. It is a standard 1½-storey structure with steeply pitched gables to the main body and its single-storey projecting hallway. The rendered rubble walls contain openings with hood mouldings to segmental pointed arches, that to the hall set in an equivalent recess. Recently rehabilitated with the loss of some of its previous character.

Coote 1802; Bence-Jones 1988.

66. LARCH HILL, Mountrath; pre-1839; *demolished.*
An early seat of the Despard family; the bat's-wing paterae on the surviving gate pillars suggest that its gatekeeper's lodge may have been of late eighteenth-century origin.

67. LAURAGH, Mountmellick (2).

West entrance; pre-1839; *demolished.*

East entrance; pre-1839; *demolished.*

Replaced by a bungalow, the stumps of two chamfered ashlar rusticated gate pillars remain.

Another seat, in the early nineteenth century, of Revd Sir Erasmus Dixon Borrowes, 8th baronet of Gilltown, Co. Kildare (*q.v.*).

68. LAUREL HILL, Mountrath; pre-1839; *demolished.*
A property in the late eighteenth century of the Despard family, who were succeeded here early the following century by James Bradish.

69. LAWNSDOWN, Portarlington (3).
A once-noble landed estate, now devastated, the state of its gate lodges reflecting the ruinous mansion beyond.

Principal entrance; *c.* 1820.
The remains of a standard single-storey

cottage with harled walls below a shallow-pitched hipped roof with carved paired soffit brackets to oversailing eaves. The stone stack is a late Victorian rebuild. Of the once-grand gatescreen only two of its fine ashlar pillars survive with their fluted friezes. The carriage gates have gone, to be pathetically replaced by a modern farm gate, but the flanking ironwork screens with spear, husk and quatrefoil motifs, and containing matching postilion gates, remain; rustic harled outer convex quadrant walls. The screen being identical to that at Ballyfin (*q.v.*), it is doubtless significant that in 1748 Lady Sarah Moore married William Pole of that place, whilst the lodge would seem to post-date it and to have been built during the occupancy of Lieutenant-Colonel Robert Moore (1789–1879) of the Moorefield, Co. Kildare (*q.v.*), family.

Inner lodge; *c.* 1880.
Only a few yards up the same eastern approach is this later lodge in similar condition. The roofless shell of a single-storey standard structure with toothed red-brick dressings in rendered walls below what was previously a hipped roof.

Rear entrance; pre-1914; *demolished.*
A lost lodge on the western avenue within County Offaly.

BPB (1929).

70. LEVALLY, Rathdowney; *c.* 1780.

An elegant and antique entrance comprising deep ogee quadrant walls in rubble, perhaps originally harled and limewashed, the coping of which is continuous as a band into the four containing tall slender cut-stone pillars, which have moulded plinths and cappings crowned by unusual fluted egg finials. A less than elegant cattle grid replaces the old gates. Intriguingly secreted behind the right-hand wall are the remains of a unique survivor—the fabric of a hexagonal brick-built gate lodge, presumably originally two-roomed single-storey, with special bricks to the angles and lancet openings, now blocked up. Its hexahedral roof, probably rising to a central chimney-stack, now supplanted by a concrete flat one. A property in 1777 of the Vickers family. An important entrance ensemble well worthy of restoration.

Taylor and Skinner 1778.

71. LISDUFF, Errill (2).
Two lodges possibly built by the Rt Hon. John Wilson Fitzpatrick (1811–83) upon his elevation to the title of Lord Castletown in 1869, neither of which survives, although that to the rear entrance may be incorporated in a twentieth-century bungalow not quite opposite the gates. Castletown's main seat was at nearby Grantstown Manor (*q.v.*).

BPB (1929).

72. LODGEFIELD, Cullahill; *c.* 1800.
A single-storey symmetrical three-bay cottage with door to the right-hand side in harled rubble walls, and an off-centre chimney-stack to a hipped roof with tiny slates. Presumably a property of the Lodge family, in 1837 that of Lodge Phillips.

Lewis 1837.

73. MAIDENHEAD, Ballylynan; pre-1839; *demolished.*
A seat in the late eighteenth century of the Bambrick family that passed to the Kidds.

74. MIDDLEMOUNT, Rathdowney; pre-1839; *demolished.*
Although let for most of the nineteenth century to the Roes, it was a lodge and property of the Flood family 'which has beautiful gardens and finely improved demesne belonging to it'. Thus found the *Post chaise companion* of 1786.

Wilson 1803.

75. MONORDREE, Mountmellick; pre-1909; *demolished.*
A house and flour mill in 1850 of Joseph Beale.

Griffith 1848–60.

76. MOUNT EAGLE, Ballyroan; pre-1839; *demolished.*
A property in the first half of the nineteenth century of Owen McMahon.

77. MOUNTMELLICK BREWERY, Mountmellick; pre-1850; *demolished.*
A lodge identified by the Griffith valuation, but not obvious on the OS maps, to a premises in Church Lane of James Sheane, the 'Old Brewery' listed as being vacant in 1850.

Griffith 1848–60.

78. MOUNTMELLICK MILL, Mountmellick; pre-1850; *demolished.*
A concern, recorded by Griffith in 1850 on Pound Street (now Wolfe Tone and O'Moore Streets), of the Neale family.

Griffith 1848–60.

79. MOYNE, Durrow; *c.* 1810.

A late Georgian Gothic lodge, single-storey, with its short front to the avenue canted and containing a flat-arched doorway flanked by pointed-arched Y-traceried windows in stone facings. Twentieth-century reroofing of synthetic slates, not inappropriately canted, and two octagonal brick chimney-stacks. Occupied. Built for Robert Stubber. The gates are contrastingly Classical in flavour, in rough stone and cast ironwork which looks to be of *c.* 1845, probably when the public road was rerouted in the time of Robert Hamilton Stubber, whose father, Revd Alexander Chetwood Hamilton, had inherited the estate and assumed the Stubber surname.

LGI (1904).

80 OLDDERRIG, Carlow; pre-1839; *demolished.*
A property of many various owners, in 1814 of Benjamin Galbraith.

Leet 1814.

OLDGLASS (see GRANTSTOWN MANOR)

81. OLDTOWN, Cullahill; pre-1839; *demolished.*
A gatekeeper's lodge opposite the gate that had gone by 1908. In 1837 a seat of the Delany family.

Lewis 1837.

82. PHILLIPSBURGH, Cullahill; pre-1839; *demolished.*
An estate of the Phillips family.

83. POLESBRIDGE, Stradbally; *c.* 1835.
The ruinous remains of a standard 1½-storey gabled English Picturesque cottage-style lodge with a gablet feature above the front door. Smothered in vegetation. An early nineteenth-century property occupied by Pierce Moore.

Leet 1814.

84. RAHEENAHAWN, Timahoe; pre-1839/*c.* 1860.
A neat mid-Victorian 1½-storey English Picturesque cottage-style lodge, multi-gabled with decorative foiled bargeboards. Perfectly symmetrical with a pair of gablets over the three-bay ground-floor main front, a central

single-storey hall breaking the main eaves. Two-over-two sash windows in rendered walls with quoins. Occupied. Probably built for J.W. Dunne, it is a replacement for a predecessor on the site.

85. RAHEENDUFF, Stradballly; pre-1909; *demolished.*
For long a seat of the Caulfeild family, its lodge may have dated from the time of Commander Edwin Toby Caulfeild RN (1793–1881), who inherited the property as a seven-year-old and in whose minority and absence at sea it was let to the Baldwins.
BPB (1929).

86. RAHIN, Ballylynan (2).
Another property of the Weldons of nearby Kilmorony (*q.v.*), both of the lodges to which date from before 1839, one demolished, the other ruinous.
BPB (1929).

87. RATH, Ballybrittas; *c.* 1860.
A standard 1½-storey gabled structure with similarly treated hall breakfront that has a mouth-organ fanlight. Eight-over-eight sash windows with stone surrounds in roughcast walls. Perforated earthenware crestings and spiky finials. Probably received a make-over at a later date but built for Edmund Gerald Dease (1829–1904), who had come to the place on the death of his uncle in 1856.
LGI (1904).

RATHDARE (see BELLEGROVE)

88. RATHDOWNEY RECTORY, Rathdowney; pre-1839; *demolished.*
A once-prosperous parish, upon which Johnstown glebe house was built in 1814 for £1,700, to which the rector, Revd Marcus Monck, had subscribed £400, a sum that may have included the provision of a pair of gate lodges, which had gone by 1908.
Lewis 1837.

89. RATHLEAGUE, Port Laoise (2).
'... of Sir John Parnell ... the mansion house is very old and indifferent ... an extensive lake ... and a Grecian temple, which is executed with taste.' Thus reported Coote in 1801, without making mention of the gate lodges, one of which was in place by 1839, the other having been built by 1850. Neither has survived. Sir John died in the very year of publication of Coote's survey, to be succeeded by his sons, one of whom, Sir Henry Brooke Parnell (1776–1842), became the 1st Baron Congleton in 1841.
Coote 1802; Griffith 1848–60; *BPB* (1929).

90. RATHLEAGUE LODGE, Port Laoise (2).
Both lodges, dating from before 1839, have gone. This was home to the Clarke family, one of whose gatekeepers in 1850 was John Garrett.
Griffith 1848–60.

91. RATHMOYLE, Abbeyleix (2).
Neither the pre-1839 gate lodge, which was here in the time of E.B. Handcock, nor that built by his successor, the splendidly named Horatio Uniacke Townshend (1826–97), has survived.
Lewis 1837; Griffith 1848–60.

92. RATHSARAN RECTORY, Rathdowney; pre-1839; *demolished.*
A glebe house dating from 1820, the gate lodge to which may have been contemporary.
Lewis 1837.

93. ROCKVIEW, Port Laoise; *c.* 1845.
Now at the entrance to a modern housing development is this modest single-storey gabled structure with a two-window-bay elevation to the road and a hall projection to the old avenue. Built in rubble stone, it has new wave and foil bargeboards and delicate turned finials. Occupied and much modernised, to the original estate of Robert Groves.

94. RYNN, Mountmellick (2).
An estate of the Croasdaile family, an earlier house on which was replaced in 1855 by the present one after a fire. There being no gate lodges shown on the OS map of 1839, they may well have been contemporary with this rebuilding by John Croasdaile (1830–89). Neither has survived.
LGI (1904).

95. SABINE FIELD, Monasterevin; pre-1839; *demolished.*
A property alternatively recorded, correctly or not, as 'Saline Fields', 'Sally Park' and 'Ballintogher', probably to satisfy the whims of its various occupants, who included Michael Lloyd in 1814, a Captain Lloyd in 1816, Michael L. Apjohn in 1824 and Dawson French in 1837, any of whom may have built the lodge.
Leet 1814; Mason 1814–19; Pigot 1824; Lewis 1837.

96. SCOTCHRATH, Shanahoe; pre-1839; *demolished.*
A house belonging to the White family, the porter's lodge to which had gone by 1909.

97. SHAEN, Port Laoise (5).
A generously lodged estate, the ancestral home of the Kemmis family had two of pre-Victorian date.
East lodge; pre-1839; *demolished.*
West lodge; pre-1839/*c.* 1850.
The early lodge has gone but is survived by a very fine late Georgian gatescreen comprised of a pair of V-jointed rusticated ashlar

carriage pillars flanked by flat-arched postilion openings with tall ashlar quadrant walls beyond, unusually angled at 45° rather than curved. The replacement lodge is a commodious 1½-storey gabled affair with a two-bay front façade and a pair of gablets breaking the eaves, with a later single-storey addition partly obscuring the ground floor; rendered walls, wavy bargeboards and a pair of diagonally positioned chimney-stacks on a rectangular base. Occupied.
North-east lodge; *c.* 1880.
A single-storey four-bay gabled late Victorian cottage with asymmetrically placed hall projection; quoins but otherwise plain. Occupied.
South-west lodge; *c.* 1880.
Differs only from the north-east lodge in having a hip-roofed hall and no quoins.
Tower lodge; *c.* 1840; architect perhaps W.D. Butler.

On the south-eastern approach is this striking Romantic Castellated composition in very fine ashlar stone. Dominated by a tall octagonal battlemented stair-tower with mock cross arrowloops and slit windows. Between this and a square turret is the hood-moulded Tudor-style carriage archway, the centre-piece framed by tall crenellated curtain walls, terminating in great pillars in similar vein. To the rear are the sad remains of a single-storey porter's lodge with battlemented parapet, hood-moulded window and circular turret. Thomas Kemmis (1798–1844) had inherited the property in

1827 and employed architect William Deane Butler to redesign the house four years later. This impressive entrance may be part of his commission that did bear fruit. There is a similar design at Camlin Castle, Co. Fermanagh, by J.B. Keane.

The later lodges were built for Thomas's son of the same name.

LGI (1904); Dean 1994; Williams 1994.

98. SHANAHOE, Shanahoe; *c.* 1860.
A property that was offered for sale at auction as an incumbered estate and purchased in 1859 by William Mooney, who leased it to Robert H. Tilly, who may have been the builder of the gate lodge. Much modernised and extended to give the appearance of a twentieth-century bungalow but retaining original features in its wide oversailing eaves with soffit brackets.

Lyons 1993.

99. SHANDERRY, Mountrath; pre-1839; *demolished.*
A property in the early nineteenth century of the Despard family but subsequently leased to various tenants. Its porter's lodge was sited opposite the gates.

100. SHANVAGHEY, Rathdowney; *c.* 1855.
A single-storey gabled structure with a three-window-bay main avenue elevation. There are intricately moulded paired brackets to eaves and verges. A seat in 1850 of John Short. Occupied.

Griffith 1848–60.

101. SHEFFIELD, Port Laoise; pre-1839; *demolished.*
The ancestral seat of the Cassan family; the builder of the gatekeeper's lodge may have been Major Matthew Cassan (1754–1838), who succeeded to the place on his father's death in 1773.

LGI (1904).

102. SPRINGMOUNT, Shanahoe; *c.* 1810.

A noble entrance screen of deeply V-jointed rusticated stone pillars with oversailing moulded cappings, good iron entrance gates and flanking postilion openings. Deferentially not quite opposite the entrance is a contrastingly modest standard single-storey porter's lodge with harled walls and shallow-pitched gabled roof. Unsophisticated but pleasantly proportioned. Chimney-stack rising off the rear wall. A demesne in the late eighteenth century of Edward Brereton, from whom it passed by the marriage in 1783 of his daughter and co-heir Sackvilla to Sir John Allen Johnson Walsh (1735–1831), but one Henry Bourne is recorded as the occupant in 1814 and Mrs Bourne 23 years later.

Leet 1814; Lewis 1837; *BPB* (1929).

103. STRADBALLY HALL, Stradbally (5).

Ulster Museum

This has been the ancestral home of the Cosby family since the sixteenth century. A charming oil painting of *c.* 1740 in the time of Pole Cosby depicts the demesne in its maturity, peppered with playful and functional garden buildings, much subdivided by the formal paths of the time, and sporting a plethora of gates with lofty wide-capped pillars, some with ornate finials, and a first generation of gate lodges at some of the entrances. At an access from the town was a pair of single-storey sentry-boxes with pyramidal roofs rising to central chimney-stacks and centred on an axis with the front door of the old house, which was replaced in 1768. Another formal avenue leads south-east to a secondary lodged gate breaking the boundary wall.

The eighteenth and nineteenth centuries saw dramatic changes on the estate, the mansion being rebuilt further south in 1772 and completely transformed almost a century later into the present Italianate pile by Sir Charles Lanyon. The landscape of the park had also taken on a completely new appearance in a fashionable informal Romantic style, with serpentine avenues leading to five later widely dispersed entrances to the demesne, all now in dilapidated condition and here treated as they appear on a clockwise tour of the perimeter from Abbeyleix.

Campion's Wood gate; pre-1909; *demolished.*

Town gate; *c.* 1870; *demolished.*

Surviving, and worthy of mention, off the main street is a fine example of cast ironwork in the form of ornate straight screens and matching gates framing a pair of carriage piers with elaborate foliated work, each bearing a Cosby crest—a proud griffin, surrounded by anthemion motifs.

Polesbridge gate; *c.* 1840.

A once-impressive entrance screen in the shape of an extensive semicircular gate sweep comprised of four V-jointed rusticated pillars that contain high rendered walls with architraved pedestrian openings on each side of the carriage gateway. The left-hand quadrant terminates in the lonesome shell of a single-storey lodge in stucco with stone quoins and a square window opening with moulded lugged surround. Missing is its hipped or pyramidal roof. It seems that the lodge never had the companion that the entrance demands to balance the composition.

South gate; pre-1909; *demolished.*

Timahoe gate; pre-1839/*c.* 1865; architect possibly James F. Kempster.

At this south-easterly extremity of the estate was the only lodge shown on the first OS map. The peculiar structure that survives today is its replacement. Single-storey and built off a butterfly plan, each of its identical gables containing paired round-headed Y-traceried four-over-four sash windows with underpanels, all contained in moulded surrounds. Over these are bizarre double mouldings, apparently without architectural precedent. From the internal angle projects a flat-roofed canted hallway flanked by semicircular-headed narrow recesses. In stucco finish with clipped gables, this is a gauche composition, not quite unique, for there is an almost identical lodge on the Rockingham estate, Co. Roscommon. Robert Ashworth Godolphin Cosby, who succeeded to the estate in 1851 on the death of his uncle, invited designs from no fewer than three architects to transform the house: Lanyon, John Louch of Dublin and James Kempster of Ballinasloe. This is a design of which the latter would have been quite capable. Derelict.

LGI (1904); Bence-Jones 1988; Cosby Papers at PRONI; Malins and Glin 1976.

104. THORNBERRY, Abbeyleix; pre-1839; *demolished.*

An early eighteenth-century house, in 1814 of Francis Evans, which by 1837 was owned by the Corker family, the lodge to which may have been contemporary.

Leet 1814; Lewis 1837.

105. WOODBROOK, Portarlington (2).

Jonathan Cope Chetwood succeeded to Woodbrook on the death of his father in 1771 and came to live here after army service, only for the house to be destroyed by fire in the early nineteenth century. He set about rebuilding it *c.* 1815 to designs of architect James Shiel, whose commission extended to providing plans for at least one of the estate's gate lodges. Drawings for various alternatives survive which probably relate to the south entrance, for none of the proposals are for a gate lodge opposite its gates.

North entrance; pre-1839; *demolished.*

A lodge across the road from the entrance that had been removed by 1910.

Design no. 1; *c.* 1820.

Irish Architectural Archive

Irish Architectural Archive

A delightfully naive composition, perhaps by Chetwood himself, comprised of a perspective sketch and an eccentric hexagonal plan containing three regular hexagonal rooms forming a central triangular chimney—all quite quirky but nevertheless practical. Its single-storey main three-bay symmetrical front projects beyond flanking entrance gates.

Design no. 2; *c.* 1820; architect probably James Shiel; *unexecuted.*

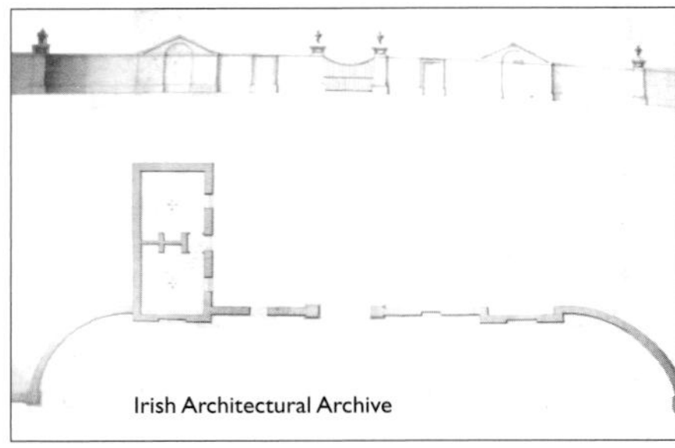
Irish Architectural Archive

An intended extensive and symmetrical walled gatescreen of four pillars, with urn finials and swagged friezes, containing concave quadrants, architraved pedestrian openings and projecting elevations in the form of blind semicircular-arched recesses breaking pedimented gables. That to the left-hand side was to be the front to a long two-roomed porter's lodge behind, and that to the right-hand side merely a balancing façade.

Design no. 3; *c.* 1820; architect probably James Shiel; *unexecuted.*

An elevation drawing has not come to light for this proposal, which shows a plan of deep concave quadrant walls, relieved by recesses and niches, framing a pair of rectangular lodges with doors to the forecourt and sturdy piers to their carriage access walls, suggesting a central triumphal archway. Unsigned and undated.

Design no. 4; *c.* 1820; architect James Shiel; *unexecuted.*

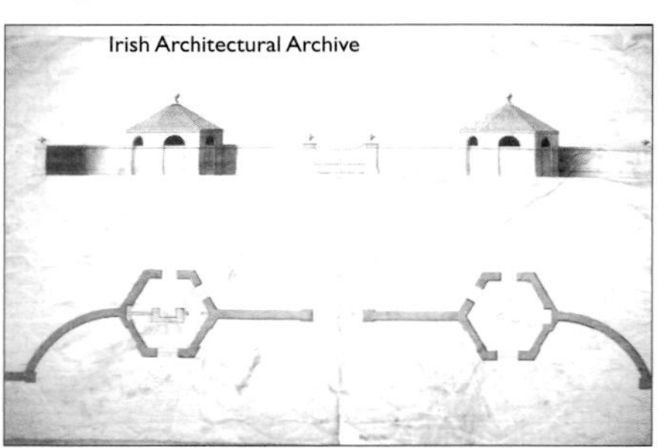
Irish Architectural Archive

A signed drawing indicating a fine composition of a pair of single-storey hexagonal 'day and night' lodges with equivalent roofs rising to ball finials. Their walls are arcaded with part-blind recesses having round-headed lunette windows over, divided by a string-course as sills which is a continuation of the lengthy wall copings, which extend over outer concave quadrants, and inner straight curtain walls, which terminate in pillars with dainty urn finials.

Design no. 5; *c.* 1820; architect James Shiel.

A drawing that displays the gatescreen as executed at the southern entrance, entitled 'A Design for an Entrance Gate for Jonathan Chetwood Esq. Portarlington' and signed by

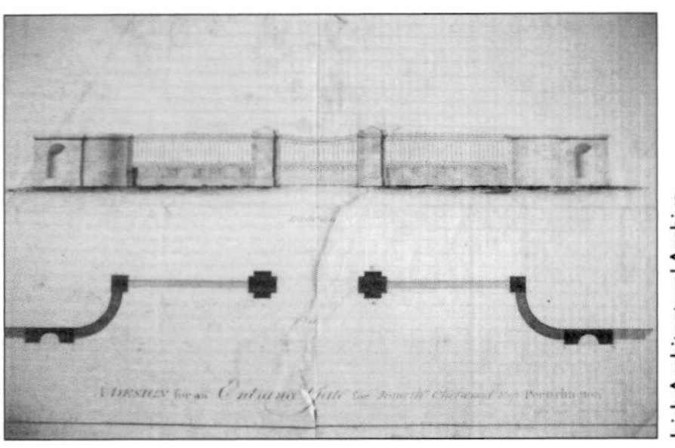
Irish Architectural Archive

the architect. Beautifully presented in ink and watercolour.

South entrance; *c.* 1820; architect possibly James Shiel.

The gatescreen differs from the architect's initial intentions only in having postilion gates breaking the dwarf walls of railed screens. Hefty ashlar cluster carriage pillars with concave cappings carry gates of matching ironwork with spear tops. Beyond are convex quadrant walls stopped by piers with round-headed niches. This layout is not unlike those at Lawnsdown (*q.v.*) and Ballyfin (*q.v.*). There is no documentary evidence of this quirky little lodge being by Shiel. Single-storey, its shorter main façade to the avenue has a wide ashlar stylised pediment which embraces a narrow window wall flanked by deep recesses, one a porch, to be supported rather uneasily, two centuries later, by slender cast-iron posts. On the ridge is an octagonal stone chimney-stack and later scalloped earthenware cresting which is reflected in the modern fascia boards.

LGI (1912); *JASCK* Vol. 9 (1920); IAA (Woodbrook Drawings Collection).

106. WOODVILLE, Port Laoise; *c.* 1825.

A charming rose- and ivy-clad single-storey standard lodge below a hipped roof with harled walls behind low box hedge enclosures. Squared casement windows, sheeted door and red-brick chimney-stack are clues to a twentieth-century make-over. A property in 1824 of William Kelly, also recorded here 26 years later as proprietor of house, offices, flour mill and 49 acres.

Pigot 1824; Griffith 1848–60.

COUNTY LONGFORD

1. AGHAREAGH, Longford; pre-1914; *demolished.*
A property in 1854 of John O'Beirne, the porter's lodge to which was built opposite the gates after 1837 but was swept away to accommodate twentieth-century road-widening.

Griffith 1848–60.

2. ARDAGH, Ardagh (5).
Ardagh model village is the charming vision of an improving landlord in Sir Thomas John Fetherston, 5th baronet (1824–69), who had inherited the old family home nearby in 1853 on the death of his uncle and his father in the space of a month. Before his own premature demise he had transformed the place with the help of his architect, J. Rawson Carroll, who from 1862 created estate workers' cottages in the medieval English Picturesque style, arranged about the focal point of a Gothic clock tower that Sir Thomas had erected as a memorial to his uncle. The redevelopment of the property extended to the replacement of three earlier entrance lodges to the old house of *c.* 1744 by the present two in a rather more reticent and contrasting Italianate manner.

Longford gate; *c.* 1865; architect probably J.R. Carroll.

An 1877 photograph of the lodge shows how effective was the contrast between the cut stone of the dressings and that of the darker random rubble walls. Now mellowed, the stark contrast is between stone and the white plastic replacement windows and fascia boards. Single-storey standard below a hipped roof, with a projecting pedimented hallway flanked by paired windows which have individually, segmentally arched heads and bracketed sills. The front door is similarly arched, with a keystone and framed by prominent 'Irish pilaster' quoins repeated on all external corners. The pediment and fascia have now sadly been picked out in white PVC and the original tall brick cluster-stack reduced. The fine concave-walled quadrants and six cut-stone pillars with layered cappings and scallop motifs remain unscathed, but the fine timber and iron carriage gates have gone, to be replaced by a twentieth-century overthrow announcing 'Convent of Mercy'. The earlier lodge opposite this entrance, recorded as vacant in 1854, was removed.

Edgeworthstown gate; *c.* 1865; architect probably J.R. Carroll.

In detailing and materials as the above but built off a less formal L-plan. Missing any distinctive quoin features, the hipped roof catslides as a canopied porch over the front door, located in the internal angle. There is rather less PVC intrusion here, the two-over-two sash windows remaining but the very tall brick corbelled chimney-stacks dramatically reduced. There is the most extensive and ornate of entrance sweeps in the form of shallow concave ashlar quadrant walls with decorative ironwork in a repetitive spiky quatrefoil motif extending into the carriage gates and single postilion gate. All relieved by as many as a dozen pillars with pyramidal cappings and diamond features. There was an earlier lodge on this site, which was similarly unoccupied in 1854.

Griffith 1848–60; *BPB* (1923); Bence-Jones 1988; Casey and Rowan 1993.

3. BALLYMULVEY, Ballymahon (2).
A property in the eighteenth century of the Molyneaux family which, owing to the failure of the male line, passed by marriage to Lemuel Shuldham in 1772. Both its lodges, in place before 1837, have been demolished.

LGI (1904).

4. BRIANSTOWN, Longford; pre-1837; *demolished.*
A 1731 house of the Achmuty family, in whose hands it remained until the mid-nineteenth century. Surviving at the entrance are two mid-Georgian limestone pillars with ball finials on squat pedestals with crude corniced caps and friezes.

Bence-Jones 1988.

5. CARRICKMOYRAGH, Newtownforbes; *c.* 1850.
Severed from its demesne by a realigned public road is this standard structure with steeply pitched roofed, a chimney-stack to each gable and a breakfront hallway. Built in harled rubble, it lies a roofless shell. Probably 1½-storey. Erected for Thomas Gregory.

Griffith 1848–60.

6. CARRIGGLAS MANOR, Longford (5).
A grand landed estate of two architectural phases that display the tastes of the times of two discerning families and their two respective architects of differing temperaments, both English but domiciled here under very different circumstances. James Gandon (1742–1823) chose to live and work in Ireland in the public sector after being invited to design the Dublin Custom House, but this commission for Sir William Gleadowe-Newcomen in 1792 was to have been one of his rare excursions into country-house work. He was to be thwarted, however, for owing to the subsequent collapse of the Newcomen Bank the house was never built, although, strangely, his designs for stables and farmyards and a main entrance to the demesne were realised.

The Grand Gate; *c.* 1800; architect James Gandon.

On this once-important main approach, now a quagmire, lies Gandon's only, if not executed, surviving estate entrance, its lodges lying vacant and neglected. These form a pair of single-storey twin pavilions below hipped roofs, their long elevations facing each other behind the gatescreen as asymmetrical three-bays below segmental arches with six-over-six sash windows. To the visitor each presents a single blind façade with round-headed recess and a string-course that continues as a coping to straight screen walls with postilion gate openings. These link the lodges to the grand carriage archway, similarly in limestone ashlar, not as triumphal as could be expected of a pupil of

Sir William Chambers but rather understated and Soaneian in feel. A simple die surmounts a fine dentil course above the semicircular archway with, in the spandrels, paterae draped with Gandon's characteristic lop-sided husk drapes. A mutuled spring cornice course sits over piers relieved by blank rectangular panels above round-headed niches. A fine composition by one of Ireland's most prominent architects in a squalid setting, the positioning of an electricity pole symptomatic of the general attitude towards it.

Deer-park gate; *c.* 1770.

The earliest of the Carrigglas lodges, a cubic sentry-box, its single-storey three-bay symmetrical façade addresses the road, the narrow windows little more than sidelights to the doorway in a stucco wall framed by pronounced V-jointed stone quoins. Probably once hip-roofed, it lies derelict and sealed up. Alongside, linked by a short, lofty wing wall, is a pair of noble ashlar gate pillars with mouldings to plinths and sharply chiselled capping cornices. Not unlike those at the other Newcomen seat of Mosstown (*q.v.*).

Sir William Gleadowe-Newcomen died in 1825 without legitimate male issue and the estate was leased to the Rt Hon. Thomas Langlois Lefroy (1776–1869), in whose family it has remained ever since. He and his son Anthony between 1837 and 1845 replaced the old house with a brand-new mansion, something that had been beyond their predecessor. Their architect was the unpredictable Daniel Robertson, who had arrived in Ireland in 1829, having left his employment in Oxford under a cloud. Unsurprisingly, the design was in his favourite collegiate Tudor style, to which his little gatekeeper's lodge is an appropriate prelude.

North-west gate; pre-1837/*c.* 1840; architect Daniel Robertson.

Replacing an earlier lodge on the site is this characterful little 1½-storey gabled Tudor Gothic cottage (*below*). Built off a simple rectangular plan but with castellated appendages rendering it irregular in a canted bay window to the leading gable forward of the gatescreen and, facing the avenue, an outsized breakfront porch with four-centred archway. Otherwise there are label-moulded chamfered mullioned bipartite openings with margined sash windows in limestone ashlar walls. There are simple perforated scalloped bargeboards. Alongside is a wing wall containing a pointed-arched postilion gate and a pair of large Classical ashlar carriage pillars. Good chunky contemporary cast-iron gates.

North gate; pre-1837/*c.* 1860.

An affected single-storey standard lodge, rendered with big punched ashlar quoins, and a central breakfront hall below a catslide roof, to each side of which the four-over-four sash windows have gablets over. These and the main gables are ornamented by continuous carved bargeboards; perforated scalloped earthenware cresting. The entrance sweep is considerably more antique, with a pair of towering plain ashlar pillars flanked by rubble quadrant walls, one containing a segmentally headed pedestrian gate. Possibly contemporary with the previous porter's lodge on the site.

Creeve lodge; *c.* 1850.

On the eastern approach by the Creeve River and banished to the exterior of a plain gatescreen is this pleasant 1½-storey standard lodge with chimney-stacks to each steeply pitched gable. Two-over-two sash windows painted bright red in limewashed harled walls. Tiny loft window; occupied.

LGI (1904); Colvin and Harris 1970; McParland 1985; O'Dwyer 1999; Casey and Rowan 1993; Colvin 2008.

7. CARTRON, Ballymahon; pre-1837/*c.* 1865.

National Inventory of Architectural Heritage

In 1787 Revd D.A. Beaufort noted here 'Ned Malone's', whose early porter's lodge was replaced by the surviving structure built for Thomas S.B. Wright. Now derelict is this single-storey standard hip-roofed roughcast cottage with a gabled breakfront hall displaying mid-Victorian embellishments in scalloped bargeboards terminating in a wooden apex feature.

D.A. Beaufort (1787); Slater 1856; *Land Owners in Ireland 1876; NIAH.*

8. CASHEL RECTORY, Lanesborough; pre-1837; *demolished.*

The lodge may have been contemporary with the building of the glebe house in 1817 during the incumbency (1813–38) of Revd

Richard Hartley Sinclair (1787/8–1838).

Lewis 1837; Leslie and Crooks 2008.

9. CASTLECOR, Ballymahon; pre-1837/*c.* 1845.

'Castlecor of Thomas Hussey has been justly termed "one of the most singular mansion houses in the province of Leinster"—was erected by the late Rev. Cutts Harman, dean of Waterford.' The dean, whose principal seat was nearby Newcastle (*q.v.*), indeed created a remarkable octagonal house, but after his death in 1784 it passed out of that family and by 1825 was being rented by Captain Thomas Hussey, who was still here in 1856, having by then purchased the place. He was probably responsible for extending it into a more habitable form and replacing its old gate lodge with one across the road, opposite a new set of entrance gates. This is in the form of smooth stone Greek stelae-type pillars with moulded plinths, huge homogeneous tapering shafts with recessed moulded panels and hefty cappings, all contrasting nicely with high-quality punched random ashlar quadrants. Precisely opposite the contemporary chunky iron gates is the lodge, which is where the symmetry ends, for it is a Picturesque design built off an L-plan. Single-storey with punched stone quoins contrasting with whitewashed walls below a hipped roof, its main front projects gabled to frame a semi-hexagonal bay window with equivalent roof and pretty trefoil cluster-posts to the corners. Crude modern wavy bargeboards and original corbel blocks to eaves below unusual decorative lion-mask gutter brackets; staged chimney-stack. Modern lead-effect glazing points to the loss of cast-iron latticed originals. Occupied and contained behind a simple iron fence.

Brewer 1825; Slater 1856; Bence-Jones 1988.

10. CASTLE FORBES, Newtownforbes (5).
Mostly an extraordinarily bland and disappointing series of lodges dating from the turn of the twentieth century, when work was carried out for Bernard Arthur William Patrick Forbes, 8th earl of Granard, by Frederick W. Foster of London.

Town lodge; *c.* 1820.
A relatively interesting Regency survivor, although much modernised. Single-storey and rendered below a hipped roof, its short three-bay elevation addresses the avenue with a central round-headed door opening. Tucked in behind an extensive mid-Georgian stone gate sweep of six pillars, containing flanking concave quadrants, inner wing walls with postilion openings and carriage opening. All probably built for the 6th earl, George Forbes (1760–1837), who inherited the place in 1780.

Sadly, none of the lodges were designed by J.J. McCarthy, 'the Irish Pugin', who was commissioned by the 7th earl to extend the castle in the 1860s.

North lodge; *c.* 1910; architect possibly F.W. Foster.
A substantial roughcast gabled gatehouse.

East lodge; *c.* 1910; architect possibly F.W. Foster.
Similar to the north lodge but regular three-bay with a two-storey projecting hall with room over. Now separated from the property by a realigned road.

West lodge; pre-1837/*c.* 1910; architect possibly F.W. Foster.
Replacing an earlier lodge at this entrance is this gatehouse, much as the preceding.

Inner lodge; pre-1837/*c.* 1910; architect possibly F.W. Foster.
As the above, a gatehouse replacing a predecessor on the site.

Lacy 1863; *BPB* (1929); Sheehy 1977; Bence-Jones 1988.

11. CASTLE WILDER, Ballymahon; pre-1837; *demolished.*
An estate founded by the Wilder family, briefly occupied by Hugh Pollock in the early nineteenth century. The first OS map refers to the property as 'Cloghdoo'.

Lewis 1837.

CLOGHDOO (see CASTLE WILDER)

12. CLONFIN, Ballinalee (2).
Two charming late Georgian porters' lodges built by William Thompson, both lying abandoned.

West lodge (*below*)**;** *c.* 1810.
Located opposite and remote from its entrance gates is this single-storey harled rubble-built cottage with its leading face canted three-bay, the central doorway flanked by two tiny Gothic lancet windows. Semi-octahedral roof.

East lodge; *c.* 1820.

A standard single-storey structure with bow ends and equivalent roof over, and with rectangular-paned transomed and mullioned casement windows. There is an unfortunate later gabled hall projection that may conceal a sophisticated entrance doorway.

LGI (1904).

13. CLONGESH RECTORY, Newtownforbes (2).

Front gate; *c.* 1820.
A lodge that post-dates the 1810 glebe house later known as 'St Anne's Hill', perhaps built by the incumbent (1798–1821) Revd George Crawford (1775/6–1846). Situated opposite and obliquely to the entrance gates is this derelict and overgrown gatekeeper's lodge. Single-storey gabled with two wide bipartite sash windows in harled rubble walls; a single diagonally set chimney-stack breaks the ridge. Good square Georgian gate pillars falling to ruin, as is the rectory.

Back gate; pre-1837; *demolished.*
A lodge lost by 1900.

Lewis 1837; Leslie and Crooks 2008.

14. CLONWHELAN, Edgeworthstown; pre-1837; *demolished.*
A property in 1814 of Miss Godley and eleven years later of William Murray. Its lodge had gone by 1914.

Leet 1814; Brewer 1825.

15. CLOONBONY, Lanesborough; pre-1837; *demolished.*
A seat from early times of the Davys family.

16. CLOONCALLOW, Ballymahon; *c.* 1820.

A simple standard hip-roofed lodge built in rubble with brick dressings and finished in harling; clipped eaves; derelict. Earlier mid-Georgian and very grand ashlar carriage pillars with scroll-topped gate stops and crisply chiselled pineapple finials. Later iron gates. All probably for Daniel Murray.

CLOONSHANNAGH (see COOLAMBER MANOR)

17. COOLAMBER MANOR, Lisryan (4).
Situated in the townland of Cloonshannagh, after which the house was also known, it was built *c.* 1820 to designs by the Cork architect John Hargrave for Major Blackhall. It survives but there is no trace of any of its gate lodges, although thanks to the Griffith valuation the names of all of its gatekeepers in 1854 are recorded for posterity: Joseph Miller, Patrick McKenter, William Fife and Thomas Gilligan. The latter occupied the lodge on the northern approach, one of four lodges indicated on the first OS map, all thus pre-dating 1837; the structure on the main approach is shown as cruciform on plan and may have been of some presence, perhaps forming part of Hargrave's commission.
Griffith 1848–60; Bence-Jones 1988.

18. CORABOLLA, Ballymahon; pre-1914; *demolished.*
The house, built *c.* 1840, was auctioned in 1861 as an incumbered estate, prior to which it had been the property of Hugh Morrow. Its porter's lodge thus post-dated 1837 and was demolished in 1967.
Slater 1846; Lyons 1993.

19. CORNADRUNG COTTAGE, Lough Gowna; pre-1910; *demolished.*
On the banks of the lough, a fishing-lodge acquired as a retreat by the wealthy Dublin barrister and judge Henry George Hughes (1810–72), the future fourth baron of the exchequer. After 1837 he created a new avenue at the entrance, of which all that remains are railings with lancet tops.
Griffith 1848–60; Wikipedia.

20. CREEVAGHMORE, Ballymahon; pre-1837; *demolished.*
A substantial Georgian farmhouse of the Sandys family with very fine contemporary stone gate pillars, much as those to neighbouring Clooncallow (*q.v.*) but without the pineapple finials.
Casey and Rowan 1993.

21. CROWDRUMIN LODGE, Drumlish; pre-1914; *demolished.*
A lost gate lodge, built by Samuel Galbraith or, after his death in 1864, by his son John Samuel Galbraith (1828–1903), whose main seat was Clanabogan, Co. Tyrone.
LGI (1904).

22. CURRYGRANE, Ballinalee (2).
Inner lodge; pre-1837; *demolished.*
Located deep within an estate in the early nineteenth century of William L. Galbraith.
Outer lodge; *c.* 1860.
Probably built by the public road as a replacement lodge when James Wilson (1832–1907) acquired the property and employed William Hague as his architect in 1866 to design alterations and additions to the house. Whether he was responsible for the lodge is difficult to assess, as it lies a ruinous four-bay single-storey hip-roofed shell.
IB (1 April 1866); *IFR*.

23. DERRYCASSAN, Lough Gowna (2).
Like neighbouring Erne Head (*q.v.*), a lakeside home of a branch of the Dopping family.
East entrance; pre-1837; *demolished.*
West entrance; *c.* 1865.

A dual-function building at an access to the demesne, also serving as a post office. Originally built off an L-plan in quarry-faced stone facings with contrasting punched ashlar quoins and toothed chamfered window dressings below tall eaves with exposed rafter toes to its hipped roof. An extensive addition in cement rendering contains a bipartite window with arrowhead arches repositioned from the original structure. In the internal angle is a later pretty arcaded Tudor-style glazed porch. Built in the time here of Ralph Anthony Dopping-Hepenstall (1823–87), who succeeded to the property in 1855.
Brewer 1825; *LGI* (1904).

24. DOORY HALL, Ballymahon (2).
An early nineteenth-century house, designed by John Hargrave of Cork for John Jessop, with which the main lodge may be contemporary.
Front entrance; *c.* 1820/*c.* 1860.
A wide, straight, railed screen with spear tops incorporating a carriage gate and postilion gates and stopped to the left-hand side by a simple single-storey two-bay cottage with its gable to the road. Derelict and looking mid-Victorian but perhaps worked over in that period.
Rear entrance; *c.* 1870.
Opposite the gates and looking like an early twentieth-century labourer's cottage is this four-bay single-storey gabled structure with a flat-roofed hall projection. Probably originally three-bay standard and built by Francis John Jessop (1837–75).
LGI (1904); Bence-Jones 1988.

25. DROMING or DRUMING PARK, Ardagh; *demolished.*
A seat of the Newcomen family, the lodge to which had gone by 1914.

26. DRUMNACOR, Ballymahon; *c.* 1820.
Like nearby Creevaghmore (*q.v.*) a property of the Sandys family, of whom John inherited the place by marrying a Jessop heiress and built the late Georgian house, although the lodge dates from the time of William Sandys. Opposite the entrance is a standard single-storey hip-roofed cottage with oversailing eaves. Its central doorway is now a window, with entry now via a later lean-to hall to the left-hand side.
Mason 1814–19.

27. EDGEWORTHSTOWN, Edgeworthstown (3).
The erstwhile home of the talented Edgeworth family, the inventor Richard Lovell Edgeworth (1744–1817) and his authoress daughter Maria (1767–1849), who would have been able to describe the estate's three porters' lodges, all of which pre-dated 1837 but none of which survive.

That the family was content with at least one of their gatekeepers is manifest in a letter home from Maria on 31 March 1813, when she was *en route* with her father for her first visit to London. Impressed as she was with the lodge to Kinmel Park in north Wales and its 'two neat old women who shewed us the inside', she 'would not change our own good Margery Woods for any porter-ess in Christendom'.

The only survivor is at the main entrance by the town, a most singular creation, a replacement of about 1880 for Antonio Eroles Edgeworth (1842–1911), who inherited the place in 1864. Single-storey standard, almost a caricature, with a very steeply hipped roof rising to an outsized diagonally set chimney-stack with a corbelled capping. Two lofty windows in smooth rendered walls flank the main delight—a most extraordinary extravaganza of a cast-iron porch below its own hipped roof. Indian in flavour, with highly ornate perforated over-panels carried on six slender barley-twist posts and Corinthian capitals, two pairs and two engaged to the walls, remarkably it is not unique, for there is an almost identical example on the side lodge to the Newcastle estate (*q.v.*). The lodge has been most sympathetically extended to the rear.

LGI (1912); Colvin 1971; Williams 1994; Hicks 2012.

28. EDGEWORTHSTOWN or MOSTRIM RECTORY, Edgeworthstown; pre-1914; *demolished.*
A post-1837 lodge, which proved rather less durable than the early eighteenth-century rectory, perhaps built during the incumbency (1843–63) of Revd John Hugh Johnston Powell (1806/7–73).

Leslie and Crooks 2008.

29. ERNE HEAD, Lough Gowna; pre-1837.
Like neighbouring Derrycassan (*q.v.*), a lakeside property of the Dopping family, of whom Ralph (1766–1818) may have been the lodge-builder.

LGI (1904).

30. FAIR VIEW, Cloondara; pre-1913; *demolished.*
An Irish seat in the mid-nineteenth century of Sir Robert Henry Gunning (1795–1862) of Eltham, Kent, its lodge probably of that period.

BPB (1929).

31. FARRAGHROE, Ballinalee (3).

Schoolhouse entrance; *c.* 1815; architect possibly John Hargrave.
At the crossroads on the eastern avenue is this lovely three-bay symmetrical house below a hipped roof with squared sash windows, reducing from six-over-six panes on the ground floor to three-over-six above, in Georgian manner. There is a later gabled porch. Recorded as a schoolhouse in 1837, it may also have functioned as a lodge. Perhaps by the Cork architect who considerably enlarged the house from a shooting-box for Willoughby Bond (1790–1875), who succeeded to Farraghroe in 1811 upon his father's death.

Main entrance; *c.* 1855.
A lodge plain but for its punched random ashlar finish, it is single-storey below a hipped roof with banded chimney-stack. Three-bay with a gabled central hall projection that has a side-entry doorway. Chunky carriage pillars are flanked by straight wing walls and convex quadrants beyond, the chief interest of which is a novel three-up/three-down stepped pedestrian stile access.

West entrance; *c.* 1875.
A single-storey commodious structure built with random quarry-faced stone below a hipped roof with chimney-stacks in punched ashlar. Two-bay elevation to the road and symmetrical three-bay to the avenue, with unfortunate flat-roofed central hall projection. Occupied. Layered gate pillar cappings like those at Lismoy Upper (*q.v.*) and Lissard (*q.v.*). Perhaps dating from the time of James Willoughby Bond, second son of Willoughby Bond.

LGI (1904); Bence-Jones 1988.

32. FERNSBOROUGH, Abbeylara; pre-1837; *demolished.*
Prior to becoming home to Thomas Gosselin *c.* 1846, it was an estate of generations of Alexander Burrowes, descended from that family of Stradone, Co. Cavan.

IFR.

33. FOX HALL, Carrickboy (2).

Inner lodge; pre-1837; *demolished.*
The earlier of two lodges on the same avenue, located deep within an estate belonging since the sixteenth century to the Fox family.

Outer lodge; *c.* 1880.
By the public road, a two-storey hip-roofed three-bay gatehouse with central two-storey projection, and a further single-storey flat-roofed hall extension beyond that again. Plain, rendered and modernised. Probably built by Richard Edward Fox (1846–85).

LGI (1904).

GORTEEN (see LARK FIELD)

34. GRANARD RECTORY AND CHURCH, Granard; pre-1836; *demolished.*
The lodge marked on the 1914 OS map was shown as a school on the first edition of 1836, perhaps having a double role. It may have been contemporary with the glebe house, which was erected in 1825 during the incumbency (1811–37) of Revd Christopher Robinson (1762/3–1837).

Lewis 1837; Leslie and Crooks 2008.

35. GRANARD UNION WORKHOUSE, Granard; *c.* 1842; architect probably George Wilkinson; *demolished.*
An institution that opened its doors on 30 September 1842 to a potential 600 unfortunates.

O'Connor 1995.

36. HERMITAGE, Ballymahon; pre-1837; *demolished.*
A house, later called 'Knockagh', that was home to William Fox in 1814. On the 1914 OS map the lodge is shown unhatched, suggesting that it was by then a shell like the house, which was recorded as being in ruins.

Leet 1814.

37. THE HERMITAGE, Drumlish; *c.* 1860.
A standard single-storey lodge in harled rubble with a chimney to each gable. Derelict. A property in 1837 and 1854 of Thomas Ellis.

Lewis 1837; Griffith 1848–60.

38. HIGGINSTOWN, Granard; pre-1836; *demolished.*
An estate in 1814 of John Judkin Butler, which ten years later had passed to Francis Tuite.

Leet 1814; Pigot 1824.

39. KEEL DEER PARK, Ballymahon; *c.* 1825.
By the roadside is this sizeable 1½-storey gabled cottage with Regency Tudor

Picturesque features. The two-bay leading front has squared windows in round-arched recesses. To the ridge is an impressive triple bank of diagonally set chimney-stacks. Addressing the park is a standard three-bay front with central single-storey gabled entrance hall, all in a roughcast finish. To one end is a single-storey gabled addition, whilst by the entrance gateway is a lean-to extension with latticed casement windows. All in a generosity of accommodation which, with adjacent outbuildings, suggest that the occupant's duties, rather than solely attending to the gates, extended to managing a park that formed part of the estates of the Harmans of nearby Newcastle (*q.v.*), the doyenne of whom in the early nineteenth century was Lady Frances Parsons-Harman (d. 1841), who had succeeded her father in 1807 and eight years previously had married the 1st Viscount Lorton.

LGI (1904).

40. KILCOMMICK RECTORY, Keenagh; *c.* 1850.
At the entrance to a rectory built in 1827 was added this relatively social and commodious 1½-storey lodge. Built in harled rubble, set well back from the gates, its one-bay short gabled front faces the avenue, the doorway with a crude brick label moulding below a tiny attic window. Presumably erected during the incumbency (1848–66) of Revd Thomas Henry (1809/10–66).

Leslie and Crooks 2008.

41. KILLASONA, Abbeylara; pre-1914.
A property of the Nugent family, its lodge, built after 1837, so derelict and altered as to make visual dating almost impossible. Opposite the gates, it now has a mono-pitched roof with a blank shield to its leading front, sited behind a hoop-topped railing. Gate sweep rebuilt in concrete blockwork—a sorry scene.

42. KILSHRULEY, Ballinalee (3).
All three lodges to an estate of the Edgeworth family have gone. Both that to the north and one opposite the west gate post-dated 1836, that on the southern approach being earlier.

KIRKVIEW (see ST ALBANS)

43. KNAPPOGE, Ballymahon; pre-1837; *demolished.*
A property in 1854 of Robert Wallace, the lodge to which had gone by 1914.

Griffith 1848–60.

KNOCKAGH (see HERMITAGE)

44. KNOCKMARTIN, Newtownforbes; *c.* 1845; *demolished.*
A gatehouse situated distant from the public road, identified in 1854 as a property of Michael Cody.
Griffith 1848–60.

45. LARK FIELD, Ballinalee; pre-1837; *demolished.*
A seat in 1837 and 1854 of Robert Grier, later called 'Gorteen'.
Lewis 1837; Griffith 1848–60.

LEAMORE PARK (see LONGFORD JAIL GOVERNOR'S HOUSE)

46. LEDWITHSTOWN, Ballymahon; pre-1837; *demolished.*
A lovely Palladian villa, built by the Ledwith family in the mid-eighteenth century, at the entrance to which only a pair of contemporary low square ashlar pillars survive, with corniced cappings and scroll-topped gate stops.
Casey and Rowan 1993.

47. LISGLASSICK, Ballymahon (2).
Both lodges, dating from before 1837 and possibly contemporary with the Regency house built by John R. Robinson, have gone.
Brewer 1825.

48. LISLEA, Keenagh; *c.* 1860.
A standard 1½-storey gabled lodge with high eaves having carved modillion brackets over random rubble walls with brick dressings. Six-over-six squared sash windows on each side of the doorway, which has a moulded stone lintel. Occupied. A seat in 1854 of Elizabeth Bickerstaff.
Griffith 1848–60.

49. LISMOY UPPER, Newtownforbes; *c.* 1870.

A spacious single-storey standard lodge, three bays wide by two deep, in a nice cream rubble stone with brick dressings and grey limestone quoins. A gabled hall projection with serrated ornamental bargeboards nestles below the high main eaves, with exposed joist ends to its steeply hipped roof. The chimney-stack is layered to imitate the carriage pillar cappings. There are similar features to the gates at Farraghroe (*q.v.*) and Lissard (*q.v.*), and Bachelors' Lodge, Co. Meath (*q.v.*). A property in 1870 of John Quinn, coroner, who succeeded a Mrs Fitzgerald to the place.
Griffith 1848–60; Slater 1870.

50. LISSARD, Edgeworthstown (3).

The estate had three lodges in 1837 in the time of John Lewis More O'Ferrall (1800–81). He had inherited from his kinsman Edward O'Ferrall, who had died five years previously. Both the south and central lodges have been removed, to be survived by a structure on the northern approach. This is single-storey, completely reconstructed and extended, with segmentally headed openings in dark random rubble facings below hipped roofs. The carriage pillars are original, with layered cappings just like those at Farraghroe (*q.v.*) and Lismoy Upper (*q.v.*), and Bachelor's Lodge, Co. Meath (*q.v.*). Good chunky cast-iron gates with striking meeting rail finials.
IFR.

51. LONGFORD COUNTY INFIRMARY, Longford; *c.* 1845.

Still being maintained to perform its original role is this endearing little lodge, though now at the entrance to the police barracks rather than the old infirmary and physician's residence. An enduring piece of townscape, single-storey, built in rubble stone off a cut-stone plinth with brick dressings to openings. The windows are narrow sashes set in round-headed recesses, a single bay to the road and two to the approach, whilst that to the rear lights a room within a canted exterior below an equivalent roof, which is otherwise hipped with carved soffit modillion brackets, though now lacking its chimney-stack.

52. LONGFORD JAIL GOVERNOR'S HOUSE, Longford; *c.* 1870; architect not known.
A quite sophisticated little single-storey porter's lodge built off an L-plan in a type of High Victorian Tudor Gothic style, faced in very fine coursed limestone. Both leading gables are skew-tabled with moulded kneelers, that to the avenue containing a pair of round-headed narrow lights below a Tudor relieving arch, whilst that to the road has a triple window. The elevation addressing the house has two bipartite windows with arrowhead lintels. To the ridge is a tall,

banded brick chimney-stack. In the internal angle is a glazed hallway of the twentieth century. Located at the gate to the imposing governor's residence, which later became 'Leamore Park' in its own right and now serves as a day centre.

53. LONGFORD PRESBYTERIAN CHURCH, Longford; pre-1914; *demolished.*
The old Meeting House on Battery Road and its later porter's lodge, built after 1837, are things of the past, both having been removed in the 1950s.

54. LONGFORD UNION WORKHOUSE, Longford; *c.* 1842; architect probably George Wilkinson; *demolished.*
An institution that opened for admissions on 24 March 1842, one of 163 such workhouses built around the country at this time, for the design of most of which the English architect George Wilkinson was responsible. Longford workhouse was burnt down in 1909.
IB (3 April 1909); O'Connor 1995.

55. MEELTANAGH, Keenagh; pre-1837; *demolished.*
The lodge to the property had been removed by 1914. The house in 1854 was occupied by Richard Taylor.
Griffith 1848–60.

56. MIDDLETON, Lanesborough; pre-1837; *demolished.*
An estate originally belonging to Wesley Harman, from whom it was purchased in 1764 by Henry Montfort (1709–76) and sold by his great-grandson of the same name *c.* 1837. The gatekeeper's lodge had gone by 1914.
IFR.

57. MILL VIEW, Carrickboy; pre-1914; *demolished.*
A property occupied in 1854 by Francis Diamond.
Griffith 1848–60.

58. MONASCALLAGHAN, Keenagh; pre-1837; *demolished.*
Another property of Colonel Wray Palliser of Derryluskan, Co. Tipperary, in the mid-nineteenth century, the gate lodge to which had gone by 1914.

59. MONEYLAGAN COTTAGE, Longford; *c.* 1845; *demolished.*
A gatehouse identified in the 1854 valuation as belonging to the property of General James Hey, leasing from John Crawford. Dr Forbes Crawford is recorded here in 1837, the date of the first OS map, on which no gatehouse is identifiable.

Lewis 1837; Griffith 1848–60.

60. MOSSTOWN, Keenagh (3).
Originally the seventeenth-century ancestral home of the Newcomen family; sadly, their huge plain mansion was demolished in 1959, and its main lodge has fared little better.

Principal entrance; *c.* 1760.

Irish Architectural Archive

Irish Architectural Archive

Sir Thomas Newcomen, the 8th baronet, succeeded his father in 1759 and was probably responsible for this quite unique prelude to the big house. It was a single-storey Georgian Gothic structure built in pitted rubble masonry, with bowed ends containing lancet-headed openings with Y-traceried windows below a steeply pitched thatched roof. One bowed front projects beyond the straight right-hand wing wall, which is finished in large pebble-dash. In complete contrast are the noble sophisticated carriage gate pillars in limestone ashlar with moulded plinths and projecting corniced cappings, which bear a pair of rather grand eagles. Alas, the lodge lies a shell. Traditionally it once served as a Methodist chapel, where inevitably John Wesley is supposed to have preached.

Sir Thomas Newcomen died without male issue in 1789 and the property passed to Alexander Crawford Kingston, whose descendant, Arthur Johnston Kingston, added a large rear lodge.

Secondary entrance; *c.* 1830.

A 1½-storey Tudor Picturesque-style gabled lodge, built originally off an L-plan but since much added to, is finished in modern roughcast with cast-iron latticed casement windows. The shallow-pitched roof has curved ornamental bargeboards and two pairs of diagonally set tall chimney-stacks. Its generous proportions are explained by its once functioning additionally as a laundry. Occupied and beautifully situated by the Royal Canal and an aqueduct.

Mill entrance; *c.* 1865.
At the head of the north-western approach, preceded by a charming bridge crossing by the considerable remains of an old flour mill, is the latest of the lodges built for Arthur Johnston Kingston. On an L-plan formed by a single-storey projection below a catslide roof. From the leading elevation of the main rectangular 1½-storey block, both front and rear elevations gabled with two-window bays below oculi lighting attic rooms. The original rendered finish has been removed to reveal a pleasant rubble-built fabric with brick-dressed openings. Modernised with replacement windows and a lean-to elevation out of sight.

Burke's *Dormant and extinct peerages* (1883); English 1973; IAA photographs (7/62 Z 2&3); NIAH.

MOSTRIM RECTORY (see EDGEWORTHSTOWN RECTORY)

61. MOUNT JESSOP, Longford (2)
An old estate of the Jessop family until about 1850. Both the house and its lodges, dating from before 1837, have been demolished.

62. MOYGH, Ballymahon; *c.* 1830
A Regency house and its gate lodge built by Molyneux William Shuldham (1784–1846), of the family whose main seat was at Ballymulvey (*q.v.*). A single-storey standard lodge, now derelict and approaching ruin. With a fabric of rubble and brick dressings, it was finished in harling with a brick eaves corbel course to its hipped roof. Square carriage pillars flanked by postilion openings with flat coping arches in straight screen walls, terminating in convex quadrants beyond.

LGI (1904); Casey and Rowan 1993.

63. MULLAGH, Longford; *c.* 1800.
A single-storey porter's lodge with a symmetrical three-bay front in limewashed harled walls below a high hipped roof, with

stone eaves course, half-conical to the avenue over a bowed end elevation. Derelict. A property of the Kennedy family in the late eighteenth and early nineteenth centuries.

64. NEWCASTLE, Ballymahon (3).
A house built *c.* 1750 which, after the death of the Very Revd Cutts Harman in 1784, seemed destined never again to be the main residence of the senior member of a family, passing as it did through the failure of male issue to three of Ireland's most prominent ones. Dean Harman's nephew, Laurence Parsons-Harman (1749–1807), who inherited the property, was created earl of Rosse of Birr Castle, Co. Offaly (*q.v.*), a year before his death, upon which his widow lived here until her demise in 1838, when the place was effectively a dower house. She was a daughter of the 1st earl of Kingston of Mitchelstown Castle, Co. Cork. Through the marriage of her daughter in 1799 to the 1st Viscount Lorton of Rockingham, Co. Roscommon, the place eventually became that family's secondary residence and home to their second son, the Hon. Laurence Harman King-Harman (1816–75), who from about 1840 was responsible for many improvements on the estate, including the building of two gate lodges. The significance of this genealogy is that it points to the identity of the architects responsible. The Forgney parish church nearby, with its 1813 front, is very similar to St Beadh's Church by the Rockingham demesne. James Pain worked at the latter and with his brother George Richard Pain in designing the vast Mitchelstown Castle, so both branches of the King-Harman family would have been familiar with these erstwhile pupils of John Nash.

'Forge Cottage' lodge; *c.* 1840; architect possibly James Pain.

Opposite the entrance on the eastern approach and so called after the now-ruined neighbouring smithy is this standard gabled 1½-storey cottage with a pair of gablets breaking the eaves over attic windows and, below, a central single-storey gabled porch

64. Newcastle, church lodge.

with pointed-arched entrance having a smooth surround in roughcast walls. Over the entrance is a cruciform motif in perforated bricks and to each side a minuscule arrowhead opening. Later serrated bargeboards and modern plastic windows with squared lead-effect panes. The lodge has the feel of a John Nash-designed cottage at the entrance to the Moccas estate in Herefordshire. The entrance gates have gone.

Church lodge; *c.* 1840; architect perhaps James Pain.

Located behind an extensive railed entrance sweep of concave quadrants and six slender stone pillars with outsized four-sided pedimented cappings is this delicious Georgian-style cottage, standard single-storey but of generous proportions below a hipped roof. Roughcast with creeper, it has pretty cast-iron lozenge-pattern glazed windows below elliptical arches on each side of a bowed projection with panelled double-leaf doorway below a round-headed spoked fanlight; flanking narrow slit lights. To both end elevations are further bowed projections with three-bay six-over-six sash windows; rear return. Immaculately maintained at the now-redundant southern access.

North lodge; pre-1837.

The oldest of the three lodges, much altered and extended, with two distinctive and incongruous features. One is an Eastern-style cast-iron highly decorative porch of *c.* 1880, just like that to the Edgeworthstown House lodge (*q.v.*), with paired barley-twist columns, Corinthian capitals and under-panels. Rosette cresting and a spiky finial

crown its lead roof hips. To each overthrow is a personalised monogram, probably of Wentworth Henry King-Harman, who inherited the property in 1875, and his wife, Annie Kate Smith. In contrast, the doorway has an Adam-style surround of modern creation, with paterae, vases, swags and husks. Pathetic remains of a gatescreen in the shape of an ashlar carriage pillar with moulded plinth and cornice capping with simple ball finial.

LGI (1904); *BPB* (1929); Davis 1960; Casey and Rowan 1993.

65. NEWTOWNBOND, Edgeworthstown; pre-1837; *demolished.*

A property of the Bond family, the porter's lodge to which was opposite its entrance gates.

66. PARK PLACE, Ballymahon; *c.* 1830.

A once-proud little park, in the late eighteenth and early nineteenth centuries of Revd Robert Moffett, rector of Tashinny, of which little survives but for a small square single-storey single-bay cottage in harled rubble and big cut limestone quoins, having a multi-square-paned cast-iron casement window with centre pivot opener; chimney-stack to one gable. Probably built by John R. Robinson of Lisglassick (*q.v.*), who was here in 1837.

Leet 1814; Lewis 1837; Leslie and Crooks 2008.

67. RATHCLINE, Lanesborough (2).

South lodge; *c.* 1830.

A much-altered structure, with only a Tudor-style label moulding to a window in a flat-arched recess to suggest its age but not its original form.

North lodge; pre-1837.

Now a four-bay single-storey gabled building with a projecting flat-roofed hall. Modest, derelict and sited outside its entrance, which has a pair of good squat rusticated pillars. This entrance seems to have been shared with neighbouring Salisbury Lodge. An estate recorded as early as 1824 to be that of Luke White, the third son of a father of the same name, from Woodlands, or Luttrellstown, Co. Dublin (*q.v.*), who died unmarried in 1854.

Pigot 1824; *BPB* (1929).

68. RATHMORE, Ballymahon; pre-1837; *demolished.*

A property in 1837 of Robert C. Barber.

Lewis 1837.

69. RICHFORT, Ardagh (2).

The lodges to a seat of the Richardson family have gone. Both were in place by 1837, that to the north having been removed before 1914. Surviving is a pair of big square limestone gate pillars.

70. ST ALBANS, Longford; *c.* 1850.

The manse is first recorded *c.* 1850 as home to the Presbyterian minister Revd Samuel McCutcheon. Its lodge, what remains of it, seems also to have been shared with neighbouring Kirkview. It lies a roofless shell with a not-quite-symmetrical three-bay elevation to the road, its opening sealed up in rubble walls, the windows wider than high. The house has a decorative cast-iron porch like those to the Edgeworthstown (*q.v.*) and Newcastle (*q.v.*) gate lodges.

Slater 1856.

ST ANNE'S RECTORY (see CLONGISH RECTORY)

71. ST MEL'S SEMINARY, Longford; *c.* 1865; architect probably John Bourke.

The great Italianate institution on the hill, built to designs of John Bourke of Dublin, was opened in September 1865 to 48 boarders and 25 day-boys. Bourke's commission may have included plans for the lodged entrance. The relatively modest single-storey standard rendered hip-roofed porter's lodge with a gabled hall breakfront flanked by six-over-six sash windows contrasts with a considerably grander

National Inventory of Architectural Heritage

gatescreen. Railed ogee quadrants are contained by four Classical stone pillars with recessed panels and ball finials.

IAA; NIAH; Williams 1994.

SALISBURY LODGE (see RATHCLINE)

72. SHRULE, Ballymahon; *c.* 1860.
A standard structure, tiny but lofty, built of stone with cream brick dressings and stone eaves corbel course to its hipped roof; door with mouth-organ fanlight. Well maintained and within a stone's throw of the flour-mill owner's house, in 1854 of Michael Murtagh.

Griffith 1848–60.

73. SHRULE RECTORY, Ballymahon; pre-1837; *demolished.*
The gatekeeper's lodge, which had been removed before 1914, may have been contemporary with the glebe house, which was built in 1813, 'a good residence', by Revd Francis Maguire (1775/6–1844), rector here from 1806 until his death.

Mason 1814–19; Lewis 1837; Leslie and Crooks 2008.

74. TEMPLEMICHAEL RECTORY, Longford; pre-1837; *demolished.*
'The glebe-house is beautifully situated about half a mile from the church, and near the river Camlin, which flows through the demesne; it was built in 1760, and for its improvements various sums were expended between 1763 and 1795, amounting together to £2314', a sum which may have covered an eighteenth-century gate lodge. The first incumbent was Revd John Ryder, from 1756 until his death in 1791.

Beaufort Revd D.A.; (1787); Lewis 1837; Leslie and Crooks 2008.

75. TIR LICKEEN, Ballymahon; pre-1837; *demolished.*
A mansion built by Lord Annaly of the first creation was in the late eighteenth century home to Henry Gore, after which it was occupied by Matthew Crawford. By 1914 both the house and its lodge, situated opposite the entrance, were in ruins.

Taylor and Skinner 1778; 1969 [1783]; Wilson 1803; Mason 1814–19; *Parliamentary Gazetteer* (1845).

76. WHITE HILL, Edgeworthstown; pre-1837/pre-1882; *demolished.*
An estate to which Henry Bevan Wilson-Slator (1785–1857) succeeded in 1832 on the death of his father-in-law, previously of this place. He duly assumed the additional surname of Slator and perhaps replaced the gate lodge to the property. That successor is shown on later OS maps as a carriage archway flanked by accommodation, described by Bence-Jones in 1978 as an 'Imposing castellated gatehouse', since having gone the way of its big house, unrecorded.

LGI (1904); Bence-Jones 1988.

COUNTY LOUTH

1. ANAVERNA, Ravensdale (2).
Beautifully set on the slopes of Black Mountain is the house of Baron McClelland, built *c.* 1790 to designs of Thaddeus Gallagher. It has two pleasant porters' lodges placed opposite their gates.

South gate; *c.* 1800; architect possibly Thaddeus Gallagher.
A single-storey three-bay hip-roofed cottage with harled walls in which are two tripartite Wyatt windows that help to date its construction.

North gate; *c.* 1850.

After Baron McClelland's death, his widow lived on here until the property was acquired about 1850 by Acheson Thompson, who probably added this second lodge. Single-storey standard with foiled bargeboards to shallow main gables and that to the breakfront hall, which has a segmentally arched doorway below a wide flimsy label moulding. On each side, in harled walls, are wide tripartite windows. Across the road is a quite charming vast iron gate sweep comprised of urn-topped gate piers framed by *étoile*-topped latticed screens terminating in fan stops.

Tempest 1920; Casey and Rowan 1993.

2. ARDEE, Ardee; pre-1835; *demolished.*
A lodge to an estate of the Ruxton family.

3. ARDEE MENTAL HOSPITAL, Ardee; *c.* 1933; *demolished.*
A short-lived gatekeeper's lodge to St Brigid's Mental Hospital, an extensive red-brick complex designed by H.T. Wright in 1933.

Casey and Rowan 1993.

4. ARTHURSTOWN, Tallanstown; *c.* 1810.
An awkward single-storey standard lodge, its high eaves to steeply pitched hipped roof catsliding briefly over a central breakfront, flanked by a pair of large square windowless openings in harled stone walls. Built by Thomas William Filgate, descended from that family of nearby Lisrenny (*q.v.*).

LGI (1904).

5. ASHVILLE, Ardee; *c.* 1845.
Opposite the gates is this commodious and conspicuous gatehouse, two-storey, three-bay

under a steeply hipped roof and a full-height gabled central projection with side-entry doorway and modern continuous bracket bargeboards. Rendered with Irish pilaster quoins, matching those on the main house, and striking bipartite casement windows with most ornate cast-iron octagonal glazing pattern. The latticed chinoiserie cast-iron gates are carried on similar 'cage' posts with very fine anthemion motifs over. There are like gates at Red House (*q.v.*) nearby. A property in 1854 of Laurence Kieran.

Griffith 1848–60.

6. ATHCLARE, Dunleer; pre-1835; *demolished.*
A bungalow now occupies the site of the lodge to a seat in the early nineteenth century of the Plunketts.

7. BALLINREASK, Drogheda; *c.* 1820.
A nice little two-roomed single-storey lodge being maintained as a store, with roses trained up its harled walls below an almost pyramidal roof. Minute narrow windows to each side of the front door. Harled convex quadrant walls frame simple low ashlar gate pillars that lead to the lovely single-storey Georgian villa, in 1854 occupied by Samuel McClintock. Later in the nineteenth century renamed 'Beltichbourne Cottage'.

Griffith 1848–60.

8. BALL'S GROVE, Drogheda; *c.* 1810; architect not known; *demolished.*
Surviving is this most sophisticated of entrance gateways, a grand Classical triple archway in fine punched limestone ashlar comprised of a central round-headed carriage opening crowned by a pediment, the tympanum of which contains the Ball family arms, over *oeil-de-boeuf* niches flanking the spandrels above a Greek key-pattern impost course which continues across wrought-iron gates in flat-arched postilion openings. One wing wall contains an oval plaque inscribed 'The Bell'. To the central keystone is an iron lantern bracket. Built in 1801 as a gift from the grateful Drogheda town corporation to John Ball, MP for the borough, in grateful recognition in 1799 of his stance against the Act of Union. This handsome structure now stands out of context, having lost its tree-

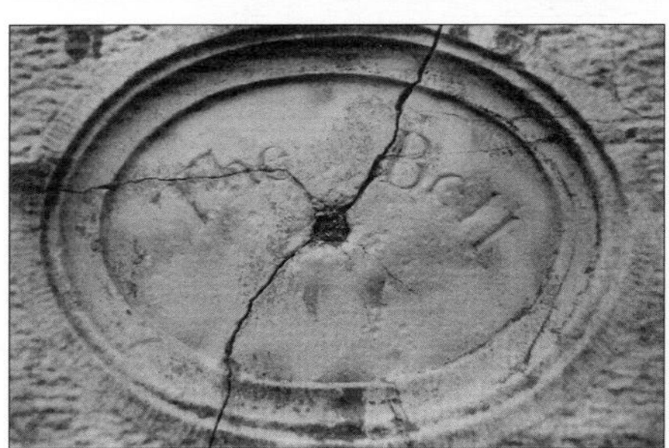

lined driveway and accompanying gate lodge, which was sited forward of its gates; it was a relatively modest rubble-built single-storey hip-roofed cottage, with a two-window bay elevation addressing the approach. The archway design seems to owe something to that at Summerhill, Co. Meath (*q.v.*).

Craig and Glin 1970; Bence-Jones 1988; Garner 1986; Casey and Rowan 1993; Howley 1993.

9. BALLYBARRACK, Dundalk; pre-1835; *demolished.*
A lost lodge to a property in the mid-nineteenth century of the Coleman family.

10. BALLYMAKENNY RECTORY, Drogheda; *c.* 1800.
A typically spare Church of Ireland rectory lodge with no hint of architectural pretension, despite the involvement of Thomas Cooley and Francis Johnston in the design of the church. This is nevertheless a delightful ensemble of entrance, mature trees and cottage, disregarding the intrusions of an appallingly sited telegraph pole and modern windows. Single-storey, two-window bay to the road, in limewashed harling below a steeply hipped roof, the lodge sits forward of

the gates. It would have been added not long after the building of the rectory in 1785 under the patronage of Lord Primate Richard Robinson, 1st Lord Rokeby of nearby Rokeby Hall (*q.v.*), and during the incumbency of Revd John Graves. The house is now in private ownership under the name of 'East Rand'.

Lewis 1837; Leslie 1911; Malcomson 2003.

11. BALLYMASCANLON, Dundalk (3).
A plain Georgian house transformed into the present Tudor-style manor house after it passed in 1854 from the ownership of James Wolfe McNeill through the incumbered estates court, with which sale went three attractive gate lodges.

Main entrance; *c.* 1850; architect not known.

A charming standard 1½-storey English Picturesque cottage with a projecting porch having a segmentally headed opening and all gables decorated with carved foiled bargeboards. Below Tudor label mouldings are pretty bipartite casement windows with wooden latticed glazing pattern, in white harled walls which have recently been stripped in modernisation to reveal the fabric of brick porch and dressings to rubble walls. Attractive wooden picket fencing and octagonal carriage posts.

Secondary entrance; pre-1835/*c.* 1840.
On the southern approach by a pretty terrace of estate cottages is this delightfully naive Picturesque cottage, two-window bay to the avenue in harled walls and presenting an eccentric gabled front to the road, with simple wavy bargeboards above an attic casement window, below which, asymmetrically placed, is a single-storey canted bay window with equivalent roof and lattice-paned lights. The wavy barges continue as fascia boards. A replacement lodge now abandoned, overgrown and doomed.

Rear entrance; *c.* 1840.
A very fine late Georgian-style villa outside the gates. Standard 1½-storey with a shallow-pitched roof having high oversailing eaves with paired brackets. In harled walls are six-over-six sash windows on each side of an original panelled front door below a spoked round-arched fanlight. Occupied.

11. Ballymascanlon, rear entrance.

Lyons 1993; Casey 2002.

BALLYMASCANLON CHURCH OF IRELAND CHURCH (see ST MARY'S)

12. BARMEATH CASTLE, Dunleer; *c.* 1830.

Irish Architectural Archive

Sir Patrick Bellew (1798–1866), the future 1st baron, succeeded to the old Pale castle and its mid-eighteenth-century additions on the death of his father in 1827 and, after taking a Spanish bride in 1830, embarked upon a major transformation of the house into a rambling neo-Norman mansion to designs of Thomas Smith of Hertfordshire. The works on the demesne extended to the provision of a new entrance, which presents itself to the public as a pair of plain single-storey astylar boxes but they face the park with three-bay symmetrical Georgian Gothic elevations. The present Lord Bellew opines that this disparity arose because, his being a Roman Catholic landed family, it was considered politic not to give offence to Protestant neighbours and to confine any ostentation to within. These single-roomed 'day and night' lodges, labelled 'Sea Lodge' and 'Dunleer Lodge' on the 1911 OS map, have lancet-headed openings with Y-traceried windows in harled walls below hipped roofs. Almost square on plan, they are linked by a modest gatescreen of two postilion openings and a pair of carriage pillars with concave cappings. All sadly overgrown and derelict.

BPB (1929); Casey and Rowan 1993; IAA photograph (61/36).

13. BEAULIEU, Drogheda (4).
In an Irish context this is the most singular of grand houses, apparently dating from the 1660s, and is a property peculiar in the proximity of public roads to it, the porters' lodges being but a stone's throw away, one of which was of particular interest. Samuel Lewis in 1837 found '... the seat of the Rev. A.J. Montgomery, was built by the lady of Sir H. Tichborne: it is a stately mansion, situated in an extensive and finely planted demesne, bounded on the south by the Boyne, and contains an ornamental sheet of water; a very handsome entrance lodge has been recently erected.' It is highly unusual for him to have taken notice of a gate lodge unless something exceptional excited him. Indeed, only seven years later John d'Alton was moved to record that 'on grounds near the shore, a handsome Swiss-cottage has lately been built'. The object of their admiration was the lodge next to that 'ornamental sheet of water'.

Pond lodge; *c.* 1830; architect not known; *demolished.*
This was the most desirable and decorative of Picturesque English cottages in the pioneering P.F. Robinson manner—indeed, it may have had as its source design no. 4 in his *Rural architecture or designs for ornamental cottages*, which first appeared in 1823, its popularity taking it to four further editions. It was 1½-storey, raised off a fairly regular plan, and owed its irregular outline to ornamental gables with robust carved foiled and cusped bargeboards variously perforated by trefoils and mouchettes. The attic floor was jettied on chunky wooden corbels, one gable displaying a lancet light, the other a canted oriel window, transomed with delightful trefoiled heads. The multi-paned ground-floor casement windows were sheltered beneath a charming wrap-around single-storey verandah, its lean-to hipped roof carried on rustic branched tree trunks,

Buvinda

13. Beaulieu, pond lodge.

Garry

broken only by a little gabled porch with a Tudor-style entrance archway. To one side was a monumental chimney-stack, partly obscured by a single-storey extension. A splendid cottage, obviously created to accommodate rather more than a lowly gatekeeper. Indeed, Griffith in 1855 reveals a hefty £10 valuation and its occupant to have been Revd Edward G. Groome, the lodge serving as his rectory for the parish. Tragically, this was all removed in 1980 after vandals set fire to the roof.

Fort lodge; pre-1825; *demolished.*
North-west of the mansion the 1907 OS map shows a structure, circular or perhaps octagonal on plan, of which there remains no trace in the undergrowth.

Drogheda lodge; pre-1855; *demolished.*
Erected after 1835, its gate porter in 1855 was Henry Reid.

Garden lodge; *c.* 1790.

Beryl Dean

Presenting a blind front to the road and standing sentinel over a carriage doorway in the garden wall is this brick-built two-storey gatehouse, square on plan, its upper floor once slate-clad and containing Georgian Gothic pointed-arched windows. The pyramidal roof, now felted, is 'blunted', suggesting the loss of an ornamental lantern, ventilator feature or belfry. Alongside is a gabled single-storey adjunct with a lean-to multi-paned bay window facing the garden. Presumably built for Revd Robert Montgomery (1754–1825), to whom the property had descended from the Tichbornes by a series of marriages, he having wedded the daughter of Thomas Tipping (1735–76) of Beaulieu and Bellurgan Park (*q.v.*). It was his son, Revd Alexander Johnston Montgomery (1782–1856), who would have been responsible for the three lodges, since lost.

Lewis 1837; d'Alton 1844; Griffith 1848–60; *LGI* (1904); *Country Life* (15 and 22 Jan. 1959); Casey and Rowan 1993; Garry 1996; Buvinda 1999.

14. BEECH GROVE, Drogheda; *c.* 1845; *demolished.*
A lodge built by Charles White sometime between the 1835 OS map and the valuation of 1854.

Griffith 1848–60.

15. BELLURGAN PARK, Ballymascanlon; *c.* 1840.
A long, plain, single-storey standard gatekeeper's lodge with harled walls below a hipped roof. It looks considerably older but does not appear on the 1835 OS map. Built for Edward Tipping.

BELLVIEW (see CARSTOWN)

BELTICHBOURNE COTTAGE (see BALLINREASK)

16. BELTICHBOURNE, Drogheda; *c.* 1860; architect probably William Caldbeck.
A pretty mid-Victorian porter's lodge, probably similar to how that to Williamstown

(*q.v.*) used to look and presumably by William Caldbeck for Francis William Leland, timber merchant of Drogheda. Single-storey standard in pleasant mellow brickwork, having a semi-octagonal hall projection with sidelights. Small round-headed windows are set in flat-arched recesses. Hip-roofed, it depends for decorative effect on a jolly embracing serrated fascia board, like bunting. There is a paired brick chimney-stack with stone band and capping. The gatescreen is equally ornate but Classical in feel, its cast-iron gate pillars with anthemion and palmette motifs. These are linked by railed ogee quadrants to outer stone pillars with semicircular cappings framing more anthemion features. Terminating in delightful fan railings.

17. BLACK HALL, Termonfeckin; pre-1835.
A very fine early nineteenth-century villa in the manner of Francis Johnston, built for George Pentland, the contemporary lodge to which is an overgrown ruin. In harled stone, with gables tall enough for it to have been 1½-storey. Its condition defies further description.

Pigot 1824; Casey and Rowan 1993.

18. BOYNE MILLS, Drogheda; *c.* 1865; architect possibly John McCurdy.
A very fine industrial complex from *c.* 1865 of the Boyne Mill Manufacturing Co. Ltd of Benjamin Whitworth and Brothers. The Italianate complex of cotton mills is comprised of a stately brick chimney in the guise of a Doric column, grand main factory building and its porter's lodge of equal consequence, prominent as it fronts the road

with its asymmetrical Italianate façade in a cubic box with pyramidal roof and bracketed eaves band over distinctive quarry-faced limestone, which contrasts with the smooth dressings. The main front displays a semicircular-arched doorway of noble proportions with impost blocks and keystone, alongside a tripartite window in the form of a round-headed arcade. The Whitworth Hall in the town is a building commissioned by Benjamin Whitworth from W.J. Barre after an architectural competition which also drew an entry from John McCurdy. The mill complex buildings have all the forthright characteristics of the latter's work.

Garner 1986; Casey and Rowan 1993.

19. BRAGANSTOWN, Castlebellingham; pre-1835; *demolished.*
Revd Anthony Garstin succeeded his father, Christophilus Garstin (1766–1821), the likely builder of the now-missing lodge. The Mansfieldstown rector added offices in 1824, and in the 1840s transformed the old Georgian residence into a Tudor Gothic manor house to designs of Thomas Smith of Hertfordshire. No evidence survives to show whether these improvements extended to the estate entrance.

LGI (1904); Leslie 1911.

20. BRIGHTON VILLA, Dundalk; 1886.
A tall-eaved hip-roofed single-storey three-bay lodge, symmetrical but for its off-centre chimney-stack. Probably originally brick-faced, now rendered over, with Irish pilaster quoins to reflect the main house, which is now 'Windwood Lodge Nursing Home', having been built in 1867 by Henry Harden, its lodge added later by pawnbroker James Dougan.

21. CARRICKEDMOND, Forkhill (2).
Both lodges, to a property in the early nineteenth century of Colonel John Ogle, dated from prior to 1835 and have gone, suffering the same fate as the big house.

Tempest 1920.

22. CARSTOWN, Termonfeckin (2).
A remarkable old house of the Plunkett family, who built it in 1612, which by the eighteenth/early nineteenth century was owned by the Brabazons. After the death in 1828 of Philip Brabazon, also of Mornington, Co. Meath (*q.v.*), the property passed to Henry Chester, who added the two gate lodges, one of which has proved considerably less durable than the surviving house.

Secondary lodge; *c.* 1850.
Opposite its gates, built in a pleasant orange brick, is this standard single-storey structure with a hipped roof, atop which is a pair of brick diagonally set chimney-stacks; wide windows to each side of an unusual projecting gabled hall.

Principal lodge; *c.* 1850; architect not known.

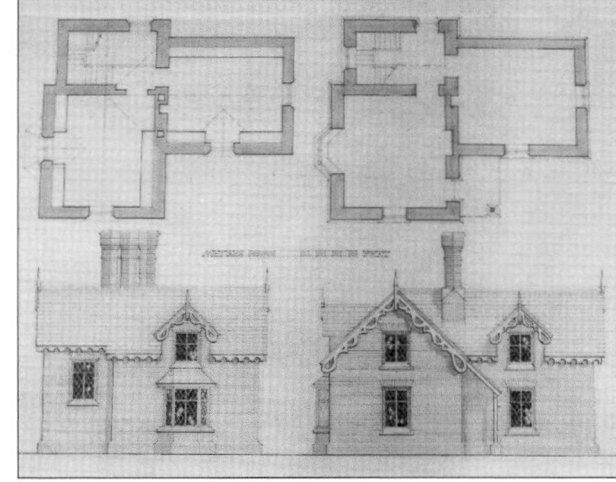

A most conspicuous and once-desirable 1½-storey English Tudor Picturesque-style cottage, which despite being two-up/two-down is of considerable size with a generous staircase, built in Flemish bond mellow brickwork off a T-plan. Of irregular outline, its gables were decorated with carved continuous bracket bargeboards perforated with little quatrefoil motifs. To the road was a large canted bay window, whilst to one internal angle at the rear the roof catslides to form a porch over the front door, and in the other is a lean-to outhouse. Its crowning glory is a towering trio of diagonally set brick corbelled pots. Sadly and mysteriously, it now lies in an advanced stage of dilapidation.

Casey and Rowan 1993.

23. CASTLEBELLINGHAM, Castlebellingham (2).
Originally the ancestral seat of the Bellinghams, it took on its present castellated appearance through a series of remodellings in the nineteenth century, at least the first of which in 1834 was by Thomas Smith of Hertfordshire, who had a considerable clientele in County Louth. As it was one member of the family, Sir Alan Edward Bellingham, 3rd baronet (1800–89), who had inherited the estates in 1826, it would not be unrealistic to suppose that he kept faith in his architect to provide a design for an appropriate introductory entrance at the far end of the old straight avenue on an axis with his front door.

Front entrance; *c.* 1850; architect possibly Thomas Smith.
A conspicuous landmark for travellers on what was once the hectic main Belfast–Dublin road, it offers, with the neighbouring church and the 1826 Elizabethan-style alms cottages, a wonderful village-scape. It is a hefty but rather two-dimensional structure in contrasting masonry, heavy with toothed dressings, label-moulded slit windows and mock machicolated crenellations. This castellated gatehouse is comprised of a central elliptically arched carriage gateway,

with hood moulding and sculpted foliated dripstones, below three windows to an upper room under a battlemented rampart. On each side is a pair of three-storey square towers with postilion doorways, cross arrowloops and stepped castellated parapets. Flanking these are two single-storey gatekeeper's rooms, but beyond these the original convex quadrant walls have given way to rerouted access to what is now a hotel beyond.

Rear entrance; *c.* 1840.
A standard single-storey roughcast structure with an oversailing hipped roof, lacking any fancy features.

Lewis 1837; *BPB* (1929); Bence-Jones 1988; Casey and Rowan 1993.

24. CHARLEVILLE, Drumcar; *c.* 1850/*c.* 1910.

A single-storey standard lodge with shallow-hipped roof, certainly built after 1835 following the death of Lieut.-Col. Tisdall, when the property was acquired by Matthew O'Reilly Dease. Its precise date is disguised by an early twentieth-century make-over of roughcast walls with smooth rendered bands and dressings to steel window casements. There is a later hall projection and an extension to the rear, to form a double pile.

LGI (1904).

25. CHRISTIANSTOWN, Mansfieldstown; pre-1835; *demolished.*
An estate in the early nineteenth century of James Bell.

CHURCH PARK (see SILVER PARK)

26. CLERMONT PARK, Blackrock (3).

Main entrance; pre-1835; *demolished.*
The access at the eastern gate was guarded by a pair of lodges sited obliquely. By 1911 only one survived at what became known as the 'Green Gate'.

North entrance; *c.* 1835.

A welcome survivor is this 1½-storey gabled cottage with front door to the left-hand side of a three-bay front in roughcast finish to rubble fabric. There are some Tudor features applied in label mouldings to tiny bipartite casement windows and doorway and diagonally placed flues off a rectangular base. Occupied.

West entrance; pre-1911; *demolished.*

A demesne of the Fortescue family, Barons Clermont, which by 1920 had been sold to the estate commissioners and broken up to be divided amongst small farmers.

Tempest 1920.

27. CLONMORE RECTORY, Dunleer; *c.* 1792; architect possibly Francis Johnston.
Just as the glebe house built in 1782 to the designs of Francis Johnston for £905.4.11 is modest, so too is its gate lodge, probably of slightly later date. Standard single-storey with hipped gables, that to the road blind,

whilst the avenue front has two-over-two sash windows on each side of a sheeted door in roughcast walls. Two punched ashlar carriage pillars with concave cappings and unusual corbelled friezes. Built during the incumbency of Revd John Gibson. Johnston seems to have set up an office at Rokeby Hall (*q.v.*), where he was employed, for there are designs of cottages for Clonmore by him from there dated 1792 and 1793.

Lewis 1837; Leslie 1911; *IGS Bulletin* (1987); Casey and Rowan 1993.

28. CONVENT OF MERCY, Ardee; *c.* 1858; architect John Neville.

An apt prelude to the Convent complex within, designed by the Louth County Surveyor John Neville, here in a newfangled Pugin manner, a deviation from his more familiar Italianate style. It is 1½-storey with steep gables decorated with continuous bracket bargeboards and ornamental carved fascia boards, which are set off nicely by rubble facings with limestone trimmings. Arrowhead window to attic room, two-window bay front to the avenue and entrance door out of sight. To the ridge is a paired chamfered stone chimney-stack. A distinctive pair of octagonal limestone carriage pillars with quatrefoil decorated friezes and layered cappings support good chunky contemporary fleur-de-lis-topped gates and matching railings framed by rubble quadrants, the left-hand one of which is broken by a little gabled, arched pedestrian gate.

Bassett 1886; Casey and Rowan 1993; Williams 1994.

29. CORBOLLIS, Mansfieldstown (3).
The sad remains of a once-fine demesne built up in the late eighteenth and early nineteenth centuries by the Lee family, later the Lee-Normans. The main entrance is ruinous, its lodge, like the big house, has gone and another lies derelict.

Main entrance; *c.* 1830; *demolished.*
A single-storey standard harled lodge below a hipped roof, its sheeted doorway flanked

by a pair of eight-over-eight square-paned sash windows. A plain affair when compared to its gatescreen, which was notable for its fine railings and matching gates, those to the carriageway hung on a pair of trabeated postilion opening archways in ashlar alongside. To each extremity were pillars with recessed panels. A pleasant group of structures, which graced a picturesque spot at a twist in the road by the Glyde River, now lost.

Tallanstown gate; *c.* 1855.
A two-roomed single-storey lodge with high eaves to its semi-octahedral roof over a canted main front, a sashed window to each face with segmental heads and moulded surrounds in rendered walls. Probably a grander replacement for an earlier pre-1835 cottage, itself now doomed.

Middle entrance; *c.* 1800/*c.* 1850.

Perhaps of two ages is this partly two-, partly 1½-storey commodious double pile with high hipped roof and wide eaves above a three-bay front. Nice little square windows to end elevations, with tiny panes in pink roughcast walls. Pretty and well maintained. All three entrances for Thomas Lee-Norman.

LGI (1904).

30. CORDERRY, Louth; pre-1835; *demolished.*
By 1911 the lodge, to a seat in 1814 and 1837 of Faithful Fortescue, had gone.

Leet 1814; Lewis 1837.

31. CORDERRY LOWER, Louth; pre-1835; *demolished.*
John McCann is noted as landowner in the townland in 1814.

Leet 1814.

32. CURRAGHBEG, Ardee; pre-1835; *demolished.*
A lodge to a property in 1814 of George Boylan, replaced by a bungalow. Later a seat of the Lewers family.

Leet 1814.

33. DARVER CASTLE, Readypenny X; pre-1835.
What may have been originally standard single-storey gabled porter's accommodation, since much extended and improved out of all recognition. Roughcast with stone quoins at the extremities. Distant from its entrance to a property from 1799 of Joseph Booth (1784–1857).

LGI (1958).

34. DELLIN, Dromiskin; pre-1911; *demolished.*
An estate created after 1835, in the mid-nineteenth century of Gordon Holmes. A short-lived lodge.

Land owners in Ireland 1876; Bassett 1886.

35. DERRYFALONE, Inniskeen; pre-1835; *demolished.*
Home in 1814 to William Foster, which had passed in 1837 to George McGusty.

Leet 1814; Lewis 1837.

36. DRAKESTOWN, Ardee; pre-1835; *demolished.*
A seat in the early nineteenth century of Nathaniel Manning.

37. DROGHEDA RAILWAY STATION, Drogheda; *c.* 1850; architect probably George Papworth.
Standard single-storey Italianate-style lodge with brick walls and limestone architraves to the windows, now 'blandified' by coats of paint. Bays defined by plain pilasters below a hipped roof. Extended by a bay to the right-hand side. Presumably part of George Papworth's commission to design the station in 1844–52.

38. DROMIN, Dunleer; *c.* 1840/*c.* 1910.

The valuation of 1854 records a gatehouse here to the property of Patrick Brennan, built after 1835, as was the main house, which looks to date from *c.* 1840. The present lodge is from the early twentieth century, a neat single-storey four-bay structure below a hipped roof with two brick chimney-stacks. Finished in roughcast with smooth-rendered plinth and eaves band, it is dominated by a typical Edwardian porch of carved wood, leaded sidelights and half-timbered-effect gable. Occupied. Earlier gatescreen of four octagonal iron posts and postilion gates terminating in nice fan features, just as at Beltichbourne (*q.v.*) and presumably from the same local iron foundry. By 1910 Dromin had become home to John Quinn.

Griffith 1848–60; *Thom's*.

39. DRUMCAR, Drumcar (2).
Both lodges dating from before 1835 to the house, flour and corn mills of John McClintock have gone.

40. DRUMCASHEL, Ardee (2).
Thomas Macan purchased Drumcashel in 1838 but it was not until 1851 that his son Richard developed the place, building himself a miniature 'castle', now a ruin, and two lodges at its gates.

West lodge; *c.* 1851; architect possibly William Caldbeck.

A derelict single-storey affair, its canted short main front facing the avenue is below a hipped roof. What are probably walls of facing brick and corbelled eaves course are now rendered over. Giving a clue to the house within is a pair of crenellated turrets as carriage pillars.

East lodge; *c.* 1851; architect possibly William Caldbeck.

Opposite the gates is a pleasant single-storey standard hip-roofed cottage constructed in rubble facings with brick to its gabled porch projection, a pair of Tudor-style diagonally placed chimney-stacks and dressings to windows of wooden latticed casements. Admirably extended in the twentieth century to the right-hand side in sympathetic manner. Around the whole is a serrated fascia board, just as at the lodges to Willamstown (*q.v.*) and Beltichbourne (*q.v.*), which may be a hallmark of architect William Francis Caldbeck.

Leslie 1908; Casey and Rowan 1993.

41. DRUMLECK, Castlebellingham; *c.* 1850.
Standard 1½-storey gabled lodge with high eaves and single-storey projecting flat-roofed hall. Plain and roughcast. Built for Francis Jeffers.

Griffith 1848–60.

42. DRUMMULLAGH, Omeath; pre-1835; *demolished.*
A delightful late Georgian villa, sometime home to the Stannus family.

43. DRUMSHALLON, Termonfeckin; *c.* 1830.
A modest single-storey gabled cottage built on an L-plan by the Henzell famly. Occupied.

44. DUNANY, Togher (3).
Another seat of the Bellingham family of Castlebellingham (*q.v.*), one of the early lodges to which, sited within the demesne, has gone.

Inner front gate; pre-1835; *demolished.*
Situated up the main avenue and probably superseded by the surviving lodge at the public road.

Outer front gate; *c.* 1845.
A 1½-storey gabled structure with its short main front to the avenue. Built in rubble stone with brick dressings, it has an attic room to the rear, there being a blind recess to the first-floor front elevation that should contain the family coat of arms. Lean-to single-storey extension to right-hand side. Derelict. Built for Alan O'Bryen Bellingham (1805–57), an eminent physician and third son of the 2nd baronet.

Rear gate; *c.* 1830.
A single-storey hip-roofed lodge, its main single-bay façade to the avenue has a bipartite window divided by a sash box, set in a flat-arched recess. Finished in roughcast, there is a later two-storey rear extension and single-storey hall projection to the right-hand side under a catslide roof. Occupied. Built in the time here of the widow of the 2nd baronet, after 1827.

BPB (1929).

45. DUNDALK DISTRICT HOSPITAL, Dundalk; *c.* 1850.
A single-storey porter's lodge on an L-plan built in random rubble facings with brick dressings and soldier arches. Plain bargeboards to gables. Occupied.

46. DUNDALK GRAMMAR SCHOOL, Dundalk; *c.* 1845.
A 1½-storey gabled lodge, its ground-floor windows set in segmentally arched recesses in rendered walls; two modern dormer windows to the leading front. There is a fine extensive cast-iron gatescreen with posts like those favoured by architect William Watson. An institution founded in 1816, with subsequent additions over that century.

Bassett 1886; Tempest 1920.

47. DUNDALK, Dundalk (2).
A town house initially of the Lords Clanbrassil and, like their country seat of Tollymore Park, Co. Down, later of the earls of Roden, to whom the properties descended by marriage. It faced the street that disguised

an ornamental demesne of 373 acres behind.

South entrance; pre-1785/pre-1863.
At the base of a lime-tree-lined avenue at Park Street, the early Brownrigg map of 1785 and the first OS map of 1835 show there to have been a lodge with cruciform plan, which suggests that it may have been of some presence. No photographs of it have come to light, and one can speculate that it may have been influenced by the remarkable Thomas Wright, the 'Wizard of Durham', who was a guest here of Lord Limerick in the early eighteenth century. Later in the century Robert Adam is known to have designed a 'Chinese bridge' for Dundalk House. This lodge by 1863 had a successor near the street, which in turn succumbed to later developments.

North entrance; pre-1863; *demolished.*
A later lodge with an L-imprint, erected after 1835 on the approach from Castletown Road, has also gone.

The house was demolished in 1911 and its demesne built over.

Lewis 1837; Fraser 1838; Malins and Glin 1976.

48. DUNGOOLY LODGE, Forkill; *c.* 1845.
A single-storey rubble-built gabled structure, part of a complex of outbuildings, lies derelict. A seat in the mid-nineteenth century of the McArdle family.

Griffith 1848–60.

EAST RAND (see BALLYMAKENNY RECTORY)

49. FAIRHILL, Dundalk; pre-1835; *demolished.*
Tucked in behind the Cambricville Brewery was a gatekeeper's lodge to a demesne that was home to a succession of occupants, from the Mercers in the late eighteenth century, the Hon. John Jocelyn MP, fourth son of the 1st earl of Roden of Dundalk House (*q.v.*), until his death in 1828, and later in the century Mrs Rebecca Foster.

Taylor and Skinner 1778; 1969 [1783]; Wilson 1803; Pigot 1824; Lewis 1837; *BPB* (1929).

50. FALMORE HALL, Dundalk; pre-1835; *demolished.*

A good late Georgian house in the John Hargrave manner, which was occupied in 1814 by James Johnston and ten years later by Francis Eastwood. At the secondary gate is a pretty iron gatescreen, its gate posts with Gothic tops, liberally decorated with anthemion motifs.

Leet 1814; Pigot 1824.

51. FANE VALLEY, Louth; *c.* 1770; *demolished.*
Sadly removed was a delightful single-storey Gothic gatekeeper's lodge with at least one ogee-arched opening in the Batty Langley manner, built in the time here of a Mr Smith, when it was called 'Grange House'. By 1814 it was the residence of the Fitzgerald family.

Taylor and Skinner 1778; 1969 [1783]; Wilson 1803; Leet 1814.

52. FAUGHART, Faughart; pre-1835; *demolished.*
A lodge to a property in 1814 and 1837 of Neill McNeill, which had gone by 1938.

Leet 1814; Lewis 1837.

FAUGHART RECTORY (see PARSONAGE)

FORT HILL (see PARSONAGE)

53. GLYDE COURT, Mansfieldstown; *c.* 1830.
At a respectful distance from the extensive late Victorian gatescreen with ogee railed quadrants is this modest standard single-storey hip-roofed porter's lodge, notable for its finish of orange facing brick. Derelict. Probably built by Thomas Fortescue, who was to become 1st Baron Clermont in 1852, in contrast with his prolonged Tudor-style mansion, previously known as 'Rosy Park'.

LG (1972); Casey and Rowan 1993.

54. GRANGE, Dromiskin; *c.* 1835.

A property in the early nineteenth century of the Byrne family which by 1837 had become home to Mrs Fortescue, perhaps the widow of Chichester Fortescue, late of Dromiskin, who was given the security of this characterful lodge by her gates. Single-storey with a hipped roof that extends over the short principal elevation to the avenue, to be carried on square wooden posts to each corner, displayed in recesses on both sides of the main living room with its bipartite casement window, which has distinctive octagonal-patterned cast-iron glazing. Greatly extended and reroofed in synthetic slates. Pretty spear-topped wooden picket railings and later Arts and Crafts gates.

Lewis 1837; *LG* (1972).

GRANGE (see FANE VALLEY)

55. GREENHILLS, Drogheda; pre-1835; *demolished.*
A seat in 1783 of Mr Ogle and in 1814 of William Sinnott, which subsequently became the residence of the Smiths of nearby Newtown (*q.v.*).

Taylor and Skinner 1778; 1969 [1783]; Leet 1814.

56. GREENMOUNT LODGE, Castlebellingham; *c.* 1825.
A seat in the early nineteenth century of Turner Macan and his son of the same name, and his grandson Major Thomas Macan, who was probably responsible for this porter's lodge. It is a sizeable single-storey structure with main short canted elevation to the avenue, which has been subsequently elongated from the original two-roomed accommodation. Plain, rendered and occupied.

Leslie 1908.

57. HEYNESTOWN RECTORY, Dromiskin; *c.* 1860.
One of the later glebe houses, its lodge unusually commodious for a Church of Ireland rectory but derelict, overgrown and barely visible. It is 1½-storey, steeply gabled and brick-built, probably dating from the incumbency of Revd Alexander Rowley Miller.

Leslie 1911.

58. HOATHSTOWN, Ardee; *c.* 1840.

Alongside the gates facing the road is a pleasant pair of single-storey three-bay symmetrical semi-detached harled estate cottages sharing a steeply hipped oversailing roof and central chimney-stack. A property in the mid-nineteenth century of the Gray family.

Griffith 1848–60.

59. HOLLYMOUNT, Dundalk; *c.* 1845; *demolished.*
A lodge built between 1835 and 1854, when the valuation identified John Hale as the immediate lessor of the place.

Griffith 1848–60.

60. JANEVILLE, Dunleer; *c.* 1820.
A single-storey lodge with a semi-octahedral roof over the canted main short front facing the avenue, which has a sheeted front door flanked by pretty little square windows, each with a pair of cast-iron margined latticed casements. Roughcast and derelict, it was a property in 1854 of Robert Harrison.

Immediately opposite is the lodged gate to Rathcoole House (*q.v.*).

Griffith 1848–60.

61. KILCURLY COTTAGE, Dundalk; *c.* 1830.
Not quite opposite the gates is this standard 1½-storey structure with rendered walls and clipped verges to its gables. Probably raised by an attic storey later in the nineteenth century; derelict. This may also have been to the site of the corn mill of Messrs McKeon, which ceased operation about 1835.

Hogg 2000.

62. KILCURLY, Dundalk; *c.* 1830.
Probably originally standard single-storey gabled, it has been subjected to many alterations over the years, including a little gabled hall to the avenue front. Now very derelict. In the first half of the nineteenth century a seat of the McKeon family.

63. KILDEMOCK RECTORY, Ardee; *c.* 1785.

A glebe house built in 1781 for the Revd Dr Disney at an expense of £1,010.1s.6d, a sum which may have covered this accompanying charming vernacular Gothic cottage. Single-storey gabled and sited with its back to the road in limewashed harled finish, a pair of square latticed cast-iron windows facing the avenue are probably a later insertion. The main elevation to the glebe is naïve two-bay, both door and window with pointed heads; lofty brick chimney-stack to the ridge. Derelict but maintained.

Lewis 1837; Leslie 1911.

64. KILLANY RECTORY, Essexford; pre-1835; *demolished.*
A lodge that was located well within Drumgarvey Glebe to a parish that lay predominantly in County Monaghan, in the diocese of Clogher. A wealthy incumbent from 1806 until his death was Revd Sir Harcourt Lees (1776–1852).

Leslie and Crooks 2006.

65. KILLINCOOLE, Readypenny X; *c.* 1845; *demolished.*
A lodge identified by the valuation of 1854 to a house, offices and land of Travers Wright, of which there is no sign on the 1835 OS map.

Griffith 1848–60.

66. KILLINCOOLE RECTORY, Readypenny X; *c.* 1835.

A delightful rustic cottage—too late to be by Francis Johnston, to whom the rectory is attributable—is single-storey of standard format with a clipped-eaves hipped roof and limewashed harled walls which have some Tudor-style features. To the ridge are the stumps of a pair of diagonally set brick chimney-stacks on a rectangular base, whilst the tiny windows are bipartite cast-iron latticed casements. There also seems to be evidence of there having been a porch to the front door. Built for the long-time incumbent Revd Joseph Wright, who was rector here (1815–48). The comparatively delicate gatescreen has perforated spear-topped cast-iron rails.

Leslie 1911; Casey and Rowan 1993.

67. KILLINEER, Drogheda; *c.* 1840; architect not known.
George Evans is the first to be recorded as living here in 1824, although the lodge and the neo-Classical house both post-date the first OS map of 1835, when the property had passed to George Harper, salt merchant of Drogheda, who was in occupation in 1854. This lodge (*below*) is the perfect introduction to its big house, reflecting as it does the rendered walls, a Doric portico with flat entablature and identical thinly margined six-over-six sash windows to each side. Of considerable presence though hardly chaste, it is standard single-storey with slender Irish pilaster quoins and lofty eaves to the steeply hipped, almost pyramidal, roof. Sometime since extended into a double pile, it lies well tended and secure behind a fine contemporary gatescreen of ogee iron railings with matching carriage and postilion gates framed by six V-jointed rusticated stone pillars with four-pedimented cappings.

Pigot 1824; Griffith 1848–60.

68. KILSARAN, Castlebellingham; pre-1835/*c.* 1850.
A nice little standard single-storey cottage under a shallow-hipped roof and gabled breakfront with scalloped carved bargeboards over the front door. Occupied, it was built by Michael Chester of the Williamstown (*q.v.*) family as a replacement for a predecessor on the site of the Bellingham family, whose house is now a shell.

Lewis 1837; Leslie 1908; Casey and Rowan 1993.

69. KILSARAN RECTORY, Castlebellingham; pre-1835/*c.* 1850; *demolished.*
A grand mid-eighteenth-century house, known initially as 'Spencer Hill' after its builder, Hannah Spencer, and subsequently purchased in 1798 as a rectory. The later porter's lodge was erected for Revd Robert Le Poer McClintock (1810–79), of the nearby Drumcar (*q.v.*) family, rector from 1835 until his death. Sited at the opposite side of the gate from its predecessor, it has suffered a like fate.

Lewis 1837; *LGI* (1904); Fleming 2001.

KNOCK ABBEY (see THOMASTOWN CASTLE)

70. LISNAWULLY FARM, Dundalk; *c.* 1905; *demolished.*
A short-lived lodge that first appears in the valuation books in 1908, built for Richard D. Cox at the entrance to his house and 136 acres.

71. LISNAWULLY, Dundalk; *c.* 1830.
A large plain single-storey gabled standard lodge with wide openings on each side of a

breakfront hallway below oversailing eaves; rendered. A property between the 1820s and 1879 of the Byrne family.

Pigot 1824; Lewis 1837; *Land owners in Ireland 1876*.

72. LISRENNY, Tallanstown (4).
The venerable old mansion of the Filgate family since the seventeenth century is still occupied, having in 1854 survived being offered for sale as an incumbered estate. In the event it was saved from this indignity and retained by William Filgate (1781–1875). He in 1830 had succeeded to 'a handsome residence in an extensive and well-planted demesne, and the grounds and hedge-rows are exceedingly well kept', as it was described seven years later, when he would have known the three early lodged gates in his hedgerows, all of which are indicated on the 1907 OS map.

'Tallanstown lodge'; pre-1835; *demolished.*
Of this structure on the northern approach there is no trace.

'Middle lodge'; pre-1835.
Recorded on the first OS map as a schoolhouse, its sorry remains can still be uncovered as a sizeable single-storey ragstone-built shell with shallow-pitched gables.

'Ardee lodge'; pre-1835; *demolished.*
A pair of lodges distantly flanking a wide entrance screen that would have marked the principal avenue on the southern approach from Dublin.

In 1916 William Filgate's granddaughter, Eileen Georgina (1879–1971), inherited the property. In 1902 she had married Richard Alexander Bailie Henry, who assumed the Filgate surname under the terms of her father's will, and they set about creating a fourth and more conspicuously sited arrival from Tallanstown, which effectively doomed its predecessors.

Modern lodge; 1922; architect not known.
Inheriting in a singularly inauspicious year, the couple must have delayed building this extraordinary entrance complex until relative calm had returned to the country. This strikingly gauche lodge is an innovative twentieth-century interpretation of the Tudor Castellated style. Single-storey standard with a crenellated parapet stepped to form a gable behind the central breakfront hall, which has a balustraded parapet of its own over a pseudo-three-centre-arched fanlit doorway in a V-jointed rusticated wall. To each side is a pair of transomed and mullioned bipartite windows with round arches framed by smooth label-moulded dressings in roughcast panels contained by quarry-faced toothed quoins. Latterly doubled in size, in like form and detailing, it is raised on a man-made terrace and approached by a flight of steps. Equally impressive and in contrast is the extensive railed gatescreen with its stylised Classical pillars, remarkable for their unsurpassed workmanship. Beautifully sculpted, four central pillars are as columns with fluted shafts rising to gadrooned cappings which frame cast-iron carriage gates and matching straight railed wings, by R. Turner of Dublin, which in turn extend as ogee quadrants to stop against square limestone pillars. These again boast gadrooned caps, their friezes with Greek key patterns and the shafts having recessed panels with unusual upturned fan motifs. All looking to date from about 1870 and appearing to be by the same designer as those at Mount Hanover, Co. Meath (*q.v.*).

LGI (1904); Lyons 1993; Wikipedia.

73. LISTOKE, Drogheda; pre-1835/*c.* 1880.

A generously sized single-storey standard late Victorian lodge built in brick, those as toothed opening dressings left unpainted for effect. The four-over-four sash windows with round-arched glazing pattern are framed in recessed panels formed by plain eaves band and pilasters. The central breakfront hall contains a fanlit double-leafed door below perforated wavy bargeboards. The soffit brackets to eaves extend to the main gable verges. On the red earthenware ridge is a pair of symmetrically placed slender chimney-stacks. Occupied, well maintained and prettily rose-embowered. Built by Major-General John Prevost Battersby (1826–1917), whose father, Colonel Francis Battersby, acquired the property about 1830, inheriting the previous lodge on the site, the gatescreen to which survives, with its convex railed quadrants meeting in similar iron postilion and carriage gates with hooped tops, palmette finials and good scroll-topped meeting rails. Probably dating from the time here of Peter van Homrish in the early nineteenth century.

Leet 1814; Pigot 1824; *LGI* (1904).

74. LOUTH HALL, Tallanstown (6).
A classic example of a palimpsest is this home to the same family spanning seven centuries, evolving from the fourteenth-century tower-house of the Plunkett family, their now great crenellated pile lying abandoned and forlorn in bare surroundings. Two of its gatekeepers' lodges remain, occupied, both of which comprise the final phase of the demesne's development.

Cherrywood Walk gate; pre-1835; *demolished.*

Lodge Wood gate; pre-1835/*c.* 1845; *demolished.*
Thankfully there survives a photograph of this thoroughly quirky affair at what was the principal entrance by the village (*below*). Replacing a predecessor at the opposing side of the avenue, it was 1½-storey, built in ragstone, harled, its gables castellated over *oeil-de-boeuf* lights, contained by finialled pilasters. At the intersection of the crested ridges was a quite unique castellated octagonal chimney-stack. A delight, its site is not improved by a twentieth-century bungalow replacement. Surviving is a good railed concave-quadrant gatescreen and matching gates with fleur-de-lis finials and

Irish Architectural Archive

swag motifs between six concave-capped pillars. Built for the 12th Lord Louth, Thomas Oliver Plunkett (1809–49), who succeeded his father of the same name in 1823.

There followed two lodges erected in the time of his grandson, Randal Pulgrim Ralph Plunkett (1868–1941), the 14th Lord Louth, after he inherited in 1883.

Spring Hill gate; pre-1835/*c.* 1885.
Succeeding an earlier lodge on an adjacent site is this elevated 1½-storey gabled lodge, a like-roofed single-storey hallway projecting from the right-hand side of its three-bay main front. Constructed in a pleasant ragstone, nicely set off by feature red-brick toothed dressings to openings with chamfered reveals.

Graveyard gate; *c.* 1885.
At a new approach formed from the south-east extremity of the demesne, identical to that at the Spring Hill gate but here imaginatively and admirably extended into a home for modern family living.

BPB (1929); IAA photograph (62/25).

MARLAY FARM (see ROKEBY HALL)

75. MILESTOWN, Kilsaran (2).
A property that was granted to Henry Bellingham and passed through many hands before being acquired in about 1830 by John Woolsey (1782–1853), who may have built its two pre-1835 porters' lodges, neither of which has survived.

LGI (1904).

76. MONASTERBOICE, Collon (3).
'... of W. Drummond Delap, Esq., who has a large estate here and is planting on an extensive scale, is undergoing great improvement, and a spacious mansion is now being erected by the proprietor.' Lewis was recording in 1837 the mere beginnings of a lengthy period of development by the long-lived William Drummond Dunlop (*c.* 1780–1875), who changed his name in 1861. He certainly made his mark on the estate, endowing it with a variety of buildings—both folly, in a tower and an archway dated 1862, and functional, in the shape of three porters' lodges. That he pursued his passion for building over the span of his life is clear from these lodges.

Main entrance; *c.* 1835; architect not known.

A lovely 1½-storey Tudor/Italianate hybrid so popular in early Victorian times, it is the most sophisticated of the lodges but ironically the least cared for, lying roofless and overgrown. Built in random stone facings which contrast well with punched ashlar plinth and dressings, the only evident elevation displays a shallow-pitched oversailing bracketed verge over a tripartite attic window above a little single-storey canted living-room bay with hefty wooden mullions and transoms containing latticed leaded lights. To the sides are window gablets, and to the ridge a brick base carrying a pair of diagonally set stacks in Tudor fashion. This seems to have replaced a much earlier Georgian drum lodge on the site.

East entrance; *c.* 1850/*c.* 1900.
What is now a commodious two-storey house has clearly been much extended from its original hip-roofed form to an irregular plan, with transomed and mullioned casement windows with mellow brick dressings in random uncoursed stone facings. Above is a lofty pair of diagonally set brick chimney-stacks with corbelled cappings. This feature is duplicated on the extensive gabled additions carried out in like materials, the brick more conspicuously red and the windows sliding sash. Prettily clad in Virginia creeper. Occupied.

West entrance; *c.* 1870.

Like the other lodges, constructed in random uncoursed rubble but with steeply pitched gables and on a regular plan, apart from a single-storey hallway projecting from the avenue gable, the front door not being where it should be—on the central projection, which is blind below the staircase landing window. Conspicuous brick dressings and again a pair of Tudor-style chimney-stacks. A back return completes the cruciform plan. Pretty and lovingly maintained.

Poor Mr Drummond would turn in his grave if he saw the condition of his house and main lodge today.

Lewis 1837; *LGI* (1904); Bence-Jones 1988; NLI/Lawrence photograph (1742 R).

77. MONAVALLET, Louth; pre-1835; *demolished.*
A property in 1854 of James McCann, the gate lodge to which had gone by 1911.

Griffith 1848–60.

78. MOOREMOUNT, Dunleer (2).
Sometime after 1835 the early lodge opposite the entrance was replaced by a successor by the gates. Neither has survived. A seat in 1854 of Owen Kieran.

Griffith 1848–60.

79. MOUNT REILLY, Dundalk; pre-1835; *demolished.*
To a property in 1854 of William McCullagh which was later named 'Mullaharlin', after its townland. Only two big round cone-topped pillars remain at the entrance.

Griffith 1848–60.

MULLAHARLIN (see MOUNT REILLY)

80. NEWTOWN, Drogheda (3).
All three lodges built after 1835, two by the coast and the other inland, which led to the outbuildings, have gone. Built by Francis Donagh, a name which is recorded here between 1837 and 1876.

Lewis 1837; *Land owners in Ireland 1876.*

81. NEWTOWN, Termonfeckin (2).
Main entrance; pre-1835; *demolished.*
Of the pair of lodges on the western approach to the old Georgian mansion of the McClintock family there is no sign. What remains here, in part, is a later gatescreen, probably erected about 1852 after a Ralph Smyth had purchased the property. This is in the shape of four square ashlar entablatured pillars with recessed panels to shafts and, in contrast, concave outer quadrants in quarry-faced stone with crenellated copings. Some good mid-Victorian cast-iron railings and gates survive.

Side entrance; *c.* 1890.

Beryl Dean

A pretty pair of semi-detached 1½-storey estate cottages, each presenting a three-bay doorless façade to the road, in coursed rubble stone contrasting with red-brick dressings and ashlar quoins. Brick is also employed in the two pairs of intricately designed, diagonally set chimney-stacks which flank the ridge above two dormer windows with ornamental bargeboards and hip-knobs. To each end gable is a pair of attic windows with segmental heads in a highly ornamental brick surround. The house is now 'An Grianan', home to the Irish Countrywomen's Association.

Casey and Rowan 1993.

82. OMEATH PARK, Omeath (2).
Two lodges built for John Bell, which display none of the pomposity of the new Victorian age; rather they look back to an earlier time in their modest vernacular appearance.

North entrance; *c.* 1840.
Forward of an extensive rustic gatescreen is this unsophisticated single-storey standard cottage with a shallow-pitched hipped roof.

It has a nasty later mono-pitched central hall extension.

South entrance; *c.* 1840.
Behind its gates, as simple as its counterpart, but having an original hip-roofed projecting hallway with a round-headed doorway.

A property that later in the century became home to the Woodhouse family.

83. ORIEL TEMPLE, Collon (2).

Revd Daniel Augustus Beaufort in 1788, as the parish rector, paid a visit to the demesne of John Foster (*c.* 1740–1828), later to be created Baron Oriel of Ferrard, to find it adorned with several frivolous buildings, a rustic cottage, a grotto and the temple which became a feature of the later extended house. By 1813 Curwen reported that Colonel Foster was 'making very material additions to the place', which a quarter of a century later did not impress Fraser: 'The lodge of Viscount Ferrard, called Oriel Temple is a plain small building, and (contrary to what its name implies) presents nothing to attract the attention of the admirer of domestic architecture'. In 1853 it was recorded that there were growing in the demesne the greatest number of trees in any one park in Ireland. So much is written about the place down the years but, frustratingly, there is no mention of the gate lodge by the main gate at the head of the village street, which was in place by 1835 but of which there is now no trace.

The improvements continued into the twentieth century, and a gate lodge was added opposite the gates to the eastern approach at White River Cross on the site of an earlier structure by the 12th Viscount Massereene and 5th Viscount Ferrard, Algernon William John Clotworthy Skeffington of Antrim Castle. It is a 1½-storey roughcast house below a steeply pitched hipped roof with concrete roof-tiled finish and a tall brick chimney-stack. Its eaves are broken on the short main front by a gablet with a touch of 'Stockbroker Tudor' in its bracketed mock half-timbered finish, which sits above a single-storey canted bay window in roughcast walls. Occupied. The place is now a Cistercian Abbey.

Curwen 1818; Fraser 1838; Tempest 1920; *BPB* (1929); Bence-Jones 1988.

84. PARSONAGE, Dundalk; *c.* 1830.
A nice plain little harled single-storey gabled lodge, its brick chimney-stack with sawtooth slate flashings matching the coping of the adjoining yard wall. Simple recessed-panel gate pillars with fancy concave cappings. Although the 1835 OS map names it 'Parsonage', Lewis two years later records the property as "Fort Hill of Rev. G. Tinley ... having in the demesne a Danish fort, from which it takes its name ...'. It was essentially, though, until about 1850 the rectory for Faughart parish, before being united with that of Baronstown. Revd Gervais Tinley was the rector here from 1808 to 1841.

Lewis 1837; Leslie 1911.

85. PIPERSTOWN, Termonfeckin (2).
A house of 1842 for Henry St George Smith, to which he added two lodged entrances not long after, presumably built by James McCullen, contractor of Beamore, Co. Meath (*q.v.*).

Main entrance; *c.* 1845; *demolished.*
The lodge is survived by a screen with squat stone pillars on which are the concave cappings so familiar in the county.

Secondary entrance; *c.* 1845.

In contrast to the mildly Classical house is this pleasant 1½-storey cottage opposite the gates in a subdued Tudor Picturesque style. Raised in ragstone off a symmetrical three-bay plan with smooth stone quoins and well-chiselled label moulding to ground-floor bipartite casements. Mellow brickwork is seen in the chimney-stack, dressing and single-storey gabled hall, which projects with carved ornamental bargeboards below the central attic gablet—like the main gables, its verges supported by chunky expressed purlin ends. A desirable building that in 2000 lay mysteriously abandoned and blocked up.

Griffith 1848–60; *JCLAHS* (1993); Casey and Rowan 1993.

86. PROSPECT, Knockbridge (3).
An estate recorded between 1814 and 1856 as home to William H. Richardson, who ensured that it was well served by porters at its entrances.

Rear entrance; *c.* 1845; *demolished.*
Listed by Griffith but not appearing on the 1835 OS map, it is lost without trace.

Dundalk entrance; *c.* 1835.
On the northern approach off the Dundalk–Ardee road is this modest single-storey standard cottage, Georgian in feel and square on plan below an almost pyramidal roof, with two relatively commodious rooms accessed via an internal hall with a quirky semicircular rear wall. Unusually sophisticated are the internal shutters to wide windows and the sheeted front door. It lies derelict, with nasty modern sand/cement-rendered walls. A 1850s cast-iron gate lies rusting and askew, one surviving carriage pillar with concave stone cap. The rubble quadrants complete a sorry scene.

Ardee entrance; *c.* 1850.
Another simple standard single-storey lodge of early Victorian appearance, with limewashed harled walls below a hipped roof which catslides over the central hall breakfront. Occupied. Rustic farmyard gates alongside.

Leet 1814; Griffith 1848–60; Slater 1856.

87. RAHANNA, Ardee; *c.* 1825.
One is met at the entrance by nice latticed iron gates, just like those at another Ruxton family property of nearby Red House (*q.v.*)—hardly surprising, as Rahanna was built about 1820 by Clarges Ruxton, fifth son of William of that place. He was also responsible for the single-storey three-bay wide-eaved hipped-roof gatekeeper's residence opposite the gates. It is much modernised, rendered, with a later shallow-pitched gabled porch.

LGI (1904); Bence-Jones 1988.

88. RATH COTTAGE, Dundalk; pre-1907; *demolished.*
What looks like a mid-Victorian *cottage orné*, probably built by Revd John Marmion, who was here between 1854 and 1870, survives its lodge, built after 1835.

Griffith 1848–60; Slater 1870.

89. RATH, Termonfeckin; pre-1835; *demolished.*
A country estate of the Brabazon family, scion of the earls of Meath of Killruddery, Co. Wicklow (*q.v.*), the gate lodge to which may have been built by either William Brabazon (1732–93), who married his cousin Catherine Frances Brabazon of Carstown (*q.v.*), or their only child, Wallop Brabazon.

BPB (1929).

90. RATHCOOLE, Dunleer; *c.* 1825.
Opposite the entrance to Janeville (*q.v.*) is this standard single-storey lodge of generous proportions, built of harled rubble with brick-dressed openings and punched ashlar quoins below a hipped roof, now minus its chimney-stack. Blocked up and in an advanced stage of dereliction, having been in 1837 'situated in a neat demesne of Edward Tisdall'.

Lewis 1837.

91. RATHESCAR LODGE, Dunleer (4).
Although built by Baron Anthony Foster of Oriel Temple (*q.v.*) merely as a hunting-lodge, it became of greater significance when inherited as a main seat by his younger son, Bishop William Foster (1744–97), sufficient to warrant the addition of no less than four gate lodges, not one of which was durable enough to survive until today. These were built either by the cleric or by his elder son, the Hon. John Leslie Foster (1781–1842).

BPB (1929); Casey and Rowan 1993.

92. RATHMULLEN, Drogheda; pre-1836; *demolished.*
A seat in 1814 of Graves Chamley Graves but

offered for sale on his behalf as an incumbered estate and purchased by Thomas Kelly in 1854.

Leet 1814; Lyons 1993.

93. RAVENSDALE PARK, Ravensdale (3).
This great house and its embracing estate are no more. The former evolved through three major stages of development. Initially 'of the family of Fortescue. The present well-wooded and improved demesne was created from a tract so wild that it might be denominated a waste, by James Fortescue who died 1782. The house seldom affords a residence to its noble owner.' Thus noticed Brewer in 1825, and as early as 1788 the Revd Daniel Augustus Beaufort mentioned 'Mr Fortescue's beautiful lodge'. By 1837 Lewis was able to describe 'a handsome mansion, situated in an extensive and beautiful demesne, with a well stocked deer park', of Thomas Fortescue, later created 1st Lord Clermont, which referred to sweeping works carried out by the Newry architect Thomas J. Duff. In 1859 Thomas's younger brother, Chichester Fortescue, subsequently raised to the title of 1st (and last) Lord Carlingford, engaged the Belfast practice of Lanyon and Lynn to transform the house into a large Italianate mansion. These years of progressive improvements on the property included the building of three gatekeepers' lodges, all of which, although architecturally unworthy, were at least unusually socially conscious, being relatively commodious.

Flurrybridge gate; *c.* 1830; *demolished.*
A plain gabled two-storey house of three-bay irregular ground-floor front with two bays over, in roughcast walls. Removed *c.* 2000 to make way for a chalet bungalow.

Middle gate; *c.* 1830.
A two-storey three-bay gatehouse with gablets over first-floor openings. Roughcast and gabled to the main road, with an ornamental balcony. Occupied.

Ravensdale gate; *c.* 1835; architect possibly T.J. Duff.
Made plain by later modernisation is this 1½-storey gabled porter's lodge with foiled bargeboards and diagonally set brick chimney-stacks. Three-bay and roughcast, situated outside a ruined stone entrance screen. Perhaps a survivor of the commission of Duff, like the beautiful Picturesque schoolhouse nearby.

The big house was burnt and demolished in the 1920s.

D.A. Beaufort (1788); Brewer 1825; Lewis 1837; *DB* (1 Aug. 1859); Bence-Jones 1988; Casey and Rowan 1993.

94. RED, Ardee (2).
The late eighteenth-century brick house of the Parkinson family was inherited in 1806 by William Parkinson Ruxton, who furnished the property with two gate lodges.

Main entrance; *c.* 1820.
A standard 1½-storey rustic Regency cottage with white harled walls. Two wide tripartite windows, which reflect the Wyatt windows of the big house, flank the doorway below bracketed eaves to a roof which is hipped to the park and half-hipped to the road to

permit an attic window. Simple octagonal pillars carry pretty iron lattice postilion and carriage gates. Occupied.

Side entrance; *c.* 1825.

A basic single-storey gabled lodge with simple replacement carved bargeboards, roughcast walls and basic single-bay elevations of multi-paned casements. Occupied.

LGI (1904); Bence-Jones 1988.

95. RICHARDSTOWN CASTLE, Ardee; *c.* 1885; architect not known.
A highly individual example of a single-storey standard gate lodge in the distinctive polychromatic brickwork so beloved of late Victorian architects (*below*). Situated opposite its gates, it is gabled with bold stone skew-tables and kneelers, the breakfront porch notable for a pair of diagonal buttresses, Tudor-arched entrance and a blank shield over, above which is a lion crest and the motto 'Honor Et Virtus', presumably of the lodge's builder, John Henry. On each side are bipartite casement windows with chamfered reveals and lintels. To the gable

ends are Gothic versions of Palladian windows. All raised off a stone plinth. There are corbelled gutter brackets, ornamental earthenware crestings and a soaring and articulated brick chimney-stack. Nicely presented behind a cast-iron railed screen on a masonry plinth. Across the road is a contemporary gate sweep with variegated brickwork pillars, those to the carriage opening having decorative lanterns on masonry cappings. The gates are well conceived in hardwood and fine foliated ironwork combination. Beyond are equally fine straight iron-railed screens. Within the demesne is an intriguing house that has evolved over the years with many stages of development, none of which is as late as the building of its lodge.

Bassett 1886; Casey and Rowan 1993.

96. ROESTOWN, Ardee; *c.* 1850.
A standard single-storey building of brick construction finished in harling with Irish pilaster quoins and a central canted hall projection with equivalent roof and sidelights. Gabled, with paired casement windows. Built for Peter McLoughlin.

Griffith 1848–60.

97. ROKEBY HALL, Dunleer (3).
Richard Robinson (1709–94) became Anglican primate of all Ireland in 1765 and remained so until his death. He is credited with the architectural transformation of Armagh into an archiepiscopal city worthy of the name. Initially in this task his chosen architect was Thomas Cooley (1740–84), who is credited with providing designs of the archbishop's new Irish country seat here at 'Marlay'. Sadly, Cooley was not to see its execution, and it was left to Francis Johnston, Cooley's assistant and Robinson's protégé, to supervise completion of the building and furnish the demesne with gate lodges and Marlay model farm. Following his elevation as 1st Lord Rokeby, the primate was to rename the property after his ancestral seat of Rokeby Park in Yorkshire.

Barmeath Road gate; 1788; architect Francis Johnston.

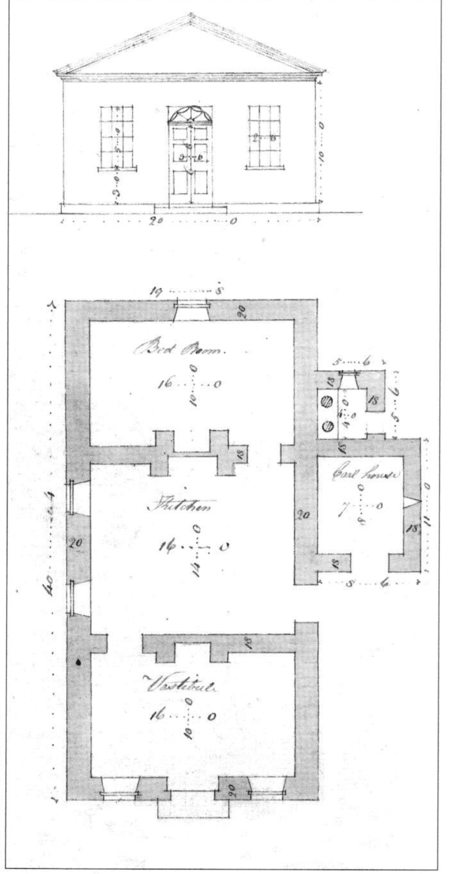

Irish Architectural Archive

This main entrance on the eastern approach is distinguished by a grand Classical gatescreen dominated by a pair of V-jointed rusticated carriage pillars with unusual fluted-panel friezes, projecting corniced cappings and elegant pedestalled ball finials with Greek key-pattern rustication. These are closely related to Cooley's pillars at the Armagh palace gates and, if not by him, Johnston had them very much in mind. Beyond these are screen walls, containing postilion openings, stopped by pillars with gadrooned cappings, a Johnston trademark. The great sweep extends further in convex quadrants. Attending on all this is Johnston's lodge, for which the original sketch design survives, dated November 1788 and signed 'Francis Johnson' before the addition of the 't'. That Robinson approved is clear from another drawing, dated one month later, without any significant alteration. But in reality what exists is a very much watered-down version, losing in its building a pretty leaded Georgian fanlight, through the eaves line being lowered, and the pediment which was intended to crown the main avenue front. Over the short three-bay symmetrical elevation is substituted a stone parapet with mutuled, moulded cornice that does not even extend down the sides, and the stuccoed front becomes exposed rubble beyond. A hipped roof covers this single-storey three-roomed cottage, with four-over-two sash windows on each side of a sheeted door that the architect conceived as being two-leaved and panelled. Already Robinson was losing interest in the project. Derelict.

South entrance; *c.* 1788; architect Francis Johnston.

Here the architect's original concept is almost realised, with the gabled version of his lodge boasting a pediment embracing the three-bay symmetrical harled front, which here does not lurk behind the gates but rather proudly stops the left-hand side of another noble gatescreen. Without any pedestrian gates, the great segmental ashlar sweep has tall quadrant walls framed by lofty square corniced carriage pillars with gadrooned tops, and outer cylindrical pillars with domed cappings similarly carved, much as Johnston employed at the Park Gate to Phoenix Park, north Dublin (*q.v.*). There are good contemporary modest wrought-iron carriage gates. This entrance is well maintained.

It must be significant that there is an earlier and very similar Classical lodge to Ardbraccan Palace, Co. Meath (*q.v.*), where Thomas Cooley was involved.

Dunleer Road entrance; *c.* 1787/*c.* 1860; architect Francis Johnston.

On the northern avenue from the Dunleer Road is a similar lodge but as basic as Johnston intended, built to serve Robinson's model farm of Marlay. The architect's surviving drawing shows a modest single-storey two-roomed cottage below a hipped roof, its short main three-bay symmetrical façade facing the avenue, flanked by convex quadrant walls and rusticated ashlar pillars with concave cappings and farm gate. Today on the same footprint is a two-storey hip-roofed gatehouse, its upper doorway accessed by a bridge from the raised avenue. But Johnston's original porter's lodge survives, now serving as a basement to the mid-Victorian addition. It seems that this was necessitated by its being low-lying and in close proximity to the 'Great Drain' indicated on the undated drawing. The second storey shows a little more sophistication than below, having Doric pilasters as quoins in its harled limewashed walls. Occupied in 1854 by Margaret Reilly, whose landlord was Sir John S. Robinson.

Mason 1814–19; Griffith 1848–60; *IGS Bulletin* (July–Dec. 1969); Casey and Rowan 1993; Malcomson 2000; NLI drawings (AD 1554, 1555 & 1843).

98. ST ANDREW'S CHURCH OF IRELAND CHURCH, Omeath; *c.* 1838; *demolished.*
Principally a sexton's lodge by the gate, it may have been contemporary with the founding of the church in 1838. Taken down in the late 1990s. A chapel of ease in Carlingford parish, with a succession of perpetual curates until 1860.

Leslie 1911.

99. ST MARY'S CHURCH OF IRELAND CHURCH, Ballymascanlon; *c.* 1850.
Partially built in 1819, the church preceded its lodge by about 30 years. A good, solid

rather than elegant English Picturesque Cottage, 1½-storey gabled, with perforated continuous bracket bargeboards to main roof and that of the little single-storey hall projection tucked in below high eaves with its pointed heads to doorway and sidelights. Bipartite four-over-four sash windows in roughcast walls with smooth toothed dressings and quoins. Occupied. From 1851 to 1890 Revd John Thomas Warren was the long-serving perpetual curate.

Leslie 1911.

100. SANDYMOUNT, Blackrock; *c.* 1845.
A fine marine villa in Italianate style built for James Shekleton, coach-maker, iron-founder, millwright and farm implement manufacturer of Dundalk, whose business allowed him the added luxury of a porter's lodge by his gate, albeit a tiny structure. Single-storey and hip-roofed, its later gabled hall projection with arrowhead-arched doorway protecting against icy blasts. Extended to one side, rendered and occupied. Gatescreen comprised of carriage pillars with ball finials; secondary cast-iron posts with anthemion motifs and striking *étoile*-topped railings.

Slater 1846; Griffith 1848–60.

101. SEAFIELD, Togher; pre-1835; *demolished.*
'... the neat and pleasantly situated residence of Henry L. Brabazon.' This 'Harry' Brabazon, listed in 1837, was also in residence here 23 years earlier.

Leet 1814; Lewis 1837.

102. SILVER PARK, Tallanstown; pre-1835; *demolished.*
A lodge that served an older house on the site than the present replacement, now known as 'Church Park'. Its proprietor in 1837 was Neale Thomas Coleman, whose gatekeeper eighteen years later was James Mathew.

Lewis 1837; Griffith 1848–60.

103. SMARMORE CASTLE, Ardee; *c.* 1780.
In a romantic setting is the old fourteenth-century keep of the Taaffes, with many eighteenth-century additions, from which latter era its lodge dates. A main two-bay elevation greets the visitor, fronting the road

in the form of a pair of brick-dressed Georgian Gothic pointed-arched windows in lichened rubble, long sealed up. This is all that remains of what may have been single-storey below a hipped roof, for it now forms part of a concrete-block, corrugated-iron-roofed shed. Built originally by John Taaffe (1746–1825).

LGI (1904); Casey and Rowan 1993.

SPENCER HILL (see KILSARAN RECTORY)

104. SPRINGHILL, Tallanstown; pre-1835; *demolished.*
An early nineteenth-century home of William McMahon.

105. STEPHENSTOWN, Louth (3).
A late eighteenth-century house built by Mathew Fortescue with a pair of lodges at its main gates, which had gone by 1911. His son, of the same name (1791–1845), added two further lodged entrances.

Rear gate; *c.* 1830/*c.* 1850.

A single-storey hip-roofed structure, later remodelled with an extension to the front which doubled it in size to form an L-plan. Rendered, with pretty carved Tudor-style fascia boards embracing the whole, a feature much favoured in the county and perhaps indicating the hand of architect William Caldbeck. In 2000 it lay roofless, awaiting removal. Quarry-faced masonry pillars with farm gate.

Front gate; *c.* 1830.

Equally dilapidated is this once-charming single-storey harled rubble cottage, the steeply hipped roof to which extended over the short two-bay avenue front to create a verandah with wooden posts.

LGI (1904); Casey and Rowan 1993.

106. STICKILLIN, Ardee; pre-1835; *demolished.*
A property in 1824 of John Norris, which later passed to Alexander Henry.

Pigot 1824; Slater 1846.

107. STONE, Dunleer; *c.* 1820.
Alongside the gates facing the road is this gawky 1½-storey standard stone-built gabled cottage with lofty eaves, below which is a lean-to central hall projection. The house had passed from a Mr Owens in 1783 via J.T. Foster in 1800 to William McClintock by 1814.

Taylor and Skinner 1969 [1783]; Wilson 1803; Leet 1814.

108. STRANDFIELD, Dundalk; pre-1835.
A property in 1837 of James Moore.

Lewis 1837.

109. THE SYCAMORES, Drogheda; *c.* 1880; architect not known; *demolished.*
A big late Victorian brick house, multi-gabled with terracotta features, its grounds spoilt by being broken up for modern housing, the gate lodge removed. It was built of coursed rubble limestone with red-brick dressings to round-headed windows and had high-pitched gables. All created by William Whitworth MP.

Garner 1986.

110. THISTLE LODGE, Ravensdale; pre-1835; *demolished.*
A property in the mid-nineteenth century of Patrick Moore.

Griffith 1848–60.

111. THOMASTOWN CASTLE, Tallanstown (4).
Alternatively known as 'Knock Abbey', this is a classic example of a palimpsest, with its fourteenth-century keep of the Bellews allied to an eighteenth-century house of the Tenison family of Loughbawn, Co. Monaghan. The place was acquired about 1800 by Matthew O'Reilly (d. 1817); his grandson, Myles William O'Reilly (1825–80), inherited in 1844 and in 1862 further extended and altered the old castle into a Castellated Gothic-style composition. He had commissioned architect William Caldbeck, who was responsible for one of the gate lodges.

Inner lodge; *c.* 1800.

Still apparent despite subsequent twentieth-century rehabilitation and additions is the nucleus of a standard single-storey hip-roofed Georgian Gothic lodge. In crisp modern rendering are original pointed-arched openings with feature rubble dressings and Y-traceried windows on each side of a later central gabled hall projection with crude wavy bargeboards. Doubtless originally dating from the advent of Matthew O'Reilly.

Outer lodge; *c.* 1860; architect probably William Caldbeck.

A most uncommon single-storey lodge with partial basement and steep gables, built in striking Flemish bond red brick and contrasting limestone quoins and plinth off an L-plan formed by a rear return. The tall eaves accommodate a series of canted bay windows with their own roofs to the main two-bay front and two further elevations. In each main gable is a most peculiar blank oval limestone plaque, both seemingly still awaiting sculpted O'Reilly coats of arms. Big dominant brick and stone chimney-stacks on plinths. Much modernised and extended in imaginative haphazard fashion to form a unique independent dwelling. There are four good octagonal limestone entrance pillars with concave cappings and fleur-de-lis-topped cast-iron railings and gates.

LGI (1904); McCullough 1994; Casey and Rowan 1993.

112. THORNFIELD, Inniskeen; *c.* 1830.
A very modest single-storey gabled affair, harled and boarded up. A seat in the mid-nineteenth century of the Kenny family.

TOWNLEY GLEBE (see TULLYALLEN RECTORY)

113. TOWNLEY HALL, Drogheda (3).
Blayney Townley Balfour (1769–1856), the third in a succession of four of that name to be masters of the estate, inherited old Townley Hall in 1788 on the death of his grandfather. On reaching his majority he set about planning its replacement, which culminated in the acclaimed neo-Classical masterpiece of architect Francis Johnston, the

Irish Architectural Archive

113. Townley Hall, Francis Johnston (1802), unexecuted.

Irish Architectural Archive

113. Townley Hall, Francis Johnston (1802), unexecuted.

Irish Architectural Archive

113. Townley Hall, B.T. & F. Balfour, Boyne gate.

spare grey exterior of which disguises wonders within. After the discarding of designs of James Playfair (1792), whom Blayney met on his 'Grand Tour', Johnston was called in to assist in its creation for a client and his sister, Anne Dawson, who both had 'ideas' and no little flair as amateur architects. To further complicate matters, Johnston had to deal with Lady Florence Cole of Florence Court, Co. Fermanagh, whom Blayney married in 1797 and who was also 'very accomplished in pencil-drawing'. Despite there being so many cooks, the architect was still active on the estate as late as 1823, the house having reached completion in 1800. That an appropriate grand entrance to the demesne was being considered is evident from a design of April 1802 by Johnston for a noble archway. This is depicted in no less than two beautiful watercolours, a design which shows distinct similarities to a drawing of an entrance for Emo Court, Co. Laois (*q.v.*), by James Gandon (1780), with his trademark draped paterae, which Johnston repeats in the spandrels of the segmentally arched carriage opening, the use of prominent mutules and not least in the crowning coat of arms, which he amends to a draped tondo, a device employed at the same time in a chimney-piece at the Bank of Ireland, Dublin. Like Gandon's design, Francis Johnston's did not find favour and was not executed, but he did assist in what materialised at the main entrance.

Boyne gate; 1819; architects Blayney Townley Balfour and Florence Balfour (*above*).

An undated drawing for the entrance screen, as executed but for the lions on the carriage pillar cappings, signed by the Balfours, survives. The four hefty square ashlar pillars have deep panel recesses and corniced cappings, and contain straight railings incorporating postilion gates. The design was reproduced as a working drawing by Francis Johnston in 1810 and its construction may have preceded the addition of the gate lodge by almost a decade. One Richard Mallet of 9 Marlborough Street, Dublin, quoted £237.17.8d for the ironwork. The splendid little temple lodge has a pedimented tetrastyle portico of a sort of hybrid Tuscan/Doric order, which screens a three-bay symmetrical elevation to the avenue. It extends as a simple single-storey two-roomed cottage to the rear. Andrew Boyd, who is recorded as working on the big house as early as 1797, also laid out the pediment, made moulds for the cornice and measured the stonecutter's work. This important and durable little lodge has been demoted to the status of a single-cell shelter, shorn of its windows, door and softening contextual landscape.

Schoolhouse lodge; *c.* 1820; architect possibly Francis Johnston.

To the north of the demesne is this dual-function building in a sort of Hiberno-Italianate style on a T-plan, with 1½-storey teacher's accommodation and single-storey classroom wing at right angles, a feature brick chimney-stack at their intersection in the form of a pair of diagonally placed flues on a rectangular base. The shallow-pitched roofs have, or had, paired brackets to eaves and verges over a main front recessed behind corner piers containing bipartite multi-pane casements. To the classroom is a tripartite Wyatt window. All originally in traditional limewashed harling, which has recently been removed and a fabric of rubble construction and red-brick dressings laid bare, naked as unintended and at the mercy of the elements. Occupied.

Slane gate; *c.* 1835.

On the western approach in the same Irish/Tuscan manner as the school lodge is another 1½-storey two-up/two-down structure, but without a wing; its single-bay short main front has the ground-floor window set in a square recess under a loft light below oversailing shallow-pitched verges with paired brackets; roughcast. Too late to be by Francis Johnston.

LGI (1904); *IGS Bulletin* (July–Dec. 1969 and 1987); Howley 1993; IAA (Murray Collection).

114. TULLYALLEN RECTORY, Drogheda; pre-1835; *demolished.*

A lodge that may have been contemporary with the glebe house built in 1816 during the incumbency (1812–28) of Revd Thomas Rice Fosbery (1788–1828).

Lewis 1837; *LGI* (1904); Leslie 1911.

115. WALSHESTOWN, Clogherhead; pre-1835; *demolished.*

The porter's lodge was perhaps of an age with where Nicholas Markey 'has lately built a most comfortable house', noted in 1814.

Mason 1814–19.

116. WILLIAMSTOWN, Castlebellingham (2).
The estate was acquired by the Chester family in about 1800, being greatly improved, extensively planted and the demesne enclosed by a wall nearly three miles long. Finlay Chester engaged architect William Caldbeck in 1858–60 to design a large Italianate villa, so typical of his work. His commission extended to plans for at least one of the lodges.

Front entrance; *c.* 1860; architect probably William Caldbeck.
A commodious two-storey gatehouse (*above*) built in a symmetrical Picturesque Italianate style with some Tudor features thrown in, its verges and eaves carried on carved brackets. Central doorway in a projecting gabled single-storey hall with spiky hip-knob. Finished in white rendering with stone quoins and modern casement windows. Well served by three chimney-stacks. Occupied and well tended.

Rear entrance; *c.* 1860; architect William Caldbeck.

In contrast is this forsaken ornamental Picturesque cottage, single-storey standard under a hipped roof with decorative pierced and foiled fascia board taken about the semi-octagonal central hall projection which has a semi-octahedral roof with scalloped slates. The hall is flanked by round-headed narrow windows in square recesses, a feature repeated to end elevations. The whole is now spoiled by a cloak of dreary grey sand/cement rendering. A clue to its original finish is in its paired brick chimney-stack. How this lodge could, and did, look can be seen in the same design to be found at Beltichbourne (*q.v.*), a stark example of differing attitudes to, and treatment of, these little buildings. There are beautifully crafted curvilinear scrolled iron carriage gates with fleur-de-lis finials, all displayed in a sea of mud.

Leslie 1908; Williams 1994.

117. WILVILLE, Greenore; pre-1835; *demolished.*
A seat in 1800 of Brabazon Brabazon, which ten years later had passed to John Gernon.

Wilson 1803; Leet 1814.

WINDWOOD LODGE (see BRIGHTON VILLA)

118. WOODTOWN, Mansfieldstown; pre-1835; *demolished.*
A property in the mid-nineteenth century of the Marlay family of Belvedere, Co. Westmeath (*q.v.*).

LGI (1904).

COUNTY MEATH

1. ACLARE, Drumcondra (2).

North Lodge; pre-1836; *demolished.*

The original avenue approach served the previous house on the property, home in 1814 to Francis Corbet (1770–1825), who in 1820 assumed the Singleton surname and whose eldest son succeeded him. The lodge has been replaced by a twentieth-century bungalow.

South Lodge; post-1836; *demolished.*

Henry Corbet Singleton (1796–1872) replaced the old house in 1840 with the present fine neo-Classical villa and added another porter's lodge, which has met the same fate as the earlier one.

LGI (1904); Bence-Jones 1988.

2. ACLARE LODGE, Drumcondra; *c.* 1840.

In 1837 'the neat residence of G. Moore Adams', whose gatekeeper's lodge survives as a roughcast single-storey standard hip-roofed structure, its three-bay asymmetrical front with a later off-centre flat-roofed hall projection; diagonally set chimney-stack in Tudor fashion.

Lewis 1837.

3. ADAMSTOWN, Laracor; *c.* 1830.

A modest standard single-storey gabled building with a two-window bay elevation to the road; roughcast. Derelict, windowless, forlorn and appreciated only by the cattle sharing the same field. A property which changed hands many times over the years: in 1783 of a Mr O'Reilly, in 1814 of Richard Crawford and in 1837 of T. Disney, perhaps the same as noted then at neighbouring Rock Lodge (*q.v.*).

Taylor and Skinner 1969 [1783]; Leet 1814; Lewis 1837.

4. AGHER, Summerhill (3).

John Pratt Winter (1768–1846), who inherited Agher on the death of his father Samuel in 1811, was generally agreed by his contemporaries to be one of the great social improvers: 'The excellence of this mansion, and the beauty of its demesne, are contemplated by the examiner with unalloyed admiration when he beholds the numerous peasantry, on the surrounding estate, living in eligible dwellings, and with decency and comfort, under the judicious protection of its esteemed and exemplary proprietor'. These 1825 observations were reiterated twelve years later by Samuel Lewis, who noted 'the neat appearance of the cottages on the estate'. This neatness no doubt extended to add to the comfort of his gatekeepers, but did not guarantee durability.

North lodge; pre-1836; *demolished.*

All that remains is a once-fine gatescreen, now dilapidated.

Middle lodge; *c.* 1820.

A modest single-storey standard lodge with shallow-hipped roof, a survivor of J.P. Winter's cottage improvements.

South lodge; *c.* 1880; architect not known.

Opposite its gates is this 1½-storey mid-Victorian affair built by James Sanderson Winter, grandson of the improver, who succeeded to the property in 1867 and whose monogram is incorporated in the nearby extravagant national school. Gabled with high eaves, there is a string-course at attic-floor level and stone quoins to an irregularly fenestrated front, its low gabled projecting hallway flanked by a narrow bipartite light and a rectangular bay window with its own hipped roof. Now all rendered drab with a coat of sand/cement, which probably obliterates decorative polychromatic brickwork. Rundown entrance screen with palmette-topped railings of earlier date.

Brewer 1825; Lewis 1837; *LGI* (1904).

5. ALLENSTOWN, Bohermeen; pre-1836; *demolished.*

William Waller (1710–96) built the original house and also later considerably extended and refaced it in 1785 to the designs of Revd Daniel Augustus Beaufort, who had become his son-in-law in 1767. That ubiquitous cleric and talented amateur architect in 1789 noted in his diary that he was laying out foundations for 'Allenstown Lodge' and in 1791 ordered a 'Wyatt window'. Can this refer to a lodge at the gates? Tantalisingly, all the evidence has been removed.

LGI (1904); *IGS Bulletin* (Jan.–March 1975).

6. ANNESBROOK, Duleek (6).

Henry Smith in 1821, in expectation of hosting George IV *en route* to dally with his mistress at Slane Castle (*q.v.*), glorified his house with the addition of a grand oversized portico, a banqueting-room extension and, for his further delectation, a new gate lodge opposite the main gates. The demesne had four lodges in 1836, which were supplemented thereafter by another two, only one of which survives in reality, while another two can be considered from photographs.

Middle entrance; *c.* 1821; architect probably Francis Johnston; *demolished.*

'We waited for the coach at the beautiful lodge and gate of Annsbrook; and one of the sons of the house coming up, invited us to look at the domain, which is as pretty and neatly ordered as—as any in England.' Whether the king was as appreciative of this entrance as the novelist William Makepeace Thackeray clearly was in 1842 is a moot point, given that he had just left behind his Royal Pavilion, Brighton, which was nearing completion in 1821. Standard single-storey in what was to be perceived as the Regency style, not that his majesty would have been aware of that, with its three-over-three sash windows set in elliptically arched recesses to the main front, framed by toothed quoins and on each side of a central breakfront comprised of an open pediment above Ionic columns *in antis* with equivalent flanking pilasters, which screen a semicircular recessed entrance porch, all below a hipped roof. Nicely exhibited behind a railed screen, which tragically proved to be no protection.

Irish Architectural Archive

River entrance; *c.* 1835; architect possibly William Murray; *demolished.*

Irish Architectural Archive

Often attributed to Francis Johnston, this design is much too audacious to have been by him. The gadrooning of the chimney capping, a feature beloved of the architect, may well have been perpetuated here by his cousin and erstwhile partner William Murray (1787–1849). Single-storey hip-roofed standard but of considerable presence, in stucco contrasted with stone pilasters which framed innovative convex curved corners containing round-headed niches and supported a heavy eaves entablature which met an equally robust central portico with two pairs of Doric columns. On each side and to end elevations were bipartite casement windows with decorative glazing pattern. Another inexcusable loss, once sited south of the house.

North entrance; 1845.

Built at the access to the stable yard, which displays an '1845' date-stone, this peculiar little composition now serves at the main approach to the house from the east. Built by Henry Jeremiah Smith (1783–1857) in what would be described as the Castellated Romantic style were it in fact crenellated, which it may once have been. Symmetrical and stone-faced, it is comprised of two

particularly mean rooms, 9ft 6in. by 6ft 6 in., separated by a double elliptically arched carriage opening, with pronounced voussoirs, flanked by a pair of mock arrowlooped square turrets, all with flat parapets. Basic wing walls behind iron-fenced convex quadrants. Derelict.

The lodges described are three of four located in the townland of Boolies Little, whilst one in Lundestown townland opposite an old entrance and another distant to the south-east in Deenes townland have also disappeared. Given the architectural quality of these known losses, it doesn't bear imagining what else has vanished.

Brewer 1825; Thackeray 1879; *LGI* (1904); Bence-Jones 1988; Casey and Rowan 1993; IAA photographs (S/90/12 & S/91/1).

7. ANTYLSTOWN, Navan; pre-1836; *demolished.*
Replaced by a bungalow with Irish pilaster quoins, which may reflect its predecessor. Surviving are nice square ashlar pillars with primitive decorative motifs. The proprietor in 1854 was John Burgess, leasing from William Morgan.

Griffith 1848–60.

ARCHDEACONRY (see MEATH ARCHDEACONRY)

8. ARCH HALL, Wilkinstown (2).
The sad remains of the big house and grotesque archway on the axis of its approach, both by one of Ireland's greatest architects, Sir Edward Lovett Pearce, which have nevertheless fared better than the two demolished lodges which pre-dated 1836. A seat of the Garnett family.

9. ARDAGH, Kingscourt; pre-1913; *demolished.*
A mid-Victorian lodge, to a property of the Shekleton family, which has been replaced by a council cottage.

10. ARDBRACCAN RECTORY, Navan; pre-1836.
Probably built during the incumbency (1818–43) of Revd the Hon. Henry Pakenham (1781–1863) is this 1½-storey gabled affair, three-bay symmetrical, its wide windows with quarry-faced stone lintels over, in rendered walls with toothed quoins. A central hip-roofed dormer window is part of modernisation that has transformed the lodge out of all recognition. Simple square limestone gate pillars to a fine Classical glebe house now in private hands and known as 'Ardbraccan Lodge'.

Leslie and Wallace 2009.

11. ARDBRACCAN PALACE, Navan.
A grand Palladian palace for the bishops of Meath was designed in 1734 by Richard Castle, but only the wings were executed and, for whatever reason, it was 30 years before a main centre block was completed to unite them, and this only after three further architects were consulted by the then (1766–98) bishop, the Hon. Henry Maxwell: James Wyatt, Thomas Cooley and Revd Daniel Augustus Beaufort. Their respective contributions would seem to have been proportionate to their availability, Wyatt never having visited these shores, Cooley having an increasingly busy practice in Armagh and Dublin, whilst that aspiring amateur Revd Beaufort was rector of the neighbouring parish of Navan and had the ear of his bishop. Curwen in 1813 had no doubts as to the persevering cleric's responsibility, but Brewer twelve years later confuses matters by attributing the plans to Wyatt, 'performed under the superintendence of the late Dr Beaufort'. The source of the designs for the entrance gates and lodge is just as equivocal, although what is clear is that Cooley and Beaufort were involved. In the Farnham Papers held in the National Library of Ireland are undated proposals for two lodged entrance gates by the former, which remained unrealised.

Design no. 1; *c.* 1770; architect Thomas Cooley; *unexecuted.*

National Library of Ireland

A design at the centre of which is an impressive Classical Triumphal archway, pedimented over a round-headed carriage opening flanked by a pair of postern doorways framed by lofty rusticated pillars with flaming urn finials. Rather less happy is the arrangement of a pair of lodges advancing behind blind concave quadrants, apparently below flat roofs, terminating awkwardly in rusticated niches.

Design no. 2; *c.* 1770; architect Thomas Cooley; *unexecuted.*

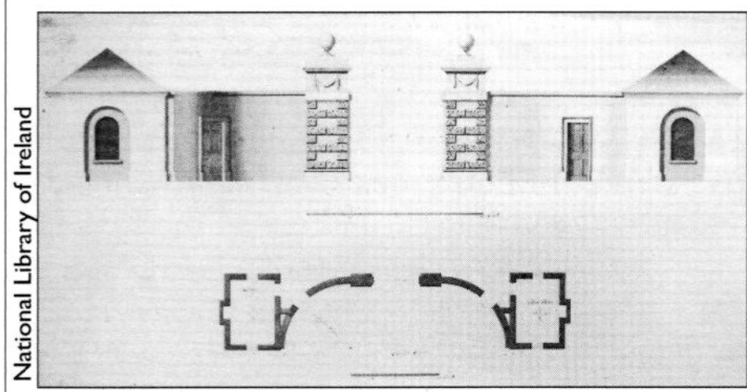
National Library of Ireland

Presumably chronologically the second of the two proposals, being the more successful, the single-storey lodges with hipped roofs less dependent on the concave quadrants and with outward-looking round-headed windows in equivalent recesses. Centrally are grand pillars in the Chambers manner, with vermiculated shafts, swagged friezes and ball-finialled cappings.

In the event plans for a pair of lodges were abandoned.

Main entrance; *c.* 1772; architect possibly Thomas Cooley.

National Library of Ireland

Plans and elevations for a grand Classical gatescreen signed by Beaufort (*above*) and dated 1772 survive as built, but for the ball finials. This design, however, is almost as erected at Armagh archiepiscopal palace to a 1771 drawing by Thomas Cooley featuring

the same swagged friezes and V-jointed rustication to carriage and secondary pillars. It seems that Beaufort adapted an original design by Cooley, introducing intermediate piers to the postilion gates. Significantly, there is an identical gatescreen to the Armagh example at nearby Drewstown (*q.v.*), which was commissioned by the Hon. Barry Maxwell, the future 3rd Baron Maxwell of Farnham, Co. Cavan, older brother of the bishop of Meath. At a distance from the gates is a single-storey lodge having a sophisticated three-bay ashlar short front to the avenue with moulded architraved doorway. Three-roomed and extending in rubble finish, its four-bay side elevation ending below a hipped roof. The Tudor-style latticed glazing bars may be fashionable alterations of the 1830s.

It may be relevant that this is a design much akin to one at Rokeby Hall, Co. Louth (*q.v.*), by Francis Johnston, once assistant to Thomas Cooley.

Curwen 1818; Brewer 1825; *BPB* (1929); *IGS Bulletin* (Jan.–March 1975); Bence-Jones 1988; Casey and Rowan 1993; Dean 1994; NLI drawings/Farnham Collection (AD 2992, 2993 & 3440); Mulligan 2001.

12. ARDMULCHAN CASTLE, Navan; pre-1836; *demolished.*
Of the previous house of the Taaffe family and its gate lodge there is no sign, the former having been replaced in 1904, by a mansion in the Scots Baronial style, the latter not.

Bence-Jones 1988.

13. ARDSALLAGH, Navan (3).
A demesne associated over the years with leading English aristocracy. Having been laid out by the Lopes family, earls of Ludlow, by 1838 it had become the 'delightfully situated but neglected demesne' which was acquired by Francis Russell (1788–1861) on his succession in 1839 as 7th duke of Bedford of Woburn Abbey. He set about revitalising the estate by building a new house and two gatekeepers' lodges, one of which replaced an earlier one of the Ludlows. The house has a feel of the English architect Edward Blore about it, and he certainly worked for the 5th duke at Woburn in the early 1830s, so both lodges could conceivably be from his office.

South lodge; *c.* 1845; architect possibly Edward Blore.

By the River Boyne is this 1½-storey English Picturesque Cottage-style lodge rising off an L-plan to ornamental foiled bargeboards and spiky hip-knobs. There are attractive bipartite Tudor-arched casement windows in roughcast walls. Neglected.

North lodge; *c.* 1845; architect perhaps Edward Blore.

In contrast to the above is a regular single-storey gabled cottage with similar foiled bargeboards, here taken beyond as fancy fascias. Bipartite rectangular-paned casements in modern roughcast to walls. The central projecting gabled hallway has been disfigured by a flat-roofed addition.

Fraser 1838; *BPB* (1929); Casey and Rowan 1993; Colvin 2008.

14. ASHFIELD, Slane; *c.* 1850; architect possibly William G. Murray.

To a restrained neo-Classical villa designed by William G. Murray for his uncle, Arthur George Murray, is this charming little doll's house by the gates. Standard single-storey and small-scale, its gables have carved bargeboards and hip-knobs; the projecting central hall, with a deeply chamfered stone door-surround, is flanked by wide windows in roughcast walls. Vacant, but maintained and secured, its windows sealed with mock painted glazing bars and curtains. Good cast-iron contemporary gatescreen with ogee-railed quadrants repeated beyond in stone.

Casey and Rowan 1993.

ATHBOY CHURCH OF IRELAND CHURCH (see ST JAMES')

15. ATHBOY RECTORY, Athboy; pre-1836; *demolished.*
A lodge that may have been contemporary with the building of the glebe house in 1818 at a cost of £1,700 during the incumbency from 1811 until his death of Revd Robert Tronson (1743–1831).

Lewis 1837; Healy 1908; Leslie and Wallace 2009.

16. ATHLUMNEY, Navan (2).
A seat of the Metge family.

Main entrance; pre-1836; *demolished.*

Secondary entrance; *c.* 1850.
Alongside the gates facing the road is a 1½-storey pair of semi-detached estate workers' cottages with an array of gablets to tiny attic windows above two gabled single-storey halls, rather unadvisedly sharing a common gutter as they project together. Harled, rubble-built, they also share a great brick chimney-stack. Modest entrance pillars with concave cappings. Built for Peter Ponsonby Metge.

LGI (1904).

17. BACHELOR'S LODGE, Donaghpatrick; pre-1836/*c.* 1890.

A thoroughly dilapidated late Victorian porter's lodge, which had a predecessor. Single-storey standard, gabled in roughcast with starkly contrasting red-brick toothed dressings and segmental window arches with stone keystones. Centrally are the sad remains of a low gabled porch with perforated earthenware cresting, repeated on the main ridge; paired brackets to verges. The quarry-faced masonry quadrant walls and carriage pillars with their unusual layered cappings are also to be found in County Longford at Farraghroe (*q.v.*), Lismoy Upper (*q.v.*) and Lissard (*q.v.*). A property of the earls of Essex, probably retained as a hunting-lodge and occupied by their tenants or agents, in the persons of John Wade in the early nineteenth century and Joseph Lowry in 1890.

Mason 1814–19; Lewis 1837; *Thom's*; Casey and Rowan 1993.

18. BALAMARINO, Drogheda; pre-1912; *demolished.*
A lodge built sometime after 1836 by a member of the McEvoy family.

19. BALBRIGH, Robinstown; *c.* 1860.

Built by William Tisdall, who succeeded his father to the place in 1835, opposite the gates is this remarkably commodious gatehouse, its central gabled two-storey two-bay block strikingly flanked by a pair of single-storey lean-to wings behind screen walls with carved tops. An imaginative composition in pleasant rubble finish with brick soldier arches to cast-iron latticed windows. What may have originated as semi-detached cottages now lies abandoned.

LGI (1904).

20. BALFESTOWN, Dunboyne (2).

South lodge; *c.* 1880.

A single-storey hip-roofed cottage, roughly harled, with projecting gabled hall having plain bargeboards. Complicated casement windows with an Arts and Crafts feel. Substantial but derelict.

North lodge; *c.* 1835.

A single-storey structure with paired exposed joist ends to eaves taken around to form a suggestion of open-pedimented gables. In harled stone, with gabled central hall projection and generous contemporary back return forming a cruciform plan.

A property in 1854 of Stephen T. Mathews.

Griffith 1848–60.

21. BALLAIR or BELLAIR, Moynalty; pre-1913; *demolished.*

A lodge built after 1836 to a seat in the mid-nineteenth century of Alexander Walker.

Griffith 1848–60; *Land owners in Ireland 1876.*

22. BALLINACREE, Oldcastle; pre-1913; *demolished.*

Opposite the gates, dating from after 1836, was a gatekeeper's lodge to a property which in 1854 included a woollen factory of Joseph Forde.

Griffith 1848–60.

23. BALLINDERRY, Enfield; pre-1836; *demolished.*

In 1837 Ballinderry was 'The property of the Hon. R.T. Rowley, and the residence of Thomas Murphy'. At the entrance all that survive are outer rendered pillars with heavily moulded cappings, similar to those of 1906 at Owenstown (*q.v.*). The carriage pillars have succumbed to farm traffic.

Lewis 1837.

24. BALLINLOUGH, Ballinlough; pre-1836; *demolished.*

A property in 1854 of Willoughby Bond, the lodge to which was removed in the 1930s.

Griffith 1848–60.

25. BALLINLOUGH, Dunshaughlin; *c.* 1835.

A single-storey lodge with four-bay elevation to the road, gabled, with a similarly treated breakfront hall. Rendered, with a nice original casement window to the avenue. Being rehabilitated in 1997. The proprietor in 1854 was James Mulvany.

Griffith 1848–60.

26. BALLYBEG, Kells (2).

North entrance; *c.* 1810.

A single-storey standard structure with hipped roof, clipped eaves and limewashed, harled rubble construction. The simplest of vernacular lodges, were it not for a touch of sophistication to one end in the shape of a central window flanked by a pair of Classical round-headed niches. These are reflected in contemporary loop-topped iron gates. Derelict. Built by Patrick O'Reilly.

South entrance; *c.* 1850.

Fast becoming choked by ivy is this two-

Ballybeg, north entrance.

roomed symmetrical five-bay single-storey lodge, roughcast below a hipped roof with a flat-roofed porch to the front door, its canopy once carried by six cast-iron posts with moulded wooden capitals. Erected in the time here of Terence O'Reilly, who in 1837 had a nursery of 100 acres, 'affording employment to about 80 persons'.

Leet 1814; Lewis 1837; Griffith 1848–60.

27. BALLYBOY, Athboy [1]; pre-1912; *demolished.*

The lodge was built after 1836, presumably for the proprietor in 1854, John C. Clifford, whose estate lies 4km south-west of the town.

Griffith 1848–60.

28. BALLYBOY, Athboy [2]; *c.* 1825; architect possibly Francis Johnston.

Three kilometres north-east of the town is this attractive complex of gatescreens, identical to those at Roristown (*q.v.*) and Rockview, Co. Westmeath (*q.v.*), the main entrance being of tall fluted octagonal carriage posts with ball finials, coordinated on the opposite side of the road in a lower screen of gate posts carrying iron pedestrian gates with delightful Catherine-wheel pattern, behind which is the original gate lodge. Single-storey of single-bay main façade, much modernised and extended into an exercise in duality by a repeat structure to the left-hand side, joined by a central block with a verandah of concrete columns, all quite innovative but doing little for the previous symmetry of the concept. Built for Nicholas Gannon.

29. BALLYFALLON, Athboy; pre-1836; *demolished.*

A pleasant entrance of railed quadrants and gates with octagonal posts, the gate lodge to which opposite has gone. A seat in the early nineteenth century of J. Bartley.

Lewis 1837.

30. BALLYHACK, Ratoath; *c.* 1845.

Parallel to the road and alongside a narrow gated access is a standard commodious lodge in whitewashed rubble fabric below a hipped roof. Vacant.

31. BALLYMACOLL, Dunboyne (2).

Front entrance; *c.* 1820/*c.* 1890.

A late Georgian lodge originating in the time here of Henry Hamilton (1760–1844) as a simple standard single-storey structure in harled rubble. This was given a late Victorian facelift by his grandson, Revd James Hamilton, who inherited the estate in 1861, with the application of fleur-de-lis cresting,

fish-scale slate banding, decorative carved fascias and bargeboards, a pretty canopied porch to the front door with chinoiserie-patterned rails, matching the chunky wooden gatescreen, and unusual ornate pelmet hoods to the windows, a feature to be found on the main lodge to the neighbouring Hamwood demesne (*q.v.*), a property of an unrelated Hamilton family.

Rear entrance; *c.* 1890.

Apparently another of Revd Hamilton's improvements is this single-storey Picturesque building built off an L-plan in quarry-faced masonry with brick highlights in its toothed quoins and dressings. Above the windows are label mouldings in Tudor fashion but elaborated with strange Victorian motifs over to relieve the steep gables. As in the front lodge, there are fish-scale slate bands to the roof and incongruously delicate spiky hip-knobs.

LGI (1904).

32. BALLYMAGARVEY, Duleek; pre-1836; *demolished.*

An estate of the Osborne family, to which a fine low gatescreen survives but no lodge.

33. BALLYNADRIMNA, Athboy; pre-1836; *demolished.*

William Thorogood was the proprietor of this holding in the first half of the nineteenth century. Its gate lodge opposite the gates has gone.

34. BALRATH BURY, Kells (4).

For three centuries the home of the Nicholson family, whose eighteenth-century mansion—the pre-1836 gate lodge to which has gone—was replaced by the present house *c.* 1930. In the interim, Christopher Armytage Nicholson (1768–1849), his son, John Armytage Nicholson, and his grandson, who shared his name, built a series of porters' lodges about the estate.

Main entrance; *c.* 1845; architect not known.
At a crossroads on the Kells approach, the lodge (*above*) presides imposingly over a large forecourt outside the gates in an Italianate style. Standard 1½-storey with shallow-gabled roof in the form of open pediments, dominated by a pair of tall chimney-stacks which form an important element of the design. In stuccoed walls, three-over-three segmentally arched sash windows in similar recesses flank the stone frontispiece, accommodated below tall eaves, the pediment to which has a glazed tympanum to light the hall, probably a later innovation. Wide railed gatescreen of ogee quadrants, contained by octagonal stone pillars, the gates hung on iron carriage piers with lanterns. Occupied.

South entrance; *c.* 1845.
At the Clonmellon road access, aside from and outside the gates is the two-storey gatehouse in the form of a two-bay cube below a hipped roof with carved rafter toes. Windows with small squared lights under Tudor-style label mouldings in roughcast walls. Occupied. Two stone octagonal gate pillars, smaller versions of those to the main entrance.

North entrance; 1875.
A solid, ungainly composition built in coursed random quarry-faced masonry with an ashlar finish to the lower storey of the gabled front, extending as quoins and dressings to the two windows over. Three-bay symmetrical ground-floor elevation with two-over-two sashes and a date-stone in the gable. Calcium silicate brick stack with corbelled capping.

Side entrance; *c.* 1880; architect William I. Chambers.

On the previous main avenue is this extravagant design, with all the early trappings of the Arts and Crafts movement in its half-timbered work, tile-hanging, stone and elaborately carved woodwork. Commodious, 1½-storey and arranged on an L-plan, one projection is in the form of a semi-octagonal bay with equivalent roof covered in earthenware plain tiles, the main pitch of which catslides over the internal angle to form a fine verandah porch supported on turned posts. The main gable has a timber-framed apex with serrated clay-tiled bands to the attic storey, bellcast and projecting on great chiselled corbel stones on each side of a canted bay window in a random uncoursed rubble ground floor. There is a grand ashlar chimney-stack with moulded capping and a mono-pitched dormer window. The overall effect is not helped by the intrusion of plastic windows and glazing of the porch.

LGI 1904; Bence-Jones 1988; Williams 1994.

35. BALTRASNA, Oldcastle; 1800.
Here is a fine late Georgian entrance of railed screens between V-jointed rusticated stone pillars, those of the carriage opening having fluted friezes and scroll-topped gate stops. The plain two-roomed single-storey lodge with high eaves to its hipped roof may be contemporary, but lies derelict and almost obscured by a peculiar later stone-built canted room to its front, and itself now roofless. The original dates from the time of Thomas O'Reilly (1741–1805) or his son James.

LGI (1904).

36. BALTRASNA, Ratoath; pre-1836; *demolished.*
A seat in 1854 of the Bryan family.

Griffith 1848–60.

37. BARONSTOWN, Skreen; *c.* 1850.
Opposite the entrance is a solid little single-storey standard lodge, built in big random stone blocks under a hipped roof which catslides over the central front door breakfront. A property created between 1836 and 1854 by Edward T. Wilkinson.

Griffith 1848–60.

38. BARROCKSTOWN, Maynooth; pre-1836; *demolished.*
An estate in 1814 of John Brown.

Leet 1814.

39. BEAMORE, Drogheda; *c.* 1855.
A simple single-storey standard gabled cottage built in pleasant rubble stone with some brick dressings, limewashed front elevation, brick skew-table and clipped eaves. Fronting the road and sited forward of its basic gatescreen with concave quadrants, which has late eighteenth-century gates salvaged from Bellewstown church in the 1880s. The lodge probably dates from when the house was built in 1850–1 by James McCullen (1817–77), jobbing builder and farmer, whose gatekeeper in 1854 was probably Patrick Fay. Vacant.

Griffith 1848–60; *CLAHJ* (1993).

40. BECTIVE, Bective (3).
Not worthy of notice by late Georgian travellers, this beautiful estate on the banks of the River Boyne realised its present appearance and was put on the map by Richard Bolton, who began its improvement about 1836. He enlarged it by extending to the north and westwards, thus rendering redundant an earlier porter's lodge, and created the beech plantation through which the driveway meanders towards his new, rather restrained early Victorian house. By 1849 the demesne was walled in and Bolton then added two more extravagant and contrasting lodges.

Front entrance; 1852; architect possibly W.G. Murray.
Attributable to Murray on the basis of its similarity in form to his father's north lodge at Rockfield House (*q.v.*) is this striking

composition (*above*) in Tudor manor house style, single-storey with prominent skew-tables having bold moulded kneelers and exaggerated stone hip-knobs. Fundamentally a rectangular block with two projections to the avenue, in a Tudor-arched porch with a plaque containing the family's crest: a hawk, their motto, 'Deus Providebit', and helpfully the date of construction. Alongside extends a living-room annexe with grand transomed and mullioned multi-paned window in a parapeted frontispiece. To the park gable is an undersized semi-octagonal bay window with equivalent roof, and off the rear wall survives a 'P.F. Robinson' octagonal chimney-stack. Lying abandoned and rendered over in dull cement cloak, it is in stark disparity with its gatescreen. This is an imposing Classical design, splendidly located on an axis with the Trim approach; its four giant V-jointed rusticated stone pillars with moulded cornice cappings contain fine iron carriage gates and

ashlar quadrants, their postilion openings with dies to the copings over. Sadly disused.

Rear entrance; *c.* 1850; architect possibly W.G. Murray.

More tranquilly situated is a gatescreen similar to the above, in less pretentious masonry but with equally decorative ironwork, behind which lies a more appropriate and refined Classical lodge built in stone, curiously mixing punched ashlar and cruder quarry-faced finish. Single-storey below a shallow oversailing hipped roof with paired soffit brackets. Raised off a T-plan, the downstroke displays an entrance in the form of a loggia of two Roman Doric columns and two quarter ones *in antis* framing a panelled front door and sidelights. The large square windows are subdivided into round-headed

quadripartite casements. Occupied and appreciated.

Lewis 1837; Wilde 1850; Casey and Rowan 1993.

BEECHVILLE (see THURSTIANSTOWN)

41. BELLMOUNT, Navan; pre-1836; *demolished.*

A property of the Nelligan family in the first half of the nineteenth century.

42. BELLVILLE, Castletown; pre-1836; *demolished.*

A seat in 1854 of Revd Patrick Gibney, his gatekeeper then Peter Kelly, whose lodge had gone by 1900.

Griffith 1848–60.

43. BELVIEW, Ballinlough; pre-1836; *demolished.*

The lodge to this very fine mid-Georgian villa of the Daniell family is lost without trace.

44. BEN'SFORT, Kells; *c.* 1825.

Originally a three-bay cottage, sometime later extended by a bay. Single-storey roughcast with a steeply gabled roof repeated in the projecting hall. Completely blind rear elevation. V-jointed rusticated stone mid-Georgian gate pillars. A property with a variety of occupants over the years, of whom the Booker family seems to have been longest in residence in the early nineteenth century.

Lewis 1837.

45. BESHELLSTOWN, Naul; *c.* 1870.

A single-storey standard hip-roofed structure, its walls harled, with brick as dressings and soldier arches to openings. Much extended, the door now a window. Located remote from the entrance to a place in 1854 occupied by a Miss White.

Griffith 1848–60.

46. BETAGHSTOWN, Bettystown (2).

An earlier pre-1836 lodge to the right-hand side of the entrance was superseded *c.* 1850 across the avenue by the present structure. Robert Shepherd's replacement to the estate of his predecessor, the Hon. Capt. Jones, is itself since much altered out of all recognition. The previous hip-roofed standard single-storey lodge is still detectable through many extensions and improvements, the whole having been clothed in reconstituted stone. The original roof extends to the road in a catslide and serrated fascia board carried around to a gabled breakfront with continuous bracket bargeboards. The mid-nineteenth-century gatescreen is untouched, with four stone ball-finialled pillars containing concave quadrants broken by nice postilion gateways. In an adjoining screen wall is an Edward VII postbox.

Leet 1814.

47. BLACKCASTLE, Navan (2).

Richard Fitzherbert (b. 1775) inherited the estate on the death of his father in 1825, replacing the old cottage with 'a square, modern building, designed more for comfort than architectural beauty', and added two gatekeepers' lodges at different dates.

Slane lodge; *c.* 1835.

In the English Picturesque Cottage style so popular at the time, this 1½-storey gabled affair in random stone has been modernised almost out of all recognition, with an oriel window to the attic room.

River lodge; *c.* 1850.

On an elevated site is the sad shell of a once-pretty standard 1½-storey English Picturesque Cottage. Gabled and built in harled rubble, there are the remains of dainty label mouldings to square windows on each side of a canopied front door. There was an attic oriel window to the leading gable. In 2007 awaiting the approach of invading apartment blocks, the big house having already succumbed.

Wilde 1850; *IFR.*

48. BLOOMSBERRY, Kells; pre-1836.

Only a single one-window elevation of the original lodge, built off an L-plan, survives alongside late Georgian gate pillars with scroll-topped stops. Beside this again is a later, early Victorian gatescreen with concave cappings, perhaps dating from the time of architect William Caldbeck's involvement here in the employment of Richard Barnewall around 1850.

Craig 1984; Casey and Rowan 1993.

49. BOB'SVILLE, Crossakiel; *c.* 1800.

A property named by Robert Battersby (b. 1720), who built his villa *c.* 1765, to which there was the epitome of a vernacular Irish gate lodge. Originally single-storey standard, its symmetrical three-bay front to the park with six-over-three sash windows, built in harled rubble below a steeply hipped roof that may have been thatched. Subsequently altered, with two bipartite windows inserted in the road elevation and the door moved to an end wall. Probably built by William Battersby, it now lies derelict.

Wilson 1803; Casey and Rowan 1993.

50. BOYNAGH HILL, Nobber; pre-1836; *demolished.*

A seat in 1854 of Edward Kellett.

Griffith 1848–60.

BOYNE (see STACKALLEN)

51. BOYNE HILL, Navan (2).

Two porters' lodges that were in place by 1836 have both been demolished. At least a most striking gatescreen remains at the southern entrance to an estate of the Gerrards of Gibbstown (*q.v.*) and Liscarton Castle (*q.v.*). In cast iron and extensive, the gates and wide-railed screen are chinoiserie in style, with rose bosses and fleur-de-lis finials. The main carriage posts have ivy-entwining rosettes climbing toward lanterns atop.

LGI (1904).

52. BOYNE LODGE, Trim (2).

East lodge; *c.* 1810.

Irish Architectural Archive

A most unorthodox lodge opposite the gates, with its almost blind front façade, the windows confined to the bow ends, with a central lean-to hall below the tall eaves of its semi-conical-ended roof. Single-storey and with harled finish to rubble construction bordering on the ruinous, it lies derelict.

West lodge; *c.* 1825.

Single-storey square on plan, two-bay by two-bay, its squat pyramidal roof rises to a central brick chimney-stack. Harled and derelict.

A demesne in 1814 of James A. O'Reilly.

Leet 1814; IAA photograph (S/238/4).

BOYNE VALLEY (see STAMEEN [1])

53. BOYNE VIEW, Navan; pre-1836; *demolished.*

The lodge to a property of the Williams family had gone by 1912 but is survived by its nice wrought-iron gate posts and railing with palmette motifs.

54. BRANGANSTOWN, Kilmessan; pre-1836; *demolished.*

A seat in the mid-nineteenth century of Nicholas Madden.

55. BRAYMOUNT or BREEMOUNT, Trim; pre-1836; *demolished.*

Remaining are V-jointed rusticated pillars and cast-iron gates of *c.* 1850. A Georgian-style bungalow now occupies the site of the lodge to a place of James Murphy in 1814.

Leet 1814.

56. BRIDE'S STREAM, Kilcock; *c.* 1825.

Just detectable through the undergrowth is a derelict plain single-storey harled cottage, hip-roofed with corbelled eaves, its single-window-bay elevation forming the main front. The disused entrance has palmette-topped railed concave quadrants framing nasty modern steel gates. The fine Palladian villa became home to the Coates family about 1800, of whom John would have been responsible for lodge and entrance.

Bence-Jones 1988.

57. BRITTAS, Nobber (3).

A pleasant mansion, home to the Bligh family since the seventeenth century. Just as it realised its present layout over the years with additions and alterations initiated by succeeding members of the family, so too were changes made at the demesne entrances, for none of the three survivors relate to those shown on the 1836 OS map.

North lodge; pre-1836/*c.* 1870.

On the same site as its predecessor is this single-storey gabled structure with smooth red-brick quoins, dressings and eaves course to otherwise roughcast walls. Derelict and choked with rampant laurel.

Middle lodge; pre-1836/*c.* 1845.

This is 1½-storey, built off an L-plan, with gablets to each of its hip-roofed extremities. Harled, with a string-course at attic-floor level. Pretty but derelict and inaccessible through the undergrowth.

South lodge; pre-1836/*c.* 1845.

Escaping dereliction is this agreeable rubble-built structure on a T-plan. A recess to its single-storey wing forms a porch giving access to the two-storey main body of the lodge, which has a hipped gable; carved brackets to soffits and cut-stone first-floor string-course. Well restored with rectangular-paned casement windows.

All three gatekeepers' lodges look to have been built for Edward Bligh (1779–1872), who inherited the estate on the death of his father in 1830.

LGI (1904); Bence-Jones 1988.

58. BROE, Slane; *c.* 1840.

A modest single-storey standard gabled porter's lodge, extended by a bay to the right-hand side and rendered over. A property in the mid-nineteenth century of Thomas Maguire.

Griffith 1848–60.

59. BROWNSTOWN, Kentstown (3).

Three gate lodges are revealed by the 1854 valuation to a property of John Cornwall, two of which can be identified on the 1912 OS map and on site but were not marked on the 1836 first edition. Formerly a seat of the Somervilles, the house was being 'put in order' in 1837.

North lodge; *c.* 1845.

Standard 1½-storey gabled, its high eaves with plain paired soffit brackets over the single-storey hall projection. Almost identical to the neighbouring Staffordtown (*q.v.*) lodge, presumably by the same local jobbing builder. Occupied.

South lodge; *c.* 1845.

A standard single-storey lodge now boasting a flat roof and similar hall projection. Not pretty.

Lewis 1837; Griffith 1848–60; Casey and Rowan 1993.

60. BRYANSTOWN, Kilcock; *c.* 1950.

A single-storey three-bay by two-bay cube lodge with pyramidal roof.

CABRA CASTLE (see *THE GATE LODGES OF ULSTER*)

61. CALGATH, Kilcock; pre-1836; *demolished.*

A pleasant gentleman farmer's house in the early nineteenth century of the Tronson family.

62. CANNONSTOWN, Kells; pre-1836; *demolished.*

One of the two neighbouring estates of the Rothwell family, the other being Rockfield (*q.v.*), by which it was eventually absorbed.

63. CARROLLSTOWN, Trim; *c.* 1885; architect John P. Davis.

Opposite the gates is this amply proportioned 1½-storey gabled gatehouse, perfectly symmetrical with a pair of eight-over-four sash windows in gablets to the attic, on each side of a full-height gabled breakfront hall with fanlit doorway in random stone contrasting with otherwise white rendered walls containing eight-over-

eight sash windows to living rooms; modern louvred shutters. Four striking ashlar pillars with recessed panel shafts in the shape of pylons under distinctive bracketed cappings. Highly ornate railed screens and matching carriage gates with humorous hinges in the form of fists. There are identical pillars at Kilcarn House Lower (*q.v.*). All presumably part of a commission of John P. Davis, architect of Trim, who designed the residence for Patrick J. Dunne in 1883, the contractor being Mr A. Hammond of Sheephouse, Drogheda.

IB (15 Jan. 1883).

64. CASTLEPARKS, Slane; *c.* 1850.

Tucked in behind a tight rubble-built concave quadrant with concave capped pillars, its back to the road and stopping a range of outbuildings, is this solid single-storey standard lodge below a hipped roof. Constructed of pleasant random uncoursed rubble with brick dressings to cast-iron latticed casement windows. Not in use and missing its chimney-stack. A property in 1854 of John L. Cornwall, probably the same as at Brownstown House (*q.v.*).

Griffith 1848–60.

65. CASTLERICKARD, Ballivor; *c.* 1835.

Opposite the entrance to a property in 1814 and 1837 of George Lucas Nugent is a modest single-storey lodge, its short window and door two-bay gabled front facing the gates. There is a later two-storey extension to the rear. Derelict.

Leet 1814; Lewis 1837.

66. CAUSESTOWN, Kilberry; pre-1836; *demolished.*

A property in the late eighteenth century of a Mr Tooke that passed *c.* 1810 to John M. Grainger, in whose family it remained until it was auctioned as an incumbered estate in 1860.

Taylor and Skinner 1778; 1969 [1783]; Leet 1814; Lyons 1993.

67. CHARLESFORT, Kells (3).

A house was originally built here by Charles Tisdall *c.* 1750, but it was his son Michael (1755–94) who added the early lodges.

South entrance; *c.* 1790.

A familiar pattern of Georgian Gothic porter's lodge with lancet lights to a centred main front. Single-storey, it has been much extended in like manner.

North entrance; *c.* 1790/*c.* 1860.

What probably originated as single-storey standard, harled with a hipped roof, was later extended to the left-hand side and united by a central canted projection below a catslide roof to abut a stub of the old gatescreen. A most ungainly affair, now abandoned.

Side entrance; 1860.

John Tisdall (1815–92) succeeded to the property on the death of his father, Charles Arthur, in 1835 and erected this single-storey hip-roofed structure. Harled, its short gabled front addresses the avenue with a single squared-light window. The door on the park elevation has a date-stone over; brick chimney-stack with sawtooth band.

LGI (1904).

68. CHERRYMOUNT, Moynalty (2).

South lodge; pre-1913; *demolished.*

North lodge; pre-1913.

A single-storey affair, elongated and modernised out of all recognition.

Extensive alterations and additions were being carried out to the mansion house and offices in 1875 by A. McAlister, architect, for Claude C.C. Hamilton, who had succeeded the Smith family to the property.

IB (15 May 1875).

69. CLIFTON LODGE, Athboy (4).

An urbane Regency villa of the Bligh family, earls of Darnley, the property named after a lesser of their English titles and occupied by their agents. The author of the house design may be the Cork architect John Hargrave, for two of its gatekeepers' lodges can safety be attributed to him. His client was probably Edward Bligh, the 5th earl (1795–1835), who succeeded to the title on his father's death in 1831, so his reign was very short. He did, however, outlive the unfortunate architect by two years, for Hargrave drowned in a yachting accident in 1833.

Athboy gate; *c.* 1832; architect John Hargrave.

An attractive and chaste single-storey Classical composition in ashlar, its main elevation to the road perfectly symmetrical, with the central segmental bow containing a Wyatt window flanked by a pair of round-headed niches, all below a shallow-hipped roof underlined by bracketed eaves. There is an identical lodge at Ballynegall, Co.

Westmeath (*q.v.*), where Hargrave is also known to have worked. Beautifully maintained but suffering the intrusion of plastic windows.

Middle gate; pre-1836; *demolished.*

The first OS map suggests that a pair of substantial lodges flanked the gates.

Trim gate; *c.* 1832; architect John Hargrave.

There is a very similar design to this by the architect at Fota, Co. Cork. A two-storey gatehouse in random coursed limestone ashlar with a canted main front below a semi-octahedral-cum-hipped roof. To one side is a gabled single-storey hall, probably once balanced by a similar accretion on the opposing front, now supplanted by a larger modern extension in matching manner. The oversailing eaves and entrance verge are emphasised by prominent brackets or mutules. A large chimney-stack rises off the rear wall. Plinth and string-course identical to the Fota example.

Kildalkey gate; *c.* 1825.

Situated on the western approach beyond the Tremblestown River is this substantial two-storey three-bay hip-roofed gatehouse with a single-storey breakfront door feature. Symmetrical, in roughcast finish with stone quoins. Having its own yard and outbuildings, it is identified on the 1912 OS map as a 'Lodge' but was avenueless in 1836.

LGI (1904); Guilt (1912); *BPB* (1929).

70. CLONABREANY, Crossakeel (2).

A seat since 1684 of the Wade family, the only structure on which remaining intact is the stable block, both lodges, one of which was in place by 1836, having been demolished.

LGI (1904); Glin *et al.* 1988.

71. CLONCARNEEL, Ballivor; pre-1836; architect possibly Francis Johnston; *demolished.*

An understated but striking gatescreen comprised of octagonal stone posts with fluting and postilion gates on each side of the carriage opening. Across the road where the porter's lodge was located is a matching straight screen, all very much like the layouts at Ballyboy (*q.v.*), Roristown (*q.v.*) and Rockview, Co. Westmeath (*q.v.*). The house, previously called 'Clown', was designed in 1801 by Francis Johnston for Walter Dowdall.

Mulligan 2001.

72. CLONGILL RECTORY, Wilkinstown; *c.* 1880.
A late Victorian gatekeeper's lodge to a glebe house of 1811. Single-storey symmetrical and built in red brick with an ogee eaves course to its gabled roof. Wide windows on each side of a canopied front door. Later single-bay extension. By about 1880 the house had ceased to be a rectory, after the parish was combined with others under the Union of Donaghpatrick, and was bought by Thomas Martin.

Lewis 1837; Healy 1908.

73. CLONLEASAN HILL, Clonmellon; pre-1913; *demolished.*
A property in 1854 of the Booker family.

Griffith 1848–60.

74. CLONLEASAN, Clonmellon; *c.* 1845.
Like neighbouring Clonleasan Hill, a mid-nineteenth-century seat of the Bookers, whose gate lodge survives. Originally a standard gabled single-storey structure, harled, with a catslide roof to the breakfront hall, the front door to which has become a window in modernisation that saw it extended by a bay. Still a charming cottage, well maintained as a holiday let.

Griffith 1848–60.

75. CLOONEY, Castletown; *c.* 1850.
What was probably erected as a standard single-storey gabled lodge is now four-bay. A property in 1854 of James Reilly.

Griffith 1848–60.

76. CLOWANSTOWN, Skryne (2).

'J.P. Pile carrying out extensive alterations and additions at Clownstown of L. McCreery. Work besides house itself, will embrace a motor house, coach house and new lodge. The roof of the latter will be thatched, rather unusual nowadays, but adding considerably to the picturesqueness of the approach. Plans prepared by A.E. Murray.' Built to replace an earlier pre-1837 gate lodge to a seat of the Maher family at this new entrance to serve the house of a new owner and oversee the arrival of the motor car, the development was complete by October 1908. This is an outstanding Arts and Crafts design by the third in line of an architectural dynasty, Albert E. Murray (1849–1924). Single-storey, of the simplest of concepts, built in random coursed rubble off a square plan capped by a steeply pitched bellcast pyramidal roof rising to a sturdy central chimney-stack. The intended thatch seems never to have materialised; rather it was finished in the surviving small slates with leaded hips. But the principal feature is the semicircular entrance hall advancing from the leading front with the finest of latticed cast-iron glazing wrapped around below a semi-conical roof. Occupied.

IB (25 Jan. 1908; 4 April 1908; 17 Oct. 1908); ffolliott 1971b.

CLOWN (see CLONCARNEEL)

77. COOPERHILL, Julianstown; *c.* 1810.
A two-storey hip-gabled cottage with whitewashed harled walls attached to outbuildings. Nearby is a pair of grand stone entrance pillars with unpedestalled ball finials. Flanking are screen walls containing flat-arched architraved postilion openings, extended further by tall rendered convex quadrant walls. All probably built for Nathaniel Cooper, who succeeded his father John to the property in 1808.

LGI (1904).

78. CORBALLIS, Laytown; pre-1836; *demolished.*
A lodge perhaps added to the estate by J. Smith Taylor, who came to the place after Hugh Rothwell between 1814 and 1837.

Leet 1814; Lewis 1837.

79. CORBALTON HALL, Skreen (3).
A house, originally named 'Cookstown', in the late eighteenth century of the White family, which was purchased and amalgamated *c.* 1800 with the Corballys' neighbouring estate of Sydenham. Elias Corbally then extended Cookstown to designs of Francis Johnston, and it is mainly his elegant cut-stone villa that survives. Nothing in the lodges suggests his influence.

Rear lodge; pre-1836/*c.* 1890.
Of late Victorian appearance, two-storey, roughcast with red-brick toothed dressings, its gables with replacement carved bargeboards; single-storey gabled hall projection. Probably incorporating an earlier lodge on the site, which may have been one of a pair. Lately much extended as rear return in like style.

South lodge; pre-1836.
What was apparently a single-storey hip-roofed structure conceivably by Johnston but overcome by twentieth-century additions, thankfully screened by foliage. In contrast, across the road is a modern elegant Classical archway in beautifully worked limestone with pretty floral paterae in its spandrels and 'MMIII' inscribed in a die. Wholly appropriate to what lies within and a welcome enhancement to the run-down perimeter of the place.

North lodge; *c.* 1890.
Likewise opposite its entrance is this clumsy substantial 1½-storey structure in English Picturesque Cottage mode with multi-paned windows, that to the ground-floor leading gable segmentally arched. Roughcast walls and modern mono-pitched canopy to the front door combine with coarsely carved bargeboards, earthenware cresting and two large chimney-stacks in an attempt at the quaint.

This late Victorian work was carried out after the death of Matthew Elias Corbally in 1870, the property then being inherited by his only child, Mary Margaret (1845–1925), who in 1865 had married Alfred Joseph Stourton, Baron Mowbray, Seagrave and Stourton (1829–93), living on here as his widow with her second son, Major Alfred Edward Corbally Joseph Stourton (1872–1926); after their deaths the estate fell on hard times before experiencing a recent renaissance.

BPB (1929); Bence-Jones 1988.

80. CORBOY, Navan; pre-1836/*c.* 1860.
A simple standard single-storey gabled stone dwelling, the predecessor to which was at the other side of the entrance to a property in 1854 of Edward Casey.

Griffith 1848–60.

CORNANSTOWN (see CURNIAGHANSTOWN)

81. COURTHILL, Dunboyne (2).
A house and its lodge, both of *c.* 1835, built by Henry Greene. About 1900 the former was remodelled for John L. McCarthy, who replaced the latter with the surviving structure on a different site. It is a pleasant standard single-storey lodge of traditional format under a hipped roof, but with a pair of canted oriel windows, flat-roofed and supported on big carved scrolled brackets flanking a flat-roofed porch with more scroll features and supporting pretty climbing roses. Rendered, as is the bulky chimney-stack. Modest entrance with narrow access.

Casey and Rowan 1993.

82. COWSLIP LODGE, Bettystown (2).

To a prettily named demesne is a pretty little single-storey standard gatekeeper's lodge of *c.* 1840, which lies mysteriously abandoned and prey to vandals below a hipped roof. There extends from the side elevation a bow with bipartite timber latticed casements, repeated on the main front. Smooth-rendered, it has unfortunately lost its original chimney-stack in modernisation and extension. A property in the early nineteenth century of George H. Pentland, which had an earlier pre-1836 lodge.

Leet 1814; Slater 1846.

83. CROSSDRUM, Oldcastle (2).

Outer gate; pre-1836; *demolished.*

Inner gate; *c.* 1850.

Built by Edward Rotheram (1789–1881) and situated well within the demesne was a single-storey standard lodge, raised by a storey *c.* 1945, with a hipped roof and the addition of a strange recessed elevation to the avenue containing a little bay window. Avenue discontinued.

LGI (1904).

84. CRUICESTOWN, Nobber; *c.* 1845.

Originally a house of the Cruice family, it was rebuilt by Alexander Shaw *c.* 1845, which must be the date for its porter's lodge. Standard single-storey with a hipped roof, it is fenestrated in the manner of half a century earlier, as the pointed-arched windows suggest. There is a later flat-roofed hall projection. Derelict and lurking behind a contrasting castellated entrance screen of tall rubble-built curtain walls with Welsh copings and Gothic arched postilion openings alongside tall square turrets as carriage pillars with crenellations, mock machicolations and cross arrowloops. The latter was apparently work for Sir Lionel Alexander about 1874.

Lewis 1837; Casey and Rowan 1993.

85. CULLEN, Slane (2).

East entrance; *c.* 1830.

Originally a single-storey standard roughcast gabled cottage, later extended by a bay. Vacant.

West entrance; pre-1912; *demolished.*

A property that passed from the Aiken family in the early nineteenth century to a John Bolton.

Leet 1814; Slater 1856.

86. CULMULLIN, Dunshaughlin; *c.* 1860.

A most curious amalgam of styles, conflicting proportions and detailing allied to superior workmanship and materials. A 1½-storey lodge built in random ashlar facings with fancy carved English Picturesque Cottage

bargeboards to main gables and that of the central breakfront hallway below the tall eaves. This contains a remarkable door-case with a finely chiselled architrave, shouldered with a matching swelling to the base. Above the lintel springs a shallow pointed-arched fanlight with similar moulded surround. To add to the discordance is a modern contribution of the most hideous 'multi-paned' plastic windows in its large openings. The generous scale might be explained by its pre-1837 predecessor on the site having been a schoolhouse 'of 18 boys and 5 girls for which Mr Dopping allows a house and garden rent-free', which function this may have continued. A concoction for James Kearney, who succeeded Dopping to the property.

Lewis 1837; Griffith 1848–60.

87. CURNIAGHANSTOWN, Kilberry; *c.* 1845.

A basic single-storey standard gatekeeper's cottage with a hipped roof which catslides over an off-centre breakfront hallway with curved corners. Built in harled rubble, limewashed, below brick eaves course; tiny and derelict. Probably erected for Andrew Flynn, who is recorded here in 1854.

Griffith 1848–60.

88. DALTONSTOWN, Duleek (2).

East lodge; *c.* 1875.

A pleasant mid-Victorian 1½-storey gabled lodge on an L-plan with a later single-storey wing built in coursed dark rubble contrasting with red-brick toothed quoins and dressings to six-over-six sash windows; carved ornamental bargeboards much as those at Culmullin (*q.v.*).

West lodge; *c.* 1875; *demolished.*

An estate created from adjoining land of the Somerville family, the house dating from *c.* 1865; Alexander Clegg added the lodges later.

89. DANCE'S COURT, Athboy; pre-1836; *demolished.*

A property in 1837 of H. Biddulph Warner.

Lewis 1837.

90. DANGAN CASTLE, Summerhill (3).

Although best known for being if not the birthplace then at least the childhood home of Arthur Wellesley, duke of Wellington (1769–1852), Dangan was once the most extraordinary eighteenth-century estate in the country. After inheriting in 1728 from a cousin, Richard Colley, who later assumed the surname Wellesley, and his descendants as Lords Mornington initially shaped the place as an Arcadia, dotting the park with statues of Greek gods, temples, obelisks and ornamental canals. By 1776 Arthur Young on tour found, created in the heart of Ireland, a naval playground with man-made lakes, one as big as 100 acres, with islands, promontories, earthwork forts and batteries. But in 1793 the Wellesleys sold out to Colonel Thomas Burrowes, who, after improvements and additions to the house, himself disposed of Dangan in 1803; thereafter it went into decline to its present state, whereby a substantial shell of a durable mansion and stable block survive but only two of its original 25 obelisks, little of its planting and nothing of its statuary, temples or gate lodges. Of one of the latter a surprising record remains.

Summerhill gate; *c.* 1770; *demolished.*

Perhaps not so surprising, as it appears to have been quite singular, as Mr and Mrs Hall in the early 1840s found amongst the dereliction of the once-fine demesne: 'The great iron gate would not open; and the carriage-drive is overgrown with grass. We alighted, therefore, and entered through a small passage to the exquisite little lodge, which, unhappily, is falling into decay, although occupied by a man who called himself "caretaker". A low line of cottages stretch to the right outside the gate; and the dwellers therein came forward, as usual, to look at "the quality".' These cottages were located on a southern approach on an axis of the main road from Dublin, along which the Halls took their leave and were moved to make further observations: 'The entrance gates to the park of Dangan still exist—one of

Irish Tourists' Handbook

the gates, that is to say, for another is placed before a Roman Catholic chapel recently erected at Navan. The gate that remains is of wrought iron of very costly workmanship and great beauty, the lodge yet stands beside it—an exquisite example of architecture.' The illustration in an 1854 railway tourists' handbook (*previous page*) reveals their appreciation to be understandable and it to have been a quirky combination of rustic thatched charm attached to a lofty sophisticated distyle Roman Doric portico. If the relative scale of the figures shown is not artistic licence, it was of considerable presence, although the 1836 OS map indicates it to have been minuscule on plan and set apart from its entrance gates, and to have been intended as one of the many architectural ornaments about this ideal rustic paradise. It is indicated on William Larkin's Road Map of 1806–10.

Trim gate; pre-1836; *demolished.*

Rear gate; pre-1836; *demolished.*

Sadly, nothing remains of the other entrances, although tradition has it that the Corinthian columns and equivalent pilasters incorporated into the gatescreen to nearby Springvalley (*q.v.*) were salvaged from a Dangan lodge.

Young 1780; Lewis 1837; Hall 1841–3; *APSD*; *The Irish tourists' illustrated handbook for visitors in Ireland*; Bence-Jones 1988; Malins and Glin 1976; Mulligan 2001; Horner 2007.

91. DARDISTOWN CASTLE, Julianstown; *c.* 1890.

Elevated and opposite the entrance is a substantial pair of late Victorian semi-detached hip-roofed two-storey cottages in rough modern rendering and red-brick dressings and quoins. Now knocked into one to form 'Dardistown Cottage'. A seat in the nineteenth century of the Osborne family.

92. DEER PARK, Kells; pre-1912; *demolished.*

A property of the Jones family of nearby Jonesborough (*q.v.*).

93. DELVIN LODGE, Gormanstown; *c.* 1830.

An unassuming standard white-rendered gabled lodge by the roadside, with later extension to the right-hand side, towards the gates of a property of the Jameson family.

94. DOGHTOG, Ratoath; *c.* 1825.

Alongside the gates is a single-storey plain hip-roofed four-bay cottage finished in roughcast, the original front door now converted into a window. An estate in the nineteenth century of the McCabes.

95. DOLANSTOWN, Kilcock; pre-1836; *demolished.*

An early eighteenth-century house, in 1814 of Cunningham Jones.

Leet 1814.

96. DOLLARDSTOWN, Yellow Furze (2).

Like the big house of the Meredyth family, both gate lodges have been demolished.

97. DOLLY'S GROVE, Carton (2).

A delightful late Georgian villa, in 1814 of James Hamilton.

Side entrance; pre-1836; *demolished.*

Front entrance; *c.* 1850.

What presumably started life as a standard three-bay single-storey porter's lodge has since been elongated to form a five-bay elevation, symmetrical under a hipped roof, with a gabled hall projection containing a hood-moulded Gothic fanlit doorway; roughcast, its windows one-over-one sashes from the period of its modernisation. Occupied. Nearby is an early modest late Georgian gatescreen comprised of roughcast concave quadrants framed in cut stone, and square ashlar pillars with friezes. The lodge was built by Henry Meade Hamilton (1820–95), who succeeded to the property in 1847.

Griffith 1848–60; *LGI* (1904).

98. DONACARNEY, Drogheda; *c.* 1900.

A standard single-storey twentieth-century lodge built in Flemish bond red brick, with continuous bracket ornamental bargeboards to main gables and that of its main accent, a porch with strikingly contrasting Tudor-style half-timbered work carried on turned wooden posts on dwarf wing walls. Abandoned, with its windows boarded up. Entrance pillars and convex quadrants in big quarry-faced stone blocks. The proprietor in 1890 was Robert Bedford Daly. There are lodges of a similar date and style at nearby Stameen (*q.v.*) by W. M. Mitchell and Sons.

Thom's.

99. DOOLISTOWN, Rathmoylan; pre-1836; *demolished.*

A property in 1808–55 of Joseph Fox, whose father Mathew had inherited it through marriage to Elizabeth Grierson. The fine Georgian house is now a ruin.

LGI (1904).

100. DOWDSTOWN, Navan (2).

Replacing an earlier house of the Taylor family of Headfort (*q.v.*) and Ardgillan Castle, Co. Dublin (*q.v.*), an estate that was lodgeless, is this Baronial pile of *c.* 1870 by W.H. Lynn of the Belfast architectural practice of Lanyon, Lynn and Lanyon. Both its lodges appear to be later again and by different hands.

Main entrance; *c.* 1890; architect not known.

A pair of gargantuan ashlar gate pillars with moulded cappings and pedestalled ball finials greets the visitor, carrying very ornate cast-iron scrolled gates. Flanking are concave rubble quadrants with sloped copings, all

looking like a twentieth-century rebuild to accommodate road-widening. Behind is an Arts and Crafts 1½-storey lodge built off an irregular plan in coursed random rubble with toothed brick dressings below a great expanse of roof catsliding over single-storey projections.

Side entrance; *c.* 1880.

A 1½-storey gabled lodge finished in roughcast with red brick as toothed dressings, quoins and two gablets breaking the front eaves over a three-bay ground floor with glazed porch to the right-hand side.

Both lodges were built for General Sir Richard Chambré Hayes Taylor (1819–1904), who inherited Dowdstown on his mother's death in 1859 but spent little time here, it being rented out to various tenants.

BPB (1929); Williams 1994; Casey and Rowan 1993.

101. DOWTH HALL, Drogheda (2).

Eastern entrance; pre-1836; *demolished.*

Effectively sited off a right-angle bend was an early lodge of the Viscounts Netterville to their mid-eighteenth-century house. The avenue is now disused and overgrown; all that survives is a later nineteenth-century gatescreen with fine ironwork and distinctive stone pillars built up in blocks of raised panels, alternately reticulated and topped by four-gabled copings. Perhaps a design by George Ashlin, who worked on the neighbouring Netterville Almshouses.

Western entrance; *c.* 1865; architect possibly William Caldbeck.

A very fine gatekeeper's lodge in hardly understated Italianate style built for Richard Gradwell (1824–84), whose family of nearby

Platten Hall (*q.v.*) had come by the property. Single-storey standard in stucco finish with prominent open pediments to main gables and that of the breakfront hall, all having distinctive verge mutules extending as eaves brackets with ogee guttering. V-jointed toothed quoins and segmentally arched windows with banded surrounds and bracketed sills. The fine panelled double-leaf door, flanked by recessed panel pilasters, has a hood-moulded head with bulky reticulated keystone. Centrally placed on the ridge is an ashlar chimney-stack with plinth and moulded capping.

LGI (1904); Williams 1994; Casey and Rowan 1993.

102. DREWSTOWN, Clonmellon; pre-1836; *demolished.*
What remains at the entrance to the estate is a fine gatescreen comprising postilion openings flanking a pair of magnificent Classical carriage pillars identical to those of 1771 at the archiepiscopal palace in Armagh (*below*), by Thomas Cooley. Here are the same V-jointed rusticated stone shafts, Greek key-patterned bands, swagged friezes and ball finials, commissioned by Barry Maxwell during his short occupancy, which terminated unexpectedly when he succeeded as 3rd Baron Farnham on the death of his elder brother in 1779. His younger brother, Henry Maxwell, whilst bishop of Meath had very similar pillars erected at Ardbraccan Palace (*q.v.*), where Cooley was also employed, so attribution is easy. Not so the missing gate lodge, which could have been built after Maxwell's departure by the purchaser of Drewstown, Joseph McVeagh, or his son, Ferdinand Meath McVeagh (1789–1866).

LGI (1904); *BPB* (1929).

103. DRUMBARAGH or DRUMBARROW, Kells.
A late Georgian house of the Woodward family, whose most famous son was the architect Benjamin Woodward (1816–61), to whom is attributed one of the gate lodges, despite its being unlike anything else he is known to have done.

East lodge; *c.* 1840; architect probably Benjamin Woodward.

A bulky 1½-storey gabled lodge in English Picturesque Cottage style built off an L-plan, with tight wavy bargeboards and fascias carried about the tall hallway set awkwardly into the internal angle. Two-over-two sash windows in walls with bland rendering, which probably hides an original stone or brick finish. To the road gable is a single-storey projecting bay window, and an impressive pair of diagonally set chimney-stacks breaks the ridge. Replacing a contemporary entrance is an extensive screen of railed concave quadrants contained by four stone pillars with four-pedimented cappings, presumably built for John Sweetman, who had purchased the property.

West lodge; *c.* 1830.

A barn-like two-storey gabled gatehouse built in rubble with harled finish and segmentally arched openings. Erected for Henry Woodward.

O'Dwyer 1997b; IAA photograph)8/57).

104. DULEEK, Duleek; *c.* 1770.
An antique and substantial gabled structure with a blind façade to the road and a lancet window facing the house. Probably built in the time here of Thomas Trotter MP.

Casey and Rowan 1993.

105. DUNBOYNE CASTLE, Dunboyne (2).
The big house took on its present appearance in the mid-1760s, when it was substantially remodelled for Sarah Hamilton by George Darley of Drogheda, to whom can be credited the contemporary entrance screen and perhaps its attendant porter's lodge.

Main entrance; *c.* 1765; *demolished.*

A segmental entrance screen of tall stuccoed quadrant walls, each pierced by a postilion opening with moulded flat lintel relieved by a segmental arch over in V-jointed voussoirs as a continuation of the toothed dressings. The keystone is in the form of a floral patera. The four V-jointed masonry pillars have rusticated ball finials, those to the carriage opening with Greek key-pattern bands, just like those at Headfort (*q.v.*).

Side entrance; *c.* 1870.

Severed from its original context by a surround of council housing is this remarkable survivor, standing elevated in a garden oasis. Single-storey, built off an L-plan, with a tiny hall set into the internal angle below the high bracketed eaves of the hipped roof, with two rebuilt banded red-brick chimney-stacks breaking the ridge. Segmentally arched openings to the panelled front door and one-over-one sash windows arranged in pairs in modern roughcast walls. Built for Richard Moore Sadleir (1841–77), whose father had inherited Dunboyne through marriage to a Butler daughter of the Barons Dunboyne.

IFR; Casey and Rowan 1993.

106. DUNSANY CASTLE, Dunshaughlin (5).

With neighbouring Killeen Castle (*q.v.*) one of the medieval Meath properties of the Plunkett family, Dunsany, of the earls of that name, is a castle which has experienced much architectural change over the centuries, as more recently have its estate entrances, three of its gatekeepers' lodges having had predecessors dating from before 1836. Four lodges surviving can be dated to the time of the improving 14th baron, Edward Wadding Plunkett (1773–1848), who inherited the place on the death of his father in 1821 and probably employed the architect James Shiel, to whom can be attributed two lodges, to carry out extensive alterations to the ancestral home.

Killeen gate; pre-1836/*c.* 1840; architect probably James Shiel.
Replacing an earlier lodge on the site is this perfect prelude to the big house (*above*). In the form of a square keep, appearing two-storey to the visitor but presenting a more imposing three-storey elevation to the park, it is built in uncoursed rubble facings with label-moulded mullioned bi- and tripartite windows below a heavy castellated stage with Irish crenellations. Alongside, strangely carried out in contrasting ashlar, is a sturdy gatescreen with great battered piers flanking the carriage opening below a four-centred Tudor arch containing decorative impenetrable ironwork, with quatrefoils, mouchettes, cusped arcaded tracery and a battleaxe atop the carriage gate meeting rails below a mock portcullis. To one side is a smaller-scale postilion opening with hood-moulded archway. Stretching beyond are extensive convex quadrant walls. Above the carriage arch is a cut-stone Plunkett coat of arms and their motto, 'Festina Lente'—diligently but not hurriedly.

Folly gate; pre-1836/*c.* 1840; architect possibly James Shiel.

There are some examples of Romantic ruins in Ireland, notably those at Belvedere, Co. Westmeath, and Heywood, Co. Laois, but none combined with domestic accommodation as here. There is widespread dereliction to estate entrance gates throughout the country but here it is intentional and unique. This sham ruin was doubtless inspired by the abbey ruins nearby within the demesne; it is comprised of a square tower built in random rubble with 'crumbling' parapet and mock arrowloops haphazardly distributed. Adjoining is a pair of pointed entrance arches, the lower to the pedestrian opening, apparently decaying. Within, not seemingly associated, is a single-storey stone three-bay structure with paired sash windows. An earlier building by the entrance has gone.

North gate; *c.* 1840.

Built solely to monitor a pedestrian opening in the estate wall is this forgotten lodge. Now a roofless shell, it was a single-storey standard affair in Regency style, with windows and doorway in the hall breakfront set in segmentally arched recesses. Originally hip-roofed, it retains a later sand/cement rendering to resemble stucco. Capacious with a diminutive back return.

Warrenstown gate; *c.* 1840.
Opposite the redundant entrance in a mild Tudor style with crude label mouldings in roughcast is this single-storey porter's lodge, its main front single-bay gabled.

West gate; pre-1836/*c.* 1870; architect probably Sir George Gilbert Scott.

The most forbidding of compositions, built in unusual slender horizontal courses of apparently continuous rock-faced masonry, which extends parallel to the road's edge as a curtain wall with crenellated top terminating in a pedestrian opening to the left-hand side, remote from a great gaunt two-storey carriage gate tower, similarly castellated, with a segmentally arched opening containing a pair of doors, their studded horizontal planks corresponding with the stone coursing, over which is a sham metal portcullis. These could be opened or closed by mechanisms in rooms to each side of the archway. Above this again is a tripartite chamfered window to the first-floor apartment, its central light now accommodating a carved coat of arms from elsewhere which doesn't quite fit. It bears the mysterious motto 'Destin Letit'. Abutting the tower and protected by the screen wall is a single-storey lodge in the same materials, extending to the chimney-stack, with a crenellated parapet. There is no design in the country akin to this, which suggests an outside influence, and the main contender must be the English architect Sir George Gilbert Scott (1811–78), who designed the stables for the 16th baron, Edward Plunkett (1808–89), in about 1874. All this replaced a pre-1836 lodge located behind the left-hand quadrant of a less extensive gatescreen.

BPB (1929); Craig and Glin 1970; Humphreys 1979; Casey and Rowan 1993; Stamp 2002.

107. DURHAMSTOWN CASTLE, Navan; pre-1836; *demolished.*
An old fortified residence, alternatively spelt 'Dormstown', which passed from the Gerrards to the Roberts family in the early nineteenth century and to which the gate lodge had gone before 1912.

108. EDEN VIEW, Drogheda; *c.* 1860; *demolished.*
Now home to Drogheda Grammar School, the finely proportioned mid-Victorian villa dates from the time here of John Chadwick and the gate lodge was probably contemporary.

Griffith 1848–60.

109. ELM GROVE, Ballivor (2).
A decimated demesne of the Browne family, now without entrance gates but remarkably retaining two good gate lodges.

Rear entrance; *c.* 1870.
Opposite its missing gatescreen is a 1½-storey hip-roofed structure with a pair of gablets above a symmetrical three-bay ground floor, its central hall projection similarly hipped. Built in high-quality random limestone ashlar. Well maintained.

Front entrance; pre-1836/*c.* 1870; architect possibly John McCurdy.

Replacing a predecessor, opposite a now non-existent avenue, is this excellent mid-Victorian single-storey lodge built off an L-plan, with hallway and porch in the internal angle below a hipped roof supported by a conspicuous squat column with a generous composite capital. Constructed in good punched ashlar with contrasting smooth dressings. To one gable is a canted bay with chamfered mullions and a stone bellcast roof rising to the Browne crest of a double-headed eagle. Some of the original multi-paned slit windows remain and there is evidence of carved sawtooth bargeboards; triple stone chimney-stack. Much of this design is redolent of the work of architect John McCurdy, there being similar lodges by him at Pollerton, Co. Carlow (*q.v.*), and Harristown, Co. Kildare (*q.v.*).

Both lodges were built during improvements for Anthony Browne.

Land owners in Ireland 1876.

110. ELM GROVE, Gormanstown; pre-1836; *demolished.*
All that remains of the lodge to an estate in 1854 of William A. McKenna is a solitary stone gable wall.

Griffith 1848–60.

FARM (see GLENMORE)

111. FERGANSTOWN, Navan; pre-1836; *demolished.*
A property in 1814 of Denis Branagan.

Leet 1814.

112. FERRANS, Kilcock; *c.* 1850.
An orderly little standard single-storey porter's lodge below a hipped roof with a gabled breakfront hallway. Recently much improved and rendered, it is framed by concave wing walls, perfectly reflecting the entrance screen opposite. Built for Isaac North-Bomford (d. 1866).

Slater 1856; *LGI* (1904).

113. FLEENSTOWN, Ashbourne (2).
North lodge; pre-1912; *demolished.*
South lodge; *c.* 1870.
A commodious standard single-storey lodge with a steeply hipped roof rising to a red-brick chimney-stack with plinth and sawtooth corbelled capping. Roughcast with a flat-roofed hall breakfront but a modern conservatory across the whole front.

Michael Kennedy was the proprietor in 1854.

Griffith 1848–60.

114. FLEMINGSTOWN, Naul; *c.* 1850.
Once watching over two adjacent entrances, but now vacant, is this not-quite-symmetrical standard single-storey lodge with minute windows in roughcast walls below a gabled roof. A property in 1854 of John Curtis.

Griffith 1848–60.

115. FOSTERSTOWN, Trim; *c.* 1750.
A delightful and surprising surviving example of a vernacular cabin as gate lodge and, since the demise of that at nearby Spring Valley (*q.v.*), unique in the country. Admirably and lovingly maintained in its setting of five majestic beech trees is this almost symmetrical single-storey standard lodge, with tiny casement windows on each

side of a large planked door in limewashed harled walls below a very steeply pitched hipped thatched roof. Presumably built on a property once of the Foster family, an early recorded occupant of which was William Carshore in 1814, although he was probably a tenant of the Wellesleys of Dangan Castle (*q.v.*) prior to their selling it two years later. The place was subsequently called 'Wellington' in celebration of the Iron Duke's reputedly having resided here in the 1790s when he was MP for Trim. He would not have known the present house, which is an 1843 replacement, but would have recognised the porter's lodge in its pristine state. Rustic gatescreen.

Leet 1814; Bence-Jones 1988; Mulligan 2001.

116. FOXBROOK, Ballivor; pre-1836; *demolished.*
A seat in the nineteenth century of the Fox family.

117. FRANKVILLE, Athboy; pre-1836; *demolished.*
The property in the early nineteenth century of Francis Welsh.

118. FREFFANS, GREAT, Laracor; *c.* 1850.
Located 150m up the avenue from modern gates is a once-standard single-storey hip-roofed affair with a gabled central projecting hall. Now extended to the rear to double it in size, its roof rising ever upwards to isolate the original chimney-stack from its ridge. Rendered and occupied. The 1854 valuation records that the farm offices were built in 1852, presumably not long after the house, which does not appear on the 1836 OS map. A development by Henry Law.

Griffith 1848–60.

119. GALLOW HILL, Kilcock; pre-1836; *demolished.*
An estate in the late eighteenth century of a Mr Flanagan which by the early nineteenth century was home to the Maher family.

Wilson 1803; Lewis 1837.

120. GALTRIM, Summerhill; *c.* 1805; architect Francis Johnston.
A delightful villa designed by Francis Johnston as a glebe house for Revd Thomas Vesey Dawson after his marriage in 1793 to Anna Maria, only daughter of Blaney Townley Balfour of Townley Hall, Co. Louth (*q.v.*), where Johnstown was working at that time. The wealthy incumbent included a gate lodge as part of the architect's commission. His three-bay single-storey hip-roofed cottage

was not to have its fairest face wasted on the visitor but rather to be admired across the miniature park. Its central bay is three-bay on its own, nine-over-nine sash windows arranged in a central bow, flanked by Wyatt windows, all nearly full height, worthy of a grander house and reflecting the rear façade of the house. The harled walls are finished in a pretty pastel shade. The rear entrance front is rendered less coherent by modern alterations and additions. There is a very similar version of this design at Lagore (*q.v.*), where the bow serves as the entrance hall. Galtrim remained a rectory until 1815 with the arrival of the Fox family.

BPB (1929); Craig 1976; Bence-Jones 1988; Casey and Rowan 1993.

121. GERNONSTOWN, Slane; *c.* 1860.
Now a four-bay single-storey hip-roofed structure with a gabled hall breakfront containing a segmentally arched door. Paired modillion brackets to soffits carried around singly to bargeboards. Roughcast walls with stone quoins to create a pleasant mildly Italianate feel. Originally three-bay standard and extended by a bay, judging by the cruder quoin stones to the right-hand side. Alongside squat pillars with the concave stone cappings so common in County Louth and north Meath. A property in 1854 of Henry Blackburne.

Griffith 1848–60.

122. GIBBSTOWN, Donaghpatrick; 1883; architect probably W.H. Lynn.
There was already an old Plunkett castle and an early Gerrard house here before Thomas Gerrard (1834–1913) inherited the property as a four-year-old on the death of his uncle of Boyne Hill (*q.v.*). He commenced a massive redevelopment of the demesne 36 years later, the foundation stone for a vast ill-fated Italianate palazzo complete with belvedere tower to designs of the Belfast architect W.H. Lynn being laid in 1870. Ten years in the building, it was approached via an equally monumental gatescreen from Crasulthan crossroads, which strangely remained unattended. Preceded by an extraordinary circular enclosure of a copse of English yews, its robust decorative railings repeated in the convex entrance quadrants behind, which frame similar ironwork to a triple gateway marked by huge square Classical stone pillars with recessed panel shafts and pronounced projecting cornices.

This deficiency in lodges to the estate was only remedied in 1883, when Lynn was plying the Tudor Revival, but strangely at a

secondary access which was little more than a hole in the hedge. Across the road is a severe two-storey gabled gatehouse in red brick, its three-bay façade having a central full-height breakfront, the windows previously six-over-nine sashes with deep stone sills and label-moulded lintels. In the leading gable is a stone chiselled with the date of construction and Thomas Gerrard's monogram.

A year before his death poor Thomas was to see his great 'Irish Osborne' burn down in 1912; he ordered its rebuilding, only for it to be dismantled later in the century.

IB (13 April 1912); *LG* (1937); Bence-Jones 1988; McFadden 2001; Mulligan 2001.

123. GINNETS PARK, Summerhill; *c.* 1820.
A modest single-storey hip-roofed roughcast cottage presenting a four-window-bay elevation to the road. Probably much altered and extended from its original form. An estate in the early nineteenth century of Captain John Mockler.

Leet 1814; Pigot 1824.

124. GLEN, Drogheda (2).
Originally a modest holding, it was much improved around 1855 by George Chadwick, who built a grander house and gave it a gatekeeper's lodge, the new entrance at which points to work by architect John P. Davis.

Main gate; *c.* 1855; architect probably John P. Davis.

An altogether agreeable mid-Victorian single-storey standard lodge built in mellow orange brick facings. Its gables display conflicting styles: those to the main pitches have mutules to their verges and gutters returning to suggest an open pediment in Classical style, whilst that over the breakfront hall sports Picturesque carved foiled bargeboards which are reflected in the scalloped slate roof. Extended by a bay in like manner with two-over-two sash windows. In contrast are the convex quadrant walls, of quarry-faced random uncoursed stone, which frame ashlar pillars in the shape of tapered pylons with outsized cappings, much as those to Carrolstown (*q.v.*) and Kilcarn Upper (*q.v.*) by architect John P. Davis. Highly decorative chunky iron gates.

Secondary gate; *c.* 1895; architect probably W.M. Mitchell and Sons.

About 1885 the property was acquired by Alan Thomas Cairnes (1859–1902), younger brother of the proprietor of neighbouring Stameen (*q.v.*), the gate lodge to which is replicated here. Occupied and immaculately maintained behind a simple screen of hoop-topped railings and pedestrian gate is this delightful single-storey lodge on an asymmetrical butterfly plan, its black-and-white Elizabethan Revival gable features contrasting effectively with the red-brick façades which contain multi-paned casement and sash windows. The gabled porch projects from the internal angle at 45°. Red-brick chimney-stacks break the red terracotta ridge.

Griffith 1848–60; *IFR*.

125. GLENMORE, Drogheda; *c.* 1855.
A 1½-storey cottage built in pleasant coursed random rubble finish, its steep gables with subtly carved bargeboards, ground-floor label-moulded windows and hoods to round-headed attic lights giving a Tudor Revival feel. Basically rectangular on plan, with a back return and later ill-conceived single-storey hall projection; its hipped roof sports scalloped slates, lending an informal touch. A property in 1836 called 'Farm' of the Coddingtons of Oldbridge (*q.v.*), it was

acquired by Blaney T. Balfour (1769–1856) of Townley Hall, Co. Louth (*q.v.*), and apparently renamed after his death by the subsequent owner, Captain Gilbert Nicholson.

Slater 1870; *LGI* (1904).

126. GORMANSTOWN CASTLE, Gormanstown (2).
Sadly, a pair of lodges on the northern approach and a single one to the east, shown on the 1836 OS map, to the great castellated pile of the Preston family, Viscounts Gormanstown, have been swept away, probably by the Franciscans as surplus to requirements when the place became a school.

127. GRANGE, Dunshaughlin (3).
All three porters' lodges built *c.* 1850 for James George Murphy were removed after his house became the centre of an agricultural college.

128. GRAVELMOUNT, Castletown (2).
Successively, between 1783 and 1837, home to the families of Weldon, Moore, Longfield and O'Connor, to which both gate lodges are no more.

129. GREEN PARK, Dunshaughlin; *c.* 1830.
A standard single-storey gabled cottage built in rubble stone, with evidence of there having been pediment features to the windows. Now a shell. Seat of the Garnetts, descended from that family of Williamstown (*q.v.*), of whom Cope Garnett may have been the builder.

Lewis 1837; *LGI* (1904).

130. THE GROVE, Balrath; *c.* 1820.
A nondescript lodge, much altered and extended, with its short gabled elevation to the avenue. One-time estate of the Tandy family.

131. HAMLINSTOWN, Crossakeel; pre-1836; *demolished.*
A seat in 1814 of Edward Kearney with, unusually, what appears to have been a pair of lodges opposite its entrance gates.

Leet 1814.

132. HAMWOOD, Dunboyne (2).
A pretty property founded in the mid-eighteenth century and owing its name to the union of Charles Hamilton and his wife Elizabeth Chetwood, who would seem also to have been responsible for the main gatekeeper's lodge.

Front entrance; 1783.

A charming, unusual and generous four-bay single-storey lodge, probably based on the plan of a vernacular linear three-roomed cottage, dominated by a steeply pitched hipped roof which must originally have been thatched, judging by the eyebrow effect to each end elevation, a feature to be found to the Fosterstown (*q.v.*) lodge and many other traditional County Meath cottages. The small cottagey windows, now lattice-paned, substantiate the '1783' date-stone on the road front. A century after its inception, Charles Hamilton's great-grandson Charles Robert, who had succeeded on his father's death in 1880, clearly did not relish a peasant hovel at his gate. He dressed it in late Victorian Arts and Crafts manner, replacing the thatch with an expanse of earthenware tiles with decorative scalloped courses and bonnets, and added a delightful gabled porch to the front door and ornamental canopies to the windows, just like those to the Ballymacoll (*q.v.*) lodge nearby. There is a nice wooden picket fence entrance screen stopped by granite gate pillars.

Side entrance; *c.* 1845.
A two-storey single-bay cubic gabled roughcast gatehouse with single-storey gabled hall projection and a later single-storey lean-to on the opposing front. Added to the demesne by the second Charles Hamilton (1772–1857) to live here.

LGI (1904); Casey and Rowan 1993.

133. HARBOURSTOWN, Naul (4).
The early gatekeeper's lodge, like the fine Georgian mansion of the Caddells, has gone. Those later three surviving, probably built by Robert Caddell (1810–87), who had inherited in 1856, are somewhat less refined than the big house.

West gate; *c.* 1860.
A very substantial gabled house built in a mellow brick with a peculiar three-window-bay main front over which are equivalent blind recesses, giving the impression of a compact two-storey lodge but the gable revealing it to be a lofty 1½-storey structure with large attic windows. Brick relief in a sawtoothed eaves band, dentil course to the shallow-pitched lean-to single-storey entrance hall, and corbels stepping up the main verges. Derelict. Contrasting squat ashlar entrance pillars with moulded copings.

East gate; *c.* 1860.
Sited at a crossroads is this modest single-storey gabled roughcast cottage with two-bay road front and lean-to entrance hall to one end. Occupied. Earlier big ashlar corniced carriage pillars and contemporary ironwork of *c.* 1845.

South gate; *c.* 1860.
Another commodious two-storey structure, two-bay front to the road and supporting single-storey lean-to annexes on each gable. Deserted.

LGI (1904).

134. HAYES, Yellow Furze (2).
A secondary seat of the Bourke family, Lords Mayo of Palmerstown, Co. Kildare (*q.v.*). The earlier porter's lodge was built by Robert Bourke (1797–1867) before he succeeded to the title as the 5th earl in 1849.

South entrance; *c.* 1835.

What would be an unremarkable little single-storey standard hip-roofed cottage were it not for the *orné* verandah about the front and sides created by the exaggerated soffit oversail carried on chamfered octagonal wooden posts. Constructed in random rubble facings with cut-stone rusticated door surround and brick window dressings. Saved from dereliction in 1997 to be rehabilitated, extended and cleared of vegetation. Located distant from its entrance.

North entrance; *c.* 1890.
Originally a standard single-storey lodge, roughcast, later extended by two bays to the left-hand side and a gabled porch projection added.

BPB (1929).

135. HEADFORT, Kells (3).
It was the 3rd Baron Headfort, 1st earl of Bective, Sir Thomas Taylour (1724–95) who developed this magnificent estate. He and his father, who died in 1757, engaged an array of architectural talent—Castle, Ensor, Chambers, Semple and Adam—but it is unfortunate that, for whatever reason, Semple's pedestrian elevations were chosen. It was probably Semple's death *c.* 1782 that led to yet another architect, Thomas Cooley, being commissioned to complete the furnishing of the property, which he did by designing the bridge over the Blackwater River and doubtless the estate entrances.

Main entrance; *c.* 1783; architect probably Thomas Cooley.
Cooley's bridge from the town carries the public road, which leads obliquely to the main access, dominated by two majestic V-jointed rusticated Classical pillars with moulded plinths and cornices below foliated urns. To each side are postilion openings in similar masonry that contrasts with the extensive tall rubble screen wall, which terminates to the right-hand side in a plain ashlar pillar crowned by a ball finial with Greek key-pattern band, much as the secondary gates. The wall is punctured by three windows, all with modern casements, lighting the lodge, which lies parallel. Single-storey gabled, its main short front faces the avenue, with an open pediment in cut stone contrasting with white walls. Much extended and modernised.

Secondary entrance; *c.* 1783; architect probably Thomas Cooley.

Another pair of grand Classical carriage pillars crowned by ball finals with Greek key-pattern bands, a device which Cooley favoured, for the same are to be seen at St Columba's in the town, at Armagh Palace and at Drewstown (*q.v.*). These are mirrored opposite in the entrance to the park. Within is what originated as a simple little single-storey gabled Classical lodge with parapeted side elevations and an open pediment in the form of a cut-stone skew-table to the avenue façade. This subtle Georgian design is confused by the addition of wings and the insertion of a canted bay window in the principal elevation. Now finished in whitened roughcast. Thomas Cooley died prematurely in 1784, so this Headfort commission would have been some of his last work.

Park entrance; *c.* 1783; *demolished.*
Good ashlar gate pillars, corniced but lacking finials, framed by ogee quadrants stopped by lower pillars. The gate lodge opposite had been removed by 1913.

BPB (1929); *Country Life* (21 and 28 March 1936; 5 April 1973); Casey and Rowan 1993.

136. HERBERTSTOWN, Ratoath; *c.* 1916; architect unknown.

A house and its lodge built for Captain H. Whitworth in Queen Anne Revival manner by an unidentified architect. The latter is 1½-storey, built off a square plan, with sill-high plinth and rusticated quoins in brick framing pebble-dashed panels. Main elevation three-bay symmetrical of six-over-six sashes on each side of a semi-octagonal, flat-roofed, glazed hall projection. A steeply pitched pyramidal roof rises from conspicuous multi-bracketed eaves to an octagonal, banded and corbelled brick stack; contemporary flat-roofed dormers. A competent and incongruous design in the Irish countryside.

Casey and Rowan 1993.

137. HILLTOWN, Bellewstown (2).
A good neo-Classical house built as part of a considerable mid-nineteenth-century redevelopment of the estate by the brothers Boylan, Nicholas (1797–1852) and Thomas (1808–72). This included two tasteful porters' lodges that are deprived of the roles to which they owe their being, thanks to the house being dismantled a century later and offered for reassembly elsewhere.

Side entrance; *c.* 1850; architect possibly William Farrell.

A charismatic little building in the shape of a single-storey standard lodge with a very shallow hipped roof and exaggerated oversailing eaves with finely carved modillion brackets arranged in pairs. Rendered walls with toothed quoins and moulded surrounds to windows and a front door with sidelights. The modern windows strike a discordant note. Unusually, the chimney-stack rises off the rear wall, which may be significant, as this was a feature of lodges designed by architect William Farrell. There is a very similar building at the entrance to Kells Rectory, Co. Kilkenny (*q.v.*), in both form and proportion.

Main entrance; *c.* 1850; architect possibly William Farrell.

Overlooking Bellewstown racecourse is this splendid gatekeeper's dwelling, single-storey and built off a cruciform plan, capped by hipped roofs with a deep frieze carried by wide ashlar Doric pilaster quoins that frame contrasting white wall panels containing bipartite windows with minimal plain surrounds and decorative margined casements. Expertly restored by architect Dawson Stelfox, who designed the two-storey extension to one side. Four stone pillars with recessed panels and bold cappings frame good contemporary straight railed screens and matching carriage gates.

IFR.

138. HILLTOWN, Clonee (3).
Hollway Steeds acquired the estate about the turn of the twentieth century from Patrick Boylan and improved security at the gates.

Front lodge; *c.* 1900.
Single-storey standard with roughcast walls, cotoneaster-clad, and steeply pitched roof with mock half-timber effect to gables. Minimal label mouldings to openings.

Back lodge; *c.* 1900.
A plain roughcast gabled symmetrical three-bay structure.

Railway lodge; *c.* 1880.
A modest two-bay single-storey cottage under a hipped roof, now serving as stables, built by the Midland Great Western Section of the Great Southern Railway Company at a crossing where the line bisected the property.

139. HURLESTOWN, Kells; pre-1836; *demolished.*
A lodge to a seat in late Georgian times of the Lowther family has been swept away in the interests of road improvements.

140. JANEVILLE COTTAGE, Slane; *c.* 1840.
A single-storey four-bay harled hip-roofed cottage with a gabled breakfront doorway; wooden carved modillion brackets to the soffit. Derelict and choked in ivy. A property of Andrew Tiernan in 1854.

Griffith 1848–60.

141. JOHNSBROOK, Clonmellon; *c.* 1820.
Remote from its gates is a two-storey gabled gatehouse with later mildly ornate

bargeboards. Walls probably originally brick facings, now rendered over, containing square-paned windows. Extensive gatescreen with concave quadrants between V-jointed rusticated pillars in a variety of different sizes with moulded unblocked cappings. Built for Thomas Tandy.

Leet 1814; Lewis 1837.

142. JOHNSTOWN, Duleek; *c.* 1790.

A delightful single-storey standard rustic lodge with a hipped roof. Entered below a wide three-centred arch giving into a recessed porch, flanked by small windows in harled rubble walls. Derelict but maintained. Modest gatescreen. The place is recorded in 1814 as being of Mr W. Madden.

Leet 1814.

143. JOHNSTOWN, Dunshaughlin; *c.* 1830.
A simple single-storey standard cottage below a hipped roof, its main roughcast front facing the park; a later flat-roofed projecting hall is probably contemporary with the rebuilt brick chimney-stack with a sawtooth course of about 1870. Occupied. A seat in 1843 of John Morrin.

Griffith 1848–60.

144. JOHNSTOWN, Enfield; *c.* 1810.

Presiding over the forecourt at right angles to its gatescreen is this pleasant standard single-storey gate lodge, presenting a hipped roof to the visitor but a canted end to the demesne. Georgian-style windows on each side of a round-headed doorway with crude hood moulding. Impressively sited to stop a vista from the village are the fine ashlar mid-Georgian gates, with two tall carriage pillars having projecting moulded cornices over friezes ornamented with pretty petalled paterae. A seat in the late eighteenth century of a branch of the Forde family of Seaforde, Co. Down, which by 1814 had passed to James Halpin. Thereafter in the nineteenth century of the Rorkes.

Taylor and Skinner 1778; 1969 [1783]; Leet 1814; *LGI* (1904).

145. JONESBOROUGH, Kells; pre-1836; *demolished.*
A property in the late eighteenth and early nineteenth centuries of Frederick Edward Jones.

Taylor and Skinner 1778; 1969 [1783]; Leet 1814.

146. JULIANSTOWN, Nobber; pre-1836; *demolished.*
The lodge to the early nineteenth-century gentleman farmer's house of Simon Owens has gone.

147. KEERAN, Lobinstown; pre-1836/*c.* 1860/2000.

Opposite the gates is a site that has seen three stages of gate-lodge development. First was that to the lovely villa which passed from the ownership of James Joseph Norris in 1855 through the incumbered estates court to John J. Taaffe of the Smarmore Castle, Co. Louth (*q.v.*), family, who rebuilt it as a 1½-storey three-bay lodge with high eaves to its gabled roof. Local tradition has it that this had a distyle Doric pedimented portico, perhaps salvaged from its predecessor. By the late twentieth century it had become a wreck, with its portico spirited away, but in 2000 it was transformed in a mild Picturesque manner with a single-storey gabled hall projecting from rubble walls with brick dressings and original punched ashlar quoins. Good cast-iron railed sweep from the second phase, having noteworthy stone pillars with unusual Egyptian-style recessed panels, a feature to be found also at neighbouring Moorestown (*q.v.*).

Lyons 1993.

148. KILALLON RECTORY, Clonmellon; pre-1836; *demolished.*
Opposite the gates was a porter's lodge that may have been contemporary with the 1812 glebe house. If so, it was built during the incumbency (1796–1821) of Revd George Leslie Gresson (1769–1842).

Lewis 1837; Leslie and Wallace 2009.

149. KILBEG, Moynalty (2).

Main entrance; *c.* 1850; *demolished.*
Surviving are good mid-nineteenth-century tall square pillars with concave railed quadrants.

Secondary entrance; *c.* 1870.
Located alongside and forward of the gates is a gabled 1½-storey lodge with high eaves to accommodate a gabled breakfront entrance feature flanked by a pair of segmentally arched windows in harled walls. Intricate carved bargeboards. Derelict.

A property in 1854 of Charles Reilly, succeeded by Farrell Reilly in 1870.

Griffith 1848–60; *Land owners in Ireland 1876.*

150. KILBREW, Curragha; *c.* 1800.
A minuscule standard single-storey lodge with a projecting gabled doorway, its hipped roof now finished in corrugated iron. Derelict. Built either by the Gorges family or by William Murphy of Mount Merrion, Dublin, who succeeded to the place in the early nineteenth century.

Lewis 1837.

151. KILBREW RECTORY, Curragha; *c.* 1845; *demolished.*
The glebe house was erected in 1817 but its lodge was of later date, built during the incumbency from 1836 until his death of Revd Thomas Houston Barton (1801–62).

Lewis 1837; Leslie and Wallace 2009.

152. KILBRIDE, Trim (2).
A classic instance of a palimpsest is the medieval tower-house and its attached mid-Victorian house, which itself is of two periods. It was added by John Dutton, 1st Baron Sherborne of Gloucestershire (1779–1862), after whose death it was acquired by George Augustus Rotheram of the Crossdrum (*q.v.*) family. He remodelled the house, probably to designs of William Caldbeck, and possibly the earlier of the porters' lodges, the architect having died in 1872.

Western entrance; *c.* 1865; architect possibly William Caldbeck.

Not quite opposite the gates is a curious and commodious two-storey gatehouse remarkable for its short two-bay main front being recessed below the hipped roof and between extended side walls built in very high-quality punched ashlar arranged randomly in courses with subtly contrasting smooth cut-stone dressings. It extends rearwards with sparse fenestration and lies abandoned.

Eastern entrance; *c.* 1875; architect not known.

A 1½-storey standard gabled lodge clearly by the same unidentified hand as almost identical ones in the county at Posseckstown (*q.v.*), Rockfield (*q.v.*) and Rosnaree (*q.v.*), all of which have in common the main roof catsliding centrally over a projecting hallway, and a pair of windows lighting the attic room. Built in rubble stone with yellow brick dressings. Occupied. There are two panelled, anthemion-topped entrance pillars.

Lewis 1837; *LGI* (1904); *BPB* (1929); Casey and Rowan 1993.

153. KILCARN LOWER, Navan (3).

A couple of very smart little late Victorian lodges to a property of the Murphy family, both attributable to architect John P. Davis of Trim through a pair of gate pillars being identical to those at Carrollstown (*q.v.*).

Rear entrance; pre-1836/pre-1912; *demolished.*

Only a brick gable survives of a later lodge which itself had a predecessor closer to the gates.

Side entrance; 1886; architect John P. Davis.

A standard single-storey gabled lodge principally constructed in coursed rubble facings, ashlar quoins and brick features in the plinth, with toothed dressing to two-over-two sash windows, corbelled and bracketed eaves band and the gabled breakfront hall with a round-headed fanlight, above which is a cut-stone quatrefoil device as keystone over that again. Below the terracotta hip-knob is a date-stone with the monogram for Francis O'Morchoe. Seemingly indifferent to and distanced from the gates, which have striking entrance pillars in the form of ashlar pylons with recessed panels tapering to distinctive bracketed cappings.

Front entrance; 1886; architect John P. Davis.

Identical to the side lodge but for being a hip-roofed variant and having the date-stone and motto as keystone, with a carved Murphy crest over and their motto, 'Fortis Et Hospitalis'. Well maintained and extended, located opposite its gates and separated by the main Navan–Dublin racetrack.

154. KILCARN UPPER, Navan; pre-1836; *demolished.*

A late eighteenth-century seat of the Barry family.

155. KILCARTY, Kilmessan; pre-1836; *demolished.*

To Thomas Ivory's Palladian-style farmhouse and yard, designed for Dr George Cleghorn *c.* 1780, all that remains at the entrance is a pair of square stone carriage pillars with pedestal-less ball finials atop.

Craig 1976.

156. KILCOOLY, Trim; *c.* 1830.

Succumbing to nature is this overgrown abandoned lodge, single-storey with its short front to the avenue in the shape of a single square window in harling on rubble stone plinth below a hipped roof. The only show is the occasional carved modillion bracket to the eaves. Restrained, which is more than can be said for the vulgar late Victorian gatescreen. A property in the nineteenth century of the Purdon family.

157. KILLARKIN, Dunboyne (2).

North gate; *c.* 1820.

A quaint whitewashed roughcast single-storey steeply gabled four-bay cottage, its entrance to the right-hand side. Tiny squared-pane windows aplenty.

South gate; *c.* 1845.

A dapper single-storey standard gabled lodge with Tudor-style label-moulded cast-iron latticed casement windows in roughcast walls. Continuous bracket carved main bargeboards but scalloped to those of the projecting hall. The corbelled red-brick chimney suggests a make-over of *c.* 1880. Probably built for Jonathan Nugent, who was here in 1854.

Griffith 1848–60.

158. KILLEAGH RECTORY, Oldcastle; pre-1836; *demolished.*

The gate lodge to an early nineteenth-century glebe house, probably built during the perpetual curacy (1809–43) of Revd Thomas O'Rorke (d. 1854), had gone by 1913.

Leslie and Wallace 2009.

159. KILLEEN CASTLE, Dunshaughlin (3).

Although two of its lodges have been removed, Killeen was never as blessed with them as that other great Plunkett stronghold, neighbouring Dunsany Castle (*q.v.*).

West entrance; pre-1836; *demolished.*

South entrance; pre-1912; *demolished.*

Replaced by a twentieth-century bungalow that sits alongside a gatescreen of *c.* 1890 in the form of round pillars carrying wooden gates.

North entrance; *c.* 1890; architect perhaps George C. Ashlin.

A highly distinctive composition, with its gay polychromatic brickwork as dressings, banded chimney and string-course contrasting starkly with the grey stone construction. Symmetrical, with one-over-one sashes on each side of a little projecting hallway with its hipped roof below the lofty main eaves, which accommodates loft rooms; scalloped slate banding to the steeply pitched main hip. Dilapidated. Built for

Arthur James Plunkett, 11th earl of Fingal, who inherited the ancestral home in 1881 and may have employed George Ashlin as his architect, as he had at the Netterville Almshouses.

BPB (1929).

160. KILLEEN RECTORY, Dunshaughlin; pre-1836; *demolished.*
A lodge possibly contemporary with the building of this generous glebe house about 1810, which would have occurred on the arrival of Revd William Henry Irvine (1763–1839), rector of this parish of Tara from 1810 until his death.

LGI (1904); Casey and Rowan 1993; Leslie and Wallace 2009.

161. KILLYON MANOR, Ballivor (3).
Well up the southern avenue approach to the house of the Loftus family, beyond the fine masonry bridge over the River Deal, in early times was a gate lodge, now gone. Dudley Loftus died in 1807, when the property passed through his daughter Eliza's marriage to the Magans. It was she and her husband, William Henry Magan (1790–1840) of Clonearl, Co. Offaly (*q.v.*), who added another porter's lodge at that avenue's junction with the public road.

South lodge; *c.* 1830.
Located opposite the gates and seemingly paying no heed to them is a standard single-storey hip-roofed cottage with a projecting similarly roofed hallway with its door set in a square-headed recess. Originally flanked by a pair of small lattice-paned cast-iron windows, one of which has been replaced by a large mullioned light, an alteration which must date from its joining to a large house to the rear. The Tudor Revival mood extends to the pair of diagonally placed chimney-flues.

North lodge; *c.* 1845.
A plain two-storey hip-roofed gatehouse, three-bay with roughcast walls and quarry-faced stone quoins. Presumably built for Eliza Magan, who lived on here for many years.

LGI (1904); Mulligan 2001.

KILMAINHAM WOOD (see WOODVILLE)

162. KILMER or KILMUR, Ballivor (2).
A property which, after the death of Lieutenant-Colonel T. Lowther Allen, was inherited about 1815 by his cousin, Alexander Shirley Montgomery, who would have added at least one of the lodges to the estate.

North lodge; pre-1836; *demolished.*
South lodge; *c.* 1825.
Opposite the entrance is a much-altered single-storey lodge, roughcast, under a hipped roof. It seems to have started life with a principal elevation comprised of a central window bow flanked by recesses, that to the left-hand side perhaps having contained the doorway. Now altered and extended on that side to spoil the original symmetrical concept.

Leet 1814; *LGI* (1904).

163. KILSHARVAN, Julianstown (2).
On the banks of the River Nanny lay an 1845 bleach-mill and a mill-owner's house, which 'occupies a situation of calm, quiet, sylvan solitude; and has been much improved in both mansion and demesne by its proprietor Andrew Armstrong'. The late eighteenth-century gate lodge to this mansion remarkably survives intact.

West lodge; *c.* 1790.

For its age this is an extraordinarily commodious Georgian Gothic lodge, single-storey standard and three-bay but elongated, with its pointed Y-traceried windows sparely distributed in its white harled walls. A pair of brick chimneys are symmetrically placed on the undulating ridge of the hipped gable roof. A hip-roofed hall projects centrally. Occupied and lovingly maintained. The secure gatescreen is later, comprised of punched ashlar carriage pillars and dressings to the postilion openings set in cruder rubble walls. In lieu of gates are studded doors.

East lodge; *c.* 1880.
Almost a century later and probably contemporary with the new grand villa built by James McDonnell (1826–1904) is this single-storey four-bay lodge on an elevated site opposite the gates. Roughcast with red-brick highlights as dressings, quoins and chimney-stacks, with ornamental earthenware corbels to the eaves of its hipped roof. The hipped-roof breakfront doorway has been replaced by a window.

Lewis 1837; *Parliamentary Gazetteer*; *LGI* (1904); Casey and Rowan 1993.

164. KILSKYRE RECTORY, Kilskyre; pre-1836; *demolished.*
Probably yet another example of a Church of Ireland glebe house gate lodge so basic and unsocial as to guarantee its early demise. Probably built during the incumbency from 1806 until his death of Revd Thomas De Lacy (1773–1844).

Leslie and Wallace 2009.

165. KING'S FORT, Moynalty (2).
North lodge; pre-1836; *demolished.*
South lodge; pre-1836.
A thoroughly overgrown single-storey gabled lodge with rubble walls and brick-dressed openings.

The fine mid-eighteenth-century house built by John Chaloner (1700–78) has fared little better than its lodges, lying ruinous. An architect called Keegan in 1813 gave it a rear extension, and it could be speculated that his commission stretched to the addition of lodges in improvements to the property.

Chaloner (1985); Casey and Rowan 1993.

KINGSMOUNTAIN (see MOUNTAINSTOWN, Clonmellon)

166. KNIGHTSBROOK, Trim (2).
The lodges have been removed to a house described in 1837 as 'formerly the handsome residence of the Perceval family', a year when both were in place.

Lewis 1837.

167. KNOCKMARK, Dunshaughlin; *c.* 1908; architect probably R.C. Orpen.
A property that started life in 1814 as a rectory, and is reputed to have been developed by architect James Franklin Fuller in 1879. It took on its present appearance in 1907, when Thomas Barrington Donnelly employed R. Caulfield Orpen to transform it into the present Edwardian pile. The little lodge, or bungalow, is probably contemporary, displaying the same roughcast finish, yellow brick chimney-stack and toothed quoins. Single-storey standard with a bellcast hipped roof rising from wooden bracketed eaves. There are flat-roofed bay windows with nasty modern inserts and an equally unpleasant projecting hallway between.

Lewis 1837; *IB* (10 Aug. 1907).

168. LAGORE, Dunshaughlin; *c.* 1800; architect probably Francis Johnston.

A beautiful lodge, a composition much more worthy of Johnston than his Dunshaughlin courthouse of 1799–1802, for which commission Patrick Thunder of Lagore would have been one of his clients. He had married Elizabeth Taafe of Smarmore Castle, Co. Louth (*q.v.*), in 1798 and this represents part of a tidy-up of his property to make it presentable to his new bride. Easily attributable to Johnston for its resemblance to his lodge at Galtrim (*q.v.*), it lies opposite the gates. Single-storey and perfectly symmetrical below a shallow hipped roof with small slates extending over the central bowed hall projection, which contains a double-leafed door with pretty original applied ironwork decoration. On each side the hall is lit by a pair of four-over-four sidelights, beyond which are Wyatt tripartite windows in harled walls. To the ridge is a pair of perfectly balanced but slightly quirky diagonally set chimney-stacks. Indicated on Larkin's Road Map of 1812.

LGI (1904); Casey and Rowan 1993; Horner 2007.

169. LAKEFIELD, Crossakeel; pre-1836/*c.* 1850.
Replacing an earlier pair of lodges is this

shell of a once-Picturesque 1½-storey structure. Stone-built, with a hipped roof to the road but gabled to the park, having foiled bargeboards over a single-storey canted bay window. Below the carved wavy rafter toes at the eaves is a symmetrical three-bay façade with gabled projecting single-storey hall. Built for Robert H. Battersby, who inherited the property in 1839.

LGI (1904).

170. LANSDOWNE LODGE, Kinnegad; *c.* 1840.
A standard single-storey lodge, low and not quite symmetrical, harled and limewashed below a hipped roof. Square ornamental limestone pillars with ironwork all of an age. A holding in 1854 of James Fenelon, leasing from the marquis of Lansdowne.

Griffith 1848–60.

171. LARCH HILL, Kilcock; *c.* 1820.
The remarkable *ferme ornée* that is this demesne was probably created in the mid-eighteenth century by the Prentice family. None of the flippancy of its follies extends to the gate lodge, which does not enter into the spirit of things, being relatively conventional but an appropriate introduction to the modest gentry farmhouse. Standard single-storey, built off a square plan, having a pyramidal roof rising from clipped eaves to the central stunted chimney-stack. Finished in roughcast, like its unprepossessing gatescreen. Probably dating from the time of Samuel Watson, who was here in 1824.

Pigot 1824; Howley 1993; *Country Life* (8 April 1999).

172. LEGGAGH, Castletown; pre-1836; *demolished.*
A property in the early nineteenth century of the Kieran family, its lodge has been replaced by a labourer's cottage.

173. LEIGHSBROOK, Navan; pre-1836; *demolished.*
A property in 1814 of Revd George Brabazon (1780–1851), rector of Painestown and of the same family as the earls of Meath, who had married into the Leighs of Rosegarland, Co. Wexford (*q.v.*), in 1758. By the mid-nineteenth century the place was inhabited by Alfred Hudson.

BPB (1929).

174. LIONSDEN, Ballivor; pre-1836; *demolished.*
A house built in 1788 by Revd Godwin Swift of Swiftsheath, Co. Kilkenny (*q.v.*), who died in 1815, to be succeeded here by his grandson, Godwin Meade Pratt Swift.

LGI (1904).

175. LISCARTON CASTLE, Navan; pre-1836; *demolished.*
The medieval castle in 1633 belonged to Sir William Talbot but was later developed into a dwelling house, perhaps by Thomas Gerrard, who is recorded here between 1814 and 1856.

Leet 1814; Wilde 1850; Slater 1856.

176. LISMULLEN, Skreen (4).

The seat of the Dillons, baronets, the two lodges to which, existing in 1836, have gone. Three brothers succeeded to the place in quick succession, but it was probably the youngest, Sir William Dillon (1774–1851), who inherited in 1845 as the 4th baronet, who was responsible in his short tenure for the two replacement surviving porters' lodges.

Rear gate; *c.* 1845.
On an elevated site is a modest 1½-storey two-bay gabled structure, later increased in size to a double pile.

Front gate; *c.* 1845.
A highly distinctive feature on the Navan–Dublin road (*above*) is this two-storey gatehouse built in pleasant rubble with an oversailing hipped roof, the bracketed eaves broken by gablets and a prominent chimney-stack to the front elevation. Below this, advancing uneasily below an equivalent roof, is a hefty single-storey semi-octagonal entrance room. A perfectly symmetrical composition, with a double-leafed panelled front door and striking windows with margined glazed casements. Occupied.

BPB (1929).

177. LODGE PARK, Ballivor; *c.* 1850.
A ruinous single-storey cottage built in stone rubble with brick dressings to an irregular three-bay entrance front. To the left-hand side of the doorway is an arbitrarily placed slit window. Now missing its hipped roof. A property that had a succession of different owners, in 1846 home to John O'Reilly.

Slater 1846.

178. LORETO CONVENT, Navan; *c.* 1830.
A single-storey three-bay lodge, probably contemporary with the 1830 house, which projects within the perimeter rubble wall in the shape of a canted wing with equivalent roof and pointed heads to openings. Little more than a sentry-box.

NIAH.

179. LOUGHAN, Moynalty; pre-1836; *demolished.*
A property in 1854 of John Keating.

Griffith 1848–60.

180. LOUGH CREW, Oldcastle (8).
'Loughcrew House, the residence of Jas. L.W. Napier [*sic*], is a magnificent structure in the Grecian Ionic style, erected from designs by Mr Cockerell of London; it is faced entirely with hewn limestone, has a noble portico, and contains some good paintings by the old masters. The mansion, the out-offices (which are of a superior order) and the improvements to the demesne are stated to have cost upwards of £80,000. The demesne comprises about 900 plantation acres of which nearly 200 are planted; the principal approach is by a lodge of elegant design ...' This is what Samuel Lewis had to record in 1837, probably after a visit the year before, the same date as the first OS map, which shows that James Lenox William Naper (1791–1865) was an inveterate builder and improver, for he was still to erect half a dozen more porters' lodges to decorate the periphery of his demesne. He was but a babe of nine months, an only son, when his father died, and it was surely no coincidence that the great neo-Classical mansion was built a year before his marriage in 1824. Sadly, it was destroyed by a devastating fire and mostly demolished in 1968, but it has been survived by its majestic lodge, which remains to oversee the principal gate as the finest neo-Classical gate lodge in the land, a testimony to the ability of its architect.

Main entrance; 1825; architect Charles R. Cockerell.
Located opposite the gates on an elevated site as a Greek temple approached by a crepidoma, or stepped base, to its pronaos below a pedimented tetrastyle Doric portico, which screens a single opening in a double-leafed door with margined glazing, as have its windows to the side elevations. Built in high-quality limestone ashlar above a tall

plinth of channelled masonry to the sill course. Across the rear elevation, to form a T-plan, is a lower hip-roofed block, which may have been a later addition before 1836. The column capitals are unusual in having a narrow band of fluting that does not extend down the shafts; its English architect, C.R. Cockerell (1788–1863), who had travelled widely in Greece as a young man, was perhaps influenced by the Temple of Apollo, Delos. Rather peculiarly, a dummy chimney-stack to the fore acts as a sort of acroterion. This composition is completed by an extensive framing railed screen on a stone plinth, which is repeated across the road with wrought-iron carriage pillars that support tall braziers and with a single postilion gate to one side. Cockerell's biographer David Watkin describes the scene eloquently: 'Cockerell's designs for the lodge were approved on 3 August 1825. The lodge must be considered as one of the most brilliant small monuments of the Greek Revival. No photograph can convey the compelling, almost imperious presence of this tiny building in the midst of a vast landscape, nor the manner in which it dominates the whole journey down the long drive from the house to the entrance gates. It stands not timidly flanking the gates but facing them centrally from the opposite side of the road. Cockerell brilliantly contrived to make of the public road at this point a kind of piazza or Baroque enclosure by lining it with railings which curve forward towards the road at each end of the enclosed space. The absolute inevitability of the lodge is achieved not only by its masterly siting but by its blending of Doric and Tuscan forms. It does not give the impression of a sacred Doric temple caught unawares in a landscaped park because the broad eaves and the absence of a frieze give it the authentic vernacular or rustic stamp of the Tuscan order. Yet the Greek Doric is hinted at in the curious fluting which ends abruptly just below the capitals.'

Berry's lodge; *c.* 1835.

A structure notable for both its precocious appearance, as being from the 1850s, and its bulk: it must have had a dual role, perhaps doubling as the estate agent's house. Located on the Kells approach, it is a two-storey gatehouse, gabled and built off a T-plan with single-storey lean-to in each internal corner. Harled with stone as quoins, dressings, label mouldings, skew-tables and big banded chimney-stacks to give it an ungainly Tudor Revival feel.

Chattan's lodge; *c.* 1845; architect possibly C.R. Cockerell.

A most singular and attractive gatehouse, which lies abandoned and decaying. Two-storey gabled and built off a T-plan with much the same footprint as Cockerell's main lodge, in this case in a Tudor Revival manner, the cross of the T formed by catslide roofs to the rear. Constructed in rubble stone with chamfered dressed surrounds to tiny-paned windows, some bipartite mullioned. From the leading gable advances an independently gabled outset with a most curious and elaborately created first-floor mock window over the remains of what may have been a canopied rustic sitting-out area.

Lake lodge; *c.* 1845.

By Creeve Lough on a beautiful site is this neglected and overgrown 1½-storey Picturesque cottage. Built in an uncoursed quarry-faced masonry with hewn-stone first-floor string-course. Extensive eaves overhang to a gabled roof with carved timber brackets and a gablet to the avenue front that has a little square-paned sash window.

Drumone lodge; *c.* 1850.

A relatively plain single-storey gabled structure in roughcast finish, with a gablet breaking the front eaves above the central doorway.

Rustic lodge; *c.* 1830/*c.* 1880; architect not known.

Irish Architectural Archive

What a sorry sight is this scene, particularly when compared with an early photograph of it in its heyday. Quite why such a potentially desirable structure was allowed to descend to this state of dereliction is inexplicable. It was a highly decorative two-storey gabled gatehouse, three up/two down, the carriage opening being bridged by a room approached via an easygoing spiral stairs. The roof is ornamented by a pair of rock-faced chimney-stacks, fleur-de-lis cresting, diaper sawtooth tiles and wavy carved bargeboards. The upper storey was clad in rustic timber posts, arranged vertically above a band of chevron work, and containing bipartite windows with cast-iron fancy hexagonal glazing. In the central gable is a faintly Oriental-style canted oriel window with bellcast rooflet. The lower storey is three-bay, defined by rock-faced pilasters 'carrying' tree trunks in the form of applied three-centred arches with rendered panels containing more lozenge-glazed windows. Once a striking introduction to the demesne but now barely discernible through the undergrowth. The first OS map of 1836 shows it either to have had a predecessor, which also spanned the entrance, or to be a recasting.

Mahon's lodge; *c.* 1845/*c.* 1880.

On the western approach is this delightful little gatekeeper's lodge, single-storey and built off a square plan, with an unusual high rubble plinth to sill level and a shallow pyramidal roof rising to the chimney-stack, which is rock-faced, just as to the rustic lodge, and extending as a feature in a central

pilaster to the two-bay road front and as surround to the windows on the avenue elevation. The latter is a margined bipartite casement in an opening that must originally have been the front door, for a threshold step survives. The rock-faced features may be later affectations applied to otherwise harled walls. Recently much extended and saved from dereliction.

Oldcastle lodge; *c.* 1860.

A dapper little single-storey standard gabled lodge with back return built off a tall plinth in solid uncoursed stone facings; banded ashlar chimney-stack. No decorative features survive, there being plain bargeboards and modern windows inserted.

Lewis 1837; *LGI* (1904); Fletcher 1961; Watkin 1986; Howley 1993.

181. LOUGH CREW RECTORY, Oldcastle; pre-1836; *demolished.*
The lost lodge may have been contemporary with its glebe house, which was built in 1821 at an expense of £1,879, part of which was defrayed by the incumbent, Revd Richard Blackhall Vincent (1766–1834), rector from 1815 until his death.

Lewis 1837; Leslie and Wallace 2009.

182. LOUGHER, Duleek; *c.* 1820.
All that remains is a corrugated-iron-roofed, gabled, whitewashed, stone-built cottage to a property in 1837 of Walter Coyle.

Lewis 1837.

183. MACETOWN, Rathfeigh; *c.* 1850.
Opposite the gates lies a fine solid single-storey standard lodge, a typical mid-nineteenth-century Irish architectural blend of styles, with Classical carved paired modillion brackets to eaves of the hipped roof, traditional pilaster quoins and tripartite sash windows with Tudor label mouldings over, placed high in surprise at its present

desolation, as it lies abandoned and vandalised. Framed by railings and quadrant walls, across the road are squat V-jointed rusticated stone carriage pillars. A seat in 1854 of Patrick Leonard.

Griffith 1848–60.

184. MAPERATH, Moynalty (5).
Although the big house of the Rowley family was demolished in the 1960s, remarkably all but one of its lodges live on, relieved of their duties. Thomas Taylor Rowley, who inherited Maperath in 1807 on the death of his father Henry, could have been responsible for the four that were in place in 1836 and might have built the fifth before his passing in 1859.

North lodge; pre-1836; *demolished.*
Surviving are high harled convex wall quadrants with one postilion opening, of *c.* 1820.

Upper middle lodge; *c.* 1850.
A modest three-bay single-storey hip-roofed lodge with scalloped and sawtooth slate bands and rendered walls.

Middle lodge; pre-1836/*c.* 1880.
Replacing a predecessor at the other side of the entrance is this single-storey three-bay structure, built in stone with brick features in dressings, quoins and chimney-stack. Gabled, as is the breakfront hall. Built by Henry Rowley, who died without issue in 1881.

Lower middle lodge; pre-1836/1891.
Again succeeding an earlier lodge, similarly opposite its gates, is a typical late Victorian lodge, quite unsubtle in the choice of materials. Single-storey standard, of generous proportions below a hipped roof, constructed in rubble facings with contrasting smooth V-jointed hewn quoins and striking red brickwork to soldier arches, bold corbelled eaves band and chimney-stacks (one now removed). From the centre advances a modern gabled brick-built room, which continues the eaves course and contains the relocated date-stone with the monogram of Henry Rowley Crawford, who had inherited Maperath.

South lodge; *c.* 1800.

A quite delightful Georgian Gothic lodge, single-storey standard below a steeply pitched pyramidal roof rising to a central chimney-stack. Pointed-arched openings in limewashed rubble walls, the main front behind a colonnade of four slender Tuscan columns, the eaves over being contrived to accommodate a deep entablature. Admirably maintained behind a contemporary gatescreen of spear-topped railed quadrants and matching carriage gates hung on grand V-jointed rusticated Classical pillars with finely chiselled moulded cornices.

LG (1882); The Irish Bomfords (www.bomfords.net).

185. MEADESBROOK, Garristown (2).
A seat in the early nineteenth century of the Madden family to which both pre-1836 lodges have gone.

186. MEADESTOWN, Robinstown; pre-1912; *demolished.*
A property in the first half of the nineteenth century of Christopher Barnewall, who died in 1849; he was succeeded by his son Charles, who probably then added the gate lodge and the gate sweep with neat octagonal limestone gate posts.

BPB (1929).

187. MEATH ARCHDEACONRY, Kells; *c.* 1820.
'Stonebrook of Rev. Archdeacon of Meath ... one of the principal ornaments of this neighbourhood. We are not aware that a finer spot for the erection of a villa is to be found in this part of the county.' So in 1825 did Brewer consider this setting of the big plain square house built *c.* 1780 by the Venerable Charles Stone, archdeacon from 1759 until his death in 1798, who named it accordingly. The single-storey hip-roofed roughcast cottage for the gatekeeper was added somewhat later by his successor, Archdeacon Thomas De Lacy (1773–1844), rector of Kilskyre (*q.v.*), but has subsequently been much improved and extended, now monitoring the entrance to a property since renamed 'Blackwater' after the river running by.

Taylor and Skinner 1778; 1969 [1783]; Brewer 1825; Leslie and Wallace 2009.

MEATH EPISCOPAL PALACE (see ARDBRACCAN PALACE)

188. MILLBROOK, Navan; pre-1836; *demolished.*
A big mill-owner's house and his 'Paper and Frieze Manufactory' nearby, in the early nineteenth century of John McDonnell, the porter's lodge to which has gone.

Lewis 1837.

189. MILLBROOK, Oldcastle; pre-1836; *demolished.*
A once-vibrant but now derelict complex of flour and flax mills and mill-owner's house known as 'Henry's Mill', named after William Henry, who is noted here in 1802 and 1837.

Thompson 1802; Lewis 1837; Mulligan 2001.

190. MILLTOWN, Kilskeer; pre-1836.
A single-storey stone-built gabled gatekeeper's cottage, now ruinous and overgrown, a property *c.* 1800 of a Mr Smith which by 1814 had passed to John Kearney.

Wilson 1803; Leet 1814.

191. MOORETOWN, Lobinstown; pre-1828/*c.* 1835.

An 1828 estate map shows there to have been an earlier lodge to this fine late eighteenth-century house, in 1814 and 1819 home to Philip Pendleton; it would seem to have been replaced by George Henzill. The present owners have embarked on an admirable programme of restoration of the estate's buildings, which has initially made the present lodge available as a holiday let. Effectively sited on a right-angled bend in the road, it presides over both entrance gates, to house and farm buildings, despite discourteously turning its back on visitors in presenting its best face to the park. Standard single-storey below a hipped roof with banded chimney-stack, it retains its tiny square-paned cast-iron casement windows in what were harled walls. This finish has been incorrectly removed in rehabilitation works but is none the worse for that, in revealing the highest-quality fabric of rubble walls with brick-dressed openings. The good contemporary fleur-de-lis-topped ironwork to carriage gates, with poppy finial to meeting rails, and convex railed quadrants has been repaired to complement this pleasant place.

Leet 1814; Mason 1814–19; Lewis 1837.

192. MOORTOWN, Kilberry; *c.* 1900; *demolished.*
A property comprised of house, offices, gate lodge and 190 acres of Edward McGlue, first recorded as such in a valuation book of 1902. Its lodge was short-lived.

193. MOSNEY, Laytown; pre-1836/*c.* 1900.
An unremarkable two-storey gatehouse with symmetrical three-bay ground-floor front, two-bay over, in rendered walls with red brick as quoins, dressings and chimney-stack to a steeply pitched hipped roof. Long a property of the Pepper family, whose earlier lodge has been demolished.

194. MOUNTAINSTOWN, Clonmellon; *c.* 1820.
A tiny two-storey gabled gatehouse with a symmetrical three-bay entrance elevation with two-bay fenestration above. Sturdy stone construction. One-time seat of a branch of the Battersby family which was later renamed 'Kingsmountain'.

195. MOUNTAINSTOWN, Wilkinstown (2).
The delightfully naive Irish Queen Anne house built by the Gibbons family now lacks both of its gate lodges, each in place before 1836. They may have dated from the coming here of the Pollocks and have been contemporary with the identical remaining entrance screens. Each is comprised of elegant wrought-iron-railed concave quadrants that contain pedestrian gates and have four square ashlar pillars with fluted friezes relieved by pretty floral paterae. All from *c.* 1780.

Mulligan 2001.

196. MOUNT HANOVER, Julianstown; *c.* 1850; *demolished.*

The loss of the lodge built by James Mathews would be regrettable if it had any of the quality and originality of the gatescreen opposite. The four pillars, all topped by ball finials clasped by gadrooned 'eggcups', are crisply sculpted with similar gadrooning to cappings, the outer ones square with oval 'cobweb' paterae to the friezes, the carriage pillars in the form of fluted column shafts which are monolithic cylinders. The fine ironwork, with spiky fleur-de-lis finials and quatrefoil motifs, is contemporary mid-nineteenth-century work. There is very similar masons' craftsmanship at the entrance to Lisrenny, Co. Louth (*q.v.*), by an unidentified designer.

197. MOYGLARE, Maynooth; *c.* 1910; *demolished.*
Arthur Edward Kinahan (d. 1946) of the Roebuck, Co. Dublin (*q.v.*), family acquired this property from Joseph Chapman in 1899, further developing it with a new steward's house, gardener's house and a porter's lodge across the road from its entrance gates, which proved short-lived.

IFR.

198. MOYGLARE HOUSE, Maynooth; *c.* 1840.

Considerably later in date than the big late eighteenth-century house, its lodge was added by Charles Cannon. A standard single-storey affair on a square plan below a shallow pyramidal roof with scalloped coursed slate bands rising to its central chimney-stack. The three-bay main front faces the park, as an object to be appreciated from within. Pretty lattice-glazed casement windows in whitewashed roughcast walls are highlighted by later shutters, much as on its counterpart to Moyglare Rectory (*q.v.*) nearby.

199. MOYGLARE RECTORY, Maynooth; *c.* 1840.
A single-storey standard hip-roofed lodge finished in white roughcast with modern external shutters like the neighbouring lodge to Moyglare House (*q.v.*). Somewhat later than the glebe house of 1815, though both were built during the incumbency from 1814 until his death of Revd Arthur Ardagh (1775–1846).

Lewis 1837; Leslie and Wallace 2009.

200. MOYNALTY LODGE, Moynalty; *c.* 1825.
Outside the gates and fronting the road is this charming pair of semi-detached English Picturesque-style cottages now forming one dwelling. All part of a development inspired by the improving landlord John Farrell (1784–1870), who upon his marriage in 1820 had been given Moynalty by his wealthy Dublin brewer father. 'The present village,

which is of recent erection, was, till within the last four years, comprised of cabins; it is now clean and well-built, and comprises 33 detached houses ...' So recorded Samuel Lewis in 1837; he would also have noticed nearby the 1½-storey estate houses with steeply pitched gables and gablets adorned with faintly carved foiled and cusped bargeboards and hip-knobs, all in the P.F. Robinson manner. To the ridge is a shared brick chimney-stack with diagonally set flues in the Tudor style, as are the latticed cast-iron casement windows, some set below segmental arches. The original doorways, now with matching windows inserted, have label mouldings over, all set in roughcast walls. Nice square cast-iron entrance posts with anthemion decoration.

Lewis 1837; *LGI* (1904); Casey and Rowan 1993.

201. MOYNALTY RECTORY, Moynalty; *c.* 1825.
A simple single-storey hip-roofed lodge with harled walls and brick eaves course; three-bay standing elevated from the gates. Somewhat later in date than the glebe house of 1792 and built for the long-lived rector Revd William Kellett (1769–1851), incumbent from 1803 until his death.

Lewis 1837; Leslie and Wallace 2009.

202. MUCKERSTOWN, Dunboyne; *c.* 1840.
A single-storey standard lodge, not quite symmetrical, with the doorway off-centre between two-over-two sash windows in limewashed harled walls below corbelled clipped eaves to the steeply hipped roof. Derelict but in use, built in the time here before 1854 of Thomas Kennedy.

Griffith 1848–60.

203. MULLAGHDILLON, Slane; *c.* 1870.
To the pleasant late Georgian villa of the Blackburne family is this later single-storey standard gabled cottage constructed in rubble facings contrasting nicely with the red-brick dressed openings, with the remains of Georgian-style sash windows and foiled bargeboards to the steep verges. Derelict.

204. MULLAGHFIN, Duleek; pre-1836; *demolished.*
A late eighteenth-century gentleman farmer's house, owned in 1814 by Henry Swift.

Leet 1814.

205. MULLAGHWILLIN CORN MILL, Lobinstown; pre-1836; *demolished.*
A property in the early nineteenth century of A. Sallary Esq., which in 1854 was vacant and by 1913 had lost its lodge.

Leet 1814; Lewis 1837; Griffith 1848–60.

206. NAVAN UNION WORKHOUSE, Navan (2).
Now St Brigid's Hospital, the former workhouse had two lodges, both demolished, which were presumably also designed by the tireless George Wilkinson about 1842, when the institution opened for the admission of 500 unfortunates.

O'Connor 1995.

207. NEVINSTOWN, Navan; pre-1836; *demolished.*
A seat in the first half of the nineteenth century of the White family.

208. NEWBRIDGE MILLS, Navan; *c.* 1855.
A commodious rubble-built gabled gatehouse fronting the road, two storeys over a basement, linked to a lofty segmentally arched carriage gateway with a tiny pedestrian opening between. 'Improved' with plastic windows to its two-bay front, synthetic slates and minus a chimney. This would seem to be a survival from the previous complex of miller George Mullen, much of which was burnt down on 7 March 1871, before the flour mill and stores were restored by John Spicer.

209. NEWCASTLE, Innfield; pre-1810/*c.* 1860.
A single-storey standard lodge, square on plan, finished in roughcast with stone dressings, keystones and quoins; shallow pyramidal roof with scalloped slate bands rising to a central chimney-stack. Either a make-over of an old structure or a mid-nineteenth-century replacement. The early lodge is shown on Larkin's Road Map (1806–10) to a property of one Ryan Esq., which by 1837 was home to the Lennons.

Wilson 1803; Lewis 1837; Horner 2007.

210. NEW GROVE, Kells; *c.* 1800.

What must have been an attractive Georgian Gothic *cottage orné* is this single-storey lodge, which looks as if its steeply hipped roof was once thatched, now replaced by corrugated iron. Two-window bay to the park. There is evidence of there having been a gabled canopy over the lancet-headed front doorway, which occupies the single-bay avenue elevation. Simply two-roomed and built in ragstone, limewashed with Irish pilaster quoins. In complete contrast but probably contemporary is the towering pair of V-jointed rusticated ashlar Classical carriage pillars flanked by postilion gates. All built in the time here of Mary Reilly or her uncle Hugh before her.

Mulligan 2001; NIAH.

211. NEWHAGGARD, Trim; *c.* 1850; *demolished.*
A lodge probably built by John Conolly, who came to live here after the tenure of Charles Nangle before him.

212. NEWRATH, Slane; *c.* 1845.
A house and lodge in 1854 on the property of Thomas Macken. The latter is sited alongside and facing the carriageway, single-storey standard with a hipped roof, roughcast and boarded up. Of the entrance screen all that survives is a lonesome pillar with recessed panel and entablatured capping.

Griffith 1848–60.

213. NEWTOWN, Carlanstown; pre-1836; *demolished.*
Surviving is a gatescreen comprised of four big random stone pillars with a flat-arched postilion gate and a balancing recess in the opposing quadrant. Probably built by the Smith family of Annesbrook (*q.v.*) and Beabeg after they acquired the property from the Meredyths after 1802.

LGI (1904); *BPB* (1929).

214. NEWTOWN, Dunboyne; *c.* 1870.
An unusual single-storey roughcast hip-roofed lodge with the chimney-stack rising off the rear wall and an irregular main front, half-forming a porch recess with what is probably a later projecting glazed hall below a catslide roof; the left-hand side has a two-over-two sash window. Occupied. Probably built by Patrick Brady when the property was created about 1870 from Dunboyne Castle (*q.v.*) lands.

215. NEWTOWN GIRLEY, Athboy; pre-1836/*c.* 1840.
A nice little low single-storey standard cottage with a hipped roof and gabled breakfront doorway, finished in white roughcast. There was probably a predecessor dating from before 1836 opposite the entrance. A seat in 1854 of Eliza Brady.

Griffith 1848–60.

216. NEWTOWN KELLS CHURCH OF IRELAND CHURCH, Carlanstown; *c.* 1850; *demolished.*
The old church is now a ruin, in latter times it not having been a viable living; despite this, a gate lodge was built between 1829 and 1854 during the incumbency of Revd Joseph Stevenson (1800–79).

Griffith 1848–60; Casey and Rowan 1993; Leslie and Wallace 2009.

217. NEWTOWN PARK, Trim; pre-1836; *demolished.*
In 1854 a vacant corn mill and the house of Patrick Daniel, which looks to date from *c.* 1830.

Griffith 1848–60.

220. Oakley Park.

218. NEWTOWN PROSPECT, Kilcock; pre-1836/*c.* 1915.
The previous lodge to a property of the Coates family has been replaced by a good Arts and Crafts affair; single-storey, roughcast, with small-paned windows below eaves supported by hefty joist ends and a gabled hipped roof with louvres to its gambrels. Apparently built for Revd M.F. Coates when the family returned to a property tenanted for many years.

219. NORMAN'S GROVE, Dunboyne; pre-1836.
At a disused entrance is a modest single-storey gabled stone-built cottage in harled finish; overgrown and derelict. A property that constantly changed hands over the centuries but received its present name when bought by the Lee Norman family in 1748.

Casey and Rowan 1993.

220. OAKLEY PARK, Moynalty; pre-1836/*c.* 1839; architect possibly W.V. Morrison.
The first lodge to the property would date from the time here of the Crawfords but was replaced by George Bomford (1811–86), who had purchased Oakley and almost doubled the size of the old eighteenth-century house around 1829. He clearly commissioned an architect of some standing, for this porter's accommodation is one of the finest neo-Classical lodges in the province. An unsigned drawing survives of the principal storey for doubling the size of the house as built, with printing in a hand attributable to the architect William Vitruvius Morrison (1794–1838), and if the lodge is also by him this could be his final commission before his premature death. Single-storey standard below a hipped roof with tall eaves having a frieze that is a continuation of the cut-stone entablature of the pedimented distyle portico. This has fluted Doric columns and corresponding pilasters applied to stuccoed walls with round-headed sash windows; solid banded chimney-stack. In 2000 this important building lay derelict. The complementary gatescreen comprises four identical ashlar pillars with little breakfronts

in the form of tapering Greek stelae with recessed panels and semicircular pedimented cappings; contemporary ironwork to carriage and flanking postilion gates with low curtain walls beyond.

LGI (1904);The Irish Bomfords (www.bomfords.net).

221. OATLANDS, Navan (2).
A small estate of the Thompson family which had to wait until well into the residence here of William Thompson (1767–1851) for lodges to be added at its entrances.

Main entrance; *c.* 1840.

A charismatic little single-storey gatekeeper's lodge with a delightful mix of rustic in the crude roughcast walls and sophistication in the outline of a moulded cut-stone pedimented gable, V-jointed toothed quoins and Classical dressing of the tripartite windows to the short leading elevation, which addresses the gates across the road. This quirky window with its own miniature pediment has been compromised by the intrusion of modern plastic windows but in contrast the extension to the rear is unobtrusive. Equally unusual is the eccentric gatescreen; its railed convex entrance quadrants continue beyond the gates to describe semicircles, stopped by octagonal stone posts with fluted friezes, just like those at Ballyboy (*q.v.*) and Roristown (*q.v.*).

Schoolhouse entrance; pre-1912.
To the rear of the estate on the southern approach is a dual-function building erected after 1836, so overgrown as to defy description or precise dating. It could have been built by George Annesley Pollock, who came to Oatlands after William Thompson's death.

Griffith 1848–60; *LGI* (1904).

222. OLDBRIDGE, Drogheda; pre-1836/1890.
Splendidly sited on a right-angled bend in the road by the River Boyne is an orderly straight late Georgian-style gatescreen to the earlier neglected mansion of the Coddington family. Comprised of four dignified punched ashlar pillars containing two pairs of carriage gates and a central matching railing, it may date from *c.* 1832, when architect Frederick Darley was employed by Nicholas Coddington (1793–1837) to enlarge the house. The 1836 OS map appears to show an early porter's lodge incorporated into the entrance. Its late Victorian replacement, a 1½-storey gabled affair, sits at a discreet distance. Roughcast with label mouldings to windows, the projecting hip-roofed hallway is accommodated below high eaves with corbels. The date-stone reflects the end to a final prosperous era of the property in the time of John Nicholas Coddington (1828–1917).

LGI (1958); Bence-Jones 1988.

OLDCASTLE GLEBE (see KILLEAGH RECTORY)

223. OWENSTOWN, Maynooth; 1906; architect F.W. Higginbotham.

'Estimates are being obtained for a handsome gate entrance and lodge at Owenstown, for W. McGrath; F.W. Higginbotham T.C., architect.' Thus did the *Irish Builder* magazine herald the coming of the bungalow to these shores. Single-storey, four-bay, neatly roughcast, with stone features in the shape of moulded window surrounds, sill and head courses, plinth, channelled toothed quoins and infrequent corbels to the eaves of the hipped roof, now with replacement synthetic slates and a large banded rendered chimney-stack, probably the survivor of two. The projecting glazed porch reflects the transomed and mullioned windows, with their leaded and coloured glass lights; gabled with carved bargeboards, hip-knob and curly brackets. Contemporary Edwardian decorative ogee iron quadrants and Classical rendered moulded pillars, much as at nearby Ballinderry (*q.v.*).

IB (14 July 1906).

224. PARKSTOWN, Ballivor; pre-1836; *demolished.*
A large mid-Georgian house, in 1837 of one J. Campbell.

Lewis 1837.

225. PARSONSTOWN, Lobinstown (2).

Irish Architectural Archive/Craig Collection

A lost house inhabited by the Blackburne family in the early nineteenth century, when it was served by a lodge on the northern approach which has since been replaced by a labourer's cottage. Around 1840 the property passed from Revd A. Blackburne (1804–74), rector of Kilshine, to the ownership of Matthew Brinkley (1797–1855), who added a second lodge to the southern avenue. This is a pretty single-storey standard structure below a steeply hipped oversailing roof, conspicuous for its doorcase, consisting of a pair of engaged Tuscan columns set in a recess, or *in antis*. On each side were bipartite casement windows, with striking cast-iron glazing arranged in a hexagonal pattern, in harled walls. These have been replaced in modernisation by latticed panes in a roughcast finish. The carriage pillars have recessed panels and the concave cappings beloved of masons in south Louth and north Meath; gates and screens have chinoiserie pattern. All dating from *c.* 1845.

Lewis 1837; Slater 1846; *LGI* (9104); Leslie and Wallace 2009.

226. PEACOCKSTOWN, Ratoath; pre-1836; *demolished.*
A house, offices, gate lodge and land in 1854 of Patrick Leonard.

Griffith 1848–60.

227. PHILLISTOWN, Trim; *c.* 1850.
A tiny derelict single-storey standard cottage, its corrugated-iron gabled roof catsliding centrally over the front door projection. A property in 1854 of Aaron Moffett.

Griffith 1848–60.

228. PHILPOTSTOWN, Robinstown; pre-1836; *demolished.*
A seat established by the Philpot family but from the early nineteenth century home to the Youngs.

229. PILTOWN or PILLTOWN, Drogheda; *c.* 1835; architect W.D. Butler.

A development of house, porter's lodge and entrance gates for Thomas Brodigan to designs by William Deane Butler in 1834. His entrance screen displays beautifully crafted pillars of ashlar in Classical manner, with mouldings to plinths and recessed panel shafts below cappings with friezes and cornices. The contemporary ironwork to gates and matching railings are spear-topped with fine poppy-finialled meeting rails. Opposite is the splendid neo-Classical lodge, which is in fact a sophisticated ashlar front façade applied to a basic standard single-storey hip-roofed structure. Framed by Tuscan pilasters, as is the centre-piece with plinth, sill course and lugged surrounds to openings, that to the doorway tapered in faintly Egyptian pylon fashion. The entablatured parapet is crowned by a central chiselled antefixa feature with voluted palmette. Nicely flanked by ogee railed quadrants stopped by distant pillars, it is proudly maintained but with ill-advised modern window replacements.

Casey and Rowan 1993.

230. PLANTATION, Kingscourt; *c.* 1845.
A thoroughly decent little single-storey standard lodge with a steeply pitched hipped roof over pleasant random stone-faced walls with brick lintels to bipartite two-over-two sash windows flanking the sheeted fanlit doorway. Strangely deserted. Simple range of spear-topped gates and fluted cast-iron posts. A seat in 1846 occupied by George Irwin and Thomas George Irwin. [Fig. 4, p. 1.]

Slater 1846.

231. PLATTEN HALL, Donore (2).
The most hideously mutilated of once-fine Irish demesnes that is also missing its handsome early eighteenth-century mansion, which always lacked a settled family connection down the years. Remarkably, there is some surviving evidence of its past glory in the remains of its main entrance gates.

North entrance; *c.* 1820.
Impressively sited on the axis of the public road approach is this once-imposing mid-Georgian entrance screen of V-jointed rusticated ashlar pillars flanked by harled concave quadrant walls, each containing flat-arched postern openings with moulded architraves. Forward of this is a dilapidated and overgrown single-storey standard lodge with paired windows in wide openings on either side of the doorway with three-centred archway. Presumably built in the time here of Robert Reeves.

South entrance; pre-1836; *demolished.*
A lodge that was located opposite the gates of that part of the seat now occupied by a monstrous cement factory complex.

Leet 1814; Bence-Jones 1988.

232. PORTMANNA, Dunboyne; 1912.
A two-bay symmetrical roughcast early twentieth-century bungalow with liberal use of earthenware features in red-brick toothed quoins and dressings, chimney-stack, roof tiles, perforated crestings to ridge and hips of the half-hipped gables and terracotta date-plaque. Ornamental paired soffit brackets; inappropriate late twentieth-century window replacements. Built for the proprietor, Patrick Moore.

233. POSSECKSTOWN, Enfield; *c.* 1870.
A mildly Picturesque roughcast 1½-storey standard gabled commodious lodge with significantly similar features to those at Rosnaree (*q.v.*) and Kilbride (*q.v.*) in the paired attic windows and catslide roof over the projecting porch which retains Georgian-style sash windows, highlighting the unfortunate loss of those elsewhere; basic

wavy bargeboards. Contemporary Classical entrance pillar with bold cornice mouldings. A property in 1870 of Thomas Russell.

Slater 1870.

234. PRIEST'STOWN, Dunboyne; *c.* 1800.
A seat of the Butler family throughout the nineteenth century. At what is now the rear entrance is a derelict three-room vernacular linear thatched cottage, probably built in the time here of Revd Richard Butler (1758–1841).

LGI (1904); Leslie and Wallace 2009.

235. RAHINSTOWN, Summerhill (2).
Originally there was a large Georgian house of the Bomford family at the heart of the estate, which was Tudorised by Robert George Bomford (1802–46), who probably also furnished the property with one gate lodge, built sometime between 1836 and his premature death.

Front entrance; *c.* 1870; architect probably Sandham Symes.
A decent unassuming little single-storey lodge with an oversailing hipped roof and a two-bay front to the avenue of six-over-six sash windows in roughcast walls framed by smooth corner strips and plinth; later lean-to hall extension to the road. Looking to be around 40 years older, but not so the contemporary brasher gatescreen.

R.G. Bomford died without leaving issue and his sister disposed of the place through the incumbered estates court; it was purchased by Robert Fowler (1797–1868), but it was his son of the same name (1824–97) who replaced the old house *c.* 1870 with the present Italianate-style mansion to designs of Sandham Symes. Towards the end of the century he also commissioned an extraordinary replacement porter's lodge at the other approach.

Rear entrance; *c.* 1890; architect possibly W.M. Mitchell.
Built in random rubble facings but deserving of its local sobriquet 'Red Lodge' for its preponderance of red-brick toothed quoins and dressings, colossal corbelled chimney-stacks and the earthenware tiles of roof and cladding. This is a remarkable example of Elizabethan Revival Arts and Crafts style on a grand scale, raised off an irregular plan in 1½ storeys; its steeply pitched roof has hip-roofed dormers and scalloped tile-hanging to three of its gables and, for relief, the other in half-timbered work. To the leading gable is a single-storey canted bay window and alongside, in an internal angle, a catslide-roofed entrance canopy. The multi-paned windows are in red livery with brick sills and segmental arches. All in the forthright manner of architect William Mansfield Mitchell (1842–1910).

Griffith 1848–60; *LGI* (1904); *IFR*; Lyons 1993; Casey and Rowan 1993; Kavanagh 2006.

236. RAHOOD, Nobber; *c.* 1800.

Opposite the gates is a standard single-storey hip-roofed late Georgian lodge with block rusticated surrounds to lancet windows flanking the doorway with a semicircular fanlight. Modernised with less than appropriate new door-case and windows, its protective harled finish stripped to reveal immaculate rubble construction, now left to withstand the elements. Perfectly symmetrical but for the off-centre chimney-stack. For long the home of the Cruise family, in 1814 of Richard Cruise.

Leet 1814.

237. RANDALSTOWN or RANDLESTOWN, Navan (2).

Irish Architectural Archive

The valuation of 1854 records gate lodges to the property; only one is evident on successive OS maps and it survives as a photographic record only. The estate, ancestral home to the Everard family since the 1300s, lies a scene of devastation, both the big house and this lodge having been demolished in the 1970s. These images show a most peculiar lodge dating from about 1800 which was, for whatever reason, contrived to look like a single-storey structure from road and avenue, with high eaves to its hipped roof and unusual chamfered corners. From the park it was revealed as a two-storey gatehouse with a symmetrical façade featuring a large segmentally arched recess with moulded surround and keystone. To the short avenue front was applied an idiosyncratic three-bay frontispiece with a pediment over a doorway with semicircular fanlight containing Gothic tracery. Flanking it were slit windows; stuccoed with a large chimney-stack shaped to restate the main theme. There was an extensive gatescreen of fine railed shallow concave quadrants. All work for Thomas Everard, after whose death the place was tenanted for many years by Henry Meredith, his sons having left to serve in the church, army and navy.

Griffith 1848–60; *LGI* (1904); Bence-Jones 1988; IAA photograph (S/348/6).

238. RATHALDRON, Navan; pre-1836/*c.* 1845; architect possibly James Shiel.
William Wilde visited here in 1850 and found a 'castellated mansion, partly ancient and partly modern, approached by one of the finest avenues of lime trees in Meath, perhaps in Ireland; it consists of a strong, well-built quadrangular tower, of very considerable antiquity, to which a handsome castellated dwelling-house has lately been added'. What he noticed was a medieval tower-house of the Cusack family, extended after the death of Christopher Cusack by Fleming P. O'Reilly, the county treasurer in 1843. What he chose not to notice was an

235. Rahinstown, rear entrance.

appropriate and daunting curtain-raiser at the bottom of the avenue in this Picturesque castellated gatehouse spanning the access (*above*). Two-storey and built in good punched ashlar, the tall Tudor carriage archway is surmounted by a mock machicolation projecting from the Irish crenellated ramparts, which are approached via an octagonal stair turret which has a balancing square buttressed counterpart. The accommodation is lit by label-moulded chamfered openings and to the right of the main carriage opening is a tiny pedestrian

access. The room above the archway is lit to the rear by a quatrefoil window, a motif repeated in the good cast-iron gates. Replacing a predecessor, the O'Reilly arms sculpted centrally dates it to after their arrival. Cautiously attributed to architect James Shiel by Christine Casey. Derelict between concave quadrant crenellated rubble walls.

Slater 1846; Wilde 1850; Casey and Rowan 1993.

239. RATHBEGGAN, Dunboyne; *c.* 1845.
A property in the late eighteenth century of the Tighe family which by 1837 had passed to John Standish. The lodge was built sometime between 1836 and 1854 by him or his successor, Edward F. Standish. It is a standard single-storey harled steeply hip-roofed cottage, which now lies derelict.

Taylor and Skinner 1778; 1969 [1773]; Lewis 1837; Griffith 1848–60.

240. RATHCORE, Rathcore (2).
This estate of the Kennedy family remained lodgeless in the nineteenth century, but P.J. Kennedy remedied this with considerable ostentation in commissioning a striking gatescreen and two porters' lodges from an architect not known for his reticence. Sadly, a century after their creation both buildings show a lack of appreciation from later owners, as both lie abandoned, approaching ruin.

Main entrance; 1906; architect James Franklin Fuller.

Apparent is a splendidly maintained and durable gatescreen comprised of four tall pillars, all ball-finialled, the outer crenellated and those to the carriage opening with buttressed faces in granite, as are the concave rubble quadrants, all by Mr McEvoy of Ballyknockan. Contemporary carriage and both postilion gates are wrought iron by J. and C. McGloughlin Ltd. Barely visible within is the little derelict lodge in dense undergrowth. Single-storey below a hipped roof, with a central gabled hall projection having decorative half-timbered work to the apex with pebble-dashed panels. Otherwise highly conspicuous for its finish of channelled rustication with beaded surrounds to two-over-two sash windows.

Secondary entrance; *c.* 1906; architect probably J.F. Fuller.

On an elevated site and more brazenly neglected is this similarly boldly rusticated rendered 1½-storey standard affair. Gabled with sufficiently tall eaves to easily accommodate the central projecting hallway, over the doorway of which is an entablature carried on a pair of fluted console brackets. Crowning it all, the rustication extends to the chimney-stack.

IB (29 Dec. 1906).

241. RATHKENNY, Rathkenny; *c.* 1865.
To the 'handsome and sophisticated' mid- to late eighteenth-century home of the Hussey family is a rather less urbane but pleasant two-storey gabled, roughcast gatehouse from a century later. Of generous proportions, it looks across the modest gates from without, with a symmetrical front of two-over-two sash windows on each side of a flat-roofed hall breakfront, and two equivalent windows above. Eaves and verges are articulated by ornamental brackets, whilst to the leading gabled elevation is a canopied doorway and a curiously antique-looking little lancet sash window over. Probably a development for Edward Horatio Hussey (1807–76).

LGI (1904); Casey and Rowan 1993.

242. RATHMORE, Athboy; pre-1836.
A property of the Blighs, earls of Darnley, of nearby Clifton Lodge (*q.v.*), the gate lodge to which had gone by 1912.

243. RATOATH MANOR, Ratoath; pre-1836; *demolished.*
A gatekeeper's lodge probably built by James Corballis of Roebuck House, south Dublin (*q.v.*), after he acquired the manor house in 1813 and prior to his death in 1842.

IFR.

244. RATOATH RECTORY, Ratoath; pre-1836; *demolished.*
A lodge that may have been contemporary with the building of the glebe house in 1813 during the incumbency from 1794 until his death of the rector Revd Launcelot King Conyngham (1772–1820).

Lewis 1837; Leslie and Wallace 2009.

245. ROCK BELLEW, Julianstown; pre-1836. The lodge, a seat in 1814 of Peter Sherlock, is now ruinous and overgrown.

Leet 1814.

246. ROCKFIELD, Kells (4).

Richard Rothwell (1799–1853), who inherited the property on the death of his father in 1817, is likely to have added the two early lodges to the estate between then and his marriage in 1824. Both, in any case, are shown on an estate survey map of 1830 by George Plunkett.

South gate; *c.* 1820.

Kevin Mulligan

A charming standard lodge in harled rubble construction, its high cut-stone eaves band and offset chimney permitting a loft room lit by a window in the hipped gable end to the road. The opposing elevation to the park is bowed below an equivalent roof configuration and contains a tripartite lattice-paned casement window, a pretty feature repeated on each side of the sheeted front door. Admirably restored and extended in 1999, sufficient to warrant an award from An Taisce.

East gate; *c.* 1820; *demolished.*

A harled single-storey lodge with short two-bay front to the avenue, below a hipped gable roof, comprised of a window and doorway each set in individual flat-arched recesses. Replaced by a bungalow.

Richard Rothwell continued to spend money on improvements to house and estate, as recorded in an account book between 1838 and 1841, presumably under the superintendence of architect William Murray, who exhibited designs to the RHA in 1841. It is safe to attribute the lodge at the Kells avenue to him.

North gate; 1843; architect William Murray.

Now lying derelict and boarded up on an abandoned approach is this very fine Tudor Revival lodge built in random uncoursed stone facings off an informal plan, having an abundance of gables with paired verge brackets, crowned by a dominant trio of octagonal chimney-stacks. There is a mixture of label-moulded bi- and tripartite mullioned cut-stone windows and a Gothic-arched front door to the hall, which extends alongside the main avenue gable, which houses a semi-octagonal bay window. To the apexes are shields, one obligingly inscribed with the date of construction. Largely single-storey but for an attic room to the rear. There is a good and extensive straight railed entrance screen with palmette finials and cast-iron carriage posts which have pretty anthemion motifs, all contained by outer stone pillars with innovative cappings. There is a lodge with a similar irregular layout at Bective House (*q.v.*).

West gate; *c.* 1865.

Probably originally in a rendered finish is this 1½-storey gabled lodge, now with its ragstone fabric and brick dressings exposed. Asymmetrical three-bay main front with doorway to left-hand side below a gabled bracketed canopy; pair of windows to loft rooms. Built by Richard Rothwell's eldest son, Thomas.

LGI (1904); Mulligan 2001.

247. ROCK LODGE, Laracor (2).

Neither of the lodges, that to the eastern gate seeming to have doubled as a schoolhouse, survives. Both dated from before 1836 in the time of Thomas Disney, probably the same as owned neighbouring Adamstown (*q.v.*).

Lewis 1837.

248. ROESTOWN, Dunshaughlin; *c.* 1850; *demolished.*

A lodge located opposite the gates that was built sometime between 1836 and 1854, probably by James Maher.

Griffith 1848–60.

249. RORISTOWN, Trim; *c.* 1825; architect possibly Francis Johnston.

Opposite the entrance is a distinguished small building in the manner of a Classical temple. Single-storey, originally raised off a cruciform plan, with a tetrastyle pedimented portico having, uncommonly, octagonal limestone columns screening a three-bay façade comprised of a segmentally arched window flanked by a pair of round-headed niches. From a side elevation extends a distyle pedimented entrance portico to the doorway, which presumably had a balancing projection to the opposing side; stuccoed with toothed quoins. Extended unobtrusively to the rear and well maintained behind a straight railed screen with a pair of delightful 'Catherine wheel' postern gates carried on octagonal stone posts with some fluting and convex cappings. These features repeat in the gatescreen across the road, with matching railings but shaped as ogee entrance quadrants. There are estate entrances akin to this at Ballyboy (*q.v.*), Cloncarneel (*q.v.*) and Rockview, Co. Westmeath (*q.v.*). The big house was built in 1787 by Cornelius Drake, with the porter's lodge dating from a couple of generations later and added by Christopher Drake.

D.A. Beaufort (1787).

250. ROSNAREE, Slane; *c.* 1875; architect not known.

For Charles W. Osbourne is this sturdy standard 1½-storey gabled lodge built in random coursed quarry-faced stone with striking cream brick highlights of toothed quoins and dressings. The front door has dwarf flanking walls and a canopied catslide roof with railway architecture in the scalloped sheeting as spandrels and fascia; perforated scalloped cresting and pairs of windows to the loft rooms, which identify the design to be by the same hand as the lodge at Posseckstown (*q.v.*). Contemporary cast-iron gates, finialled carriage posts and ogee quadrant railings by Kennan and Sons of Dublin.

Slater 1870; *Land owners in Ireland 1876.*

251. ROSS, Finneas; pre-1836/*c.* 1900; architect not known.

By Lough Sheelin is a distinctive single-storey standard hip-gabled lodge of considerable presence and the perfect introduction to the contemporary big house, many of whose details it reflects in the stylised door and window surrounds, all of which break the eaves line. The door-case comprises a pair of engaged square Doric columns supporting an entablature with miniature triangular pediment, which harks back to James Paine. The windows have segmental pediment variants, lugged architraves and corbelled sills, all contrasting effectively with roughcast walls. The perfect symmetry is maintained by the considered positioning of the chimney-stacks. The replacement windows reflect their six-over-six wooden sash predecessors, but the nasty aluminium doorscreen grates. Located opposite the gates, where there was an earlier lodge of the Somerville family. A development from the turn of the twentieth century, when William Ahern was listed as owner.

252. RUSK, Dunboyne; pre-1836; *demolished.*
The early eighteenth-century house of the Wilson family lies in ruins, its lodge gone.

253. RYNDVILLE, Innfield (2).
An old estate of the Rhynds, both of whose lodges and entrances have gone without trace.

254. ST CLOUD, Slane; *c.* 1890.
A plain single-storey four-bay hip-roofed roughcast lodge with a gabled return forming an L-plan. Good railed entrance quadrants with nice anthemion motifs and carriage pillars with 'St Cloud' chiselled into each below concave cappings crowned with gadrooned tops. The outer pillars are cylindrical on outsized plinths, all looking as if cobbled together at different dates. A property in the nineteenth century of the Russell family. There may have been an earlier pre-1836 lodge located off the secondary road.

255. ST JAMES CHURCH OF IRELAND CHURCH, Athboy; *c.* 1845.

Dwarfed by the sixteenth-century church tower is a little single-storey hip-roofed cut-stone sexton's lodge, its short three-bay front outside the gates. Openings are lancets, the windows tiny and antisocial, the doorway below a gablet with a crowning stone finial, an unusual feature that is repeated on the hip corners. Now minus its chimney-stack but revitalised by library use. Built for Revd Robert Noble (1796–1870), long-serving rector between 1831 and his death.

Leslie and Wallace 2009.

256. SILVERSTREAM, Gormanstown; *c.* 1860.
A sturdy, neat and well-kept standard single-storey lodge, built in dark random rubble finish contrasting with lighter cut-stone dressings and V-jointed rusticated quoins; capped by a shallow oversailing hipped roof. Erected for the Hon. Thomas Preston (1817–1903), seventh and youngest son of the 12th Viscount Gormanstown of the nearby castle of that name.

BPB (1929).

257. SION, Navan; *c.* 1860; *demolished.*
A mid-nineteenth-century property created by John Charles Metge (d. 1870) of the nearby Athlumney estate (*q.v.*).

LGI (1904).

258. SKREEN, or SKRYNE, CASTLE, Skreen; *c.* 1865.
A solid, no-nonsense, square single-storey lodge built in dark stone with mellow brick dressings to two- by two-bay elevations below a pyramidal roof rising to a central chimney-stack. The twentieth-century metal windows, flat-roofed hall protuberance and general dilapidation spoil the effect. Built by the Wilkinson family.

259. SLANDUFF, Kentstown; *c.* 1870.
A single-storey gabled lodge, stone-built with brick dressings and a tall round-headed Georgian-style window to one end. A property in 1854 of Peter Austin.

Griffith 1848–60.

260. SLANE CASTLE, Slane (3).
The great estate of the Conyngham family since 1703, when Henry Conyngham came into possession of it, is a show-piece of the Romantic Castellated style, which extends from the castle itself to its three demesne entrances. Although the architectural evolution of the big house is complex, with many practitioners, such as Wyatt, Gandon, Brown and Francis Johnston, attempting to satisfy their clients, it was the latter, arriving here in 1792, who was entrusted to create important preludes to the place. Writing at the end of his life, he recorded that he had 'planned and executed several detached works, about the castle of Slane, as the Gothic gate opposite the mill', all for Henry Burton Conyngham, 3rd baron and 1st marquis (1766–1832), who had inherited the estate on his father's death in 1787. The property has become a home to pop concerts, and this precedent was set in its accessibility to the public as early as 1883, when Wakeman advised: 'Tourists should leave their cars at the Slane gate, giving directions to the driver to meet them at the opposite entrance to the demesne, on the road to Navan. The walk from gate to gate will occupy but a short time. Almost everything that could be imagined attractive in green sward and sylvan glory may be here found.'

Dublin gate; *c.* 1800; architect Francis Johnston (*below*).
Approached up Millhill by the Dublin road is a familiar landmark to travellers, considered by Odlum to be arguably one of the most impressive 'castle-style' entrances ever erected in Ireland. Of that there is no doubt, although Sir Richard Colt Hoare on tour in 1806 was a bit stuffier and found it to be 'slender and meagre according to the Gothic costume of modern architects'. Viewed from a certain angle it can appear as attenuated as a stage set, but from the main approach it is truly effective, surviving precisely as Johnston intended on his drawing; in rubble construction with cut-stone dressings, the great carriage archway, now lacking the intended studded wooden doors, is crowned by the family coat of arms below a machicolated and crenellated

National Library of Ireland

parapet, all flanked by the similarly topped hexagonal towers with postilion doorways and relieved by mock arrowloops. To each side the castellated curtain walls step according to the contours between the road and river-bank to terminate in square turrets. There is little inkling of gatekeeper's accommodation, but it is there, tucked in behind the right-hand screen wall, a simple two-roomed single-storey structure, not integrated into the scheme of things but rather as an afterthought. It is nevertheless built as indicated on the architect's design. A very appropriate introduction to the estate, 'In pale golden stone, it has a lightness and charm that recalls a conventional fairytale castle', as Rosemary ffolliott observed.

Slane gate; *c.* 1805; architect possibly Francis Johnston.

Next to the village is a single-storey hip-roofed structure on an L-plan, the generous accommodation explained by its early nineteenth-century dual function as a schoolhouse. Like the Dublin gate, another example of the porter's quarters being disguised behind a screen wall. Built in pleasant random rubble with a crenellated parapet, it is perforated by a Tudor-arched entrance porch and a pair of two-over-two tall sash windows. The lodge itself has been extended and sanitised in modernisation, losing a Picturesque canted bay to the avenue elevation in the process. Shown on the William Larkin Road Map of 1806–10.

Navan gate; *c.* 1810; architect probably Francis Johnston.

Located by an old road junction, from which it has now been removed by realignment that creates a generous forecourt to this quirky two-storey gatehouse in the form of a medieval barbican. Square on plan, built in random rubble, it is penetrated by a large Tudor-arched carriage access and surmounted by machicolated and deeply crenellated ramparts, which, like the first floor, are approached via a spiral staircase housed in the dominant round tower. This upper room is lit by little lancet windows alongside carved Conyngham shields. Elsewhere there is further relief in mock arrowloops, but the main idiosyncrasy is the circular bartizan, which, rather than being correctly placed on a corner of the structure, is corbelled centrally above the main archway. As with the other entrances, the gate-porter's accommodation is subservient to the general scheme of things. This is relegated to the left-hand side as a single-storey lodge behind a parapeted wall that also serves as a quadrant of the main sweep and is pierced by pointed-arched windows. As ever, little consideration was given to the convenience of the gatekeeper, sacrificed as it was to effect, but it was still preferable to a thatched hovel.

Hoare 1807; Wakeman 1883; *BPB* (1929); ffolliott 1970; *Country Life* (17, 24 and 31 July 1980); Howley 1993; Casey and Rowan 1993; Rothery 1997; NLI drawing (AD 3420); Horner 2007.

261. SLANE FLOUR MILLS AND HOUSE, Slane; *c.* 1800.

William Burton of Slane Castle (*q.v.*) and Townley Balfour of Townley Hall, Co. Louth (*q.v.*), jointly in 1763 established this, then the largest flour mill in Ireland, at a cost of £20,000. The miller's house alongside pales in scale if not in sophistication, but the lodge outside the gates is relatively plain and diminutive, having been a single-storey standard structure below a hipped roof with a corniced limestone eaves band. What was once an agreeable building has been most grotesquely extended and effaced by later additions, its chimney-stack rising ever higher in search of draw. Shown on William Larkin's Road Map of 1806–10.

Young 1780; Mulligan 2001; Horner 2007.

262. SMITHSTOWN, Dunshaughlin; pre-1912; *demolished.*

A lodge built after 1836 by the Logan family.

263. SOMERVILLE, Duleek (3).

A house, originating from *c.* 1730 after Sir James Somerville succeeded to his uncle's Meath estates, which owes its present late Georgian form to a reconstruction by Sir Richard Morrison a century later for Sir William Meredyth Somerville, 5th baronet and later 1st Lord Athumney (1802–73). He had inherited the estate in 1831 and may have been prompted into the improvements by his marriage the following year to Lady Harriet Maria Conyngham of Slane Castle (*q.v.*). If there were any doubts as to the safety of the attribution of these works to Morrison they are surely dispelled by the lodge and gatescreen at the previous main entrance.

Balrath gate; *c.* 1835; architect Sir Richard Morrison.

Irish Architectural Archive/Robert Raley

Irish Architectural Archive/Robert Raley

'... a fine mansion in an extensive demesne, has been recently enlarged and improved, and a handsome entrance lodge erected.' This handsome building, appreciated by Samuel Lewis in 1837, has been subjected to the most horrific and ignorant alterations at the hands of a twentieth-century moderniser.

Morrison has graced the country with a series of gate lodges, all of which evolved from Sir John Soane's 'Greek Cottage', presented as a design in his *Sketches in architecture* (1793) [Fig. 6, p. 7]. This Morrison adapted with little alteration at Killruddery, Co. Wicklow (*q.v.*), and Castlecoole, Co. Fermanagh, through the Classical temple variants at Ballyfin, Co. Laois (*q.v.*), and Fota, Co. Cork, to this, his ultimate neo-Greek solution. Whereas the earlier examples were based on a cruciform plan with a short front for impact with side-entry hall and balancing closet wing, here these hip-roofed projections are to the fore, creating a T-plan with a pedimented breakfront entrance that, for effect, has a crepidoma or stepped approach. The pediment was supported on sturdy recessed-panel pilasters, with the architect's trademark laurel wreaths, and a pair of unfluted Ionic columns *in antis*. An Irish flavour is introduced in the channel-rusticated pilaster quoins. All in fine limestone ashlar with stucco panels. Sadly, the whole roof configuration has been altered, with the loss of the pediment and the introduction of concrete-roll roof tiles and full-height louvred shutters to the front door, all in search of that gay 'hacienda' feel. As in his other estate entrances, Morrison accompanies the lodge with a gatescreen hardly deviating from plate 20 of J.B. Papworth's *Rural residences* (1818) [Fig. 7, p. 7], with characteristic Greek stelae-type main carriage pillars, to which are added Morrison's signature laurel wreaths to the friezes. As Papworth recommends, there are secondary posts to carry the gates in highly decorative ironwork, by Richard Turner of Dublin, with repeating anthemion and rosette motifs—all to be found in an identical entrance at Castle Morres, Co. Kilkenny (*q.v.*).

Kentstown gate; *c.* 1790.

Probably the original principal entrance to the demesne from the village is this impressive double rustic Triumphal archway incorporating a pair of 'day and night' lodges; giving the impression of generous two-storey accommodation, it is in fact a bit of a sham, as it is comprised of two giant screen walls sandwiching only two tall rooms. Built in random rubble facings with three bays, front and back defined by two-stage pilasters carrying entablatured parapets. The lofty central round-headed carriage archway is flanked by panels with blind *oeils-de-boeuf* over rusticated Gibbsian windows to the approach and semicircular-arched niches to the park. All now rather less effective since the original limewashed harling was removed.

School lodge; *c.* 1835; architect possibly Sir Richard Morrison.

Labelled a 'schoolhouse' on the 1836 OS map, by 1912 it was classified as a gate lodge. Difficult to disentangle through a jumble of single-storey extensions but just discernible is the nucleus of a two-storey structure, below a shallow-hipped roof with paired carved eaves brackets, faced in stone rubble. A central single-storey verandahed projection with a canted bay window may form part of the original scheme of things.

Lewis 1837; Debrett (1920); Casey and Rowan 1993; IAA photographs (8/99).

264. SPRING VALLEY, Summerhill; *c.* 1810.

Irish Architectural Archive/Rossmore

What was the most quaint of estate entrances would now be but a memory had it not been much photographed. Sited on a right-angled bend of the public road at what, in the days of the horse-drawn carriage and cart, must have seemed the most propitious of accesses, the gatescreen has now succumbed to modern wayward traffic, whilst the charming lodge has fallen victim to the philistine. The former was a delightful mishmash incorporating, probably from about 1870, two Corinthian columns as gate pillars and responding pilasters that traditionally had been salvaged from a portico to a gate lodge at Dangan Castle (*q.v.*). The lodge here was probably built when the property passed through marriage from the Dennis family to the Bryans about 1810. Single-storey standard and traditional, with white harled walls and steeply thatched roof with a suggestion of hipped gables, much as at Hamwood (*q.v.*) and probably influenced by the Fosterstown (*q.v.*) lodge nearby. The doorway had a flat-roofed porch projection, but all that now survives of a favourite landmark is a chimney-stack.

Mulligan 2001; IAA photographs (46/2).

265. SPRINGVILLE, Kells; pre-1836; *demolished.*

A property in the late eighteenth century of a Mr Kellet which passed from Edward Bradley, who is noted here in 1814, to Philip O'Reilly from about 1824.

Taylor and Skinner 1778; 1969 [1783]; Leet 1814; Pigot 1824.

266. STACKALLEN, Slane (4).

The noble Queen Anne-style mansion built by the Williamite general Gustavus Hamilton, 1st Viscount Boyne, as 'Boyne House' had two lodges dating from before 1836, both subsequently replaced by those surviving.

Front entrance; *c.* 1845; architect possibly Frederick Darley Jr.

The house was briefly leased for school use in the mid-nineteenth century as St Columba's College; Frederick Darley Jr was employed to adapt it, and he may then have designed the new porter's lodge. Superseding a predecessor opposite the gates is this very fine example built off a T-plan in excellent random limestone ashlar. The hipped roof oversails to form a verandah about the downstroke with a range of supporting posts. Facing the avenue is a rectangular bay window with tripartite Georgian-style four-over-four sash window, repeated in single and bipartite form elsewhere. The bold cornice of the stone chimney-stack is repeated in the gatescreen pillars, those to the carriage gates octagonal, which originally stopped low ogee walled quadrants. The estate boundary has recently been realigned to exclude the lodge.

Rear entrance; *c.* 1875.

A spacious and perfectly symmetrical single-storey five-bay building below a hipped roof opposite the gates. The central pedimented porch to a double-leafed sheeted door is flanked by brick-dressed bipartite casement windows in pleasant random rubble walls; mellow brick banded and corbelled chimney-stack. Replacing an earlier lodge by the gates. For Gustavus Hamilton-Russell, 8th Viscount Boyne (1830–1907), after he inherited the property in 1872.

BPB (1929); Casey and Rowan 1993; Mulligan 2001.

267. STAFFORDSTOWN, Kentstown (2).

The earlier eighteenth-century house of a branch of the Rothwell family had its main lodged approach from the south.

South entrance; *c.* 1800.

Approaching ruin is what was a simple gabled single-storey lodge with a small hall projection from the avenue façade, which is, unusually, otherwise blind. Equally curious is an appendage on the road elevation in the shape of a semi-octagonal addition with the remains of lancet windows, brick-dressed in rubble walls. Probably built by John Rothwell (1763–1826), upon whose death without issue the property passed through marriage to Whitwell Butler (1790–1877), who built what is now the main mid-nineteenth-century house and added a secondary lodge to the northern avenue.

North entrance; *c.* 1850; architect perhaps W.G. Murray.
An unremarkable 1½-storey standard gabled affair, its main eaves, with paired plain soffit brackets, sufficiently high to accommodate the central gabled single-storey hall. Deserted and enshrouded in ivy. The neighbouring lodge at Brownstown House (*q.v.*) is very similar.

LGI (1904); Casey and Rowan 1993.

268. STALEEN, Donore; *c.* 1845/*c.* 1890.
A single-storey gabled standard brick-built lodge with Wyatt windows, seemingly erected across the face of its predecessor and much extended in unsympathetic manner. A property for much of the nineteenth century of the Sharman-Crawford family of County Down. There is a nice earlier railed gatescreen with ogee quadrants and cast-iron posts with anthemion tops.

269. STAMEEN, Drogheda; *c.* 1895; architects probably W.M. Mitchell and Sons.

William Elliot Cairnes of Killyfaddy, Co. Tyrone, acquired Stameen in 1825, and it was probably his younger son, Thomas Plunket Cairnes (1830–94), a wealthy Drogheda brewer and banker, who developed the property with the assistance of his architect, W.F. Caldbeck, to whom is attributed the big Italianate-style villa. An early gate lodge to the estate, inherited from the previous owners, served until the turn of the new century and the advent of Thomas's son, William Plunket Cairnes (1857–1925). This can be credited to the Dublin architectural practice of W.M. Mitchell and Sons, both on stylistic grounds and on the fact that the firm is known to have worked here in 1930. It is a very pleasing Arts and Crafts Elizabethan Revival design in the form of a not-quite-symmetrical single-storey lodge raised off a butterfly plan in a pleasant orange brick laid in an uncommon English cross-bond. This contrasts nicely with the mock half-timbered effect to main gables and that of the ornamental porch, which projects invitingly from the internal angle with its finely carved woodwork. The windows are small square-paned casements. Red earthenware ridge tiles are interrupted by banded and corbelled chimney-stacks. In 2000 pathetically abandoned, caught in the inexorable advance of modern housing development. There is an identical porter's lodge to nearby Glen House (*q.v.*).

IFR; Casey and Rowan 1993; IAA.

270. STAMEEN VILLA, Drogheda; *c.* 1770.
A property in 1814 of E. Sherlock Esq., in whose family it remained until late in the century. Their lodge on the main northern approach survives as an antique and vernacular-looking three-bay single-storey cottage with a high-pitched hipped roof, its corrugated-iron roof having replaced the original thatch. Rendered and limewashed white. Deserted. The gate porter in 1855 was Patrick Doner.

Leet 1814; Griffith 1848–60.

271. STEDALT, Stamullin; pre-1911; *demolished.*
A seat for much of the nineteenth century of the Walsh family; its short-lived gate lodge opposite the gates was perhaps contemporary with the house of *c.* 1870, which is now a nursing home.

272. STIRLING, Clonee (2).
Francis MacFarlane settled here in the mid-eighteenth century and built the delightful pair of cottages at what may then have been the main gate.

West entrance; *c.* 1780.

Now converted into one home, these two semi-detached single-storey Georgian Gothic gabled cottages would each originally have had symmetrical three-bay façades. Well restored, with pretty pointed heads to windows with Y-traceried glazing in white walls.

Francis MacFarlane's son Henry inherited Stirling and nearby Huntstown, Co. Dublin (*q.v.*), and seems to have lived in the latter after his marriage in 1815. The County Meath property was subsequently inhabited by his sister Mary and her husband Richard Barker, whom she wed in 1817. The new splendid entrance must date from then.

East entrance; *c.* 1817.
Strikingly sited at a road junction is a pair of Classical lodges closely modelled on the entrance screen to the Viceregal Lodge in the Phoenix Park (*q.v.*), the design of which is attributable to John Nash, based on its similarity to that at Caledon House, Co. Tyrone. Originally each lodge would have had a wide tripartite Wyatt window with Georgian glazed sashes below the stone moulded pediments. These are linked by screen walls with postern openings, flanking octagonal carriage pillars crowned by

lanterns, just as in the Phoenix Park. Whilst modernisation has shown appreciation for the symmetry of the composition with balancing wings to each building, there has not been the same respect for original materials, previous stone and stucco having been obliterated by pebble-dash finish, and the new windows are sadly inappropriate.

LGI (1904).

273. SUMMERHILL, Summerhill (3).
The greatest loss to Ireland's domestic architectural heritage came in the 1950s with the shameful demolition of Pearce's and Castle's great Baroque palace. Built in 1728 for Hercules Rowley, it was dramatically sited on a height, its straight avenue on an axis with the centre of the sleepy village of the same name. The main entrance here, like others to the demesne, is of rather less architectural consequence, dating from developments of later generations of the Rowley family, Barons Langford.

Village entrance; *c.* 1820.

Kevin Mulligan

An unspectacular gatescreen in limestone ashlar of plain square carriage pillars flanked by a pair of pedestrian gates and concave-walled quadrants beyond. At an uncomfortable distance for the gatekeeper is a 1½-storey late Georgian lodge, three-bay symmetrical with tall eaves and hipped gables sufficient to accommodate attic rooms. Later indignities include the addition of a flat-roofed hall projection and roughcast finish over the stone construction. In 2008 it was being subjected to a major extension to the rear, certainly not deferential to the original. Built for Clotworthy Taylor Rowley, 1st Baron Langford (1763–1825), after the

Irish Architectural Archive/Craig Collection

estate had suffered a period of neglect following a fire in the great house *c.* 1800 and the death within two years of the 1st and 2nd viscounts.

Kilcock entrance; *c.* 1780; *demolished.* The most engaging and unique of buildings (*above*) was the two-storey gatehouse built at the base of the southern avenue on an axis with the road from Kilcock. Square on plan, its standard three-bay ground floor with advancing central gabled hall was flanked by a pair of Y-traceried Georgian Gothic lancet windows. Above was a similar single window below a parapet, the crowning glory to which was, matching the window heads, a metal-covered convex-pitched roof or dome, rising to the central chimney-stack, attracting the sobriquet 'Balloon Lodge'. A wonderful oddity, probably erected by Hercules Langford Rowley before his death in 1794, now lost. Shown on Larkin's 1812 Road Map of Meath.

Moy entrance; pre-1836/*c.* 1850. Replacing an earlier lodge on this western approach is a two-bay 1½-storey structure with hipped gables built in rubble stone alongside a pair of ashlar gate pillars. Modern concrete-tiled roof finish.

Hoare 1807; D.A. Beaufort (1808); Fraser 1838; *BPB* (1929); Colvin and Harris 1970; Casey and Rowan 1993; Horner 2007; IAA photographs (11/6).

274. SUTHERLAND, Ratoath; *c.* 1800.
A tiny, square, two-bay single-storey lodge built in harled rubble below a now-missing pyramidal roof. The gates to this property, in 1814 of Christopher Rooney, have also gone.

Leet 1814.

275. SWAINSTOWN, Kilmessan; pre-1836/*c.* 1880.
An ancestral property of the Preston family, the eldest sons of which were invariably called Nathaniel. Their early gate lodge was replaced by a late Victorian successor. The single-bay gabled main front to the avenue has its window dressed in red brick and a dentil course over the soldier arch. Above that, in a rendered finish, was a feature destroyed to accommodate a burglar alarm. Much extended and modernised. Presumably built by Nathaniel Francis Preston (1843–1903), who succeeded to the estate in 1853 and whose death ended the direct male line.

LGI (1904).

276. SYLVAN PARK, Kells; pre-1836; *demolished.*
A lodge built either by the Grattan family or by Walter Kearney, who succeeded them *c.* 1810. The big house has likewise gone.

Wilson 1803; Leet 1814.

277. TEAGUESTOWN, Trim (2).
Both lodges were added to the property of Hugh Hanbury between 1836, the date of the first Ordnance Survey map, and their recording in the valuation of 1854. That to the west has been demolished, whilst the eastern lodge lies ruinous and overgrown.

Slater 1846; Griffith 1848–60.

278. THOMASTOWN, Duleek; pre-1836/*c.* 1850.
On the site of an earlier long narrow structure is a highly Picturesque 1½-storey gabled lodge with ornamental carved bargeboards to its steeply pitched roof. Built in stone facings with red-brick dressings. Home in the early to mid-nineteenth century of the Kettlewell family.

279. THURSTIANSTOWN, Yellow Furze; *c.* 1850.
A property that became known as 'Beechville' was home to the Russell family in the mid-nineteenth century. The lodge is a modest single-storey standard harled gabled affair.

280. TOBERTYNAN, Rathmoylan; pre-1836; *demolished.*
The lodge is survived by a good mid-Georgian gatescreen comprised of four square ashlar pillars with pretty eight-petalled paterae, or rosettes, to the friezes; simple railings. Probably dating from the time here of the Nugent family. The lodge may have been temporary or an addition by Francis McEvoy or his brother James, who succeeded him in 1808.

Lewis 1837; *LGI* (1904).

281. TRAMMONT, Rathmoylan; *c.* 1845; architect not known.

An early Victorian development by James Williams for himself, which included the 'Hansel and Gretel'-style house and its pretty gate lodge. Williams, who did not live long to enjoy his creations, dying in 1853, would be appalled to see the state of the latter. It lies abandoned and in an advanced state of decay. Single-storey standard, built in rubble stone, with much use of bull-nose bricks as opening dressing and in the chimney-stack with its sawtooth corbelling. Under a steeply hipped roof with carved soffit brackets, the gabled frontispiece hall projection has the remains of ornamental wooden bargeboards with a type of quatrefoil perforation. The margined glazing to the double-leaved door gives a clue as to the nature of the wide windows, now boarded up.

Slater 1846; Casey and Rowan 1993.

282. TRIERMORE, Clonmellon; pre-1836/*c.* 1845.

283. Trim Military Barracks.

A smart lodge opposite the gates, still occupied, probably a replacement for a predecessor on the site. Standard single-storey below a hipped roof with oversailing eaves and carved paired soffit brackets. Roughcast with Irish pilaster quoins and smooth surrounds to margined sash windows which flank a projecting flat-roofed door-case. Atop the ridge is a banded octagonal stone stack. Nicely framed behind an extensive railing with recessed-panel pillars that reflect the entrance screen opposite. Built for Thomas Rotheram (1793–1861), whose elder brother was responsible for a lodge to nearby Crossdrum (*q.v.*).

LGI (1904).

283. TRIM MILITARY BARRACKS, Trim; *c.* 1845.
Now in service as a hotel is this old 'barracks for infantry, adapted to the reception of 3 officers and 80 non-commissioned officers and privates'. The forecourt is bounded to the road by a tall rubble screen wall broken by an ashlar semicircular-arched carriage opening with entablatures, flanked by a pair of flat-arched pedestrian openings. Hidden within are twin single-storey sentry-box lodges, their two-bay façades facing each other across the gateways. Each presents a wide gabled front to the barracks in the form of a pair of sash windows in a recess with segmental arch, creating an open pediment defined by cut-stone skew-tables and spring courses that return as eaves. All in an undisciplined mix of limestone and brickwork probably post-dating the barracks by about twenty years.

Lewis 1837.

284. TRIMLESTOWN CASTLE, Trim; pre-1836; *demolished.*
The main seat of the Barnewall family, Lords Trimlestown, lies in ruins, its lodge gone. Later twentieth-century gate lodges, said to be by the Belfast architectural practice of Blackwood and Jury, identified by Jeremy Williams were not found by the writer.

Williams 1994.

285. TRUBLEY, Bective; *c.* 1847; *demolished.*
A small landed estate formed by Matthew Fulham just after the first Ordnance Survey, the gate lodge being identified in the 1854 valuation.

Lewis 1837; Griffith 1848–60.

TUBBERTINAN (see TOBERTYNAN)

286. WALTERSTOWN, Moynalty (2).
A late Georgian house in 1783 of the Smith family which twenty years later was in the hands of Robert Kellett. The lodges, however, are from much later.

North lodge; *c.* 1900.
A rather ungainly 1½-storey commodious gabled affair on an L-plan, with a single-storey lean-to timber porch in the internal angle. Lower floor roughcast with brick quoins below a mock jettied half-timbered attic storey. Deserted, well beyond the entrance.

South lodge; *c.* 1900.
Sited facing and on the roadside is a standard 1½-storey building, central hipped dormer in a roof with rows of scalloped slates. Brick stacks and quoins to roughcast walls.

A property in 1876 of Thomas Kearney.

Taylor and Skinner 1778; 1969 [1783]; Leet 1814; *Land owners in Ireland 1876.*

287. WARRENSTOWN, Dunshaughlin (2).

West lodge; pre-1836; *demolished.*
An early lodge to a property long of the Johnston family had gone by 1913, to be replaced by a bungalow.

East lodge; pre-1913; *demolished.*
This may have dated from the late nineteenth century, when the Leonards arrived.

288. WATERLOO LODGE, Trim; pre-1836; *demolished.*
Both house and lodge probably just post-date the famous battle. In 1846 home to John Hynds.

Slater 1846.

WELLINGTON (see FOSTERSTOWN)

289. WESTLAND, Moynalty (2).

Front entrance; pre-1836; *demolished.*
Built by Thomas Barnes, long associated with the property.

Side entrance; *c.* 1810.
An antique long, low, single-storey three-bay lodge with tiny square-paned lights on each side of a later nasty flat-roofed hall projection. White harled walls below a very shallow-pitched hipped roof.

290. WESTON, Duleek; pre-1836/*c.* 1850.
An earlier house and its lodge, sited on the other side of the entrance, were replaced by Francis James Kelly (b. 1819) not long after succeeding to the estate on the death of his father in 1846. Both buildings are Regency in style, with windows set in segmentally arched recesses and carved modillion brackets to their eaves. Single-storey standard below a hipped roof oversailing to cover the hall breakfront. Later flat-roofed canted bay to the road; harled and derelict.

LGI (1904).

291. WHITEWOOD LODGE, Nobber; *c.* 1835; architect Arthur Creagh Taylor.

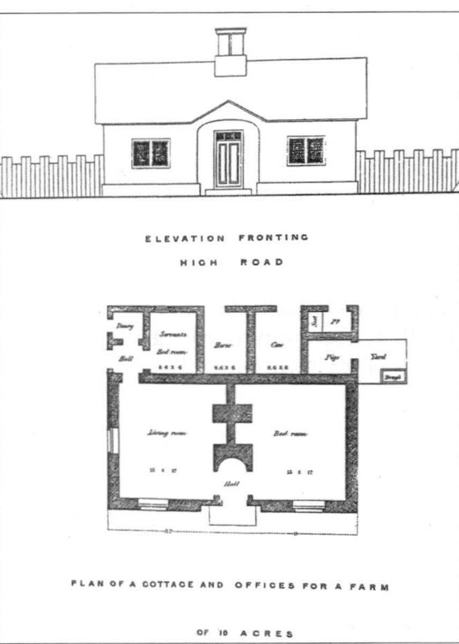

A rare and stylish example of a small house of 1735 by Richard Castle, a hunting-lodge for the Preston family of Gormanstown Castle (*q.v.*). Its gatekeeper's lodge is from a century later, to a design by A.C. Taylor prior to its inclusion in his pattern book of 1841, *Designs for agricultural buildings suited to Irish estates*, to which the 12th Viscount Gormanstown was a subscriber. In fact a 1½-storey variant of his published model in a sort of reticent Tudor Revival manner. Single-storey standard and gabled, with a pair of rectangular ashlar stacks coupled by the capping. Below is a gablet over the front fanlit doorway, which is set in a three-centred arched recess flanked by square window openings with keystones in uncoursed squared masonry walls. Located well within the property, it lies derelict and unwanted.

Taylor 1841; *BPB* (1929); Casey and Rowan 1993.

292. WILLIAMSTOWN, Clonee; *c.* 1845.
Situated on the boundary with County Dublin, both house and lodge form part of a development by William Johnston between 1836 and 1854. This is a tiny single-storey standard roughcast building with clipped eaves to the hipped roof, a diagonally set chimney-stack and modern window replacements. Vacant. There is a pair of drum entrance pillars.

Griffith 1848–60.

293. WILLIAMSTOWN, Kells; pre-1836; *demolished.*

An estate established in the mid-eighteenth century by William Williams, upon whose death it passed, through the marriage of his daughter and co-heir Esther, to Revd Hamilton Cuffe, third son of the 1st earl of Desart, on whose death it was inherited in 1811 by his son, John Conway Cuffe. On the latter's demise in 1833 Williamstown was acquired by Revd George Charles Garrett (1764–1841). From which era the gate lodge originated cannot be identified. What is clear is that the impressive gatescreen that survives dates from 100 years after the building of the big Classical house of *c.* 1780. It is very much a late Victorian design, with two big cut-stone gate pillars with bold plinths, scroll-topped buttresses and small recessed panels. Matching iron screens and gates with repeating roundel motifs and quarry-faced stone convex quadrants beyond.

LGI (1904); *BPB* (1929); Leslie and Wallace 2009.

294. WILMOUNT, Kells; *c.* 1830.
Alongside and forward of the gates is a single-bay gabled elevation having a most peculiar roof of its own, with mildly ornate bargeboards. Stretching behind is a long, low single-storey porter's accommodation. Built in boulder masonry, now hideously housing a garage door in its front. A property in 1814 of William Tallon, after whom it may have been named, which by 1837 had passed to John Radcliffe.

Leet 1814; Lewis 1837.

295. WOODFARM, Slane; pre-1836; *demolished.*
A seat in the nineteenth century of the Drew family, leasing from the earl of Sheffield.

296. WOODPARK, Dunboyne; pre-1836; *demolished.*
A lodge opposite the gates to a property in the late eighteenth century of a Mrs Shields, followed there by the Preston family.

Taylor and Skinner 1778; 1969 [1783]; Lewis 1837.

297. WOODTOWN, Athboy; pre-1836; *demolished.*
The very fine Palladian-style gentry house in the early nineteenth century of the Read family.

298. Woodview.

298. WOODVIEW, Kilberry; *c.* 1890.
A distinctive single-storey late Victorian lodge, with much effective use made of red clay materials in brick gabled breakfront dressings, corbelled eaves band and chimney-stack and earthenware hip tiles, perforated cresting and hip-knobs. Otherwise built in contrasting random grey stone below a hipped roof. A pair of wide windows to the road elevation overlook an older cast-iron gatescreen of spear-topped railings and posts with pretty anthemion motifs. To the park elevation is a later extension with half-timbered effect below a catslide roof. Previously the Donaghpatrick rectory of 1812, which was given over to secular use *c.* 1868 by John Richards Roberts before he succeeded to Durhamstown Castle (*q.v.*) in 1880, Woodview was then taken by Miss Mary Fahy, leasing from the Everards of Randalstown (*q.v.*).

Lewis 1837; Casey and Rowan 1993.

299. WOODVILLE, Kells; pre-1836; *demolished.*
The long-time residence of the Hill family.

300. WOODVILLE, Nobber; pre-1836; *demolished.*
Previously known as 'Kilmainham Wood', a property associated with the Hussey family of Westown, north Dublin (*q.v.*).

COUNTY OFFALY

1. ACRES HALL, Tullamore; pre-1838; *demolished.*
Now Tullamore town hall, this graceful town house was built for himself in 1786 by Thomas Acres, then the leading property developer in the area. He died in 1836, leaving his home to his daughter Ellen and her husband George Pierce, physician and surgeon, also of Clunagh (*q.v.*), who is identified in the 1851 valuation as the occupant of a property with a gate lodge, which seems from the first OS map to have been located at the rear gate by a walled garden rather than on the street front.

Griffith 1848–60; Nolan and O'Neill 1998.

2. AGHANVILLA, Clonygowan; pre-1838/*c.* 1850.
The early lodge was to a property at the beginning of the nineteenth century of William Newcombe. Situated outside the gates is a 1½-storey gabled structure with high eaves to accommodate a lean-to hall projection. Roughcast with modern windows but deserted. This appears to be of mid-nineteenth-century origin, when Samuel Ridgeway occupied the property, and is either a replacement or raised by an attic storey off the original.

Leet 1814; Griffith 1848–60.

3. ALDERBOROUGH, Geashill; *c.* 1870; *demolished.*
Much altered and derelict is this single-storey porter's lodge below a steeply hipped roof with fish-scale slates and ornamental cresting. Lost to road-widening. A seat in 1853 of William Warren.

Griffith 1848–60.

ANNAGHBRACK (see KILLOUGHY RECTORY)

4. ANNAGHMORE, Tullamore; pre-1838/*c.* 1890.
A bland single-storey gabled affair with a flat-roofed hall projection. Derelict. Built for Captain Maxwell Fox (1826–99), whose father, Major Barry Fox, had acquired the place *c.* 1830, as a replacement for an earlier lodge to a property in 1824 of Francis H. Biddulph or of his predecessor, William Curtis.

Coote 1801; Pigot 1824; Lewis 1837; *LGI* (1904).

5. ANNAVILLE, Shinrone; pre-1838; *demolished.*
A lodge located well within the boundary of an estate of John Smith in the first half of the nineteenth century.

6. ANNE GROVE, Roscrea; pre-1836.
A property that has seen regular changes of ownership over the centuries, perhaps reflected in the appearance of the gatekeeper's lodge. Single-storey, once standard, hip-roofed but now extended by a bay in modernisation, which also included pebble-dashing the walls, a new brick chimney-stack and the invasion of synthetic slates, all of which banish its original character. Gate pillars with a faintly Gothic flavour. In the early nineteenth century Anne Grove had three different owners in Lieutenant-Colonel White (1814), Joseph Canter (1824) and Revd William Minchin (1837).

Leet 1814; Pigot 1824; Lewis 1837.

7. ARDNURCHER RECTORY, Horseleap; pre-1838/*c.* 1880.
A glebe house built in 1815 during the incumbency of Hemsworth Usher (1758–1821), from when the original porter's lodge may have dated. What appears on site today must be a late Victorian replacement, built when the rector was George Samuel Greer (1848–1921) between 1880 and 1885. Standard single-storey gabled with harled walls. Gabled breakfront hall and red-brick chimney-stack. Derelict.

Lewis 1837; Leslie and Wallace 2009.

8. BALLINAMINTON, Tober; pre-1838; *demolished.*
A fine mid-eighteenth-century house of the Marsh family briefly outlasted its gate lodge, which had gone by 1912.

English 1974.

9. BALLINCOR, Shinrone; *c.* 1835.
A modest single-storey standard building with steeply gabled roof and a nasty flat-roofed hall projection. A seat in 1814 of Ruddock Gregg.

Leet 1814.

10. BALLINTEMPLE, Moneygall (2).
Both lodges to a property of the Percys at the turn of the nineteenth century, followed by the Burrowes by 1837, have gone, one having been removed before 1911.

Coote 1801; Lewis 1837.

11. BALLYCUMBER, Ballycumber; *c.* 1850.
A rather goofy single-storey standard gabled building with tall eaves, opposite a good gatescreen with postilion openings and convex quadrants beyond. All for John Warrenford Armstrong.

Slater 1846; Griffith 1848–60.

12. BALLYDERMOTT, Clonbulloge; pre-1913; *demolished.*
A big house that for much of the nineteenth century was home to one John Ridgeway, its lodge built after 1838.

13. BALLYEIGHAN, Birr; *c.* 1880; architect not known.

A villa that the civil engineer-cum-architect Bernard Mullins (1772–1851) built for himself in 1815 with a fashionable neo-Greek cut-stone porch, which is reflected in the gatescreen. The ashlar pillars are in the shape of Greek stelae with recessed-panel tapering faces containing iron railings and postern gates. Strangely, there was no attendant gate lodge until after the property changed hands with the coming of Joseph Studholme about 1880. Even then the gatehouse is far removed, outside the demesne boundary and appearing indifferent to it. This is a 1½-storey, lofty, incongruous, quirky, Hansel-and-Gretel affair, with very steeply pitched roofs sporting fleur-de-lis cresting, mock Gothic lucernes and bold bracketed eaves and verges to main gables and that of the central breakfront, which contains an oriel window above the recessed porch with three-centred archway. Other eccentric features include a dentil course at first-floor level, cut-stone quatrefoil motifs and decorative quoins and window dressings. Just visible, rising off the back wall is a triple chimney-stack with ornamental capping. The effect could be described as unique were it not for a lodge to Castle Bernard (*q.v.*) clearly by the same unidentified innovative hand. The sense of independence is further emphasised by its railed enclosure with chunky Gothic-capped pillars.

LG (1885; 1912); IAA.

14. BALLYLIN, Ferbane (3).
Home to the family since John King acquired it in 1762; it was probably his son of the same name (1760–1820) who built the late eighteenth-century house, the east gate lodge to which was probably contemporary.

Rear entrance; *c.* 1780.
A plain single-storey gabled building with limewashed walls. Derelict.

Revd Henry King (1799–1857) succeeded to the property on his uncle's death and seems soon after to have added another lodge on the western approach, the main gate.

Front entrance [1]; *c.* 1825.

'... the handsome house, and well-improved demesne, of the family of King' is what Brewer found in 1825, along with a newly built porter's lodge which today presents a modest one-bay short front to the avenue, extending to the rear below a hipped roof. The wide rectangular opening is now occupied by an unfortunate twentieth-century metal casement, which may have replaced a more appropriate tripartite Wyatt window. Sometime later in the century it was extended towards the road, to form an L-plan, with a pretty small-paned casement window and fashionable wavy wooden fascia boards applied to embrace the whole; roughcast.

Front entrance [2]; *c.* 1880.

As an only son, John Gilbert King (1822–1901) inherited Ballylin and, for whatever reason, perhaps simply to house another estate worker (the property having extended to nearly 4,000 acres), added a third lodge. This he located at the same main gate but made no attempt to create a matching pair, it being an exercise in duality, facing its predecessor across the avenue. Single-storey, its nucleus hip-roofed, from which gabled wings advance, both with flat-roofed canted bay windows. Between is an entrance verandah, its bracketed eaves carried on two Tuscan columns. Perhaps starting life on an L-plan, the left-hand wing a later extension. Roughcast, one smooth red-brick late Victorian chimney-stack betrays its age. Three contemporary cut-stone tall entrance pillars survive, with unorthodox cappings and octagonal shafts broached off square bases.

Surprisingly, all the lodges survive the big house.

LGI (1904); Sheil 1998.

15. BALLYNACARD, Kilcormac; *c.* 1800.
The ruins of a single-storey harled rubble-built gabled structure to a property in the mid-nineteenth century of the Maxwell family.

16. BALLYRIHY, Dunkerrin; pre-1838; *demolished.*
A seat in the early nineteenth century of the Lewis family which was alternatively known as 'Myrtlegrove'. Its lodge opposite the gates had gone by 1911.

17. BALLYSTANLEY or BALLYSTONELLY, Roscrea; *c.* 1845.

Rosemary ffolliott

A problematic property, its name corrupted down the years, having seen a variety of owners and with its gatekeeper's lodge located marginally over the county boundary in Tipperary. A standard single-storey cottage, its three-bay front not quite symmetrical and chimney-stack off-centre. Below a hipped roof with clipped eaves, the walls in limewashed harling finish containing pretty cast-iron small-paned bipartite casement windows. Probably built by one John Franks, who is recorded here in 1853.

Griffith 1848–60.

18. BARN, Moate; pre-1838; *demolished.*
A seat in 1853 of John Griffith, the lodge to which had gone by 1912.

Griffith 1848–60.

19. BARNAGROTTY, Moneygall; *c.* 1840.

Strangely removed from the entrance opposite is the single-storey standard lodge built in harled rubble, its three-bay elevation not paying heed to the gates but with a large window to the road in a bowed end below a corresponding roof with tiny slates. Very derelict, it looks to date from much earlier in the century, built by Jonathan Tydd Abbott.

20. BARROWBANK, Portarlington; pre-1838; *demolished.*
A seat in 1837 of J.W. Johnstone.

Lewis 1837.

21. BAWN, Clara; pre-1838; *demolished.*
A property in the mid-nineteenth century of Captain John B. Thornhill.

22. BEECH PARK, Birr; *c.* 1845.
A pretty little lodge, single-storey gabled, its main short front to the fore, three-bay below wave and foil bargeboards. Entrance screen of small railed concave quadrants with four square stone corniced pillars. Mid-nineteenth-century premises which were previously of Whiteford Mills and House of Thomas Hackett, whose brother Richard lived at nearby Elm Grove (*q.v.*).

IFR.

23. BELLAIR, Ballycumber; *c.* 1825.

Opposite the gates is a standard single-storey porter's lodge with a shallow-hipped roof and unusually wide windows with basic label mouldings in roughcast walls; derelict. Nothing in this is attributable to Sir Richard Morrison, who designed the house about twenty years earlier, in his familiar villa style, for Thomas Homan Mulock (1770–1843), who inherited on his father's death in 1803. The entrance screen is fine, with harled concave quadrants framing postilion gates flanking tall carriage pillars with fluted friezes and cappings crowned by lanterns.

LGI (1904); McParland *et al.* 1989.

24. BELLEFIELD or BELFIELD, Shinrone; *c.* 1825.
A tiny standard single-storey hip-roofed lodge, presenting its symmetrical three-bay façade to the road in limewashed harled walls. To the avenue front is a cast-iron latticed window. Probably built by Joseph Walker, whose gatekeeper in 1854 was Jane Lamb.

Lewis 1837; Griffith 1848–60.

25. BELLMOUNT or BELMONT, Clonony; pre-1838/*c.* 1860.
Replacing an earlier lodge at an entrance further south is this exceptionally

commodious gatehouse (*above*) of 1½ storeys below a steeply hipped roof, the eaves of which are broken by gablets with skew-tables and bold kneelers, one to the road front and two to the avenue, carefully arranged over a five-bay ground floor to present a perfectly symmetrical façade with small-paned casements in roughcast walls. A lodge that may have lost many original Tudor features in modernisation, for it stands behind a gatescreen of wide railed quadrants framing a surviving pair of striking castellated octagonal stone turrets as gate pillars, now lacking their gates. The house and attendant mills were owned from the late 1700s to the mid-1800s successively by Gilbert Holmes, Charles Atkinson, Robert Baker and John Collins.

Taylor and Skinner 1778; 1969 [1783]; Leet 1814; Lewis 1837; Griffith 1848–60; *LGI* (1904).

26. BIRDVILLE, Ballycumber; pre-1838; *demolished.*

A property in 1814 of Robert Adamson and in 1854 of Edward Holmes, who leased the lodge then to Margaret Connolly.

Leet 1814; Griffith 1848–60.

27. BIRR CASTLE, Birr (3).

The town of Birr—or Parsonstown, as it has been alternately and alternatively known—owed its name and elegance to the settling here in 1620 of the Parsons family, who over succeeding centuries replaced the old stronghold of the O'Carrolls. Having survived a number of sieges, by the end of the 1798 Rebellion the castle gradually took on a less defensive cloak. Sir Laurence Parsons (1758–1841), who succeeded his grandfather in 1807 as 2nd earl of Rosse and who forsook politics after being thwarted in his opposition to the Act of Union, turned his attention to giving castle and demesne a more decorative frock, much admired by visitors and tourists, not least by Fraser in 1838: 'It has been completely modernised by the present proprietor, and the high embattled walls, towers and gateways, which surround the offices and grounds, are all in keeping; and while they maintain the character of the mansion, add much to the general appearance of the town'.

Town gate; *c.* 1845.

That the 2nd earl was a considerable influence on the design of the main gate can be seen in a series of sketch proposals by him, from about 1801, one of which is very close to the finished article. The amateur architect had a professional, John Johnston, who translated his client's thoughts into coherent working drawings, the result of which can be seen today at the end of Oxmanstown Mall, precisely as described by Lacy in 1855: 'The demesne is entered from Oxmanstown Mall by a spacious and massive gateway, which is flanked on each side by a strong, circular, embattled turret. Beyond each of these turrets is a nice wicket, the intermediate walls, which extend on each side of the grand entrance, and on each extremity of which rises a square tower, being, like the connecting walls, decorated with embrasures and embattled ornaments, the whole presenting an imposing defensive appearance. On writing his name in the visitor's book the stranger is permitted to enter.' What that visitor failed to notice behind the left-hand ashlar screen wall was the later porter's accommodation, which then would have been in the form of a single-storey double pile built in random cut-stone facings, each gable having a bipartite label-moulded window with cast-iron small-paned lights with horizontal pivot openers. Over these are blind lancets and perforated ornamental curved bargeboards. To the postern gate the roof extends to form a canopied verandah with a carved wooden arcade to monitor visitors. Subsequently the structure was doubled in size to form a quadruple pile. There is a similar arrangement, peculiar to King's County, at both Castle Bernard (*q.v.*) and Gloster (*q.v.*).

2nd earl of Rosse

27. Birr Castle, town gate.

Tipperary gate; *c.* 1825.
Across the River Camcor in County Tipperary and the Province of Munster, well out of the way is this badly abused little lodge which, despite unspeakable things having been visited upon it, is in use and lovingly maintained. Surviving are label mouldings to modern six-over-six sash windows in roughcast walls.

Inner gate; 1848; architect probably Mary, Countess of Rosse.

David H. Davison (Countess of Rosse c. 1856)

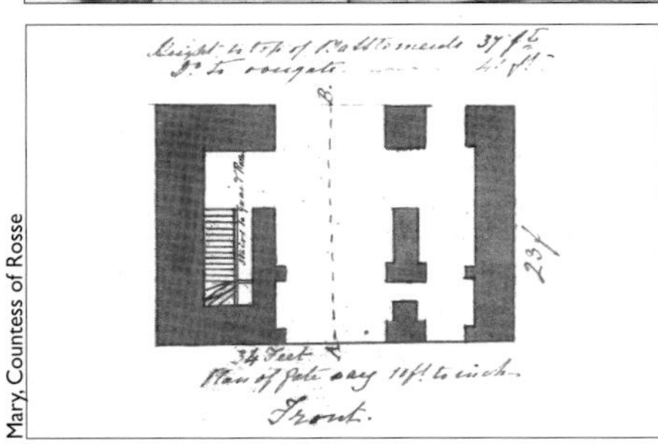

Mary, Countess of Rosse

Mary, Countess of Rosse

Mary, Countess of Rosse

On a boundary within the demesne separating the park from the castle precincts is an impressive barbican or gatehouse, again described by the reliable Lacy in 1855: 'On approaching the castle, the visitor enters the extensive and surrounding area by a splendid and lofty arched way, formed in the lower part of the strong, castellated gate tower. The ceiling of this entrance, being enriched with nice groinings, has a very fine appearance. While here, he becomes informed that the massive iron gates and side wickets, which are of strong, yet fanciful character, and emblazoned with the escutcheon and arms of the noble proprietor, are all the products of his furnaces and workshops; and that all the articles of iron manufacture used upon his extensive concerns, including his farms, are wrought and fashioned in his own forges, and under his immediate inspection.' That noble proprietor was the 'Astronomer Earl', William Parsons (1800–67), who had succeeded as 3rd earl of Rosse in 1841. He had, significantly, five years earlier married Mary Field of Heaton Hall, Yorkshire—significantly because it has become clear that she was not only a pioneer photographer but also an aspiring amateur architect who produced proposals for the inner gate, and also brought useful funds to Birr to finance such a scheme at a time when the Famine was at its height. The Rosse Papers contain preliminary drawings by her of elevations showing rather predictable round flanking towers, which were not realised, but a ground-floor plan much as built, indicating a staircase access to the first-

Mary, Countess of Rosse

floor 'guard room'. The side elevation playfully suggests a drawbridge approach over the 'defensive' ditch. In fact, the main elevations are much simplified, perhaps showing the influence of a restraining hand. The front façade is subtly articulated by a central stepped machicolation, containing carved family bearings above a slit window and flanking blind niches over the grand carriage archway. The rear elevation is dominated by a corbelled Tudor-style transomed, mullioned and crenellated oriel window, all set in very fine limestone ashlar walls. Just as her father-in-law had John Johnston as a mentor, so might Mary's have been the English architect Anthony Salvin (1799–1881), who is recorded as working on the castle. Alternatively, it could have been her uncle, Captain Wharton-Middleton. The gates remain truly as splendid as the day Lacy described them.

Brewer 1825; Fraser 1838; Lacy 1863; *BPB* (1929); *Country Life* (25 Feb., 4 March and 11 March 1965); Rosse Papers; Colvin 2008.

28. BIRR RECTORY, Birr; *c.* 1845.
The old rectory of Birr parish was replaced by the present plain Regency villa in 1826 to

designs by James Pain. Its pretty gate lodge was added about twenty years later during the long incumbency (1833–75) of Revd Marcus McCausland (1802–81). Single-storey standard, built in harled rubble, with bipartite latticed casement windows on each side of a gabled projecting hall with carved wavy bargeboards. The main gables contain relieving Gothic slits, while there are scalloped slate bands to the roof.

Lewis 1837; *LGI* (1904); Leslie and Crooks 2010.

29. BIRR VIEW, Birr; *c.* 1840.
A standard single-storey gatekeeper's lodge with paired carved modillion brackets to oversailing eaves. Modern window inserts and a nasty curved roof to the hall projection. Built for Bartholomew Warburton.

Fraser 1838.

30. BROGHILL or BROUGHALL CASTLE, Kilcormac; pre-1838; *demolished.*
A property in the late eighteenth century of Dr Daly which passed about 1810 to N. Fitzsimmon, who was here for 40 years.

31. BROOKFIELD, Tullamore; pre-1838; *demolished.*
Today there is no evidence of an estate entrance, never mind a gate lodge. At the turn of the nineteenth century, then called 'Merryfield', of the Crofton family, thereafter of Revd Ralph Coote (d. 1868).

Wilson 1803; Leslie and Wallace 2009.

32. BUSHERSTOWN, Moneygall (2).
Originally called 'Bouchardstown', this was long the residence of the Minchin family, both porters' lodges to which were opposite their gates.

Dunkerrin entrance; pre-1838; *demolished.*
Removed before 1911.

Moneygall entrance; *c.* 1825.

Single-storey standard under a steeply hipped roof covered in canted slates and tall eaves with paired modillion brackets. The rendered front has two-over-two sash windows with Tudor label mouldings on each side of an impressive centre-piece, the parapet of which breaks the eaves and contains a panelled door with a delicate lead Classical round-headed fanlight. A really quite grand lodge of generous proportions, given greater impact by framing straight railed screens terminating in stone pillars with recessed panels and moulded cornices. Built by George Minchin.

Brewer 1825; ffolliott 1971b Bence-Jones 1988.

33. CANGORT, Shinrone (2).

The ancestral home of the Atkinson family since 1600, the present surviving lodge to which replaced a predecessor to the older house of 1801. Guy Atkinson II (1800–59) built a new Tudor Revival cut-stone addition after the death of his father, Jackson Wray Atkinson, in 1846 and complemented it with this striking cottage. Single-storey three-bay with the doorway to the right-hand side of mullioned Gothic windows with chunky stone-dressed hood-moulded lancet lights with Y-tracery over little casement lights; rendered, with fancy carved perforated continuous bracket bargeboards to steeply pitched gables. Located remote from the entrance, which has circular stone pillars with square cappings, much as at Grenane, Mooresfort and Lismacue, Co. Tipperary, and Kilfrush, Co. Limerick, where there is work attributable to architect C.F. Anderson.

Coote 1801; *LGI* (1904); Bence-Jones 1988.

34. CANGORT PARK, Shinrone; *c.* 1840
A 1½-storey three-bay Picturesque cottage with sheeted door to the right-hand side of squared casement windows. Occupied, *Pyracantha*-clad and pretty. Unlike the villa, not attributable to Sir Richard Morrison, it dating from 1807 for William Trench (1769–1849), who would also have commissioned the lodge.

BPB (1929).

CARMEL (see GREEN HILLS, Kilcormac)

35. CASTLE ARMSTRONG, Ballycumber; pre-1838; *demolished.*
A residence in 1814 of A. Bagot Armstrong.

Leet 1814.

36. CASTLE BERNARD, Kinnitty (2).
It seems that Thomas Bernard MP (1769–1834) just a year before his death had resolved to transform the old family seat of 'Castletown' into the fine Tudor Revival mansion manifest today as the Kinnitty Castle Hotel, to designs of the brothers Pain. As early as 1811, however, plans were already afoot to improve the estate, for Samuel Beazley had exhibited plans in the RA for a school and park entrance for the same client—a scheme that was apparently realised.

South gate; *c.* 1811/*c.* 1885; architect S. Beazley/architect not known.
Just to be seen peeking through a late Victorian make-over is evidence of a pretty Georgian Gothic entrance in the shape of a

double-leafed doorway below an ogee archway set in a two-centred arched recess supported on dainty cluster-columns, all in a breakfront to a symmetrical three-bay front to what is a ground-floor plan sufficiently generous to suggest a function other than accommodation for a gatekeeper alone. To each end elevation is a wide label-moulded latticed tripartite classroom casement window. Remarkably, this is apparently the first recorded architectural commission of the fascinating Westminster-based Samuel Beazley, Peninsular War volunteer, novelist, playwright and architect. His creation was to be seriously revamped with the succession to the property in 1882 of Thomas Scroope Wellesley Bernard (b. 1850), two years after he had married a Danby of nearby Leap Castle (*q.v.*). All in a stucco-effect rendered finish with quoin stones, the structure was raised by half a storey off a double corbelled band to form a conspicuous triple-gabled attic floor with steeply pitched carved pendant bargeboards over tri- and bipartite label-moulded sash windows. Relieving the spandrel area of the original front door is a pair of quatrefoil features. To the main ridge are two bulky chimney-stacks completing a fairy-tale composition probably by the unidentified author of the lodge to Ballyeighan (*q.v.*) and now revitalised in its new role as 'Gate Lodge Spa'.

North gate; pre-1838/*c.* 1866; architect probably James Pain.
Replacing an earlier pair of lodges flanking the old approach is this appropriate introduction to the new house within, in like

Tudor Gothic style (*above*). A grand carriage archway and curtain walls are crowned by crenellated parapets supported by paired corbel brackets. The right-hand screen wall contains a label-moulded postern gate, balanced to the left-hand side by a similarly hooded tripartite window to the porter's lodge behind, which accommodation appears as a single-storey double-gabled pile, much as at Birr Castle (*q.v.*) and Gloster (*q.v.*) in the county. One ridge of the shallow-pitched roofs is broken by a choice pair of octagonal brick and stone chimney-stacks. Stucco walls are enhanced by pretty label-moulded, chamfered stone-dressed windows with charming foiled and cusped lights. The Tudor-arched doorway is hood-moulded with reeded pilasters, while the gables are relieved by sculpted shields.

LGI (1904); ffolliott 1970; Williams 1994; Colvin 2008.

37. CASTLE GARDEN, Banagher (2).
Both pre-1838 lodges to a seat unoccupied in 1814 and owned by Edward Kennedy in 1853 have gone.

Leet 1814; Griffith 1848–60.

38. CASTLE IVOR, Banagher (2).
All that survives at the two estate entrances is a good early Victorian gatescreen with fluted friezes to moulded cornice-capped pillars. The lodges in place by 1838 were built by the Armstrong family.

CASTLE VIEW (see GARRYCASTLE)

39. CEDAR HILL, Roscrea; 1871; *demolished.*
Previously a lodgeless property known as 'Brosna', with its great flour mills, later converted to maltings; in about 1870 Robert Dowd sold them, renamed his home and added the gate lodge.

40. CHARLESTOWN, Charlestown; pre-1838; *demolished.*
The flour mills, kiln and miller's house in 1837 of Marcus Goodbody, the gate lodge to which on the main street had gone by 1912.

Lewis 1837.

41. CHARLEVILLE FOREST, Tullamore (4).
Francis Johnston's great Romantic Castellated masterpiece lies close to the town of Tullamore in an ancient oak forest. Built by 1812 for Charles William Bury, 1st earl of Charleville (1764–1835), its three pre-1838 gatekeepers' lodges were traditionally by Johnston and dated from 1818. For whatever reason, these were all removed and replaced by the 3rd earl, Charles William George Bury, although he would hardly have enjoyed their completion, having died in 1859. These original lodges must all have been minimal, for the 1st earl had been almost bankrupted after lavishing so much money on his castle and outbuildings. That he did have equally grand but unfulfilled plans for his estate entrances is evidenced by some unsigned and undated surviving drawings by his architect. One of these is a plan indicating a buttressed castellated two-storey gatehouse integrated to carriage and postern arches, with elaborate groin vaulting intended over. Sadly, an elevation drawing has not emerged. The other shows a Classical variant on a similar plan in the form of a triumphal archway, two-storey and of three bays, defined by four engaged Tuscan columns with a tall carriage opening containing a pair of panelled doors and complementary round-headed over-panel. This design is not very far removed from Francis Johnston's Ely Gate to Rathfarnham Castle, south Dublin (*q.v.*). These proposals having been discarded, a further design was commissioned in 1829

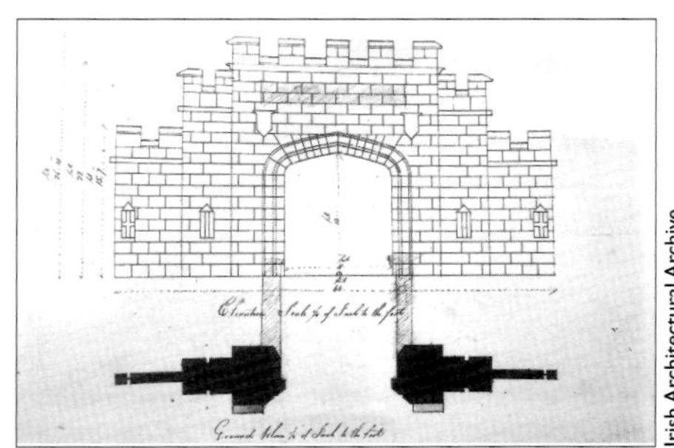

Irish Architectural Archive

41. Charleville Forest, unexecuted design—R. Meath.

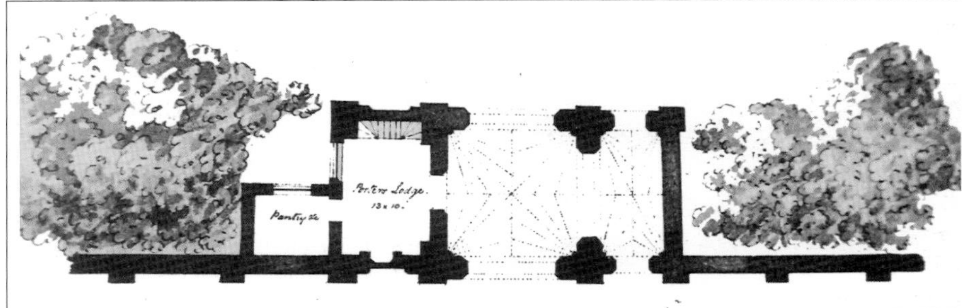

41. Charleville Forest, unexecuted design—F. Johnston (Irish Architectural Archive).

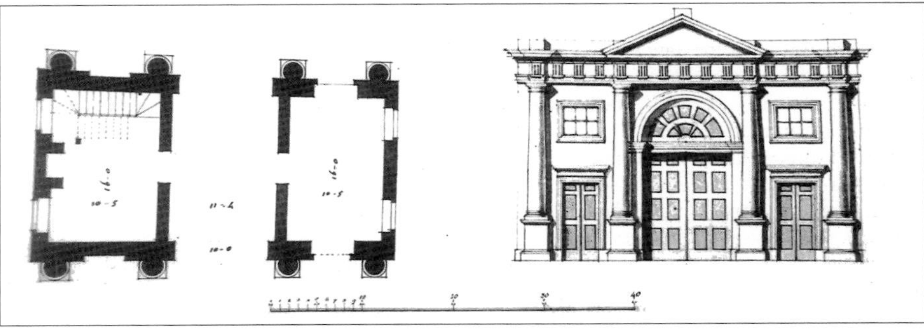

41. Charleville Forest, unexecuted design—F. Johnston (Irish Architectural Archive).

from Richard Meath for a Tudor Castellated gateway, likewise rejected.

Tullamore gate; pre-1838/1860; architect not known.

Beryl Dean

An attractive single-storey Tudor Picturesque cottage built in quarry-faced coursed limestone off an L-plan, its openings dressed in smooth chamfered masonry with tripartite cast-iron latticed casement windows. To the leading gable is a shield displaying the Charleville monogram, coronet and the date of construction, over which are elaborately carved wavy bargeboards with cusped perforations rising to a spiky hip-knob.

Main gate; pre-1838/*c.* 1845; architect not known.

'The demesne is entered by a large and handsome gateway, with a nice gate-lodge within its slightly curved sweep, and the mansion approached by a broad and well-laid-out avenue.' The nice lodge apparent today may well be that observed by Lacy in 1855. It is 1½-storey with minimal attic space, built in tooled limestone on a T-plan, its gables clipped. Openings with minimalist Tudor label mouldings over what were originally quadripartite and tripartite chamfered casements, now horribly

41. Charleville Forest, Mucklagh gate.

modernised to admit more light. To the central leading gable is a tiny bipartite loft window, and from the ridge emanates a pair of diagonally set stone stacks. The extensive railed screen contains two individual Gothic pillars with elaborately carved traceried cusped recessed panels, both surmounted by crocketed pyramidal cappings. Alongside are pedestrian openings for 'little' people, the gates with quatrefoil motifs. The screen is possibly a survival of Johnston's work.

Mucklagh gate; *c.* 1800/1860.

The lodge lies a shell of a single-storey, gabled, stone-faced, Tudor Revival structure on an L-plan; inscribed on a lintel is 'A.D. 1860'. The main feature of this country entrance at a road junction on the Kilcormac road is the original impressive but simple castellated composition of a Tudor-arched carriage gateway below a crenellated, machicolated parapet running between a pair of castellated round towers. Built in pleasant rubble with convincing 'medieval' arrowloops and a pedestrian doorway in the left-hand tower, it has recently been admirably restored. This may well also be a survivor of Johnston's work.

As early as 1785 architect John Pentland had been engaged to offer designs for gatescreens (*below*), two drawings for which display a wide Classical vocabulary of V-jointed rustication, draped urns, ball finials, fluting, key patterns, paterae and swags. These apparently came to nothing.

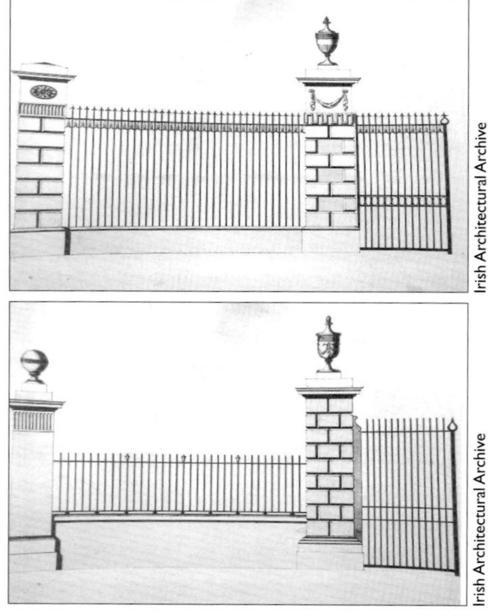

Irish Architectural Archive

Irish Architectural Archive

Lacy 1863; *Country Life* (27 Sept. 1962); IAA photographs (13/53R 5, 6, 10, 14, 21 & 23).

42. CHESTERFIELD SCHOOL, Birr; pre-1912; *demolished.*

Once another property of the earls of Rosse, it lay vacant in 1853 before being run as a school from around 1870 by Richard Biggs.

Griffith 1848–60.

43. CLARA, Clara (3).
A seat of the Cox family, proprietors of the adjoining town, two pre-1838 lodges to which have gone. A third built within the park, probably in the time of a later owner, Richard Goodbody, has also been taken down.

Bence-Jones 1988; *IADS* (2000).

44. CLAREEN, Shinrone; *c.* 1825.

An example of an inspired restoration of a quintessential little standard single-storey hip-roofed harled lodge with latticed windows on each side of a splendid replica panelled door. Discourteously presenting its rear to the road, there is a wide casement to the avenue, with the main front to be admired by its creator, in this case doubtless Henry Birch Smith (1776–1849), who probably built it after his father's death in 1820.

IFR.

45. CLAREMOUNT, Banagher; *c.* 1835.

John Priaulx Armstrong (1802–79) acquired the late Georgian villa in the 1830s and added what was a highly individual little porter's lodge, not enhanced by a later lean-to addition across its short main front to the road, which obscures a conspicuous façade. This three-bay elevation is comprised of the doorway flanked by a pair of intricate Tudor Gothic windows containing leaded latticed and Y-traceried lights. Above in the shallow-pitched gable is a little pointed loft window. The avenue elevation, with decorative corbelled eaves, has been altered accordingly to contain the repositioned front door, with a basic canopied porch and Gothic slit windows in limewashed rubble walls. To the park the roof hips toward the stump of a chimney-stack. Maintained in a derelict state but crying out for return to its original form. Good contemporary gatescreen of four ashlar pillars and spear-topped carriage gates with short matching railings. There are identical Tudor Gothic windows to lodges in the vicinity of Cork City, suggesting the work of Sir Thomas Deane.

LGI (1904).

46. CLARKVILLE, Edenderry; *c.* 1845.
A three-bay single-storey harled and limewashed cottage, gabled and simply skew-tabled; derelict. A residence in 1853 of Henry Clarke.

Griffith 1848–60.

47. CLOGHAN, Clareen; pre-1838; *demolished.*
A property in 1824 of William Minnitt (1777–1841), who by marrying a daughter of John Palmer of Glenacurragh Castle (*q.v.*) made that his main house.

Pigot 1824; *LGI* (1904).

48. CLONBEALE, Birr; pre-1838; *demolished.*
All that remains of the gatekeeper's lodge to the seat of the Molloy family is its rectangular base in forest opposite its gates. These are in the form of small stone octagonal pillars with fluted shafts and panelled plinths; railed convex quadrants beyond.

49. CLONBRIN, Rathangan; pre-1838; *demolished.*
An estate in the mid-nineteenth century of William Gresson, whose predecessor here in 1814 was John Corry.

Leet 1814; Griffith 1848–60.

50. CLONEARL, Daingean (3).
Brewer in 1825 found that Clonearl, 'however repulsive in natural circumstances, has been gradually formed into one of the finest demesnes to be seen in this county. Great improvements of the mansion are now in progress.' William Henry Magan (1790–1840) was then completing his fine neo-Classical house to designs by architect William Farrell, whose commission may also have included the provision of three gate lodges. From this period of building only one lodge and some gatescreens survive, the house having been burnt down as early as 1846.

Killeshil gate; pre-1838; *demolished.*
The first OS map indicates a lodge of some consequence in annotating a 'gatehouse', presumably two-storey, and shows a plan with projecting hall and bowed ends. Nothing remains of it, but there are two huge ashlar carriage pillars and tall concave quadrant walls.

Inner gate; pre-1838; *demolished.*
Here on the southern approach from Philipstown, as it was called, are the remnants of an imposing straight stone entrance screen.

West gate; *c.* 1825; architect possibly William Farrell.
A generous-sized single-storey three-roomed harled lodge below a hipped roof. Perfectly symmetrical, its central room advancing as a canted projection; derelict. Yet another set of noble entrance pillars.

Brewer 1825; *IFR*; Bence-Jones 1988.

51. CLONOGHILL CEMETERY, Birr; *c.* 1870; architect possibly W.F. Kempster.

A fine commodious single-storey caretaker's lodge built off an L-plan, gabled with a little hallway projecting from the internal angle, its doorway and window having pointed heads, the latter with Y-tracery. Otherwise wide small-paned casement lights with label mouldings in Tudor style, as are the tall chamfered chimney-stacks. Plain bargeboards over mock pointed-arched arrowslits. The original roughcast finish has been removed in renovation to reveal good-quality rubble construction with brick dressings. There is a good entrance screen of four ashlar pillars with postilion gates. The identical lodges and gates at Coolfin House (*q.v.*) and a handed version at Dungar Cemetery (*q.v.*) are clearly a design by the same unidentified architect, this having pre-dated them by twenty years, the graveyard being first valued in 1869.

52. CLUNAGH or CLOONAGH, Tullamore; *c.* 1840.

A simple single-storey limewashed, harled porter's lodge below an oversailing hipped roof. Two-window-bay short elevation to the avenue, the road front relieved only by the doorway. Wide contemporary straight gatescreen of four squat tooled square pillars and spear-topped railings. The lodge, probably built by George Pierce MD, to a property previously of the Curtis family lies abandoned.

Griffith 1848–60.

53. CLYDUFF, Roscrea; *c.* 1850.
Opposite the entrance is a solid single-storey cottage with hipped roof and bold stone dressings to openings in roughcast walls. Three-bay front elevation with doorway to right-hand side and a tripartite window to an end gable, all with keystones. A seat in 1853 of Thomas Spunner, whose gatekeeper was Jane Burgess. Delightful Disneyland gate pillars in the form of tapering drums with crenellated cone cappings.

Griffith 1848–60.

54. COOLDERRY, Shinrone; *c.* 1810.
A late eighteenth-century house, recently restored, in the nineteenth century of the Robinson family, whose two-storey gatehouse is a good late Georgian structure of single bay to the road and two bays to the park of roughcast walls with limestone quoins below a shallow-pitched hipped roof with oversailing eaves. Four simple punched limestone ashlar pillars with railed screens.

55. COOLFIN, Banagher (2).

South gate; *c.* 1890; architect possibly W.F. Kempster.
'Cummeen Lodge' is a pretty single-storey gabled lodge built in limestone rubble with punched ashlar quoins and cream brick dressings off an irregular L-plan with a hall protruding from the internal corner, it having lancet heads opposed to flat-arched windows elsewhere. Having the appearance of a mid-nineteenth-century structure were it not for its being identical to those at Dungar (*q.v.*) and Clonoghill graveyards (*q.v.*), the former of which dates from *c.* 1894. It was erected for Arthur Hugo Florian de Burdet Burdett (1863–1917), who succeeded to the place on the death of his father in 1884, it first being recorded in the valuation book in 1891. Occupied and lovingly maintained.

North gate; *demolished.*
The third OS map indicates that this was a twin of its counterpart to the southern avenue.

IFR.

56. COOLYGAGAN, Rathangan; *c.* 1800.
A tiny ruinous standard single-storey hip-roofed cottage with breakfront hall, tucked in alongside the left-hand gatescreen quadrant, fronting the road. Presumably built for Isaac Gatchell, its gate porter in 1853 was John Broy.

Leet 1814; Griffith 1848–60.

57. COROLANTY or CURRALANTY, Shinrone; *c.* 1840.
Totally overgrown in brambles is this derelict single-storey standard cottage with limewashed harled walls below a hipped roof. Built for Richard Hammersly, who seems to have acquired the place from Henry Spunner.

Leet 1814; Lewis 1837.

58. CRINKILL COTTAGE, Birr; pre-1838; *demolished.*
A small estate in the early to mid-nineteenth century of the Warburton family.

59. CUBA COURT, Banagher; pre-1838; *demolished.*
A house that was once one of the most important early eighteenth-century residences in the country is now preserved only in photographs, whilst the age and appearance of its porter's lodge may remain a mystery. It was built probably either by the Rt Hon. Denis Bowe Daly of the County Galway Dalystown family or to serve at the entrance to a military hospital, as the house had become in 1814, prior to being converted to school use. Today the site of the lodge, beyond the old rustic stone entrance, is occupied by a bungalow with aggressively coloured brickwork.

Leet 1814; *LGI* (1904); Craig 1976.

60. CUSHINA, Cushina; pre-1838; *demolished.*
A property in the nineteenth century of the Tabuteau family, the lodge to which had gone by 1913.

61. DAVISTOWN, Kilcormac; pre-1838; *demolished.*
The lodge had been removed before 1912, serving as it had as a seat of the Davis family.

62. DERRINBOY, Kilcormac; pre-1838; *demolished.*
The residence at the turn of the nineteenth century of the Clarkes, from whom it was leased by the Gamble family of Killooly Hall (*q.v.*) in 1837 until into the twentieth century.

Taylor and Skinner 1778; 1969 [1783]; Wilson 1803; Lewis 1837.

63. DERRY, Shinrone; *c.* 1825.
A lodge that originated as a standard single-storey three-bay cottage, gabled with harled walls. Sometime later in the century extended by a bay to the left-hand side to include a Wyatt window and embellished with ornamental fretted bargeboards, now derelict and sporting a corrugated-iron roof. An estate for much of the nineteenth century of the Doolan family.

64. THE DOON, Ballynahown; pre-1838; *demolished.*
Francis Enraght-Moony (1744–1802) assumed his mother's name of Moony in 1789 and nine years later a new mansion was built. The porter's lodge was built not quite opposite the gates but by 1912 was a shell, as suggested by the OS map of that year, it being unhatched.

LGI (1904); Bence-Jones 1988.

65. DOVE HILL, Kilcormac; pre-1838; *demolished.*
A residence, previously of the Molloys, which passed through marriage to Charles Holmes in the early nineteenth century.

LGI (1904).

66. DRUMBANE or DRUMBAWN, Birr; pre-1912; *demolished.*
A property, originally named 'Prospect', which between 1837 and 1870 was occupied by John Julian, its lodge erected after 1838.

Lewis 1837; *Land owners in Ireland 1876.*

67. DUNGAR CEMETERY, Roscrea; *c.* 1894; architect possibly W.F. Kempster.

A caretaker's lodge in the form of a single-storey gabled Tudor Picturesque cottage built off an L-plan with label-moulded windows; tucked into the internal angle is a little Gothic hallway with pointed heads to front door and Y-traceried window; dominant chimney-stacks and spiky hip-knobs to gables. Good ashlar gate pillars with plain friezes and straight railed screens to match carriage gates. All the same as the lodges and entrance gates at Coolfin House (*q.v.*) and Clonoghill Cemetery (*q.v.*), other than being a handed version. Resplendent in primrose-painted roughcast. A commemorative plaque records the opening of the graveyard by the Rt Revd P.J. McRedmond, bishop of Killaloe, in 1894.

68. DUNGAR, Roscrea; pre-1838/*c.* 1890; architect possibly J.F. Kempster.

Joseph Fade Hutchinson, the sixth of nine brothers, succeeded his brother James here in 1839 and a quarter of a century later commissioned the Ballinasloe architect James Forth Kempster to design him a new villa, in the Italianate style, in which Kempster was obviously proficient, rather than in his obligatory Picturesque mode. The striking gate lodge, a replacement for a predecessor perhaps built by a previous proprietor, Captain Chetwyn, is in a later railway type of Italianate, with its dressings and chimney-stack in a conspicuous cream calcium-silicate brick. It is 1½-storey on an

L-plan with an arcade entrance porch filling the internal angle, constructed in a grey uncoursed random limestone with bold cut-stone bracketed eaves to the shallow-pitched gabled roof. The two-over-two sash windows have a variety of segmentally arched heads. To the road elevation at attic-floor level is a curious pair of horizontal slit windows overlooking the gates, probably there more for aesthetic relief. The entrance screen is contemporary, comprised of big cast-iron carriage pillars linked to outer stone equivalents by postilion gates. The elderly Kempster may have returned here to design the lodge for Turner Oliver Read, it first appearing in the valuation book in 1891.

LGI (1904); *Thom's*.

69. DUNGAR PARK, Roscrea (2).
Both lodges dating from before 1835 have been demolished, that to the northern approach being deleted from the valuation books as early as 1870. A seat until *c.* 1865 of George Evans.

70. DUNKERRIN DEANERY, Dunkerrin; *c.* 1790.

Affectionately known locally as 'the Inkpot' is this delightful perfectly circular single-storey porter's lodge with a conical roof rising to a drum chimney-stack. Two-roomed, the eaves, with exposed rafter toes, are sufficiently tall to accommodate attic bed space. Constructed in harled rubble, a basic sheeted door in a Gothic pointed-arched opening faces the avenue, flanked by a pair of semicircular-arched minuscule windows. Sadly derelict, demanding restoration as a maintained garden folly. Accompanying rustic railed entrance screen. Probably built during the incumbency of Revd Charles Knox, rector here until 1807.

Leslie and Crooks 2010.

71. DURROW ABBEY, Tullamore (3).
Hector John Graham Toler (1781–1839) unexpectedly succeeded his older brother in 1832 to become 2nd Lord Norbury just six months after their father's death. He promptly set about extensive building improvements on the estate to the designs of William Murray, who fashioned a new mansion and porters' accommodation at two entrances, all in the Tudor Revival manner.

Kilbeggan gate; *c.* 1837; architect William Murray.
Low-lying beyond a beautiful and curvilinear ironwork entrance screen (*above*) with

OPW

postilion gates flanking the carriage opening is this fine Tudor-style single-storey gabled lodge (*top*). Built in good-quality punched ashlar off a cruciform plan, with all the characteristics of that style in label mouldings, mullioned bi- and tripartite small-paned windows, and skew-tables with hip-knobs. The leading gable to the avenue

OPW

contains a label-moulded family shield in the apex, and a pair of diagonally set chimney-stacks project where the ridges meet. Being rehabilitated.

Tullamore gate; pre-1838/*c.* 1855.
Probably the original main access to the estate, alongside the road is a replacement lodge. Single-storey and hip-roofed, with a three-bay window front of three-over-three sashes in boulder-faced walls with orange brick dressings and soldier arches and a cut-stone eaves band; projecting hall to the rear. Vacant.

Schoolhouse lodge; *c.* 1837; architect William Murray.

An excellent and decorative dual-function 1½-storey Tudor Revival composition in uncoursed random cut limestone. Built off an L-plan with label-moulded chamfered mullioned windows having pretty small-paned cusp-topped casement lights. The structure is enhanced by a breakfront window to the park gable, a single-storey canted bay window projecting from the avenue gable with an unusual sawtooth parapet, and in the internal angle a little crenellated hall with a hood-moulded Tudor-arched doorway. The steeply pitched roofs are contained by skew-tables and deep kneelers, one of which was embellished by a carved bust of Queen Victoria, probably commemorating her accession to the throne. Sadly, this was vandalised during 'the troubles' and subsequently removed. From the rear rises a pair of octagonal chimney-stacks in the guise of Tudor finials. Proudly maintained by the present owner.

The unfortunate 2nd earl did not enjoy

71. Durrow Abbey, schoolhouse lodge.

his new creations for long, being murdered in his demesne; the house lay vacant for many years thereafter, the valuation books recording that 'since the death of the late Lord Norbury these premises are unoccupied with the exception of a housekeeper and four police constables who reside in the basement storey'. The property was to suffer further tribulations with the burning of the mansion in the 1920s but has subsequently been restored.

Lewis 1837; *BPB* (1929); Bence-Jones 1988; Nolan and O'Neill 1998.

72. EGLISH CASTLE, Birr; pre-1838; *demolished.*
A property which between 1814 and 1837 passed from the Berry family to a Captain English, whose big house now lies a ruin.

Leet 1814; Lewis 1837.

73. ELM GROVE HOUSE AND DISTILLERY, Birr; pre-1838; *demolished.*
One of two new distilleries that had been set up in Birr by 1818, the proprietor of which was Michael Hackett. On his death in 1856 his son Richard was in residence, but the business appears to have failed. The first OS map suggests a lodge of some substance.

Slater 1856; *LGI* (1904); Townsend 1999.

74. EMMEL CASTLE, Cloghjordan; *c.* 1825.
A model case of a palimpsest is the combination of the seventeenth-century tower-house of the O'Carrolls and the Georgian residence built on by Captain Robert Johnstone, who had purchased the place in 1782. He was also responsible for the wide gatescreen with concave quadrants between circular pillars with his winged-spur family crest adorning the friezes and a beautiful flower sculpted to bloom from the moulded cornice. Sadly, only two of these pillars survive intact. The attendant lodge seems to date from slightly later, presumably from the time of Johnstone's nephew, Thomas Stoney (1748–1826), who had inherited on his uncle's death in 1803, for there are paired carved brackets in Regency

fashion to the tall eaves of its steeply hipped roof, which extends to reflect the canted avenue front below. Single-storey and roughcast with rendered angle pilasters, it has been disfigured by modern windows and a hideous flat-roofed hall projection.

Bence-Jones 1988; *IFR.*

75. FOXBURROW, Moneygall; *c.* 1830.
A single-storey gabled structure horribly adapted to agricultural use. A property in 1814 of Francis Talbot that passed to his son-in-law, Revd James George Purcell (b. 1795/6), who in 1836 left for England.

Leet 1814; Lewis 1837; Leslie and Crooks 2010.

76. FRANKFORT CASTLE, Dunkerrin; pre-1838; *demolished.*
An early nineteenth-century Romantic development that incorporates an earlier medieval castle, the gate lodge to which, of the Rolleston family, along with the big house has gone.

Bence-Jones 1988.

77. GAGEBOROUGH, Horseleap; pre-1912; *demolished.*
A property in 1853 of John C. Judge.

Griffith 1848–60.

78. GALLEN PRIORY, Ferbane (2).
A Georgian Gothic mansion of the Armstrong family, who were raised to the baronetcy in 1841, now serves as a much-extended nursing home. Both the original approaches are now lodgeless, but the 1838 OS map shows there to have been one to the south by the Grand Canal and a pair set back from the road at the main entrance, near the town.

79. GARRYCASTLE, Banagher; pre-1912; *demolished.*
A seat of the Armstrong family, whose lodge was erected after 1838.

80. GARRYHINCH, Mountmellick (3).
A property since the seventeenth century of the Warburton family whose residence was burnt in 1914 and since demolished, to be survived by just one of its gate lodges.

West entrance; pre-1913; *demolished.*
Presumably one of two new lodges built for Richard Warburton III (1846–1921), who succeeded upon his father's death in 1862.

Middle lodge; pre-1838; *demolished.*
Atkinson, who visited during his tour of 1813, recorded that 'The light aspect of the entrance corresponds with the lodge and improvements'; he could have been describing either of the two earlier lodges.

East entrance; pre-1838/*c.* 1870; architect not known.

A fine mid-Victorian gatekeeper's lodge now almost overcome by extensions to cope with its elevation to the status of golf clubhouse. Still discernible is a 1½-storey structure built in good-quality random punched limestone facings with featured relieving arches over cut-stone chamfered dressed openings. Informal English Picturesque Cottage in style, built off an L-plan, its steeply pitched roofs have a variety of carved perforated decorative bargeboards. From the old avenue gable projects a single-storey hip-roofed bay window, alongside which, advancing from the internal angle, may have been an ornamental porch, now superseded by a modern extension. Some original rectangular-paned casements survive, whilst rising from the muddle is a Tudor-style chimney in the shape of a cluster of three brick flues. To one gable is a bull's-eye feature with trefoil insert. At the entrance is a pair of carriage pillars with chamfered shafts and concave layered cappings. A replacement for an earlier lodge on the site.

Atkinson 1815; *LGI* (1958).

81. GEASHILL CASTLE, Geashill; pre-1838/*c.* 1860.
A single-storey standard gabled lodge with similar projecting hall. Roughcast and derelict, it is a replacement for a predecessor on the site, built for Edward St Vincent, 9th Baron Digby (1809–89), who at this time was carrying out additions and alterations at his house to designs by J. Rawson Carroll. It now lies in ruins.

DB (1 July 1860); *BPB* (1929).

82. GEASHILL RECTORY, Geashill; pre-1838; *demolished.*
A lodge that may have been built *c.* 1780 by the well-connected incumbent, the Very Revd Dean William Digby (1730–1812), brother of the 6th and 7th Barons Digby of neighbouring Geashill Castle (*q.v.*).

Taylor and Skinner 1778; 1969 [1783]; Wilson 1803; *BPB* (1929); Leslie and Wallace 2009.

83. GLASSHOUSE, Shinrone (2).
Early lodge; *c.* 1825; *demolished.*

National Inventory of Architectural Heritage

The home in the early nineteenth century of Thomas Spunner to which was a most peculiar little lodge. Single-storey, long and narrow below a hipped roof with a semi-octagonal leading front, which may have been a later addition, having a window flanked on the angles by round-headed niches and doorways on opposing façades behind that; rendered with limestone quoins. In 1853 the lodge was vacant and it has lately succumbed.

Later lodge; *c.* 1865; architect probably Denis Hanly.

The property passed by marriage to Charles Rolleston, who assumed in 1867 the additional name of Spunner under the terms of the will of Thomas Spunner. He left his stamp on the place by adding this commodious and striking single-storey gatekeeper's lodge, built off an L-plan. Its leading gable contains a canted bay with scalloped slate roof over, which has a limestone shield in the apex with a crest of the Rolleston-Spunners: an eagle's head pierced through the neck by an arrow. The

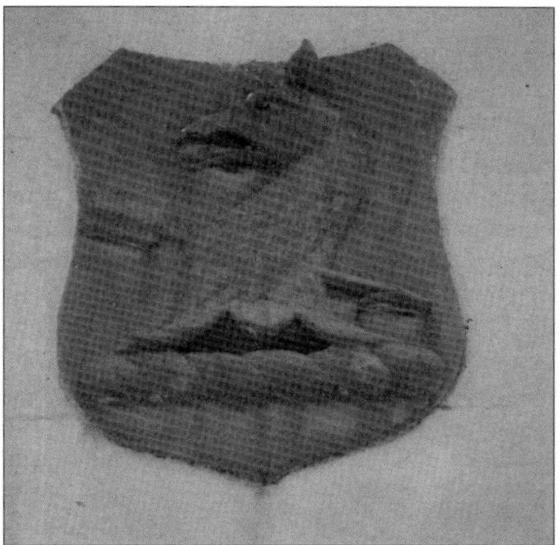

right-hand wing has a three-bay elevation of round-headed sash windows recessed behind an entrance verandah, the carved ornamental wooden arcade to which supports the extended hipped roof; rendered with toothed quoins. There is an identical gate lodge at Solsborough House, Co. Tipperary, one of the stone gate pillars to which is inscribed 'Denis Hanly, builder, Nenagh, 1863'. By 1870 he was recorded as 'builder (& architect)' in Slater's *Directory*. Here the property is entered through a contemporary cast-iron gatescreen with highly ornamental carriage posts with foliated decoration and spear-topped rails, recently removed.

Griffith 1848–60; *LGI* (1904); Bence-Jones 1988; NIAH.

84. GLENACURRAGH CASTLE, Birr; *c.* 1820.
A single-storey linear cottage with minimal skew-tables to an estate in the earlier nineteenth century of Thomas Palmer.

85. GLOSTER, Shinrone (2).
A great house best known for its associations with Sir Edward Lovett Pearce and his wonderful eye-catcher archway within the park, designed for his cousin Trevor Lloyd. Just a memory is the herald to this in its grand entrance, now sadly and badly modernised.

Main entrance; *c.* 1845.

Sister Mary C. Merriman

The great concave-walled quadrants remain but now minus their previous limewashed stuccoed finish, which contrasted pleasantly with the big limestone carriage pillars with their bold moulded cappings and ball finials. These are lost, along with the obelisk replicas of those of the eye-catcher that terminated the entrance screen, rising off bases containing round-arched niches. Also alien to modern requirements and sensitivities were the pair of postilion openings, each with panelled doors below keystoned lintels. The 'improvements' do not deserve notice. Behind and against the left-hand quadrant, and relatively unscathed, is the porter's accommodation. Probably from a century later and unique were it not for a similar arrangement at Birr Castle (*q.v.*) is the single-storey lodge arranged as a triple pile with Tudor-style label mouldings to openings in rubble walls. The roof is ornamented with cresting and carved finials to ridges and

Sister Mary C. Merriman

85. Gloster, main entrance.

gutters, and perforated foiled and cusped bargeboards which extended along a delightful curved canopy over the front door and gave shelter to visitors and gatekeeper alike, with access under from one of the postilion doors. This was supported on wooden posts with Gothic pendants between, in the manner of a railway halt. Created for Lt.-Col. Hardress Lloyd.

Side entrance; *c.* 1865; architect possibly W.F. Kempster.

John Lloyd (1832–83) succeeded to Gloster on the death of his father in 1860 and added this two-storey gatehouse in a correct Italianate style. Built off an L-plan with shallow-pitched gables arranged as open pediments supported on V-jointed Irish pilaster quoins, which contrast with painted rendered walls containing a mix of openings: flat, segmental and round-arched, and, for variety, a hood-moulded *oeil-de-boeuf.* In the internal angle nestles a single-storey hip-roofed hallway. To the road elevation a pair of unusual segmentally roofed gablets break the eaves.

IFR; Bence-Jones 1988.

86. GOLDEN GROVE, Roscrea (2).

Offaly gate; pre-1838; *demolished.*

Tipperary gate; *c.* 1840.

Over the county boundary, to an estate whose avenues are now public roads, with no entrance apparent, is what was a single-storey standard lodge, roughcast below a hipped roof, now extended by a bay and sporting two chimney-stacks. Plain and occupied. Built for William Piesley Vaughan (1774–1842).

LGI (1904).

GORTNAMONA (see MOUNT PLEASANT)

87. GRANGE, Clareen (2).

Both lodges to a demesne of the Harding family have gone. Each dated from before 1838. That to the main entrance on the western approach was opposite the gates. The other, to the southern avenue, was removed before 1912 but is survived by a rustic entrance screen with concave quadrants terminating in pillars with deep-set round-headed niches. The property is now known as 'Manor House'.

88. GREENHILLS, Edenderry; *c.* 1800.

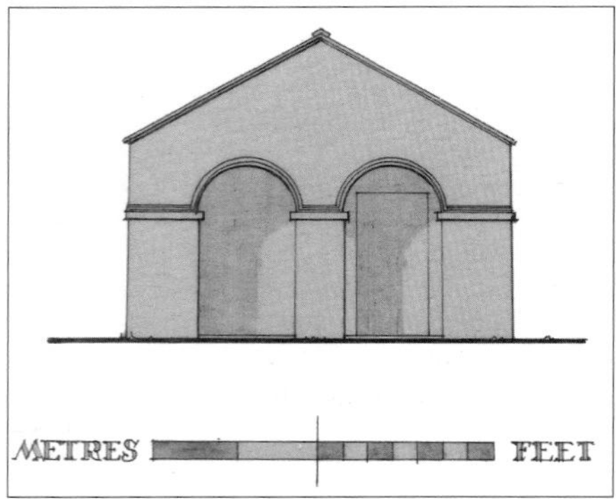

What started life as the most fundamental of single-storey three-roomed lodges, probably built for Thomas Longworth-Dames (1768–1825), was given some presence and sophistication by his son Francis (1789–1863) by the simple device of the application to its short avenue front of a chunky Italianate *porte-cochère* of a pair of round-headed arches with moulded plastered spandrels and soffits above the imposts. Today it lies approaching ruin and overgrown, having lost its role, the big house having been demolished to be survived by its outbuildings.

LGI (1904).

89. GREEN HILLS, Kilcormac; pre-1838; *demolished.*

A house, later called 'Carmel', owned by Captain Thomas Hobbs (1791–1842), who fought and was wounded at Waterloo; its lodge had gone by 1912.

Pigot 1824; *LGI* (1904).

90. HIGH PARK, Birr; *c.* 1810.

A tiny gabled cottage, its short three-bay front to the avenue, 'much improved' in grey rendering; unoccupied but maintained. A seat in the early nineteenth century of the Smith family.

HILLBROOK (see ROSSE VILLA)

91. HILLSBOROUGH HOUSE, MILLS AND CLOTH FACTORY, Roscrea; *c.* 1820.

The premises in 1814 of William Bridge, which ten years later had become a business of William Buckley, in whose family it remained for most of the century. In a beautiful setting by the entrance bridge and mill-race is the generously proportioned gatehouse. Two-storey, two-bay, with three-over-six sashes in harled walls below a hipped roof, it lies derelict.

Leet 1814; Pigot 1824.

92. HILLSIDE VILLAS, Birr; *c.* 1885; *demolished.*

A fine tree-lined avenue leads from the now-lodgeless entrance screen, which incorporated red-brick highlights, to the twin detached houses beyond in the same material. A development that seems to have been undertaken by one John Sweeny, appearing first in the valuation books in 1881.

93. HUNTSTON or HUNSTANTON, Clonony; pre-1838; *demolished.*

Like nearby Moystown (*q.v.*), a seat in the early nineteenth century of the L'Estrange family, which passed to the Burdetts on the death of Christopher Carleton-L'Estrange in 1843.

IFR.

94. JONESTOWN, Edenderry; *c.* 1865; *demolished.*

An old house of *c.* 1780 given a castellated

face-lift in the mid-nineteenth century when a Mrs Beasley was followed here by the Robinsons, who also added a lodge and a decorative gatescreen, which survives the crossroads realignment. The outer pillars incorporate their crest (out of a mural coronet a demi-buck) carved in the tympanums of the semicircular pedimented cappings. The carriage pillars in elaborate cast iron have *étoile* and fan motifs.

KEARNEYVILLE (see WOODLANDS)

95. KILCLARE, Clara; pre-1854; *demolished.*
A house in 1814 called 'Bellview', home to Andrew Armstrong, to which the valuation of 1854 associates a gatehouse probably built after 1838 and identifies the porter as Anne Fallon, leasing from John Herbert Armstrong. Surviving are big harled rustic concave-walled quadrants with contrastingly decorative iron gates.

Leet 1814; Griffith 1848–60.

96. KILCONCORKRY, Rathangan; *c.* 1855.

An attractive early Victorian standard single-storey lodge with a hipped roof and gabled breakfront hall containing a sheeted stable door, flanked by unusual bipartite casement windows with tiny rectangular panels and shouldered heads, all set in segmentally arched recesses in harled walls with high plinth to sill level. Derelict. Crude unremarkable gatescreen. Built for Captain John C. Nelson.

Griffith 1848–60.

97. KILCOURSEY, Clara; *c.* 1911; architect probably L.A. McDonnell.

The most delightful and restrained of Arts and Crafts-style lodges. Single-storey standard with a shallow-hipped roof of plain earthenware tiles and a minimal scalloped crested ridge on each side of a hefty chimney-stack. The oversailing soffit is at head height of tiny-paned casement windows in smooth roughcast walls above a bold plinth. Contrasting coarse stone gatescreen and refined Arts and Crafts wooden carriage gates. The valuation book of 1911 records that a new house and offices for Joseph Harold Goodbody (1880–1947) were complete.

IFR; Williams 1994.

98. KILDUFF, Daingean; pre-1912; *demolished.*
The grand gatescreen that survives probably pre-dates the lodge but post-dates the 1775 house, built for Roger North, by about 30 years. Comprised of three limestone pillars, two of which retain their corniced cappings, containing screen walls with architraved postern openings. Beyond are deep concave rubble quadrant walls. The spear-topped gates have repeating quatrefoil motifs. The missing lodge could have been added by John Hussey Walsh (1791–1863), who acquired the property around 1850.

Griffith 1848–60; *LGI* (1904); NIAH.

99. KILFOYLAN, Tober; pre-1838; *demolished.*
An estate of the Birmingham family, whose lodge, located well within the property, had gone by 1912.

KILLAGALLY GLEBE (see TESSAURAN RECTORY)

100. KILLAVILLA, Roscrea; pre-1838; *demolished.*

Francis Jackson in the 1830s redeveloped the estate with a building programme that included a new mansion and complementary entrance, probably with a contemporary gate lodge. What is on the site today is a modern look-alike lodge but the gates are original. An impressive screen comprised of railed ogee quadrants on dwarf walls leading to four stone pillars with corniced cappings supporting matching spear-topped carriage and postern gates.

101. KILLEENDUFF, Clonygowan (2).
Both the pre-1838 porter's lodge opposite the gates and its replacement have been demolished. A property in 1853 of John G. Wilson.

Griffith 1848–60.

102. KILLOOLY HALL, Kilcormac; pre-1838; *demolished.*
The lodge opposite the gates to a seat of the Gamble family was swept away by road-widening.

103. KILLOUGHY RECTORY, Clonaslee; pre-1838; *demolished.*
Situated in Annaghbrack glebe, the porter's lodge on which had been removed before 1912.

104. KILLURIN, Blue Ball; pre-1838; *demolished.*
A property in 1814 of James Whitestone and in 1853 home to William Sutherland, the gate lodge to which had gone by 1912.

Leet 1814; Griffith 1848–60.

105. KILMORE, Ferbane; pre-1838; *demolished.*
A gatekeeper's lodge to an estate in 1814 of James Bagnal.

Leet 1814.

106. KILNAGARNAGH, Ferbane; *c.* 1830.
Thomas Mulock III (1795–1860) succeeded to the property in 1827 on the death of his father and erected the fine neo-Classical villa and a contemporary gate lodge. Whilst his home was demolished a century later, it is survived by its lodge, now derelict. Single-storey standard below a hipped roof with small original slates, the openings having Tudor-style label mouldings in roughcast walls framed by big cut-stone quoins, located forward of a pair of octagonal stone entrance pillars.

LGI (1904); English 1974.

KINNITTY CASTLE (see CASTLE BERNARD)

107. LARCH VALE, Moneygall; pre-1838; *demolished.*
A late Georgian house, in 1837 home to Revd William Reynell Gresson (1798/9–1873), rector of Bourney, Co. Tipperary.

Lewis 1837; Leslie and Crooks 2010.

108. LEAP CASTLE, Clareen; *c.* 1845.

Originating as a tower-house of the O'Carrolls, Leap chiefly owes its present appearance to Jonathan Darby (1713–76), who extended it in Georgian Gothic fashion, 'which have highly ornamented that ancient building, preserving the antique, where it was proper externally, and giving all the elegance and convenience of modern architecture to the interior'. So recorded Charles Coote in his *Statistical survey* of 1801, and had it been built he could not fail to have noticed the grand arched entrance to the demesne. In a Romantic Castellated style, built in rubble stone, the lofty elliptical carriage archway is flanked by a pair of square turrets with mock arrowloops. To each side is a wing wall, one containing a pointed-

110. Lettybrook (Offaly Historical Society).

arched postern gate and the other a matching blind recess. Beyond are convex quadrants. Within is a perky little Tudor Gothic porter's lodge from the time of Jonathan's great-grandson, William Henry Darby (1790–1880). Single-storey standard below a steeply hipped roof, the main three-bay front has high-quality tooled dressings to openings strikingly set off by white walls. A pair of label-moulded bipartite windows with chamfered reveals flank a beautiful pointed-arched doorway with chiselled cluster-column surround, clearly intended to reflect the Gothic Venetian doorway in the big house, in the Batty Langley manner of a century earlier. Lovingly maintained in pristine state.

Coote 1801; *LGI* (1904); Bence-Jones 1988; McCarthy and O'Neill 2008.

LECARROW GLEBE (see REYNAGH RECTORY)

109. LEIPSIC, Shinrone; pre-1838; *demolished.*
An early nineteenth-century property of a branch of the Smith family.

110. LETTYBROOK, Kinnitty; *c.* 1825.
A perfectly charming little porter's lodge, presumably the creation of John Armstrong Drought (*c.* 1762–1839). Single-storey with a hipped roof, it presents a short front to the avenue, with a tripartite entrance of a sheeted doorway flanked by sidelights with Gothic trefoil heads. Of harled rubble construction, it lies dilapidated and dejected. There is very similar tracery to the lodge at neighbouring Castle Bernard (*q.v.*).

LGI (1904).

111. LISDERG, Clonony; *c.* 1895.
A standard 1½-storey late nineteenth-century lodge on a site well elevated from the avenue, gabled with perforated scalloped earthenware cresting. Wide windows on each side of a gabled canopy carried by curved stone brackets off the pilastered door-casing. A house previously called 'Woodland', which about 1875 was purchased by Thomas Perry on the death of Thomas L'Estrange. The lodge was built by Wilfred Perry.

112. LOUGHTON or LAUGHTON, Moneygall (3).
A seat which passed about 1828 to Benjamin, 1st Lord Bloomfield (1762–1846), from Thomas Ryder Pepper, who, according to Brewer, three years earlier had 'a handsome mansion and well-improved demesne'. Bloomfield by 1835 was carrying out further extensive additions and improvements to the house and demesne, his architect being James Pain, whom he was also employing at his other seat of Ciamaltha, Co. Tipperary. At the three estate accesses all that can be confidently attributed to him is one gatescreen, thanks to a combination of demolition, alterations and dereliction.

Main entrance; pre-1838.

Extended over the years to form a cruciform plan, it may have originated in a simple rectangular plan presenting a short front to the avenue. This elevation now has a gablet feature projecting from the steeply hipped roof over a wide window. Harled, overgrown and approaching ruin. Four stone pillars with chamfered recessed panels may be Pain's work, but the novel iron trellis gates with spear-tops and *étoile* motifs must be later.

Side entrance; pre-1838.

What may have started as a simple single-storey standard gabled affair now forms an L-plan created by the addition of a late Victorian wing containing a hip-roofed hall-cum-porch projection with a pair of circular rustic stone columns as support. Some original leaded casement lights survive, one in a round-headed recess below a nominal skew-table gable; roughcast.

South entrance; pre-1838; *demolished.*
A building at the gate, which is noted on the first OS map as a 'school'.

Brewer 1825; Lewis 1837; *LGI* (1904).

MANOR HOUSE (see GRANGE)

113. MEELAGHANS, Tullamore; pre-1838; *demolished.*
A miller's house of Owen Owens in 1854, when the valuation notes that the mill had not been working for seven years.

Griffith 1848–60.

114. MEELAGHANS HOUSE, Tullamore; pre-1838; *demolished.*
A property in 1814 of Patrick Molloy, which by 1854 had passed to John Rigby.

Leet 1814; Griffith 1848–60.

115. MEELAGHANS LODGE, Tullamore; pre-1912; *demolished.*
A seat in the mid-nineteenth century of Nicholas M. Delamere.

116. MILLBROOK COTTAGE, Birr; pre-1838; *demolished.*
The lodge opposite the gates to a residence in 1824 of Henry Hobbs had been removed before 1912.

Pigot 1824.

117. MILLTOWN, Shinrone.
Opposite the gates is a plain single-storey hip-roofed cottage, altered and extended to form an L-plan. A property in the early nineteenth century of the Spunners of Glasshouse (*q.v.*).

118. MONASTERORIS, Edenderry; pre-1838/*c.* 1855.
A fine late Georgian house, which strangely escaped the notice of Samuel Lewis and later of Bence-Jones, to which there was an early lodge probably built by Mark Synott (1777–1838). His two sons outlived him by only three years and by 1853 the place had passed to Joshua Manly. His replacement lodge is a sturdy single-storey standard structure built of limestone rubble facings with cut-stone quoins, brick dressings to small-paned casement windows and a continuous label

moulding embracing its three-bay front. Maintained below a shallow-hipped roof, its doorway sealed up. There is a contemporary chunky cast-iron gatescreen and hooped carriage gates, flimsier and probably surviving from the time of the earlier lodge.

Griffith 1848–60; *LGI* (1904).

119. MONASTERORIS HOUSE, Edenderry; *c.* 1830.

A most irregular little lodge, single-storey below a hipped roof but built off a cranked plan, loosely following the meandering of the ogee quadrant screen wall, to which it presents a blind façade relieved by a pair of round-headed recesses. Harled but enhanced by cut-stone quoins and chamfered surround to a bipartite mullioned window with cast-iron latticed casements, the lintel to which has a pretty sculpted fringe. Nearby, the V-jointed rusticated carriage pillars have an equally unusual lozenge-chiselled frieze, presumably the same mason amusing himself. Nice, no-nonsense spear-topped carriage and postern gates. This whole complex would date from the time here of Revd William George Wakely, rector of Ballyburly, who died in 1836. His lodge lies abandoned.

Pigot 1824; Lewis 1837; *LGI* (1904).

120. MONEYGUYNEEN, Kinnitty; *c.* 1880.
A gabled 1½-storey gatekeeper's lodge with a single-storey projecting wing and alongside it a tiny hall in the internal angle. Originating as a Picturesque cottage but now rendered bland by 'improvements'. Occupied. Part of a major redevelopment of the property after 1878, when it was purchased by Assheton Biddulph of Rathrobin (*q.v.*).

LGI (1904).

121. MOOROCK, Ballycumber; pre-1838; *demolished.*
A porter's lodge opposite the entrance to an estate in the early nineteenth century of George Arbuthnot Holmes (1788–1847). It had gone by 1912.

LGI (1904).

122. MOOR PARK, Birr; pre-1838; *demolished.*
A property before 1850 of Thomas Robinson, the lodge to which was opposite the gates.

Slater 1846.

123. MOUNT BRISCOE, Daingean (2).

Main entrance; pre-1838; *demolished.*
Surviving is a good late Georgian gatescreen comprised of harled rubble concave quadrants, each containing a now-sealed postern opening, contrasting with four ashlar pillars, those to the carriage gates having fluted friezes with paterae below moulded corniced cappings.

Secondary entrance; pre-1838; *demolished.*

A seat in 1814 of Nugent Briscoe that by about 1840 had passed to the Dooley family.

Leet 1814; Slater 1846.

124. MOUNT BUTLER, Roscrea; pre-1838; *demolished.*
Like its lodge, what was in 1824 '... the handsome and pleasant residence of Capt. Smith', and recorded as such by Lewis in 1837, is no more. Prior to that, it had been occupied by Arthur Molloy in 1814 and by a Mr Cox at the end of the eighteenth century.

Taylor and Skinner 1778; 1969 [1783]; Leet 1814; Pigot 1824; Lewis 1837.

125. MOUNT HEATON, Roscrea (2).
A property with a chequered history, which started life as a delightful Georgian Gothic country house of the Armstrong family, of whom William Henry Armstrong (1774–1835), who inherited from his father in 1791, is popularly said to have lost it in a game of cards with the prince regent in 1817. It seems to have been purchased by a General Taylor but remained in the occupancy of the Hutchinsons of Timoney Park, Co. Tipperary, until *c.* 1855, after which it was sold to the Reid family. It was purchased in 1878 by Count Arthur Moore. He gave it to the Cistercian Order, who established a monastery and school, renamed it 'Mount St Joseph's Abbey' and replaced the two original gate lodges in 1903.

West gate; pre-1838/1903; architect not known.

A commodious 1½-storey replacement structure in ornate Picturesque manner with opulent and highly decorative fretted bargeboards in variety, all painted black, in striking contrast to the white rendered walls. The embellishments extend to earthenware fleur-de-lis crestings to ridges and fancy fascia board to the single-storey canted bay on the avenue gable. Occupied and immaculate. The contemporary railings and carriage gates carry the 'MSJ' monogram, while the stone pillars may be the original from the days of Mount Heaton.

East gate; pre-1838/1903; *demolished.*

The early lodge and its replacement have gone but are survived by a most splendid gatescreen of extensive quadrant walls framing four V-jointed rusticated cut-stone pillars flanking a pair of ornate cast-iron postilion gates and railings. The carriage pillars are crowned by a noble pair of eagles, the crest of the Reid family, probably dating from the 1850s.

Pigot 1814; Lewis 1837; Slater 1846; 1856; Griffith 1848–60; Bence-Jones 1988; Lyons 1993.

126. MOUNT LUCAS, Daingean; *c.* 1865.
Now lacking its gatescreen is this solid single-storey gabled lodge constructed with uncoursed cut-stone facings, the doorway set into a segmentally arched recess. There is a pair of central chimneys and modern plastic windows. Occupied. Built for John Lucas (1812–65) or his widow, who lived on in the place.

LG (1875).

127. MOUNT PLEASANT, Blue Ball (2).
An estate, which originated as 'Gortnamona' and has since reverted to that name, of the O'Connor family. Upon the death of Maurice Nugent O'Connor in 1818 the property was vested through his youngest daughter, who married Revd Benjamin Morris in 1822; their son, the Hon. William O'Connor-Morris, assumed that name, and he replaced both of the earlier lodges, which were opposite their gates.

East entrance; pre-1838/*c.* 1860.
A 1½-storey gabled lodge built off an L-plan with a single-storey hallway extending from the right-hand leading gable. Roughcast and modernised.

West entrance; pre-1838/pre-1912; *demolished.*
Even the replacement has been superseded, by a twentieth-century bungalow, and has gone the way of the big house, which was burnt in 1922.

LGI (1904); Glin *et al.* 1988.

MOUNT ST JOSEPH'S ABBEY (see MOUNT HEATON)

128. MOYALLY, Moate; pre-1838; *demolished.*
A seat of the Marsh family until the mid-nineteenth century, the gate lodge to which was already a shell by 1912. Remains of an impressive gatescreen.

129. MOYSTOWN, Clonony; pre-1838/*c.* 1845.
Home to the L'Estrange family from the seventeenth century until 1853, when it was sold as an incumbered estate, Moystown was entered between a pair of lodges, which were replaced in the mid-nineteenth century by the present structure. This was either because the predecessors were particularly antique or owing to their inferior construction; certainly the OS name books state that Col. L'Estrange's tenants in the townland of Clonbronniff lived 'miserably'. This was Colonel Henry Peisley L'Estrange (1793–1847), whose son of the same name parted with the property, which by 1946 had been acquired by the Land Commission, with the inevitable consequences. The gate lodge survives.

Single-storey gabled on an L-plan, whitewashed with mock arrowloops to each leading front and a pair of octagonal chimney-stacks. Extended to the rear in a hipped-roof double pile but much abused, with a shed door opening punched in the front elevation. There is a pointed arch in one entrance wall that may remain from the lost pair.

IFR; Lyons 1993; Sheil 1998.

MYRTLEGROVE (see BALLYRIHY)

130. NEWTOWN, Tullamore (2).

Main entrance; pre-1838; *demolished.*
Surviving are the mysteriously truncated remains of the gatescreen in the form of four ashlar pillars with bold corniced cappings and oval paterae to the friezes, much as those at Racecourse Hall, Co. Tipperary. For whatever reason, these seem to have been shortened in reconstruction and the architraved postilion openings reduced in height and sealed. Probably, with its lodge, built for Sir William Cusack-Smith (1766–1836) as an appropriate introduction to a country seat of the solicitor-general and baron of the court of the exchequer, which he became successively from 1800 onwards.

Secondary entrance; pre-1838; *demolished.*
Another missing lodge which was opposite its gates.

BPB (1929).

131. OAKLEY PARK, Clareen (2).
'There is a beautiful demesne called Oakley ... it belongs to George Stoney, who has expended large sums of money, adorning, with all the diversities of water and landscape his mansion here ...' Thus did the *Parliamentary Gazetteer* report in 1845. Stoney inherited the estate in 1824, and his adornments perhaps included the furnishing of the two porters' lodges. They present a pitiable sight today.

South gate; pre-1838; *demolished.*

North gate; pre-1838.
A lodge that appears a hodgepodge through alterations and additions over the years. A single-storey structure with a degree of design detectable in a recessed triangle on the leading single-bay gable, suggestive of a crude pediment. There are the sad remains of entrance quadrants and gate pillars with recessed decorative Italianate panels in their plinths, shafts and friezes.

Parliamentary Gazetteer; *LGI* (1904).

132. PALLAS PARK, Blue Ball; *c.* 1800; *demolished.*

Offaly Historical Society (I.A.A.)

All that remains of a once-fine wooded landed estate is a crumbling boundary wall and ruined outbuildings. Much was the creation of the Malone family of Baronstown, Co. Westmeath (*q.v.*), whose mansion and gate lodge have gone, the latter preserved only in an old photograph that shows an eccentric little structure nearing its end. Single-storey with a short gabled elevation to the avenue that was comprised of an arcade of three round-headed arches, the recesses to which presumably contained the doorway flanked by windows. Rubble-built with brick dressings, probably harled. The gatescreen is relatively intact and extensive, of four grand ashlar pillars with moulded bases and friezes with crude fluting of almost niche proportions, but now lacking their cappings.

The original screen railings contain postern gates with repeating spear, husk and quatrefoil motifs, whilst the carriage gates are later replacements. Lodge and gates were part of the improvements of Henry Malone.

LGI (1904); IAA photograph (62/20 Z1).

133. PHILIPSTOWN BARRACKS, Daingean; *c.* 1820.
In 1837 '... a large cavalry barracks, containing accommodations for 12 officers, 131 non-commissioned officers and privates, and 82 horses, with a hospital for 16 patients ...', but currently unused. Tucked in safely and snugly behind the tall protective barracks wall is this standard single-storey late Georgian lodge with a steeply pitched hipped roof. Occupied, well maintained in roughcast finish, but with unfortunate plastic windows on each side of a round-headed doorway with an apology for the original spoked fanlight.

Lewis 1837.

PROSPECT (see DRUMBANE)

134. RAHAN LODGE, Rahan; *c.* 1800.
A single-storey three-bay lodge, its door to the right-hand side, below a shallow-pitched oversailing hipped roof; eight-over-four sash windows in limewashed boulder walls. There is a ghastly flat-roofed room obscuring the front door, spoiling the whole effect. Vacant. A property at the turn of the nineteenth century of the O'Brien family.

135. RAHAN RC COLLEGE, Rahan; *c.* 1818; *demolished.*

The complex, '... founded in 1818 for the education of young gentlemen, under a rector and seven professors belonging to the order of Jesus, and a Presentation Convent', is announced by a splendid late Georgian entrance screen of shallow concave-walled quadrants containing postern openings and finished in white harling, contrasting beautifully with the Classical V-jointed rusticated masonry carriage pillars, which have finely moulded cappings over friezes, each face of which is decorated with paired festoons, a feature also to be found at Whigsborough (*q.v.*). The gates are more recent.

Lewis 1837.

136. RATHENNY, Moneygall (2).

South entrance; *c.* 1825.

Consciously and impressively sited as a vista stop on a kink in the public road is a wide straight estate entrance screen of four tall ashlar pillars with alternate fluting and rosette motifs to leading friezes. Between are railed screens with postilion gates and carriage gates with spear-topped rails. Beyond is a sturdy single-storey lodge with steeply hipped roof and tall eaves, its short front to the avenue containing a tripartite lattice-paned casement window. On opposing side elevations are small wings under catslide roofs. Occupied and well maintained. Mansell Andrews's gatekeeper in 1854 was Darby Donohoe.

North entrance; pre-1838; *demolished.*

A seat in the nineteenth century of the Andrews family.

Griffith 1848–60.

137. RATHMORE, Birr (2).
A property of a junior branch of the Synge family from nearby Syngefield (*q.v.*). Both its pre-1838 lodges, built for George Synge (1757–1837), have gone.

LGI (1904).

138. RATHMOYLE, Daingean; *c.* 1855.
Built off an irregular plan by the roadside on a right-angled bend, single-storey, finished in roughcast with highly ornamental carved bargeboards: foiled, pendulous and cusped. Occupied and extended to the right-hand side. Alongside is a gatescreen of squat V-jointed rusticated Classical pillars, which pre-date the lodge. The proprietor in 1856 was Sylvester Rait.

Slater 1856.

139. RATHROBIN, Black Lion; *c.* 1835.
Opposite the gates is a single-storey gabled gatekeeper's lodge with a double-pile room to rear and a flat-roofed hall projection to the front. Derelict, approaching ruin, like architect Sir Thomas Drew's great house within. The lodge was built for Francis Marsh Biddulph (1802–68), who inherited the place on his father's death in 1827.

LGI (1904).

140. REYNAGH or RYNAGH RECTORY, Banagher; *c.* 1842.
On Lecarrow glebe, set forward of its gates, is a tiny single-storey gabled cottage, rather basic, as is typical of lodges to rectories of the Church of Ireland. Derelict and probably dating from the incumbency (1841–3) of Revd Robert Mitchell Kennedy (1798–1864), who succeeded the long-serving Revd John Burdett.

Lewis 1837; Leslie and Crooks 2010.

141. RIDGEMOUNT, Kilcormac; pre-1838; *demolished.*
A seat throughout the nineteenth century of the Drought family.

142. ROBINSON'S DISTILLERY, Birr; pre-1854; *demolished.*
A gatehouse recorded in the Griffith valuation as beside a 'dilapidated distillery' of the representatives of Robert and Simpson Robinson. This would seem to have been one of two distilleries started up by 1818 but which folded in the 1840s.

Griffith 1848–60; Townsend 1999.

143. ROCKFIELD, Horseleap; pre-1912; *demolished.*
A property that passed from the Higgins family between 1837 and 1853 to Adam Fuller, its lodge post-dating 1838.

Lewis 1837; Griffith 1848–60.

144. ROSS, Tullamore; pre-1838/*c.* 1860.
A pleasant two-storey gabled gatehouse built in good coursed rubble with polychromatic toothed brick dressings to openings of a three-bay ground floor and two windows over. Apparently a replacement for a predecessor on the site to a property of the Briscoe family, which was let in 1854 to a Denis Helion.

Griffith 1848–60.

145. ROSSE VILLA, Birr; pre-1838; *demolished.*
Later named 'Hillbrook', a home to a succession of occupants, one of whom was William Justin O'Driscoll in 1837, presumably the same barrister to be found later living at Bellcourt, Co. Wicklow (*q.v.*).

Lewis 1837.

RUSSAGH (see GAGEBOROUGH)

146. RUTLAND, Roscrea; pre-1838; *demolished.*
A property of Croker Wright, whose daughters married the brothers Revd William Minchin and Charles Humphrey Minchin of the nearby estate of Greenhills, Co. Tipperary, and upon whose death without male issue Rutland passed to the latter of the brothers. Two years before his wedding in 1817 he had served under Wellington at Waterloo, living on until 1884. His gate lodge is survived by a good gatescreen of six slender square pillars, only the outer pair of which retain the ball finials on their pedestals.

IFR.

147. ST CATHERINE'S CHURCH OF IRELAND CHURCH, Tullamore; *c.* 1850.
A standard single-storey lodge with a hipped roof in pleasant grey rubble construction with cream brick soldier arches to openings. Square casements now replaced by plastic, with synthetic slates to the roof. Occupied. At the entrance to Francis Johnston's earlier church of 1818 and the rectory of three years before, the lodge dates from the incumbency (1843–61) of Revd Edward Fleetwood Berry (1817–75).

Lewis 1837; Leslie and Wallace 2009.

148. ST COLUMBA'S ROMAN CATHOLIC CHURCH, Tullamore; pre-1854; *demolished.*
A lodge identified in the Griffith valuation as being occupied by Anne Egan; it was probably replaced by the National School on the site in 1888.

Griffith 1848–60.

ST KILDA (see WILLIAMBROOK)

149. SCREGGAN, Tullamore; pre-1838; *demolished.*
All evidence of there having been a lodge opposite the gates has been erased, and the 1912 OS map shows the avenue as having gone. Probably built for Edward John Briscoe (1770–1815), whose main seat was Riversdale, Co. Westmeath (*q.v.*).

LGI (1904).

150. SHANEVALLEY, Edenderry; *c.* 1860.
A plain single-storey mid-Victorian affair, to a property in 1853 of Pilkington Homan, which served for a while as a smithy. Occupied.

Griffith 1848–60.

151. SHARAVOGUE, Birr (3).
A secondary seat of the Westenras and in the same Tudor Gothic style as their main one of Rossmore Park, Co. Monaghan. Both are but memories, the latter having been demolished whilst Sharavogue lies in ruins, eventually falling victim to the Land Commission. It is survived by some outbuildings and its two later lodges, sited opposite their gates in similar Tudor Revival manner. These could well be to a design by William Deane Butler, whom the family favoured following the death of William Vitruvius Morrison. Built by John Craven Westenra (1798–1874), third son of the 2nd Baron Rossmore, they were identical but now are contrasting examples of how and how not to maintain and restore a historic building.

Inner lodge; pre-1838; *demolished.*

West lodge; *c.* 1845; architect perhaps W.D. Butler.

Built off an L-plan is a single-storey gabled structure, its apexes having ornamental wooden pendant features and carved paired soffit brackets to eaves. Particularly conspicuous are the stone-dressed chamfered mullioned bipartite windows with label mouldings and very decorative cast-iron hexagonal-patterned casements in rendered walls. In the internal angle is the pointed-arched doorway. Sympathetically rehabilitated.

East lodge; *c.* 1845; architect perhaps W.D. Butler.

As the west lodge but with a steeper roof line, roughcast, lacking some of its original

154. Syngefield, main entrance.

architectural features and suffering the intrusion of inappropriate modern casements.

BPB (1929).

152. SILVER HILLS, Moneygall; *c.* 1850; *demolished.*

A lodge identified in the valuation of 1854 to a property of Charles Rolleston (1768–1820), of that family whose main seat was at ffrankfort Castle (*q.v.*) nearby.

Griffith 1848–60; *LGI* (1904).

153. STRAWBERRY HILL, Cloghan; pre-1838; *demolished.*

The lodge to the delightful rambling Georgian Gothic house has gone, but remaining are main pillars with round-headed panels containing lion heads and vase finials with frolicking cupids in relief. The place in the late eighteenth century belonged to Thomas Coghlan, who was succeeded here *c.* 1800 by Major John Molloy.

Wilson 1803; Leet 1814; Brewer 1825.

154. SYNGEFIELD, Birr.

Main entrance; pre-1838; *demolished.*

A once-magnificent gatescreen (*above*) that forebodes the scene of dilapidation beyond. The mid-eighteenth-century house built by the Very Revd Edward Synge (1726–92) is approached through a lofty pair of contemporary ashlar gate pillars rising off moulded plinths to bold corniced cappings below ball finials on sturdy pedestals. To each side is a wide postilion opening with blocked dressings, that to the right-hand side sealed up. Recently restored by Birr Town Council.

Secondary entrance; pre-1838; *demolished.*

BPB (1929); ffolliott 1970.

155. TEMORA, Kilcormac; pre-1838; *demolished.*

All that remains at the entrance to an estate in the early nineteenth century of the Magawley family is a simple straight entrance screen with small postilion openings.

156. TESSAURAN or TISARAN RECTORY, Ferbane; *c.* 1820.

A single-storey porter's lodge with its single-bay short front to the avenue, which used to face a schoolhouse at the other side of the entrance and now has a grand extension to the rear. It presided over the gates to a rectory built in 1812 on Killagally glebe by Revd Henry Mahon (1771–1838) of the Castlegar, Co. Galway, family, who was incumbent here from 1802 until his death.

Lewis 1837; Leslie and Wallace 2009.

157. THOMASTOWN PARK, Kilcormac (2).

A big house, built in 1730 by a Mr Leggat, which at the turn of the following century was occupied by the Bennett family, who would have added at least one of the porters' lodges.

Main entrance; *c.* 1800.

Lying derelict is a charming cottage with amateur design interpretations of Georgian Gothic and just an overtone of Palladian. Single-storey gabled, its short front contains a pair of lancet windows flanking a larger opening, which may have been the doorway, and in the peak is a blind lunette, all in harled walls. Later ornamental bargeboards of *c.* 1860 were added to the concoction. By the road are the dilapidated remains of a fine contemporary gatescreen comprised of shallow concave quadrant walls containing dressed postilion openings, flanking a pair of tall ashlar carriage pillars with their simple original iron gates; across the road is an almost matching entrance which led to more Bennett land. All presumably built by Francis Bennett.

Secondary entrance; pre-1838; *demolished.*

This lodge on the western approach, like the big house, has gone.

Burke 1854–5; *LGI* (1904).

158. THORNVALE, Moneygall (2).

An early nineteenth-century house of the Garvey family.

Tipperary lodge; pre-1840/*c.* 1860.

A gabled 1½-storey gatekeeper's lodge with a symmetrical three-bay ground-floor front and gablets to attic over with, like its main gables, carved ornamental bargeboards. These and the canted slates suggest a mid-Victorian reworking of an earlier cottage, which may have been raised to create loft accommodation, presumably by George Garvey.

Offaly lodge; pre-1838; *demolished.*

At the northern approach survives a gatescreen of *c.* 1875 of stone chamfered pillars with layered cappings beyond ornate inner cast-iron carriage pillars with fancy 'gabled' tops.

Slater 1856.

159. TOBERDALY or TUBBERDALY, Daingean (2).

North entrance; *c.* 1800.

Not quite opposite the entrance is a standard single-storey three-bay gabled lodge and similar projecting porch with lancet-headed openings. Roughcast and occupied. Across the road is an entrance screen of four stone pillars, chamfered to create almost octagonal shafts with domed cappings, and all framed by dwarf ogee walled quadrants. Built in the time here of James Nesbitt.

South entrance; *c.* 1865.

Also opposite its gates is a typical mid-Victorian single-storey standard porter's lodge below a shallow-hipped roof with a

160. Tullamore Gaol.

pedimented porch breakfront. Built in solid coursed rubble facings with brick dressings and soldier arches to windows, which have corbelled sills. A segmental brick arch spans the porch recess. Modern windows and inappropriate concrete interlocking roof tiles. The gatescreen has been removed. All for Catherine Thamison Downing Nesbitt (d. 1886), who succeeded to the estate on the death of her brother in 1857.

LGI (1904).

160. TULLAMORE GAOL, Tullamore; *c.* 1830; architect probably James Pain.
'The first Stone of this Prison was laid by Charles William Baron Tullamoore on the 13th day of September in the year of our Lord 1826 under the 7th Year of the Reign of His Most Gracious Majesty George the Fourth. Commissioners Lord Baron Tullamoore M.P., Colonel Thomas Bernard M.P., William Trench, John Head Drought, Valentine Bennett and Francis Berry Esquires. Engineer John Killay. Contractors Henry Mullins and McMahon, John Rafter Sculp.' Thus runs the inscription on a plaque over the arched entrance in the monumental gatehouse, which screens the radiating cell blocks behind. Although no architect is credited with its design, this plan form is a clue to its author, as it repeats the pioneering layout at Limerick prison planned by James Pain. Constructed with coursed random punched masonry, the gatehouse is dominated by a pair of great square castellated towers with false arrowloops and would-be machicolations to recesses. To each side are similarly treated lower wings, whilst access is through a four-centred arched gateway below a mock machicolation feature. A railed screen to the road has beautifully cast iron fasces and battleaxe pillars. The cell blocks behind were destroyed in 1922 and reconstructed for industrial use fifteen years later.

Nolan and O'Neill 1998; Lee 2005. IAA photograph (3/46).

TULLANISK (see WOODFIELD)

161. WALCOT, Birr; pre-1838/*c.* 1860.
Lying ruinous and overgrown, what appears to have been a single-storey standard lodge below a hipped roof. Minuscule with a projecting gabled hall, it is raised off a moulded plinth, with chamfered stone to opening jambs, lintels, external corners and gate pillars. Altogether, with its stuccoed finish, once a quite pretentious little building, which makes its present condition all the sorrier. This would seem to be a reworking of or even a replacement for a structure shown on the site on the first OS map. The house had a succession of occupants in the nineteenth century, the earliest recorded of whom was John Drought in 1814, followed a decade later by attorney W.L. Hobart. Its mid-Victorian appearance may be attributable to its 1856 owner, Laurence Parsons, presumably the third son (1805–94) of the 2nd earl of Rosse of Birr Castle across the road.

Leet 1814; Pigot 1824; Slater 1856; *BPB* (1929).

162. WHIGSBOROUGH, Birr; pre-1838.
Atkinson visited the estate in 1811 and was impressed: 'I have seen much more extensive concerns than this, but very few that were laid out to more advantage: here the frame and position of the house—the gates—the little wooden bridge—the water and the verdant sod, all conspire to make a pleasing impression upon the beholder'. Perhaps significantly, however, he makes no mention of a lodge. At the entrance is a pair of splendid Classical gate pillars, only differing from those at Rahan College (*q.v.*) in being a few courses higher. Raised in V-jointed rusticated punched ashlar with bold moulded corniced cappings over friezes with double swags to each face. These must be late eighteenth-century, which would make those at Rahan copies rather than by the same architect or mason. Tucked in behind the left-hand quadrant wall is a tiny ruinous single-storey gabled lodge, its short front to the avenue containing a single round-headed doorway. Probably all built for John Drought, who was the proprietor in 1801.

Coote 1801; Atkinson 1815.

WHITEFORD (see BEECH PARK)

163. WILLIAMBROOK, Birr (2).
Both lodges have been demolished. That on the northern approach was opposite its gates in 1838 but had been removed before 1912, when the house was renamed 'St Kilda', the later lodge to which was at the end of a tortuous avenue off the Military Road. The latter was probably built by James Rolleston, who is recorded here in 1870. A good cast-iron gatescreen survives.

Slater 1870.

164. WOODBROOK, Shinrone; pre-1838.
A property in the mid-nineteenth century of the Woods family, the lodges to which had gone by 1911.

165. WOODFIELD, Birr (2).
A secondary residence of the Parsons family of Birr Castle (*q.v.*), which seems to have served as an overflow for younger sons. The first occupant from *c.* 1800 was Revd William Parsons (1764–1838), third son of the 4th baronet. His successor furnished the estate with two new gate lodges, one a replacement at the main gate.

South entrance; pre-1838/*c.* 1840.
A standard single-storey structure below a hipped roof with paired carved eaves brackets. The panelled door is flanked by square lattice-paned casement windows in rendered walls. Its predecessor was at the other side of the avenue. Good Classical gatescreen of four ashlar pillars with fluted friezes and moulded cornice cappings. Railed screens containing postern gates. All

perhaps the work of William Parsons before he succeeded as 3rd earl of Rosse in 1841 and returned to his ancestral home.

North entrance; *c.* 1840.

A single-storey standard gabled cottage, harled, with six-over-nine sash windows. Abandoned.

The estate was alternatively known as 'Woodville' and is now called 'Tullanisk'.

Coote 1801; *BPB* (1929).

166. WOODLANDS, Birr; pre-1912; *demolished.*

Previously called 'Kearneyville' after its owner, it was from the mid-nineteenth century tenanted by George Heenan.

167. WOOD OF O, Tullamore; pre-1838; *demolished.*

A property in 1814 of a Major Warburton, which later passed to the Slator family.

Leet 1814; Griffith 1848–60.

168. WOODVILLE, Shinrone; pre-1838; *demolished.*

The proprietor in 1814 was John Delahunt.

Leet 1814.

169. WRAYMOUNT, Birr; pre-1838; *demolished.*

A seat in the early nineteenth century of Major Wray.

COUNTY WESTMEATH

1. ANNASKINNAN, Killucan; *c.* 1850.
Built for William Garty is this standard hip-roofed lodge constructed in rubble stone with red-brick toothed dressings, quoins and soldier courses, and diagonally set stacks in the same material. Derelict.

Griffith 1848–60.

2. ANNEVILLE, Mullingar; pre-1837; *demolished.*
A good middle-sized Classical house built about 1750, probably for the Rochforts of nearby Belvedere (*q.v.*), from whom it passed *c.* 1785 to John Smith, letting to the rector from 1814 until his death of Mullingar parish, Revd Thomas Robinson (1748–1828), in whose family it remained until the mid-nineteenth century. Its lodge was removed before 1914.

Taylor and Skinner 1778; 1969 [1783]; Wilson 1803; Leslie and Wallace 2009.

3. ARCHERSTOWN, Delvin; *c.* 1820.

A good late Georgian Gothic single-storey porter's lodge with its short canted elevation to the avenue, below a corresponding roof, having lancet-headed openings to each face of harled walls. In 2000 gutted in planned renovation, which included lifting the roof to permit attic accommodation, with roof windows and a scalloped slate band. Fundamental gatescreen to a property in 1815 'a new-built seat of Mr Battersby'.

Atkinson 1815.

4. ARCHERSTOWN HOUSE, Delvin (2).
An estate in 1783 of a branch of the prolific Smith, or Smyth, family of Westmeath, who were here until 1836, when it was acquired by Samuel Arthur Reynell (1814–77) from Killynon (*q.v.*) in the year of his marriage.

Main gate; *c.* 1790.
A once-impressive entrance comprised of six tall ashlar pillars containing contrasting harled screen walls, the outer shallow concave quadrants, the inner relieved by lancet windows, now blind, each of which permitted observation from the porters' lodges behind. A matching pair of single-storey Georgian Gothic hip-roofed twins, each three-bay harled front facing the other across the avenue, all openings having pointed heads presumably once containing Y-traceried sashes. Now both terminally derelict, that to the right-hand side in 1837 was designated a police barracks and in 1854 was let to the 'constabulary force', probably since the 1798 unrest.

Irish Architectural Archive

Secondary gate; pre-1837.
A simple standard hip-roofed lodge, occupied, much modernised and extended.

Taylor and Skinner 1778; 1969 [1783]; Lewis 1837; Griffith 1848–60; *LGI* (1904); IAA photograph (21/29).

5. AUBURN COTTAGE, Athlone; pre-1837; *demolished.*
A property in 1846 of John Martin of the Excise Office.

Slater 1846.

6. AUBURN, Athlone; pre-1837; *demolished.*
A seat in the early nineteenth century of the Bruce family, the lodge to which was opposite the gates.

7. AUBURN, Glassan (2).
The house was either built by John Hogan about 1805 or was a comprehensive remodelling of an earlier one of the Naper family, the gatekeeper's lodge to which has survived.

Main entrance; *c.* 1760.

A building of antique appearance with minuscule square windows in limewashed harled walls, the three-bay avenue front irregular, with its contrasting wide sheeted doorway to the left-hand side; steeply pitched hipped roof. The windows have later margined casements of *c.* 1840 that may be contemporary with the elegant gatescreen, comprised of four stone posts in the form of Tuscan columns carrying carriage gates and flanking postilion gates with fleur-de-lis finials. A once-fine lodge now approaching ruin.

Side entrance; pre-1837; *demolished.*
A secondary lodged approach, which had gone by 1914.

The whole property now a sorry mess.

LGI (1904); English 1973.

8. BAGSHOT LODGE, Athlone; pre-1914; *demolished.*
A lodge apparently built in the mid-nineteenth century, when the proprietress was Mary Anne Cheevers.

Griffith 1848–60.

9. BALLAGHKEERAN, Athlone; *c.* 1880.
A standard single-storey roughcast structure with hipped roof, atop which is a polychromatic brick stack with corbelled capping, which reveals its age. The Murtaghs lived here in the late nineteenth century.

BALLARD (see LAUREE)

10. BALLINALACK, Multyfarnham; pre-1914; *demolished.*
A lodge built after 1837, probably in the time here of the Casey family sometime after succeeding the Reynells.

Griffith 1848–60.

BALLINACLOON (see BALLYNACLONAGH)

11. BALLINLOUGH CASTLE, Clonmellon (2).
The beautiful property of the Nugent family, previously O'Reilly, Sir Hugh having assumed his mother's maiden name in 1812. There is nothing in its lodges with the same charm as castle and demesne (which remarkably survived the clutches of the Land Commission in the early twentieth century and remains with the family), both apparently the creation of Sir James Nugent, 2nd baronet.

Side entrance; *c.* 1830.
Facing the road, alongside its gatescreen, is this single-storey plain roughcast gabled affair, now extended to four-bay with six-over-six sash windows and having a flat-roofed projecting hall. Unoccupied.

Main entrance; *c.* 1830.
A nondescript single-storey roughcast structure, its short gabled one-bay front to the avenue. Far more worthy of note are the fine

gate pillars, which look to date from the 1780s, when Sir Hugh O'Reilly, 1st baronet, transformed his old house into the Irish castle of today. These rise strikingly in contrasting alternating smooth block and rock-faced rustication to cappings crowned by vases complete with ringed handles. Scroll-topped stops to good later iron gates with decorative meeting rail finial.

BPB (1929).

12. BALLYGLASS, Mullingar; pre-1837; *demolished.*
A lodge not quite opposite the gates to a seat of the McLoughlin family.

13. BALLYHANDY, Castletown Geoghegan; pre-1837; *demolished.*
A porter's lodge to a 74-acre holding in the mid-nineteenth century of parish priest Fr Andrew McGuire, leasing from John Savage Nugent.

Griffith 1848–60.

14. BALLYHEALY, Devlin; *c.* 1835.
Impressively located to stop a road vista but deprived of its entrance screen is this much-abused Regency lodge. Built by Philip Batty, it was originally a single-storey standard pyramidal-roofed structure, probably harled to set off bold stone dressings with prominent keystones and quoins. Sadly, the coursed rubble fabric has been exposed, plastic 'Georgian' windows inserted and the roof re-covered in soulless synthetic slates. Square on plan and extended to the rear.

15. BALLYLOUGHLOE RECTORY, Moate; pre-1837; architect perhaps Francis Johnston; *demolished.*
Francis Johnston in 1820 wrote that he erected a glebe house near the town of Moate. Mount Temple glebe, as it is better known, 'was built by a gift of £100 and a loan of £675 from the late Board of First Fruits in 1809'. His commission may well have extended to providing a contemporary gate lodge for the rector, Revd Thomas English (1738–1816), incumbent from 1800 until his death.

Lewis 1837; English 1973; Leslie and Wallace 2009.

16. BALLYNACLONAGH, Multyfarnham (2).
An early lodge indicated on the 1837 OS map to a property of the Murphy family was removed before 1914, leaving a later one to the west, which has since suffered the same fate.

17. BALLYNAHOWN COURT, Ballynahown (2).
Once the principal seat of the Malone family, a fine Palladian mansion built in 1746, unusually in red brick, at the entrance to which was an early lodge.

Malone entrance; pre-1837; *demolished.*
The 1854 valuation notes that the 'old gate-lodge' was unoccupied, about to be superseded. The family forsook their ancestral home on the death in 1836 in his youth of an elder son, Edward Malone, the last in a long line of that name associated with Ballynahown. They retired to their other property of Baronston (*q.v.*) and sold Ballynahown to John Ennis (1800–78), a Dublin merchant created a baronet in 1866, who amended the estate access.

Ennis entrance; *c.* 1850.

Diverting the avenue southwards, Ennis replaced the earlier lodge with this striking little building on a perfect axis with the gates opposite. It consciously replicates the materials of the big house, with fine white mortar joints under a shallow pyramidal roof that extends to cover the projecting hall, which creates recesses with slender cast-iron corner columns. Single-storey standard, there are brick pilasters to all corners, evidence of latticed windows, a pretty carved fascia of pendants and a central staged chimney-stack. Behind its own wide railed screen, which terminates in V-jointed ashlar pillars matching those across the road, its gate is framed by a pair of *Taxus baccata* 'Fastigiata'. Now lying abandoned and derelict.

Griffith 1848–60; Foster 1882; *LGI* (1904); Bence-Jones 1988.

18. BALLYNEGALL, Mullingar (3).
'... Ballynagall, until a recent period termed Castle-reynell, was formerly property of the Reynell family, off whom it was purchased by the present proprietor, James Gibbon. By this gentleman a splendid mansion has been erected, after the designs of Mr Francis Johnston, at the expense, as we believe, of more than 30,000L.' When Brewer wrote this in 1825 the handsome house had been built for seventeen years and the landscape gardener-cum-architect Alexander McLeish was creating the setting for a place that included three early porters' lodges, only one of which survives.

Main entrance; *c.* 1825; architect John Hargrave.

Often understandably credited to Francis Johnston, this chaste lodge is in fact too late to have been by him and is safely attributed to the Cork architect, for he is documented to have designed the nearby Church of Ireland church in 1828 and stables for James Gibbons in 1836. Furthermore, there is an identical lodge to Clifton Lodge, Co. Meath (*q.v.*), where, as Kevin Mulligan pointed out, John Hargrave is also known to have worked. Single-storey and built off an L-plan in ashlar below a shallow-hipped roof with a distinctive bracketed eaves course over a main façade comprised of a central bow containing a mullioned tripartite Wyatt window with Georgian sashes, on each side of which are round-headed niches.

Inner lodge; pre-1837/*c.* 1860.
Within the demesne on the Lough Owel approach is a gawky gabled 1½-storey affair. Built in random smooth stone, symmetrical, with a full-height breakfront hall. Occupied and much modernised. There was a predecessor on the site. Presumably a replacement by Thomas James Smyth, who succeeded to the property on the death of his cousin J.W.M. Berry in 1855.

North lodge; pre-1837/*c.* 1880.

A replacement for an earlier lodge opposite the entrance is this most singular and generously proportioned 1½-storey gatekeeper's lodge. A wide gable to the avenue with prettily fretted bargeboards embraces an attic window over a two-bay ground floor comprising round-arched openings from which project, rather awkwardly, a pair of canted bay windows with equivalent rooflets. All built in high-quality random uncoursed rough masonry with brick dressings. Most quirky is the left-hand corner, which is chamfered to accommodate a distyle Classical pedimented portico that faces the gates with octagonal columns perhaps salvaged from its predecessor. To the ridge are sawtooth earthenware crestings stopped by decorative fleur-de-lis hip-knobs.

These three lodges have outlived the big house, which tragically now lies an empty shell.

Brewer 1825; *APSD*; *LGI* (1904); Casey and Rowan 1993.

19. BARBAVILLA, Collinstown (3).
The antique mansion of the Smyth family, which survives all its lodges. Two of these, one of which lay opposite its entrance, were in position by 1837 and have been replaced by modern structures. The southernmost and latest may be incorporated in the present Picturesque composition.

20. BARONSTON, Ballynacarrigy (3).
'The house is a very large handsome, modern building ... the domain spacious, and adorned with much fine timber, planted by

his Lordship's grand-father, about eighty years ago.' His lordship, to whom Curwen alluded on 6 October 1813, was the first and last Baron Sunderlin, Richard Malone (1738–1817), who succeeded to the property in 1776 on the death of his uncle. Prior to his demise he built the magnificent pavilioned Palladian-style mansion and beautified the demesne with at least one of the lodged entrances. Thanks to two fires and the invasion of the Land Commission in the 1920s, very little domestic architecture survives and the property has become one of the great unlamented lost demesnes. That the baron was a man of considerable refinement has recently been underlined by the revelation that Kilbixy parish church, within the demesne by the main entrance gates and to the construction of which he contributed several thousand pounds, was completed in 1793 to designs by the eminent English architect James Wyatt, who may also have been responsible for the Sunderlin mausoleum alongside, where his lordship rests. Whether he designed anything else about the estate is not clear, although the architect was certainly an avid specifier of Coade stone, some of which features at one gate.

South gate; *c.* 1800; architect perhaps James Wyatt.

Here are the ruins of a rubble structure with an L-plan, having brick dressings to a round-arched leading window. The main interest, however, is a small but sophisticated gatescreen comprised of a pair of Classical piers, both with a truncated Doric pilaster to each corner, which support plain cappings with dies as bases to a pair of Coade stone urns possibly to Wyatt's design, very like those at Pakenham Hall (*q.v.*) but here there are husks as swags. These rare survivals are clearly from a consignment ordered by Lord Sunderlin in 1799, as recorded in Coade's Gallery.

North gate; *c.* 1810; architect not known.

Only a quarter of a mile from the southern entrance and with the grand gate in between is a distinguished Classical porter's lodge, still standing imperious in a farmyard in a clutter of agricultural paraphernalia, gates and sheds, some tacked on. Generously proportioned, which probably accounts for its survival as a barn, it had an attic storey behind its main single-bay front of limestone ashlar, the windows set in a semicircular-arched recess with an impost course, all crowned by a shallow pediment. The first OS map shows it to have had side wings in 1837.

Grand gate; 1810; architect not known; *demolished.*

Watson Mills

Located as an impressive vista stop on an axis with the approach from the little village of Ballynacarrigy was an extensive and elegant Classical entrance screen with an appropriate matching lodge behind in attendance. Sadly, this is all now a thing of the past but can be described from an old photograph in the possession of Mr Watson Mills. What tantalising glimpse there is of the lodge suggests that it was much as that at the northern gate, certainly having a pedimented main front facing the avenue. The gatescreen is dominated by a pair of *aedicules*, really repeats of the lodge frontispieces but with the added elaboration of recessed supporting panels, paterae to the spandrels and mutules to the pediments. These ashlar structures act as giant gate pillars to the main spear-topped carriage gates and the flanking postern gates. The composition continues in more conventional fashion with pillars and convex quadrant walls with further recessed panels.

Curwen 1818; *LGI* (1904); *IGS Bulletin* (Oct.–Dec. 1970); Kelly 1990; Casey and Rowan 1993; *IADS* (2007); Robinson 2012.

21. BELLANALACK, Moate; pre-1837/*c.* 1860.
A modest rendered single-storey hip-roofed lodge with an elongated three-window main front below eaves with exposed rounded rafter toes. It would appear to be a reworking of, or a replacement for, an earlier structure on the site at the entrance to a property in the mid-nineteenth century of the Adamson family. Derelict.

22. BELLMOUNT, Mullingar (2).
A seat of the O'Reilly or Reilly family to which neither of the earlier gatekeepers' lodges appears to have survived.

North lodge; pre-1837; *demolished.*

South lodge; pre-1837/*c.* 1890.
Single-storey, built off an L-plan, its canted projection below an equivalent roof that is otherwise hipped. Roughcast with a later extension to the left-hand side. Occupied. A late Victorian replacement for an earlier lodge on the site.

23. BELLVIEW, Mullingar (2).
Both lodges indicated on the 1837 OS map have gone almost without trace; very tall convex quadrants in rubble stone are all that remain at one entrance, minus their central carriage pillars and probably flanking postilion openings. A property of Robert Walsh in 1814 and of Thomas Walsh in 1837.

Leet 1814; Lewis 1837.

24. BELMORE PLACE, Ballymore; pre-1914; *demolished.*
An estate in the mid-nineteenth century of John Fetherstonhaugh Lowry (1819–83), who was of that family of Pomeroy House, Co. Tyrone.

LGI (1904).

25. BELVEDERE, Mullingar (3).
The magical property by the banks of Lough Ennell created by the notorious Robert Rochfort, 1st earl of Belvedere, from the 1740s as an adjunct to his main seat of Gaulston (*q.v.*). His choice of architects was clearly sounder than that of his unfortunate wives, the result of which was Castle's delightful Palladian villa, a Thomas Wright Gothic folly and the extraordinary Jealous Wall, all from an era prior to that of the gate lodge becoming widespread, although the first OS map of 1837 does suggest a pair situated well within the demesne, now gone. Hereabouts is a good early Victorian gatescreen with cast-iron piers having anthemion tops. Beyond these are walls over which are Rochfort lions with shields in paws.

Intermediate lodge; *c.* 1860.
Again remote from the public road is a derelict single-storey standard cottage with a hipped roof and matching hall projection; roughcast with Tudor-style label mouldings and toothed stone dressings. Probably built for Charles Brinsley Marlay (1831–1912), who had inherited Belvedere in 1847. It was

he who greatly improved the estate and altered the house over his lengthy occupation, commissioning a succession of architects.

Outer entrance; *c.* 1890; architect possibly Walter Glynn Doolin; *demolished.*
The late Victorian lodge has gone but is survived by an ostentatious gatescreen comprised of a pair of carriage pillars in quarry-faced stone crowned again with lions holding shields (Marlay had assumed the Rochfort crest and name without using the latter), which are linked by concave quadrants to two lesser pillars carrying vermiculated rusticated ball finials. The whole extends yet further in straight screens to terminate in outer pillars with plain ball finials. Walter Glynn Doolin had been employed to terrace the front lawn and his commission may have been broadened to include the demesne boundary.

LGI (1904); *Country Life* (22 and 27 June 1961); *IAR* (Autumn 2002).

BELVEDERE LODGE (see BLOOMFIELD)

26. BELVILLE COTTAGE, Mullingar (2).
A property identified by the 1854 valuation as having two gatekeepers' lodges of Florence Mahony, one of which existed in 1837; both now removed.

Griffith 1848–60.

27. BELVILLE, Athlone; *c.* 1825.
At some distance from its gates is a delightful single-storey porter's lodge, its short three-bay symmetrical avenue front with round-headed openings, the sash windows having spoked glazing. The hipped roof originally extended to create a verandah, with four spindly iron columns for support but subsequently reduced to two *in antis*, formed by wing wall projections. Roughcast, occupied but derelict like the big house, in 1824 home to William Jones and thirteen years later to Gustavus Jones. Spear-topped gates with quatrefoil motifs.

Pigot 1824; Lewis 1837.

28. BENISON LODGE, Castlepollard; pre-1837; *demolished.*
A seat in 1814 of Thomas Hutchinson Smyth, upon whose death in 1830 it passed to his son, Revd Thomas Smyth (1796–1874). Their home lies derelict, its gate lodge having been removed before 1914.

Leet 1814; *LGI* (1904).

29. BENOWN, Glassan (2).
'Harmony Hall', as this place has alternatively been called, is a house of *c.* 1788, built by Colonel William Caulfeild, who also added two lodged entrances before his death in 1831, one quite unique.

East gate; *c.* 1800.
The public road from Glassan bisects a circular forecourt comprising two great harled segmental walls, that to the park containing widely spaced postilion openings with moulded granite architraves flanking the central carriage gates, their pillars having sculpted stone corniced cappings and a continuous moulded plinth. Opposite, a single-storey curved porter's lodge lay mostly hidden, only a few openings piercing the equivalent wide screen wall. Now a modern extension has spilled into the forecourt, spoiling the effect.

West gate; *c.* 1820.
Not quite opposite its entrance is this modest standard gabled cottage.

LGI (1904); English 1973.

30. BLOOMFIELD, Mullingar; pre-1837; *demolished.*
A property in the early nineteenth century of Abraham Boyd (1760–1822), who in 1815 married as his second wife the widow of the 2nd earl of Belvedere of the neighbouring estate, from which liaison originated the Boyd-Rochforts of Middleton Park (*q.v.*). In 1842 Bloomfield was purchased by Col. John Caulfeild, who renamed it 'Belvedere Lodge'. A modern house has been built on the site of the lodge.

LGI (1904); *BPB* (1929).

BRACCA CASTLE (see COOLALOUGH)

31. BRACKLYN CASTLE, Delvin; 1821; architect possibly Francis Johnston.
An extraordinary fantasy (*below*) to encounter on a quiet Irish secondary road is this inappropriate introduction to the understated late Georgian villa within: basically a pair of grottoes brought together as porter's 'day and night' rooms linked by a covered carriage archway. Constructed in selected limestone boulders in a sort of rustic Baroque manner, with the emphasis on a pyramidal theme to create a Gothic roofscape. Each 3.7m² room has a brick vaulted ceiling below a delightful bellcast slated roof, the external corners strengthened by sturdy finialled turrets framing windows with segmental heads and relieving arches repeated in the main carriage archway, which is crowned by a pointed belfry with some brick dressing, a cut-stone shield and date-stone. To the rear the windows are reduced to lunettes with mock arrowloops. Beyond, a pair of postern gates is flanked by scaled-down versions of the porter's rooms, with relieving niches and pyramidal roofs, much as the little mausoleum in the demesne. The composition is completed by low concave-walled quadrants terminating in miniature obelisks. Now restored and maintained as a folly—when did the last gatekeeper escape the drip, drip, drip?

James Fetherstonhaugh had commissioned this and seen its completion just one year before his death in 1822. He had also been responsible for the house, which looks to pre-date the lodge by about twenty years and which bears a resemblance in form to Francis Johnston's Ballynegall (*q.v.*). Being a habitual builder, he had also created Rockview (*q.v.*) and its attendant lodge nearby, either as a retirement home or dower house. Both these are attributable to the architect, which raises the questions of whether Fetherstonhaugh would have gone elsewhere for design work on his remarkable new entrance and whether it offers a new insight into another side of Johnston's personality.

IFR; Howley 1993; Casey and Rowan 1993.

32. BRYANSTOWN, Mullingar (2).

West lodge; *c.* 1850.

A tiny derelict standard lodge with steeply hipped roof and projecting gabled hall under the eaves; harled rubble walls.

East lodge; pre-1914; *demolished.*

A lodge that was located opposite the entrance to a property in 1854 of Hugh Duignan.

Griffith 1848–60.

33. CALVERSTOWN, Tyrellspass; *c.* 1850.

A modest single-storey gabled cottage, derelict and lacking its avenue. A seat in the mid-nineteenth century of the Hornidge family.

34. CARN PARK, Moate (2).

South lodge; *c.* 1820.

A pleasant and commodious 1½-storey vernacular gabled cottage, built by Travers Adamson. Roughcast, occupied, improved and located opposite its gates by the crossroads.

North lodge; pre-1914; *demolished.*

A later lodge, built after 1837, perhaps for William Gustavus Adamson, has been removed.

Leet 1814; Lewis 1837.

35. CARRICK, Collinstown; *c.* 1845.

Derelict and lying low to the road is a 1½-storey symmetrical gabled structure with a single-storey breakfront gabled hall. Roughcast with ornamental foiled bargeboards in Picturesque English cottage style. Erected, to a house also known as 'Lough Bawn', for George Battersby (1802–80), a Dublin barrister who succeeded his father here in 1839.

LGI (1904).

36. CARRICK, Rochfortbridge; pre-1837; *demolished.*

Another of the many seats in the county of the Fetherstonhaugh family; its lodge was located opposite the gates and the first OS map suggests that it had a central hall projection.

37. CARTONTROY, Athlone; pre-1913; *demolished.*

A property in the mid-nineteenth century of the Sproule family.

38. CASTLE DALY, Ballynahown (2).

An estate from the seventeenth century of the O'Daly family, of whom Joseph Morgan Daly created the earlier of its entrances.

Main gate; *c.* 1835.

Prominently located at a crossroads is a wide screen of rubble walls containing carriage and flanking postilion gates with four squat ashlar pillars, probably reduced in height, judging by the scale of the bold plinth mouldings, and carrying dainty outer ball finials and puny toy lions to the carriage pillars. Within, an abandoned and crumbling lodge, still of some presence and not beyond saving. Single-storey below a steeply pitched hipped roof, which extends beyond the short main front to form a portico of, most peculiarly, three dumpy cylindrical Classical

columns, the central of which is plonked in front of the large single window opening. Stucco-finished and sporting a continuous serrated fascia board suggestive of a later make-over.

Secondary gate; *c.* 1855.

A ruinous single-storey rubble-built structure, again with its short front addressing the avenue. Presumably erected for George McDonnell, who bought the place when it was offered for sale as an incumbered estate in 1852, when its name was altered to 'Kilcleagh Park'.

Fraser 1838; Griffith 1848–60; Casey and Rowan 1993.

39. CASTLELOST RECTORY, Rochfortbridge; pre-1837; *demolished.*

A glebe house built in 1810, the gate lodge to which may have been contemporary. The former lies a roofless shell. Built during the incumbency of Revd Samuel Lucas (1768–1850), who was rector here from 1801 until his death.

Lewis 1837; Leslie and Wallace 2009.

40. CASTLETOWN-KINDALEN RECTORY, Castletown Geoghegan; *c.* 1850.

Alternatively known as Vastina parish, its gate lodge post-dates the glebe house built in 1813 and looks to be from the incumbency (1844–76) of Revd John Francis Battersby (1809–77). A modest single-storey cottage, its short two-bay elevation faces the avenue immediately behind the gates. Hip-roofed and rendered, a longer two-bay front is parallel to the road, set back from the boundary wall to accommodate a pedestrian gate. Occupied.

Lewis 1837; Leslie and Wallace 2009.

41. CHARLEVILLE, Rathconrath; pre-1837/*c.* 1880.

A property purchased in the early nineteenth century by Charles Kelly, the gate lodge to which was replaced by his grandson of the same name, who inherited in 1881, the successor opposite its gates. This is a commodious single-storey gabled Italianate-style building, raised off an L-plan, with a hallway below a catslide roof in the internal corner. Rendered with neat toothed brick dressings to round-headed windows under foil- and wave-carved bargeboards and a dainty brick corbelled chimney-stack on a stone base. In its abandoned state it too awaits replacement. The place for some reason was renamed 'Lunestown' in the mid-nineteenth century by John Hubert Kelly.

LGI (1904).

CLARE ISLAND **(see DERRYMACEGAN)**

42. CLONDRISSE, Killucan; *c.* 1877.

Seemingly dating from the arrival here of Richard Reynell Jr, when the property valuation rose by £2, is this enchanting little forerunner of the twentieth-century double-fronted bungalow. Single-storey of standard format, below its hipped roof is a cluttered front of a pair of semi-octagonal bay windows with equivalent roofs flanking the projecting gabled hall, its door having a charming trefoil fanlight and intricately carved bargeboards; the whole in a stucco-effect rendered finish.

43. CLONHUGH or CLANHUGH, Ballynafid (4).

Until the mid-nineteenth century this was a lodge by Lough Owel of the Forbes family, earls of Granard of Castle Forbes, Co. Longford (*q.v.*), to which was a solitary gatekeeper's cottage opposite the gates.

Early lodge; pre-1838; *demolished.*

The first OS map indicates a rectangular building with a central projecting hall.

The Forbes seem to have let the place until it was purchased by Colonel Fulke Southwell Greville-Nugent (1821–83), who commissioned architect William Caldbeck to build him one of his typical Italianate villas on the site. It was completed by 1867, in good time to be an appropriate seat of the 1st Baron Greville, to which honour he was raised in 1869. The estate was also suitably furnished with two new porters' lodges in addition to 'extensive farm-offices and stabling'.

Main entrance; *c.* 1867; architect William Francis Caldbeck.

In a decidedly more flamboyant Italianate

style than the house is this single-storey two-roomed lodge, built in good random ashlar with an abundance of bold woodwork highlights in carved corbels to eaves, decorative mock purlin ends to the verges and, to the short avenue elevation, an entrance porch having ornamental brackets with pendants carrying a bellcast roof with scalloped slates. The road front has two segmentally headed two-over-two sash windows in matching recesses; to the ridge is a corbelled cut-stone chimney-stack on a plinth. Recently rescued from dereliction by the present owner and his architect Martin Reynolds with sensitivity, extended to a double pile.

Inner gate; *c.* 1867; architect probably William Francis Caldbeck.

By way of variety is this Tudor Revival 1½-storey affair, within the estate by a railway crossing. Constructed in similar random uncoursed stone with label mouldings to the two-window-bay façade and other openings. To the side is a single-storey hall below a catslide roof. Modernised with inappropriate windows and plain bargeboards. Occupied and well tended.

Ballynafid gate; *c.* 1910.
A single-storey gabled lodge with big porch projection. Roughcast with Edwardian mock-Elizabethan half-timbered-effect apexes over roughcast-finished walls. Occupied. Probably built for the 3rd baron, Charles Beresford Fulke Greville, who succeeded to the estate on the death of his father in 1909.

IB (1 Feb. 1864 and 15 Dec. 1867); *BPB* (1929); Casey and Rowan 1993.

44. CLONLOST, Killucan (4).
An estate of the Nugent family, whose grand house now lies in ruins, its importance underlined by the number of porters' lodges it boasted, only one of which survives. Of the three existing in 1837, that to the northern gate has been demolished, along with its replacement opposite. That remaining of the southern lodges is a modest standard roughcast structure with a wide-eaved hipped roof. Attached is a gabled extension; derelict. Appearing to date from *c.* 1830, in the time of James Nugent.

Brewer 1825; Lewis 1837.

45. CLONMOYLE, Mullingar (2).
Both lodges, one of which pre-dated 1837, have gone. An estate in 1814 of David Jones, which by 1846 had passed to Charles Joly.

Leet 1814; Slater 1846.

46. CLONYN CASTLE, Delvin (4).
The ancient seat since the twelfth century of the Nugents, later earls of Westmeath, whose seventeenth-century house cloaked in Georgian Gothic mantle remains. This had in 1837 two lodged entrances on the north and south approaches but, strangely, that from the village of Delvin stayed unmanned until the demesne had passed to Fulke Southwell Greville-Nugent, who had come to it as son-in-law of the 8th earl of Westmeath (1785–1871), who died without leaving male issue. Greville-Nugent assumed that surname in 1866 and by 1869 was created 1st Earl Greville. He was by 1854 already ensconced here with his wife Rosa, whom he married in 1840, and commenced an extensive programme of redevelopment of the demesne, which included new and replacement gatekeepers' lodges, and culminated in the great Victorian castellated mansion designed by John McCurdy and his partner William Mitchell in the late 1860s and early 1870s.

Delvin entrance; pre-1914.

The lodge, built after 1837, lies a ruin behind all that survives contemporary with the late eighteenth-century improvements of the old Nugent house in the form of a very fine Gothic gatescreen. Rubble-walled quadrants frame screen walls with pointed-arched postilion gates, on each side of a pair of lofty octagonal carriage pillars embellished with delicately sculpted engaged cluster-columns linked by a Gothic-arched arcade surround. The cappings carry pedestals now lacking their ball finials. A very fine introduction to the demesne, which has been allowed to deteriorate disgracefully. There is an almost identical pair of pillars to the County Kildare demesne of Leixlip Castle (*q.v.*).

North entrance; pre-1837/*c.* 1850.
Here are the remnants of an old rubble-stone screen wall with a single postern gate. This may have been contemporary with the earlier lodge on the site. Its replacement is a standard 1½-storey gabled Picturesque cottage with carved continuous-bracket bargeboards and a central projecting single-storey hall. Occupied.

South entrance; pre-1837; *demolished.*
West entrance; pre-1914; *demolished.*
BPB (1929); Casey and Rowan 1993.

47. CLOONAGH, Castletown Geoghegan; *c.* 1840.
Alongside the gates is a pair of single-storey harled gabled semi-detached cottages with brick eaves corbel course. Vernacular, derelict, now serving as byres. Probably built in the time here of John Logan.

48. COOKESBOROUGH, Killucan (2).
The Cooke mansion and its two pre-1837 gate lodges are things of the past, the latter having gone by 1914.

49. COOLA COTTAGE, Kilbeggan; pre-1837; *demolished.*
A property in the late Georgian period of Gustavus Lambert, which by the early nineteenth century was let to the Conolly family.

50. COOLALOUGH, Kilbeggan; pre-1837; *demolished.*
Otherwise known as 'Bracca Castle', described in 1825 as a handsome modern seat of the Handy family.

Brewer 1825.

51. COOLAMBER, Lismacaffry (2).
Not to be confused with Coolamber Manor (*q.v.*) just across the County Longford boundary is this large house, home to a succession of owners named Philip O'Reilly, which, like nearby Daramona (*q.v.*), displays mid-nineteenth-century features reminiscent of the work of the Lanyon and Lynn architectural practice of Belfast. At that same period both lodges may have been updated.

North gate; *c.* 1830.
Terminating the shallow right-hand quadrant of the entrance screen, forward of the carriage gates, is a standard single-storey porter's lodge, its pair of canted bay windows flanking the doorway looking like Victorian additions, as on the house. Ruinous and ivy-covered.

South gate; *c.* 1830.
Behind the decorative gatescreen with octagonal stone posts is a lodge similar to that above, its bay windows in rendered walls accommodated below the high eaves of a hipped roof.

LGI (1904).

52. COOLURE, Castlepollard (2).
A big plain Georgian house of *c.* 1775, built for the future Admiral Sir Thomas Pakenham (1757–1836) on the banks of Lough Derravaragh, part-financed from an inheritance of his brother, the 2nd Baron Longford of neighbouring Pakenham Hall (*q.v.*). Neither of its gatekeepers' lodges, which may date from the building of the house or improvements carried out in 1821, has survived.

Casey and Rowan 1993; Pakenham 2000.

53. CORBETSTOWN, Killucan; *c.* 1855.
In a sad state of advanced dilapidation is this highly decorative little lodge with a plethora of ornamental features. Single-storey standard, its shallow-pitched gabled roof is embellished with the most delicate of cast-

53. Corbetstown.

iron cresting to a roof of scalloped slates with exposed rafter toes and pretty perforated foiled and cusped carved bargeboards rising to pendant hip-knobs. The stone-dressed front door is flanked by lattice-paned bipartite casement windows in walls finished in harling, which has fallen away to reveal high-quality brickwork dressings in rubble construction. Lighting the attic rooms are surprising Georgian Gothic-style pointed windows with Y-traceried sashes. When John D'Arcy died unmarried, the place devolved on a kinsman who lived in England, and Joseph E. Purser is recorded as proprietor in 1854.

Griffith 1848–60; *LGI* (1904).

54. CORNAHER, Kilbeggan; pre-1837; *demolished.*
A late Georgian house, for long the seat of the Very Revd Charles Vignoles, dean of Ossory, and his sons, situated at the end of a long avenue through pleasant parkland, at the foot of which was a 'gatehouse', according to the 1837 OS map.

LG (1886).

55. CORNAMAGH CEMETERY, Athlone; *c.* 1870.
A standard 1½-storey gabled cottage with a canopied front door below eaves with exposed rafter toes, broken by two attic gablet windows. Roughcast, occupied and immaculately maintained at the entrance to a graveyard which first accepted burials in 1871.

CORR (see GLENCARA)

56. CORREAGH COTTAGE, Kilbeggan; pre-1837.
At the gates is a stone ruin to a property in the early nineteenth century of Colonel Hearn.

Pigot 1824; Lewis 1837.

57. THE COTTAGE, Rochfortbridge; pre-1837; *demolished.*
Another seat of the Shiel family of Mahonstown (*q.v.*), the lodge to which had gone by 1914.

58. CRADDANSTOWN, Raharney; pre-1837.
Forming part of, and alongside, the entrance screen are the roofless remains of a lodge in rubble construction, fronting the road in a three-bay elevation, with doorway to right-hand side.

In the first half of the nineteenth century an estate of Lockhart Ramage.

Leet 1814; Lewis 1837.

59. CREGGAN CASTLE, Athlone (2).

The sorry remnants of a once-proud demesne of the Longworth family. All that survive of the house are two early nineteenth-century Gothic towers and, at the now lodgeless entrances, a pair of once-magnificent ashlar carriage pillars in chunky Baroque manner with outstanding sculpted mouldings, now horribly disfigured.

60. CULLEEN, Mullingar; *c.* 1845 *demolished.*
The gate lodge may have been added to the property after it passed *c.* 1840 from Thomas McEvoy to Godfrey Levinge.

Fraser 1838; Slater 1846.

61. CURRISTOWN, Killucan; pre-1837/*c.* 1860.
A seat of the Purdon family since the early eighteenth century, the original gate lodge to which was replaced by the present structure not long after the 1854 valuation records its predecessor as being unoccupied and its immediate lessor as being Augustus C. Purdon. What survives is a lovingly maintained 1½-storey four-bay gabled building in coursed stone with a breakfront single-storey hall, similarly gabled, having ornamental woodwork. Modernised with rendered toothed dressings about neat new square casements; single-storey lean-to on right-hand side.

IFR.

62. DARAMONA, Rathowen (2).
A good mid-nineteenth-century Italianate villa, built for William Wilson, a noted astronomer of Lark Hill, south Dublin (*q.v.*), which shows characteristics of the work of the Belfast architectural firm of Lanyon and Lynn, perhaps of their erstwhile assistant Thomas Turner. These features can also be seen at neighbouring Coolamber (*q.v.*). Not enough survives of the gate lodge to allow attribution to anyone.

Main entrance; *c.* 1855; *demolished.*

Side entrance; *c.* 1855.

Only a front elevation in stone remains, good inner cast-iron posts and railings framed by outer ashlar pillars.

LGI (1904).

63. DARLINGTON LODGE, Rathconrath; pre-1837.
Of the lodge, to a property in 1837 of A. McDonnell, only one gable wall survives.

Lewis 1837.

64. DERRYMACEGAN, Finnea (2).
A seat previously called 'Clare Island' and lately 'Gore Point', after the peninsula on which it is situated in Lough Sheelin and after the Gores who founded it. Their lodge, located on the original road that skirted the estate, has been isolated by a new route to the north.

Outer lodge; *c.* 1770.

A mid-Georgian two-storey gatehouse, remarkable both for its survival and for its size, its generous proportions probably being explained by its description on the 1837 OS map as a 'Police Office'. Perfectly square on plan and built in rubble stone, harled and limewashed, it is placed forward of the gates, its road front with a two-window bay to the ground floor and a single loft light tight to the eaves. A rare example of late eighteenth-century vernacular architecture, it lies boarded up. There are various mono-pitched additions.

Inner lodge; pre-1913; *demolished.*
Probably built by Captain Alexander Walker, who is recorded as living here between 1837 and 1856.

Lewis 1837; Slater 1856.

65. DERRYMORE, Killucan; pre-1837; *demolished.*
An estate that had a succession of proprietors: the Nugents in the eighteenth century, a Captain Daly in 1814 and the Fetherstonhaugh family of Bracklyn Castle (*q.v.*) in the mid-nineteenth century. Their house lies a ruin.

Leet 1814; *LGI* (1904).

66. DONORE, Multyfarnham (3).
When the Revd D.A. Beaufort visited the property on the banks of Lough Derravaragh on 13 October 1808 he found 'a noble house in wretched repair, the offices almost ruinous—alas'. The cleric had discovered an estate neglected after the death without issue of Sir Peter Nugent, 2nd baronet, eleven years before and the absence of his nephew and heir, who was to drown in 1810. Happily for the place, it was resurrected by the latter's son, Sir Percy Nugent (1797–1874), 1st baronet of the second creation, who also furnished it with at least two of its porters' lodges to grace what in 1845 was described as 'a handsome, substantial Grecian mansion'.

North entrance; pre-1837; *demolished.*
Located well within the demesne, this early lodge has gone without trace.

West entrance; pre-1914; *demolished.*
The lodge has been replaced by a twentieth-century bungalow, but there are the remains of a once-extensive gatescreen in square outer ashlar pillars with recessed panels.

East entrance; *c.* 1845.
Built in coursed rubble, harled, is a 1½-storey gabled lodge with high eaves and central gabled hall breakfront. Three-bay symmetrical, with dentil ornament to the bargeboards, and a stone chimney-stack. It lies derelict as a manifestation of the property's final demise, the big house having been demolished.

TCD (Beaufort MS 4033); *Parliamentary Gazetteer*; *BPB* (1929).

67. DORRINGTON, Ballymore; pre-1914; *demolished.*
Only the stables survive, both the big house and its lodge having gone. Robert St George Gray (1797–1856) seems to have acquired the property from Robert Jones about the 1840s, and his son William Henry Gray commissioned architect Thomas Drew in 1887 to plan alterations to the house.

IFR; IAA.

68. DRUMCREE, Collinstown (2).
Yet another fine Classical mansion of the eighteenth-century Westmeath Smyths with which they blessed the county but which has since gone unappreciated. Drumcree was a distinguished house of *c.* 1750 that now lies derelict, and its gatekeepers' lodges have fared no better.

West entrance; pre-1813; *demolished.*
A lodge removed before 1900, perhaps that which Atkinson in 1813 described as 'the grand entrance to this villa' and 'that beautiful gate-house which stands beside it'.

East entrance; *c.* 1830.
A good sculpted stone gate sweep with round inner carriage pillars and spear-topped railings. Across the road by the church at a T-junction is a ruinous three-bay single-storey gabled lodge in roughcast finish with the remains of decorative rectangular margined glazing, which dates the windows, and perhaps the structure. If so, the builder was Robert Smyth, who succeeded to the place on the death of his father William in 1827.

Atkinson 1815; *LGI* (1904).

DRUMCREE RECTORY (see KILCUMNEY RECTORY)

69. DRUMMAN, Rochfortbridge; pre-1914; *demolished.*
A property in 1853 of George Bagnall, the gate lodge to which was erected after 1837.

Griffith 1848–60.

70. DRUMMAN or DROMMIN LODGE, Rochfortbridge; pre-1837; *demolished.*
A seat in the late eighteenth century of the Tyrrell family, which by 1837 was occupied by T.M. Carew.

Taylor and Skinner 1778; 1969 [1783]; Lewis 1837.

71. DUNBODEN PARK, Rochfortbridge (3).
A Georgian house, now a ruin, of the Cooper family, which in 1837 had two lodged gates. It was remodelled in 1866 by architect Sandham Symes, who may also have been responsible for the third lodge on the eastern approach, commissioned by Colonel Joshua Henry Cooper (1831–1901), who had inherited the property on the death of his father in 1850.

West entrance; pre-1837; *demolished.*
Here at the old main gate was the consequence and symmetry of a pair of Georgian lodges, now lost without trace.

Middle entrance; *c.* 1835.
A derelict single-storey three-bay gabled rubble-built cottage, its door to the right-hand side.

East entrance; *c.* 1860; architect perhaps Sandham Symes.
At a narrow disused gateway behind a tall wall is a derelict mid-Victorian single-storey lodge in rendered finish, built off an L-plan. In the internal angle is an entrance porch supported on two cast-iron posts.

DB (15 Aug. 1866); *LGI* (1904).

DURROW ABBEY (see COUNTY OFFALY)

72. DYSART, Delvin; *c.* 1840.
A distinctive country house built in 1757 by Nicholas Ogle, the gate lodge to which was erected for his grandson (1768–1849) of the same name. It is deceptive, being roofless and rubble-built, with the gable to the park containing a dressed-stone pointed-arched doorway, giving it the feel of a tiny antique abandoned church. Single-storey, blind to the visitor and its gates, the avenue elevation has two latticed cast-iron casement windows. It pays no heed to the distant gatescreen of four excellent cast-iron posts in the form of Greek stelae with anthemion and sunflower motifs more indicative of the period. The Ogle family still lives at Dysart.

IFR; Casey and Rowan 1993.

73. EAST HILL, Glassan; *c.* 1845.
The charming late Georgian cottage residence, though built in 1803 by the Temples of nearby Waterston (*q.v.*), was home from 1807 until 1862 of the Cuppaidge family, of whom it was probably John L. Cuppaidge who added the presentable little porter's lodge. Square on plan, single-storey standard with exposed rafter toes to the oversailing eaves of its pyramidal roof, which rises to a central chimney-stack. Roughcast and immaculately maintained.

English 1973; Casey and Rowan 1993.

74. EDMONDSTOWN, Collinstown (2).
Another seat of the Reynell family of Killynon (*q.v.*), of whom Robert Reynell lived here until his death in 1834.

Main entrance; pre-1837.
A nondescript blocked-up single-storey gabled structure.

Rear entrance; pre-1837.
An extensive derelict and ivy-shrouded 1½-storey gabled lodge.

LGI (1904).

75. FARDRUM, Athlone; *c.* 1845.
Four good square pillars with side railings to match its gates. Opposite is a two-bay single-storey lodge built in rubble stone off an L-plan; hipped roof with a brick eaves course. Ruinous. Built for Edwin Thomas Mathews.

Lewis 1837.

76. FARNAGH, Moate; *c.* 1860.
A single-storey gatekeeper's lodge, square on plan with a two-bay rendered front, door and window below a pyramidal roof, central chimney-stack and a pretty decorative perforated wavy fascia board to its eaves.

Probably built by Adam Fairbrother, to whom the property passed from the Wynne family about 1860.

Griffith 1848–60.

77. FARRA, Bunbrosna; *c.* 1850.

Built in random ashlar to form a solid single-storey standard lodge below a steeply hipped roof rising to a pair of stone diagonally set chimney-stacks on a rectangular base. Central projecting hip-roofed hallway with side windows. Well maintained but with plastic Georgian-effect lights. An estate in 1854 of Patrick Cormick.

Griffith 1848–60.

78. GARROW, Athlone; pre-1876; *demolished.*
A lodge built after 1837 by Jonas Swaine, corn merchant and miller of Connaught Street, Athlone.

Slater 1846; 1856; Griffith 1848–60.

79. GARTLANDSTOWN, Collinstown; *c.* 1845.
A modest roughcast standard lodge below a hipped roof springing from a corbelled clipped eaves course. Sheeted door and margined glazing to windows. Vacant. A property in 1854 of Michael Hope.

Griffith 1848–60.

80. GAULSTOWN, Castlepollard; pre-1837; *demolished.*
The delicious Palladian cottage built by the Lill family about 1730, which a century later was home to Hubert De Burgh.

81. GAULSTON PARK, Rochfortbridge (4).

Leo Daly

Now a past glory is the demesne of the Rochforts, earls of Belvedere, with its grand winged eighteenth-century house and formal garden, notable for being beloved of Swift and Dr Delany but notorious as a place of incarceration for 30 years of Mary by her husband Robert Rochfort, 1st earl of Belvedere. Purchased in 1784 by John Browne, later 1st Baron Kilmaine (1730–94), the place was sold in 1918 and burnt down in 1920. Its gate lodges of various indeterminate dates have all gone, a record of but one of which survives in a photograph of *c.* 1980. It shows what was little more than a sentry-box, probably dating from about 1790, after the Browne family had acquired the property. Square on plan in harled rubble with a dressed pointed window and stone eaves band to a shallow pyramidal roof, but no chimney-stack evident. Without physical evidence it would be difficult to refute that it witnessed the famous visitors and tragic events of the early eighteenth century.

LGI (1904); *BPB* (1929); Bence-Jones 1988; Malins and Glin 1976.

82. GAYBROOK, Mullingar (2).
In 1786 Mr and Mrs Smyth were 'Choosing site for new house' with the assistance of Revd D.A. Beaufort. Ralph Smyth (1751–1817) had just purchased the place from John Gay and construction began the following year. But it was his son Robert Smyth (1801–78), who had succeeded to the place on the death of his elder brother in 1827, who was responsible for the two gate lodges at different stages in his life.

East entrance; *c.* 1835.

Rather earlier than its appearance suggests is this 1½-storey lodge, generous in plan and proportions, its main front elevation masquerading as single-storey with a series of round-headed arches, those to the main rooms forming recesses for flat-arched windows, flanking those to a projecting canted bay which rise full height along with the fanlit double-leafed panelled doors. Within, this bay extends to form an extraordinarily extravagant feature for a gate lodge in an octagonal hallway rising 1½ storeys to a delicately vaulted plaster ceiling. Built in good cut-rubble facing, it has tall eaves with corbel blocks to a hipped roof accommodating loft rooms lit by windows to opposing ends. In 2000 this fine building lay disgracefully derelict and neglected. There is a good gatescreen of cast-iron railings flanking matching carriage gates and posts, to the left-hand side of which the estate wall is pierced by a pedestrian opening.

West entrance; *c.* 1850.

Conspicuously located at a crossroads and similarly abandoned and sealed up on a disused avenue is another good solid porter's lodge, which sometime also served as a post office. Single-storey standard below a hipped roof with a prominent projection in its gabled front hall. To the road elevation is a tripartite window to look out for visitors. Built off a cruciform plan in a fabric of neat rubble dressed with cream brick that is now

exposed, probably having been harled. Straight-walled gatescreen with decent modest ashlar pillars.

TCD (Beaufort MS 7941); Burke 1854–5; *IFR.*

83. GIGGINSTOWN, Collinstown; pre-1837/*c.* 1855; architect probably J.S. Mulvany.

A property for many years of the Dardis family, whose gate lodge it may have been, shown on the first OS map, or perhaps of their successor, Capt. Brabazon O'Connor. In any case, the present elegant neo-Classical villa and its splendid entrance complex are replacements built for Miss Elizabeth Busby, who inherited the estate from O'Connor in 1853. Frederick O'Dwyer has attributed both on stylistic grounds to J.S. Mulvany. The fact that the gate lodge shares a distinctive characteristic with half a dozen such buildings in counties Cork, Limerick, Tipperary and Waterford, then unique to architect C.F. Anderson, can only be explained by Mulvany's being aware of them, for Anderson emigrated to North America in 1849. This singular characteristic is in the form of four stylish Doric columns, one to each recess on the main corners of an otherwise single-storey gabled lodge that has a projecting front hall to form a standard plan. The columns, rising off a bold plinth, contrast with the relatively crude gable pediments with their mutules that carry around the eaves extending from an

84. Glenanea, Samuel Woolley perspective (Castletown Trust Collection).

entablatured band. This stonework compares with white harled walls containing a series of narrow round-headed windows to main elevation and hall sides. The larger flat-arched windows to the end gables had dividing sash boxes to form bipartite lights. To the ridge is a stone-banded paired stack. The gatescreen is extensive, innovative and less than graceful, with a strange mix of shapes, comprising carriage pillars tapering to four-faced pedimented cappings on which are peculiar barrel-topped protrusions which are reflected on a series of secondary pillars in railed screens which extend to concave quadrant walls terminating in more agreeable tapering pillars.

Leet 1814; Lewis 1837; Griffith 1848–60; *IGS Journal* (2000).

84. GLENANEA, Collinstown (2).
Previously called 'Ralphsdale' after its builder, Ralph Smyth, who before his death in 1797 had commissioned the English architect Samuel Woolley to design his relatively restrained Classical house. No such inhibition is evident in his scheme for the main entrance to the demesne.

Main entrance; 1796/*c.* 1860; architect Samuel Woolley.

Here was the most opulent Classical gatescreen in the country, the centre-piece of which was based on a design by Robert Adam for that at Syon House, Middlesex. This became known to Woolley through being illustrated in the Scottish architect's *The works in architecture* (1778). What was realised was like a display for Mrs Coade's Stone in a variety of unique cream earthenware products from her Lambeth works in London. In 1799 Mrs Coade described it as 'a Colonade and Gateway with a crest on it, Statues in niches'. The great

central round-headed carriage archway is flanked by giant pilasters with, in their recessed panels, lion masks emitting branches of foliage. The Corinthian capitals carry an entablature with an ornate frieze of paterae, swags, fluting and a carved dentil course, while crowning the whole, on a swagged plinth, was a splendid unicorn. The archway was flanked by four-bay screens of rails and Ionic columns stopped by, where Adam had sentry-box lodges, grand pillars niched to receive beautiful statues of Flora and Pomona (the base of each inscribed COADE LONDON 1792), with plaques over and their cappings topped by decorative urns. Not content with the pretension of Adam's design, Smyth and Woolley extended it with tall concave-walled quadrants containing postilion doors and terminating in great blind archways with round-headed recesses, plaques and more urns above. That this extravaganza was executed is borne out by the first OS map, which also indicates a

structure behind the right-hand 'archway' that may even have originally had a balancing twin lodge. The complex, in much-reduced and vandalised form, can be seen at the entrance to Rosmead (*q.v.*), the reason for which may be explained by that oft-quoted tale whereby to distinguish the family from so many other Smyths in the county the proprietor became known as 'Smyth with the gates'. Irritated by this, it would have been Ralph's great-grandson, William Edward Smyth (1830–90), who had them dismantled, and thereafter the family became 'Smyth without the gates'. The Flora and Pomona statutes have been taken away for safekeeping. Woolley also provided a watercolour for an identical gatescreen (never realised) for the Fordes of Seaforde in County Down.

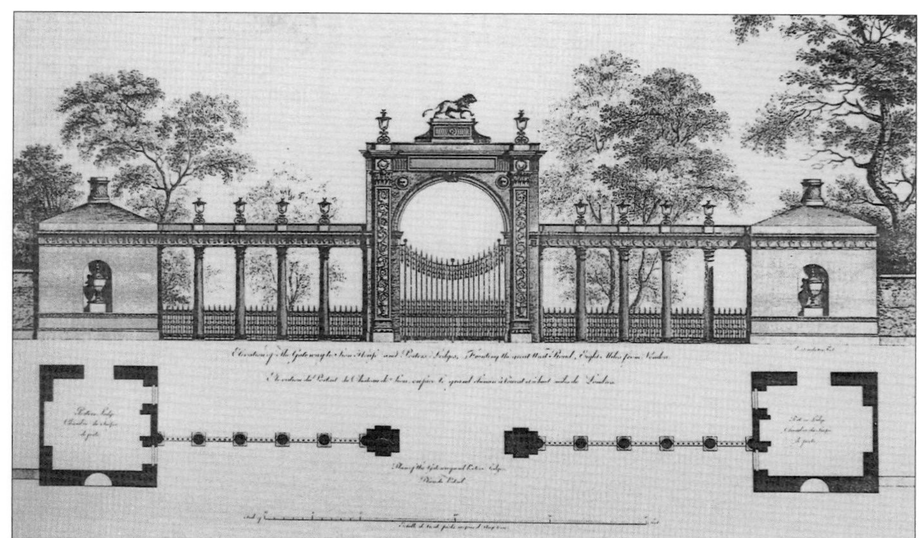

84. Glenanea, Robert Adam design.

In about 1860 W.E. Smyth, having had the grand entrance removed, built a replacement 1½-storey standard lodge in a naive mix of Tudor and Classical styles, with a pair of diagonally set chimney-stacks and ornamental foiled bargeboards in the former and moulded architraved window and door surrounds in the latter, and even a touch of the Gothic in its pointed attic windows, which have peculiar dentil courses to their sills. Finished in random ashlar with prominent toothed quoin stones, there are round-headed niches to each gable end, probably influenced by those on the missing pillars. Occupied.

South entrance; *c.* 1860.
As the above, 1½-storey standard and gabled with similar foiled bargeboards, but in a more basic rendered finish and with a pair of octagonal brick chimney-stacks in Picturesque English Cottage manner. Derelict.

Adam and Adam 1778; *LGI* (1904); Guinness and Ryan 1971; Mowl and Earnshaw 1984; Kelly 1990; Dean 1994.

85. GLENCARA or GLENCARRY, Rathconrath (2).
Charles Kelly purchased the estate, then named 'Corr', and in 1824 built the present house and the southern gatekeeper's lodge.

South entrance; pre-1837; *demolished.*
The lodge had been removed by 1914.

North entrance; *c.* 1840; architect possibly J.B. Keane.
Opposite the gates is what was once an impressive lodge but is now spoiled by dereliction and the insertion of a nasty steel window in the leading front. Single-storey square on plan below a pyramidal roof rising to a stumpy octagonal chimney-stack broaching off a square base. Main front in random stone with a cut-stone chamfered surround to that rogue window. Across the road the stack is echoed by six good octagonal pillars framing carriage and postilion gates and matching railings extending in convex quadrants beyond. Possibly all to designs of architect J.B. Keane, who is recorded as working here around 1840 for Robert Hume Kelly (1800–68), who had succeeded on his father's death in 1839.

LGI (1904); Bence-Jones 1988; NIAH.

86. GLYNWOOD, Athlone; *c.* 1855.

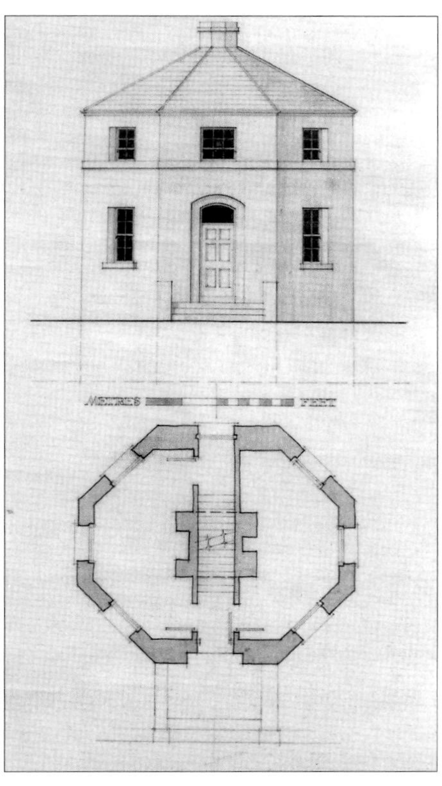

The pathetic remains of a once-proud Victorian estate, initially created by Francis Longworth in the early nineteenth century. When his son John died without issue in 1881, the property passed to a cousin, Francis Travers Dames-Longworth, who greatly improved the place and extended the mansion. It would seem to have been John, however, who built the unorthodox lodge in his time here. Now barely visible in the undergrowth, and little more than a shell by a muddy track that was once a busy avenue, is a two-storey lodge over a basement of an octagonal plan. The entrance storey is treated as a *piano nobile*, approached over a miniature perron or stepped bridge. Within, the space was sufficient to accommodate a central staircase flanked by a pair of chimney-breasts that rise to meet at first-floor ceiling level to form a central stack which crowned the octahedral roof. Unlike the Italianate excesses on the big house, the lodge is devoid of ornament, depending for impact upon its form, the rendered walls being relieved only by a stone course at first-floor sill level and the fanlit front door set in a segmentally arched recess. The windows reduced upwards from six-over-six to six-over-three sashes. In keeping with the general scene of devastation, the entrance gates have disappeared.

LGI (1904); English 1974.

GORE POINT (see DERRYMACEGAN)

GORTMORE (see LONGFIELD)

87. GRANGE BEG, Raharney; pre-1913; *demolished.*
A lodge built after 1837 to a property in 1854 of Thomas Gibson.

Griffith 1848–60.

88. GRANGE MORE, Raharney (3).
The grand house of the Briscoe family is an overgrown shell, with two of its lodges gone.

West entrance; pre-1837; *demolished.*

Inner lodge; *c.* 1830; architect not known; *demolished.*

Irish Architectural Archive

The good taste of Edward Briscoe (1799–1842) was displayed in this outstanding and innovative single-storey Classical design which presented a busy short front to the avenue, comprised of a decoratively glazed bipartite cast-iron casement window flanked by a pair of round-headed niches in a harled wall recessed behind a delicate tetrastyle portico of four Tuscan columns supporting a flat entablature, below a high-eaved hipped roof with prominent paired corbel blocks to the soffit and a banded chimney-stack. Sadly, the lodge is no more, but the portico lives on as an ornament at Butterstream Gardens, Co. Meath.

East entrance; pre-1837.
Although two round-headed windows are recognisable as original on each side of an entrance breakfront, this building has been altered dramatically, probably raised by a storey and extended to the right-hand side. Occupied and immaculately maintained, as is the late Victorian gatescreen with excellent chunky iron railings and gates with repetitive anthemion and sunflower motifs. The carriage gates are retained by clenched iron

fists set in grand cut-stone pillars incised with Soaneian decoration, with moulded plinths and curved corniced cappings. Erected for John Fetherstonhaugh Briscoe (1830–82) about 1875. During his minority after he succeeded to the seat it was let to Capt. William Graham, one of whose gatekeepers in 1854 was Patrick Hearne.

Griffith 1848–60; *LGI* (1904); IAA photograph (25/9).

89. GREENPARK, Mullingar; pre-1838; *demolished.*
Surviving their lodge is a fine pair of carriage pillars in V-jointed rusticated stone with ball finials on pedestals. In 1814 this was another seat of Hartley Hodson of Old Connaught, Co. Wicklow (*q.v.*), and of his son, Sir George Frederick John Hodson of Hollybrooke (*q.v.*) in the same county. A place previously known as 'Tuitstown'.

Leet 1814; *BPB* (1929).

90. GRIFFINSTOWN, Kinnegad; pre-1837; *demolished.*
An estate, initially of the Griffin family, which subsequently passed successively to two prolific Westmeath families, the Smyths and the Fetherstonhaughs. It was the Revd John Fetherstonhaugh (1796–1874) who built the present Regency villa and perhaps the porter's lodge shown on the first OS map, which seems to have been of standard plan with a central projecting hallway, built on an axis of the gates, the avenue splitting to pass on both sides of it, to reunite behind and continue within.

Taylor and Skinner 1778; 1969 [1783]; Leet 1814; Fraser 1838; *LGI* (1904); Casey and Rowan 1993.

91. GUILDFORD, Mullingar; pre-1837; *demolished.*
The seat in 1814 of Christopher Coffie Jr.

Leet 1814.

92. HALL, Ballynahown; pre-1837; *demolished.*
The lodge, situated well off the public road, to a property in the early nineteenth century of James Clibborn.

Leet 1814; Fraser 1838.

93. HALSTON, Ballymore; *c.* 1810.
Henry Gamble about 1810 took an old house called 'Becksborough', doubled it in size, renamed it 'Henrystown' and added a gate lodge to the estate as part of his improvements. It survives behind the right-hand convex entrance quadrant as a single-storey bow-fronted cottage below a semi-conical roof and with smooth stone dressings to openings in roughcast walls. Lovingly restored and extended in many directions.

Taylor and Skinner 1778; 1969 [1783]; Leet 1814; Casey and Rowan 1993.

HARMONY HALL (see BENOWN)

94. HAWTHORN COTTAGE, Athlone; pre-1837; *demolished.*
A property in 1837 of William Cooke, recently renamed 'Woodville'.

Lewis 1837.

95. HEATHSTOWN, Clonmellon (2).
North lodge; pre-1914; *demolished.*
South lodge; *c.* 1840.
Derelict and boarded up, opposite its gates, is a standard hip-roofed structure with roughcast walls and large Picturesque octagonal chimney-stacks. Decorative gatescreen with anthemion motifs.

Both lodges were built after 1837, one being recorded in the 1854 valuation to a property of Richard Dyas, who was also noted here six years earlier.

Slater 1846; Griffith 1848–60.

96. THE HERMITAGE, Athlone; *c.* 1908; *demolished.*
A very short-lived lodge to an Edwardian property created by Lieutenant Harry Davis.

97. HUNTINGDON, Killucan; *c.* 1835.
Another estate of the Purdon family, descended from those at neighbouring Lisnabin Castle (*q.v.*), of whom Robert (*c.* 1773–1855) added a gatekeeper's lodge on the eastern approach. Single-storey, constructed in good uncoursed random stone, two-window bay to the road and single to the avenue, below a steeply hipped roof with a smooth stone eaves band containing paired corbel blocks to its gutters. Sturdy but deserted.

IFR.

98. HYDE PARK, Killucan; *c.* 1810.
A gentleman farmer's house built by James D'Arcy in 1775, complemented by a modest gate lodge, presumably built after his death in 1803 by his son John (1767–1846). Single-storey with a two-window-bay main front in harled rubble construction below hipped roof. Derelict.

LGI (1904).

99. JAMESTOWN COURT, Castletown Geoghegan (2).
In 1825 'a spacious and handsome mansion, partly built by Kedah Geoghegan but enlarged with wings by Sir Richard Nagle his maternal grandson'. It would have been his son of the same name, the 2nd baronet, who established the porters' lodges.

Deer-park gate; pre-1837/*c.* 1870.
A 1½-storey gabled affair in rendered finish with single-storey gabled front hall and back return. Cream brick dressings to the latter suggest a mid-Victorian remodelling of an earlier structure.

Main gate; *c.* 1845.

Looking distinctly antique but probably prompted by the arrival of the adjacent railway cutting is this two-storey gabled gatehouse tacked onto the end of the right-hand of two straight rubble-built screen walls tall enough for each to accommodate delightful pointed-arched postilion openings, a feature repeated in pointed heads on the lodge, which has a single-storey wing. Occupied.

Brewer 1825.

100. KEOLTOWN, Mullingar; *c.* 1860.
A property previously called 'Lakefield' of the L'Estrange family that passed to the Swifts, of whom John built the present dull mid-Victorian house and lodge. Single-storey standard, built in rubble stone with red-brick dressings below an oversailing hipped roof. Derelict.

Griffith 1848–60; *IFR.*

101. KILBEGGAN RECTORY, Kilbeggan; pre-1837; *demolished.*
A lodge that may just have post-dated the glebe house of 1800 during the incumbency of Revd William Marshall (b. 1755), rector from 1801 to 1831.

Lewis 1837; Leslie and Wallace 2009.

KILCLEAGH PARK (see CASTLE DALY)

102. KILCOOLEY, Castletown Geoghegan; pre-1854; *demolished.*
A property in 1854 of Richard Wade, the lodge to which was built after 1837.

Griffith 1848–60.

103. KILCUMNEY RECTORY, Collinstown; pre-1837; *demolished.*
Comprising part of the Anglican Union of Drumcree formed in 1818, the gate lodge may well have been built by Michael De Courcey DD (1787–1860), rector from 1818 until his death.

Leslie and Wallace 2009.

104. KILDEVIN, Lismacaffry (2).
The novel bow-fronted house is obligingly inscribed 'Robert Sproule 1833' and the lodges, both demolished, were built within four years of that date; one of them was also serving as a 'police barrack' in 1837. There was a family of architects of that name who may have been responsible.

ffolliott 1971a; Bence-Jones 1988.

105. KILLINURE, Glassan; pre-1837; *demolished.*
A property in 1783 of the Hall family, thereafter until 1837 a home to the Murrays.

Taylor and Skinner 1778; 1969 [1783]; English 1973.

106. KILLUA CASTLE, Clonmellon (5).
Sir Benjamin Chapman inherited a place called 'St Lucy' in 1779; by 1782 he had been elevated to the baronetcy and had completed his big plain house to replace the old castle. Before his premature death in 1810 he had also furnished the demesne with decorative porters' lodges, one of which survives in its original form.

The temple gate; *c.* 1802; architect not known.
Opposite the gates of the south-eastern approach, on a manicured grassy mound is this splendid little single-storey tetrastyle temple lodge (*below*), its columns supporting a steeply pitched pediment and screening the front door, which is flanked by a pair of round-headed niches. Local legend has it that the latter once housed busts of Nelson and Wellington while the acroterion blocks had statues of angels at the three angles, recently replaced by two urns. Now a cosy home in an idyllic garden, lovingly maintained.

The 2nd baronet, Sir Thomas Chapman (1756–1837), continued the improvement of the property with gusto but was clearly less conservative than his brother, for he embraced the new Picturesque Romantic Castellated fashion that was sweeping the county and neighbouring Meath, clothing his house in Tudor Gothic detailing, crenellations and towers. That he and his architect, or architects, considered an apt prelude at the entrances to the estate to be important is obvious from the gatekeeper's lodge at the other southern avenue then created. Quite who Sir Thomas's architect was is not entirely clear, for while there is early accreditation to Alexander McLeish there is much in the house recently attributed to James Shiel. McLeish arrived in Ireland as a landscape gardener in 1813 but died in 1829 a recognised architect, having also been recorded as the designer of Lisnabin Castle (*q.v.*) for the Purdons. Although they may have collaborated here, as they are thought to have done at nearby Knockdrin Castle (*q.v.*), it is probable that Shiel was called in to complete the interiors at Killua after the Scotsman's demise.

The Gothick gate; 1828; architect possibly Alexander McLeish.

A splendid eye-catcher that in 2000 lay in an advanced state of dilapidation, but not beyond salvation. Built in coursed limestone, it is a composition of five bays defined by dividing pilasters that emerge on high as crenellated square turrets. Central is the tall carriage opening with four-centred archway below a little quatrefoil motif and a castellated parapet. Flanking is a pair of two-storey one-over-one apartments, lit on the lower storey by dressed hood-moulded pointed windows and crowned by crenellated gables. Beyond, on each side, are accompanying label-moulded postern gate openings, slightly angled, the whole extending further in shallow concave quadrant walls. The design is bound together

by moulded string-courses, relieved by mock arrowloops and Cross of Lorraine motifs and enhanced by high-quality ironwork. Although front and back elevations match, and the upper rooms must have been accessed by steep stairs and are lit by minuscule end windows, it is not beyond the ingenuity of the modern architect to create a striking but sympathetic conversion for contemporary living.

The Picturesque or Clonmellon gate; *c.* 1804/1855; architect not known.

J.A.W. Humphreys

Just such a scheme has transformed this delightful little toy castle, enlarging it into a desirable property. Quite the most appropriate prelude to the big house, equalling it in dishonesty as a shameless sham castle, but in miniature. Built in random limestone facings with dressed label- and hood-moulded openings to square and pointed-arched openings forming a two-storey screen to the most modest of lodges behind, consisting of a central square tower flanked by tall screen walls to tall outer turrets with mock windows. At least the central tower and flanking windows had the function of serving the dwelling behind, the entrance hall probably having been double-height. Recently this toy castle, with its curious cobweb plaque ornaments, has been given substance by an imaginative extension in like manner at right angles to the original and fronting a home of generous accommodation. Whether the first lodge on the site of where the 1st baronet created the Clonmellon avenue is the one that was subsequently replaced is not obvious, but what is clear is that the later deceit was for his nephew, Sir Benjamin James Chapman (1810–88), who succeeded to the estate as 4th baronet after the early death of his brother in 1852. He subsequently created a fourth porter's lodge in complete contrast.

Kells gate; 1856.
Opposite the gates of the northern approach is this relatively plain creation in coursed limestone ashlar, its appearance not helped by the intrusion of modern windows. Single-storey standard below a hipped roof with paired expressed rafter toes and a gabled hall breakfront, the bargeboards of which have applied serrated ornament. Occupied.

For most of the building dates I am indebted to the copy in the Irish Architectural Archive of notes by the widow of the 7th baronet, upon whose death in 1919 the baronetcy became extinct and thereafter the estate and mansion slid into dereliction. Nevertheless, the castle, from being an ivy-covered shell for decades, is currently being gloriously rehabilitated by the present inspired owners.

Brewer 1825; *BPB* (1917); Malins and Bowe 1980; Casey and Rowan 1993; Howley 1993; *IAR* (1996); IAA (RP.D.141.10); IAA photographs (25/13 Z1–3); Humphreys 1979.

107. KILLYNON, Killucan; pre-1837.
A ruinous three-bay single-storey structure in which only the basic fabric of brick-dressed rubble can be discerned. Built for Richard Reynell (1768–1834), who succeeded to the seat in 1788.

LGI (1904).

108. KINTURK, Castlepollard (3).
An estate of the Pollard family, of whom William Dutton Pollard (1789–1839) in 1821 engaged the English architect Charles Cockerell to enlarge and remodel his house. This commission may have extended to the main entrance.

Town gate; *c.* 1825; architect possibly C.R. Cockerell.

Sited well forward of its entrance gates is this charming naive Classical single-storey standard gatekeeper's lodge below a hipped roof, its breakfront porch fronting the footway with two flimsy cast-iron Doric columns *in antis* supporting a bargeboarded pediment. Finished roughcast with modern windows and an unhappy roof covering of concrete tiles. Occupied.

Side gate; pre-1837; *demolished.*
Unlike the above, located well within the demesne was a pair of lodges giving access to the outbuildings.

Country gate; *c.* 1850.
At the southern extremity of the demesne, with its back turned on the impressive perimeter wall, is an abandoned jasmine-covered single-storey standard gabled cottage of generous proportions. Pleasantly finished in brick dressings to rubble facings, and mildly ornamental bargeboards. A highly desirable property, whose dereliction is a mystery. Built for William Pollard (1815–71), who assumed the Urquhart surname of his wife after their marriage in 1846.

LGI (1904); Bence-Jones 1988.

109. KNOCKDRIN CASTLE, Mullingar (3).
In 1796, at the age of eleven, Richard Levinge (1785–1848) succeeded his father as 6th baronet and inherited an extensive estate of over 5,000 acres. About 1815 he proceeded to replace the old house, called 'High Park', with a vast and imposing castellated Gothic Revival mansion to designs by James Shiel, after discarding earlier plans by Sir Richard Morrison. Of the lodges at the three demesne entrances, which he either built or inherited, none survive in their original form.

East lodge; pre-1837/*c.* 1900.
On the Killucan road opposite the gates is an exercise in duality, a single-storey building whose main function in 1837 and 1914 was to serve as a 'Constabulary Barrack'. The entrance porch is flanked by a pair of gabled projections, each of one bay. Probably about the turn of the twentieth century it received a face-lift with the application of rendered toothed quoins to otherwise roughcast walls and mock 'black and white' work to the apexes.

Fifteen years after succeeding as 7th baronet, Sir Richard George Augustus Levinge (1811–84) replaced two of the porters' lodges that he had inherited, one in spectacular form.

North lodge; pre-1837/*c.* 1860.
A perky little single-storey standard affair, raised in random ashlar below a hipped roof with oversailing eaves. The left-hand bay is a canted projection to view the older square Georgian entrance pillars with scroll-topped stops, which were associated with the earlier lodge. Vacant.

West lodge; pre-1837/1862; architect John McCurdy.
To replace a previous lodge on the site, 'A new principal entrance is to be erected at Knockdrin Castle, the picturesque seat of Sir Richard Levinge, Bart., M.P. The baronial character of the mansion is to be adhered to in the proposed structure, which will be built on the Mullingar side of the demesne, commanding the main road leading from that important town. A tower of 55 feet in height will form its principal feature. An arched portal, surmounted by crenellated parapets, will be filled with ornamental wrought iron gates and portcullis, typical of the period of the building. It is to be executed in limestone. Mr McCurdy archt.' But for the gates and portcullis, which appear from a photograph of *c.* 1871 never to have been realised, this *Dublin Builder* entry is an accurate preview of what is manifest today (*below*). A wholly appropriate prelude to the great mansion within, the four-centred arched carriage opening below a machicolated stepped gable, which houses a plaque with the family's arms, is flanked on one side by a three-stage octagonal tower that accommodates the gatekeeper's rooms, lit by label-moulded openings, and on the other side by a sham square turret, all crowned by bold machicolated and battlemented parapets. To each side are lower wing walls, that to the right-hand side containing a postern opening. A sturdily built structure likely to survive another 150 years, despite lying abandoned and boarded up.

Irish Architectural Archive

DB (1 Feb. 1862); NLI/Lawrence photograph (6953C); *BPB* (1929); Casey and Rowan 1993; IAA photograph (25/14 Z2).

LAKEFIELD (see KEOLTOWN)

110. LADESTOWN or LEDESTOWN, Mullingar; pre-1837/*c.* 1865; architect possibly John McCurdy.

An early lodge to the estate, probably contemporary with the 1823 house, to which the Lyons family came in 1715, has been replaced by the existing building, presumably built for John Charles Lyons (1792–1874). It has characteristics of the work of architect John McCurdy, rather like a simplified version of his lodges at Harristown, Co. Kildare (*q.v.*), being on an L- or butterfly plan, with a hallway at 45° across the internal angle, the canopy over supported on a pair of carved wooden brackets with pendant features. Single-storey, built in Flemish bond facing brick contrasting with toothed stone quoins and dressings to segmentally headed windows, the avenue wing being canted with semi-octagonal roof and the other simply gabled with basic bargeboards which may have had decorative predecessors, probably discarded when the matching extension was built in the twentieth century. The tall chimney-stack has been rendered bland in sand/cement.

LGI (1904); Bence-Jones 1988.

111. LADYWELL, Glassan; *c.* 1845; architect Sandham Symes.

An Italianate lakeside villa built in 1845 for the Mahon family, whose main seat was at Castlegar, deep in the heart of County Galway. Designed by architect Sandham Symes, who was also responsible for its contemporary gatekeeper's lodge. This displays on its leading elevation a most peculiar feature in a raised and fielded panel, characteristic of Symes and also to be found in his lodges at Whitestown, Co. Dublin (*q.v.*). Single-storey and roughcast below a shallow-hipped roof, the two-bay avenue elevation has tripartite Wyatt windows with corbelled sills, its doorway out of sight. Plinth, eaves course and corniced chimney-stack are in contrasting cut stone. A smart little Classical lodge, strangely lying abandoned. Presumably a development enjoyed by Sir James Fitzgerald Mahon, 3rd baronet (1812–52), rather than his older brother, Sir Ross Mahon, who was the client but died in 1842.

BPB (1929); Casey and Rowan 1993.

112. LA MANCHA, Mullingar; *c.* 1835.
A single-storey lodge with steeply hipped roof over a three-bay roughcast main front, the doorway to the right-hand side in a tiny gabled projection. Occupied. Nice cast-iron entrance posts decorated with a wealth of anthemion motifs. A property in the early nineteenth century of a Mr Hudson, leasing from the Swift family, who owned much in this townland of Lynn. The lodge was probably given a face-lift in the 1850s when they reoccupied their house.

Pigot 1824; Lewis 1837; Fraser 1838; Griffith 1848–60.

113. LARKFIELD, Mullingar (2).
A seat of Francis Pratt Smith in the first half of the nineteenth century, when there was a lodge entrance on the southern avenue. From about 1860 it came into the possession of Edward Battersby, who added a second lodge on the northern approach. Both have been demolished.

Leet 1814; Griffith 1848–60; *LGI* (1904).

114. LAUREE, Kilbeggan; *c.* 1820.
A modest single-storey gabled two-bay roughcast cottage, now below a corrugated-iron roof. Derelict. Now renamed 'Ballard', in the early nineteenth century it was a property of H.W. Battersby.

Leet 1814; Pigot 1824.

115. LEMONGROVE, Mullingar; *c.* 1830.
A seat in 1814 of Joseph Lemon to which survives a standard single-storey hipped-roof cottage with oversailing eaves over roughcast walls, with smooth lugged surrounds to tripartite windows with intermediate sash boxes. Derelict. Hooped iron screen railings.

Leet 1814.

116. LEVINGTON PARK, Mullingar; *c.* 1800.

Another big house of the Levinges of Knockdrin Castle (*q.v.*), built in 1748 by Richard Levinge (1724–86), who became 4th baronet in 1762. Thereafter it became a dower house and home to a junior branch of the family. At the entrance to the demesne, fronting a minor public road, is an unusually generous pair of lodges in the form of gabled two-storey gatehouses, each of a single bay with a Gothic glazed upper sash window over a considerably larger twelve-paned casement, set in harled walls. Both seem to have been improved in the 1850s with the application of carved continuous-bracket bargeboards and fancy exposed rafter toes. To one gable a little slit window monitors the gatescreen, comprised of stone pillars containing a wide carriage opening flanked by a pair of flat-arched postilion gates. Good original Georgian ironwork survives. All probably built for the widow of the 5th baronet, Elizabeth Frances (née Reynell), after his death in 1796.

Leet 1814; *BPB* (1929); Casey and Rowan 1993.

117. LISNABIN CASTLE, Killucan (2).
This is the perfectly charming toy castle created in 1825 for Edward Purdon (1774–1867) by the Scottish landscape gardener-cum-architect Alexander McLeish. Judging by his little lodge to Knappagh, Co. Armagh, it is unfortunate that this disciple of J.C. Loudon did not live after 1829. The two porters' lodges to the demesne are of later date.

Main entrance; *c.* 1840; architect probably Sandham Symes.

A pretty single-storey standard hip-roofed lodge with a gabled hall breakfront. As is common at this period, there is a confusion of styles in the central pediment in Classical manner and the Tudor bipartite cast-iron lattice-paned casements and carved wooden cusped fascia board taken into the tympanum. Rendered and derelict. What identifies it as a Sandham Symes design is his singular and mysterious recessed blind panel to the avenue elevation, an idiosyncrasy to be found at his Ladywell (*q.v.*) lodge and those by him at Whitestown, north Dublin (*q.v.*). There is a good railed gatescreen containing postern openings with four bold ashlar turrets as pillars, chamfered and squinched to square crenellated cappings embellished with chiselled shields, redolent of the architect's castellated style for the Warren family in south County Dublin. It may not be a coincidence that Geraldine, a sister of the Mahon brothers of Ladywell, married a Purdon in 1842. The gatekeeper in 1854 was Maria Curtis.

Secondary entrance; *c.* 1850.
Opposite the gates is a much 'improved' cottage with very rough roughcast, inappropriate modern windows and concrete tiles to the gabled roof. Single-storey, now four-bay with gabled hall projection and original toothed limestone dressings. Occupied. The gate porter in 1854 was Patrick Downes.

Griffith 1848–60; *LGI* (1904); Malins and Bowe 1980; Dean 1994.

118. LISSYWOLLEN, Athlone; pre-1837; *demolished.*
A property of the Cooke family which had a succession of tenants, Sir George Tuite of Sonna (*q.v.*) in 1814 and H. Malone by 1837. Its lodge had been removed by 1952.

Wilson 1803; Leet 1814; Lewis 1837.

119. THE LODGE, Castletown Geoghegan; pre-1837; *demolished.*
A seat of the Dillon family later renamed 'Togherstown'.

120. LONGFIELD, Ballymore; pre-1837; *demolished.*
In the early nineteenth century this was an estate of James Longstaff; its name was changed to 'Gortmore' on the arrival of Arthur Hill Griffith.

Leet 1814; Lewis 1837; Griffith 1848–60.

LOUGHAN (see MOUNT DALTON)

LOUGH BAWN (see CARRICK)

121. LOUGH REE LODGE, Glassan; *c.* 1830.
A standard single-storey lodge, the hipped roof to which catslides beyond the front to form a verandah carried on four iron posts that have replaced earlier ones, the wooden capitals of which survive. Roughcast and occupied, opposite the entrance. A lakeside retreat in 1837 of Gustavus Handcock Temple, whose older brother lived at nearby Waterston (*q.v.*).

Lewis 1837.

122. LOUGH PARK, Castlepollard; pre-1837; *demolished.*
The lodge, which had gone by 1914, may have been built after the property passed from John Hill Foster after 1814 to Nicholas Evans (1795–1879), perhaps on his marriage in 1819. He lived on here until his death.

Leet 1814; *LGI* (1904).

123. LOWTOWN, Kinnegad; pre-1837; *demolished.*
Neither house nor gate lodge of the Dopping family has survived.

LUNESTOWN (see CHARLEVILLE)

124. LYNN, Mullingar; pre-1854; *demolished.*
In the late eighteenth and early nineteenth centuries a seat of a branch of the Swift family which later adopted the surname Dennis. No lodge is apparent on the 1837 OS map but one is recorded in the valuation, when the house was occupied by John L. Cronin.

Griffith 1848–60; *LGI* (1904).

125. LYNN LODGE, Mullingar; *c.* 1835.
A bland single-storey structure, probably rendered so by subsequent modernisation and extension to the right-hand side, starting life as a four-bay lodge, its original front door now blocked up. Roughcast with clipped verges. Occupied. The interest in this entrance lies in the rustic rubble-built round-headed carriage archway, its piers and apex surmounted by elegant pedestalled ball finals. Presumably built by Richard Swift not long after inheriting the place from his father, Meade.

LGI (1904).

126. LYNNBURY, Mullingar (2).
Yet another property in Lynn townland of the Swift family but which by 1824 was occupied by William Bourne, who was probably responsible for at least one of the porters' lodges.

Secondary entrance; pre-1837; *demolished.*

Main entrance; *c.* 1815; architect possibly Sir Richard Morrison.

A single-storey standard roughcast lodge with one-over-one sashes that have lost their late Georgian glazing bars. Under a shallow-hipped roof with oversailing eaves is the conceit of a distyle pedimented portico with Roman Doric columns and equivalent pilasters. This degree of sophistication, along with the gatescreen, suggests an attribution to Sir Richard Morrison, or might this be another appearance of his shadow from County Galway, the shady Dominick Madden? The entrance format is precisely that which he habitually distributed about the country at the turn of the nineteenth century. The cylindrical inner carriage pillars and the intermediate square pillars with recessed panels contain spear-topped postern gates. The convex-walled quadrants beyond that again are stopped by more pillars with fluted friezes—all in beautifully tooled ashlar with moulded cornices.

Pigot 1824.

127. MAHONSTOWN, Mullingar; pre-1914; *demolished.*
A property in the early nineteenth century of the Shiel family, let in 1854 to Robert Rathburn.

Griffith 1848–60.

128. MEARESCOURT, Ballynacarrigy (3).

A very Irish Palladian mansion, built around 1760 by John Meares, to which there were two gatekeepers' lodges in place before 1837, both of which had been demolished by 1914. That which survives dates from about 1860, at a time when much seems to have been expended about the estate in the building of workers' cottages by John Devenish Meares (1795–1876). This is a functional 1½-storey hip-roofed lodge with high eaves in random rubble construction, with cream brick as dressings to modern eight-over-eight sash window openings and to the single-storey gabled hall projection. Immaculately maintained. Of greater interest are the older square entrance pillars with their scroll-topped stops, fluting to friezes and rusticated ball finials; concave rubble quadrants. But the real jewel is an extraordinary postilion opening punched in the estate wall beyond, with the most opulent of Baroque-style casing: a moulded stone architrave with scrolled keystone is further framed by fluted pilasters rising to grand console brackets, with luxuriant acanthus leaves, carrying an entablature decorated with a band of egg-and-dart moulding. Unlike the carriage entrance of *c.* 1780, this may be a mid-Victorian extravagance.

LGI (1904); Casey and Rowan 1993.

129. MEELDRUM, Kilbeggan; pre-1837; *demolished.*
A property of the Clarke family to which there was a large lodge, indicated on the first OS map, which had been removed by 1914.

130. MIDDLETON PARK, Castletown Geoghegan (4).
John Bernard Burke was so taken with this estate that he granted it two entries in his *Visitation of the seats and arms of the noblemen and gentlemen of Great Britain and Ireland.* That in his 1854 volume is informative: 'the seat of George Augustus Boyd, Esq., D.L. and J.P. is situated about the centre of Ireland, on the western shore of Lough Ennell, or Belvedere Lake ... This

place formed a portion of the territory of the McGeoghegans, a powerful sept in that district, but was sold in the last century to John Berry, Esq., in whose family it remained up to 1841, when it was added by purchase, by its present proprietor to his estates in the neighbourhood, as it appeared to offer a more desirable site on which to erect a suitable mansion than his family residence on the eastern shore of the lake. The former house was accordingly removed, and the present one erected under the superintendence of George Papworth, Esq. It affords a good example of the adaptation of Greek architecture to modern dwellings ...' George Augustus Rochfort-Boyd (1817–87), for he assumed the additional surname of his mother, the countess of Belvedere, in 1867, inherited a gate lodge of the Berry family and replaced it with another to the north-west.

East lodge (*above*); *c.* 1845; architect possibly Sandham Symes.

Despite displaying many modern synthetic materials introduced in rehabilitation, the original form and detailing are still evident. On the old main approach is a very smart single-storey standard lodge with a shallow-hipped roof having carved modillion brackets to the soffits. These are carried under and into the tympanum of the pediment over the central hall projection. Front door and windows are set in segmentally arched recesses, the latter once cast-iron latticed casements, bipartite to the main front, tripartite to one end, and significantly to the opposing elevation a blind recess. This is a feature characteristic of the work of architect Sandham Symes, to be found at Ladywell (*q.v.*) and perhaps more importantly at Whitestown, Co. Dublin (*q.v.*), a seat of the Woods family, also of Milverton Hall (*q.v.*) in that county, where Symes also worked. G.A. Boyd had in 1843 married Sarah Jane Woods of the latter property and may have had to look beyond George Papworth as architect, for his last known commission was in 1853. Occupied and sharply rendered.

South lodge; *c.* 1855.

Now in pleasant exposed rubble finish and plain bargeboards is this once-Picturesque cottage built off a T-plan, 1½-storey and generous in accommodation, with a full-height gabled hallway in the front internal angle. Modern squared casement windows with rendered surrounds and a three-flue chimney-stack reduced from something more dominant.

West lodge; 1895; architect not known.

A surprise in the heart of the Irish countryside is this suburban 'Stockbroker Tudor' affair, with its conspicuous half-timbered-effect upper storey; the contrast with the ground floor may have been great, it having been red-brick, like the chimney-stack, but now rendered over. Built off a T-plan, 1½-storey with single-storey glazed canted bay windows to its leading gables. Associated outbuilding in the same manner with perforated earthenware cresting. The contemporary gatescreen has highly ornate curvilinear ironwork to carriage gates, postilions and the extensive ogee railed quadrants on dwarf walls, which are stopped by tall decorative carved late Victorian gate pillars with plinths, moulded recessed panelled shafts and complex cappings. Probably built for the widow of Rochfort Hamilton Boyd-Rochfort, whose son was a minor on his death in 1891.

Burke 1854–5; *LGI* (1904); Williams 1994.

131. MITCHELSTOWN, Delvin (2).

Along with the neighbouring estate of South Hall (*q.v.*) this was a property from the early 1700s of the Tighe family, the main entrances to which faced one another across the Athboy–Delvin road, in 1818 'a road completely shaded with trees'.

South gate; pre-1837; *demolished.*

North gate; *c.* 1860.

Opposite the entrance is 'Blackstone Lodge', so-called for its dark limestone blotchy random facings to a standard single-storey gabled structure with a similar projecting hallway. Square main windows and little round-headed lights to end elevations and sides of hall. Much modernised and extended, the additions well considered and sympathetic, but badly let down by the choice of modern materials: synthetic slates, lead-effect glazing and a plethora of plastic in bargeboards, fascias, soffits, rainwater goods, windows and front door. St Lawrence Robert Morgan Tighe (1838–95) had succeeded to the property as a fifteen-year-old on the death of his father in 1853, and the place was then leased to Captain John Roden until his coming of age, which he marked on his return by building the new porter's lodge. The entrance screen, which is identical to that at South Hill, is comprised of four Classical pillars with recessed panels flanked by straight railings.

Atkinson 1815; *LGI* (1904).

132. MONTEVIDEO, Mullingar; pre-1837; *demolished.*

More recently renamed 'Prospect', in the early nineteenth century the house was occupied by proprietors Andrew Dudgeon in 1814 and Henry Wilton ten years later.

Leet 1814; Pigot 1824.

133. THE MOORINGS, Athlone (2).

A very fine small suburban park that has suffered over the years on account of its setting and the increasing demands of public transport. The coming of the railway in the mid-nineteenth century required relocation of the pre-1837 entrance and lodge further north. That replacement lodge seems to have been swept away in twentieth-century road-widening that necessitated the re-siting of an excellent gatescreen, the quality of which suggests that its companion may have been of some architectural pretension. In a format favoured by Sir Richard Morrison, probably influenced by entrances to the demesnes of Thomastown Park and Johnstown nearby in County Roscommon, a pair of cylindrical limestone carriage pillars with square corniced cappings are flanked by postilion openings framed by square Classical pillars, repeated beyond in terminating rubble concave quadrants. The contemporary gate ironwork of *c.* 1850 has good spear and palmette finials. The name of the property, inscribed on the outer pillars, betrays the career of its owner until his death in 1851: Commodore James Caufeild RN, who also lived at Benown (*q.v.*). It may be significant that in 1823 he had married the Hon. Augusta Crofton of Mote Park, Co. Roscommon, where the architect Morrison was employed.

BPB (1929).

134. MORNINGTON, Multyfarnham; pre-1837/*c.* 1860.
Patrick O'Hara (1826–60) purchased Mornington in 1858 but had little time to enjoy it. He may just have furnished the estate with a replacement porter's lodge opposite the gates. Like the asymmetric house, as rebuilt many years later by his son, the lodge is irregular in elevation, the three-bay front having doorway and one window in a porch recess to the right-hand side, the high eaves being carried on a pair of cast-iron post columns. Single-storey in stucco finish with modern plastic windows. Occupied.

LGI (1904).

135. MOSSTOWN, Ballymore; pre-1914; *demolished.*
Both house and lodge have gone. The former was a seat of a branch of the Fetherstonhaugh family of Bracklyn Castle (*q.v.*), the gatekeeper's lodge, dating from after 1837, built either by Widenham Francis Fosbery (1837–89) or his predecessor, William James Perry, from whom he acquired the property in 1867.

LGI (1904).

136. MOUNT DALTON, Rathconrath; *c.* 1810.
In a delightful situation is this neat single-storey lodge, built off a square plan in roughcast finish that sets off the stone of plinth, eaves band and channelled toothed quoins. With a two-window-bay elevation to the park, it has been tastefully extended and improved. Pleasant contemporary straight rubble-built entrance screen, with good ironwork to carriage opening and flanking postern gates. Built either by Richard D'Alton, count of the Holy Roman Empire, whose house dates from 1784, or his successor here, Oliver William Costello Begg. The gatekeeper in 1854 was Timothy Nolan.

Lewis 1837; Griffith 1848–60.

137. MOUNT MURRAY, Multyfarnham; pre-1838.

Either a mid-Victorian replacement for or a reworking of an early lodge for Henry Murray. In any case, this is an unusual affair, single-storey, the three-window-bay elevation to the avenue gabled with, in its apex, a sculpted sandstone plaque containing the family coat of arms and their motto, 'Tout Prest'. On another front is a gabled hall projection with a flat-arched niche. Roughcast finish. Vacant.

MOUNT TEMPLE GLEBE **(see BALLYLOUGHLOE RECTORY)**

138. MOYDRUM CASTLE, Athlone (5).
The pathetic remains of a once-proud property created in the main about the first quarter of the nineteenth century when William Handcock, 1st Baron Castlemaine (1761–1839), commissioned Sir Richard Morrison to transform the 'Willbrook House' of his father, the Very Revd Richard Handcock, into the very latest of Castellated Tudor Gothic mansions. Architecturally there is little left to savour from this inspired period of building, nor is there much evidence of the magnificent, extensive and tastefully laid-out grounds with their undulations clothed with oak woods over which Neale eulogised in 1820. In those early heady days two new lodged entrances were created.

'Grand gate'; *c.* 1815; architect probably Richard Morrison; *demolished.*
Of this main entrance from the west on the main approach from Athlone, and so called on the OS maps, little remains. Presumably forming part of Morrison's commission, its lodge has been replaced by a modern structure, while all that survives of the gatescreen is a postilion gate with side railings in good wrought iron between a pair of stone pillars, one of which retains its moulded capping; fine moulded plinth.

Secondary gate; *c.* 1825.

On the northern avenue, by the ruined Moydrum chapel, where it met an early public road, against all the odds survives a single-storey three-bay gate lodge built off an L-plan, its main front recessed below a hipped roof to form a verandah with four iron Gothic quatrefoil cluster-posts for support. The roof retains its covering of scalloped slates but the roughcast finish and modern window insertions are not so happy. One should be thankful for small mercies. Occupied.

Richard Handcock (1791–1869) succeeded as 3rd Baron Castlemaine in 1840 but his taste in architecture is difficult to determine, for of the three porters' lodges associated with his tenure one remains an unexecuted design and another has gone, while he would not wish to be judged upon the third.

Annaghgortagh gate; *c.* 1855.
A thoroughly unprepossessing single-storey roughcast cottage below a hipped roof. Originally three-bay, later extended by a further bay, a flat-roofed hall protrudes from its main front. Occupied. An entrance created when rerouting of the public road marooned the 1st viscount's secondary gate.

Crosswood gate; pre-1876; *demolished.*
A barn occupies the site of what seems to have been a lodge of generous proportions on the southern approach, which was probably rendered redundant by the coming of the railway track.

Although Jeremy Williams states that the Castlemaines called in William George Murray to embellish their demesne with Baronial entrance gates, now vanished, there is nothing on the 1876 OS map to suggest that any design was ever realised on site. The frustrated architect was to submit no fewer than four proposals for lodged entrances. These are in the form of the most beautifully crafted ink and watercolour drawings depicting elaborate stone-built Tudor-Gothic structures, reducing, probably on financial grounds, from a most grandiose proposal to that of the relatively modest approved scheme.

Design no. 1; Oct. 1859; architect W.G. Murray; *unexecuted.*

IAA/Murray Collection

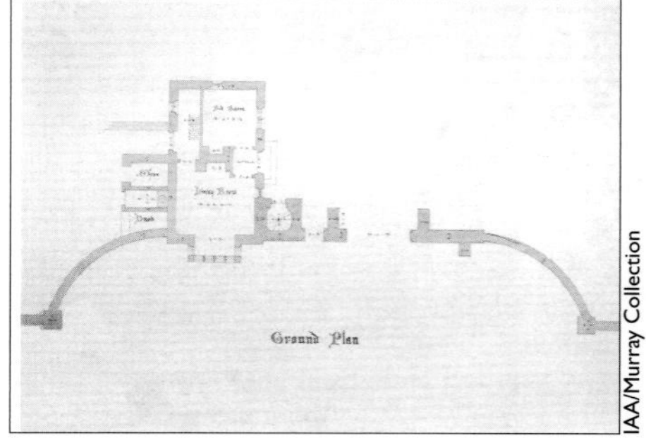

IAA/Murray Collection

In High Victorian Gothic manner, flanked by tall concave-walled quadrants is a Tudor-arched carriage gateway surmounted by a coat of arms in its stepped gable. Alongside is a little pointed-arched wooden postern gate, and the 1½-storey porter's accommodation with its projecting two-stage rectangular bay window and flag-carrying carved beast to the apex. But dominating the whole is a lofty steepled tower without any apparent function other than to astonish, for its spiral stair does not lead anywhere in particular.

Design no. 2; Dec. 1859; architect W.G. Murray; *unexecuted.*

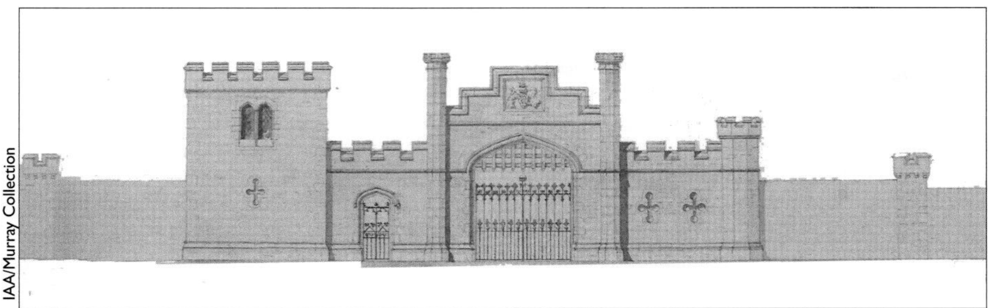
IAA/Murray Collection

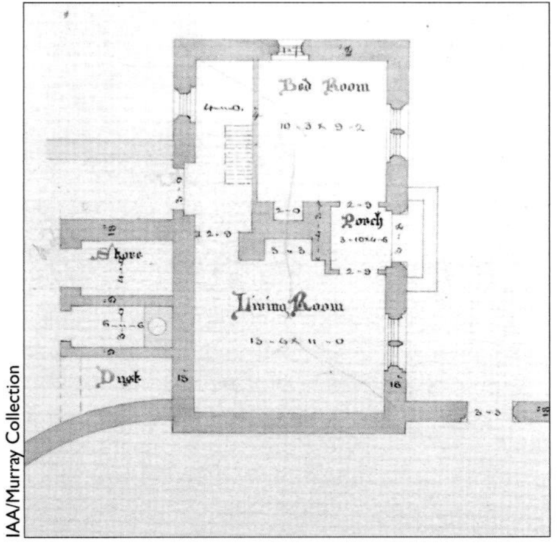

IAA/Murray Collection

A variation on the above, with an identical floor plan but two-storey within a castellated cloak, like a miniature keep, alongside a 'portcullised' gateway with a stepped parapet, again containing a coat of arms, all framed by a pair of slender octagonal turrets. The composition is balanced by a squat octagonal tower stopping the crenellated straight curtain wall, which is relieved by mock arrowloops.

Design no. 3; Dec. 1859; architect W.G. Murray; *unexecuted.*

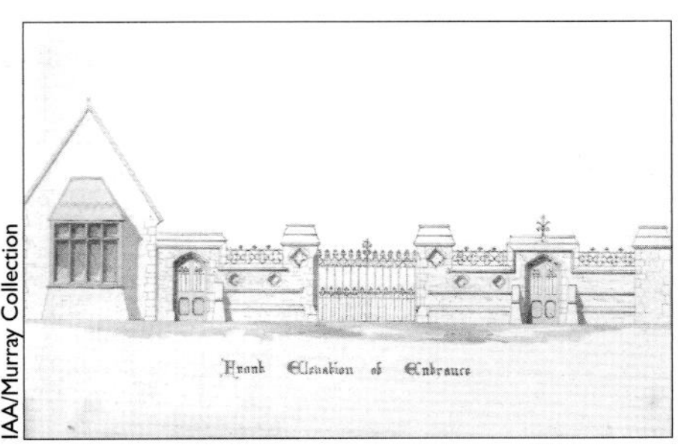

IAA/Murray Collection

IAA/Murray Collection

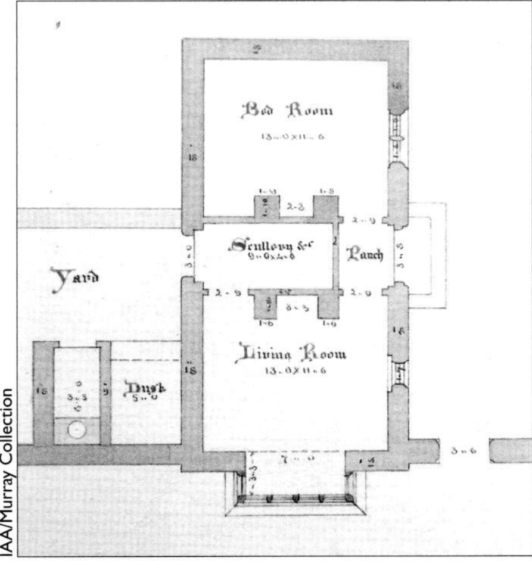

IAA/Murray Collection

A scaled-down version of design no. 1, the lodge reduced to single-storey and the bay window with battered base. The tower and carriage archway give way to a highly decorative gatescreen with quatrefoil motifs, which makes much use of fancy ironwork in its postilion gates and copings. Behind the gatescreen is a three-bay façade with cusp-headed windows, hood-moulded pointed-arched doorway and more ironwork in ornamental hinge straps and cresting to a skew-tabled roof with scalloped slate bands.

Design no. 4; Dec. 1859; architect W.G. Murray; *unexecuted.*

IAA/Murray Collection

Apparently the approved scheme, the lodge is reduced to a pleasant single-storey standard detached cottage behind the gates, with a pair of bipartite mullioned latticed windows on each side of a Tudor-arched doorway below a steeply pitched hipped roof. The attached architect's note records his reservations in that 'The Gate House quite too modern for the Stile of the Gate'. He identifies one of three alternative gatescreens in Castellated style, all with identical ironwork, as being that selected, but even that would have to be subject to some modification. It seems that all this effort (and

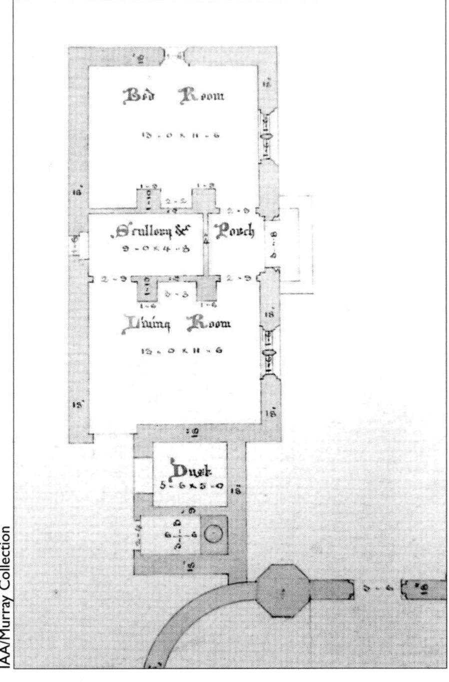

IAA/Murray Collection

any speculation over its planned location) was quite irrelevant, as nothing materialised. The demesne lies a shadow of its former self.

Neale 1820–3; *BPB* (1929); English 1974; McParland *et al.* 1989; Williams 1994; IAA (Murray Collection 3/959–974).

139. MOYLISKER RECTORY, Mullingar; *c.* 1813.

An undistinguished single-storey cottage with a main two-window-bay front, hipped gables to principal block and its back return, and a later catslide roof to a porch facing the park. Roughcast and vacant. The glebe house was built in 1813 for the considerable sum of £1,055.18.7½d, which may also have funded a contemporary porter's lodge. The rector from 1809 until his death was Meade Swift Dennis (d. 1837), whose grandfather had abandoned the surname Swift, a family once much in evidence in this townland of Lynn. The rectory is now a private house called 'Ardlynn'.

Lewis 1837; *LGI* (1904); Leslie and Wallace 2009.

140. MULLINGAR INFIRMARY, Mullingar; pre-1837; *demolished.*

Now the County Library, in 1837 the County Infirmary was described as 'a spacious and well-arranged building, situated on the Dublin road'.

Lewis 1837.

141. MULLINGAR LUNATIC ASYLUM, Mullingar; 1898; architects Joyce and Parry.

The original asylum of 1847–55 was designed in the Gothic style by J.S. Mulvany. Joyce and Parry were commissioned to remodel it in 1890–6 and to provide a gate lodge. This is a typical late Victorian blowsy affair on an L-plan, with hefty banded, fluted and moulded chimney-stacks breaking the ridge with its fancy cresting. The gables are accentuated by paired wooden verge brackets, that to the old avenue containing a canted glazed bay window with semi-hexagonal roof over. Alongside, projecting from the internal angle, is the hall with date-stone in the apex and the monogram 'M.D.A.', presumably Mullingar District Asylum. Below this was the doorway, now relocated to the side below a glazed lean-to verandah that leads to a contrasting Gothic-arched pedestrian gate in rubble stone by the side of the footpath. Finished in painted smooth rendering with fussy applied quoins. In use. Now St Loman's Hospital.

IADS (2000); Casey and Rowan 1993.

142. MULLINGAR ASYLUM FARM ANNEXE, Mullingar; *c.* 1910.
A single-storey lodge built off an L-plan, with carved serrated bargeboards to a shallow-pitched roof. Roughcast and occupied. In the internal angle is a small lean-to hallway.

143. MULLINGAR NEW CEMETERY, Mullingar; *c.* 1860.

Were it not in a setting of tarmac this would be a more obviously attractive building. Cruciform in plan, the main body 1½-storey, flanked by balancing single-storey wings. Gabled, with plain unadorned continuous bracket bargeboards and constructed in an attractive coursed rubble stone with toothed dressed stone to a peculiar mix of openings—pointed, round-headed and segmentally arched. In use. Good contemporary Classical entrance pillars and ornate iron gates.

144. MULLINGAR UNION WORKHOUSE, Mullingar; *c.* 1845; architect probably G. Wilkinson.

Now St Mary's Hospital, as a workhouse it opened in 1841 to a standard design of the industrious George Wilkinson. This is a neat little no-nonsense design with a touch of the Picturesque in its wavy unperforated bargeboards set off nicely by the mellow limestone uncoursed rubble of the walls. There is a chamfered dressed surround to the four-over-four sash window, while from the main body of the lodge alongside projects a little hallway with a deeply recessed panelled door below a round-headed archway. Scruffy but in use.

Slater 1870; Casey and Rowan 1993.

145. NEWCASTLE, Coole; pre-1837; *demolished.*
An old tower-house that remained a residence into the mid-nineteenth century of W.H. Keating, whose lodge had gone by 1914.

Casey and Rowan 1993.

146. NEWCASTLE, Tyrellspass (2).
There was a house here before the present mid-nineteenth-century affair, a seat of the Coffey family, which had two lodged entrances.

North gate; *c.* 1810.
Opposite the entrance is a single-storey standard lodge with hipped gables. Later extended by a further two bays in like manner and also perhaps gaining a projecting gabled hall with clipped verge over a tripartite window. Occupied.

South gate; pre-1837/*c.* 1860.
The present lodge is probably a replacement. Single-storey with gabled roof, sufficiently steep to accommodate loft rooms, constructed in rubble facings with cream brick dressings; mildly ornamental modern bargeboards and exposed rafter toes. Sympathetically extended and restored, with a gabled projecting hall. Presumably rebuilt in the time of Richard Coffey.

Slater 1856; Casey and Rowan 1993.

147. NEW COURT, Athlone; *c.* 1855.

A development for William Potts on the outskirts of the town, a house and its contemporary lodge in an English Picturesque Tudor style. The latter is a pretty little single-storey cottage, two-bay with a projecting hall having Tudor arches. Gabled, with fancy carved bargeboards, and finished in roughcast with applied smooth plinth, quoins and dressings. To the main gable is a tripartite cast-iron latticed casement window. Occupied. In contrast, the gatescreen has a pair of fine granite Classical cluster carriage pillars with prominent moulded cornices and gadrooned cappings. Simpler outer pillars contain concave rubble quadrants with crenellated coping, which reflects an extension to the house. Decorative twentieth-century carriage gates. Charles Papworth in 1863 carried out works for a Mr Potts at Correen Castle, Co. Roscommon, and may well have been employed here.

Thom's.

148. NEW FOREST, Kilbeggan; *c.* 1800.

This remains a truly remarkable vision, even lying as it does the roofless shell of a once-exceptional lodge. Assuming it to be contemporary with its adjacent gatescreen, it may date from the time of purchase of the quintessential mid-eighteenth-century Irish Palladian mansion, with a striking resemblance to Meare's Court (*q.v.*), by Henry Daniel (1767–1843) about 1800. Alternatively, they could be part of the improvement and beautifying of the house by Mr Garden, noted by Revd Beaufort in 1787. Single-storey, built off a simple rectangular plan in harled rubble finish with stone eaves course to a hipped roof, its extensive avenue elevation has a window to each end flanking a central feature of an arcade of three round-headed niches. Significantly, to the front of this is a stone platform that must have been the base for a decorative portico, like the roof a thing of the past. Originally two-roomed, the end elevation to the park has a round-headed window, with a doorway to the opposing road front. Rustic harled quadrants frame square ashlar carriage pillars with faintly recessed panels, friezes, sparsely fluted to reflect the lodge's niches, and unusual bapstone finials. Alas, at the time of survey, a sorry crumbling ensemble.

D.A. Beaufort (1787); Wilson 1803; *LGI* (1904).

149. NEWPASS, Rathowen (2).
A property since the late seventeenth century of the Whitney family, from whom it passed through marriage to Sir Thomas Fetherston, 2nd baronet, of Ardagh, Co. Longford (*q.v.*). His son, Sir Ralph George Fetherston, 3rd baronet (1784–1853), succeeded to the place in 1819 and may have been responsible for at least one of the gate lodges, although the place seems to have been home to a junior branch of the family which appended the Whitney surname to their own.

Main entrance; *c.* 1825.
On an elevated position from the gates is this most desolate sight in the remains of a quirky little lodge. Single-storey standard and square on plan, with a three-bay avenue front

Irish Architectural Archive

149. Newpass.

of three round-headed openings with spoked glazing to six-over-six sashes and in the door fanlight, the striking feature of which is the projecting portico. Heavy in appearance but in lightweight construction is the open pediment with a barrel vault soffit leading to the front door. Pluckily supported by four wooden posts, there are fragments of a dentil ornament to the verges. Hipped to the rear, an outsize stack straddles the ridge.

Side entrance; pre-1837; *demolished.* Situated on the eastern approach.

BPB (1923); Casey and Rowan 1993; IAA photograph (S/251/8 & 25/20 Z1).

150. NICHOLASTOWN, Mullingar; pre-1838; *demolished.*
This seems to have been another seat of the Fetherston family, previously called 'Feelstown', the lodge to which had gone by 1914.

Taylor and Skinner 1778; 1969 [1783]; Wilson 1803.

151. NOUGHAVAL, Ballymore; pre-1837; *demolished.*
The gatekeeper's lodge was located opposite the gates to a residence in the nineteenth century of William Dawson.

152. PAKENHAM HALL, Castlepollard (9).
Alternatively and alternately known today as 'Tullynally Castle', this is a generously lodged estate, as befits its status as home since 1655 to the noble family of Pakenham, Lords Longford, in whose hands it remains to this day. The core of the mansion is a plain, mid-Georgian pile which from about 1800 received its fashionable Romantic Castellated Gothic garb, in which idiom it was dramatically extended by a succession of eminent Irish architects: Francis Johnston, his erstwhile assistant James Shiel and, in 1842, the aged Sir Richard Morrison. To only one of these practitioners can a single lodge be confidently ascribed. There is also some evidence of two early lodges, which were subsequently superseded by what survive.

Main entrance; *c.* 1790/*c.* 1825; architect James Shiel.
There are tantalising references to what preceded the present gatehouse on the Castlepollard approach. Its Classical predecessor, built by William Michael Pakenham, 2nd Baron Longford (1743–92), was clearly considered unfashionable by his eldest son, the 2nd Lord Longford, Thomas Pakenham (1774–1835), who summarily removed it, though not before some of its embellishments were salvaged. These are in the form of that very desirable and expensive Coade stone manufactured in Lambeth by Elizabeth Coade, who noted in her 1799 Gallery notebook: 'Sphinxes etc. at Lord Longford's'. The 'etc.' would seem to refer to two swagged urns of Sir William Chambers pattern that survive along with the pair of delectable female sphinxes stamped 'Coade's Lithodiptera', each wearing a Pharaonic headdress with a knot atop. These may have

adorned the cappings of gate pillars or perhaps the parapet of a lodge or lodges, which must have been of some architectural sophistication. No doubt this entrance was created before Francis Johnston worked here, for it is difficult to imagine Shiel being party to its removal.

Today one is met by a formidable Tudor Castellated gatehouse, with a central carriage opening surmounted and flanked by porter's accommodation. The sturdy rectangular rubble-built block is rendered articulate and asymmetrical by a circular tower to the right-hand side, which contains a spiral stair giving access to the upper floor. The park elevation has single label-moulded windows with pretty lozenge-patterned cast-iron glazing and a shield above the carriage arch, while facing the visitor there are bipartite windows and relieving mock cross arrowloops. Occupied. Shiel's drawing survives, hung in the castle's main hall.

Pakenham Papers

School lodge; *c.* 1790; *demolished.*
The 1837 OS map shows a schoolhouse by the outbuildings at the head of the Portjack avenue from the south, which was still in existence in 1914. This may be the dual-function building founded by the socially conscious Catherine, wife of the 2nd baron from 1768, recorded for posterity in a charming sketch by one of the Edgeworth girls, with whom the Pakenham family were

152. Pakenham Hall, school lodge, sketched by 'one of the Edgeworth girls'.

very close. This indicates a single-storey rustic cottage with thatched hipped gables and centrally projecting thatched porch, probably simply harled, with wide lattice-paned casement windows. It catered for 'about twenty scholars who came after their breakfast & rec.d at noon potatoes and milk—and stayed till half-past three in Winter and 6 in summer, being of different persuasions mostly Romanist taught Writing & arithmetic ... all the protestants well instructed in catechism & psalm singing & taken to church by the mistress'. There is no mention of whether she had also to open and close the gates.

Carn lodge; pre-1837/*c.* 1910; architect not known.

Within the demesne, north of the walled garden, at the gate to the farm in Carn townland is this 1½-storey villa straight from Edwardian suburbia, with its fancy carved woodwork to the little glazed gabled hall flanked by a pair of flat-roofed canted bay windows in grey sand/cement-rendered walls. Between the main gable hip-knobs a serrated terracotta cresting is broken by two symmetrically placed chimney-stacks. A specification for this replacement structure is retained in the Pakenham Papers, unsigned and undated.

Kinturk demesne lodge; pre-1837/1904; architect not known.

Replacing an earlier lodge is this commodious 1½-storey building in roughcast finish with red-brick toothed quoins, its

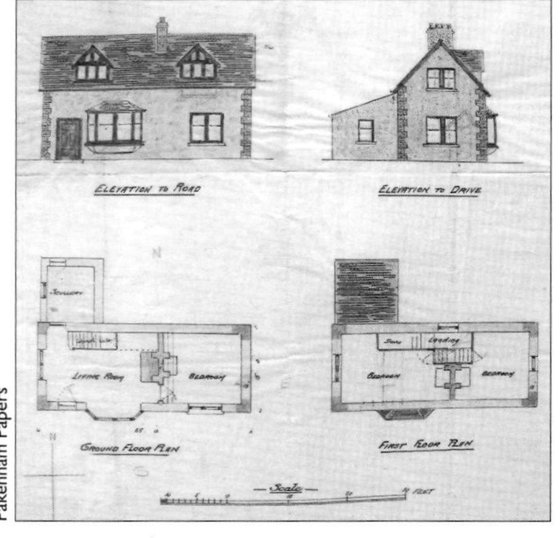

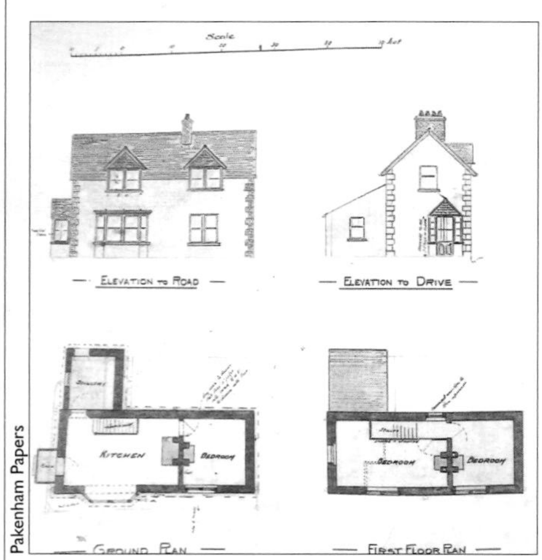

eaves broken by gablets with scalloped earthenware apex tile-hanging. Below are a single-storey canted bay window and gabled hall projection, all very much as shown on the surviving drawings, dated but unsigned. There are other contemporary drawings for estate cottages in the Pakenham archive by J.O. Moynan, archt., of Nenagh.

Clonteen lodge; pre-1837.

The first OS map shows a simple rectangular lodge opposite the entrance, but this must

have been extended *c.* 1840 with the addition of a semi-octagonal single-storey room with equivalent roof and an ornate carved cusped fascia board right around. The double-leafed sheeted front door is flanked by a pair of small-paned bipartite casement windows in harled walls. In 2006 unobtrusive single-storey wings were added.

Portjack lodge; pre-1837; *demolished.*

There are reports of tragic goings-on in several of the gate lodges in the early 1900s, including two murders. This one on the southern approach to the farmyard became ominously referred to as the *maison du pendu*, which may have contributed to its demise in the 1950s. Of its appearance nothing is recalled.

Coole lodge; pre-1837/1925; architect not known.

At the north-west extremity of the estate is this single-storey bungalow built off an informal plan with mock half-timbered-effect gables, carved serrated bargeboards and a little hall tucked into an internal corner below a catslide roof. Finished in roughcast, with paired windows and a date-stone to the leading gable. Occupied, with later twentieth-century additions, replacing an earlier lodge on the site.

North lodge; pre-1837; *demolished.*

A lodge on the Coole road that was taken down in the 1980s.

Tromora lodge; *c.* 1860.

A modest 1½-storey commodious affair on a symmetrical plan with gables and projecting single-storey hall. Located to the north and beyond the demesne proper but linked to it by a long, straight, tree-lined avenue, the creation of which seems to have been commenced about 1840 and which was known as 'Ladies' Drive'.

There is also in the Pakenham Papers a watercolour design (*top of facing page*), undated and unsigned, in the form of an elevation for a pair of single-storey Classical lodges, each with two round-headed windows, screen wall and gate pillars with fluted friezes. The drawing has been cut out of a larger one that may have identified its

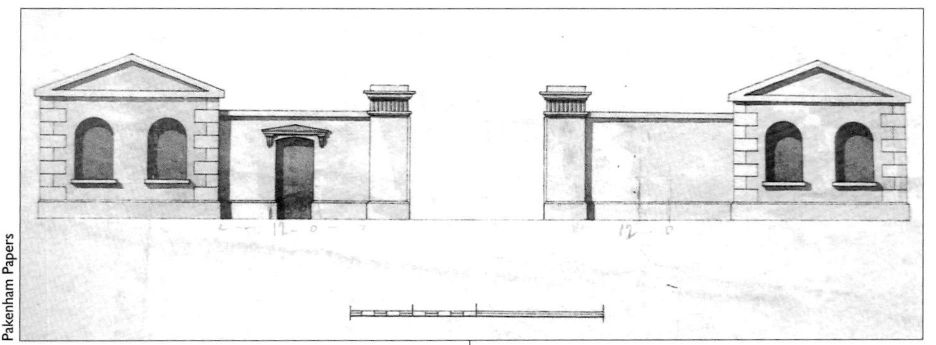

intended location. Perhaps it was an alternative to James Shiel's Tudor gatehouse.

Country Life (23 and 30 Dec. 1971); Kelly 1990; Casey and Rowan 1993; Pakenham 2000; IAA drawing (S/1807/14); Pakenham Papers.

153. PORTLICK CASTLE, Glassan; pre-1837; *demolished.*
A Dillon stronghold that went through a succession of owners before the Smyth family occupied it for much of the nineteenth century and probably added the porter's lodge, which had been removed before 1914.

Bence-Jones 1988; Casey and Rowan 1993.

154. PORTLOMAN or PORTLEMON, Mullingar; pre-1838; *demolished.*
A seat of the de Blaquiere family, of whom the 2nd baronet, Sir John (1776–1844), may have built a lodge, which had gone by 1914.

BPB (1917).

155. PRESENTATION CONVENT, Mullingar; *c.* 1870; architect probably W.F. Caldbeck.

A new convent and schools built for the Rt Revd Dr Nulty, lord bishop of Meath, at a cost of £5,000–£6,000, which included boundary walls and the lodge to plans furnished by W.F. Caldbeck—one of the architect's final works, for he died in 1872, aged only 47. Single-storey, Italianate in style, but unusually built off an L-plan below a hipped roof. A leading corner to the avenue is recessed to form an entrance porch, its corbelled eaves carried by a square pillar with recessed panels and responding pilasters and a moulded entablature. Heavily roughcast with a gabled extension and three banded and cornice-capped chimney-stacks. Occupied. Some of the gatescreen survives in short railed concave quadrants and iron Gothic posts with crenellated tops.

IB (1 Dec. 1869).

PROSPECT (see MONTEVIDEO)

RALPHSDALE (see GLANANEA)

156. RATHCASTLE, Ballynacarrigy; *c.* 1810.
A tiny three-bay single-storey hip-roofed cottage with clipped eaves corbel course and doorway to right-hand side. Roughcast and derelict. In contrast are less rustic late Georgian ashlar gate pillars with fluted friezes. Rubble wing walls beyond contain postilion gates. A seat in 1814 of Thomas Barron.

Leet 1814.

157. RATHCONNELL COURT, Mullingar (2).
A late eighteenth-century Gothic house of the Adams family which in 1837 had two entrance lodges, of which there are only the remains of one to the southerly gate. Single-storey, modest and derelict, with a hipped roof having clipped eaves and corbel course. Its main front has been gouged out for farm use. Probably dating from *c.* 1820, when Francis Adams was the proprietor.

Pigot 1824.

158. RATHCONRATH RECTORY, Rathconrath; pre-1838.
Sited outside its gates is a ruinous cottage with three-bay front built in rubble stone. Perhaps contemporary with the 1818 glebe house that cost £1,569, to which the incumbent from 1811 until 1837, Revd Frederick Augustus Potter (b. 1783), subscribed £831.

Lewis 1837; Leslie and Wallace 2009.

RATHWIRE (see RIVERSTOWN)

159. REDMONDSTOWN, Castletown Geoghegan; pre-1837; *demolished.*
The first OS map indicates a minuscule square structure at the left-hand side of the gates to a property in 1814 of John Tisdall.

Leet 1814.

160. THE RETREAT, Athlone (2).
A property in both 1824 and 30 years later of a William Cooke, across which the intervention of the railway *c.* 1850 called for the building of a secondary entrance and lodge.

Outer gate; *c.* 1820.
Situated on the public road, its avenue now also of that status, is a small single-storey standard hip-roofed harled cottage with its original sheeted front door. Of the gates all that remains is the stone left-hand concave quadrant.

Inner gate; *c.* 1850.

On each side of the railway track are identical cast-iron carriage gates with decorative spear and palmette motifs and iron posts with fine anthemion features. There is the ruin of a single-storey hipped-roof roughcast lodge with a two-window-bay main front, probably erected by the railway company.

Pigot 1824; Griffith 1848–60.

161. REYNELLA, Delvin (3).
The Scottish landscape gardener-cum-architect Alexander McLeish is said to have created Reynella in its entirety, designing house, gardens and grounds, despite Curwen's statement in 1813 that the house had been built twenty years previously. What is likely is that he was responsible for ancillary buildings on the estate, which included the three porters' lodges, before his death in 1829. He would have been commissioned by Richard Molesworth Reynell (1791–1824), who had inherited the place in 1807 as a minor. Curwen also commends his father's widow for her energetic continuation of her late husband's work on the property.

East lodge; pre-1837; *demolished.*

Middle lodge; *c.* 1825; architect possibly Alexander McLeish.
A 1½-storey mildly Picturesque cottage finished in roughcast with foiled bargeboards to main gables and that of the central breakfront hall.

West lodge; *c.* 1825; architect possibly Alexander McLeish.
Much as the middle lodge but now relegated to use as stables serving a twentieth-century bungalow nearby. Surviving is a pair of stone octagonal entrance pillars.

Curwen 1818; *LGI* (1904); Malins and Bowe 1980.

162. RIVERDALE, Raharney (2).
Edward John Briscoe (1770–1815) inherited this property from his uncle, the probable builder of the early lodge. This was replaced

later in the nineteenth century by one opposite the gate, presumably by his grandson of the same name, who succeeded to the place in 1854. It has suffered the same fate.

LGI (1904).

163. RIVERSTOWN, Killucan; *c.* 1875.

An early property of the Purdon family, then lodgeless and known as 'Rathwire'. The striking mid-Victorian lodge opposite the gates is single-storey standard but ruggedly built in a variety of quarry-faced random and coursed stone, with contrasting smooth masonry as string-course, quoins, end window dressings and moulded surround to the depressed-arched doorway, which is sheltered by the exaggerated gabled canopy projection. This feature is repeated in the advancing hipped gables of the main roof with its carved rafter ends. Modernisation has seen a large back return extension, new windows and chevron-sheeted front door. Built for Benjamin Hannan, who lived here in the mid- to late nineteenth century.

Griffith 1848–60; *Thom's*.

164. ROBINSTOWN, Castletown Geoghegan; *c.* 1845; *demolished.*

A lodge built not long after the Fetherstonhaugh family of Carrick (*q.v.*) had acquired the property from the D'Arcys *c.* 1840.

Lewis 1837; Slater 1846; Griffith 1848–60.

165. ROCHFORT, Mullingar (3).

The great Castle-attributed Palladian shell built about 1742 still stands proud. The 1837 OS map indicates one gate lodge, built either by Gustavus Hume-Rochfort or by Sir Francis Hopkins, to whom he sold it *c.* 1836, despite fathering seven sons and five daughters. The apparent undesirability of the place continued when Hopkins left it to his sister Anna Maria, who in 1835 had married Nicholas Loftus Tottenham of Glenfarne Hall, Co. Leitrim. She proceeded to improve the property, which she renamed 'Tudenham', with the advice of the Dublin architect John McCurdy, who designed a gatekeeper's lodge that survives, as conspicuous a landmark as the big house. There is an unexecuted proposal (*bottom of page*) for a grand neo-Classical lodge and gatescreen, unsigned and undated, probably by McCurdy and rejected in favour of what was built. It was to have been a cube in channelled rusticated masonry with a pedimented breakfront having a pair of Doric columns *in antis*, the whole to be crowned by a dome and flanked by wide gatescreens with iron posts containing anthemion motifs.

Church lodge; pre-1914; *demolished.*

Inner lodge; pre-1914.

A 1½-storey building, gabled, with gablets, so extensively modernised and extended as to make it unclear what is original.

Main entrance; 1865; architect John McCurdy.

The most ostentatious of compositions in the Italianate manner. Single-storey lodge, built off a cruciform plan, with a strapwork parapet concealing the roof of a structure faced in punched ashlar. On a grand scale, which displays the architect's eclecticism, it rises off a sturdy plinth with a moulded course at the spring line of round-headed paired windows and the splendid arches of the entrance porch, the archivolts of which rise centrally off an impressively chiselled composite capital with flowers, scrolls, shamrocks and scallop shells. In the spandrels are plaques with laurel wreaths,

one containing the date of construction. The lodge forms part of an extensive gatescreen of highly ornate ironwork and towering stone pillars with recessed panels and concave curved cappings. Sadly, all marooned by road realignment. It had a predecessor on the site.

LGI (1904); Bence-Jones 1988; Williams 1994; NLI drawing (AD 3311).

National Library of Ireland

166. ROCKBROOK, Ballinacarrigy; *c.* 1800.

The most perfectly delightful piece of village-scape located as a vista stop at the head of the main street is this naive composition, a mixture of the rustic and the sophisticated. The pair of ashlar carriage pillars, with moulded plinths and rusticated ball finials on unusual curved cappings, contrast with whitewashed harled concave quadrants, the left-hand one of which is contrived to be the leading front of a single-storey gate lodge with a single squat pointed-arched window monitoring the gates below a curved pediment, the crude cornice to which is mirrored as a coping on the right-hand quadrant. This also forms a lintel to the postilion opening, which contains a charming loop-topped iron picket gate. This important example of Irish heritage is maintained, though sadly the ball finials have gone and the lodge lies a shell. A seat in the late eighteenth and early nineteenth centuries of the Isdell family.

Taylor and Skinner 1778; 1969 [1783]; Wilson 1803.

167. ROCKFIELD, Castletown Geoghegan; pre-1914; *demolished.*
A property in 1854 of Marcus Colgan.
Griffith 1848–60.

168. ROCKFIELD, Rathowen; pre-1837; *demolished.*
A residence in the first half of the nineteenth century of Matthew Crawford, the lodge to which had gone by 1914.
Leet 1814; Lewis 1837.

169. ROCKVIEW, Delvin (2).
A villa described by Brewer in 1825 as 'lately erected by James Featherston, father of Mr Featherston of Bracklyn'. He was in fact James Fetherstonhaugh (d. 1822) of the latter place (*q.v.*), whose architect may have been Francis Johnston, a commission which could also have included the early porter's lodge.

East entrance; *c.* 1820; architect possibly Francis Johnston.

Irish Architectural Archive

Opposite the gates, retained as a garden folly in the garden of a bungalow, is the pale shadow of a once-refined porter's lodge now lacking its previous tetrastyle pedimented portico and stripped of its original harled finish to reveal the startled rubble fabric and the three-bay front comprised of a central large lattice-paned window flanked by a pair of round-headed niches. This was contained behind a spear-topped railing framed by two charming 'Catherine wheel' pedestrian gates hung on stone octagonal fluted posts, which are repeated across the road on the entrance screen. What is interesting is that there is a similar lodge opposite the gates to Roristown, Co. Meath (*q.v.*), with identical pillars and ironwork, a similar arrangement at Ballyboy, Co. Meath (*q.v.*) (its lodge much altered), and most significantly at Cloncarneel (*q.v.*) in the same county, which Francis Johnston is known to have designed, the entrance gates there with the same fluted octagonal gate posts and matching screen opposite but now lacking its gate lodge.

West entrance; *c.* 1845.
Now isolated by modern road realignment and bordering on the ruinous are the remains of a 1½-storey harled lodge, gabled to the old road, with a round-headed opening to the attic room, and hipped to the demesne; some evidence of latticed glazing to windows of the avenue elevation. Built in the time here of Richard Steele Fetherstonhaugh (1823–96) after coming of age, having succeeded to the estates on the death of his father in 1834, and perhaps having improved them on his marriage in 1846.
Brewer 1825; *LGI* (1904); Casey and Rowan 1993; IAA photograph (25/22 Z1).

170. ROSEMOUNT, Moate; pre-1837; *demolished.*
A lodge, perhaps contemporary with 'a well-improved demesne, mansion lately built by the late Owen Geoghegan', noted by Brewer in 1825, had been removed before 1914. The fine Palladian-style villa, later home to a branch of the Nugent family, remains.
Brewer 1825; English 1973.

171. ROSMEAD, Delvin (2).
The now-ruined demesne of what was the seat of Henry Woodman Wood in the summer of 1811, when the tourist A. Atkinson was much impressed by the place and particularly taken with the arrangement of its entrance.

East gate; pre-1811; *demolished.*
'The approach to the house, and of a neat porter's lodge, sheltered in a meadow just opposite ... This little lodge, which, in proportion to its size, had as perfect marks of neatness and architectural skill as the lordly edifice on the lordly ground above it. The approach through the avenue to the house, indicates the open and hospitable temper of the owner.' This lodge lay across the road, considerably removed from its gates. By 1900 it had been greatly extended prior to its demise.

West gate; *c.* 1853; architect possibly Sandham Symes; *demolished.*
The estate is now best known for a subsequent proprietor, George Charles Mostyn, 6th Baron Vaux of Harrowden (1804–83), who purchased it in 1852 and accommodated the remains of the extraordinary entrance screen of Glenanea (*q.v.*), from where it had been removed in much-reduced form but now lies a shadow of its former self, the fine display of Coade stone unappreciated and a target for vandals. A new avenue was created on a prominent site to accommodate it and a new gate lodge built to accompany it at what became the principal entrance. From an old photograph the lodge would appear to have been relatively modest in a mild Picturesque manner, single-storey with ornamental foiled bargeboards to its shallow-pitched gables. Architect Sandham Symes had been employed at Rosmead by the baron, his commission perhaps including design of the new lodge.
Atkinson 1815; *BPB* (1929); Craig and Glin 1970; Lyons 1993.

172. ROSSANA, Athlone; *c.* 1835.
A residence in 1837 of one Captain Stubbs that subsequently went through a succession of occupants. The lodge, a 1½-storey standard gabled affair, has consequently been much altered and extended. Segmentally headed windows to the main front in roughcast finished walls, scalloped slate courses to the roof and wavy carved bargeboards with hip-knobs to original and new gables. Occupied.
Lewis 1837.

173. RUSSELLSTOWN, Mullingar; *c.* 1900.
A holding of a Thomas Allen in 1854 that was then valued as no more than a £1 herd's house; by 1900, then held by Robert J. Downes, it had been developed into a property whose status warranted a gate lodge. This is a three-roomed three-bay single-storey structure below a hipped roof, finished in roughcast but with the main avenue front articulated by the central window set back to form a small verandah. The road elevation is also given interest by a rectangular bay window projection below a catslide roof. There are the remains of small-paned casement windows in a characterful though derelict building not beyond salvation.
Griffith 1848–60; *Thom's.*

ST LOMAN'S HOSPITAL (see MULLINGAR LUNATIC ASYLUM)

174. SALLYMOUNT, Castlepollard; *c.* 1830.

A good late eighteenth-century gentleman farmer's house, in 1814 home to Walter Nugent. Sometime within the next twenty years it acquired a gate lodge, probably upon its becoming a seat of George Smith Rotheram, of the Triermore, Co. Meath (*q.v.*), family, who lived on here until his death in 1878. The lodge is single-storey in limewashed rubble construction below a hipped roof that extends along with side walls to effect a recessed two-bay avenue front comprised of a sheeted door and the window, which at some time has been halved in length to form a square two-over-two sash. Solid and unoccupied. Punched masonry chamfered carriage pillars with the plainest of bow-topped railed wrought-iron gates.

Leet 1814; Lewis 1837; *LGI* (1904).

175. SONNA, Ballynacarrigy (3).
An ancient seat of the Tuite family, none of the porters' lodges to which are intact. The northern and middle ones have been demolished and only that to the south-east is faintly recognisable as being a standard single-storey hip-roofed structure with segmentally arched openings and a chimney-stack rising off the rear wall. Probably extended into a double pile after 1837 but now almost totally obscured by a luxuriant covering of ivy.

176. SOUTH HILL, Delvin; *c.* 1845; *demolished.*
A big late Georgian pile, now home to the Sisters of Charity, built by Robert Tighe, which was lodgeless until the Chapmans of Killua Castle (*q.v.*) inherited it about 1835. William Chapman (1811–89) added one opposite the entrance, which survives in the form of a straight railed screen with four low pillars having recessed panels, identical to that to the other Tighe seat of neighbouring Mitchelstown (*q.v.*).

Leet 1814; Lewis 1837; Griffith 1848–60; *LGI* (1904); Bence-Jones 1988.

177. SPRINGPARK, Athlone; *c.* 1860.
On an elevated site by the railway embankment is a single-storey bungalow either replacing or developed from a mid-Victorian gate lodge, to a property in 1854 of William Potts, presumably the same as at nearby New Court (*q.v.*).

178. STANEMORE, Ballynacarrigy; pre-1914; *demolished.*
A seat in 1854 of James Austin.

Griffith 1848–60.

179. STREETE RECTORY, Streete; pre-1837; *demolished.*
A glebe house built in 1812 by the Revd James Webster (b. 1765/6), with which the gatekeeper's lodge may have been contemporary.

Lewis 1837; Leslie and Crooks 2008.

180. TEMPLEORAN, Tyrellspass (2).
Two lodges were added to the seat after it was acquired by Edward Fetherstonhaugh.

Main gate; 1887.
A standard single-storey lodge, its steeply hipped roof having a gabled central hall projection with perforated foil bargeboards, dentil course to the verges and a date-stone in the apex. On each side in rendered walls are bipartite one-over-one sash windows. Catslide roof to rear return; quaint but derelict.

Secondary gate; *c.* 1880.
Outside its gatescreen is a shallow hip-roofed single-storey two-bay cottage built in coursed rubble with yellow brick dressings and punched stone quoins. Bordering on the ruinous.

180. Templeoran, main gate.

TOGHERSTOWN (see THE LODGE)

181. TORE or TORR, Tyrellspass; *c.* 1800.

Hidden behind one of the concave entrance quadrant walls is the decaying fabric of a little Georgian Gothic lodge. Single-storey and two-roomed, its leading short gabled front to the avenue contains a tripartite doorway—the entrance flanked by a pair of sidelights, all three below pointed arches. Rubble-built, creeper-covered and roofless, it would make a delightful controlled eye-catcher ruin from the house, were the latter not in the same state. A demesne inherited on the death of his father, Abraham, in 1799 by Henry Pilkington, who only lived on for another eleven years.

LGI (1904).

TUDENHAM PARK (see ROCHFORT)

182. TULLAGHAN, Mullingar; pre-1837; *demolished.*
A property in the early nineteenth century of the Talbot family, which the first OS map shows to have had a pair of lodges at an inner gate.

Leet 1814; Griffith 1848–60.

TULLYNALLY CASTLE (see PAKENHAM HALL)

183. TURBOTSTOWN, Coole (2).
Although the Dease family has been here since the early seventeenth century, the present villa is of Regency creation and its main lodge contemporary.

Castlepollard gate; *c.* 1825.
A single-storey plain standard porter's lodge, remote from its carriage gates but linked to them by a straight screen wall. Facing the approach below an oversailing hipped roof with long uncarved soffit brackets. Derelict. Built by Gerald Dease (1790–1854).

Coole gate; *c.* 1880.

A quirky structure on the western approach, it would be square on plan and pyramidally roofed were one corner not chamfered with the roof cut accordingly, to leave a sort of irregular 'quintagon'. Rendered with brick toothed quoins, dressings and soldier aches below high eaves, the roof rising steeply to a banded brick chimney-stack. Brick breakfront porch with on one side a tripartite window and on the other a playful canted bay window with its own roof on the chamfered face. Derelict. Erected for Gerald Dease's grandson of the same name, who succeeded to the estate in 1874.

LGI (1904).

184. TWYFORD, Athlone; pre-1837; *demolished.*
A seat of the Handcock family of neighbouring Moydrum Castle (*q.v.*) until the 1790s, after which it was home to the Hodsons, who probably then added its gate lodge. The big house is a shell.
English 1973.

185. TYRRELLSTOWN, Mullingar; pre-1837; *demolished.*
A property in 1814 and 1837 of Benjamin Briggs.
Leet 1814; Lewis 1837.

VASTINA GLEBE (see CASTLETOWN-KINDALEN RECTORY)

186. VIOLETSTOWN, Mullingar; pre-1914; *demolished.*
A lodge probably built by Edward Lewis, who is recorded as living here in 1837 and 1876. Both it and the big house have gone.
Lewis 1837; *Land owners in Ireland 1876.*

187. WALSHESTOWN, Mullingar; *c.* 1800.
Set well back from its gates is a minuscule standard single-storey hip-roofed lodge in random rubble construction with brick eaves band and tiny windows. To a lovely mid-Georgian house in 1854 occupied by Maurice Ham.
Griffith 1848–60.

188. WARDENSTOWN, Killucan; pre-1837; *demolished.*
A property in the early nineteenth century of the Webb family, who built the lodge prior to the arrival of the Vandeleurs *c.* 1845.
Leet 1814; Lewis 1837.

189. WATERSTOWN, Glassan (3).
Yet more tragic remains of a once-proud County Westmeath landed estate, with another noble mansion, here designed by Richard Castle for Gustavus Handcock (1693–1751), reduced to half a shell of its former self, forlornly surveying its lost demesne dotted with derelict outbuildings, an eye-catcher dovecote and extensive walled gardens. To one of these, the orchard, survive gardeners' quarters in the form of a pair of single-roomed, pyramidal-roofed cubes linked by a pedimented entrance archway, the tympanum of which is pierced by a Palladian lunette, and all as a very early example of polychrome brickwork. All very much in the mood of twin porters' entrance lodges and more worthy of such a property than the two gate lodges that survive.

Main entrance; pre-1837; *demolished.*
Neither gates nor lodge of what may have been an appropriate prelude survive.

South entrance; *c.* 1810.
A modest single-storey gabled roughcast three-bay cottage lying derelict. 'Molly's Cottage'.

North entrance; *c.* 1820.
Another unassuming gatekeeper's lodge; single-storey, hip-roofed and three-bay, its sheeted doorway to the left-hand side of bipartite casement windows. Located and abandoned opposite what was an extensive semicircular entrance concourse, now the site of a twentieth-century bungalow.

Three lodges built during the time here of Robert Handcock Temple.
English 1974; Casey and Rowan 1993.

190. WEBBSBROOK, Coole; pre-1837; *demolished.*
A seat in the early nineteenth century of John Webb, the lodge to which had been removed before 1914. Now called 'Lickba'.
Leet 1814.

191. WILLIFIELD, Ballynacarrigy; *c.* 1870.
Opposite the ornamental mid-Victorian cast-iron gatescreen is a contemporary 1½-storey gabled gatehouse in roughcast finish to an irregular three-bay front, the doorway to the right-hand side. A property called 'Willybrook' in 1838 that belonged to James F. Eivers in 1876.
Land owners in Ireland 1876.

192. WILSON'S HOSPITAL, Multyfarnham; *c.* 1800.
A surprising apparition in the Irish landscape is this Palladian-style building; founded in 1759 by Andrew Wilson as a home for elderly Protestant men and a school for Protestant boys, it remains a school to this day. Not quite as antique but proving as durable is the Georgian Gothic porter's lodge by the gate (*below*). Single-storey, now roughcast, contrasting with stone dressings, quoins and skew-tables, it presents a symmetrical three-bay short gabled front to the avenue. A pair of pointed-arched windows flank the flat-arched blocked doorway, over which are two awkwardly placed stone plaques, one bearing the Wilson crest and the other their coat of arms.

Immaculately maintained but suffering from modern plastic windows. The striking gatescreen has a towering pair of corniced-capped Classical pillars with pineapple finials, flanked by wing walls containing postilion door openings, all perhaps originating from that period after the hospital was destroyed in 1798 and subsequently rebuilt.
Casey and Rowan 1993.

193. WOODFORT, Killucan; pre-1914; *demolished.*
A pair of lodges that were probably built after the property passed from Cooke Reynell, who died in 1841, to Edmond R. Nugent.
Griffith 1848–60; *LGI* (1904).

194. WOODLAND, Ballynafid; *c.* 1855.
A pretty little single-storey standard gatekeeper's lodge by a railway crossing. Square windows flank a sheeted front door built in rubble stone with brick soldier arches below the tall eaves of an oversailing hipped roof, atop which is a cut-stone chimney-stack. Built by the Great Midland and Western Railway Company, it was originally harled and gave access to a residence of the Maxton family, who were agents to the neighbouring Clonhugh estate (*q.v.*) of the Forbes family, earls of Granard.
Griffith 1848–60; NIAH.

WOODVILLE (see HAWTHORN COTTAGE)

COUNTY WEXFORD

ADAMSTOWN (see KNOCKREIGH)

1. AHARE, Castletown; pre-1840; *demolished.*
A lodge that was shown unhatched on the 1940 OS map, indicating that it was already ruinous by then. The property, in 1790 of a Col. Deaken (Deacon?), passed by marriage after the death in 1802 of Edmond Rice to the Beauman family of nearby Hyde Park (*q.v.*), who thereafter let it out to a succession of tenants. In 1853 the gatekeeper was Thomas Jordan, leasing from Joseph Gilbert. The house has also gone, having been in decline since the mid-nineteenth century.

Wilson 1803; Griffith 1848–60; *LGI* (1904).

2. ALMA, Wexford; *c.* 1854.

The house and its lodge appear to be contemporary, built by Robert Allen of R.M. and R. Allen, corn merchants and shipowners. Single-storey standard, its high oversailing eaves with moulded frieze below give it a jaunty feel. Tall one-over-one bipartite sash windows flank the sheeted front door in newly rendered crisp finish. Occupied. Simple railed concave entrance quadrants and stone posts with recessed panels.

Slater 1856.

ARCHERTON (see PROSPECT VIEW)

3. ARDAMINE, Courtown; *c.* 1880.

A short-lived house, built up by three generations of the Richards family from 1818 to its burning in the Troubles of the 1920s. It is survived at a secondary entrance by a substantial structure, which is in fact a pair of semi-detached estate workers' houses. They are 1½-storey, each on an L-plan and perfectly symmetrical, with a double gable advancing towards the avenue, both having a catslide roof in the internal angle forming a canopied porch with flimsy cast-iron post support. All pleasantly faced in ragstone with relief in polychromatic brickwork to segmentally arched windows and string-course. Steeply pitched roof with a variety of sawtooth and scalloped slating and a big sturdy central brick chimney-stack. Built for Arthur William Mordaunt Goddard Richards, who inherited the place on his brother's death in 1879 and seems to have been responsible for an extensive building development about the estate. The site of the house has been reduced to the ignominy of being a caravan park.

LGI (1904); Rowe and Scallan 2004.

ARDARA (see WELLINGTON COTTAGE)

4. ARNESTOWN, New Ross; pre-1840; *demolished.*
As early as 1783 the proprietor was one Corbet Esq., but for much of the nineteenth century it was home to the Carr family.

Taylor and Skinner 1778; 1969 [1783]; Griffith 1848–60; Bassett 1885.

5. ARTRAMON, Castlebridge; pre-1840; *demolished.*
A late eighteenth-century house described in 1837 as the elegant seat of G. Le Hunte. This was George Le Hunte (1815–91), who bought it from his cousins. Its lodge had gone by 1941.

Lewis 1837; *LGI* (1904).

BALLINAPARK (see BROWN PARK)

6. BALLINCLAY, Camolin (2).
Both lodges to the property were in place by 1839 but have been demolished, that towards Camolin having gone by 1902, the other ruinous. They were either built by the Wrights, founders of the estate, or after Joseph Waring acquired it in the early nineteenth century.

Rowe and Scallan 2004.

7. BALLINGLY, Wellingtonbridge; *c.* 1800.
Off the beaten track, in perfect seclusion by the Corock River, are a ruined church and family graveyard, opposite whose gates are the remains of a modest gate lodge, put to use in an agricultural capacity, gutted, a wide opening gouged out of one gable. Single-storey standard, its front door blocked up and flanked by painted mock window inserts in harled rubble walls, the steeply pitched gabled roof covered in corrugated asbestos. Perhaps built in the brief time here of a Dr Harper before the coming of the Corish family.

Rowe and Scallan 2004.

8. BALLINKEELE, Ballymurn; *c.* 1839; architect Daniel Robertson.

The estate was purchased from Edward Hay in 1825 by the young John Maher (1801–60), who commissioned Daniel Robertson to design him a new house. Although the drawings are dated 1840 and are in the architect's less familiar Italianate style, the new gate lodge was already in place by then, opposite the entrance, almost as if prepared to monitor the major building works within. This 1½-storey cottage in contrasting Tudor cloak is of standard symmetrical elevation with, in harled walls, stone-dressed openings and conspicuous label mouldings to tripartite lattice-paned casements and the central doorway. The high eaves and gabled ends oversail with carved brackets and accommodate attic rooms lit by bipartite windows. A pretty, well-maintained building. The extensive railed gatescreen is wholly cast iron, with decorative pillars containing anthemion motifs, presumably selected by the architect.

At the lodgeless Ballymun entrance is another ornate gatescreen of six granite pillars with moulded recessed panels and a range of beautifully cast and elaborate ogee quadrants with matching carriage and postilion gates. It would seem that there was to have been an attendant lodge here, as there exists a dimensioned proposal dated July 1843 by Robertson for an ornamental 1½-storey cottage on an irregular plan with unusually low-pitched roofs having decorative fretted bargeboards. Intended were two attic bedrooms over a kitchen and lobby (or porch) and a single-storey scullery

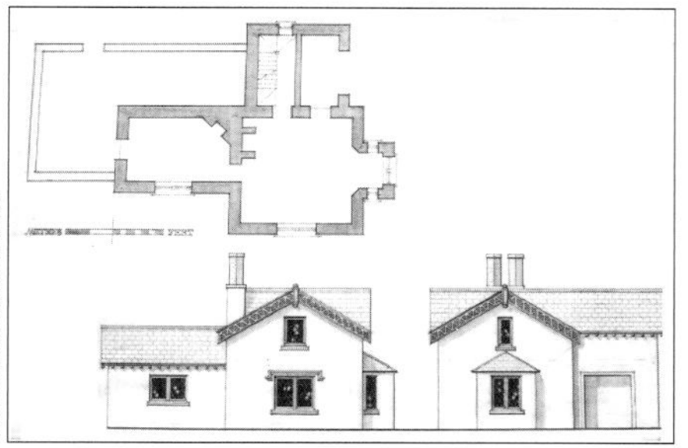

Irish Architectural Archive

back return with yard area. The avenue elevation shows a single-storey hip-roofed bay window, and a large chimney-stack rising off the back wall with two diagonally set Tudor-style flues. The illustration is a redrawing of Robertson's original.

Lacy 1863; *LGI* (1904); Williams 1994; *IAR* (1999); IAA drawing (S00152/98/105[70]).

9. BALLINROOAUN LODGE, Screen; pre-1853; *demolished.*

A property of Richard Samuel Guinness in 1837 that by 1853 he was leasing to Henry Goold according to the valuation, which also refers to a gatehouse, unclear on the OS maps or on site, assumed removed.

Lewis 1837; Griffith 1848–60.

10. BALLYANNE, New Ross (2).

A poignant illustration of how a once-prosperous estate can fall from grace. Once home to Henry Houghton, who died about 1800, but not before endowing the Fever Hospital in New Ross (*q.v.*), creating a 'handsome seat' and furnishing the demesne with two fine lodged entrances. His house has gone, along with its fine interiors, but its porters' lodges survive—just.

North gate; *c.* 1790.

A rare survivor is this charming 1½-storey Georgian Gothic cottage with high eaves to the hipped roof. Finished in harling, it turns its blind elevation to the road and a pair of pointed sash windows on the opposing park front. To one end is a stunted sort of Gothic Venetian window with pointed head, Y-tracery and sidelights. Very derelict, in keeping with the dilapidated concave stone quadrants and redundant avenue.

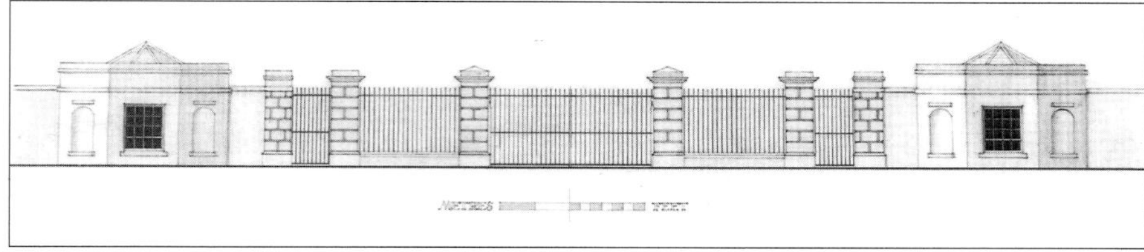

10. Ballyanne, south gate.

South gate; *c.* 1790.

Here is the most perfect prelude to the contemporary house, which had a three-storey double-canted bay front. Still in use, the old main entrance comprised an impressive wide-ranging straight gatescreen consisting of six V-jointed rusticated ashlar pillars with moulded cappings, the centre pair of which have scroll-topped gate stops. Between are railings and matching spear-topped iron postern gates, while the whole terminates in two matching porters' lodges, of which only the leading elevations remain. These have canted fronts with central windows (now blocked up), each flanked by a pair of segmentally arched niches with basic dripstones above. Harled finish, with parapets to screen the roofs.

Henry Houghton's widow, Mary O'Ferrall, married for a second time but died in 1812, when the property was inherited by her brother.

Lewis 1837; *LGI* (1904); Walsh 1996; Rowe and Scallan 2004.

11. BALLYBOGGAN, Wexford; pre-1840/1905; architect not known.

The present gatekeeper's lodge is a replacement for that which existed in the time of the Harvey family, one of whom, James William Harvey (1798–1873), is noted here in 1837 but later moved to Broomley Cottage (*q.v.*). The property was later renamed 'Park House'. The present structure is a very smart Edwardian affair, 1½-storey by dint of a basement which elevates the principal floor off an L-plan, with a flight of steps leading to a glazed entrance hall in the internal angle. The main interest is a vast corbelled chimney-stack and the gables with their carved and perforated wooden features to the eaves and turned hip-knobbed apexes, features all to be found in the lodge to Healthfield (*q.v.*) by the same unidentified designer. Crisply rendered with modern plastic windows. There are four contemporary stone gate pillars with moulded cappings in the form of four-faced pediments on pulvinated friezes. Built by Martin Pierce, who arrived about the turn of the twentieth century and replaced the old lodge on precisely the same footprint. There is an almost identical structure at Healthfield (*q.v.*).

Lewis 1837; *LGI* (1904); Rowe and Scallan 2004.

12. BALLYCONNICK, Cleristown; *c.* 1870.

A two-storey harled gabled gatehouse with two-bay attic storey over a four-bay ground floor. Perhaps this was part of the continuing improvements nearing completion in 1868 being carried out by John Sparrow, who was a tenant of Anthony Cliffe of Bellevue (*q.v.*).

Doyle 1868.

13. BALLYCOURCY or BALLYCOURSEY, Enniscorthy; *c.* 1835.

A single-storey cottage of four bays (reduced from five) with steeply pitched gabled roof. Roughcast, with unusual eight-over-twelve squared cast-iron windows with openers pivoting. Built in the time here of Anthony Hawkins.

Leet 1814; Lewis 1837.

14. BALLYCROSS, Bridgetown; pre-1840/*c.* 1860; *demolished.*

Long-time seat of the Rowe family, whose early house and its pair of gate lodges by the entrance have gone, as has the replacement porter's cottage, although its contemporary house survives, originally built by John Rowe.

LG (1863); Lacy 1863.

15. BALLYCRYSTAL, Kiltealy; *c.* 1850.

An intriguing building group at the entrance to the now-demolished big house, in 1837 'of Thomas James Esq., romantically situated on the mountainous confines of the county of Carlow'. It consists of a fine pair of lofty ashlar pillars of *c.* 1750 with moulded cornices and elegant ball finials, with what appear to be original simple wrought-iron carriage gates. These are linked by a rubble screen wall, with dressed postilion opening, to an antique two-storey hexagonal sentry tower with equivalent roof and having genuine gunloops defending the entrance. To the right-hand side is a smart gabled structure in sharp rendering, in occupation, so modernised as to be of indeterminate age. This may be the building referred to in 1853 as a gatehouse occupied by Lewis Richards, leasing from Revd John James. The gates would have given onto an early house destroyed in the '98; the gatehouse belongs to its rebuilt successor. The tower may be a survivor from the time here of the Colcloughs of Tintern (*q.v.*) in the 1500s.

Lewis 1837; Griffith 1848–60; Rowe and Scallan 2004.

16. BALLYFAD, Coolgreany; *c.* 1820.
A tiny single-storey standard gabled cottage with projecting gabled hall. Rendered and occupied. Presumably built by Mr Andrew Forde, resident in 1814.

Leet 1814.

17. BALLYHEALY, Bridgetown; pre-1925; *demolished.*
Probably a mid-Victorian gatekeeper's lodge to the property in the nineteenth century of the Tench family.

18. BALLYHIGHLAND, Enniscorthy (3).
James Howlin was recorded here in 1814, but it was probably his younger son John (1797–1857), who inherited in 1823, who added two porters' lodges to complement the house and outbuildings, which date from the early 1830s. These have gone but a third survives, perhaps built *c.* 1870 by James Moffatt, who had purchased the property a couple of years before. This was a single-storey solid structure with a symmetrical three-bay front, having a central breakfront hall with a rudimentary pediment breaking the fascia of the hipped roof. Built off an L-plan in squared stone block construction, exposed in rehabilitation by removal of a harled finish which would have highlighted the dressed stone of its quoins and chamfered window surrounds. Modernisation has seen the insertion of inappropriate plastic windows and the covering of the roof in synthetic slates.

Leet 1814; Doyle; *LGI* (1904).

19. BALLYMACKESY, Clonroche; *c.* 1840.
The similarity of this little ruinous lodge to that at neighbouring Borrhill (*q.v.*) suggests that it was built by the Fitzhenry family just before Lawrence Sweetman came to the property. Standard single-storey hip-roofed and constructed in brick-dressed rubble with harled finish. Later catslide-roofed extension to right-hand side.

Rowe and Scallan 2004.

20. BALLYMORE, Camolin; *c.* 1815.

Part of the 1670 house was built by a Major Dennison, but most of the other surviving architecture on the estate is the work of the Donovan family. This includes the delightful little Georgian Gothic porter's lodge, which was perhaps part of the improvements carried out by Richard Donovan (*c.* 1757–1816). It is a single-storey harled rubble-built cottage with steeply pitched hipped roof, having its long two-bay front, of lattice-paned bipartite casement windows, to the base of the 1km-long avenue. Facing the road is a Y-traceried sashed pointed light with, squeezed in alongside and surely of later date, a flat-arched doorway. Occupied and proudly maintained. There are simple rubble-stone entrance quadrants and square carriage pillars with rusticated ball finials.

LGI (1904); Rowe and Scallan 2004.

21. BALLYNABOLA or BALLINABOOLA, Old Ross; *c.* 1820.
To a late Georgian house of the Browne family is a ruinous ivy-shrouded single-storey standard lodge, three-roomed and square on plan below a pyramidal roof. Harled, with six-over-six sash windows.

Rowe and Scallan 2004.

22. BALLYNADARA, Enniscorthy; *c.* 1900.
Opposite the gates is a standard gabled lodge in nice random rubble facings with brick dressings, arches and quoins. Extended and occupied. House and lodge comprise a development at the turn of the century by John Connor.

23. BALLYNAGEE, Wexford; pre-1941; *demolished.*
A seat in 1853 of James Crosbie.

Griffith 1848–60.

24. BALLYNAPIERCE, Enniscorthy; *c.* 1845.
A pretty English Picturesque Cottage-style lodge built by Overington Bolton. Single-

storey standard with ornamental continuous-bracket bargeboards and spiky carved hip-knobs to the main gables and that of the projecting porch, which is carried on a pair of basic wooden posts. Cast-iron latticed casement windows bipartite to the road gable, which may have lost their original Tudor label mouldings in a modern rendering scheme. To the ridge is a pair of chimney-stacks united by a common capping. Good concave quadrant dwarf walls and decorative railings with matching gates on plain pillars.

Lewis 1837; Griffith 1848–60.

25. BALLYNASTRAW COTTAGE, Bunclody; pre-1839; *demolished.*
A small estate, in 1814 home to Laurence Doyle, the gate lodge to which had been removed by 1923.

Leet 1814.

26. BALLYNESTRAGH, Killinierin (2).
The ancient seat of the Esmondes, which remains that family's property to this day. The present house was built in 1937 to replace the previous one with sixteenth-century foundations after it was burnt in the

Troubles. Only one of the earlier two lodges barely survives.

East gate; *c.* 1825.

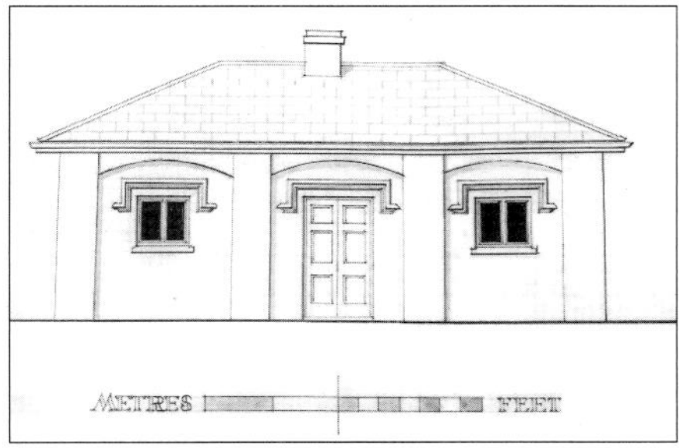

This may have formed part of the improvement to the house and demesne instigated by the 9th baronet, Sir Thomas Esmonde (1786–1868), who succeeded his uncle to the estate in 1803. The lodge is a typically naive Irish Regency affair by his jobbing builder, displaying a confusion of styles. Single-storey standard and hip-roofed, with openings below the popular new Tudor label mouldings, rather crudely executed, all set in segmentally arched Classical recesses. Tiny windows set in harled walls. It now lies derelict and overgrown. Postilion gates flank simple square carriage pillars with ball finials.

West gate; pre-1940; *demolished.*

BPB (1929); Bence-Jones 1988; Rowe and Scallan 2004.

BALLYOWEN (see ROSEGARLAND COTTAGE)

BALLYRANKIN (see NEWLANDS)

27. BALLYRANKIN, Clohamon (2).

Major John Devereux (1768–1841) lived just long enough to appreciate the radical new building works on his estate, which saw the erection of a fine Classical villa and two gatekeepers' lodges opposite their entrances, both virtually identical.

Main gate; *c.* 1835; architect not known.

At the northern approach, now disused, is a fine railed gatescreen of decorative ironwork, its convex quadrants and matching carriage gates all set off by four stone pillars with moulded recessed panels and gadrooned cappings. Across the road, deprived of its original role, is the conspicuous lodge. Standard but having a hipped roof with paired carved wooden modillion brackets to the unusually tall eaves, sufficient to accommodate loft rooms. The rendered main front has its openings contained in rectangular recesses, the casement windows particularly ornate, with cast-iron hexagonal glazing pattern. Occupied.

Secondary gate; *c.* 1835; architect not known.

Once guarding the southern avenue was what an old photograph shows to have been an almost identical lodge to the above, differing only in its chimney-stack being off-centre and its panelled doorway set in a smaller recess. It now lies pathetically derelict, its original striking windows replaced by hideous twentieth-century steel casements. These scenes at the gates are sadly indicative of past tragic events within, the house having been lost in the Troubles.

LGI (1904); Walsh 1996.

28. BALLYSESKIN, Bridgetown; pre-1840; *demolished.*

A gate lodge opposite the gates that may have been built by Henry Archer (d. 1836), who had come into the property by marriage to a Bunbury.

Lewis 1837; Rowe and Scallan 2004.

BANNOW (see GRANGE)

29. BARGY CASTLE, Tomhaggard; *c.* 1840.

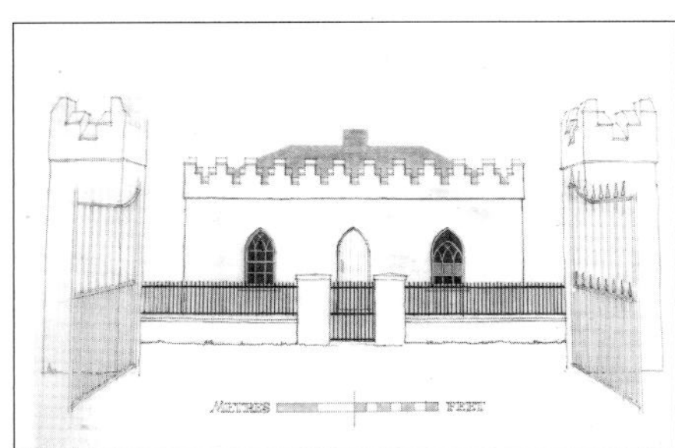

Other than in its symmetry, this entrance and lodge are the perfect prelude to their big house. Single-storey standard, the harled rubble construction, Gothic pointed openings and Irish crenellations to parapet and gate pillars reflect the finish and details of the mansion. Located opposite the entrance screen, the old porter's accommodation is now little more than a shell. Having medieval foundations, Bargy Castle evolved to its present informal appearance through centuries of alterations and additions, mainly during three centuries of ownership by the Harvey family, of whom Major John Harvey (1816–80) added the lodge after succeeding to the property in 1834, when it was still home to his grandmother.

Heaney 1999; *LGI* (1904); Rowe and Scallan 2004.

30. BARNADOWN, Ballycanew (2).

A property, from 1798 and in the first half of the nineteenth century of the Brownrigge family, to which both pre-1839 lodges have been demolished.

Lewis 1837; Rowe and Scallan 2004.

31. BARNTOWN, Wexford; pre-1905; *demolished.*

Now known as 'Slaney Manor' is what was in 1837 'the newly erected residence of James Perceval'. He died in 1843, so it may have been his son, John James Perceval (b. 1843), who added the lodge sometime after coming of age.

Lewis 1837; *LGI* (1904).

32. BEAUFIELD, Bunclody; pre-1839; *demolished.*

A seat in 1837 of Thomas Braddell, the lodge to which, opposite the gates, by 1923 was close to ruin, a fate which has befallen the big house.

Lewis 1837.

BEECHVILLE (see MARYVILLE)

33. BELLEVUE, Wexford (4).

An estate of important architecture created over a century by two families but largely devastated by the efforts of 'Sinn Féin pyromaniacs' in 1923. The fine original coordinated composition that was the house, now reduced to a hodgepodge, was home to George Ogle, who built it in 1737 and complemented it with one of the oldest remaining pairs of entrance lodges in the country.

Baroque gate; *c.* 1740.

At the head of the northern approach, which followed the River Slaney, was an impressive and extensive entrance screen as an introduction to the mansion. Comprised of two single-storey gabled two-roomed lodges, 166ft apart and originally linked by shallow concave quadrants (now gone). Unusually, the single-bay fronts do not face each other but continue the quadrant angles and consist of a single round-headed keystoned opening, subsequently reduced to a window flanked by bold banded pilasters of brickwork alternating with harling, all below a pediment containing a blind lunette. Otherwise finished in stucco, the chimney-stacks rise off the opposing gables, and one can speculate that the gate pillars matched the pilasters, crowned by blocked ball or pineapple finials. A unique survival of rustic Baroque, perhaps contemporary with the house.

North lodge; pre-1840; *demolished.*
Another gate on the main avenue probably dating from the Ogle era.

Following the death in 1814 of George Ogle's son of the same name, the estate was purchased in 1825 by Anthony Cliffe (1800–78), who added a new entrance from the south monitored by a neo-Classical lodge.

South lodge; *c.* 1845; architect probably C.F. Anderson or Daniel Robertson.

The visitor is confronted by a bridge before the spear-topped carriage gates flanked by tall straight brick screen walls and integral square pillars with stone plinth and continuous corniced cappings and copings. Behind is a pretentious little lodge, its short back and front avenue elevations pedimented with acroteria, on a deep frieze carried on paired stone Doric pilasters that define the two-bay sides containing margined sash windows in what may have been brick panels to match the gatescreen but now in dreary grey rendering. Also unfortunate is the flat-roofed hallway, which extends towards the avenue similarly pilastered but probably an ill-conceived part of the original design. Despite this, it would appear to be architect-designed, quite by whom is not recorded but the two leading contenders must be Charles Frederick Anderson, who is noted as working for Cliffe on engineering the course of the Blackwater River, and Daniel Robertson, who was employed about this time by Cliffe's brother-in-law, the 1st Lord Carew, at Castleboro (*q.v.*).

Inner lodge; pre-1840.
Another porter's cottage to the north of the demesne, now unrecognisable from its original form, having been incorporated into and lost in a modern house. Its gates have been removed.

Doyle 1868; *LGI* (1904); Culleton 1994; Walsh 1996.

34. BELMONT, Wexford (2).
A large, lost Tudor Revival mansion in the manner of Daniel Robertson, presumably built on the occasion of his marriage in 1836 by Charles Arthur Walker (1791–1853) of the Percy Lodge (*q.v.*) family at what in 1835 was already described as 'a nice place, looking over the valley of the Slaney, with views over the bay and town etc.', with 'an excellent garden and both it and its pleasure grounds are stocked with a great variety of trees, shrubs and plants of every kind'. There were two gatekeepers' lodges in place by 1840, built either by Walker or by the previous proprietor, William E. Lees.

North lodge; pre-1840; *demolished.*
Located beside the church, it had gone by 1905.

South lodge; *c.* 1830.
A roughcast four-bay hip-roofed structure with a projecting gabled hall, plain but for having some fish-scale slate courses to the roof. Occupied and probably extended since its first building.

Pigot 1824;Lewis 1837; *LGI* (1904); Walsh 1996; Heaney 1999.

35. BENVILLE, Murntown (2).
Both present lodges seem to owe their appearance to Edward Acton Gibbon (1835–1920), who purchased the property from the Morroghs in 1900 and greatly improved it by also building a new house. It is first recorded on the 1811 Valentine map as 'Benville', presumably after a Benjamin of the Wilson family, who were here until about 1870. A later Benjamin Wilson by 1838 had renamed it 'Sleedagh' after its townland.

South entrance; *c.* 1850/*c.* 1900.
Now a standard and spacious 1½-storey gatehouse with fancy Picturesque carved bargeboards to main gables, two front gablets and to the single-storey central projecting hall, the upper floor now clad in more recent shiplap boarding but the ground floor perhaps revealing its earlier origins with its V-jointed toothed quoins. Occupied, with a back return.

North entrance; pre-1840/*c.* 1900.

Eithne Scallan

Built as a replacement for an earlier Wilson lodge on the site is this 1½-storey Edwardian affair with its mock Tudor 'black and white' gable feature typical of the time. From this leading one-bay front projects a single-storey canted bay window, whilst to the avenue elevation is a lean-to canopied doorway. Roughcast, occupied and smartly maintained. The carriage gate pillars in stone with layered pyramidal cappings and contrasting roughcast walled quadrants look to date from *c.* 1855, in the time here of a later Benjamin Wilson.

Griffith 1848–60; *LGI* (1904); Rowe and Scallan 2004.

36. BERKELEY FOREST, New Ross (2).
A fine house of mid-Georgian appearance on a property granted to Bishop George Berkeley, from whom it passed by inheritance to the Berkeley Deane family.

South lodge; *c.* 1800.

Prominently facing the road alongside its entrance gates is a pretty, once-quintessential Georgian Gothic porter's lodge in a dilapidated state, with evidence of subsequent alterations. Originally single-storey standard with two lancet windows flanking the doorway (now blocked up) in harled walls below a hipped roof, the eaves line of which was raised to provide additional loft space. To one side a lean-to wall attaches a basic screen wall to the carriage entrance of a pair of stone pillars with nicely moulded cappings that neatly match the chimney-stack. Deserted.

North lodge; 1854.

Built in the time of John St George Deane, who inherited the place in 1837, is this pleasant concoction of a standard 1½-storey lodge with Tudor Picturesque serrated bargeboards to main gables and that of the projecting single-storey hallway, which may be an afterthought, for it has an incongruous Classical pedimented door-case and little round-headed sidelights. On each side is a window set in Regency-style semicircular-arched recesses. To the park gable is a single-storey canted bay with corresponding roof; rendered with modern window inserts. Occupied. Four ashlar pillars with moulded cappings contain the carriage gates, with contemporary ironwork and a pair of sealed-up postilion openings.

Slater 1846; 1856; *LGI* (1904); Walsh 1996; Rowe and Scallan 2004.

37. BETTYVILLE, Wexford; pre-1840; *demolished.*
A late eighteenth-century house, then the property of the Jacob family, from whom it passed *c.* 1800 to Walter Redmond, after whose death without male issue it was inherited by his son-in-law, John Hyacinth Talbot. It has gone the way of its lodge.

Taylor and Skinner 1778; 1969 [1783]; Wilson 1803; *LGI* (1904); Rowe and Scallan 2004.

38. BIRCH GROVE, Wexford; *c.* 1845; *demolished.*
A gatekeeper's lodge built sometime between the first OS map of 1840 and the Griffith valuation of 1853, when it is recorded as a seat of Robert Sparrow.

Griffith 1848–60.

39. BLACKSTOOPS, Enniscorthy; pre-1902; *demolished.*
A property of Lord Portsmouth, which was let to Richard N. Bennett before being documented as occupied by Thomas Pounder in 1853 and 1885; the lodge, built after 1840 not quite opposite its gates, has been swept away in modern roadworks.

Wilson 1803; Leet 1814; Griffith 1848–60; Bassett 1885.

40. BLEACHLANDS TOWNLAND, Castlebridge; pre-1840; *demolished.*
A gate lodge and garden let in 1853 to gate porter Patrick Power by Samuel Atkins of the nearby house, offices, corn mill and bleach green. Removed before 1905.

Griffith 1848–60.

41. BLOOMFIELD, Enniscorthy (2).
A very fine example of architect Daniel Robertson at his most able in the Tudor Revival manner in this villa for William Russell Farmar (1802–71) in about 1835, to which he added two lodges in a similarly informal outline but in a characteristic Picturesque style, which he also produced for a very similar cottage on the Castleboro estate (*q.v.*).

East entrance; *c.* 1838; architect Daniel Robertson.

A highly distinctive design for a 1½-storey lodge which, although having symmetrical façades, displays an irregular outline by the placing of a single-storey wing and the position of a prominent pair of octagonal stone chimney-stacks. The road elevation has a little gabled single-storey breakfront window below a label-moulded attic window with chamfered dressing, over which are the most decoratively carved bargeboards to the steeply pitched gables. On the avenue front is the entrance doorway with the most deeply chamfered of granite surrounds, over which, breaking the high eaves with moulded corbel blocks, is an eccentric gablet simply contrived to contain a blank shield and emphasise the doorway under. The whitewashed roughcast finish contrasts effectively with what granite highlights haven't been painted over. The striking squat ashlar gate pillars have moulded and crenellated cappings, identical to those at another Robertson house: Wells (*q.v.*).

West entrance; *c.* 1840; architect Daniel Robertson.

A handed version of the above, with a variation in its beautiful bargeboards, fretted as Pugin would have approved, but with disastrous modern plate-glass windows in the leading gable.

Lewis 1837; *LGI* (1904); Walsh 1996; *IAR* (1999).

42. BORLEAGH MANOR, Killinierin (2).
In 1868 Doyle records that 'The house, formerly but a small lodge has been converted into a spacious modern mansion in the Italian style', probably referring to that which was intended to be built in 1837 by Revd T. Quin (1756–1841), according to Lewis. So it was presumably his successor, Henry Quin, who continued the estate improvements with the addition of two lodges, neither of which has survived despite being erected after 1840 and at least one of which was in place by 1853.

Lewis 1837; Griffith 1848–60; Doyle 1868.

43. BORODALE, Enniscorthy; pre-1840; *demolished.*
The house that was the birthplace of Admiral of the Fleet David Beatty, of WWI fame, and in 1837 was described as 'an elegant modern villa' of his ancestral namesake, was demolished 100 years later, to be barely outlived by its gate lodge, which may have been contemporary.

Lewis 1837; Walsh 1996.

44. BOROHILL, Clonroche; *c.* 1840.
The exiled '98 rebel Jeremiah Fitzhenry returned to his seat in 1811 after being pardoned by the duke of Wellington, and seems to have added a gate lodge to the property in his old age. Looking much like that to neighbouring Ballymackesy (*q.v.*), it was a standard hip-roofed affair, built in rubble stone, brick-dressed and finished in harling. Now ruinous and engulfed in laurel.

Rowe and Scallan 2004.

45. BORRMOUNT MANOR, Enniscorthy (2).
The house as it stands was built by James Gethings *c.* 1841 after marrying the widow of its previous owner, Parsons Frayne. In Italianate style, it contrasts with the pretty surviving Picturesque lodge. Both lodges were built after the sale of the property through the incumbered estates court in 1854, when it subsequently passed through three other hands, and formed part of the improvement works that included a new kitchen and stable offices *c.* 1880 under the direction of architect John McCurdy for Loftus A. Bryan.

Front lodge; *c.* 1880; architect possibly John McCurdy.

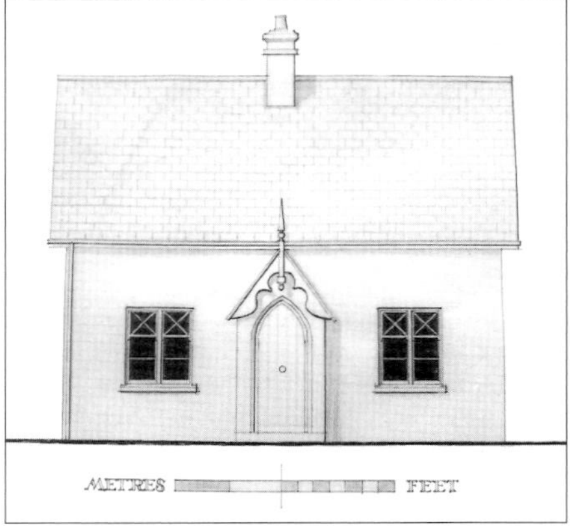

A standard single-storey gabled cottage with high eaves to accommodate the projecting hall, with its pointed-arched doorway and mildly decorative bargeboards with spiky hip-knobs, like the main gables. The bipartite sash windows in rendered walls had chinoiserie upper panes. Nicely canopied in *Clematis montana*. The highly ornate and sturdy cast-iron gate pillars had anthemion motifs and little pineapple finials, while the carriage gates were suitably chunky. By 2008 the whole entrance complex had taken a turn for the worse, the cast-iron pillars and gates having been removed, as had the original windows, to be replaced by nasty modern plastic. The clematis had also fallen foul of the 'improvers'.

Back lodge; *c.* 1855; *demolished.*
All that survives is an overgrown entrance sweep of small ogee railed quadrants with stop posts displaying nice anthemion motifs.

Lacy 1863; Lyons 1993; Walsh 1996; IAA.

46. BRICKETSTOWN, Taghmon; pre-1840; *demolished.*
A property in the early nineteenth century of Thomas Stannard.

47. BROOK HILL, Wexford; *c.* 1850; architect not known.

A highly decorative little lodge, tragically abandoned and overgrown, precocious in its detail, appearing to date from twenty years later. The present house was built by the Revd Thomas Bell (1802–81), curate of Ferns parish (1844–7), after he married into the Bury family, previous proprietors of Brook Hill; the lodge is recorded in the 1853 valuation. Single-storey standard and rendered, with round-headed openings in matching recesses with hood mouldings and having Irish pilaster quoins, all below an oversailing hipped roof with eaves band and multiple soffit brackets.

Slater 1846; Griffith 1848–60; Lacy 1863; Leslie and Knox 2008; Rowe and Scallan 2004; NIAH.

BROOKVILLE (see JANEVILLE)

48. BROOMLEY COTTAGE, Crossabeg; *c.* 1835.
Samuel Lewis in 1837 informs us that 'Some handsome cottage residences have lately been erected on the Kyle estate, of which that called Broomley is occupied by C. Huson', and in 1868 Doyle goes on to record that 'the seat of Mr Solly Flood, J.P. is a new structure, conspicuous for magnitude', and accurately predicts that it 'is not yet relieved by the plantations, which, in a succeeding generation, will embellish it'. Charles Huson

of the Springfield (*q.v.*) family and Mr Flood were in fact long-term tenants here of the Harvey family of Kyle (*q.v.*), who in their philanthropy provided on the park perimeter a pair of schoolhouses, one for each sex, one of which remains at the gate with the dual role of a porter's lodge. Although of generally three-bay format, it is suitably sized to fulfil both functions, and characterful, with bowed ends below a conspicuously oversailing shallow-pitched hipped roof, the eaves of which are sufficiently high to permit teacher's loft space, and, below, a single-storey projecting hall with its own hipped roof. Despite the inappropriate modern windows flanking and in the bows, it is easy to imagine Picturesque latticed casements on each side of a pretty open porch and rustic harled walls. The eaves are now broken by a pair of flat-roofed 'gablet' windows. There survive contemporary cast-iron hoop-topped gate posts with anthemion motifs, and spoked-pattern postern and carriage gates.

Lewis 1837; Doyle 1868; Rowe and Scallan 2004.

49. BROWN PARK, Bunclody; pre-1839/*c.* 1875.
Contrary to the spelling on the early OS map and in the directories, this was in the first half of the nineteenth century home to the Browne family, who by 1837 seem to have renamed it 'Ballinapark' after its townland. Their lodge to the right-hand side of the entrance could have been built by G. Browne, noted here by Lewis, or by a predecessor, Revd John Browne, in 1814. In any case, it was supplanted to the other side of the gate by the Hall-Dares of neighbouring Woodfield (*q.v.*). This perky and pretty survivor (*below*) would be perfectly symmetrical were it not for its offset chimney-stack. It is 1½-storey with a steeply hipped roof and high eaves interrupted at opposing ends by matching gablets—all very English, and almost Nash-like, were it not so regular. The Westmoreland green slate roof and secret hips tell of a twentieth-century rehabilitation. Constructed in haphazard ragstone with chunky granite blocks as quoins to the main block and its single-storey projecting gabled hall, the openings having orange brick segmental arches. Occupied and beautifully tended, with a trim hedge and picket fence enclosure.

Leet 1814; Lewis 1837; Rowe and Scallan 2004.

50. BROWNSWOOD, Enniscorthy (3).
Here was a perfectly polite Georgian gentry house acquired by Capt. Jeremiah Lonsdale Pounden, swept away *c.* 1894 by his daughter Eveleen in favour of an ill-mannered neo-Jacobean pile. Married since 1863 to the painter James McLaren Smith, she clearly felt that this new dwelling reflected her newly acquired status as Baroness Gray, a title she inherited on the death of her uncle, the 14th earl of Moray and 18th Lord Gray. Her daughter, the furniture designer Eileen Gray, was so appalled at the loss of her childhood home that she fled to Paris, never to return, although she may have had fonder memories of the new gate lodges. As mere Mrs Smith in 1889 Eveleen had engaged the Dublin architect William Mansfield Mitchell to alter and add to the old house and design two gate lodges, but about five years later she employed his friend Sir Thomas Drew and local builder William Fortune to create the present pile and a third porter's lodge.

Main entrance; *c.* 1890; architect W.M. Mitchell.
Happily, on the centenary of their completion this striking lodge and its entrance were saved from advanced dereliction by a faithful restoration scheme.

Approached through a wide gatescreen of tall concave quadrant walls in red brick, relieved by red sandstone plinth banding and pillar cappings, on an elevated site is a dominating 1½-storey 'Stockbroker Tudor' creation built off a cruciform plan. Its attic storey is jettied out to the sides and projects over the entrance to form a verandahed porch, with picket fence, carried on wooden posts with curved pelmets between. Over is a carved dentil course and, above that, serrated terracotta tile-hanging with half-timbering in the gable apexes. There is more 'black and white' work to the ground floor, but the recurring theme is of red earthenware in the brick walls, Rosemary roof tiles and perforated cresting to the ridges, which meet at a bold brick chimney-stack. There are similar lodges by the architect at Ashfield Lodge, Co. Cavan, and Connellmore, Co. Kildare (*q.v.*).

South entrance; *c.* 1890; architect W.M. Mitchell; *demolished.*

Probably swept away by the demands of the neighbouring concrete-works blight.

Rear entrance; *c.* 1895; architect Sir Thomas Drew.

The architect at his most original in this charming single-storey bungalow on a rambling plan but with a regular entrance elevation where the hipped roof catslides to cover a pair of multi-paned bay windows, which project to create a recessed entrance porch with the same curved fascia as the main lodge but with perforated motifs. A coved stone eaves band surmounts roughcast walls above an exaggerated red-brick plinth, which rises to sill level.

LGI (1904); *BPB* (1929); Williams 1994; Walsh 1996; Dean 1994.

51. BUTLERSTOWN CASTLE, Tomhaggard; *c.* 1850.

A property named for the old Butler tower-house that adjoins the late Georgian villa, which obviously had a later make-over,

probably when the lodge was added by John Boxwell (d. 1859), who succeeded to the seat in 1825. Single-storey standard and rendered, with label mouldings to openings below a hipped roof surmounted by a conspicuous pair of square chimney-stacks on a rectangular plinth. Occupied, with modern windows and a lean-to structure to the left-hand side. Modest stone gate pillars with curious cut-stone 'bullet' finials.

IFR; Walsh 1996.

52. CAHORE, Donaghmore; *c.* 1845; architect Daniel Robertson.

Carlow and Wexford gentry were lifeblood for that enigmatic architect Daniel Robertson, those counties being enriched by his creations, mainly in the fashionable early Victorian Tudor Castellated Revival style, such as this mansion for Judge John George (1804–71). Although there is no documentary evidence of Robertson's working for him, on stylistic grounds this is easily attributable, not least through its similarity to his Carrigglas, Co. Longford (*q.v.*), for another of the Dublin legal profession. His 1½-storey gabled lodge in red brick with stone chamfered and label-moulded dressings is raised off a cruciform plan with what appears to be a standard entrance elevation, but what should have been the projecting hall is not so, the whole having been reoriented, with a bipartite double-arched and mullioned window, below a shield, where the door should be. With pronounced eaves and verge brackets and a pair of brick octagonal chimney-flues, it pays scant attention to the gatescreen. Distant are four octagonal granite entrance pillars on moulded plinths and having cushion cappings with 'topknots', framing good cast-iron carriage gates and matching railings.

Walsh 1996; *IAR* (1999).

53. CAMOLIN, Camolin; *c.* 1866; architect possibly T.N. Deane.

A house alternatively called 'Valentia' after a lesser title of the Annesleys, earls of Mountnorris of nearby Camolin Park (*q.v.*), with whom it was associated. It had a succession of occupants before Arthur William Grattan Guinness (1827–69) had plans for a new house drawn up in 1864–6 by architect T.N. Deane. Although it has been demolished, the remaining lodge may be contemporary with it. In immaculate condition, with modern windows and a covering of concrete tiles to its gabled roof, which retains paired carved verge brackets. Single-storey, three-bay and rendered, with a breakfront gabled hall to the right-hand side of two wide brick-dressed and segmentally arched windows with fundamental label mouldings. Plain, older harled ogee entrance quadrants and stone pillars.

O'Dwyer 1997b; Rowe and Scallan 2004.

54. CAMOLIN PARK, Camolin (3).

An important Classical brick mansion probably created by Richard Annesley, 6th earl of Anglesey, just after he came into the property through his third marriage in 1741. In the autumn of 1814 A. Atkinson was here on tour to record that Viscount Valentia 'was actively engaged in opening a respectable and indeed very needful approach to his seat from the Gorey road', to which no doubt was appended one of the porters' lodges. His descendants, who became earls of Mountnorris, eventually sold it in the incumbered estates court in 1852 and thereafter its decline continued, leading to the loss of its three pre-1839 gate lodges before 1905 and demolition of the big house by 1974.

Atkinson 1815; Bence-Jones 1988; Walsh 1996.

55. CARNAGH, New Ross (2).

After inheriting the estate in 1808, Henry Lambert (1786–1861) lived long to enjoy the fruit of his labours, which included adding a new front to the house, doubling it in size and building at least one gate lodge.

North lodge; pre-1840; *demolished.*

South lodge; *c.* 1820

Opposite the gates, what was a single-storey standard Regency-style lodge with its openings set in semicircular-arched recesses on a plinth, which probably originated with a hipped roof. This seems subsequently to have had the eaves raised and clipped gables created to accommodate loft rooms.

LGI (1904).

56. CASTLEBORO, Clonroche (6).

In 1814 Mason found the property of 'Robert Shapland Carew ... but no improvements about it except trees'. This scene 50 years later had been spectacularly remedied by Carew, as the first of three successive generations of that name. There is little doubt that most of the credit for this transformation should go to his son, Robert Shapland Carew II (1787–1856), who inherited the estate in 1829 and was created 1st Lord Carew in 1834. Much of the subsequent building is thought to have been prompted by the burning of the old house in 1839. This may not have been the tragedy it first appears, for the 1840 OS map shows the north gate lodge

Irish Architectural Archive

to have already been in place, perhaps intended as an introduction to a new house being considered much earlier than previously thought. If anything, this looks like a product of the 1820s.

Temple gate; *c.* 1825; architect not known.

Built on the northern approach is this Greek temple lodge (*above*), its pureness such that it cannot have been envisaged as an introduction to the immoderate pile that was to transpire years later, but rather to what was earlier intended or already in place. In any case, this is as grand a little building as any in the county, nobly elevated on a grassy mound by Boro bridge at the head of a long flight of steps from which it commanded the entrance gates (now gone). It is in essence a single-storey three-roomed porter's lodge on a T-plan, done up in a Classical cloak faced with ashlar, having a three-bay leading elevation behind a pronaos formed by a pedimented distyle Greek Doric portico with antae. Like all else of architectural significance on the demesne it lies an empty shell—not totally inappropriate for a Greek temple. It should be secured and protected now for posterity as an important ruin.

It seems that the 1st Lord Carew inherited another two gatekeepers' lodges on the estate, which have since gone. He engaged as his architect the exiled Englishman Daniel Robertson, of whose work there is so much to admire in the county. Although more comfortable in the newfangled Tudor Revival Castellated manner, he was to prove here his eclectic ability, if not as author of the Greek temple lodge then in the great Roman mansion and two Picturesque lodges safely attributable to him through being identical to those at Bloomfield (*q.v.*).

South gate; *c.* 1845; architect Daniel Robertson.

Rendered bland by modern 'improvement' in which it lost its Tudor features of ornamental octagonal paired chimney-stacks, decorative bargeboards and label mouldings, it retains

the bold eaves corbel brackets and the conspicuous Carew monogram shield contained in a gablet blatantly created to display it centrally on the avenue elevation above the single-storey gabled porch projection. Basically this is a 1½-storey cottage with steep gables on a rectangular plan, with a single-storey wing to the park gable and a single-storey gabled breakfront bay window feature to the road front.

Inner gate; *c.* 1845; architect Daniel Robertson.

Originally much as the south lodge and similarly abused over the years, with a large twentieth-century addition to one end creating a rather ungainly whole. It may have varied in having a considerably larger porch with dentil course, ornamental bargeboards and crude hip-knob.

Robert Shapland Carew III (1818–81), the 2nd Lord Carew, carried on the embellishments to the estate commenced by his grandfather and so vigorously continued by his father, with the addition of a once truly imposing entrance lodge and gates to the eastern avenue.

Grand gate; 1862; architect possibly John McCurdy.

This was an object of much admiration. Lacy in the summer of 1862 was moved to record: 'A new and fine approach to the grand mansion, with a splendid gate-lodge, is now being constructed on that part of the demesne which is in the immediate vicinity of the road leading to the railway station at Ballywilliam'. Similarly, in 1885 Bassett states that 'A broad clearing reveals a "grand gateway" and handsome granite lodge. Free

56. Castleboro, the grand entrance..

admission is given to visitors, and the drive in the demesne is through ferny woods, and across the Boro ...' This is a noteworthy and extravagant single-storey commodious four-roomed lodge in the most beautiful and crisply tooled granite ashlar. Two-bay sides and three to the avenue front; each bay is defined by Doric pilasters with recessed panels, each of which frames an aedicule or window with moulded sill, dressings and scrolled console brackets with acanthus leaf motifs supporting a triangular pediment. The entrance front is dominated by a pedimented tetrastyle Doric portico screening the front door, which is flanked by a pair of round-arched niches. This sumptuous design now lies, like much else on this once-proud property, a shell, with its parapet crumbling and the chimney-stack, its four-pot capping supported by paired brackets, emphasised by its rooflessness. The huge complementary railed gatescreen with great granite entrance pillars, the recessed pylon panels of which still contain the Carew monogram, has been salvaged and re-erected at Farmleigh (*q.v.*). This important structure is well capable of being restored to its former glory and dignity, and—with little imagination or extension—of being adapted to modern living needs. Attribution to McCurdy is based on knowing that his surviving and erstwhile partner in practice, W.M. Mitchell, was employed here by the 4th Earl Carew in 1908 and on there being like gates by him at Harristown, Co. Kildare (*q.v.*).

Mason 1814–19; Lacy 1863; Bassett 1885; *IB* (8 Feb. 1908); *BPB* (1929); Bence-Jones 1988; Malins and Bowe 1980; *IAR* (1999); IAA photograph (4/55).

57. CASTLETOWN, Coolgreany; pre-1840; *demolished.*

A property from the late eighteenth century of the Grogans of Johnstown Castle (*q.v.*), the gate lodge to which in 1837 was at the gates to 'a destitute mansion'. Surviving are nice rustic slate stile steps. There is a record in 1885 of a John Newton at Castletown Gatehouse. It had been removed before 1905.

Lewis 1837; Bassett 1885; Rowe and Scallan 2004.

58. CHARLESFORT, Ferns; pre-1839.

Opposite the gates, a once-standard single-storey hip-roofed cottage, sometime extended to four-bay to the left-hand side. Now ruinous. A seat in 1814 until his death in 1833 of Charles Dawson, after whom it may have been named. He was succeeded by his son Walter, who died here in 1859.

Leet 1814; *LGI* (1904).

CLIFTON (see WELLINGTON COTTAGE)

59. CLOBEMON HALL, Cohamon (2).

A delightful small estate created on the banks of the Slaney River by Thomas De Rinzy, who built the fine house *c.* 1820 to designs by Thomas A. Cobden, as well as two gate lodges, at least one of which may have been by him. Both were in place by 1840 but neither survives, which is a shame, given the known quality of his lodges elsewhere and of the surviving main gatescreen, the lodge to which was opposite. The two square granite carriage pillars have fluted friezes and moulded cornices with concave cappings. These are flanked by extensive concave quadrant walls, the copings of which slope upwards to accommodate the postern opening, with cut-stone architraves.

Lewis 1837; *LG* (1849); Bence-Jones 1988.

CLOHAMON GLEBE (see ST MARY'S RECTORY)

60. CLOHAMON FLOUR MILL AND COTTON FACTORY, Clohamon; 1819.

Alongside the gate and facing the road is a generously proportioned standard 1½-storey gabled gatehouse with a pair of gablets breaking the eaves, the soffit to which has iron brackets. Previously harled, with nicely contrasting chamfered granite dressings and label mouldings, as can be seen surviving on an attic window. Unfortunately now rendered rather bland in modernisation, having been refenestrated with modern casement windows; the front door has also been blocked up, but its label moulding and segmentally arched lintel survive. The latter has 'MDCCXIX' beautifully chiselled in relief, a date which would seem to reveal when Clohamon was founded as 'a neat and thriving village of recent origin, and the population is chiefly employed in the large flour and cotton-mills of Mr William Lewis', as described in 1837 by Samuel Lewis. It 'gave employment to upwards of one hundred hands. Mr Lewis died in 1868, and the machinery soon afterwards was broken up and sent to England as scrap iron' and 'the operatives have been scattered to Portlaw, Cork, Limerick, Liverpool, and America'. Only workers' cottages and the gatehouse survive as testimony to this once-bustling and prosperous concern.

Lewis 1837; Doyle 1868; Bassett 1885.

61. CLONARD GREAT, Wexford; pre-1840/*c.* 1860.

What is manifest at the gate today is not what was here in the time of the Kellet family from 1793 to about 1857. Rather it is a replacement by Joseph McQuillan, whose standard, solid, no-nonsense two-storey gabled gatehouse has a single-storey gabled central hall projection with the suggestion of ornamental bargeboards and a turned hip-knob. Finished in stucco with toothed quoins, there are more elaborate carved main bargeboards of repeating pendulous fleurs-de-lis, the same as those on the lodge to Kerlogue (*q.v.*). Occupied. Drab, unpainted, sand/cement-finished gate pillars and short concave quadrants give no hint of the delightful old mid-Georgian house within.

Slater 1856; *Land owners in Ireland 1876*; Rowe and Scallan 2004.

62. CLONARD LITTLE, Wexford; pre-1840/*c.* 1860.

Very tall, old, concave, limewashed, harled quadrants and pillars, probably dating from the time of the early lodge of the Richards family, are accompanied by a nondescript 1½-storey gabled later lodge, presumably built as a replacement for William Brown, who was the proprietor in 1870.

Lewis 1837; Slater 1870; Rowe and Scallan 2004.

63. CLONATTIN, Gorey (2).

In 1786 'the seat of Andrew Ram, Esq., the demesne of which is most highly improved, and laid out in the very best manner'. Much of the good work till then must have been destroyed in the devastation wrought on the estate by the 1798 rebellion, and it would have been his son, Lt.-Col. Abel Ram, who succeeded his father in 1793, who rebuilt the house and perhaps added the two gate lodges before his demise in 1830. Both had gone by 1905.

Wilson 1803; Brewer 1825; *LGI* (1904).

64. CLONGANNY, Ballygarrett; *c.* 1840.

A distinctive single-storey lodge, its short front gabled in the form of a wide pediment defined by cut stone in roughcast walls. Below this is a three-bay façade with a full-length Y-traceried window flanked by a pair of niches, all having pointed heads, masquerading as Georgian Gothic from 50 years earlier and the time of the White family but probably built by their tenant, one John Groome, before 1853. Three-bay plain avenue front. Occupied.

Griffith 1848–60; Rowe and Scallan 2004.

65. CLONHASTON MANOR, Enniscorthy (2).

A pleasant small estate in the early nineteenth century of the White family to which its lodges were added after 1840, probably by Samuel White.

North lodge; *c.* 1850; *demolished.*

South lodge; *c.* 1850.

Across the road from the entrance is a once-proud and decorative gatekeeper's lodge, now abandoned and dilapidated. Single-storey standard but sufficiently lofty for its hipped roof to permit attic space. Stucco-finished, the elliptically arched fanlit door is set in a recess flanked by crude label-moulded bipartite casements, which have the

remains of ornamental hexagonal-paned glazing and are internally framed in architraved recesses. From the ridge rises a pair of diagonally set Tudor-style chimney-stacks.

Griffith 1848–60; Walsh 1996.

66. CONVENT OF MERCY, Rosslare; *c.* 1911; *demolished.*

The core of the complex is a house called 'Mervin' of the Irvine family, acquired by the Order for religious use in 1911. The gate lodge that was then built has proved particularly short-lived.

Rowe and Scallan 2004.

67. COOLBAWN, Clonroche; pre-1905; *demolished.*

The very fine but ill-fated Tudor Revival mansion built in the early 1830s for Francis Bruen (1800–67) to designs of Frederick Darley Jr was outlived by its later lodge, built after 1840, which itself succumbed in 1997 (three weeks before the arrival of the author), to be survived by some lonesome mushroom-capped entrance posts.

LGI (1904); Bence-Jones 1988.

68. COOLCLIFFE, Taghmon; pre-1840.

Presiding over the gatescreen from without is a standard three-bay hip-roofed lodge, stripped of all original character in enthusiastic 'improvements', it being covered in modern boulder-effect rendering, making it impossible to date visually with any accuracy. Relatively unscathed are the good mid-Georgian square granite entrance pillars, which contain date-stones: to the left-hand side '1727' and something illegible; to the right-hand side '1784' and 'John Cox'. These would appear to indicate respectively the date of erection of the house and that of the gates (and perhaps lodge) and their builder—John Cox (d. 1793).

Walsh 1996.

COOLMELAGH (see PROSPECT, Bunclody)

COOLNASTUD (see FARM HILL)

CORBET HILL (see TALBOT HALL)

69. COURTOWN, Courtown (5).

The English tourist Henry D. Inglis visited here in the spring of 1834 and was impelled to describe 'The domain of Lord Courtown which is small, but very beautiful. It is a little green Paradise, sloping up from the sea, with fine avenues of old wood, and with clumps of evergreens, laurel especially—the luxuriant growth of which, I had never seen equalled in England.' The hodgepodge of a house that evolved thereafter was no huge loss when it was burnt down in 1950, but some of its charming gate lodges have thankfully survived, built by the Stopford family, from 1762 earls of Courtown.

North gate; pre-1839; *demolished.*

Middle gate; pre-1839; *demolished.*

Kiltennel gate; *c.* 1810/*c.* 1835; architect perhaps William Burn.

The visitor is met by what appear to be two generations of gate lodges, a delightful late Georgian cottage and, beyond, its successor, an early Victorian lodged archway (*below*). James George Stopford (1765–1835) succeeded as 3rd earl of Courtown on the death of his father in 1810, and this single-storey thatched hip-roofed lodge, with a three-bay front to the avenue of six-over-six sash windows set in elliptically arched recesses in harled walls, must have been one of his first improvements. The central window may originally have been the doorway. The 4th earl, James Thomas Stopford (1794–1858), clearly felt that he could improve upon his father's contribution

Irish Architectural Archive

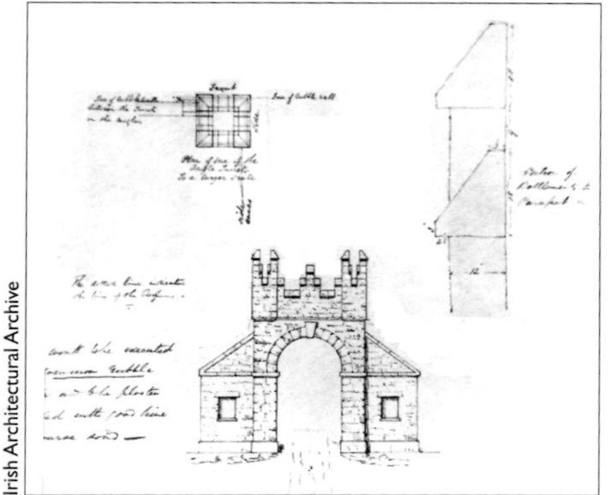
Irish Architectural Archive

and commissioned this Classical pedimented round-headed archway flanked by a pair of single-storey 'day and night' lean-to lodges. Constructed in stone rubble with brick dressings, which may have been finished in 'plaster dashed with good lime and coarse sand', for it is just such harling that is described on a drawing dated August 1844 which appears to show this entrance with the pediment intended to be replaced by an Irish crenellated parapet with corner tourelles. Quite who the architect was is not clear, for the signature is sketchy. In 1822 the 4th earl had married his cousin, a daughter of the 4th duke of Buccleuch, a family which for years employed that prolific Scottish practitioner William Burn (1789–1870) as their architect. The 5th earl of Courtown was later to engage Burn (in 1865–7) to remodel the house and design another lodge, so it is not unreasonable to conclude that he was involved 30 years earlier, in his prime.

Gorey lodge; *c.* 1867; architect William Burn.

James George Henry Stopford, the 5th earl (1823–1914), put his considerable stamp on the estate with yet more building works and a third-generation gatekeeper's lodge. This is an enchanting and generously proportioned 1½-storey standard cottage, Burn at his most innovative in old age, having cast off his habitual neo-Jacobean method. The exposed rubble fabric with brick dressings beautifully sets off the startling white of the chunky woodwork of his two-tier tripartite oriel-cum-gablets, with their latticed casement windows and continuous bracket bargeboards, which are repeated on the central, equally hefty gabled porch with two heavy chamfered post supports. Conspicuous are the Y-effect gable features and originally carved hip-knobs. Markedly missing its chimney-stacks and having an extension to one side with an unfortunate flat roof and inappropriate front door replacement—otherwise immaculate. Walls with brick-lined recessed panels and Welsh coping, framing a pair of ashlar carriage pillars. Mysteriously the lodge seems to have escaped valuation until 1892, but it is surely of earlier date.

Inglis 1835; Lacy 1863; *BPB* (1929); Colvin 2008; Williams 1994; IAA photographs (15/10 R53and S39/12).

70. CROMWELL'S FORT, Wexford; pre-1840; *demolished.*

A fine house built in 1783 by Isaac Cornock (1739–1804) which has suffered the indignity of being abandoned for many years, being converted into flats and having its park built over, with the loss of its lodge. Isaac was succeeded here by his only son, Revd Zachariah Cornock (1770–1858).

LGI (1904); Walsh 1996.

71. CROSSTOWN CEMETERY, Wexford; 1892.

A substantial late Victorian standard single-storey lodge built off a square plan in the Gothic style. Gabled with a similar projecting hallway, its rafter toes exposed and bargeboards perforated with Maltese crosses; all openings have pointed arches with hood mouldings, their dripstones patiently await sculpting while a slate plaque high in the leading gable gives the date of construction. With its pair of centrally placed chimney-stacks, it makes a depressing sight in its drab cement rendering with boarded-up windows and roofless hall. In similar grey finish is the Classical gatescreen with moulded recessed panels to pillars and concave quadrant walls.

CULLENSTOWN (see ROCKVIEW)

72. CULLENTRA, Wexford; *c.* 1855.

The pretty early nineteenth-century cottage residence probably built by Sir John Judkin Fitzgerald of Lisheen, Co. Tipperary, which was leased for most of the century to the Little family of solicitors, of whom Simon may have built the lodge opposite the gates after the death of George Little in 1852. A Picturesque English Cottage-style structure, partly 1½-storey, partly single-storey, raised off an irregular T-plan with a hall projecting from an internal angle, its gables decorated with foiled bargeboards and a hefty chimney-stack dominating the roof. Sensitively enlarged to the rear but having lost its original sliding sash windows to plastic replacements.

Lewis 1837; *LGI* (1904); *BPB* (1929); Rowe and Scallan 2004.

73. CURCLOGH, Blackwater; pre-1840.

A ruined cottage with the remains of a steeply pitched thatched hipped roof at the gates to a property in 1853 of John Prendergast.

Griffith 1848–60.

74. CURRACLOE, Curracloe; pre-1905; *demolished.*

A villa of 1831 built by the Toole family, whose main seat was then Edermine (*q.v.*). The lodge opposite the gates, possibly added by William J. Toole after the death of his father in 1859, is survived by a good cast-iron gatescreen, which may have had an earlier lodge alongside.

Lacy 1863; Rowe and Scallan 2004.

75. DAPHNE CASTLE, Enniscorthy; *c.* 1800.

Once an apt prelude to the Georgian Gothic home of the Pounden family beyond, this little single-storey hip-roofed porter's lodge has its main short front to the avenue with a pointed-arched doorway, now derelict but part of a car repair business at the now-redundant entrance to the demolished home. The lodge was built either by John Pounden, prior to his being killed in the 1798 Rebellion, or by one of his sons: Joshua, who is recorded here in 1800, or John Colley Pounden by 1814.

Wilson 1803; Leet 1814; Walsh 1996.

THE DEEPS (see NEWTOWN)

76. DRINAGH SOUTH, Wexford; *c.* 1880.

Eithne Scallan

A perfectly proper little lodge of 1½-storey standard format, but rather than having high eaves to permit attic rooms it has a precipitous roof, the verges of which project boldly over two-over-two sash windows in smooth rendered walls. Occupied. Plain entrance pillars with concave railed quadrants. Contemporary with the new house built in 1881 by Henry J. Cooper on the

proceeds from his nearby limestone works.
Rowe and Scallan 2004.

77. DUFFREY HALL, Kiltealy; pre-1839; *demolished.*
Another seat of the Colcloughs of Tintern Abbey (*q.v.*), which from being described as the most insignificant seventeenth-century building in County Wexford was 'in a state of ruin' by 1845; in 1905 both it and its gate lodge had gone.
Parliamentary Gazetteer; Rowe and Scallan 2004.

78. DUNBRODY PARK, Duncannon (4).
The period 1860–70 saw Henry Spencer Chichester, 2nd Baron Templemore (1821–1906), undertake major additions to his house and extensive improvements on the estate, all of which were rather unassuming and included the provision of four new gate lodges to replace two existing ones built by his predecessor before 1840. All are in an understated but pleasant English Picturesque cottage manner, none of which can be likened to a style favoured by the architect J.S. Mulvany, who appears to have carried out works to the house about 1862.

Duncannon gate; pre-1840/*c.* 1865.
A 1½-storey structure, its two-bay main elevation of wide windows with smooth surrounds in roughcast walls below a gabled roof having wavy bargeboards. The gate pillars are diagonally set with ball finials. Its predecessor was opposite the gates.

Clonsharragh gate; *c.* 1865.
Both lodge and gates as above. Situated on the southern approach.

Coleman gate; pre-1840/*c.* 1865.
Finished in an attractive local rubble stone, 1½-storey with a shallower-pitched roof than the other lodges. The ground-floor avenue front is three-bay, with the central doorway sheltered by a mono-pitched bracketed canopy over which a gablet breaks the main eaves. The original perforated wavy bargeboards have given way to modern over-simple replacements but retain delicate hip-knobs; two-over-two sash windows. Matching rubble entrance pillars with dainty ball finials. A replacement lodge.

Arthurstown gate; pre-1840/*c.* 1865.
By far the most substantial of the gatekeepers' cottages, it probably having also served as a post office, like its predecessor. Faced in agreeable rubble stone with brick dressings to six-over-six sash windows, it is 1½-storey standard, its three-bay front having three gablets corresponding to the openings below and having, like the main gables, geometrically carved perforated bargeboards. To the avenue gable, monitoring the gates, is a single-storey canted bay window. With sawtooth-pattern slated roof, repeated on the modern single-storey gabled hallway. Lord Templemore's gatekeeper in 1853 in the earlier building is recorded as Martin Whelan. As befits a main entrance, the screen is extensive, with railed concave quadrants on dwarf walls framing octagonal ashlar pillars with more ball finials sitting snugly on their cappings. Occupied and well maintained like all the lodges, which lend themselves to holiday accommodation.
Griffith 1848–60; Doyle 1868; *BPB* (1929); *IADS* (2000).

79. DUNISHAL, Carnew; pre-1839; *demolished.*
A lodge that graced the entrance to a large farm in the early nineteenth century of Richard Bookey.
Leet 1814; Lewis 1837.

80. DUNSINANE, Enniscorthy; pre-1840; *demolished.*
A seat acquired by Capt. John Baker Graves after the death in 1826 of the previous proprietor, Hugh Hovell Farmar, who in turn had inherited it from his father of the same name in 1812.
Lewis 1837; *LGI* (1904).

EARLSWOOD (see MOUNT NEBO)

81. EDERMINE, Enniscorthy (2).
A property previously of Laurence Toole, from whom it was purchased in 1837 by Sir John Power (1771–1855) of the whiskey family for his only son and heir, James (1800–77). They wasted little time in transforming the estate by building a new mansion house, for which the foundation stone was laid in 1838, and providing it with a fitting main entrance and porter's lodge, all to the designs of architect John B. Keane.

North entrance; pre-1840/*c.* 1910.

At the secondary gate, which may have served as the main approach to the Toole house, is a little single-storey hip-roofed lodge which possibly originated as a standard early nineteenth-century structure but which owes its present appearance to alterations and additions carried out a century later. Now forming an L-plan with a small hall and porch in the internal angle, it displays distinct Arts and Crafts features in the small square upper panes of the casement windows below segmental heads in roughcast walls and the finely carved turned post supports to the porch roof. The oversailing eaves have modillion brackets decorating the soffits.

South entrance; *c.* 1839; architect J.B. Keane.
Opposite the gates is this single-storey lodge, standard but obviously, from its presence and detailing, designed. Sash windows with margined glazing flank the central round-headed fanlit doorway in rendered walls below oversailing eaves with paired soffit brackets to a hipped roof which rises sharply to a ridge with a commanding pair of stone chimney-flues on a rectangular base. Nicely

exhibited behind a cast-iron screen of entrance piers and railings, exactly mirroring that opposite. The main carriage pillars are in granite with moulded recessed panels and corniced cappings. This is a rare example of an important gatescreen surviving the demands of modern road-widening, it having been dismantled and carefully rebuilt.
Lewis 1837; Fraser 1838; Lacy 1863; *BPB* (1929); Bence-Jones 1988.

82. ELLERSLIE, Wexford; *c.* 1850.
A plain single-storey hip-roofed rendered lodge, much extended, to a property in 1853 of John Jackman.
Griffith 1848–60.

83. ENNISCORTHY DISTRICT ASYLUM, Enniscorthy; *c.* 1868; architects possibly Farrell and Bell; *demolished.*
A lodge probably to a design by architects Farrell and Bell, as was the vast St Sennan's Hospital, and presumably in the same brick and stone finish.
O'Dwyer 1997a.

ENNISCORTHY RECTORY (see TEMPLESHANNON RECTORY)

84. FARM HILL, Gorey; *c.* 1865.
Built in nice random rubble with red-brick dressings and chimney-stack is this single-storey gabled lodge with mildly ornamental bargeboards and long two-window-bay front to the road. A property that now takes the name of its townland, 'Coolnastud', and was

in 1856 home to one Ponsonby Moore.
Slater 1856.

85. FARMLEIGH MANOR, Enniscorthy; pre-1839/1874; *demolished.*
Neither the early lodge, possibly built by George Rawson Richards, nor its replacement of 1874 opposite the entrance survives. The latter dates from the time here of Richard Williamson. The entrance now provides a home for the magnificent gatescreen taken from Castleboro (*q.v.*).
Lacy 1863; Lyons 1993.

86. FERNS DEANERY, Ferns; *c.* 1805.
A tiny, quaint, single-storey standard lodge with harled walls and simple clipped verges to a steeply pitched roof. Now serving as a garden centre shop, it may be contemporary with the building of the deanery in 1805 during the incumbency of Revd Peter Browne, from 1794 until his death in 1842.
Lewis 1837; Leslie and Knox 2008.

87. FOLLY COTTAGE, Tagoat; pre-1840; *demolished.*
A small estate in 1814 of Matthew Hughes, which by 1853 was home to Fanny Hughes, whose gatekeeper was Matthew Coghlan.
Leet 1814; Griffith 1848–60.

88. FUDDLETOWN, Mayglass (2).
A property associated with the Mayler or Meyler family, both lodges to which, one dating from before 1840, have been demolished.
Griffith 1848–60.

89. GLANDORAN, Gorey; pre-1939; *demolished.*
A seat in the mid-nineteenth century of William Woodroofe.
Griffith 1848–60.

90. GLEANN-NA-SMÓL, Enniscorthy; *c.* 1855.
Opposite the gates is a single-storey hip-roofed lodge with a two-bay elevation, now much improved and extended. Probably contemporary with the building of the house, 'the neat and modern residence of Mr James Davis' referred to by Doyle in 1868, home to the milling family of Enniscorthy.
Doyle 1868; Rowe and Scallan 2004.

91. GOBBINSTOWN, New Ross; pre-1840; *demolished.*
An antique house, from early times of the Fitzhenry family, a Mary Fitzhenry being recorded in residence as late as 1876. The porter's lodge opposite the gates is shown on the 1840 OS map as square on plan, whereas, perhaps significantly, it appears as a rectangle on the 1905 edition. Now gone, as is its big house.
Land owners in Ireland 1876; Rowe and Scallan 2004.

92. GRAIGUE, Wellingtonbridge; pre-1840; *demolished.*
The property until his death in 1821 of George Carr, which thereafter passed back to the Boyse family of neighbouring Grange (*q.v.*). The childhood home of Mrs S.C. Hall (née Fielding), which was demolished along with its lodge in the twentieth century.
Doyle 1868.

93. GRANARD VILLA, Wexford; pre-1905; *demolished.*
A lodge that may have been contemporary with the house, which was built in 1856 by the McDonald family.
Rowe and Scallan 2004.

94. GRANGE, Killann; *c.* 1810.

For its age an unusually substantial hip-roofed two-storey Georgian Gothic gatehouse, built in rubble with a harled finish; prominent granite dressings in its bold V-jointed rusticated quoins and surrounds to openings, all of which have pointed heads, in an almost symmetrical three-bay façade. Built by Revd John Richards (1757–1827) after he inherited the property, also known as 'Monksgrange', on his father's death in 1795. Now lying abandoned and windowless, it still has the potential to be returned to its former glory.
LGI (1904).

95. GRANGE, Wellingtonbridge (2).
An estate also known as 'Bannow' with its late Georgian house was mainly the creation in 1816 of Samuel Boyse, when in whose care it was united with the neighbouring demesne of Graigue (*q.v.*). The gate lodge, then opposite the front entrance, was later replaced when improvements to the property were carried out in the time of Henry Samuel Hunt Boyse (1809–80), who succeeded his uncle in 1864.

Front entrance; *c.* 1865.
This was a single-storey standard affair, built off a square plan with a pyramidal roof and central lean-to roofed hall projection. All now rendered plain by modernisation with nasty concrete roll-tiled roof finish. Big square gate pillars with moulded recessed panels and exaggerated cornices to cappings and concave balustered quadrants beyond.

Back entrance; pre-1905; *demolished.*
A lodge built after 1840, probably as part of the later mid-Victorian improvements.
Doyle 1868; *LGI* (1904); Rowe and Scallan 2004.

96. HARPERSTOWN, Taghmon; pre-1840; *demolished.*
Atkinson in the autumn of 1814 described 'the seat of Captain Hoar, a neat modern edifice, enriched with copious plantations', and the only one 'of distinction on that road'. Likewise, Doyle in 1868 paints a very different picture to the scene today: 'the demesne lands, is the type of a well-ordered English manor residence: the approaches to the mansion house, and the drives through the demesne, which contains some noble timber, and many plantations, and much oak-wood around, are quite in the English park style'. Now the house and castle of the Hore family lie in ruins, the timber felled and the gate lodge removed.
Atkinson 1815; Doyle 1868.

97. HEALTHFIELD, Wexford (2).
Although a property of ever-changing owners down the centuries, it is chiefly to two that it owes its present appearance, not least in its gatekeepers' lodges, which are separated in time by about a century. Edward Beatty had acquired the estate from the Sweetmans about 1810; ten years later he greatly enlarged the house and subsequently added a lodge at the main entrance.

North gate; *c.* 1840; architect not known.

Originally the most delightful of lodges and highly original, were there not others to an identical pattern at Long Graigue (*q.v.*), Raheenduff (*q.v.*) and Stokestown (*q.v.*) in the same county and at Ballycurry (*q.v.*) in County Wicklow. All are single-storey standard and hip-roofed, but what sets them apart are the uncommon ogee arches to their openings. Here the original sheeted door has been retained, as has the Y-traceried window frame arrangement, but not the intricate glazing pattern, and this has combined with the sanitised re-rendering of the walls, the new soulless synthetic roof slates and its extension by a bay to one side to deprive the lodge of its character. Its consequent survival as a home is a consolation. Thanks to a nineteenth-century public road realignment it now occupies a secluded site.

Healthfield was purchased in 1890 by the White family, of whom Lt.-Col. Henry Jervis Jervis-White replaced a previous lodge.

South gate; pre-1840/*c.* 1900; architect not known.
A striking Edwardian Picturesque single-storey lodge on an L-plan, with two-over-two sash windows in rendered walls and decorative carved wooden triangular features with quatrefoil perforations to gables at eaves and apexes, the latter containing elaborate hip-knobs. The ridges are highlighted by trefoil-perforated earthenware cresting meeting at a lofty chimney-stack with corbelled capping. Immaculately maintained and sympathetically extended. There is an

97. Healthfield, south gate (Eithne Scallan).

almost identical lodge to Ballyboggan (*q.v.*) by the same unidentified hand. The first OS map shows there to have been a circular 'drum lodge' on the site, probably dating from the time here in the late eighteenth century of John Grogan of the Johnstown Castle (*q.v.*) family.

Wilson 1803; *LGI* (1904); Rowe and Scallan 2004.

98. HEATHPARK, Old Ross; pre-1905; *demolished.*
A lodge built after 1840 to a property of the Whitney family.

99. HILL CASTLE, Rossclare (2).
The old house, like the Nunn family, here since they built it in 1675, has gone, its outbuildings in ruins, but remarkably there are still remains of the two Georgian Gothic lodges. Joseph Nunn died in 1803 without male issue, leaving the property to his elder daughter Frances, who in 1784 had married her cousin Joshua, of St Margaret's, thus reuniting the family. The lodges look to date from that period.

Back gate; *c.* 1805.
Only two cottage walls still stand, containing little pointed openings, and a single small rubble-built convex quadrant.

Front gate; *c.* 1805.

The quintessential Georgian Gothic porter's lodge in almost pristine condition, having recently been restored. Single-storey standard, its three-bay front of pointed openings with Y-traceried glazing below a hipped roof, now pyramidal since the accommodation was increased to a square on plan, and rising to a central chimney-stack. The roof is covered with clinical synthetic slate, whilst the walls are appropriately roughcast with smooth rendered dressings. The delightful contemporary spear-topped gates and railed concave quadrants survive with modest carriage pillars, contrasting with harled screen walls with Welsh copings.

IFR.

100. HILLVIEW, Tinahely; pre-1840.
Opposite the entrance gates, only the front wall of a standard single-storey lodge in rubble stone remains to an estate listed in 1837 as of Sandham Symes.

Lewis 1837.

101. HOLLYFORT, Gorey; pre-1839; *demolished.*
A gatekeeper's lodge remembered as being hip-roofed; both it and its big house have been demolished, not even leaving evidence of the entrance. In 1853 the proprietor, Henry Atkins, had William Rickaby as his porter.

Griffith 1848–60.

HOLLYMOUNT (see GLEANN-NA-SMÓL)

102. HOUGHTON'S FEVER HOSPITAL, New Ross; 1809.

A distinguished Classical piece of townscape gifted by the Houghton family of Ballyanne (*q.v.*), the estate on the outskirts of town. The two-storey hip-roofed gatehouse is three-bay with single-bay wings beyond. In stuccoed walls, the tall ground-floor windows with round-arched heads (now sealed up) probably have spoked glazing to the sashes. These flank the grand granite frontispiece, which contains an elliptically arched carriage opening crowned by a plaque proclaiming: 'Haughton Hospital / Founded by the munificence of the Late Henry Haughton of Ballyane House Esquire. Erected and Opened for the Reception of Patients by Mary his wife Anno 1809'. Atop this again is a pedestalled ball finial. The generous accommodation clearly provided for more than a gatekeeper, probably including reception and offices. The complex served also as an infirmary, with a capacity of 72 beds in 1844.

Parliamentary Gazetteer; NIAH.

103. HYDEPARK, Coolgreany; *c.* 1805; architect probably Richard Morrison; *demolished.*

A regulation late Georgian villa of Richard Morrison, which, together with his familiar gatescreen, makes attribution of the long-lost lodge fairly safe. It was probably one of those hip-roofed cottages with a single-bay short front to the avenue that he based on a Soane model. Intact is Morrison's recognisable entrance, which he repeatedly used in the early part of his career. Drum carriage pillars are flanked by railings contained by square squat ashlar pillars, with recessed panels and exaggerated cornices, beyond which in contrast are whitewashed stuccoed convex quadrant walls terminating in another pair of square pillars. There are more railings beyond that again to create a most extensive introduction to the house built by John Christopher Beauman, who wasted no time in redeveloping the demesne after inheriting it in 1802.

Soane 1793; *LGI* (1904); McParland *et al.* 1989.

104. INGLEWOOD or ENGLEWOOD, Enniscorthy; pre-1840; *demolished.*
A villa of *c.* 1840, long known as 'Johnville', the lodge to which may have served an earlier house on the site. Thomas Greene was the proprietor in the 1850s.

Griffith 1848–60; NIAH.

105. ISLAND, Kilmuckridge; pre-1840; *demolished.*
A property in the nineteenth century of the Boltons, of whom William must have built the lodge, for there was a succession of the family of that name here. The gatescreen

opposite survives in the form of four rusticated pillars with ball finials.

LGI (1904).

106. JANEVILLE, Wexford; *c.* 1840.

A dinky single-storey standard cottage having a projecting hipped roof with tiny slates over squared sash windows in harled walls. Derelict. Now known as 'Brookville', in 1837 it was a property of D. Jones Esq.

Lewis 1837.

107. JOHNSTOWN CASTLE AND DEER-PARK, Murntown (6).

The jewel in Wexford's crown and the county's finest attraction, it remains strangely disregarded by the large-format coffee-table books on 'Irish houses and castles'. The magnificent 50-acre wooded ornamental park with its three artificial lakes was created in the 1830s and '40s as an idyllic setting for the vast and spectacular castellated pile of masonry to be enjoyed today. The transformation of the old Georgian house of the Grogans seems to have been commenced *c.* 1810 by John Knox Grogan (1760–1814), probably to designs of the London architect Thomas Hopper. But it is to his son, Hamilton Knox Grogan-Morgan (1807–62), and his wife Sophia Maria, whom he married in 1829, that it owes its present appearance. They proved to be serial builders and the house evolved into its present vastness in a series of building phases mainly to plans of Daniel Robertson and his executant assistant Martin Day. Suitable complementary lodged entrances to the demesne appeared apace, as noted by Thomas Lacy about 1860: 'There are four entrances to that portion of the demesne on which the castle stands, to three of which are appropriate gate-lodges, and an equal number to the deer park, with gate-lodges to two of them'.

Grand entrance; *c.* 1825; architect possibly James Pain.

Lacy continues: 'The grand entrance (*below*), which is near the church of Rathaspick, is formed by an ample and widely-spreading gentle curve, with a handsome, well-proportioned gate in the centre, and a corresponding wicket on each of its sides. Beyond each wicket is a beautiful lodge, which displays a semi-hexagonal front with a fine Gothic window of three lights in each of its three sides, in the lower story, and a handsome circular window above each of the former, in the upper story. The summits of each lodge, and those of the sweeping side extension, are decorated with embattled ornaments which are partially concealed by the clustering luxuriant ivy by which they are enveloped. The visitor becomes greatly struck with the peculiarly rich appearance of this entrance, that leads into a lawn of great extent and beauty, through which the castle is approached by a fine spacious avenue, on each side of which are trees of great magnitude, and of a healthy and vigorous appearance.' That this description did not match what is manifest on site today was not fully realised until the recent publication of a series of Victorian photographs, one of which reveals the full outrage visited on this entrance, the onset of which is described by Bassett in 1885: 'The old castle gate, or the one nearest Wexford, was formerly a very picturesque structure with two castellated lodges, and an amount of well trained and trimmed ivy, unequalled in the whole county. One of these lodges has been remodelled in a different style, and the ivy has been removed from lodges and walls.' The old image shows a pair of two-storey octagonal lodges with hood-moulded Tudor-Gothic sash windows below centre-pivot *oeil-de-boeuf* lights to the upper storeys and crowned by crenellated parapets, behind which the roofs rose to octagonal stone chimney-stacks. The lodges were linked by a tripartite castellated archway, the carriage opening having been flanked by square turrets. Today the archways have gone, as have the parapets, to be replaced by projecting eaves, with all the windows sporting square heads in the most drab grey sand/cement livery. A remodelling prompted by leaks owing to a combination of parapets and ivy, or by a change in fashion? An undated drawing survives by architect James Pain for work to the castle, doubtless prior to the advent of Daniel Robertson, and the entrance is just the sort of Nash-inspired design attributable to him.

Irish Arts Review

Back gate; *c.* 1835; architect possibly Martin Day.

Opposite a now-redundant avenue is this perfectly symmetrical toy castle, its two-storey entrance tower projecting beyond the main single-storey body of the lodge, all having Irish crenellated parapets. Constructed in pleasant rubble, setting off the dressed chamfered openings with enveloping label mouldings. Just visible above the upper castellations is a pair of stone octagonal chimney-stacks in the Tudor manner. All looking too regular to be by Robertson, and perhaps by the Wexford practitioner Martin Day. Sealed up and derelict.

Garden gate; 1846; architect Daniel Robertson.

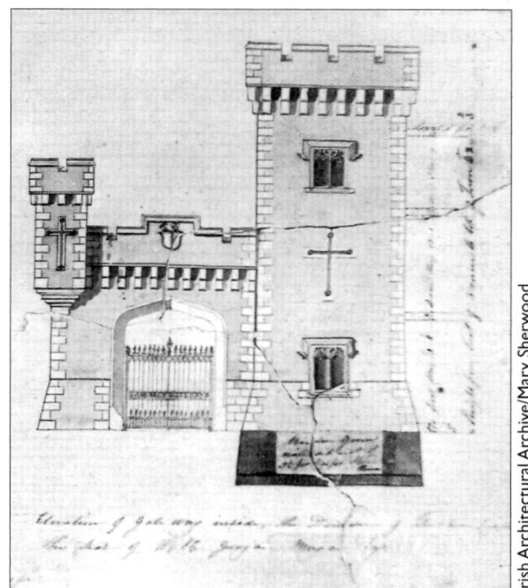

Irish Architectural Archive/Mary Sherwood

107. Johnstown Castle and Deer-park, garden gate. Part of a Martin Day/Daniel Robertson drawing (1846).

Lacy continues his tour of the demesne: 'The entrance to the gardens at which are a new castellated gate-lodge, and an ample gateway beneath an elliptic Gothic arch, is about half a mile from the grand approach just mentioned. Opposite the entrance to this part of the demesne is the castellated gateway leading into this portion of the deer park.' Ample indeed is this dramatic entrance, curiously filling a relatively minor role. Raised in random rubble with the most finely chiselled dressed granite, the Tudor-arched carriage gateway is dominated to one side by a towering three-storey 'keep' with a highly ornamental first-floor oriel window with elaborate Gothic tracery in stone. The porter's accommodation extends in a projecting single-storey room alongside. The other carriage pier carries a square corbelled bartizan, the whole composition relieved by

107. Johnstown Castle and Deer-park, garden gate.

mock cross arrowloops and crowned by sham machicolated battlements; decorative iron gates with pikestaff rails. Although a fine dated drawing by Martin Day shows the rear elevation and section of the entrance as built, he must have been working to Daniel Robertson's direction, as there is a gatehouse by the latter at Shankill, Co. Kilkenny (*q.v.*), very much akin to this.

Middle gate; pre-1840; *demolished.*
Between the grand and garden entrances was an early lodge that presided over a grand semicircular forecourt and matching area opposite but had been removed by 1905.

The two pre-1840 gate lodges to the deer-park, one in Kildavin Upper and the southern one in Kildavin Lower townlands, have been demolished, the latter serving for a while the twentieth-century Kildavin House.

There survives an undated proposal, perhaps for Johnstown, by Martin Day, dimensioned but unrealised, for a mammoth gatehouse of Hampton Court Palace scale. Two single-storey apartments with square battered turrets flank a central carriage archway surmounted by an oriel window to first-floor accommodation contained by octagonal towers. The whole medieval-style scheme displays all the Tudor Castellated vocabulary of machicolated battlements, Gothic tracery and hood mouldings, shields and arrowloops.

Irish Architectural Archive/Mary Sherwood

Lacy 1863; *LG* (1863); Malins and Bowe 1980; Howley 1993; Williams 1994; *IAR* (1999; 2001); IAA photographs (15/2R2+N and 15/2R3+N).

JOHNVILLE (see INGLEWOOD)

108. KERLOGUE, Wexford; *c.* 1885.

A late Victorian development for Francis Boxwell, whose monogram and '1884' are inscribed on a plaque on his Tudor Revival house. Its contemporary single-storey lodge, raised in a mellow orange brick off an L-plan, has contrasting white carved ornamental bargeboards of repeating pendulous fleurs-de-lis, just as on the Clonard Great lodge (*q.v.*). There are decorative hip-knobs, perforated terracotta crestings and six-over-one sash windows with minimal earthenware drip-shelves. There appears to have been some fenestration rearrangement, the front door having been moved from the internal corner; elaborate banded and corbelled chimney-stack. There survive two granite gate pillars, chamfered with pyramidal cappings.

Rowe and Scallan 2004.

109. KILCARBRY, Enniscorthy; *c.* 1820.
The huge flour mill complex illustrated in 1885 by Bassett is now much reduced, with the loss of many buildings and the huge chimney. What remains in this idyllic spot by the Boro River include the mill-owner's house and its gate lodge, probably dating from the arrival of Francis Davis, who built

the concern up to its mid-nineteenth-century importance. Prior to this, Thomas Barrington is recorded here in 1814 and may have been the builder of the lodge. Within a stone's throw of the house behind a tall plain concave quadrant wall is a charming Georgian Gothic single-storey standard gatekeeper's cottage, with pointed-headed openings and admirable Y-traceried replacement windows in rubble walls, probably once harled. In use, with a peculiar new roof.

Leet 1814; Lewis 1837; Bassett 1885.

110. KILLABEG, Enniscorthy; pre-1840; *demolished.*
A property in 1814 of Bartholomew Sparrow.

Leet 1814.

111. KILLOUGHRUM, Enniscorthy (2).
Yet another Wexford example of the work of Daniel Robertson, whose hand is not evident at either of the gates. A seat in the mid-nineteenth century of Robert William Phaire. One lodge has been demolished, while the other, dating from after 1840, is ruinous but reveals a stucco finish and central breakfront.

PRONI (Rathdonnell Papers); *IAR* (1999).

112. KILLOWEN, Wexford; *c.* 1800.
A Georgian Gothic porter's lodge that may have been built by one Brown Esq., recorded here in 1783, or by his successor, John Henry Glascott, the proprietor in 1810. Single-storey standard, hip-roofed with tiny slates, but much modernised, with new windows to its pointed lights, an unsightly hall projection and stucco-effect sand/cement rendering.

Taylor and Skinner 1778; 1969 [1783].

113. KILMACOE LODGE, Castlebridge; pre-1840; *demolished.*
Of the delicious *cottage orné*, in 1837 of Cadwallader Waddy, and its gatekeeper's lodge opposite the gates nothing remains, the latter having gone by 1905 and the house being demolished in 1990.

Lewis 1837; Rowe and Scallon 2004.

114. KILMANNOCK, Campile; 1879; architect Sir Thomas Drew.
A seat for many years of the Houghton family which did not warrant the cachet of a porter's lodge until the advent of Capt. Samuel Barrett-Hamilton (1838–1906). It is a splendidly ornate and solid Picturesque High Victorian affair, almost identical to that at Ashfield Lodge, Co. Cavan, by the same architect. Beautifully constructed in

contrasting masonry, it is basically 1½-storey gabled but having a single-storey canted projection with corresponding roof, which forms an L-plan. A porch in the internal angle is formed by a catslide roof carried on a squat neo-Norman column and corbel bracket with flower and foliage motifs, all richly chiselled, as is the informative plaque with scrolled frame which reveals the date of erection and its builder from the monogram 'S.B.' (he did not assume the additional surname until 1887). A diagonally set brick corbelled chimney-stack breaks a ridge with earthenware ridge and fancy hip-knobs.

LGI (1912); Bence-Jones 1988; Dean 1994.

KNOCKMULLEN (see MARYVILLE)

115. KNOCKREIGH, Adamstown; pre-1910.
Long home to the Downes family, it did not acquire a lodge opposite the gates until the early twentieth century, when the property was improved by Philip Thomas Murphy. What survives must have been a single-storey hip-roofed structure, now extended and modernised out of all recognition. Previously called 'Adamstown' after its townland and parish.

Rowe and Scallan 2004.

116. LANDSCAPE, New Ross; pre-1840; *demolished.*
A seat in 1837 'of John Ussher, Esq., derives its name from the beautiful view it embraces'. He died in 1844, but his family continued to reside here for several more generations; their lodge was removed in the early twentieth century.

Lewis 1837; *LGI* (1904).

117. LARAHEEN, Hollyfort; *c.* 1825.
A peculiarly asymmetrical three-bay front and very off-centre chimney-stack to this otherwise single-storey standard pleasantly rustic lodge with oversailing eaves and small slates to its steeply hipped roof. The whole appropriately crudely re-rendered in modernisation but with blatantly plastic windows, the lead-effect glazing of which may reflect cast-iron latticed predecessors. Built for the Charles family. Occupied. Plain entrance screen.

Rowe and Scallan 2004.

118. LESKINFERE RECTORY, Gorey; pre-1839; *demolished.*
The glebe house was built in 1805 by Revd Wensley Bond (d. 1820) at an expense of £1,400, which may have covered the erection of its gate lodge.

Lewis 1837; Leslie 1936.

119. LOFTUS HALL, Fethard (3).
The great institutional neo-Classical house dates from 1871, designed by an as-yet-unknown architect engaged by John Henry Wellington Graham Loftus (1849–89), 4th marquis of Ely, who had succeeded to his father's extensive estates as a minor in 1857 but wasted little time in commencing improvements upon his coming of age. 'Redmond Hall', as it was then called, after its previous owners, had been acquired by the Loftus family sometime between 1669 and 1703, when they may have found the main entrance further to the north-east of the present gate, in Porter's Gate townland. This they replaced by a more direct approach from the main road, which was certainly in place by 1771. In 1783 the Rt Hon. Charles Tottenham (1738–1806) succeeded to his uncle's vast properties and assumed the additional Loftus surname. That he did not find the old Hall and his newly acquired Wexford property sufficiently grand for one who in 1785 was elevated to Baron Loftus of Loftus Hall is clear from his commissioning the renowned Scottish architect Robert Adam that same year. We know this from surviving sketches for a noble demesne entrance, which surely was only part of a greater scheme of things. For whatever reason, nothing materialised.

Unexecuted design (*below x 2*); 1785; architect Robert Adam.
The drawings, entitled 'Design of a Gateway for the Park of the Right Honourable Charles Loftus', signed by the architect and dated 19 February 1785, proposed a spectacular Roman triumphal archway with round-headed carriage opening framed by a pair of engaged Doric columns supporting a heavy entablature, complete with guttae, triglyphs and balustered parapet. This was to have been flanked by small-scale versions of the main gate as postilion openings crowned by dies with vases and having a uniting fluted frieze that continues in the parapet to a single-storey single-roomed octagonal porter's lodge. The 'Back front' to the park was to have been plainer, shedding the column embellishments, the lodge

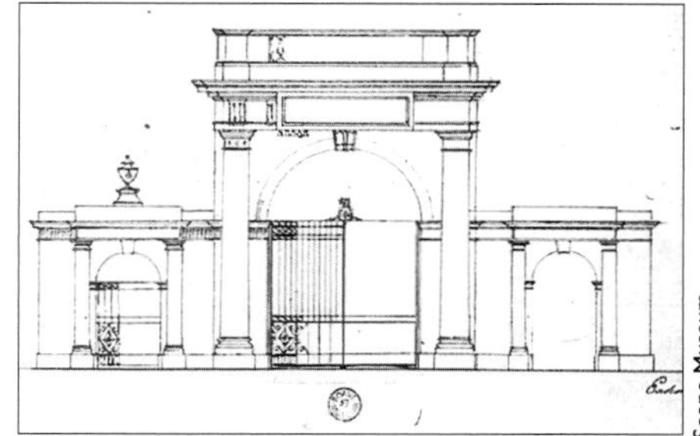
Soane Museum

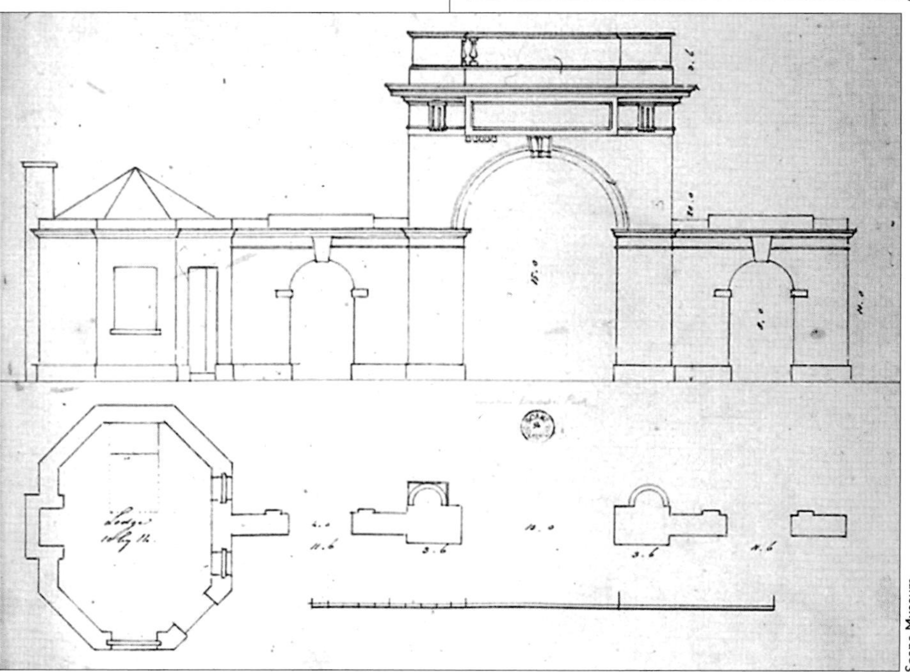
Soane Museum

accommodation displaying Adam's social indifference. That Charles Loftus, later to be further elevated as 1st marquis of Ely, had intentions for the place which did not stop at the perimeter of the demesne is clear from another Adam drawing in the Soane Museum entitled 'A Gate across a walk in the Park'. That the grand entrance was never realised is obvious from the OS map of 1840, and three generations of marquises (two of them absentees) and almost a century passed before the 4th marquis was to fulfil his great-grandfather's ambitions for Loftus Hall.

Main entrance; pre-1840/1876; architect not known.

The first OS map shows, at the base of the direct avenue, a structure forward of and to the left-hand side of the gates, linked by a straight angled screen. In 1871 this was swept away to make way for a more appropriate introduction, probably by the same unidentified architect responsible for the big house. The lodge is of considerable presence, single-storey standard and hip-roofed but with a central Classical portico in the form of a pair of slender Doric columns, lacking entases, now with a simple gable projecting beyond the fanlit panelled door, which is flanked by two-over-two sash windows. Finished in stucco with plinth, plain dressings and toothed quoins, nicely exhibited behind its own railed screen, it faces the entrance, which is comprised of four great ashlar pillars, with distinctive ball finials, joined by concave quadrant walls. An illustration of 1835 indicates many more of just such pillars about the old house, and also to be found at the other entrance.

Secondary entrance; pre-1840.

At the southern gate is a plain and simple gabled single-storey cottage, with its own pair of noble carriage pillars and ball finials precariously perched on flimsy pedestals. These may well date from the very early eighteenth century, unlike those copies at the main entrance.

Brewer 1825; *BPB* (1929); Bence-Jones 1988; Colfer 2004; Kavanagh and Murphy 1996; Sir John Soane's Museum drawings (Adam 51/55–57).

120. LONGGRAIGUE, Foulksmills (2).

The early lodge, located remote from the public road, to an estate in the early nineteenth century of Caesar Sutton was replaced in the 1840s, when Longgraigue was acquired by Joseph Deane. It is built to a design identical to the lodges at Healthfield (*q.v.*), neighbouring Raheenduff (*q.v.*), Stokestown (*q.v.*) (also associated with the Deanes) and Ballycurry, Co. Wicklow (*q.v.*), all by an unidentified architect in a distinctive Gothic style. Single-storey standard, harled and with an oversailing hipped roof, its openings have the most attractive ogee-arched heads. The casement windows contain the most intricate of geometric glazing patterns topped by Y-tracery, which is repeated in the fanlight of a doorway framed by pairs of delicate pencil-thin, engaged cluster-columns with peculiar 'bugle' capitals. Sadly derelict.

Lewis 1837; Griffith 1848–60; *LGI* (1904).

121. LYMINGTON, Enniscorthy; *c.* 1885.

A property with a lengthy medical association, the Classical villa having been built in 1839 by the physician Richard

Cranfield. About 40 years later the pretty gate lodge was added by Dr F. Furlong. Single-storey gabled on an L-plan in a late Victorian Tudor Gothic Picturesque style, with hood-moulded pointed-arched openings and ornate carved bargeboards. The terracotta ridge tiles, red-brick specials to chimney-stack and eaves course and decorative woodwork to the gabled porch set in the internal angle betray its age. Lovingly maintained but with plastic windows.

Bassett 1885; Rowe and Scallan 2004; NIAH.

122. MACMINE CASTLE, Enniscorthy (2).

Graham's description of what he found on 8 June 1835, 'an old ruin by the river', could well be the observation of a current visitor. What has transpired in the interim is ably described by Lacy in 1862: 'The fine old castle which constituted a portion of the mansion was kept in excellent preservation by the King family, its former proprietors; but on the estate coming into the possession of Mr Richards, the eldest son of the Rev. George Richards, of Coolstuffe, who became the purchaser of it under the Incumbered Estates Commission, he at once commenced improvements on a very extensive scale ... A new avenue has been laid out by the spirited proprietor, with a splendid gateway and an elegant gate-lodge in the Elizabethan style of architecture.' This mock castle was eventually abandoned in the 1940s, to remain an evocative shell to this day in the most heavenly of locations. It was survived by its lodges, only the later of which is still there.

North lodge; pre-1840; *demolished.*

A modern bungalow incongruously occupies the site of the Kings' gate lodge, behind a substantial castellated gateway with an elliptical carriage arch below a sham machicolated and battlemented parapet flanked by a pair of square turrets. Probably an addition of *c.* 1855 by John Richards (1808–81) after he bought the place, it incorporates a plaque which reads: 'Magh-Mayne Castle Erected 1290'.

South lodge; *c.* 1855.

The porter's lodge to which Lacy referred lies opposite its entrance and is a substantial 1½-storey affair with mild Tudor Revival features. Gabled, as is the projecting hall with room over, it is perfectly symmetrical, in roughcast finish with bracketed eaves and two pairs of chimney-stacks diagonally set. Occupied.

Heaney 1999; Lacy 1863; *LGI* (1904); Bence-Jones 1988; Williams 1994.

123. MACMURROUGH, New Ross; *c.* 1820.
A standard 1½-storey limewashed rubble-built cottage, lying very derelict. Built not long after the house was erected in 1810 for Henry Loftus Tottenham (1770–1826), whose son Charles's gatekeeper in 1853 was David Thorpe.

Griffith 1848–60; *LGI* (1904); Rowe and Scallan 2004.

124. MARLFIELD, Gorey; *c.* 1852.
A house built by James Thomas Stopford (1794–1858), 4th earl of Courtown, as a dower house to the main seat of nearby Courtown House (*q.v.*). Dating from 1852, occupied initially by the family's agent, it is in a Regency style, retarded by about a quarter of a century, like its mildly Italianate lodge. Single-storey on a T-plan below a shallow-pitched gabled roof, its main front to the park being two-bay with six-over-six sash windows in rectangular recesses. Rendered in a pink pastel finish, the blind gable to the road relieved by a banded surround and central niche.

BPB (1929); Walsh 1996.

125. MARYVILLE, New Ross; pre-1840; *demolished.*
A property, now called 'Knockmullen', occupied in 1824, the year of his marriage, by James Talbot (1794–1852), fourth son of Mathew Talbot of Talbot Hall (*q.v.*).

LGI (1904).

126. MARYVILLE, Wexford; pre-1840; *demolished.*
In 1853 a seat of Caroline Woffington, whose gatekeeper was Thomas Doyle. Sometime after 1905 the place became 'Beechville'.

Griffith 1848–60; *Land owners in Ireland 1876.*

127. MEDOP HALL, Camolin; pre-1839; *demolished.*
Both the gatekeeper's lodge and its big house, in 1814 of George Doran and in 1837 of Thomas Smith, have gone.

Leet 1814; Lewis 1837.

128. MERRION, Gorey; *c.* 1855.

The valuation books reveal the house to be as late as *c.* 1870 and its then occupant to be John B. Allen, from whom it passed about 1890 to William J. Weldon, who built the pretty porter's lodge. It is a simple Picturesque rectangular 1½-storey two-up/two-down structure, with a single-bay front to the avenue surmounted by ornamental geometrically carved bargeboards and very fine hip-knob with ogee finial and turned pendant. To the park is a single-storey gabled hall projection with an elliptically arched doorway, and later lean-to extension to the road. There are some surviving casement windows in stucco-effect walls, attractively painted. Contemporary decorative entrance screen, posts and gates. The valuation books also give the gatekeeper in 1898 as Sarah Hogan, followed by Kate Hogan.

129. MERTON, Enniscorthy; *c.* 1860.
A standard 1½-storey two-up/two-down white roughcast lodge with a hipped roof, its main elevation facing the park. Nice ogee quadrants to entrance screen. Built by Thomas Annesley Whitney (1794–1876), who succeeded his father here in 1831.

LGI (1904).

MERVIN (see CONVENT OF MERCY)

130. MILLMOUNT, Gorey; pre-1840; *demolished.*
A property in 1824 of Capt. Robert Sovereign Owen, a pair of lodges to which had gone by 1905.

Pigot 1824.

131. MONART, Enniscorthy; pre-1840; *demolished.*

A splendid mid-eighteenth-century Palladian-style house in 1783 of Edward Rogers, which was inherited by his son-in-law Nathaniel Cookman. The lodge is survived by a very fine and singular gatescreen. Two towering brick carriage pillars with moulded stone plinths and cappings are flanked by shallow convex plain railings on dwarf walls leading to smaller-scale pillars on each side containing a pair of granite door-cases with moulded architrave surrounds to postern gates, the pediments over broken to accommodate grand keystones. Probably dating from about 1820 in the time of Edward Rogers Cookman.

Taylor and Skinner 1778; 1969 [1783]; *IFR.*

132. MONEYLAWN COTTAGE, Gorey; pre-1839; *demolished.*
A seat in 1837 'of R. Brownrigge, Esq., a very pleasant villa'.

Lewis 1837.

MONFIN (see ST ANNE'S)

133. MORETON, Wexford; *c.* 1830.
A property later known as 'Mount Henry' which in the early nineteenth century was home to a branch of the Talbot family. A plain standard single-storey lodge with clipped eaves to its hipped roof. Much modernised and extended in the late twentieth century.

Griffith 1848–60.

MOUNT CORBETT (see TALBOT HALL)

134. MOUNT ELLIOTT, New Ross; *c.* 1800.

A big house with a troubled history, having been burnt twice, reduced by a storey, losing its founding family and being renamed 'Rosemount'. Built by the Elliotts in 1761, its lodge was not added until the turn of the nineteenth century. This is a pretty Georgian Gothic-style cottage, single-storey standard with a very shallow hipped roof oversailing a unique elliptically curved façade recessed behind a pair of slim iron columns *in antis*. The openings have pointed heads with latticed glazing in new stucco-effect walls. Sympathetically modernised and extended, awaiting a renewed patina.

Taylor and Skinner 1778; 1969 [1783]; Wilson 1803.

135. MOUNT FOREST, Ballycanew; *c.* 1820.

A house of the Fitzsimmons family was demolished in the 1940s, to be survived by its gate lodge opposite the entrance. Now derelict, it is a standard single-storey structure in harled rubble, with large round-headed window openings flanking a flat-arched doorway below a steeply pitched hipped roof with some bands of canted slates.

Griffith 1848–60.

136. MOUNT GEORGE, Ferns; pre-1839.
The simple single-storey lodge lies ruinous, its big house demolished. A property in the late eighteenth and early nineteenth centuries of the Lee family.

Rowe and Scallan 2004.

137. MOUNT HANOVER, New Ross; pre-1905; *demolished.*
A lodge built perhaps as compensation *c.* 1850 for the railway dividing the estate of Henry Williams, created on a new approach to his villa.

MOUNT HENRY (see MORETON)

138. MOUNT NEBO, Gorey (3).
In its earlier days as Mount Nebo this was the estate of the Gowan family, whose lodge within the property, now demolished, was home to William Devitt, gatekeeper in 1853 when William Adams was proprietor. In 1855 Arthur Wyatt (1829–87), a wealthy Welsh slate quarry-owner, married Margaret Louisa Bonham of Ballintaggart, Co. Kildare (*q.v.*), and about nine years later acquired the place, renaming it 'Earlswood'. As part of sweeping improvements, he initially added new offices before commissioning a grand house to cost £3,000, which he sadly never saw completed. His architect has not been identified but it is difficult to look beyond the Wyatt architectural dynasty from which he came, his grandfather being Benjamin Wyatt and his great-uncle the celebrated James Wyatt, and he had many cousins in the profession. Thereafter his widow persevered with the building programme, doubtless employing Richard Orpen, the architect favoured by her brother at Ballintaggart, where there are two very similar lodges. As there, they are in a fashion of half a century before.

South lodge; *c.* 1900; architect probably R.F.C. Orpen.

Differing from the average Irish gate lodge in its two-bay main elevation to the avenue, with a gabled ornamental wooden porch having geometrical perforated bargeboards and fancy hip-knobs, just as those to the main gables. It is 1½-storey and built in pleasant dark rubble facings with subtly contrasting ashlar dressings and quoins; there is a canted oriel window to the road front monitoring the entrance. Immaculately maintained, with modern lead-effect windows. Nice simple stone entrance screen with convex quadrant walls and railings over.

North lodge; *c.* 1900; architect probably R.F.C. Orpen.

A charming rustic version of the above, harled with tiny casement windows and studded front door framed in a breakfront stone porch with decorative bargeboards, as those to the main lodge. Fronted by a pretty picket fence, it once doubled as a post office.

The property was acquired in 1907 by the order of monks who established Mount St Benedict's School here, though it has since reverted to a private house and its original name.

Leet 1814; Pigot 1824; Griffith 1848–60; Bassett 1885; *LGI* (1904); *LG* (1912); Robinson 1979.

MOUNT ST BENEDICT (see MOUNT NEBO)

139. NEWBAWN, Newbawn; pre-1840; *demolished.*
A property in 1837 of Tobias Rossiter.

Lewis 1837.

140. NEWBAY, Wexford; pre-1840/*c.* 1870.
The house was built in 1822 for Henry Hatton to designs of the Dublin architect William Farrell, but the gatekeeper's lodge looks to be slightly later, perhaps as a result of later reworking if not replacement. Softened by a cloak of ivy, it is a standard single-storey cottage with oversailing shallow-hipped roof, its eaves marked by carved pairs of brackets. Uncommon horizontal sliding sash windows are installed in rendered walls with tell-tale mid-Victorian moulded quoins. Concave walled quadrants and pillars have moulded recessed panels.

Thomas Jeffries, who bought the property in 1869, was probably responsible for these improvements.

Bence-Jones 1988.

141. NEWBRIDGE LODGE, Camolin; pre-1839; *demolished.*
A date-stone in the outbuildings indicates a period of development by the Kenny family in 1810.

Rowe and Scallan 2004.

142. NEWFORT, Screen (2).

A seat in 1783 of Turner Esq., the early lodge to which, situated within the demesne, has gone. The Turner family remained here as lessees of the Lords Kilmaine until well into the nineteenth century. Their later lodge survives by the public road, abandoned as a home but robust and maintained. A delightfully rustic Palladian composition mysteriously not appearing on the 1839 OS map, it must have been built soon after. It is 1½-storey gabled, its single-bay principal front having a recessed entrance porch with two basic columns *in antis*, above which is a small lunette window lighting the loft, which is accommodated by high eaves. In whitewashed harled finish with a single-storey lean-to room at the rear. Built by Edward Turner.

Taylor and Skinner 1778; 1969 [1783]; Lewis 1837; Doyle 1868.

143. NEWLANDS, Clohamon; pre-1839.
In 1868 the house was 'an especially pretty cottage orné, occupied by Capt. Esmonde White', the porter's lodge to which lies indifferently not quite opposite its gates. The gable to the road of the single-storey cottage has foiled bargeboards, probably added by White to an early structure, in 8 June 1835 to 'The revd Mr Hoare's cottage'. The latter was the eldest son of Capt. Walter Hore of Seafield (*q.v.*), Revd Walter Hore, prebendary of Kilrush parish until his death in 1843. The property is confusingly renamed as its neighbouring estate, 'Ballyrankin' (*q.v.*).

Doyle 1868; *LGI* (1904); Heaney 1999.

144. NEWTOWN, Wexford (2).
A property which down the years has been alternately and alternatively called 'The Deeps', with a truly singular house in the form of a Classical pavilion, mainly the creation of two families, each of whom contributed remarkable lodges 40 years apart and in contrasting styles. The Wexford banking Redmonds had been here since the late eighteenth century, and John Edward

Redmond (1806–65) succeeded to the place in 1822 after his father's death. The year of his coming of age, 1827, coincided with the publication of an architectural pattern-book, *Retreats*, by the little-known architect James Thomson. There is no knowledge of Thomson's ever having visited Ireland, so it is more likely that Redmond, or his builder, was familiar with plate XLI for a 'Rustic Lodge', a design faithfully reproduced at an inner gate.

Inner lodge; *c.* 1830; architect James Thomson.

It is worth repeating Thomson's commendation for the design. 'The subject of the present plate is a gardener's cottage or porter's lodge; and designed not merely to provide for the absolute necessities to human existence, but to characterise the hospitable hand for which the English country gentleman is so eminently distinguished; to embrace those comforts which are seldom lost upon the destined inhabitant, and even to contribute to his humble but unqualified enjoyments. In its own construction the walls should be of free stone or brick and rough-casted, the covering of thatch in either case, and the eaves decorated with oak borders cut into scallops or other appropriate forms. On one side of the octagon a pair of large grotesque cantilevers are made to support a lean-to covering, under which is placed a bench for the recreation of its owner. A little scullery and larder should be added, when the occupant is not intended to fare at the tables of the domestics.' What tenuously survives is the main octagonal living room with an octahedral roof and lower rectangular bedroom wing, all in stuccoed finish to walls and slates to the roof. The openings have Tudor label mouldings, while the integral arbour may or may not have been as designed but has now a corrugated-iron canopy. There is no longer any evidence of the entrance gates on a now-redundant avenue.

Not long after Redmond's death without issue the property was acquired by Charles Stephen Walker (b. 1840), colonel of the 3rd Hussars and of the Percy Lodge (*q.v.*) family, who left his mark on the estate in the form of another delightful lodge.

144. Newtown inner lodge. The design faithfully reproduced at an inner gate from an architectural pattern-book, *Retreats*, by the little-known architect James Thomson (above and below).

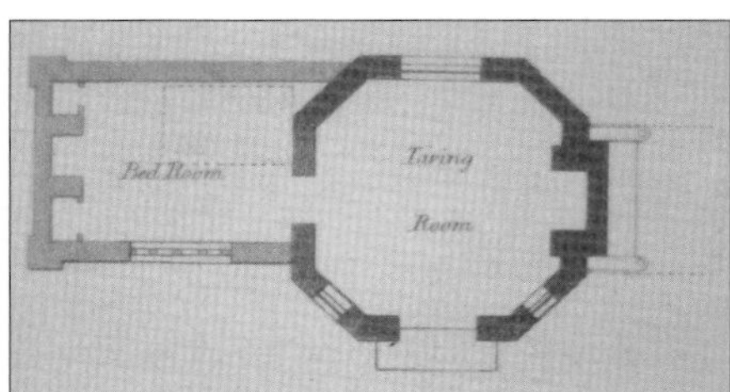

Outer lodge; *c.* 1890; architect not known.

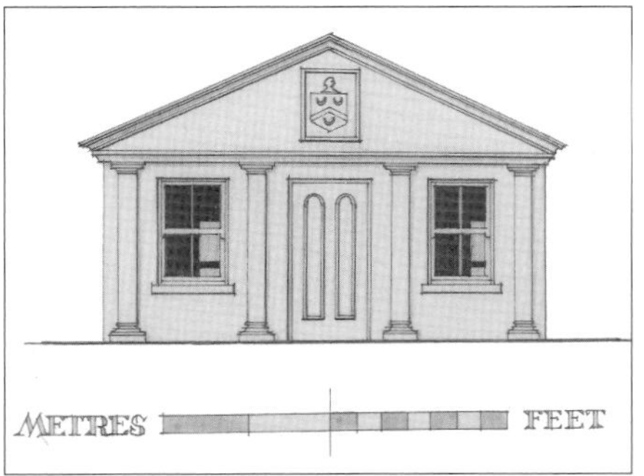

Located outside its gates and facing the public road is a sophisticated single-storey three-bay Classical façade of four Doric pilasters supporting a wide pediment, the tympanum of which contains a sculpted stone plaque with the Walker arms: *Arg., on a chevron gu., between three crescents az., as many annulets or.* The two-over-two sash windows flank a nice mid-Victorian door with round-headed moulded panels.

Both these gems lie overgrown and in an advanced stage of dereliction but neither is beyond salvation. Frustratingly and ironically, they lie beyond the boundary of a reduced demesne that is now owned by the building conservation expert and artist Peter Pearson.

Thomson 1827; *LGI* (1904); *IFR*.

NEWTOWNBARRY (see WOODFIELD)

NEWTOWNBARRY RECTORY (see ST MARY'S RECTORY)

145. NORRISMOUNT, Camolin; pre-1839; *demolished.*

The house, named by the Annesley family, earls of Mountnorris from nearby Camolin Park (*q.v.*), has gone along with its lodge. The property was in 1814 home to Henry Brownrigg and in 1837 to Robert Brownrigg.

Leet 1814; Lewis 1837; Rowe and Scallan 2004.

146. OAKLANDS, New Ross (2).

The house and one of its lodges have gone, but that which survives was probably built by Lt.-Col. Richard Jones Sankey, who is recorded as living here in 1814 and 1837.

Front lodge; pre-1840; *demolished.*

Back lodge; *c.* 1820.

A typical little single-storey standard Regency lodge with a series of round-headed openings, including the fanlit doorway, set in equivalent recesses. Hip-roofed, the walls are now rendered and it has an unfortunate modern flat-roofed hall projection. Occupied.

Leet 1814; Lewis 1837; *LGI* (1904).

147. PALACE, New Ross; pre-1840; *demolished.*

Samuel Harman (1748–1816) was succeeded here by his only son, Revd Thomas Harman (1788–1871), and it may have been work for him, described in 1837 as 'a neat villa, recently much enlarged and improved', that included the addition of a gate lodge. Both it and the house have gone.

Lewis 1837; *LGI* (1904).

148. PARK COTTAGE, Wexford; *c.* 1865.

The valuation of the property rose by £1.5.0d about 1870, when it was in the ownership of John A. Cooper, which may indicate the addition of the porter's lodge. It is a simple single-storey gabled structure with mildly ornamental bargeboards and exposed rafter toes, presenting its main single-bay front to the avenue. Considerably more modest than the pretty villa. Derelict.

PARK (see BALLYBOGAN)

149. PEPPARD'S CASTLE, Kilmuckridge; pre-1839; *demolished.*
In 1837 'the seat of Henry White, Esq., is a handsome modern mansion', the year of that proprietor's death. He may have been the builder and perhaps also provided the gate lodge, which had gone by 1924, demolished sometime in the previous nineteen years.

Lewis 1837.

150. PERCY LODGE, Wexford (2).
A seat initially named after Percy Evans Freke (1774–1844), who settled here from Castle Freke, Co. Cork, after marrying Dorothea Harvey of nearby Kyle (*q.v.*) in 1797. The earlier of the two lodges on the southern approach would have been of his creation. Following his death, the property was acquired by the Walker family, of whom Charles Arthur Walker built another lodge to the northern avenue and renamed the place 'Tykillen'. He was clearly a caring and improving landlord, as described by Doyle in 1868: 'The labourer's dwellings on it are of a superior description, consistent with this gentleman's long-established reputation for generous and encouraging treatment of the tenants on his estate'. Both lodges have been demolished.

Doyle 1868; *BPB* (1929).

151. POLEHORE, Wexford; *c.* 1885.
Although the house was erected in the early 1840s by Herbert Hore, and his family lived here until 1872, it had no gatekeeper's lodge until it was bought in 1883 by Richard Spring. The lodge survives as a smart 1½-storey standard affair, gabled and constructed in orange brick facings. It has recently been competently rehabilitated, the width of the window openings being reduced to accommodate attractive tripartite four-over-four wooden sashes.

Rowe and Scallan 2004.

152. PROSPECT, Bunclody; pre-1839; *demolished.*
Also known as 'Coolmelagh' after its townland, its lodge was probably built in the time here of George Braddell, who is listed as owner in 1814 and 1837. Both house and lodge have gone, the latter by 1905.

Leet 1814; Lewis 1837.

153. PROSPECT, Wexford; pre-1840; *demolished.*
A seat in the early nineteenth century and before of the Hatton family which by 1855 was sub-let to Anne Archer by John Stafford. A few years later the property's value had reduced by £2.0.0d, which perhaps reflects the removal of its gate lodge.

Rowe and Scallan 2004.

154. PROSPECT VIEW, Wexford; pre-1840/1902; *demolished.*
By 1876, in the time here of Charles Taylor, the house had become known as 'Archerton', which may reflect the name of a previous owner. The valuation at the turn of the twentieth century suggests the building of a replacement lodge by Lett Sealy Jeffares, grocer in the town.

Land owners in Ireland 1876; Bassett 1885.

155. RAHEEN, Adamstown; *c.* 1875.
On an elevated site with a fine view of the gates opposite is a thoroughly solid single-storey standard gabled lodge with a shallow-pitched roof displaying a repetitive perforated shamrock or trefoil motif to both earthenware crestings and decorative bargeboards. In drab grey rendered walls with raised quoins are two-over-two sash windows, two being gathered in one gable with a central sash box. Rising off the rear wall is a pair of square brick stacks with a common capping. It lies uninhabited, having been built by Matthew Furlong, the proprietor in 1876.

Land owners in Ireland 1876.

156. RAHEENAGURREN, Gorey; pre-1839; *demolished.*
A property in the nineteenth century of the Byrne family, the lodge to which had been removed by 1905.

157. RAHEENDUFF, Foulksmills; *c.* 1840; architect not known.
The most exquisite of lodges, unusually sited within but on the axis of the entrance screen—symmetrical, welcoming yet controlling. Replacing an earlier lodge to one side, it addresses the visitor with a backdrop of mature trees, single-storey standard with an exceptionally shallow-pitched hipped roof, roughcast with stone quoins. Its delight is the fenestration of Gothic ogee openings with the most intricate of margined geometrical cast-iron glazing pattern to the windows, which are crowned by delicate Y-tracery. The sheeted front door is faintly inscribed with the window pattern but, unlike that at nearby Longgraigue, lacks a fanlight. Framing the opening is a pair of slim fluted engaged columns, and within the hall is a pretty glazed vision panel. The entrance screen would have been relatively plain were it not for inspired twentieth-century gates, their ironwork imitating that of the windows. The architect irritatingly remains unidentified, as he does for identical lodges in the county at Longgraigue, Healthfield and Stokestown, and that to Ballycurry, Co. Wicklow (*q.v.*). Built for Joseph Fade Goff.

LGI (1904).

Barry Watson postcard

158. RAINSFORD, Bunclody; *c.* 1835.

Across the road from the gatescreen, with its squat octagonal V-jointed, ball-finialled carriage posts, is a pair of 1½-storey semi-detached estate cottages. Generously proportioned and finished in roughcast below a hipped roof with high eaves interrupted by two gablets; two-bay ground floor with modern squared casements, doorways to each end and lacking their chimney-stacks. Built by William Ryland Rainsford and probably contemporary with the big house.

Lewis 1837.

159. RAMSFORT, Gorey (3).

A fascinating rambling house which owes its appearance and evolution in the main to two persons, Stephen Ram (1819–99), who inherited the estate from his father in 1832, and William Kirk, to whom he sold it about 1870. They engaged a succession of architects, but it was the Rams who were responsible for the porters' lodges.

North lodge; *c.* 1835; *demolished.*

An old and indistinct photograph shows what appears to have been a Picturesque single-storey structure on an irregular plan with a gabled front to the avenue containing a label-moulded window. Just apparent, the Tudor theme continues in a pair of diagonally set chimney-stacks. In contrast, framed by low rubble screen walls, is a pair of Classical carriage pillars of V-jointed rusticated masonry topped by ball finials. On these were hung the most decorative of late Victorian iron gates, obviously an improvement of W.M. Kirk, perhaps to the design of Walter Glynn Doolin, whom he commissioned in 1874.

Middle lodge; pre-1840; *demolished.*

South lodge; *c.* 1835; architect possibly Daniel Robertson.

Here is today what to all appearances is a thoroughly forgettable late Victorian or Edwardian gabled gatehouse with disparate soaring rendered chimney-stacks and concrete tiled roof, a description which could be left at that were it not for the revelation of another old image, of 1866, which exposes it in a previous life and the twentieth-century outrage visited on it. This is a scene (*below*) from a Helen Allingham picture, a ravishing English Picturesque cottage complete with a steeply pitched undulating thatched hipped roof from which gablets grow organically to light the attic rooms, one containing an oriel window. Piercing the thatch were carved wooden hip-knobs and the same chimneys that survive, but displaying their brick construction in an original context. The idyll is completed by a rustic wooden boundary fence and pretty garden. The architect Daniel Robertson reputedly worked on the first phase of the main house, and if anyone was capable of such an informal delight it was him. Until 1971 the huge carriage pillars, upon which hung the main gates, and gate entry to the avenue, were re-positioned, permitting wider access to what is now a public road. Again contrasting with their lodge, they are blatantly Classical, with V-jointed rusticated stone shafts crowned by pediments. A scene that continues to bear testimony to another appalling example of desecration of our architectural heritage.

Michael Fitzpatrick (view of 1866)

Michael Fitzpatrick

LGI (1904); Fitzpatrick 1987; Williams 1994; Walsh 1996.

160. RAMSGRANGE CHURCH, CONVENT AND SCHOOL, Ramsgrange; *c.* 1871; architect possibly E.W. Pugin.

A sleepy hamlet associated with that tragic genius A.W.N. Pugin, for the *Catholic Directory* of 1838 records that 'to him the Revd George Murphy and his parishioners are indebted for the plan of the church of St James at Ramsgrange'. Although not officially listed in his works, such was his frenzied output that he forgot much of it. The convent added by the St Louis nuns in 1871 has been attributed to his son, Edward Welby Pugin, and the little gate lodge appears to be contemporary with this period of building. It is certainly distinctive, with certain quirks that can be associated with a discerning hand. Built in attractive rubble stone, standard 1½-storey with very steep roofs to accommodate attic rooms. The gables in the course of time have probably lost decorative bargeboards, although very ornate crestings to ridges just survive. Over the hood-moulded pointed front door of the projecting hallway is a clock, while all windows are exceptionally narrow lancets, allowing little light to penetrate within. A pretty little Picturesque Gothic composition. Occupied. The ogee entrance quadrant walls have ecclesiastical ironwork over, terminating in pillars with pointed-arched recesses.

Atterbury 1995; Williams 1994.

161. RATHASPICK, Wexford; pre-1840/1900; architect not known.
Nothing can prepare one for the shock of coming across this extraordinary apparition in the Irish countryside—a building of 'unparalleled craziness', as Jeremy Williams described it. It is a replacement lodge to the most restrained of seventeenth-century houses of the Richards family, in the French Renaissance style, like a compressed Loire

château but in the most garish of livery. Timber-framed, it is solid only in its polychromatic brick base and chimney-stack. The variegated theme extends to the tiles on its remarkable roofscape, which is dominated by a pyramid with *oeil-de-boeuf* dormers and intricate ironwork finials. Wooden-clad with shiplap boarding as would-be channelled rustication, there is a variety of projecting bay windows and lean-tos, some with turned wooden corner columns, and much else. Some of the mullioned and transomed casements have ornate pediments over, while eaves and verges have bold carved brackets. The date '1900' on the main gable probably gives a clue as to its origin, that being the year of the great Paris Exhibition, from which it may have been transported in fabricated form to be assembled for Edmund Moody. His family had acquired Rathaspick about 1880 and had an interest in the technology in their capacity as proprietors of the neighbouring sawmills and 'woodworks'. What would normally be considered an ostentatious gatescreen pales into insignificance in comparison. It is extensive, with wide concave balustraded quadrants interrupted by piers, and pillars with ball finials, moulded recessed panels and cappings with fluting and guttae. The gates have gone.

Bassett 1885; Williams 1994; Walsh 1996.

162. RATHJARNEY VILLA, Murntown; *c.* 1840.

Eithne Scallan

A standard single-storey hip-roofed whitewashed harled lodge masquerading as Georgian Gothic but which does not appear on the first OS map. On each side of a simple square-headed sheeted front door are the narrowest of lancet windows. Boarded up and derelict. Built for the Browne family.

Rowe and Scallan 2004.

163. RATHMACKNEE, Murntown; pre-1840; *demolished.*
On 9 June 1835 Robert Graham noticed 'a nice modern residence inhabited by Mr Armstrong, Mr Grogan Morgan's agent'. This was William Andrew Armstrong, employed to manage the neighbouring Johnstown Castle estate (*q.v.*).

Lewis 1837; Heaney 1999.

164. ROBINSTOWN, New Ross; pre-1840; *demolished.*
A lodge built either by the Giles family or after it was purchased in 1837 by John Redmond.

Lewis 1837.

165. ROCHFORT, Enniscorthy; pre-1840; *demolished.*
An early eighteenth-century house, occupied in 1837 by J. Jervis Emerson, the porter's lodge to which had been removed before 1905.

Lewis 1837.

166. ROCKFIELD, Wexford; pre-1840; *demolished.*
A lodge built either by the Nunn family, whose town house this was, or by Patrick Walter Redmond (1803–69), who was living there in 1837.

Lewis 1837; *IFR*; Rowe and Scallan 2004.

167. ROCKLANDS COTTAGE, Wexford; pre-1840; *demolished.*
An early Victorian villa and gate lodge, the former noted in 1846 as home to Lt. William Sterne; the latter, described as 'quaint', was removed to permit road improvement.

Slater 1846; Rowe and Scallan 2004.

168. ROCKLANDS, Wexford; pre-1840; *demolished.*
A seat in the early nineteenth century of Joseph Kearney, which thereafter had a succession of occupants. The lodge succumbed to road-widening.

IFR.

169. ROCKVIEW, Taghmon; *c.* 1810.
A standard single-storey hip-roofed lodge with whitewashed harled walls and granite chimney-stack. Derelict. A property in 1814 of John Heatley. Recently renamed 'Cullenstown'.

Leet 1814.

170. ROCKVIEW, Wexford; 1887; *demolished.*
A nicely proportioned villa built in 1848 for local merchant Robert Stafford, which remained unlodged until acquired by William O'Keeffe around 1800. His lodge proved short-lived, though the house survives as 'St Magdalene's'.

Rowe and Scallan 2004.

171. ROSEGARLAND COTTAGE, Wellingtonbridge; *c.* 1860.
A mildly Picturesque irregular gabled cottage on an L-plan with plain bargeboards and rendered walls. A seat in 1837 and 1853 of Ralph Hinks. Now called 'Ballyowen'.

Lewis 1837; Griffith 1848–60.

172. ROSEGARLAND, Wellingtonbridge (4).
This must have been an attractive property in its time, pleasantly located on the banks of the Corock River, but now thoroughly run-down, to judge from the appearance of the surviving gate lodges. At least three of these were built as improvements by Francis Leigh (1755–1839), who as eldest son inherited the place on the death of his father in 1803 and may have been behind the realignment of the public road to take it clear of the house and considerably enlarge his demesne accordingly, as recorded by Atkinson after visiting the property in the summer of 1814.

North lodge; pre-1840; *demolished.*

Middle lodge; *c.* 1835.

Once a fine Regency cottage but now lying abandoned. Single-storey standard, of larger than normal size, with harled walls and hipped roof. Unusually wide tripartite small-paned sash windows on each side of a flat-arched fanlit doorway.

Main lodge; *c.* 1835.

Identical to the above, with carved soffit brackets; similarly derelict and overgrown. Opposite, forming a forecourt across the avenue, is a peculiar structure which may have been an arbour. Stone-built and harled is a Gothic-arched recess flanked by a pair of diagonally placed square castellated turrets, which are repeated beyond to stop concave-walled quadrants.

South lodge; *c.* 1830.
Another standard single-storey gatekeeper's lodge, almost totally choked by ivy, but just recognisable is a flat-arched doorway flanked by pointed-arched windows with cast-iron Y-traceried glazing pattern. Ruinous. All very depressing.

Atkinson 1815; *LGI* (1904); Walsh 1996.

ROSEMOUNT (see MOUNT ELLIOTT)

173. ROSSDROIT RECTORY, Enniscorthy; *c.* 1815.

A lodge probably contemporary with the erection of the glebe house in 1814 during the incumbency of Revd William Hinson (1765–1842), rector here from 1806 until his death. Little more than a roofless shell is this once-pretty single-storey standard hip-roofed structure with Georgian Gothic pointed-arched openings.

Lewis 1837; Leslie and Knox 2008.

174. ST AIDAN'S, Ferns (2).
The mansion began life in 1785 as the episcopal palace of the bishops of Leighlin and Ferns, a role which ceased in 1835 when the see was united to Ossory, and it later became a private house.

Town gate; pre-1839; *demolished.*
From the remains of the Georgian gatescreen it may be assumed that the lodge served the bishops.

Country gate; *c.* 1835.
A lodge which, unlike its entrance gates opposite, has survived road-widening. Large three-roomed symmetrical with a hipped roof, its eaves high to accommodate attic rooms. The central entrance bay is in the shape of a canted projection with a moulded string-course and a semi-octahedral roof. Occupied. Probably built by Robert B. Brien, the first secular owner.

Walsh 1996.

175. ST ANNE'S, Enniscorthy (2).
The house now known as 'Monfin' dates from 1823, but its lodges, now both demolished, were built after 1840, perhaps added by John F. Lane, who was here in 1846 and 1853. By 1870 it was occupied by Mrs Lane, presumably his widow.

Slater 1846; 1870; Griffith 1848–60; Rowe and Scallan 2004.

176. ST AUSTIN'S, Coolgreany (2).
The house of 1763 has seen a succession of families as occupants down the years. The Bolgers, recorded here between 1786 and 1837, may have been responsible for building the lodges, but by 1853 James Perrin was listed as proprietor, his two gatekeepers being James Keegan and John Murphy. The lodges' present irregular and plain appearance might, however, be due to remodelling or replacement at the hands of T.C. Ellis in the 1870s.

North gate; pre-1840/*c.* 1870.

The single-storey core of the original lodge may survive as the rear of the surviving gabled double pile, created by the later addition of a 1½-storey extension across its front to form a commodious unprepossessing whole. Grey roughcast finish with external sheeted shutters. Rather more appealing are the late eighteenth-century ashlar carriage pillars, with their thin fluted friezes framed by tall concave quadrant walls.

South gate; pre-1840/*c.* 1870.
Another grey roughcast lodge but minuscule and single-storey, one end gabled, the other hipped. Two-bay, with a gabled hallway projecting from the left, and the chimney-stack rising off the rear wall. Shuttered, like its counterpart, but in use.

Wilson 1803; Lewis 1837; Griffith 1848–60; Slater 1870; *Land owners in Ireland 1876.*

177. ST EDMOND'S, Castlebridge (2).
Part of the Le Hunte of Artramon (*q.v.*) estates but much tenanted, its pre-1840 lodges both having been demolished.

Rowe and Scallan 2004.

ST JAMES'S CHURCH (see RAMSGRANGE)

ST JOHN OF GOD NOVITIATE (see ROCKFIELD)

ST MAGDALENE'S (see ROCKVIEW, Wexford)

178. ST MARY'S CEMETERY, Enniscorthy; 1898; architect not known.
An ornamental late Victorian single-storey affair built off an L-plan in brick facings, its steep gables having their apexes highlighted with carved joinery crowned by fancy finials. To the avenue gable is a rectangular bay, with

a pair of segmentally headed keystoned windows, below its own hipped roof. The lower wing extending to the road contains a little hallway and verandah with more decorative woodwork in chamfered posts and brackets. Breaking the perforated ridge cresting is a chimney-stack with elaborate brickwork.

179. ST MARY'S, Wexford; pre-1905; *demolished.*
A property that consistently failed to register in directories, either in its previous guise of 'South Hill' or later, when it was absorbed into the neighbouring Summerhill (*q.v.*), becoming a bishop's palace and renamed. The valuation of 1853, however, gives the occupier as Nicholas Whitty, listed seven years earlier as a tanner in the town. Its gate lodge, built after 1840, was short-lived.

Slater 1846; Griffith 1848–60.

180. ST MARY'S RECTORY, Bunclody; pre-1839; *demolished.*
The lodge to 'a handsome residence, built in 1808', had been removed before 1905. Perhaps contemporary with the glebe house erected during the incumbency of Revd James Morgan, rector of Newtownbarry parish from 1799 until 1810.

Lewis 1837; Leslie and Knox 2008.

181. ST PETER'S COLLEGE, Wexford; *c.* 1850; architect possibly Richard Pierce Sr.

A large religious complex which originated in the 1818 purchase of a Georgian house and land of the Redmond family, and grew over the nineteenth century to include the main collegiate block designed by local architect Richard Pierce Sr, who then in 1838 acted as superintending architect for that tragic genius A.W.N. Pugin, architect of the chapel, and may well have been retained to plan the gate lodge and entrance screen added a few years later. Behind a set of carriage and postern gates with severe granite Classical pillars with recessed panels and crenellated quadrant walls is a cheerful little 1½-storey standard lodge in Picturesque Gothic style. Its steep gables boast foiled bargeboards over windows with segmental pointed arches but having inappropriate modern casements. The projecting porch has a pointed doorway with hood moulding, its dripstones uncut. Lacy in 1862 was impressed: 'A new entrance gate, with panelled Tuscan pillars of fine granite, has also been recently erected immediately adjoining the handsome lodge, which some years since was built within the demesne'. In 1853 the gate porter was Robert Hughes.

Lewis 1837; Griffith 1848–60; Lacy 1863; Bassett 1885; Atterbury 1995; McCarthy and O'Neill 2008.

ST SENNA'S (see ENNISCORTHY DISTRICT ASYLUM)

182. SAVILLE, Enniscorthy; pre-1840; *demolished.*
A seat at the turn of the nineteenth century of Thomas Sparrow.

183. SAUNDERS COURT, Crossabeg (5).
One of the great unlamented lost demesnes, of which precious little architecture survives other than some outbuildings and the substantial remains of a huge double-lodged triumphal entrance archway. The Gore family had come by the place through the marriage in 1730 of the 1st earl of Arran, as Sir Arthur Gore became, to a daughter of the Saunders family. He set about building a new mansion and enthusiastically planting the estate, elevating it to a place of note. But his immediate descendants in the title lost interest and it went into decline through their absenteeism, its maturing noble oak woods and hedgerows being felled. Interest in it was revived by the 4th earl, Philip Yorke Gore (1801–84), who succeeded to Saunders Court on his uncle's death in 1837. He displayed the same fervour as his great-grandfather and commenced a renaissance of the demesne, employing the renowned landscape gardener James Fraser, who was then working at nearby Castleboro (*q.v.*), in tandem with the architect Daniel Robertson. Sadly, this proved to be a false dawn and the same disaffection with the place seems to have afflicted the 4th earl, for he sold it *c.* 1860 to Arthur Giles, who effected a modernisation of the house. Nevertheless, from about 1880 the demesne went into terminal decline to arrive at its present tragic state. As early as 1815 Atkinson had noted an obvious deterioration in the property: 'I felt my heart impelled by a sentiment of sympathy … by the neglected and ruinous aspect of Sanderscourt, no longer the seat of nobility, nor of that munificence and national hospitality for which it was once so remarkable'.

Main entrance; *c.* 1780; architect possibly John Roberts.
A magnificent towering Palladian carriage gateway in the form of a round-arched opening, double-sided, flanked by Tuscan engaged columns rising from unusually tall plinths to carry the crowning pediments. Beyond, in pleasant Flemish bond brickwork, are wings and pavilions, the former as concave quadrant walls with round-headed niches, creating yard areas, linked to generously proportioned hip-roofed gatehouses, appearing as single-storey but raised off basements. Their principal elevations to the park are two-bay windows with six-over-six sashes framed by keystoned Gibbsian block surrounds. Atkinson's visit of 1815 confirms what is suggested by the 1840 OS map, that this impressive complex never realised the purpose for which it was intended: 'When I arrived within view of the splendid arch and lodges, which, on an elevated position above the public road, form a grand outpost to this concern, and through which, though never carried into effect, an approach was meditated by the late Earl, my mind became unexpectedly introduced into a train of reflection on the ruinous consequences to this country, of that absentee

system, which since our union with England has become so much the fashion. This splendid portal, with the degraded state of the mansion-house and offices, (now wholly deserted by the proprietor and his family,) and which form a striking contrast to each other, were well calculated to impress this subject upon the mind.' Presumably built by Arthur Saunders Gore, 2nd earl of Arran (1734–1809), who had inherited the estate on the death of his father in 1773, it is attributable to architect John Roberts of Waterford. Given its unfortunate history, having lain vacant in 1853 and subsequently suffering years of neglect and abuse, it is comforting that this magnificent structure is now subject to a plucky restoration by the Irish Landmark Trust, despite still forming part of an unsightly farmyard.

Galbally Bridge gate; pre-1840; *demolished.*
By the now-lost northern approach, a lodge that had been removed by 1900.

Kavanaghspark gate; *c.* 1845.
A much-extended single-storey structure with oversailing hipped roof on an L-plan.

Killeen gate; 1889.
A 1½-storey late Victorian cottage in pleasant rubble facings with red-brick dressings. Sympathetically extended, by the entrance to a southern approach created during the tenure of Crosbie W. Harvey (1831–96) of nearby Broomley Cottage, to a previously extensive but lodgeless gatescreen.

Atkinson 1815; *Parliamentary Gazetteer*; Griffith 1848–60; Lacy 1863; Malins and Bowe 1980; Walsh 1996.

184. SEAFIELD, Gorey; pre-1840; *demolished.*
A house that looked to date from *c.* 1800 is said to have been built as a dower house by the Stopfords, earls of Courtown, but was occupied for the first half of the nineteenth century by the Hores of Harperstown (*q.v.*). Both the big house and its lodge have gone.

Leet 1814; Slater 1846.

185. SEA VIEW, Castlebridge; pre-1905; *demolished.*
A gentleman farmer's house occupied by the Culleton family in 1853 and 1885; their lodge, built after 1840, perhaps replaced a predecessor opposite the gates.

Griffith 1848–60; Bassett 1885.

186. SION, Castlebridge; *c.* 1845; *demolished.*
A lodge built sometime between the first OS map of 1840 and the 1853 valuation, when it was the property of Francis Lee, or Leigh (1808–82), who acquired it from the Lyster family about 1840.

Lewis 1837; Griffith 1848–60; *LGI* (1904).

187. SLANEY HILL, Wexford; *c.* 1820.
A 1½-storey three-bay gabled porter's lodge, its chimney-stack and door to the left-hand side. Compact, it has buttresses on the front elevation to prevent its collapse into the road. In use. The earliest family known to be associated with the property were the Scallans.

SLANEY MANOR (see BARNSTOWN)

SLEEDAGH (see BENVILLE)

188. SOLSBOROUGH, Enniscorthy (3).
Yet another example of a noble Wexford landed estate lying forsaken, minus its big house. Home to the Richards family since the 1660s, it was burnt down accidentally in 1933 but remarkably retains its three porters' lodges, occupied and much as built. They and the mansion, as last manifest, would have been part of a grand rebuilding programme instigated shortly before or after his father's death in 1871 by General George Solomon Richards (1817–1905).

South gate; pre-1840/*c.* 1870; architect not known.
At the main entrance, and replacing an earlier lodge that lay vacant in 1853, is this mid-Victorian Picturesque Gothic design. Typical of the period, being built off an L-plan, single-storey with steep roofs, its gables ornamented with apex joinery and fancy finials. Faced in a pleasant ragstone with toothed brick dressings and quoins, the avenue gable contains a splendid 'church' window with mullioned Y-tracery and latticed glazing pattern below a pointed arch. From the internal angle springs an inviting decorative gabled entrance porch. Admirably rescued from dereliction, restored and sympathetically doubled in size in 1997 by its new owners, who also created a garden out of wilderness, a feature of which is the splendid pair of carriage pillars. These are presumably contemporary with the previous lodge, of mid-Georgian construction with V-jointed rusticated masonry and intricately moulded cappings topped by peculiar apologies for ball finials.

North gate; pre-1840/*c.* 1870; architect not known.
Identical to the main lodge and equally well

rehabilitated. It similarly had a predecessor on the site.

Middle gate; pre-1840/*c.* 1870; architect not known.

Mary Doyle

Differing from its neighbouring lodges only in being bigger in plan and situated opposite the gates, presiding over an access to the River Slaney, as did its predecessor.

Griffith 1848–60; *LGI* (1904); Walsh 1996.

189. SOMERTON, Wexford; pre-1840; *demolished.*

A house built *c.* 1800 by John Redmond (1770–1822), banker of the town. Like its lodge, a thing of the past, removed to make way for a hospital.

IFR.

SOUTH HILL (see ST MARY'S)

190. SPRINGFIELD, Wexford; *c.* 1820.

A simple unassuming two-up/two-down gabled gatehouse to the back of the footway, in grey rendered finish. Vacant and boarded up. Alongside is a postilion gate linking it to the carriage opening with a pair of granite V-jointed rusticated pillars. Once a seat of the Huson family.

191. STOKESTOWN, New Ross; *c.* 1835; architect not known.

A lovely lodge, built when this was the seat of George Drake (1776–1852) but occupied by his brother-in-law, Joseph Deane. Deane is also listed at Longgraigue (*q.v.*), where there is an almost identical lodge, as there are at Raheenduff and Healthfield in the same county and at Ballycurry, Co. Wicklow (*q.v.*). Single-storey standard with an oversailing shallow-hipped roof, it is notable for the ogee heads to its openings, which are dressed by chamfered granite in roughcast walls with stone quoins. There is also a feel of the Gothic in its unusual circular chimney-pot. Sadly, this important cottage lies disgracefully neglected and missing its characterful margined glazing pattern, though the six-panel door survives.

Lewis 1837; Slater 1846; *LGI* (1904).

192. SUMMERHILL, Wexford; *c.* 1830.

For about a century this was home to the

Devereux family, by whom it was virtually gifted *c.* 1900 as a palace for the Roman Catholic bishops of Ferns, who had only to move from neighbouring St Mary's (*q.v.*). There is evidence of both interests at the entrance to the property. The lodge is standard single-storey with modern windows in drab grey rendering below a hipped roof with a replacement brick chimney-stack and late Victorian pots. The sole architectural feature is a continuous label moulding embracing the three openings. The gates from the turn of the twentieth century are rather more pretentious, with four tall granite pillars having recessed moulded panels and Maltese cross motifs below exaggerated corniced cappings, on which have been deposited balls praying for pedestals to introduce some degree of grace. Beyond are convex quadrant walls with railings over, matching the four gates.

Rowe and Scallan 2004.

193. SUMMERVILLE, Wexford; pre-1840; *demolished.*

One of those suburban villas in proximity to the town that has been temporary home to a succession of residents, the earliest of whom recorded here is a Mary Howlett in 1853.

Griffith 1848–60.

194. SWEETFARM, Enniscorthy; *c.* 1840.

An astylar two-storey gatehouse, three-bay symmetrical, its two first-floor windows tucked in below the deep soffit of a steeply hipped roof with a central chimney-stack. Harled and occupied at the entrance to a delightful Regency villa, in 1837 home to William Jones.

Lewis 1837.

195. SWEETMOUNT, New Ross; pre-1905; *demolished.*

The house is twin to the other Sweetman property of Ballymackesy (*q.v.*), dating from *c.* 1810. Its lost lodge is much later, probably built in the time here of F.M. Sweetman.

Slater 1870.

196. TALBOT HALL, New Ross (2).

A large mid-Georgian gentry house built by the Corbet family and known as 'Corbet Hill'. More of their fine architectural legacy is to be found on the southern approach.

Back gate; pre-1840.

In contrast to an incoherent undatable gatekeeper's structure is a charming Georgian Gothic triple archway in the Batty Langley manner (*bottom of page*). The main pointed opening spans the avenue, to be flanked by similarly arched posterns, all crowned by a crow-stepped gable with relieving trefoil and cross arrowloop motifs in the harled surface. This is all contained by a pair of square turrets with dentil courses as mock machicolation but, like the arch apex, apparently missing finishing finials.

By 1814 the Corbets had vacated the place, and ten years later the famous John Hyacinth Talbot had commenced a lengthy occupation of the property, changing its name. While he also owned the lodgeless estates of Mount Talbot and Ballytrent in the county, here he seems to have acquired a property with two. That which was demolished in the late twentieth century at the main gate was a replacement, however, built for his daughter and son-in-law. On his death he bequeathed Talbot Hall to Anne Eliza, who in 1824 had married Sir Thomas Redington of Kilcornan, Go. Galway, and she lived here long after her husband's death in 1862.

Front gate; pre-1840/*c.* 1860; architect not known; *demolished.*

Irish Architectural Archive/Craig Collection

This was a typically pretentious little mid-Victorian composition with a decorative avenue front. Single-storey standard below a shallow-hipped roof, its three bays treated as an arcade of round-arched openings linked by a string-course at spring level, the panelled front door was fanlit and flanked by recesses containing chunky transomed and mullioned Y-tracery with intricate cast-iron hexagonal glazing pattern. Stucco-finished with raised quoins, it was shamefully swept away, with its pretty contemporary iron gatescreen, in the interests of road improvements.

Taylor and Skinner 1778; 1969 [1783]; Leet 1814; *LGI* (1894; 1904); IAA (Maurice Craig photo 4/1546).

197. TAULAGHT, Wellingtonbridge; pre-1840; *demolished.*
A house in 1814 of Bagenal Colclough and in 1837 of George Hughes, which by 1925 was in ruins and its gate lodge gone.

Leet 1814; Lewis 1837.

198. TEMPLE SHANNON RECTORY, Enniscorthy; *c.* 1896.
To what became Enniscorthy parish is this very fine early nineteenth-century Palladian-style rectory built by the prosperous incumbent, Revd Richard Radcliff. What he would have thought of its gatekeeper's lodge, added later in the century by a subsequent rector, Revd Arthur Robinson Barton (1848–1900), might be profane. Now severed from the main house as an independent property is this substantial 1½-storey gatekeeper's lodge with steeply pitched gables, having the remnants of a 'Stockbroker Tudor' style in a carved half-timbered feature in the apex of the avenue elevation. Probably once a perfectly decent example of the taste of the times, it is now much watered down in modern improvement.

Lewis 1837; Leslie and Knox 2008.

199. TEMPLESHELIN COTTAGE, Adamstown; *c.* 1875.
A lodge built for William M. Gibbon, who greatly improved the property in the 1870s, has been developed into a twentieth-century bungalow.

200. THORNVILLE, Bridgetown; pre-1840; *demolished.*
A noteworthy development, commenced after its purchase in 1816 by John Lloyd, who in 1818 began draining, fencing and planting it, and in 1826 built the outbuildings, followed by the house, which he had completed by 1836. His gate lodge would have dated from that period.

Heaney 1999; Doyle 1868.

201. TINTERN ABBEY, Saltmills; pre-1840; *demolished.*
An extraordinary property, since the Dissolution the seat of the Colclough family, who converted the old Cistercian abbey into their residence, which it remained until 1959. The gate lodge, mentioned in passing by Lacy in 1862, may have been built by the regally named Caesar Colclough (1766–1824), who succeeded to Tintern in 1794.

Lacy 1863; *LGI* (1904).

202. TOMDUFF, Ballycanew; *c.* 1835.
A standard 1½-storey nondescript affair, the gables of its very steeply pitched roof clipped. The gatescreen is similarly very basic. Derelict. A Mr Lyndon is recorded here in 1786, but he was probably a tenant of the Jones family.

Wilson 1803; Rowe and Scallan 2004.

TYKILLEN (see PERCY LODGE)

203. UPTON, Kilmuckridge (2).
An early nineteenth-century house of William Morton, recorded here in 1814 and 1837, was burnt down in 1923. Both its porters' lodges, in place by 1839, have also gone.

Leet 1814; Lewis 1837.

VALENTIA (see CAMOLIN)

204. WELLINGTON COTTAGE, Wexford; *c.* 1855; architect not known.
'... the traveller, whether native or stranger will pause in astonishment and delight, to view the rich and ornamental grounds of Wellington Cottage, the unique residence of Joseph Harvey, Esq. The new and beautiful gate-lodge, which is in the enriched Tudor style, excites in an especial manner the admiration of the visitor; while the conservatory and green-house are also creditable to their proprietor.' This is well-founded admiration from Thomas Lacy, that mid-Victorian chronicler of old Wexford and regarder of gate lodges, writing in 1863. A pleasant, rambling suburban Regency villa built in 1820 by Arthur Meadows, which boasted the splendid conservatory in the grounds, now sadly removed. The house, disappointingly renamed 'Ardara', remained lodgeless until the advent of Joseph Harvey, who had married Meadows's daughter Barbara in 1807. He doubtless waited until his father-in-law's demise before building the lodge and installing his own family's arms

over the front door. By an as-yet-unidentified designer, this is a very decorative and expensive little building. Single-storey and raised off an L-plan, with stuccoed walls terminating in moulded cut-stone skew-tabled gables with hefty kneeler blocks and very ornate finials, there are tripartite round-arched sash windows below label mouldings, over which the main gables are relieved by semicircular-arched niches. From the internal angle projects a little gabled hall with Tudor-arched doorway. The double-leaf door has beautifully carved panels with Tudor Gothic foiled tracery, a theme which is repeated in the broached octagonal chimney-pot, which breaks the crested ridge, and in the four square granite entrance pillars. Remarkably, the contemporary iron gates and railings also survive intact. The chiselled arms over the front door comprise the Harvey crest of three crescents below their crest of a dexter arm embowed in armour, grasping a sword. In 1895 the grounds of Wellington Cottage were divided and a new house, 'Clifton', was built, which now claims this handsome entrance as its own.

Lacy 1863; *LGI* (1912); Rowe and Scallan 2004.

205. WELLS, Kilmuckridge (2).
Yet another example in the county of the work of Daniel Robertson is this beautiful manor house plucked from the English countryside, in his favourite Tudor Gothic style. Built in 1836 for Robert Doyne (1782–1850), 'the grounds around it have been elaborated into appearances of decoration somewhat in keeping with the new style of the mansion'. This landscaping, noted in 1845, included the creation of a straight avenue to the public road on an axis with the front door, facing which was a gate lodge.

Main entrance; *c.* 1839; architect possibly Daniel Robertson; *demolished.*

Exactly the same as the entrance to Bloomfield (*q.v.*) is this pair of sturdy square granite pillars with moulded crenellated cappings upon which hang a pair of gates, ahead of their time, in wood and iron combined and containing Tudor Gothic foiled tracery motifs. If the missing lodge opposite is to be judged by the standard of design and workmanship of the gates and their big house, it is an unfortunate loss.

Church gate; *c.* 1830/*c.* 1860.
A once single-storey standard lodge, sometime raised to 1½-storey, in rubble construction. Gabled, with perforated foiled bargeboards that also decorate the projecting single-storey hall. Small squared cast-iron casement windows. Now having the function of a post office.

Lewis 1837; *Parliamentary Gazetteer*; *LGI* (1904); *IAR* (1999).

206. WEXFORD GAOL, Wexford (*below*); pre-1840/*c.* 1845; architect not known.
'The jail ... enclosed by a high boundary wall, which is entered in the north side, which faces the Spawell Pond, by a large and strong door, which is formed within a massive arch, whose projecting and very deep mouldings arrest the particular attention of the visitor. The whole contour of this entrance, with its castellated and formidable adjuncts, conveys to the mind a lively impression of its strength and security.' Thus in 1862 did Thomas Lacy describe this impressive and dramatic piece of townscape, which, as Samuel Lewis informs us, had a predecessor in 'two turnkeys' lodges'. Although the first impression is of an imposing and impenetrable medieval gatehouse, viewing it from the rear reveals it to be a sham, little more than a vast stage-set against which the disparate working accommodation leans. The unidentified architect has failed to express its function in favour of initial impact. Constructed in random squared red Park sandstone, with granite dressings to relieving mock arrowslits, corbelled battlements and a grand round-arched deeply chamfered opening with hood moulding. A perfectly symmetrical composition comprising three towers, that containing the central entrance with a window over, linked by short curtain walls to outer ones, and all battered or tapering upwards to give an added feel of solidity. The original 'strong door' has given way to gates and a panel over them proclaiming its new municipal use, no longer a place of 'incarceration for petty criminals, idiots and lunatics'.

Lewis 1837; *Parliamentary Gazetteer*; Slater 1846; Lacy 1863; NIAH.

207. WILMOUNT, Castlebridge; *c.* 1810.
Opposite the entrance is a plain standard gabled structure with tiny-slated roof finish and little attic window. Occupied. A property in the nineteenth century of the Goodall family. In 1853 it was let to Denis Kehoe, whose gatekeeper was one James Murphy.

Lewis 1837; Griffith 1848–60.

208. WILTON CASTLE, Enniscorthy (2).
The *Parliamentary Gazetteer* in 1845 considered Wilton to be 'one of the most perfect and beautiful examples of a modern castle to be found in the country'. Harry Alcock (1792–1840) commenced improvements to the property upon inheriting it on his father's death in 1812, but sadly did not live to see the house transformed from 'the dull style of the period of William and Mary' into a Romantic rambling Tudor castle created for him by Daniel Robertson. Despite being burnt down in 1923, it remains today an evocative and spectacular sight on a bluff above the River Boro. Nothing at the gates dates from that inspired period of building, relating rather to the old, 'dull' Wilton House.

West gate; pre-1840; *demolished.*

East gate; *c.* 1750.
A pair of majestic Classical ashlar mid-eighteenth-century carriage pillars marking the main entrance to the estate rise off moulded plinths to sculpted cornices and friezes with triglyphs and guttae below pedestalled cappings, now missing their crowning finials—ball or pineapple? Framing

them are wide-ranging tall rubble quadrants with sealed postern openings and a window with chamfered stone dressing piercing the right-hand quadrant from the little lodge modestly placed behind but having a sophisticated door-case to the park with architraved surround and scrolled keystone. It now lies an overgrown shell, the remains of a two-window-bay front to the avenue, a porter's lodge venerable in Irish terms. It may have been redundant from an early date, for a valuation book note of 1899 identifies a lodge for the first time, perhaps suggesting a replacement that has fared worse.

Parliamentary Gazetteer; Doyle 1868; *LGI* (1904); *IAR* (1999); Walsh 1996.

209. WOODBROOK, Kiltealy (2).
Two lodges, both built after 1840, have gone. One of them was recorded in the 1853 valuation, and it, at least, was erected in the time here of William Jacob Blacker (1823–69), who succeeded his father in 1831. Its site has now been invaded by *Rhododendron ponticum*.

LGI (1904).

210. WOODFIELD, Bunclody (2).
The house and village previously called 'Newtownbarry', after the Barry family who owned the place, passed by marriage to the Maxwells, becoming a secondary seat of the Lords Farnham. That mansion in 1862 was described by Thomas Lacy as being 'of long standing, and of cottage-like character, in the Grecian style of architecture' and it had two lodged entrances.

Wexford gate; *c.* 1835.

Sited below the level of the road are the pathetic remains of what was once a highly decorative 1½-storey Tudor Picturesque adornment to the demesne. Gabled and built in ragstone with crude granite quoins, there are gablets back and front, that to the rear lighting the stairs, and alongside a tall feature, diagonally set chimney-stack taken down with the breast expressed externally. To the back gable was a doorway over which is a stone-corbelled block that looks to be the remains of an oriel window there for the porter, blessed to admire the confluence of the rivers Clody and Slaney from his bedroom. There are peculiar drip mouldings to the windows, while a later single-storey hall shelters the front door. A shell. Commissioned by the 5th Baron Farnham, John Maxwell Barry Maxwell (1767–1838). Adjacent is a set of tall entrance pillars in quarry-faced masonry, giving a flavour of the austere mansion within.

Carlow gate; pre-1839/1920.
An unprepossessing but pleasant and generously proportioned three-bay symmetrical gatehouse, with its end gable fronting the road forward of the gates. This displays carved bargeboards, below which are a first-floor window with granite entablature and moulded surrounds and a date-stone indicating the time of its being raised a storey, or the replacement of a predecessor.

About 1855 the estate was sold through the incumbered estates court and was subsequently acquired by Robert Westley Hall-Dare (1817–66), who commissioned architect William Henry Lynn of the Belfast practice of Lanyon, Lynn and Lanyon to replace the old Barry house with the surviving Italianate-style residence. He barely lived long enough to appreciate it.

Lacy 1863; *DB* (15 April 1864); Doyle 1868; *LGI* (1904); *BPB* (1929); IAA photograph (S/37/3).

211. WOOD VIEW, Taghmon; pre-1905; *demolished.*
A property in the mid-nineteenth century of a branch of the Beatty family, the lodge to which is indicated on the 1905 OS map as a long and narrow structure opposite the gates.

212. WOODVILLE, New Ross (2).
An attractive early nineteenth-century villa recorded in 1814 as home to William A. Minchin, who probably added the early lodge.

North entrance; *c.* 1815.

This is a standard two-storey Georgian Gothic gatehouse below a hipped roof with pointed-arched windows, the chimney-stack rising off the rear wall. Finished in roughcast to the ground floor, which may indicate that at some stage it was raised by a storey, when the gabled single-storey hall was perhaps added. There is an original cast-iron latticed casement to one window. Occupied and well tended.

The property was on long lease to Edward William Tottenham (1779–1860), who is first noticed here in 1837, until his

death. By 1870 the Minchins were back in residence in the person of George Minchin, but six years later it was leased again and then sold to Patrick James Roche, malter of New Ross and Enniscorthy, who added the later lodge, probably through compensation from the railway company whose track intruded on the property.

South entrance; 1887; architect possibly Albert Edward Murray.
A striking High Victorian entrance complex with all manner of architectural devices to attract the attention. The sturdy standard 1½-storey porter's lodge has half-hipped gables with ornamental pierced bargeboards. Its quarry-faced masonry has smooth stone highlights as quoins, dressings to shouldered windows, pointed relieving arches, plinth and string-courses. To the park gable is a single-storey rectangular bay window, and the main roof catslides over the hall projection with scalloped slates and carved eaves brackets. The earthenware-crested ridge with decorative hip-knobs is broken by a large battered chimney-stack. The equally conspicuous gatescreen is comprised of wide banded ogee quadrant walls, carriage and postilion gates contained by six ornate granite pillars sculpted with fluting, paterae and Greek key pattern. The design of the lodge is akin to one at Annaghmakerrig, Co. Monaghan, designed by the practice of Henderson and Murray, of whom the latter may have been the architect here, following the breakup of the partnership, although it may owe not a little to the 'Single Cottage' in John Vincent's *Country cottages* (1861). Its first porter was Robert Gunning.

Leet 1814; Lewis 1837; Vincent 1861; Slater 1870; *LGI* (1904); *Land owners in Ireland 1876*; Walsh 1996; NIAH.

COUNTY WICKLOW

1. ABBEY, Wicklow; pre-1838; *demolished.*
The *Parliamentary Gazetteer* of 1844 sums up the history of the site: 'The ruins of the Franciscan friary founded in the reign of Henry III by the O'Byrnes and the O'Tooles, stands a little north-east of the Roman Catholic chapel, opposite to the parsonage-house, but in a garden which formerly belonged to the family of Eaton, but is now attached to the house of the Roman Catholic parochial clergyman; and, together with some old yews and other trees which shade them, they are carefully preserved'. Unsurprisingly, it does not record from what period the gate lodge dated.

Parliamentary Gazetteer.

2. ALTIDORE, Newtown Mount Kennedy (2).
A house and its lodge that reflect change of ownership and architectural taste of the times. Initially a relatively plain Georgian house in a naturally beautiful setting, it additionally 'acquired rich embellishments from the taste and care at once of Col. Carey, Lady Jane Carey and Mr Blackford ... reels in the scenic luxuries of cascades, alpine bridges, rustic seats, and serpentine walks'. The *Parliamentary Gazetteer* gushes further in its appreciation of the improvements of the aptly named Careys, who would seem to have been the tenants of John Blackford, an absentee who eventually offloaded the place to the Revd Lambert Watson Hepenstall (*c.* 1788–1859). He probably purchased it about the time of his first marriage in 1809, acquiring a property with its sole lodged entrance on the northern approach.

North gate; *c.* 1800.

The original entrance to this earthly paradise was in the affected form of a pair of lodges, a symmetry beloved of the Georgians, now lost by the removal of one, giving a lop-sided effect. The survivor is a simple single-storey Classical cottage, presenting its single-window-bay main front to the road with a pedimented gable underlined by a brick header dentil course. Roughcast walls rise from a stone plinth. Its two-bay side elevation searches across the forecourt divide for its lost companion, no longer linked to it by its original gatescreen; the incompatible replacement of about a century later is set well back. Of typically brash late Victorian design, the two stone gate pillars display a rich Classical vocabulary of moulded plinths, recessed panels, friezes with triglyphs and guttae below boldly bracketed moulded cappings. The gates are very fine, with decorative scrollwork, fern leaves and finials with coronets to denote an aspiration.

South gate; *c.* 1840.

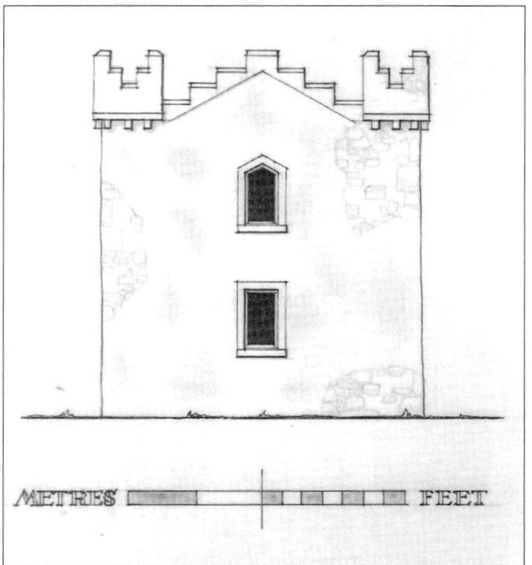

Looking rather more antique than is suggested by its absence from the 1838 OS map is this eccentric gatehouse, clearly designed to reflect the Romanticising of the house, which was given the appearance of a toy fort by the addition of round corner towers. Two-storey gabled in harled rubble, the park front is two-bay with arrowhead openings, while the elevations to rear and avenue have crow-stepped gables, the latter with quirky corbelled castellated turrets to each corner. Now sadly derelict and bordering on ruin. Equally dilapidated, in similar construction but in a contrasting Classical manner, is a gatescreen of concave quadrants with simple cut-stone carriage pillars and postilion openings, dressed, with keystones. Unlike the lodge, which dates from the time of the Revd Hepenstall, the gates appear to be of mid-Georgian origin.

Lewis 1837; *Parliamentary Gazetteer*; Bence-Jones 1988; Leslie and Wallace 2001.

3. ARDBRAY, Bray; pre-1885; *demolished.*
A lodge to a property built in the 1850s for Ellen Weldon, which was added not long after by Henry T. Vickers.

Slater 1870.

4. ARDMORE, Bray; *c.* 1870; architects probably McCurdy and Mitchell.

Although the architectural practice of Lanyon, Lynn and Lanyon was engaged to design a new marine villa for Thomas Paul Lefroy QC (1806–91) of Carrigglas Manor, Co. Longford (*q.v.*), in 1861, the lodge looks to date from a later phase of development, when McCurdy and Mitchell were commissioned by the same client fourteen years later. This is a standard lodge, appearing as single-storey but with high eaves permitting roof-lit attic rooms in a hipped roof with exposed rafter toes. Stuccoed walls with V-jointed stone quoins contain segmentally headed windows on each side of a gabled breakfront hall with a curious mix of half-hearted half-timbered apex and delicate Doric pilasters. Occupied. There are the remains of a gatescreen, two pillars of which have recessed panels and friezes.

DB (15 Feb. 1861); *Thom's*; Williams 1994.

5. AUGHRIM FLOUR MILLS, Aughrim; *c.* 1880.

Norman Campion

Although there has been a mill on the site since about 1730, this vast concern was mainly the foundation of the Fogarty family a century later. At the entrance is this sturdy Picturesque-style Victorian single-storey standard lodge in a drab grey stuccoed finish, lifted by lighter detailing in raised quoins, perforated foiled bargeboards to its main steeply pitched gables and that of the projecting hall, and sawtooth terracotta cresting with spiky hip-knobs. The fanlit hall door and its sidelights have round-headed arches, while to the road gable is a canted glazed bay window with equivalent roof, over which is the peculiar feature of a large recessed blank shield.

Milling magazine (25 April 1936).

6. AVOCA LODGE, Avoca; *c.* 1830.
A plain and much 'improved' two-storey gabled affair to a property in 1854 of Henry Hodgson of Ballyraine (*q.v.*).

Griffith 1848–60.

7. AVONDALE, Rathdrum; *c.* 1820/*c.* 1850.
A distinguished gentry house built for himself by Samuel Hayes in 1779; he bequeathed it to William Parnell (1780–1821), who assumed the additional surname of his benefactor. He may have built what was an average single-storey hip-roofed porter's lodge set well back from the gates (*below*). It seems that his son, John Henry Parnell (1811–59), was of more carefree disposition, for after coming of age he transformed it with a delightfully absurd addition. Showing no respect for the form of the existing structure is a 1½-storey room describing a sort of semi-octagon on plan, rising to a parapet with exaggerated Irish crenellations and flimsy mock machicolations. The ground-floor openings on each face are granite dressed in roughcast walls with the suspicion of ogee heads. As relief over is a series of motifs, quatrefoil, cross arrowloops and, over the door, a blind tripartite window or arcade. Equally silly is a towering chimney-stack rising as a pair but bridged to form one below the capping. Now enjoying a new life as a ticket office and reception to the attraction of the ancestral home of Charles Stewart Parnell.

Brewer 1825; *LGI* (1904); Bence-Jones 1988.

8. BALLINACOOLEY, Glenealy; pre-1910; *demolished.*
A seat in the nineteenth century of the Hayes family, the lodge to which was built after 1838.

9. BALLINACOR, Rathdrum; *c.* 1835.

William Kemmis (1777–1864) about 1830 purchased the property on a bank of the Avonbeg River, rebuilt the old house of Lord Moira, created beautiful grounds with planting of rhododendrons by the mile-long avenue and added a porter's lodge at its distant entrance gate. Probably later extended by a bay to the left-hand side onto an original standard single-storey structure with a canted entrance front below a corresponding roof having conspicuous carved soffit brackets, which continue even more prominently below the verge of the breakfront hall gable that contains a tripartite doorway. In roughcast walls are pretty cast-iron casements with octagonal glazing pattern. Occupied.

LGI (1904); Bence-Jones 1988; Heaney 1999.

10. BALLINROAN, Baltinglass; pre-1854; *demolished.*
A lodge built about 1850, probably after the seat passed from George Cummins to the Green family.

Griffith 1848–60.

11. BALLYARTHUR, Avoca; *c.* 1835; architects probably R. and W.V. Morrison.

Irish Architectural Archive

In 1814 A. Atkinson was here on tour and opined that 'The approach through Ballyarthur demesne to the dwelling-house, when put into competition with the beauties of that place and of the neighbouring valley, was very shocking also [with the local roads], but Mr Symes, in the autumn of 1814, was opening a new approach through the plantations on his demesne, which when complete will no doubt quadrate with the character and consideration of that seat'. But it was to be a generation before the property was lodged. Brewer in 1825 notes on his travels: 'Ballyarthur, formerly of Mr Symes, now the residence of Rev. Henry Lambert Bayley. The house is a substantial and commodious structure, but has, in itself, no claims on the attention of the traveller.' Ten years later Graham notices the property as 'an extensive place and covered with fine woods which they are cutting very fast. It belongs to a young man of the name of Bayly who is just going to be married to a daughter of the knight of Kerry. His mother and some brothers live in the house with him at present. The house is a plain one, and ill-placed, being considerably above the trough of the river.' The young man was Edward Symes Bayley (1807–84), who succeeded his reverend father in 1827 and indeed married Catherine Fitzgerald in 1835. He made a mark on his inheritance and again claimed the attention of the traveller, for Lewis in 1837 records 'The avenue leading to the house, which is through a turreted archway ...'. Nineteen years later Thomas Lacy was impressed by 'a very remarkable gate-lodge, standing within a capacious archway, which is ornamented on the west by a light and fanciful turret'. Young Bayley had clearly availed himself of the services of Richard and William Vitruvius Morrison whilst they were supervising their works on the neighbouring

Irish Architectural Archive

estate of Shelton Abbey (*q.v.*). Situated to the north, near the village, at the head of a two-mile avenue is this remarkable group of buildings in the Romantic Castellated Tudor Gothic style. The buttressed Tudor-arched carriage opening is surmounted by a mock machicolated and crenellated parapet, flanked to one side by a lower postilion doorway with label mouldings, and on the other by a tall octagonal watch-tower broached off a square base, relieved by sham arrowloops and housing a spiral staircase which leads solely to a view from the battlements. Behind, in a similar rubble construction but contrasting in a downright quirky concoction, is the gate lodge. Basically 1½-storey gabled, built off a cruciform plan with its main short elevation to the avenue; the latter has a large hood-moulded Tudor-arched recess, within which is the parlour window in the form of a highly ornate tripartite Gothic window with label moulding, tracery and cast-iron latticed glazing. This is all contained below a crow-stepped gable with eccentric cylindrical finials to the base steps and apex, below which are three little lancet lights. To the side walls are single-storey battlemented wings. This is a plan form pioneered in Ireland by the Morrison office, in which the main body of the lodge is two-roomed, flanked by an entrance hall or porch to one side, and balanced by a closet on the opposing front, but normally done up in a Classical cloak. A delightful composition, often wrongly associated with the Shelton Abbey estate.

Atkinson 1815; Brewer 1815; Lewis 1837; Lacy 1863; *BPB* (1929); Howley 1993; Heaney 1999; Lawrence photograph (5703C); IAA photographs (S/2226/3 & 4).

12. BALLYBEG, Tinahely (2).
The ancestral home of the Symes family.

Tinahely gate; pre-1838.
A ruined single-storey standard lodge, possibly dating from the time of Revd Henry Symes, who was proprietor in 1783 and 1814.

Aughrim gate; pre-1910; *demolished.*
A short-lived lodge, built after 1838 during the occupancy of Arthur Rowley Symes, attorney.

Taylor and Skinner 1778; 1969 [1783]; Leet 1814; Fraser 1838; Slater 1856.

13. BALLYCURRY, Killiskey (5).
This estate of the Boswells passed through marriage in 1766 to Charles Tottenham I of New Ross (1743–1823), who in 1805, like his neighbour at Glanmore Castle (*q.v.*), engaged Francis Johnston to build him a new house, a commission which may have included the design of a gate lodge to the property.

Killiskey gate; *c.* 1805.
A tiny 1½-storey rendered gabled cottage with a Georgian Gothic Y-traceried pointed-arched window, the one visible clue as to its age, as much is obscured by extensions and foliage. Occupied.

Charles Tottenham II (1768–1843) on succeeding to Ballycurry continued improvements with the addition of another lodge.

Glanmore gate; *c.* 1825; architect perhaps Francis Johnston.

On the south-western approach is this most delightful of Regency lodges. Single-storey standard, roughly harled below a shallow-pitched oversailing hipped roof, it is distinguished by its openings. All have delicate ogee-arched heads, the windows in matching recesses with cast-iron latticed casements with spoked tops, whilst the double-leaved door with its Y-traceried fanlight is framed by a moulded surround meeting in a shamrock motif at the apex. Conceivably a late work by Francis Johnston, there are four further examples of this design, all of later dates at four County Wexford estates of Healthfield (*q.v.*), Longgraigue (*q.v.*), Raheenduff (*q.v.*) and Stokestown (*q.v.*), presumably admiring copies.

Charles Tottenham III (1807–86) maintained a programme of development, which included a further two gatekeepers' lodges.

Glen gate; *c.* 1845.
The Tottenham estates extended westwards beyond the public road to land on the north side of the famous Devil's Glen, down which tumbles the Vartry River, a beauty spot to which the Tottenhams magnanimously gave the public access and marked with a lodge at the entrance, noted by Mr and Mrs S.C. Hall in the 1840s: 'Mr Tottenham requires that all visitors shall leave their names at his lodge, where an order for admission into the glen is given by the lodge-keeper, a kindly and gossiping dame in whose company the stranger may pass a few minutes very profitably'. Her accommodation, described in 1856 by Thomas Lacy as 'Mr Tottenham's unique gate-lodge', is in the shape of a 1½-storey English Picturesque cottage with decorative foil and wave bargeboards to very steep gables. Roughcast, its windows have tiny squared cast-iron casements on each side of a double door with elliptical fanlight. The gate is marked by anthemion motifs to the cast-iron pillars.

Inner gate; *c.* 1845.

On the south-eastern avenue to the demesne proper is a decent early Victorian Classical entrance with V-jointed rusticated granite pillars having corniced cappings and containing good contemporary ironwork to carriage and postern gates. Within is a beautifully tended single-storey standard lodge with oversailing hipped roof, its soffit with carved brackets broken by a small pediment carried on a pair of slender Tuscan columns marking the front door. On each side, set in rectangular recesses to ground level, are casement windows with delicate hexagonal glazing pattern in walls of modern smooth rendering.

Not to be outdone by his father, grandfather and great-grandfather, Charles George Tottenham (1835–1918) thirteen years after succeeding to Ballycurry erected the fifth and final lodge.

Ashford gate; 1899.

He took as his model the nearby inner lodge, for the form is identical and has the same portico, though with fluted columns and the date in the tympanum. Otherwise the windows are less elaborate plate glass, late Victorian in drab grey stuccoed walls with Tudor label mouldings and carved paired modillion brackets to the soffit. The sombre rendering is more than offset by its setting of colourfully planted elevated site and backdrop of conifers.

Hall 1841–3; Lacy 1863; *LGI* (1958); Bence-Jones 1988.

14. BALLYDONAREA, Kilcoole; pre-1838; *demolished.*

What appears from the OS maps to have been a commodious elongated structure to a property in 1814 of John Revel.

Leet 1814.

15. BALLYFREE, Glenealy; *c.* 1825.

Forward of its gates is this pleasant single-storey standard gatekeeper's lodge, with hipped roof projecting over plain bracketed eaves. Replacement two-over-two sash windows flank the pointed-arched doorway in stuccoed walls. Occupied, at the entrance to the delightful contemporary villa that was home to Joseph Dickson in the early nineteenth century.

Lewis 1837.

16. BALLYGANNON, Kilcoole; *c.* 1800.

To the charming old thatched house of the Scott family is a mid-Georgian gatescreen of granite ashlar carriage pillars flanked by contrasting rendered concave quadrant walls containing postilion gate openings. The left-hand wall is connected to the overgrown ruins of the lodge forward of the gates. A watercolour of September 1913 by Alma Burton shows it to have been a simple single-storey standard cottage, harled, with a chimney-stack to one of its gables. The painting also reveals ball finials to the gate pillars and a well-wooded setting—now, like the big house, all gone.

Taylor and Skinner 1778; 1969 [1783]; Leet 1814.

17. BALLYHENRY, Ashford; *c.* 1850.

A dapper 1½-storey standard English Picturesque cottage, the bargeboards and fascias of the main block and its single-storey projecting hallway being perforated and carved with a repeating trefoil motif. Replacement windows and smart modern rendering contrast with the original mellow brick chimney-stack. In conflict is the hefty Classical but contemporary gatescreen of ashlar masonry with exaggerated corniced cappings, scroll-topped stops and iron fists gripping the ornamental carriage and postern gates. A property in the mid-nineteenth century of Livingston Thompson, whose immediate lessors were the Truell family.

Griffith 1848–60; Slater 1856.

18. BALLYHOOK, Stratford (2).

Front lodge; pre-1910; *demolished.*

Built after 1838 by either Edward Nolan, recorded here in 1854, or Thomas Nolan, recorded in 1876.

Back lodge; *c.* 1860.

A standard 1½-storey building with steeply pitched gables. Faintly Picturesque, with ornamental bargeboards, harled walls and brick quoins. Located opposite the entrance to ancillary buildings but not facing it.

Griffith 1848–60; *Land owners in Ireland 1876.*

19. BALLYHORSEY, Newtown Mount Kennedy; *c.* 1840; *demolished.*

A gatehouse manned in 1854 by John Fitzpatrick as porter to Elizabeth Ireland, presumably the widow of William W. Ireland, who is recorded on this 55-acre holding in 1837, prior to his adding the lodge.

Lewis 1837; Griffith 1848–60.

20. BALLYKEANE, Redcross; *c.* 1850; *demolished.*

A lodge whose gatekeeper in 1854 is identified by the valuation as John Byrne, to a property of Francis Wright.

Griffith 1848–60.

21. BALLYMORRIS, Bray; pre-1885; *demolished.*

The gatekeeper's lodge, built after 1838, has gone without trace. A property that was home to a succession of families in the mid-nineteenth century: Graydons, Maxwells and Crawfords.

22. BALLYNURE, Grangecon (2).

Walter Bagenal Carroll died in 1801, to be succeeded here by his son Henry, a minor who did not come of age until 1820 and married two years later. Both lodges appear to date from that period.

North lodge; *c.* 1820.

A simple, suave little building, its harled walls in pastel pink wash livery. Single-storey, its main single-bay elevation to the avenue in the form of a sash window, now unfortunately lacking its squared Georgian glazing bars, framed in a segmentally headed recess below a pedimented gable. The composition is balanced by lean-to projections on each side. Extensive modern iron gatescreen.

South lodge; *c.* 1820.

A single-storey structure below a shallow-hipped roof with the long avenue elevation of two tiny windows, that to the road two-bay with the doorway to the right-hand side. Finished in whitewashed stucco, with carved paired modillion brackets to the soffit and a stone chimney-stack.

Leet 1814; Lewis 1837; *LG* (1871).

23. BALLYORNEY, Enniskerry; pre-1838; *demolished.*

A dower house of the Monck family of nearby Charleville (*q.v.*) but occupied for periods in the early nineteenth century by the Quins, with whom they intermarried.

Bence-Jones 1988.

24. BALLYORNEY or BALLYORNAN HOUSE, Enniskerry; 1873.

Very derelict and lying low to the avenue is this tiny single-storey standard hip-roofed lodge of harled rubble. Plain and looking more antique than the OS map evidence suggests. In fact built by March 1873, when Humphrey M. Bourne was carrying out 'improvements inside and some small additions' to the house that he had just acquired from Major Edward Kenny.

25. BALLYRAHEEN, Tinahely; pre-1838; *demolished.*

A seat of the Chamney family, of whom Henry Chamney was resident in 1814.

Leet 1814.

26. BALLYRAINE, Arklow; *c.* 1845.

A house built *c.* 1810 by Henry Atkins, in whose family it remained until about 1840, when it became home to Henry Hodgson, builder of the porter's lodge. An uncommon structure, two-storey, or single-storey over a basement, constructed of rubble stone but having a brick-built short canted front to the avenue below a corresponding roof. Dilapidated, boarded up and obscured by undergrowth, it appears to have a projecting hip-roofed hall at the upper level facing the park. A Henry Hodgson was still proprietor in 1876; the gatekeeper in 1854 was Patrick Williams.

Mason 1814–19; Griffith 1848–60.

27. BALLYROGAN, Redcross; pre-1910; *demolished.*
Built after 1838, the lodge, to a property in the nineteenth century of the Byrne family, has been replaced by a modern bungalow. Mysteriously, it receives no notice in the valuation books but may date from *c.* 1870, with the advent of Edward P. Byrne.

28. BALLYRONAN TOWNLAND, Kilcoole; *demolished.*
An anonymous property in 1854 of Thomas Yelverton, the lodge to which was erected sometime thereafter but by 1929 was, along with the big house, described in the valuation book as 'down'.

Griffith 1848–60.

29. BALLYWALTRIM GROVE, Bray; pre-1885; *demolished.*
An estate in 1837 of John Ormsby, from whom by 1846 it had passed to Capt. Croasdaile, whose family remained here until the end of the century and built a porter's lodge after 1838. In 1885 simply called 'Waltrim'.

Lewis 1837; Slater 1846.

30. BALTIBOYS, Ballymore Eustace; *c.* 1890; *demolished.*
A lodge erected probably for Capt. T.R.A. Stannus, who had acquired the old house of the Smith family about 1830. It was an extensive single-storey hip-roofed structure on an L-plan, with a dominant heavily corbelled brick chimney-stack. This was to be demolished along with many other houses in the area to make way in 1940 for the Blessington lakes created by the Poulaphouca dam.

31. BALTINGLASS UNION WORKHOUSE, Baltinglass; *c.* 1860.
The lodge is of somewhat later date than the main block, to which first admissions were in 1841, and thus too late to have been the work of George Wilkinson. Built in rough coursed granite with cream brick dressings, the lodge is single-storey three-bay with two chimney-stacks to the hipped roof. Later aluminium windows and a cement-rendered projecting hip-roofed hall.

O'Connor 1995.

32. BARRADERRY, Kiltegan; *c.* 1830.
A very derelict standard single-storey lodge with a steeply hipped roof with clipped brick eaves. Otherwise constructed in harled rubble with granite-dressed and keystoned openings. A seat in 1837 of Vaughan Pendred.

Lewis 1837.

33. BAY VIEW, Bray; *c.* 1845; *demolished.*
The lodge was probably contemporary with the impressive pair of granite carriage pillars, now gateless, which survive. Classical and composite, with Greek stela frontispieces having moulded tapering recessed panels and gadrooned half-cappings. Subsequently renamed 'Novara', or 'Navarre', its lodge and gates were possibly a development for P.W. Jackson. The lodge had been removed in 1885.

An Old Inhabitant 1907.

BEECHURST (see RICHVIEW, Bray)

34. BELFIELD, Newtown Mount Kennedy; pre-1838; *demolished.*
A seat in 1837 of John Dick.

Lewis 1837.

35. BELLCOURT, Bray; 1864; architect Sir George Hodson.

A hip-roofed variant of the lodge at Hollybrook (*q.v.*) that Sir George Hodson designed for himself, which it otherwise replicates in every elaborate detail. Of standard format, it appears as single-storey but its high eaves accommodate loft rooms now lit by modern gablets. Rich in ornamental carved carpentry, with intricate perforated foiled fascias repeated as bargeboards to the porch, which has a decorative apex supported by a pair of voluptuous posts with responding pilasters. Like its Hollybrook variant, there is a steep approach to the Tudor-arched front door, which has a roundel over and is flanked by label-moulded windows, now lacking their original elaborate glazing pattern. The raised V-jointed stone quoins are painted black in stark contrast to a later crude roughcast finish. To the ridge is a diagonally set chimney-stack in the Tudor tradition. Surviving its big house at the entrance to a modern development, it was built by barrister William Justin O'Driscoll after he had acquired the place from Thomas Smythe, when he 'much improved' the house.

36. BELLEVUE, Delgany (3).
The once-grand landed estate of the immensely rich banking family of La Touche, whose house was commenced in 1754 by David La Touche (1703–75) and added to in 1780 by his son Peter to designs by Thomas Cooley. It was his nephew, however, also Peter La Touche (1777–1830), and his wife Charlotte Maud who did most to ornament the demesne with all those necessities of the wealthy: Swiss cottage, chapel (by Richard Morrison), Gothic dining room, Turkish tent and three lodged entrances. Of the latter, only one remains relatively intact.

Back entrance; *c.* 1820; *demolished.*

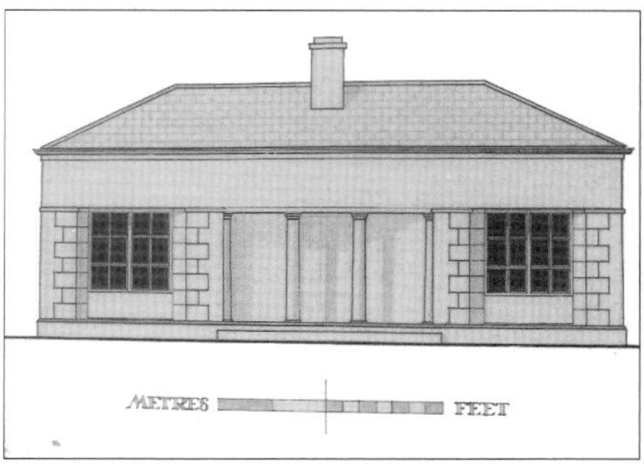

Below a hipped roof with high eaves and exceptionally deep frieze band, which probably accommodated loft rooms, was a symmetrical three-bay front, unusual in that wide squared casement windows with chamfered reveals flanked a broad segmental recess behind a pair of wooden Doric columns with responds, *in antis.* A harled finish was set off by granite plinth, toothed dressings and a string-course. A striking structure that was removed in the late twentieth century, survived by the remains of a fine mid-Georgian gatescreen of granite pillars with friezes below concave cappings.

Middle entrance; pre-1838; *demolished.*

Front entrance; *c.* 1800; architect not known.

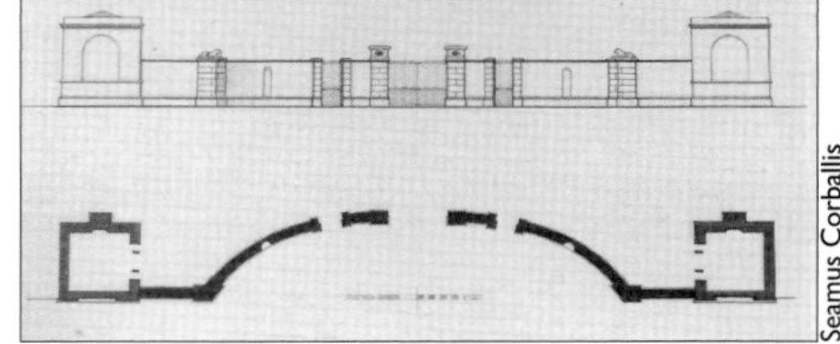

Seamus Corbally

A spectacular gate sweep comprised of an unusually wide segmental walled screen, originally harled, relieved by round-headed niches and granite ashlar pillars and dressings to postern openings. The inner square carriage pillars have to their friezes fine oval paterae with leaves radiating from lion masks, whilst the outer cranked pillars are crowned by lazy lionesses couchant in Coade stone, not purpose-made for their cappings. Beyond all this, and linked by short straight walls, is a pair of lodges in the form of big Classical single-roomed cubes as inconveniently distant 'day and night' accommodation, but creating the required dramatic impact on the visitor. Elevations with semicircular-headed recesses face the road on a stone string-course and under a parapet concealing their roofs. Now without a practical role, they lie abandoned but maintained, the carriage opening widened to give access to Delgany Golf Club.

Brewer 1825; Lewis 1837; *LGI* (1904); Bence-Jones 1988; Flannery 1990; Kelly 1990.

37. BELMONT, Greystones; pre-1838; *demolished.*
Another property of the Meaths of Killruddery (*q.v.*), which in 1814 was leased to a Colonel Keating.

Leet 1814.

38. BELVEDERE HALL, Greystones; pre-1856/*c.* 1865; *demolished.*
Previously a property called 'Templecarraig', sold in 1856 by Edward Massey and purchased by Major D'Oyly William Battley (1808–87), who built a new Italianate villa. From the valuation books it seems that he acquired a property that had a gate lodge and that a new one was built, probably as a replacement, about 1865. It must have been of some consequence, for the surveyor as a result raised the value of the property by £6-0-0d and noted that it cost £1,500! Sadly, all that remains at the entrance are some tapering pillars. The place was renamed in memory of the family's descent from the Rochforts, earls of Belvedere.

LGI (1904); Lyons 1993.

39. BIRCHVILLE, Kilcoole; *c.* 1830.
A single-storey gabled structure, much 'improved' to include lumpy boulder-effect rendering. Gabled porch projection and back return. Isolated by the creation of a new northern approach before 1900. Sometime seat of the Birch family, and by 1854 of William H. Redmond.

Griffith 1848–60.

40. BLAINROE, Wicklow; pre-1910; *demolished.*
An estate of William J. Smith to which the lodge may have been added after it was acquired by William Newland *c.* 1875.

Griffith 1848–60.

41. BLESSINGTON, Blessington; pre-1760; *demolished.*
A great brick William and Mary mansion existed here, built by Michael Boyle, archbishop of Armagh, who also founded the village to which it was linked by a formal avenue, at the base of which Rocque on his map of 1760 indicates a structure by the gates. In 1778 the house devolved upon the Hill family, marquises of Downshire, but was burnt down in 1798 by insurgents and never restored. The 1838 OS map shows the ruins still in place and nothing by the entrance.

Lewis 1837; Bence-Jones 1988; Ferguson 1998.

42. BONABROCKA, Wicklow; *c.* 1850.
A modest single-storey gabled cottage, rendered, of four bays, one of which may have been a later extension. Vacant. The proprietor noted here in 1854 and 1876 was Anne Farrell.

Griffith 1848–60; *Land owners in Ireland 1876.*

BRAYHEAD (see SANS SOUCI)

43. BROMLEY, Kilpedder; 1893.

An attractive little mid-Victorian lodge built for E.H.C. Wellesley, who had acquired the estate. Single-storey, three-bay and gabled, with red brick as dressings to segmentally headed windows and an embracing string-course contrasting nicely with the random granite facings. From the left-hand opening projects a glazed gabled entrance hall, and to the leading gable a canted bay window monitors the entrance, which is earlier and probably dates from the time of the previous owners, the Daly family from Dunsandle, Co. Galway. A pair of stone carriage pillars with slim fluted friezes and boulder finials are flanked by plain harled concave-walled quadrants.

Leet 1814; Lewis 1837; Slater 1870.

44. BROOMFIELD, Ashford; *c.* 1845.

An estate in the late eighteenth century until *c.* 1840 of the Majoribanks family, by whom it was then let to Robert Bride. He added the gatekeeper's lodge sometime between the OS map of 1838 and the Griffith valuation sixteen years later. It is a fair-sized single-storey standard structure, notable for a verandah about three sides created by its hipped roof extending to be carried on chamfered wooden posts. Wide bipartite casement windows in harled walls, rubble-built, all now too obvious, as they and the roof have been stripped of their finishes.

Taylor and Skinner 1778; 1969 [1783]; Leet 1814; Slater 1846; Griffith 1848–60.

45. BURGAGEMOYLE COTTAGE, Blessington; pre-1838; *demolished.*
A seat in 1824 of George Hornidge, the lodge to which was opposite its entrance.

Pigot 1824.

46. BURNABY PARK, Greystones; *c.* 1850.
A standard single-storey rendered gabled lodge with a similarly roofed entrance lobby having a porthole window. Much improved with a later big back return.

47. BUSHY PARK, Enniskerry; *c.* 1825.

A comfortable seat, found so by a variety of aristocratic families over the years. It was the residency of the Howards that produced the porter's lodge, in the person of the Hon. Col. Hugh Howard (1761–1840), fourth son of the 1st Lord Wicklow, who came here after the death of Sir Hercules Langrishe in 1811. What probably began as single-storey standard three-bay hip-roofed and plain Classical in origin has since been very much altered to eventually appear as it does today, as a home suitable for modern living. Still single-storey below the original hipped roof, it has small-paned casement windows in roughcast walls; the avenue elevation has been reduced to two-bay by the addition of a gabled hall projection, the front door of which (recently converted to a window) has a Tudor label moulding below carved Picturesque bargeboards and intricate pendant hip-knobs. This work may be dated to *c.* 1850 and attributed to that active amateur architect Sir George Hodson of Hollybrook (*q.v.*), for a solitary surviving octagonal wooden gatepost here, with fancy

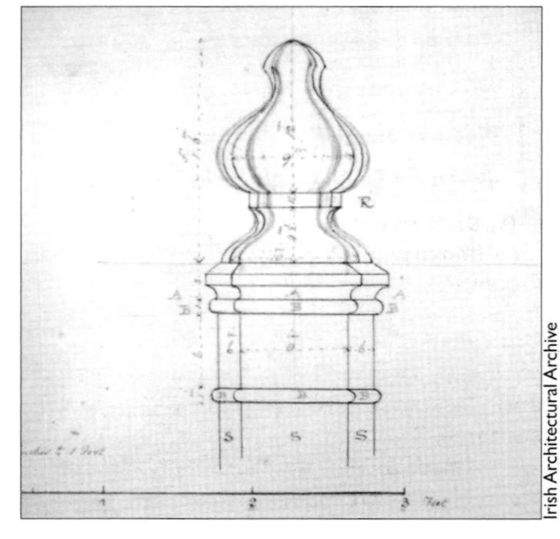

Irish Architectural Archive

finial, is just as he sketched and intended for his own house. The lodge has been further improved with a large and sympathetic extension to the rear.

A later occupant of the property, the Rt Hon. Judge John Keogh, who took up residence in 1857, had plans either to replace the existing lodge or add another, for in a bundle of drawings by architect Charles Geoghegan is a rough plan for what was intended to be a Picturesque Tudor cottage off an informal plan. Unsigned, undated and unannotated but identifying the client, what is clear is that it was never executed at Bushy Park.

Leet 1814; An Old Inhabitant 1907; *BPB* (1929); IAA drawing (87/55, 22/1).

CARRIGBRAE (see PROSPECT COTTAGE)

48. CASTLE GRANGE, Killiskey; pre-1838; *demolished.*
An estate in the first half of the nineteenth century of the Vicars, or Vickers, family.

49. CASTLE HOWARD, Avoca (3).
A spectacular site for a house which Lt.-Col. Robert Howard, younger brother of the 1st earl of Wicklow of Shelton Abbey (*q.v.*), purchased in 1811 from the director of the local copper mines. He adorned it with a new mansion in the medieval castellated abbey style, much admired in his *Views of seats* by J.P. Neale, who, as ever, was enthusiastic about a design by Richard Morrison. He was, however, less enamoured of the lack of architectural quality beside the new entrance.

Main gate; pre-1838/*c.* 1860.
'... a new approach to the Castle has been executed with considerable judgement; to connect which with the public road, a Bridge of a single Arch has been thrown across the River, in a well chosen situation. But we regret that the same good taste which directed the other improvements, was not consulted in this. An Arch of a very unsightly appearance, crowned with a Lion, discordant alike with the Castle to which it forms the approach, and with the scenery which environs it has been lately erected on this Bridge; and though doubtless intended as an embellishment, its effect is highly injurious.' Neale, who visited in the 1820s, would be grateful to know that the situation has been remedied. Replacing an earlier lodge is this decent 1½-storey standard three-bay structure in the English Picturesque Cottage manner, with decorative carved perforated foiled bargeboards to main gables, that of the single-storey door canopy and two symmetrically placed dormers. There is further enhancement in the sawtooth crestings, exposed rafter toes and three-over-six sash windows with label mouldings in roughcast walls. Occupied and immaculate. Built for Richard Howard Brooke (1801–77), who had inherited the place through his aunt and assumed the additional Howard surname.

Inner lodge; pre-1910; *demolished.*

North entrance; *c.* 1820.
Opposite the gates is a single-storey gabled cottage with no architectural pretensions. Occupied and much extended.

Neale 1820–3; 1824–9; Brewer 1825; Barrow 1836; *BPB* (1929); McParland *et al.* 1989.

50. CASTLE KEVIN, Laragh; *c.* 1870; *demolished.*
To an early Georgian villa a lodge was added by Charles Frizell; it has been replaced by a 1990s bungalow.

51. CHARLEVILLE, Enniskerry (6).
A Palladian-style mansion, set in beautiful surroundings, which had to be rebuilt five years after a disastrous fire in 1792 by Charles Stanley Monck, who narrowly claimed a viscountcy a year before his death in 1802 for voting in favour of the Union. It was presumably he who built the solitary early lodge to the demesne, opposite the entrance to the family dower house of Ballyorney (*q.v.*), which had been removed by the late nineteenth century. It was his grandson and namesake, the 4th viscount (1819–94), who inherited the property in 1849 after his uncle and father had died in quick succession. He adorned the immediate park and the adjoining Dargle Glen walk with a series of four lodges over a period of 30 years to an identical design by an unidentified architect, but conceivably by the talented amateur Sir George Frederick Hodson of nearby Hollybrook (*q.v.*). Surviving amongst drawings by him is one for an ornamental gatepost, unfortunately undated but entitled: 'Present Entrance to Dargle—Lord Monck's side—Planned and drawn for Lord Monck and carried out by him'.

South demesne lodge; *c.* 1860; architect possibly Sir G.F. Hodson.
On a generous plan is this single-storey standard lodge (*below*) with a shallow-hipped roof and roughcast walls but highlighted by bold paired soffit brackets and much use of granite in plinth, V-jointed quoins, window architrave and a sturdy pair of Doric columns *in antis* and lintel to frame the front door recess. Totally Classical were it not for bipartite cast-iron lattice casements in the Tudor manner.

North demesne lodge; *c.* 1860; architect possibly Sir G.F. Hodson.

As the above but better tended, and protected behind an impressive gatescreen befitting the main entrance to a landed estate. Four tall granite pillars frame straight curtain walls, all in V-jointed rusticated masonry, with round-headed postilion openings having, like the main carriage gates, ornate scrolled ironwork, all of mid-Victorian origin.

Upper Dargle lodge; *c.* 1872; architect possibly Sir G.F. Hodson.

Immediately opposite the Charleville main entrance by Tinnehinch Bridge, sited romantically in a clearing is the same design, much extended sympathetically to the rear but unfortunately now deprived of its chimney-stack and re-rendered in a smooth grey finish.

Lower Dargle lodge; pre-1805/*c.* 1890; architect possibly Sir G.F. Hodson.
Almost two miles downriver by Dargle Bridge lies the fourth of these matching

gatekeepers' lodges, again quite sensitively extended but lacking its distinctive glazing pattern. This building may have superseded an earlier lodge depicted in an illustration of 1805 by Sir John Carr. It shows a hip-roofed thatched rustic cottage, its short elevation to the road alongside the gatescreen.

Inner Dargle lodge; pre-1885.
At an intermediate gate on the glen walk lie the ruins of a lodge and outbuildings, built after 1838 and probably contemporary with the 4th viscount's extraordinary building schedule.

Carr 1806; Lewis 1837; Griffith 1848–60; *BPB* (1929); Bence-Jones 1988; Lawrence photograph (2134R); IAA drawings (87/55,22/1).

CHERRYMOUNT (see TIGRONEY)

52. CLERMONT, Rathnew; *c.* 1830.

A single-storey standard lodge with stuccoed walls, stone quoins and label mouldings to tiny windows below a hipped roof. From the centre projects an oversized gabled hall with side entry, hip-knob and perforated serrated bargeboards which mirror the red earthenware crestings to ridge and hips, the latter added in a later phase of improvements. Since much extended and renovated, with the loss of any characterful glazing pattern. An overflow estate for members of the Leeson family of Russborough (*q.v.*), which suggests that the naivety of this composition can be attributed to a long-term tenant of the property, John A. Leonard, who was here in the 1830s.

Lewis 1837.

53. CLONMANNON, Rathnew; pre-1838.
The ancestral seat of the Truell family, at the entrance to which is a 1½-storey gabled roughcast structure, either an early lodge transformed in modernisation or a replacement.

54. COOKSTOWN, UPPER, Enniskerry; pre-1838.
A remarkably interesting though scarcely beautiful little building which now serves as rectory for the Anglican parish of Powerscourt, having been much reworked and extended to that role from modest proportions as porter's lodge to the nearby big house, in 1814 of John Stanley, itself much altered in the later nineteenth century to become three dwellings. Since 1857 located by the Gothic Revival church of St Patrick, the lodge appears as a single-storey shallow hip-roofed structure, its irregular main front of four bays in a roughcast finish. Articulated by a projecting gabled hallway with some Italianate detailing, the rectangular fanlit panelled door with chamfered stone surround is flanked by unequal canted bay windows of two-over-two sashes below equivalent roofs in synthetic slate finish. In 1889 much extended to the rear; presumably further converted during the long incumbency of Revd Henry Galbraith (1827–1905) from 1874 until his death.

Leet 1814; Leslie and Wallace 2001.

55. COOLAGAD, Greystones; *c.* 1860.
A standard single-storey hip-roofed cottage, derelict and overgrown. A property in the nineteenth century of the Fox family.

56. COOLATTIN, Shillelagh (4).
The only known example in Ireland of a country house designed by John Carr of York, built *c.* 1804 for William, the 4th Earl Fitzwilliam (1748–1833), who was lord lieutenant of Ireland in 1795, as a replacement for an earlier building destroyed in 1798. An early pre-1838 lodge was superseded when a portion of public road was subsequently absorbed into the estate; it was replaced by the present building.

South entrance; *c.* 1850.
A single-storey five-bay gabled cottage, its limewashed stucco walls with three-over-three sash windows in its articulated main front, the doorway with sidelights in a central hall projection. Probably originating as a standard three-bay structure.

Middle entrance; *c.* 1870.

A commodious two-storey Tudor Revival gatehouse. Three-bay but not quite symmetrical, the gabled single-storey hall projection slightly off-centre to accommodate a tripartite living-room window. All other windows are bipartite with label mouldings and chamfered dressings in pleasant square-coursed random rubble walls. The gables are decorated with perforated foil and wave bargeboards, while the eaves have fancy carved fascia boards. To the ridge are two pairs of dainty diagonally set brick chimney-stacks.

North entrance; *c.* 1890; architect not known.

By Greenhall bridge is this highly ornamental 1½-storey Picturesque cottage, like the middle lodge part of improvements carried out by the 6th earl, William Thomas Spencer Fitzwilliam (1815–1902), who succeeded his father in 1857. The central hall projection has side entry and a steeply pitched roof with perforated foil and wave bargeboards, repeated on the main gables and gablets. To the ground floor are label-moulded tripartite windows, each one-over-one sashes with chinoiserie glazing patterns. Rendered with stucco effect, the decorative features extend to exposed rafter toes, spiky turned hip-knobs and distinctive roofs with red terracotta scalloped tiles and tall banded brick chimney-stacks. Appropriate modern picket fencing.

BPB (1929); Bence-Jones 1988.

57. COOLAWINNIA MILL, Rathnew; *c.* 1825.
A concern in the early nineteenth century of the Cotter family to which survives a single-storey standard lodge with hipped gables having serrated fascias and bargeboards. Modern windows in rendered walls. Occupied.

Leet 1814; Lewis 1837.

58. COOLBALLINTAGGART LODGE, Aughrim; pre-1910; *demolished.*
A porter's lodge built after 1838 to a property in the mid-nineteenth century of the Tate family, which has succumbed to afforestation.

Slater 1846; 1856.

59. COOLMONEY, Donard; *c.* 1850.
In 1837 'the residence of Lady Louisa Hutchinson, a handsome and newly erected mansion'. She was a daughter of the 3rd earl of Donoughmore, and lived here after being widowed in 1833 until her death in 1876. Margaret Byrne is recorded as (probably the first) gatekeeper by the valuation of 1854. Opposite the gates is her single-storey four-bay gabled cottage with similarly roofed breakfront hall, resplendent in steeply pitched corrugated iron over modern squared casement windows in bland cement-rendered walls. Occupied.

Lewis 1837; Griffith 1848–60.

60. COPSE, Rathdrum; pre-1838/1881; architect H.R. Newton.

The mountainous hunting-lodge of the Brabazon family of Killruddery (*q.v.*). The English architect Henry Robert Newton exhibited his design for this replacement porter's lodge in 1881 at the Royal Hibernian Academy. His client was William Brabazon, the 11th earl of Meath (1803–87), who survived him by but one year. This is a sturdy 1½-storey typically late Victorian affair, constructed in rubble facings with bold red-brick quoins and toothed dressings to wide segmentally headed transomed and mullioned windows. Gabled, with sawtooth earthenware cresting and scalloped slate bands to its roofs, the lower wing has suffered a ghastly bricking-up of its original open porch to display a modern Crittall steel window, losing one of that architect's splendid trademark designs of carved joinery in the process.

BPB (1929); IAA.

61. CRONROE, Rathnew (2).
The seat of the Eccles family before the coming of the Casements *c.* 1860.

North entrance; *c.* 1835.
Presumably built by Isaac Ambrose Eccles is this standard single-storey hip-roofed cottage, now revealing its rubble construction with brick dressings, attractive but probably originally harled. A pair of modernised tripartite 'Wyatt' windows flank a tiny later glazed gabled porch tucked in below the eaves. Vacant. Very tall granite entrance pillars and concave-walled quadrants.

South entrance; pre-1838; *demolished.*
A modern twentieth-century four-bay hip-roofed bungalow with gabled hall projection in gate-lodge manner as replacement. Basic square granite pillars survive.

Lacy 1863; Slater 1870.

62. CRONYBYRNE, Rathdrum (2).
Although described by Atkinson in 1815 as 'a mansion highly deserving of notice', it was nevertheless replaced on an adjacent site in mid-century by Andrew William Byrne (1815–74), in improvements to the property that included the addition of two new porters' lodges.

South gate; pre-1838/*c.* 1850; *demolished.*
Neither the original lodge nor its successor at the other side of the gateway survives.

North gate; *c.* 1850.

Opposite its entrance is this charismatic little building in a blend of styles. Although standard in configuration and apparently single-storey, it is effectively on two floors, being raised off a basement. Approached by a flight of steps to a *piano nobile* through a small portico, the gable of which sports mildly Picturesque carved bargeboards supported by a pair of Tuscan columns. Gabled, rendered and finished brilliant white, its narrow pointed-arched openings looking earlier than its actual date of construction.

Atkinson 1815; Griffith 1848–60; Bence-Jones 1988; *IFR*.

63. THE DARGLE, Enniskerry (2).
A delightful small estate, previously 'Dargle Cottage', belonging to the Sandys family in the mid-nineteenth century, to which two porters' lodges were added after 1838.

East lodge; 1860; *demolished.*

West lodge; 1859.
A perfectly formed lodge, beautifully maintained in its own pretty garden setting. Single-storey standard below a hipped roof, in roughcast walls a fine six-panelled front

door is flanked by a pair of tripartite windows, each section divided into small panes having rounded heads with a faintly Gothic feel. Built for Henry Sandys. Extended into a double pile to rear.

64. DARGLE COTTAGE, Enniskerry; *c.* 1840.
An attractive small gentry villa, in the mid-nineteenth century taken on long lease by Henry Joseph Monck Mason, to which its lodge is proportionate in size. A tiny roughcast hip-roofed cottage with a canted bay on its leading short elevation. Occupied.

An Old Inhabitant 1907.

DARGLE VALE (see KILLARNEY WOOD)

DARGLE WALK (see CHARLEVILLE)

65. DARRAGHVILLE, Kilcoole (2).
Although now serving as a convent, this graceful late eighteenth-century villa was for much of the nineteenth century home to a George Newton.

South lodge; pre-1838; *demolished.*

North lodge; *c.* 1820.
A tiny standard single-storey structure, roughcast below a steeply pitched hipped roof with chimney-stacks to each end. The exaggerated gabled hall projection, the serrated perforated crestings and replacement windows would be alterations executed when the property became a religious institution.

Leet 1814; Slater 1870.

66. DERRYBAWN, Laragh; *c.* 1865.
Despite James Critchley's being recorded here in 1814, the Regency house would seem to have been the creation of the Bookey family, of whom William E.T. Bookey later added a gatekeeper's lodge. Opposite the entrance is a single-storey standard lodge, larger than the average, with an elongated well-proportioned main front of two segmentally arched bipartite casement windows in harled walls on each side of a gabled entrance breakfront with basic wavy bargeboards. The hipped roof has carved modillion soffit brackets. Derelict.

Leet 1814; Slater 1870.

67. DERRYLOSSORY RECTORY, Annamoe; pre-1838; *demolished.*
The glebe house was built in 1816, its gate lodge perhaps contemporary. If so, it was built during the long incumbency from 1813 until his death of Revd Lambert Watson Hepenstall (*c.* 1788–1859), a wealthy rector

who had as his seat Altidore (*q.v.*).

Lewis 1837; Griffith 1848–60; Slater 1870; Leslie and Wallace 2001.

68. DONARD, Donard (2).

A house built in 1813 for William Heighington I, whose son and grandson of the same name each built a lodge during their residency.

Front entrance; *c.* 1850.

A single-storey standard lodge with roughcast walls and a hipped roof. Modern metal window frames spoil the effect. Vacant. Built in the time of William Heighington II (1814–67) sometime after 1822, when he inherited Donard as a minor.

Back entrance; pre-1838/1897.

Replacing an earlier lodge is this late Victorian cottage built by William Heighington III, who, like his father, succeeded to the place as a minor in 1867 when sixteen years old. A standard structure, gabled, with red-brick quoins and dressings to segmentally headed openings in pleasant contrast to random rubble facings. Occupied and sympathetically extended, with a date-stone to one gable.

LGI (1904); Bence-Jones 1988.

69. THE DOWNS, Delgany; *c.* 1880.

Although a single-storey standard gabled lodge, it is a remarkable and fussy creation, typical of the late Victorian period, with a clutter of features. Mainly finished in stucco but with toothed brick dressings and granite quoins; decorative hexagonal cast-iron glazed casement windows flank the central hall projection with chamfered Classical posts which support a gable, like those of the main roof ornamented with carved perforated and cusped wavy bargeboards with spiky hip-knobs. To the roof are bands of scalloped slates and intricate cresting; chimney-stack missing. The gate pillars are of a single material. Stone in V-jointed rustication, with fluted friezes and ball finials and, like the leading gable of the lodge, displaying a variety of armorial bearings relating to Lt.-Col. Francis Sadleir Stoney (1834–1927), who doubtless added the entrance upon acquiring the property around 1880 from John Radley, who had built the house only about five years before.

LGI (1958).

70. DROMIN, Delgany; 1899; architect Frederick Batchelor.

Unlike its contemporary big house, this is a delightfully understated Arts and Crafts composition. Single-storey on an L-plan below a hipped roof of earthenware plain

tiles and exposed rafter toes. Simple whitened rendered walls display mullioned, leaded casement windows, while the entrance is emphasised in the internal corner by a flat-roofed portico with a pair of fluted Doric columns. A development from 1898 for the Hon. Judge Joseph Hamilton Moore by Frederick Batchelor of Carroll and Batchelor, the building contractor for which was Patrick Hanway.

IB (15 Feb. 1900); Williams 1994.

71. DRUMKEY CHURCH OF IRELAND CHURCH, Wicklow; pre-1838; *demolished.*

On a long approach from the west, which continued past a large, mysterious and, on the first OS map, unannotated building with gardens; now lost, like its lodge, neither being valued in 1854 by Griffith and both certainly gone by 1890. This avenue nevertheless went on to access the church of St Livinius and its parochial schools beyond, on Church Hill.

Griffith 1848–60.

72. DUNGANSTOWN, Wicklow; *c.* 1845.

A standard single-storey gabled lodge in random rubble construction with a contemporary back return. Unusual Greek stela-type chimney-stack. A modern door and windows spoil the effect. Perfectly round entrance pillars, with moulded 'beret' cappings, contain rustic concave quadrant walls. Built soon after 1835, when Matthew Wright acquired the property previously of John Hoey.

Lewis 1837; Fraser 1838; Griffith 1848–60.

73. DUNRAN CASTLE, Killiskey (3).

A residence in the mid-nineteenth century of Revd Dr Joseph J. Fletcher, whose property was 'as to both site and architectural character, a modern structure of superior taste'. There is little surviving today to suggest that its lodges were of similar quality.

South entrance; pre-1838/*c.* 1860.

A plain two-storey three-bay replacement gatehouse with a chimney to each gable, subsequently extended into a greater scheme of things.

Middle entrance; *c.* 1845.

A simple single-storey gabled cottage built in limewashed rubble with square-glazed casement windows. Derelict. Crude stone entrance pillars and tall concave quadrant walls.

North entrance; pre-1910.

Dating from after 1838 is this square three-bay structure below a pyramidal roof, much modernised and perhaps dating from the time of the Atkinson family's ownership.

Parliamentary Gazetteer.

74. EAST HALL, Greystones; *c.* 1845.

Contemporary with the lovely Regency-style villa is this minuscule doll's house of a lodge. Single-storey gabled with a modern back return and squared casement windows. Occupied and immaculate. A property in 1854 of Revd Samuel Eccles DD (1795–1876).

Griffith 1848–60; Leslie and Wallace 2001.

75. EASTHILL, Newtown Mount Kennedy; *c.* 1885.

A property purchased in 1859 by Joseph Fulton Meade from George Wynne. The lodge is a single-storey gabled affair of four bays and two chimney-stacks, with feature 'black-and-white' gables, slender hip-knobs, canted slate bands to the roof and moulded window architraves. The projecting gabled hall contains a '1907' date-stone, which presumably was the time of a make-over for Mrs Bertha Meade.

Lyons 1993.

EDEN VIEW (see CARRIGBRAE)

76. ELSINORE, Delgany; *c.* 1904.

A modest single-storey standard hip-roofed lodge, finished in grey rendering and suffering replacement casement windows on each side of a modern flat-roofed glazed hall extension. The lodge is first mentioned in the valuation books in 1904, when it was occupied by a Mr Kinsella to the house of Justin McCarthy.

77. EMMA VILLE, Arklow; pre-1838; *demolished.*

A seat in the early nineteenth century of William Christmas, by whom it was much improved and enlarged before coming into the possession of David Wright by 1837. Both house and lodge had vanished by 1910.

Mason 1814–19; Lewis 1837.

78. ENNISKERRY LODGE, Enniskerry; *c.* 1850.

A pretty four-bay roughcast single-storey cottage with modern wide square-paned casement windows below a hipped roof. Projecting glazed gabled hall. A property in the mid-nineteenth century of Dr Dennis Murray. Decorative gatescreen modelled on those of Charleville (*q.v.*) and Powerscourt (*q.v.*), which points to the influence of the amateur architect Sir George Hodson.

Griffith 1848–60; Slater 1856.

79. FAIRWOOD PARK, Tinahely (2).

The first OS map of 1838 suggests that there may have been a pair of lodges to the forecourt of the house in the time here of Francis H. Morton. What survives is a standard 1½-storey cottage with rendered walls and punched stone quoins. Gabled, with similarly treated entrance breakfront fitted below the main eaves. Dating from about 1855, when the proprietor was James W. De Butts, who was also to be found in the county as proprietor of Favouretta (*q.v.*).

Another lodge added by Annesley De Butts in 1900 has also gone.

Leet 1814; Griffith 1848–60.

80. FAIRY HILL, Bray; pre-1838; *demolished.*
A property that by 1837 had become home to barrister Peter W. Jackson after the occupancy of Michael Blackly.

Leet 1814; Lewis 1837.

81. FARRANKELLY, Delgany; *c.* 1840.
A much-modernised and extended single-storey three-bay lodge, roughcast with squared casement windows, and evidence of turn-of-the-twentieth-century work in 'black-and-white' features to its gables. An estate for much of the nineteenth century of the McDonnell family.

82. FASSAROE, Enniskerry (2).
A property in the first half of the nineteenth century of the Crampton family of neighbouring St Valery (*q.v.*), who initially let it to Edward Barrington. He eventually purchased it around 1860 and built lodges at its two entrances.

Back entrance; *c.* 1860; *demolished.*

Front entrance; *c.* 1860.
Now labelled 'Hunter's Lodge', this is a small villa in its own right, snuggled into a beautiful site in the glen of the Cookstown River. Generously proportioned, built off a T-plan in the English Tudor Picturesque style of pleasant random rubble with granite quoins, it is 1½-storey with steep gables having intricate crested ridges and fancy hip-knobs but plain bargeboards. The avenue gable has a single-storey canted bay window with corresponding roof. The effect is unfortunately spoiled by the arrival of plastic in inappropriate replacement windows and a nasty modern conservatory intruding where a canopy used to be by the front door in the internal angle. To the rear is what may be a later Victorian extension, creating a double pile.

Griffith 1848–60; An Old Inhabitant 1907.

83. FAVOURETTA, Glenealy; pre-1838/*c.* 1860.

What seem to have been a pair of lodges flanking the entrance have been replaced by a more fashionable mid-Victorian Tudor Gothic cottage. Originally a 1½-storey three-bay standard steeply gabled structure, later extended by a bay to the left-hand side and a dormer window added to compensate for the consequent loss of a gable window to an attic room. The opposing loft window is a lancet with hood moulding, while the ground-floor windows are bipartite sashes with their sash-box dividers below label mouldings. The gabled hall projection has a chamfered Tudor-arched doorway. All plain-rendered with simple bargeboards and a no-nonsense gatescreen with roughcast concave quadrants. Occupied.

Listed in 1837 as a seat of Revd Leek McDonnell, by 1854 it had passed to James W. De Butts of Fairwood Park (*q.v.*) and is now named 'Glenealy Lodge'.

Lewis 1837; Griffith 1848–60.

84. FORT FAULKNER, Aughrim; pre-1910; *demolished.*
An estate of the Faulkner family, the lodge to which was built after 1838.

85. FORT GRANITE, Kiltegan (2).
A property with the most charming and unusual of porters' lodges, both entrances created by the long-lived Thomas Stratford Dennis (1781–1870), who remodelled the house in 1810 when it came to him through his marriage that year to his cousin Katherine Saunders of Saunders Grove (*q.v.*).

East entrance; 1810/1819 (*below*).

'A castle with two towers ar., from each tower a banner floating to the sinister gu.' Such is the Dennis crest, ingeniously and entertainingly created here to a large scale as an appropriate introduction to their aptly named seat. A pair of two-stage circular crenellated and machicolated rubble-built towers flank the entrance, which is spanned between by a large pointed-arched carriage gateway. Behind and to one side is what seems to be an earlier lodge, probably dating from the works to the house, although the chronology is far from clear. This is a simple rectangular rubble-built hip-roofed cottage, apparently later given a crenellated parapet on two sides only, in a not-entirely-seamless link with the inspirational gateway. At this time, too, it may have been given pointed heads to its openings. A little castellated store across the avenue awkwardly attached to the other tower is also an afterthought.

West entrance; *c.* 1845.

A most delightful and unorthodox little lodge, raised as a single-storey L-plan off a part-basement. A festive foiled fascia board extends right around on the eaves to a hipped roof which oversails sufficiently to cover the canted entrance breakfront, the front door of which has a dainty ogee chiselled lintel, flanked on the other faces by small chamfered sidelights with Gothic inserts. Finished in harling with granite chamfered dressings and quoins. The gatescreen is comprised of simple dwarf-walled concave quadrants with hooped railings and ball-finialled iron carriage posts.

JASCK (1891/5); *IFR*; Bence-Jones 1988.

86. FORT TOWN, Tinahely; *c.* 1830.
Seemingly once a single-storey standard lodge, subsequently raised in the later nineteenth century by an attic storey, with a pair of gablets to the front of its hipped roof. Later corniced chimney-stack. An estate in the nineteenth century of the Morton family.

87. FRIARSHILL, Wicklow; *c.* 1855.
A much-modernised and extended mid-nineteenth-century Picturesque Gothic lodge built to a property of the Leeson family, Lords

Milltown of Russborough (*q.v.*). It is 1½-storey with steeply gabled roof and, now, plain bargeboards. Surviving to one gable are decorative windows: to the attic room is a slim lancet light with latticed glazing and a quatrefoil motif, while a bipartite casement window below has pretty hexagonal-pattern divisions.

Griffith 1848–60.

88. GLANMORE CASTLE, Rathnew (5).
Whereas architect Francis Johnston provided the Tottenhams of Ballycurry (*q.v.*) across the road with a Classical design for their house, here in 1805 Francis Synge (1761–1831) was completing to his plans 'a handsome and spacious castellated mansion with embattled parapets'. Regrettably, as there, no porters' lodges by Johnston survive at Glanmore, if there ever were any.

North lodge; *c.* 1845.
A standard single-storey gabled cottage, rendered with stone quoins. There is a small canted bay to the road elevation and a later catslide hall projection to the main front. Occupied.

Inner lodge; pre-1838; *demolished.*

East lodge; pre-1838; *demolished.*

West lodge; pre-1838/*c.* 1870.
A 1½-storey structure built in pleasant rubble stone, the irregular two-bay elevation comprised of a large gable to the left-hand side alongside a steeply pitched gablet, both decorated with bargeboards perforated by a pretty ivy motif; two-over-two mid-Victorian sashes. Occupied and replacing an earlier lodge.

School lodge; 1807.
Kilfee schoolhouse was 'Erected 1807 by Sir Fran. Hutchinson Bart.', an uncle of Francis Synge. Located opposite another estate entrance, its schoolmaster, or schoolmistress, no doubt had the secondary role of gatekeeper.

Carr 1806; Lewis 1837; *IFR*; Bence-Jones 1988.

89. GLENAIR, Delgany; pre-1911.

Another of those attractive Regency-style hip-roofed single-storey-over-basement villas in which Wicklow abounds, this one home in the nineteenth century to the Greene family. At its entrance gates is a less discreet prelude in what seems to be a subsequently refaced post-1838 lodge. Single-storey standard in form with a hipped roof, it has been clad in vertical granite crazy paving, starkly dressed with red-brick plinth, segmental arches and toothed dressings and quoins. Front-door sidelights and main casements have bold wooden latticed glazing patterns. Time should mellow it.

90. GLENART CASTLE, Arklow (5).
The grand Irish estate of the Probys of Elton Hall, Huntingdonshire, which began as the modest hunting-lodge of 'Poolahony'. It was transformed in a series of building phases in the nineteenth century by succeeding earls of Carysfort, through its Regency manifestation as 'Kilcarra Castle' before burgeoning into the vast, rambling battlemented mansion of today. With all this expenditure it is strange that none was allocated to lodge-building until *c.* 1870. This omission was to be remedied by the creation of a series of outstanding and entertaining examples that appeared here at different stages. The Dublin architect John McCurdy was commissioned in 1869 by Granville-Leveson Proby, the 4th earl (1825–72), to carry out major additions and alterations to the house. Two adjacent porters' lodges look to date from that period.

East lodge (1); *c.* 1870; architect probably John McCurdy.
A sturdy and decorative 1½-storey gabled English Picturesque cottage with a very steep roof having foiled cresting and carved bargeboards. It is faced, as are all the Glenart lodges, in a distinctive polygonal granite finish, with cut-stone quoins and dressings to segmental pointed-arched openings. To the avenue gable is a single-storey canted bay window and corresponding roof. Derelict.

East lodge (2); *c.* 1870; architect probably John McCurdy.

Sharing much with its slightly larger neighbouring lodge, including dereliction, this 1½-storey standard structure differs otherwise in having flat-headed windows and a segmentally arched doorway. Here are the same exposed rafter toes and bulky granite ashlar chimney-stack. There are the remains of a gatescreen with shallow ogee dwarf-walled quadrants and railings over.

Upon inheriting from his brother, William Proby, the 5th earl (1836–1909), continued improvements to the estate but for some reason or other did not retain McCurdy, rather engaging the relatively obscure London-based architect John Birch, who was to achieve some recognition as a pioneer in the reintroduction of concrete as a building material. In two gatekeepers' lodges, here and that to Tollymore Park, Co. Down, he was to prove himself as a master in the composition of a Romantic cottage. That he was content with his designs for the earl of Carysfort is obvious from their reproduction in his pattern-book, *Picturesque lodges*, published in 1879.

Ballydough lodge; 1876; architect John Birch.

John Birch

Situated at the southernmost gate to the estate is this single-storey lodge (*top*), basically square on plan and dependent for its Picturesque effect upon breakfronts, a projecting hall, a varied roofscape and its pair of diagonally set Tudor-style chimney-stacks. Plate XIV (*above*) in Birch's book paints an idyllic and accurate picture of what was built, and it is accompanied by a brief description of the plan which finishes: 'It consists of a porch, living room, scullery, and two bedrooms, with out offices. The walls having been built in random rubble work of local stone, with dressings to doors, windows, and angles of Aughrim granite, and the roofs are slated. The entrance gate is of oak and iron, with ornamental iron railings, and Aughrim granite piers, walls, and copings.' Whilst the quadrants survive intact, the decorative gates have not stood the test of time. The gables are ornamented with iron finials, perforated foiled bargeboards and half-timbered effect to apexes. To the main road gable is a tripartite window with a stepped label moulding over, containing a plaque with a sculpted coronet and the Carysfort monogram. The avenue gable contains a pretty canted bay window with a bellcast lead roof, while that to the park displays a date-stone above the bipartite window. All faced in Glenart polygonal rubble. The years and occupants have been kind to this striking lodge, which has suffered only replacement squared casement windows for more intricate originals and a synthetic slate roof finish. Otherwise the additional porch carried on four plain round pillars and other extensions are discreet.

Poolahony lodge; 1875; architect John Birch.

Located within the demesne on the southern approach is this delightful and desirable little Picturesque 1½-storey lodge, with eccentric and innovative features, which lies mysteriously unoccupied and vandalised. Fundamentally built off a rectangular plan with two attic bedrooms, and a lower hip-roofed back return. The leading elevation has canted corner windows, the chamfers of which extend up the steeply hipped roof to meet a tripartite gabled gambrel loft window. Between the quirky ground-floor windows Birch intended there to be a Tudor-arched recess to accommodate a garden seat. Not executed; there is only a Carysfort monogram and coronet. What did materialise, extending towards the avenue, is a gabled porch with rustic tree trunk support and perforated scalloped bargeboards which are repeated on the gambrels. Back and front, sheeted doors have big ornamental hinge straps. Surviving are a date-stone, cast-iron latticed casements and the remains of a big, square, diagonally

John Birch

set stone chimney-stack. The beautiful iron and oak gates depicted in plate XIII of Birch's pattern-book (*above*) have been destroyed.

Kilcarra lodge; 1888; architect possibly John Birch.

NLI/Lawrence Collection

Far to the north at Woodenbridge is this conspicuous architectural group consisting of a large carriage archway attached to a 1½-storey lodge. Again finished in the polygonal rubble beloved of the Probys, it is in essence built off an L-plan disguised by the addition of eye-catching devices which give it a Scots Baronial feel, particularly in the corbelled bartizan to one corner and the circular entrance tower in the internal angle, both of which sport conical roofs culminating in ball finials. The most inventive feature is the treatment of the leading corner, which begins as a right angle but, as at the Poolahony lodge, reduces to a canted tripartite window, which thereafter corbels to a 45°-angled attic gablet, skew-tabled and ball-finialled, with its own leaded casement tripartite window, below which is contained a date-stone. Alongside is the hood-moulded round-headed entrance arch, flanked by mock arrowslits and surmounted by a crow-stepped gable, which inevitably houses the Carysfort monogram and coronet. All framed by extensive concave quadrant walls embracing a big forecourt. This dramatic complex lies inexplicably dilapidated and

apparently unloved. John Birch, who flourished between 1864 and 1897, may well have been recalled, for it would be peculiar if the 5th earl was not delighted with the architect's contribution at the other gates. Since William Proby died without male issue, the titles became extinct and the family lost interest in their Irish estate, which is reflected in the present condition of its gate lodges.

Mason 1814–19; *IB* (15 Oct. 1869); Birch 1879; *BPB* (1903); Debrett's *Peerage* (1911); Williams 1994; Dean 1994; Lawrence photograph (5687C).

91. GLENCARRIG, Glenealy (2).
The archetypal example of the dilemma facing an early Victorian improving landlord, of what architectural style to exhibit at his gate. Here it is solved by displaying the old-fashioned Classical at one entrance and the newfangled Tudor Picturesque at another. The proprietor was Revd John William Fairbrother Drought (1809–91), who succeeded to Glencarrig on his father's death in 1844.

Ballyfree East gate; *c.* 1845.

Approached obliquely from the road is a fine pair of ashlar carriage pillars, squat with bold plinths and tapering recessed panels below heavy cappings. Good cast-iron gates and matching curved railings survive with pretty repeating anthemion motifs, all contemporary with the good single-storey Classical lodge behind. Parallel with the road is a regulation symmetrical three-bay front, the front door round-headed. The main elevation to the visitor is a single-bay façade, its large window incongruously below a basic label moulding under a pedimented gable, the tympanum of which contains a spoked and framed *oeil-de-boeuf*. Now finished in roughcast with quoins. Bargeboards and a modern replacement window spoil the effect. Occupied and kempt.

Ballyfree West lodge; *c.* 1845.

In contrast to the main lodge is this standard 1½-storey Tudor Gothic Picturesque cottage, with a steeply pitched roof decorated with foiled bargeboards and fascias. Finished in ragstone with brick dressings and granite quoins. To the main front, segmentally headed windows flank a little glazed gabled porch with dwarf walls, while a lancet attic window to the leading gable is the principal feature. Pleasant but not helped by recent window 'improvements'.

LGI (1904).

92. GLENCARRIG, Greystones; 1857.

In 1838, as a property called 'Kindlestown' and lodgeless, it was another house belonging to the La Touche family of Bellevue (*q.v.*), but the lodge would seem to have been added later by Alexander Montgomery. It would be a solid single-storey standard mainly Italianate affair were it not for the conflicting Tudor label mouldings above the windows on the main front. Hip-roofed, as is the projecting porch with its architraved opening surround, within which is a nice surprise in the fine Classical doorway, with entablature supported on scrolled brackets and a rectangular fanlight. Stucco-finished with prominent V-jointed quoins, there is a round-headed window with moulded surround to the road elevation. In keeping with the general Italianate theme are square gadrooned granite cappings to the gate pillars, much as those to Mount John (*q.v.*). Ironwork to carriage and postilion gates and railings match, with a recurring palmette motif.

93. GLENCORMAC, Kilmacanoge; *c.* 1880; architects Millar and Symes.

The great High Victorian house, built in 1877 for James Jameson of the whiskey distilling family, which was destroyed by fire, is survived by its gatehouse in similar style. Generously proportioned in mellow polychromatic brickwork, it is 1½-storey and gabled, raised off an L-plan. The roof is embellished with scalloped slate bands, sawtooth cresting and heavily decorative carved perforated bargeboards with a repeating quatrefoil motif. There is further ornamental carpentry in apex features and brackets to the main gables and to the single-storey hallway below a catslide roof in the internal angle. Square-headed windows to the canted bay window in the leading gable; elsewhere they have segmental pointed arches.

IB (15 Oct. 1877).

94. GLENDALOUGH, Annamoe (3).
A delightful seat by the banks of the Avonmore River, which in the early nineteenth century belonged to the Hugo family. Known then as 'Dromeen' or 'Drummin', it had two lodged gates.

Annamoe entrance; *c.* 1825.
A nice little single-storey roughcast lodge with shallow-pitched gables, latticed casement windows and a projecting gabled hall with a mouth-organ fanlight to its front door. Extended by a bay to one side. Occupied.

Drummin entrance; pre-1838; *demolished.*
A lost lodge that was located opposite the gates.

Around 1838 the estate was purchased by Thomas Johnston Barton (1802–64) of that family of Straffan, Co. Kildare (*q.v.*). He proceeded to transform the house with extensive additions and outbuildings in the Tudor Revival fashion favoured by his architect Daniel Robertson, who can have been little more than executant architect for the new lodge on the northern approach.

Oldbridge entrance; *c.* 1840/*c.* 1850; architect T.F. Hunt.
Next to Lough Dan is this charming and wholly appropriate *cottage orné* prelude to Barton's new Tudor Gothic mansion. Thomas Frederick Hunt (*c.* 1791–1831) was a pioneer of the Picturesque, but most of his designs were purveyed through his series of architectural pattern-books, which were widely read by landowners and architects. Here, on the opposite page, is his plate XXVI from *Exemplars of Tudor architecture*, first published in the year of his death, with a second edition in 1840. It was presumably Daniel Robertson who faithfully reproduced it, though without its intended accompanying grand Tudor gateway. It is easy to understand Robertson's altering of Hunt's intended square chimney-stacks to octagonal to tally with the big house, but it is more difficult to accept that he had anything to do with the extraordinarily inept juxtaposition of the ridges. The mainly single-storey standard body has a steeply pitched hipped roof and latticed casement windows flanking the central Tudor-arched doorway, over which projects a gabled attic

T. F. Hunt

room with quadripartite window, supported on a pair of Tuscan columns to form a porch and having an intermediate slated canopy. Finished in stucco with bold granite quoins, there is a gabled dormer window to one end, while Hunt's spectacular gabled and bracketed oriel window, which overlooked the park on the opposing elevation, has been relocated. Not long after its completion, a remarkable addition was made in the form of an octagonal schoolroom, presumably to cater for children of the estate workers. It now forms a fine living room, with its octahedral roof and Hunt's oriel facing forwards. At right angles, now viewing the park, is a grand bipartite cut-stone window with round-headed lights. It is not clear whether Hunt's intricately designed bargeboards ever materialised or whether they succumbed to the Irish climate, but the prominent soffit brackets did. That the schoolroom is clearly an attachment somehow does not seem important, given all the other irregularities. It is interesting to quote Hunt's description of his design:

> 'The Gate House, or Park Entrance
>
> Designed rather to produce an agreeable and picturesque effect, than to accord with any fixed rules or customs of art: such, indeed, was the practice towards the latter end of the sixteenth century, when it would appear that—like the fashion of the present day—every man wished to display his taste and learning in architecture. The Porter's lodge being a detached rustic cottage, is applicable to any other situation or purpose—such as a gamekeeper's dwelling, or a "garden-house"; but it should be "—Over canopy'd with luscious woodbine, with sweet musk-roses, and with eglantine".'

John Claudius Loudon in his *Encyclopaedia of gardening* illustrated Hunt's perspective a few years later, informing us that 'The bailiff's cottage, serving also as a porter's lodge, was erected in Ireland'.

Hunt 1836; Loudon 2000 [1846]; Lewis 1837; *LGI* (1904); *IAR* (1999).

95. GLENDARRAGH, Newtown Mount Kennedy; pre-1838.
Originally a single-storey hip-roofed structure, left undatable through a variety of unsightly later protuberances. Roughcast with evidence of some original casement windows. A property in 1814 of Lt.-Col. C.S. Williams, which for many years thereafter became home to St George Knudson and his widow.

Leet 1814; Lewis 1837; Slater 1856.

GLENEALY LODGE (see FAVOURETTA)

96. GOLDENFORT, Stratford (2).
In 1837 'the seat of Lieut.-Gen. Saunders, who has very much improved the estate', when the improvements may have extended to the provision of the two gate lodges. Much has altered in the interim.

South lodge; pre-1838.
A cottage opposite the gates with stone quoins, transformed into a twentieth-century bungalow.

Inner lodge; pre-1838/*c.* 1860.
Located half a mile off the public road is this replacement gatekeeper's lodge, 1½-storey standard with a jettied gable and finished in modern boulder-effect rendering. Presumably built for Morley Caulfield Saunders, who succeeded on his brother's death in 1854 to a secondary property of that family of neighbouring Saunders Grove (*q.v.*).

Lewis 1837; *LGI* (1904).

97. GRANGECON, Grangecon (3).
An estate granted by Queen Elizabeth I to Sir J. Harrington remained in that family until *c.* 1840, by which time the property had seen the building of three porters' lodges, one of which survives.

Middle entrance; *c.* 1790.

Parallel to the road is this good, straight, late Georgian Classical gatescreen of four crudely chiselled square pillars with fluted friezes containing a pair of postilion openings in high walls, and pleasant contemporary spear-topped wrought-iron gates. Of an age is a pair of semi-detached cottages within; 1½-storey with bowed ends and equivalent roof over, the eaves of which are lofty to accommodate attic rooms. Roughcast in recent improvements which saw the conversion to one dwelling and the introduction of a fancy carved fascia board and scalloped slate bands in re-roofing.

The new owners were the Mahony family, of whom David Mahony (1820–1900), after inheriting the place in 1853, replaced two of the old Harrington lodges on the extremities of the estate. The architect William Francis Caldbeck makes undated mention in his Account Book of Grange Con, which surely confirms that these lodges were by him, for there is a very similar one of his at Eaton Brae, Co. Dublin (*q.v.*).

North lodge; pre-1838/*c.* 1865; architect W.F. Caldbeck.

This is a bold single-storey standard gabled Italianate building with prominent Irish pilaster quoins to main corners and those of the gabled entrance breakfront, which contains a fanlit segmentally arched doorway with moulded surround. The windows are similarly treated in grey rendered walls. The leading gable with a banded apex frames a shield with lion rampant. To the road is a good contemporary gatescreen with Classical pillars and railed ogee quadrants.

South lodge; pre-1838/*c.* 1865; architect W.F. Caldbeck.

Identical to the north lodge, and also with conspicuous wooden brackets to eaves and verges. The gatescreen varies in being straight.

Lewis 1837; *LGI* (1904); Craig 1984.

98. GREY FORT, Kilcoole; pre-1838; *demolished.*
A lodge built to a property previously called 'Ballydonarea', in 1854 of John H. Dunne.

Griffith 1848–60; Slater 1870.

99. GRIFFINSTOWN, Colbinstown; *c.* 1890.

A typically quirky late Victorian Arts and Crafts Elizabethan composition. Single-storey, raised off an L-plan, its gabled roof is finished in plain earthenware Rosemary tiles, from the ridge of which rises a great panelled and corbelled red-brick chimney-stack. The leading gables are particularly eccentric, their oversailing verges containing minimal half-timbering effect over a brick lean-to breakfront framing a round-headed opening with a small rectangular-planed tripartite casement window over which is scalloped tile-hanging. To each side are lower roughcast lean-tos with brick quoins. There is an unfortunate later flat-roofed hall in the internal angle, which probably replaced a more appropriate canopied porch. All very confusing, and accompanied by a contemporary monkey-puzzle tree. A property long associated with the Cooke family, which by 1884 had passed to John Gailey. The valuation book first notes a lodge here in 1893.

GROVE PARK (see WHALEY ABBEY)

100. HIGH PARK, Kiltegan (3).
An estate whose house is a replacement for that burned down in the insurgency of 1798. A seat of the Westby family, to which only one of its porters' lodges remains.

West lodge; pre-1838; *demolished.*

Middle lodge; pre-1838; *demolished.*
Probably once the main entrance, to which a sophisticated gatescreen survives in the shape of outer ashlar pylon or Greek stela-type tapering pillars framing a straight railed screen on a dwarf plinth, and decorative cast-iron carriage posts from which springs a modern round-arched overthrow announcing its new ownership: 'St Patrick's Missionary Society'. The screen looks to date from *c.* 1845.

East lodge; *c.* 1825.
Originally a plain standard single-storey gabled cottage, now extended to each side by a bay, that to the right-hand side gabled at right-angles. Rendered and occupied. Built in the time of Edward Westby (1755–1838), who succeeded his brother Nicholas in 1800.

Lewis 1837; *LGI* (1904).

101. HOEYFIELD, Delgany; pre-1838; *demolished.*
The Hoey family was certainly here as far back as 1783, and their gatekeeper's lodge is survived by a much more recent gatescreen. Concave quadrant walls in polygonal masonry frame two great chunky granite gate pillars of rusticated blocks topped by cappings with quarry-faced semicircular pediments, each inscribed with the name of the place and crowned with electric lantern lights. Equally impressive and forthright cast-iron carriage gates.

Taylor and Skinner 1778; 1969 [1783].

102. HOLLYBROOKE, Bray (3).
'The last of the Adairs, Mr Foster Adair of Hollybrooke, M.P., left an only daughter and heir Anne, who became the first wife of Robert Hodson, Esq., created a Baronet of Ireland, 28th August 1787, and brought with her this fine estate.' Hodson died in 1809, to be followed by two sons as 2nd and 3rd baronets, who inherited an old house with a sole gate lodge at the southern gate. Sir Robert Adair Hodson (1802–31) engaged the young architect William Vitruvius Morrison—who, like himself, was to die young—to design him a magnificent granite-built Tudor Revival house. It was completed in 1835, to be enjoyed by Sir George Frederick John Hodson (1806–88), who was to prove a talented artist and amateur architect and as such was involved in the design of the outbuildings and at least one of the gate lodges after Morrison's death in 1838.

North entrance; *c.* 1842; architect Sir G.F. Hodson.

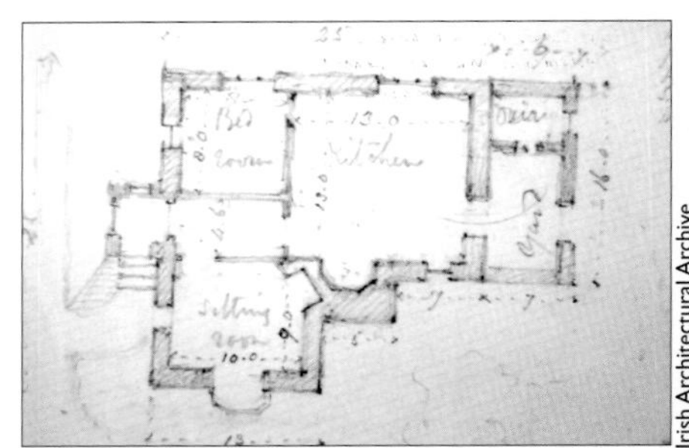

Irish Architectural Archive

Irish Architectural Archive

A competent pencil drawing of perspective, plan and elevation survives, entitled 'first sketch of Gate Lodge Hollybrooke May 1842', with Sir George's monogram signature. It shows a highly decorative Picturesque English cottage design, single-storey off an L-plan, with an oriel window, ornamental

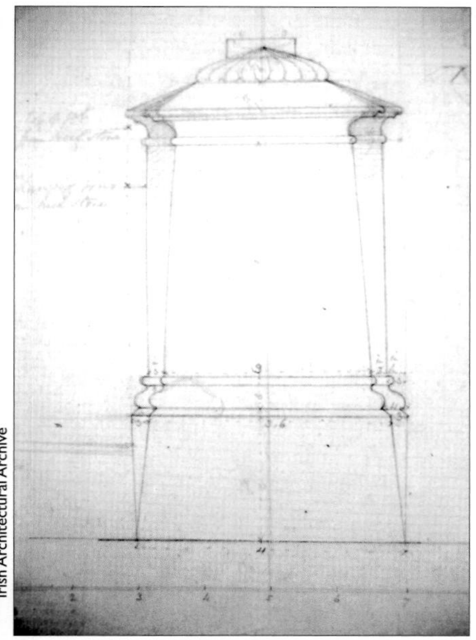

entrance porch and prominent staged chimney-stack. In the event this proposal was discarded in favour of what materialised, which is a 1½-storey standard alternative, raised on a platform with a stepped approach to the elaborate central gabled porch, with its pair of sensual curved octagonal-sectioned wooden posts with a remarkable 'screen' overthrow. Over the hood-moulded, Tudor-arched sheeted front door with studs and strap hinges is a delightful spoked *oeil-de-boeuf.* On each side in stuccoed walls are label-moulded chamfered window openings with delicately glazed margined octagonal-paned casements. To the steeply pitched roof are canted slates and intricately carved perforated cusped wavy bargeboards and fascias. Just visible, on the rear return, are elaborate chimney-pots, reflecting those on the big house. There is a hip-roofed version of this lodge at Bellcourt. Adjoining is Sir George's personalised gatescreen, for which a working drawing survives, clearly influenced by the Morrison/Papworth pillars at Killruddery (*q.v.*). Four ashlar pillars with tapering frontispieces, moulded plinths and gadrooned pedestals, two carrying ball finials, contain ogee quadrants of dwarf walls and railings to match the carriage gates. The lodge now lies behind a high stockade and security gates, protected from the stare of the great unwashed. A change from the relaxed times of mid-Victorian days, when Thomas Lacy described 'the beautiful demesne of which is open to respectable strangers, on writing their names and addresses in the visitors' book, which is kept at the gate-lodge'.

Giltspur gate; pre-1854; *demolished.*
The gate lodge recorded in the 1854 valuation in this townland, with the porter identified as Johanna Roche, must be the 'Giltspur Cottage' on the OS map. Located on an avenue linking Hollybrooke with the neighbouring estate of Kilruddery (*q.v.*) to the east, and built after 1838, it has been replaced by a twentieth-century bungalow, to be survived by Classical granite entrance pillars with recessed panels.

South entrance; pre-1838/*c.* 1855; architect probably Sir G.F. Hodson.

Replacing an earlier lodge on the site, this decorative cottage was initially severed from the estate by road realignment, became abandoned and was eventually removed in 1997. Bearing a close resemblance to Sir George Hodson's design of the lodge at Golden Gate, Powerscourt (*q.v.*), it was a 1½-storey standard rendered English Picturesque cottage, with steeply pitched gables having ornamental cusped bargeboards and diagonally set chimney-stacks in the Tudor manner. To the central gabled breakfront was a wide hood-moulded opening below a shield, flanked by a pair of crude label-moulded windows.

Lewis 1837; Griffith 1848–60; Burke 1854-5; Lacy 1863; *BPB* (1929); McParland *et al.* 1989; IAA drawings (87/55:18/1 & 87/55:19/1).

103. HOLLYWOOD, Glenealy (2).
A seat in 1837 of A.S. Broomfield, which by 1854 had become home to the Tombe family of neighbouring Ballyfree (*q.v.*).

Rear entrance; pre-1838; *demolished.*
Front entrance; *c.* 1835.

A distinctive 1½-storey Regency Tudor Gothic cottage with a symmetrical three-bay main front, the eaves of its hipped roof broken by gablets to give light to attic rooms, but that to the front blind to accommodate the projecting single-storey gabled hall below. The latter is flanked by label-moulded openings with bipartite pointed-arched openings. To the road elevation is a tripartite variant light. Over newly rendered walls are carved modillion brackets to eaves and verges, while a pair of banded octagonal flues rise from a square stack central to the ridge. The proportions of the lodge have been considerably altered by the recent raising of the roof to give greater loft headroom, at the same time as the previous fine window-frames were replaced by the present simplified versions. The adjacent contemporary gatescreen, in contrast, is Classical and comprised of four very fine stone pillars with recessed panels and oversailing corniced cappings containing elaborate straight iron railings and matching carriage gates.

Lewis 1837; Griffith 1848–60.

104. HOLYWELL, Delgany; pre-1838; *demolished.*
A lodge possibly built for Revd Lewis Rowland Delamere (*c.* 1800–65) upon his coming to a property in 1814 of George Morgan Crofton.

Leet 1814; Lewis 1837.

105. HUMEWOOD CASTLE, Kiltegan (5).
Other than in the quantity of gate lodges to the estate there is nothing at an individual entrance to prepare the visitor for the extravagance within. The great rambling undecorated granite sculptural pile that is Humewood Castle and its outbuildings is one of the most spectacular Victorian mansions on these islands. Its construction, however, is infamous for the refusal of the client, the Rt Hon. William Wentworth Fitzwilliam Hume Dick (1805–92), to pay the bill, having been presented in 1870 with a final account for the work that was £10,000 over his budget. Six years later the court found in the contractor's favour, with a matching amount in costs. This whole episode proved to be the high and low point of the architect's career, and it is fair to assume that William White (1825–1900) was not retained to embellish the property further with the required ancillary buildings, such as porters' lodges. It is known that his friend, exact contemporary and fellow architect James Brooks was engaged to tidy up the mess and that some, if not all, of them are his designs, which may explain why none is an appropriate prelude for what lies beyond, despite all being of a quality of which most Irish estates would be proud. Brooks is known to have worked here between 1873 and 1877.

Graigue lodge; pre-1838/*c.* 1875; architect possibly James Brooks.

At the north-western approach is this one of three identical lodges, near the site of a pair of porters' lodges marking the entrance to the old Humewood House. The gatekeeper in 1854 is recorded as being John Birmingham, who was succeeded by Garrett Byrne about 1862. Solid, standard and single-storey, looking like a forerunner of the twentieth-century bungalow, with its double-fronted elevation of two canted bay windows, with corresponding roofs, in dressed stone projecting from pleasant uncoursed random rubble granite walls. Between is a segmentally arched fanlit front door, below eaves of exposed rafter toes to a shallow gabled roof with a pair of square brick chimney-stacks and pretty, over-delicate bargeboards. Recently installed casement windows spoil the effect. The straight gatescreen is comprised of four square cut-granite pillars with striking pyramidal layered cappings crowned with stylistic thistles. Between are unpretentious railed screens and matching carriage gates.

North-eastern lodge; *c.* 1875; architect possibly James Brooks.

As Graigue Lodge, but retaining its original cast-iron latticed glazing to windows and fanlight, and having stone chimney-stacks. Here, too, is the same distinctive gatescreen.

Barraderry lodge; *c.* 1875; architect possibly James Brooks.

On the south-western avenue are gates and lodge identical to those to the north, in pristine condition.

Kiltegan lodge *(below)*; *c.* 1875; architect possibly James Brooks.

The main entrance by the village has the same characteristic gatescreen as elsewhere but, as befits a principal approach, has a gatekeeper's house of greater presence and more generous accommodation. Constructed in random uncoursed granite, it is 1½-storey on an L-plan, with the familiar single-storey canted bays to each leading gable. Peculiarly, to the internal angle are both a flat-roofed hallway and a separate gabled porch with a pair of square columns which seems to serve no function other than as a focal point or arbour. There are carved sawtooth bargeboards to the shallow-pitched roof and the distinctive cast-iron latticed casement windows.

Feddan lodge; *c.* 1860; architect not known.

Although displaying the same uncoursed random granite facings as the castle, outbuildings and other lodges, this cottage is a puzzle in not sharing any architectural detailing in common, perhaps explained by dating from before the main excesses. It is 1½-storey standard gabled with high eaves, which are just broken off-centre by a charming steeply pitched gabled ashlar Tudor Gothic frontispiece with mildly ornamental bargeboards and segmentally pointed-arched doorway with relieving quatrefoil motif over. To each side are casement windows with pretty cast-iron octagonal glazing pattern and plain cut-stone dressings. Like the front door, the cut-stone chimney-stack with plinth and corniced capping is asymmetrically placed, while the

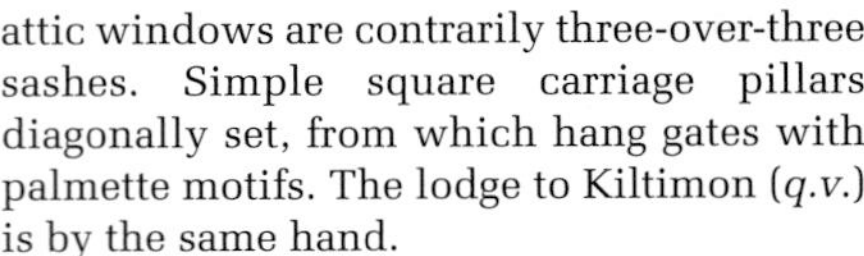

attic windows are contrarily three-over-three sashes. Simple square carriage pillars diagonally set, from which hang gates with palmette motifs. The lodge to Kiltimon (*q.v.*) is by the same hand.

As an alternative to the Brooks attribution, it may be significant to note very similar layered pyramidal cappings to entrance pillars at St Patrick's Cemetery, Clonmel, Co. Tipperary, which could be credited to architect Walter Glynn Doolin.

Griffith 1848–60; *LGI* (1904); *Country Life* (9 and 16 May 1968); Bence-Jones 1988; Girouard 1979; Williams 1994.

106. INCHANAPPA, Rathnew; pre-1838/*c.* 1875.

An estate of the Earbery family, which passed by marriage to the Croftons of County Leitrim. The early lodge built by Revd Henry William Crofton was probably given a dramatic make-over by his son, Henry Morgan Earbery Crofton (1840–78). Until recently it could be seen as a 1½-storey structure developed into an L-plan, with an original cast-iron latticed loft window and later fancy perforated bargeboards mirrored in mid-Victorian earthenware cresting. Recent owners have transformed it into a quite convincing gabled English Picturesque Cottage-style villa that replicates the intermediate features of bargeboards and cresting. The hexagonal ashlar entrance pillars with ogee cappings of *c.* 1835 have seen many changes down the years.

LGI (1904).

107. JOHNSTOWN, Arklow; *c.* 1840.

Originally a plain single-storey hipped-roof affair set forward of its gates, now much extended into an L-plan. In 1854 a seat of Edward Byrne, whose gate lodge then lay vacant.

Griffith 1848–60.

108. KILBRIDE MANOR, Kilbride (2).

The previous house on the site was transformed about 1835 by the Moore family into a Tudor Revival manor house in a development that extended to the building of two gate lodges.

West lodge; *c.* 1840; architect not known.

Probably by the same unidentified architect of the house, being in a similar, if watered-down, style. It is 1½-storey, and its leading gable and that to the left-hand breakfront have skew-tables with deep kneelers. Otherwise unembellished, with roughcast walls, the lodge was unfortunately not blessed with the window area afforded the

big house, which a later owner has attempted to remedy, with disastrous effect on its fenestration. Sufficiently commodious to serve as a post office, which it did for many years. In contrast is a very ornate cast-iron gatescreen comprising four fine posts with Tudor Gothic decorative motifs: cusped tracery, crenellated tops and quatrefoils, which extend across gates and railings.

East lodge; *c.* 1845.
A pretty single-storey three-bay cottage tucked away below road level. Faced in random rubble, the shallow-pitched gables have scalloped bargeboards, with a tiny Gothic lancet window to the leading apex. Occupied and much modernised, with a conservatory applied over the left-hand bay.

Both built for Joseph Scott Moore (1796–1884).

LGI (1904).

109. KILBRIDE TOWER, Bray; *c.* 1889; architect not known.

Even though it post-dates the house, previously called 'Mayfield Tower', this is very much a chip off the old block, or rather brick, as this distinctive lodge displays the same finish as the big house. Single-storey standard and hip-roofed, with a corbelled eaves band of specials broken by the shallow gable of the entrance breakfront containing the double-leafed front door. Cream brick as bands and voussoirs to the segmentally arched openings enhances the red-brick Flemish bond facings. Now extended to the right-hand side with a far-from-invisible join. Cast-iron carriage posts with Celtic cross motif to shafts and crowned by banded ball finials. All apparently for the splendidly named Marcus Tertius Moses, wholesale tea merchant of Dublin, who is recorded here in 1889.

Thom's.

KILCARRA (see GLENART CASTLE)

110. KILCRONEY, Bray (3).
A great, rambling granite Tudor Revival house which evolved on the site of the old Kilcroney Cottage, being transformed initially by Revd Dr Humphrey Lloyd (1800–81) about 1850 to designs attributed to the English railway architect Sancton Wood by Jeremy Williams. Until Lloyd moved to Victoria Castle, Co. Dublin (*q.v.*), *c.* 1870 the property appears to have been lodgeless. This was remedied by the new owner, Matthew P. D'Arcy, a wealthy brewer who moved here from Shanganagh House, Co. Dublin (*q.v.*), and who engaged Dublin architect John McCurdy to carry out alterations to the house and add a main entrance screen and attendant lodge.

Main gate; *c.* 1870; architect John McCurdy.

Located on the northern extremity of the estate is a pretentious gatescreen and pretty lodge. Extensive concave railed quadrants, with ironwork of differing dates, are broken by six highly ornate and expertly sculpted pillars with Gothic recessed panels, bossed chamfers and corbelled pyramidal layered cappings. The decorative Tudor Picturesque cottage is raised off a T-plan in random rubble facings with cut-stone dressings to single, bipartite and tripartite lattice-paned casement windows. Single-storey and gabled, with intricate perforated cusped wavy bargeboards and a tall chimney-stack cluster

to the ridge. From the leading gable projects a lower gabled porch, now glazed, with elegant curved post supports. There is a very similar lodge to this at Paradise Hill, Co. Clare, by the same architect.

Tower lodge; pre-1912; *demolished.*
Replaced by a modern bungalow.

Secondary gate; *c.* 1870.
Situated to the south of the property at the entrance to the farmyard is an altogether more modest cottage, as befits its role. Single-storey standard, built in quarry-faced uncoursed squared granite below a hipped roof. To the front door is a hip-roofed porch with flimsy post support, now glazed in. Chimney-stack in matching stone. Occupied and affectionately named 'Tudor Cottage'.

Thom's; *LGI* (1904); An Old Inhabitant 1907; Williams 1994.

KILGARRAN (see SEAVIEW)

111. KILLARNEY HILL, Bray; *c.* 1885; *demolished.*
A property whose lodge was built in the time here of Colonel Edward Bayley, who succeeded the Reid family to the place.

112. KILLARNEY, Bray; *c.* 1886; *demolished.*
Home to William Henry Jackson in the latter half of the nineteenth century, its porter's lodge being added for Mrs Ruth Jackson.

113. KILLARNEY WOOD, Bray; 1871; architect probably E.H. Carson.

Markedly subtler than the polychromatic house is the durable Flemish bond red-brick livery of its lodge. It is 1½-storey with steeply pitched roof, the ornamental bargeboards to main gables and dormer windows intricately pierced with a repeating quatrefoil motif and sawtooth trimming. Three-bay entrance front, the left-hand one breaking forward and gabled, containing a pair of windows, as elsewhere having arrowhead arches with one-over-one sashes. To the wall-plate level are pairs of decoratively carved brackets. Immaculately rehabilitated and sympathetically extended but pointedly detached from its big house by an unsightly barricade wall. Designed for David Richard Pigot (*c.* 1803–73), chief baron of the Irish exchequer, to a property previously called 'Dargle Vale'.

Thom's; Williams 1994.

114. KILLINCARRIG FARM, Greystones; pre-1838/*c.* 1845.

A standard lodge with steeply pitched hipped roof, now clad in concrete tiles, with clipped eaves to rendered and whitewashed walls. Occupied and much modernised. A seat in 1846 of Arthur Jones. There was an earlier lodge by the gate that may have served the proprietor in 1783, a Mr Bunn.

Taylor and Skinner 1778; 1969 [1783]; Slater 1846.

115. KILLINCARRIG, Greystones; *c.* 1860.

An estate in the mid-nineteenth century of Sir St Vincent Keene Hawkins Whitshed, who added a porter's lodge with a shallow-pitched roof and pretty bargeboards displaying perforated wave and fleur-de-lis motifs, extending to pierced fascias to eaves which oversail to cover a breakfront hall. Occupied and roughcast, with modern windows.

Griffith 1848–60; Bence-Jones 1988.

116. KILLOUGHTER, Killiskey; pre-1838; *demolished.*

In 1837 'the pleasing villa of H.T. Redmond'. Presumably the gate lodge was contemporary with the late Georgian house. By 1910 it had been removed.

Lewis 1837.

117. KILLRUDDERY, Bray (5).

Brewer in 1825 wrote: 'until lately, a low and rather old building, quite destitute of architectural interest; but a new and very estimable structure is now in progress, after the designs of Messrs. R. & W. Morrison'. John Chambré Brabazon (1772–1851) succeeded to the estate in 1797 and as 10th earl of Meath on the death of his brother. As early as 1814 he had planned a transformation of his house, but discarded proposals by Francis Johnston in favour of an Elizabethan Revival scheme by the Morrisons six years later. Their commission included designs for at least one of two gate lodges at entrances from the direction of Bray, neither of which has survived the expansion of that town.

North lodge; *c.* 1829; architects probably R. and W.V. Morrison.

The early OS maps show a large square imprint of a lodge, derelict in 1989, when it was tentatively attributed to the Morrisons by McParland *et al.*

North-east lodge; *c.* 1829; architects R. and W.V. Morrison; *demolished.*

Without any regard to the principle of a lodge serving as an introduction to the architecture of the big house, and in a twofold act of blatant plagiarism, the architects chose a design by John Soane from his *Sketches in*

J. Soane

architecture of 1793 (*above*), which he 'Intended for an Entrance to a Gentleman's Seat'. Father and son offered this design with varying success to noblemen throughout the country to adorn their demesnes. It remained an unexecuted proposal for Baronscourt, Co. Tyrone, but materialised for Lord Belmore at Castlecoole, Co. Fermanagh, while there is also a ruined example of it at Kinlough, Co. Leitrim, probably by the Morrison assistant J.B. Keane. Single-storey below a shallow-

hipped roof with bracketed soffits, it was cruciform on plan, its main single-bay front facing the avenue in the form of a segmentally arched tripartite window, with intricate octagonal glazing pattern, dressed in bold granite frame with distinctive voussoirs that break a deep stone band. This stone and that of the plinth contrasted with the otherwise stucco finish. To the road was a granite-built porch with a segmental head accommodated by an open pediment with mutules. This was balanced on the opposing side by a matching closet. In 1854 its proud porter was Patrick Dowling. This important lodge, which the architects estimated to cost £600, became a late twentieth-century victim to an appalling case of vandalism when it and its gates were dismantled, apparently to facilitate road improvements. To add insult to injury, its front façade is provocatively and preposterously displayed on an elevation to its bungalow replacement. As an accompanying gatescreen the Morrisons chose the neo-Classical 'Park Entrance' that is plate 20 of J.B. Papworth's *Rural residences* of 1818 [Fig. 7, p. 7]. This design they offered with success to great landowners throughout Ireland and here copied with only minor adaptations. The main carriage pillars are in the shape of Greek stelae with tapering frontispieces having recessed panels and carrying cornices below plinths inscribed with the Brabazon motto, 'Vota Vita Mea', flanked by gadrooned half-cappings and crowned by beautifully sculpted family falcons. On each side were postern gates with, like the main carriage gates, secondary iron piers, just as Papworth recommended.

J. B. Papworth

Beyond were concave-walled quadrants, the distant pillars with full gadrooned cappings.

William Brabazon (1803–87) succeeded in 1851 as the 11th Lord Meath and wasted little time in planning additions to his father's house and further lodges to the estate. His architect was the prolific Scottish practitioner William Burn, who designed the exquisite orangery and certainly one gate lodge, for which sample drawings were prepared, although, strangely, it seems not to have been built.

Unexecuted design; 1852/3; architect William Burn.

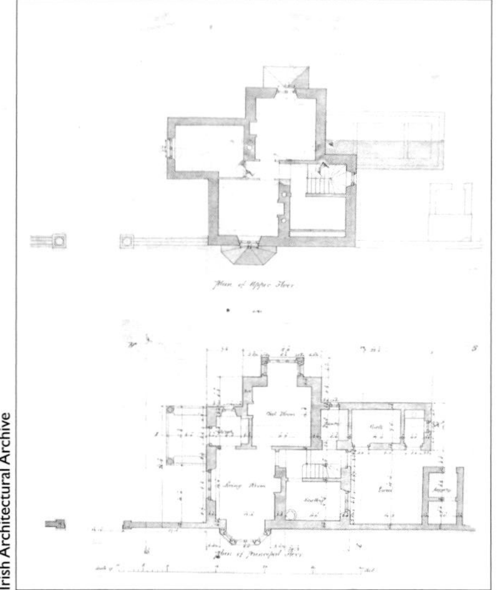

Irish Architectural Archive

Irish Architectural Archive

Irish Architectural Archive

This was to have been a typical 1½-storey rubble-built English Tudor Picturesque Cottage design on an irregular plan, with perforated wavy bargeboards, single-storey canted bay window, an attic room carried on a pair of columns to form a porch to the front door—surely influenced by T.F. Hunt's lodge to Glendalough House (*q.v.*)—and an impressive array of Tudor-style chimney-pots. It may have been a preliminary proposal for what was built at the southern gate, for Burn's drawing shows a pair of Classical pillars with rusticated ball finials, as appear there. The architect did have a porter's lodge akin to this erected on the Clandeboye estate, Co. Down.

'Wicklow lodge'; *c.* 1852; architect possibly William Burn.

A highly ornamental and generously proportioned affair, built off an L-plan in random rubble facings, with relieving arches to quadripartite and tripartite cut-stone mullioned windows with the most decorative of latticed cast-iron glazing patterns. To one gable is a single-storey canted window. The steeply gabled roof is adorned with beautifully carved perforated bargeboards, of which Pugin would have been proud, a pair of hexagonal brick chimney-stacks and an earthenware-tiled roof with sawtooth bands, a finish which may be a later innovation. More recent still are modern additions, which are generally circumspect but for a glazed hall that has done away with the original entrance in the internal angle.

East lodge; pre-1885; *demolished.*
Built sometime after 1838, a building with a short lifespan.

Inner lodge; *c.* 1890; architect probably J.F. Fuller.
The 11th earl had employed James Franklin Fuller to work on the estate in the 1860s and '70s, and he was retained by his son, Reginald Brabazon (1841–1929), the 12th earl, as a design for an elaborate gate by the architect contains the monogram 'R.B.' This hefty lodge at an inner gate is just the sort of forthright, solid affair one would expect of

the Kerryman. Seemingly also home to the estate gamekeeper, it rises off an informal plan to 1½ storeys with very steeply pitched main gables and gablets with mock half-timberwork to the apexes. Constructed in random stone facings relieved by a moulded string-course at first-floor level, prominent quoins and a variety of cut-stone mullioned casement windows. Above are bulky rectangular brick chimney-stacks.

Soane 1793; Papworth 1818; Brewer 1825; Hunt 1836; Griffith 1848–60; *BPB* (1929); Bence-Jones 1988; *Country Life* (14 and 21 July 1977); McParland *et al.* 1989; Dean 1994; Williams 1994; IAA (014/38CS365; 14/38 R9+N).

KILMACURRAGH (see WESTASTON)

118. KILMANOGE, Glenealy; pre-1910; *demolished.*
A lodge, to a property in 1854 of James Bowe, built after 1838.

Griffith 1848–60.

119. KILMARTIN, Killiskey; pre-1838; *demolished.*
A seat in 1814 of Thomas Fox, which by 1837 had passed to John Matthews.

Leet 1814; Lewis 1837.

120. KILPOOLE, Wicklow; *c.* 1845; *demolished.*
An estate of the Ellis family, the gate lodge to which was built after 1838 and was recorded in the Griffith valuation.

Griffith 1848–60.

KILQUADE HILL (see ST PATRICK'S PAROCHIAL HOUSE)

121. KILQUADE, Kilcooley (2).
A property that passed around the turn of the nineteenth century from the Boyd family to John T. O'Reilly.

North lodge; pre-1838; *demolished.*
A modern house occupies the site, alongside an early gatescreen comprised of four chamfered granite pillars with wide gadrooned cappings.

South lodge; pre-1838; *demolished.*

A small structure, shown on the early OS maps to have been circular on plan or bow-ended.

Taylor and Skinner 1778; 1969 [1783]; Leet 1814; Slater 1856; 1870.

122. KILRANELAGH, Baltinglass (2).
A seat in the late eighteenth century of the Greene family, then called 'Greenville', which by 1814 was home to Francis William Greene, who was probably responsible for at least one of its gatekeepers' lodges.

Back gate; pre-1838; *demolished.*

Front gate; *c.* 1800.

Irish Architectural Archive/Knight of Glin

That the assistance of a practised hand was probably not enlisted may have resulted in this absolute joy of an entrance by an inspired jobbing builder, or even by F.W. Greene himself. Cleverly resolving the Georgian dilemma of applying symmetry and balance at the park gate, circumventing the expense of a pair of lodges or the inconvenience of one opposite the gates, here the single lodge faces the road, flanked by matching gateways in concave quadrant walls. In a sort of delightful naive Palladian style is a single-bay façade comprised of a round-arched sash window of squared panes with spoked head set in a segmentally arched recess. Above is a stepped parapet, containing a relieving blind plaque, crowned by three ball finials on pedestals. All finished in a basic roughcast, behind which is a gabled lodge, partly single-storey, partly two-storey. Sadly this splendid composition lies derelict, part-tended but lacking its ball finials. Alongside is a charming and antique milestone.

Taylor and Skinner 1778; 1969 [1783]; Leet 1814; IAA photograph (49/78).

123. KILTIMON, Killiskey (2).
O'Neill Segrave acquired the demesne and its well-wooded glen from Hugh Eccles around the date of his marriage in 1848, replacing the main gate lodge and adding another further north.

South entrance; pre-1838/*c.* 1860.
Bearing a distinct resemblance to the Feddan lodge at Humewood Castle (*q.v.*), with the same mildly ornamental bargeboard to its main gables and that to the similar steeply pitched hall frontispiece, which breaks the high eaves and contains a segmental pointed-arched front doorway. This contains double-leafed sheeted doors with ornamental iron hinge brackets. Standard 1½-storey with simple one-over-one sash windows to the main front and the single-storey canted bay windows on the road elevation, the roof of

which rises to a tiny chinoiserie balconette below an attic window which discordantly exhibits a nasty twentieth-century steel casement.

North entrance; *c.* 1860.
A plain single-storey hip-roofed affair extended into a double pile.

Parliamentary Gazetteer; Griffith 1848–60; *LGI* (1904).

KINDLESTOWN (see GLENCARRIG, Greystones)

124. KINDLESTOWN LOWER, Delgany; *c.* 1850.
A single-storey standard hip-roofed lodge with two-over-two sash windows, in whitened rendered walls, flanking a projecting gabled hallway; an extension to each end, with a bull's-eye window to one. A property in 1855 of William Orpin.

Griffith 1848–60.

KINDLESTOWN UPPER (see UPLANDS)

125. KINGSTON, Rathdrum; pre-1838/*c.* 1845.
A five-bay single-storey symmetrical cottage with whitewashed roughcast walls, hipped gables and a central extending gabled hall. Located opposite the entrance, having superseded its predecessor by the gates. Long the property of the King family, of whom Thomas Mills King may have replaced the older lodge.

Lewis 1837.

126. KIPPURE LODGE, Kilbride; *c.* 1830.
A single-storey cottage with a shallow-pitched roof having low skew-tables and sturdy granite kneelers; wide bipartite casement windows. Occupied. Presumably built for George Moore, whose family were also at nearby Kilbride Manor (*q.v.*).

Lewis 1837.

127. KNOCKARIGG, Grangecon; pre-1838; *demolished.*
A property in 1814 and 1837 of James Wall, the lodge to which was opposite its gates.

Leet 1814; Lewis 1837.

128. KNOCKROBIN, Rathnew; *c.* 1880; architect perhaps Sandham Symes.

A big mid-Victorian villa of the Edwards family that has the appearance of a work by architect Sandham Symes wearing his Italianate hat. The singular little 1½-storey gabled Picturesque lodge built on an L-plan would be contemporary were it not for the carved posts and apex feature of its pretty gabled porch, which looks to be from about twenty years later. Finished in harling with big granite quoin stones and high eaves, the main front is two-bay, both of which are concentrated on the right-hand side, the window alongside the front door, leaving the remainder blind. The inappropriateness of the modern casement is relieved by the latticed internal security grille, giving a Tudor touch. Possibly a late work by Symes from the office of Millar and Symes. Occupied and immaculate in a pretty garden setting.

Griffith 1848–60; Slater 1870.

129. LAKE VIEW, Roundwood; pre-1838; *demolished.*
Alternatively known as 'Lake Park' down the years, in 1814 it was occupied by John Webster, though by 1837 it was 'the admired residence of Gerard Macklin'. It may never be known whether this was the same Mr Macklin for whom the architect George Papworth designed a new Gothic entrance.

Leet 1814; Lewis 1837; IAA.

130. LAMBERTON, Arklow; 1898; architect possibly John Birch.

Another seat of the Probys of Glenart Castle (*q.v.*), which they let for much of the nineteenth century, firstly to Revd Henry Lambert Bayly, briefly of Ballyarthur (*q.v.*), and from 1825 to Capt. Samuel Hore RN and his widow. William Proby, the 5th and last earl of Carysfort (1836–1909), added this lodge to the property late in the century to a design whose quirkiness is redolent of those at Glenart Castle (*q.v.*), there known to be by the architect John Birch. It is 1½-storey gabled, built in immaculate quarry-faced coursed granite with cut-stone dressings; its two-bay main front is dominated by an eccentric canted bay window which reduces via hipped cheeks to a skew-tabled gablet attic window, mullioned and leaded as below. To the right-hand side under high eaves is a wide round-headed, studded and sheeted door with hood moulding, above which is the date-stone, finely chiselled with the Carysfort monogram and coronet.

Leet 1814; Pigot 1824; Debrett's *Peerage* (1911).

131. LARAGH, Annamoe (3).
A beautiful mountainous estate which came into the possession *c.* 1850 of George Booth, who within twenty years had given the property porters' lodges at three of its entrances.

East entrance; *c.* 1855.
A pretty 1½-storey standard Picturesque cottage in coursed granite rubble with perforated foiled bargeboards to main gables and that of the central porch, which is supported by a pair of square posts. The front door is flanked by a pair of windows with chamfered dressings and label mouldings. To the park elevation is a single-storey canted bay with round-headed sash windows, and over is an unfortunate modern window replacing a more appropriate predecessor to the attic room; cut-stone banded chimney-stack.

West entrance; *c.* 1855.
A two-storey gatehouse with shallow gabled roof having wavy bargeboards. Symmetrical ground-floor elevation, with label mouldings and chamfered dressings to openings and a pair of square matching windows over. Constructed in granite rubble with exposed rafter toes and bland modern plate-glass windows.

Middle entrance; *c.* 1875.
A tidy Classical-style single-storey standard lodge with a hipped roof in coursed granite facings, with brick toothed dressings to six-over-six sash windows on each side of a

correct portico with a pair of fluted Doric columns and triglyphed frieze to a little pedimented gable. Clashing in scale, it may have been salvaged from elsewhere; two symmetrically placed chimney-stacks. An entrance severed from the demesne by public road realignment.

Griffith 1848–60.

132. LA VALLEE, Bray; *c.* 1885; *demolished.*
A lodge built for William Hopkins, swept away by roadworks.

Thom's; Slater 1870; *LGI* (1904).

133. LEAMORE, Newtown Mount Kennedy; pre-1838; *demolished.*
A seat in 1837 of John Smith.

Lewis 1837.

134. LORD POWERSCOURT'S PLEASURE GROUNDS, Enniskerry; 1886.
On the northern bank of the Dargle River is this idyllic walk, opened to the public for their enjoyment and provided with accommodation for a gatekeeper at the western gate. It appears from its outline on the OS map to have been of some presence and obviously intended by the 7th Viscount Powerscourt (1836–1904) to be admired. Built two years after he succeeded to the title and a year after being created a peer, today it is a pitiable sight, revealed as the shell of a harled rubble-built single-storey cottage with toothed brick dressings and quoins. The first porter was James Malone.

BPB (1929).

LORETO CONVENT, Bray (see SANS SOUCI)

135. LOUGHBRAY COTTAGE, Enniskerry; pre-1838/*c.* 1870.
In 1838 Frazer wrote: 'The surgeon general has built a picturesque cottage suited to the character of the place, to which from the fatigues of his professional duties, he occasionally retreats'. This charming Swiss cottage had been designed by William Vitruvius Morrison for Dr Philip Crampton (1779–1858) and reputedly built at the expense of his friend the duke of Northumberland around 1830, when he was lord lieutenant, as replacement for its predecessor, which had been burnt down. This successor suffered the same fate in 1868 and was again rebuilt. This may be the date when the present lodge was erected to supersede a predecessor on the site. It is a relatively uninteresting long single-storey four-bay gabled affair, constructed with granite boulders and having brick bull-nose dressings and segmentally arched heads to windows. A projecting gabled porch has a round-headed opening. Derelict.

Fraser 1838; *Irish Penny Journal* (1840–1); McParland *et al.* 1989.

136. LUGGALA, Roundwood (2).
Neither lodge prepares one for the delights of the architecture within—the Georgian Gothic shooting-box of the La Touche banking family, whose main seats were at Bellevue (*q.v.*) and Marlay, Co. Dublin (*q.v.*).

High lodge; pre-1838.
A gabled stone shell.

Low lodge; *c.* 1835.
Probably given a make-over in about 1850, this is a pleasant 1½-storey standard gabled cottage with six-over-six sash windows, in smooth rendered walls, on each side of a later projecting gabled hall with ornamental hip-knob and little round-headed sidelights. To the leading gable is a pair of attic windows overlooking a lean-to garage. Occupied and well maintained.

Carr 1806; Lewis 1837; Bence-Jones 1988.

MAGHERAMORE (see SEA PARK)

137. MARLTON HALL, Wicklow; pre-1838; *demolished.*
A seat in 1814 of one John Price.

Leet 1814.

MAYFIELD TOWER (see KILBRIDE TOWER)

138. MONALIN, Newtown Mount Kennedy; *c.* 1893; *demolished.*
A lodge built and located within the property for Revd John Alexander Stamper (1826–1901) shortly after his retirement from ministry in Lincoln.

Leslie and Wallace 2001.

139. MONASTERY HOUSE, Enniskerry; pre-1838; *demolished.*
An estate in 1854 of Charles Stronge, the gatekeeper's lodge to which had gone by 1912.

Griffith 1848–60.

140. MOUNT AVON, Avoca; pre-1910.
A lodge built after 1838, so modernised and extended as to make dating difficult. Single-storey gabled, lengthened into a dog-leg on plan. A demesne in the mid-nineteenth century of Charles West, which by 1885 had passed to William Bolton.

Griffith 1848–60; *Land owners in Ireland 1876.*

141. MOUNT CORBALLIS, Rathdrum; *c.* 1945.
A solid square single-storey Arts and Crafts composition, below a pyramidal roof of small slates rising to a central stack. Built in rubble facings with a two-window-bay front to the avenue and a road elevation relieved by the entrance door. An estate long associated with the Manning family, who built a new house in 1877, which passed *c.* 1945 to a Miss Eastwick, who added the porter's lodge.

142. MOUNT JOHN, Newtown Mount Kennedy; *c.* 1855.

In contrast to the graceful late eighteenth-century Classical villa of the Archer family is a pleasant English Tudor Picturesque lodge. Standard 1½-storey, gabled, now with plain bargeboards, finished in whitewashed harling and having label mouldings to bipartite casement windows. The single-storey gabled hall projection has sidelights and the doorway a mouth-organ fanlight. A stone string-course defines the first-floor level, while the gutters are supported by iron brackets and a sturdy granite chimney-stack tops the ridge. To the road is a fine pair of cut-stone granite carriage pillars with recessed panels, fluted friezes and gadrooned cappings, just like those at Glencarrig, Greystones (*q.v.*). These carry good contemporary cast-iron gates with anthemion finials. Plain harled screen walls, the right-hand one of which contains an Edward VII postbox.

143. MOUNT KENNEDY, Newtown Mount Kennedy (2).
In this fine sylvan setting is the mansion built in 1782 to designs by the prominent English architect James Wyatt. The client was Lt.-Gen. Robert Cuninghame, who had acquired the property, previously owned by the Kennedy family, in 1769. Wyatt never visited the site and its supervision was left in the hands of executant architect Thomas Cooley, another Englishman who was domiciled in Ireland but died prematurely in 1784. His last task may have been the design of the front gate lodge.

Main entrance; *c.* 1784; architect Thomas Cooley.

Surviving is the undated architect's drawing of the front elevation of the lodge, which itself surprisingly remains much as Cooley intended. Single-storey standard but substantial, with a back return making it an L-plan, the three bays to its main front having

rounded openings set in equivalent recesses below a hipped roof with clipped eaves. Cooley showed the windows and fanlight to the panelled door with unusually meagre Gothic Y-tracery, today interpreted in a rather more generous lead-effect application. Finished in harled-like rendering and well tended, it presides over a forecourt to the contemporary gatescreen comprised of Classical pillars in V-jointed rusticated granite with fluted friezes.

Secondary entrance; pre-1838; *demolished.*

Parliamentary Gazetteer; *Country Life* (4 and 11 Nov. 1965); Bence-Jones 1988; *IFR*; NLI drawing (A.D. 3568/25).

144. MOUNT PLEASANT, Delgany; *c.* 1820.
A property with ever-altering families down the years and consequent name changes, it being alternatively called 'Prospect' and more recently 'Struan Hill'. The pleasant mid-Georgian villa is complemented by a generous gatehouse of two storeys below a hipped roof, with a chamfered corner to the avenue which contains a round-headed doorway with spoked fanlight in white harled walls. Much improved and extended. Granite gate pillars with those gadrooned cappings so common in the county. All perhaps for Richard Smith, who is recorded at Prospect in 1814.

Leet 1814.

145. MOUNT USHER, Ashford; 1906; architect George Tighe Moore.

The famous river garden created by the Walpole family on the banks of the Vartry from an old estate of the Ushers, which was extended in 1889 and 1905. The original *Pinus montezumae* here and a gate lodge for George Walpole date from this latter phase of improvements. A striking single-storey Edwardian gabled lodge, built off a T-plan in Flemish bond orange brickwork, with geometrically decorative half-timber effect applied to the leading gable apexes over projecting glazed canted bay windows with partially tiny-paned Arts and Crafts glazing. To an internal angle is the flat-roofed hallway. Occupied and smartly maintained.

IB (6 April 1907); *Country Life* (23 May 1974).

NAVARRE or NOVARRA (see BAY VIEW)

NEWCOURT (see SANS SOUCI)

146. NEWCOURT, Bray; pre-1838; *demolished.*
Despite being situated in Old Court townland, this seat seems to have assumed its name when the neighbouring property of the same name (see Sans Souci) was acquired by the Loreto nuns in 1850. A small estate in 1814 of James Kirkwood, which became home in 1837 to Mrs McMahon.

Leet 1814; Lewis 1837.

147. OLD COURT, Bray (3).
The Welshman Richard Edwards was granted the old tower-house called 'Mulso's Court' about 1685 and built himself a new house in proximity. To this residence was an early porter's lodge, since removed. The Edwards family may have fallen on hard times, for in 1811 they removed to outbuildings, taking the Old Court name with them. A new residence appears within the curtilage of the old estate called 'Vevay', which thereafter was occupied by a succession of ladies called Weldon. To this was attached a lodge.

Inner gate; *c.* 1845.

A conspicuous little building in an Italianate manner; single-storey standard under a hipped roof extending over a back return that forms an L-plan. The oversailing eaves are broken to the front by a central gabled hall projection that contained a round-headed fanlit doorway, now grotesquely converted into a window. To each side are paired semicircular-arched narrow windows with raised surrounds in modern stucco-effect drab grey sand/cement rendering. Adjacent is a good contemporary railed gatescreen of concave quadrants and matching carriage gates carried on anthemion-topped iron piers.

Outer gate; pre-1838/1862.
A standard 1½-storey gabled affair, with a lean-to canopy and tiny sash windows with an off-centre dormer window over. First valued in 1862 as a replacement for Mrs West after she leased the property from John Brennan.

Leet 1814; *Parliamentary Gazetteer*; Griffith 1848–60; Burke 1854–5; An Old Inhabitant 1907.

OVOCA COTTAGE (see VICTORIA COTTAGE)

148. PALMTREE COTTAGE, Coolgreany; pre-1838; *demolished.*
A property in 1854 of William Nulty, the gatekeeper's lodge to which had been removed by 1909.

Griffith 1848–60.

149. PARKNASILLOGE, Enniskerry; *c.* 1880.
The single-storey gabled lodge lies derelict, conspicuous for its brick toothed quoins and dressings in whitewashed walls and an unusual arrowhead bay window projecting from its short avenue frontage. To the road a catslide extension contains the entrance hall. Sundry other additions disguise its date of origin, but it was probably built for Edward Ebenezer Barrington after he acquired the estate from the Buckley family around 1860.

150. POLLAPHUCA, Ballymore Eustace; pre-1838; *demolished.*
A lodge located opposite the entrance to a property in 1854 of John Moore, which by the early twentieth century had become the 'Pollaphuca Hotel'.

Griffith 1848–60.

151. POWERSCOURT, Enniskerry (7).
The jewel in Wicklow's architectural crown is this magnificent mansion, designed by Castle in 1731, and its stunning estate and setting, the restoration of which disguises a troubled past. Apart from the calamitous burning of the place in 1974, planned improvements to the demesne were understandably disrupted in the first half of the nineteenth century by the increasing 'shortevity' of the 4th, 5th and 6th viscounts. Their successors inherited as minors of ever-decreasing ages, which accounts for the state of the property as related in 1835 by John Barrow: 'the domain of the young Earl of Powerscourt. It is undoubtedly a noble place, but the house is under repair, the furniture packed up, and everything in confusion. I went over it, however, but saw nothing worth particular mention.' Robert Graham also describes 'a large ugly house, with a good deal of dressed grounds, but, in the absence of the proprietor, not kept in the best order. As he is expected home, the house is undergoing a thorough repair and is in great disorder, and they are very unwilling to show it.' This all seems a little harsh and was perhaps influenced by the tourists' reception. Neither made mention of the splendid main entrance noted by Samuel Lewis a year later. It would be fascinating to know what influence the dowagers had over the piecemeal building developments of this era.

Eagle gate; *c.* 1820; architect probably Richard Morrison.
So called for the eagle 'displayed' sculpture by Thomas Kirk, added *c.* 1840 to crown the pediment over a great round-headed carriage archway, the whole conspicuous for singular pulvinated joints which also define the voussoirs and extend through scroll-topped piers and beyond the postern openings into pillars with ball finials, below which are friezes containing sculpted laurel wreaths, a feature much favoured by architect Richard Morrison. Thomas Lacy, who visited Powerscourt, described the entrance screen as having eagles also on the secondary pillars and urns beyond. Attribution of Morrison's involvement here is strengthened by the design of the sturdy gate lodge, which is almost identical to his steward's house at Castlecoole, Co. Fermanagh. Single-storey standard below an oversailing hipped roof, the white rendered bays defined by stone pilasters that frame architraved six-over-six segmentally arched sash windows with recessed under-panels. The six-panelled front door has a plain over-panel, just as at Castlecoole, whilst to the end elevations are tripartite 'Wyatt' windows. Elevated from the gates, it is a design that confers an appropriate sense of *gravitas* on a main entrance to an estate of such importance from the estate village. Presumably Morrison was commissioned by Richard Wingfield, the 5th Viscount Powerscourt (1790–1823), who had succeeded to the estate in 1809. The architect was certainly working on Enniskerry cottages in 1818.

Kilmalin gate; pre-1838; *demolished.*
The gatekeeper is recorded in 1854 as John Wright.

Parknasilloge gate; *c.* 1820.
A plain single-storey hip-roofed lodge, much modernised.

Tinnehinch gate; 1856; architect Sir George Hodson.
This Tinnehinch Avenue was one of three drives created as Famine relief. Emerging at the bridge over the Dargle River, it was some years before lodge and gates were added. Mervyn Wingfield (1836–1904), the 7th viscount, succeeded to Powerscourt as an eight-year-old and so it was ten years before he turned to his near neighbour and talented amateur architect, Sir George Frederick Hodson of Hollybrooke (*q.v.*), to provide the design for the lodge. It was to be a quintessential Tudor Picturesque Cottage in the manner pioneered by the architectural pattern-books of T.F. Hunt and P.F. Robinson. Faithfully built as per Sir George's drawings of 1854, it is 1½-storey standard with limewashed harled walls and steeply pitched roofs highlighted by a pair of octagonal chimney-flues, scalloped slate and perforated foiled bargeboards to main gables and that to the projecting central porch, which has a hood-moulded Tudor-arched opening, the

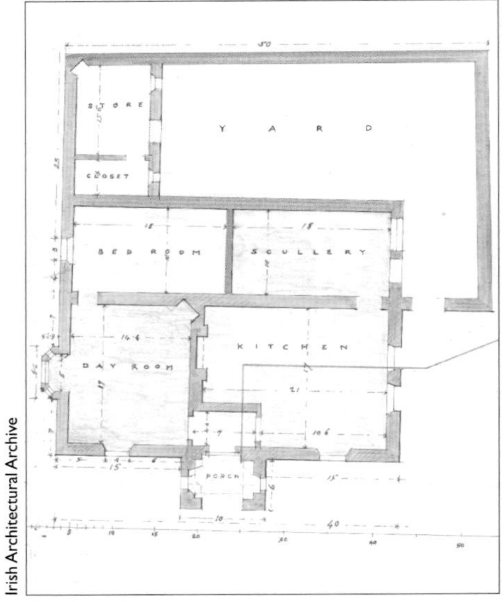

Irish Architectural Archive

Irish Architectural Archive

date of completion in a shield over. On each side are label-moulded bipartite casement windows below ornamentally carved fascia boards. To the road gable is a medieval canted oriel window overlooking the gates. These magnificent 'Golden Gates', as they are known, arrived here in 1867 from the Paris Exhibition. Highly decorative scrolled ironwork to overthrow, main carriage gates, postilion gates and railed screens are framed by six stone pillars, reducing in size from the towering carriage pair, all of which are built off tall plinths in rusticated blocks with recessed panels. These pillars were to a French design, executed in granite by Matthew Noble, a local mason from Glencree. Mighty impressive but for the strangely dilapidated lodge, of which there was an almost identical example at Hollybrooke.

Bahana Bridge gate; 1868; architect not known.

Afar, at the end of a tortuous avenue following the Dargle, at a bridged crossing, is another very fine Tudor Revival lodge on the southern approach. This is a single-storey standard version with plain bargeboards to steep main and porch gables and cut stone rationed to the hefty ashlar stack, front elevation and rectangular bay window on the leading gable; else whitened roughcast. The projecting hall has little round-headed sidelights and a hood-moulded pointed entrance opening below a date-stone shield. To each side is a pair of label-moulded bipartite one-over-one sash windows. A very smart little building, raised on a little embankment with a stepped approach. At a distance is a fine low pair of mid-Victorian carriage gates in a sort of Gothic chinoiserie mix, hung on squat quarry-faced stone pillars. Could the lodge be another contribution of Sir George Hodson and, if so, what arrangement was there for remuneration from the young 7th viscount?

Earlier, two new avenues had been created as Famine relief to the south-west in the deer-park: Earl's Drive and Lady's Drive. Both received porters' lodges to monitor their gates, created in the minority of the 7th viscount and presumably overseen by his mother, the dowager Lady Powerscourt, who in 1846 took the future 4th marquis of Londonderry as her second husband.

North deer-park gate; *c.* 1840.

A pretty single-storey *cottage orné*; its canted leading front, with cast-iron latticed bipartite casements, is recessed under the semi-octahedral oversailing roof carried on iron posts to form a verandah which extends past the avenue elevation. Finished in white harled finish, it has a 1½-storey gabled extension of *c.* 1860 to the rear with architraved sash windows. Enclosed by a picket fence and in use.

South deer-park gate; *c.* 1850.

A rendered single-storey two-bay gabled structure, extended in two storeys beyond with a single-storey gabled hall link, decorated by deeply waved perforated bargeboards throughout. Occupied.

Brewer 1825; Griffith 1848–60; Lacy 1863; Powerscourt 1903; *BPB* (1929); Malins and Bowe 1980; McParland *et al.* 1989; Bernelle 1992; Williams 1994; IAA drawings (87/55: 24/1–5); Lawrence photograph (1684R).

152. PRESENTATION COLLEGE, Bray (see SANS SOUCI)

153. PROSPECT COTTAGE, Bray (2).

Lodges built in 1871 and 1881 to a property previously called 'Eden View', which became 'Carrigbrae', have been demolished. Home in 1881 to James Scott Robertson, letting from the O'Reilly family.

154. RAHEENGRANEY, Shillelagh; *c.* 1845.

A standard 1½-storey gabled cottage with high projecting eaves, much altered, with widened window openings and concrete tile reroofing in modernisation. Occupied. A seat of the Braddell family in the mid-nineteenth century, opposite the entrance to which it is sited.

155. RATHCLAREN, Bray; *c.* 1880; *demolished.*

A lodge to a property in the late nineteenth century of the Oswalds.

156. RATHDRUM WORKHOUSE, Rathdrum; 1910; architect G.T. Moore.

A neat little Edwardian cottage in Classical style and in pristine condition. Relieved of its duties, the workhouse of 1842 having been demolished. Single-storey below a hipped roof with chunky chimney, it is smooth-rendered with a pair of square-paned tripartite Wyatt sash windows flanking a simple central breakfront doorway. Designed by George Tighe Moore, in contrast to his Picturesque Arts and Crafts lodge to Mount Usher (*q.v.*). Occupied.

Wicklow Newsletter (1 Oct. 1910); O'Connor 1995.

157. RATHNEW AND WICKLOW CEMETERY, Rathnew; *c.* 1905.

Some materials on this lodge, such as the perforated terracotta scalloped ridge tiles and hip-knobs, reveal it as not being the Georgian Gothic cottage it initially appears. The uniform stucco-effect drab grey rendering with raised quoins also confirms its early twentieth-century origin. Single-storey standard on an L-plan below a hipped roof, all its openings have pointed heads, including the doorway in the gabled hall projection that fits below the main clipped eaves. Being abandoned and blocked up, it would seem to be suffering the penultimate indignity had it not latterly seen service as a public toilet. Built to accommodate a caretaker as its main function.

NIAH.

158. RATHSALLAGH, Colbinstown; *c.* 1830.

A distinctive single-storey standard lodge below a shallow-hipped roof, notable for its long low lines and meagre window-to-wall ratio. In immaculate whitened rendered walls are tiny bipartite casement lights, like the doorway below Tudor label mouldings. To the roof is a pair of chimney-stacks and bold paired modillion brackets to the oversailing soffits. Equally striking entrance screen, with carriage pillars in the shape of trabeated postilion openings in granite masonry with moulded cornices and dies carrying lanterns. Good contemporary matching ironwork to gates with repeating husk motif. A seat in the early nineteenth century of Edward Pennefather until his death in 1847. The gatekeeper of his son of the same name in 1854 was John Norris.

Griffith 1848–60; *LGI* (1904).

159. RAVENSWELL, Bray; pre-1838; *demolished.*
A lodge built for Isaac Weld, the noted antiquary, after he purchased the property in 1813. In 1849 his gate porter was Mary Bryan.

Griffith 1848–60; An Old Inhabitant 1907.

160. RICHVIEW, Bray; pre-1910; *demolished.*
The lodge was probably added by William Bachelor after he came to the property *c.* 1855. Subsequently renamed 'Beechurst', both it and its lodge are remembered in the name of a modern housing avenue.

161. RICHVIEW, Delgany; *c.* 1830.
A plain roughcast two-storey two-bay hip-roofed gatehouse to a small estate in the nineteenth century of the Archer family.

162. RIVERSDALE, Bray; *c.* 1830/1890.
A single-storey standard hip-roofed porter's lodge built on the property of the La Grange family. The original Regency-style carved paired modillion soffit brackets survive, but the wide window openings with moulded surrounds look like later modernisation, probably when it was extended for Ethelbert Collins into a double pile and the chimney-stack was moved to one end; roughcast.

163. ROANCRUAGHAN, Bray; *c.* 1911; architects probably O'Callaghan and Webb; *demolished.*
A lodge that did not see out the century, presumably contemporary with the house built in 1911 for William F. Figgis and designed by O'Callaghan and Webb.

IB (24 June 1911).

164. ROCKBRAE, Bray; *c.* 1890.
Set in a development of late Victorian suburban villas and vying for attention is this conspicuously plain single-storey four-bay gabled cottage at the gate to a newly built property in 1890 of Andrew McCullagh.

Thom's.

165. ROUNDWOOD PARK, Roundwood; pre-1838; *demolished.*
A seat in 1783 of one Hatch Esq., which for much of the nineteenth century became home to the Gower family.

Taylor and Skinner 1778; 1969 [1783].

166. ROYAL DRUMMOND INSTITUTION, Bray; *c.* 1918.
Not contemporary with the original 1892 building of the Institute for Girls, which from 1917 became a House for Blind Soldiers, in 1918 the Duke of Connaught's Hospital for fitting artificial limbs, by 1920 an orphanage for daughters of dead soldiers, and finally to its present function as National Schools of the Loreto Sisters. A large lodge, single-storey with a hipped roof and front verandah supported on four columns screening a wide segmentally arched window with tiny squared lights. Tapering chimney-stack and exposed rafter toes. In use.

167. ROYAL NATIONAL HOSPITAL, Newtown Mount Kennedy; *c.* 1892; architect possibly T.M. Deane.
A big 1½-storey gable-on affair, perhaps contemporary with the 'Newcastle Hospital' commissioned in 1892 by the government from architect Thomas Manley Deane in half-timbered Elizabethan Revival manner.

Williams 1994.

168. RUSSBOROUGH, Blessington (3).
Richard Castle's magnificent Palladian mansion was being built in the 1740s for Joseph Leeson (1701–83), who was created 1st earl of Milltown in 1763. With its projecting wings and pavilions and further extending frontage, perhaps the need for the additional security of a lodge at the main gates was felt unnecessary; certainly Rocque's map of 1760 only suggests that there may have been one by the back entrance. Those that were eventually added were short-lived and the place is now lodgeless. Recent owners may have regretted their demolition, given the infamous late twentieth-century art thefts.

Main entrance; pre-1838; *demolished.*

The post-1760 lodge built very much as an afterthought has been survived by a noble granite-built triple archway located at the head of the principal and original avenue to the east. Perhaps to a design by Francis Bindon, for Castle had died in 1751, it is preceded by a forecourt and tall convex quadrant walls. The central pedimented round-headed carriage archway with lion statues as acroteria is flanked by a pair of smaller postern gates, similarly pedimented over flat arches. Relief is achieved by chamfered toothed dressings continued as voussoirs and keystones over.

Front entrance; pre-1838; *demolished.* All that remains are V-jointed rusticated masonry pillars with unblocked moulded cornices of mid- to late eighteenth-century origin.

Rear entrance; pre-1838; *demolished.* Perhaps the earliest of the porters' lodges, as suggested by the Rocque map of 1760, but now lost without trace.

Brewer 1825; *BPB* (1873); *Country Life* (5, 12 and 19 Dec. 1963); ffolliott 1970; Craig and Glin 1970; Howley 1993; Ferguson 1998.

169. RYECROFT, Bray; *c.* 1860; *demolished.* A nineteenth-century property of the Scovell family, the lodge to which is survived by a very fine neo-Classical gatescreen with Greek stela-type pillars, a feature much favoured by architects Richard Morrison and Daniel Robertson, which they sourced from J.B. Papworth's *Rural residences* of 1818.

Papworth 1818.

170. ST ANNE'S CONVENT, Newtown Mount Kennedy; *c.* 1870.
Set well back from its entrance gates is this single-storey standard lodge with steeply pitched hipped roof having clipped eaves, scalloped slate courses, perforated scalloped terracotta cresting and an off-centre chimney-stack; modern windows. Occupied.

171. ST HELEN'S, Bray; 1909; architects O'Callaghan and Webb.

A dapper little example of the Arts and Crafts Elizabethan Revival style. Single-storey, built with white-finish roughcast off a T-plan, from the steeply hip-roofed cross of which a gabled wing extends to the avenue with a striking 'black-and-white' gable, over a glazed canted bay window, carried on a pair of wooden brackets. In an internal angle is a porch with carved balustrade and posts. In contrast, a big ribbed red-brick chimney-stack rises from the ridge. Erected, as a mirrored version of the perspective design published in the *Irish Builder*, for Mrs F.E. Gilmore to a house that is semi-detached with 'Rahan'. Much extended and lovingly maintained. Built by H. Pemberton, builder of Ballybrack. The lodge to Templecarrig (*q.v.*) has much in common with this.

IB (17 April and 1 May 1909).

ST LIVINIUS (see DRUMKEY CHURCH OF IRELAND CHURCH)

172. ST PATRICK'S PAROCHIAL HOUSE, Kilcoole; *c.* 1860.
An unprepossessing standard three-bay lodge with clipped eaves to its steeply hipped roof. Occupied. The house is now a private residence called 'Kilquade Hill'.

173. ST VALERY, Enniskerry; pre-1838; *demolished.*
A lodge built after the time here of the Walker family and contemporary with the creation of architect W.V. Morrison's villa for their successor, the Rt Hon. Philip Cecil Crampton (1782–1866), about 1825.

McParland *et al.* 1989.

174. SANS SOUCI, Bray (5).
A once-important landed estate in the heart of Bray, which inevitably was overrun and broken up by the spread of the town. The Georgian Gothic house of the Putland family became 'Newcourt' and in 1850 was sold, with the northern portion of the property, to the Loreto nuns for a convent. Of the four pre-1838 lodges, that to the south was circular on plan. When Charles Putland built his new house of 'Brayhead' on the part of the property that he retained, a fifth lodge was added on the new road which split his original estate. Brayhead has since become the Presentation College and not one lodge has survived.

An Old Inhabitant 1907; Williams 1994.

175. SAUNDERS GROVE, Baltinglass; pre-1838; *demolished.*
Of the fine early Georgian mansion and large gate lodge of the Saunders family nothing remains. Surviving is a good entrance screen with two large carriage pillars in V-jointed rusticated masonry with scroll-topped stops, surmounted by outsized ball finials in cups. New dwarf wing walls lead to matching outer pillars.

Craig and Glin 1970; Bence-Jones 1988.

176. SEAPARK, Wicklow (4).
Robert Francis Ellis (1822–99) inherited Seapark on the death of his father, Henry, in 1848, along with a sole gate lodge on the southern approach. Twenty years later he rebuilt the house and gave it three new lodged entrances, removing the original. His architect was William George Murray, whose commission included at least one entrance.

East lodge; pre-1910; *demolished.*

South lodge; *c.* 1870; architect possibly W.G. Murray.
A standard gabled affair raised in coursed rubble facings with brick as quoins, dressings, segmental opening arches and the gabled breakfront hallway. Mid-Victorian two-over-two sashes; derelict. Railed concave entrance quadrants frame rough vermiculated stone pillars.

North lodge; *c.* 1870; architect W.G. Murray.

Very much the principal entrance is this ostentatious Italianate gateway and lodge, the latter single-storey standard but commodious and richly endowed with Classical detailing. Gabled, with ogee guttering and fascias returning sufficiently to hint at open pediments to each end and the central projecting hall. The main eaves are emphasised by paired modillion brackets over a moulded string-course. In rendered walls, the paired windows have moulded surrounds carried around segmental heads, a feature repeated about the fanlit panelled doorway. The whole sits on a plinth, as do the pair of chimney-stacks with their banded shafts and corniced cappings. Occupied. The gatescreen is equally pretentious and extensive in its convex railed quadrants framed by four conspicuously vermiculated stone pillars with disc-ornamented friezes. The heavy decorative ironwork of the carriage gates extends to lanterns on the main cappings.

The place now goes under the name of 'Magheramore' and is in use as a convent.

IB (1 April 1868); *LGI* (1904); Bence-Jones 1988.

177. SEASON PARK TOWNLAND, Newtown Mount Kennedy.
The townland was comprised of three major lots in the valuation books, each of which may have been served by a gate lodge at some stage in the nineteenth century, none of them named.

Lot 1; pre-1838; *demolished.*
The first OS map shows a structure by the gate to a seat in 1854 of Denis McClements that had gone by 1910.

Lot 2; pre-1903; *demolished.*
There is specific reference in the 1903 valuation book but only to record its removal from a property then of Edward Cullen.

Lot 3; pre-1838; *demolished.*
Surviving is a late Georgian villa next to the village on a one-acre holding, in 1854 of Richard McClelland, with an unannotated building by the entrance in 1838, which had been demolished by the turn of the twentieth century, when the house was in use as a rectory.

Griffith 1848–60.

178. SEAVIEW, Enniskerry (2).
A property which over the nineteenth century saw a succession of owners come and go, as have its lodges. The earlier was in place by 1838, when the Revd A. Wynne was the proprietor. The eastern lodge was built *c.*

1860 for Echlin Montgomery to a place subsequently renamed 'Kilgarran'.

Lewis 1837.

179. SEAVIEW, Kilcoole; pre-1838; *demolished.*

A seat in the late eighteenth century of Captain Robert Gore, which by 1837 was occupied by a Mrs Barry.

Taylor and Skinner 1778; 1969 [1783]; Leet 1814; Lewis 1837.

180. SHELTON ABBEY, Arklow (4).

Although the mansion is recorded as taking on its present magnificent Gothic abbey cloak in the reign of the 4th earl of Wicklow, William Forward-Howard (1788–1869), the modernisation and eleven-bay front is noted by Mason as early as 1816, only a year after the death of the 2nd earl and two years before the demise of his brother, the 3rd earl. Sadly, nothing survives to suggest that the commission of Richard and William Vitruvius Morrison extended to furnishing plans for porters' lodges.

Only one survives, that being a plain standard three-bay cottage with hipped roof and wide windows, extending to one side to form an L-plan, and dating from *c.* 1825. Two other pre-1838 lodges on the Arklow–Avoca road served as schoolhouses, one of which formed half of a pair of structures flanking one gate. The fourth gatekeeper's lodge, added after 1838 to an access from the south, has also been demolished.

Mason 1814–19; *BPB* (1929); McParland *et al.* 1989.

181. SIDNEY LODGE, Bray; pre-1838; *demolished.*

A suburban property doubtless named by its mid-nineteenth-century owner Sidney Herbert (1810–61), eminent politician and statesman, secretary of state for war, third son of the 11th earl of Pembroke, who was created 1st Lord Herbert of Lea in the year of his death.

BPB (1929).

182. SLANEY PARK, Baltinglass (2).

South gate; pre-1838/1885; *demolished.*

An early lodge that may have been contemporary with the Georgian house of the Grogan family was replaced by a short-lived successor, which itself was 'down' according to the 1931 valuation.

North gate; 1885.

A perfectly symmetrical late Victorian standard 1½-storey Tudor Picturesque-style cottage. Built in random quarry-faced stone with label mouldings to its bipartite and tripartite one-over-one sash windows. Carved foiled bargeboards decorate the main gables and those of both dormer windows. To the front door is a lean-to canopy supported on wooden posts. Occupied and well tended. Built by William Edward Grogan (1863–1937).

Leet 1814; Slater 1856; 1870; *LGI* (1958); Bence-Jones 1988.

183. SPRING FARM, Kilcoole; pre-1838; *demolished.*

An estate whose occupant in 1814 was Revd Brownrigg and in 1837 Richard Hudson.

Leet 1814; Lewis 1837.

184. SPRING FARM, Redcross; *c.* 1840.

A tiny basic roughcast gabled single-roomed one-bay cottage with an eaves band, doorway to the front elevation and a minuscule window to the road. Derelict. The proprietors in the mid-nineteenth century were the Wright family.

Griffith 1848–60.

185. SPRINGFIELD, Bray; pre-1838; *demolished.*

A property in 1814 of J. Odell and by 1837 of Alderman West, which by 1846 had been renamed 'Westmoreland' by the Hore family.

Leet 1814; Lewis 1837; Slater 1846.

186. STRATFORD COTTON WORKS, Stratford-on-Slaney; pre-1838; *demolished.*

The extensive cotton and calico-printing works in 1837 of Messrs Orr and Co., established in 1792, which employed up to 1,000 persons, who were housed in the purpose-built squares and streets created by the earl of Aldborough but which by 1845 were already experiencing hard times. The lodge has a bungalow on its site.

Lewis 1837; *Parliamentary Gazetteer.*

187. STRATFORD LODGE, Stratford-on-Slaney; pre-1838; *demolished.*

In 1837 Samuel Lewis records that 'At Stratford Lodge are two schools, one an infants' school, and both supported by Lady Elizabeth Stratford'. Stratford Lodge is one of the earls of Aldborough's three lost Irish mansions. The infants' school, as the 1838 OS map states, shared the function of gate lodge at its entrance gates. Lady Elizabeth Stratford, who died in 1837, was an unmarried sister of the 2nd, 3rd and 4th earls of Aldborough.

Lewis 1837; *BPB* (1861).

STRUAN HILL (see MOUNT PLEASANT)

188. SUMMER HILL, Enniskerry; *c.* 1820.

Originally a single-storey gabled cottage, much modernised and extended, with a hip-roofed projection to the avenue and perforated canted terracotta cresting. A late Georgian seat in the early nineteenth century of the Flood family.

Lewis 1837.

189. SWEET BANK, Newcastle; *c.* 1890; *demolished.*

A lodge built on a 122-acre holding for Alexander Parker Keene.

Griffith 1848–60.

190. TALBOTSTOWN, Brittas; *c.* 1830.

In 1912 a visitor described going 'through a gateway beside an unoccupied gate lodge, into an avenue of yews leading up to Talbotstown House ... an old country residence, with extensive gardens and orchards, now in a somewhat neglected condition'. Since then the once-quintessential little three-bay Regency lodge still lies abandoned but has suffered much abuse in the interim, with extension and half-hearted modernisation. Originally single-storey with an oversailing hipped roof carried on paired wooden eaves brackets over harled walls, in which the fenestration has been rearranged for the worse. A seat in the first half of the nineteenth century of the Paramour family.

Joyce 1912.

191. TEMPLECARRIG, Greystones; *c.* 1910; architects probably O'Callaghan and Webb.

A single-storey Edwardian lodge, the leading gable of which is so akin to that at St Helen's (*q.v.*) for it to be attributable to the architectural practice of O'Callaghan and Webb. The steeply pitched half-timbered Elizabethan Revival apex projects over a tiny canted bay window and is supported on a pair of flanking carved wooden brackets which are repeated to carry the gabled front-door canopy at the centre of the symmetrical three-bay avenue elevation. In modernisation it has unfortunately lost its chimney-stack, been smooth-rendered and gained a back return. From about 1850 an estate of the Hudson family. First record of the lodge in the valuation books is in 1912, by which time Lt.-Col. James Reid had acquired Templecarrig.

192. TEMPLELYON, Redcross; *c.* 1875; *demolished.*

A gatekeeper's lodge built probably by William Law Bestall or his widow Catherine, who lived on here after around 1873.

Slater 1870.

193. TIGRONEY, Avoca (2).

In 1825 Brewer found 'Cherrymount, a villa inferior in magnitude to many seats on the borders of the Ovoca, but surpassed by few in charms of situation'. What he did not find were the gate lodges, which were added a few years later by John Dudley Oliver (1809–

70), who succeeded to the place on his father's death in 1832 and saw fit to alter the previous pretty name of the place.

South lodge (*above*); *c*. 1840.
The builder cleverly took advantage of the site contours to create a single-storey standard three-bay lodge over a part-basement at one end for it to be in part effectively two-storey. Constructed in crude squared coursed granite with bipartite cast-iron latticed casement windows below a hipped roof. Occupied.

North lodge; *c*. 1845.
Standard single-storey in rough coursed cut stone, plainer than the above, with clipped gables. Surrounded by a hodgepodge of appendages with a variety of roofs. In use.

LGI (1904).

194. TINAKILLY, Rathnew (2).
A seat in the late eighteenth century of the Radcliffe family, from whom it passed to Joseph Leigh through his marriage in 1797 to a Radcliffe daughter. He was here until *c*. 1830 and was probably responsible for the pre-1838 gate lodge. Thereafter the place was home to Revd John Dickson for about 30 years before a new house was erected for Commander Robert Charles Halpin RN (1836–94), captain of the steamship *Great Eastern*. Designed in 1875 by James Franklin Fuller, who was not noted for his delicate touch, it was not completed until 1883. Thus the two surviving lodges could be by him.

North lodge; pre-1838/*c*. 1880; architect probably J.F. Fuller.
A replacement for an earlier lodge on the site is this bulky 1½-storey steeply gabled structure, its roof decorated with a red-brick chimney-stack in a crested ridge, bands of canted slates and perforated foil and wave bargeboards. Gothic-style pointed windows are dressed in toothed brickwork. Derelict and overgrown.

South lodge(*below*); *c*. 1880; architect probably J.F. Fuller.
A generously proportioned 1½-storey standard structure in smooth rendered finish, most windows being one-over-one sashes below segmental heads. The roof displays perforated scalloped bargeboards and, paradoxically, rather too delicate spiky hip-knobs. Banded chimney-stack to a synthetic-slated roof; the central single-storey gabled hall projection fits below the high main eaves. Occupied.

Taylor and Skinner 1778; 1969 [1783]; Leet 1814; Lewis 1837; Slater 1856; *LGI* (1904); Bence-Jones 1988; hotel information brochure.

195. TINNAPARK, Newtown Mount Kennedy; pre-1838/*c*. 1862.
A ruin marks the site of the old gate lodge to a seat in 1783 of Sir Skeffington Edward Smyth, from whom it seems to have passed by marriage to James Daly MP of the Dalystown, Co. Galway, family. Myles Staunton was resident here in 1837. By 1862 William Clarke had taken the place and was building a new house, apparently also extending or replacing the gate lodge.

Taylor and Skinner 1778; 1969 [1783]; Leet 1814; Lewis 1837; *LGI* (1904).

196. TINNEHINCH, Enniskerry (2).
An estate noted for its connections with the Rt Hon. Henry Grattan MP, for whom a grateful Irish parliament fitted up an old inn, a place of his 'frequent resort', to be his permanent residence. Both lodges added by his descendants after 1838, one in 1886 for Lady Lavoa Grattan, have been demolished, as has the house.

Lewis 1837.

197. TINODE, Brittas; 1872; architect probably George C. Ashlin.
William Logan was the first of his family to come to live here in 1764 in what was then 'Horseshoe House', but it was exactly a century later that his grand-nephew William Henry Ford Cogan (1823–94) realised a brand-new house on the site. The estate had devolved upon him on the death of his uncle in 1851, and his wedding seven years later prompted the engagement of architect W.F. Caldbeck to design the house, its out-offices and stables. By 1870 he had embarked on a

197. Tinode.

further phase of development with the building of a farm steading to designs of George C. Ashlin, Caldbeck apparently having given up practising the year before. Ashlin's brief seems also to have included the provision of a gate lodge, which survives as a smart little 1½-storey building, perfectly symmetrical three-bay but with Ruskinian Gothic detailing in its segmental-pointed arches to paired one-over-one sash windows and to the fanlit doorway in its central frontisipece. It, like the main gables, has skew-tables and deep moulded kneelers and is topped by a delicate iron finial. Built in coursed granite facings; the front door is emphasised by contrasting coloured masonry, while to the leading gable is a small, quasi-Gothic lunette attic window. The eaves are highlighted by decorative sculpted gutter brackets, and the ridge is broken by a central ashlar chimney-stack with plinth and moulded cappings. Occupied and immaculately maintained. Somewhat distant is its contemporary gatescreen, with chamfered ashlar carriage pillars and innovative ornate gates with a hint of chinoiserie and floral bosses.

DB (1 Sept. 1859); *IB* (1 Feb. 1864 and 15 May 1870); Wikipedia.

198. TITHEWER or TITTOUR, Newtown Mount Kennedy; pre-1838; *demolished.*
George Barker Nutall (1738–1806) was the first of that family to live here, and either he or his son, John Christopher Nutall (1774–1849), built the porter's lodge, which had been removed by 1911.

LGI (1904).

199. TOBER, Dunlavin; pre-1838; *demolished.*
An estate of the Powell Leslie family of Glaslough, Co. Monaghan, which was let out over the years. The big house has gone the way of its lodge.

Bence-Jones 1988.

200. TOMDARRAGH, Roundwood; pre-1838; *demolished.*
Samuel Edge is recorded as proprietor in 1814.

Leet 1814.

201. TOOMAN, Kilpedder; pre-1838; *demolished.*
A seat in 1837 of Lawrence Graydon, whose gatekeeper's lodge had gone by 1911.

Lewis 1837.

202. TRUDDER, Newtown Mount Kennedy (2).
A property in the first half of the nineteenth century of the Henry family, both the lodges of which have been demolished, that on the western avenue having been built before 1838, the other from the east added as late as 1905 for Revd John Maher.

203. TRUDDER LODGE, Newtown Mount Kennedy; *c.* 1865; architect not known.
In contrast to the restrained Classical villa and its outbuildings of 1840 is the later Tudor Picturesque-style cottage with exaggerated steeply pitched roofs covered in fish-scale slate finish and set off with delicate cresting and elegant perforated undulating bargeboards. Built off an L-plan in 'crazy-paved' granite facings, a single-storey glazed canted bay window with leaded casements projects from each leading front, and a delightful lean-to verandah fills the internal angle as an entrance porch carried on rustic posts. Very decorative and appreciated by its owners. Probably built for John Joshua Nunn,

who had acquired the property *c.* 1860 from Revd Crompton Henry Keogh.

Slater 1870.

204. TULFARRIS, Ballymore Eustace (2).
While the big house of the Hornidge family survives as a hotel, no lodges remain.

South gate; pre-1838; *demolished.*

North gate; pre-1838/*c.* 1900; *demolished.*

Dept. of Arts, Heritage, Regional, Rural and Gaeltacht Affairs

Both the earlier porter's cottage and its replacement have gone, the latter having succumbed to the rising waters of the Blessington lakes created by the Poulaphouca dam, built in 1944. This short-lived structure was a single-storey standard gabled affair, rendered, with brick dressings to windows and its round-headed fanlit door. To the leading gable was a bipartite window. Built by Richard Joseph Hornidge (1863–1911).

LGI (1912).

205. TYNTE PARK, Dunlavin (2).
Lewis in 1837 wrote: 'A splendid mansion and out-offices have been lately built at a very great expense by Lady Tynte, on part of the estate called Loughmogue, now Tynte Park; and her grandson and heir, Mr Tynte, who resides with her, has considerably improved the grounds by planting and fencing'. These were Hannah, widow of Sir James Stratford Tynte, presumably the builder of the Regency villa, and Joseph Pratt Tynte (1815–96), who had assumed that surname in 1836. He was to vigorously continue the embellishment of the property, including the addition of two porters' lodges, during his long occupancy.

South gate; *c.* 1840.
Opposite its entrance is a single-storey three-bay cottage below a shallow-hipped roof with a banded cut-granite chimney-stack. Built

with exposed rubble walls containing latticed casement windows, it has been much 'improved', having a modern conservatory built across its front.

North gate (*above*); *c.* 1845.

Also opposite the gates is this tidy exercise in duality, its spaciousness explained by its main role as a school. Single-storey and built in a fabric of ragstone with brick dressings and pilasters, exposed and pleasing but probably originally stuccoed or harled. It takes the form of a couple of single-bay gables as open pediments, with paired verge brackets or mutules which carry across recessed central eaves above the round-headed fanlit doorway; fundamental drip-shelves over windows, which would have been small-paned sliding sashes.

Lewis 1837; *LGI* (1904); Bence-Jones 1988.

206. UPLANDS, Greystones; *c.* 1855.

A standard stuccoed steeply gabled 1½-storey lodge with a tiny gabled porch projection flanked by two-over-two sash windows. Occupied and in 2000 being extended. A property previously called 'Kindlestown Upper' but now 'Delgany House', which in 1854 was owned by James Evans.

Griffith 1848–60.

VALLOMBROSA (see COUNTY DUBLIN, SOUTH)

207. VARTRY LODGE, Roundwood; *c.* 1890.

A standard single-storey lodge with a shallow-hipped roof having moulded brick eaves corbels, tucked below which is a small hall projection similarly hip-roofed. Probably later extended by a bay to the left-had side; the chimney-stack rises off the rear wall. Occupied. The house itself, in contrast, is a commodious and attractive High Victorian Ruskinian Gothic villa of about 1865, when the adjacent reservoir was close to completion for the Corporation of Dublin, and may have been intended as rather grand accommodation for the superintendent of the works.

VEVAY (see OLD COURT)

208. VICTORIA COTTAGE, Avoca; *c.* 1800.

A charming Georgian Gothic lodge. Originally single-storey standard below a hipped roof finished in small early slates, its openings with pointed arches in a harled finish. In 1814 it served 'Ovoca Cottage' of Major Arthur Miller, which was subsequently removed and replaced by 'Victoria Cottage' on a different site. Latterly the lodge has been considerably extended, by a bay to the left-hand side and a forward projecting wing to the other, with sympathetic fenestration.

Leet 1814.

209. VIOLET HILL, Bray (2)

A pretty Picturesque Gothic Revival house designed for Edward Lysaght Griffin in 1868 by the Limerick architect William Fogerty, who also provided plans for an appropriate introductory lodge.

North lodge; *c.* 1869; architect William Fogerty.

Single-storey on an L-plan in the same style as the house, repeating many of its features in the pretty canted oriel window on the leading gable below fancy fretted cusped bargeboards, spiky hip-knob and brick chimney-stacks to match. Finished in white roughcast. The main roof projects over the internal angle to form a verandah porch, its eaves carried on carved wooden posts and segmental pointed arches. The sheeted front door in the recess is similarly arched, with a pair of flanking narrow windows. Occupied.

South lodge; *c.* 1860.

What appears to be an earlier lodge, probably built in the time of the Williamson family, is single-storey on a T-plan, with roof part-hipped and part-gabled with trefoil-perforated bargeboards.

IB (1 April 1868).

210. WESTASTON, Rathdrum (2).

The setting for one of the most tragic of Ireland's architectural sights: the ruins of Thomas Acton's beautiful Queen Anne-style house of 1697, otherwise known as 'Kilmacurragh'. An early pre-1838 lodge has gone, but marking the other entrance is a sturdy two-storey standard gatehouse below a gabled roof with carved modillion eaves brackets, constructed in pleasant rubble facings, its openings emphasised by brick toothed dressings and soldier arches. All of about 1855, with modern small-paned casement windows. Probably built by a later Thomas Acton (1826–1908), who inherited the place on the death of his father in 1854.

LGI (1912); Bence-Jones 1988.

WESTMORELAND (see SPRINGFIELD)

211. WHALEY ABBEY COTTAGE AND HOUSE, Ballinaclash (4).

The main seat of the Whaley family, to whom the famous Georgian character Thomas 'Buck' Whaley belonged. They built their mansion on the site of a ruined medieval monastery, but by 1838 it had been forsaken by Richard William Whaley for the Regency cottage nearby called 'Abbeyview'. He was still in residence in 1876 and thus must have been responsible for the two gate lodges to the property, which he may have had in mind at entrances to a new house that was never realised.

West entrance; pre-1910; *demolished.*

A lodge built after 1838.

East entrance; *c.* 1860.

A 1½-storey gabled Picturesque lodge built in pleasant coarse rubble with brick dressings. The perforated and foiled decorative bargeboards are as those on the nearby Castle Howard lodge (*q.v.*), complete with the unusual carved rafter toes. Shallow-pitched gabled hall projection in brick construction. Occupied.

Two further lodges were built, perhaps in the final years of the nineteenth century, when William F. Littledale was in residence.

North entrance; pre-1910.

A lodge built after 1838 lies in ruins.

South entrance; pre-1910; *demolished.*

A property now known as 'Grove Park'.

Fraser 1838; *Parliamentary Gazetteer.*

212. WHITEHALL, Baltinglass; pre-1838; *demolished.*

A property which between 1824 and 1837 passed from James Palmer to William Butler, but the original house was in ruins by 1885 and its lodge gone, its attendant bleach mill by 1854 no longer considered for valuation.

Pigot 1824; Lewis 1837.

213. WICKLOW RESERVOIR, Wicklow; *c.* 1881.

A tiny standard single-storey lodge with a steeply hipped roof, dominated by a gabled hall projection, with flanking segmentally arched windows. Cement-rendered in stucco effect and reroofed with concrete interlocking roof tiles in a half-hearted modernisation, despite which it lies derelict and abandoned. In 1881 the town commissioners constructed waterworks to provide an abundant and pure water supply for the town of Wicklow.

Hannigan and Nolan 1994.

214. WINGFIELD, Enniskerry (2).

Named after the family of the Viscounts Powerscourt as their dower house, but surplus to that requirement for much of the nineteenth century. In the early part of that century it was home to the Quinn family, and until 1870 it was occupied by Henry Darley. The two lodges have gone, that to the north having pre-dated 1838.

215. WOODMOUNT, Arklow; *c.* 1840.

A dinky single-storey standard lodge below an oversailing hipped roof with a scalloped fascia board. Much modernised with synthetic slates, rendering and lead-effect glazing. A late Georgian gentleman farmer's house, recorded as home to Peter Murray in 1816 and 30 years later occupied by Michael Hudson.

Mason 1814–19; Slater 1846.

216. WOODSTOCK, Kilcoole (3).

A grand house, further aggrandised after 1827, when it was purchased from the Knox family by Revd Lord Robert Ponsonby Tottenham (1773–1850), bishop of Clogher, who added an Ionic porch and wings with pavilions. He further embellished the estate with the addition of three gatekeepers' lodges. In his role as bishop of Clogher from 1822 to 1850, Robert Tottenham had employed David Henry in the completion of his new palace, so there is little doubt that when the name of the architect-cum-builder crops up again, coupled with Mullins and MacMahon, as working at a Woodstock House that this was the bishop's new country seat.

Main entrance; *c.* 1830; architects probably Henry, Mullins and MacMahon.

Quite a polished little single-storey Regency design, having a not-quite-symmetrical three-bay elevation to the avenue, comprised of a gabled hall projection with double-leafed door and side windows, flanked by a single casement to one side and a bipartite one to the other, all below faintly segmental heads in stuccoed walls. The margined glazing pattern is repeated, with a hint of Y-tracery, in the semi-octagonal canted bay with corresponding roof to the road front, which extends below a main gable, like the hall, in the form of an open pediment. Paired soffit brackets continue around the eaves of the hipped end to the park. Behind the ridge rises a chimney-stack diagonally set in conflicting Tudor style.

East entrance; *c.* 1830; architects probably Henry, Mullins and MacMahon.

A typically hybrid design of the period is this perfectly delightful little single-storey building in a smooth whitewashed rendered finish, with newfangled Tudor-style details applied to a symmetrical Classical front. Originally built off an L-plan, a hall breakfront with open pediment projects from the hip-roofed main body of the lodge with its bold soffit brackets to the tall eaves. The breakfront contains a relieving rectangular recess over the front door, where a date-stone should be, whilst flanking are two minuscule windows with prominent label mouldings and latticed lights. Off the rear wall rises a pair of diagonally set squat chimney-stacks on a rectangular base. Much extended, occupied and lovingly tended.

West entrance; *c.* 1845.

A two-storey three-bay hip-roofed gatehouse with, below a blind 'window', a single-storey gabled hall projection with a round-headed doorway.

The mansion and demesne are now home to Druid's Glen Golf Club.

LGI (1904); Bence-Jones 1988; IAA.

216. Woodstock, main entrance.

GLOSSARY

A GOTHIC *COTTAGE ORNÉ* LODGE

1. Pent
2. Cluster-column
3. Pinnacle
4. Crockets
5. Finial
6. Eyebrow eaves
7. Diocletian window
8. Lancet head
9. Y-tracery
10. Harling
11. Hexagonal
12. Ogee arch
13. Arrowloop or loophole (mock)
14. Trefoil window
15. Half-hipped gable
16. Broach
17. Diagonally set chimney-stack

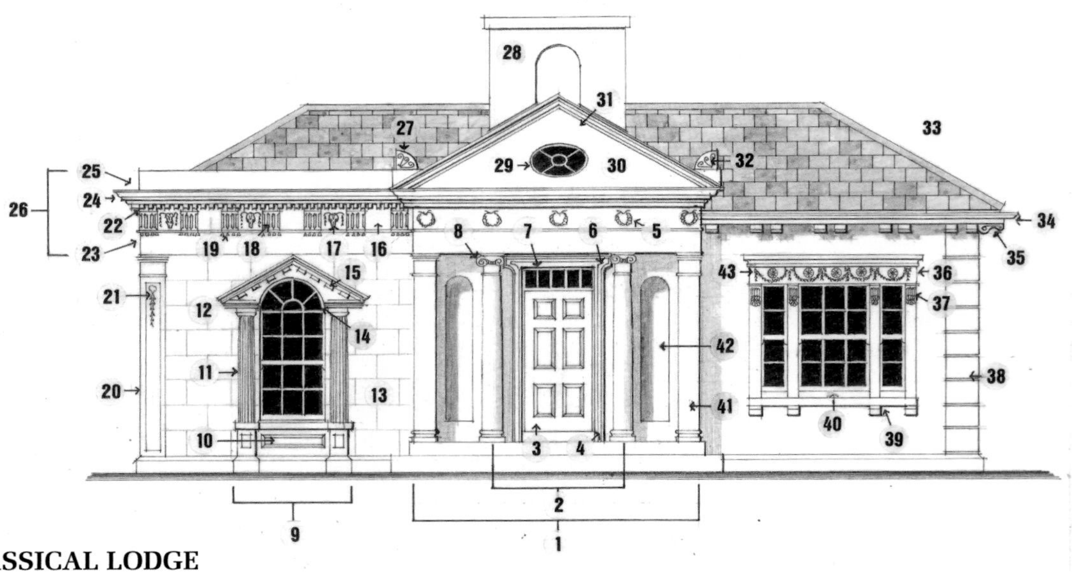

A NEO-CLASSICAL LODGE

1. Portico
2. Columns *in antis*
3. Panelled door
4. Architrave surround
5. Laurel wreath or garland
6. Lugged head
7. 'Mouth-organ' fanlight
8. Ionic capital
9. Aedicule
10. Under-panel
11. Doric column (fluted)
12. Open pediment
13. Ashlar (masonry) or stucco (applied)
14. Spoked head
15. Mutules
16. Metope
17. Bucrania (oxhead) or aegricane (ram's head)
18. Triglyph
19. Guttae
20. Pilaster
21. Margent
22. Dentil course
23. Frieze
24. Cornice
25. Blocking course
26. Entablature
27. Acroterion
28. 'Vanburgh' or bridged chimney-stack
29. *Oeil-de-boeuf* or ox-eye opening
30. Tympanum
31. Pediment
32. Anthemion motif
33. Hipped roof
34. Eaves
35. Modillion bracket
36. Flat entablature
37. Crossette
38. 'Irish pilaster' (quoins)
39. Bracketed sill
40. 'Wyatt' or tripartite window
41. Antae
42. Niche
43. Patera and festoon (or swag) ornament

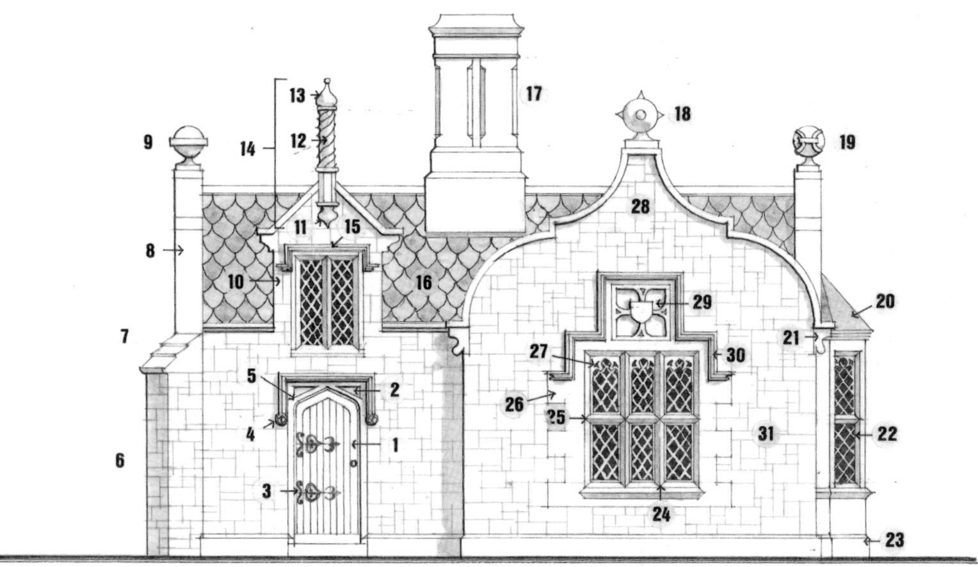

A 'TUDORBETHAN' LODGE

1. Sheeted door
2. Spandrel
3. Strap hinges
4. Dripstone
5. Tudor arch
6. Buttress
7. Weathering
8. Skew-table
9. Rusticated ball finial
10. Gablet
11. Pendant
12. 'Barley-twist' shaft
13. Finial
14. Hip-knob
15. Label moulding
16. Fish-scale slates
17. Coupled chimney-stack
18. 'Morgenstern' ball finial
19. Strapped ball finial
20. Half-umbrello roof
21. Kneeler
22. Latticed glazing
23. Plinth
24. Mullion
25. Transom
26. Dressing
27. Cuspidated head
28. Shaped or curvilinear gable
29. Foiled quarter with blank shield
30. Stepped label moulding
31. Squared, uncoursed masonry

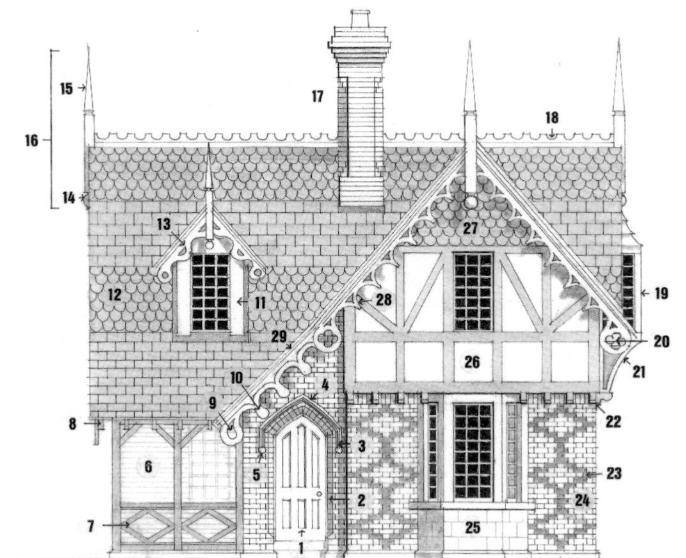

A PICTURESQUE ENGLISH COTTAGE LODGE

1. Panelled door
2. Chamfer
3. Hood moulding
4. Segmentally pointed arch
5. Dripstone
6. Verandah
7. Lozenge-pattern balustrade
8. Exposed rafter ends
9. Mouchette motif
10. Lobed bargeboard
11. Dormer window
12. Scalloped slates
13. Waved bargeboard
14. Pendant
15. Finial
16. Hip-knob
17. Modelled chimney-stack
18. Cresting (serrated)
19. Oriel window
20. Quatrefoil motif
21. Corbel
22. Jettying
23. Diaper work
24. Flemish bond brickwork
25. Canted bay window
26. Black-and-white work or half-timbering
27. Tile-hanging
28. Foiled bargeboard
29. Catslide roof

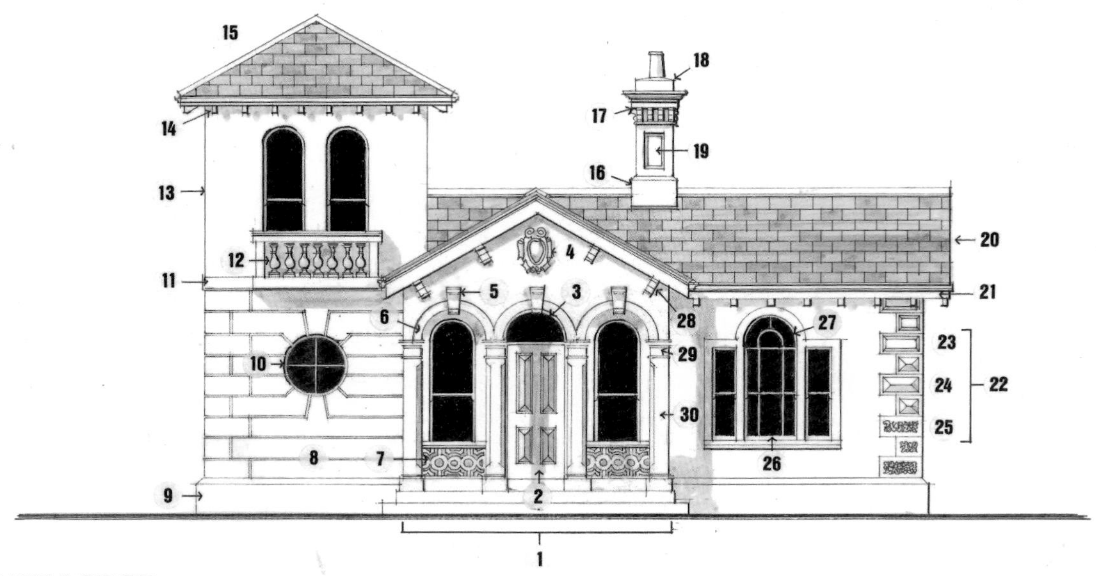

AN ITALIANATE LODGE

1. *Porte-cochère*
2. Raised and fielded panelled door
3. Fanlight
4. Cartouche
5. A cone (scrolled keystone)
6. Archivolt
7. Balustrade (fretted)
8. Channelled rustication
9. Plinth
10. Oculus
11. String-course
12. Balconette (balustrade)
13. Belvedere tower
14. Exposed rafter ends
15. Pyramidal roof
16. Plinth
17. Bracketed cornice
18. Blocked capping
19. Recessed panel
20. Gabled roof
21. Fascia
22. Quoins
23. Raised
24. Diamond-pointed
25. Vermiculated or reticulated
26. Venetian window
27. Margined glazing
28. Purlin ends
29. Impost
30. Pier

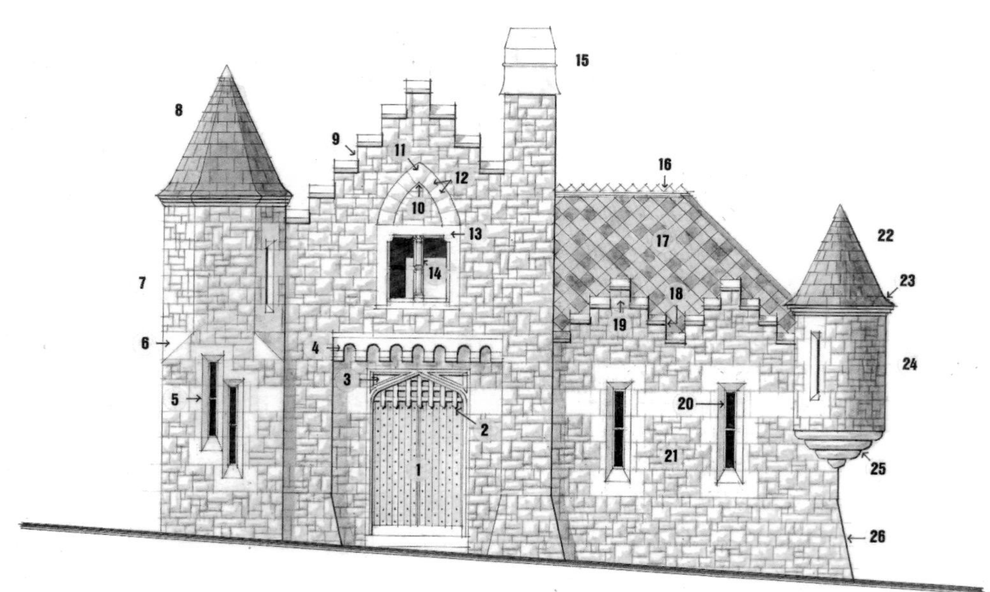

A CASTELLATED SCOTS BARONIAL LODGE

1. Studded doors
2. 'Portcullis'
3. Spandrel
4. 'Machicolation'
5. Batement window
6. Broach
7. Turret
8. Octahedral roof
9. Crow-stepped gable
10. Relieving arch
11. Keystone
12. Voussoirs
13. Shouldered arch
14. Colonette (banded)
15. Chimney capping
16. Cresting (sawtooth)
17. Lattice-pattern slating
18. Allure or ramparts
19. Crenellations (Irish)
20. Chamfered slit opening
21. Squared course masonry (quarry-faced)
22. Conical roof
23. Bellcast
24. Bartizan
25. Corbel
26. Batter

BIBLIOGRAPHY

Abbreviations

BPB = Burke's *Peerage and baronetage* (various editions; London, 1861, 1873, 1903, 1906, 1917, 1923, 1929, 1949, 1970).

DB = *Dublin Builder* (various articles, 1850–66).

IAA = Irish Architectural Archive, drawing and photograph collections.

IADS = *Irish Arts and Decorative Studies: Journal of the Irish Georgian Society* (various articles, 1998–2011).

IAR = *Irish Arts Review* (1984–2011).

IB = *Irish Builder* (various articles, 1867–1979).

IFR = Burke's *Irish family records* (London, 1976).

IGS = *Irish Georgian Society Bulletins* (1958–97).

JASCK = *Journal of the County Kildare Archaeological Society* (various articles, 1891–9).

JCLAHS = *Journal of the County Louth Archaeological and Historical Society* (1993).

LG = Burke's *The landed gentry of Great Britain* (various editions; London, 1849, 1863, 1871, 1875, 1882, 1886, 1912, 1958, 1972).

LGI = Burke's *The landed gentry of Ireland* (various editions; London, 1886, 1904, 1912, 1958).

NAIOPW = National Archives of Ireland, Office of Public Works Deposit.

NIAH = National Inventory of Architectural Heritage (available at http://www.buildingsofireland.ie/).

NLI = National Library of Ireland, Drawings Collection.

RIBA = Royal Institute of British Architects.

A

Adam, R. 1990 *Classical architecture: a complete handbook.* Viking, London.

Adam, R. and Adam, J. 1778 *Works in architecture of Robert and James Adam*, Vol. I. London.

An Old Inhabitant 1907 *A hundred years of Bray and its neighbourhood: from 1770 to 1870.* Hodges and Figgis, Dublin.

Archer, J. 1801 *A statistical survey of County Dublin.* The Dublin Society, Dublin.

Atkinson, A. 1815 *The Irish tourist: in a series of picturesque views.* Courtney, Dublin.

Atterbury, P. (ed.) 1995 *A.W.N. Pugin: master of Gothic Revival.* Yale University Press, New Haven and London.

B

Ball, F.E. 1995 [1902–20] *A history of the County Dublin* (6 vols) (reprint). Criterion Press, Dublin.

Ball, F.E. and Hamilton, E. 1895 *The parish of Taney: a history of Dundrum.* Hodges and Figgis, Dublin.

Barrow, J. 1836 *A tour around Ireland in the Autumn of 1835.* J. Murray, London.

Bassett, G.H. 1884 *Kilkenny city and county guide and directory.* Sealy, Bryers and Walker, Dublin.

Bassett, G.H. 1885 *Wexford county guide and directory.* Sealy, Bryers and Walker, Dublin.

Bassett, G.H. 1886 *Louth county guide and directory.* Sealy, Bryers and Walker, Dublin.

Beaufort, Revd D.A. 1764–1808 Unpublished travel journals. Trinity College Dublin Library.

Beaufort, L. 1781–1820 Unpublished travel journals. Trinity College Dublin Library.

Beckett, S. 1958 *Malone dies.* Calder and Boyars, London.

Bence-Jones, M. 1987 *The twilight of the Ascendancy.* Constable, London.

Bence-Jones, M. 1988 *A guide to Irish country houses.* Constable, London.

Bernelle, A. (ed.) 1992 *Decantations: a tribute in honour of Maurice Craig.* The Lilliput Press, Dublin.

Birch, J. 1879 *Picturesque lodges.* W. Blackwood and Sons, Edinburgh and London.

Blau, E. 1982 *Ruskinian Gothic: the architecture of Deane and Woodward (1845–1861).* Princeton University Press, Princeton NJ.

Brewer, J.N. 1825 *The beauties of Ireland.* Sherwood, Jones and Co., London.

Bunbury, T. and Kavanagh, A. 2004 *The landed gentry and aristocracy of Kildare.* Irish Family Names, Dublin.

Burke, B. 1844; 1883 *Dormant and extinct peerages* (various editions). London.

Burke, H. 1993 *The Royal Hospital, Donnybrook: a heritage of caring (1743–1993).* The Royal Hospital, Donnybrook, Dublin.

Burke, J.B. 1854–5 *A visitation of the seats and arms of the noblemen and gentlemen of Great Britain and Ireland* (2 vols). Hurst and Blackett, London.

Buvinda 1999 *Drogheda: a walk in the past.* Buvinda Historical Publications, Drogheda.

C

Carr, J. 1806 *The stranger in Ireland in 1805.* Richard Phillips, London.

Casey, C. 2005 *The buildings of Ireland—Dublin.* Yale University Press, New Haven and London.

Casey, C. and Rowan, A. 1993 *The buildings of Ireland—north Leinster.* Penguin Books, London.

Casey, S. 2002 *Dundalk in old photographs.* Gill and Macmillan, Dublin.

Chaloner, D. 1985. John Chaloner. *The Irish ancestor* 17 (2), 59–63.

Chambers, Sir W. 1862 *Treatise on civil architecture* (revised by W.H. Leeds). The Building News, London.

Cobbe, A. and Friedman, T. 2005 *James Gibbs in Ireland: Newbridge, his villa for Charles Cobbe, archbishop of Dublin.* The Cobbe Foundation and the Irish Georgian Society, Surrey.

Colfer, B. 2004 *The Hook Peninsula.* Cork University Press, Cork.

Colgan, J. 2005 *Leixlip, County Kildare.* Tyrconnell Press, Leixlip.

Colvin, C. (ed.) 1971 *Maria Edgeworth: letters from Ireland 1813–1844.* Clarendon Press, Oxford.

Colvin, N. 1995 *A biographical dictionary of British architects 1600–1840.* Yale University Press, New Haven and London.

Colvin, Sir H. 2008 *A biographical dictionary of British architects 1600–1840.* Yale University Press, New Haven and London.

Colvin, H.M. and Harris, J. (eds) 1970 *The country seat: studies in the history of the British country house.* Allen Lane, London.

Coote, Sir C. 1801 *A statistical survey of King's County.* The Dublin Society, Dublin.

Coote, Sir C. 1802 *A statistical survey of Queen's County.* The Dublin Society, Dublin.

Corballis, C. 1996 *In the Shadow of the Steeple* **5**. Journal of the Tullaherin Heritage Society, Kilkenny.

Corish, P.J. 1995 *Maynooth College 1795–1995.* Gill and Macmillan, Dublin.

Costello, C. 1996 *A most delightful station: the British Army on the Curragh of Kildare, Ireland, 1855–1922.* The Collins Press, Cork.

Costello, P. 1989 *Dublin churches.* Gill and Macmillan, Dublin.

Costello, S., O'Dwyer, M. and White, K. 1995 *Kilkenny city and county: a photographic record.* College Books, Kilkenny.

Craig, M. 1976 *Classic Irish houses of the middle size.* The Architectural Press, London.

Craig, M. 1980 *Dublin 1660–1860.* Allen Figgis, Dublin.

Craig, M. 1982 *The architecture of Ireland: from the earliest times to 1880.* Batsford, London.

Craig, M. 1984 The account book of William Caldbeck, architect. *Architectural History* **27**, 421–8.

Craig, M. and Fewer, M. 2002 *The new neighbourhood of Dublin.* A. and A. Farmer, Dublin.

Craig, M. and Glin, The Knight of. 1970 *Ireland observed*. Mercier Press, Cork.

Crofton, D.H. 1980 *The children of Edmonstown Park: memoirs of an Irish family*. Volturna, Peterhead.

Crookshank, A. and Glin, The Knight of. 1994 *The watercolours of Ireland*. Barrie and Jenkins, London.

Culleton, E. (ed.) 1994 *Treasures of the landscape: County Wexford's rural heritage*. Wexford Organisation for Rural Development, Wexford.

Curl, J.S. 1993 *Encyclopaedia of architectural terms*. Donhead, London.

Curren, L. and Pegley, S. 2001 *Aspects of Leixlip: four historical essays*. LPSV Publishers, Dublin.

Curwen, J.C. 1818 *Observations on the state of Ireland* (2 vols). Baldwin, Cradock and Joy, London.

D

d'Alton, J. 1844 *The history of Drogheda* (2 vols). J. d'Alton, Dublin.

d'Alton, J. 1976 [1838] *The history of Dublin* (reprint). Tower Books, Cork.

Davis, T. 1960 *The architecture of John Nash*. Studio Books, London.

de Breffny, B. 1977 *Castles of Ireland*. Thames and Hudson, London.

de Breffny, B. and ffolliott, R. 1975 *The houses of Ireland*. Thames and Hudson, London.

Dean, J.A.K. 1994 *The gate lodges of Ulster: a gazetteer*. Ulster Architectural Heritage Society, Belfast.

Dearn, T.D.W. 1811 *Designs for lodges and entrances*. J. Taylor, London.

Debrett's *Peerage and titles of courtesy* (various editions) (Dean and Son, London, 1911, 1920).

Devine, J. 2003 *The house of Corkagh*. South Dublin Libraries, Dublin.

Doyle, M. 1868 *Notes and gleanings relating to the county of Wexford: its past and present conditions*. Dublin.

Dublin Almanac and General Register of Ireland (1841, 1843). Pettigrew and Oulton, Dublin.

Dublin City Council 2006 *The Georgian squares of Dublin: an architectural history*. Dublin City Council, Dublin.

Duffy, H. 1999 *James Gandon and his times*. Gandon Editions, Kinsale.

E

Elsam, R. 1803 *An essay on rural architecture*. E. Lawrence, London.

English, N.W. 1973 Some country houses near Athlone. *The Irish Ancestor* **5** (1), 17–23.

English, N.W. 1974 Some lost country houses near Athlone. *The Irish Ancestor* **6** (2), 79–84.

F

Fairbairn, J. 1986 *Crests of the families of Great Britain and Ireland*. New Orchard Editions, London.

Ferguson, P. (ed.) 1998 *The A to Z of Georgian Dublin: John Rocque's maps of the city in 1756 and the county in 1760*. Harry Margary, Kent.

Fewer, M. 2001 *By swerve of shore: walking Dublin's coast*. Gill and Macmillan, Dublin.

ffolliott, R. 1958 *The Pooles of Mayfield*. Hodges Figgis, Dublin.

ffolliott, R. 1970 Entrance gates. *The Irish Ancestor* **2** (2), 128–30.

ffolliott, R. 1971a Some lesser known country houses in Munster and Leinster. *The Irish Ancestor* **3** (1), 49–50.

ffolliott, R. 1971b The charm of Irish gate lodges. *The Irish Ancestor* **3** (2), 102–4.

Fitzgerald, E. 2000 *Lord Kildare's Grand Tour (1766–1769)*. The Collins Press, Cork.

Fitzpatrick, M. 1987 *Historic Gorey: a pictorial view*. M. Fitzpatrick, Wexford.

Flanagan, B. 1991 *Stately homes around Stillorgan*. B. Flanagan, Dublin.

Flannery, J. 1990 *Christ Church, Delgany, 1789–1990: between the mountains and the sea: a parish history*. Select Vestry of Delgany Parish.

Fleming, Revd W.E.C. 2001 *Armagh clergy 1800–2000*. Dundalgan Press, Dundalk.

Fletcher, Sir B. 1961 *A history of architecture on the comparative method* (17th edn). The Athlone Press, London.

Flynn, M.P. [n.d.] History of the Flynn family and Skerries. Unpublished.

Foster, J. 1882 *Baronetage and knightage of the British Empire for 1882*. Nichols and Sons, London.

Fraser, J. 1838 *Guide through Ireland*. Wm Curry Jr and Co., Dublin.

Friel, P. 2000 *Frederick Trench (1746–1836) and Heywood, Queen's County*. Irish Academic Press, Dublin.

G

Gandy, J. 1805a *Designs for cottages, cottage farms, &c.* John Harding, London.

Gandy, J. 1805b *The rural architect*. John Harding, London.

Garden History (Journal of the Garden History Society) **28** (1) (Summer 2000).

Garner, W. 1986 *Drogheda: architectural heritage*. An Foras Forbartha, Dublin.

Garry, J. 1996 *The streets and lanes of Drogheda*. J. Garry, Drogheda.

General alphabetical index to the townlands and towns, parishes, and baronies of Ireland: based on the census of Ireland for the year 1851 (first published Dublin, 1861; Genealogical Publishing Co., Baltimore, 2000).

Gibbs, J. 1728 *A book of architecture*. London.

Girouard, M. 1979 *The Victorian country house*. Yale University Press, New Haven and London.

Glin, The Knight of, Griffin, D. and Robinson, N.K. 1988 *Vanishing country houses of Ireland*. Irish Architectural Archive and Irish Georgian Society, Dublin.

Goodwin, F. 1850 *Rural architecture* (2 vols). Henry G. Bohn, London.

Gorham, M. 1990 *Dublin yesterday*. Fitzhouse Books, London.

Griffin, D. and Pegum, C. 2000 *Leinster House (1744–2000)*. Irish Architectural Archive, Dublin.

Griffith, R. 1848–60 *The general valuation of rateable property in Ireland* (Leinster). The Valuation Office, Dublin.

Guide through Glasnevin Cemetery (M.H. Gill, Dublin, 1879).

Guinness, D. and Ryan, W. 1971 *Irish houses and castles*. Thames and Hudson, London.

Guilt, J. 1912. *An encyclopedia of architecture*. Longmans, Green and Co., London.

H

Hall, Mr and Mrs S.C. 1841–3 *Ireland, its scenery, character &c.* (3 vols). Jeremiah How and Parsons, London.

Hannigan, K. and Nolan, W. (eds) 1994 *Wicklow history and society: interdisciplinary essays on the history of an Irish county*. Geography Publications, Dublin.

Harris, J. and Snodin, M. 1997 *Sir William Chambers: architect to George III*. Yale University Press, New Haven and London.

Harrison, W. 1890 *Memorable Dublin houses: a handy guide*. W. Leckie and Co., Dublin.

Harvey, J. 1949 *Dublin: a study in environment*. Batsford, London.

Haughey, C.J. 1996 *Abbeville*. Town House, Dublin.

Healy, Revd J. 1895 *Maynooth College: its centenary history (1795–1895)*. Browne and Nolan, Dublin.

Healy, J. 1908 *History of the diocese of Meath*. Dublin.

Healy, P. 2004 *All roads lead to Tallaght*. South Dublin Libraries, Dublin.

Healy, P. 2005 *Rathfarnham roads*. South Dublin Libraries, Dublin.

Heaney, H. (ed.) 1999 *A Scottish Whig in Ireland 1835–38*. Four Courts Press, Dublin.

Hicks, D. 2012 *Irish country houses: a chronicle of change*. The Collins Press, Cork.

Hill's guide to Blackrock, with a description of the neighbourhood and excursions to the numerous objects of interest and attraction 1892 (facsimile edition) (Carraig Books, Dublin, 1976).

Hoare, R.C. 1807 *Journal of a tour in Ireland 1806*. W. Miller, London.

Hogg, W.E. 2000 *The millers and the mills of Ireland of about 1850*. W.E. Hogg, Dublin.

Horner, A. 2005 *Irish Historic Towns Atlas No. 7: Maynooth*. History Publications, Bray.

Horner, A. 2007 *Mapping Meath in the early 19th century*. Wordwell, Bray.

Howley, J. 1993 *The follies and garden buildings of Ireland*. Yale University Press, New Haven and London.

Humphreys, J.A.W. 1979 The phenomenon of the grand entrance: an analysis of the development of Irish entrance gateways between 1660 and 1921. Unpublished thesis, University of East Anglia.

Hunt, T.F. 1836 *Exemplars of Tudor architecture* (2nd edn). Longman, Rees, Orme, Brown, Green and Longman, London.

I

Inglis, H.D. 1835 *A journey throughout Ireland* (2 vols). Whittaker and Co., London.

Institute of Landscape Horticulture of Ireland Journal (1988). [Article on Phoenix Park.]

Irish Georgian Society 1969 *The Georgian Society records of eighteenth century domestic architecture and decoration in Dublin* (5 vols) (first published Dublin, 1909–13). Irish University Press, Shannon.

Irish Penny Journal (various articles, 1840–1).

The Irish tourist's illustrated handbook for visitors in Ireland (J. McGlashan, London, 1852).

J

Johnston, L. 1989 *Dublin—then and now*. Gill and Macmillan, Dublin.

Jones, B. 1974 *Follies and grottoes*. Constable, London.

Joyce, W. St J. 1912 *The neighbourhood of Dublin*. M.H. Gill and Sons, Dublin.

K

Kavanagh, A. 2006 *The landed gentry and aristocracy of County Meath*. Irish Family Names, Dublin.

Kavanagh, A. and Bunbury, T. 2004 *The landed gentry and aristocracy of Kilkenny: the Kilkenny gentry*, Vol. I. Irish Family Names, Dublin and Bunclody.

Kavanagh, A. and Murphy, R. 1994 *The Wexford gentry*, Vol. I. Irish Family Names, Enniscorthy.

Kavanagh, A. and Murphy, R. 1996 *The Wexford gentry*, Vol. II. Irish Family Names, Enniscorthy.

Keane, R., Hughes, A. and Swan, R. 1995 *Ardgillan Castle and the Taylor family*. Ardgillan Castle, Dublin.

Kearns, S. 1995 *Dublin in old picture postcards*. European Library, the Netherlands.

Kelly, A. 1990 *Mrs Coade's Stone*. Self-Publishing Association, Upton-upon-Severn.

Kelly, D. 1995 *Four roads to Dublin: a history of Rathmines, Ranelagh and Leeson Street*. O'Brien Press, Dublin.

Kenny, C. 1995 *Kilmainham: the history of a settlement older than Dublin*. Four Courts Press, Dublin.

Killanin, Lord and Duignan, M.V. 1962 *Shell guide to Ireland*. Ebury Press, London.

L

Lacey, J. 1999 *A candle in the window: a history of the barony of Castleknock*. Marino Books, Dublin.

Lacy, T. 1852 *Home sketches on both sides of the Channel*. London and Dublin.

Lacy, T. 1863 *Sights and scenes of our fatherland*. London and Dublin.

Lalor, B. (ed.) 2003. *The encyclopedia of Ireland*. Gill and Macmillan, Dublin.

Land owners in Ireland 1876 (reprint). Genealogical Publishing Co., Baltimore.

Langley, B. and Langley, T. 1747 *Gothic architecture, improved by rules and proportions*. John Millan, London.

Lanigan, K.M. and Tyler, G. (eds) 1987 *Kilkenny: its architecture and history*. Appletree Press, Belfast.

Lawrence Photographic Collection (1870–1914), National Library of Ireland, Dublin.

Leask, H.G. 1964 *Irish castles and castellated houses*. Dundalgan Press, Dundalk.

Lee, D. 2005 *James Pain, architect*. Civic Trust, Limerick.

Leet, A. 1814 *A directory to the market towns, villages, gentlemen's seats, &c.* Brett Smith, Dublin.

Leo Daly Photograph Collection, Westmeath County Library.

Leslie, Canon J.B. 1908 *History of the parish of Kilsaran*. William Tempest, Dundalk.

Leslie, Canon J.B. 1911 *Armagh clergy and parishes*. William Tempest, Dundalk.

Leslie, Canon J.B. 1933 *Ossory clergy and parishes*. Fermanagh Times, Enniskillen.

Leslie, Canon J.B. 1936 *Ferns clergy and parishes*. Church of Ireland Printing and Publishing, Dublin.

Leslie, Canon J.B. and Crooks, Canon D.W.T. 2006 *Clergy of Clogher*. Ulster Historical Foundation, Belfast.

Leslie, Canon J.B. and Crooks, Canon D.W.T. 2008 *Clergy of Kilmore, Elphin and Ardagh*. Ulster Historical Foundation, Belfast.

Leslie, Canon J.B. and Crooks, Canon D.W.T. 2010 *Clergy of Killaloe, Kilfenora, Clonfert and Kilmacduagh*. Ulster Historical Foundation, Belfast.

Leslie, Canon J.B. and Knox, Revd I. 2008 *Clergy of Waterford, Lismore and Ferns*. Ulster Historical Foundation, Belfast.

Leslie, Canon J.B. and Wallace, W.J.R. 2001 *Clergy of Dublin and Glendalough*. Ulster Historical Foundation, Belfast.

Leslie, Canon J.B. and Wallace, W.J.R. 2009 *Clergy of Meath and Kildare*. The Columba Press, Dublin.

Lewis, S. 1837 *Topographical dictionary of Ireland* (3 vols). Samuel Lewis, London.

Liddy, P. 1987 *Dublin be proud*. Chadworth, Dublin.

Lightbown, R.W. 2008 *An architect earl: Edward Augustus Stratford, 2nd Earl of Aldborough*. OLL Editions, Kilkenny.

Loeber, R. 1981 *A biographical dictionary of architects in Ireland 1600–1720*. John Murray, London.

Lohan, R. 1994 *Guide to the archives of the Office of Public Works*. OPW, Dublin.

Longfield map Collection *c.* 1770–1840. National Library of Ireland.

Loudon, J.C. 1833 *An encyclopaedia of gardening*. Longman, Hurst, Rees, Orme and Brown, London.

Loudon, J.C. 2000 [1846] *An encyclopaedia of cottage, farm and villa architecture* (reprint). Donhead, Shaftesbury.

Luckombe, P. 1790 *A tour through Ireland in 1779*. Whitestone, Dublin.

Lyall, S. 1988 *Dream cottages*. Robert Hale, London.

Lyons, M.C. 1993 *Illustrated incumbered estates*. Ballinakilla Press, Whitegate.

M

McCarthy, M. and O'Neill, K. (eds) 2008 *Studies in the Gothic Revival*. Four Courts Press, Dublin.

McCartney, D. 1999 *A national idea: the history of UCD*. Gill and Macmillan, Dublin.

McCullen, J.A. 2009 *Phoenix Park*. Government Publications, Dublin.

McCullough, N. 1994 *Palimpsest: change in the Irish building tradition*. Anne Street Press, Dublin.

MacDonnell, R. 2002 *The lost houses of Ireland: a chronicle of the great houses and the families who lived there*. Weidenfeld and Nicholson, London.

McFadden, O. 2001 *Know where we live*. O. McFadden, Gibbstown.

MacLoughlin, A. 1979 *A guide to historic Dublin*. Gill and Macmillan, Dublin.

McParland, E. 1985 *James Gandon: Vitruvius Hibernicus*. A. Zwemmer, London.

McParland, E. 2001 *Public architecture in Ireland 1680–1760*. Yale University Press, New Haven and London.

McParland, E., Rowan, A. and Rowan, A.M. 1989 *The architecture of Richard Morrison and William Vitruvius Morrison*. IAA, Dublin.

McVeagh, J. 1996 *Irish travel writing*. Wolfhound Press, Dublin.

Malcolm, E. 1989 *Swift's Hospital: a history of St Patrick's Hospital, Dublin (1746–1989)*. Gill and Macmillan, Dublin.

Malcomson, A.P.W. 2000 *The Irish peerage and the Act of Union 1800–1971*. Cambridge University Press, Cambridge.

Malcomson, A.P.W. 2003 *Primate Robinson 1709–1794*. Ulster Historical Foundation, Belfast.

Malcomson, A.P.W. 2005 *Nathaniel Clements: government and the governing elite in Ireland 1725–75*. Four Courts Press, Dublin.

Malcomson, A.P.W. 2009 *Virtues of a wicked earl: the life and legend of William Sydney Clements, 3rd Earl of Leitrim*. Four Courts Press, Dublin.

Malins, E. and Bowe, P. 1980 *Irish gardens and demesnes from 1830*. Barrie and Jenkins, London.

Malins, E. and Glin, The Knight of. 1976 *Lost demesnes 1660–1845*. Barrie and Jenkins, London.

Malton, J. 1978 *A picturesque and descriptive view of the city of Dublin*. Dolmen Press and IGS, Dublin.

Mansbridge, M. 1991 *John Nash: a complete*

catalogue. Phaidon Press, Oxford.
Mason, W.S. 1814–19 *Statistical account or parochial survey of Ireland* (3 vols). John Cunningham, Dublin, Edinburgh and London.
Maxwell, C. 1949 *Country and town in Ireland under the Georges*. Dundalgan Press, Dundalk.
Maxwell, C. 1956 *Dublin under the Georges*. Faber and Faber, London.
Meagher, J. (ed.) 1998 *Conaghy*. St Colman's Heritage Association, Kilkenny.
Miller, J. 1789 *The country gentleman's architect*. I. and J. Taylor, London.
Miller and Robertson, 'Collection of Kilkenny views'. Unpublished notebooks, Royal Society of Antiquaries of Ireland.
Milling Magazine (25 April 1936).
Morrison, R. 1793 *Useful and ornamental designs in architecture*. Robert Crosthwaite, Dublin.
Mowl, T. 1984 The evolution of the park gate lodge as a building type. *Architectural History* **27**, 467–80.
Mowl, T. and Earnshaw, B. 1984 *Trumpet at a distant gate*. Waterstone, London.
Mulhall, M. 1996 *Lucan and Lucanians: a revised history of Lucan*. Leinster Leader, Naas.
Mulligan, K. 2001 *Buildings of Meath*. The Fieldgate Press, Kells.
Murphy, É. 2003 *A glorious extravaganza: the history of Monkstown Parish Church*. Wordwell, Bray.
Musgrave, Sir R. 1801 *Memoirs of the different rebellions in Ireland*. John Milliken, Dublin.

N
Neale, J.P. 1820–3 *Views of the seats of noblemen and gentlemen*, 1st series (6 vols). Sherwood, Neely and Jones, London.
Neale, J.P. 1824–9 *Views of the seats of noblemen and gentlemen*, 2nd series (6 vols). Sherwood, Gilbert and Piper, London.
Nelson, E.C. and McCracken, E.M. 1987 *The brightest jewel: a history of the National Botanic Gardens*. Boethius Press, Kilkenny.
Nolan, J. 1982 *Changing faces*. St Vincent's Tontine, Dublin.
Nolan, W. and O'Neill, T.P. (eds) 1998 *Offaly history and society*. Geography Publications, Dublin.

O
O'Connor, J. 1995 *The workhouses of Ireland: the fate of Ireland's poor*. Anvil Press, Dublin.
O'Donoghue, B. 2007 *The Irish county surveyors 1834–1944*. Four Courts Press, Dublin.
O'Dwyer, F. 1981 *Lost Dublin*. Gill and Macmillan, Dublin.
O'Dwyer, F. 1996 A.W.N. Pugin and St Patrick's College, Maynooth. *Irish Arts Review* **12**, 102–9.
O'Dwyer, F. 1997a *Irish hospital architecture*. Department of Health and Children, Dublin.
O'Dwyer, F. 1997b *The architecture of Deane and Woodward*. Cork University Press, Cork.
O'Dwyer, F. 1999 'Modelled muscularity': Daniel Robertson's Tudor manors. *Irish Arts Review* **15**, 87–97.
O'Flanagan, J.R. 1870 *The lives of the Lord Chancellors and Keepers of the Grand Seal of Ireland* (2 vols). Longmans Green, Dublin.
O'Kane, F. 2004 *Landscape design in eighteenth-century Ireland*. Cork University Press, Cork.
O'Kane, F. 2012 *William Ashford's Mount Merrion*. Churchill House Press, Tralee.
O'Sullivan, J. 1987 *The book of Dún Laoghaire: the evolution of Ballybrack and Killiney*. Blackrock Teachers' Centre.
O'Toole, J. 1993 *The Carlow gentry*. J. O'Toole, Carlow.
OSI 1991 *An illustrated record of Ordnance Survey in Ireland*. Ordnance Survey of Ireland, Dublin.

P
Pakenham, V. 2000 *The Big House in Ireland*. Cassell and Co., London.
Papworth, J.B. 1818 *Rural residences*. Ackerman, London.
Parliamentary Gazetteer of Ireland 1844–1845 (3 vols; A. Fullerton and Co., Dublin, London and Edinburgh, 1846).
Pearson, P. 1981 *Dún Laoghaire/Kingstown*. The O'Brien Press, Dublin.
Pearson, P. 1998 *Between the mountains and the sea*. The O'Brien Press, Dublin.
Pearson, P. 2000 *The heart of Dublin*. The O'Brien Press, Dublin.
Pearson, P. 2002 *Decorative Dublin*. The O'Brien Press, Dublin.
Pevsner, N. and Sherwood, J. 2002 *The buildings of England: Oxfordshire*. Yale University Press, New Haven and London.
Pigot, J. 1824 *Dictionary of Ireland*. Pigot and Co., London.
Pike, W.T. and McDowell, C. 1908 *Dublin and County Dublin in the 20th century*. W.T. Pike, Brighton and London.
Powerscourt, Viscount. 1903 *A description and history of Powerscourt*. Mitchell and Hughes, London.
Pugin, A.W.N. 1839 *Ornamental gables* (2nd edn). Henry G. Bohn, London.

R
Rawson, T.J. 1807 *A statistical survey of County Kildare*. Graisberry and Campbell, Dublin.
Reilly, P.A. 1993 *Wild plants of the Phoenix Park*. OPW, Dublin.
Robertson, J.G. 1983 [1851] *Antiquities and scenery of County Kilkenny* (reprint). Boethius Press, Kilkenny.
Robertson, W. 1800 *Designs in architecture*. R. Ackermann, London.
Robinson, J.M. 1979 *The Wyatts: an architectural dynasty*. Oxford University Press, Oxford.
Robinson, J.M. 2012 *James Wyatt: architect to George III*. Yale University Press, New Haven and London.
Robinson, P.F. 1833 *Designs for lodges and park entrances*. Priestley and Weale, London.
Rothery, S. 1997 *A field guide to the buildings of Ireland*. Lilliput Press, Dublin.
Rowe, D. and Scallan, E. 2004 *Houses of Wexford*. Ballinakella Press, Whitegate.
Royal Institute of British Architects 1993 *Dictionary of British architects 1834–1900*. Mansell Publishing, London.
Ryan, C. and Hayes, O. 2002 *Dundrum, Stillorgan and Rathfarnham: gateway to the mountains*. Cottage Publications, Dublin.

S
Savage, P.D. 1980 *Lorimer and the Edinburgh craft designers*. Paul Harris Publishing, Edinburgh.
Seymour, Ven. St J.D. and Leslie, Canon J.B. 2012 *Clergy of Cashel, Emly and Leighlin*. Ulster Historical Foundation, Belfast.
Shaffrey, P. and Shaffrey, M. 1985 *Irish countryside buildings: everyday architecture in the rural landscape*. The O'Brien Press, Dublin.
Sharkey, J.U. 2002 *St Anne's: the story of a Guinness estate*. Woodfield Press, Dublin.
Shaw, H. 1988 *The Dublin pictorial guide and directory of 1850* (reprint). Friar's Bush Press, Belfast.
Sheehy, J. 1977 *J.J. McCarthy and the Gothic Revival in Ireland*. Ulster Architectural Heritage Society, Belfast.
Sheil, H. 1998 *Falling into wretchedness: Ferbane in the late 1830s*. Irish Academic Press, Dublin.
Slater, I. 1846 *National commercial directory of Ireland*. Slater, Manchester.
Slater, I. 1856 *National commercial directory of Ireland*. Slater, Manchester.
Slater, I. 1870 *Royal national commercial directory of Ireland*. Slater, Manchester and London.
Smith, C.F. 2001 *Newtownpark Avenue: its people and their houses*. Albany Press, Dublin.
Smyth, H.P. 1994 *The town of the road: the story of Booterstown*. Beyond the Pale Publications, Dublin.
Snodin, M. 1996 *Sir William Chambers*. V&A Publications, London.
Soane, J. 1793 *Sketches in architecture*. Taylor, London.
Somerville-Large, P. 1995 *The Irish country house: a social history*. Sinclair-Stevenson, London.
Wright, G.N. 1839 Ireland illustrated. H. Fisher, Son and Co., London.
Stamp, G. 2002 *An architect of promise: George Gilbert Scott Junior (1839–1897) and the late Gothic Revival*. Shaun Tyas, Donington.

T
Taylor, A.C. 1841 *Designs for agricultural buildings suited to Irish*

estates. Grant and Bolton, Dublin.
Taylor, G. and Skinner, A. 1778 *Maps of the roads of Ireland* (1st edn). W. Wilson, London and Dublin.
Taylor, G. and Skinner, A. 1969 [1783] *Maps of the roads of Ireland* (2nd edn) (reprint). Irish University Press, Shannon.
Tempest, W. 1920 *Descriptive and historical guide to Dundalk and district.* Dundalgan Press, Dundalk.
Temple, N. 1979 *John Nash and the village picturesque.* Alan Sutton, Gloucester.
Thackeray, W.M. 1879 *The Irish sketchbook.* Smith Elder and Co., London.
Thom's Irish Almanac and Official Directory (various editions; Alexander Thom, Dublin, 1844–1910).
Thompson, R. 1802 *Statistical survey of County Meath.* Dublin Society, Dublin.
Thomson, J. 1827 *Retreats: a series of designs.* J. Taylor, London.
Townsend, B. 1999 *The lost distilleries of Ireland.* Neil Wilson Publishing, Glasgow.
Twiss, R. 1776 *A tour in Ireland in 1775.* R. Twiss, London.

V

Vincent, J. 1861 *Country cottages.* Robert Hardwicke, London.

W

Wakeman, W.F. 1883 *The tourist's picturesque guide to Ireland.* Dublin.
Walsh, D. 1996 *100 Wexford country houses.* Mill Park Publications, Enniscorthy.
Walsh, W. 2009 An architectural study of Kilfane House. *In the Shadow of the Steeple* **10**. Journal of the Tullaherin Heritage Society, Kilkenny.
Warburton, J., Whitelaw, J. and Walsh, R. 1818 *History of the city of Dublin.* Cadell and Davies, London.
Watchorn, F. 1985 *Crumlin and the way it was.* O'Donoghue Print, Dublin.
Watkin, D. 1986 *The life and work of C.R. Cockerell.* Zwemmer, London.
Whelan, K. and Nolan, W. (eds) 1987 *Wexford history and society: interdisciplinary essays on the history of an Irish county.* Geography Publications, Dublin.
Whyte, T.J. 2007 *The story of Woodstock.* Cappagh Press, Dublin.
Wilde, W.R. 1850 *The beauties of the Boyne, and its tributary, the Blackwater.* McGlashan, Dublin.
Williams, J. 1994 *A companion guide to architecture in Ireland 1837–1921.* Irish Academic Press, Dublin.
Wilson, W. 1803 *The post chaise companion, or, Traveller's directory through Ireland* (3rd edn). J. and J.H. Fleming, Dublin.
Wright, G.N. 1831 *Ireland illustrated.* H. Fisher, Son and Jackson, London.
Wright, G.N. 1839 *Ireland illustrated.* H. Fisher, Son and Co., London.

Y

Young, A. 1780 *Tour in Ireland, 1776–1779.* T. Cadell and J. Dodsley, London.

APPENDIX

ORDNANCE SURVEY OF IRELAND: SIX-INCH COUNTY SERIES MAPS

County	1st edition	2nd edition	3rd edition
Carlow	1840		1905–6
Dublin	1844	1871–5	1906–9
Kildare	1839		1907–9
Kilkenny	1842	1899–1902	
Laois	1841		1908–9
Longford	1838		1911–12
Louth	1836		1907–9
Meath	1837		1908–11
Offaly	1840	1900–4	
Westmeath	1838		1910–13
Wexford	1841	1902–5	
Wicklow	1839		1910–11

ARCHITECTS, BUILDERS (B), LANDSCAPE ARCHITECTS (L) AND MANUFACTURERS/CRAFTSMEN (M)

Letters and numbers in italics refer to counties and entries. Numbers set in bold refer to pages in the chapter on the history of the gate lodge in Leinster pp 1–20.

Cw = Carlow
Dn = Dublin, north
Ds = Dublin, south
Ke = Kildare
Kk = Kilkenny
Ld = Longford
Lh = Louth
Ls = Laois
Mh = Meath
Oy = Offaly
Wm = Westmeath
Ww = Wicklow
Wx = Wexford

PATRONS, PROPRIETORS AND PORTERS (P)

Letters and numbers in italics refer to counties and entries. Numbers set in bold refer to pages in the chapter on the history of the gate lodge in Leinster pp 1–20.

Cw = Carlow
Dn = Dublin, north
Ds = Dublin, south
Ke = Kildare
Kk = Kilkenny
Ld = Longford
Lh = Louth
Ls = Laois
Mh = Meath
Oy = Offaly
Wm = Westmeath
Ww = Wicklow
Wx = Wexford

C

E

M

Y